Introduction to Accounting: An Integrated Approach

Introduction to Accounting: An Integrated Approach

CHAPTERS 1 TO 25

Penne Ainsworth
Kansas State University

Dan Deines
Kansas State University

R. David Plumlee
University of Kansas

Cathy Xanthaky Larson
Middlesex Community College

Irwin

Chicago • Bogotá • Boston • Buenos Aires • Caracas
London • Madrid • Mexico City • Sydney • Toronto

Irwin Book Team

Publisher: *Michael W. Junior*
Executive editor: *Jeff Shelstad*
Developmental editors: *Kelly Lee and Leslye Givarz*
Marketing manager: *Heather L. Woods*
Senior project supervisor: *Denise Santor-Mitzit*
Senior production supervisor: *Bob Lange*
Director, Prepress Purchasing: *Kimberly Meriwether David*
Designer: *Matthew Baldwin and Maureen McCutcheun*
Coordinator, Graphics and Desktop Services: *Keri Johnson*
Compositor: *Times Mirror Higher Education Group, Inc., Imaging Group*
Typeface: *10/12 Jansen*
Printer: *Von Hoffmann Press, Inc.*

Library of Congress Cataloging-in-Publication Data

Introduction to accounting : an integrated approach / Penne Ainsworth
 . . . [et al.]. — 1st ed.
    p.   cm.
   Includes index.
   ISBN 0–256–12383–7 (combined vols.). — ISBN 0–256–23308–X (vol.
1). — ISBN 0–256–23374–8 (vol. 2)
   1. Accounting.   I. Ainsworth, Penne.
  HF5635.I655   1997
  657—dc20   96–20987

▼▼ Times Mirror
M Higher Education Group

Printed in the United States of America
1 2 3 4 5 6 7 8 9 0 VH 3 2 1 0 9 8 7 6

First, and foremost, we dedicate this text to our families without whose love and support we never could have completed this project. To our spouses, **Scott Ainsworth, Linda Deines, Marlene Plumlee, and Doug Larson,** *and to our children,* **Heather, Dusty, Jennifer, Jeff, Matt, Sarah, Ashley, J. D., and Robyn,** *we love you and we thank you for your patience. We would also like to thank the students of Kansas State University who used previous drafts of this textbook and gave us valuable suggestions for improvement. Finally, we would like to thank our development editors, Leslye Givarz and Kelly Lee, our executive editor, Jeff Shelstad, and the production and marketing departments at Irwin.*

About the Authors

Penne Ainsworth
Kansas State University

Penne Ainsworth, CPA, CMA, and CIA, received her Ph.D. from the University of Nebraska. She is an associate professor in the accounting department at Kansas State University and co-authored the original application for the grant KSU received from the Accounting Education Change Commission (AECC). She won the Kansas State Bank Outstanding Teacher Award in 1993. She is a member of the AAA and the IMA. Penne's research focuses on managerial accounting and accounting education. Her work has been published in *Issues and Accounting Education* and other journals.

Dan Deines
Kansas State University

Dan Deines earned a B.A. in history from Fort Hays State University and his Ph.D. from the University of Nebraska. Dan is the Ralph Crouch, KPMG Peat Marwick Professor of accounting at Kansas State University, where he won the College of Business Outstanding Teaching Award in 1988 and the Outstanding Advisor Award in 1994. He was a co-author of the AECC grant proposal and was the co-coordinator of administering the grant. He is nationally recognized for his work on recruiting high quality students to the accounting profession. Dan's research interests are in financial reporting. He is a member of the AICPA, the AAA and the Kansas Society of CPAs.

R. David Plumlee
University of Kansas

R. David Plumlee earned both his Bachelors and Masters degrees from the University of Oklahoma, and is a CPA. After receiving his Ph.D. at the University of Florida, David taught at the University of North Carolina and Kansas State University before moving to the University of Kansas where he is currently the Baird, Kurtz and Dobson Faculty Fellow. He has published research in a number of scholarly journals including *Journal of Accounting Research* and *The Accounting Review*. David is currently serving as Associate Editor of *The Accounting Review*.

Cathy Xanthaky Larson
Middlesex Community College

Cathy Xanthaky Larson, CPA, received her BS in Business Administration from Salem State College and her MBA from Bentley College. Cathy is a tenured professor at Middlesex Community College and an adjunct professor at both Salem State and Bentley. She is a member of the AICPA, AAA, Massachusetts Association of Accounting Professors, and Teachers of Accounting at Two Year Colleges (TACTYC). She is currently serving as vice president of TACTYC. Cathy received Middlesex's Faculty Member of the Year Award in 1985 and 1990.

Preface

WHY DID WE WRITE THIS TEXT?

This text is based on the philosophy that an introductory accounting text should emphasize the type of information that the language of business provides for decision makers. Learning only the mechanics of the accounting process is no longer adequate for understanding the critical role of accounting information in effective business decision making. On the other hand, learning the basic mechanics of the accounting process allows users of accounting information to understand how events are operationalized in the accounting system. Understanding the decision relevance of accounting information as well as the mechanics of the system is what we offer in *Introduction to Accounting: An Integrated Approach.*

Introduction to accounting courses serve a very diverse group of students, only a small percentage of which will continue as accounting majors. Therefore, these students need to understand that accounting is a vital link between business events and business decisions in a complex environment. Understanding this important concept better serves the needs of this student population and is the first step in attracting a more creative, broader thinking student into the accounting major.

A NEW AND RESPONSIVE PHILOSOPHY

The Bedford Report, the Big Eight White Paper, and the Accounting Education Change Commission all call for accounting education to keep pace with the dynamic changes occurring in the business world. Accounting, the authors of these documents argue, has become a broadly based information system limited only by the needs of the information user. These professionals urge accounting educators to turn from their rules-driven curricula to adopt a new approach to the instruction of accounting. *Introduction to Accounting: An Integrated Approach* is a timely response to this call for change.

HOW HAVE WE SPECIFICALLY RESPONDED?

As you become more familiar with this text, you will note that it provides an innovative approach to familiar topics. In other words, we have taken topics traditionally taught in the first year-long accounting course at most two- and four-year institutions and presented them within a different context and organizational structure. Specifically, *Introduction to Accounting: An Integrated Approach* is built around three very important themes:

1. **Accounting is an information system that serves two diverse sets of users**—those internal to the organization and those external to the organization. Traditionally, accounting has addressed these two major audiences separately by segregating the financial accounting discipline, which primarily serves external users, from the managerial accounting discipline, which addresses the needs of internal users. *Introduction to Accounting: An Integrated Approach* exposes its readers to the idea that the accounting system provides information which is beneficial to both groups. Therefore, we integrate the coverage of managerial and financial accounting topics.

2. **The cash flow statement is a model to sequence information.** We organize information around operating, financing, and investing activities. We chose to focus on operating activities first for three primary reasons: (*a*) Businesses first address issues concerning products/services and customers, then financing and investing activities are considered. (*b*) Students are more familiar with operating

activities and, therefore, these activities are inherently easier to understand, reinforcing our idea of moving from simple to complex issues. (*c*) Classroom experience shows that students understand financing and investing activities better after grasping the issues surrounding operating activities.

3. **The approach taken to accounting is a business cycle perspective.** Within the operating, as well as the financing and investing, parts of this text, we discuss business events according to the logical way businesses function. Businesses first plan activities (events), then they perform those activities, and finally they evaluate the results of those activities. Within this framework, the performance phase is when information is captured and recorded in the financial accounting system.

These last two organizational themes lead to a very straightforward and logical presentation of material within *Introduction to Accounting: An Integrated Approach*. Chapters 1–13, (the operating "half"), is organized as follows:

- Introduction to business and accounting

- Planning for operating activities (events)

- Performing (recording) operating activities

- Evaluating and controlling operating activities

Chapters 14–25, (the financing and investing "half"), is organized similarly:

- Introduction to financing and investing activities

- Planning for financing and investing activities (events)

- Performing (recording) financing and investing events

- Evaluating and controlling business—financing, investing, and operating activities

Just as Chapters 1 and 2 serve as an introduction to the business world and accounting's role in it and set the stage for the entire book, Chapters 22–25 evaluate the firm's overall performance, and really serve as a summary and analysis for the entire text presentation.

WHAT ARE OUR OBJECTIVES?

This text is designed to be used in a year-long financial/managerial, introductory, or principles of accounting course. *Introduction to Accounting: An Integrated Approach* is designed to benefit all students, regardless of their chosen major. In designing the text, we incorporated these six objectives:

1. **To focus on the use of accounting information by internal and external stakeholders.**

We maintain a consistent focus throughout this text on the use of accounting information, rather than the preparation of accounting information. As mentioned earlier, the process of recording, adjusting, and closing events and their impact on financial statements is covered, but it is not the primary focus. This more balanced approach will benefit all students. Non-accounting majors will gain an appreciation for the use of accounting information, and accounting majors will better understand what users need while at the same time gaining a complete preparation for future courses in accounting.

2. **To integrate financial and managerial accounting.**

Introduction to Accounting: An Integrated Approach consistently emphasizes the business event and analyzes the event from both an external (financial reporting) and an internal (managerial decision making) perspective. Financial and managerial accounting are subsystems of the same accounting information system, and while these subsystems serve different user groups, we do not feel one is more important than the other.

3. **To order content elements in a logical manner.**

Student learning is obviously enhanced by presenting topics in a logical and coherent sequence. We follow three simple tenets: Simple topics are presented before more complex topics; Events are presented before transactions; and Accounting is presented within a business cycle context.

4. To promote active learning on the part of the student.

Various pedagogical devices are used to stimulate active learning experiences for the student. Most obvious are the Pause and Reflect questions posed at various times throughout each chapter. These questions serve as a checkpoint for the student's understanding of the material, as well as a critical thinking stimulus. Additionally, the Cases, Computer Applications, Critical Thinking, and Ethical Challenge sections at the end of all chapters give the students the opportunity to apply their accounting knowledge to a broader business setting, and virtually always require learning and exploring outside of the book.

5. To promote effective communication by the student.

Again, many of the end of chapter materials can and should be used to encourage written and oral communication on the part of the student. The *Instructor's Resource Manual*, prepared by Penne Ainsworth, contains many useful suggestions for incorporating communication into your classes.

6. To stimulate interest in the field of accounting.

Classroom experience has shown that the approach of *Introduction to Accounting: An Integrated Approach* will serve as the greatest way to motivate interest in the discipline of accounting. As students gain an understanding and appreciation of the broader role of accounting in the business world, they are more likely to express interest in accounting as a field of study.

HOW DO WE HELP YOU PREPARE AND EXCEL?

We provide the following supplements for you in order to ease your transition to *Introduction to Accounting: An Integrated Approach.*

Instructor's Resource Manual Prepared by Penne Ainsworth and subtitled "How to Teach an Integrated Approach," this manual contains very detailed teaching notes for each chapter. It includes the learning objectives cross-referenced to the end-of-chapter materials, additional considerations and cooperative learning suggestions for the end-of-chapter materials, a discussion outline, two test/retest quizzes, two on-demand problems, and a unique continuing cooperative learning case following the organization of the text that can be copied for classroom use.

Solutions Manual Prepared by the authors and verified for accuracy by Barbara Schnathorst, C.P.A. of Colorado Springs, CO, this manual contains detailed solutions to all end of chapter material.

Solutions Transparencies Exercises and problems from the Solutions Manual are reproduced in acetate format for maximum instructor efficiency.

PowerPoint Slides Prepared by David Vicknair of Rockhurst College in Kansas City, MO, these electronic teaching acetates consist of approximately 30 slides per chapter. Accompanied by an Instructor's Manual demonstrating how to use them, these initial slides give you great freedom to build a more lively and modern classroom presentation.

Test Bank Prepared by Cathy Xanthaky Larson, this manual consists of approximately 1,100 multiple choice questions and problems.

Computerized Test Bank Available in DOS, Windows, and Macintosh versions, this option provides you more flexibility in designing your assessment tools.

Financial Accounting Video Series and Managerial Accounting Video Series These short, action oriented videos provide the impetus for lively classroom discussion.

Instructor's Manual for Video Use Prepared by Jeannie Folk of the College of DuPage in Wheaton, IL, this comprehensive guide will show specifically how to integrate the two video series described above into your introductory accounting classroom.

We provide the following supplements for your students as they study and learn from *Introduction to Accounting: An Integrated Approach*.

Study Guide   Prepared by Debra Kerby and Scott Fouch of Northeast Missouri State Univ., this manual will reinforce the concepts found in the text through additional Pause and Reflect questions, short essay assignments, and additional chapter by chapter review.

PowerPoint Ready Notes   Prepared by David Vicknair of Rockhurst College, this useful student tool will allow for a more efficient classroom setting by giving the students a master template for note taking. Mirroring the PowerPoint slides available to the instructor, students will have a beginning point so they can concentrate on the classroom presentation instead of furiously taking notes.

General Ledger Applications Software (GLAS)   This general ledger program, available in both DOS and Windows formats, will solve selected end of chapter material from the recording chapters (7–10 and 18–21). It also will allow for any problem requiring journal entries (in the recording chapters) to be solved via its custom feature.

Annual Report Booklet   Nine annual reports will appear in the Annual Report Booklet. They include Walt Disney (Chapter 2), The Boston Celtics (Chapter 7), Wal-Mart (Chapter 8), Anheuser-Busch (Chapter 10), Archer Daniels Midland (Chapter 18), Genentech (Chapter 21), Harley-Davidson (Chapter 22), Southwestern Public Service Company and Entergy Corporation (Chapter 24). Students will use the Annual Report Booklet to answer some of the questions in the end of chapter material in the text.

Practice Set   This manual practice set, prepared by Cathy Xanthaky Larson will allow for additional reinforcement of the accounting cycle presentation in Chapter 7.

***The Wall Street Journal* Edition of the textbook**   For a nominal fee, students can purchase a version of the text that will entitle them to a 10 week subscription to *The Wall Street Journal*. Additionally, if at least 10 students at a school utilize this benefit, the adopting instructor will get a free subscription for one year.

Accounting Cycle Software   Prepared in conjunction with the Graduate Management Admissions Council, this multimedia software product will provide an interactive, independent learning review of the entire accounting cycle.

WE HAVE LISTENED TO YOU

The market research and developmental process employed to ensure the quality of *Introduction to Accounting: An Integrated Approach* was extensive. For more than 48 months, this manuscript has gone through four complete drafts, and has been tremendously aided by the comments of the following people, who provided insightful comments/criticisms/enhancements along the way.

Mark Alford
The University of Texas—San Antonio

Sue Atkinson
Tarleton State University

Andy Barnett
San Diego State University

Peter E. Battelle
University of Vermont

Sheila Bradford
Tulsa Junior College

Clifford D. Brown
Bentley College

Sarah Brown*
University of North Alabama

Tom Buchman
University of Colorado—Boulder

Bruce Cassel*
Dutchess Community College

Barbara Chiappetta*
Nassau Community College

Rosalyn Cranor
Virginia Polytechnic Institute

Louann Hofheins Cummings*
Siena Heights College

Karel Ann Davis
Butler University

Doris deLespinasse
Adrian College

Jane B. Wells
University of Kentucky

Jack E. Wilkerson
Wake Forest University

Jack Zeller*
Kirkwood Community College

Gil Zuckerman*
North Carolina State University

*A very well orchestrated focus group run by Irwin in November of 1994 provided tremendous guidance as we headed into the final, most important draft prior to the release of the Preliminary Edition in August of 1995.

Sarah Brown
University of North Alabama

Bruce Cassel
Dutchess Community College

Barbara Chiappetta
Nassau Community College

LouAnn Hofheins Cummings
Siena Heights College

Terri Guttierez
University of Northern Colorado

Patty Holmes
Des Moines Area Community College

Thomas Knoll
DeVry Institute of Technology

Marilyn Okleshen
Mankato State University

Martha Rassi
Glendale Community College

Jack Zeller
Kirkwood Community College

Gill Zuckerman
North Carolina State University

Over the last 2½ years, we have been aided by the efforts of Leslye Givarz of Williamsburg, VA. Leslye has worked with Kelly Lee at Irwin to champion the entire developmental process. Leslye's skills at assimilating many reviewer comments into a cohesive plan for revision have been appreciated. Most importantly, Leslye has spent hours upon hours working to ensure that the individual writing styles of the four text authors attain consistency from Chapters 1 to 25. We would not have achieved such a well-written first edition without the efforts of Leslye.

The publication of the Preliminary Edition (Volume 1 in August, 1995 and Volume 2 in December, 1995) has allowed for an additional step of customer feedback. We thank the Preliminary Edition class-test sites for believing in the product enough to adopt "sight unseen." We also thank these users for their continuous feedback which has led to a better First Edition.

Kathy Brockway
Kansas State University

Joyce Griffin
Kansas City Kansas Community College

Anne T. Kostorizos
Middlesex Community College

Jennifer Lima
Kansas State University

Johanna Lyle
Kansas State University

Ken Mark
Kansas City Kansas Community College

Cheryl Miles
Kansas State University

Barbara Shiarappa
Trenton State College

Fred W. Smith
Kansas State University

Finally, the enthusiasm for the ideas expressed in *Introduction to Accounting: An Integrated Approach* has been verified by the many schools and conferences at which the authors have been invited to present. Over the last four years, some of those schools and conferences include: Mankato State University, Salem State University, University of Wyoming, Illinois State University, West Virginia University, North Carolina State University, University of South Dakota, Missouri Southern State University, Minnesota Council of Accounting Educations, Rhode Island Accounting Convention, and the Teachers of Accounting at Two-Year Colleges.

HOW WILL THE TEXT COME TO YOU?

The First Edition of *Introduction to Accounting: An Integrated Approach* will be available in two volumes as well as a full-text option. We are publishing the book in two volumes so we can more effectively integrate the class-test site feedback. Individuals who have used the second volume of the Preliminary Edition in the spring of 1996 provided us valuable feedback, and we will utilize that feedback to improve the second volume of the book, which is due in October of 1996. At the time we release that second volume, we will also publish a full 1–25 text. Users will then have the option of purchasing the book in volumes or as a full version.

Penne Ainsworth
Dan Deines
R. David Plumlee
Cathy Xanthaky Larson

Brief Road Map

Road Map

PART TWO

PLANNING AND DECISION MAKING

CHAPTER 4

PART THREE

RECORDING WITHIN THE OPERATING CYCLES

CHAPTER 7

Recording and Communicating in the Accounting Cycle

CHAPTER 8

Recording and Communicating in the Expenditure Cycle

PART FOUR

CONTROLLING WITHIN THE CYCLES

PART FIVE

PLANNING AND DECISION MAKING

CHAPTER 14

The Time Value of Money: A Tool for Decision Making ... 468

PART SIX

RECORDING WITHIN THE FINANCING AND INVESTING CYCLES

CHAPTER 18

Recording and Communicating Long-Term Debt Financing Activities

CHAPTER 19

Recording and Communicating Equity Financing Activities

PART SEVEN

FIRM PERFORMANCE: EVALUATION AND CONTROL

CHAPTER 22

Introduction to Accounting: An Integrated Approach

PART ONE

Introduction to Business and Accounting Information

This part of the text, the operating activities segment, presents an overview of business as the framework for viewing more specific business and accounting activities. Accounting and business, after all, are inextricably linked, as the history of business illustrates in the first chapter. Accounting has traditionally fostered communication of important business information, serving as the language of business. This language is important for users of business information, both inside and outside the business organization. Chapter 2 tells us why.

Business operations and the communication of operations information are better understood if they are viewed in terms of three important business cycles: expenditure, revenue, and conversion. Chapter 3 introduces business cycles and illustrates their significance. This part of the text provides the "big view" of how accounting has functioned and changed to keep pace with the needs of users today.

CHAPTER 1

Business and Accounting

Learning Objectives

1. Describe the development of accounting and business, the four basic concepts of accounting, and the role of risk and reward in business.
2. Explain the differences among business industry types and business organizational structures.
3. Define external and internal stakeholders and explain the interest each type of stakeholder has in business in the 1990s.

In 1962, Philip Knight and Bill Bowerman, Knight's former track coach at the University of Oregon, each invested $500 to create a company called Blue Ribbon Sports. The company distributed athletic shoes designed by Bowerman and manufactured by Onitsuka Tiger in Japan. Initially the shoes were shipped out of Bowerman's garage and distributed at track meets. In 1966, Blue Ribbon Sports opened its first retail store in Santa Monica, California. In 1971, Blue Ribbon Sports changed its name to Nike who was the Greek goddess of victory.

Today, Nike is a multinational company that sells shoes throughout the world and has investors on many continents. In fact, Nike communicates its financial results to shareholders (owners) in five languages!

Nike's pattern of development is typical of many businesses—starting out as a small enterprise and growing into a multinational corporation. Nike, Apple Computers, and Microsoft all began as garage-based small businesses.

In this chapter, we explore the development of accounting and business as well as their roles in the 1990s and beyond. It is important to understand the history of business in order to understand the future of business. In addition, we explore the fundamental concepts of accounting, which provide the framework for modern accounting systems. Finally, we examine accounting and related careers in the 1990s.

BUSINESS AND ACCOUNTING: A PARTNERSHIP AS OLD AS TIME

Business is the exchange of goods, services, and money, on an arm's-length (objective) basis, that results in mutual benefit or profit for both parties involved. An individual engages in business because he or she believes that the **rewards,** or possible future benefits, of business are greater than the **risks,** or possible future sacrifices, of business.

For as long as there have been people who engaged in buying and selling goods, there has been a need for ways to hold other people accountable for their actions—to provide some assurance that they will behave or perform as expected. In the broadest sense, **accountability** is responsibility. When we hold someone accountable for his or her actions, we assume that the individual is responsible or answerable for certain actions.

This need for accountability has evolved over time into the need for accounting systems that provide information to hold people and, therefore, businesses accountable for the resources entrusted to them by others. An **accounting system** is a set of methods, plans, and procedures used to identify, analyze, measure, record, summarize, and communicate relevant economic information to interested parties.

For example, if you were a merchant 1,000 years ago and needed goods to sell, you might send a trusted friend to make a trade for you and to arrange for the delivery of the traded goods. In order to protect your investment in these goods, you would need a way to determine how much you have invested, who has control of the goods you are trading, and how much you are receiving in return for your investment. Likewise, your trusted friend needs a way to determine the amount of goods traded and how much is received in trade. Finally, the person with whom you are trading needs a way to indicate how much they received in the trade as well as what they have given to you. A system that protects these business parties by providing the economic information necessary to evaluate and control business transactions is called an accounting system.

Accounting systems have evolved over many centuries as the needs for information about business have changed. It is important to understand the evolution of accounting because accounting is not a science such as physics. Rather accounting is a discipline that changes as the needs of its users change. The accounting systems used hundreds of years ago are not adequate today. Likewise, today's accounting systems will be inadequate at some point in the future.

To understand the evolution of accounting, we will travel back in time, making six stops, to consider important business and accounting eras. These six eras illustrate the changes that have occurred in business and accounting.[1]

Early Business Development

The first leg of our journey takes us to the first dynasty of Babylonia (2285–2242 BC), a rich farming area located between the Tigris and Euphrates rivers in what is now the country of Iraq. Babylonia is ruled by the Code of Hammurabi, which requires that a merchant selling goods must give the buyer a sealed memorandum quoting prices, or the trade is not legally enforceable.[2] However, there is one problem—most of the citizens of Babylonia are illiterate.

---

[1]For a more thorough study of accounting history, read A. C. Littleton, *Accounting Evolution to 1990* (New York: American Institute Publishing Company, 1993); and Michael Chatfield, *A History of Accounting Thought* (Huntington, NY: Robert E. Krieger Publishing Company, 1977).

[2]Michael Chatfield, *A History of Accounting Thought*, p. 5.

Early business failures

Assume you are a merchant in Babylonia. How will you conduct business? You are operating as a **sole proprietorship,** that is, a business owned by one person, and your personal belongings are at risk if your business fails. You also are operating as a **merchandising company,** that is, a company that obtains and distributes goods to consumers, so you must find both a supplier of and a buyer for your goods. Since the chances are very good that all of you are illiterate, how will you record your business transactions?

First, you must find a scribe who is probably sitting outside the city gates. Next, you explain to him your agreed-upon transaction and he records it in a small mound of clay. Then, since neither you nor your buyer can read or write, you affix your "signatures" to the agreement by impressing your signature amulet on the clay document. This holds both parties accountable for the transaction.[3]

The clay record is allowed to dry in the sun, or, if the transaction must be carried out quickly, the records can be kiln-dried. Obviously, the scribe's integrity is crucial. This scribe is the predecessor to the 20th century accountant.

Venture Trading

The next stop on our journey is the trading centers of medieval Italy, which developed partly as a result of the Crusades from the 11th to the 13th centuries. Literacy is more widespread, arabic numerals are beginning to be used, an international banking system exists, and the use of credit is prevalent. Banks are also business enterprises operating as **service firms,** which exist to provide services such as loaning money and performing other services for their customers.

At this time, it is commonplace for a partnership to be formed for a single venture. A **partnership** is a business owned by two or more individuals who agree to share both the risks and rewards of the business. How would you conduct business in such an environment? First you must find a partner. Then, each of you would contribute goods to be traded with others in foreign countries. Note that your personal belongings are still at risk if the business fails, but now you share this risk with one or more additional individuals.

Next, you hire an agent to ship the goods to the foreign land. When the ship returns from trading, it is loaded with goods of the foreign land, which you and your partner divide between yourselves. How do you determine the proper allocation of the goods acquired? You need a **partnership agreement,** which stipulates the rights and obligations of each partner and describes how to divide the goods (partnership profits).

Then, your accounting system provides the information to help you determine your individual share of the goods received by the partnership. The accounting system also

---

[3]Every male citizen was required to have a signature amulet to conduct business. Only male citizens had amulets because women were not allowed to conduct business. The amulet was a charm worn around the man's neck that gave him a legal identity. It was buried with him when he died.

reflects the information to hold the trading agent accountable for making a profitable trade. However, your accounting records do not distinguish between business and personal affairs, so at the end of each individual trading venture, it is necessary to terminate the business and divide the goods between the partners.

Growth of Commerce

Gradually, such one-venture partnerships gave way to businesses organized with the idea of continuing for more than one venture. In addition, businesses grew in size and became more geographically dispersed as the population became more mobile. At that time accounting systems were required to (1) measure each partner's share of the ongoing business and (2) control business associates in remote locations.

At this point, we begin to see the development of two very important accounting concepts (theories): (1) the business entity concept and (2) the going concern concept. The **business entity concept** requires that an accounting system reflect information that identifies and summarizes only those economic events that pertain to a particular entity. That is, business and personal affairs should be kept separate. This concept is particularly important so that each partner can receive the correct share of the business's profit.

The **going concern concept** assumes that, absent any information to the contrary, the business will continue into the foreseeable future. That is, the business does not terminate at the end of a venture. This concept is important because it allows business records to continue from one venture and time period to another.

Pacioli and the Method of Venice

Next, we venture to 15th century Venice, Italy, where business is commonly conducted using currency rather than barter (goods). The arabic number system is widely used, enabling addition and subtraction to be done easily, and illiteracy is greatly reduced, allowing more people to become involved in business. The double-entry accounting system[4]—in which for every "debet dare" there is a "debet habere"—has evolved to the point where it is very much like the present-day system. *Debet dare* and *debet habere* are Latin terms meaning "should give" and "should have," respectively.

The first published work on the double-entry accounting system occurs in 1494 when several chapters concerning accounting are included in a mathematics book written by Luca Pacioli, who is commonly called the father of accounting.[5] Pacioli is well respected in Italy and his book is one of the first printed works using movable type. Pacioli does not invent double-entry accounting. Rather, he reports what merchants are commonly doing. This accounting method becomes known as the method of Venice. Because movable type allows easy reproduction, the availability of Pacioli's work encourages the use of the double-entry system throughout Europe. (We discuss the double-entry system in more detail later.)

At this point, two other important accounting concepts emerge: (1) the monetary unit concept and (2) the periodicity concept. The **monetary unit concept** asserts that money is the common measurement unit of economic activity. This concept is crucial to accounting because it enables records to be kept based on a common denominator. For example, rather than recording the number of cows and sheep available for trade, the accounting system reflects the monetary value of the livestock, whether it is lira, pesos, francs, yen, or another designated monetary unit. This makes determination of profit easier because monetary values, unlike sheep and cattle or other bartered goods that differ, can be added and subtracted.

The **periodicity concept** requires that the profits of the business be determined at regular intervals throughout the life of the business. This means the business does not have to end before determining its profits. This concept makes admission of new

---

[4]The double-entry system is a bookkeeping system that records two sides of each economic event. Appropriate numbers are entered into the accounting records twice, hence, the term *double entry*.

[5]Luca Pacioli, *Summa de Arithmetica, Geometria, Proportioni et Proportionalita.*

partners and departure of old partners easier because business profits are calculated at regular intervals. Thus, partners and potential partners can evaluate the success of the business while the business remains in operation.

Advent of the Corporation

Now we travel to the end of the 18th century when important economic and institutional changes have taken place. The Industrial Revolution, which started during the latter part of the 18th century in England, has been responsible for technological developments that eventually lead to changes in the systems of production, marketing, and financing.

Manufacturing firms that produce products from raw materials for sale to consumers are commonplace and distribution systems for these products are increasingly sophisticated. The development and use of machinery allow for mass production of inexpensive goods. Revolutions in transportation, such as railroads, create access to new markets for the goods. These changes precipitate the need for additional sources of funds, and financial institutions grow to meet this need. More elaborate accounting systems evolve in order to respond to the requirements of management and owners as well as those of the financial institutions that provide funds to the business.

As business increases, it is possible to accumulate wealth and have funds available for investment purposes. Corporations emerge to provide opportunities for investing in businesses without the obligation to oversee the day-to-day business operations. A **corporation** is a business entity that is legally separate and distinct from its owners. Corporations are attractive business ventures because they provide investors with **limited liability,** that is, the investors are not personally liable for the debts of the business. If the business fails, the most an investor can lose is the amount of his or her investment because the corporation's creditors cannot demand any additional monies from investors.

The advent of the corporation places additional requirements on the accounting system because investors, called *shareholders* or *stockholders*, have invested primarily for the return (profit) that the business operations generate. Thus, there is a need for frequent, periodic reporting on the status of the business and its operations since it is not feasible for investors to personally oversee operations. Therefore, investors must rely on the information generated by the accounting system to hold the managers accountable.

The evolution of the corporation also firmly entrenches the concepts of business entity, going concern, and periodicity because the corporation is *legally separate and distinct* from its owners. Furthermore, as the number and size of corporations grow, it becomes necessary to standardize external reporting practices—those communicated outside the organization—to ensure that all investors have access to information that allows comparisons among different investment alternatives.

PAUSE & REFLECT	Did the advent of the corporation help or hinder the development of accounting? Why?

Standardization of Accounting

The last leg of our journey brings us to the 20th century when two principal events propel standardization of accounting in the United States: (1) the Sixteenth Amendment to the Constitution in 1913 and (2) the stock market crash of 1929.

Sixteenth Amendment   The Sixteenth Amendment establishes a system of federal income taxation, which requires the periodic determination of income by individuals and businesses. It has a profound effect on the accounting profession because it requires records to support the determination of taxable income, which essentially makes accounting systems mandatory. It propels standardization in accounting because it limits the number of reporting options to make income determination more uniform across companies. However, it conflicts in many ways with generally accepted accounting practices of the time. For example, it requires businesses to report income on a calendar-year basis, which conflicts with the acceptability of reporting income on a fiscal-year basis in the accounting profession. A **fiscal year** is a year-long period that encompasses a natural business cycle and allows a business to prepare its required accounting information during its slowest business period. All businesses must compute and report income for tax purposes; however, only corporations are actually taxed on business income. Sole proprietorship and partnership income is taxed at the individual owner's level.

Stock Market Crash The stock market crash of 1929, followed by the Depression of the 1930s, leads to federal regulation of the securities market. Such regulation appears in the form of the Securities and Exchange Act of 1933, which requires that all companies issuing capital stock (shares of companies that indicate ownership rights) to the public must register with the Federal Trade Commission (FTC) and file and disclose to the public certain financial information. The Securities and Exchange Act of 1934 requires the submission of annual financial information for all publicly owned corporations[6] to a new commission called the Securities and Exchange Commission (SEC). This regulation limits the reporting options available for companies and requires full disclosure of financial results so that investors can compare companies. In general, the SEC allows the accounting profession to determine accounting rules for businesses.

Exhibit 1.1 shows the principal developments in accounting standardization from 1913 to 1973. Partly because of the controls that were instituted in the 1930s as a result of the stock market crash of 1929, the more recent stock market decline of 1987 had only a short-term impact on the U.S. economy. On October 19, 1987, the Dow Jones Industrial Average (a barometer of stock market movement) lost 508 points, nearly 20 percent of its value. Within a few months, however, the Dow recovered everything that it had lost. There was no depression. In fact, the economy of the late 1980s was quite strong.

PAUSE & REFLECT	Why is standardization in accounting practice necessary? Does it limit a company's ability to describe its financial results in a meaningful way? Why or why not?

GENERALLY ACCEPTED ACCOUNTING PRINCIPLES

As Exhibit 1.1 shows, the **Financial Accounting Standards Board (FASB)** is the third accounting rule-making body. The FASB is a full-time, paid group of professionals who are responsible for developing accounting standards for reporting to external financial statement users (investors and others outside the business). The FASB actively seeks input from businesspersons outside the accounting profession who are affected by its pronouncements as well as from practicing accounting professionals. This has not always resulted in smooth sailing for the FASB. Its pronouncements often generate great controversy within the business community. However, the FASB believes that outside input is important. Its predecessors, the APB and CAP, did not use outside input and were criticized because of this.

The pronouncements of the FASB are referred to as *Statements of Financial Accounting Standards (SFAS).* In addition to numerous accounting standards, the FASB has developed six *Statements of Financial Accounting Concepts*, which serve as a common framework for the development of future *Statements of Financial Accounting Standards.* The *SFAS*s, as well as the bulletins, opinions, and principles issued by the CAP and APB, comprise what are known as **generally accepted accounting**

---

[6]A corporation that issues ownership rights to the general public is commonly referred to as a *publicly owned corporation.*

EXHIBIT | 1.1

Standardization in
Accounting

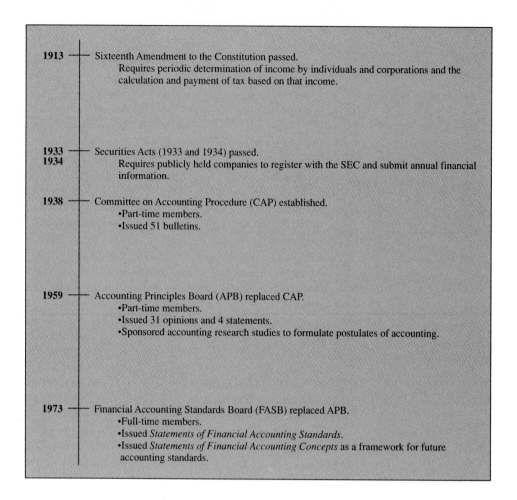

1913 ── Sixteenth Amendment to the Constitution passed.
          Requires periodic determination of income by individuals and corporations and the
          calculation and payment of tax based on that income.

1933 ── Securities Acts (1933 and 1934) passed.
1934   Requires publicly held companies to register with the SEC and submit annual financial
          information.

1938 ── Committee on Accounting Procedure (CAP) established.
          •Part-time members.
          •Issued 51 bulletins.

1959 ── Accounting Principles Board (APB) replaced CAP.
          •Part-time members.
          •Issued 31 opinions and 4 statements.
          •Sponsored accounting research studies to formulate postulates of accounting.

1973 ── Financial Accounting Standards Board (FASB) replaced APB.
          •Full-time members.
          •Issued *Statements of Financial Accounting Standards.*
          •Issued *Statements of Financial Accounting Concepts* as a framework for future
           accounting standards.

principles (GAAP). These principles direct acceptable accounting practice and are based on the four basic concepts (business entity, going concern, monetary unit, and periodicity) described previously.

The SEC officially recognizes GAAP as being authoritative and requires that the information filed with the SEC comply with GAAP. If a company's financial information is audited by a certified public accountant, it must comply with GAAP. **Auditing** is the process of examining a company's financial records by a CPA to ascertain whether they complied with GAAP. (See . . . of Interest Accounting Careers.)

The **American Institute of Certified Public Accountants (AICPA)** is a national organization which is actively involved in the development of accounting standards and sets auditing standards for public accounting firms. The AICPA, which administers the CPA examination, is the professional organization for all certified public accountants.

In recent years, the idea of standardization in financial accounting for external users has become internationalized. The **International Accounting Standards Committee (IASC)** is leading the way toward standardization of international accounting for external reporting. To date, compliance with international standards is voluntary, but a growing number of companies and countries are complying to improve comparability among international companies operating in various countries throughout the world.

PAUSE & REFLECT

Why do you think the SEC allows the accounting profession to establish generally accepted accounting principles (GAAP)?

BUSINESS IN THE 1990s

The basic purpose of business and therefore accounting has stayed the same throughout the centuries. People go into business to achieve their monetary and personal goals. They use accounting to measure their success by looking at their scorecard at the end of the year: What were sales? What were profits? Has the company paid off its debts? Is the company increasing its share of the market? How can the company improve its goods and services? How can the company attract the best people to be employees? Is it engaged in an endeavor that benefits society?

Advances in computers and telecommunications have made it easier for U.S. companies to do business around the world and for foreign companies to do business in the United States. In addition, the fall of Communism has opened up the emerging markets of Asia, Latin America, and Eastern Europe. Now, more than ever, accounting information is needed to enable businesses to compete and to allow investors to evaluate business results.

Investing in Business in the 1990s

While the basic purpose of business has not changed, the business world is very different today than it was a thousand years ago. For one thing, there were no **stock exchanges** (markets for buying and selling stocks) then. Take a look at your local newspaper and turn to the business section. Here, you can follow the "stocks" of literally thousands of companies organized as corporations. A **share of stock** is a certificate that represents ownership in the corporation. You'll see thousands of companies listed along with their stock prices, highs and lows for the year, ratio of price of the stock to earnings of the company, and so forth. Some of these companies trade on the New York Stock Exchange, the American Stock Exchange, and various regional stock exchanges. Other stocks trade on NASDAQ, the National Association of Securities Dealers Automated Quotations, a stock market essentially run by computer networks and brokerage firms.

Billions of shares of stock trade every year in these markets. If you have as little as a few hundred dollars, you can buy shares of stock in your favorite company and follow its progress every day in the newspaper. You are part owner of that company, whether it is a huge conglomerate such as General Electric Company with manufacturing operations throughout the world, or a fast growing new company, such as Fore Systems (makers of networked computer systems), which grew from a $100,000 investment in 1990 to a company with $75.6 million in sales in 1995.

With your shares of stock, you may have voting rights that allow you to express your opinion on major issues facing the company. To make sure that your interests are represented, public companies are audited by CPA firms, and the results are published in the company's annual report, which is mailed to shareholders. We examine an annual report in Chapter 2.

If you buy a share of stock at $100 and sell it for $120 in one year, there is a **return of investment,** or the receipt by the investor of the original amount invested, of $100. In addition, the investor would receive a **return on investment** of $20, the profit received on the owner's investment in the corporation. When the return on investment is stated as a percentage—for example, a 20 percent return ($20/$100)—this is known as the **rate of return** of the investment. Most stocks pay **dividends** (a distribution of corporate profits), offering shareholders an immediate return on investment. Typically, utility companies pay the highest dividends, as much as 5 percent, or $5 on a $100 stock. In contrast, fast growing companies typically do not pay dividends. Instead, management of such companies often reinvest the company's profits in the company rather than paying out dividends.

Companies also issue bonds to the public. A **bond** is a certificate, usually in denominations of $1,000, that represents the debt of the company. An **initial issue** (original sale) of bonds (or stocks) is typically accomplished through an investment banker who assists the company in selling the bonds to investors. Bonds pay interest—a series of payments that compensate the lender for the risk and the trouble of making the loan. Bonds can be held to maturity, or they can be traded in the secondary market, like stocks. A **secondary market** is an exchange where bonds (also stocks) are bought and sold after the initial issue. Although the bond's interest payments are fixed, the market value of a bond can fluctuate in value, depending upon the credit quality of the issuing company or the general level of interest rates. When interest rates rise, bond prices fall, because the fixed cash flow stream that the bond offers is less desirable compared to that offered by new bonds.

Because of the booming number of companies with bonds outstanding and shares of stock, another industry has arisen in recent years: **mutual funds.** A mutual fund is an investment company that pools the money from many individual investors and invests it for the common goal of receiving a quality rate of return. A mutual fund is an excellent vehicle for many people who would not be able to buy bonds or shares of stock on their own. In addition to having professional management, a mutual fund offers diversification to shareholders, which is an important investment principle. From a risk standpoint, it is better to invest in many different companies than just one. Finally, a mutual fund offers investors the ability to buy and sell shares with as little as a $50 investment thus providing access to stock exchanges for small investors.

Manufacturing, Merchandising, and Service in the 1990s

As discussed previously, a manufacturer takes a raw material such as steel and turns it into a finished product, such as a car. A merchandiser, such as an automobile dealer or a clothing retailer, buys finished goods from a manufacturer and sells them to consumers. A service company does not actually manufacture anything, rather, it performs a service. For example, an advertising agency develops a marketing strategy for the automakers and implements it by, among other things, buying commercial time on television.

Accounting firms, banks, hospitals, hotels, and utilities are other examples of companies that provide a service. Retailers such as Nordstrom and Bloomingdales are merchandise companies. Bristol-Meyers Squibb is a manufacturer of pharmaceuticals. Other manufacturers include defense contractors, furniture makers, and homebuilders.

Certain types of businesses are more susceptible to swings in the economy than others. Manufacturers tend to do as well as the economy. That means that their successes are cyclical. As a result, their stocks sell for a lower price than companies that are less affected by the economy. Another economic variable that affects big-ticket manufacturers such as automakers and homebuilders is the level of interest rates. Interest rates are the costs of borrowing money for a variety of time periods. As interest rates rise, automakers and homebuilders tend to suffer slower sales. The reason: People usually need to borrow money to buy their goods.

To a lesser extent, retailers are impacted by a sluggish economy. If, for example, the general population is lacking confidence in the future, then consumers will be less likely to spend a lot of money during the holiday season. In addition, retailers slash prices when business is slow. Although this stimulates sales, it cuts profitability.

Service companies tend to weather changes in the economy the best. Certainly, hospitals see just as many sick people when the economy is slow as when it is booming. Entertainment companies such as Disney tend to sell just as many movie tickets when the economy is slow.

What about This Service Economy?

Although much has been written about how the United States is becoming a service economy rather than a manufacturing economy, a glance at the 10 largest U.S. companies ranked by size shows a strong mix of manufacturing and service firms. According to *Business Week* of the five largest companies ranked according to stock market value, only AT&T is considered primarily service.[7] The largest company is General Electric, a multinational conglomerate (holding company) with 1994 profits of $5.9 billion. Second is AT&T (telecommunications) with 1994 profits of $4.7 billion. Other big manufacturers include the third largest company, Exxon (fuel), and the

---

[7]*Business Week*, March 27, 1995, p. 104.

fourth largest company, Coca-Cola (consumer products), which had profits in 1994 of $5.1 billion and $2.6 billion, respectively. Wal-Mart Stores (retailing) rounds out the top five largest companies with 1994 profits of $2.7 billion. Some large, primarily service companies include American International Group (1994 profits of $2.2 billion) and Bellsouth (1994 profits of $2.2 billion), both of which are telecommunications companies. Other large manufacturing companies include Procter & Gamble (1994 profits of $2.4 billion) and IBM (1994 profits of $3 billion). Large merchandising companies include Home Depot and Sears, Roebuck with 1994 profits of $604 million and $1.2 billion, respectively. True, most of these huge companies have been around for decades. But the ability to access the public markets has also made it possible for Microsoft, the eleventh largest company in 1994, to become an industry powerhouse.

Ownership Structures

The world of business is not just the giant public company with offices around the world. It is also the free-lance artist working at home, the innkeeper in Maine, and the lawyer, doctor, dentist, accountant, bricklayer, and candlestick maker earning a living as a sole proprietor. Small business throughout the country accounts for the lion's share of job growth. According to the Bureau of Labor Statistics, 74 percent of all businesses were operated as sole proprietorships in 1990.

Many professionals such as doctors, lawyers, and accountants, form partnerships in which they split the profits as well as the workload. A business partnership is like a marriage in many ways. Each partner has to compromise regarding the other person's strengths and weaknesses. In a partnership, as in a marriage, each partner has the power to act for all other partners, which is known as **mutual agency.** Mutual agency together with unlimited liability make partnerships risky ventures. A partnership agreement, therefore, is essential to protect the rights of the individual partners. If the partners do not draw up a partnership agreement, the affairs of the partnership are addressed in the **Uniform Partnership Act,** which governs the rights and obligations of partners. Partnerships sometimes "end in divorce" because the partners have a falling out, at which point one or more of the partners may become a sole proprietor. Partnerships are the least common form of business, accounting for only 8 percent of businesses in 1990 according to the Bureau of Labor Statistics.

Rather than raising money through the public markets, the sole proprietor usually starts a business with personal savings or money from friends and family. Just like a public company, a sole proprietor must be concerned with sales, profits, recruiting, market share, and so on. And the sole proprietor must keep track of cash flow, produce year-end financial reports, and have systems in place to make sure employees are accountable. The delicatessen owner must have a way to make sure the employee at the cash register isn't putting money in his own pocket when no one is looking. The doctor must make sure the clerical staff is sending the proper forms to the insurance companies so that the office is properly reimbursed.

Sometimes, it is advantageous for a small business to incorporate. Being a corporation has certain advantages, including limited liability for owners and tax advantages. But most corporations are privately held in this country—that is, there is no public stock, just private stock in the hands of a few owners. In 1990, corporations accounted for 18 percent of businesses in the United States.

Exhibit 1.2 illustrates the basic differences among sole proprietorships, partnerships, and corporations. Notice that although a partnership must have at least two owners, size does not distinguish business ownership structures. Also note that the corporation is the only form of business that is required to pay income taxes. This results in a situation commonly known as **double taxation** in which the profits of the corporation are taxed twice—once at the business level and again at the stockholder level (if the profits are distributed as dividends).

There are a number of other business forms that combine various characteristics of sole proprietorships, partnerships, and corporations. For example, a **limited partnership** is a partnership composed of one or more general partners and one or more limited partners. The general partner(s) are personally liable for the business,

EXHIBIT	1.2	Characteristics of Primary Ownership Structures		
		Sole Proprietorship	**Partnership**	**Corporation**
Unlimited life		no	no	yes
Limited liability		no	no	yes
Business taxation		no	no	yes
Legal entity		no	no	yes
One owner allowed		yes	no	yes
Service firms		yes	yes	yes
Merchandising firms		yes	yes	yes
Manufacturing firms		yes	yes	yes

while the limited partners' personal risk is limited to the amount of their investment in the partnership. An **S corporation** is a small business corporation owned by no more than 35 individuals in which the profits earned by the business are not subject to income tax at the corporate level. Rather, an S corporation's profits are taxed at the individual shareholder level regardless of whether the profits are distributed as dividends. A **limited liability partnership (LLP)** is a partnership in which the individual partners are responsible only for their own acts and the acts of those individuals under their control. Therefore, one partner in an LLP cannot be held responsible for the negligence of another partner. Many public accounting firms are organized as LLPs.

PAUSE & REFLECT

Economists often state that corporations do not pay income taxes because they pass the taxes on to the consumer. What do economists mean by this? Do you think this is true? Why?

Although there are several major forms of business, all of them have a common challenge when it comes to various ethical considerations. Now we turn our attention to some of these considerations.

A Host of Ethical Dilemmas

Many manufacturers actually make their goods in places such as Asia and Latin America where wages are lower. Nike, based in a suburb of Portland, Oregon, makes all of its shoes in the Far East. That raises the first of many interesting ethical dilemmas in business. Is it ethical to pay people $0.30 an hour in their country, rather than paying $10.00 an hour in the United States for the same labor? Critics would say that Nike and others are exploiting the people of the local country. Nike would counter by saying that the wages paid are at the going rate in the local market, and that it is serving its stockholders best by making the most profitable shoe possible.

Another ethical dilemma facing companies is the degree to which the stockholders' stake in the business has priority over other **external stakeholders.** External stakeholders are parties outside an organization who have an interest, or stake, in the organization. They include, in addition to stockholders, creditors, governmental units, suppliers, customers, and the general public. In addition, companies must also consider the priority of external stakeholders over **internal stakeholders.** Internal stakeholders are parties inside the organization who have a stake, or interest in the organization, such as employees and managers. (See Chapter 2 for more on both types of stakeholders.) Sometimes the interests of these groups of stakeholders collide. For example, should television companies that produce and broadcast violent or sexually suggestive programming take into account the impact of such programs on the general audience? If the answer is no, then these companies are favoring the interests of their shareholders over the interests of society in general. Should a company that is posting significant losses avoid massive employee layoffs? Here, the interests of the stockholders for profits conflict with the interests of employees for job security. Should an American company engage in bribery to secure a customer overseas, even though paying such "commissions" is a common practice in that local country? By doing so, the shareholders are being favored over the government.

Fortunately, in the vast majority of cases, the various stakeholders have similar goals. When the company is doing well, shareholders benefit with a higher stock price, creditors benefit by not having to worry about being paid, suppliers are kept busy, employees get raises, and the customer gets the best product possible. If the company tries to skimp on the product for short-term profitability, the customer will begin to look elsewhere. If the company treats its employees poorly, they will leave and, therefore, weaken the company. For Nike, the company is in the fortunate position of being extremely profitable—rewarding stockholders, creditors, the government, suppliers, employees, and customers with a shoe and other products that are most desired.

A Formula for Success

Regardless of the form or size of a business, there are certain attributes that most successful businesses possess. The business has to define a market and serve that market. It has to have a competitive advantage—a patent, a superior technology, or special skills. It has to sell or market itself to that market. And most importantly, it has to spend less money than it takes in.

For example, Susan T. is a CPA in solo practice. She is also a nurse by training. She believes that she has a competitive advantage in serving medical practices because she understands the unique needs of that market. In order to market her services, she attends local medical conventions and advertises in local medical publications. Because she has a special niche, she has a thriving practice. To take her practice to a higher level, she will eventually want to hire an associate, paying that associate a lower hourly rate than she charges her clients.

Successful businesses are using technology to become more efficient. Instead of hiring several accountants to run a business, many owners have installed accounting software that can be run by one person. By using technology, labor costs fall, and the company can price its products more competitively. Of course, technology, while good for business, is not necessarily good for workers, unless they are able and willing to be retrained.

Sometimes, unlike Susan T.'s case, a business has to change the definition of its market in order to survive. Some of the most successful U.S. corporations have created new markets in other parts of the world. By viewing their potential customers as being located throughout the world, they have vastly expanded their business opportunities. For example, Hewlett-Packard is successful because it has been able to reinvent itself as necessary in the highly competitive and rapidly changing environment of computer technology.

Finally, to be successful, a business must have capable employees empowered to do their jobs successfully. These employees provide five basic functions for business—marketing; human resources; production and operations; finance; and accounting and information systems.

The **marketing** functional area determines the wants and needs of consumers and devises a system for distributing the goods and services the customers demand. It is customer focused and governed by the four P's—product, price, promotion, and physical distribution. Marketing is concerned with issues such as global markets and customer satisfaction.

Human resources management is the function responsible for ensuring that capable employees are given the opportunities to succeed in the workplace. Human resources must be concerned with issues such as diversity in the workplace and employee empowerment.

The **production and operations management** function is responsible for planning, organizing, directing, and controlling the operations of the business. Production and operations occur at all levels throughout the company, from line managers responsible for overseeing production to the chief executive officer responsible for overseeing the entire company.

Finance is the functional area responsible for managing the financial resources of the business. It is concerned with issues such as when and how to raise money for the company and where to invest that capital.

Finally, **accounting and information systems** is the functional area responsible for providing the information for the other functional areas to enable them to do their jobs and for reporting the results to interested parties. This function is crucial since, without it, the other functional areas cannot operate. This is why accounting is commonly called the *language of business.*

ACCOUNTING AND CAREERS IN THE 1990s

Accounting is a career that involves, but is not limited to, numbers. Accountants are in demand by many different types of industries and perform diverse duties, ranging from preparing accounting reports to overseeing a company's quality control program. (See . . . of Interest Accounting Careers.)

Crunching the Numbers

There is a misconception that computers make accounting, traditionally referred to as *crunching the numbers,* unnecessary. True, there is software available that will perform some accounting functions. But in order to get the most out of software, it is still important to understand the accounting process itself and to have had the experience of doing the accounting tasks manually. Just because you have a calculator doesn't mean you don't need to understand the multiplication process.

Why Accounting?

An accounting course is like a course in English or history—it provides general knowledge that will make it easier for you to understand the world when you graduate from college. After taking this course, you should be able to use accounting software programs for your business and understand the impact of accounting transactions. On a more personal level, you should be able to gain insights and skills in handling your own business decisions. And you should be able to read an annual report so that you can be an intelligent consumer of various companies' stocks.

By taking this course, you may be embarking on the first of many accounting courses leading up to the certified public accountant (CPA) exam, the certified management accountant (CMA) exam, or other professional exams. You may use your accounting background as a lawyer, an engineer, a management consultant, a real estate broker, a hospital administrator, a professional athlete, a doctor, an entrepreneur, or someone with a financial responsibility of some kind. A larger dose of accounting is required for bankers and stockbrokers. The banker needs to be able to read financial statements with a critical eye to make sure that it is prudent to loan a company money. The stockbroker has to be able to read a company's financial statements to decide whether the company would be a wise investment. Are sales growing? Are profits growing? The answers to these and many other financial questions are provided by the accounting function.

Accounting: Useful for All Professionals

Accounting courses are certainly useful for a variety of careers within a company—purchasing agents, sales and marketing specialists, human resource managers, computer experts, and operations managers. All of these people need to understand the impact of their decisions on the company's profitability. The purchasing agent's skill in negotiating the prices of raw materials has a direct impact on the cost of goods produced. The degree to which the sales and marketing people cut prices in order to close deals has a direct impact on the company's total sales in dollars for the year. The human resource manager's decisions regarding employee benefits has a direct impact on the company's ability to attract key people, as well as the cost of hiring them. The computer specialists—otherwise known as management information services professionals—have a direct impact on the efficiency of the organization by providing top management with timely reports with which to make crucial business decisions. Finally, the operations manager must be familiar with budgets and how

One way to choose a career in accounting is by attending career fairs where professionals spend time talking with students about their occupations.

they relate to the quantity and price of raw materials, labor, and other costs. The information necessary to make these crucial business decisions is provided to these internal users by the accounting function.

If you decide to take even more accounting courses, then you'll be preparing yourself for several financial careers within the business environment. The **controller** is the company's chief accounting officer, responsible for preparing the company's financial statements, tax returns, payroll, and operating budgets. The **treasurer** is responsible for investing the company's money and for securing financing from creditors. The **chief financial officer (CFO)** is the member of top management of the company to whom the controller, treasurer, and internal auditor report. He or she works hand in hand with the company's chief executive officer. Even the CEO needs to understand accounting.

Regardless of what career you choose, accounting can be one of the most valuable disciplines to study because it provides a good foundation for many occupations.

SUMMARY

Business has evolved as technology has changed and as the population has become more mobile. Accounting, likewise, has developed over time as the needs of its users, both internal and external to the organization, have changed. Business in the 1990s is a dynamic environment characterized by global markets and rapidly changing technology. Accounting in the 1990s, as throughout history, is an integral part of business, providing the information necessary for businesses to operate in a constantly changing environment.

- There are four concepts crucial to accounting: (1) the business entity concept, (2) the going concern concept, (3) the monetary unit concept, and (4) the periodicity concept.

- The accounting profession determines generally accepted accounting principles (GAAP), and the Financial Accounting Standards Board (FASB) is currently the standard-setting body of the accounting profession.

- There are five functional areas in business: (1) marketing, (2) human resources management, (3) production and operations management, (4) finance, and (5) accounting and information systems.

ccountants are in demand by many different companies. Some accountants work for private companies, some work for public accounting firms, and others work in government or other not-for-profit entities.

PRIVATE ACCOUNTING

Private accounting refers to accounting in the individual business unit. For example, an individual may be employed as an accountant for Walt Disney Company. More accountants devote their time to private accounting than to either of the other two groups. IBM, United Telecom, Hartford Insurance, and other large companies employ thousands of people who perform accounting duties. On the other hand, the smallest organizations also have accounting needs that may be fulfilled by one or two individuals.

The CMA (Certified Management Accountant) designation is issued by the Institute of Management Accountants to persons demonstrating competence in the subject areas included in the field of management accounting. **Management accountants** provide information to internal stakeholders. The CIA (Certified Internal Auditor) designation is issued by the Institute of Certified Internal Auditors to persons demonstrating competence in internal auditing. **Internal auditors** are private accountants who assess the company's internal control system (discussed in Chapter 3), help external auditors (discussed next), and provide assistance in designing and implementing accounting information systems. Private accountants frequently possess one or both of these certifications as well as the certified public accountant designation discussed below.

PUBLIC ACCOUNTING

Public accounting refers to a variety of accounting services provided by an accounting firm for many different types of businesses. Instead of working for one particular business, a public accountant most often provides his or her services to a variety of clients. Public accountants provide three primary services—auditing, taxation, and management consulting.

Auditing services involve an independent assessment of whether a company's financial statements are prepared in accordance with generally accepted accounting principles. External auditors issue an opinion, which is part of the annual report that companies provide to external users. A "clean" opinion means that, in the opinion of the auditor, the financial information has been fairly presented in accordance with GAAP. Taxation services include tax preparation and planning. Management consultants provide advice on the design of accounting systems, evaluation of computer systems, and evaluation of controls used to safeguard the company's resources.

Public accountants who provide auditing services must possess a **certified public accountant (CPA)** certificate issued by the American Institute of Certified Public Accountants. A CPA certificate demonstrates competence in the field of public accounting, although many accountants in private as well as governmental accounting also possess a CPA certificate. Only a CPA can attest to the presentation of a publicly held company's financial information.

GOVERNMENTAL AND OTHER NOT-FOR-PROFIT ACCOUNTING

Governmental and other not-for-profit accounting includes accounting for governmental units (federal, state, or local) and other not-for-profit enterprises, such as the American Red Cross, educational institutions, and hospitals. The nature of these types of organizations, the sources and restrictions on their funds, and the requirements imposed on them by law present unique problems in accounting.

In the governmental accounting sector, opportunities exist for accountants to help administer the tax laws, investigate tax returns, and/or provide cost-benefit analysis of proposed and existing legislation. Some accounting opportunities are available with federal government agencies such as the Office of Management and Budget (OMB), the Securities and Exchange Commission (SEC), the Internal Revenue Service (IRS), and the Federal Bureau of Investigation (FBI). Although there is not a special certificate for government and not-for-profit specialization, many accountants in this field hold CPA, CMA, and/or CIA certifications.

KEY TERMS

accountability Responsibility

accounting and information systems function The functional area of business responsible for providing information to the other areas to enable them to do their jobs and for reporting the results to interested parties

accounting system A system used to identify, analyze, measure, record, summarize, and communicate relevant economic information to interested parties

American Institute of Certified Public Accountants (AICPA) The professional organization for all certified public accountants that is actively involved in the development of accounting standards and sets auditing standards for public accounting firms

auditing The process of examining a company's financial records by a CPA to ascertain whether they comply with generally accepted accounting principles

bond A certificate that represents the debt of a company

business The exchange of goods, services, and money, on an arm's-length basis, that results in mutual benefit or profit for both parties involved

business entity concept The concept that requires that an accounting system reflect information that identifies and summarizes only those economic events that pertain to a particular entity

certified public accountant (CPA) An accountant who can attest to the presentation of financial information of a publicly held company

chief financial officer (CFO) A member of top management to whom the controller, treasurer, and internal auditor report

controller The company's chief accounting officer

corporation A business entity that is legally separate and distinct from its owners

dividends A distribution of corporate profits

double taxation A situation in which the profits of corporations are taxed twice—once at the business level and, again, at the stockholder level if the profits are distributed as dividends

external stakeholders Parties outside an organization who have an interest, or stake, in the organization, such as stockholders, creditors, suppliers, customers, and the general public

finance function The function responsible for managing the financial resources of the company

Financial Accounting Standards Board (FASB) The standard-setting body responsible for developing accounting standards for reporting to external financial statement users

fiscal year A year-long period that encompasses a natural business cycle and allows a business to prepare its required accounting information during its slowest business period

generally accepted accounting principles (GAAP) The *Statements of Financial Accounting Standards,* bulletins, opinions, and principles that direct acceptable accounting practice

going concern concept The concept that assumes that, absent information to the contrary, the business will continue into the foreseeable future

human resources management function The function responsible for ensuring that capable employees are given the opportunity to succeed in the workplace

initial issue The original sale of stocks or bonds to investors

internal auditor A private accountant responsible for assessing the company's internal control system

internal stakeholders Parties inside the organization who have an interest, or stake, in the organization, such as employees and management

International Accounting Standards Committee (IASC) The group that is leading the way toward standardization of international accounting for external reporting

limited liability The condition which indicates that investors are not personally liable for the debts of the business

limited liability partnership (LLP) A partnership in which the individual partners are responsible only for their own acts and the acts of those individuals under their control

limited partnership A partnership composed of one or more general partners and one or more limited partners

management accountant An individual who provides information to internal stakeholders

manufacturing firm A company that produces products from raw materials for sale to consumers

marketing function The function responsible for determining the wants and needs of consumers and devising a system for distributing the goods and services they demand

merchandising company A company that obtains and distributes goods to consumers

monetary unit concept The concept that asserts that money is the common measurement unit of economic activity

mutual agency A situation in which each partner has the power to act for all other partners

mutual fund An investment company that pools the money from many individual investors and invests it for a common goal

partnership A business owned by two or more individuals who agree to share both the risks and rewards of business

partnership agreement An agreement that stipulates the rights and obligations of each partner and describes how to divide the partnership profits

periodicity concept The concept that requires that the profits of the business be determined at regular intervals throughout the life of the business

private accounting Accounting in the individual business unit

production and operations management function The function that is responsible for planning, organizing, directing, and controlling the operations of business

public accounting A variety of accounting services provided by an accounting firm for many different types of businesses

rate of return A return on investment stated as a percentage of the investment

return of investment The return of the amount invested

return on investment The return, or profit, received on the owner's investment

reward Possible future benefits of an action

risk Possible future sacrifices of an action

S corporation A small business corporation owned by no more than 35 individuals in which the profits earned by the business are not subject to income tax at the corporate level

secondary market An exchange where bonds and stocks are bought and sold after the initial issue

service firm A company that provides services to customers

share of stock A certificate that represents ownership in a corporation

sole proprietorship A business owned by one person whose personal possessions are at risk

Statements of Financial Accounting Standards (SFAS) Pronouncements of the Financial Accounting Standards Board

stock exchanges Exchanges for buying and selling stocks; for example, New York, American, and various regional exchanges

treasurer The individual responsible for investing the company's money and securing financing from creditors

Uniform Partnership Act The act that governs the rights and obligations of partners when a partnership agreement does not exist

QUESTIONS

1. Explain what a business is and why it exists.
2. Explain the concepts of risk and reward. How are they related?
3. Explain the concept of accountability. How can someone be held accountable?
4. What is an accounting system? How does information generated by an accounting system hold individuals and businesses accountable?
5. Explain the differences among sole proprietorships, partnerships, and corporations and give an example of each.
6. Explain the differences among service companies, merchandisers, and manufacturers and give an example of each.
7. Why is the business entity concept important to accounting?
8. Why is the going concern concept important to accounting?
9. What is the monetary unit concept and why is it important to accounting?
10. Does the monetary unit concept imply that a company must keep its accounting records in one currency? Why or why not?
11. What is the periodicity concept and why is it important to accounting?
12. How does a partnership agreement protect partners from mutual agency? Are partners protected if they do not prepare a partnership agreement? Why or why not?
13. Explain the concept of limited liability. Is it a positive or negative concept for the owner? Why?
14. Why were the Sixteenth Amendment and the stock market crash important to the development of accounting?
15. What is GAAP and why is it important?
16. What is the difference between a stock and a bond? Which is better for the investor? Why?
17. What is the difference between return on investment and return of investment?
18. Is an individual safer investing $1,000 in a mutual fund or $1,000 in General Motors? Why?
19. Does the economy affect service companies, merchandisers, and manufacturers differently? Why or why not?
20. Who are the external and internal stakeholders of business?
21. What are the five functional areas of business and what is the purpose of each?

22. What are customer satisfaction and employee empowerment?

23. Why did limited partnerships, S corporations, and LLPs develop?

24. Explain what is meant by the term *ethical dilemma* in business.

25. Business industry types are not mutually exclusive. Describe a business that is both a service and a merchandising firm. Describe a business that is both a merchandising and a manufacturing firm. Describe a business that is both a service and a manufacturing firm. Are there any businesses that play all three roles? Why or why not?

EXERCISES

E 1.1 Identify the risk and reward in the following situations.
   a. Skipping class to play golf.
   b. Skipping class for a club field trip.
   c. Computerizing your business or personal financial records.
   d. Going to graduate school instead of accepting a job offer.
   e. Telling an accounting client that you have found proof that an upper-level manager in the client's firm is embezzling the firm's money.
   f. Borrowing money from a bank (at the current interest rate) to purchase items for your business.

E 1.2 Identify the reward and risk of the following activities.
   a. Bunge jumping.
   b. Taking $5,000 to Las Vegas to gamble.
   c. Opening a fast-food restaurant.
   d. Skipping work.
   e. Borrowing money from a relative.
   f. Starting a private investigation business.

E 1.3 There are three primary ownership structures discussed in this chapter. List the advantages and disadvantages of each. If you were a business owner, which ownership structure would you choose? Why?

E 1.4 Dillards is major department store chain with locations in 20 states. In 1993, women's clothing and accessories made up 36 percent of its sales, men's clothing and accessories accounted for 18 percent of sales, children's and juniors' clothing was 12 percent, cosmetics sales amounted to 13 percent, and housewares, shoes, furniture, and other items made up the remaining 21 percent of sales. Dillards is a corporation traded on the New York Stock Exchange. Describe the stakeholders of Dillards, whether they are internal or external, and the stake each has in the business.

E 1.5 Walt Disney Company is a corporation traded on both the New York and Tokyo stock exchanges. Its sales are generated from theme parks, such as Walt Disney World, filmed entertainment, such as *The Lion King*, and consumer products, such as Mickey merchandise. Describe the stakeholders of Disney, whether they are internal or external, and the stake each has in the business.

E 1.6 The chapter discusses three business industry types (service, merchandising, and manufacturing). Classify the following businesses according to their business types.
   a. Sears, Roebuck & Co.
   b. Fisher-Price.
   c. Wal-Mart discount store.
   d. Your local grocery store.
   e. Taco Bell restaurant.
   f. Dugan & Sons Construction (residential construction).
   g. Coldwell Banker Real Estate.
   h. Dillards department store.
   i. Nike Athletic Shoes.

E 1.7 The chapter discusses three business industry types (service, merchandising, and manufacturing). Classify the following businesses according to their business types.
   a. Kraft.
   b. Peachtree Windows and Doors.
   c. First National Bank.

d. Flint Hills Legal Services.

e. Coopers and Lybrand accounting firm (a "Big Six" accounting firm).

f. Toyota Motors.

g. International Business Machines (IBM).

h. Microsoft, Inc.

i. Pizza Hut.

E 1.8 Describe companies from your hometown that have the following ownership structures; (1) sole proprietorship, (2) partnership, (3) corporation.

E 1.9 List as many well-known companies as you can think of that have the following ownership structures: (1) sole proprietorship, (2) partnership, (3) corporation.

E 1.10 Interview a marketing, management, or finance instructor to determine the role that individuals with these particular backgrounds play within an organization. Describe what you have discovered.

E 1.11 Interview a marketing, management, or finance instructor to determine the information used by individuals with these particular backgrounds within an organization. Describe what you have discovered.

E 1.12 The four basic accounting concepts (business entity, going concern, periodicity, and monetary unit) are related. Describe how.

E 1.13 Describe why the four basic accounting concepts (business entity, going concern, periodicity, and monetary unit) are necessary in order for corporations to exist.

E 1.14 Go to the library and investigate the Committee on Accounting Procedure and the Accounting Principles Board. Why were these bodies superseded? What did they accomplish while in existence?

E 1.15 Go to the library and investigate the Financial Accounting Standards Board. How many members does it have? What is the composition of its membership? How many *SFAS* has it issued? What is the process that the FASB uses to issue a standard?

PROBLEMS

P 1.1 Find, from a local or national news source, a business that has recently failed or has recently achieved great success. Answer each of the following questions regarding the business.

a. According to the source, what was the reasons(s) for the failure or success?

b. Did management cite anything they could have done to prevent the failure, or anything in particular that led to success?

c. Using 20/20 hindsight, identify some things that could have been done to prevent the failure or that might have led to the success.

P 1.2 Gretchen saved a portion of her earnings from the job she held during high school to help pay for college. Gretchen was very diligent about putting her money in the bank, but realizes that she is not going to have enough to pay for the five years of school she will need to prepare for a career in accounting. She is considering various other ways of financing her education. The options include:

1. Getting a part-time job, and working during school and breaks to earn the additional money.

2. Investing the money in her own small business. During high school she made tie-dyed shirts, brightly colored "baggy pants," and other popular clothing items for friends and family and believes she can turn this hobby into a business venture.

3. Obtaining loans through the financial aid office at her school. (These would be education loans with low interest rates and deferral of payments, but there are limits on the amount that can be borrowed each school year.)

Answer each of the following questions:

a. Choose one of the options above, considering the risks and rewards of each and your personal risk preference.

b. Is there a *combination* of options (those listed above or other options you've determined) that would better satisfy your risk and reward preferences?

c. Suppose the money Gretchen had available for school consisted not only of her personal savings, but also money from a relative (spouse or parent). How does this affect your risk and reward preferences and your final choice of option(s)?

P 1.3   In 1989, the *Exxon Valdez* ran aground off the shore of Alaska. Review news accounts of the accident to determine Exxon's stakeholders who were affected by this accident and how they were affected. Describe your findings.

P 1.4   In 1994, Dow Corning was subject to a class-action lawsuit. Review news accounts of the lawsuit to determine Dow Corning's stakeholders who were affected by the lawsuit and how they were affected. Describe your findings.

P 1.5   Obtain and review the January issue of *Forbes*, which contains the "Annual Report on American Industry." Answer each of the following questions:
   a. How many different industry types are listed?
   b. Which companies within each industry showed the largest sales for the 12-month period?
   c. Which industries created jobs during the 12-month period?
   d. Which industries suffered declines during the 12-month period?
   e. How does *Forbes* calculate growth?

P 1.6   Consult the January issues of *Forbes* for two consecutive years. Find the "Annual Report on American Industry" and answer the following questions:
   a. Were the same companies listed in each industry for the two years?
   b. Which companies stayed at the top of their respective industries for two years?
   c. Which companies experienced a turnaround in the two-year period?
   d. What companies were featured in the older of your two-year survey? How did these companies do in the most recent period?

P 1.7   Obtain the latest edition of *The Wall Street Journal*. Find the New York Stock Exchange information. Answer the following questions:
   a. What was the change in General Motors' stock price for the day?
   b. What was the change in IBM's stock price for the day?
   c. What information is given in the other columns?

P 1.8   Review *The Wall Street Journal* each day for one week. Find a company you are interested in and answer the following questions:
   a. What was the change in the company's stock price for the week?
   b. What were the highest and lowest selling prices for the company's stock during the week?
   c. Graph the changes in stock price for each day during the week. What does this graph indicate?

P 1.9   Assume you and some friends are going to start a new business. Determine the products or services you will offer. Write a plan for your business that describes the products or services you will offer, the prices you will charge, and how you will finance your business.

P 1.10   Assume you invest $1,000 for one year. Determine your return on investment and your return of investment in each of the following situations.
   a. You receive $980 at the end of the year.
   b. You receive $1,000 at the end of the year.
   c. You receive $1,050 at the end of the year.

COMPUTER APPLICATIONS

CA 1.1   Assume you invest $5,000 for one year. Use a computer spreadsheet package to determine how much money you will receive at the end of one year in each of the following situations.
   a. You receive a 100 percent return of capital and dividends of 5 percent.
   b. You receive a 100 percent return of capital and dividends of 8 percent.
   c. You receive a 90 percent return of capital.
   d. You receive a 100 percent return of capital and a 10 percent return on capital.
   e. You receive a 100 percent return of capital and a 12 percent return on capital.

CA 1.2   Assume you have taken a part-time job as a clerk in a local business. Mr. Gumble, the boss, hired you because you are taking an accounting class and he would like your help setting up an accounting system. Currently he is running the business out of his personal checking account and does not prepare any business financial reports. Use a computer word processing package to prepare a memo to Mr. Gumble explaining how and why his current business practices could be improved.

CASES

C 1.1   Select a company you are interested in and obtain a copy of its most recent annual report. Keep this report for your use while reading this textbook. Based on the information in the annual report, answer the following questions:
 a. What organizational structure does this firm use?
 b. What is the industry type (service, merchandising, or manufacturing) of the business?
 c. Who wrote (or is responsible for) the annual report and to whom is it addressed?
 d. Does the company do business domestically and/or internationally?

C 1.2   Consider the businesses in the town where your college is located. Select one that interests you (or one your instructor has selected) and prepare written responses to the following questions. Be sure your responses are specific to the business you have selected.
 a. Describe the function of the business. What products or service does it provide?
 b. What is the organizational form of the business? What do you think the owners considered as their risks and rewards?
 c. What do you think this company's strategic plan is? What type of intermediate goals should it have to achieve its strategic plan?

CRITICAL THINKING

CT 1.1   In the 1980s, much was written in the financial press about the inability of U.S. companies to compete with businesses from other nations such as Japan and Germany. Some of the arguments given were that American workers are lazy, American managers don't care about quality, and American business focuses too much on the short term. Prepare an argument supporting or refuting these claims.

CT 1.2   Critically evaluate the following argument:
"The business of business is business. Business should not be involved in social issues. It is the role of the government to control pollution and unemployment. It is the role of business to make a profit for its stockholders."

ETHICAL CHALLENGES

EC 1.1   In 1994, the tobacco industry came under attack by antismoking activists. Discuss the ethical dilemma faced by the tobacco industry. Be sure to consider all the stakeholders involved.

EC 1.2   In the early 1990s, the federal government began closing military bases in an effort to trim the defense budget. Discuss the ethical dilemma faced by Congress as it considers which bases to close. Be sure to consider all the stakeholders involved.

CHAPTER 2

Accounting and Its Role in Business

Learning Objectives

1. Distinguish between external and internal stakeholders and their respective needs for accounting information.
2. Describe how a company uses accounting subsystems to meet the needs of external and internal users.
3. Describe how a company uses the financial accounting subsystem to identify, analyze, measure, and classify accounting events.
4. Describe how a company uses the financial accounting subsystem to communicate the results of accounting events to external users.
5. Describe how a company uses the management accounting subsystem to communicate information to internal users.

The Walt Disney Company is a multinational corporation whose profits come from three major sources—theme parks and resorts, filmed entertainment, and consumer products. Disney has had great success with ventures such as Disney World in Orlando, Florida, and with films such as *The Lion King* and *Pocahontas.* It has also had some setbacks, such as Euro Disney in Paris, which underwent a financial restructuring in 1994.

With record revenues of $10.06 billion in 1994, Disney continues to be an international giant in filmed entertainment, theme parks and resorts, and consumer products. In 1984, Disney's revenues from countries other than the United States totaled $142 million, or 8.4 percent of total revenues. In 1994, Disney's overseas revenues, excluding Euro Disney, totaled $2.4 billion, or 23 percent of total revenues.[1] Disney's domestic and international revenue sources have changed over the years. In 1984, theme parks accounted for 75 percent of Disney's income, and filmed entertainment accounted for only 1 percent of income. By 1993, however, filmed entertainment accounted for 36 percent of income, while income from theme parks dropped to 43 percent.[2] In 1994, for the first time, revenues from filmed entertainment exceeded those from theme parks and resorts, accounting for $4,793.3 million (48 percent) of Disney's $10,055.1 million total revenues.

[1] The Walt Disney Company, 1994 Annual Report, p. 21.
[2] Maggie Mahar, "Not So Magic Kingdom," *Baron's*, June 20, 1994, pp. 29–33.

The success of Disney, particularly in the area of filmed entertainment, has also aided other companies. In 1988, Disney struck an alliance with Mattel, making it the official toy licensee for Disney. Due to the success of *The Lion King* and other projects, Mattel experienced skyrocketing sales of stuffed animals, figurines, and games with little or no advertising. Its Disney licensing division generates approximately $300 million in annual sales.[3]

Many different stakeholders, including the managers of Disney businesses, owners of Disney stock, creditors, business partners such as Mattel, and employees, are interested in the financial activities of the Disney Company. The accounting information system tracks these activities and communicates them to interested parties.

As discussed in Chapter 1, accounting is the language of business whose purpose is to provide relevant information to stakeholders. What does this mean, and why is it important? **Relevant information** has a logical connection to the ideas under consideration and, therefore, is capable of making a difference in the user's decision. Thus, what is relevant for one stakeholder group may be less important to another group. The needs of various stakeholders determine what information they deem relevant; therefore, in order to understand what relevant information is, first it is important to understand the information needs of external and internal stakeholders.

ACCOUNTING AND THE INFORMATION NEEDS OF EXTERNAL STAKEHOLDERS

Although external stakeholders include a broad set of people and organizations, they all have a common need for information. External stakeholders, for example, stockholders, creditors, governments, suppliers (vendors), and customers, do not see the day-to-day activities of managing the business. As a result, they, instead, must rely on information the business provides to communicate important events.

Businesses provide information to external stakeholders in a variety of forms, as shown in Exhibit 2.1. For example, stockholders and creditors receive financial statements, government authorities receive corporate income tax returns (Form 1120)[4] and employee tax information (Form 941), and government regulatory agencies, such as the Securities and Exchange Commission (SEC), receive required business information, including financial statements, on Form 10K. Suppliers and customers receive a wide variety of business information specific to various business transactions undertaken. We discuss the specific information needs of these external user groups, in turn, below.

Stockholders' and Creditors' Information Needs

Stockholders and creditors need information that indicates whether management is taking undue risks or operating inefficiently. Because stockholders and creditors supply the capital needed by the business, they need information to assess the safety and growth of their investment. That is, will they receive a return of, and a return on, their investment? Surveys conducted in 1973 and again in 1991 show that stockholders have changed their investment goals, as shown in Exhibit 2.2. In 1973, stockholders purchased more risky securities (31.5 percent were interested in speculative gains), indicating that stockholders were more interested in a large return on their invested capital. On the other hand, in 1991, stockholders were looking for secure

---

[3]Kate Fitzgerald, "Disney Aids Mattel in a 2-Legged Toy Race," *Advertising Age*, September 28, 1994, p. 33.

[4]Recall that sole proprietorship and partnership income is not taxed at the business level, rather this income flows through to the individual(s) and is taxed at the individual level.

EXHIBIT | 2.1

**Accounting Information
Provided to External Users**

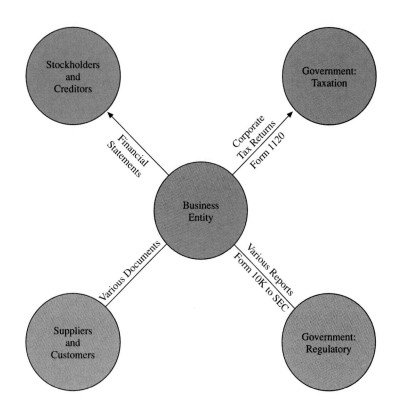

EXHIBIT | 2.2

Changing Investment Goals*

Stockholders' Investment Goals

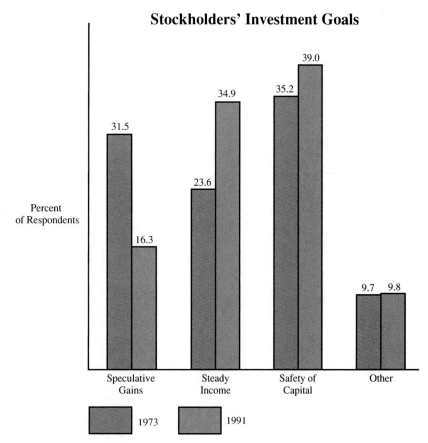

*Source: Marc J. Epstein, "Corporate Governance and Shareholders' Revolt," *Management Accounting*, August 1992, p. 33.

and stable investment opportunities (34.9 percent and 39 percent were interested in steady income and safety of capital, respectively), indicating that stockholders were more interested in a return of, and a smaller return on, their capital.

More recently, stockholders are also demanding more control over management. For example, in 1991, Sears, Roebuck & Company's stockholders voted to allow full confidentiality in stockholder voting and determined that all directors must own at least 1,000 shares of stock.[5] This allowed Sears' stockholders to vote for changes in the company's operations without undue pressure from management to vote a certain way. In addition, it required those individuals who serve on the board of directors to have a substantial direct financial interest in the consequences of their votes. Thus, Sears' stockholders increased their control over management by protecting themselves from undue management influence and by making members of the board of directors become owners who have a personal stake in Sears' business.

A principal source of information for stockholders and other external users is the corporate annual report sent by management to stockholders and available to other external stakeholders. **Annual reports** contain general information about the company as well as more specific, accounting-related information in the form of **financial statements.** *Financial statements* is a collective term used to describe the information communicated to external users by the financial accounting subsystem (discussed later). See the annual report of Walt Disney Company.

The annual report begins with a letter from Michael D. Eisner, chairman of Disney, to the owners and employees of Disney in which he discusses Disney's future. Following his letter is a section entitled "1994 Disney Year in Review," which highlights Disney's achievements during 1994 as well as its coming attractions. For example, it highlights major events by quarter and discusses Disney's growing international presence.

The "Financial Review" begins on page 39 of the annual report and contains Disney's financial statements and the notes to those statements. Disney includes three financial statements in its annual report: (1) the consolidated statement of income, (2) the consolidated balance sheet, and (3) the consolidated statement of cash flows, which we discuss in detail later in this chapter. The annual report ends with a statement of management's responsibility for financial statements and the report of the independent auditor.

Government's Information Needs

Communication with governments involves accounting in two important areas: taxation and regulation. Corporations pay income tax to various levels of government, particularly federal and state governments. In addition, both sole proprietorship and partnership income must be reported to the Internal Revenue Service on the individual owner's personal income tax return. The federal government bases its assessment of a corporation's income taxes on a set of rules found in the Internal Revenue Code. Tax authorities rely on businesses to provide supporting information to confirm the amount of taxes they owe to the government. This information is generated by the business's tax accounting subsystem (discussed later). Governments also require business to provide information about other taxes that are not obligations of the business itself, such as employee taxes. We discuss these taxes in later chapters.

In addition to taxes, businesses use accounting information to support their compliance with government regulations. For example, businesses submit Form 10K to the SEC. This report contains financial statements as well as other information required by the SEC such as disclosure of changes in the board of directors or major stockholders. Documentation submitted to the SEC is important to ensure that all stockholders have equal access to information about the company. Other regulatory requirements such as the documentation of expenditures for pollution prevention or cleanup also come from the regulatory accounting information subsystem (discussed later).

---

[5]Marc Epstein, "Corporate Governance and the Shareholders' Revolt," *Management Accounting*, August 1992, pp. 32–35.

Customers' and Vendors' Information Needs

Management uses the business's accounting information system to communicate with customers and vendors in different ways than it communicates with stockholders, creditors, and government. Because customers and vendors are regularly involved in transactions with the business, communications with them include many different types of documents on a frequent basis for these external parties. We discuss several of these documents in Chapter 3.

Communications in the Future

Even as we move toward a world where electronic messages replace paper ones, businesses and the external parties with whom they transact will continue to communicate using accounting information. The technological changes from a paper-based communication system to an electronic system of communication affect the speed and form of the communication about transactions between the business and its external stakeholders. However, the substance of the communications, that is, information about the business, its products and services, and its success or failure, remains essentially the same in most accounting information systems.

ACCOUNTING AND THE NEEDS OF INTERNAL STAKEHOLDERS

Internal stakeholders such as managers and employees need accounting information to help plan the business activities required to meet the business's goals and to evaluate whether the goals are being met. Thus, internal stakeholders use accounting information primarily to make decisions about future business operations. This contrasts with the primary use of information by stockholders and other external parties whose decisions are made primarily about how the business operated in the past.

Internal stakeholders have wide-ranging needs for accounting information. Although they have access to and use the same information generated by the accounting subsystems for external stakeholders, much of their information needs are not captured in the financial statements generated for external stakeholders. Their information needs are met by the management accounting subsystem (discussed later).

For example, assume that the production management team at Walt Disney studios has to make decisions about what costumes and sets to use for a new motion picture. The team needs information to determine whether to make the costumes and sets internally or whether to hire an outside company to provide these items. This decision requires the accounting department to gather the relevant information, such as the expected cost of making the sets internally versus the expected cost of buying them from an external supplier. Regardless of the decision reached by the production managers, it is necessary, at some point, to evaluate their decision to assess the results and determine whether the correct decision was made. This type of evaluation requires accounting information as its basis. For example, assume the production team decides to make the costumes and sets internally. The evaluation process would include comparing the actual cost of making these items to the estimated cost of buying them. Such evaluation of the actual results becomes an important part of planning effectively for the future.

THE ACCOUNTING INFORMATION SYSTEM

To ensure that users get the type of information they need, when they need it, the accounting information system has four related subsystems designed to provide relevant information to external and internal users. The accounting subsystems are:

- The **financial accounting subsystem,** designed to communicate financial information to external users, primarily stockholders and creditors.
- The **management accounting subsystem,** designed to provide information to internal users, primarily employees and managers.
- The **tax accounting subsystem,** designed to provide tax and other information regarding taxes to governments.
- The **regulatory accounting subsystem,** designed to provide required information (reports) to regulatory agencies such as the SEC.

EXHIBIT | 2.3

The Subsystems of an
Accounting Information
System

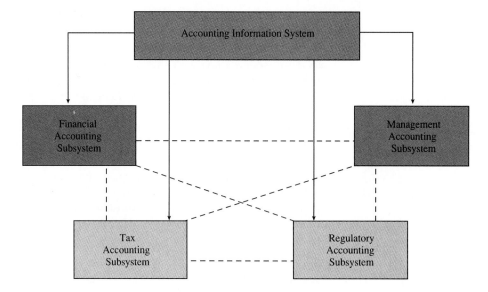

Exhibit 2.3 illustrates the relationship among these subsystems of the accounting information system. These subsystems share some of the same information and have the same primary purpose—to provide users with relevant information. Thus, they interact as denoted by the dashed lines connecting the subsystems shown in the exhibit. Yet, each subsystem also has a slightly different purpose based on the respective users' needs. This enables the company to provide information to users without maintaining redundant accounting records. For example, all four accounting subsystems extract information concerning customers; however, customer-related information is communicated to various users in different ways.

We focus on the financial and management subsystems of accounting because these systems provide the basic information used by the other two subsystems. The additional required information generated by the tax and regulatory subsystems is beyond the scope of this book; however, it is important that you are aware of their primary purposes.

FINANCIAL ACCOUNTING SUBSYSTEM

The financial accounting subsystem is designed to provide relevant information to external stakeholders. The information provided by this subsystem is commonly referred to as **financial accounting information.** Since external stakeholders need information to evaluate how the business, as a whole, performed in the past, the financial accounting subsystem must capture, record, and report the effects of past economic events on business. In order to do this, the financial accounting subsystem is used to identify, analyze, measure, and record economic events. The events are then summarized and communicated to external stakeholders. For example, Disney records the amount of daily attendance receipts at Walt Disney World and reports its theme parks' income, in total, for a period of time to stockholders and other interested parties.

How Do Companies Use the Financial Accounting Subsystem to Identify and Analyze Relevant Events?

To answer this question, we must first understand economic events themselves. Then, we can discuss how to identify and analyze accounting events.

Economic Events   An **economic event** describes a situation that occurs which, when acted on, affects an entity's wealth. For example, a decision to rent or buy a house, is an economic decision. There are benefits and sacrifices related to each decision alternative that affect the renter or purchaser's rights and obligations. The benefits of buying a house include the right to live in the house, pride of ownership, and the right to sell the house at a later date. The sacrifices of buying the house include the obligation to pay property taxes, the monthly mortgage payments, and the obligation to maintain the property. Alternatively, the benefits of renting include the right to leave at the end of the lease term, the lack of long-term financial commitments, and the lack of obligation for routine repairs. The sacrifices of renting include the obligation to make rental payments, potential disputes with the landlord, and the chance that the lease may not be renewed. Since the benefits and sacrifices affect your wealth, the decision, when acted on, becomes an economic event. The same is true regarding the economic events of a business.

Identifying and Analyzing Accounting Events **Accounting events** are economic events that possess three special qualities. An accounting event must:

1. Be specific to an economic entity.

2. Be capable of being measured in financial terms.

3. Have two effects that create or change the rights and/or obligations of the entity.

If the event does not possess *all three qualities*, it does not qualify as an accounting event. We describe each of these qualities, in turn.

Specific to an Economic Entity

This quality stems from the business entity concept discussed in Chapter 1. For an accounting event to be specific to an economic entity, it must have a direct impact on the economic entity for which accounting records are kept. For example, assume that Disney sells the movie, *The Lion King, Part 2* to video stores throughout the country. This is an accounting event for Disney because it is specific to Disney and also has the other two qualities presented above. On the other hand, for Time Warner, a competitor of Disney, it is not an accounting event because it is not specific to Time Warner.

Capable of Being Measured in Financial Terms

Second, an accounting event must be measurable in financial terms. This results from the monetary unit concept. For example, assume that Disney has agreed to sell 100,0000 copies of *The Lion King, Part 2* to Blockbuster Video, but it has not determined a selling price for the video. Since this event cannot yet be measured in financial terms, it would not be an accounting event even though it is specific to Disney.

PAUSE & REFLECT   If Disney gave Blockbuster *The Lion King, Part 2* in exchange for a building site for a new theme park, would this be an accounting event?

Two Effects That Create or Change the Rights and /or Obligations of the Entity

Last, an accounting event must have two effects that create or change the business's rights and/or obligations. We analyze this final quality by using the performance test. Most accounting events involve exchanges between two accounting entities. (We discuss exceptions later.) These exchanges consist of two stages—the promise stage and the performance stage. In the promise stage, one party offers to do a specific thing, and the other party accepts the offer. In the performance stage, one or both parties do what was promised in the promise stage. An accounting event does not occur until the exchange results in performance by one or both parties.

For example, assume that Disney offers to sell 100,000 copies of *The Lion King, Part 2* to Blockbuster Video for $1 million and Blockbuster accepts the offer. This is not an accounting event because it is merely an exchange of promises. However, as soon as Disney delivers the movie to Blockbuster, which indicates performance, an accounting event has occurred. As soon as Disney performs, its rights to 100,000 copies of the movie *The Lion King, Part 2* are reduced, and it creates a right to receive $1 million from Blockbuster. On the other hand, Blockbuster has created the right to receive 100,000 copies of the movie *The Lion King, Part 2* and has a related obligation to send Disney a check for $1 million when it accepts delivery of the videos.

Comprehensive Example of an Accounting Event Assume that Blockbuster Video sends Disney a check for $1 million prior to the delivery of 100,000 copies of *The Lion King, Part 2*. Since all three qualities are present, this is an accounting event. The event is specific to both Blockbuster and Disney (quality 1); it is measurable in financial terms (quality 2); and it has changed the rights and/or obligations of the specific entities (quality 3). Blockbuster has reduced its rights to cash by $1 million and has created a right to receive the movie from Disney. On the other hand, Disney has an obligation to send Blockbuster 100,000 copies of *The Lion King, Part 2* and has increased its rights to cash by $1 million.

How Is the Financial Accounting Subsystem Used to Measure and Classify Accounting Events?

We cannot talk about rights and obligations without a better understanding of how to measure and classify them. We measure the effect of an accounting event, like those described previously, at the cash or cash equivalent[6] cost of the item at the time the event takes place. That is, if an amount of cash is exchanged, the event is recorded at that amount. However, if cash is not exchanged, the event is recorded at the cash equivalent amount.

For example, assume that Disney purchases a new theme park by issuing shares of stock. In this case, there has been no exchange of money, so the event is recorded at the cash equivalent amount of the shares of stock issued. Assuming that 100,000 shares of stock with a current selling price of $45 were given in the exchange, the event would be recorded at $4.5 million.

In addition to measuring accounting events, the effects of these events must be classified so that they can be communicated to external parties. We classify the effects of accounting events as:

- **Assets,** the rights to use resources with expected future economic benefits.

- **Equities,** the obligations to transfer resources to others in the future.

Assets: The Rights to Use Resources **Assets** are rights to use resources (goods or services) that are expected to result in future economic benefit for the accounting entity. An asset represents the firm's exclusive *right to control* an expected future benefit. For example, if Disney has cash in the bank, it has the right to use that cash for any legal purpose; therefore, cash is an asset. If a company such as Blockbuster Video owes money to Disney Company, Disney has the right to receive that money. This right to receive money from a customer, an asset, is commonly referred to as **accounts receivable.** Disney also has an inventory of costumes, movie sets, and movie props. Disney has the right to use or sell these items as it desires; therefore, these items are assets, commonly known as **inventory** or **supplies.** Typically, we use the term *inventory* to denote assets that the company intends to sell to customers, while *supplies* are assets the company intends to use, such as office supplies. Finally, Disney owns theme parks, such as Disney World, and the copyrights (legal rights to produce and sell literary or artistic work) to motion pictures and television shows. See Disney's annual report for a description of these items. Since Disney has the right to use or sell these items, they are assets. Assets, such as theme parks that have physical substance and expected useful lives of many years are commonly called **property, plant, and equipment.** Assets, such as copyrights that are legal rights expected to last many years are commonly known as **intangibles** because they have no physical substance. Many companies classify their assets as **current assets,** which are those expected to be converted to cash or consumed within a year, or **long-term assets,** which are assets that are expected to be used for more than a year. Therefore, assets such as cash, accounts receivable, and inventory are current assets while property, plant, and equipment and intangibles are long-term assets.

---

[6]The cash equivalent amount is the amount of cash *that would have been exchanged* had the event been conducted for cash.

Equities: The Obligations to Transfer Resources **Equities** are a business's obligations to transfer resources to other parties at some future date. Equities are commonly divided into two groups:

- **Liabilities,** the obligations to transfer a measurable amount of resources or services in the future to providers of goods (money and other property) and services other than owners.

- **Owners' equity,** the obligation to transfer the company's residual resources to owners in the event the company ceases operations.

A liability is an obligation to transfer a measurable amount of resources to employees and other providers of goods and services, such as creditors, government agencies, or customers. For example, assume that Jeremy Irons provided the voice of Scar in *The Lion King, Part 2* but Disney did not immediately pay him the $750,000 he required for his services. In this case, Disney has a liability because it owes a salary to an employee, Jeremy Irons. **Salaries payable** is a liability representing the company's obligation to employees for salaries and wages.

As another example, assume that Disney has purchased costumes and sets costing $675,000 from a costume supplier, but has not yet paid for the items. Disney has a liability, known as accounts payable, because it is obligated to pay the costume supplier. **Accounts payable,** then, is a liability representing the company's obligations to external suppliers of goods or services.

Finally, assume that Disney borrowed money from the bank to finance its next movie. Disney has an obligation to repay the bank at some point in the future.[7] This liability is commonly referred to as **notes payable** and represents the company's obligation to repay amounts borrowed from outside parties.

Companies commonly classify liabilities as **current liabilities,** or those expected to be discharged within a year, or **long-term liabilities,** which are those expected to be discharged after a year. Thus, accounts payable and salaries payable are current liabilities while notes payable due in five years is a long-term liability.

PAUSE & REFLECT

How is the accounts receivable of the seller related to the accounts payable of the buyer when a sale is made on account? Explain.

---

[7]Disney is also obligated to pay the bank any interest charged on the loan. Interest on loans is discussed in detail later in this text.

Owners' equity is an obligation to transfer the company's **residual resources** (resources remaining after all liabilities have been met) to the owners of the business in the event the business ceases operations. This obligation is represented in two ways: (1) the potential return of capital and (2) the potential return on capital.

First, the owners contribute resources to the business, referred to as **contributed capital,** which entitles them to receive any assets remaining after business liabilities are met. It does not, however, *guarantee* that owners will receive assets, therefore, the amount and timing of this obligation are uncertain.

Second, the business exists to provide a return on capital contributed by its owners. This return (profit) is generated by business operations, discussed below in the section "Revenue, Expense, and Income." If the business chooses to use this profit rather than give it to the owners, it is known as **retained earnings.** Recall that the profits the business distributes to its owners are called *dividends.* Retained earnings, then, is the accumulated profits of the entity less dividends distributed to owners. Businesses are not required to give owners a return, so both the amount and timing of the obligation to owners represented by retained earnings are uncertain.

The Effects of Accounting Events   Notice from these examples that every accounting event has *two* monetarily equal effects on the business entity, which results in the creation or changes in assets and/or equities. Notice also that the monetary measurement of the event occurs at the time of the event by using the cash or cash equivalent amount. The design of the financial accounting subsystem allows the company to capture and communicate *both* monetary effects of accounting events. This duality results in the following equality:

$$\text{Assets} = \text{Equities}$$

This equality means that the total assets of the company must, at all times, equal the total equities of the company. Therefore, for each and every accounting event, the *total change in assets* must equal the *total change in equities.* Since equities are divided into two components (liabilities and owners' equity), we can also state the following, which is known as the **accounting equation:**

$$\text{Assets} = \text{Liabilities} + \text{Owners' equity}$$

To illustrate, assume that Disney Corporation borrows $500,000 from a bank to open a new Disney Outlet store. This is an accounting event because it is specific to Disney, measurable, and changes the business's rights and/or obligations. Disney receives an asset, the right to cash, $500,000, and incurs an equity, the obligation to repay $500,000 to the bank. Thus:

$$\text{Assets} = \text{Liabilities} + \text{Owners' equity}$$
$$+500,000 = +500,000 + \qquad 0$$

Now, assume that Disney issues capital stock to raise an additional $300,000. This is also an accounting event. Disney increases its assets, the right to cash, by $300,000, and increases its owners' equity, the obligation to return capital to its owners, by $300,000. This latter event has the following effects on the accounting equation:

$$\text{Assets} = \text{Liabilities} + \text{Owners' equity}$$
$$+300,000 = \qquad 0 \quad + \quad +300,000$$

Now that you know how to identify, analyze, measure, and classify accounting events, we look more closely at owners' equity events and the return generated by business operations. The discussion of how to record accounting events in the financial accounting information subsystem takes place in Chapter 7.

Revenue, Expense, and Income Simply stated, a **revenue** is the amount earned by a company for providing goods and services to customers, while an **expense** is the amount incurred in an attempt to generate revenue. The difference between revenue and expense in a certain time period is called **accounting income** or **net income** (profit).

The net income is the return on the capital provided by creditors (liabilities) and owners (owners' equity). After all the liabilities have been met, that is, after there is a return of and return on creditor's capital, any remaining profit belongs to the company's owners. This is why owners are said to have a **residual interest,** which is the interest remaining after all the company's obligations have been met.

Revenues, which increase income, increase the firm's obligation to its owners. On the other hand, expenses, which decrease income, decrease the firm's obligation to its owners. We measure income periodically based on the business's fiscal year, which is an application of the concept of periodicity discussed in Chapter 1.

Analyzing and Measuring Revenue and Expense Events Recall that the financial accounting subsystem analyzes two sides of every accounting event. Since a revenue is the amount earned by a company for providing goods or services, we define a **revenue event** as (1) *either* an increase in assets or a decrease in liabilities *and* (2) an increase in owners' equity resulting from the operations of the business. Since an expense is the amount incurred by a company attempting to generate revenue, we define an **expense event** as (1) *either* a decrease in assets or an increase in liabilities *and* (2) a decrease in owners' equity resulting from the operations of the business.

For example, assume that the ticket receipts of Disney World are $50,000 for one week and that theme park employees have earned, but have not been paid, wages of $12,000. The effects of these events are shown below:

	Assets	=	Liabilities	+	Owners' equity
Revenue event:	+50,000	=	0	+	+50,000
Expense event:	0	=	+12,000	+	−12,000
	+50,000	=	+12,000	+	+38,000

Note that in the revenue event, there is an increase in assets *and* an increase in owners' equity, and that in the expense event, there is an increase in liabilities *and* a decrease in owners' equity. Also observe that after each event the equation balances, that is, total assets equal total liabilities plus owners' equity.

PAUSE & REFLECT	Refer to the example above. If these are the only two events during the period, how much is Disney's income?

As another example, assume that the Disney sells merchandise inventory such as Mickey Mouse sweatshirts, which cost $50,000, to customers for $87,500 cash. In this case, two measurable events occur. One event concerns the revenue generated from the sale of the merchandise. In this case cash increases by $87,500 and owners' equity increases by $87,500.

	Assets	=	Liabilities	+	Owners' equity
Revenue event:	+87,500	=	0	+	+87,500

The other event concerns the merchandise inventory that Disney used up (sold) to generate the revenue. This expense is known as **cost of goods sold,** which represents the company's cost of the products sold to customers. Cost of goods sold decreases owners' equity.

	Assets	=	Liabilities	+	Owners' equity
Expense event:	−50,000	=	0	+	−50,000

Finally, consider the revenue-generating events that take place in a manufacturing company. In companies such as Ford Motor Company, the company purchases raw materials, such as steel, and converts these materials into cars by using labor and other resources. When the products are finished, they can be sold to car dealerships.

The amounts incurred to obtain the raw materials and convert them into cars are assets to the company until the cars are sold. For example, assume that Ford purchases $75,000 of steel from U.S. Steel and that U.S. Steel will send Ford a bill next month. This event results in an increase in **raw materials inventory** and an increase in accounts payable of $75,000 and, therefore,

$$\text{Assets} = \text{Liabilities} + \text{Owners' equity}$$
$$+75,000 = +75,000 + 0$$

Raw materials inventory is an asset that represents the company's right to use raw materials. This asset is inventory because the company intends to use the raw materials to make products that are sold to customers.

Subsequently, Ford uses $50,000 of steel, $25,000 of labor, and $80,000 of other resources to produce cars. Assume that Ford has paid for other resources in cash, but has not yet paid its employees. When Ford uses the steel, labor, and other resources in production, it creates a new asset called **work-in-process inventory**, which represents the company's right to use partially completed products. The event results in an increase in work-in-process inventory of $155,000 ($50,000 + $25,000 + $80,000), a decrease in raw materials inventory of $50,000, a decrease in cash of $80,000, and an increase in salaries payable of $25,000 and, thus,

$$\text{Assets} = \text{Liabilities} + \text{Owners' equity}$$

+155,000		
− 50,000		
− 80,000		
	+25,000	
+ 25,000 =	+25,000 +	0

Now assume that cars costing $120,000 are finished and transferred to the warehouse. This event creates another asset known as **finished goods inventory**, which represents the company's right to use finished products. Finished goods inventory increases by $120,000 while work-in-process inventory decreases by $120,000. Hence,

$$\text{Assets} = \text{Liabilities} + \text{Owners' equity}$$

+120,000		
−120,000 =	0 +	0
+0 =	+0 +	0

Again, the asset effects are off-setting and the accounting equation remains in balance. Note also that this accounting event is not an exchange between two parties—it is an internal exchange.

Finally, assume that cars costing $60,000 are sold to dealerships for $90,000 on accounts receivable. As with a merchandising company, this event results in two measurable events—one that is a revenue event, and one that is an expense (cost of goods sold) event. These events are reflected below:

	Assets =	Liabilities +	Owners' equity
Revenue event:	+90,000 =	0 +	+90,000
Expense event:	−60,000 =	0 +	−60,000
	+30,000 =	+0 +	30,000

Notice that this revenue event results in an increase in assets *and* an increase in owners' equity, while this expense event results in a decrease in assets *and* a decrease in owners' equity. Thus, the accounting equation is in balance.

Now that you understand how to analyze asset, liability, and owners' equity events, we look at how companies communicate their effects to external users.

How Does the Financial Accounting Subsystem Communicate Accounting Events?

The purpose of the financial accounting subsystem is to communicate relevant information to users through a company's financial statements. Both the form and content of these financial statements is determined by generally accepted accounting principles, as discussed in Chapter 1. The four primary financial statements of concern to external users are (1) the income statement, (2) the statement of owners' equity, or the statement of retained earnings, (3) the balance sheet (statement of financial position), and (4) the statement of cash flows. In addition, the annual report, which contains the financial statements, also includes notes to the financial statements, which provide supplementary information vital to the understanding of the statements.

Income Statement   The purpose of the **income statement** is to report to external users the revenues, expenses, and resulting net income for a particular period of time. External users often want to compare the results of one time period with those of previous periods. Therefore, companies often publish comparative financial statements that show the results of operations for three to five consecutive periods. Exhibit 2.4 shows Disney's consolidated income statements for 1992–94. Notice that the most recent period is presented first.

This statement is called a *consolidated statement of income* because it represents the income generated from many different companies in the Disney corporate family in one total set of (consolidated) numbers.

The 1994 income statement shows that the revenues of Disney from theme parks and resorts, filmed entertainment, and consumer products were $10,055.1 million for the fiscal year ended September 30, 1994. The expenses of Disney for this same time period were $8,089.4 million. This results in income, which is labeled operating income, of $1,965.7 million. Operating income is the return generated from Disney's operations during the 1994 fiscal year.

Notice that the income statement reports other revenue and expense items such as interest expense and investment and interest income. These items represent revenues and expenses from sources other than continuing business operations. The resulting 1994 net income was $1,110.4 million. We discuss these other sources of income later in this textbook.

Several notes contain information relevant to the income statement. For example, note 1 (see Walt Disney Company's annual report) describes when Disney recognizes revenue, and note 6 discusses income taxes. We discuss the content of notes in more detail later in this textbook.

Statement of Owners' Equity   The **statement of owners' equity** is designed to show external users the changes that occurred in owners' equity for the period of time covered by the income statement. The statement of owners' equity provides a link between the income statement and the balance sheet. The income (loss) shown on the income statement is also presented in the statement of owners' equity as an increase (decrease) in owners' equity during the period. The ending balance in owners' equity is shown on the balance sheet (discussed next). Sometimes companies do not present the changes in owners' equity (called *stockholders' equity* for corporations) as a formal statement. Rather, they present such information in the footnotes to the financial statements.

Exhibit 2.5 shows the information concerning changes in stockholders' equity for Disney Company as presented in note 8, "Stockholders' Equity." Notice that it indicates the amounts of contributed capital, referred to as *common stock* and *paid-in capital*, which we discuss later in this textbook, and the retained earnings at the beginning of the period. These amounts increase or decrease by the amount of changes that occurred during the 1994 fiscal year, resulting in the ending balances. In this case, retained earnings decreases by the payment of dividends ($153.2 million in fiscal 1994) and increases by the net income generated during the 1994 fiscal period ($1,110.4 million), resulting in an ending balance of $5,790.3 million. Notice that the amount of net income that increases retained earnings is the same amount shown on the income statement in Exhibit 2.4.

EXHIBIT | **2.4** | **Walt Disney Company's Income Statement**

Consolidated Statement of Income
Years Ended September 30, 1992, 1993, and 1994
(in millions, except per share data)

	1994	1993	1992
Revenues:			
Film entertainment	$ 4,793.3	$3,673.4	$3,115.2
Theme parks and resorts	3,463.6	3,440.7	3,306.9
Consumer	1,798.2	1,415.1	1,081.9
	10,055.1	8,529.2	7,504.0
Costs and expenses:			
Filmed entertainment	3,937.2	3,051.2	2,606.9
Theme parks and resorts	2,779.5	2,693.8	2,662.9
Consumer products	1,372.7	1,059.7	798.9
	8,089.4	6,804.7	6,068.7
Operating income:			
Filmed entertainment	856.1	622.2	508.3
Theme parks and resorts	684.1	746.9	644.0
Consumer products	425.5	355.4	283.0
	1,965.7	1,724.5	1,435.3
Corporate activities:			
General and administrative expenses	162.2	164.2	148.2
Interest expense	119.9	157.7	126.8
Investment and interest income	(129.9)	(186.1)	(130.3)
	152.2	135.8	144.7
Income (loss) from investment in Euro Disney	(110.4)	(514.7)	11.2
Income before income taxes and cumulative effect of accounting changes	1,703.1	1,074.0	1,301.8
Income taxes	592.7	402.7	485.1
Income before cumulative effect of accounting changes	1,110.4	671.3	816.7
Cumulative effect of accounting changes:			
Pre-opening costs	—	(271.2)	—
Postretirement benefits	—	(130.3)	—
Income taxes	—	30.0	—
Net income	$ 1,110.4	$ 299.8	$ 816.7
Amounts per common share:			
Earnings before cumulative effect of accounting changes	$ 2.04	$ 1.23	$ 1.52
Cumulative effect of accounting changes			
Pre-opening costs	—	(.50)	—
Postretirement benefits	—	(.24)	—
Income taxes	—	.06	—
Earnings per share	$ 2.04	$ .55	$ 1.52
Average number of common and common equivalent shares outstanding	545.2	544.5	536.8
Pro forma amounts assuming the new accounting method for pre-opening costs is applied retroactively			
Net income		$ 571.0	$ 672.7
Earnings per share		$ 1.05	$ 1.25

Other corporations present a **statement of retained earnings** rather than a statement of owners' equity. The statement of retained earnings shows only the changes that affected retained earnings during the period. Those changes affecting contributed capital are not shown.

Balance Sheet (Statement of Financial Position)   The purpose of the **balance sheet,** or **statement of financial position,** is to show the assets, liabilities, and owners' equity that exist at the end of the period covered by the income statement. The balance sheet, then, is a snapshot of the company at a particular point in time. The balance sheet illustrates the accounting equation: Assets = Liabilities + Owners' equity.

EXHIBIT	2.5	Walt Disney Company's Stockholders' Equity

Stockholders' Equity
(in millions)

	Shares	Common Stock	Paid-in Capital	Retained Earnings
Balance at September 30, 1991	548.6	$13.7	$536.0	$3,950.5
Exercise of stock options, net	3.6	.1	70.1	—
Dividends ($.20125 per share)	—	—	—	(105.3)
Net income	—	—	—	816.7
Balance at September 30, 1992	552.2	13.8	606.1	4,661.9
Exercise of stock options, net	12.4	.3	256.2	—
Dividends ($.24 per share)	—	—	—	(128.6)
Net income	—	—	—	299.8
Balance at September 30, 1993	564.6	14.1	862.3	4,833.1
Exercise of stock options, net	2.4	.1	68.8	—
Dividends ($.2875 per share)	—	—	—	(153.2)
Net income	—	—	—	1,110.4
Balance at September 30, 1994	567.0	$14.2	$931.1	$5,790.3

Exhibit 2.6 illustrates Disney's balance sheets for the fiscal years ended September 30, 1993 and 1994. Again, the most recent year is shown in the first column. Assets are presented first, followed by liabilities and stockholders' equity. Also notice that the total assets ($12,826.3 million) equal the total liabilities plus stockholders' equity.

Take a moment to look at the asset section of the balance sheet. Notice the line denoted "theme parks, resorts, and other property, at cost: attractions, buildings, and equipment." This amount, $7,450.4 million, represents the total cash or cash equivalent cost of these items. Directly beneath this amount is a line denoted "accumulated depreciation." **Accumulated depreciation** represents that portion of the cost of these assets that has been used in an effort to generate revenues. When assets such as properties are used to generate revenues, a portion of the cost of the assets is deducted from the revenues of the period as **depreciation expense,** which is included in the expenses of the income statement. The amount of each year's expense is accumulated (combined) with that of previous years on the balance sheet. In this way, the user can ascertain both the amount originally incurred for the assets as well as the estimated amount of the assets used to generate revenues. Notice that accumulated depreciation and depreciation expense do not refer to a loss in value or usefulness of the asset. Rather, they are simply the recognition that the asset has been used in an attempt to generate revenues.

Now look at the liabilities and stockholders' equity section of Disney's balance sheet. Disney reports accounts payable and other accrued (summed) liabilities of $2,474.8 million at the end of fiscal 1994. Also notice that under the heading "stockholders' equity" Disney reports preferred stock of $0 and common stock of $945.3 million. Preferred and common stock are two classes of stock, which we discuss in more detail later in this text. Disney has been authorized to issue preferred stock; that is, it has permission to do so, but it has not yet issued any stock of this type. On the other hand, it has issued 567 million shares of common stock. Finally, there is an amount shown on the balance sheet as "retained earnings." This amount represents the accumulated income of the company that has not been distributed to owners in the form of dividends. This amount agrees with the amount shown in the last line of Exhibit 2.5.

Statement of Cash Flows The **statement of cash flows** is designed to show the business's cash inflows and cash outflows as well as the net change in the business's cash balance for the same time period as the income statement. The cash inflows and outflows are divided into three sections depending on their source: (1) net cash flows from operating activities (activities required for the actual operations of the business), (2) net cash flows from investing activities (activities resulting from investing innonoperating[8]

---

[8]Nonoperating assets and liabilities are not directly connected to the generation of revenues and expenses.

EXHIBIT | 2.6 | Walt Disney Company's Balance Sheet

Consolidated Balance Sheet
At September 30, 1993, and 1994
(in millions)

	1994	1993
Assets		
Cash and cash equivalents	$ 186.9	$ 363.0
Investments	1,323.2	1,888.5
Receivables	1,670.5	1,390.3
Merchandise inventories	668.3	608.9
Film and television costs	1,596.2	1,360.9
Theme parks, resorts and other property, at cost:		
Attractions, buildings, and equipment	7,450.4	6,732.1
Accumulated depreciation	(2,627.1)	(2,286.4)
	4,823.3	4,445.7
Projects in progress	879.1	688.2
Land	112.1	94.3
	5,814.5	5,228.2
Investment in Euro Disney	629.9	—
Other assets	936.8	911.3
	$12,826.3	$11,751.1
Liabilities and Stockholders' Equity		
Accounts payable and other accrued liabilities	$ 2,474.8	$ 2,530.1
Income taxes payable	267.4	291.0
Borrowings	2,936.9	2,385.8
Unearned royalty and other advances	699.9	840.7
Deferred income taxes	939.0	673.0
Stockholders' equity:		
Preferred stock, $.10 par value; Authorized—100.0 million shares;		
issued—none		
Common stock, $.025 par value; authorized—1.2 billion shares;		
issued—567.0 million shares and 564.6 million shares	945.3	876.4
Retained earnings	5,790.3	4,833.1
Cumulative translation adjustments	59.1	36.7
	6,794.7	5,746.2
Less treasury stock, at cost—42.9 million shares and 29.1 million shares	1,286.4	715.7
	5,508.3	5,030.5
	$12,826.3	$11,751.1

assets from the period), and (3) net cash flows from financing activities (activities relating to amounts received from, or paid to, owners and received by, or paid for, nonoperating liabilities for the period). We discuss the differences among operating, investing, and financing activities in more detail in Chapter 3.

Exhibit 2.7 shows Disney's consolidated statement of cash flows. It shows cash inflows and outflows (the latter is denoted with parentheses) from operating investing, and financing activities. Cash inflows from operating activities were $2,807.3 million during fiscal 1994, while cash outflows from investing activities were $2,886.7 million. Take a moment to look at the financial section. It indicates that Disney received $1,866.4 million from borrowing activities during fiscal 1994 and used $153.2 million to pay dividends to owners.

PAUSE & REFLECT	What other activities are indicated in the financing section on the statement of cash flows?

Finally, the statement of cash flows indicates the net change in cash and cash equivalents (see note 1 in Walt Disney Company's annual report, which explains how Disney defines a cash equivalent). This amount is added to the beginning balance of cash and results in the ending balance of cash ($186.9 million), which is the same amount of cash shown on the balance sheet in Exhibit 2.6.

EXHIBIT | 2.7 | Walt Disney Company's Statement of Cash Flows

Consolidated Statement of Cash Flows
Years Ended September 30, 1992, 1993, and 1994
(in millions)

	1994	1993	1992
Cash provided by operations before income taxes	$3,127.7	$2,453.9	$2,132.0
Income taxes paid	(320.4)	(308.7)	(293.9)
	2,807.3	2,145.2	1,838.1
Investing activities:			
Film and television costs	(1,433.9)	(1,264.6)	(606.0)
Investments in theme parks, resorts, and other property	(1,026.1)	(813.9)	(599.1)
Euro Disney investment	(971.1)	(140.1)	(68.3)
Purchases of investments	(952.7)	(1,313.5)	(1,008.5)
Proceeds from sales of investments	1,494.1	841.0	409.0
Other	3.0	31.4	(50.8)
	(2,886.7)	(2,659.7)	(1,923.7)
Financing activities:			
Borrowings	1,866.4	1,256.0	182.8
Reduction of borrowings	(1,315.3)	(1,119.2)	(184.6)
Repurchases of common stock	(570.7)	(31.6)	—
Dividends	(153.2)	(128.6)	(105.3)
Other	76.1	136.1	71.4
	(96.7)	112.7	(35.7)
Decrease in cash and cash equivalents	(176.1)	(401.8)	(121.3)
Cash and cash equivalents, beginning of year	363.0	764.8	886.1
Cash and cash equivalents, end of year	$ 186.9	$ 363.0	$ 764.8

The difference between income before taxes and cumulative effect of accounting changes as shown on the consolidated statement of income and cash provided by operations before income taxes is explained as follows.

	1994	1993	1992
Income before income taxes and cumulative effect of accounting changes	$1,703.1	$1,074.0	$1,301.8
Cumulative effect of accounting changes	—	(514.2)	—
Charges to income not requiring cash outlays:			
Depreciation	409.7	364.2	317.3
Amortization of film and television costs	1,198.6	664.2	442.3
Euro Disney	110.4	350.0	—
Other	121.1	163.5	155.4
Changes in:			
Receivables	(280.2)	(211.0)	(161.5)
Merchandise inventories	(59.4)	(146.1)	(151.2)
Other assets	(81.5)	197.0	(121.3)
Accounts payable and other accrued liabilities	146.7	544.4	335.9
Unearned royalty and other advances	(140.8)	(32.1)	13.3
	1,424.6	1,379.9	830.2
Cash provided by operations before income taxes	$3,127.7	$2,453.9	$2,132.0
Supplemental cash flow information:			
Interest paid	$ 99.3	$ 77.3	$ 62.5

See notes to consolidated financial statements.

How Do Financial Statements Reflect Accounting Events? An Example

To illustrate the connection between accounting events and the financial statements, we will follow a company through three fiscal periods. We show the effects of the accounting events on the company's assets, liabilities, and owners' equity on a spreadsheet. Immediately following the spreadsheet, we show the effects of the events on the financial statements. We illustrate the statement of retained earnings rather than a statement of owners' equity to highlight the changes in retained earnings due to net income and dividends.

Note that for purposes of the income statement, the labels for events are:

(R) for revenue

(E) for expense

For purposes of the statement of cash flows, the labels for events are:

(O) for operating activities

(I) for investing activities

(F) for financial activities

Any returns given to the owners are labeled (D) for dividends.

Period 1   The following events occur:

1. The owners invest $10,000 cash in the business.

2. The business pays $500 rent on office space for the period.

3. Customers pay the business $6,000 for services the business rendered during the period.

4. The business pays $4,000 for employees and other services used during the period.

5. At the end of the period, the business buys a computer for $3,000.

Exhibit 2.8 illustrates these events in a spreadsheet format; it also presents the related financial statements. Take a moment to study the connection between the spreadsheet and the financial statements. Notice that all the events listed in the cash column are reported on the statement of cash flows. The cash flows are divided into three sections—cash flows from operations ($1,500), cash flows from investing (–$3,000), and cash flows from financing ($10,000). The total of the assets and liabilities and owners' equity columns on this spreadsheet appears on the balance sheet resulting in total assets of $11,500 ($8,500 + $3,000) and total liabilities plus owners' equity of $11,500. All of the events labeled (R) and (E) in the retained earnings column appear on the income statement, resulting in net income of $1,500 ($6,000 – $4,500), which also appears on the statement of retained earnings.

PAUSE & REFLECT	Why is there no depreciation expense shown for period 1?

Period 2   The following events occur:

1. The company borrows $5,000 from the bank.

2. Customers pay $3,500 for services received from the business.

3. The company performs $4,500 of services and bills the customers.

4. Employees earn $4,000 but are only paid $3,000 because the last week's paychecks have not been processed.

5. At the end of the period, the company recognizes one-quarter of the cost of the computer ($3,000 × 1/4 = $750) as depreciation expense.

Exhibit 2.9 illustrates these events in a spreadsheet format followed by the related financial statements. Notice that the ending balances of the assets, liabilities, and owners' equity from period 1 carry over to period 2 as beginning balances. This reflects the going concern concept introduced in Chapter 1. Therefore, period 2's ending balances for assets, liabilities, and owners' equity are calculated as the beginning balances plus and minus the changes that occur as a result of events during period 2. The accumulated depreciation column appears in the asset section of the spreadsheet as a negative amount because it is reflected as a deduction from the cost of the computer shown on the balance sheet.

Take a moment to be sure you understand the connection between these accounting events and their reporting in the financial statements. In particular, notice that the net cash flow from operations ($500) *does not* equal the net income of the period ($3,250) because operating cash flows result from collections from customers and payments made to suppliers for services, while net income results from the amount of revenues less expenses.

EXHIBIT 2.8

Example Company:
Accounting Events of Period 1

	Assets		=	Liabilities	+	Owners' Equity	
	Cash	Computer				Contributed capital	Retained earnings
Beginning balance	$ 0	$ 0				$ 0	$ 0
Events:							
1	+10,000 (F)					+10,000	
2	− 500 (O)						− 500 (E)
3	+ 6,000 (O)						+ 6,000 (R)
4	− 4,000 (O)						− 4,000 (E)
5	− 3,000 (I)	+ 3,000					
Ending balance	$ 8,500	$ 3,000	=		+	$10,000	$ 1,500

Example Company
Income Statement

Revenue	$6,000
Less expenses	4,500
Net income	$1,500

Example Company
Statement of Retained Earnings

Beginning balance	$ 0
Add net income	1,500
Ending balance	$1,500

Example Company
Balance Sheet

Assets		Liabilities and Owners' Equity	
Cash	$ 8,500	Contributed capital	$10,000
Computer	3,000	Retained earnings	1,500
Total assets	$11,500	Total liabilities and owners' equity	$11,500

Example Company
Statement of Cash Flows

Cash flows from operations:	
Cash collections from customers	$ 6,000
Cash paid for services	(4,500)
Net cash flow from operations	1,500
Cash flows from investing:	
Cash paid for computer	(3,000)
Cash flows from financing:	
Cash received from owners	10,000
Net increase in cash	8,500
Beginning cash balance	0
Ending cash balance	$ 8,500

EXHIBIT 2.9

Example Company:
Accounting Events of Period 2

	Assets				=	Liabilities		+	Owners' Equity	
	Cash	Accounts receivable	Computer	Accumulated depreciation		Wages payable	Notes payable		Contributed capital	Retained earnings
Beginning balance	$ 8,500		$ 3,000						$10,000	$ 1,500
Events:										
1	+ 5,000 (F)						+ 5,000			
2	+ 3,500 (O)									+ 3,500 (R)
3		+ 4,500								+ 4,500 (R)
4	– 3,000 (O)									– 4,000 (E)
5				– 750		+ 1,000				– 750 (E)
Ending balance	$14,000	$ 4,500	$ 3,000	– $ 750	=	$ 1,000	$ 5,000	+	$10,000	$ 4,750

Example Company
Income Statement

Revenue	$8,000
Less expenses	4,750
Net income	$3,250

Example Company
Statement of Retained Earnings

Beginning balance	$1,500
Add net income	3,250
Ending balance	$4,750

Example Company
Balance Sheet

Assets		Liabilities and Owners' Equity	
Cash	$14,000	Wages payable	$1,000
Accounts receivable	4,500	Notes payable	5,000
Computer	3,000	Contributed capital	10,000
Less: Accumulated depreciation	(750)	Retained earnings	4,750
Total assets	$20,750	Total liabilities and owners' equity	$20,750

Example Company
Statement of Cash Flows

Cash flows from operations:	
Cash collections from customers	$ 3,500
Cash paid for services	(3,000)
Net cash flow from operations	500
Cash flows from financing:	
Cash received from bank loan	5,000
Net increase in cash	5,500
Beginning cash balance	8,500
Ending cash balance	$14,000

PAUSE & REFLECT

Refer to Exhibit 2.9. What are the specific items resulting in the differences between cash flows from operations and net income? Why?

Period 3 The following events occur:

1. The company buys $600 of office supplies from ABC Supplies. ABC will send a bill for the supplies at the beginning of the next month.

2. The company pays the employees their remaining wages from last period ($1,000).

3. The customers who were billed last period pay the company the entire amount owed ($4,500).

4. The company provides $8,000 in services to customers of which $3,000 is paid in cash.

5. Employees are paid $5,000.

6. Services costing $1,200 cash are used to generate revenue.

7. The company pays owners $500.

8. At the end of the period, the company recognizes one-quarter of the cost of the computer ($750) as depreciation expense.

9. At the end of the period, the company has used one-third of the supplies purchased this period ($600 × 1/3 = $200), which results in supplies expense.

PAUSE & REFLECT

Take a moment before moving on and check your understanding of the effects of period 3's events. Set up a spreadsheet and record the ending balances from Exhibit 2.9. Then enter the events of period 3 and present the resulting financial statements.

Exhibit 2.10 illustrates the events of period 3 along with the resulting financial statements. Again, observe the difference between cash flows from operations on the statement of cash flows ($300) and net income on the income statement ($850). There are no dividends shown on the income statement because they are not expenses of the business. Rather, dividends are a return on capital for owners and are not incurred in an effort to generate revenue. However, when supplies are used in an effort to generate revenue, it is referred to as *supplies expense*. Finally, observe that the total accumulated depreciation amount has increased to $1,500 because it now represents two periods' depreciation expense.

Now that you understand how the financial accounting subsystem operates, we turn our attention to the management accounting subsystem.

MANAGEMENT ACCOUNTING SUBSYSTEM

The management accounting subsystem is designed to provide relevant information to internal stakeholders. The information provided by this subsystem is commonly referred to as **management, or managerial, accounting information.** Since internal stakeholders need information to make decisions about future business operations, the management accounting subsystem must identify and report information which is relevant for the particular decision maker. For example, have you ever wondered how a corporation determines what items to sell and the number of items to order and distribute to its stores? For such planning decisions, companies use the management accounting subsystem to identify, analyze, and communicate relevant information that is measured in terms of its expected future value. When evaluating actions previously taken, the company uses the management accounting subsystem to identify, analyze, and communicate relevant information that is measured in terms of its past value. Typically, management accounting information is not provided to external users because the nature of its content is confidential and the company may not want competitors to have access to it.

How Is Management Accounting Information Classified?

Management accounting information is commonly classified as follows:

- **Cost,** something that requires the use of business resources.

- **Benefit,** something that provides business resources and/or reduces resource consumption.

EXHIBIT 2.10 Example Company: Accounting Events of Period 3

		Assets				=	Liabilities			+	Owners' Equity	
	Cash	Accounts receivable	Supplies	Computer	Accumulated depreciation	=	Wages payable	Accounts payable	Notes payable	+	Contributed capital	Retained earnings
Beginning balance	$14,000	$4,500		$3,000	− 750	=	$1,000		$5,000	+	$10,000	$4,750
Events:												
1	− 1,000 (O)											+ 8,000 (R)
2			+ 600				− 1,000	+ 600				− 5,000 (E)
3	+ 4,500 (O)	− 4,500										− 1,200 (E)
4	+ 3,000 (O)	+ 5,000										− 500 (D)
5	− 5,000 (O)											− 750 (E)
6	− 1,200 (O)											− 200 (E)
7	− 500 (F)											
8					− 750							
9			− 200									
Ending balance	$13,800	$5,000	$400	$3,000	− 1,500	=	$ 0	$ 600	$ 5,000	+	$10,000	$ 5,100

Example Company
Income Statement

Revenue	$8,000
Less expenses	7,150
Net income	$ 850

Example Company
Statement of Retained Earnings

Beginning balance	$4,750
Add net income	850
Deduct dividends	(500)
Ending balance	$5,100

Example Company
Statement of Cash Flows

Cash flows from operations:

Cash collections from customers	$ 7,500
Cash paid for services	(7,200)
Net cash flow from operations	300

Cash flows from financing:

Cash paid to owners	(500)
Net decrease in cash	(200)
Beginning cash balance	14,000
Ending cash balance	$13,800

Example Company
Balance Sheet

Assets		Liabilities and Owners' Equity	
Cash	$13,800	Wages payable	$ 0
Accounts receivable	5,000	Accounts payable	600
Supplies	400	Notes payable	5,000
Computer	3,000	Contributed capital	10,000
Less Accumulated depreciation	(1,500)	Retained earnings	5,100
Total assets	$20,700	Total liabilities and owners' equity	$20,700

A cost may be incurred to obtain assets or expenses or to fulfill obligations. For example, if Disney plans to purchase a new theme park by issuing stock of $200 million, the *cost* of the park is $200 million. On the other hand, if Disney pays its employees $30,000 for their services, the *cost* of the employees' wages, an expense, is the $30,000 given up to obtain the services. Likewise, if Disney pays its stockholders a dividend of $500,000, the *cost* of the dividend is the $500,000 cash given up.

A benefit is an increase in assets or revenues or decrease in obligations. For example, Disney's new theme park would include benefits such as the revenues from ticket sales and the increase in the market value (what the assets could be sold for) of the park.

In general, in business, if the financial benefits of a particular action outweigh the costs, the general recommendation would be to take the action. For example, if Disney plans to purchase a new theme park, it will determine the expected future benefits of the park, such as revenues from ticket sales and the value of the assets of the park, and compare this amount to the cost of purchasing and maintaining the park. If the expected benefits are greater than the costs, the company should consider purchasing the theme park. Sometimes, however, costs and benefits are not measurable solely in financial terms. For example, in 1994 Disney considered building a historical theme park in Virginia. However, the citizens of the area did not support the idea. Many believed that Disney would mar the natural beauty of the area and increase traffic congestion and air pollution. The efforts of the citizens caused Disney to reevaluate its decision. In this case, the costs to Disney's reputation if it built the Virginia theme park outweighed the benefits to be gained from the park, so Disney did not build the park.

How Is Management Accounting Information Different from Financial Accounting Information?

The information provided to internal stakeholders by the management accounting subsystem differs from that provided to external parties on four primary dimensions: (1) the type of information, (2) the level of detail needed, (3) the type of report provided, and (4) the time frame for the decision. We will look at each of these dimensions separately.

Type of Information Provided   The management accounting subsystem, unlike the financial accounting subsystem, often communicates nonfinancial data, that is, quantitative information not stated in dollars and cents. For example, managers often need information about the number of hours worked on a particular project, the quantity of raw materials expected to be used in production, and the number of defective units produced in a day. Each of these items can be stated in dollars, for example, the cost of labor used, the cost of raw materials, and the cost of defective units. Yet, using dollars may not be relevant in these circumstances.

If the business decision maker is trying to determine whether a particular project can be completed on time, he or she should consider the number of hours required to complete the project. Which information is more relevant to this decision maker—the number of hours worked on the project to date or the cost of labor incurred on the project to date? In this case, the number of hours (nonfinancial quantitative information) is more relevant.

If Disney is deciding whether to open a new theme park, the number of customers expected may be more relevant than the amount of expected ticket receipts because the number of customers may be a better indicator of future success than ticket prices, which can change. Finally, if the marketing manager of Disney is evaluating the success of its latest movie, the number of tickets sold may be a better measure of success than the revenues generated from ticket sales because ticket prices vary across the country.

Level of Detail   The level of detail needed by internal users varies widely. Some internal users need information that is very specific and detailed, while others need more general information. The level of detail needed depends on the nature of the decisions being made.

For example, if Disney is attempting to increase the sales of Mickey Mouse collectibles, an individual salesperson needs specific information about sales at each of the *stores within the salesperson's territory* because this person is responsible for sales in each thical business decisions sometimes relate to issues in which the interests of a company's various business stakeholders conflict. For example, is it ethical for a company operating in another country to offer bribes to local government officials if this is acceptable business practice in that country? If an employee overhears that his or her company plans to take over another company, can this employee ethically act on this information by purchasing the stock of the target company?

Many companies have codes of ethical conduct, which employees are expected to understand and follow, to help individuals deal with situations such as these. Often a company's internal auditors are asked to review the company's policies and determine whether systems are in place that encourage employee compliance with the ethical standards. While company policies regarding ethical conduct vary, there are three general models of ethical decision making commonly used as the framework for corporate ethics.

The **utilitarian model** indicates that the company should undertake actions that result in the greatest good for the greatest number of stakeholders. Under this model, the company must determine the benefits and sacrifices of a given action and its effect on various stakeholders and choose the action with the most benefits and the least amount of sacrifices. The practical difficulty of using this model is determining if an action that benefits many stakeholders and harms other stakeholders is ethical. For example, if a domestic company moves its manufacturing facilities to another country in order to take advantage of less expensive labor, is this ethical? This action benefits consumers by providing them with less expensive products but hurts the local economy where the manufacturing facilities had been located.

The **rights model** states that the company should undertake actions that do not violate the basic, inherent rights of *any*

stakeholder. These rights include the right to equal protection, privacy, and due process. The rights model requires that the company determine the effects of a given action on the rights of the various stakeholders. The practical difficulty of this model lies in determining whether one individual's rights can be violated in order to protect the rights of others. For example, does a company have the right to test its employees for drug use if this violates their rights to privacy?

Finally, the **agency model** states that the managers of the business are the agents of the stockholders and, therefore, should undertake those actions that are in the stockholders' best interests. Under this model, the company must determine the impact of a given action on the stockholders. The practical problem presented here is that often the interests of the manager and the stockholders conflict. Therefore, the manager might undertake actions that are, in the short run, in the manager's best interests, but are, in the long run, possibly detrimental to the stockholders. For example, is it ethical for a manager to increase sales during the current period by selling on accounts to customers whose credit rating is unknown if there is a chance that these sales will be uncollectible in the future?

As you can see, these types of ethical decisions confronting personnel in various organizations are complex and give rise to the need for ethical guidelines rather than stringent rules. The internal auditor must determine whether the company has policies regarding ethical conduct in place, whether employees are aware of the policies, and the extent to which accounting and other systems support and encourage ethical decision making. The internal auditor reports his or her opinions regarding the existence of ethical policies to the appropriate member(s) of management with the authority to enforce such policies. Internal auditors do not establish ethical policies, nor do they enforce ethical guidelines—those actions are the responsibility of management.

---

individual store. On the other hand, the salesperson's boss, the sales manager, needs sales information concerning each *territory within his or her district* because this manager is responsible for the district, not for individual stores' sales. Finally, the marketing manager needs aggregated (summary) sales information about each *district within the region* because he or she cannot oversee each individual territory or store.

As you can see, the level of detail needed decreases as the span of responsibility increases. In general, there is a greater need for more aggregated data when there is a wide span of responsibility and a greater need for more detailed data at lower organizational levels.

Type of Report   The type of report provided to internal users also differs from the reports required by external users. Individual companies are free to choose the best method of presenting their internal accounting information because there are no regulations governing its format. Rather, the form and content of internal reports vary with the user, the decisions, and company policy. No two companies prepare identical internal accounting reports.

Exhibit 2.11 illustrates an example of the type of internal report that might be prepared for the marketing manager whom we just described. This report lists the

EXHIBIT 2.11 | Accounting Report for Marketing Manager

District Sales July 1—December 31, 1995

District	Units Sold	Total Sales
A—Northeast	323,679	$ 3,884,148
B—Northwest	437,921	4,817,131
C—South	554,064	5,569,199
Total	1,315,664	$14,270,478

units sold and total dollars of sales made in each district within the region. In contrast, a report prepared for an individual salesperson might show sales in each store, by item. We illustrate other examples of internal reports in later chapters.

PAUSE & REFLECT

Should owners have access to the same information as managers in order to hold the managers accountable? Why or why not?

Time Frame The time frame for generating internal accounting reports also depends on the specific needs of the respective users. In contrast to external financial statements, which are required periodically, internal reports are needed at various times. Some internal users need daily information, while others may need accounting information less frequently. For example, the production manager of a company would need daily production reports indicating the number of units produced, the number of defective units, and the number of additional orders received. (Some companies produce these status reports more than once a day!) The CFO of the company, however, does not need this daily information because he or she is not involved in the daily production decisions. Rather, periodically (perhaps monthly), she or he would need a summary production report to review and use for evaluation of the production department.

As you can see, unlike the financial accounting subsystem, the management accounting subsystem uses information from any source and in any form suitable for its intended purpose. Thus, the goal of the managerial accounting subsystem is to provide relevant information at appropriate levels of detail, in the right type of report format, to the right person at the appropriate organizational level, at the right time. Exhibit 2.12 shows a comparison of the financial and management accounting subsystems.

EXHIBIT 2.12

Comparison of Financial and Management Accounting Subsystems

	Accounting System	
	Financial Accounting Subsystem	Management Accounting Subsystem
User	External	Internal
Measure	Cash or cash equivalent	Expected future value or actual past value
Classification	Assets Liabilities Owners' equity	Costs Benefits
Communication	Income statement Statement of owners' equity Balance sheet Statement of cash flows	Management reports

SUMMARY

Businesses have many stakeholders, who have various needs for information. Accounting meets these various information needs through four related subsystems: the financial accounting subsystem, the management accounting subsystem, the tax accounting subsystem, and the regulatory subsystem. The financial and management accounting subsystems are considered the primary subsystems of accounting.

The financial accounting subsystem is designed to provide financial accounting information to external stakeholders, primarily stockholders and creditors, while the management accounting subsystem is designed to provide management accounting information to internal stakeholders. Financial accounting information is commonly classified as assets, liabilities, and owners' equity. Management accounting information is commonly classified as costs and benefits.

- Accounting events have two effects, which are indicated by changes in assets and/or equities. Assets are rights to future economic benefits, while equities are obligations to provide economic benefits in the future.

- Equities are commonly classified as liabilities and owners' equity. A liability is an obligation to transfer a measurable amount of resources in the future to providers of goods and services. An owners' equity is an obligation to transfer the company's residual resources to owners in the event the business ceases operations.

- A revenue is the amount earned by a company for providing goods and services. A revenue event results in either an increase in assets, or a decrease in liabilities and an increase in owners' equity. An expense is the amount incurred by a company for attempting to generate revenues. An expense event results in either a decrease in assets, or an increase in liabilities and a decrease in owners' equity. The difference between revenue and expense in a particular time period is referred to as *net income* (profit).

- The results of accounting events are reported to external users on four interrelated general-purpose financial statements—the income statement, the statement of owners' (stockholders') equity, the balance sheet, and the statement of cash flows.

- The management accounting subsystem provides internal users with information that is not available in the financial accounting subsystem, such as future costs and benefits and nonfinancial data.

KEY TERMS

accounting equation Assets = Liabilities + Owners' equity

accounting event An economic event that is specific to the entity, is measurable, and changes the entity's rights and/or obligations

accounting income See **net income**

accounts payable A liability representing the company's obligation to external suppliers of goods or services

accounts receivable An asset representing the company's right to receive money from customers

accumulated depreciation The portion of the cost of an asset that has been used in an effort to generate revenue

agency model An ethical decision-making model which states the managers of the business are the agents of the stockholders and, therefore, should undertake those actions that are in the stockholders' best interests

annual report The report provided to stockholders and other external users that contains general information about the company as well as the financial statements for the fiscal period

asset A right to use resources that are expected to have future economic benefits for the entity

balance sheet (statement of financial position) The financial statement designed to show the assets, liabilities, and owners' equity of the entity at the end of the period covered by the income statement

benefit Something that provides business resources or reduces resource consumption

contributed capital The resources contributed by the owners that gives the owners the right to receive assets remaining after business liabilities are met

cost Something that requires the use of business resources

cost of goods sold An expense that represents the company's cost of the products sold to customers

current asset An asset expected to be converted to cash or consumed within a year

current liability A liability expected to be discharged within a year

depreciation expense The portion of the cost of an asset that is deducted from the revenues of the period

economic event A situation that occurs which, when acted on, affects an entity's wealth

equity Obligations of the business to transfer resources of the company to other parties at some time in the future

expense The amount incurred in an attempt to generate revenue

expense event Either a decrease in assets or an increase in liabilities *and* a decrease in owners' equity resulting from the operations of the business.

financial accounting information The information provided by the financial accounting subsystem

financial accounting subsystem The accounting subsystem designed for communicating with external users, primarily stockholders and creditors

financial statements A collective term used to describe the information communicated to external users by the financial accounting subsystem

finished goods inventory An asset that represents a company's right to use finished products

income statement The financial statement designed to show the revenues, expenses, and the resulting net income for a period of time

intangibles Assets that represent legal rights that are expected to last many years and have no physical substance

inventory An asset that the company intends to sell to customers

liability An obligation of a business to transfer a measurable amount of resources or services to providers of goods and services other than owners

long-term asset An asset expected to be used for more than a year

long-term liability A liability expected to be discharged after a year

management (managerial) accounting information The information provided by the management accounting subsystem

management accounting subsystem The accounting subsystem designed to provide information to internal users, primarily employees and managers

net income (accounting income) The difference between revenue and expense in a certain time period

notes payable A liability representing the company's obligation to repay amounts borrowed from outside parties

owners' equity The obligation of a business to transfer residual resources to owners in the event that the business ceases operations

property, plant, and equipment Assets that have physical substance and expected useful lives of many years

raw materials inventory An asset representing the company's right to use raw materials

regulatory accounting subsystem The accounting subsystem designed to provide required information (reports) to regulatory agencies such as the SEC

relevant information Information that is capable of making a difference in the user's decision

residual interest The interest remaining after all the company's obligations have been met

residual resources Business resources remaining after liabilities have been met

retained earnings The accumulated profits of the entity less dividends distributed to owners

revenue The amount earned by a company for providing goods and services to customers

revenue event Either an increase in assets or a decrease in liabilities *and* an increase in owners' equity resulting from the operations of the entity

rights model An ethical decision-making model that states that the company should undertake actions that do not violate the basic, inherent rights of any stakeholder

salaries payable A liability representing the company's obligation to its employees for salaries and wages

statement of cash flows The financial statement designed to show a business's cash inflows and outflows as well as the net change in the cash balance for the same time period as the income statement

statement of owners' (stockholders') equity The financial statement designed to show the changes that occurred in owners' equity for the period of time covered by the income statement

statement of retained earnings The financial statement designed to show the changes that occurred in retained earnings (not contributed capital) for a period of time

supplies An asset that is expected to be used by the company

tax accounting subsystem The accounting subsystem designed to provide tax and other information regarding taxes to governments

utilitarian model An ethical decision-making model which indicates that the company should undertake actions that result in the greatest good for the greatest number of stakeholders

work-in-process inventory An asset representing the company's right to use partially completed products

QUESTIONS

1. Describe the four accounting subsystems.
2. Who are the users of the two primary accounting subsystems?
3. How does the financial accounting subsystem differ from the management accounting subsystem?
4. How does the financial accounting subsystem communicate accounting events to users?
5. What is meant by "every accounting event has two effects"?
6. Define an accounting asset. Give three examples of the types of assets Ford Motor Company is likely to have.
7. Define an accounting equity. Give three examples of the types of equities Southwest Airlines is likely to have.
8. Why is an owner's interest in a company called a *residual interest?*
9. Does net income increase the company's obligations to its owners? Why or why not?
10. What, in general, is a revenue? What is a revenue event? Provide an example of a revenue event for a service firm.
11. What, in general, is an expense? What is an expense event? Provide an example of a expense event for a merchandising firm.
12. What are the four primary financial statements and what is the purpose of each?
13. Describe how the four financial statements are related.
14. What is accounting depreciation? Is it different from physical depreciation? Why or why not?
15. How are events communicated in the management accounting subsystem?
16. Discuss the types of information provided by the management accounting subsystem.
17. Discuss the importance of the level of detail in management accounting communications.
18. Discuss the importance of timeliness in management accounting communications.
19. What are the financial statements presented to external users by Disney Company?
20. What is the purpose of the notes to consolidated financial statements?
21. What independent accounting firm audits Disney Company financial statements?
22. What stock exchanges list Disney Company stock?
23. What is the importance of the other nonfinancial information presented in the Disney annual report?
24. Who is responsible for the financial statements of Disney Company?
25. How can businesses use ethical decision-making models?

EXERCISES

E 2.1 Following is a list of events that occurred in the first month of business at a local hair salon. Indicate which of the events are accounting events and provide a short justification for your answer.
  a. The owner purchases supplies (combs, brushes, shampoo) on open account.
  b. The salon manager hires a receptionist and several stylists. The receptionist will be paid on an hourly basis. Stylists will receive commission and tips.
  c. A customer pays for a haircut and permanent that she just received.
  d. The customer makes another appointment for six weeks from now.

e. The owner contacts a supplier to be the exclusive provider of hair-care products for the salon.

f. All employees have worked for two weeks. Employees are paid on a monthly basis.

g. The owner finds out that a competitor across the street is offering 20 percent off on all permanents for the next week.

E 2.2   Specify in the space provided the effect of each of the following accounting events on assets and equities. Use (I) for increase, (D) for decrease, and (NC) for no change.

Asset	Equity	
_____	_____	*a.* Issued stock for cash.
_____	_____	*b.* Purchased supplies on open account.
_____	_____	*c.* Purchased office equipment for cash.
_____	_____	*d.* Returned some of the supplies purchased on open account to the seller because the wrong items were received.
_____	_____	*e.* Paid for the supplies purchased above.
_____	_____	*f.* Purchased additional office equipment by making a cash down-payment with the balance owed on open account.

E 2.3   Specify in the space provided the effect of each of the following accounting events on assets and equities. Use (I) for increase, (D) for decrease, and (NC) for no change.

Asset	Equity	
_____	_____	*a.* Owner withdrew cash from the business.
_____	_____	*b.* A customer returned merchandise previously purchased on open account.
_____	_____	*c.* Paid an obligation to the IRS for taxes.
_____	_____	*d.* Employees earned, but were not paid, one week's salary.
_____	_____	*e.* Supplies are used in the business.
_____	_____	*f.* Made a sale on open account.

E 2.4   Specify the effect (increase or decrease) of each of the following accounting events on assets and equities. Indicate the specific asset and/or equity affected by each event.

a. Borrowed cash from the bank.

b. Purchased machinery for cash.

c. Paid an obligation resulting from a purchase of inventory on open account.

d. Collected money from a customer who owed for a purchase made on open account.

e. Purchased office supplies on open account.

f. Signed a note to replace an obligation that was in the form of an open account.

E 2.5   For each of the accounting events shown below (*a–f*), indicate in the space provided the appropriate number designating the effect of that event. If none of the options applies, use NA for not applicable.

1. Increases assets, increases revenues.
2. Increases assets, decreases assets.
3. Decreases assets, decreases liabilities.
4. Decreases assets, increases expense.
5. Increases liabilities, increases expense.
6. Increases assets, increases liabilities.

_____   *a.* Sent a bill to a customer for service performed.

_____   *b.* Purchased an advertisement in the local newspaper for cash.

_____   *c.* Collected cash from a customer for merchandise previously purchased on open account.

_____   *d.* Made a cash purchase of supplies for use in the business.

_____   *e.* Paid the telephone bill that had not been recorded as a liability.

_____   *f.* Received a bill from the electrician for repairs to the interoffice communications system.

E 2.6   For each of the accounting events shown below (*a–f*), indicate in the space provided the appropriate number designating the effect of that event. If none of the options applies, use NA for not applicable.

1. Increases assets, increases revenues.
2. Increases assets, decreases assets.
3. Decreases assets, decreases liabilities.

4. Decreases assets, increases expense.
5. Increases liabilities, increases expense.
6. Increases assets, increases liabilities.

_____ a. Performed services for a customer and received cash immediately.
_____ b. Paid the electrician's bill for repairs to the intercom system (see E 2.5f).
_____ c. Paid employees' wages for the week.
_____ d. Issued stock in exchange for a parcel of land.
_____ e. Purchased furniture and equipment totaling $18,000 by making a $5,000 downpayment and signing a note payable for the balance.
_____ f. Returned $200 of the office supplies and obtained a cash refund.

E 2.7 For each of the accounting events shown below (*a–f*), indicate in the space provided the appropriate number designating the effect of that event. If none of the options applies, use NA for not applicable.
1. Increases assets, increases owners' equity.
2. Increases assets, increases liabilities.
3. Increases assets, decreases assets.
4. Decreases assets, decreases liabilities.
5. Decreases assets, decreases owners' equity.

_____ a. Purchased a large neon sign as an advertising display. The sign cost $600 and was purchased on credit.
_____ b. Purchased raw materials for $15,000 on open account.
_____ c. Issued raw materials of $10,000 into production.
_____ d. Used direct labor of $3,000 and overhead of $6,000 in production. Assume that both the labor and overhead items were paid in cash.
_____ e. Finished products costing $55,000.
_____ f. Sold products that have a production cost of $64,000 to a customer for $83,000 cash.

E 2.8 Refer to E 2.7. For each of the accounting events (*a–f*), indicate which financial statement(s) will reflect the event at the end of the period. Give a short justification for your answer in each case.

E 2.9 For each of the accounting events shown below (*a–f*), indicate in the space provided the appropriate number designating the effect of that event. If none of the options applies, use NA for not applicable.
1. Increases assets, increases owners' equity.
2. Increases assets, increases liabilities.
3. Increases assets, decreases assets.
4. Decreases assets, decreases liabilities.
5. Decreases assets, decreases owners' equity.

_____ a. Paid an obligation on open account of $1,300.
_____ b. Paid rent of $4,200 for the year.
_____ c. Purchased office supplies costing $1,500 for cash.
_____ d. Obtained a loan of $5,000 from 1st Local State Bank.
_____ e. Issued stock for cash.
_____ f. Collected $500 cash from one of its customers for merchandise previously purchased on open account.

E 2.10 Refer to E 2.9. For each of the accounting events (*a–f*), indicate which financial statement(s) will reflect the event at the end of the period. Give a short justification for your answer in each case.

E 2.11 Determine which of the following events result in a revenue or expense event. Use (R) for revenue, (E) for expense, or (N) for neither.
_____ a. A customer buys merchandise and pays cash.
_____ b. A customer buys merchandise and charges the purchase on open account.
_____ c. A customer pays for merchandise previously purchased on open account.
_____ d. A utility bill is received from local electric company.
_____ e. The utility bill received in *d* above is paid after 20 days.
_____ f. Income taxes are owed to the state treasurer.

E 2.12 Determine whether each of the following events results in a revenue or expense event. Use (R) for revenue, (E) for expense, or (N) for neither.
_____ a. A customer pays for legal services to be provided over the next six months.
_____ b. Insurance for the next year is purchased with cash.
_____ c. One month of legal services paid for in *a* above is provided to the client.

_____	*d.* One month of insurance coverage purchased in *b* above expires.
_____	*e.* Cash is used to purchase a machine for use in the factory.
_____	*f.* The machine purchased in *e* above is depreciated for one year.

E 2.13 Refer to E 2.12. For each of the events determined to be "N," neither a revenue or expense event, indicate the effect of the event on assets, liabilities, and owners' equity.

E 2.14 For each of the accounting elements shown below (*a–f*), indicate in the space provided the appropriate number designating the financial statement(s) where the element would appear.

1. Income statement
2. Statement of owners' equity
3. Balance sheet
4. Statement of cash flows

_____ *a.* Sales on account
_____ *b.* Accounts receivable
_____ *c.* Accounts payable
_____ *d.* Supplies expense
_____ *e.* Property, plant, and equipment
_____ *f.* Depreciation expense

E 2.15 For each of the accounting elements shown below (*a–f*), indicate in the space provided the appropriate number designating the financial statements where the element would appear. Some elements may appear on more than one statement.

1. Income statement
2. Statement of owners' equity
3. Balance sheet
4. Statement of cash flows

_____ *a.* Inventory purchases on account
_____ *b.* Cash sales
_____ *c.* Utilities payable
_____ *d.* Note payable, due in five years
_____ *e.* Interest expense
_____ *f.* Interest payable

E 2.16 On March 1, 1995, Simmons Company sold merchandise inventory to Broad Street Company. Broad Street Company agreed to pay Simmons Company $7,500 for the merchandise on April 1, 1995. The merchandise cost Simmons Company $6,300. What is the effect of the March 1 event on Simmons's assets, liabilities, and owners' equity? What is the effect of the April 1 event on Simmons's assets, liabilities, and owners' equity?

E 2.17 Describe the types of management accounting information the marketing manager of a large retail clothing chain needs. How frequently is this information desired? Is this information primarily financial or nonfinancial in nature? Why?

E 2.18 Describe the types of management accounting information the production manager of a large automobile manufacturer needs. How frequently is this information desired? Is this information primarily financial or nonfinancial in nature? Why?

E 2.19 Describe the types of management accounting information the human resources manager of a large travel agency needs. How frequently is this information desired? Is this information primarily financial or nonfinancial in nature? Why?

E 2.20 What are the total revenues for Disney Company for the fiscal year 1994? Are revenues higher or lower than in 1993? Is this good? Why or why not?

E 2.21 What is the net income for Disney Company for the fiscal year 1994? Is it higher or lower than 1993? Is this good? Why or why not?

E 2.22 What is the amount of total assets, liabilities, and owners' equity of Disney Company at the end of fiscal 1994?

E 2.23 What was the amount of cash generated by Disney's operating activities during fiscal 1994? Is this good? Why or why not?

E 2.24 Did Disney Company pay dividends or borrow any money during fiscal 1994? Explain.

E 2.25 Did Disney use cash to purchase any theme parks during fiscal year 1994? Explain.

PROBLEMS

P 2.1 For each of the following items (*a–l*), indicate on which financial statement you would expect to find it and briefly explain why you chose that particular statement. Some items may appear on more than one statement.

           1. Income statement
           2. Statement of owners' equity
           3. Balance sheet
           4. Statement of cash flows

_____ *a.* Cash paid to suppliers
_____ *b.* Accounts payable
_____ *c.* Sales, both cash and credit
_____ *d.* Dividends paid during the year
_____ *e.* Buildings
_____ *f.* Net income
_____ *g.* Cash received from sales
_____ *h.* Common stock
_____ *i.* Operating expenses
_____ *j.* Inventory
_____ *k.* Patents
_____ *l.* Beginning retained earnings

P 2.2 For each of the following items (*a–l*), indicate on which financial statement you would expect to find it and briefly explain why you chose that particular statement. Some items may appear on more than one statement.

           1. Income statement
           2. Statement of owners' equity
           3. Balance sheet
           4. Statement of cash flows

_____ *a.* Cost of merchandise sold during the period.
_____ *b.* Accumulated depreciation on equipment.
_____ *c.* Depreciation expense.
_____ *d.* Capital stock issued for cash during the period.
_____ *e.* Ending retained earnings.
_____ *f.* Ending cash balance.
_____ *g.* Note payable, due in 10 years.
_____ *h.* Interest payable, due in 30 days.
_____ *i.* Interest revenue.
_____ *j.* Note receivable, due in 60 days.
_____ *k.* Interest receivable.
_____ *l.* Cash paid for buildings during the period.

P 2.3 Domino Company has the following information available from fiscal 1995. Use the relevant information to determine the income for the year ending October 31, 1995, for Domino Company.

a. Cash sales, $56,000.
b. Employee salary expense, $34,000.
c. Capital stock issued for cash, $100,000.
d. Depreciation expense, $1,500.
e. Sales on open account, $85,000.
f. Long-term loan received, $50,000.
g. Interest earned on short-term investments, $300.
h. Income tax expense, $10,100.
i. Inventory purchased for resale, $120,000.
j. Inventory sold, $60,000.
k. Insurance purchased for the next year, $3,600.
l. Rent expense, $12,000.

P 2.4 The accounting events listed below (*a–i*) affected assets and equities of Domino Company during fiscal 1995.

a. Purchased office supplies of $250 on open account.
b. Borrowed $1,000 from the 1st State Bank and signed a note payable for that amount.

c. Billed a client $450 for services rendered.
   d. Paid the utility bill for the month, $320. No obligation for the bill has been recorded.
   e. Collected $200 from a client immediately upon rendering services.
   f. Paid for office supplies purchased in event *a* above.
   g. Collected $150 from a client who had previously been billed.
   h. Recorded, but did not pay, the telephone bill for the month, $180.
   i. Issued capital stock for cash, $10,000.

Required:
   a. Using the form shown below, specify the effect of each event on the assets, liabilities, and owners' equity of the company. Use + for increases or – for decreases. Event *a* is shown as an example.
   b. Determine the total assets, liabilities, and owners' equity that would appear on the balance sheet at the end of fiscal 1995.
   c. Determine the net income that would appear on the income statement for the fiscal period ending 1995.
   d. Determine the cash inflows and outflows that would appear on the statement of cash flows for the fiscal period ending 1995.

		Equities	
Event	Assets	Liabilities	Owners' Equity
a	+250	+250	

P 2.5   The accounting events listed below (*a–i*) affected assets and equities of Ellington Company during the fiscal year ending December 31, 1996.
   a. Purchased $18,000 in merchandise inventory on open account.
   b. Sold $35,000 in merchandise inventory on open account to a customer for $49,700.
   c. Purchased $13,000 in merchandise inventory for cash.
   d. Sold $26,800 in merchandise inventory for $37,520 cash.
   e. Received the monthly utility bill, $575.
   f. Paid employees $4,600 for wages earned.
   g. Received a partial payment from a customer on account, $29,000.
   h. Paid rent for the current month, $6,000.
   i. Recorded depreciation on store equipment, $3,000.

Required:
   a. Using the form shown below, specify the effect of each event on the assets, liabilities, and owners' equity of the company. Use + for increases or – for decreases.
   b. Determine the total assets, liabilities, and owners' equity that would appear on the balance sheet on December 31, 1996.
   c. Determine the net income that would appear on the income statement for the period ending December 31, 1996.
   d. Determine the cash inflows and outflows that would appear on the statement of cash flows for the period ending December 31, 1996.

		Equities	
Event	Assets	Liabilities	Owners' Equity

P 2.6   The accounting events listed below (*a–i*) affected assets and equities of Frybarker Enterprises during the period ending September 30, 1995.
   a. Owner contributes $50,000 in cash.
   b. Raw materials are purchased on account for $100,000.
   c. Raw materials of $84,000 are issued into production.
   d. Assembly workers' wages of $23,000 are paid in cash.
   e. Factory overhead of $35,400 is incurred, but not paid.
   f. Products costing $95,000 are finished.
   g. Products costing $72,500 are sold for $101,500 in cash.
   h. Selling expenses of $15,075 are paid in cash.
   i. Owner withdraws $5,000 in cash.

Required:
   a. Using the following form, specify the effect of each event on the assets, liabilities, and owners' equity of the company. Use + for increases or – for decreases.
   b. Determine the total assets, liabilities, and owners' equity that would appear on the balance sheet on September 30, 1995.

c. Determine the net income that would appear on the income statement for the period ending September 30, 1995.

d. Determine the cash inflows and outflows that would appear on the statement of cash flows for the period ending September 30, 1995.

			Equities	
			---	---
Event	Assets	Liabilities	Owners' Equity

P 2.7 Describe the effects of each of the following events: Use specific names for the different types of assets, liabilities, and owners' equities, use numbers to indicate the monetary amounts, and use (I) for increase or (D) for decrease to indicate the direction of the effects noted.

a. Macon Industries purchased land costing $8,000 and buildings costing $90,000 by paying $23,000 in cash and signing a note payable for the $75,000 balance.

b. Robot Manufacturing has an obligation on its books for $3,000 it owes to Simplex Systems. Robot Manufacturing Company purchases an additional $5,000 in supplies from Simplex Systems and makes an immediate cash payment of $8,000 to pay for both the current and previous purchase. What is the effect on Robot?

c. Simplex Systems has a right to receive $3,000 from Robot Manufacturing Company for purchases previously made on open account. Simplex Systems sells $5,000 in supplies to Robot Manufacturing Company and receives a check for $8,000 at that time. The supplies purchased cost Simplex $2,000. The check pays for Robot's current and previous purchase. What is the effect on Simplex?

d. Baker Company purchased merchandise on open account at a cost of $950. Baker then sold the merchandise to Simpson Company for $1,500 cash. What is the effect on Baker?

e. Baker Company paid for the merchandise it purchased above in event *d.* What is the effect on Baker?

f. Kruse, Inc., paid $3,500 cash for merchandise. Kruse then sold the merchandise on open account to Alex Supply Co. for $6,000. What is the effect on Kruse?

g. Alex Co. paid Kruse, Inc., for the merchandise purchased above in event *f.* What is the effect on Kruse?

P 2.8 Describe the effects of each of the following events: Use specific names for the assets, liabilities, and owners' equities, use numbers to indicate the monetary amounts, and use (I) for increase or (D) for decrease to indicate the direction of the effects noted.

a. Central Plains, Inc., issued 1,000 shares of stock in exchange for a building. The building appraised at $67,000. The stock is currently trading for $73 per share.

b. G. O. Law Partnership provides legal services to a local travel agency. The law office normally bills $500 for such services. Instead of paying cash for the services, the travel agency gave G. O. Law Partnership a free cruise trip. The cruise package has been advertised at $619.

c. P&H Plumbing and Heating Company provided services to the local auto dealership when the dealership was building a new facility. P&H bills $16,000 for such services. Instead of paying cash, the dealership gave P&H Plumbing and Heating Company a new truck to use in its business. The truck cost the dealership $13,000 and lists at $18,000.

P 2.9 Provide a brief explanation describing each accounting event presented below.

a. Cash decreased; obligation to supplier decreased.

b. Right to cash from customer increased; revenue increased.

c. Cash increased; owners' equity increased.

d. Obligation to employees increased; expenses increased.

e. Cash decreased; right to inventory increased.

f. Cash decreased; telephone expense increased.

g. Obligation to supplier increased; utility expense increased.

h. Right to office equipment increased; obligation to supplier increased.

i. Cash decreased; obligation to bank decreased.

j. Cash increased; right to cash from a customer decreased.

P 2.10 Each of the following situations applies one of the basic concepts of accounting discussed in Chapter 1. Determine which of the following concepts is used in each situation and indicate why for each of your responses.

1. Business entity
2. Going concern
3. Monetary unit
4. Periodicity

a. A company trades a delivery truck for computer equipment. The effects of the event are determined to be $5,000.

b. A corporation has 10,000 stockholders. Subsequently, 2,000 stockholders sell their shares. The corporation does not recognize this event.

c. A corporation continues in business even though four of its stockholders have died.

d. A company prepared annual financial statements.

e. A company carries the balances of its assets, liabilities, and owners' equity from one year to the next.

f. The major supplier for Palino Company declares bankruptcy, but Palino does not recognize this event.

g. A company issues 12,500 shares of capital stock in exchange for a parcel of land. The stock is currently selling for $10 per share on the American Stock Exchange. The event results in an increase in assets and an increase in owners' equity of $125,000.

P 2.11 What is Euro Disney? Did it have a net income or net loss for fiscal 1994? How large is Disney's investment in Euro Disney?

P 2.12 What were the quarter-by-quarter revenues of Disney Company for fiscal 1994? Is this trend good or bad? Why? Is there other information you would want in order to answer these questions? If so, what?

P 2.13 What was the quarter-by-quarter net income of Disney Company for fiscal 1994? Is this trend good or bad? Why? Is there other information you would want in order to answer these questions? If so, what?

COMPUTER APPLICATIONS

CA 2.1 Robson Company experienced the following accounting events during a month in fiscal 1996.

1. Purchased office supplies of $500 on open account.
2. Borrowed $2,000 from 1st State Bank and signed a note payable for that amount.
3. Billed a client $900 for services rendered.
4. Paid the utility bill for the month, $640. No obligation for the bill has been recorded.
5. Collected $400 from a client immediately upon rendering services.
6. Paid for office supplies purchased in event 1 above.
7. Collected $300 from a client who had previously been billed.
8. Recorded, but did not pay, the telephone bill for the month, $360.
9. Issued capital stock for cash, $20,000.

Required:
a. Set up a spreadsheet using columns for each effect and rows for each event.
b. Enter the accounting events above into the spreadsheet.
c. Determine the changes in the amounts of total assets, liabilities, and owners' equity that would affect the balance sheet.
d. Determine the net income that would appear on the income statement for the period.
e. Determine the cash inflows and outflows from operating, investing, and financing events that would appear on the statement of cash flows for the period.

CA 2.2 Stark, Inc., experienced the following accounting events during a month in 1996.

1. Purchased $36,000 in merchandise inventory on open account.
2. Sold $76,000 in merchandise inventory on open account to a customer for $99,400.
3. Purchased $26,000 in merchandise inventory for each.

4. Sold $53,000 in merchandise inventory for $75,040 cash.
5. Received the monthly utility bill, $1,150.
6. Paid employees $9,200 for wages earned.
7. Received a partial payment from a customer on account, $58,000.
8. Paid rent for the current month, $12,000.
9. Recorded depreciation on store equipment, $6,000.

Required:
a. Set up a spreadsheet using columns for each effect and rows for each event.
b. Enter the accounting events above into the spreadsheet.
c. Determine the changes in the amounts of total assets, liabilities, and owners' equity that would affect the balance sheet.
d. Determine the net income that would appear on the income statement for the period.
e. Determine the cash inflows and outflows from operating, investing, and financing events that would appear on the statement of cash flows for the period.

CA 2.3   Thomas Enterprises had the following accounting events during a month in fiscal 1996.
1. Owner contributes $100,000 in cash.
2. Raw materials are purchased on account for $200,000.
3. Raw materials of $168,000 are issued into production.
4. Assembly workers' wages of $46,000 are paid in cash.
5. Factory overhead of $70,800 is incurred, but not paid.
6. Products costing $190,000 are finished.
7. Products costing $145,000 are sold for $203,000 in cash.
8. Selling expenses of $30,150 are paid in cash.
9. Owner withdraws $10,000 in cash.

Required:
a. Set up a spreadsheet using columns for each effect and rows for each event.
b. Enter the accounting events above into spreadsheet.
c. Determine the changes in the amounts of total assets, liabilities, and owners' equity that would affect the balance sheet.
d. Determine the net income that would appear on the income statement for the period.
e. Determine the cash inflows and outflows from operating, investing, and financing events that would appear on the statement of cash flows for the period.

CASES

C 2.1   Refer to the annual report obtained in Case 1.1.

Required:
a. What financial statements does your company include in its annual report?
b. What is the company's fiscal year-end? Did it show a net income or a net loss for the fiscal period? Is this good? Why or why not?
c. What is the dollar amount of its total assets? What is the dollar amount of its current assets? Is this good? Why or why not?
d. What is the dollar amount of its total liabilities? What is the dollar amount of its current liabilities? Is this good? Why or why not?
e. How many shares of stock has the company issued? Did it pay a dividend to stockholders this year?
f. Did the company indicate a positive or a negative cash flow from operations? Is this good? Why or why not?
g. Did it borrow any money during the period? Did it use cash to purchase any property, plant, or equipment during the period? Is this good? Why or why not?

C 2.2   Painter Supplies buys paint and supplies wholesale as needed for contracting jobs, but it also maintains a stock of paint and miscellaneous supplies. The accountant for Painter Services provided the following analysis of events that occurred during July. The president cannot understand this analysis and would like you to describe the events for her.
a. Asset (Cash) increased, $920.
   Asset (Accounts Receivable) decreased, $920.
b. Asset (Supplies) increased, $75.
   Asset (Cash) decreased, $75.
c. Asset (Cash) increased, $380.
   Equity (Owners' Equity, revenue) increased, $380.
d. Asset (Inventory) increased, $425.
   Equity (Accounts Payable) increased, $425.

e. Equity (Accounts Payable) decreased, $875.
   Asset (Cash) decreased, $875.

f. Asset (Accounts Receivable) increased, $765.
   Equity (Owners' Equity, revenue) increased, $765.

g. Equity (Owners' Equity, expense) decreased, $300.
   Asset (Cash) decreased, $300.

h. Equity (Accounts Payable) decreased, $425.
   Asset (Cash) decreased, $425.

i. Equity (Owners' Equity, expense) decreased, $425.
   Asset (Inventory) decreased, $425.
   Asset (Accounts receivable) increased, $600.
   Equity (Owners' Equity, revenue) increased, $600.

CRITICAL THINKING

CT 2.1   Although employees are often considered to be a company's most valuable asset, they do not appear as assets on the company's balance sheet. Prepare an argument supporting or refuting this practice.

CT 2.2   Disney has been widely criticized for investing in Euro Disney. In fact, some analysts suggest that Disney should abandon the Euro Disney park immediately. Prepare an argument supporting or refuting Disney's decision to operate a theme park in Paris.

ETHICAL CHALLENGES

EC 2.1   The March 1994 issue of *Management Accounting* presented an article[9] describing various practices that management undertook to increase or decrease reported net income or to increase or decrease the amount reported as assets and liabilities for a particular period of time. While many of these practices are legal, some question exists as to whether they are ethical. For each of the following situations, discuss whether the action taken by the manager is ethical and why or why not.

a. On December 15, a clerk ordered $3,000 of office supplies, and the supplies were delivered on December 29. This order was a mistake because the manager had ordered that no other expenses be incurred for the remainder of the year, and the supplies were not urgently needed. The manager asked the accounting department not to record the invoice (bill) until January.

b. On December 15, a clerk ordered $15,000 of inventory to be delivered at the end of the year. Since it is not known for sure whether the inventory will be received before the end of the year, the manager asked the supplier not to bill the company for the inventory until after the first of the year.

c. On September 1, the company received $12,000 in advance from a customer for work to be performed evenly over the next 12 months. However, due to staffing problems, the work is behind schedule. The manager asked the accounting department to recognize 4/12 of the revenue this year even though 4/12 of the work has not been completed.

d. During December the sales manager made several sales on account to customers that the company has never done business with before. It is not known whether the customers are creditworthy. The manager has asked the accounting department to recognize the sales since they were made in good faith.

EC 2.2   The management accounting subsystem provides information to managers and other internal users that is not provided to external users. External users have an incentive to ask management for this information since information is provided to external users free of charge. Management, however, may not want to give this information to external users. Discuss the dilemma faced by management in determining how much information to provide to external users.

---

[9]Kenneth Rosenzweig and Marilyn Fischer, "Is Managing Earnings Ethically Acceptable?" *Management Accounting*, March 1994, pp. 31–34.

CHAPTER 3

Business Operations and Cycles

Southwest Airlines is the only major U.S. airline that can claim to have been consistently profitable since 1973. Southwest attributes its success to its low-cost approach to business operations. The management and employees of Southwest made strategic decisions about how they operate in order to maintain the lowest cost structure in the airline industry. The low costs allow Southwest to offer low fares that, in turn, attract people who might not otherwise fly.

Among the things that Southwest Airlines does to lower costs is focus on the short-haul customers and offer them direct flights to satellite or downtown airports. Other airlines use a system called *hub and spoke* where all flights travel to or from "hub" airports. This requires that their short-haul customers travel out of their way to hub airports when they make short trips. In addition, Southwest Airlines uses only one kind of plane rather than the variety of planes used by most major air carriers. This means that they have lower training costs (for pilots, flight attendants, and mechanics), maintenance costs (because they need spare parts for only one kind of plane), and scheduling costs (because there is no choice about what size plane to schedule). Based on Southwest's customer-focused, low-cost philosophy, it intends to grow and prosper despite the swelling competition from other airlines trying to copy its approach.

WHAT ARE BUSINESS ACTIVITIES?

Southwest Airlines is an example of a service firm that has risen to impressive heights based on an understanding of its industry and what it takes to operate efficiently. The company has done this without sacrificing what it is in business to provide—service to its customers. As any business strives to do, Southwest Airlines makes three major types of business decisions: operating, investing, and financing.

Chapter 2 introduced financial statements, described how they reflect accounting events, and showed how the financial statements relate to one another. This chapter shows how business activities, such as buying and selling goods or paying employees, result in accounting events that ultimately translate into financial statements. **Business activities** are events that involve making and carrying out the operating, investing, and financing decisions that deal with business assets or obligations.

In a profit-seeking business, there are three types of business activities that correspond to the three types of business decisions. **Operating activities** are the profit-making activities of the enterprise.[1] Recall from Chapter 2 that a business's profit (net income) results when revenues exceed expenses for a given period. So, operating activities include those business activities that generate revenues, such as selling merchandise for cash or on credit or providing services for a fee. They also include activities that result in increased expenses, such as purchasing goods for manufacture or resale, paying wages, or combining goods and labor to manufacture products.

Investing activities include the purchase and sale of long-term assets in addition to other major items used in a business's operations. For example, purchasing equipment and buildings that a company expects to use over two or more years is an investing activity. However, actually using the buildings and equipment to provide a service, or to make or sell a product, is an operating activity. **Financing activities** are activities that involve obtaining the cash or using other noncash means to pay for investments in long-term assets, and to repay money borrowed from creditors, and to provide a return to owners.

In this chapter, we focus on operating activities, which we divide into three cycles of events commonly found in businesses: (1) expenditure, (2) revenue, and (3) conversion. Our goal is to describe, in a coherent way, the activities that are planned, performed, and evaluated as part of business operations. We also discuss procedures that owners and managers use to ensure the accuracy of accounting information and to protect assets from theft or misuse. Then we relate operating activities to the documents found in most accounting systems to show the connection between the sources of information and the activities they describe, and how they help provide accountability. Later in the chapter, we discuss the cycle of planning, performing, and evaluating business activities as it applies to operating activities.

BUSINESS OPERATING, INVESTING, AND FINANCING ACTIVITIES

Operating decisions are made regularly and routinely; for example, when Southwest Airlines purchases fuel or sells tickets on scheduled airline flights. While it is possible to change such decisions, it is not usually necessary to do so. However, unanticipated changes due to economic fluctuations, customer needs, or vendor availability require quick adjustments. These types of adjustments are part of many operating decisions. For example, if an airport is closed due to bad weather, Southwest must revise its schedules quickly, or if a plane malfunctions, the company must find a new plane so that service continues.

Both investing and financing decisions require long and careful consideration, and are often difficult and/or costly to change. Decisions about investing in major long-term assets are made in light of economic considerations such as the nature of the competition and other market conditions where the business operates. Businesses

---

[1]In a not-for-profit enterprise, such as the American Red Cross, operating activities are the activities intended to meet the goals and objectives of the enterprise. For example, during the flood of 1993, the activities undertaken by the American Red Cross to provide food, clothing, and shelter to flood victims were operating activities.

also use information about consumer demand for their products or service to determine the amount of investment to make in certain types of equipment or the extent to which they should automate their production process. Southwest decided to invest in a fleet of Boeing 737 jets rather than a fleet of jets of various sizes because it would give them a great cost advantage over their competitors.

Financing decisions involve determining the means of paying for major assets. In Southwest's case, the airline had borrowed almost $205 million for property and aircraft as of the end of 1993.

Operating Activities Versus Financing and Investing Activities

The distinction between operating activities and financing and investing activities is sometimes blurred. Though paying interest to lenders for use of their money is a financing activity, interest is considered to be an expense when calculating periodic income, which implies that it is an operating activity.[2] In addition, financing can refer to payments for assets used in operations, such as inventory. Generally, when we refer to financing activities, we mean those activities associated with obtaining cash to pay for long-term assets and repaying amounts borrowed.

The term *investing* sometimes refers to purchasing assets used in operations as well as making operating expenditures. We use the term *investing* to refer to the purchase or sale of long-lived assets. The distinction involves whether the asset is a major resource the business intends to keep or an asset it consumes in a short period of time. Companies often buy insurance policies that cover multiple years. Although these insurance policies cover multiple years, their cost is not considered to be an investment because insurance is part of day-to-day profit-making activities rather than a major, long-lived asset.

Some operating activities have characteristics of both investing and financing activities. For example, think of a business that sells on credit to its customers. Sales on credit are like investments because the business has chosen a resource (payments due from customers) that will provide cash in the future rather than cash at the time of sale. Similarly, purchasing goods for resale, which is an operating activity, is also a financing transaction because the vendors lend the company the amount of the purchase until they receive subsequent payment from the company.

One characteristic that generally distinguishes selling and purchasing on credit from investing and financing activities is that selling and purchasing activities directly influence the amount of profit the firm makes. In addition, both selling and purchasing activities are a series of transactions that tend to be repeated regularly and frequently during business operations.

---

[2]We treat interest associated with financing long-term assets as a financing activity, though interest paid is shown on the statement of cash flows as an operating activity.

Selling equipment to make a profit is an operating activity.

Selling equipment that was used to produce a product which is sold for a profit is an investing activity.

Keep in mind that classifying activities as operating, investing, or financing depends on the nature of the company's business. When businesses sell equipment used to produce their products and receive more cash than the equipment's cost less accumulated depreciation, they increase profits due to having a gain on the equipment's sale. This is an investing transaction rather than an operating activity because it only changes the operating resources available from the asset classification of equipment to cash. However, if the business sold equipment as its main activity, like John Deere and Company which makes and sells of tractors and other heavy equipment, then the sale of equipment would be an operating activity because, in this case, the equipment is considered to be inventory. The difference in the two examples is that the first company sold the resources (equipment) used to make the products the company sells, while John Deere sells equipment it makes to earn a profit.

Exhibit 3.1 shows the interrelationship among operating, investing, and financing activities. Note that financing activities provide cash for investing, which then provides long-lived assets for operating activities. In turn, operating activities provide cash for both financing and investing activities. One implication of this dynamic interrelationship is that the ways in which a business chooses to invest affect its financing and operating decisions. For example, when Southwest's management decided to use the Boeing 737 exclusively, it was making an investing decision with operations in mind. The savings in operating costs, such as training, maintenance, and scheduling, from using only one type of plane were also an important part of its investing decision. The choice of Boeing as a plane supplier also may have been made not simply for its planes, but also because Boeing included financing that was attractive to Southwest. Another factor that might affect investing and operating decisions is the ability of investors and owners to provide cash to finance the business. If a company cannot find enough cash to finance investment in a high-tech, automated production facility, for example, it is likely to operate with more employee labor to produce its product with a lower investment in equipment and buildings.

Use of Operating Profits

Two aspects of operating activities distinguish them from investing and financing activities: (1) they are more directly associated with profit making, and (2) they involve a series of transactions or events that occur regularly and routinely.

Operating activities are the driving force of a business. As Exhibit 3.2 shows, businesses use their operating profits in three important ways: (1) to acquire goods and services for resale or to obtain materials to produce products for resale (operating activities), (2) to acquire additional major, long-term assets (investing activities), and (3) to pay for the capital provided by lenders and owners (financing activities). Profitability, in turn, affects financing activities. The ability of a business to be profitable is seen by current and potential lenders and owners as the principal source of loan repayment, interest payments, and dividends. Profits from operations also provide

EXHIBIT	3.1

Relationships among Business Activities

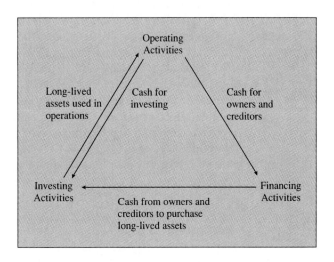

EXHIBIT 3.2

Uses of Operating Profits

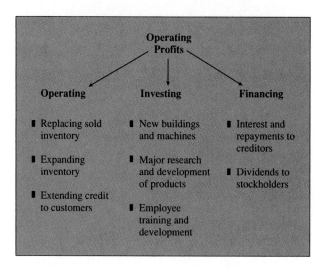

capital that the business can use to make additional investments. At the very least, profits are necessary to stay in business, even if the business never grows beyond its current level of investment.

For example, as part of its operating activities, Southwest Airlines spent $641 million for wages and salaries and $304 million for fuel and oil in 1993.[3] It also earned $2.2 billion from passengers in 1993. Together, the 1993 operating revenues and expenses resulted in an operating profit for Southwest of $292 million.[4] The company also entered into a transaction with Boeing in 1993 in which it agreed to buy 63 Boeing 737s in the years 1997 through 2001. The total capital required to fund this investment is $3,109 million.

PAUSE & REFLECT   **If a car dealer buys 10 trucks, is this an operating or investing activity? Why? If the dealer must borrow money from the bank to finance the purchase, does this change your answer? Why or why not?**

As Exhibit 3.3 shows, operating, investing, and financing activities are associated with certain parts of financial statements. The income statement, the current portion of the balance sheet, and the statement of cash flows reflect operating activities. Recall from Chapter 2 that the income statement includes sections that reflect reported revenues, cost of goods sold, and other expenses. The transactions summarized on the income statement generally result from operating activities. A section of the statement of cash flows, with a title similar to the one used by Walt Disney Company, "Cashflows Provided by Operations Before Income Taxes," shows the cash flows from operating activities. Operating activities are also associated with current assets (i.e., a customer charging purchases on account results in an accounts receivable) and current liabilities (i.e., a company charging its purchases on account results in an accounts payable). Investing and financing activities are linked more directly to most of the items found on the balance sheet. The assets shown on the balance sheet represent investments, even though we refer only to transactions involving long-term assets like buildings as investing activities. The balance sheet shows the amounts of debt and equity that result from financing activities in the long-term liability and owners' equity sections. Financing and investing activities also tie into separate sections of the statement of cash flows.

---

[3]Southwest Airlines, Inc., Annual Report, 1993.

[4]All of the operating revenues totaled $2,297 million, while total operating expenses came to $2,005 million. Thus, the difference of $292 million is the operating profit.

EXHIBIT | 3.3

Reporting Business Activities on Financial Statements

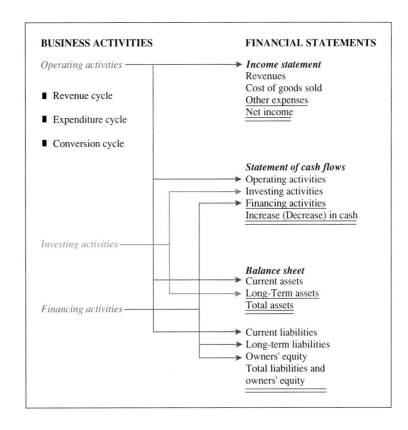

BUSINESS ACTIVITIES	FINANCIAL STATEMENTS
Operating activities	***Income statement***
	Revenues
■ Revenue cycle	Cost of goods sold
	Other expenses
■ Expenditure cycle	Net income
■ Conversion cycle	
	Statement of cash flows
	Operating activities
	Investing activities
	Financing activities
	Increase (Decrease) in cash
Investing activities	***Balance sheet***
	Current assets
	Long-Term assets
	Total assets
Financing activities	
	Current liabilities
	Long-term liabilities
	Owners' equity
	Total liabilities and owners' equity

Now that we have explained the nature of operating activities, we turn to the control system that helps to promote efficient and effective business operations. The control system set up by management incorporates procedures and techniques that ensure the accuracy of accounting information and help protect business assets.

WHAT ARE INTERNAL CONTROLS?

As part of effectively running a business, management should ensure that the business has a good system of internal controls. An **internal control system** is the set of policies and procedures designed to meet three objectives: (1) promote operational efficiency, (2) ensure the accuracy of information in the accounting system, and (3) encourage management and employees to comply with applicable laws and regulations.

While having a system of internal controls is a good business practice, it is also a legal requirement. In 1977, the U.S. government passed the Foreign Corrupt Practices Act, which requires that all publicly owned companies maintain accurate and detailed accounting records and a documented system of internal controls. In a simplified sense, the procedures employed in internal control systems include: (1) requiring proper authorization for transactions, (2) separating incompatible duties, (3) maintaining adequate documents and records, (4) physically controlling assets and documents, and (5) providing independent checks on performance.

Requiring Proper Authorization

Every business has goals that serve as a framework for its daily activities, for example, the level of profit it wants to attain or the quality level of its product. The means of achieving these goals are part of the company's policies.

One way to be sure that employees follow company policies is to ensure that those persons responsible for certain activities also have the authority to enforce the policies associated with the activities. For example, if a person is responsible for packing and shipping, he or she should be given authority to arrange shipping with independent shipping companies. For major transactions involving investing and financing activities, the authority to approve transactions often rests at the highest level of the organization. In a corporation, the authority to engage in major transactions, such as issuing stock, rests with the board of directors. While owners and boards of directors remain ultimately responsible for all business policies and related actions, they often delegate responsibility and authority for many day-to-day transactions to lower management and operating personnel.

Separating Incompatible Duties

If one company employee performs certain combinations of jobs, it sometimes makes it too easy and inviting to violate company policies. For example, assume that an employee is responsible for recording cash received in the accounting records as well as for depositing cash in the bank account. This combination of duties makes it very easy for the employee to record less cash than was received in the accounting records, to deposit the recorded lower amount, and to keep the difference. Dividing among employees the responsibilities for duties that have the potential to allow for one person to violate company policies is called **separation, or segregation, of incompatible duties.**

In order to determine which employee duties are incompatible, we divide any business transaction into four phases: approval, execution, custody, and recording. In the approval phase, an employee with authority agrees to allow another employee to initiate a transaction. The execution phase involves a person who has approval to legally commit the business to a transaction, such as when the individual makes an agreement to purchase goods or services with an outside party. Custody includes actually possessing the asset, such as cash or inventory items, and recording requires entering transactions into the accounting system.

A good system of internal controls prevents employees from performing more than one phase of any business transaction. Note that in small companies there are usually not enough employees to segregate all the incompatible duties. In such cases, there are other control procedures in place to ensure that the effect of segregation occurs, such as forcing employees to take mandatory vacations, which allows an opportunity for checks on an employee's work. Another effective control in small businesses is the usual presence of the owners at the workplace, which makes it easier to detect employee wrongdoing.

Maintaining Adequate Documents and Records

Recording transactions is an important control procedure because employees know that the actions they take on behalf of the company are recorded in the company's records. In addition, properly recording transactions allows managers to trace responsibility for transactions so that they can maintain employee accountability. Therefore, a good internal control system includes documents that capture all the necessary information about a transaction in the most efficient and effective way possible. At a minimum, necessary information includes a description of the product as well as the price, date, parties involved, and terms of the transaction.

Whether the "documents" are paper and manually completed or images of documents on a computer screen, they should make it easy for employees to provide the required information and ensure that everything necessary is included. For paper documents, one important control procedure is prenumbering them so that all numbers in a sequence must be accounted for. Therefore, an employee could not use a prenumbered document without potentially being held accountable for it. Prenumbering documents, along with securing documents so that access is limited to authorized employees, helps ensure that they are not misused as part of unauthorized transactions.

Physically Controlling Assets and Documents

Part of the role of an internal control system is to safeguard both human and physical resources. For human resources, safeguarding means enforcing policies and regulations regarding workplace safety. Companies protect physical assets and accounting records by limiting access to them by unauthorized personnel. Limiting physical access includes, for example, using cash registers that produce a written receipt and record of transactions, locking storerooms, and using fireproof safes. Even fences around company buildings and parking lots for company vehicles are examples of physical safeguards of assets.

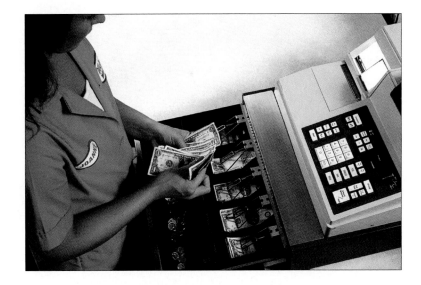

Segregation of incompatible duties is dividing responsibilities for duties in securing cash. This cashier is responsible for charging customers and receiving cash. Another employee will then have the responsibility of counting the cash and varifying the amount against the transactions recorded by the register tape.

Providing Independent Checks on Performance

Companies strengthen their internal control systems by providing independent checks on the performance of employees; this includes having another employee who was not involved in the original activity check the work. For example, when an independent person compares the amount recorded as cash receipts in the accounting records with the records of the bank, the comparison helps to ensure that all the cash the company received was deposited in the bank. Independent checks not only guard against intentional theft and fraud but also reveal cases where employees perform certain procedures incorrectly. The independence of the person providing the check is critical because people checking their own work have no reason to report any problems or wrongdoing.

In the next section, we present business transactions and the associated internal controls. By following the sequence of transactions in each of the three business transactions cycles, we show how the accounting information system uses various documents to gather and control the necessary information about the transactions. We include examples of three documents that are commonly used by employees who are not accountants.

A CYCLES' VIEW OF OPERATING ACTIVITIES

As we noted previously in this chapter, we group operating activities into three cycles: (1) expenditure, (2) revenue, and (3) conversion. The expenditure and revenue cycles represent a series of transactions between a company and another party. The conversion cycle represents a series of events that occur within a single manufacturing company. By viewing the operating activities as these cycles of related transactions or events, it is easier to understand the various transactions in which most businesses engage in pursuit of their objective of trying to earn a profit.

The **expenditure cycle** is a sequence of business events in which the business exchanges assets for goods and services provided from suppliers, such as vendors and employees. In the **revenue cycle,** customers and the business engage in a series of transactions in which the business sells goods and services to the customer and receives payment from the customer. We discuss these cycles subsequently in more detail.

Cycles in Service and Merchandising Firms versus Manufacturing Firms

Exhibit 3.4 shows that both expenditure and revenue cycles occur in service and merchandising firms. Recall that the product of a service firm is a service, such as health care or legal advice. During the expenditure cycle, a service firm acquires labor, skill, and expertise from its employees in exchange for cash, or wages paid. A service firm also acquires other goods and services necessary for business operations, such as utilities for the buildings and benefits like health insurance for employees. In the revenue cycle, service firms exchange their services for cash or for a customer's agreement to pay later.

EXHIBIT   3.4

Operating Cycles for Service
and Merchandising Firms

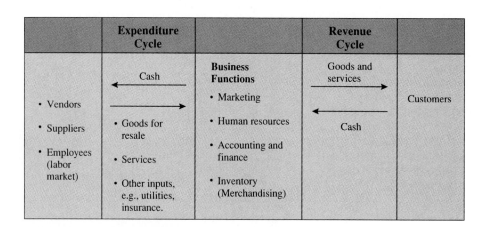

	Expenditure Cycle		Revenue Cycle	
• Vendors • Suppliers • Employees (labor market)	← Cash → • Goods for resale • Services • Other inputs, e.g., utilities, insurance.	**Business Functions** • Marketing • Human resources • Accounting and finance • Inventory (Merchandising)	Goods and services → ← Cash	Customers

Merchandising firms also have employee and other operating costs as part of their expenditure cycle, and their revenue cycle often includes providing customer services. The important difference between service and merchandising firms is that merchandising firms sell goods to customers as part of their revenue cycle and purchase the same goods for resale as part of their expenditure cycle. The purchase of goods for resale represents most of the transactions in the expenditure cycle of merchandising firms.

Cycles in Manufacturing Firms

The **conversion cycle,** shown in Exhibit 3.5, occurs in manufacturing firms as a sequence of events that combines raw materials, labor from employees, and other manufacturing resources to produce products. Most of the transactions found in service and merchandising firms are also part of the business activities of manufacturing firms. A major difference between manufacturing firms and other types of businesses exists in the expenditure cycle because the manufacturer purchases goods that are used to make other products, which it sells to customers.

The conversion cycle found in manufacturing firms differs from the expenditure and revenue cycles in that it does not involve exchange transactions between the company and external parties. Rather, the conversion cycle is a sequence of events conducted within a business. There are documents related to conversion, or production, activities that serve to maintain employee accountability for various facets of the production process itself. We discuss this cycle in more detail below.

A part of a merchandising firm's revenue cycle is providing customer service. The purchase of those same goods for resale is part of their expenditure cycle.

PAUSE & REFLECT

Classifying firms into service, merchandising, and manufacturing can be challenging. How would you classify a fast food restaurant like McDonald's? Or a company that sells appliances with warranties for the appliances' parts? Would your answer change if the warranty was sold separately as a service contract?

EXHIBIT | 3.5

Operating Cycles for Manufacturing Firms

	Expenditure Cycle	Conversion Cycle	Revenue Cycle	
• Vendors • Suppliers • Employees (labor market)	Cash ← → • Raw materials • Services • Other inputs, e.g., utilities, insurance.	Combine raw materials, labor and other inputs to make products	Goods and services → ← Cash	Customers

As we expand our discussion of each operating cycle, we describe some of the source documents that serve as inputs into the accounting system, with a focus on the documents often used or discussed by employees who are not accountants. All of these documents communicate information about transactions between a business and outside parties. For example, some documents indicate both the types and quantities of goods a customer wants to buy or the amount of money the customer owes to the business. We also explain the role of documents that a company sends between employees of the business, such as those used to communicate between the employees who need a product or service and the employees who are responsible for purchasing that product or service.

Even if most of you who read this book do not become accountants, you need to understand how to use accounting information in your organization. Thus, the discussion focuses on how to interpret the information in the documents rather than on how to prepare them. Understanding what information is communicated and where it originates enhances your understanding of the transactions and will allow you to answer questions like, When was this shipped? or What price did we agree to?

We illustrate the sequence of communications in the three business cycles by explaining the **paper trail** required, in most cases, for each cycle. The paper trail is the series of documents created to record information regarding various business transactions. Visualizing documents can provide a more concrete picture of the operating activities involved in each business cycle. However, today virtually all businesses have computerized accounting systems that perform the function of one or more of these documents electronically.

PAUSE & REFLECT

What aspects of transactions will change when they are communicated electronically instead of manually by paper documents? What aspects will not change? Is it better to communicate documents electronically rather than manually to avoid unwanted tampering in communication? Why?

Expenditure Cycle: Acquiring Merchandise, Services, or Raw Materials

We begin our discussion of the three transaction cycles with the expenditure cycle. We know that the expenditure cycle is a sequence of transactions, or activities, between a business and the suppliers from whom it acquires goods and services. The business's suppliers include vendors who provide merchandise for resale (merchandising firms) or raw materials for production (manufacturing firms). In addition, other external parties provide services to a business, such as utility and advertising companies. We also consider payments for services provided by employees as part of the expenditure cycle, though the detailed discussion is deferred until Chapter 8.

For most businesses, purchasing activities that lead to business expenditures are important because of their sheer volume and the dollar amount involved. For example, in

1993 Southwest Airlines operated 178 airplanes that served 52 airports, and each plane was in operation an average of 10 hours and 56 minutes a day.[5] Each time Southwest bought fuel, it engaged in a purchasing activity. In total, those purchases translate into fuel and oil purchases for 1993 totaling almost $304 million. This was equivalent to 13.3 percent of Southwest's revenues from ticket sales and charter flights.

There are two business goals accomplished during the expenditure cycle: (1) to receive the best quality goods and services, when needed, at the lowest possible price and (2) to ensure timely payment for the goods and services.

In this chapter, we focus on the purchase of goods for resale. However, purchases of other goods and services used by businesses, such as buying supplies and hiring business consultants, follow a similar sequence. The steps involved in paying employees for services (are examined in Chapter 8).

The expenditure cycle includes four primary activities: (1) determining the business's needs for goods and services, (2) selecting a vendor and placing the order, (3) receiving, securing, and storing the goods, and (4) paying for the goods and services received. The complexity of each of these activities depends on the nature of the business, its size, and the degree of geographic dispersion. For example, a small retailer with a single shop does not have the same complexity as a broadly scattered chain of stores such as J. C. Penney whose store managers order goods that are paid for from a central headquarters. However, the sequence of purchasing activities is basically the same for both types of organizations. Remember these important considerations for each activity in the expenditure cycle.

Determining the Business's Need for Goods   It would create chaos if everyone in a business were to order goods and services from vendors. There would be times when orders would be duplicated, and other times when orders were never placed. Small companies, usually those with less than 40 or 50 employees, can use less formal procedures for ordering goods or services than larger companies. In a small company, it may be sufficient to tell the person authorized to make the purchase to do so. However, as companies increase in size and become more geographically dispersed, their purchasing procedures need to become more formalized.

Large companies, like J. C. Penney and Southwest Airlines, have separate purchasing departments managed by people who are experienced in both the legal and logistical aspects of purchasing for large organizations. To make sure that proper ordering procedures are followed, the purchasing department is given authority to purchase on behalf of the other areas within the business. So how does the department know what to order, how many items to order, and when the items are needed?

When various business departments need items, they request them by using a purchase requisition to communicate their needs to the purchasing department. The purchasing requisition includes the type and quantity of items needed. Exhibit 3.6 describes the function and sources of purchase requisitions and the other three primary documents found in the expenditure cycle: purchase order, receiving report, and vendor's invoice. The purchase order indicates the items required. Purchase orders are sent to vendors or other suppliers who will provide the goods or services in accordance with the shipping instructions included on the purchase order. The other documents complete the communications necessary to buy and pay for goods and services.

Selecting Vendors and Ordering Goods   Exhibit 3.7 presents an example of a *purchase requisition*, a document that includes information about the type and quantity of goods or services needed and the date they are required by the requesting department. Notice the control features incorporated in the purchase requisition: They are serially

---

[5]Southwest Airlines, Inc., Annual Report, 1993.

EXHIBIT	3.6	Documents Found in a Typical Expenditure Cycle

Document Name	What Is Its Function?	Where Does It Originate?
Purchase requisition (see Exhibit 3.7)	Provides an approved list of goods and services by someone who is authorized to make purchases	Anyone within the business who needs goods or services—usually a department
Purchase order (see Exhibit 3.8)	Provides the vendor with a list of what items are needed and their quantities, in addition to other terms, like shipping dates	The purchasing department, or someone authorized to buy for the business
Receiving report	Shows a record of the type and quantity of goods received and their condition upon receipt	Receiving department
Vendor's invoice	Requests payment for goods or services delivered to the business	The vendor or supplier

numbered so that the person responsible for them knows if documents are missing. Also, the authorized person must sign the request so that the purchasing department can verify the signature to avoid unauthorized requests.

Once the purchasing department receives the purchase requisition from the requesting department, it selects the vendor to supply the needed goods or services. As a result of the recent emphasis on product quality, relationships between businesses and their vendors have become even more important than they were in the past. Businesses want the goods they purchase to be exactly as specified and to be as free from defects as possible. Also, businesses need to ensure that goods are available when needed and in the quantities needed. Thus, the business vendor selection process assesses service and quality as well as price. In the 1980s, it was more typical for purchasing managers to shop for vendors with an emphasis on price; more recently, however, quality and service have become equally important goals.

As a result of these closer relationships, businesses and vendors often work together in areas such as product design and production scheduling. When Chrysler Motors designs new cars, designated employees consult with the vendors who will supply parts like seats, windshields, and headlights and discuss production issues like the ease of assembly and quality control. Although purchasing jets is not an operating activity, Southwest Airlines and Boeing have a cooperative business-vendor relationship. As part of the recent purchase of 63 Boeing 737s, Southwest participated in the design of those jets, which resulted in a quieter, more fuel-efficient, and more easily maintainable aircraft. Herb Kelleher, CEO of Southwest Airlines, referred to Boeing as "our partner for 22 years."

Often the business goal of getting the right quantity and quality of goods when needed conflicts with the goal of buying those goods at the lowest possible price. For example, vendors usually offer lower prices per unit for larger quantities purchased (volume discounts). However, purchasing larger quantities may require the business to receive more goods than it actually needs. This could lead to lost, damaged, or stolen goods. In addition, large amounts of goods may require warehouse space for excess inventories. Managers who are responsible for purchasing must balance these conflicts when determining the timing and quantity of goods to purchase. We discuss this issue in Chapter 5.

Once the vendor is selected, the purchasing department sends a *purchase order* (shown in Exhibit 3.8) to the vendor. The purchase order stipulates the quantity and description of the goods or services requested as well as other terms such as the delivery date.

By accepting the purchase order, two important things occur: (1) the vendor enters into a legal contract binding the vendor to provide the goods or services and (2) the purchaser agrees to pay the vendor the agreed-upon price. Thus, the purchase

EXHIBIT **3.7** **Purchase Requisition**

It is important for purchasing personnel to know when goods or services are needed by the department that placed the request.

Only persons within the department with proper authority approve requisitions.

Once a vendor is selected, that information plus the purchase order number is added to the requisition.

Items must be described in detail so that purchasing personnel can determine what is needed and the quantity desired.

COMPANY		CO. NO.	SHIP TO		DATE ORIGINATED	BU	CO. NO.	BILL OF MAT'L NO.	REQUISITION NO.
PURCHASE ORDER NO.	SHIPPING DATE				DATE REQUIRED	ORIGINATED BY			9467

VENDOR (PURCHASING USE ONLY)

USED FOR

MARK FOR		PHONE		MAIL	CONFIRMING TO
VIA					Items Listed on This Document Rec'd by:
F.O.B.					

Signature _____ Date

Item No.	Quantity	Unit of Meas.	Description of Material	Account Coding Block						Purchasing Use Only	
				BU	Loc	Acct/WO	Sub	Var./Stock No.		Unit Price	Amount

Total Amount:

Est. Order Value (Originator):

Buyer: .

PURCHASING USE ONLY

PREFERRED VENDOR (OPTIONAL)

APPROVALS			
MANAGER	DATE	SUPERINTENDENT/SUPERVISOR	DATE
MANAGER (DIRECT)	DATE	MATERIALS REVIEWED BY	DATE
VICE PRESIDENT	DATE	PURCHASING DEPARTMENT	DATE

DISTRIBUTION: Original to Purchasing   Copy to Numeric and/or Work Order File

EXHIBIT | **3.8** | **Purchase Order**

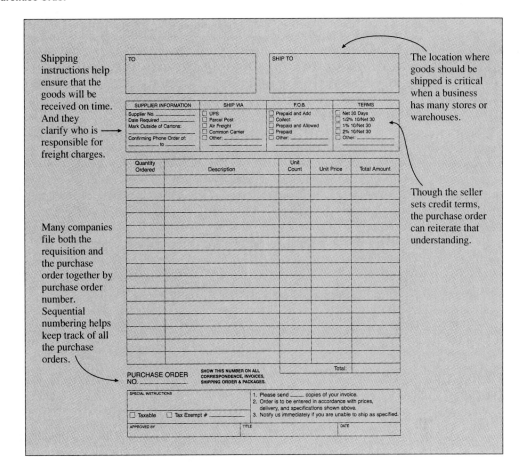

Shipping instructions help ensure that the goods will be received on time. And they clarify who is responsible for freight charges.

The location where goods should be shipped is critical when a business has many stores or warehouses.

Though the seller sets credit terms, the purchase order can reiterate that understanding.

Many companies file both the requisition and the purchase order together by purchase order number. Sequential numbering helps keep track of all the purchase orders.

order is not only a means of communicating but also has legal standing as a contract. Purchase orders can also communicate other terms of the agreement, such as the delivery date and credit terms.

Receiving, Securing, and Storing Goods   After the vendor delivers the requested goods to the business, the business must inspect, store, and secure the assets. The inspection process ensures that (1) the goods meet the agreed-upon terms of the transaction, including the type and quantity of items, and (2) the goods are in acceptable condition. The business's employees in the receiving department record this information on the receiving report and send it to the department responsible (usually accounting) for making payments to the vendor.

Another result of the closer relationships between vendors and businesses today is that we now find vendors working to provide goods that are free of defects so that they do not need to be inspected. Receiving goods for production that are free of defects means that manufacturers do not have production delays due to inferior goods. It also reduces the chance that the business's customers will receive goods that are not high quality.

Once goods are inspected, strong internal controls require that they be secured and stored so that only certain people have access to them. In addition, it is often necessary to consider storage under certain special physical conditions, such as appropriate temperature and humidity. For example, electronic components may be damaged by heat and dust, so manufacturers must store them in a cool clean place prior to shipment.

he revolution in electronic technology has had a profound effect on the ways that companies purchase goods and services. Today, it is common to find companies that use purchase requisitions and receiving reports that are electronic—that is, they never exist on paper!

Many businesses now use a process called *electronic data imaging (EDI)*, which requires that users complete "forms" on their computer screens. The information generated is stored and then transmitted electronically when necessary. Among the many advantages of EDI is the ability of employees to check information instantly, thus reducing errors and delays that are inherent in a manual purchasing system.

Gerard D. O'Connell, CEO of Structured Computer Systems, Avon, Connecticut, cites three ways that automated purchasing systems help his company's operations:

- *Increase efficiency.* End users at more than 300 district offices use a system to generate requisitions without involving purchasing staff. As a result, the vast majority of purchase orders require no manual attention at corporate headquarters.
- *Reduce inventory.* Another purchasing operation uses a computerized materials management system to manage discrepancies between the demand for goods and their inventory levels. The system updates the inventory levels of raw materials and finished goods and automatically generates requisitions, when needed, for products that need to be restocked. This system has reduced stockouts and, at the same time, allowed the company to reduce its inventory, which made it possible to defer building another warehouse.
- *Contain costs.* By having a computerized purchasing system, the company can easily and quickly see the level of expenditures committed to its suppliers. This allows for timely comparisons of actual spending to amounts budgeted, which helps various departments stay within their spending limits.

Adapted from *Purchasing,* December 12, 1995.

Paying for Goods and Services Received Paying vendors for the goods and services received is the final activity in the expenditure cycle. The *vendor's invoice* is a bill that the vendor sends after shipping the goods. It shows the quantity of goods sent, the description of the goods, and the price billed to the customer. The person responsible for paying the invoice (in the accounting department) cross-checks the quantity and description of the goods or services on the purchase order, the completed receiving report, and the vendor's invoice to ensure that only goods ordered, received, and authorized for payment are paid for.

Purchase Discounts One critical aspect of paying invoices is the timing of the payment. Vendors offer **purchase discounts,** which are reductions from the invoice price for payment by customers made within a period of time, often 10 to 30 days. These discounts are incentives for the business to pay early. The business should delay payment of the invoice until the latest possible time in the discount period, yet pay it early enough to be able to take the discount. Although paying early requires that the business give up the use of cash before it legally has to, there is a significant advantage to the business in taking purchase discounts, as we now illustrate.

Critical Timing for Payment Assume that J. C. Penney receives an invoice for goods from a vendor with a total price of $150,000. The terms on the invoice state 2/10, n/30. This means that J. C. Penney may deduct 2 percent from the total $150,000, or $3,000, if it pays the full amount due within *10 days* of either the receipt of the invoice or the invoice date, even though the invoice is not due for 30 days. Thus, if J. C. Penney pays the invoice within 10 days, the goods will cost only $147,000 [$150,000 − ($150,000 × .02)].

Purchase discounts often deceive managers because their amount, usually 1 or 2 percent, seems small. However, 1 or 2 percent on a large purchase can be thousands of dollars. We can find the annualized interest cost of not taking a discount by using the following general formula:

$$\frac{365 \text{ days}}{\text{Invoice period} - \text{Discount period}} \times \frac{\text{Discount \%}}{100\% - \text{Discount \%}}$$

The first term in this formula finds the number of times the interval from the end of the discount period to the end of the invoice period occurs in a year. The second term is the interest rate on the discounted amount—the discount percentage divided by the invoice as a percentage (100%) less the discount percentage. Then, multiplying the number of intervals by the interest rate results in annual interest rate incurred by the purchaser if it does not pay within the discount period.

In the J. C. Penney example, the 2 percent discount is for only a 10-day period. So, paying at the end of the invoice period is like paying interest for the remaining 20 days (30-day invoice period less the 10-day discount period), which is equal to the dollar amount of the discount. Therefore, the effective annualized cost of *not* taking a 2 percent discount is:

$$\frac{365}{30 - 10} \times \frac{.02}{1.00 - .02} = 37.2\%$$

As you can see, the cost of not taking a discount is very high. For most businesses, the best policy is to pay all invoices within the discount period, even if the company has to borrow the money from a bank and pay interest at an annual rate of 12 or 14 percent. In our example, if J. C. Penney owed an average of $2 million throughout the year and paid within the discount period instead of at the end of each invoice period, it would have saved $744,000 ($2,000,000 × 37.2%), quite a considerable sum!

In summary, the expenditure cycle occurs every time a business acquires a good or service from someone outside the business. In the revenue cycle, described next, businesses engage in a sequence of activities that provide cash from operating activities.

PAUSE & REFLECT

Do the events involved in paying employees require the same documents as other transactions with vendors in the expenditure cycle? If not, what other documents might be found in transactions with employees?

Revenue Cycle: Selling Goods and Services

The revenue cycle involves a business and its customers in a series of transactions where the customer receives goods and pays for them. The two primary goals of the revenue cycle are: (1) to sell the products the customer wants, in the quantities they want, at a competitive price, and (2) to receive payment from the customer within the invoice period.

There are five primary activities in the revenue cycle: (1) generating customer orders, (2) approving customer credit for credit sales, (3) shipping goods to customers, (4) billing credit customers, and (5) collecting from customers. The complexity of the revenue cycle depends mainly on the customer-credit policies the business establishes. A company such as McDonald's, which does not extend credit to its customers, has a much less complex revenue cycle than a company, such as J. C. Penney, which allows its customers to use J. C. Penney charge cards. Next, we discuss some important aspects of the activities in the revenue cycle for a company that extends credit to its customers.

Generating Customer Orders Changes in business practices are revising the nature of generating customer orders, which is the beginning of the revenue cycle. Until the mid-1980s, companies made products first and then began the process of marketing them to potential customers. Increasingly, in today's business environment, marketing a product begins even before it is developed.

Companies often use two important sources of information to determine which products and services will meet customers' needs: the marketing department's analysis of customer buying habits and surveys of customer preferences. Related customer-focused issues, such as quality of the products and services, are essential to successful marketing of products and, consequently, to the profitability of the business.

Although sales transactions between the business and its customers occur in a variety of forms, the two basic forms are cash sales and credit sales. Customers often initiate cash sales when they go to the business, but cash sales also occur in other settings. For example, consider door-to-door book sales made by students or cosmetic sales made by cosmetic company representatives, or personal fitness trainers who visit clients' homes. Cash sales are the simplest sales transactions in that they require a direct exchange of cash for goods or services. In such cases, there is no need for shipping products and billing, or for subsequent collections from customers.

Credit sales are made when goods are delivered to the customer before the customer pays for them. Credit sales can result from personal contact, either with the customer in a retail store or with a sales representative who calls on the customer at his or her business. When making credit sales, an employee writes a *sales order*, which starts the process of filling the customer's request. Customers initiate credit sales by placing an order in person, by mail, or by telephone.

Some transactions that appear to be credit sales from the customer's perspective may, in fact, be cash sales from the business's perspective. When the customer uses an outside credit card, such as VISA, Mastercard, or American Express, the business, such as J. C. Penney, treats the transaction as a cash sale. When a customer uses the business's charge card, such as using a J. C. Penney card at J. C. Penney, the transaction is treated as a credit sale.[6] The reason for the distinction between the outside credit card sale being treated as a cash sale and the company's credit card being treated as a credit sale is that the business is not subject to the risk of nonpayment with an outside card. When a customer uses an outside charge card, the credit card company pays the business in cash for the amount of the sale less the card company's fee. Then the credit card company assumes the risk of collection.

Typically, credit cards like VISA charge businesses fees ranging from 1 to 7 percent to cover the cost of collecting from the customer and other costs of their operations like advertising and uncollectible amounts. When a business issues its own credit cards, it bears the risk of nonpayment and all costs of collection, which can be significant.

Another form of sale results from bidding by a variety of competitors. In these cases, the customer invites bids and specifies what he or she wants to buy, which can range from major construction projects, such as ships or buildings, to large lots of supplies used in offices or in production. The advantage of the bidding process to the customer is that it explicitly encourages competition among vendors who are vying to make the sale and, therefore, who are focused on the customer's specific needs. This approach to sales transactions is very common in service industries like architecture and engineering, or even for contracts involving services such as janitorial services.

Approving Customer Credit Businesses face a risk of being unable to collect the amounts due from customers when they allow credit sales to be made. Thus, an important step in the credit sales approach is making sure that the customer can pay for the goods.

---

[6]Many businesses allow customers to charge purchases without using a charge card (known as *charging on open account*).

The best way to reduce the risk of nonpayment is to obtain credit approval. This usually involves a background check of how well the potential customer has paid debts in the past by reviewing the customer's credit history. Obtaining credit approval for customers usually is necessary only for the initial sale. After that, the customer is preapproved and can make purchases for amounts within approved limits without additional credit checks.

Shipping Goods to Customers   Many sales occur where the customer is not present, such as when the customer places phone orders. In such cases, it is necessary to remove goods from storage, such as warehouses, and ship them to the customer. Shipping can be done on "common carriers" like freight companies or on the business's own trucks. When using a common carrier, the business includes the freight charges as part of the sales agreement between the business and the customer. To determine who pays freight charges, it is necessary to first determine who owns the goods during transit. Ownership in transit depends on the shipping terms.

Shipping Terms   The shipping agreement between the business and the common carrier is known as a *bill of lading*. It sets out the rates that the carrier will charge and the degree of responsibility that each party has for lost or damaged goods. This document can be used to trace lost shipments using the carrier's accounting system.

The terms of the bill of lading may indicate that the goods were shipped **free on board (FOB) destination,** which means that the legal title to the goods does not pass to the customer until he or she *receives* the goods. Therefore, goods sold FOB destination implies that the seller of the goods pays any related freight charges required to move the goods to the customer.

On the other hand, goods shipped **FOB shipping point** legally belong to the customer when they are picked up by the common carrier because that is the point at which legal title transfers. In such cases, the customer would be responsible for payment of freight charges.

Implications of Shipping Terms   The term of shipment—FOB destination or FOB shipping point—have two important implications. One implication involves measuring a period's income. If goods are sold FOB destination at the end of an accounting period, then the sale is not included in determining the seller's current year's income because the transaction is not complete until the customer has title to the goods. If the same goods are sold FOB shipping point at the end of the accounting period, the seller would include the sale as part of the current year's income. As an example, suppose a company ships $200,000 of merchandise on December 31, 1996. If the merchandise is shipped FOB shipping point, the company has a $200,000 sale in 1996. However, if the goods are shipped FOB destination, the company cannot recognize this sale until 1997 when the goods are received by, and legal title passes to, the buyer.

Shipping terms also have another implication for goods damaged or lost during shipping. If title does not pass until the customer receives the goods, then goods that are damaged or lost during shipping are the seller's responsibility. The seller must deal with the shipping company to find the lost items or file the required insurance claims with its insurance company. When title passes at the shipment point, the buyer has responsibility for dealing with these problems.

Billing Credit Customers   Billing is an essential step in the process of making credit sales. Exhibit 3.9 shows an example of the type of *sales invoice* that sellers send to customers as "bills." The seller includes on the invoice information about the quantity and type of goods the customer is expected to pay for, and the price and terms of the sales agreement. The invoice often includes the customer's purchase order number, which the customer can easily use to trace the order from its inception through the receipt of the goods to approval of the invoice for payment.

EXHIBIT | **3.9** | **Sales Invoice**

It is important for
the company to
fill customers'
orders completely,
including
back-ordered
items.

Two copies of an
invoice are often
sent and the
duplicate is
returned with the
payment as a
remittance advice.

Prices of items on an
invoice should be
taken from an
approved price list.

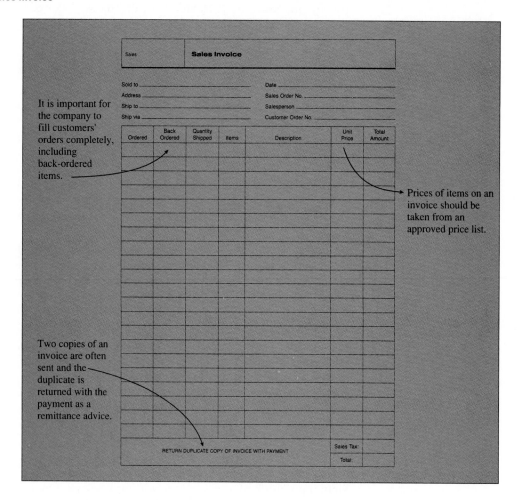

Note that the revenue cycle for one business (the seller) is the expenditure cycle for another (the customer). When the business sends an invoice to be paid, the customer receives the invoice and goes through the process described previously in the expenditure cycle. Exhibit 3.10 shows the customer and business in a related series of events that reflect a business's sale of goods to its customer. As part of its revenue cycle, the business receives the customer's purchase order (A), then sends the goods and invoice to the customer (B), and then receives payment (C). The customer's expenditure cycle begins with issuing the purchase order (A). After the customer receives the goods and invoice (B), it pays the invoice (C).

PAUSE & REFLECT

Sometimes sellers have some, but not all, items that a customer ordered. Should they wait until they have all the goods, or ship a partial order to the customer? Why? How would billing be affected?

In addition to determining which customers are allowed to purchase goods and services on credit, the business must also determine its discount policies. When a company wants to induce its customers to pay their bills early, it offers a **sales discount.** The sales discount works just like a purchase discount: It allows the customer to pay less than the full amount of the invoice if the customer remits the payment within a prespecified period of time. A business receives purchase discounts in the

EXHIBIT	3.10

Two Sides of the Same Transaction: Customer's Expenditure Cycle and Business's Revenue Cycle

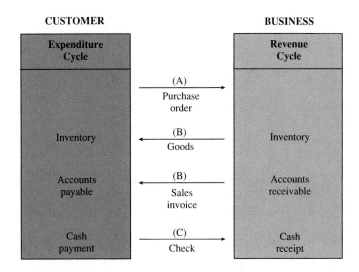

expenditure cycle that reduce its cost of purchases if it makes payments within the discount period, and offers sales discounts in the revenue cycle for the items that it sells.

Suppose a $20,000 sales transaction between two companies has terms of 3 percent discount for payment within 30 days, with the entire amount due in 60 days (i.e., 3/30, n/60). The buyer pays within the discount period and sends the seller $19,400 [$20,000 × (1.0 − .03)]. The buyer has a purchase discount of $600, and the seller records the same $600 as a sales discount!

Sales discounts are more common in wholesale industries where companies make sales to retailers like J. C. Penney, rather than in businesses which sell the goods to the consumer. Exhibit 3.11 presents a summary of the functions and sources of the sales order, bill of lading, and sales invoice documents we have discussed. In addition, it presents information about the sales slips given to customers at the point of sale and the remittance advice that customers include when they send payments for credit sales, both of which are important to the revenue cycle.

EXHIBIT	3.11	Documents Found in a Typical Revenue Cycle

Document Name	What Is Its Function?	Where Does It Originate?
Customer or sales order	Initiates the process of filling the customer's order; the request for specific products (type, amounts, etc.) or services	The customer or a salesperson
Bill of lading	Serves as a contract between a freight carrier and the selling company indicating carrier company rates and responsibility for lost or damaged goods	The business contracts with a common carrier for carrier to deliver the goods to the customer
Sales invoice (see Exhibit 3.9)	Requests payment from the customer for goods or services supplied by the business	Company sends it to the customer after goods are shipped or services are provided
Sales slip	Serves as initial record of a cash sale and as a receipt for the customer	Produced at the time of a cash sale by the cash register or handwritten by the salesclerk, who gives it to the customer
Remittance advice	Ensures that the business records the customer's payment properly; a list of the customer's account-related information (date, account number, amount of payment, etc.)	Part of the sales invoice the customer detaches and returns with his/her payment

Even providing services under a long-term contract that resulted from winning a competitive bid requires that a company engage in periodic billing and collection. Typically as part of the contract, the parties agree to "progress billings." The firm providing the service, like an architecture or accounting firm, periodically sends invoices during the term of the contract to cover a portion of the total amount due, which equals unbilled work performed to date. In addition, the firm providing the service and the business receiving the service agree on the measures to use regarding the service provided, like hours worked, because receipt of services is harder to measure than receipt of goods.

Collecting from Customers It is important to both the customer and the business that the business records payments properly to give the customer credit for payments made. The customer does not want to be billed more than once for purchases that he or she has paid for. Double billing does not reflect well on the business, and it hurts customer relations. So the business wants an internal control system that avoids the expense of trying to straighten out problems caused by double billing and lost customers due to billing problems.

Regardless of whether a business is a service, merchandising, or manufacturing firm, it has expenditure and revenue cycles. However, manufacturing firms make the products they sell. In the next section, we describe the processes involved in making products.

Conversion Cycle: Manufacturing Products

The conversion cycle, as previously described, is found *only* in manufacturing businesses. It requires the use of machines and other equipment along with employee labor to convert raw materials into products to be sold. The raw materials are acquired through the expenditure cycle, and the finished goods produced by the business are, in turn, sold during the revenue cycle.

We know that, unlike the other two cycles, the events of the conversion cycle do not directly involve outside parties. However, vendors are linked to the conversion process through the expenditure cycle. Recall that vendors affect the quality of the goods and the timing of their receipt and, thus, introduction into the conversion process. Customers also are connected to the conversion process directly through the products sold to them as part of the revenue cycle.

Recently businesses have begun to use their customers as a source of information for the conversion process, so that products manufactured meet customers' needs and, thus, compete effectively in the marketplace. The goal of the conversion cycle is to manufacture quality products that customers want at the time they want them at the lowest possible cost.

There are four primary activities in the conversion cycle: (1) scheduling production, (2) requisitioning raw materials, (3) combining labor, machines, and other resources to make the goods, and (4) storing finished goods. The length and complexity of the conversion cycle vary greatly among manufacturing firms. For example, clothing manufacturers like Levi Strauss make their products in a short (less than one year), repetitive conversion cycle. Other manufacturers, like Boeing, require a much longer conversion cycle to manufacture products because their products are so large and complex. In the following sections, we describe some important aspects of each activity in the conversion cycle.

Scheduling Production Manufacturers try to process raw materials in a systematic and controlled way that minimizes costs. Since it is often necessary to use machines to make a wide variety of products, scheduling the use of machines and the arrival of materials is an important part of controlling and reducing costs. Production managers who understand the details of the production process make these scheduling decisions using estimates of product demand from the sales and marketing departments. These are important decisions that have significant bearing on the manufacturer's profitability.

Why Is Scheduling Important?   Scheduling production would not be a problem if a business made only one product, knew when customers wanted the product, and had only a few vendors from which it had to arrange delivery. Because most manufacturers have many products, many vendors, and do not know exactly when a customer wants the product, scheduling production is not a simple problem. How well scheduling is done can greatly affect the cost of the product. For example, a company with 800 production workers, each paid $18 an hour, will lose $14,400 for every hour that it has to stop production due to shortages of raw materials.

Many manufacturers use each of their machines to make a variety of different products. Using the same machine to make different products requires changing its "setup." **Machine setups** are adjustments made to machines to get them ready to manufacture the next type of product; for example, changing parts like drill bits so that the machine meets the design requirements of the next product. When machines were manually operated, this process took hours, or even days. Increasingly we find that computers control machine setups, and, because of this, required setup times are dropping. Dramatic reductions in setup times have been reported. For example, one company reported reducing setup time for one machine from 6 hours to 1.7 minutes.[7]

In addition, manufacturers are organizing their production floors into "cells" so that machines related to the production of certain products or types of products are located close to each other, which reduces travel time between machines for goods in production. Traditionally, machines that served the same purpose (e.g., drills) were clustered together.

In manufacturing facilities organized in the **cells,** the machines related to products or groups of products are clustered. For example, consider a pharmaceutical firm that makes antibiotics sold in capsules. The firm could organize its production into cells by locating the machines for mixing the compounds, putting the mixed product into the capsules, and packaging the capsules close together on the production floor. This would make the production process more efficient. Another company that reorganized its facility reported a reduction in the travel distance for one product from 2,000 feet to 18 inches.[8] Schedulers also use mathematical models to determine the optimal length of production runs (the number of a given product made at one time) based on factors like setup times and the organization of the production floor.

Factors Affecting Scheduling   The overriding factor in scheduling production is the demand for the product. A manufacturer wants inventories of both raw materials and finished goods to be as small as possible. So, it wants to produce the amount of product required when the product is needed. Predictions of customer demand for the product based on sources such as surveys conducted in places that sell the product play a critical role in production scheduling. Customer demand for products can fluctuate with the season, or even daily, and the production process needs to adapt its output to the expected level of demand. Chapter 5 discusses planning for operating activities, including production, in more detail.

The complexity of the products and the production process itself, as well as the number of different products produced, can affect scheduling. Products like cars and appliances make production complicated because of the number of different parts they require. In manufacturing products such as these, getting the parts where they are needed, and when they are needed can be a difficult scheduling task. Products that require a complicated sequence of processes also can make the production scheduling difficult. For example, refining crude oil into gasoline involves a complicated series of chemical transformations and, consequently, sophisticated scheduling of production activities.

---

[7]Reported by Robert Kaplan in "Accounting Lag: The Obsolescence of Cost Accounting Systems," *California Management Review*, Winter 1986, pp. 174–99.

[8]Ibid., p. 180.

In addition to making a wide array of products, manufacturers sometimes must package a product, or products, in a variety of different forms. Pharmaceutical companies like McNeil Consumer Products, maker of Tylenol, package a brand like Tylenol in a variety of different strengths and package sizes, all of which complicate scheduling the production process. Other factors affecting scheduling include the availability of raw materials, the length of production runs, the time and complexity of machine setups, and lead times for delivery, including packaging and shipping time.

Obtaining Raw Materials Raw materials and other supplies (inventories) used in the production process are acquired through the expenditure cycle and stored in a secure place until they are needed on the production floor. Raw materials, such as the steel used in making cars or the crude oil used in making gasoline, and supplies, such as the glue used in making furniture or the solder used in making electric appliances, are then requisitioned into the manufacturing process as they are needed.

Every product, whether it is produced by a chemical process, such as gasoline, or assembled from parts, such as cars, has a list of ingredients similar to a recipe. We call this a *bill of materials*, which is produced by the design engineers and lists every part or ingredient necessary to make the product. Engineers also develop an *operations list* which shows the sequence of activities required to manufacture the product. Using the bills of materials, the operations list, and production schedules, purchasing departments can coordinate schedules with production and inventory control personnel to have the right materials available for production when they are needed.

When there is a need for raw materials in production, an authorized employee from the production department obtains the needed materials from storage. In order to maintain control over the materials, the person getting the materials uses a materials requisition form. This document indicates what is needed in production and shows that the person requesting the goods has the authority to do so. Thus, the accountability for these materials shifts from storage to production at the time of materials requisition. Therefore, any damage or theft after the materials leave storage and before they are moved to finished goods is the responsibility of the production department.

Making Products Manufacturing processes for making products are as varied as the products we see every day. Actual production begins when the scheduler of production issues a production order. Production orders provide information to the production workers about the required schedule and identify the products or batches of products as they go through the production process. Being able to identify when and where defective products were produced allows quality control, that is, monitoring quality to ensure adherence to standards, to be included in the production process. In addition, knowing where specific items or batches are in the process improves prediction of the need for raw materials and machine time, as well as the completion time for the goods.

The Role of Labor Businesses hire the individuals to supply the labor required to make products. These employees provide a variety of human resources for the production of goods. Employees provide labor for operating manufacturing machines or for transforming the raw materials into finished products manually. In addition, employees provide labor in the form of supervisory services, janitorial services, and other labor services used in the manufacturing process. Exhibit 3.12 shows the required combination of production inputs in the conversion cycle to manufacture finished products.

Manufacturing Overhead **Manufacturing overhead** is the cost of all manufacturing resources used to make products that are not directly associated with production. Manufacturing overhead includes items such as the rent on the manufacturing

EXHIBIT | 3.12

The Production Process and the Conversion Cycle

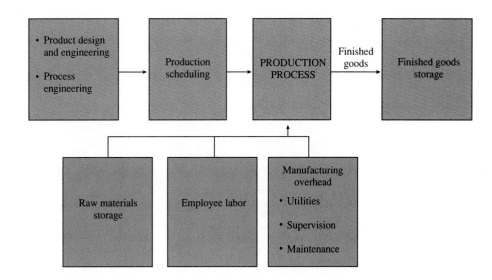

facilities; insurance on the raw materials inventory; and heat, light, and power used to manufacture products. A growing category of overhead costs includes the engineering costs of designing products and scheduling the production process. Associating engineering and other overhead costs with products helps make the operating and strategic decisions about those products more economically sound. Nonmanufacturing cost includes rent, utilities, and insurance costs for the parts of the business *not directly associated with production*, such as the sales and human resources departments.

Effects of Automation As companies become more automated, the amount of manufacturing overhead relative to direct materials and direct labor increases. For many manufacturing companies, manufacturing overhead is 70 percent or more of the costs of total production.

Until the mid-1980s, direct labor was a large part of the costs of making products. As a result, the costs included in manufacturing overhead were assigned to products based on the amount of labor that products required. The more labor time that a product took to manufacture, the more overhead costs were included in its total costs. Thus, goods that required large amounts of labor also had large amounts of overhead added to their cost, regardless of the amount of overhead the product might have actually required.

Now, in mass production industries like consumer electronics, we find that direct labor is only 5 percent or less of the total product cost. Therefore, adding overhead costs based on direct labor distorts the cost of products and can lead to bad business decisions. Today to allocate overhead costs more realistically, businesses are using activity-based costing, which we discuss in more detail in Chapter 10.

Storing Finished Goods After the manufacturing process is complete, finished products move from the production floor to storage. An efficient business stores these products for as short a time as possible to minimize the storage costs and the investment in finished, unsold goods. Selling finished goods involves activities previously described in the revenue cycle.

Exhibit 3.13 shows the functions of the primary documents in the conversion cycle. The bill of materials and the operations list are created by engineers as part of designing the product. The production of a product is initiated by the production schedulers with the production order. Materials requisitions authorize the release of raw materials to the production floor, while time tickets record the amount of time that production workers spend on various products or conversion activities.

EXHIBIT	3.13	Documents Found in a Typical Conversion Cycle	
Document Name	**What Is Its Function?**		**Where Does It Originate?**
Bill of materials	Shows the quantities of materials and parts necessary to make a specific product; the "recipe" for a product		Product design engineers
Operations list	Shows the sequence of production operations (e.g., cutting, welding, grinding)		Engineers who design a process to make the product as efficiently as possible
Production order	Identifies the job or batch of products as it goes through the process; includes information about the items, schedules, etc.		Production schedulers
Materials requisition	Authorizes the type and amount of raw materials to be removed from storage; shifts responsibility to employees on the production floor		Production personnel take the raw materials and supplies, and sign the requisition prepared by storage personnel as confirmation of receipt
Time ticket	Records employees' time as they work on various activities or batches of production		Employees; more recently, they use magnetic cards scanned by "readers"

RECENT BUSINESS CHANGES AND THEIR EFFECTS ON MANUFACTURING

It is important that you understand how recent changes in the business environment have had significant impacts on the way businesses operate. The greatest effects of these changes have been on the manufacturers' conversion cycle. We can group changes into three related areas: (1) the move toward the global markets, (2) customer-focused operations, and (3) advances in manufacturing and communications technology. Here we present a brief description of the impact of these changes on how manufacturers operate today.

Global Markets

The world is getting smaller in the sense that communication and transportation between countries are faster and cheaper than ever. Products made anywhere in the world can be sold almost anywhere else. Another effect of globalization is the formation of free trade blocks where member countries eliminate tariffs within the block and, thus, permit goods to be traded without restrictions. In 1992, the United States joined with Mexico and Canada to create the North American Free Trade Agreement (NAFTA), and many countries in Europe operate as a free trade block known as the European Economic Community. While these arrangements offer free trade among member countries, trade with nonmember countries remains restricted. These restrictions allow member countries to protect industries within the trading block by implementing tariffs for outside purchases, which effectively raise the price of goods from nonmember countries. However, the main effect of these trade agreements is increased trade among countries.

A major impact of globalization is that manufacturers must consider cultural differences when they design and market products. For example, when they design cars for global markets, U.S. automakers have had to consider the significance of gasoline costs, which are much higher outside the United States. Consequently, auto manufacturers assume that customers in those markets expect better fuel efficiency than U.S. customers, so cars intended to be sold in those markets must be more fuel efficient to compete effectively.

Labor markets are also becoming global. International companies like Nike can use labor in Mexico and China to make products. Then, Nike sells its products all over the world. In general, as countries with relatively low wage rates enter the worldwide manufacturing arena, countries with higher wage rates like the United States are disadvantaged because of higher labor costs and, therefore, manufacturing costs. As a result, manufacturers in high-wage countries have two alternatives: (1) they can move production to the low-wage countries, or (2) they can shift to more automated production processes. For manufacturers like Sony who have chosen to automate production, labor cost is a small and decreasing part of the costs of goods manufactured.

The impact of global markets is likely to continue for many years. As countries enter the global economy, they begin a cycle of improvement, beginning as producers. As sales of these countries' products increase, so does their wealth, which, in turn, allows them to also become consumers and raise their standard of living.

Customer-Focused Operations

Another major change in the business environment is the advent of customer-focused operations. The customer focus means that the whole operation of the business is aimed at providing the customers with what they want. Products need to be "user friendly" so that they meet the needs of consumers, are easy to use, and are reliable. Not only should the product be good, but the related product services like warranties and repairs should also meet customers' needs. Quality of goods and services has become the principal goal of customer-focused operations.

For manufacturing firms, this means setting the goal of zero defects for the goods they produce. The idea of zero defects has translated into designing products for quality rather than using inspections to determine quality of products. Before the product quality movement brought the concept of zero defects to manufacturing, product quality depended on inspections conducted during and after the production process. Now, quality results from changes in the production process, such as stopping production when defects are found and correcting the problem before any more defective items are produced. Other changes include designing products with fewer parts to assemble and simpler designs, thus creating less opportunity for production mistakes. Because vendors now get involved in the design process of the final product, they can actually see how their supplied parts/ideas fit into the final product. Companies allow vendors to have input into the design so that the final product can be made more easily and also can be more cost effective. At the same time, design engineers have to consider the production process itself, so that the product design makes it easy to assemble and allows the cost-efficient use of people and machines in production.

Advances in Manufacturing and Communications Technology

The most important recent changes in the production process involve technology. These technological changes are computer based and include

1. Computer-assisted design (CAD) of products, so that product designs can be "tested" before a single item is produced.

2. Computer-assisted manufacturing (CAM), which improves the speed and precision of activities like machine setups.

3. Computer-integrated manufacturing (CIM), in which the computer controls every aspect of production, beginning with requisitioning materials from vendors through scheduling flow of goods and materials through production.

New manufacturing technology also includes the use of robotics and other machines for producing goods with little human labor.

Automation requires more precise coordination of when the inputs, such as component parts and raw materials, arrive from vendors. In addition, changes in communications allow links to customers, which can control the production schedule. These links to customers, as well as to vendors, allow the amount produced to be as close to the amount demanded as possible, with no extra raw materials awaiting production. For example, one of Wal-Mart's vendors is Procter & Gamble, which manufactures a number of products including personal-care products like toothpaste. When Wal-Mart sells a tube of toothpaste and scans it at a checkout counter in its store, a series of computers communicate that event into Procter & Gamble's production schedule for toothpaste. This means that Wal-Mart has an automated requisition and purchase order, and that the replacement toothpaste orders, schedules for production, and shipment occur with little or no human intervention.

Increasing automation also is leading to the earlier involvement of customers and vendors in product development, which we already have mentioned. A more automated manufacturing process leads to increased investment in machines to do the work. Thus, it is important for businesses to gather a lot of quality information from customers and vendors as products are developed. This helps create the products that the customers want and also helps ensure that vendors can supply the necessary parts when they are needed. Determining customers' wants will help ensure that the expensive, specialized machines designed to automatically manufacture products are good investments. Then, with a good marketing strategy, companies can expect their products to sell well enough to pay for the required investment in automation and, as a result, to provide a good return.

The three factors discussed above—globalization, customer-focused operations, and technology—have radically changed manufacturing practices since the early 1980s. The markets for products now encircle the globe. The competition for customers has forced manufacturers to focus on the wants and needs of the customer. And computer-based technology has allowed new levels of production and product quality. The effects of these factors on manufacturing firms are likely to increase in the future.

In spite of these advances, not even products that are popular with customers sell well forever. Changes in customers' tastes and preferences as well as competitive pressures force businesses to develop new products. Next we discuss factors that affect the time span from the initial idea for a product through the time that it is no longer viable.

Product Life Cycle

The increased involvement of customers and vendors in the design process is due to shortened product life-cycles and increasing automation in the manufacturing process. The **product life cycle** is the course of product-related events that begins with the idea for a new product and ends when the product is no longer sold.

Exhibit 3.14 shows the level of costs incurred and revenues earned during various stages of the product life cycle. The **start-up phase** begins with initial product design and continues through the initial manufacture to delivery of the product to the first customer. This involves many costs, most of which involve marketing research and engineering costs, and no sales revenues. After the initial sale, the product enters a **development phase,** which follows the initial product sale, where product costs are still fairly high as the company explores new markets for the product. Once these markets are established, successful product sales climb throughout the **maturity phase** to the point where most of the potential customers have the product. Product costs are lower during the maturity phase because there is no longer a need for product and market development. Following the maturity phase, the product enters the **decline phase** where sales begin to decrease. Costs are lowest at this point. Once sales reach the point where the resources required to produce and sell the product would be better spent on other products, the company usually diverts resources to more lucrative ventures, and the life cycle of the product ends.

EXHIBIT | **3.14**

Product Costs, Sales Revenues, and the Product Life Cycle

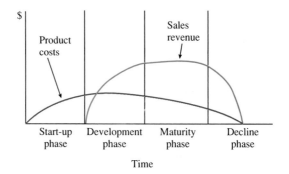

EXHIBIT | 3.15

The Management Cycle

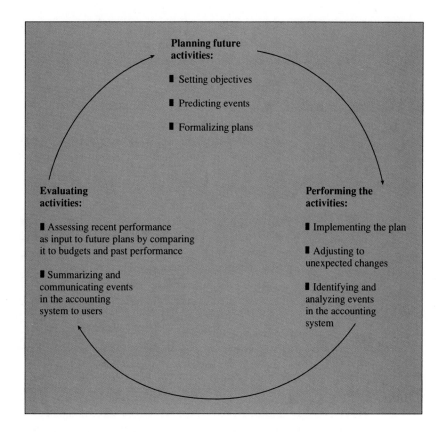

Planning future
activities:

■ Setting objectives

■ Predicting events

■ Formalizing plans

Evaluating
activities:

■ Assessing recent performance
as input to future plans by comparing
it to budgets and past performance

■ Summarizing and
communicating events
in the accounting
system to users

Performing the
activities:

■ Implementing the plan

■ Adjusting to
unexpected changes

■ Identifying and
analyzing events
in the accounting
system

As product life cycles shorten, a business must have new products ready to take the place of those for which demand has declined or disappeared. Therefore, the development of new products or substantial changes in existing products must happen faster.

THE MANAGEMENT CYCLE

The activities in each of the three operating activity cycles do not just happen at the right time with the right people. To make things work well, businesses must plan carefully. Then, after performing the planned activities, businesses must evaluate the results. This is yet another cycle of events called the **management cycle.**

Businesses make and implement decisions in the management cycle in three phases (shown in Exhibit 3.15). In the **planning phase,** management determines its objectives and the means of achieving those objectives. The **performing phase** occurs when management implements the plans by actually doing the planned activities. Finally, in the **evaluating phase,** management compares the results of performing activities with the plan to determine whether it achieved the company's objectives.

Regardless of their ownership structure or the economic market in which they operate, businesses have management cycles that follow this sequence of planning, performing, and evaluating decisions. In this chapter, we focus on operating decisions in the management cycle.

Planning Phase

Planning is an essential part of a successful business. Without plans, a business might not get goods produced, or customers might not get the goods or services they want. **Strategic plans** set the broad course for the business in terms of its objectives, for example, what products to sell, whether to build the facilities to make what they sell, or whether to buy products for resale from someone else. Strategic plans cover a relatively long period of time (5 to 10 years), while **operating plans,** which are plans for business activities to accomplish objectives, usually apply to only a year at a time.

Successful management of a business requires both strategic and operating planning—for the overall strategy of the business and for the shorter time periods, including day-to-day functioning of the business. Once strategic plans are set, they become a framework within which management formulates its operating plans to guide shorter-term decisions.

Operating plans must be compatible with the strategic plans of the firm. For example, projected sales for the coming period cannot exceed the productive capacity of the firm plus the inventory the business has on hand. Productive capacity is determined during strategic planning when management chose the size of the production plant.

In order to make planning manageable, businesses should begin by setting **objectives** which are results it wants to accomplish. However, setting objectives that are too general, such as "to make a lot of money," is not very useful. Such objectives do not serve as guides for what actions to take. Good operating plans lay out specific actions that must be taken in the near future.

Operating plans include the business activities previously described for each of the three operating activity cycles. In the revenue cycle, planned objectives would include actions such as selling a certain number of items this year, or selling a certain portion of the total market's sales for a given product. This is known as *market share*. For example, Sony could set as their objective to have 30 percent of the 31-inch television market next year. The operating plans for the expenditure cycle could include objectives like hiring a certain number of salespeople or purchasing a certain quantity of goods for resale. The production scheduling previously discussed takes place as part of planning in the conversion cycle. The next management cycle phase involves actually performing (implementing) the operating plans.

Performing Phase

As we mentioned previously, in the performing phase, a business actually completes its planned activities. All three operating cycles function to generate the profit needed to stay in business and grow. Throughout the performance phase of the management cycle, the accounting system identifies and analyzes the events that occur. For example, the system would monitor collection from customers to see if any customers are late in making payments for their credit sales. If a customer is considered to be too slow in making payments, the credit manager might contact him or her, or the business might stop making credit sales to the late payer until he or she catches up on payments.

A business also uses other information from the accounting system during the performance phase for activities. For example, the system would reflect bills paid on time, in the right amount, or for the right customer, or it would ensure that there is proper recording of customer orders, among other things.

Evaluation Phase

The evaluation phase is the final phase of the management cycle. Evaluating operations involves comparing the actual operating activities results with planned results and with other standards to assess performance. Differences between planned and actual or standard activities can stem from two sources: (1) The plan was good but the activities were not performed well, or (2) the plan was not very good and the activities were done well.

These two sources have different implications for planning future activities. If the plan was bad, there is a need to examine the assumptions and bases of the plan to improve them and thus provide for better predictions. On the other hand, if the plan was good, then management and employees need to identify any performance problems they observed or experienced in order to make the necessary changes for improvement.

Although operating activities are constantly monitored during the performance phase, events are not formally summarized and communicated until the evaluation phase. The nature of the communicated information varies depending on the level of detail a person needs and his or her level within the organization. Generally, as we mentioned in Chapter 2, individuals who have more responsible positions in the organization are likely to use aggregated, or more summarized and less detailed, information.

The information provided by the accounting system is used in the evaluation phase for two important business functions: (1) to evaluate operating activities and (2) to use as a basis for planning activities in the next iteration of the management cycle. In the evaluation phase, there is a merger of these two functions of the management cycle. While one is evaluated, the next is planned. For example, it is necessary to examine activities that did not turn out as planned to determine why they did not work. Also, those activities that worked better than planned are examined to see why they worked so well.

Suppose that a business finds that they did not sell as much of a product as planned. To evaluate the difference between the number projected for sale in the plan and the actual result, evaluations would include questions like: Was the product what the customers wanted? Did the company do enough advertising? Did the salespeople call on enough customers? Did the company not produce enough?

Accounting reports that summarize the activities of the period provide information to help answer these questions. Answers to the questions are, in turn, used to plan the next period's activities. If the amount of advertising was not sufficient, perhaps it would be possible to plan to spend more money on advertising during subsequent periods. However, if the problem turns out to be that the business did not produce enough of the product and could not fill all the orders received, spending more on advertising would be a waste of time and money. The solution, in the second case, would be to find a way to increase production capacity for the next period.

Since the evaluation phase happens when a period's events are summarized and communicated, you might ask how long a period is. The period, or length of the management cycle, depends on the activity being evaluated. Typically, operating activities are evaluated monthly or quarterly. That length of time reduces the effects of natural variation in factors like cash collections and sales, and makes it possible to see general trends. That is, really good days' sales and really bad days' sales balance out against each other so that it is possible to assess the general level of sales activity more realistically.

The length of the management cycle varies significantly, even within a single business. The nature of the specific business activity determines the length of the management cycle. For example, a company might not want to reprimand a vendor for being late with a delivery if it only happens once a year. So, evaluating vendors' performance works well on a quarterly or annual basis. On the other hand, if a production process is producing too many defective products and customers are returning products too often, then weekly or daily evaluations might be required.

In computerized production environments, evaluation becomes continuous. Certain processes are monitored constantly for variations that sometimes are smaller than the diameter of a human hair! On the other hand, variations in activities like sales are normal and expected, so the length of the management cycle must be a longer period than those for production goods where even small variations are unacceptable.

SUMMARY

Business activities can be divided into three types: operating, investing, and financing. In this chapter, we focus on operating activities, which form three cycles of transactions or events found in businesses trying to make a profit. In addition to performing these activities, owners and managers must plan for them and, following performance, evaluate the activities to see if they were successful.

- Business activities associated with the day-to-day profit-making activities are called *operating activities*. Operating activities are organized into three cycles: (1) expenditure, (2) revenue, and (3) conversion.

- The policies and procedures found in the internal control system are designed to (1) promote operational efficiency, (2) ensure the accuracy of accounting information, and (3) encourage compliance with applicable laws and regulations.

- The expenditure cycle is a series of transactions between a business and its vendors. These transactions involve acquiring and paying for goods and services necessary to run a business.

- In the revenue cycle, the business and its customers engage in a series of transactions. These include activities involving selling goods and services to customers and collecting payment from customers.

- The transactions of the conversion cycle are all internal to the business. This cycle involves the combination of raw materials with labor and overhead inputs to make products for sale. Recent changes in the business environment have had the most impact on the conversion cycle.

- The management cycle requires activities to be planned, performed, and then evaluated. The evaluation phase allows determination of the level of performance and provides input into the next iteration of the management cycle.

KEY TERMS

business activities Events that involve making and carrying out operating, investing, and financing decisions that deal with business assets or obligations

cell A manufacturing facility where machines related to products or groups of products are clustered

conversion cycle The sequence of manufacturing events that combines raw materials with labor and other manufacturing resources to produce products

decline phase The final phase of the product life cycle, when sales begin to decrease

development phase The second phase of the product life cycle, which follows the initial sale where the company seeks new markets for the product

evaluating phase The final phase of the management cycle, in which management compares the results of performing activities with the plan to determine whether it achieved the company's objectives

expenditure cycle The sequence of business events in which the business exchanges assets for goods and services provided from suppliers

financing activities Business activities that involve obtaining the cash or noncash other means to pay for investments in long-term assets, to repay borrowed money from creditors, and leave in owners

free on board (FOB) destination Shipping terms where the legal title to goods passes to the customer when he or she receives the goods

free on board (FOB) shipping point Shipping terms where the legal title to purchased goods passes to the customer when the goods are picked up by the common carrier

internal control system The set of policies and procedures designed to promote operational efficiency, ensure the accuracy of accounting information, and encourage compliance with laws and regulations

investing activities Activities involving the purchase and sale of long-term assets and other major items used in a business's operations

machine setups Adjustments made to machines to get them ready to manufacture the next type of product

management cycle Three phases of business events in which decisions are made. The phases are: (1) planning, (2) performing, and (3) evaluating

manufacturing overhead The cost of all manufacturing resources used to make products that are not directly associated with production

maturity phase The third phase of the product life cycle, during which successful product sales climb until most potential customers have the product

objectives Results the business wants to accomplish

operating activities The profit-making activities of a business enterprise

operating plans Plans for business activities to accomplish objectives, usually apply to only a year at a time

paper trail The series of documents created to record information regarding various business transactions

performing phase The second phase of the management cycle, where the business implements the plans by actually doing the planned activities

planning phase The first phase of the management cycle in which management determines its objectives and the means of achieving them

product life cycle The course of product-related events, that begins with the idea for a new product and ends when the product is no longer sold

purchase discounts Price reductions offered by vendors for payment made by customers within a period of time

revenue cycle The series of transactions in which businesses sell goods and services to customers and receive payments from customers

sales discount A purchases discount from the seller's perspective. It allows the customer to pay less than the full invoice amount if the customer remits (sends in) payment within a prespecified period of time

segregation of incompatible duties Dividing among employees the responsibility for duties that have the potential for one person to violate company policies

start-up phase The first phase of the product life cycle, which begins with the initial product design and continues through delivery of the product to the first customer

strategic plans Plans that set a broad course for a business in terms of its objectives; they cover a relatively long period of time (5 to 10 years)

QUESTIONS

1. Describe operating, financing, and investing activities of a business and give an example of each which did not appear in the text.

2. Explain the distinction between operating activities and financing and investing activities in a business.

3. Describe the three primary uses of operating profit for a business.

4. Explain the three objectives of an internal control system.

5. Explain the five procedures employed in an internal control system. Why are these procedures important?

6. Describe, in general terms, the expenditure cycle and the primary activities that take place in this cycle. Why are these activities important?

7. What is the purpose of each of the following documents in the expenditure cycle: (*a*) purchase requisition, (*b*) purchase order, (*c*) receiving report, and (*d*) vendor's invoice?

8. Explain why businesses should take available purchase discounts.

9. Describe, in general terms, the revenue cycle and the primary activities that take place in this cycle. Why are these activities important?

10. What is the purpose of each of the following documents in the revenue cycle: (*a*) sales order, (*b*) customer order, (*c*) bill of lading, (*d*) sales invoice, (*e*) sales slip, and (*f*) remittance advice?

11. Explain why obtaining a credit history is important.

12. Contrast FOB shipping point with FOB destination. Why is this distinction important?

13. How does a company treat a sale when a customer uses a bank charge card? How does a company treat a sale when a customer uses a company-issued charge card? Why is this distinction important?

14. Describe, in general terms, the conversion cycle and the primary activities that take place in this cycle. Why are these activities important?

15. What is the purpose of each of the following documents in the conversion cycle: (*a*) bill of materials, (*b*) operations list, (*c*) production order, (*d*) materials requisition order, and (*e*) time ticket?

16. What is manufacturing overhead and why is it important in today's business environment?

17. Explain how the conversion cycle is linked to the expenditure and revenue cycles in a manufacturing company.

18. What are the impacts of global markets, customer-focused operations, and advances in manufacturing technology on manufacturers?

19. What are the phases of the product life cycle and why are they important?

20. What are the phases of the management cycle and why are they important?

EXERCISES

E 3.1 The following selected activities occurred in Kostner and Weber Legal Services during the period. Determine whether each of the activities is operating, financing, or investing. Use (O) for operating, (F) for financing, and (I) for investing.

_____ *a.* Computer equipment is purchased for billing clients.
_____ *b.* Clients are billed.
_____ *c.* Payments are received from clients.
_____ *d.* Interest is charged to clients whose payments are overdue.
_____ *e.* A partner contributes money to the company.

E 3.2 The following selected activities occurred in Shuster and Sons Men's Clothing, a merchandising company. Determine whether each of the activities is operating, financing, or investing. Use (O) for operating, (F) for financing, and (I) for investing.

_____ *a.* Merchandise inventory for resale is purchased.
_____ *b.* A bank loan is obtained to purchase a delivery truck.
_____ *c.* The delivery truck is purchased.
_____ *d.* Gasoline for the delivery truck is purchased.
_____ *e.* Products are sold to customers.
_____ *f.* Interest is paid on the bank loan.

E 3.3 The following are selected operating activities of Procter & Gamble, a manufacturing company. Determine in which cycle the activities occur. Use (R) for revenue, (E) for expenditure, and (C) for conversion.

_____ *a.* Raw materials are purchased for use in manufacturing.
_____ *b.* Raw materials are stored until needed in manufacturing.
_____ *c.* Raw materials are requested for manufacturing.
_____ *d.* Employees are involved in manufacturing activities.
_____ *e.* Overhead is used in manufacturing.
_____ *f.* Products are completed and stored until sold.
_____ *g.* Products are sold and customers are billed.
_____ *h.* Customers remit payment.
_____ *i.* Raw materials are paid for.

E 3.4 Describe how the revenue cycle for the selling company mirrors the expenditure cycle for the purchasing company. Be sure to discuss the document flow between the two companies.

E 3.5 Assume that you work in the headquarters of a large merchandising company such as Sears, Roebuck and Company. Write a memo to be used in the training manual for new employees that describes the flow of documents during the expenditure cycle. Limit your discussion to merchandise purchases.

E 3.6 Assume that you work in the headquarters of a large wholesale company. Write a memo to be used in the training manual for new employees that describes the flow of documents during the revenue cycle. Assume that goods are shipped to customers, such as local Wal-Mart stores, FOB shipping point.

E 3.7 Assume that you work for a manufacturing company such as Levi Strauss and Company. Write a memo to be used in the training manual for new employees that describes the flow of documents during the conversion cycle.

E 3.8 On December 29, 1996, Specialty Products Company ships merchandise by common carrier to Bidwell Company. The terms of the sale are 2/10, n/30, FOB shipping point. It takes five days for the merchandise to reach Bidwell Company. Specialty Products Company has a December 31 year-end. Can Specialty Products consider this a sale in 1996? Why or why not?

E 3.9 Refer to E 3.8. Assuming Bidwell Company also has a December 31 year-end, can Bidwell Company consider this a purchase in 1996? Why or why not?

E 3.10 J. C. Penney accepts VISA, Mastercard, Discover, and American Express cards as well as its own J. C. Penney charge cards. Assume the VISA and Mastercard charge a 3 percent processing fee while Discover and American Express charge a 5 percent processing fee. During the period, the following charge card sales occurred but no customers paid their charge bills:

VISA	$ 8,650
Mastercard	9,245
Discover	1,360
American Express	1,100
J. C. Penney	12,930

What is the net amount of cash received from charge sales during the period?

E 3.11 Strings and Things, a local jewelry store issues its own charge cards to customers. It bills its customers on the first of every month for purchases made during the previous month. In addition, the store accepts major credit cards, such as VISA and Mastercard, personal checks, and cash. Assume that VISA and Mastercard both charge a 3 percent processing fee. The following sales were made during the month of June 1997:

Strings and Things credit card sales	$8,700
VISA and Mastercard	5,460
Cash sales	3,575
Sales paid by check	2,700

What amount is considered to be cash sales for the month?

E 3.12 Hutchinson Company orders its raw materials from a variety of suppliers. Most of its suppliers offer credit terms of 2/15, n/60. What is the annual interest cost to Hutchinson of not paying its suppliers in time to take advantage of the credit terms?

E 3.13 Assume that you are the purchasing manager for a large grocery store. How will you decide the timing and quantity of goods to purchase? What is the cost, in general terms, of making a poor decision?

E 3.14 The following selected activities occurred in Hamburg Incorporated, a manufacturing company. Determine in which phase of the management cycle the activities occur. Use (PL) for planning, (PR) for performing, or (E) for evaluating.
_____ *a.* Management decides to produce widgets.
_____ *b.* Raw materials are purchased for production.
_____ *c.* Finished widgets are stored until sold.
_____ *d.* Management decides to discontinue widget production.
_____ *e.* Labor is used in production.
_____ *f.* Vendors are selected for raw material purchases.

E 3.15 The following selected activities occurred in Globe Life Company, a service firm. Determine in which phase of the management cycle the activities occur. Use (PL) for planning, (PR) for performing, or (E) for evaluating.
_____ *a.* Clients are billed.
_____ *b.* Management decides to expand the geographic area in which services are offered.
_____ *c.* Management decides to expand the types of services offered.
_____ *d.* Management decides to terminate certain services.
_____ *e.* Services are rendered to clients.
_____ *f.* Remittance is received from clients.

PROBLEMS

P 3.1 Assume you are the inventory manager at J. C. Penney. You receive merchandise from a variety of different suppliers. Regardless of the source, all merchandise is received at a central loading dock. After the merchandise shipment is checked, it is distributed to the appropriate stores within the region. Design a receiving report to be used by employees who work on the loading dock.

P 3.2 Describe the internal control problem(s) in the following situation. If you find internal control to be lacking, describe how you would improve the situation.

The receiving department is given a completed copy of all purchase orders for merchandise. The receiving department supervisor uses this copy as the receiving report. When the supervisor signs and dates that copy, it is sent to the accounting department. Based on this receiving report, the accounting department pays the vendor.

P 3.3 Describe the internal control problem(s) in the following situation and your recommendation for improving it.

One of your employees has fictitious invoices printed, which she then mails to your company. The invoices are paid and sent to a post office box. She obtains the checks from the post office box and deposits them in the bank in the name of the fictitious company. Later, she withdraws the money for her own use.

P 3.4 Describe the internal control problem(s) in the following situation. If you find internal control to be lacking, describe how you would improve the situation.

The mail clerk opens the mail, records the receipts, and turns this record and the receipts over to the bookkeeper, who deposits the receipts in the bank. The bookkeeper then records the receipts to the individual customers' accounts. The bookkeeper has been stealing the cash receipts.

P 3.5 Copies Now is a printing company that produces pamphlets, handbills, and other paper products made to customers' orders. Some orders are large and require many hours of time to complete as well as the use of large, specialized printing presses. Other orders are smaller, requiring only photocopying, which can be completed in a short period of time. Design a production order for such a company.

P 3.6 On May 1, 1996, Target Company received a sales order from Hammond Company requesting 1,000 units of product. On May 3, Target Company filled the order and sent the goods to Hammond, FOB destination. On June 1, Target Company sent Hammond a sales invoice for $6,500 (1,000 units at $6.50 per unit) with the following terms 1/15, n/30.

Required: *a.* Describe the document flow that occurs at Hammond Company with regard to this purchase.
  b. Describe how Target will respond to the sales invoice, for example, when you will pay the invoice and for what amount.

P 3.7 Your company is experiencing a shortage of cash and this month can only pay up to $75,000 of invoices. You received the following invoices on the first of the month. (The invoice numbers are provided for reference only and do not correspond to the numbers on the actual invoices.)

Number	Amount	Terms
1	$22,400	2/10, n/30
2	13,750	3/15, n/30
3	33,600	n/60
4	41,900	1/10, n/45
5	9,875	5/15, n/30
6	19,500	2/10, n/60
7	26,440	1/10, n/30
8	14,100	n/30

Required: *a.* Determine which invoices to pay this month, when to pay them, and how much to pay for each.
  b. Would your answer to *a* change if any of the suppliers charged a late fee of 1 percent for overdue invoices? Why or why not?

P 3.8 Assume that you are the credit manager of a merchandising company that sells directly to the public. Currently the company accepts cash, VISA, and Mastercard. Your company is deciding whether to issue its own credit cards.

Required: *a.* What information do you need to make this decision and where will you obtain this information?
  b. What are the risks and rewards to your company if it decides to issue its own credit cards?
  c. Write a memo to the general manager in favor of or against this action.

P 3.9   Go to the library and find an article concerning one of the following topics in this chapter.
1. Internal control.
2. Customer credit and/or credit cards.
3. Quality control.
4. Product life cycle.

Write a one-page synopsis of the article. You may find the following sources helpful:

CPA Journal
Journal of Accountancy
Management Accounting
The Practical Accountant
Journal of Marketing

P 3.10   In the 1980s, Japanese automobile manufacturers were generally considered to produce high-quality products while their American counterparts lagged behind. Write a 2–3 page paper supporting or refuting this generalization. You may find the following sources helpful:

The Wall Street Journal
Business Week
Forbes
Management Accounting

COMPUTER APPLICATIONS

CA 3.1   On March 3, 1997, Felton Company purchased $15,875 of merchandise from Gray Company. The terms of the sale were 3/10, n/30. Gray Company bills its customers on the first of the month.

Required: Use a computer spreadsheet.
a. What is the cost of the merchandise if Felton Company pays for it on April 2?
b. What is the annualized interest cost of paying for the merchandise on April 15?
c. If the terms of sale are changed to 2/10, n/60, what is the cost of the merchandise if Felton pays for it on April 2?
d. What is the annualized interest cost of paying for the merchandise on April 15 when the selling terms are 2/10, n/60?

CA 3.2   On September 14, 1997, Gray Company sold merchandise to Felton Company for $25,980. The terms of the sale were 3/10, n/30. Gray Company bills its customers on the first of the month.

Required: Use a computer spreadsheet.
a. What is the net selling price of the merchandise if Felton Company pays for it on October 5?
b. What is the annualized interest earned by Gray Company if Felton pays for the merchandise after the discount period?
c. If Gray Company changes the terms of the sale to 4/15, n/45, what is the net selling price of the merchandise?
d. What is the annualized interest earned by Gray Company if Felton pays for the merchandise after the discount period when the terms of the sale are 4/15, n/45?
e. What other factors should Gray Company consider when deciding whether to change its selling terms?

CASES

C 3.1   Kitchens Plus manufactures custom kitchen cabinets. The company employs a general manager, two production designers, 45 cabinet makers, a bookkeeper, and three office assistants. Customers place orders in consultation with one of the production designers. Each order is then assigned to one or more cabinet makers depending on the size of the order. The selling price of the order is determined by totalling all the costs of completing the order and adding a percentage markup.

Required: *a.* Explain the information needed to operate this business.
               b. Describe the documents needed to control the conversion process.
               c. Describe how the total costs of completing an order will be determined.

C 3.2   Based on your knowledge of the company you chose in C 1.2, summarize their revenue, expenditure, and conversion (if applicable) cycles.

CRITICAL THINKING

CT 3.1   Lynn Duncan, controller of Lankar Company, has decided that the company needs to redesign its purchase order form and design a separate document to record the receipt of goods. Currently, a copy of Lankar's purchase order is serving as a receiving report, and the receiving clerk records the quantities received on the copy of the appropriate purchase order. Duncan has decided to implement these changes because there have been a number of inconsistencies and errors in ordering materials for inventory and in recording the receipt of goods. She believes these mistakes have resulted from the poor design of the current purchase order and the use of a copy of the purchase order as a receiving report. In addition to improved reporting, these new forms will provide Duncan with an excellent opportunity to reinforce the need for accuracy and thoroughness among the employees in the purchasing department.

Presented in Exhibit 3.16, in the left column, is the revised purchase order and in the right column is the new receiving report.

CMA December 1989 Adapted

Required: Review the new forms that Lynn Duncan has designed for Lankar Company and explain what should be added to or deleted from each of them.

EXHIBIT | 3.16

Lanker Company Forms

CT 3.2   Jem Clothes, Inc., is a 25-store chain that sells ready-to-wear clothes for young men and women. Each store has a full-time manager and an assistant manager, both of whom are paid on a salary basis. The cashiers and sales personnel are typically young people working part time who are paid an hourly wage plus a commission based on sales volume. The company uses unsophisticated cash registers with four-copy sales invoices to record each sales transaction.

On the sales floor, the salesperson manually records his or her employee number and the transaction details (clothes class, description, quantity, and unit price). She or he then totals the sales invoice, calculates the sales tax, and determines the grand total. The salesperson then gives the sales invoice to the cashier and retains one copy in his or her sales book.

The cashier reviews the invoice and inputs the sale into the cash register at which time the sales invoice is automatically numbered by the cash register. The cashier is also responsible for getting credit approval on charge card and personal check sales. The cashier gives one copy of the invoice to the customer, retains a second copy of the invoice as a store copy, and retains the third copy for a bank card deposit if needed. Returns are handled in a reverse manner with the cashier issuing a return slip when necessary.

At the end of the day, the cashier sequentially orders the sales invoices and records cash register totals for cash, bank card, and check sales less returns. These totals are reconciled by the assistant manager to the cash register tapes, the total of the consecutively numbered sales invoices, and the return slips.

Daily sales are reviewed by the general manager who prepares the daily bank deposit. The manager makes the deposit and files the validated deposit slip. The cash register tapes, sales invoices, and return slips are forwarded to corporate headquarters for processing.

CMA June 1988 Adapted

Required: Identify six strengths in the Jem Clothes system for controlling the revenue cycle. For each strength identified, provide a brief description of why it is important.

ETHICAL CHALLENGES

EC 3.1 In recent years, many companies have increased the amount of automation they use in manufacturing in an effort to increase quality. However, increasing automation has caused many companies to lay off workers. From a manager's point of view, discuss the ethical dilemma of replacing people with machines. Be sure to include all the stakeholders in your analysis.

EC 3.2 Many companies have adopted slogans that suggest that quality is their primary concern. Yet, very few companies have achieved a manufacturing environment where there are zero defects. Many people suggest, and in fact there are mathematical models that calculate, that some optimal number of defects is acceptable. The argument is that achieving zero defects is too expensive and would cause the price of products to increase, thereby limiting the number of customers who could afford to buy them. From a manager's point of view, discuss the tradeoff between cost and quality. Be sure to include all the stakeholders in your analysis.

PART TWO

Planning and Decision Making

Part Two sets the framework for moving ahead into broad functional areas of managing business enterprises, beginning with planning and using accounting as the link between business events and decision making. The planning function is critical to the survival of businesses today and for the years to come. Chapter 4 addresses the basic elements required for effective planning to take place: cost estimation, revenue estimation, and expected resulting profits. Chapter 5 addresses the budgeting process for operations, focusing on short-term operating plans. Accounting systems provide the information that decision makers need to make such short-term planning decisions. Chapter 6 illustrates planning and related decision making for short-term operating decisions—what is required and why.

CHAPTER 4

Pricing, Costs, and Profit Planning

Learning Objectives

1. Explain the four primary influences on selling price and how a company determines its pricing strategy.
2. Describe the three cost behavior patterns and use the formula for a straight line to define each.
3. Demonstrate how to predict costs using the high/low method.
4. Predict costs using linear regression analysis.
5. Use cost-volume-profit analysis to determine the relationships among selling price, cost, volume, and profit for a single-product firm.

Appendix

6. Use multiproduct cost-volume-profit analysis to determine the relationships among selling price, cost, volume, and profit for a multiproduct firm.

Wendy's International is a very visible part of America's fast food culture, with sales that represent about 10 percent of the current fast food sandwich market. Wendy's ranked number five in total sales in *Restaurant & Institutions'* top 400 restaurants in 1994[1] and number four in total sales in *Nation's Restaurant News'* annual top 100 sandwich chains.[2] It opened 124 new restaurants in the first six months of 1994. This trend is likely to continue. The goal is to open between 350 and 400 new stores per year.

Dave Thomas, the founder of Wendy's, began his restaurant career in the Army, where he operated an officers' club. After leaving the Army, he had a business association with Harlan Sanders founder of Kentucky Fried Chicken. Finally, he started Wendy's with an idea for an "old fashioned hamburger" and a logo inspired by his daughter, Melinda.[3]

Wendy's strategy is to distinguish itself from its competitors in the fast food market by offering customers a higher quality product and quick service. In order to offer quality products, yet keep costs down, the original menu consisted of only four items (aside from the standard selection of soft drinks): hamburgers,

---

[1]"R&I 400: Overview," *Restaurants & Institutions*, July 1, 1994, pp. 44–45, 56.

[2]Carolyn Walkup, "Wendy's Scores 22% Gain in Net Income for 2nd Quarter," *Nation's Restaurant News*, August 29, 1994, p. 14.

[3]Michael Bartlett, "R&I Interview: Dave Thomas," *Restaurants & Institutions*, February 15, 1994, pp. 34, 38, 44, 46.

chili, french fries, and Frosties (dairy drinks). Wendy's demonstrated its emphasis on quality to customers by allowing them to order hamburgers prepared the way they wanted, made fresh while they waited.

The menu has grown since 1969 and now includes many types of sandwiches and other items like salads. But the effort to maintain quality at a competitive price continues.

In Chapter 2, we saw that the role of management accounting was to provide information for internal decision makers. To the extent that the accounting system contributes to the needs of management, we must consider what managers do. Since one of management's most significant functions is planning, the management accounting system must provide information that serves that purpose. As noted in Chapter 3, planning decisions include what products to offer for sale, what prices to charge, how much to produce and sell, and what materials and other resources to use in production.

This chapter presents tools that companies can use to determine prices, predict costs, and combine selling prices and costs to determine expected profits. All of these tools are situation-specific. That is, they are useful in some situations, but have limitations and assumptions that require judgment about the particular business, its markets, and the circumstances surrounding the decisions.

FACTORS TO CONSIDER WHEN DETERMINING SELLING PRICE

Setting the selling price is an operating decision that has strategic (long-term) consequences.[4] The selling price may affect the quantity demanded by customers; it may affect the quantity supplied by competitors; it may have legal, social, or political effects; and it must cover the company's costs in the long run. For example, if companies set their prices too high, customers may not buy the products and services offered, but, instead, may purchase them from competitors. On the other hand, if companies have prices which are too low, profits may not be sufficient to cover operating costs. In addition, some companies face certain legal restrictions concerning selling prices.

Normally, the marketing department or individuals who are responsible for the marketing function set selling prices after extensive analysis of the market in which the company's products and services are offered. Perhaps you have answered questionnaires about your buying habits or the availability of certain goods in your area. Such questionnaires are tools used by market analysts to understand consumers' wants and needs, because understanding the customer is critical to setting selling prices in today's market. The market analyst also must be aware of actions taken by the company's competitors that may affect the company. If McDonald's and Burger King, for example, lower their prices by 15 percent, Wendy's may be forced to lower its prices or face losing some customers to the competition. As you have probably noticed, in the airline industry when one company lowers its prices, other companies often respond in kind. Often, it is also necessary to obtain pricing feedback from the company's legal department to ensure that selling prices meet all legal requirements. And, finally, the marketing manager must consult the purchasing and/or production departments and the accounting department to ensure that selling prices are set high enough to cover the company's cost of buying (or making) and selling the products and services. We examine these four primary influences on selling prices—customers, competition, legal constraints, and costs—next.

---

[4]Once selling prices are set, many companies have a difficult time changing them in light of changing conditions, especially when prices appear in published catalogues or selling contracts.

Customers and the Quantity Demanded

A customer's willingness to purchase goods and services depends on the selling prices a company charges for them. In simple terms, if the selling price of the product increases, the quantity of the product demanded decreases. On the other hand, if the selling price of the product decreases, the quantity of the product demanded increases.

These rules do not apply equally to all products, however. A company may be able to increase the selling price of a product if customers are loyal and unwilling to substitute other products. If the price of coffee, for example, increases substantially due to a crop failure like the one experienced in Brazil in 1994, the quantity of coffee demanded may not fall if people are unwilling to substitute another product, such as tea, for coffee.

Also, consider the case of a product that is considered to be a staple (necessity) versus one that is considered to be a luxury. A staple's selling price does not affect the quantity demanded as much as the price of a luxury item does. Consider a staple grocery product, such as ground hamburger meat, versus a luxury item such as filet mignon (steak). The quantity of hamburger demanded does not decrease dramatically in response to increases in selling price. However, the quantity of filet mignon demanded is more sensitive to price increases because people are willing to forgo purchasing such a luxury food item and may purchase a substitute product instead when its price increases dramatically.

Finally, the quantity demanded is influenced heavily by product quality and service. Products with perceived high quality and service are in greater demand than products with lower quality and service that sell at the same, or perhaps even slightly lower, prices. Recall that in the 1980s, Japanese automobiles, such as Toyota and Honda, sold at much higher prices than comparably equipped American automobiles due to the perceived high quality of Japanese cars.

Most companies try to differentiate their products in terms of quality and service. Wendy's, for example, markets its sandwiches as "made-to-order" and "served hot and fast" because it believes that this policy differentiates its products from other fast food companies. According to Dave Thomas of Wendy's, "If we don't give people the best product and we're not nice to people and the restaurants are not clean, we're not going to stay around."[5]

Competitors and the Quantity Supplied

The selling price charged by a particular company is also influenced by the quantity of the product supplied by competitors and/or the selling prices charged by those competitors. Some companies operate in an environment where there is an abundance of suppliers whose products are almost identical. Companies in this situation are **price takers,** that is, the company "takes" the selling price from the market that establishes the price based on total supply and demand. In these markets, an individual company has little or no influence on the selling price. In the agricultural industry, for example, wheat produced by each wheat farming operation is almost identical. Therefore, wheat sellers are price takers who receive the price for wheat that the market determines. This type of environment where a large number of sellers produce and distribute virtually identical products and services is called **pure competition.**

Other companies operate in an environment in which there are many companies whose products are similar, but not identical. In this environment, called **monopolistic competition,** the market has a large impact on, but no control over, prices. Individual companies operating within this type of market can influence selling prices by advertising quality and service as well as price. For example, the selling prices charged for a hamburger at Wendy's and Burger King may differ, not so much because the hamburgers themselves differ, but because Wendy's and Burger King try to differentiate their products through advertising. It is important for a firm in a monopolistic environment to constantly monitor its competitors to note changes in their operating strategies that might affect the firm's sales.

[5]Bartlett, "R&I Interview," p. 34.

Legal, political, and social forces also impact selling prices, usually by constraining the price that can be charged for products. These forces affect all companies, but there is a greater impact on large companies that have the ability to restrain trade and on companies in certain industries.

The government imposes legal constraints on companies that control a product, service, or geographic market. These companies are called **monopolies.** In certain circumstances, monopolies are allowed to operate because competition is not in the best interests of consumers. Consider utility companies that often are given monopoly rights because the cost of starting and operating a utility is so high that few companies are willing to undertake such a venture. The danger posed by monopolies is that the monopoly company can set any selling price it chooses since it is the sole provider of that particular product or service. Therefore, the government has stepped in to regulate monopolies in an attempt to ensure that they do not overcharge customers or discriminate in terms of their products, service, or distribution.

Legal and political constraints also are imposed on companies that operate in an environment known as an **oligopoly.** This type of business environment exists when a few firms control the market of a particular good or service, that is, the types of products and services and their distribution. The government monitors companies in an oligopolistic market to ensure that they do not form a **cartel,** which is a monopolistic combination of businesses, and practice **price fixing.** Price fixing occurs when companies agree to limit supply and charge identical (usually high) prices for their goods and services. For example, in the early 1970s, an oil embargo by OPEC (Oil Exporting and Producing Countries) caused the price of gasoline to skyrocket when the OPEC cartel limited supply and raised crude oil prices.

Finally, there are social constraints placed on businesses due to the products they sell or the market in which they sell their products. For example, during the flood of 1993 in the Midwest, some retail stores were accused of charging extremely high prices for items such as flashlights and drinking water. Once this practice was discovered, the public outcry was so great that the stores were forced to lower their prices. Likewise, individuals concerned about the spotted owl have placed social constraints on the timber industry in the Northwest in an attempt to limit timber production in this area.

Cost and the Long-Term Survival of the Company

The cost to produce and distribute a product also has an impact on selling price. Ultimately, a company must set a selling price for its products that is high enough to both cover all its costs and provide a profit to owners. By all costs, we mean the costs to buy or produce and distribute the product as well as the costs incurred to operate the company, such as building and equipment costs, wages and salaries, and interest on debt. To ensure that they earn a profit, companies add a **markup,** or an additional amount, to the cost of their products and services. When a company sets its selling price based on cost, it is using a cost-based pricing policy where,

$$\text{Selling price} = \text{Cost} + (\text{Cost} \times \text{Markup percentage})$$

The size of the markup percentage varies among industries. For example, jewelry is typically marked up over 100 percent, while grocery items may be marked up as little as 10 percent due to the nature of their costs, which we discuss later in this chapter.

Suppose a clothing store determines that it must mark up its clothing an average of 75 percent. Therefore, if the cost of a particular item of clothing is $20, the selling price will be:

$$\text{Selling price} = \$20 + (\$20 \times .75) = \$35$$

At this selling price, the **selling margin** (selling price less cost) percentage for the clothing item is shown below:

$$\frac{\text{Selling margin}}{\text{Selling price}} = \frac{(\$35 - \$20)}{\$35} = 43\%$$

The selling margin allows the company to cover other costs such as interest on debt, investment in assets, and research and development. If, due to supply and demand or legal, political, and social forces, the company cannot sell its products at a price that yields a sufficient selling margin, it may choose not to offer the products. We discuss pricing strategies next. Then we address the factors involved in determining costs.

PRICING STRATEGIES

In most industries, selling prices are heavily influenced by both external or market factors, such as customers, competitors, and legal/social factors, and internal factors such as cost. In most cases, companies determine prices based on one of two strategies:

1. They set prices based on the market, subject to the constraint that it is necessary to cover the long-run costs of the company.

2. They set prices based on costs, subject to the constraints of customers, competitors, and legal/social factors.

Within these two strategies, there are a variety of pricing schemes that companies use to compete in the marketplace. We look at three of these schemes, which are based on the product life cycle discussed in Chapter 3.

Penetration Pricing versus Price Skimming

Early in the product's life cycle, the company may set its selling price low in an attempt to gain a share of the total market for its goods and services. Such a pricing strategy is known as **penetration pricing** because the company tries to penetrate the market to gain a share of the market from its competitors. Later in the product's life cycle, after establishing the market for the product, the company may be able to increase its selling price. In the latter stages of the life cycle, the selling price may again be lowered as the quantity demanded decreases. This type of pricing is common in the household products industry. For example, if Procter & Gamble introduced a new dishwashing detergent, it might set the initial selling price low to entice individuals to try the product and gain a share of the market.

Penetration pricing is the opposite of **price skimming,** a pricing strategy in which a company initially sets a high price for its product. The idea behind price skimming is to appeal to those individuals who want to be the first to own a product and are willing to pay more for it. Later, when the novelty of the products wears off, the company lowers the selling price. This type of pricing is common in industries such as electronics and fashion in which products change frequently. For example, when Sony first introduced the Betamax (beta cassette recorder) in the 1970s, the selling price was high, but many people bought the product because it was different from anything else on the market at the time.

Life-Cycle Pricing

With the pricing strategy known as **life-cycle pricing,** a company may set its selling prices below its initial costs based on the idea that costs will decrease over the product's life cycle. This pricing strategy is different from penetration pricing because the company does not intend to raise its prices once there is an established market for its products or services. Life-cycle pricing attempts to establish a price that can be maintained throughout the life of the product. Since a product normally becomes less expensive to produce and sell in the latter stages of its life, the selling margin in a life-cycle pricing system increases as the product's cost declines.

Target Pricing

Finally, companies are increasingly using a pricing strategy known as **target pricing** to determine whether to introduce a product or service. Target pricing requires that the company determine the selling price of the product based on market factors and then decide *how* to produce the product so that product costs are low enough to maintain a selling margin that returns profit to the owners. The idea behind target pricing is to produce products in a cost effective manner in order to achieve an adequate return for the owners.

For example, suppose that an electronics company is planning to introduce a new compact disc recorder. Through market research it determines that it is possible to sell such a recorder for $800. Further assume that the company desires an 80 percent selling margin. Then, it must find a means of producing the recorder for $160 [($800 – Cost)/$800 = .8], or it should not produce the recorder at all.

Notice that all of these pricing strategies depend on the company's prediction of its future costs as well as market forces. In order for a company to predict its costs, it must understand how those costs behave, a subject we investigate next.

PAUSE & REFLECT | **What type of pricing strategy do you think Wendy's would use when introducing a new sandwich? Why?**

COST BEHAVIOR

Cost behavior refers to how a cost reacts to changes in the level of operating activity (discussed later in this chapter in the section on activity measures). In order to predict costs in the future, a manager must understand how costs change. Furthermore, in order to set a selling price based on cost, a manager must know what the cost is.

Why Is Cost Behavior Important?

Understanding cost behavior is important because *costs behave differently* when operating activity levels change. Understanding how costs behave is critical to estimating the amount of a particular cost at different levels of operating activity. For example, if Wendy's sells 20 percent more hamburgers during a certain period, do its costs increase by 20 percent? The answer is no, because some costs do not change with increases in operating activity, which is selling 20 percent more hamburgers in this case. To determine how much costs will increase, a manager must understand cost behavior patterns.

How Do Companies Define Cost Behavior Patterns?

Cost behavior patterns are reflected as straight-line relationships between operating activity and total cost. Recall that the formula for a straight line is $Y = m(X) + b$, where m represents rise (change in Y) divided by run (change in X), also known as the slope, and b represents the intercept on the Y-axis. We will use this formula to define cost behavior. Keep in mind, however, that many costs do not exhibit a straight-line behavior over a wide range of operating activity. Rather, due to efficiencies in production resulting from experience and specialization or due to the inefficiencies that may occur as organizations become very large, costs may exhibit a different behavior response. However, over a given range of activity, known as the *relevant range*, we can define costs as having a straight-line relationship with respect to activity level.

Relevant Range   In establishing cost behavior patterns, we limit the description to a specific range of operating activity called the **relevant range.** The relevant range is the span of operating activity that is considered to be normal for the company. Assume, for example, that a particular Wendy's store normally sells between 1,000 and 9,000 hamburgers in a month. If we define operating activity as the number of hamburgers sold, the relevant range is 1,000 to 9,000. The cost behavior pattern established is applicable *only* to the relevant range of operating activity from which the data are drawn. In other words, $Y = m(X) + b$ is relevant only for that range of operating activity—selling 1,000 to 9,000 hamburgers, in this case.

Exhibit 4.1 illustrates the concept of the relevant range. The Y-axis of the graph represents cost and the X-axis represents activity. Note that, overall, the cost line curves, but within the relevant range, the cost line is almost linear (straight). Since we assume that cost behavior patterns are linear within the relevant range, we can define costs using $Y = m(X) + b$, when X is operating activity.

EXHIBIT 4.1

Graphical Depiction of the
Relevant Range

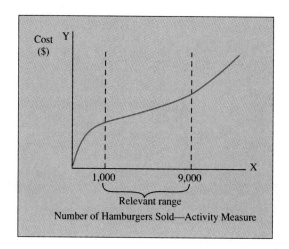

Activity Measures

Recall that operating activities are the profit-making activities of the company. Understanding operating activities is crucial to profit planning because *activities consume resources*, which causes costs to change.

Different costs change in relation to different operating activities. For example, shipping costs may change with the number of orders shipped, while receiving costs may change with the number of orders received. Operating activity is action, or something that is being done, for example, receiving, shipping, storing, or producing. The action, or activity, itself actually consumes resources.

We measure activity using different bases that reflect the consumption of resources, such as the number of orders shipped, the weight of the orders shipped, the number of units stored, or the number of machine hours used during production. These bases, which reflect the consumption of resources, are called **cost drivers.**

Exhibit 4.2 illustrates the relationship among activities, resources, cost drivers, and costs. Because activities, as measured by cost drivers, consume resources, which are measured by costs, changes in the amount of the cost driver ultimately cause, or drive, changes in cost. For example, if a company wanted to measure the resources consumed by the *activity, purchasing*, it might use a *cost driver* such as *number of purchase orders processed*. If a company wanted to measure the resources consumed by the *activity, setting up production equipment*, it might use a *cost driver* such as *number of production runs*. If a company wanted to measure the resources consumed by the *activity, using warehouses*, it might use a *cost driver* such as *number of square feet*. Notice that in all cases the cost driver is the numerical measurement of the activity. The activity consumes resources; therefore, the cost driver is assumed to consume (cause) costs.

Now that we understand the relationship between costs and cost drivers, we focus our attention again on defining cost behavior patterns. We discuss three identifiable linear cost behavior patterns: (1) fixed costs, (2) variable costs, and (3) mixed costs.

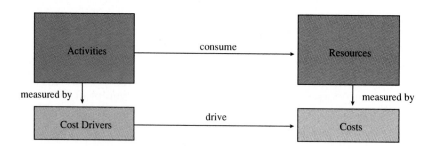

EXHIBIT | 4.3

Graphical Depiction of Fixed Cost

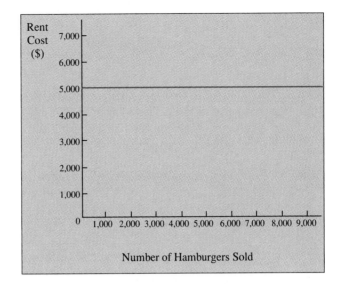

Number of Hamburgers Sold

Fixed Costs

A **fixed cost** *does not change in total as the amount of cost driver changes.* Consider the cost of monthly rent for a Wendy's restaurant, and assume that the *operating activity of selling hamburgers* is measured using the *cost driver, number of hamburgers sold.* Rent is a fixed cost because it does not change if Wendy's sells more, or fewer, hamburgers.

Exhibit 4.3 shows how a fixed cost, such as $5,000 for rent, looks throughout a range of operating activity. In Exhibit 4.3 the point where the cost line intersects the *Y*-axis represents fixed costs of $5,000. Notice that throughout the relevant range from 1,000 to 9,000 hamburgers, the total cost remains at $5,000, and the slope of the line is zero. If the number of hamburgers sold changes, the total rent cost remains the same.

The fixed cost formula, which describes the line illustrated in Exhibit 4.3, is $Y = (0)X + \$5,000$, or simply $Y = \$5,000$, which indicates that rent cost equals $5,000 per month.

Although the amount of a fixed cost does not change in total as the amount of cost driver changes, when *measured on a per unit basis, the amount of fixed cost does change.* Exhibit 4.4 shows that when 1,000 hamburgers are sold in a month, the cost of rent per hamburger is $5 ($5,000/1,000). If Wendy's sells 9,000 hamburgers in a month, the cost of rent per hamburger decreases to only $0.56 ($5,000/9,000). Exhibit 4.4 illustrates that a *fixed cost decreases per unit of cost driver as the cost driver*—the number of hamburgers sold in this case—*increases throughout the relevant range* (1,000 to 9,000 hamburgers). Other common fixed costs that exhibit the same type of behavior pattern as rent include the cost of managers' salaries, cost of fire insurance, and the cost of the cooking equipment.

EXHIBIT 4.4	Fixed Cost Behavior	
Cost Driver	**Fixed Cost**	
(Number of Hamburgers Sold)	**Total**	**Per Hamburger**
1,000	$5,000	$5.00
2,000	5,000	2.50
3,000	5,000	1.67
4,000	5,000	1.25
5,000	5,000	1.00
6,000	5,000	0.83
7,000	5,000	0.71
8,000	5,000	0.63
9,000	5,000	0.56

Variable Costs

A **variable cost** *changes in total in direct proportion to the change in the level of cost driver.* Consider the cost of wages for Wendy's employees and assume that the *operating activity of working* is measured using the *cost driver, number of hours worked.* The cost of wages is a variable cost because it changes in direct proportion to the number of hours worked.

We represent a variable cost by the formula $Y = m(X) + 0$, or simply $Y = m(X)$ because a variable cost changes in direct proportion to changes in the cost driver. Therefore, if the cost driver is zero, that is, if there is no activity, the variable cost also must be zero.

Exhibit 4.5 illustrates how such a variable cost looks throughout the relevant range of operating activity. Take a moment to examine Exhibit 4.5. Notice that throughout the relevant range, assumed to be 2,000 to 3,000 hours in this case, wage costs increase and the slope of the line is constant; that is, the slope is not steeper or flatter at any point on the line. The cost line intersects the Y-axis at the origin, which indicates that, unlike a fixed cost, there is no variable cost when there is no activity.

To determine the variable cost formula that describes the cost illustrated in Exhibit 4.5, we divide rise (change in Y) by run (change in X) to calculate m, or the slope of the line. Since the slope is assumed to be constant, it can be measured using any two points on the line. Using 2,000 hours and 3,000 hours in Exhibit 4.5, we calculate the slope as:

$$\frac{\text{Rise}}{\text{Run}} = \frac{\text{Change in cost}}{\text{Change in cost driver}} = \frac{\$15,000 - \$10,000}{3,000 - 2,000} = \frac{\$5,000}{1,000} = \$5$$

The cost of wages illustrated in Exhibit 4.5 is $Y = \$5(X) + 0$, or simply $Y = \$5(X)$, which denotes that total wage cost equals $5 multiplied by the number of hours worked.

A variable cost increases or decreases in total in direct proportion to increases or decreases in the cost driver, but when *measured on a per unit basis, variable costs are constant.*[6] Exhibit 4.6 shows that if there are 2,000 labor hours worked, the total

---

[6]The term *unit* as used here does not mean a unit of product. *Unit* is a generic term that denotes a single measurement of cost driver.

EXHIBIT | **4.5**

Graphical Depiction of a Variable Cost

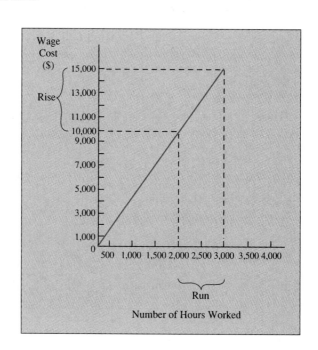

wage cost is $10,000, and the cost per hour is $5; when there are 3,000 labor hours worked, the total wage cost is $15,000, and the cost per hour is still $5.

As illustrated in Exhibit 4.6, *a variable cost varies in total, but remains constant per unit of cost driver throughout the relevant range.* Other examples of variable costs include the costs of hamburger, hamburger buns, and condiments when measuring activity as the number of hamburgers sold.

Mixed Costs

A **mixed cost** *varies in the same direction as the change in cost driver, but not in direct proportion to the change in the level of cost driver.* A mixed cost has both a fixed and a variable component, and is also known as a **semivariable cost.**

Assume that an accident insurance company charges Wendy's $2,000 per month plus $20 per employee shift (one employee working one shift). In this case, accident insurance is a mixed cost. The *number of employee shifts* is the cost driver measuring the *operating activity, providing for employees* because insurance costs increase as the number of employee shifts increases. However, the increase is not in direct proportion to the cost driver because of the fixed cost component of $2,000.

A mixed cost is represented by the formula $Y = m(X) + b$. The fixed cost component, b, represents the point where the cost line intersects the Y-axis, and the variable component, m, is the slope of the line. Exhibit 4.7 shows that throughout the relevant range, which is assumed to be 80 to 200 employee shifts, the total cost increases and the slope of the line is constant. The mixed cost line intersects the Y-axis at $2,000 and the slope of the line is:[7]

$$\frac{\Delta \text{ rise}}{\Delta \text{ run}} = \frac{\$6,000 - \$3,600}{200 - 80} = \frac{\$2,400}{120} = \$20$$

Exhibit 4.7 shows how a mixed cost, such as accident insurance, looks throughout the relevant range. The total mixed cost formula, which represents the line illustrated in Exhibit 4.7, is $Y = \$20(X) + \$2,000$, or accident insurance cost = $20 multiplied by the number of employee shifts + $2,000 per month.

---

[7]Again, the slope of the line can be measured using any two points because the slope is constant.

EXHIBIT	4.6	Variable Cost Behavior	

Cost Driver (Number of Hours Worked)	Variable Cost	
	Total	Per Hour
2,000	$10,000	$5.00
2,100	10,500	5.00
2,200	11,000	5.00
2,300	11,500	5.00
2,400	12,000	5.00
2,500	12,500	5.00
2,600	13,000	5.00
2,700	13,500	5.00
2,800	14,000	5.00
2,900	14,500	5.00
3,000	15,000	5.00

EXHIBIT | 4.7

Graphical Depiction
of a Mixed Cost

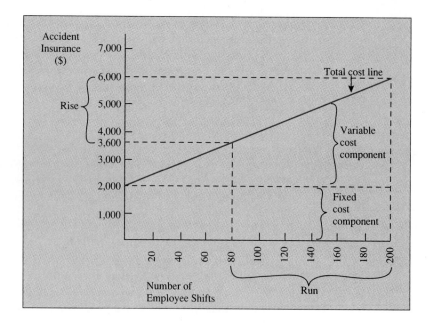

Now review Exhibit 4.8 to determine what happens to the total cost and the cost per cost driver as the amount of the cost driver (number of employee shifts) increases. When there are 80 employee shifts worked, the total insurance cost is $3,600 [($20 × 80) + $2,000], and the cost per employee shift is $45 ($3,600/80). When there are 200 employee shifts worked, the total insurance cost is $6,000 [($20 × 200) + $2,000], and the cost per employee shift is $30.

Exhibit 4.8 indicates that *a mixed cost increases in total but decreases per unit as the cost driver increases.* Other examples of mixed costs include the cost of utilities when the cost driver is the number of kilowatts used, sales salaries that consist of a salary plus bonus when the cost driver is sales in dollars, and freight charges of a fixed amount per load plus a variable amount per pound carried when the cost driver is the number of pounds carried.

Once we identify cost behavior patterns, we can use them to estimate future costs, the subject we examine next.

PAUSE & REFLECT What happens to a mixed cost in total and per unit of activity as activity decreases?

EXHIBIT | 4.8 | Mixed Cost Behavior

| Cost Driver (Number of Employee Shifts) | Mixed Cost | |
	Total	Per Employee Shift
80	$3,600	$45.00
100	4,000	40.00
120	4,400	36.67
140	4,800	34.29
160	5,200	32.50
180	5,600	31.11
200	6,000	30.00

COST ESTIMATION METHODS

We use cost estimation techniques to determine the relationship between a cost and a cost driver in order to estimate future costs. These techniques use information about *past costs* and *past levels of cost drivers* to estimate *future costs* given *expected future levels of the cost drivers*. We examine two such cost estimation methods—the high/low method and linear regression analysis.[8]

High/Low Method

The **high/low method** of cost estimation uses only two data points to determine the total cost formula. It uses the highest and lowest levels of cost driver within the relevant range to define the total cost line because these two data points give the widest range. The widest range possible is desirable because the estimated cost relationship is only valid for the range of cost driver used. For example, if we use a cost driver range of 2,000 to 9,000 hours, we can predict costs only when the cost driver is within this range of activity in the future. In addition, the range of cost driver examined must represent normal usage of resources; that is, there should have been no unusual events that occurred during the periods examined for data collection. Unusual events may distort the cost-cost driver relationship and, therefore, the predictions made using that relationship.

Use of the high/low method requires the highest and lowest levels of the cost driver and the related costs at those levels. The change in cost divided by the change in the amount of the cost driver indicates the variable cost per unit of cost driver. The variable cost, when applied in the straight-line formula, helps to determine the anticipated fixed cost.

Using the High/Low Method   Suppose that one Wendy's branch wants to predict the cost of operating its drive-up window using the number of customers coming to the drive-up window as a measure of this activity. Wendy's would gather data on the number of customers using the drive-up window (cost driver) and the cost of operating the window for each month during the prior year[9] (see Exhibit 4.9). Wendy's wants to predict drive-up window costs for next month, when it expects 4,500 drive-up customers.

First, it is necessary to determine which months have the highest and lowest levels of cost driver, respectively. Looking at Exhibit 4.9, we determine that May was the month with the highest cost driver level (8,250 drive-up customers), and February

---

[8]In practice, there are many other methods available to estimate costs, such as scattergraph and account analysis, but we focus on the high/low method and linear regression because the high/low method is easy to use and understand and linear regression provides the best information to predict costs.

[9]Some of these costs include employee wages, cost of speaker replacement, increased utility costs, and cost of headsets worn by employees.

EXHIBIT	4.9	Cost Estimation Data

Month	Number of Drive-Up Customers	Drive-Up Window Costs
January	3,200	$19,000
February	2,980	23,086
March	4,000	20,100
April	5,800	22,100
May	8,250	26,775
June	7,500	24,000
July	7,600	24,500
August	7,480	23,600
September	6,500	23,000
October	5,370	21,700
November	4,050	20,050
December	3,250	19,500

was the month of lowest cost driver level (2,980 drive-up customers). The drive-up window costs for these two months, respectively, were $26,775 and $23,086.[10]

Next, determining the variable cost per drive-up customer, requires using the change in cost divided by the change in cost driver levels. We find that the variable cost per drive-up customer is:

$$\frac{\text{Change in cost}}{\text{Change in cost driver}} = \frac{\$26,775 - \$23,086}{8,250 - 2,980} = 0.70$$

Then, by using the variable cost per drive-up customer and applying it to either the highest or lowest level of cost driver, we determine the fixed cost per month.[11] At either the highest or lowest cost driver level, we know the total cost, the level of cost driver, and the variable cost component. Using the lowest level of cost driver, the fixed cost per month is:

$$\$23,086 = (\$0.70 \times 2,980) + \text{Fixed cost}$$
$$\$21,000 = \text{Fixed cost}[12]$$

The high/low method defines the formula for estimating the cost of operating the drive-up window as:

Drive-up window cost = ($0.70 × Number of drive-up customers) + $21,000

Now, it is possible to predict the drive-up window costs for next month using this relationship. If Wendy's anticipates 4,500 drive-up customers next month, the estimated drive-up window costs for next month would be $24,150 [($0.70 × 4,500) + $21,000 = $24,150].

Is High/Low Appropriate? The high/low method is very simple to use because it requires only two data points and very little math. However, this strength is also its weakness. If either one or both of these points is not representative of normal levels of activity, the predictions made using high/low may be flawed. For example, if Wendy's spent $2,500 replacing the glass in the drive-up window in February due to a hailstorm, the glass costs incurred during February are not representative of normal costs, and any prediction made using them may be inaccurate. Or if there was a large Boy Scout convention in the area in May so that drive-up volume was unusually heavy, the number of drive-up customers in May might not represent normal activity. Given this problem, analysts must use the high/low method with caution. One way to overcome the drawback of high/low is to use more data and statistical analysis, which we discuss next.

Linear Regression Analysis

One of the most commonly used statistical techniques for estimating costs is called **linear regression analysis** or **least squares regression.** Linear regression is a cost estimation method that uses multiple data points and statistical analysis to determine the total cost line. It is called *least squares regression* because it allows determination of the total cost line by minimizing the sum of the squared deviations of the data points around the line.[13] One benefit of linear regression is that it uses more cost driver levels and related cost data. Another advantage is that companies can use it to determine whether there is a useful relationship between a cost and a particular cost driver.

The line obtained using linear regression analysis is the most accurate representation of the linear relationship between the cost driver and the related costs. Based on

---

[10]Notice that we select the high and low points based on the cost driver, not the cost, because cost drivers measure activity and are assumed to cause cost to change.

[11]We use a month as the time period because we collected monthly cost and activity data.

[12]The same fixed cost is determined if the highest level of cost driver is used: $26,775 = $0.70 (8,250) + Fixed cost. Fixed cost = $21,000.

[13]This means that if the data are graphed, the distance between the data points and the total cost line is as small as possible, which indicates that the calculated line is as accurate a linear representation as possible.

the data used, the total cost line generated by linear regression is as dependable as, or more dependable than, the total cost lines obtained using any other cost estimation technique. Dependability indicates that the linear relationship can be relied on to predict costs in the future.

Many computer programs as well as hand-held calculators perform linear regressions.[14] Our purpose here is not to learn how the computer performs linear regression; rather, we focus on the data needed for calculation purposes and how to interpret the regression output.

What Data Are Input?   First, we must determine the activity that uses resources. Next, we determine the cost driver that represents this activity and causes costs to change. Then, we collect pairs of data points so that each pair represents a certain level of cost driver and has an associated amount of related costs. As with the high/low method, the range of the cost driver should reflect normal activity. The amount of data collected is limited only by the cost of collecting it. The more good data used, the better the regression results. Good data are representative of normal levels of activity, free from errors, and available at a reasonable cost. The benefits of information must outweigh the costs of obtaining it in order for the information to be useful.

Refer again to Exhibit 4.9. We assume that the number of drive-up customers is the cost driver measuring operating activity that causes drive-up window costs to change. The cost driver and cost data are input to the linear regression equation. When analysts enter data into a linear regression package, they refer to the cost driver as X, the **independent variable,** and to total cost as Y, the **dependent variable.** The cost driver is the independent variable because the level of cost driver is independent from the level of cost.

In Wendy's case, the number of customers using the drive-up window is not dependent on the costs incurred in operating the window. Here, cost is the dependent variable because it is assumed to be caused by the number of customers using the window.

What Information Is Output?   Depending on the computer program, the output received from linear regression analysis includes: (1) the estimated fixed cost for the period, called the *intercept* or *constant*, (2) the estimated variable cost per cost driver, called the **X coefficient,**[15] and (3) various statistical measures of how good the regression equation is.

As in the case of the high/low method, the estimated fixed cost is the proportion of total cost that does not change as the level of cost driver changes. The estimated variable cost is the slope of the total cost line or the portion of total cost that changes as the cost driver changes.

Almost all regression programs provide the user with an R-squared statistic and a standard error statistic. The **R-squared** is a measure of the strength of the relationship between the cost driver, representing activity, and the cost.[16] In other words, the R-squared value provides information to answer the question: Does this cost driver cause costs to change, and can we use it to predict costs in the future? The R-squared ranges from 0 to 1, with 1 indicating that the cost driver is a perfect

---

[14]Most computer spreadsheet programs such as Lotus 1-2-3 can perform linear regression analysis.

[15]A *coefficient* is a statistical term for a component of a linear regression equation. In this case, it refers to the independent variable, cost driver.

[16]R-squared measures the variance in the dependent variable (cost) explained by changes in the independent variable (cost driver). It is the correlation coefficient, r, squared.

The correlation coefficient is the directional relationship between the variables. That is, if the dependent variable increases when the independent variable increases, a positive relationship exists between them. However, if the dependent variable decreases when the independent variable increases, a negative relationship exists. R-squared measures the strength of this positive or negative relationship.

predictor of the cost. In business settings, an acceptable *R*-squared is generally considered to be greater than 0.5. In general, the higher the *R*-squared, the stronger the relationship between the cost driver and the cost.

The second statistic frequently reported is called the **standard error of the X coefficient,** or the **standard error,** referring to the independent variable. It is the estimate of the variability in the calculated value of the variable cost per cost driver. It gives an idea of the confidence we can have in the calculated variable cost. The lower the standard error relative to the variable cost, the less variability in the estimate. When there is less variability, predictions made using the linear regression output are more reliable.

Some regression packages also report a *t* **statistic,** which is the ratio of the variable cost (*X*) coefficient to the standard error of the *X* coefficient.[17] In general, the larger the *t* statistic, the more likely it is that the variable cost is *not* zero.[18] A good rule of thumb for business applications is that a *t* statistic greater than 2 is acceptable because the probability that the variable cost is zero in these cases is very small.[19]

Using Regression Output   When the data presented in Exhibit 4.9 were input into Lotus 1-2-3, the following output resulted:

Constant	16,781.4
X coefficient	1.00082
Standard error of coefficient	0.2037
R-squared	0.71

This output indicates that the cost formula that represents these data is:

Drive-up window cost = ($1.00082 × Number of drive-up customers) + $16,781.40

In addition, the output indicates:

1. The *R*-squared is 0.71, which signifies a strong relationship between the number of drive-up customers and the drive-up window costs.

2. The standard error of the coefficient is small, which implies that there is little variability in the variable cost estimate.

3. The calculated *t* statistic is 4.91 (1.00082/0.2037), which indicates that the variable cost is different from zero.

Thus, we conclude that this regression equation is a good predictor of drive-up window costs. As in the case with the high/low method, we can use this output to predict costs in the future. If we predict 4,500 drive-up customers next month, estimated drive-up window costs for next month would be $21,285 [($1.00082 × 4,500) + $16,781.40 = $21,285].

Comparison of the High/Low and Linear Regression Methods

Take a moment to compare the cost formulas and the predictions made using the high/low method versus those using regression. With high/low, we predicted a drive-up window cost of $24,150, but when using regression, the predicted cost is only $21,285. There is a difference because the high/low method uses only two data points and may not produce a line that represents the data well.

---

[17]The *t* statistic is calculated as the *X* coefficient divided by the standard error of the *X* coefficient, which assumes that there is a direct linear relationship between *X* and *Y*.

[18]Recall, if the variable cost is zero, it means that there is no relationship between the cost driver and the cost; in other words, the cost behavior is fixed with respect to that cost driver. In such a case, the cost driver cannot be used to predict the cost.

[19]Statistics books provide *t* tables that show the probability that the variable cost is zero when that particular *t* value is calculated.

EXHIBIT 4.10

Graphical Comparison of High/Low and Regression Results

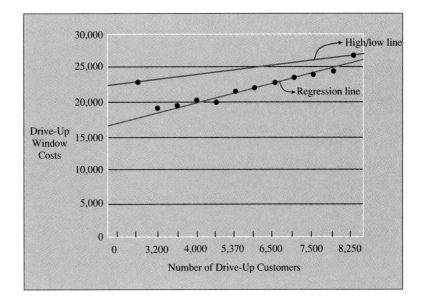

Exhibit 4.10 illustrates a plot of the data from Exhibit 4.9 and the resulting high/low and regression cost lines. As you can see, the regression line fits the data points much better—its slope is steeper, and its intercept is lower.

We can also determine the prediction error that would result from using the high/low results rather than the regression results. Exhibit 4.11 shows that, at lower levels of the cost driver (number of customers), the difference between the high/low and regression results, which is the prediction error, is larger. This occurs because fixed costs are a larger proportion of total costs at lower cost driver levels and there is a $4,219 difference in calculated fixed costs between these two methods ($21,000 high/low − $16,781 regression = $4,219). Therefore, at lower levels of the cost driver, the high/low method predicts much higher total costs than does the regression method. As the number of customers increases, this difference decreases.

PAUSE & REFLECT   Refer to Exhibit 4.11. Can we compare predictions at 2,500 or 8,500 customers? Why or why not?

Choosing Cost Drivers   Since regression programs give the user statistics that indicate how strong the relationship is between the cost driver and the cost, such programs are frequently used to find cost drivers that best represent the usage of resources. Assume that the manager of a particular Wendy's store correlates drive-up window costs to the number of

EXHIBIT	4.11	Prediction Comparison of High/Low and Regression Methods		

Number of Customers	High/Low Prediction A	Regression Prediction B	Prediction Error (High/Low − Regression) A − B
3,500	$23,450	$20,284	$3,166
4,500	24,150	21,285	2,865
5,500	24,850	22,286	2,564
6,500	25,550	23,286	2,264
7,500	26,250	24,287	1,963

A: Total cost = $0.70 + $21,000
B: Total cost = $1.00082 + $16,781

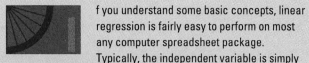

f you understand some basic concepts, linear regression is fairly easy to perform on most any computer spreadsheet package.

Typically, the independent variable is simply referred to as *X*, and the dependent variable is referred to as *Y*. Let's examine how to perform regression analysis using Lotus 1-2-3 and the following data.

Independent Variable: Number of Orders Filled	Dependent Variable: Cost of Packing Supplies
160	$18,000
250	26,000
170	20,000
240	28,000
210	24,000

First, enter all the observations of the independent variable, *X*, in column A, and the corresponding observations of the dependent variable, *Y*, in column B. (Remember, that dollar signs are not necessary when using spreadsheets.) Next, locate the "data" pull-down menu. In this menu you should see either "regression" or "analyze" depending on which version of Lotus you are using. Choose, "regression" or "analyze" and then, "regression." Now you should see a dialog box that requests certain information. First, you must indicate the location of the *X*-range. You can either enter the range where the *X* variables are located, A1.A5, in this case, or use the mouse to highlight the range. Follow the same procedure to denote the *Y* range, which, in this case, is B1.B5. Next, indicate where you want the output located using any cells other than the cells where your input is located. However, you probably want your output directly below or to the right of your input. You do not need to specify the entire range for the output, simply denote the beginning cell. Notice that in the lower left-hand corner of this dialog box is an option button for the *Y* intercept. The default is to compute the *Y* intercept, that is, to calculate a fixed cost. Alternatively, you can force the *Y* intercept to 0, but for most applications this is not necessary.

Once you are satisfied with your choices for the *X* range, *Y* range, and output range, click OK. Output, similar to that shown below, should appear on your screen.

Regression Output

Constant		2852.761
Std Err of Y Est		1315.318
R Squared		0.924561
No. of Observations		5
Degrees of Freedom		3
X Coefficient(s)	98.77301	
Std Err of Coef.	16.28947	

This is the essence of performing linear regression analysis using a computer spreadsheet. Now, it is important to know what the output indicates. First, the constant, $2,852.761, is the fixed cost. The "Std Err of Y Est" is the estimate of the error in *Y* that results from this equation. "R Squared" is the measure of the strength of the *X-Y* relationship previously discussed. "No. of Observations" refers to the number of *X* observations entered, 5, in this case. "Degrees of Freedom" is a term used in statistics that, in simple linear regression, is calculated as the number of observations minus 2. The "X Coefficient(s)" is the variable cost, $98.77301, and the "Std Err of Coef." is the standard error of the *X* coefficient discussed previously. Based on this information, what is the regression equation that can be used to estimate packing costs based on the number of orders filled? It is:

$2,852.761 + $98.77301 × (Number of orders filled)

If management estimates that 200 orders will be filled next month, the estimated packing cost is:

$2,852.761 + ($98.77301 × 200) = $22,607.36

Is this equation a good predictor of packing costs? Yes, the R-squared is .92, which is good, and the calculated *t* value is 6.0636 (98.77301/16.28947), which exceeds the minimum *t* value of 2.

Other spreadsheet packages, such as Quattro Pro and Excel, operate in a similar fashion.

hamburgers sold. Wendy's determines the number of hamburgers sold and the drive-up window costs for a period of time and uses these pairs of data as input into a linear regression package. This results in the following output:

Constant	22,450.1
X coefficient	0.3468
Standard error of coefficient	1.3442
R-squared	.36

Let's analyze this output to determine if the number of hamburgers sold is a good predictor of drive-up window costs. The *R*-squared of .36 is low, below the .5 level considered acceptable in business applications. The standard error of the coefficient is larger than the *X* coefficient itself, resulting in an unacceptable *t* statistic of 0.258 (0.3468/1.3442). Thus, we conclude that the number of hamburgers sold is not a good predictor of drive-up window costs and that the manager should not use this regression equation to predict costs in the future. The manager should investigate and use a better cost driver as a predictor of drive-up window costs, such as the number of drive-up window customers, which we discussed previously.

Now that we have discussed options for setting selling prices and methods to estimate costs, we can put these ideas together to predict profit and to see how profit changes with changes in the volume of operating activity.

COST-VOLUME-PROFIT ANALYSIS: THE RELATIONSHIPS AMONG FACTORS

Cost-volume-profit (CVP) analysis is the study of how costs and profits change in response to *changes in the volume* of goods or services provided to customers. This is a valuable tool for planning because management must assess whether its company can sell a given product in sufficient volume to cover the costs of manufacturing, or purchasing the product, and distributing it. Cost-volume-profit analysis also can be helpful in determining selling prices if it is possible to estimate the quantity demanded. However, cost-volume-profit analysis is a model that simplifies reality in order to make predictions without considering every factor connected with the decision. It is very important that users understand the assumptions under which CVP operates because the assumptions establish the limits of its applicability and its effectiveness in forecasting.

Assumptions of Cost-Volume-Profit Analysis

You already know that within the relevant range, cost behavior patterns remain constant. This same assumption applies to cost-volume-profit analysis; only *CVP assumes that cost behavior patterns are related to the volume of units produced and sold.* The assumptions of cost-volume-profit analysis are:

- *Selling price remains constant per unit regardless of the volume sold.* There are no volume discounts, nor are prices changed at various volume levels. The total revenue function is represented by a straight line, where total revenue changes in direct proportion to changes in volume of units sold and only in response to those changes.

- *Variable cost remains constant per unit regardless of the volume produced and sold.* There are no volume production efficiencies resulting from efficiencies that lower the cost per unit as more units are produced, nor are extremely high- or low-volume units more expensive to produce and sell. The variable cost portion of the total cost function is represented by a straight line where total variable costs (versus variable cost per unit) change in direct proportion to changes in the volume of units produced (or purchased, for merchandising firms) and only in response to those changes.

- *Fixed cost remains constant in total, regardless of the volume produced and sold throughout the relevant range.* Additional capacity cannot be obtained, nor can facilities be abandoned in the short run. The fixed cost portion of the total cost function is represented by a straight line where total fixed cost does not increase or decrease with changes in volume of units produced and sold.

It is important to understand the relationship between volume and fixed and variable costs—waste, theft, or spoilage may be considered a variable cost.

THE FAR SIDE   By GARY LARSON

"Well, shoot. I just can't figure it out. I'm movin' over 500 doughnuts a day, but I'm still just barely squeakin' by."

• *For manufacturing firms, the number of units produced equals the number of units sold; for merchandising firms, the number of units purchased equals the number of units sold during the period.* As a result of this assumption, there are no changes in the inventory levels from the beginning to the end of the period. Therefore, the volume number used for cost determination is the same volume number used for revenue determination.

• *If more than one product is sold, the sales mix (the relative proportions of units sold) remains constant.* At all levels of activity, the mix of product sales remains the same; that is, if twice as much product A is sold as product B at lower volume levels, then twice as much product A as product B is also sold at higher volume levels. (See Appendix 4.)

While these assumptions may seem limiting, they are sufficiently realistic within the relevant range to provide a useful first approximation of reality.

How Is Revenue Defined in CVP?

The first step in CVP analysis is to define revenue as a linear relationship between the selling price and the quantity sold. The selling price is determined after considering customers, competitors, cost, and other influences on price. We define *total revenue* as a positive straight-line relationship between the selling price per unit and the number of units sold. That is:

Total revenue = Selling price per unit × Number of units sold

or

$$TR = SPPU\,(Q)^{20}$$

In general, it is possible to increase total revenue by increasing selling price, the quantity of units sold, or both. While this may not always be true, within the relevant range, we assume that selling prices remain the same at all volumes.

How Is Cost Defined in CVP?

Next, we define total cost as having a linear relationship between the cost and the number of units purchased or produced. Analysts determine the total amount of fixed costs over the relevant range and the variable cost per unit produced or purchased by using a cost estimation technique such as the high/low method or linear regression analysis. This results in the following equation:

Total cost = Variable cost per unit × Number of units produced + Fixed costs

or

$$TC = VCPU\,(Q) + FC$$

Therefore, total cost increases beyond the level of fixed costs as the quantity of units purchased or produced increases. We assume that, throughout the relevant range, the fixed cost component remains constant in total, and the variable cost component remains constant per unit.

How Is Profit Defined in CVP?

Now that we have defined *total revenue* and *total cost*, it is possible to determine profit. **Profit,** in CVP analysis, is the excess of revenues over costs.[21] Since both revenues and costs are stated in a mathematical form, so, too, is profit.

Total revenue − Total costs = Profit

or

$$SPPU\,(Q) - [VCPU\,(Q) + FC] = P$$

We illustrate the concept of profit using the income statement of The Olde Hamburger Shoppe shown in Panel A of Exhibit 4.12. We can rearrange the income

---

[20]We use Q in cost-volume-profit analysis rather than X because we previously defined X as the cost driver that measures activity. Cost drivers are not necessarily the number of units produced and sold; however, in CVP analysis, the measure of activity occurs by using the cost driver, number of units produced and sold.

[21]There is a technical difference between *profit* and *net income*. Net income, or revenues less expenses, is reported to external users, while profit, or revenues less costs, is reported to internal users. These terms are commonly used interchangeably, and the technical difference is not important for our purposes.

EXHIBIT | 4.12 | Comparison of Income Statement and Profit Report

Panel A:

THE OLDE HAMBURGER SHOPPE
Income Statement

Sales (10,000 units @ $2.50 per unit)		$25,000
Less cost of goods sold		15,000
Gross margin		$10,000
Less operating expenses:		
Wages and salaries	$2,250	
Building depreciation	1,500	
Other expenses	2,800	6,550
Net income		$3,450

Panel B:

THE OLDE HAMBURGER SHOPPE
Profit Report

	Total	Per Unit*
Sales (10,000 units @ $2.50 per unit)	$25,000	$2.50
Less variable costs:†		
Variable cost of goods sold	6,000	.60
Variable wages and salaries	1,575	.1575
Other variable costs	560	.0560
Contribution margin	$16,865	$1.6865
Less fixed costs:‡		
Fixed cost of goods sold	9,000	
Fixed wages and salaries	675	
Building depreciation	1,500	
Other fixed costs	2,240	
Profit	$3,450	

*Variable cost of goods sold per unit $6,000/10,000 = $.60
Variable wages and salaries per unit $1,575/10,000 = $.1575
Other variable costs per unit $560/10,000 = $.056

†Variable cost of goods sold = $15,000 × .4 = $6,000
Variable wages and salaries = $2,250 × .7 = $1,575
Other variable costs = $2,800 × .2 = $560

‡Fixed cost of goods sold = $15,000 − $6,000 = $9,000
Fixed salaries and wages = $2,250 − $1,575 = $675
Other fixed costs = $2,800 − $560 = $2,240

statement information to reflect the profit equation just presented. Assume that 40 percent of cost of goods sold is variable ($15,000 × .4 = $6,000), 70 percent of wages and salaries are variable ($2,250 × .7 = $1,575), and 20 percent of other expenses are variable ($2,800 × .2 = $560). The income statement is rearranged and presented as the profit report shown in Panel B of Exhibit 4.12.

The difference between these reports is the way that they show costs (expenses). An income statement prepared for external users divides expenses into cost of goods sold and operating expenses. A profit report prepared for internal users divides costs into variable costs and fixed costs.

PAUSE & REFLECT

Refer to Exhibit 4.12. Why is building depreciation included as a fixed cost?

The amount of total sales (revenues) minus total variable costs is called the total **contribution margin** ($16,865). Likewise, the quantity represented by selling price per unit ($2.50) less variable costs per unit ($.60 + $.1575 + $.056 = $.8135) is called the **contribution margin per unit** ($1.6865). It is so named because it represents the portion of each sales dollar available to meet fixed costs. Once the fixed costs are covered, the remainder of the sales dollar is available to contribute to profit.

EXHIBIT | 4.13 | Profit Report with 20 Percent Increase in Volume

THE OLDE HAMBURGER SHOPPE
Profit Report

	Total	Per Unit
Sales (12,000 @ $2.50)*	$30,000	$2.50
Less variable costs:†		
Variable cost of goods sold	7,200	.60
Variable wages and salaries	1,890	.1575
Other variable costs	672	.0560
Contribution margin	$20,238	$1.6865
Less fixed costs:		
Fixed cost of goods sold	9,000	
Fixed wages and salaries	675	
Building depreciation	1,500	
Other fixed costs	2,240	
Profit‡	$6,823	

*$\frac{\$30,000 - \$25,000}{\$25,000} = 20\%$ increase

†Variable costs increase 20%:
    Variable cost of goods sold 12,000 × $.60 = $7,200
    Variable wages and salaries 12,000 × $.1575 = $1,890
    Other variable costs 12,000 × $.056 = $672

‡$\frac{\$6,823 - \$3,450}{\$3,450} = 97.77\%$ increase

The profit report showing contribution margin is very useful because it illustrates the relationship among revenues, costs, and volume. Now, we can answer the question asked previously: If volume is increased 20 percent, will costs increase 20 percent?

Compare Exhibits 4.12 (Pannel B) and 4.13, which show that if the number of units sold increases by 20 percent (2,000 units), sales in dollars increase by 20 percent ($30,000 compared to $25,000), variable costs increase 20 percent (total variable cost of $9,762 compared to total variable cost of $8,135), but fixed costs remain unchanged. This results in an increase in profit of 97.77 percent! (See footnote‡ in Exhibit 4.13.)

Obviously, understanding the relationships among revenues, costs, volume, and profits is critical. We examine the cost-volume-profit relationship in more detail later, but first, we turn our attention to visualizing the CVP relationship.

Graphical Approach to Cost-Volume-Profit Analysis

The relationship between costs and revenues can be presented visually in the form of a graph like the one shown in Exhibit 4.14. We represent total revenue as a linear relationship between volume and selling price, which begins at the origin. It changes in direct proportion to changes in the number of units sold because the selling price per unit remains constant throughout the relevant range. Total cost is a mixed cost, represented by a straight line that begins at a point above the origin.

Breakeven Point   The point where the total revenue line intersects the total cost line is called the **breakeven point** or the point at which total revenues equal total costs. It can be measured in dollars on the *Y*-axis or in units on the *X*-axis. Since total revenue equals total cost at the breakeven point, it is the point at which the company does not make any profit nor suffer any loss. At that point, the total contribution margin equals total fixed cost. Any volume change from this point will result in either a loss or a profit. In general, if a product cannot at least break even, it should not be produced and sold.

Profit and Loss Areas   If the company operates at the volume level above the breakeven point, such as that represented by point *A* in Exhibit 4.14, the company

EXHIBIT | 4.14

**Graphical Depiction
of Breakeven**

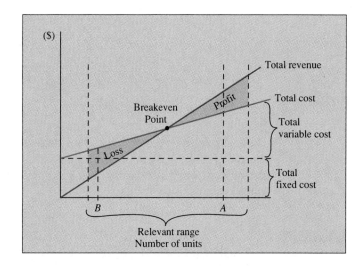

will operate at a profit. At this level, the total revenue line is above the total cost line. Therefore, total revenues exceed total costs, which results in profit. The shaded area above the breakeven point is called the *profit area* or *profit region*. The amount of the profit is represented by the distance between the revenue and cost lines on the *Y*-axis.

If the company operates at a volume level below the breakeven point, such as that represented by point *B* in Exhibit 4.14, the company will operate at a loss because the total cost line is above the total revenue line. The shaded area below the breakeven point is called the *loss area* or *loss region*.

Mathematical Approach to Cost-Volume-Profit Analysis

Graphs are useful tools for visualizing the CVP relationship because they allow us to see the breakeven point as well as the profit and loss areas. However, when managers use CVP as a planning tool, they use a mathematical model based on the relationships introduced earlier. Using *CMPU* to represent the contribution margin per unit, we represent the CVP relationship as:

$$SPPU\,(Q) - [VCPU\,(Q) + FC] = P$$
$$[(SPPU - VCPU)\,(Q)] - FC = P$$
$$CMPU\,(Q) - FC = P$$

To mathematically illustrate CVP, consider the example of starting a business that sells only hamburgers at college sporting events.

- The material cost of $0.60 per hamburger consists of one hamburger patty, a hamburger bun, condiments (ketchup, mustard, pickle), wrapping, and a napkin.

- To encourage employees to work hard, the business will pay them $0.50 per hamburger sold rather than paying them by the hour.

- The university charges a concession fee of $600 per game.

- The equipment rental (grill) costs $100 per game.

- Miscellaneous supplies (salt, pepper, etc.) are estimated at $3 per game.

- The selling price for the hamburgers is $3.00 each.

Determining the Breakeven Point   At the breakeven point, profit is zero. Breakeven, then, is represented as: $SPPU\,(Q) - [VCPU\,(Q) + FC] = 0$. Using the data above,

$$SPPU = \$3$$
$$VCPU = \$1.10\;(\$0.60 \text{ materials} + \$0.50 \text{ labor})$$
$$FC = \$703\;(\$600 \text{ concession fee} + \$100 \text{ equipment rental}$$
$$+ \$3 \text{ miscellaneous supplies})$$
$$CMPU = \$1.90\;(\$3.00 - \$1.10)$$

The number of hamburgers that the business must sell to break even is:

$$\$3.00(Q) - [\$1.10(Q) + \$703] = \$0$$
$$[(\$3.00 - \$1.10)\,(Q)] - \$703 = \$0$$
$$\$1.90Q - \$703 = \$0$$
$$\$1.90Q = \$703$$
$$Q = 370$$

Accordingly, if 370 hamburgers are sold, the profit will be zero. If 371 hamburgers are sold, profit of $1.90 results, the contribution margin per hamburger. Therefore, if the company does not believe it can sell at least 370 hamburgers per game, it should not operate.

PAUSE & REFLECT   If only 365 hamburgers are sold, what is the total amount of the loss?

Since total revenues and total variable cost both increase or decrease proportionately with changes in volume, we can use a short-cut approach to breakeven known as the *contribution margin approach*. The contribution margin approach is:

$$\frac{FC + P}{CMPU} = Q$$

The breakeven point is:

$$\frac{\$703 + 0}{\$1.90} = 370 \text{ hamburgers}$$

We can also state the breakeven point in dollars rather than units to answer the question, "How many dollars of sales are required to break even?" We express breakeven in dollars of revenue using the contribution margin ratio approach. The **contribution margin ratio** is the contribution margin per unit divided by the selling price per unit or the total contribution margin divided by the total revenue. The contribution margin ratio is 63.33 percent ($1.90/$3.00), so the breakeven point in sales dollars is:

$$\frac{\$703}{.6333} = \$1,110$$

PAUSE & REFLECT   What is the relationship between breakeven in hamburgers, 370, and breakeven in dollars, $1,110?

Determining the Target Profit Level   A company cannot survive if it only breaks even because it needs capital to grow, to pay off debt, and to distribute profits to owners as dividends. Therefore, for planning purposes, it is necessary to determine a certain targeted profit level. Using the hamburger business example, assume that its owners want to make a profit of $150 per game, how many hamburgers must it sell?

$$\$3.00Q - [\$1.10Q + \$703] = \$150$$
$$\$1.90Q - \$703 = \$150$$
$$\$1.90Q = \$853$$
$$Q = 448.95$$

Or, using the contribution margin approach:

$$\frac{\$703 + \$150}{\$1.90} = 448.95$$

Results indicate that it must sell 449 hamburgers each game to earn $150 per game. Again, the owners would use this information to decide whether to operate. If the goals of the business owners are to have a profit of $150 in order to earn an adequate return, and the owners do not believe that they can sell 449 hamburgers per game, the business should not operate.

Determining the Target Profit Level after Taxes   Corporations in the United States and many other countries must pay income taxes on profits. Fortunately, we can easily incorporate taxes into cost-volume-profit analysis.

To have a particular amount of profit after taxes, a company must earn more profit before taxes. We calculate the level of **before-tax profit,** or the amount of profit a company earns prior to the deduction of taxes, as:

$$\text{Before-tax profit} = \frac{\text{Desired profit after taxes}[22]}{1 - \text{Tax rate}}$$

Now, assuming the business owners want to make a profit of $150 per game, and that the business is subject to a 15 percent tax rate, how many hamburgers must it sell to earn $150 per game after taxes?

$$\$3.00Q - [\$1.10Q + \$703] = \$150/(1 - .15)$$
$$\$1.90Q - \$703 = \$176.47$$
$$\$1.90Q = \$879.47$$
$$Q = 462.88$$

Or, using the contribution margin approach:

$$\frac{\$703 + [\$150/(1 - .15)]}{\$1.90} = 462.88$$

According to these calculations, the business must sell 463 hamburgers to make a profit of $150 after taxes. Take a moment to examine the profit report in Exhibit 4.15, which confirms this result. It shows that total sales are $1,389 and total variable costs are $509 at this level, resulting in a total contribution margin of $880. After deducting fixed costs, the profit before taxes is $177, which, after subtracting taxes of 15 percent, results in the desired after-tax profit of $150.

PAUSE & REFLECT	What affect do taxes have on the calculation of the breakeven point? Do they increase or decrease it? Why?

---

[22]Since taxes are calculated on profits before taxes, by dividing after-tax profits by 1 minus the tax rate, we can work backwards to determine profits before taxes. For example, if profits before taxes are $100 and the tax rate is 40 percent, then profits after taxes are $60 or 60 percent. Therefore, working backwards, if profits after taxes are $60 and the tax rate is 40 percent, to calculate profits before taxes we divide $60 by 60 percent (1 − .4), which equals $100, the before-tax profit.

EXHIBIT	4.15	Profit Report—Single Product

Hamburger Business: Expected Profit from Sales	
Sales (463 × $3)	$1,389
Less variable cost (463 × $1.10)	509
Contribution margin	$ 880
Less fixed cost	703
Profit before tax	$ 177
Tax ($177 × .15)	27
Profit after tax	$ 150

EXHIBIT	4.16	Sensitivity Analysis		
Changes in Variable		**Contribution Margin Change**	**Breakeven Change**	**Units Needed for Desired Profit after Taxes Change**
Increase in selling price		Increase	Decrease	Decrease
Decrease in selling price		Decrease	Increase	Increase
Increase in variable cost		Decrease	Increase	Increase
Decrease in variable cost		Increase	Decrease	Decrease
Increase in fixed cost		No change	Increase	Increase
Decrease in fixed cost		No change	Decrease	Decrease
Increase in tax rate		No change	No change	Increase
Decrease in tax rate		No change	No change	Decrease

Using Cost-Volume-Profit Analysis— Sensitivity Analysis

Cost-volume profit analysis is a useful tool for planning because decision makers can use it to determine the breakeven point, the target profit level, and the after-tax profit level. CVP analysis provides a useful explanation of some otherwise complex interrelationships, such as analyzing the sensitivity of profit to changes in (1) selling price, (2) variable cost per unit, (3) fixed costs, and (4) tax rate. It is also possible to use CVP analysis to analyze multiple-product CVP relationships, which we discuss in the appendix to this chapter.

Sensitivity analysis is the process of changing the key variables (but *not* the assumptions) in CVP analysis to determine how "sensitive" the CVP relationships are to changes in these variables. Frequently, the values of key variables are estimates; therefore, it is useful to know how sensitive the results are to changes. Thus, analysts using sensitivity analysis increase or decrease the amount of key variables, such as selling price, variable cost per unit, fixed cost, or the tax rate, to determine the effects on profit. Generally, they change variables one at a time to isolate the sensitivity of the results to that particular variable. Be sure to review Exhibit 4.16, which shows how a change in a key variable affects breakeven, the contribution margin, and desired profit. Examples of sensitivity analysis follow.

What Is the Effect of a Change in Selling Price per Unit? A change in the selling price causes a change in both the contribution margin and the breakeven point. An increase in the selling price causes an increase in the contribution margin and, therefore, a decrease in the breakeven point. On the other hand, a decrease in the selling price triggers a decrease in the contribution margin and a subsequent increase in the breakeven point.

For example, recall our example of selling hamburgers at college sporting events. Suppose that another vendor at college games is selling hot dogs for $2.00 each, so the hamburger business owners decide to lower the hamburger selling price by $0.50 to become more competitive. Then, the new contribution margin is $1.40 ($2.50 − $1.10), so it is now necessary to sell 502 (versus 370) hamburgers to break even, as shown below:

$$\frac{\$703}{\$1.40 \text{ (new } CMPU)} = 502.14$$

A decrease in selling price per unit also requires that more units be sold to obtain a particular desired profit after taxes. Assume that the hamburger business wants to maintain a profit of $150 per game after taxes of 15 percent. Due to its reduced selling price, the business must now sell 628 (versus 463) hamburgers as shown below:

$$\frac{\$703 + [\$150/(1 - .15)]}{\$1.40} = 628.19$$

What Is the Effect of a Change in Variable Cost per Unit? A change in the variable cost per unit also causes a change in both the contribution margin and the breakeven point. An increase in the variable cost per unit causes a decrease in the contribution margin and, therefore, an increase in the breakeven point. A decrease in the variable cost per unit triggers an increase in the contribution margin and a subsequent decrease in the breakeven point.

For example, suppose the hamburger business is able to lower its variable cost per hamburger by $.05. Its new variable cost per hamburger is $1.05; therefore, its new contribution margin per unit is $1.95 ($3.00 − $1.05), resulting in a new breakeven point of 361 hamburgers, as shown below:

$$\frac{\$703}{\$1.95 \text{ (new } CMPU)} = 360.51$$

A decrease in variable cost per unit also means that fewer units need to be sold to achieve a desired after-tax profit. Assuming that $150 is the desired after-tax profit, the variable cost decrease of $.05 requires that 451 hamburgers be sold, as shown below:

$$\frac{\$703 + [\$150/(1 - .15)]}{\$1.95} = 451.01$$

What Is the Effect of a Change in Fixed Costs?   A change in fixed costs causes a change in the breakeven point but not in the contribution margin. If fixed costs increase, the breakeven point increases because it requires more unit sales to cover fixed costs. Conversely, if fixed costs decrease, the breakeven point decreases.

For example, suppose that the college, from our previous example, increases the concession fee by $50 per game. Now the business must sell 396 (versus 370) hamburgers to break even as shown below:

$$\frac{\$703 \text{ (old } FC) + \$50 \text{ (additional } FC)}{\$1.90} = 396.32$$

An increase in fixed costs also increases the number of units that must be sold to obtain a desired profit after taxes. As shown below, to obtain a profit of $150 per game after taxes of 15 percent, the company must now sell 489 hamburgers per game.

$$\frac{\$703 + \$50 + [\$150/(1 - .15)]}{\$1.90} = 489.2$$

What Is the Effect of a Change in Tax Rate?   A change in the tax rate affects only the number of units that must be sold to obtain a desired profit after taxes. If the tax rate increases, it is necessary to sell more units to obtain the same desired after-tax profit. Conversely, if the tax rate decreases, fewer units must be sold to obtain the desired after-tax profit. For example, assume the tax rate is increased to 20 percent. How many units must be sold to obtain $150 after tax?

$$\frac{\$703 + [\$150/(1 - .20)]}{\$1.90} = 468.68$$

According to our calculations, if the tax rate increases 5 percent, the number of hamburgers that must be sold to generate a profit of $150 after taxes increases to 469 (versus 463 before).

Sensitivity analysis is useful for assessing the effects of changes in the variables. Businesses often use computer spreadsheets for these analyses because they make it quick and easy to see the effects of changes in one, or several, variables.

SUMMARY

Operational planning requires the prediction of selling prices and costs. It is important to understand costs and their behavior because they are not constant. Once cost behavior patterns are understood, they can be predicted using a cost estimation technique such as high/low or linear regression. These techniques define the linear relationship between the cost driver, which represents activity, and the cost.

In cost-volume-profit analysis, the cost driver is assumed to be the volume of units produced and sold. Planners use cost-volume-profit analysis to understand the relationships among revenues, costs, volume, and profits.

- The four primary influences on selling price are: demand from customers; supply by competitors; legal, political, and social factors; and cost.

- Three common pricing strategies are penetration pricing, life-cycle pricing, and target pricing.

- The three linear cost behavior patterns are fixed, variable, and mixed. The total costs of a company consist of different types of costs that display these patterns.

- Activities consume resources (costs). A cost driver measures activity in order to define the relationship between the activity and the cost.

- Planners use cost estimation techniques such as high/low and linear regression analysis to define the relationship between the cost driver and cost in order to predict costs in the future.

- Linear regression analysis supplies statistics to evaluate the strength of the relationship between the cost driver and the cost. These statistics may be used to choose the best cost driver for a given activity.

- There are five basic assumptions of cost-volume-profit analysis that define the linear relationships among revenues, costs, volume, and profits.

KEY TERMS

before-tax profit The amount of profit a company earns prior to the deduction of taxes, calculated as net income after taxes divided by 1 − tax rate

breakeven point The point at which total revenues equal total costs, total contribution margin equals total fixed costs, and the company makes no profit and incurs no loss

cartel A monopolistic combination of businesses

contribution margin The difference between revenue (sales) and variable costs—in total, as total revenues minus total variable costs

contribution margin per unit The selling price per unit less variable costs per unit

contribution margin ratio Contribution margin per unit divided by selling price per unit, or total contribution margin divided by total revenue

cost driver The means of measuring activity that reflects consumption of resources; that which causes costs to change

cost-volume-profit (CVP) analysis The analysis of how costs and profits change in response to changes in the volume of good and services volume

dependent variable Used in linear regression to represent Y, or the total cost

fixed cost A cost that is constant in total as the amount of cost driver changes but changes per unit as the cost driver changes throughout the relevant range

high/low method The method of cost estimation that uses only two data points, the highest and lowest levels of cost driver in the relevant range, to determine the total cost formula

independent variable Used in linear regression to represent X, or the cost driver

least squares regression Another name for linear regression

life-cycle pricing A pricing strategy in which the company determines the selling price for the life of the product

linear regression analysis The cost estimation method that uses multiple data points and statistical analysis to determine the total cost line (also known as **least squares regression**)

markup The additional amount added to the cost of the product to compute the selling price

mixed cost A cost that varies in the same direction as a cost driver but not indirect proportion, and has both a fixed and a variable component (also known as a **semivariable cost**)

monopolistic competition An environment in which there are a large number of sellers with similar, but not identical, products

monopoly A company that has exclusive control over products, services, or geographic markets

oligopoly An environment in which a few firms control the types or distribution of products and services

penetration pricing A pricing strategy in which a company sets its selling price low initially to gain a share of the market

price fixing A situation in which a group of companies agree to limit supply and charge identical (usually high) prices for their goods and services

price skimming A pricing strategy in which the company initially sets a high price for its product to attract customers who are willing to pay more to receive the product first

price taker A company that must accept the price established by the market based on total supply and demand

product mix (appendix) In a multiple-product company, the total of all products sold

profit Revenues minus costs

pure competition An environment where a large number of sellers produce and distribute virtually identical products and services

R-squared Used in linear regression to indicate the strength of the relationship between the cost driver, representing activity, and the cost

relevant range The expected span of operating activity considered to be normal for the company; the range of activity used in gathering data for high/low or linear regression analysis

sales mix (appendix) The proportions of units of products sold in a multiple-product company

selling margin Selling price of a product less its cost

semivariable cost Another name for mixed cost

sensitivity analysis The process of changing the key variables in the cost-volume-profit relationship to examine the effects of the change on the other variables

standard error of the X coefficient Used in linear regression to measure the variability in the calculated value of the X coefficient

t statistic Used in linear regression to denote the ratio of the X coefficient to the standard error of the X coefficient; it is used to indicate the likelihood that the variable cost is not zero

target pricing A strategy in which the company determines whether and how to produce a product at a cost that provides a certain selling margin

variable cost A cost that varies in total in proportion to the change in cost driver level but remains constant per unit of cost driver throughout the relevant range

weighted-average contribution margin (appendix) The contribution margin used in multiple-product CVP analysis, calculated as the individual product's contribution margin weighted by (multiplied by) the relative sales mix of that product and summed

weighted-average contribution margin ratio (appendix) The weighted-average contribution margin divided by the weighted-average selling price

X coefficient Used in linear regression to denote the value of the variable cost per cost driver

APPENDIX 4

MULTIPLE-PRODUCT COST-VOLUME-PROFIT ANALYSIS

Most companies sell more than one product during a given period of time. For example, Wendy's sells hamburgers, chicken sandwiches, french fries, soft drinks, and many other products. Companies with multiple products can also use cost-volume-profit analysis for planning if they adopt one additional assumption to those outlined previously. For a multiple-product firm, the relative sales mix must remain constant within the relevant range. This assumption is important because it maintains a linear cost relationship even when many different types of products are sold. Cost-volume-profit analysis for a multiproduct company is performed similarly to that of a single-product firm, but it uses a weighted-average contribution margin.

We calculate a **weighted-average contribution margin** by multiplying the contribution margins of each individual product by the relative sales mix of that product. Then we determine the weighted-average contribution margin by adding these together. To determine the breakeven point in **product mix,** or the total of all products sold, we divide the weighted-average contribution margin into the fixed costs. To determine the quantity of an individual product sold at breakeven, we multiply the breakeven point in product mix by the relative **sales mix** (the proportion of units of products sold in a multiproduct company) for each individual product.

As with CVP analysis in a single-product firm, multiple-product CVP analysis is important for determining whether to produce the planned mix of products. If it is not possible to sell the quantity of a particular product required to break even, the product should not be sold.

Using our previous example, suppose the hamburger business is doing so well that the owners decide to open a concession stand outside the arena. Now it is possible to offer soft drinks, french fries, and ice cream cones in addition to hamburgers.

- Employees will work on a straight commission basis, receiving 20 percent of sales in dollars.
- The college concession stand fee is $700 per game.
- The rent for a stand complete with a soft drink machine, freezer, fryer, and grill is $300 per game.
- Other miscellaneous supplies are $20 per game.
- Estimated material costs are:

Hamburger (complete)	$0.60
French fries (per order)	.10
Ice cream (per cone)	.20
Soft drinks (per glass)	.05

- The business set its selling prices as follows:

Hamburger	$3.00
French fries	1.00
Ice cream	1.50
Soft drinks	1.00

The owners estimate that most people will order a hamburger and french fries, 20 percent of customers will want ice cream, and 80 percent will get a soft drink. Based on these estimates, the sales mix is:

Hamburger	1.0
French fries	1.0
Ice cream	.2
Soft drinks	.8
Total sales mix	3.0

Using this information, we can determine breakeven by calculating a weighted-average contribution margin. First, we must determine the contribution margin of each product.

	Hamburger	French Fries	Ice Cream	Soft Drinks
Selling price	$3.00	$1.00	$1.50	$1.00
Less:				
Variable cost—material	.60	.10	.20	.05
Variable cost—employees				
(20% of selling price)	.60	.20	.30	.20
Contribution margin	$1.80	$ .70	$1.00	$ .75

Now we must weight each contribution margin by the relative sales mix, as shown below:

	Hamburger	French Fries	Ice Cream	Soft Drinks
Contribution margin	$1.80	$ .70	$1.00	$.75
Sales mix	1.0/3	1.0/3	.2/3	.8/3
Weighted contribution	$ .60	$.233	$.067	$.20

Next, we add the weighted contribution margins to obtain the weighted-average contribution margin of $1.10 ($.60 + $.233 + $.067 + $.20). Then it is possible to use the weighted-average contribution margin in the same way as the contribution margin to answer questions such as how many products must the business sell to make a profit of $300 before tax? Since fixed costs are $1,020 ($700 concession fee + $300 equipment rental + $20 miscellaneous supplies), the answer is:

$$\frac{\$1,020\ (FC) + \$300\ (P)}{\$1.10\ (\text{Weighted-average } CMPU)} = 1,200$$

EXHIBIT | 4.17 | Profit Report—Multiple Products

Sales:		
Hamburgers (400 × $3.00)	$1,200	
French fries (400 × $1.00)	400	
Ice cream (80 × $1.50)	120	
Soft drinks (320 × $1.00)	320	$2,040
Less variable costs (material and labor):		
Hamburgers (400 × $1.20)	$ 480	
French fries (400 × $.30)	120	
Ice cream (80 × $.50)	40	
Soft drinks (320 × $.25)	80	720
Contribution margin		$1,320
Less fixed costs:		
Concession fee	$ 700	
Stand rental	300	
Miscellaneous supplies	20	1,020
Profit		$ 300

The business must sell *1,200 products* to make a before-tax profit of $300. To determine how many individual items must be sold, multiply the total product mix by the relative sales mix. Accordingly, the business must sell 400 hamburgers, 400 orders of fries, 80 ice cream cones, and 320 soft drinks to generate a profit of $300, as shown below:

Hamburgers (1,200 × 1.0/3)	400
French fries (1,200 × 1.0/3)	400
Ice cream (1,200 × .2/3)	80
Soft drinks (1,200 × .8/3)	320

Examine the profit report in Exhibit 4.17, which supports our analysis. It indicates that total sales will be $2,040 and total variable costs will be $720, resulting in a contribution margin of $1,320. After deducting fixed costs of $1,020, a $300 profit results.

It is possible to present multiple-product CVP analysis in sales dollars by using the weighted-average contribution margin ratio. The **weighted-average contribution margin ratio** is the weighted-average contribution margin divided by the weighted-average selling price where the individual products' selling prices are weighted by the relative sales mix. As with single-product CVP, this answers the question, "How many dollars of product sales are necessary to achieve a desired profit?"

PAUSE & REFLECT   How would Wendy's undertake a cost-volume-profit analysis?

QUESTIONS

1. How are selling prices affected by customers?

2. How are selling prices affected by competitors?

3. How are selling prices affected by legal, political, and social factors?

4. Explain how selling prices are affected by cost.

5. Describe the differences among penetration pricing, life-cycle pricing, and target pricing.

6. Define and give an example of each of the following costs for a merchandising company: (*a*) fixed cost, (*b*) variable cost, and (*c*) mixed cost.

7. Give an example of a cost that might vary with each of the following cost drivers: (*a*) number of orders placed, (*b*) number of units produced, (*c*) number of tests performed, and (*d*) number of square feet.

8. Explain the importance of the *relevant range* concept.

9. What does each element in the equation $Y = m(X) + b$ indicate in terms of costs?

10. Explain how to use the high/low method to estimate costs.

11. What are the advantages and disadvantages of the high/low method?

12. Define the following terms used in regression analysis: (*a*) independent variable, (*b*) dependent variable, (*c*) R-squared, (*d*) standard error of the X coefficient, and (*e*) *t* statistic.

13. Is an *R*-squared of .9 good? Why or why not?

14. Explain how to calculate a *t* statistic. Is a *t* statistic of 15 good? Why or why not?

15. How is activity defined in cost-volume-profit analysis?

16. Describe the five basic assumptions of cost-volume-profit analysis.

17. Explain the breakeven point in units. How is it related to the breakeven point in dollars?

18. Explain each of the following: (*a*) contribution margin per unit, (*b*) total contribution margin, and (*c*) contribution margin ratio.

19. Explain how to calculate before-tax profit by using after-tax profit.

20. How can cost-volume-profit analysis determine the number of units that must be sold to achieve a certain profit after taxes?

Appendix

21. Explain how to adapt CVP for multiproduct companies.

22. Explain why a weighted-average contribution margin is used in multiproduct CVP analysis.

23. Explain what is meant by *product mix* in multiproduct CVP analysis.

24. Explain why it is necessary to assume that the relative sales mix remains constant in multiproduct CVP analysis.

25. Explain how to determine the number of units of a particular product that must be sold to obtain a desired profit after taxes in multiproduct CVP analysis.

EXERCISES

E 4.1   Cut Above is a hair styling salon. Given below is a list of costs connected with the salon. Identify each of the costs as a variable, fixed, or mixed cost. Assume that activity is measured as the number of customers. Use (V) for variable, (F) for fixed, and (M) for mixed. Give a short justification for each of your answers.

_____   *a.* Rent on the facilities.
_____   *b.* Utilities: water, electricity, and heat.
_____   *c.* Shampoo and rinse.
_____   *d.* Laundry service for towels and gowns.
_____   *e.* Perming solution.
_____   *f.* Combs, brushes, and miscellaneous hair supplies.
_____   *g.* Hair dryers.
_____   *h.* Stylists' wages and commissions.
_____   *i.* Computer costs for inventory maintenance.
_____   *j.* Hair products sold to customers.

E 4.2   Parts Now is an automotive parts retail store. It sells motor oil, oil filters, automotive batteries, and other automotive equipment. Assume that activity is defined as the number of products sold. Identify each of the costs below as variable, fixed, or mixed costs. Use (V) for variable, (F) for fixed, and (M) for mixed. Give a short justification for each of your answers.

_____   *a.* Cost of oil.
_____   *b.* Wages paid to employees who wait on customers.
_____   *c.* Computer costs for inventory maintenance.
_____   *d.* Insurance paid on retail store.
_____   *e.* Insurance paid on shipments from the factory to Parts Now.
_____   *f.* Freight paid to receive parts from the warehouse.
_____   *g.* Utilities: water, electricity, and heat.
_____   *h.* Cost of shelving for the showroom.
_____   *i.* Wages paid to employees who deliver parts to customers.
_____   *j.* Cost of automotive batteries.

E 4.3 Bestline, Inc., is a manufacturing firm that makes ping-pong paddles. Each ping-pong paddle consists of a handle, a wooden paddle, and a rubber backing for the wooden paddle. As the paddles progress through the assembly process, workers attach the handles and glue on the rubber backing. Identify each of the costs below as a variable, fixed, or mixed cost. Use (V) for variable, (F) for fixed, and (M) for mixed. Activity is measured as the number of ping-pong paddles produced. Give a short justification for each of your answers.

_____ a. Cost of handles for the paddles.
_____ b. Wages of assembly workers.
_____ c. Rent on production facilities.
_____ d. Wages of sales personnel.
_____ e. Utilities for the production facilities: water, electricity, and heat.
_____ f. Cost of rubber backing for the ping-pong paddles.
_____ g. Production supervisor's salary.
_____ h. Cost of wooden paddles.
_____ i. Cost of glue.
_____ j. Cost of shipping crates.

E 4.4 The engineering costs and the number of machine setups for each month during the first half of the year at Gregray Company are presented below. Using the high/low cost estimation method, determine the cost equation. What do the results indicate?

Month	Engineering Cost	Number of Setups
1	$1,600	6
2	1,550	5
3	2,400	8
4	2,300	7
5	2,800	10
6	2,700	9

E 4.5 Refer to E 4.4. These data were entered into a regression program, resulting in the following output. Determine the cost equation. What do the results indicate?

Constant	157.1429
X coefficient	275.71
R-squared	.92
Standard error of X coefficient	39.3571

E 4.6 Cabbies, Inc., has incurred the following maintenance costs on its fleet of taxicabs during the past six months. Use the high/low cost estimation method to determine the expected cost if 12,000 miles are logged in one month. What do the results indicate?

Month	Total Miles Logged	Maintenance Cost
1	12,700	$13,000
2	8,300	8,500
3	10,500	10,700
4	15,600	15,800
5	9,200	9,700
6	11,700	12,000

E 4.7 Refer to E 4.6. These data were entered into a regression program, resulting in the following output. Use this output to determine the expected cost if 12,000 miles are logged in one month. What do the results indicate?

Constant	435.9561
X coefficient	0.986533
R-squared	.998
Standard error of X coefficient	0.021158

E 4.8 Use the following information to determine the profit equation for Jackson Company.

Selling price per unit	$56
Variable cost per unit	44
Fixed cost per year	620,000

E 4.9   Use the graph below to identify the items that follow.

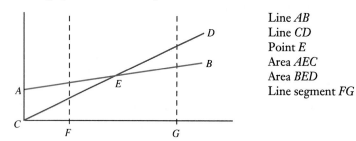

Line *AB*   _____
Line *CD*   _____
Point *E*   _____
Area *AEC* _____
Area *BED* _____
Line segment *FG* _____

E 4.10   Basic, Inc., sells its one product for $125 per unit. The variable cost per unit is $80. The fixed cost per year is $450,000.
a. What is the contribution margin per unit?
b. What is the breakeven point in units?
c. What is the contribution margin ratio?
d. What is the breakeven point in dollars?

E 4.11   Complex Company is developing a new product. The selling price has not yet been determined, nor are the variable costs per unit known. The fixed costs are $200,000. Management plans to set the selling price such that variable cost is 60 percent of the selling price.
a. What is the contribution margin ratio?
b. What is the breakeven point in dollars?
c. If management desires a profit of $30,000, what will total sales be?

E 4.12   Hill, Inc., has a product contribution margin of $40. The fixed costs are $800,000. Hill, Inc., has set a target profit of $80,000 per year.
a. What is the breakeven point in units?
b. How many units must be sold to achieve the target profit?
c. If fixed costs increase 10 percent, how many units must be sold to achieve the target profit?

E 4.13   Venus Flytrap Company distributes insect repellent. Each can of repellent sells for $2.50. The variable cost per can of repellent is $0.60. The fixed selling and distribution costs are $50,000. The after-tax target profit level is $18,000. Venus is subject to an average income tax rate of 35 percent.
a. What is the breakeven point in units?
b. What is the breakeven point in dollars?
c. To achieve the profit goal, what must before-tax profit be?
d. How many units must be sold to achieve the profit goal after tax?

E 4.14   Naval Company has the following cost-volume-profit relationships.

Breakeven point in units sold	1,000
Variable cost per unit	$1,500
Fixed cost per period	$250,000

a. What is the contribution margin per unit?
b. What is the selling price per unit?
c. What is the total profit if 1,001 units are sold?

E 4.15   Ortego, Inc., currently sells its product for $2 per unit. The variable cost per unit is $0.40 and fixed costs are $30,000. Purchasing a new machine will increase fixed costs by $5,000, but variable costs will be cut by 20 percent.
a. What is the breakeven point before the new machine is purchased?
b. What is the breakeven point after the new machine is purchased?
c. Should Ortego purchase the new machine? Why or why not?

E 4.16   Refer to the basic assumptions of CVP discussion in the chapter. Without using any numbers, prepare a graph that illustrates the first four assumptions.

E 4.17   Conway Company uses a cost-plus pricing formula for its product. The estimated cost of producing and distributing the product is $45. If the markup percentage is set at 60 percent, what is the selling price and the profit percentage?

E 4.18 Refer to E 4.17. If management wants to obtain a profit percentage of 45 percent, what selling price and markup percentage will it set?

Appendix

E 4.19 Twin Peaks Company produces two products, Alpha and Omega. The selling prices, variable costs, contribution margins, and sales mix of each product are given below:

	Selling Price	Variable Cost	Contribution Margin	Sales Mix
Alpha	$12	$8	$4	.60
Omega	10	4	6	.40

Twin Peaks Company's fixed cost is $240,000.
a. What is the weighted-average contribution margin for Twin Peaks Company?
b. What is the breakeven point in the product mix?
c. How many units of Alpha will be sold at breakeven?
d. How many units of Omega will be sold at breakeven?

E 4.20 Refer to E 4.19.
a. If Twin Peaks Company desires a net income of $40,000 before taxes, how many units of Alpha must be sold?
b. If Twin Peaks Company desires a net income of $40,000 after taxes of 30 percent, how many units of Omega must be sold?

E 4.21 Robinson Manufacturing produces and sells four types of automotive paint at wholesale to various retail companies throughout the Midwest. The selling prices and variable costs per gallon of each type of paint are given below:

	Acrylic Lacquer	Synthetic Enamel	Acrylic Enamel	Urethane Enamel
Selling price	$173	$142	$195	$373
Variable costs	69	80	117	200

On average, sales of acrylic lacquer account for 20 percent of total sales, sales of synthetic enamel account for 50 percent, sales of acrylic enamel account for 20 percent, and sales of urethane enamel account for 10 percent of total sales. Fixed costs are $1 million per year.
a. What is the weighted-average contribution margin for Robinson Manufacturing?
b. How many gallons of paint must be sold to break even?
c. How many gallons of each type of paint must be sold at breakeven?

E 4.22 Refer to E 4.21.
a. If Robinson Manufacturing desires a profit of $600,000 before taxes, how many gallons of paint must be sold?
b. If Robinson Manufacturing desires a profit of $600,000 after taxes of 40 percent, how many gallons of paint must be sold?
c. Refer to b. How many gallons of each type of paint must be sold to achieve this after-tax profit?

PROBLEMS

P 4.1 Examine the cost graphs below. Identify the cost behavior pattern shown for each graph and provide at least one example of a cost that fits the pattern.

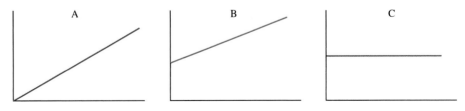

P 4.2 Ross Company is estimating costs for the last half of the year based on activity during the first half of the year. The results from January through June are:

		Costs		
Month	Units Made	Direct Material	Direct Labor	Overhead
January	2,920	$11,680	$17,520	$27,550
February	5,000	20,000	30,000	31,810
March	3,625	14,500	21,750	28,600
April	8,720	34,880	52,320	41,760
May	5,986	23,944	35,916	36,000
June	7,986	31,944	47,916	42,840

Required: a. Using the high/low cost estimation method, determine the total variable cost per unit made.
 b. Using the high/low cost estimation method, determine the total fixed cost per month.
 c. What is the cost estimation equation?
 d. Estimate the total cost if 6,000 units are made during July using the equation developed in part *c*.
 e. Estimate the total cost if 9,000 units are made during August.
 f. Explain how the concept of *relevant range* relates to part *e*.

P 4.3 Refer to P 4.2. The following are the output of a regression analysis applied to these data. (Cost is defined as total cost—direct materials, direct labor, and overhead).

Constant	18911.57
X coefficient	12.78
R-squared	.9985
Standard error of *X* coefficient	0.2465

Required: a. What is the dependent variable in the regression application?
 b. What is the independent variable in the regression application?
 c. Using the results, determine the cost equation.
 d. Estimate the total cost if 6,000 units are made during July.
 e. Estimate the total cost if 9,000 units are made during July.
 f. Explain how the concept of *relevant range* relates to part *e*.

P 4.4 Wharton Manufacturers currently uses direct labor hours to predict overhead. However, the accountant at Wharton has recently read an article on activity-based costing and has suggested that machine hours would be a better predictor of overhead cost than direct labor hours. The following data have been provided to you from the past year.

Month	Overhead Cost	Labor Hours	Machine Hours
January	$54,500	1,600	2,100
February	53,400	1,500	2,000
March	63,800	1,850	3,100
April	70,000	2,000	4,000
May	62,700	2,100	3,200
June	68,900	1,950	3,600
July	80,100	2,500	4,850
August	82,200	2,600	5,000
September	69,900	1,800	3,950
October	59,600	1,700	2,600
November	71,500	2,300	4,100
December	77,400	2,450	4,700

Required: a. Using the high/low estimation method, determine the cost equation when direct labor hours is used as the independent variable.
 b. Using the high/low cost estimation method, determine the cost equation when machine hours is used as the independent variable.
 c. What is the estimated amount of overhead if 2,200 direct labor hours are worked next month?
 d. What is the estimated amount of overhead if 4,200 machine hours are worked?
 e. Which of these variables, direct labor hours or machine hours, do you feel is the most useful? Why?

P 4.5 Refer to the information in P 4.4. The following regression results were obtained using these data:

Direct Labor:

Constant	19072.64
X coefficient	23.7194
R-squared	.8524
Standard error of X coefficient	3.121

Machine Hours:

Constant	34,986.66
X coefficient	9.124
R-squared	.987
Standard error of X coefficient	0.3277

Required: a. What is the estimated amount of overhead if 4,200 machine hours are worked next month?
b. What is the estimated amount of overhead if 2,200 direct labor hours are worked next month?
c. What are the t statistics for each regression application?
d. Which of these variables, direct labor hours or machine hours, do you feel is the most useful? Why?

P 4.6 Dirt Devils is a janitorial service that specializes in office cleaning. The charge per office averages $100 per visit. The variable costs per visit are $35. The fixed operating costs are $40,000. The management of Dirt Devils wants to maintain a profit of 10 percent of total sales revenue. (Hint: Define the desired profit as a percentage of sales rather than a dollar amount.)

Required: a. What is the profit equation?
b. How many offices must be cleaned to achieve the profit goal?
c. If the price charged for office cleaning is increased by 15 percent, how many offices must be cleaned to achieve the profit goal?
d. What are the problems that might be encountered by changing the price charged for office cleaning? Why?

P 4.7 Qualico Corporation sells widgets for $10 each. For the month of June 1996, Qualico sold 6,000 widgets and reported variable costs of $18,000 and fixed costs of $18,000. Assume that Qualico increases its selling price by 20 percent on July 1, 1996.

Required: a. How many widgets have to be sold in July 1996 to break even?
b. How many widgets have to be sold to earn a before-tax profit of $24,000?
c. If Qualico is subject to an average income tax rate of 35 percent, how many widgets have to be sold to earn an after-tax profit of $24,000?
d. How many widgets have to be sold to earn a before-tax profit of 15 percent of sales?
e. How many widgets have to be sold to earn an after-tax profit of 15 percent of sales?

P 4.8 Malden Enterprises has projected its income before taxes as shown below:

Sales (200,000)	$8,000,000
Variable costs	2,000,000
Contribution margin	$6,000,000
Fixed costs	3,500,000
Net income	$2,500,000

Required: a. What is the selling price per unit?
b. What is the variable cost per unit?
c. What is the contribution margin per unit?
d. What is the contribution margin ratio?
e. What is the breakeven point in units?
f. What is the breakeven point in dollars?

P 4.9 Think Thin is a weight control center located in Atlanta. Clients are charged a fee of $500 for the weight control, counseling, and maintenance program. The average client spends 15 weeks in the program. In addition, each client must purchase his or her weekly food allowance at the center during the 15-week program. The average cost per client per week for food is $65.

The variable costs per client per program average $100. This includes the cost of initial paperwork, insurance, and administrative costs. The variable costs per client per week average $20. This includes the cost of food, utilities, and counselors' salaries.

The fixed costs of operations including rent, property insurance, and other fixed administrative costs amount to $6,000 per 15-week period.

Required: *Assume independent situations.*

a. How many clients must Think Thin have each 15-week period to break even?

b. If Think Thin desires a profit of $8,000 per 15-week period, how many clients are needed?

c. If Think Thin has 50 clients each 15-week period, what is the profit before tax for each 15-week period?

d. If the program fee per client is increased by 15 percent, how many clients are needed to break even each 15-week period?

e. If the program fee per client is increased by 15 percent and the number of clients per 15-week period falls to 40, what is the profit before taxes each 15-week period? Should the program fee be increased? Explain.

f. If the variable costs per client per week is decreased by $2, how many clients are needed each 15-week period to break even?

g. If the variable costs per client per week are decreased as in part *f* and Think Thin has 55 clients each 15-week period, what is the before-tax profit each 15-week period?

P 4.10   Throughout history, the government has attempted to regulate selling prices and trade practices. Research one of the following topics and present your findings to the class.

a. Sherman Antitrust Act of 1890.

b. Clayton Act of 1914.

c. Robinson-Patman Act of 1936.

d. Federal Trade Commission Act of 1914.

COMPUTER APPLICATIONS

CA 4.1   Compusoft, Inc., is a computer software retailer located in Portland. Its product is state-of-the-art, so selling prices have not yet been determined. The fixed operating costs are $40,000 per period. The variable cost per software package is $100.

Required: *Use a computer spreadsheet. Assume independent situations.*

a. If Compusoft estimates demand at 500 software packages per period, what selling price must be set to break even?

b. If Compusoft estimates demand at 500 software packages per period, what selling price must be set to earn $3,000 per period before taxes?

c. If Compusoft estimates demand at 500 software packages per period, what selling price must be set to earn $3,000 per period after taxes of 40 percent?

d. Assume the selling price is determined as in part *c*, but demand declines to only 400 software packages per period, what is the effect on Compusoft's profit per period?

e. If demand is only 400 software packages per period, what selling price must be charged to earn the same after-tax profit as in part *c*?

f. What other issues are involved in changing the selling price?

CA 4.2   Biotex, Inc., anticipates the following results for its first year of operations.

Sales (600,000 units)	$24,000,000
Cost of goods sold	14,400,000
Gross margin	$ 9,600,000
Selling and administrative costs	6,000,000
Profit before tax	$ 3,600,000
Taxes	1,440,000
Profit after taxes	$ 2,160,000

An analysis of the cost records reveals that 40 percent of cost of goods sold is variable and the remaining 60 percent is fixed. The variable selling and administrative costs are $3,600,000. Taxes are calculated at an average rate based on profit before taxes.

Required: *Use a computer spreadsheet. Assume independent situations.*

a. What is the breakeven point in sales dollars? In units?

b. What is the average tax rate?

c. If fixed product costs increase by $1,000,000, what is the new breakeven point in units?

d. If variable selling and administrative costs per unit increase by 12 percent, what is the new breakeven point in units?

e. If the selling price is increased by 15 percent, how many units will have to be sold to achieve the same profit after tax as during the first year of operations?

f. If the tax rate increases to 45 percent, what is the effect on breakeven?

Appendix:

CA 4.3

Homewatch Company is a security firm that offers house-sitting services during vacations and other owner absences. Homewatch offers three types of service—basic, super, and deluxe. Basic services include mail and newspaper retrieval as well as general security. Super service includes basic service plus a once-a-day pet service. Deluxe service includes basic service plus a twice-a-day pet service. The daily fees and daily variable costs of each service are given below:

	Basic	Super	Deluxe
Customer fee	$10	$15	$20
Variable cost	3	5	7

In the past, 40 percent of customers required basic service, 30 percent of customers requested super service, and the remaining 30 percent requested deluxe service. The fixed operating costs are $970 per period.

Required:

Use a computer spreadsheet.

a. What is the breakeven point in customer days (one customer for one day)?

b. At breakeven, how many customers receive basic service?

c. If Homewatch desires a profit of $485 per period, how many customer days are needed?

d. At the sales level determined in part c, how many customers will receive deluxe service?

CA 4.4

Forms R Us is an income tax service that prepares federal income tax returns for individuals. Forms R Us offers four types of service. The fee for a 1040EZ form is $25. The fee for a 1040A form is $50. The fee for a 1040 is $100 with three or fewer schedules or $200 if four or more schedules are needed. The variable cost associated with a 1040EZ is $5. The variable cost associated with a 1040A is $10. The variable costs associated with a 1040 are $30 for three or fewer schedules and $70 for four or more schedules. Last year Forms R Us filed 8,000 tax returns. The breakdown of returns by type is given below.

1040EZ	1,000
1040A	2,000
1040 (3 schedules or less)	4,000
1040 (4 schedules or more)	1,000
Total returns	8,000

Forms R Us expects the same relative sales mix for the coming year. The fixed operating costs last year were $300,000. Management believes that fixed costs will increase by 10 percent this year.

Required:

Use a computer spreadsheet.

a. How many tax forms must be prepared to break even this year?

b. How many 1040A forms will be prepared at breakeven?

c. If management desires the same profit as last year, how many 1040 tax forms must be prepared?

d. Refer to part c. Prepare a profit report as proof of your answer.

CASES

C 4.1

Home Gyms, Inc., compiled the following information for 1997.

Sales (10,000 units)	$2,500,000
Variable costs	1,000,000
Contribution margin	$1,500,000
Fixed costs	750,000
Before-tax profit	$ 750,000
Tax (40%)	300,000
After-tax profit	$ 450,000

a. What is the breakeven point in units? What is the breakeven point in dollars?

b. How many units must Home Gyms sell to earn a profit after taxes of $90,000?

c. Home Gyms has learned that its total fixed costs will increase by $75,000 in 1998. If Home Gyms increases its selling price per unit by 10 percent in 1998, how many units must it sell to earn the same before-tax profit as in 1997?

d. What factors should Home Gyms, Inc.'s management consider prior to increasing its selling price by 10 percent?

e. If Home Gyms, Inc., can reduce its variable cost by 10 percent rather than increasing its selling price to offset the increase in fixed costs of $75,000, what is the new breakeven point?

f. If Home Gyms can reduce its variable cost by 10 percent to offset the increase in fixed costs of $75,000, should it also decrease its selling price? Why?

g. Write a memo to the president of Home Gyms explaining what she should do to offset the increase in fixed costs.

C 4.2   Refer to the annual report you obtained in C 1.2. Using your knowledge of this company and what you have learned in this chapter, classify the expenses on the income statement as costs (fixed, variable, or mixed). You may need to read some of the notes to gain a better understanding of the income statement items.

CRITICAL THINKING

CT 4.1   Wendy's was founded on the concept of "old fashioned" hamburgers. Each hamburger is a square patty, which is served directly from the grill in accordance with customer orders. During peak periods, cooks must estimate demand and have a sufficient supply of hamburgers cooking when customers arrive. Hamburgers that become too well done cannot be served because they don't meet Wendy's specifications for "hot and juicy." Thus, Wendy's invented Wendy's chili made from overdone hamburgers.

Wendy's chili is made daily by the assistant manager or an experienced crew member. It takes 4 to 6 hours to cook the chili and, during this time, it must be stirred to prevent burning, once each hour. It takes 10 to 20 minutes to prepare a batch of chili using the following ingredients:

48 ¼ pound hamburger patties (12 lbs)	$1.25/lb
1 can crushed tomatoes	1.70/can
5 cans tomato sauce	.51/can
2 cans red beans	1.32/can
1 Wendy's seasoning packet	.45/each

This recipe yields 57 bowls of chili. Ten percent of the time it is necessary to cook hamburgers specifically for the chili. The remainder of the time, overdone hamburgers, which have been refrigerated until needed, are used. It takes 10 minutes to cook 48 hamburger patties. Then, the patties must be chopped into smaller pieces, which takes about 5 minutes. Mixing the ingredients takes approximately 5 minutes.

Other chili costs include:

Serving bowls	$0.035 each
Lids for carry out	0.025 each
Spoons	0.010 each

Labor costs are:

Assistant manager	$4.08 per hour
Management trainee	3.98 per hour
Crew member	2.90 per hour

Required: Determine the cost of a bowl of chili.

CT 4.2 The shipping manager of Delta Company is concerned about the recent increase in shipping cost. He is finding it difficult to predict shipping costs from one warehouse to the next or from one month to the next. After investigation, you determine that shipping cost is driven by one of the following activities:

1. The number of shipments received.

2. The weight of the shipments received.

3. The dollar value of the shipments received.

Based on this investigation, data on each activity were gathered for regression analysis and the following results were obtained.

Regression 1: Number of Shipments

Constant 628,680	R^2 .95
X coefficient –1,127.8	Standard error 2,578.4

Regression 2: Weight of Shipments

Constant 271,610	R^2 .927
X coefficient 150.8	Standard error 22.05

Regression 3: Value of Shipments

Constant 236,790	R^2 .912
X coefficient .123	Standard error .007

Additional Information:

1. Management is expecting a 10 percent increase in product costs next year.

2. Only 80 percent of the warehouses have scales to weigh the shipments. Scales will have to be purchased for the other warehouses at a cost of $1,200 each.

3. The number of shipments varies widely between the warehouses from a low of 17 shipments per month to a high of 102 shipments per month.

Required:
a. Explain the rationale behind each of the cost driver-cost relationships.
b. Analyze this information and write a memo to the shipping manager explaining which variable (number of shipments, weight of shipments, or value of shipments) should be used to predict shipping costs in the future.

ETHICAL CHALLENGES

EC 4.1 Pharma Corporation is a pharmaceutical company that developed a drug in 1972 used in the treatment of acne. The drug recently has been found to be an effective treatment for several types of cancer. The company realizes that the demand for the new product will be very large and that the profitability of Pharma Corporation could be enhanced dramatically at a time when the financial viability of the company was in doubt. In fact, prior to the discovery of the cancer treatment, the board of directors was discussing laying off 1,500 workers.

This prescription drug is currently marketed under the trade name Skin Clear and sells for about $0.10 per tablet. The marketing department suggests that Pharma Corporation continue to sell Skin Clear, but develop a new name and dosage size for the pills that will be sold as the cancer treatment. In addition, the research indicates that the new cancer pills could be sold at a price of $4 per pill. The dosage for Skin Clear was one pill per day. The dosage for the cancer patients will be five pills per day to be taken for six months.

The cost to produce and market the cancer pill will be negligible. The sales representative will need little training to sell the new product, and the cost to produce and package the new pills will be approximately the same as the cost of producing Skin Clear.

The marketing department indicates that if the price is set at $4 per pill, many cancer patients will not be able to afford the treatment. However, the profits from the pill are needed in order to keep Pharma Corporation from going bankrupt.

Required: *a.* Name each of the major stakeholders in this scenario and discuss this situation from the viewpoint of each.

            b. If the new cancer treatment is marketed, what should the selling price be?

            c. What is your recommendation to the board of directors?

EC 4.2   Almegon is a chemical distributor that has maintained its inventory records manually for the past several years. Recently it decided to invest in an interactive computer system to replace the manual inventory system. Almegon's fixed costs were $200,000 per year and are expected to increase by $100,000 if the computer network is implemented. The variable cost per unit of inventory under the old system was $12 per unit and is expected to decrease to $5 per unit. Almegon plans to keep its current selling price of $20 per unit.

Required: *a.* What is the expected change in the breakeven point due to the computer network system?

            b. Who are the stakeholders affected by this decision and how are they affected?

            c. Should Almegon install the computer system? Why or why not?

CHAPTER 5

Planning and Budgeting for Operating Activities

Learning Objectives

1. Explain why companies use budgets.
2. Describe the various budgeting strategies companies use.
3. Explain the planning process in the revenue cycle and the resulting budgets.
4. Describe the planning process in the conversion cycle and the resulting budgets.
5. Explain the planning process in the expenditure cycle and the resulting budgets.
6. Describe the relationships of the revenue, conversion, and expenditure cycle budgets to the cash budget and pro forma financial statements.

Appendix:

7. Indicate the purpose of the economic order quantity model of inventory planning.

Henry Ford built his first car in 1892, when he was 30 years old. Just over 10 years later, he founded Ford Motor Company, which remains a world leader in automobile production today. The reasons for Ford's successes in those early years, while many other companies like Detroit Motors failed, included cutting production cost by controlling raw material use and adapting assembly-line methods. Ford standardized cars using the assembly-line approach to mass production. In October 1913, he introduced changes in the assembly line that reduced the time to assemble a car from 12-1/2 hours to 1-1/2 hours. Impetus for this change came from an engineer who saw it as the reverse of the "disassembling" lines found in the meatpacking plants in Chicago and Cincinnati.

Fiscal 1994 was a banner year at Ford Motor Company. The company's worldwide net income was $5,308 million, compared to $2,529 million the year before. Sales were up 18 percent, and operating margins improved dramatically.[1] In 1994, Ford reintroduced the Mustang. The new Mustang was designed to appeal to sportscar enthusiasts, retaining the styling of the earlier "muscle" cars, with modifications designed for the 1990s such as dual airbags, antilock brakes,

---

[1]Ford Motor Company, Annual Report, 1994, p. 23.

and an improved handling system. The new Mustang was not invented in a drawing room, however. Ford listened to its consumers and also improved its production processes. The Mustang moved from the development phase on the computer screen to the production line in a record 35 months. Now, the lessons learned during the development process are being taught throughout Ford.

Controlling costs continues to drive Ford's efforts. Alexander J. Trotman, chairman of the board, has embarked on Ford 2000, a program that will unify Ford and make it a cost-effective competitor. As part of Ford 2000, global product teams will design cars to be sold around the world. Engineers will be assigned permanently to one vehicle center to work with designers and marketers to build products for individual countries.[2] Among other things that Ford has done to get new products to the market faster is to divide the task of machining the prototype for new engines to enable development of a new engine to go from design to testing in only 100 days.

Understanding and improving the production process and listening to employees and customers continue to be the crux of Ford's success. Clearly, Ford Motor Company has come a long way from the early 1900s when Henry Ford was reported to say, "You can have your car any color you want, as long as it's black." According to Trotman, "By empowering this outstanding team [employees] to do its consistently best work, Ford will become more customer-focused, product-driven, innovative and productive. We'll be prepared not just to compete in the years ahead, but to prosper and grow as never before."[3]

Planning is crucial for any business. Without planning, a business has no direction or objectives to accomplish. In Chapter 4, we examined how to determine selling prices and the role that cost plays in profit planning. This chapter builds upon those ideas as it addresses the role of budgeting in planning for normal operating activities.

WHY SHOULD COMPANIES USE BUDGETS?

A **budget** is a plan for the future expressed in financial terms. The proper development of a budget, or **budgeting,** is the process of expressing a company's goals and objectives in quantitative terms. Budgeting is a crucial part of the planning process. Businesses, not-for-profit organizations, and individuals need budgets to plan for future activities. A business plans for the future to satisfy the needs of its customers, employees, suppliers, and owners. Not-for-profit organizations plan for the future to meet their goals in an effective and efficient manner. Individuals plan for meeting day-to-day obligations as well as for making other major less frequent expenditures, such as buying a house or car and saving for retirement. All of these groups benefit from the financial planning provided by the budgeting process. A company budgets as long as the benefits derived from budgeting exceed the costs incurred. We discuss these issues next.

[2]"Ford: Alex Trotman's Daring Global Strategy," *Business Week*, April 3, 1995, pp. 94–104.
[3]Ford Motor Company, Annual Report, 1994, p. 4.

What Are the Benefits of Budgeting?

A budget outlines how resources are expected to be received from, and used in, the operating, investing, and financing activities of the business during a specified period of time. A properly prepared budget provides a company with four primary benefits: (1) planning, (2) communication and coordination, (3) resource allocation, and (4) evaluation and control.

Planning   The primary purpose of a budget is to present and describe the financial ramifications of plans for the future. The budgeting process requires individuals to consider possible future courses of action and the resources needed to accomplish the various activities. For example, key planners of Ford Motor Company would consider the number of different models of automobiles they want to sell in the future, the number of customers they expect in the future, and the financial and physical resources needed to service those customers as part of planning. If Ford plans to sell 100 different models of automobiles, it would need to consider whether it has the physical and financial resources available to do so.

The budgeting process, which quantifies plans, would help management determine, in this case, whether selling 100 different models of cars and trucks is economically feasible. Ford Motors also has to plan where to build its various automobiles, when to begin production, how many units of each model to produce, and how to market its automobiles, both in the United States and foreign countries.

For example, Ford Motor Company produces and sells automobiles in many countries outside the United States. The models of automobiles built and sold in other countries are different from those built and sold in the United States. This requires that Ford plan both international and domestic sales and production amounts. Considering both the international and domestic markets is very important to Ford and other international companies because the types of products consumers want may differ.

In Ford's case, for example, some cars sold in Europe are designed with the right side as the driver's side. This design, however, is not popular in the United States, so any overproduction existing in Europe cannot simply be shipped to the United States for use.

Communication and Coordination   The budgeting process promotes communication and coordination among divisions or departments within a company. In order for the company to function effectively, managers and other employees must understand the interaction among the departments and how the actions of one department affect another. Then, managers must communicate their plans to each other in order to coordinate the activities of the organization as a whole. This coordination is part of the budgeting process.

For example, before Ford's production department determines the number of different models of cars to manufacture, it must consult the marketing department to determine the types of models and features that customers want. Also, when Ford plans to introduce a new model, the marketing department must plan how to promote sales of this model. Finally, if automobile production is expected to increase dramatically, the human resources department must plan for the hiring of additional workers. Such budgetary communication and coordination helps ensure that all departments are working toward common company goals. For example, when Ford introduced the new Mustang in 1994, it had a nationwide advertising campaign to promote its sales. The success of the new Mustang can be attributed, in part, to the communication and coordination that occurred among Ford's departments.

Resource Allocation   Businesses operate with limited resources, which, therefore, require some type of allocation. Budgeting aids resource allocation by ensuring that information is available to help managers determine which activities should receive the limited resources of the company. In addition, through the budgeting process, companies can analyze activities to determine if they add value to the company.

A **value-added activity** adds value to the product produced for and received by the customer. For example, manufacturing cars from raw steel is a value-added activity. Other types of activities that do not add value to the product from the customers perspective, called **nonvalue-added activities,** should be reduced or eliminated. For example, moving raw steel from one building to another does not add value to the automobile, so companies should make efforts to reduce or eliminate this type of activity. The identification and analysis of value-added and nonvalue-added activities is part of activity-based management, which we discuss in greater detail in Chapter 13.

For example, when Ford decided to produce the new Mustang, it had to determine the activities that added value to the car. It decided that equipping the car with dual airbags added value, so Ford allocated resources to cover the purchase and installation of airbags in the Mustang.

Evaluation and Control   Finally, a budget serves as a useful benchmark against which to evaluate and control actual performance. The evaluation process consists of comparing actual performance results to the budget to determine what areas deviated from planned activities and whether to take corrective actions. When actual and budgeted results do not match, the financial and operating activities of the firm may need to be adjusted, the budget may need to be revised, or both. Thus, the evaluation process serves to control operations by determining when and where a company did not achieve planned results. It is then up to management to use this information to determine the causes for budget variations.

For example, if Ford planned to produce and sell 250,000 Mustangs during 1995, but produced only 230,000 and sold only 210,000, management would need to determine why the company did not achieve its expected results. Was promotion of the Mustang inadequate? Did management overestimate the quantity demanded? Was the selling price too high? Management uses the answers to such questions when planning for the next period. Therefore, the budgeting process is circular and continuous—plans lead to actions that culminate in results. Managers and other decision makers evaluate the results and use the evaluation as input into the next period's planning process.

What Are the Costs of Budgeting?

The budgeting process requires time and other resources, such as people. The results of the process impact the activities of departments and individuals. Thus, we discuss the costs of budgeting in terms of three important aspects: (1) time and resource requirements, (2) adaptability of departments or segments of the business, and (3) motivation and behavior of individuals.

Time and Resource Requirements   Budgeting is time consuming. A typical yearly budgeting sequence may take as long as three or four months. During this time, management must coordinate its activities with others in the organization. A large organization typically appoints a **budget director,** often the controller, who determines how to collect the data and prepare the budget. The budget director works closely with various department managers who provide the information necessary to complete the budgets. The budget director typically reports to a **budget committee,** a group of key executives who are responsible for overseeing the budget process. The budget committee reports to the board of directors who approve the budget. Thus, because many people are involved in the budgeting process, the cost, in terms of human capital, is large.

Adaptability of Departments and Segments   Another cost associated with budgeting occurs when the budget is so rigidly adhered to that it inhibits a department or business segment from responding to the changes in the environment. For example, if a business segment is only allocated a specific amount of resources, it may be forced to forgo profitable opportunities due to lack of available resources.

To illustrate, suppose that after the budget process is complete, the marketing department at Ford wants to accept an order from a dealer for an additional 50,000 cars during the coming period. The production department may be reluctant to accept this order if it will cause its costs to exceed the budgeted amount for production. In this case, the department may refuse the order, not because it is unprofitable but, rather, because the budget might not be met if the company accepts the order. This type of rigid adherence to a budget limits the ability of departments or segments to take advantage of profitable opportunities as they arise.

The opposite problem may also exist if a company continues to allocate resources to product lines that are unprofitable. For example, a product line may be continued despite declining sales if the company does not consider changes in the environment during the period covered by the budget. If, instead, the company continues to follow the budgetary plans, profits may be adversely affected. For example, in the late 1950s, Ford produced an automobile known as the Edsel. This car was not very popular, yet Ford continued to produce it for several years. Many analysts think that Ford should have discontinued Edsel production after its first year.

Motivation and Behavior of Individuals The budget also has an effect on the motivation and behavior of individuals, both during the budget process and after the budget has been formalized. During the budgeting process, individuals who develop budgets (employees, lower-level managers, and/or upper-level managers) are influenced by the communication and coordination aspects of budgeting. If communication between departments is inadequate, the budgeting process can result in inaccurate departmental budgets. For example, if the marketing department and the production department at Ford do not communicate effectively, either, or both, of their department budgets may not reflect the expected activities of the coming period.

In addition, the budgeting process may lead to dysfunctional behavior on the part of those individuals involved in determining the budget numbers. Managers and other employees may be motivated to report budget numbers that they know are not accurate representations of future expectations. We call this **budgetary slack,** which is the difference between what a person with input into the budget process *chooses* as an estimate of revenues or expenses and what is *actually* a realistic estimate. In other words, budgetary slack can be viewed as a deliberately introduced bias.

For example, if the marketing manager at Ford is fairly sure that 250,000 Mustangs can be sold during the coming period, he or she might report an estimated sales number of only 200,000 Mustangs to ensure that sales are not overestimated. The difference between what the manager actually expects (250,000 cars sold) versus what the manager reports (200,000 cars sold) is budgetary slack.

Another form of introducing bias into budgets occurs when budget preparers overestimate the time or cost to complete an activity in order to protect themselves from unanticipated cost increases. For example, if the purchasing manager at Ford anticipates that automobile tires will cost $40 each, he or she might report a cost of $45 each, "just to be safe," that is, to make sure that the costs do not exceed the departmental budget. Or, if a production manager at Ford is fairly sure that it will take 20 hours to manufacture a car, she or he might report that it will take 24 hours to complete a car to allow for unanticipated delays. The additional 4 hours per car is budgetary slack.

There are many reasons why people might engage in the types of budget manipulation just mentioned. For example, top management might place emphasis on "meeting or beating" the budget to obtain bonuses or other rewards. In such cases, the person preparing the budget estimates would have an incentive to overestimate expenses or underestimate revenues to ensure meeting the budgetary goals. People also might be motivated to engage in budget manipulation because they anticipate budget number adjustments by upper-level management; that is, they might expect estimated expenses to be decreased and estimated revenues to be increased as part of upper management's budgetary input. Thus, employees might overestimate expenses or underestimate revenues to counteract management's reaction to their estimates. We discuss solutions to this problem in the section on budgetary strategies.

After the budget is formalized, individuals are also affected by budgetary requirements. The budget places certain requirements on departmental and individual work performance in order to meet budgetary goals. Individuals may resist the budget requirements for several reasons. For example, they might believe that the goals are unrealistic and, therefore, that any attempt to reach the budgetary goals is futile. Or they might resist the budgetary requirements if they think that upper management has not considered their input. We discuss solutions to these problems next.

As you can see, every budgeting process has benefits and costs. A successful budgeting process occurs when the benefits gained from budgeting exceed the costs incurred. Businesses adopt a variety of different budgeting strategies in an attempt to ensure a successful budgeting process. We discuss several of these strategies next.

WHAT ARE BUDGETARY STRATEGIES?

A budgetary strategy is the manner in which a company approaches the budgeting process. The strategy adopted by the company impacts who is involved in the budgeting process and how the budget numbers are derived. Each of the various budgeting strategies is an attempt to minimize the motivational and behavioral costs associated with budgeting. Two budgetary strategies that involve different groups of people are mandated budgeting and participative budgeting.

Mandated versus Participative Budgeting

Mandated Budgeting **Mandated budgeting** relies on predetermined standards set by upper-level managers for its budget levels. It is also known as *top-down budgeting* because top management develops the budgets and passes them down the organizational hierarchy to various divisions and/or departments without input from lower levels of management and employees.

The purpose of mandated budgeting is to set operating budgets that are in line with the goals and objectives of upper-level management. The predetermined standards on which such budgets are based are estimates of the quantity and cost of operating inputs and can be either ideal or normal. An **ideal standard** can be achieved if operating conditions are almost perfect; it does not allow for any operating inefficiencies. A **normal standard** can be achieved under practical operating conditions and allows for some "normal" operating inefficiencies.

For example, suppose the upper-level management at Ford determines that a car can be manufactured in 20 hours if the production line runs continuously. On the other hand, if normal work stoppages and estimated breakdowns are considered, it should take 24 hours to complete a vehicle. In this case, 20 hours is considered an ideal standard, while 24 hours is a normal standard.

There is a great deal of debate among psychologists, behavioral scientists, and managers as to which standard is a better motivator for employees. Some professionals think that ideal standards give employees something to aim for. Such ideal standards are viewed as being motivational, whereas normal standards are thought to be too easily achieved and, therefore, not conducive to encouraging improvement. For example, if you could achieve an A in a course without studying, how motivated would you be to study? Employees also may be unmotivated by standards that are too easy to achieve.

Others think that ideal standards do not motivate because they are too hard to achieve, causing employees to give up. They believe that normal standards that can be achieved give employees a sense of accomplishment and, consequently, serve to motivate them. For example, if you felt as though you could not achieve an A in a course no matter how hard you studied, how motivated would you be to study?

Mandated budgeting is most appropriate for divisions whose product lines are in the maturity or decline phases (described in Chapter 3). In these circumstances, the costs to produce and sell the product as well as the quantity to be sold are fairly certain. In such circumstances, it is more efficient to have upper management prepare the budget. In addition, since there is little uncertainty in this environment, employee input into the budgeting process may be unnecessary.

Participative Budgeting   **Participative budgeting** allows individuals who are affected by the budget to have input into the budgeting process. It is also known as *bottom-up budgeting* because the budgeting process begins at lower levels of the organizational hierarchy and continues up through the organization to top management. Upper-level management and the budget director are responsible for coordinating the information received from the employees and for developing a comprehensive budget plan.

For example, suppose that rather than having upper management determine the standard time allowed to produce a car, the production managers at Ford asked production employees for their input. Since the employees affected by the budget are given input into the process, this is a participative budget process.

Participative budgeting is most appropriate for divisions whose product lines are in the development or growth stages. In the development stage, the environment is particularly uncertain, and input from employees is necessary since they have a better understanding of the product than does upper management. In addition, employee input into the budgeting process may increase their motivation, which is essential to develop products and markets.

Since most companies have divisions in all the product stages from development to decline, the overall budgeting process is typically both participative and mandated. In these circumstances, employees have input into the budgeting process, the budget is revised by upper management after careful consideration of all employee input, and the final budget is prepared by the budget director and approved by the board of directors.

Incremental versus Zero-Based Budgeting

The second aspect of budgeting strategy concerns how to determine the budget numbers. Some companies begin a period's budgeting process by referring to the current period's budget, while others begin each budgeting period anew.

Incremental Budgeting   **Incremental budgeting** is a strategy whereby the company uses the current period's budget as a starting point in preparing the next period's budget. The resource requirements of the current period are increased or decreased based on the changes expected during the coming period. The advantage of this strategy is that it is less time consuming and may involve fewer individuals within the organization. The disadvantage is that an increase in resource requirements is often proposed without considering whether the increase is really necessary.

Zero-Based Budgeting   In contrast, a **zero-based budgeting** strategy in which the company begins each budget period with a zero budget requires consideration of every activity undertaken by the department or segment. Rather than beginning with the current period's budget, the manager must determine if the activity is necessary, the alternative ways of conducting the activity, and the amount of resources needed to conduct the activity.

The advantage of zero-based budgeting is that it requires managers to carefully consider the activities undertaken by their respective departments and to determine if activities add value. The disadvantage of zero-based budgeting is that it is time consuming and, therefore, requires more resources than incremental budgeting.

Many companies have adopted a budgeting strategy that is both incremental and zero-based. In this strategy, a zero-based budget strategy is followed in a two- to three-year cycle with an incremental budgeting strategy in the intervening years. In this way, it is possible to obtain the best of both strategies.

WHAT TYPES OF BUDGETS DO COMPANIES PREPARE?

The type of budgets prepared by a particular company depend on the time horizon and the nature of the business activities under consideration. The time horizon considered is a continuum between strategic and operational budgets, while the nature of the business activities determines whether there is a need for a project or master budget.

Strategic versus Operational Budgeting

A strategic budget, also known as a *forecast*, is typically prepared for a 5- to 10-year period. This type of budget considers the long-term planning of the company and is usually more general in nature than an operating budget (see next paragraph). The strategic budget is the quantification of the strategic planning process discussed in Chapter 3. A strategic budget considers questions such as: Should the company expand its product lines? Should it change its inventory policy? Should the company expand its markets?

In contrast, an **operational budget** is prepared for a much shorter period of time, typically, a year or less. An operational budget is more specific than the strategic budget. It considers questions such as: How many units should the company produce this year? How much does the company expect to spend on material purchases this year? How much labor cost is expected this year? Operating budgets are related to strategic budgets because the operating budget is the current plan for achieving the long-term goals and objectives of the company.[4]

Project versus Master Budgeting

Project budgeting is the process of ascertaining the specific resources provided by, and needed for, a specific project or activity. Often companies need to budget a particular project to determine whether it should be undertaken or to determine a bid price in a contracting situation. A company uses a project budget to determine what subset of the company's resources is necessary to complete the project. A project budget may be long term or short term in duration, but it considers only the resources required for one particular project.

In contrast, **master budgeting** is the process of compiling all the budgets prepared during the revenue, conversion, and expenditure cycles that culminates with the cash budget and pro forma financial reports as shown in Exhibit 5.1. The sales budget is related to the production budget, selling and administrative costs budget, and cash receipts schedule as well as the pro forma financial reports. The production budget, in turn, is related to the direct materials budget as well as the direct labor and manufacturing overhead budget. These budgets, in turn, are related to the cash disbursements schedule and the pro forma financial reports. The selling and administrative costs budget, which flows from the sales budget, is related to the cash disbursements schedule and the pro forma financial reports. Finally, the cash receipts and cash disbursements schedules along with the planned financing and investing cash flows become input for the cash budget and the related amount shown on the pro forma balance sheet. We discuss each of these budgets, in turn, next.

---

[4]Financing and investing activities require budgets that are longer term than operational budgets but shorter term than strategic budgets because these activities require long-range planning for the financing and acquisition of capital expenditures, such as the purchase of a building for use by the business.

EXHIBIT | **5.1**

Master Budget

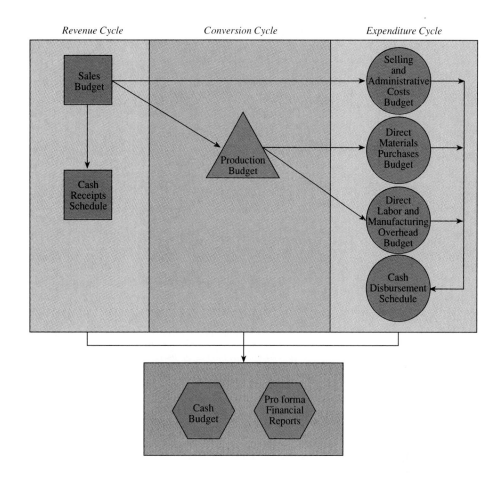

There is an emphasis on the master budget in this chapter because it is concerned with *all* the operations of the business and requires a recurring budgeting process in all businesses. Throughout the discussion of operational planning and the master budget, we consider how a large corporation such as Ford Motor Company addresses its planning issues. However, when we look at the interrelationships of the budgets, we will simplify the manufacturing process by considering, as our example, only one model of automobile and one type of raw material in an automobile manufacturer called Scott's Manufacturing.

WHAT IS OPERATIONAL PLANNING IN THE REVENUE CYCLE?

The first step in revenue cycle planning is to estimate the volume of sales of goods or services given the expected selling price. For example, a service organization must estimate how many clients it will serve in the coming period. Both merchandising and manufacturing firms must estimate how many units of products will be sold during the coming period. Government and other non-for-profit organizations must forecast the level of services to provide for the coming period. In addition, it is necessary to estimate cash receipts from customers as part of revenue cycle planning.

Sales Planning and Budgeting

Sales planning is often a difficult task requiring the input of skilled professionals. For large organizations, sales planning is usually done by the marketing department. This type of planning is important because it reflects the company's understanding of its customers' needs and wants, which is critical to the company's survival. Some of the tools used in sales planning include:

• *Analysis of past sales levels and trends.* An analysis of the past is helpful because understanding the past is often the first step to considering the future. Companies often use statistical techniques, such as least squares regression, to predict future sales levels based on past data.

- *Surveys of current and potential customers' needs.* Companies conduct surveys to determine what customers want. As previous chapters discussed, understanding the customers is crucial. For example, a survey might reveal that people are willing to pay more for a car if it has a 10-year bumper-to-bumper warranty versus a 5-year guarantee.

- *Demographic analysis of customers.* A demographic analysis tells the company where the customers are, what their disposable incomes are, and what their buying habits are. This information is also useful for understanding the customers. For example, through demographic analysis, Ford Motors might discover that in a certain geographic area, Mustangs do not sell well because they are too small for families, whereas Lincoln Continentals sell very well because they are larger and have more interior room.

- *Analysis of economic, political, legal, and social trends.* An analysis of economic, political, legal, and social trends would help determine whether there are any threats or opportunities in the external environment to address in the coming period. For example, if there is pending legislation to require dual airbags, a company like Ford Motors must use this information to determine demand for its cars that already have dual airbags as well as those vehicles that do not.

- *Analysis of competitive trends.* An analysis of the competition is critical to ensure that market share (the percentage of total worldwide sales controlled by a particular company) is not lost. In addition, actions by competitors may have an impact on the quantity of the company's products demanded by customers. For example, if General Motors lowers its base sticker price on automobiles by 20 percent, this action may have a negative impact on sales of Ford automobiles.

- *Analysis of planned advertising and promotion.* A successful advertising or promotional campaign can have a huge impact on the number of products sold. The company must anticipate the effect of any planned advertising and promotion to ensure that supply is available to meet demand. For example, when Ford Motors introduced the new Mustang, it was promoted through print and broadcast media.

After considering all of these issues, the sales budget team develops the sales budget. The **sales budget** shows the expected sales for the period in both physical (quantity) and financial (dollar) amounts (for a particular product line). Therefore, the number of sales budgets depends on the number of product lines the company has. Ford Motors might develop sales budgets for every product line in its Ford, Lincoln, and Mercury divisions, as well as its Jaguar and European divisions. The accuracy of the sales budget is important because it drives all the other operating plans.

EXHIBIT | 5.2 | Sales Budget

SCOTT'S MANUFACTURING
Sales Budget for the Budgeting Period July–December 1996
(000s)

	July	August	September	October	November	December	Total
Sales in units (cars)	15	14	13.5	14.5	15	16	88
Sales in dollars	$300,000	$280,000	$270,000	$290,000	$300,000	$320,000	$1,760,000

Note: Selling price expected is $20,000 per car ($300,000,000/15,000)

Exhibit 5.2 illustrates the monthly sales budgets of Scott's Manufacturing for the first half of the fiscal year. Notice that Scott's Manufacturing expects to sell 15,000 and 14,000 cars, respectively, in July and August. By looking at the relationship between sales in dollars and sales in units for July, we determine that the expected selling price of the car is $20,000 ($300,000,000/15,000).

Cash Receipts Planning

Once the sales budget is determined, the next step in revenue cycle planning is to estimate cash receipts. When companies sell their products on account, their cash receipts may be different from their sales. Therefore, part of revenue cycle planning includes planning the billing to and collecting from customers. To determine the expected cash receipts, the company must address two important issues: (1) what amount will be collected from customers and (2) when it will be collected.

Assume that Scott's Manufacturing offers its dealers selling terms of 2/10, n/30, and it bills its customers on the first day of every month for purchases made during the preceding month. Based on past experience, it estimates that 60 percent of sales will be collected within the discount period, 30 percent within 30 days (but not within the discount period), and 10 percent of sales will be collected in the next month after billing.[5]

Based on this information, Exhibit 5.3 shows the **cash receipts schedule,** which reflects anticipated cash collections from customers for the budgetary period of Scott's Manufacturing.

Take a moment to compare Exhibits 5.2 and 5.3. Notice that the amount of sales in Exhibit 5.2 for July is $300 million, while the amount of cash collections for July

---

[5]Some companies budget an amount of uncollectible sales that represents that portion of total sales that is not expected to be collected or that will be collected so far in the future that budgeting the timing of the receipt is not possible.

EXHIBIT | 5.3 | Cash Receipts Schedule

SCOTT'S MANUFACTURING
Cash Receipts Schedule for the Budgeting Period July–December 1996
($000s)

	July	August	September	October	November	December	Total
Sales in dollars	$300,000	$280,000	$270,000	$290,000	$300,000	$320,000	$1,760,000
Collections 60% less 2%	$132,300	$176,400	$164,640	$158,760	$170,520	$176,400	$ 979,020
Collections 30%	67,500	90,000	84,000	81,000	87,000	90,000	499,500
Collections 10%	25,000	22,500	30,000	28,000	27,000	29,000	161,500
Total collections	$224,800	$288,900	$278,640	$267,760	$284,520	$295,400	$1,640,020
Cash discounts taken	$2,700	$3,600	$3,360	$3,240	$3,480	$3,600	$19,980

Notes:
June sales = $225,000 (100% uncollected)
May sales = $250,000 (10% uncollected)

July sales are collected in August ($300,000 × .6 × .98 = $176,400 and $300,000 × .3 = $90,000) and September ($300,000 × .1 = $30,000).

(as shown in Exhibit 5.3) is $224.8 million. What is the source of this difference? Sales for July are based on the company's estimate of how many cars will be sold in July at $20,000 each. Cash collections for July is the company's estimate of how many sales from June (60 percent less 2 percent, and 30 percent) and May (10 percent) will be collected in July.

We determine the cash collections from customers for September as shown below:

August sales paid by September 10 ($280,000,000 × .6 × .98)	$164,640,000
August sales paid after September 10 ($280,000,000 × .3)	84,000,000
July sales paid in September ($300,000,000 × .1)	30,000,000
Total cash collections from customers	$278,640,000

Notice that in September, Scott's expects to collect monies from sales made in August and July. Sales made in August are billed on September 1, and Scott's collects 60 percent of these sales within the discount period; therefore, the company receives 98 percent of the sales amount. Thus, expected cash discounts are $3,360,000 ($280,000,000 × .6 × .02). Another 30 percent of the sales made during August are collected during September, but these sales are collected after the discount period. Finally, some of the sales (10 percent) made during July and billed on August 1 are collected during September. Since these sales are collected after 30 days, no discount is given.

PAUSE & REFLECT Refer to Exhibit 5.3. How are the collections during October calculated?

After completing revenue cycle planning, a manufacturing company then proceeds with conversion cycle (production) planning, while a merchandising company performs expenditure cycle planning. A manufacturer must plan production to meet the anticipated sales, while a merchandising company would plan expenditures for items such as merchandise purchases to meet anticipated sales.

PAUSE & REFLECT Think about all the different types of cars sold by Ford Motor Company. How do you think the managers at Ford estimate the quantities of each car expected to be sold for an upcoming period of time? Who are Ford Motor Corporation's customers? How do you think Ford estimates its cash collections from customers?

CONVERSION CYCLE PLANNING

Conversion cycle planning consists of four components: (1) scheduling production, (2) obtaining raw materials, (3) scheduling labor, and (4) planning manufacturing overhead. Since the raw materials, direct labor, and manufacturing overhead used during the conversion cycle are purchased and paid for during the expenditure cycle, we will consider those issues in expenditure cycle planning. However, since both production and raw materials planning depend on the inventory model adopted by the company, we discuss inventory planning next.

Planning Inventory

One of the concerns in conversion cycle planning is determining the amount and timing of finished goods, work-in-process, and raw materials inventories. Maintaining adequate supplies of inventory to meet the quantity demanded is necessary; however, holding inventory usually generates significant costs. In large organizations, inventory planning is the responsibility of the purchasing and production departments and is a process of balancing the costs of ordering inventory against the costs of carrying inventory.

Ordering Costs In the short run, inventory ordering costs are the costs incurred to place one additional order for inventory, that is, the costs that vary with the number of orders placed and received. Ordering costs include shipping costs per order, the cost incurred to fax or otherwise place an order, and insurance costs per order. In the long run, ordering costs also include the fixed costs associated with ordering, such as the cost of company vehicles used to transport inventory from the warehouse to the production facilities as well as the costs involved to maintain supplier relationships. For example, if a supplier wants to receive orders for at least 50 percent of all the company purchases, this is considered a long-run ordering cost because it limits the company's ability to choose its suppliers, but it does not vary with the number of orders placed.

Carrying Costs In the short run, inventory carrying costs are the costs incurred to carry one additional unit in inventory for the period, that is, the costs that vary with the number of units carried in inventory. Carrying costs include insurance, which is based on the number of units held in storage during the period; the estimated costs of spoilage or obsolescence during the period; and the variable costs of storing a unit, such as inspection costs. In the long run, inventory carrying costs also include the fixed costs associated with carrying inventory such as the cost of the warehouse used for storing inventory as well as the cost of the security guard for the warehouse. For example, if the company must buy or rent a warehouse in order to maintain a certain inventory level, this is considered a long-run carrying cost, but the amount of the cost does not vary with the number of units held.

There are two primary inventory models that have been developed to deal with the tradeoff between ordering and carrying costs of inventory. Companies can use these models to determine how much inventory to purchase and when to purchase the inventory. We examine the just-in-time inventory model, which is a long-run model, next. We discuss the economic order quantity model, which is a short-run model, in the appendix at the end of the chapter.

Just-in-Time (JIT) Inventory Model

The **just-in-time (JIT) inventory model** is a long-run model based on the principle that inventory should arrive just as needed for production in the quantities needed. It operates on the assumption that carrying costs should include the fixed costs of storage such as depreciation and insurance on warehouse facilities because, in the long-run, these costs are relevant. For most companies, the long-run costs of carrying inventory outweigh the long-run costs of ordering inventory, so, according to the JIT model, the best decision is to maintain zero or minimal inventories. This implies that products should be produced when needed, in the quantities needed by customers, so there is little need for work-in-process or finished goods inventories. In addition, raw materials should arrive when needed, in the quantities needed, for production. JIT is a **pull system;** that is, production is determined by (pulled by) customer demand, and the need for raw materials is determined by (pulled by) production. Accordingly, storing inventory is a nonvalue-added activity that a company should try to reduce or eliminate.

Adopting a JIT inventory model has significant implications for a company (see . . . of Interest "The Philosophy of JIT"). First, since little or no inventory is maintained, it is important that sales estimates are accurate so the production can be completed when customers demand the products. Along these same lines, it is important that production is completed with zero, or very few, defects. Since the company would carry very little inventory in a JIT system, if defects occur in the production process, customer orders may be delayed as defective products are reworked. When customer orders are delayed, a company incurs a **stockout cost.** Stockout cost is the cost incurred when a company runs out of inventory and includes the cost due to production slowdowns or stoppages and lost sales, as well as customer ill will that may result in lost sales in the future.

IT is more than an inventory management system. JIT is a management philosophy that, when successfully adopted, supports world-class business operations. The JIT philosophy is based on the idea of *kaizen,* which means "continuous improvement." This means that no matter how efficiently things are going now, a company should always strive to do better. Successful adoption of JIT requires a belief in kaizen.

Another part of the JIT philosophy is *muda,* which means "waste." The elimination of waste is crucial to JIT. Waste arises from many sources, such as the time products sit waiting for processing, the time spent moving products from one place to another for processing, the time spent reworking defective products, and the waste associated with keeping too much inventory—raw materials, work in process, and finished goods. Successful adoption of JIT requires the elimination of waste.

Finally, a successful JIT system is visual. Employees are given the responsibility for, and encouraged to find defects in products and processes. Inventory is visible; therefore, it is easy to see when inventory should be ordered. In addition, unnecessary amounts of inventory are easily seen (often they are in the way), which encourages their reduction. Scrap and waste are visible for everyone to see, which encourages reduction. Finally, employee successes in decreasing waste are visibly displayed and rewarded.

JIT is a way of life in business. It means never being satisfied with the way things are and always striving to improve the products or services offered to customers.

Third, JIT requires a company to have a strong relationship with its suppliers. Since orders are placed frequently, sometimes more than once a day, the company using JIT must choose suppliers who can meet the frequent delivery schedules on time, every time, with high-quality raw materials. The company must also have faith in the freight carriers used since a strike or accident that shuts down transportation lines also halts production.

Fourth, a company that adopts JIT must have good relationships with its employees. A JIT company often relies more heavily on its employees to detect and correct defects as soon as possible, rather than hiring a quality control inspector whose job is to inspect the final product. It is easier, and often cheaper, to correct defects early in the production process. In addition, a strike or work slowdown by employees can be devastating to a JIT company. For example, in 1996, subassembly plant at General Motors went on strike. This caused the final assembly plant to shut down within the same week because it ran out of electronic components for its automobiles.

Finally, to implement a just-in-time inventory system, a manufacturing company must have a good relationship with its customers. Since finished goods are produced only as needed by customers, and because raw material is received only as it is needed by production, customers who change their orders at the last minute cause production slowdowns for a just-in-time company. For example, a customer who, at the last minute, increases the size of its order, may cause other customers' orders to be delayed as resources are redeployed to meet the additional quantity demanded.

Companies that have successfully implemented just-in-time systems find that costs decrease because large quantities of raw materials and finished goods are not necessary. Therefore, they can eliminate many fixed storage costs. In addition, many companies have found that customer satisfaction is enhanced once a JIT system with few or no defects is implemented because customers get a defect-free product on time, every time. For example, the Oregon Cutting Systems Company found that after adopting JIT, space requirements decreased by 40 percent, defects were reduced by 80 percent, and productivity increased by 10 percent.[6]

Although adopting JIT usually results in cost savings, JIT is not desirable for every company. Typically companies in established markets where demand can be predicted fairly accurately are good candidates for JIT. For example, automobile

---

[6]Jack C. Bailes and Ilene K. Kleinsorge, "Cutting Waste with JIT," *Management Accounting,* May 1992, p. 29.

EXHIBIT | 5.4 | Production Budget

SCOTT'S MANUFACTURING
Production Budget for the Budgeting Period July–December 1996

	July	August	September	October	November	December	Total
Sales in units (cars)	15,000	14,000	13,500	14,500	15,000	16,000	88,000
Desired ending inventory (2%)	280	270	290	300	320	300	300
	15,280	14,270	13,790	14,800	15,320	16,300	88,300
Less beginning inventory	300	280	270	290	300	320	300
Car production required	14,980	13,990	13,520	14,510	15,020	15,980	88,000

Notes: July's ending inventory is 14,000 × .02 = 280 (2% of August expected sales). August's beginning inventory is July's ending inventory.

manufacturers such as Ford and Toyota have successfully adopted JIT. Those companies whose demand fluctuates greatly, whose suppliers are unreliable, or whose customers frequently change orders are not good candidates for JIT adoption. Merchandising companies such as J. C. Penney are not good candidates for JIT because if the clothing is not on the racks, the sale is lost. In addition, the selling period for a particular style of clothing is typically very short, which makes JIT adoption less desirable.

Production Planning

After establishing the inventory planning model, the next step in conversion cycle planning is to determine the quantity of finished goods to produce and when to produce them. Since production is planned to meet demand, the sales quantity information in the sales budget is a key input to the production planning process. In addition, it is necessary to determine the desired ending inventory amount of finished goods (if any). The anticipated demand plus the desired level of finished goods make up the **production budget,** which shows the expected level of production for the period, as Exhibit 5.4 illustrates for Scott's Manufacturing.

Take a moment to study Exhibit 5.4 and how it relates to Exhibit 5.2. Notice that the amounts shown in Exhibit 5.4 are stated in units (cars). Also notice that Scott's maintains a small ending inventory—2 percent of the following month's expected sales in units. Therefore, Scott's needs to produce 14,980 cars in July to meet demand (see Exhibit 5.2) and maintain its finished goods inventory level. We show how to calculate this amount below. Notice that the desired ending inventory is added to the expected sales in units while the beginning inventory is subtracted from this amount to avoid double counting.

Expected sales (in units) in July	15,000
Add desired ending inventory (August sales × .02)	280
	15,280
Less beginning inventory (to avoid double counting)	(300)
Total number of cars to produce	14,980

PAUSE & REFLECT

How do you think the managers at Ford Motor Company determine their desired ending inventories? How would they determine when to produce cars? How would conversion cycle planning be accomplished at Ford Motor Company?

EXPENDITURE CYCLE PLANNING

After completing its production planning, a manufacturing company estimates its raw materials needs for the coming period. Typically, a company separately budgets its direct materials, but it includes its indirect materials in manufacturing overhead. **Direct materials cost** is the cost of materials that can be directly traced to the finished product and are costly enough to warrant tracing. On the other hand, an **indirect material cost** either cannot be traced to the final product, or its cost is low

EXHIBIT | 5.5 | Direct Materials Purchases Budget

SCOTT'S MANUFACTURING
Direct Materials Purchases Budget for the Budgeting Period July–December 1996

	July	August	September	October	November	December	Total
Production required	14,980	13,990	13,520	14,510	15,020	15,980	88,000
Number of tires needed	74,900	69,950	67,600	72,550	75,100	79,900	440,000
Desired ending inventory (5%)	3,498	3,380	3,628	3,755	3,995	3,749	3,749
	78,398	73,330	71,228	76,305	79,095	83,649	443,749
Less beginning inventory	3,745	3,498	3,380	3,628	3,755	3,995	3,745
Tires to purchase	74,653	69,832	67,848	72,677	75,340	79,654	440,004
Purchases of tires	$3,732,650	$3,491,600	$3,392,400	$3,633,850	$3,767,000	$3,982,700	$22,000,200

Notes: Five tires are needed per car (including spare tire). July's ending inventory is 69,950 × .05 = 3,498 (5% of August's tire needs). August's beginning inventory is July's ending inventory.

enough so that tracing is not warranted. For example, steel is a direct material in car production because it can be physically traced to the final product and is expensive enough to warrant tracing. On the other hand, bolts and screws are indirect materials because they are not expensive enough to warrant determining their cost per car.

Since materials are purchased for use in production, the information from the production budget is a key input to the materials planning process. As is the case with production planning, the desired ending inventory level (if any) of direct materials is also planned. This amount together with the direct materials needed for production are combined into the **direct materials purchases budget,** which shows the expected quantity and cost of direct materials purchases for the period.[7] As Exhibit 5.5 shows, the direct materials purchases budget for Scott's Manufacturing tire purchases indicates that 74,900 tires are needed to meet July's production (5 tires per car × 14,980 cars), and the company wants to maintain an ending inventory equal to 5 percent of its tire needs for the next month (69,950 × .05 = 3,498).

Take a moment to examine Exhibit 5.5 and its relationship to Exhibit 5.4. For each month, the production required is converted into the related number of tires needed. Then, the desired ending inventory is added to determine the maximum number of tires needed. From this amount, the company subtracts the number of tires on hand, the beginning inventory, to determine the number of tires to purchase. This amount is then multiplied by the purchase price per tire, $50 in this case, to determine the purchases, in dollars, required for that month. Scott's would prepare similar budgets for its other direct materials such as steel, engines, seats, and electronic components.

PAUSE & REFLECT

How do you think direct materials planning at Ford Motor Company is accomplished? What would Ford consider to be direct materials? What would it consider to be indirect materials?

Direct Labor and Manufacturing Overhead Planning

Converting direct materials into a finished product requires labor and the use of other resources, such as machinery, facilities, and indirect materials, many of which must be acquired and paid for during the expenditure cycle. Therefore, planning these resource needs is part of expenditure cycle planning.

---

[7]A merchandising company prepares a merchandise purchases budget, which is similar to a direct materials budget. Merchandise purchases vary with the level of expected sales, so the sales budget is the primary input into the merchandise purchases budget. The merchandiser also must consider how much ending inventory is desired so the amount shown on the purchases budget is the total amount of merchandise, at the company's cost, needed to meet expected sales, plus the desired amount of ending inventory for the period.

Like materials, labor is typically divided into direct and indirect labor. **Direct labor cost** is the cost of employees whose jobs are directly related to manufacture of products. **Indirect labor cost** is the cost for other production employees who do not actually manufacture the product, but provide other needed services such as supervisory, janitorial, and security services.

It is important to estimate the number of direct laborers needed and the cost of direct labor to ensure that an adequate supply of labor is available to meet production requirements. This planning depends on the accurate determination of the amount of labor time required to complete a unit and the cost of that labor (per hour, per unit, or per period). Labor planning is typically accomplished by members of the production and human resources departments.

Since there is a need for both labor and manufacturing overhead resources to convert direct materials into finished products, the information in the production budget is input into the direct labor and manufacturing overhead planning process. The output of this process is the **direct labor and manufacturing overhead budget,** which shows the expected amount and cost of direct labor needed and the expected manufacturing overhead costs for the period.[8]

Exhibit 5.6 shows the direct labor and manufacturing overhead budget for Scott's Manufacturing. Take a moment to examine Exhibit 5.6, which shows that, like direct labor, some of the manufacturing overhead costs vary throughout the time period, while others do not. For example, indirect materials[9] and indirect labor vary with the level of production while depreciation on the building, insurance on the building, and depreciation on the machinery ($15,000, $6,000, and $57,000, respectively) do not change from one month to the next. The estimates of these resource costs are obtained using a cost estimation technique such as high/low or linear regression. In addition, by looking at the relationship between the car production required and the number of direct labor hours required for July, we determine that it should take 12

---

[8]Companies that are labor intensive, such as custom furniture manufacturing, often divide the direct labor and manufacturing overhead budget into two separate budgets.

[9]Since we have prepared only one direct materials budget, the cost of indirect materials listed in the direct labor and manufacturing overhead budget includes both direct materials, (for example, steel, seats, electronic components, and motors) as well as indirect materials (for example, trim pieces, paint, and moldings). In reality, a separate direct materials budget would be prepared for each direct material used in production.

EXHIBIT	5.6	Direct Labor and Manufacturing Overhead Budget

SCOTT'S MANUFACTURING
Direct Labor and Manufacturing Overhead Budget for the Budgeting Period July–December 1996

	July	August	September	October	November	December	Total
Car production required	14,980	13,990	13,520	14,510	15,020	15,980	88,000
Direct labor hours required	179,760	167,880	162,240	174,120	180,240	191,760	1,056,000
Cost of direct labor	$ 2,696,400	$ 2,518,200	$ 2,433,600	$ 2,611,800	$ 2,703,600	$ 2,876,400	$ 15,840,000
Other manufacturing costs:							
Indirect materials*	*179,760,000	167,880,000	162,240,000	174,120,000	180,240,000	191,760,000	1,056,000,000
Indirect labor	14,980,000	13,990,000	13,520,000	14,510,000	15,020,000	15,980,000	88,000,000
Depreciation on building	15,000	15,000	15,000	15,000	15,000	15,000	90,000
Insurance on building	6,000	6,000	6,000	6,000	6,000	6,000	36,000
Depreciation on machinery	57,000	57,000	57,000	57,000	57,000	57,000	342,000
Machinery repairs	37,450	34,975	33,800	36,275	37,550	39,950	220,000
Utilities	42,450	39,975	38,800	41,275	42,550	44,950	250,000
Miscellaneous costs	89,920	85,960	84,080	88,040	90,080	93,920	532,000
Total direct labor and overhead	$197,684,220	$184,627,110	$178,428,280	$191,485,390	$198,211,780	$210,873,220	$1,161,310,000

Note: It takes 12 direct labor hours to make a car (14,980 × 12 = 179,760), and the company pays direct labor of $15 per hour ($15 × 179,760 = $2,696,400).

*Indirect materials includes indirect materials and other direct materials because the company prepares only one direct materials budget. See footnote 9.

direct labor hours to manufacture a car (179,760 hours/14,980 cars).[10] By extending this analysis, we determine that Scott's plans to pay its direct laborers an average of $15 per hour ($2,696,400/179,760).

Selling and Administrative Costs Planning

Companies must also plan for other expenditures, salespersons' commissions, and other selling and administrative costs, such as advertising and rent. This planning is typically done by the department that supplies the resources. For example, in order to plan the labor cost of sales, the company's human relations and marketing departments might budget for the costs of salespeople. Some budget estimates for other expenses also might be based on the amount of sales, such as advertising, while others can be based on the amount of time, such as rent on the storage facilities. Therefore, knowledge of the cost behavior of these other resources is crucial to planning. The output of budgeting for such other costs is the **selling and administrative costs budget,** which shows the expected costs for the selling and administrative items for the period, as shown in Exhibit 5.7.

Study this budget and notice that some costs remain the same from month to month (administrative salaries, office equipment depreciation, and office rent), while others change (sales commissions, utilities, advertising, product warranty, and miscellaneous costs) because of their relationship to the expected level of sales for the month. For example, by looking at the relationship between sales in dollars and sales commissions in July, we determine that salespersons are paid a commission of 0.2 percent ($600,000/$300,000,000).

---

[10]This is the total time from the beginning to the end of the production process, not merely the final assembly time.

EXHIBIT	5.7	Selling and Administrative Costs Budget

SCOTT'S MANUFACTURING
Selling and Administrative Costs Budget for the Budgeting Period July–December 1996
($000s)

	July	August	September	October	November	December	Total
Sales in dollars	$300,000	$280,000	$270,000	$290,000	$300,000	$320,000	$1,760,000
Sales commissions	$ 600	$ 560	$ 540	$ 580	$ 600	$ 640	$ 3,520
Administrative salaries	80	80	80	80	80	80	480
Office equipment depreciation	12	12	12	12	12	12	72
Office rent	15	15	15	15	15	15	90
Utilities	3.5	3.3	3.2	3.4	3.5	3.7	20.6
Advertising	300	280	270	290	300	320	1,760
Product warranty	30	28	27	29	30	32	176
Miscellaneous costs	325	305	295	315	325	345	1,910
Total selling and administrative	$1,365.5	$1,283.3	$1,242.2	$1,324.4	$1,365.5	$1,447.7	$8,028.6

Note: Sales commissions are 0.2% of sales ($300,000 × .002 = $600). Advertising is 0.1% of sales ($300,000 × .001 = $300). Product warranty is 0.01% of sales ($300,000 × .0001 = $30).

Cash Disbursements Planning

Recall that the expenditure cycle concludes with the payment for goods and services. Therefore, the last step in expenditure cycle planning is to determine when and how much to pay for goods and services used. Scott's Manufacturing determines the amounts of its payments by using information from the other budgets. The direct materials purchases budget, direct labor and manufacturing overhead budget, and the selling and administrative costs budget all contain information regarding the planned operating expenditures during the period.

Management also must consider the timing of these expenditure payments. Recall from Chapter 3 that the best policy is to take advantage of purchase discounts whenever possible and to delay paying bills until the last possible date within the discount period. The output of this planning process is called the **cash disbursements schedule,** which shows the expected cash disbursements to suppliers of goods and services for the period.

Take a moment to think about all the goods and services Scott's Manufacturing plans to use during the coming period. This information is contained in the direct materials purchases budget, direct labor and manufacturing overhead budget, and selling and administrative costs budget. Examine each of these budgets, in turn. Are there any items listed in these budgets that do not require cash payments? The direct labor and manufacturing overhead budget as well as the selling and administrative costs budget contain depreciation expense. Recall that depreciation is the allocation of the cost of an asset to the time periods in which the asset is used. Therefore, depreciation expense itself does not involve a cash payment. All other items shown on the budgets do require cash payments; therefore, it is necessary to determine a cash payment schedule for them.

Assume that 80 percent of direct materials purchases are paid within 15 days of receipt of billing, thereby entitling the company to a 3 percent cash discount. The remaining purchases are paid within 30 days of billing. Billing is received on the first day of the month for purchases made during the preceding month. All other cash expenses are paid in the month incurred.

Using this payment schedule and the input information from the direct materials purchases budget, direct labor and manufacturing overhead budget, and selling and administrative costs budget, we show, in Exhibit 5.8, Scott's cash disbursements schedule. Carefully study the relationship between this budget and the other budgets in Exhibits 5.5, 5.6, and 5.7.

Exhibit 5.8 shows us that in August, the company expects to pay for all the purchases made during July. Of this amount, 80 percent is paid within the discount period ($3,732,650 × .8 × .97 = $2,896,530) while the remaining 20 percent is paid by the end of the month ($3,732,650 × .2 = $746,530). Also in August, the company

EXHIBIT	5.8	Cash Disbursements Schedule

SCOTT'S MANUFACTURING Cash Disbursements Schedule for the Budgeting Period July–December 1996							
	July	August	September	October	November	December	Total
Purchases of tires	$ 3,732,650	$ 3,491,600	$ 3,392,400	$ 3,633,850	$ 3,767,000	$ 3,982,700	$ 22,000,200
Disbursements 80% less 3%	$ 2,495,112	$ 2,896,536	$ 2,709,482	$ 2,632,502	$ 2,819,868	$ 2,923,192	$ 16,476,692
Disbursements 20%	643,070	746,530	698,320	678,480	726,770	753,400	4,246,570
Disbursements—labor and manufacturing overhead	197,612,220	184,555,110	178,356,280	191,413,390	198,139,780	210,801,220	1,160,878,000
Disbursements—selling and administrative costs	1,353,500	1,271,300	1,230,200	1,312,400	1,353,500	1,435,700	7,956,600
Total disbursements	$202,103,902	$189,469,476	$182,994,282	$196,036,772	$203,039,918	$215,913,512	$1,189,557,862
Cash discounts taken	77,168	89,584	83,798	81,418	87,212	90,408	509,588

Notes: June's tire purchases were $3,215,350 (0% paid). July's tire purchases are paid in August ($3,732,650 × .8 × .97 = $2,896,536 and $3,732,650 × .2 = $746,530).

expects to pay $184,555,110 ($184,627,110 – $15,000 – $57,000) for direct labor and manufacturing overhead and $1,271,300 ($1,283,300 – $12,000) for selling and administrative costs. Take a moment to be sure you can trace these numbers back to their respective budgets.

| **PAUSE & REFLECT** | How are the disbursements amounts for September determined? |

BRINGING IT ALL TOGETHER—THE CASH BUDGET AND PRO FORMA FINANCIAL REPORTS

The budgets prepared during revenue, conversion, and expenditure cycle planning culminate in the cash budget and the pro forma financial reports discussed next. These reports are prepared by the accounting department to illustrate the expected results of the planned activities. The cash receipts and cash disbursements schedules affect the cash budget while all the budgets affect the pro forma financial reports.

The Cash Budget

The **cash budget** illustrates the amounts of cash expected to be provided and used by operating activities during the coming period as shown in the cash receipts and cash disbursements schedules. In addition, the cash budget reflects the company's planned cash inflows and outflows from its expected investing and financing activities of the current period, which is discussed in the second half of this text.

For illustrative purposes, assume that Scott's Manufacturing plans to invest $750,000 in land during each of the first three months of the budgeting period. In addition, it plans to issue $250,000 of capital stock during October and pay dividends to its stockholders of $500,000 during December. Using this information, as well as the information from the cash receipts and cash disbursements schedules, the company prepares the cash budget shown in Exhibit 5.9.

Notice that for each month, the beginning cash balance (bottom of exhibit) is added to the net cash flow to determine the ending cash balance and that the ending balance in one month is the beginning cash balance in the subsequent month. At the end of the budget period, Scott's Manufacturing expects to have $467,962,138 of cash available as shown in Exhibit 5.9 (bottom line, last column).

EXHIBIT	**5.9**	**Cash Budget**

SCOTT'S MANUFACTURING
Cash Budget for the Budgeting Period July–December 1996

	July	August	September	October	November	December	Total
Receipts from customers	$224,800,000	$288,900,000	$278,640,000	$267,760,000	$284,520,000	$295,400,000	$1,640,020,000
Disbursements to suppliers and employees	202,103,902	189,469,476	182,994,282	196,036,772	203,039,918	215,913,512	1,189,557,862
Cash flows from operating activities	$ 22,696,098	$ 99,430,524	$ 95,645,718	$ 71,723,228	$ 81,480,082	$ 79,486,488	$ 450,462,138
Cash receipts from financing				250,000			250,000
Cash disbursements for financing activities						500,000	500,000
Cash disbursements for investing activities	750,000	750,000	750,000				2,250,000
Cash flows from financing and investing activities	($750,000)	($750,000)	($750,000)	250,000	–0–	($500,000)	($2,500,000)
Net cash flow	21,946,098	98,680,524	94,895,718	71,973,228	81,480,082	78,986,488	447,962,138
Beginning cash balance	$ 20,000,000	$ 41,946,098	$140,626,622	$235,522,340	$307,495,568	$388,975,650	$ 20,000,000
Ending cash balance	$ 41,946,098	$140,626,622	$235,522,340	$307,495,568	$388,975,650	$467,962,138	$ 467,962,138

Notes: Scott's plans to invest $750,000 in land during each of the first three months of the budgeting period. Scott's plans to issue capital stock in October and pay dividends in December.

Pro Forma Financial Reports

Pro forma financial reports are prepared by the accounting department to show the results of operations *if and only if* the planned revenues, costs, receipts, and expenditures outlined in the master budget occur. Pro forma financial reports resemble the financial statements that businesses prepare for external users. However, pro forma reports are estimates, so adhering to generally accepted accounting principles is not mandatory.

Businesses typically prepare a budgeted profit report, often called a *pro forma income statement*, to show the expected results of operations. They also prepare a pro forma balance sheet to indicate the resulting financial position anticipated.

Pro Forma Profit Report (Income Statement)

The expected revenues and expenses from the various budgets are combined in the **pro forma profit report** as Exhibit 5.10 shows for Scott's Manufacturing. Note that the pro forma profit report reflects information in the sales and selling and administrative budgets. For example, the amount of sales shown is the total of the six months' sales on the sales budget. The selling and administrative costs shown are the totals of the six months on the selling and administrative cost budget for each of the individual items. Finally, the amount shown for cost of goods sold is the total cost of producing the number of units sold (the six-month total from the sales budget).

Notice that direct materials and direct labor and manufacturing overhead costs are not listed on the profit report itself. Recall that these costs do not become expenses and, therefore, are not used in the determination of profit until the product is sold. Thus, the cost of these resources is reflected in cost of goods sold at the time of sale.

Pro Forma Balance Sheet

The **pro forma balance sheet** shows actual balances at the beginning of the budget period and the expected balances at the end of the budget period of the company's assets, liabilities, and owners' equity. Exhibit 5.11 illustrates the pro forma balance sheet of Scott's Manufacturing.

EXHIBIT 5.10

Pro Forma Profit Report

SCOTTS MANUFACTURING
Pro Forma Profit Report for the Budgeting Period July–December 1996

Sales		
Less sales discounts	$1,760,000,000	Exhibit 5.2
Net sales	19,980,000	Exhibit 5.3
Less cost of goods sold	$1,740,020,000	
Gross margin	1,182,800,412	See schedule
Less selling and administrative costs:	$ 557,219, 588	
Sales commissions		
Administrative salaries	3,520,000	
Office equipment depreciation	480,000	
Office rent	72,000	
Utilities	90,000	Exhibit 5.7
Advertising	20,600	
Product warranty	1,760,000	
Miscellaneous costs	176,000	
Net profit	1,910,000	
	$ 549,190,988	

Cost of Goods Sold Schedule:		
Beginning direct materials inventory	$ 187,250	Exhibit 5.11
Add purchases	22,000,200	Exhibit 5.5
Less purchase discounts	(509,588)	Exhibit 5.8
Less ending direct materials inventory	(187,450)	Exhibit 5.11
Direct materials used in production	$ 21,490,412	
Add direct labor and manufacturing overhead used in production	1,161,310,000	Exhibit 5.6
Cost of goods manufactured	$1,182,800,412	
Add beginning finished goods inventory	4,032,274	Exhibit 5.11
Less ending finished goods inventory	(4,032,274)	Exhibit 5.11
Cost of goods sold	$1,182,800,412	

EXHIBIT | 5.11 | Pro Forma Balance Sheet

SCOTT'S MANUFACTURING
Pro Forma Balance Sheet as of December 31, 1996

	Actual Beginning Balance	Expected Ending Balance
Assets		
Cash	$ 20,000,000	$467,962,138
Accounts receivable	250,000,000	350,000,000*
Direct materials inventory	187,250	187,450
Finished goods inventory	4,032,274	4,032,274
Machinery	6,840,000	6,840,000
Less accumulated depreciation	(1,368,000)	(1,710,000)[†]
Building	10,000,000	10,000,000
Less accumulated depreciation	(1,080,000)	(1,170,000)[†]
Office equipment	720,000	720,000
Less accumulated depreciation	(432,000)	(504,000)[†]
Land	0	2,250,000
Total assets	$288,899,524	$838,607,862
Liabilities and Owners' Equity		
Accounts payable	$ 3,215,350	$ 3,982,700[‡]
Capital stock	100,000,000	100,250,000
Retained earnings	185,684,174	734,375,162[§]
Total liabilities and owners' equity	$288,899,524	$838,607,862

*100% of December sales plus 10% of November sales.
[†]Beginning balance plus budgeted depreciation expense.
[‡]100% of December purchases.
[§]Beginning balance plus net income, $549,190,988, (Exhibit 5.10) less dividends, $500,000, (Exhibit 5.9).

Notice that Exhibit 5.11 shows the balance of the assets, liabilities, and owners' equity at the beginning of the budget period and those expected at the end of the budget period. The ending expected accounts receivable total reflects the sales for December, which will be billed on January 1, plus 10 percent of the sales in November, which is expected to be collected in January. Accounts payable is the amount that is still owed to suppliers of goods and services. This is the amount of purchases expected in December that will be billed by the company's suppliers on January 1.

Also note that the amount shown for accumulated depreciation at the beginning of the budgeting period is increased by the amount of depreciation expense expected during the budget period to determine the amount of accumulated depreciation shown on the balance sheet.

SUMMARY

Budgets are used for planning, communication and coordination, allocation of resources, and control and evaluation. Budgets affect people, and people affect budgets. Two processes to deal with these effects are participative budgeting and mandated budgeting. The purpose of participative budgeting is to involve employees in the budget process in anticipation of their acceptance of and willingness to work harder based on their involvement. The purpose of mandated budgeting is to communicate to employees the goals and objectives of upper-level management. Most companies use budgets that have characteristics of each of these processes. The number and types of budgets prepared by a company depends on whether it is a service, merchandising, or manufacturing firm. Exhibit 5.12 summarizes the types of budgets prepared by each type of firm.

- Revenue cycle planning consists of determining the amounts of expected sales revenues and cash receipts from those sales. It culminates in the production of the sales budget and cash receipts schedule.

EXHIBIT | 5.12 | **Service, Merchandising, and Manufacturing Companies' Budgets**

	Service	Merchandising	Manufacturing
Revenue cycle	Revenue budget	Sales budget	Sales budget
	Cash receipts schedule	Cash receipts schedule	Cash receipts schedule
Conversion cycle			Production budget
Expenditure cycle	Labor budget	Labor budget	Direct materials budget
	Selling and administrative budget	Selling and administrative budget	Direct labor and manufacturing overhead budget
	Cash disbursements schedule	Cash disbursements schedule	
			Cash disbursements schedule
Summarization/culmination	Cash budget	Cash budget	Cash budget
	Pro forma profit report	Pro forma profit report	Pro forma profit report
	Pro forma balance sheet	Pro forma balance sheet	Pro forma balance sheet

- Conversion cycle planning consists of determining the amount of production needed to meet the expected sales level as well as the amount of ending inventory. It culminates in the production budget.

- Expenditure cycle planning consists of determining the amounts of direct materials needed to meet production, direct labor and manufacturing overhead needed for production if applicable; and the selling and administrative costs expected in the coming period. In addition, it reflects amounts expected to be paid for these items. It culminates in the direct materials purchases, direct labor and manufacturing overhead, selling and administrative costs budgets, as well as the cash disbursements schedule.

- The budgets are prepared during the revenue, conversion, and expenditure cycle planning processes and then are combined in the cash budget and the pro forma financial reports.

KEY TERMS

budget A plan for the future expressed in financial terms

budget committee A group of key executives who are responsible for overseeing the budgeting process

budget director The person responsible for determining how to gather the budgetary data and prepare the budget

budgetary slack The difference between a chosen estimate of revenues or expenses and a realistic estimate

budgeting The process of expressing the company's goals and objectives in quantitative terms

cash budget A budget that shows the expected cash receipts and disbursements from activities for the coming period

cash disbursements schedule A schedule that shows the expected cash disbursements to suppliers of goods and services for the period

cash receipts schedule A schedule that shows the anticipated cash collections from customers for the period

daily demand (appendix) The amount of inventory required each business day; annual demand divided by the number of business days in the year

direct labor and manufacturing overhead budget A budget that shows the expected amount and cost of direct labor needed and the expected manufacturing overhead costs for the period

direct labor cost The cost of the employees whose jobs directly relate to the manufacture of products

direct materials cost The cost of the materials that can be traced directly to the finished products and are costly enough to warrant tracing them

direct materials purchases budget A budget that shows the expected quantity and cost of direct materials purchases for the period

economic order quantity model (appendix) A mathematical model used to determine the quantity of inventory in each purchase order that minimizes the total of short-term ordering plus short-term carrying costs

ideal standard A standard based on almost perfection operating conditions

incremental budgeting A budgeting strategy in which a company uses the current period's budget as a starting point in preparing the next period's budget

indirect labor cost The cost of production employees who do not actually produce the products but provide other needed services

indirect materials cost The cost of materials used in production that cannot be traced directly to the finished products or whose cost is low enough that tracing is not warranted

just-in-time (JIT) inventory model A long-run inventory model based on the principle that inventory should arrive just as needed for production in the quantities needed

lead time (appendix) The number of days elapsing from the time an order is placed until it is received

mandated budgeting A budgeting system that relies on predetermined standards set by upper levels of management that are passed down to lower levels of an organization

master budgeting The process of compiling budgets prepared during revenue, conversion, and expenditure cycle planning that culminates with the cash budget and pro forma financial statements

nonvalue-added activity Any activity that does not add value to the product from the customer's perspective

normal standard A standard based on practical operating conditions

operational budget A budget prepared for a short period of time, typically a year or less, that reflects the current plans of the company and is more specific than a strategic budget

participative budgeting A budgeting system that allows individuals who are affected by the budget to have input into the budgeting process

pro forma balance sheet A balance sheet prepared to show the expected assets, liabilities, and owners' equity at the end of the budgeting period

pro forma financial reports The financial reports prepared to show the expected results of operations

pro forma profit report (income statement) A profit report prepared to show the expected profit for the budgeting period

production budget A budget that shows the expected level of production for the period

project budgeting The process of determining the specific resources provided by, and needed for, a specific project or activity

pull system A production system in which production is determined by customers demand

reorder point (appendix) The level of inventory that, when reached, signals the need to place an order for inventory

safety stock (appendix) A small amount of inventory kept on hand to avoid stockout

sales budget A budget that shows the expected sales for the period in both physical (quantity) and financial (dollar) terms

selling and administrative costs budget A budget that shows the expected cost for the selling and administrative items for the period

stockout cost The company's cost of running out of inventory, which includes production slowdowns, lost sales, and customer ill will

strategic budget A forecast prepared for a 5- to 10-year period that reflects the long-term planning of the company and is more general in nature than the operational budget

value-added activity Any activity that adds value to the product produced for and received by the customer

zero-based budgeting A budgeting strategy in which the company begins each budget period with a zero budget and must consider all its activities proposed for the budget

---

APPENDIX 5

ECONOMIC ORDER QUANTITY MODEL

The **economic order quantity (EOQ) model** is a mathematical model that *minimizes the total of short-term ordering costs plus short-term carrying costs* for the period. It indicates the size of the order to place every time inventory is ordered. Because EOQ is a model, it is based on certain assumptions. The assumptions of the EOQ are that:

- Demand is uniform throughout the year; that is, there is no seasonal fluctuation in demand.

- Lead time (discussed below) is constant throughout the year—regardless of the supplier used, the lead time is the same.

EXHIBIT | 5.13

**Graphical Depiction
of Economic Order
Quantity Model**

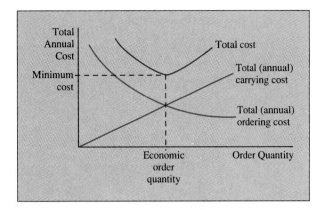

- The entire order is received at the same time; partial orders are not possible.

- No quantity discounts are offered by suppliers because EOQ assumes that inventory costs are the same regardless of the size of the order.

- Inventory size is not limited; orders of any size are possible.

- Fixed storage costs are irrelevant. EOQ is a short-term model, so it assumes that fixed costs (storage) do not change with the number of units stored.

For some companies, the assumptions of EOQ are impractical. For example, EOQ does not work well for automobile manufacturers because, among other things, fixed storage costs are not irrelevant. However, for companies whose fixed storage costs are low, and the other assumptions are not limiting, the EOQ model works very well.

The EOQ model is

$$EOQ = \sqrt{\frac{2DO}{C}}$$

where

D = Annual *demand* for inventory in units

O = Cost to place one additional *order*

C = Cost to *carry* one additional unit in inventory

We illustrate the economic order quantity model graphically in Exhibit 5.13. Notice that the economic order quantity occurs at the intersection of the total carrying cost and total ordering cost lines. At this point, the total cost is minimized. For example, assume that a company's annual demand for its product is 42,000 units, the ordering cost is $48 per order, and the carrying cost is $4 per unit in inventory per year. The economic order quantity is:

$$EOQ = \sqrt{\frac{2 \times 42,000 \times \$48}{\$4}} = 1,003.992 \text{ units}$$

This indicates that each order the company places should be for 1,004 units. If the company orders 1,004 units each time it places an order, it minimizes the total of its ordering *plus* carrying costs. The proof using 1,003.992 units, is shown in Exhibit 5.14.

Notice that, when the order size is 1,004 units, the total of carrying plus ordering costs is $4,016. The ordering costs are $2,008 because 42 orders are needed (42,000/1,004) and each order costs $48. The carrying costs are $2,008 because the average amount of inventory carried is one-half the order size, or 502 units and each unit has carrying costs of $4 per year.

If the order size decreases to 900 units in this example, the carrying cost decreases because fewer units are carried in inventory, but the ordering cost increases because more orders must be placed. The increase in the ordering cost is greater than the decrease in the carrying cost, so the total cost increases to $4,040 in this case.

Conversely, if the order size increases to 1,100 units in this example, the carrying cost increases because more units are carried in inventory, but the ordering cost decreases because fewer orders must be placed. The increase in the carrying cost is greater than the decrease in the carrying cost, so the total cost increases to $4,033 in this case.

EXHIBIT | 5.14 | **Proof of Economic Order Quantity Model**

Scenario 1—Order size, 1,004 units	**Total Cost**
Total ordering costs:	
Number of orders needed × Ordering cost	
42,000/1,003.992 × $48	
42 × $48 =	$2,008
Total carrying costs:	
Average inventory carried × Carrying cost	
(1,003.992 + 0)/2 × $4	
502 × $4 =	$2,008
Total ordering plus carrying costs at 1,004 units	$4,016

Scenario 2—Order size, 900 units	
Total ordering costs:	
Number of orders needed × Ordering cost	
42,000/900 × $48	
47 × $48 =	$2,240
Total carrying costs:	
Average inventory carried × Carrying cost	
(900 + 0)/2 × $4	
450 × $4 =	$1,800
Total ordering plus carrying costs at 900 units	$4,040

Scenario 3—Order size, 1,100 units	
Total ordering costs:	
Number of orders needed × Ordering cost	
42,000/1,100 × $48	
38 × $48 =	$1,833
Total carrying costs:	
Average inventory carried × Carrying cost	
(1,100 + 0)/2 × $4	
550 × $4 =	$2,200
Total ordering plus carrying costs at 900 units	$4,033

Once the size of the order is determined, the next issue is to determine the **reorder point,** that is, the inventory level that, when reached, indicates the need to place an order for additional inventory. To address this issue, it is necessary to determine requirements for daily demand and lead time.

Daily demand is the amount of inventory needed each business day and is calculated as annual demand divided by the number of business days in the year. To determine the reorder point, it is necessary to multiply the daily demand by the **lead time,** or the number of days elapsing from the time an order is placed until the order is received.

For example, assume that the company estimates that lead time is five days. If the company operates 300 days per year, its reorder point would be:

42,000 units (annual demand)/300 days (business days) = 140 units of daily demand

140 units × 5 days (lead time) = 700 units

The reorder point indicates that the company should place an order for 1,004 units when the quantity of inventory on hand falls to 700 units.

Earlier we discussed the issue of stockout cost, or the cost of running out of inventory. To guard against stockout costs, many companies maintain a **safety stock,** or a small amount of inventory kept on hand to avoid stockouts. The level of safety stock does not affect the EOQ calculation, but it does impact the reorder point. To calculate the reorder point when a company maintains a safety stock, we use the following formula:

(Daily demand × Lead time) + Safety stock = Reorder point

To illustrate, assume that the company wants to maintain a safety stock of 30 units. The reorder point in this case would be 730 units [(42,000/300 × 5) + 30].

PAUSE & REFLECT | If some portion of safety stock is used, how does this affect the amount of the next order or the EOQ?

1. Explain the purpose of planning and the role of budgeting in the planning process.
2. Describe the benefits of budgeting.
3. What are the costs of budgeting?
4. Describe budgetary slack and explain why employees might engage in budget padding.
5. Explain the difference between mandated and participative budgeting. When is each more appropriate?
6. What is the difference between ideal and normal standards? Which is better? Why?
7. Indicate how zero-based budgeting strategies differ from incremental budget strategies.
8. Explain the difference between operational and strategic budgeting strategies.
9. What is the difference between project budgeting and master budgeting?
10. Explain how the budgets and pro forma financial statements are related.
11. Describe how a business estimates its level of sales.
12. Explain how the estimated cash receipts are determined.
13. Indicate how companies determine inventory ordering costs and why they are important.
14. Explain how inventory carrying costs are determined and why they are important.
15. Describe the just-in-time inventory model and how businesses can most effectively use it.
16. What are the advantages and disadvantages of the just-in-time inventory model?
17. Describe the process businesses to determine the amount of production needed in a particular time period.
18. What is the difference between direct and indirect materials?
19. Describe the process businesses use to determine the amount of direct materials to be purchased in a particular time period.
20. Explain the difference between direct and indirect labor.
21. Describe the process businesses use to determine the amount of direct labor and manufacturing overhead for a period.
22. Describe the process businesses use to determine the amount of selling and administrative costs expected for a period.
23. Explain how a business determines expected cash disbursements.
24. Describe how the budgets developed in the planning phases of the revenue, conversion, and expenditure cycles are used to prepare the cash budget. What additional information is needed?
25. Explain the role and importance of the pro forma financial statements in the budgeting process.

Appendix:

26. Describe the economic order quantity model and how it is used.
27. What are the assumptions of the EOQ model?
28. Describe the reorder point and the role of stockout cost in determining the reorder point.

EXERCISES

E 5.1 Owens, Inc., operates a children's day care center in a major metropolitan area. It offers three types of child care services, full-day care, half-day care, and after-school care. Owens charges $200 per week for full-day care, $100 per week for half-day care, and $75 for after-school care. Projected enrollments for the first six weeks are shown below:

Week Number	Full-Day Care	Half-Day Care	After-School Care
1	20	15	10
2	20	20	15
3	20	16	21
4	20	20	20
5	25	15	17
6	25	17	18

What is the estimated service revenue each week for the first six weeks?

E 5.2 Refer to Exercise 5.1. Owens must employ one day care worker for every two full-time children, another for every three half-time children, and another for every five after-school children. Day care workers are paid $150 per week. What is the personnel cost per week for the six-week period?

E 5.3 Barstow Company sells two products, Dynamo and Craylon. It estimates that two Craylons are sold each period for every Dynamo sold. A Dynamo sells for $50 and a Craylon sells for $30. Barstow estimates that sales of Dynamos per quarter for the year will be 30,000, 45,000, 32,000 and 46,000 respectively. What is the estimated sales revenue each quarter for Barstow's two products?

E 5.4 Leeds Enterprises produces and sells a ceiling fan to retail outlets. Each fan costs Leeds Enterprises $40 to produce and $5 to sell. Leeds charges customers $90 per fan. Estimated sales for the first quarter are 50,000 fans, and sales are expected to increase by 10 percent per quarter for the first year, after which sales are expected to level off. What is the expected sales revenue per quarter for the first year?

E 5.5 Refer to Exercise 5.4. Leeds Company wants to maintain an ending inventory of ceiling fans equal to 25 percent of the expected sales in the next quarter. They achieved this at the end of last year. How many ceiling fans must Leeds produce each quarter?

E 5.6 Refer to Exercise 5.5. Assume it takes employees of Leeds 1/2 hour of direct labor time to produce a ceiling fan. Direct labor is $12 per hour. What is the direct labor cost per quarter?

E 5.7 To aid you in preparing its budget for March 1998, Wesley Company has provided the following information:

Amount owed by customers, March 1	$350,000
Estimated credit sales in March	400,000
Estimated amount owed by customers, March 31	225,000

What are the estimated cash receipts from customers for March 1996?

E 5.8 Chip Corporation's sales revenue is presented below:

	November (Actual)	December (Projected)	January (Projected)
Cash sales	$ 80,000	$100,000	$ 60,000
Credit sales	240,000	360,000	180,000

Management estimates that 5 percent of credit sales are uncollectible. Of the remaining credit sales, 60 percent are collected in the month of sale and the remainder in the following month. What are the expected cash collections for December?

E 5.9 Refer to Exercise 5.8. Purchases of inventory for resale each month are 70 percent of the next month's projected total sales and 30 percent of the current month's sales. The cost of purchases averages 75 percent of sales. What are the expected inventory purchases in December?

E 5.10 A firm operates 300 days per year. In the past, demand for its product has been fairly steady at 50 units per day. However, recently, customer orders have been inconsistent, ranging from 25 to 150 units per day. It costs the firm $0.50 per day to store one unit of inventory, while fixed warehousing costs are $50,000 per year. Should the firm adopt a just-in-time inventory system? Why or why not?

E 5.11 Riveria, Inc., plans to sell 50,000 units of Herbal Wash in the first quarter, 45,000 units in the second quarter, 55,000 units in the third quarter, and 48,000 units in the fourth quarter of next year at $20 each. Commission is 2 percent of sales and other variable selling and administrative costs are 7 percent of sales. Fixed selling and administrative costs consist of depreciation, rent, insurance, and salaries. The estimated total cost of these items is $15,000, $12,000, $4,000, and $20,000 per quarter, respectively. What are the budgeted selling and administrative costs per quarter?

E 5.12 Tulley, Inc., estimates that sales next year will be $450,000. Cost of goods sold is 60 percent of sales, and variable selling and administrative expenses are 10 percent. The estimated fixed selling and administrative expense for next year is $80,000. What is the projected net income for next year?

E 5.13   Engler Company projects a net income next year of $34,000. Selling and administrative expenses are projected to be $76,000. Cost of goods sold is 65 percent of sales. What is the projected sales level for next year?

E 5.14   Harrison Enterprises has a balance in its accounts receivable of $35,000 at the beginning of the period. Credit sales for the period are expected to be $675,000. It is estimated that Harrison will collect the entire beginning balance of accounts receivable plus 80 percent of the credit sales during the period. What amount should be shown on a pro forma balance sheet for accounts receivable at year-end?

E 5.15   Bestline, a firm that produces ping-pong paddles, expects to incur the costs shown below in its manufacturing process. The ping-pong paddles it manufactures consist of a wooden paddle, a handle, and a rubber backing for the paddle. Determine whether each of the following costs is direct materials, direct labor, or manufacturing overhead. Use DM for direct materials, DL for direct labor, or MOH for manufacturing overhead. Give a short justification for each of your answers.

    _____   *a.* Cost of handles for the paddles.
    _____   *b.* Wages of the assembly-line workers.
    _____   *c.* Rent on the production facilities.
    _____   *d.* Utilities for the production facilities.
    _____   *e.* Cost of the wooden paddles.
    _____   *f.* Cost of glue used to adhere the rubber backing.
    _____   *g.* Cost of rubber backing.
    _____   *h.* Cost of supervisor in production facilities.
    _____   *i.* Cost of janitorial staff in production facilities.
    _____   *j.* Cost of workers who cut the rubber backing.

E 5.16   Pegasus Shirts is a producer of men's, women's, and children's shirtware. The following is a list of production costs expected to be incurred by Pegasus. Determine whether each of the costs is direct materials, direct labor, or manufacturing overhead. Use DM for direct materials, DL for direct labor, or MOH for manufacturing overhead. Give a short justification for each of your answers.

    _____   *a.* Wages of the sewing machine operators.
    _____   *b.* Salary of the pattern cutter.
    _____   *c.* Cost of patterns used in production.
    _____   *d.* Cost of cloth.
    _____   *e.* Cost of buttons.
    _____   *f.* Cost of rent on the production facilities.
    _____   *g.* Cost of depreciation on the sewing machines.
    _____   *h.* Cost of thread used to sew shirts.
    _____   *i.* Salary of production manager.
    _____   *j.* Salary of quality control inspector.

Appendix:

E 5.17   Use the following information to determine the economic order quantity for Dynatex Company.

Units required during the year	30,000
Cost to place an order	$60
Cost of carrying a unit in inventory	$12

E 5.18   Carrigan, Inc., has determined its economic order quantity to be 500 units. Demand for the year is 27,000. Five days elapse between the time an order is placed until it is received. Carrigan conducts business 360 days per year. What is the reorder point?

E 5.19   Murray Company has calculated its economic order quantity at 200 units. The ordering cost is $40 and the carrying cost is $6. Demand for the year is 3,000 units. What is the total ordering plus carrying cost?

E 5.20   Lindquist, Inc., has calculated its economic order quantity as 500 units. The cost to place an order is $10 and the cost to carry one unit in inventory is $.25. What is the expected demand for the year?

PROBLEMS

P 5.1 Koenig, Inc., plans to produce 20,000, 22,000, 30,000, 34,000, 26,000, and 24,000 units of Quickdry in the first six months, respectively, of next fiscal year. Each unit of Quickdry produced uses four pounds of a raw material that Koenig purchases from a local supplier for $2.25 per pound. Koenig indicates that the beginning inventory of raw material is 8,000 pounds. However, next year they want to reduce ending inventories of raw materials to 5 percent of what is needed for the next month's production. Koenig pays for 80 percent of its purchases in the month of purchase, receiving a 3 percent cash discount. The remaining purchases are paid in the month following the month of purchase.

Required:
a. Determine the estimated purchases for the first three months of next fiscal year.
b. Determine the estimated cash payments for the first three months of next fiscal year assuming Koenig owes its suppliers $36,000 at the beginning of the year.

P 5.2 Rippe Company has studied the collection pattern of credit sales for the past year, and management has developed the following collection schedule for credit sales:

- 40 percent in the month of sale.
- 30 percent in the month following the month of sale.
- 15 percent two months following the month of sale.
- 8 percent three months following the month of sale.
- 5 percent four months following the month of sale.

Actual sales for the past six months are shown below:

	Sales
July	$175,800
August	194,500
September	186,300
October	210,750
November	340,000
December	375,900

Expected sales for the next six months are shown below:

	Sales
January	$200,100
February	220,450
March	300,700
April	251,200
May	275,090
June	180,460

Required:
a. Determine the expected cash receipts for January through June.
b. Determine the amount of uncollected sales during the period from January through June assuming that uncollected sales are determined after four months have passed.
c. Should Rippe tighten its credit policy? Why or why not?

P 5.3 Rosacker, Inc., shows a cash balance of $24,000 on January 1, 1997. Expected sales and purchases of Dune Buggies for the first three months of 1997 are given below

	Sales	Purchases
January	$600,000	$450,000
February	900,000	300,000
March	800,000	500,000

Sales are collected 75 percent in the month of sale and 25 percent in the month following the month of sale. Purchases are paid 20 percent in the month of purchase and 80 percent in the month following the month of purchase.

The actual sales and purchases for the last three months of 1996 were:

	Sales	Purchases
October	$500,000	$350,000
November	700,000	650,000
December	900,000	400,000

Required: *a.* Determine the cash receipts for January, February, and March, respectively.
  b. Determine the cash payments for January, February, and March, respectively.
  c. Determine the expected ending balance in cash on March 31, 1997.

P 5.4   Jasper, Inc., has hired you to help them determine the amount and timing of purchases of office supplies for resale for next year. The marketing department has forecasted sales of office supplies by quarter of $65,000, $75,000, $59,000, and $90,000 for next year. After examining last year's accounting records, you determine that the cost of goods sold is 40 percent of sales. In the past, Jasper has always maintained an ending inventory of 50 percent of the next quarter's expected cost of sales. However, due to increasing storage costs, the company decided to decrease ending inventories to 25 percent of the next quarter's cost of sales. After examining last year's purchase invoices, you have discovered that suppliers require payment within 30 days but offer a cash discount of 5 percent for payments made within 10 days.

Required: *a.* Determine the office supplies for resale purchases by quarter for next year.
  b. Determine the cash disbursements for office supplies purchases by quarter for next year.
  c. Write a letter to the president of Jasper, Inc., explaining the benefits of maintaining minimal inventories and paying for purchases within 10 days.

P 5.5   You have recently been hired by a medium-sized merchandising firm that sells T-shirts embossed with various college logos. The manager of the company has never prepared a budget and does not believe that budgeting will help the company even though it has experienced cash flow problems lately.

Required: Write a memo to the manager explaining the benefits to be derived from budgeting. Be sure to address the purposes of the budgeting process, how the different operating budgets are related and what each budget indicates, and how to use the budgeting process to analyze the recent cash flow problems.

P 5.6   Reliable Company is developing a forecast of March 1997 cash receipts from credit sales. Credit sales for March 1997 are estimated to be $640,000. The accounts receivable balance at February 28, 1997, is $600,000; one-third of the balance represents January credit sales and the remaining two-thirds is from February credit sales. All accounts receivable from months prior to January 1997 have been collected or written off as uncollectible. Reliable's history of accounts receivable collections is as follows:

In the month of sale	25%
In the first month after the month of sale	50%
In the second month after the month of sale	20%
Uncollectible and written off at the end of the second month after the sale	5%

Required: Determine the cash receipts from credit sales for March 1997.

P 5.7   Erickson has budgeted its activity for October 1997 based on the following information.

- Sales are budgeted at $450,000. All sales are credit sales, and a provision for uncollectible accounts is made monthly at the rate of 3 percent of sales.

- Merchandise inventory was $105,000 on September 30, 1997, and an increase of $15,000 is planned for this month.

- All merchandise is marked up to sell at invoice cost plus 50 percent.

- Estimated cash disbursements for selling and administrative expenses for the month of October are $60,000.

- Depreciation for the month is projected at $7,500.

Required: Prepare a pro forma income statement for Erickson for October 1997.

P 5.8   Green Thumb Lawn Care Service, a corporation located in the southeastern United States, provides lawn care services to clients. It offers two levels of service—full service that includes complete lawn care (watering, fertilizing, mowing, trimming, and hedging) and budget service, which includes only fertilizing and mowing. Clients are asked to pay for services in advance.

Each full-service customer is assigned two lawn care professionals who each work approximately 10 hours per month. Each budget service customer is assigned one lawn care professional who works approximately 15 hours per month. Lawn care professionals are paid $12 per hour.

Green Thumb pays its employees, rent, insurance, and miscellaneous costs in the quarter incurred, while chemicals, gasoline, and maintenance costs are paid in the quarter following the incurrence of the cost.

Green Thumb has prepared the following budgets for the fiscal year ending December 31, 1997.

GREEN THUMB LAWN CARE SERVICE
Professional Services Provided Budget for the Year Ended December 31, 1997

	Quarters				
	1	2	3	4	Year
Full service clients	100	300	300	150	850
Full service fee	× 1,500	× 1,500	× 1,500	× 1,500	× 1,500
Total full service revenue	$150,000	$450,000	$450,000	$225,000	$1,275,000
Budget service clients	500	510	510	505	2,025
Budget service fee	× 800	× 800	× 800	× 800	× 800
Total budget service revenue	$400,000	$408,000	$408,000	$404,000	$1,620,000
Total service revenue	$550,000	$858,000	$858,000	$629,000	$2,895,000

GREEN THUMB LAWN CARE SERVICE
Lawn Care Professional Labor Budget for the Year Ended December 31, 1997

	Quarters				
	1	2	3	4	Year
Full service clients	100	300	300	150	850
Hours of service	× 60	× 60	× 60	× 60	× 60
Total hours of full service	6,000	18,000	18,000	9,000	51,000
Budget service clients	500	510	510	505	2,025
Hours of service	× 45	× 45	× 45	× 45	× 45
Total hours of budget service	22,500	22,950	22,950	22,725	91,125
Total service hours	28,500	40,950	40,950	31,725	142,125
Wage cost per hour	× 12	× 12	× 12	× 12	× 12
Total wage cost	$342,000	$491,400	$491,400	$380,700	$1,705,500

GREEN THUMB LAWN CARE SERVICE
Selling and Administrative Budget for the Year Ended December 31, 1997

	Quarters				
	1	2	3	4	Year
Administrative salaries	$ 42,000	$ 42,000	$ 42,000	$ 42,000	$ 168,000
Rent on facilities	15,000	15,000	15,000	15,000	60,000
Insurance for business	6,000	6,000	6,000	6,000	24,000
Chemicals and gasoline	30,500	42,950	43,950	33,725	151,125
Maintenance of equipment	9,550	13,285	13,250	10,525	46,610
Depreciation of equipment	50,000	50,000	50,000	50,000	200,000
Taxes	125,000	125,000	125,000	125,000	500,000
Miscellaneous costs	10,000	11,000	11,500	10,500	43,000
Total selling and administrative cost	$288,050	$305,235	$306,700	$292,750	$1,192,735

GREEN THUMB LAWN CARE SERVICE
Cash Budget for the Year Ended December 31, 1997

| | Quarters | | | | |
	1	2	3	4	Year
Beginning balance	$ 10,500	$ 98,710	$101,260	$337,125	$ 10,500
Add receipts	550,000	858,000	858,000	629,000	2,895,000
Cash available	$560,500	$956,710	$959,260	$966,125	$2,905,500
Less disbursements:					
Professional salaries	342,000	491,400	491,400	380,700	1,705,500
Administrative salaries	42,000	42,000	42,000	42,000	168,000
Rent	15,000	15,000	15,000	15,000	60,000
Insurance	6,000	6,000	6,000	6,000	24,000
Chemicals and gasoline*	34,250	30,500	42,950	43,950	151,650
Maintenance of equipment*	12,540	9,550	13,285	13,250	48,625
Taxes	–0–	250,000	–0–	250,000	500,000
Miscellaneous costs	10,000	11,000	11,500	10,500	43,000
Total disbursements	$461,790	$855,450	$622,135	$761,400	$2,700,775
Ending cash balance	$ 98,710	$101,260	$337,125	$204,725	$ 204,725

*Amounts paid in one quarter are for costs incurred in the preceding quarter.

GREEN THUMB LAWN CARE SERVICE
Pro Forma Income Statement for the Year Ended December 31, 1997

| | Quarters | | | | |
	1	2	3	4	Year
Service revenue	$550,000	$858,000	$858,000	$629,000	$2,895,000
Less expenses:					
Professional salaries	$342,000	$491,400	$491,400	$380,700	$1,705,500
Administrative salaries	42,000	42,000	42,000	42,000	168,000
Rent on facilities	15,000	15,000	15,000	15,000	60,000
Insurance on business	6,000	6,000	6,000	6,000	24,000
Chemicals and gasoline	30,500	42,950	43,950	33,725	151,125
Maintenance of equipment	9,550	13,285	13,250	10,525	46,610
Depreciation on equipment	50,000	50,000	50,000	50,000	200,000
Miscellaneous expenses	10,000	11,000	11,500	10,500	43,000
Taxes	125,000	125,000	125,000	125,000	500,000
Total expenses	$630,050	$796,635	$798,100	$673,450	$2,898,235
Net income	$(80,050)	$ 61,365	$ 59,900	$(44,450)	$ (3,235)

GREEN THUMB LAWN CARE SERVICE
Pro Forma Balance Sheet as of December 31, 1997

Assets

Cash	$204,725
Equipment	2,000,000
Accumulated depreciation	(600,000)
Total assets	$1,604,725

Liabilities and Owners' Equity

Accounts payable	$ 44,250
Capital stock	800,000
Retained earnings	760,475
Total liabilities and owners' equity	$1,604,725

Required:
a. How many full service clients does Green Thumb expect each quarter?
b. What is the fee Green Thumb charged to budget service clients each quarter?
c. Which costs shown on the selling and administrative cost budget are fixed?
d. How often does Green Thumb plan to remit its tax payments?
e. Is the cash payment for chemicals the same as the chemical cost in quarter 1? Why or why not?
f. Where does the cash amount shown on the balance sheet originate?
g. Does management have any reason for concern about its expected financial results in fiscal 1997? Why or why not?

P 5.9 Olden Days Antiques is a partnership formed to buy and sell antiques. It buys antiques from various sources such as estate sales and auctions. The prices paid for the antiques vary, but cost of goods sold is, on average, 50 percent of sales.

Based on past experience, Olden Days estimates that 60 percent of its credit customers will pay their bills in the quarter of sale, and the remaining 40 percent will pay their bills in the following quarter. Olden Days pays its commissions, operating costs, and merchandise purchases in the quarter incurred.

Olden Days has prepared the following budgets for its fiscal year ending March 31, 1998.

OLDEN DAYS ANTIQUES
Sales Budget for the Year Ended March 31, 1998

	Quarters				
	1	2	3	4	Year
Cash sales	$500,000	$550,000	$525,000	$600,000	$2,175,000
Credit sales	300,000	330,000	315,000	360,000	1,305,000
Total sales	$800,000	$880,000	$840,000	$960,000	$3,480,000

OLDEN DAYS ANTIQUES
Personnel Budget for the Year Ended March 31, 1998

	Quarters				
	1	2	3	4	Year
Total sales	$800,000	$880,000	$840,000	$960,000	$3,480,000
Commission rate	× .05	× .05	× .05	× .05	× .05
Total commission	$ 40,000	$ 44,000	$ 42,000	$ 48,000	$ 174,000

OLDEN DAYS ANTIQUES
Purchases Budget for the Year Ended March 31, 1998

	Quarters				
	1	2	3	4	Year
Total sales	$800,000	$880,000	$840,000	$960,000	$3,480,000
Cost of sales	$400,000	$440,000	$420,000	$480,000	$1,740,000
Add desired ending inventory*	220,000	210,000	240,000	400,000	400,000
Cost of goods available	$620,000	$650,000	$660,000	$880,000	$2,140,000
Less beginning inventory	200,000	220,000	210,000	240,000	200,000
Purchases required	$420,000	$430,000	$450,000	$640,000	$1,940,000

*Desired ending inventory equal to 50 percent of next quarter's cost of sales.

OLDEN DAYS ANTIQUES
Selling and Administrative Budget for the Year Ended March 31, 1998

	Quarters				
	1	2	3	4	Year
Administrative salaries	$30,000	$30,000	$30,000	$30,000	$120,000
Insurance	15,000	15,000	15,000	15,000	60,000
Rent on facilities	18,000	18,000	18,000	18,000	72,000
Depreciation	2,000	2,000	2,000	2,000	8,000
Miscellaneous costs	21,000	24,000	22,000	28,000	95,000
Total costs	$86,000	$89,000	$87,000	$93,000	$355,000

OLDEN DAYS ANTIQUES
Cash Budget for the Year Ended March 31, 1998

| | Quarters | | | | |
	1	2	3	4	Year
Beginning cash balance	$100,000	$ 436,000	$ 743,000	$1,012,000	$ 100,000
Add cash receipts:					
Cash sales	500,000	550,000	525,000	600,000	2,175,000
Credit sales—current period	180,000	198,000	189,000	210,000	777,000
Credit sales—prior period	200,000	120,000	132,000	126,000	578,000
Total cash available	$980,000	$1,304,000	$1,589,000	$1,948,000	$3,630,000
Less cash disbursements:					
Commissions	$ 40,000	$ 44,000	$ 42,000	$ 48,000	$ 174,000
Purchases	420,000	430,000	450,000	640,000	1,940,000
Administrative salaries	30,000	30,000	30,000	30,000	120,000
Insurance	15,000	15,000	15,000	15,000	60,000
Rent on facilities	18,000	18,000	18,000	18,000	72,000
Miscellaneous costs	21,000	24,000	22,000	28,000	95,000
Total disbursements	$544,000	$ 561,000	$ 577,000	$ 779,000	$2,461,500
Ending cash balance	$436,000	$ 743,000	$1,012,000	$1,169,000	$1,169,000

OLDEN DAYS ANTIQUES
Pro Forma Income Statement for the Year Ended March 31, 1998

| | Quarters | | | | |
	1	2	3	4	Year
Sales	$800,000	$880,000	$840,000	$960,000	$3,480,000
Cost of sales	400,000	440,000	420,000	480,000	1,740,000
Gross margin	$400,000	$440,000	$420,000	$480,000	$1,740,000
Less operating expenses:					
Commissions	40,000	44,000	42,000	48,000	174,000
Selling and administrative expenses	86,000	89,000	87,000	93,000	355,000
Net income	$274,000	$307,000	$291,000	$339,000	$1,211,000

OLDEN DAYS ANTIQUES
Pro Forma Balance Sheet as of March 31, 1998

Assets

Cash		$1,169,000
Accounts receivable		144,000
Inventory		400,000
Equipment	$80,000	
Accumulated depreciation	(16,000)	64,000
Total assets		$1,777,000

Owners' Equity

Beethoven, capital	$590,000
Bach, capital	610,000
Brahms, capital	577,000
Total equities	$1,777,000

Required:
a. What is the expected cost of goods sold for quarter 1, 1999?
b. Are the expected cash receipts in quarter 2 equal to the expected sales in quarter 2? Why or why not?
c. How much cash should Olden Days collect in quarter 1, 1999, for credit sales expected in quarter 4, 1998?
d. What does Olden Days base its employees' pay on?
e. Where did the amount shown as inventory on the balance sheet originate?
f. Does management have any reason to be concerned about fiscal 1998? Why or why not?

Tykes Bykes is a sole proprietorship manufacturing tricycles for young children. These tricycles are sold to retail outlets throughout the northwestern United States. The tricycle design is fairly simple: A molded plastic body, a set of plastic handlebars, and three wheels are the only direct materials needed. Each tricycle is assembled manually requiring 3/4 of an hour, and laborers are paid $8 per hour.

All sales are on account. Direct labor, manufacturing overhead, and selling and administrative expenses are paid in the quarter incurred. Sixty percent of material purchases are paid in the quarter of purchase while the remaining purchases are paid in the quarter following the purchase.

Tykes Bykes has prepared the following budgets for its fiscal year ending September 30, 1997.

TYKES BYKES
Sales Budget for the Year Ended September 30, 1997

	Quarters				
	1	2	3	4	Year
Unit sales	10,000	12,000	9,000	15,000	46,000
Selling price per tricycle	× $16	× $16	× $16	× $16	× $16
Sales revenue	$160,000	$192,000	$144,000	$240,000	$736,000
Uncollectible accounts (1%)	$1,600	$1,920	$1,440	$2,400	$7,360
Net proceeds	$158,400	$190,080	$142,560	$237,600	$728,640

TYKES BYKES
Production Budget for the Year Ended September 30, 1997

	Quarters				
	1	2	3	4	Year
Unit sales	10,000	12,000	9,000	15,000	46,000
Add desired ending inventory*	3,600	2,700	4,500	3,300	3,300
Finished goods needed	13,600	14,700	13,500	18,300	49,300
Less beginning inventory	3,000	3,600	2,700	4,500	3,000
Production required	10,600	11,100	10,800	13,800	46,300

*Desired ending inventory equals 30 percent of next quarter's unit sales.

TYKES BYKES
Direct Labor Budget for the Year Ended September 30, 1997

	Quarters				
	1	2	3	4	Year
Production required	10,600	11,100	10,800	13,800	46,000
Hours required per tricycle	× .75	× .75	× .75	× .75	× .75
Hours required for production	7,950	8,325	8,100	10,350	34,725
Wage rate per hour	× $8.00	× $8.00	× $8.00	× $8.00	× $8.00
Direct labor cost	$63,600	$66,600	$64,800	$82,800	$277,800

TYKES BYKES
Manufacturing Overhead Budget for the Year Ended September 30, 1997

	Quarters				
	1	2	3	4	Year
Production required	10,600	11,100	10,800	13,800	46,300
Variable overhead per unit	× .90	× .90	× .90	× .90	× .90
Total variable overhead	$ 9,540	$ 9,990	$ 9,720	$12,420	$ 41,670
Fixed overhead*	15,000	15,000	15,000	15,000	60,000
Total manufacturing overhead	$24,540	$24,990	$24,720	$27,420	$101,670

*Includes depreciation of $10,000 per quarter.

TYKES BYKES
Direct Materials Purchases Budget for the Year Ended September 30, 1997

| | Quarters | | | | |
	1	2	3	4	Year
Wheels					
Production required	10,600	11,100	10,800	13,800	46,300
Wheels needed per unit	× 3	× 3	× 3	× 3	× 3
Wheels needed for production	31,800	33,300	32,400	41,400	138,900
Add desired ending inventory*	3,330	3,240	4,140	3,300	3,300
Total wheels required	35,130	36,540	36,540	44,700	142,200
Less beginning inventory	3,180	3,330	3,240	4,140	3,180
Total wheels to purchase	31,950	33,210	33,300	40,560	139,020
Purchase price per unit	× $.50	× $.50	× $.50	× $.50	× $.50
Cost of wheel purchases	$15,975	$16,605	$16,650	$20,280	$69,510
Bodies					
Production required	10,600	11,100	10,800	13,800	46,300
Bodies needed per unit	× 1	× 1	× 1	× 1	× 1
Bodies needed for production	10,600	11,100	10,800	13,800	46,300
Add desired ending inventory*	1,110	1,080	1,380	1,100	1,100
Total bodies required	11,710	12,180	12,180	14,900	47,400
Less beginning inventory	1,060	1,110	1,080	1,380	1,060
Total bodies to purchase	10,650	11,070	11,100	13,520	46,340
Purchase price per unit	× $2.50	× $2.50	× $2.50	× $2.50	× $2.50
Cost of body purchases	$26,625	$27,675	$27,750	$33,800	$115,850
Handlebars					
Production required	10,600	11,100	10,800	13,800	46,300
Handlebars needed per unit	× 1	× 1	× 1	× 1	× 1
Handlebars needed for production	10,600	11,100	10,800	13,800	46,300
Add desired ending inventory*	1,110	1,080	1,380	1,100	1,100
Total handlebars required	11,710	12,180	12,180	14,900	47,400
Less beginning inventory	1,060	1,110	1,080	1,380	1,060
Total handlebars to purchase	10,650	11,070	11,100	13,520	46,340
Purchase price per unit	× $1.00	× $1.00	× $1.00	× $1.00	× $1.00
Cost of handlebar purchases	$10,650	$11,070	$11,100	$13,520	$ 46,340
Total cost of purchases	$53,250	$55,350	$55,500	$67,600	$231,700

*Desired ending inventory equal to 10 percent of next quarter's material needs.

TYKES BYKES
Selling and Administrative Cost Budget for the Year Ended September 31, 1997

| | Quarters | | | | |
	1	2	3	4	Year
Sales revenue	$160,000	$192,000	$144,000	$240,000	$736,000
Variable cost per dollar	× .08	× .08	× .08	× .80	× .08
Total variable selling and administrative costs	$ 12,800	$ 15,360	$ 11,520	$ 19,200	$ 58,880
Fixed selling and administrative costs*	10,000	10,000	10,000	10,000	40,000
Total selling and administrative costs	$ 22,800	$ 25,360	$ 21,520	$ 29,200	$ 98,880

*Includes depreciation of $2,000 per quarter.

TYKES BYKES
Cash Budget for the Year Ended September 30, 1997

	Quarters				
	1	2	3	4	Year
Beginning cash balance	$ 65,000	$106,510	$134,550	$138,470	$ 65,000
Add cash receipts:					
Current quarter (60%)	96,000	115,200	86,400	144,000	441,600
Prior quarter (30%)	81,000	48,000	57,600	43,200	229,800
Two quarters prior (9%)	16,200	24,300	14,400	17,280	72,180
Total receipts	$193,200	$187,500	$158,400	$204,480	$743,580
Total cash available	$258,200	$294,010	$292,950	$342,950	$808,580
Less cash disbursements:					
Current purchases (60%)	$ 31,950	$ 33,210	$ 33,300	$40,560	$139,020
Prior purchases (40%)	20,800	21,300	22,140	22,200	86,440
Direct labor used	63,600	66,600	64,800	82,800	277,800
Manufacturing overhead	14,540	14,990	14,720	17,420	61,670
Selling and administrative costs	20,800	23,360	19,520	27,200	90,880
Total disbursements	$151,690	$159,460	$154,480	$190,180	$655,810
Ending cash balance	$106,510	$134,550	$138,470	$152,770	$152,770

TYKES BYKES
Pro Forma Income Statement for the Year Ended September 30, 1997

Sales (46,000 × $16)		$736,000
Less cost of goods sold (46,000 × $13.20)		607,200
Gross margin		$128,800
Less operating expenses:		
Selling and administrative expense	$98,880	
Uncollectible accounts expense	7,360	106,240
Net income		$ 22,560

TYKES BYKES
Pro Forma Balance Sheet as of September 30, 1997

Assets

Cash		$152,770
Accounts receivable		106,560
Direct materials inventory:		
Wheels (3,300 × $0.50) = $1,650		
Bodies (1,100 × $2.50) = 2,750		
Handlebars (1,100 × $1.00) = 1,100		5,500
Finished goods inventory (3,300 × $13.20)		45,560
Equipment	$768,000	
Accumulated depreciation	(144,000)	624,000
Total assets		$934,390

Liabilities and Owners' Equity

Accounts payable		$ 27,040
Tchaikovsky, capital		907,350
Total liabilities and owners' equity		$934,390

Required:
a. Does Tykes expect to collect all its credit sales? Why or why not?
b. How many tricycles does Tykes Bykes expect to sell in quarter 1, 1998?
c. How many tricycles does Tykes Bykes expect to produce in quarter 1, 1998?
d. When, and in what amounts, does Tykes expect to collect quarter 1 sales?
e. When, and in what amounts, does the company expect to pay quarter 2 purchases?
f. Where did the amounts shown as direct materials inventory on the balance sheet originate?
g. How is the ending balance in accounts receivable on the balance sheet determined?
h. How is the ending balance in accounts payable on the balance sheet determined?
i. Does management have any reason to be concerned about its financial results in fiscal 1997? Why or why not?

COMPUTER APPLICATIONS

CA 5.1 Allentown Company has studied the collection pattern of credit sales for the past year, and management has developed the following collection schedule for credit sales:

20% in the month of sale.

40% in the month following the month of sale.

20% two months following the month of sale.

15% three months following the month of sale.

5% four months following the month of sale.

Actual sales for the past six months are shown below:

	Sales
July	$351,600
August	389,000
September	372,600
October	421,500
November	680,000
December	751,800

Expected sales for the next six months are shown below:

	Sales
January	$400,200
February	440,900
March	601,400
April	502,400
May	550,180
June	360,920

Required: *Use a computer spreadsheet.*

a. Determine the expected cash receipts for January through June.

b. Determine the amount of uncollected sales during the period from January through June assuming that uncollected sales are determined after four months have passed.

c. Should Allentown tighten its credit policy? Why or why not?

CA 5.2 Bethlehem Corporation has provided the following information concerning actual purchases and sales of Peach Essence Perfume during the first four months of the year:

	Purchases	Sales
January	$168,000	$284,000
February	192,000	264,000
March	144,000	240,000
April	216,000	312,000

Collections from customers are normally 70 percent in the month of sale, 20 percent in the month following the sale, and 9 percent in the second month following the sale. The balance is expected to be uncollectible. Bethlehem takes advantage of the 3 percent cash discount allowed on purchases paid for by the 10th of the month following the purchase. Purchases for May are budgeted at $240,000, while sales for May are forecasted at $264,000. Cash disbursements for expenses are expected to be $57,800 for the month of May. Bethlehem's expected cash balance as of May 1 is $88,000.

Required: *Use a computer spreadsheet.*

a. Determine the expected cash receipts for May.

b. Determine the expected cash payment for purchases for May.

c. Determine the total cash disbursements for May.

d. Determine the ending balance in the cash account on May 31.

CA 5.3 O'Reilly's Supply, a rapidly expanding electronics parts distributor, is in the process of formulating plans for 1997. Expected monthly sales (all on account) for 1997 are:

January	$5,400,000	February	$7,000,000
March	5,400,000	April	6,600,000
May	7,500,000	June	8,400,000
July	9,000,000	August	9,000,000
September	9,600,000	October	9,600,000
November	9,000,000	December	9,900,000

O'Reilly's has an excellent record in accounts receivable collection. Eighty percent of sales are collected in the month after the sale and 20 percent in the second month after the sale.

The purchases of electronics parts (all on account) is O'Reilly's biggest expenditure. The cost of these items is 65 percent of sales. Seventy percent of the parts are received by O'Reilly's one month prior to sale, and 30 percent are received during the month of sale. Historically, O'Reilly's has paid 80 percent of accounts payable one month after the receipt of purchased parts and the remaining 20 percent two months after receipt of purchased parts.

Required: *Use a computer spreadsheet.*

a. Determine the expected cash collections by month for the second and third quarters of 1997 (April through September).
b. Determine the receipt of purchased parts by month for the period of March through September 1997.
c. Determine the cash disbursements by month for the second and third quarters of 1997.
d. Assume that the beginning cash balance on April 1 is expected to be $600,000; determine the ending cash balance as of September 1997.

CA 5.4 Bayliner Enterprises manufactures inflatable life rafts, which it sells to discount stores throughout the United States. The projected unit sales of life rafts for the first six months of the fiscal year are shown below:

Month	Unit Sales
1	475,000
2	500,000
3	487,500
4	400,000
5	425,000
6	550,000

Bayliner maintains ending inventories (raw materials and finished goods) equal to 5 percent of the next month's expected sales. Production of each life raft product requires four pounds of plastic (raw material) and three hours of direct labor. Plastic can be purchased for $0.75 per pound. Direct labor is paid $12 per hour. Manufacturing overhead per month has been estimated using the high/low method as:

Overhead = $10,000 + .2 × Direct material cost per month

Required: *Use a computer spreadsheet.*

a. Determine the expected production of life rafts by month for the first quarter.
b. Determine the plastic purchases by month for the first quarter.
c. Determine the direct labor cost by month for the first quarter.
d. Determine the manufacturing overhead costs by month for the first quarter.

CASES

C 5.1 Michael and Scott, two college roommates have decided to give a midsemester party. They will serve hamburgers, hot dogs, chips, dip, and sodas. Since their refrigerator space is limited, they do not want a lot of leftover food after the party. Scott and Michael have decided to invite 50 guests; each guest is permitted to bring a significant other to the party. They estimate that 60 percent of the guests will be accompanied by someone. Scott, Michael, and Trish (a friend) will not bring guests since they are the hosts. Scott estimates that, on average, each guest will eat one quarter-pound hamburger and two hot dogs. Michael estimates that they'll need one bag of chips for every two people and one container of dip for every two bags of chips. The roommates think that an average of five sodas per person is adequate.

After looking in their refrigerator and cupboards, they discover two bags of chips, three pounds of hamburger, 20 sodas, and one package (10) of hot dogs. Since they think they may be broke after the party, they would like to have two pounds of hamburger, one package of hot dogs, two packages of buns, one bag of chips, and six sodas left over.

Required: Estimate the costs of the party.

Appendix (requires study of Chapter 4):

C 5.2 Candibar, a wholesale distributor of candy, leases space in a warehouse and is charged according to the average number of cases stored. Management is concerned about the high ordering costs incurred last year. The company employs temporary personnel to process purchase orders and invoices upon receipt of the candy. Managers, supervisors, and shipping clerks are full-time employees.

The company placed 200 orders last year. Data for the high-activity month (30 orders) and the low-activity month (10 orders) for the purchasing and warehouse operations are shown below.

	High-Activity Month (30)	Low-Activity Month (10)
Purchasing Department		
Manager	$1,600	$1,600
Clerks	300	100
Supplies	60	20
Warehousing Department		
Supervisor	1,550	1,550
Receiving clerks	360	120
Shipping clerks	2,800	2,800
Total	$6,620	$6,190

The company purchased 160,000 cases of candy last year. Information on the high-storage month (4,000 cases) and the low-storage month (2,500 cases) is given below.

	High-Inventory Month (4,000)	Low-Inventory Month (2,500)
Warehouse charges:		
Rent	$ 6,000	$3,750
Property taxes	2,000	1,250
Insurance	4,000	2,500
Total	$12,000	$7,500

Last year it took three days to receive candy from suppliers after the order was placed. The company does business 320 days per year. They want to maintain a safety stock of 1,000 cases of candy.

Required:
a. Determine the economic order quantity.
b. Determine the reorder point.
c. Explain why ordering costs were too high last year.
d. Show proof that the economic order quantity results in the lowest possible carrying plus ordering costs. (Ignore safety stock in your calculations.)

CRITICAL THINKING

CT 5.1 Just-in-time inventory systems have been a major topic in accounting for a number of years. Conduct a library research on the topic of just-in-time inventory systems and write a 2- to 5-page paper arguing either for or against the adoption of JIT by United States manufacturing companies. Some suggested sources of information include *The Management Accountant*, the *Journal of Cost Management*, and the *Journal of Accountancy* as well as news magazines such as *Business Week*, *Forbes*, and *Fortune*.

CT 5.2 Planning and budgeting information is considered private, internal information. However, external stakeholders might benefit from knowing what management plans for the coming period. Prepare an argument supporting or refuting the release of budgeted information to external stakeholders. Be sure to consider the needs of internal as well as external stakeholders.

ETHICAL CHALLENGES

EC 5.1 You have just been hired as a sales representative for a major international advertising company. Upper-level management has requested estimated sales amounts for each sales territory. Since you have a business degree, your boss, B. G., has assigned you the task of estimating sales for the territory in which you work. You feel that this is an excellent opportunity to show your boss what you can accomplish. After talking to sales managers and examining last year's sales figures, you prepare a sales budget for the coming year and turn it in to B. G.

The next day your boss calls you into the office and tells you that your estimated sales numbers are too high. B. G. tells you that you must decrease the estimated sales or your territory may not meet the budget next year and, therefore, none of the salespeople will receive bonuses. You explain to your boss that you have talked to the sales managers, studied last year's numbers, and looked at the market growth of the company. You feel that your sales estimates are right in line with what can be accomplished by the sales staff in this territory. B. G. reminds you that you are new to the job and do not understand the ramifications of not meeting or beating the budget. B. G. also states that upper-level management will probably increase the estimated sales numbers anyway. So by lowering the numbers to begin with, the sales estimates are ultimately achieved, no one is hurt, and all the sales staff will receive their year-end bonuses.

Required: Describe what you would do in this situation and why.

EC 5.2 As discussed in the chapter, budgets affect people's behavior and people affect the reliability of the numbers on the budget. Prepare an argument supporting or refuting the use of budgets for evaluation and control purposes.

CHAPTER 6

Short-Term Operating Decisions

Learning Objectives

1. Describe the economic framework for short-term decision making.
2. Explain how to apply the economic framework to special order decisions.
3. Describe the economic framework for deletion or addition decisions.
4. Use the economic framework to solve make-or-buy problems.
5. Apply the economic framework to sell-or-process further decisions.

Appendix:

6. Describe how companies use linear programming to determine product mix.

Most people never buy steel products, such as structural I-beams used in building construction or sheets of steel used to make body parts for cars, directly from the manufacturer. But virtually every car, major building, and most houses bought contain significant portions of steel products. Prior to World War II, the United States was a world leader in the production of steel. After the war, countries whose factories were destroyed, like Japan and Germany, rebuilt their industrial base, including steel manufacturing, with newer, more efficient facilities. As a result, these countries then rendered the United States noncompetitive in the world steel market. Now, however, U.S. manufacturers have rebounded.

One company that has helped in this resurgence of U.S. steel manufacturing is Worthington Industries. Started in 1955, it has grown to become the largest specialty steel manufacturer in the United States. Specialty steel manufacturers provide their customers with products intended for specific purposes, rather than standard sizes of materials that the customer adapts to its needs.

As a specialty steel manufacturer, Worthington takes sheets of steel and transforms them into custom items like body parts for auto manufacturers. In addition, Worthington also receives special orders from customers for unusually large quantities of products or for modified products.

185

Among the factors related to its success is Worthington's commitment to quality. This includes using the latest developments in technology along with the management philosophy of the founder and long-term chief executive, John P. McConnell. McConnell believes that workers should be paid well and treated with respect and that they, in return, should work hard.

Worthington did away with timeclocks and plant supervisors and, instead, shifted responsibility to its employees. These actions have allowed Worthington to meet the needs of even the most particular end users and to deliver finished steel on time. ⚙︎

AN ECONOMIC FRAMEWORK FOR SHORT-TERM DECISIONS

Short-term operating decisions require making choices among alternatives that arise from changes in business circumstances, such as acquiring a new, large customer or responding to demand for a product that far exceeds the planned level. These decisions are short term because they assume that the business cannot modify the capacity of the machines and equipment or the number of specially trained employees in the time affected by the decision.

Short-term operating decisions are important because they present businesses with opportunities to make more money than they planned initially by either replacing planned production with more profitable items or by producing additional unplanned items that provide a positive contribution margin.

In this chapter, we discuss short-term operating decisions that companies like Worthington Industries make. These types of decisions require that management choose one alternative action from two or more possible actions. Short-term operating decisions differ from other operating decisions in that they typically are not considered in the planning phase of the management cycle. For example, when a customer offers Worthington a one-time purchase of a large quantity of a certain product at a price below the normal selling price, management has two alternative actions: (1) accept the offer or (2) do not accept the offer. Another type of short-term decision might involve a request for Worthington to produce a product that its customers want, but that Worthington does not have. Thus, Worthington would have the choice of buying the requested product from wholesalers or making it in Worthington's production facility. Worthington would have to weigh issues like whether it could forgo regular production and thereby run the risk of not producing enough of other products by accepting such an offer. In both these cases, the event was initiated by an external party and, therefore, not planned in advance.

Even small businesses face short-term decisions that could affect their profitability. Consider a local restaurant that has the chance to host the local high school athletic association's awards banquet, but will have to turn away its regular customers if it does. Or consider a small bicycle manufacturer that receives a large order of bikes from a discount retail chain and can either fill the order or keep supplying its existing customers, but not both. For any business, profitability ultimately means assessing the needs of customers and determining which products meet those needs.

In this chapter, we also explain what is unique about short-term decisions and present a simple economic framework that provides guidance for structuring and analyzing them. Then, we provide specific examples of short-term decisions and show how to apply the economic framework to short-term decisions so that management can understand the factors required to make economically sound choices.

s pressures to produce more efficiently grow, firms like Sun Microsystems Computer Corp. and 3Com Corp., both California-based manufacturers of high-tech electronics equipment, try to improve their manufacturing efficiency by using sophisticated production scheduling software. The software that Sun and 3Com use is called *ResponseAgent* produced by another California firm, Red Pepper Software.

ResponseAgent is unique in that it interacts and draws information directly from software programs that schedule materials purchases and labor availability. Because of this unique interaction, it can generate optimized production plans, monitor critical manufacturing variables, alert users to problems as they arise, and recommend optimized solutions in real time.

ResponseAgent is really decision-support software inspired by the work of Red Pepper's founder, Monte Zweben, who dealt with NASA's complex problems related to scheduling space shuttle launches and maintenance. Zweben describes how ResponseAgent functions. "The agent discovers the

constraints—such as material shortages, capacity overloads, and late orders—and can be asked to optimize the schedule automatically—as opposed to just giving you a report of what is wrong or allowing the user to fix the problem interactively." As customers of Red Pepper, both Sun and 3Com find the scheduling software a great way to improve their production flexibility and meet customer demand. Randy Heffner, a vice president at 3Com, says, "The ResponseAgent enables us to be real-time responsive to the requirements of our customers without incurring large overhead costs." Sun's chief information officer, Leon Williams, says, "The ResponseAgent is playing a key role in our efforts to integrate all our manufacturing and distribution facilities into one cohesive enterprise."

Red Pepper's software is a cutting-edge example of the next wave of manufacturing and planning technology that will allow manufacturers to constantly adapt to the uncertainties of their environment.

Source: John Teresko, "Red Pepper Software" *Industry Week*, December 18, 1995.

What Makes Short-Term Decisions Different from Other Operating Decisions?

Not all types of businesses face the need to make short-term operating decisions. Some businesses plan and perform day-to-day operations without significant unplanned events. For example, businesses like grocery retailers buy products in planned quantities with very few deviations. However, at times, maybe a couple of times a year or once every few years, most businesses encounter significant events that result in opportunities they did not anticipate.

Recall that strategic decisions set the course for businesses in the long run and that operating decisions guide the day-to-day operations of the business. Short-term operating decisions differ from both strategic and operating decisions in three very important ways. First, *they are based on the assumption that current capacity is fixed.* That is, the amount of a product that a manufacturer can make or the maximum amount of retail floor space of a merchandiser is not going to change during the time affected by these decisions. Thus, short-term operating decisions are similar to other operating decisions because they are *short run*, but they differ from strategic long-run decisions that assume that capacity can change.

Remember that in the long-run new buildings can be built, machines and equipment can be bought, and employees can be trained to do new jobs. So, if the changes in the business's operating environment that produced the short-term operating decisions are permanent, then the business can make the investment decisions to acquire additional capacity. Businesses do not undertake investment decisions lightly. They carefully assess whether the changes will last long enough to justify the additional investment. Whether the changes are permanent or not, short-term decisions are immediate and require a choice without the option of increasing capacity.

Second, *short-term operating decisions are not planned as part of the management cycle.* The need for these decisions arises after the planning phase of the cycle—during the performing phase. Events leading to these decisions either did not happen as planned—sales might be less than planned or costs might be higher—or they were not anticipated in the plans—there were unanticipated requests made by customers for new products, additional quantities of products, or changes in the prices charged by vendors.

The third distinguishing feature of these decisions is that *they are unique.* Much of the analysis of other routine operating decisions occurs during the planning phase of the management cycle. Such analysis focuses on the actual results of previous periods as a basis for planning the events of current and future periods, for example, ordering goods or selling products. During the performing phase of the management cycle, purchase and sales events are usually so routine that decision making is limited to following procedures like obtaining credit evaluations, setting production levels, or making vendor selection. Because the events that lead to short-term operating decisions are not anticipated when formulating operating plans, planners must consider each short-term operating decision by itself and analyze each in light of the circumstances at the time it arises.

In summary, **short-term operating decisions** are short-run, unanticipated operating decisions that are not included as part of planning in the management cycle. They often arise due to some unique circumstances. Choices involved in short-term operating decisions mean that managers and others who are involved in making such decisions must determine what factors are relevant and then must be able to assess their potential impact.

What Is Decision-Relevant?

Decision-relevant variables are quantities, revenues, or costs that *differ* in one or more choice alternatives. For example, if a business decides to make a new product with plastic parts, it might face the choice of buying the plastic parts or making them internally. Decision-relevant variables include the quantities of the other products that would *not* be produced if the company produces the plastic parts (that is, the difference in the quantity of other products produced as a result of the alternative to produce the plastics parts or the alternative to buy them). The cost of the parts is also decision relevant if it is different for the manufacturing alternative versus the buying alternative. Revenues become decision relevant when the sales price differs across choice alternatives, such as when a product can be sold for a higher price if it is refined more in the production process. Note that further refining makes the product's costs decision relevant because the costs also would differ across alternatives. They would be higher if the business chooses to refine the product.

An economic framework provides a way for decision makers to focus on the facets of a choice that matter, that is, the decision-relevant variables. This makes the decision-making process more efficient because no effort is wasted on variables that cannot affect the outcome. And proper application of the economic framework results in choices that maximize profit. Determining whether something is decision relevant is critical to applying the economic framework for decision making. One way to do this is by asking the question: Is it irrelevant? Let's discuss what we mean by *irrelevant* items first.

Product Aspects That Vary As a rule, aspects of products that vary, but do not have an economic effect on price or quantity, for example, patterns stamped in a sheet of steel, should not be involved in economic decisions. Assume that Worthington has a machine that can drill holes of any single size at a rate of 2,400 holes an hour, and it is considering making two products that sell for the same amount, one with five, 2 mm holes and one with six, 1.5 mm holes. All other production costs (material, labor, etc.) are the same for both products. What factors are relevant in making this choice?

The only relevant factor in this situation is the sixth hole in one of the products. The sixth hole means that Worthington can make 80 fewer units per hour of the six-hole product (2,400/5 holes = 480 and 2,400/6 = 400). If the selling price and customer demand are the same for both, Worthington should choose to make the five-hole product because it can make more of them if demand for the product is high, or use less machine time if demand is below capacity. The capacity of the machine, the other production costs, and the selling prices are irrelevant because they don't vary between the two products. In fact, five holes in each of the products are irrelevant because both products have five holes.

The sizes of the holes vary between the two products, so why are they irrelevant? Because they have no economic effect! Factors that have economic effects affect prices and/or quantities. The sizes of the holes do not affect the quantity or the price (cost) of drilling the holes; therefore, for purposes of economic decision making, the sizes of the holes are irrelevant.

There are other factors involved in short-term operating decisions, like the personal suffering of workers who lose their jobs. Such behavioral factors would be considered by most companies, but they are outside the realm of strictly economic decisions. We discuss some of these factors later in the chapter.

Sunk Costs Are Irrelevant **Sunk costs** are past costs and involve items that have already been purchased, such as buildings and equipment already owned. Sunk costs are costs that do not vary across decision alternatives. They deserve special attention here because many people tend to consider these costs in decision making even though they are irrelevant.[1] Sunk costs are irrelevant because the past cannot be changed; these costs do not vary among currently proposed alternatives.

Let's consider White Freight, a trucking company that hauls steel from a processing plant where it is made into sheets of specific sizes to a fabrication plant where it is made into finished products. Last year White Freight bought six trucks each with a six-ton capacity and paid $75,000 per truck. Over the year, White's business has grown, and now they need more hauling capacity. They are considering replacing the six trucks they purchased last year by buying eight trucks, each with a 10-ton capacity. White Freight expects that revenues from hauling will increase enough to make the decision economically rational. What about the $450,000 ($75,000 × 6) that they paid for trucks just last year? It is a sunk cost, which makes it irrelevant to this decision!

Regardless of whether White chooses to buy the new trucks, run the old ones around the clock, or forgo the potential amount of new business, the amount of money that the company has already spent on the six-ton trucks cannot be changed. The amount that White Freight has paid for the trucks is not relevant, even if the purchase occurred only yesterday. White should only consider events that can occur now and in the future. Thus, the trucks can be part of the decision, if White considers the amount of money that it would receive now by selling the old trucks to help pay for the new trucks. In any economic decision, the amounts that have been spent in the past are not decision relevant, and must be ignored.

What Are Opportunity Costs? We view decision making as a choice among alternatives, such as, choosing whether to buy products to sell or to make them. The set of alternatives available to decision makers from which they can choose the best alternative is known as the **opportunity set.** When one alternative is chosen over another, there is an **opportunity cost** of that alternative, which is the forgone benefits of the next best alternative—the one decision makers would have chosen otherwise. Opportunity costs focus on the present by addressing the question, What are our options now?

To find the opportunity cost of an alternative, determine the expected benefits for each alternative course of action in the opportunity set. White Freight's alternatives were to buy or not to buy the new trucks. The best alternative that was not chosen

---

[1] R. Hoskins, *Journal of Accounting Research* 21, no. 1 (Spring 1983), pp. 78–95.

EXHIBIT 6.1	Choice Alternatives and Opportunity Costs
Alternative	**Opportunity Costs**
1. Keep trucks and continue to haul steel	The proceeds from the sale of the trucks
2. Sell trucks	The net receipts from hauling steel using the trucks
3. Park the trucks and do not haul steel	The net receipts from hauling steel using the trucks

would yield more benefits than any of the remaining alternatives, so we assume that it is the forgone alternative. Thus, it represents the resources given up and its potential benefit represents the chosen alternative's opportunity cost. For White Freight, the opportunity cost of the alternative to keep the old trucks is the amount of profits the company would have earned from the next best alternative—hauling additional freight. In short-term decisions, the idea of an opportunity cost is an important one because these decisions always involve choices among alternatives.

In our trucking example, assume that White Freight had three alternatives regarding *what to do with the trucks it bought last year:* (1) keep the trucks, (2) sell them, or (3) park them and not use them. Each alternative would have an opportunity cost if it were chosen. Exhibit 6.1 shows the alternatives and their opportunity costs. The best alternative to keeping those old trucks was to sell them, so the opportunity cost of keeping them is the amount of proceeds that could have been received if they were sold. If White chose to sell the trucks, the opportunity cost would be the amount of net receipts they could have gotten from hauling steel (cash receipts from hauling less the amounts paid for operating expenses like fuel). In both of these cases, the third option of parking the trucks was not the better alternative of the two unchosen alternatives. Finally, the opportunity costs of parking the trucks would be the net receipts from hauling steel.[2] So, regardless of the choice situation, the opportunity cost of an alternative is the benefit that would have been received if we had chosen the best of the other alternatives.

Economists use the notion of opportunity costs, but calling them *costs* may be misleading. The term *cost*, as it is used in opportunity cost, does not fit the accounting definition of cost given in Chapter 2, which is something that requires the use of business resources. Economists refer to opportunity costs as *costs*, or *sacrifices of resources*, because they are the forgone opportunities. Thus, in a way they are sacrificed resources. However, building upon the basic idea of opportunity costs, we see that opportunity costs are really the benefits that we would have received if we had chosen the next best alternative.

Armed with knowledge of sunk and opportunity costs, and variability of an item having different values across choice alternatives, we can use these ideas to view short-term operating decisions. Next, we discuss an economic structure that is used to analyze short-term operating decisions.

PAUSE & REFLECT

Timing of short-term decisions can be critical. Can you think of circumstances in which opportunity costs become irrelevant? At times, some information that would be useful in making a short-term decision is not available, such as, the lost sales of products if their delivery was delayed. How would you decide whether to try to collect additional information?

Incremental Analysis: Comparing Alternatives

There is a known economic structure of short-term operating decisions to use as a framework in which to examine such decisions. The basis for this economic framework is *incremental analysis*. Incremental analysis answers a simple question: Which alternative in the opportunity set increases profit the most?

---

[2]This is true only because we assumed in our example that the value of the net receipts was higher than the proceeds from selling the old trucks, even when we consider that net receipts will be collected over time instead of immediately as the proceeds from a sale would be.

Unlike finding opportunity costs, incremental analysis focuses on the differences among incremental revenues, costs, and profits of the alternatives considered and does not assign a total value to one alternative based on the comparison. When considering two alternatives of a short-term operating decision, decision makers can assess the potential effect of each alternative on profit. This is the alternative's **incremental profit** which is the difference between the alternative's incremental revenues and incremental costs. **Incremental revenue (incremental cost)** is the change in total revenue (total cost) if the alternative is implemented.

For example, consider two projects whose costs and revenues include the following:

	Total Revenues and Costs		Incremental Profits	
	Project A	**Project B**	**Project A**	**Project B**
Revenue	$500,000	$450,000	$500,000	$450,000
Labor	135,000	135,000	–0–	–0–
Materials	145,000	130,000	145,000	130,000
Shipping and packaging	70,000	60,000	70,000	60,000
Costs	$350,000	$325,000	$215,000	$190,000
Profit	$150,000	$125,000	$285,000	$260,000

The opportunity cost of choosing project A is the forgone profit of project B, $125,000 ($450,000 – $325,000). Incremental analysis focuses on the incremental profits of each alternative, $285,000 for A and $260,000 for B. Since the incremental profit of project A is larger, it should be chosen. Notice that there is no incremental cost for labor. The incremental approach limits the analysis to only those items that differ across alternatives. In more complicated choices, using incremental analysis, that is, only relevant costs and revenues, makes the analysis much simpler.

Some short-term decisions offer choices that only affect costs, for example, whether to make a product or to buy it (the sales price is unaffected). Alternatives for other decisions may affect only revenues, and yet other decisions may involve both costs and revenues. Whatever the alternatives, the rule for making sound economic decisions is: *Choose the alternative with the highest incremental profit.*

Steps in Applying Incremental Analysis   The steps in applying incremental analysis to economic decision making are:

Step 1. Identify the alternative actions.

Step 2. Determine the incremental effect of each alternative on profit:
   a. Find the incremental revenue for each alternative.
   b. Determine the relevant costs for each alternative and calculate the incremental costs for each alternative.
   c. Use the difference between the incremental revenue and the incremental costs for each alternative to find the incremental profit.

Step 3. Choose the alternative that produces the highest incremental profit.

We now elaborate on each of the steps to show some of the issues that might arise in more complicated situations.

Step 1: Identify the Alternative Actions   Any decision situation can be framed as a choice with at least two alternatives. At a minimum, the choice alternatives are to do something different (e.g., make more products, work longer hours, or close a production facility) or to do nothing new (e.g., make no changes). Other situations, like product mix decisions, may offer a large number of alternatives, but the goal is still to choose the best alternative—the one with the highest incremental profit. Regardless of the situation, the first step in decision making using incremental analysis is to decide what the alternatives are.

EXHIBIT | **6.2**

Opportunity Set: Two Independent Choices

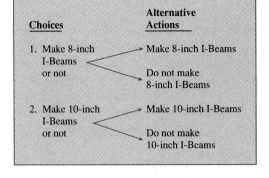

EXHIBIT | **6.3**

Opportunity Set: One Dependent Choice

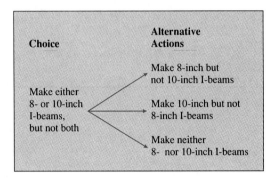

The opportunity set is limited to alternatives that involve costs, revenues, or quantities of either inputs or outputs that may vary across alternatives as a result of implementing an alternative. If Worthington Industries wants to make two products, 8-inch and 10-inch I-beams, and has enough space and a sufficient number of machines and workers to make both, what are its choice alternatives? The company has two separate choices, each with two alternatives (shown in column 1 of Exhibit 6.2). The company can (1) make 8-inch I-beams or not, and/or (2) make 10-inch I-beams or not. These are two separate choices because making one choice does not affect whether Worthington makes the other; that is, Worthington can choose to make or not make both 8-inch and 10-inch I-beams. This is typical of production decisions when businesses have excess productive capacity.

However, if the scenario changes so that Worthington can produce one or the other product, neither product, but not both, what is the choice? There is a single choice with the three alternatives shown in column 2 of Exhibit 6.3. The company can make 8-inch I-beams, make 10-inch I-beams, or make neither, but not both. The difference between this scenario and the previous one is that the products were independent in the previous scenario, so that the decision about whether to produce one did not affect the decision about the other. As soon as the two products become dependent, as they are in Exhibit 6.3, the choice becomes more complicated, with a different set of alternatives, because making both is no longer possible. The complete set of alternatives in a choice situation includes all alternatives where costs, revenues, or quantities differ for at least one other alternative.

Situations where alternatives affect each other mean that some part of the decision is limited or constrained. On the revenue side, demand for the product may be limited, or two products may compete so that sales of one affect sales of the other. Costs may be affected by factors like both alternatives requiring use of the same machine, or having an insufficient amount of skilled labor to produce both products. In production settings where resources like raw labor, materials, or machine time are limited (an economic term for this is *scarce resources*), finding the best alternative is very complicated. In order to do so, engineers and accountants sometimes use *linear programming*, a mathematical technique used in solving such complicated decision problems. (See Appendix 6.)

Step 2: Determine Incremental Effect on Profit

The second step is to find the incremental profit for each alternative. It is easier to view this step as three substeps: finding the incremental revenue, finding the incremental costs, and finding the incremental profit. Subdividing incremental profit into incremental revenue and incremental costs helps in analyzing alternatives.

Finding Incremental Revenue. The new revenue is simply the amount received from selling additional products, such as 8-inch I-beams or 10-inch I-beams. For each product, the alternatives being compared are: (1) selling and (2) not selling. To find the incremental revenue, the decision maker would compare the revenue from selling (a calculated amount) and not selling (zero). For example, if both alternatives include plans to sell 50,000 lineal feet of beams, then the incremental revenue of selling 8-inch beams is $160,000 and for selling 10-inch beams it is $170,000, as shown below:

	8-Inch I-Beams	10-Inch I-Beams
Sales price	$ 3.20	$ 3.40
Quantity (lineal feet)	50,000	50,000
Total revenue	$160,000	$170,000

Since both alternatives involve selling the same quantity, 50,000 lineal feet, quantity is *not* decision relevant. When making choices among alternatives that involve the same quantities, the alternative that produces the highest profit is the same whether the decision maker used unit prices or totals.

When quantities differ across alternatives, they become decision relevant and, thus, must be considered. The incremental revenue is still the additional revenues of each alternative. However, unit price comparisons are inappropriate if quantities differ.

Extending this example, if the alternatives are to sell either 50,000 lineal feet of 8-inch beams or 45,000 feet of 10-inch beams, the incremental revenue is as follows:

	8-Inch I-Beams	10-Inch I-Beams
Sales price	$ 3.20	$ 3.40
Quantity (lineal feet)	50,000	45,000
Total revenue	$160,000	$153,000

Now we must find the total revenue for each alternative rather than just the sales prices. The total revenue from selling the 8-inch beams is $160,000 ($3.20 × 50,000) and total revenue from selling the 10-inch beams is $153,000 ($3.40 × 45,000).

Finding Incremental Cost. Determining the incremental cost is just as important as determining the incremental revenue. Since fixed costs do not differ across alternatives because they do not change in the short run, they can always be ignored. They are the same (fixed) for every alternative. Unit-variable costs like direct labor and raw materials are decision-relevant costs because they can differ across alternatives. Other costs which vary between alternatives, such as machine setup costs are also relevant. Our analysis will focus on costs which vary per unit of product or service.

Continue the I-beam example by assuming that it requires the same amount of direct labor and unit-variable overhead to produce the two products, but 8-inch I-beams use only 80 percent of the amount of direct materials that 10-inch I-beams require. In our example, assume that direct labor is $.35 per lineal foot (labor rates are usually stated in dollars per hour, but that would just complicate our example) and unit-variable overhead is $1.05 per lineal foot. Direct materials cost $.72 for 8-inch I-beams and $.90 for 10-inch I-beams. The costs and revenues per lineal foot would be:

	8-Inch I-Beams	10-Inch I-Beams
Sales price	$3.20	$3.40
Direct materials	$ .72	$ .90
Direct labor	.35	.35
Unit-variable overhead	1.05	1.05
Total variable costs	$2.12	$2.30

Using our original assumption that the quantity of the steel is 50,000 lineal feet in both alternatives, we make our comparison in terms of each lineal foot (unit). The cost per foot for 8-inch I-beams is $2.12 ($.72 + $.35 + $1.05) compared with $2.30 per foot ($.90 + $.35 + $1.05) for 10-inch I-beams. Under the assumption that the quantities differ, the incremental cost for the 8-inch I-beams is $106,000 ($2.12 × 50,000) and for the 10-inch I-beams it is $103,500 ($2.30 × 45,000).

Finding Incremental Profit. Now we can find incremental profit for the two alternatives. Start with the situation where the quantities are equal using the following costs and revenues:

	8-Inch I-Beams	10-Inch I-Beams
Sales price	$ 3.20	$ 3.40
Total variable cost	2.12	2.30
Unit profit	$ 1.08	$ 1.10
Quantity	50,000	50,000
Total incremental profit	$54,000	$55,000

For the 8-inch I-beams, the incremental profit (Sales price – Variable cost) per foot is $1.08 ($3.20 – $2.12), and the incremental profit for 10-inch I-beams is $1.10 ($3.40 – $2.30).

When the quantities are different, incremental profit for the 8-inch I-beams is $54,000 ($1.08 × 50,000 lineal feet) and $49,500 ($1.10 × 45,000 lineal feet) for 10-inch I-beams, as shown in the following table.

	8-Inch I-Beams	10-Inch I-Beams
Sales price	$ 3.20	$ 3.40
Total variable cost	2.12	2.30
Unit profit	$ 1.08	$ 1.10
Quantity	50,000	45,000
Total incremental profit	$54,000	$49,500

Step 3: Choose the Best Alternative If steps 1 and 2 in the decision-making framework are done correctly, the third step is easy and guarantees that you'll make the best choice. The first step ensures that all the alternatives were in the opportunity set and includes only those alternatives that had decision-relevant items. The second step requires finding the incremental profit for each alternative. Now, simply compare the incremental profits and select the alternative that shows the highest profit.

In our example, when we assume that both alternatives involve selling the same number of units, the best choice is to sell the 10-inch I-beams because their incremental profit per foot is $.02 higher when compared to the 8-inch I-beams ($1.10 versus $1.08), and it is positive (greater than zero). So, if we sell 50,000 lineal feet of 10-inch I-beams, the incremental profit for the alternative is $1,000 ($.02 × 50,000).

EXHIBIT	6.4	Applying Incremental Analysis to a Customer's Offer

Incremental Step	Applied to the Steel Sale
1. Identify the alternative actions.	This situation has two alternatives: accept the offer or not.
2. Determine the incremental effect of each on net income.	Choosing to supply the steel to the customer would result in incremental revenue of $10,000, incremental cost of $9,000 (10 tons × $900 per ton), and, therefore, incremental profit of $1,000. Choosing not to supply the steel would generate no incremental revenue, no incremental costs and, thus, no incremental profit.
3. Choose the alternative that produces the highest incremental income.	The economically rational choice is to accept the offer and make the steel bars.

This may not seem like a large amount, but it is economically rational to prefer more profit to less, all other things being equal. When quantities differ, the best choice becomes the 8-inch I-beams, because its incremental profit is $54,000 which is higher than the $49,500 incremental profit of the 10-inch I-beams. As you can see, it is important to consider all of the decision-relevant factors when evaluating alternatives.

We need to be clear about a couple of points. First, choosing to do nothing is almost always an alternative. It is the standard against which all other alternatives are compared. Doing nothing always has an incremental profit of zero, since neither the revenues nor the costs change. In order to be chosen, the incremental profit of an alternative must be greater than zero; that is, the incremental revenues must exceed the incremental costs. Thus, decision makers would choose to take action/choose an alternative only if the incremental profit is greater than doing nothing. If incremental costs were higher than incremental revenues, accepting the alternative would reduce the business's profit, which would make no economic sense.

The second point that needs emphasis deals with comparing mutually exclusive alternatives—those in which only one of the possible alternatives can be chosen. In our example, there were just two alternatives. If we had a third alternative, 9-inch I-beams, we would have to compare each pair of alternatives, 10-inch compared to 8-inch and 9-inch, and 8-inch compared to 9-inch. As you can see, a large complicated decision would require time-consuming analysis. Thus, these situations benefit from using linear programming.

Exhibit 6.4 shows how to apply the steps in our economic framework to the situation in which a customer has offered to pay $10,000 for 10 tons of steel bars that cost $900 a ton to make. As you can see in the exhibit, there would be an incremental profit of $1,000. Therefore, the company should accept the offer and make the steel bars if accepting the offer would not affect things like sales to other customers or the available supply of raw materials, and if the business has the production capacity to produce them. Not all situations are as straightforward as this one. In the remainder of the chapter, we apply this economic framework to four common types of short-term decisions.

PAUSE & REFLECT

We limited the alternatives in the Worthington example to keep it manageable. Can you think of other alternatives that might have been included in the company's opportunity set? What additional information might be useful to determine whether the additional alternatives are viable?

EXHIBIT | 6.5

HEALTH EQUIPMENT COMPANY
Trampoline Cost for Production and Sales of 10,000 Units
At December 31, 1996

	Total	Variable Cost per Unit
Direct material cost	$ 750,000	$ 75
Direct labor cost	400,000	40
Unit-variable overhead cost	600,000	60
Fixed overhead cost	1,250,000	
Total product cost	$3,000,000	
Unit-variable selling cost	$ 250,000	25
Fixed selling cost	1,500,000	
Total period cost	$1,750,000	
Total cost	$4,750,000	

APPLYING THE ECONOMIC FRAMEWORK

Decision makers use the economic framework for making choices to analyze any short-term operating decision. We have chosen four of the most common types of these decisions to examine further—whether to: (1) accept a special order, (2) delete or add a product line, (3) make or buy products to sell, and (4) sell or process products further. (Decisions 3 and 4 are exclusive to manufacturing firms.)

Special Order Decisions

Special order decisions involve an opportunity for a company to accept a customer's offer to buy the company's product for an amount that is less than the normal selling price. In these situations customers also typically offer to buy more than the normal lot size of the product.[3] Management's decision is whether to accept or reject the special order.

Accepting the special order will increase revenues and costs, while rejecting the order would leave revenues and costs unchanged. Qualitative factors to consider include possible customer ill will from rejecting the proposed customer order. For example, if a company rejects a special order from a customer, it risks losing future sales to this customer and, in the long run, can lose other customers if it gets a reputation for being unwilling to negotiate prices on large orders. Ill will also might come from other customers whose orders are delayed if the special order is accepted or from those who receive less favorable prices than the price given to the special order customer.

Example 1: Special Order Decision Health Equipment Company produces and sells trampolines. Exhibit 6.5 shows the costs incurred to produce and sell 10,000 trampolines that sold for $525 each in 1996. Note that fixed overhead and selling costs are not calculated on a unit basis because these do not vary with the level of production.

It is now 1997, and Health Equipment has received a special order from Fitness Center, Inc., for 5,000 trampolines at $300 per trampoline. Health Equipment Company has the capacity to produce the 5,000 trampolines without increasing its fixed production costs, such as supervision and building space. Unit-variable selling costs do not apply to this order, as we show subsequently, but Health Equipment Company will incur additional shipping costs of $10 per unit. Assuming that production and sale of the special order does not interfere with normal production and sales, should Health Equipment Company accept the order from Fitness Center, Inc., at a selling price that is $225 below the normal selling price of $525 per unit?

We can apply the three steps of our economic framework to structure and solve this decision problem. The first step is to identify the alternative actions: to accept the offer and sell the product, or reject the offer.

---

[3]As we discuss these short-term decisions, we will use the term *product* to mean either a physical product like trampolines, or a service like legal or accounting services. We present examples of services in subsequent sections of this chapter.

The second step is to find the incremental profit. In order to do this, it is necessary to compare the decision-relevant revenues and costs of accepting the offer against zero, because not accepting the offer would affect neither revenues nor costs. We show the relevant incremental revenues and costs for this decision below:

	Alternatives	
Relevant Factors	**Accept the Offer**	**Reject the Offer**
Revenue (5,000 × $300)	$1,500,000	$–0–
Costs:		
Direct material (5,000 × $75) Exhibit 6.5	$ 375,000	–0–
Direct labor (5,000 × $40) Exhibit 6.5	200,000	–0–
Unit-variable overhead (5,000 × $60) Exhibit 6.5	300,000	–0–
Shipping costs (5,000 × $10)	50,000	–0–
Total costs	$ 925,000	–0–
Incremental profit	$ 575,000	$–0–

Notice that we did not include fixed overhead and fixed selling and administrative costs in the analysis because fixed costs do not change in the short run. That is, these fixed costs do not change if Health Equipment Company accepts the special order, therefore, they are not decision-relevant. We include the $10 per unit shipping costs that are part of the $25 unit-variable selling costs. However, we exclude the other $15 of unit-variable selling costs from the analysis because these costs will not be incurred for the units sold to Fitness Center, Inc., because Health Equipment will incur no additional selling costs due to this order. Only the costs that differ due to producing and selling the special order are relevant to the analysis.

The final step is to choose the decision with the highest incremental profit. Here, Health Equipment Company should *select the alternative with the higher incremental profit*. Because the decision to sell to Fitness Center would result in an increase of $575,000 in profit, it should accept the special order.

PAUSE & REFLECT | What qualitative information in addition to customer ill will should Health Equipment Company consider in the decision to accept or reject the special order?

Example 2: Special Order Decision Service firms also face special order decisions, though the number of relevant costs and revenues is typically limited to a few. For example, the law firm of Brooks, Sells, and Haldeman (BSH) normally charges clients $150 per hour for legal services. Recently a client approached BSH with a high-profile lawsuit. The client wants BSH to represent him for $80 per hour. BSH expects the case to take approximately 1,250 hours at a cost to the firm of $62,500, or $50 per hour. Should BSH accept this client?

As in the earlier case of the special order decision, the alternatives are to accept the order or to reject it. To find the incremental profit of accepting the special order, first find the incremental revenue generated from representing the client as opposed to turning down the offer. This amount is $100,000 ($80 × 1,250 hours) versus zero. The incremental cost is $62,500 (versus zero), so the incremental profit is $37,500 ($100,000 – $62,500). Therefore, BSH should accept the client.

In most short-run decisions, there are qualitative factors that are also important to consider. For example, the reputation of BSH would be affected, depending on whether it won or lost the case, or BSH might have to turn away other clients if the case takes more time than anticipated. So, for special order decisions, the economically sound decision rule is: Accept a special order if the additional revenue generated is greater than the additional costs incurred. However, it also is a good idea to consider other noneconomic factors as part of making such decisions.

EXHIBIT	6.6

JASON ENTERPRISES
Income Statement
For the Period Ending December 31, 1997

	Type of Coffee		
	Regular	Special Ground	Premium Ground
Sales (cases)	5,000	4,000	6,000
Sales in dollars	$355,000	$332,000	$786,000
Variable cost of sales	213,000	215,800	550,200
Variable selling cost	35,500	39,840	117,900
Fixed administrative cost (divided equally)	$100,000	$100,000	$100,000
Profit	$ 6,500	$(23,640)	$ 17,900

Deletion or Addition of Product Lines

The decision to delete a product line deals with whether to delete a particular product line that is not as profitable as expected, while addition of a product line focuses on whether it would be profitable to add a product line. Sometimes these decisions are combined as one product is added to replace another product that is being deleted. These types of short-run decisions, like the other decisions illustrated in the chapter, do not involve a change in physical capacity. Deleting a product line *and selling all the related production equipment and facilities* is an investment decision, which is long run in nature since it assumes that productive capacity changes. Adding a product line by purchasing the necessary additional productive capacity is also a long-run investment decision. We'll address the decision to delete a product line first.

Example 1: Deletion of a Product Line   Jason Enterprises currently sells three brands of coffee—regular roast, special ground roast, and premium ground roast. Exhibit 6.6 shows the operating results from the last period (December 1997) by product line. The fixed administrative cost of $300,000 is allocated equally to each product line. As shown in the exhibit, the special ground roast product line shows a net loss of $23,640. Should Jason Enterprises delete the special roast product line since it does not appear to contribute to the profits of the firm?

These kinds of decisions should not be made without analysis. It is important in such situations to consider factors such as whether customers who buy regular and premium also want special roast coffee available and might go elsewhere if it were deleted. So, the set of alternatives here is not as well defined as in the case of special order decisions. Let's assume that Jason Enterprises has limited the decision to the alternatives of eliminating the special roast or not.

We find the incremental profit for each alternative: having two products (regular and premium ground) and having all three product lines.

	Alternatives	
Relevant Factors	**Regular and Premium***	**All Three Products—Regular, Special Roast, and Premium†**
Revenue	$1,141,000	$1,473,000
Costs:		
Variable cost of sales	763,200	979,000
Variable selling costs	153,400	193,240
Incremental profit	$ 224,400	$ 300,760

*Adding the regular and premium columns in Exhibit 6.6.

†Adding all three columns in Exhibit 6.6.

Notice that the fixed administrative costs are not included in the decision because they do not differ across alternatives, therefore, they are irrelevant to the decision. Applying the final step in the analysis indicates that the product line should not be dropped because the incremental profit of all three products is higher than having just regular and premium. Thus, the total profit of the company will decline by $76,360 ($300,760 – $224,000) if Jason drops the special line.

When contemplating a deletion, the decision rule is to delete a product if it has negative incremental profit or if it is possible to replace it with a product with higher incremental profit.[4]

PAUSE & REFLECT   What qualitative information in addition to customer ill will should Jason Enterprises consider in making the decision about whether to delete a product line?

Example 2: Addition of a Product Line   Now we will turn to the topic of adding a product line. Baker and Baker, CPAs, currently offer tax and auditing services. The contribution margin generated by auditing is $100 per hour, while the contribution margin generated by tax services is $75 per hour. The firm allocates common costs, such as personnel administration, payroll, and liability insurance, equally between the tax and auditing departments. Baker and Baker's profits are:

	Departments		
	Tax	**Audit**	**Total**
Contribution margin	$144,000	$200,000	$344,000
Allocated common costs	75,000	75,000	150,000
Profit	$ 69,000	$125,000	$194,000

The firm is considering expansion into management consulting services. The partners estimate that the incremental profit from management consulting services would be $30 per hour during the current period for an estimated 1,500 hours of services. The firm also must incur common costs such as personnel administration or payroll that are not directly associated with providing any of the services. Allocating these costs to each of the service areas means that the sum of the profits for the services equals the profit for the firm as a whole. Baker and Baker would allocate firm costs equally among the three services: tax, auditing, and consulting. The following analysis shows the anticipated profit of each service line if Baker and Baker adds management consulting to its current practice.

	Alternatives	
Relevant Factors	**Tax and Audit**	**All Three Services—Tax, Audit, Management Consulting**
Total contribution margin	$344,000	$389,000
Other relevant costs	–0–	–0–
Incremental profit	$344,000	$389,000

To determine the incremental profits of tax and auditing it is necessary to compare the alternatives of having them and not having them (zero revenues and costs). The allocated costs will exist regardless of whether Baker and Baker offers

---

[4]The possibility of replacing a product line with another or expanding one of the other two lines could have been part of the analysis, but was not considered necessary for illustrative purposes here.

management consulting services; thus, they are irrelevant because they are the same in both alternatives. Note that allocated costs like payroll can become decision relevant if they actually change for one or more alternative actions. So, if the firm had to hire an additional clerk to handle payroll, that would make payroll cost decision-relevant because it would differ across alternatives.

We can see that Baker and Baker should add consulting because this alternative would result in a total firm profit increase of $45,000 ($389,000 − $344,000). This decision includes the assumption that the other two services remain and that there are no additional firm costs due to adding the management consulting service to the practice. The decision rule for an addition of a product line is to add a product line only if it has a positive incremental profit.

Special order decisions and decisions to either add or delete a product line are made in any company that creates or sells a product whether that product is a good or a service. Next we address two decisions only associated with manufacturing firms.

Short-Term Operating Decisions in Manufacturing Organizations

Manufacturing organizations encounter two additional short-term operating decisions associated with production. These decisions are commonly called *make-or-buy decisions* and *sell-or-process-further decisions*. Both decisions involve an assessment of how much effort and cost a company should put into producing a product.

Make-or-Buy Decisions   In **make-or-buy decisions,** manufacturers face the alternatives of making a product or component or buying it from an outside supplier. Making the product internally results in increases in production costs. If management decides to purchase the product from an outside supplier, there is an increase in purchasing costs.

In addition, management must consider the effects of some qualitative (noneconomic) factors like the quality of the product, the reliability of the supplier, the return policy of the supplier, and employee morale. What if the firm decided to use an outside supplier and that supplier proved to be unreliable? Production could be slowed and sales to customers lost as a result. While none of these "noneconomic" factors has direct impact on the immediate decision, each has significant potential economic impact in the future. So, considering qualitative factors has to be part of making any short-term decision.

Example: Make-or-Buy Decision   HD Corporation manufactures and sells motorcycles to dealers throughout the country. A recent report on the cost to produce its most popular model of motorcycle is shown below.

Cost Categories	Costs per Motorcycle
Direct materials	$1,500
Direct labor	1,200
Unit-variable overhead	800
Fixed overhead	2,000

These costs are based on a production level of 12,000 motorcycles per period. Recently, HD Corporation received an offer from California Motors Corporation for California to supply all the motorcycle engines HD Corporation needs for $1,900 per engine. If HD Corporation accepts this offer, it estimates reductions in direct materials, direct labor, and unit-variable overhead costs per motorcycle of 50 percent, 60 percent, and 20 percent, respectively. Should HD Corporation buy the engines from California Motors?

To answer this question, HD Corporation must find the incremental profit for the two alternatives—to make the engines or buy them. The relevant revenues and costs of the two alternatives are:

Relevant Factors	Alternatives	
	Make	Buy
Revenues	$ 0	$ 0
Costs:		
Direct material costs	$ 1,500	$750 (50%)
Direct labor cost	1,200	480 (40%)
Unit-variable overhead cost	800	640 (80%)
Purchase price of new engines	0	1,900
Incremental profit	$(3,500)	$(3,770)

This analysis indicates that HD Corporation should *not* buy the engines from California Motors Corporation. The difference in cost between the alternatives is $270 ($3,770 – $3,500) per motorcycle in favor of making the engine internally rather than buying it from California Motors Corporation. Fixed overhead costs are not relevant to the make-or-buy decision because they will not change if the HD Corporation purchases engines from California Motors Corporation.

Let's consider another scenario. Assume that HD Corporation buys the engines from California Motors Corporation, and, as a result, the facilities that are no longer required for production can be used to produce a motor scooter that will generate incremental profit of $4,000,000 per year.

Assuming production of 12,000 motorcycles per year, the opportunity cost per engine is about $333 ($4,000,000/12,000 = $333.33). Recall that an *opportunity* cost is the benefit forgone by accepting an alternative. The $333 incremental profit per engine that could be earned from producing the scooters is the opportunity cost of choosing the alternative to make the engine. That is, the incremental profit from the motor scooters can *only* be obtained if HD Corporation purchases the motorcycle engines from California Motors Corporation. If HD Corporation continues to make the engines, it forgoes this incremental profit from the motor scooters.

Now, the opportunity cost of producing the scooters is decision relevant because it differs between alternatives. The incremental cost of the buy alternative ($3,770) per year is less than the incremental cost of the make alternative due to the opportunity cost of being able to make scooters when HD purchases the engines ($3,500 plus $333 opportunity costs).[5] Now the decision between the make and buy alternatives is in favor of HD Corporation buying the engines from California Motors Corporation.

PAUSE & REFLECT | **What qualitative factors should HD Corporation consider when deciding whether to make or buy the engines? Are there any ethical issues involved in this decision?**

Sell-or-Process-Further Decisions **Sell-or-process-further-decisions** are choices between selling a product after an early stage of production or processing it more and selling it after a later production stage. Management must determine whether the incremental revenue is greater than the incremental cost of selling at an earlier or later production stage for these types of decisions. The incremental revenue is the additional revenue per unit if the product is sold *after* it has been processed further, and the incremental costs are the additional costs incurred in processing the product further.

Manufacturers who face sell-or-process-further decisions often operate production processes that result in two or more separately identifiable products called **joint products.** An example of a joint product occurs when gasoline and motor oil are refined from the same crude oil. The point in the production process where there is

---

[5]We can either subtract the incremental income from the scooters as a cost savings in the buy alternative, or add it as an additional cost to the make alternative.

identification of separate saleable products is known as the **split-off point.** The production costs incurred in production up to the split-off point are called **joint costs**. These joint costs cannot be associated specifically with any product because the products are not separately identifiable at the point where the costs were incurred.

Example: Sell or Process Further   ChemCo, Inc., produces three chemicals (A, B, and C) from a joint process. The joint costs incurred to the split-off point total $50,000, which are allocated across products based on some predetermined basis. Though allocating joint costs to products is required for financial reporting, it can mislead decision makers because joint costs are sunk and, thus, irrelevant to the decision. In this example, if each chemical is processed further before being sold, the following additional sales revenue, additional processing costs, and incremental profit result for each product.

Chemical	Incremental Sales Revenue	−	Additional Processing Costs	=	Incremental Profit
A	$132,500		$110,000		$22,500
B	165,000		150,000		15,000
C	88,000		60,000		28,000

ChemCo's alternatives are to sell chemical A and chemical C at the split-off point for $21,000 and $30,000, respectively. Should ChemCo sell chemical A and/or chemical C at the split-off point, or should the company process them further before it sells them? Here are the calculations for the incremental profit for each alternative.

	Alternative	
Relevant Factors	Sell at the Split-Off Point	Process Further
Chemical A		
Revenue	$21,000	$132,500
Costs of further processing	0	110,000
Incremental profit	$21,000	$ 22,500
Chemical C		
Revenue	$30,000	$ 88,000
Costs of further processing	0	60,000
Incremental profit	$30,000	$ 28,000

Notice that the joint production costs are not included in the decision because they are sunk costs. The incremental profit if chemical A is sold after processing further is $22,500. Since this exceeds the profit available at split-off ($21,000) by $1,500, the company should process chemical A further before it sells chemical A. The incremental profit resulting if chemical C is processed further is $28,000. This is less than the profit at the split-off point ($30,000), so chemical C should be sold at its split-off point. In general, the decision rule for a sell-or-process-further decision is: *Sell the product after further processing if the incremental profit due to further processing is greater than the incremental profit at the split-off point.*

We've seen how the economic framework applies to four common types of short-term decisions: (1) special orders, (2) adding or deleting product lines, (3) make-or-buy products or component parts, and (4) sell or process further. Though each type of decision differs in form, the overriding rule for each is to choose the alternative with the highest incremental profit. The basic consideration in each of these short-term decisions is the change in revenue and costs resulting from the alternative courses of action. Costs that do not change as a result of a course of action are not relevant in evaluating that alternative. For all short-term decisions, companies should investigate and consider both quantitative and qualitative factors.

SUMMARY

Adapting to changes in circumstances that occur after a company's planning process has occurred is essential to effective management. In order to be as profitable as possible, management must be receptive and able to analyze a variety of short-term operating decisions. The economic framework in this chapter sets out three steps that help structure short-term operating decisions so that managers can choose alternatives that make their business more profitable.

- Short-term operating decisions involve management choosing one alternative action from two or more possible actions. These actions are important because they are opportunities for the business to be more profitable. Comparisons should focus only on decision-relevant items that differ across alternatives in the opportunity set.

- Choices are economically sound when they are made within an economic framework that includes three steps: (1) identify the alternatives, (2) find the incremental profit for each alternative, and (3) select the alternative with the highest incremental profit.

- Service, merchandising, and manufacturing firms must make decisions about whether to accept or reject special orders offered by customers. Special orders may involve a customer's offer to buy more than a normal lot and/or to pay less than the normal price.

- Service, merchandising, and manufacturing firms face decisions about whether to delete or add a product line. Sometimes these decisions are combined as one product is added to replace another product that is being deleted.

- Manufacturing firms decide whether to make products or buy them from outside suppliers. They also must decide whether to sell a product at an intermediate production stage or process it further. The costs incurred up to the point where separate products are identified are known as *joint costs* that cannot be associated with any product components, and they are irrelevant in the decision about whether to process further.

KEY TERMS

constraints (Appendix) Functions stating the limits on scarce resources available

decision-relevant variables Quantities, revenues, or costs that differ in one or more choice alternatives

incremental cost The change in total cost if an alternative is implemented

incremental profit The difference between an alternative's incremental revenues and incremental costs

incremental revenue The change in total revenue if an alternative is implemented

joint costs Costs that cannot be associated specifically with any product because the products are not separately identifiable at the point where the costs were incurred

joint products Two or more separately identifiable products that result from a common production process

linear programming (Appendix) A mathematical tool used to solve complex scarce resources situations to determine optimal output given the existing constraints in the situation

make-or-buy decisions The choice between making a product or component or buying it from an outside supplier

objective function (Appendix) The profit goal

opportunity cost The forgone benefits of the next best alternative in the set of available alternatives to decision makers

opportunity set The set of alternatives available to decision makers from which they can choose the best alternative

sell-or-process-further decisions Choices between selling a product after an early stage in production or processing it more and selling it after a later production stage

short-term operating decisions Short-run unanticipated operating decisions not included as part of management's planning cycle

special order decisions The opportunity for a company to accept a customer's offer to buy the company's product for an amount which is less than the normal selling price

split-off point The point in the production process where there is identification of separate, saleable products

sunk costs A set of costs that do not vary across decision alternatives; past costs associated with items already purchased

---

APPENDIX 6

LINEAR PROGRAMMING: Helping Solve Complex Choices

Managers can solve simple choices with only two independent alternatives without sophisticated mathematical techniques by simply finding the alternative with the higher incremental profit. However, many problems involve too many alternatives, which are often dependent on one another. For example, consider a production facility that makes 20 or 30 products with the same machines and production workers. How do you determine the quantity of each product to make that will result in the highest profit? Or consider a department store that needs to decide how to allocate its floor space to the various departments to maximize profit.

When management faces these decisions where constraints, or limits, exist that affect more than one input into the purchasing, producing, or distributing process, it is possible to use a technique called **linear programming.** Linear programming is a mathematical tool used to solve complex scarce resource situations to determine the optimal output given the existing **constraints,** or the limits on scarce resources available. Under conditions involving a limited number of product and resource constraints, linear programming situations can be solved easily using only a calculator. However, for more complex situations involving multiple products and/or multiple constraints, it is necessary to use a computer program.

There are many computer programs available to solve linear programming problems. Each program is slightly different, but the key to understanding any computer program is to understand the basics of linear programming. We will therefore focus on simple linear programming problems.

Assume that Iman Cosmetics has decided to produce and distribute only two products, a cosmetics kit and a skin care kit. The proposed selling prices and unit-variable costs of the two products are shown below:

Facial Product Factors	Cosmetics Kit	Skin Care Kit
Selling price	$25	$35
Unit-variable cost	15	20
Contribution margin per kit	$10	$15

Further assume that Iman Cosmetics faces no sales constraints, but that it has two inputs: labor and machine time. Also assume that these inputs are constrained, which means there is an upper limit on the amount of the input. Labor time is limited to 20,000 minutes per production period, and machine time is limited to 15,000 minutes per production period. The time requirements for each kit are:

	Cosmetics Kit	Skin Care Kit
Labor time required	10 minutes	8 minutes
Machine time required	5 minutes	10 minutes

Mathematical Solution

Solving a linear programming problem is accomplished by expressing the relevant variables in the situation in terms of mathematical functions and solving for the optimal solution. In this case, the relevant variables are those that differ between the two products: selling price, product costs, and labor and machine time. To determine what the optimal solution is, the company must have a goal. For a profit-seeking company, the goal is often stated in terms of maximizing the contribution margin of the firm or minimizing the costs of the firm. The profit goal is called the **objective function.** However, the goal of the company is subject to the limited amounts of scarce resources available. The functions stating the limits on scarce resources are called *constraint functions.* The linear programming problem can be solved by accomplishing the following steps:

1. State the objective function (profit goal).

2. State the constraints (limits on scarce resources).

3. Solve the constraint functions.

4. Determine the optimal solution.

Step 1: State the Objective Function

Iman Cosmetics has two products, a cosmetics kit and a skin care kit. We know that the contribution margin of a cosmetics kit is $10 and the contribution margin of a skin care kit is $15. The goal of the company is to *maximize the contribution margin of the firm*, and the objective function is stated as:

$$MAX\ (CM)(CK) + (CM)(SCK)$$

where:

CM = Contribution margin per unit for each product

CK = Number of cosmetics kits produced and sold

SCK = Number of skin care kits produced and sold

So, in our example, the objective function is:

$$MAX\ 10CK + 15SCK$$

Step 2: State the Constraints

Iman Cosmetics faces constraints, or upper limits, on the amount of the inputs to the production process: labor time (LT) and machine time (MT). The most labor time available is 20,000 minutes per period, and the maximum amount of machine time available is 15,000 minutes per period. Multiplying the rate at which each product uses an input—for example, cosmetic kits require 10 minutes of labor per kit—times the number of units (cosmetic kits), gives the amount of input required for that product, which is the number of minutes required to make cosmetic kits. By adding the amount of an input required for each product and by stating that this total cannot exceed the maximum amount of input available, we can state the following constraint functions:[6]

$$LT:\ 10CK + 8SCK \leq 20,000\ \text{minutes}$$

$$MT:\ 5CK + 10SCK \leq 15,000\ \text{minutes}$$

So, for minutes of labor time, add the minutes of labor to make the cosmetic kits (10 minutes times the number of cosmetic kits, CK) and the labor for skin care kits (8 minutes times the number of skin care kits, SCK). The maximum minutes of labor that can be used is the constraint, or 20,000 minutes.

Step 3: Solve the Constraint Functions

To solve the constraint functions, we must solve each constraint for production of only one product. Then it is necessary to combine the constraint functions to solve for a product mix solution.

---

[6]There are two other constraints that are necessary when performing linear programming using a computer. These constraints are necessary to prevent a negative solution. For manual calculations, these constraints are inferred but often not stated. In our example, they are $CK \geq 0$ and $SCK \geq 0$.

Solving the Labor Time Constraint

Assuming that *only cosmetics kits will be sold* and that the entire 20,000 labor minutes are available, the solution is:

$$10CK + 8\,(0) = 20{,}000$$
$$CK = 2{,}000 \text{ (Solution A)}$$

This means that if zero skin care kits are sold, there is enough labor time available to distribute 2,000 cosmetics kits.

Assuming that *only skin care kits will be sold* and that the entire 20,000 labor minutes are available, the solution is:

$$10\,(0) + 8SCK = 20{,}000$$
$$SCK = 2{,}500 \text{ (Solution B)}$$

Thus, if zero cosmetics kits are sold, there is enough labor time available to distribute 2,500 skin care kits.

Solving the Machine Time Constraint

Assuming that *only cosmetics kits will be sold* and that the entire 15,000 machine minutes are available, the solution is:

$$5CK + 10\,(0) = 15{,}000$$
$$CK = 3{,}000 \text{ (Solution C)}$$

If zero skin care kits are sold, there is enough machine time available to distribute 3,000 cosmetics kits.

Assuming that *only skin care kits will be sold* and that the entire 15,000 machine minutes are available, the solution is:

$$5\,(0) + 10SCK = 15{,}000$$
$$SCK = 1{,}500 \text{ (Solution D)}$$

Thus, if zero cosmetics kits are sold, there is enough machine time available to distribute 1,500 skin care kits.

Solving the Combined Constraint

To solve two equations with two unknowns, we use *simultaneous solutions*. The first step in solving simultaneous solutions is to eliminate one of the unknown variables and then subtract one equation from another. Examine the two constraint functions for Iman Cosmetics Company.

$$10CK + 8SCK = 20{,}000$$
$$5CK + 10SCK = 15{,}000$$

To eliminate either the *CK* or *SCK* variable from the analysis, we can make the term for one of the products the same in both equations, then subtract one constraint equation from the other. The variable for cosmetic kits (*CK*) will be easiest to eliminate since 10 is a multiple of 5. Therefore, *every variable in the second equation is multiplied by 2*. The machine time constraint from $5CK + 10SCK = 15{,}000$, therefore, becomes:

$$10CK + 20SCK = 30{,}000$$

The next step is to subtract one equation from the other to solve for the remaining variable, which is skin care kits, in this case.

$$10CK + 20SCK = 30{,}000$$
$$\underline{-(10CK + 8SCK = 20{,}000)}$$
$$12SCK = 10{,}000$$
$$SCK = 833.33 \text{ (Solution E)}$$

Assuming no fractional distribution, 833 skin care kits will be distributed. To determine how many cosmetics kits to distribute, simply insert the number of skin care kits (Solution E) into either original function and solve for the other variable, which we do not know, *CK*.

EXHIBIT 6.7 | Linear Programming Solutions for Iman

Solution	Cosmetics Kits Distributed	Skin Care Kits Distributed	Contribution Margin
Only cosmetics kits	2,000 (Solution A)[a]	–0–	$20,000[b]
Only skin care kits	–0–	1,500 (Solution D)[c]	$22,500[d]
Both kits	1,333 (Solution F)	833 (Solution E)	$25,825[e]

[a]Select 2,000 versus 3,000 (Solution C) because there is insufficient labor time available to distribute 3,000 kits (although there *is* enough machine time available to do so.)

[b]2,000 × $10 = $20,000

[c]Select 1,500 kits versus 2,500 (Solution B) because there is not enough time available to distribute 2,500 kits—only 1,500 (although there is enough labor time available to do so).

[d]1,500 × $15 = $22,500.

[e](1,333 × $10) + (833 × $15) = $25,825.

$$10CK + 8 (833) = 20,000$$
$$10CK + 6,664 = 20,000$$
$$10CK = 13,336$$
$$CK = 1,333.6 \text{ (Solution F)}$$

Again assuming no fractional distribution, if 833 skin care kits are distributed, 1,333 cosmetics kits can be distributed with the available time. (Notice that distribution of 1,334 cosmetics kits will use more time than is presently available.) In other words, we solved the constraints to find the amount of skin care kits we could sell, then went back to see how many cosmetics kits could be distributed with the remaining time.

Step 4: Determine the Optimal Solution

There are three possible solutions to this linear programming problem. Iman cosmetics can (1) distribute *only* cosmetics kits, (2) distribute *only* skin care kits, or (3) distribute *both* cosmetics and skin care kits, as Exhibit 6.7 shows. The optimal solution is the one that produces the *highest contribution margin for the company.*

Distribute Only Cosmetics Kits

Refer to the solution illustrated in Exhibit 6.7 for only cosmetics kits. If no skin care kits are sold, there is enough labor time available to distribute 2,000 cosmetics kits (Solution A). If no skin care kits are sold, there is enough machine time available to distribute 3,000 cosmetics kits (Solution C). Are both of these solutions possible? There is enough machine time available for 3,000 cosmetics kits, but is there enough labor time available for 3,000 cosmetics kits? No, there is only enough labor time available for 2,000 cosmetics kits; therefore, the maximum number of cosmetics kits that can be distributed is 2,000 due to the labor time available. *Labor time is a binding constraint for cosmetics kit distribution.* Thus, the first possible solution (Solution A) is to distribute 2,000 cosmetics kits and zero skin care kits.

Distribute Only Skin Care Kits

Refer to the solution shown in Exhibit 6.7 for only skin care kits. If no cosmetics kits are sold, there is enough labor time available to distribute 2,500 skin care kits (Solution B). If no cosmetics kits are sold, there is enough machine time available to distribute 1,500 skin care kits (Solution D). Are both of these solutions possible? There is enough labor time available for 2,500 skin care kits, but is there enough machine time available for 2,500 skin care kits? No, there is only enough machine time available for 1,500 skin care kits. Therefore, the maximum number of skin care kits that can be distributed is 1,500 due to the machine time available. *Machine time is a binding constraint for skin care kit distribution.* Thus, the second possible solution (Solution D) is to distribute 1,500 skin care kits and zero cosmetics kits.

EXHIBIT | **6.8**

Linear Programming Graph

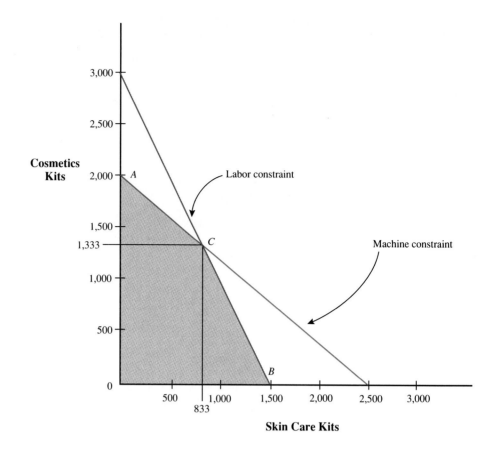

Distribute Both Cosmetics and Skin Care Kits

Refer to the simultaneous solution to produce and sell both kits presented in Exhibit 6.7. We found that 833 skin care kits (Solution E) and 1,333 cosmetics kits (Solution F) can be distributed given the constraints on both labor and machine time. Thus, the final possible solution is to distribute 833 skin care and 1,333 cosmetics kits.

Optimal Solution

The optimal solution is the one possible solution that produces the highest total contribution margin. Therefore, the optimal solution meets the objective function. Recall that the objective function is:

$$MAX\ 10CK + 15SCK$$

Exhibit 6.7 shows the three possible solutions and the contribution margin generated by each. If 2,000 cosmetics kits and no skin care kits are distributed (line 1), the total contribution margin generated is $20,000. If 1,500 skin care kits and no cosmetics kits are distributed (line 2), the total contribution margin generated is $22,500. If 1,333 cosmetics kits and 833 skin care kits are distributed, the total contribution margin generated is $25,825. Therefore, the optimal solution is to distribute 1,333 cosmetics kits and 833 skin care kits, since it provides Iman with the highest total contribution margin. Once again, remember the solution assumes that the demand for one product is independent of the other product's demand.

We present the linear programming problem graphically in Exhibit 6.8. Cosmetics kits are represented on the Y-axis, and skin care kits are shown on the X-axis. The lines connecting the Y- and X-axes represent the labor and machine hours constraints, respectively. The shaded area represents the feasible solutions; that is, any combination production level for each product that falls within this area is possible. The optimal solution, however, is located on the outer limits of the feasible area at either point A, point B, or point C. We analyze these three points to determine which produces the highest total contribution margin. In this case, point C, which represents 1,333 cosmetics kits and 833 skin care kits, is the optimal solution because it is furthest from zero. Whether you use mathematical or graphical solutions, the answer should be the same; however, complicated problems with more than two inputs are difficult to graph.

QUESTIONS

1. Explain how nonrecurring operating decisions differ from operating decisions that impact the master budget.

2. Explain the concept of being decision relevant.

3. Explain the concept of sunk cost. Are sunk costs ever relevant in decision making? Why or why not?

4. Explain the concept of opportunity cost. Are opportunity costs ever relevant in decision making? Why or why not?

5. Explain the concept of incremental analysis. When is an incremental analysis done? Why?

6. What is a special order decision? What costs are relevant in a special order decision?

7. What factors other than costs and revenues must be considered when making a special order decision?

8. What are the relevant costs when deciding whether to add a product line or delete an existing product line?

9. What factors other than costs and revenues must be considered when deciding whether to add product line or delete an existing product line?

10. What is a make-or-buy decision? What are the relevant costs when making a make-or-buy decision?

11. How are opportunity costs incorporated into make-or-buy decisions?

12. What factors other than costs and revenues must companies consider when making a make-or-buy decision?

13. What is a sell-or-process-further decision? What costs must be considered when making a sell-or-process-further decision?

14. Explain the concept of a split-off point in a sell-or-process-further decision.

15. How is the concept of sunk cost used in a sell-or-process-further decision?

16. What factors other than costs and revenues should firms consider when making a sell-or-process-further decision?

Appendix

17. Explain the concept of an objective function. How is it used in linear programming?

18. Explain the concept of a constraint function. How is it used in linear programming?

19. Explain the concept of optimal solution. How is it determined in linear programming?

EXERCISES

E 6.1   Ben Franklin Clock Company produces and sells quality wooden wall clocks that are priced at $340 each. Ben Franklin has just received a request for a special order of 1,000 clocks at a selling price of $250. The current cost to produce a clock is $260 (direct materials, $100; direct labor, $80; unit-variable overhead, $50; and fixed overhead, $30). Ben Franklin has the capacity to produce the special order without affecting current production and sales. Should Ben Franklin accept the order? Why or why not?

E 6.2   Georgio's Catering Company has received an offer from a client for a large party next month. The client has requested service (food, drinks, etc.) for 500 people at $75 per person. Georgio's normally charges $125 per person for catering services. Assuming that fixed costs will not change if Georgio's accepts the order and that variable costs are $70 per person, should Georgio's accept the offer? Why or why not? What qualitative factors should be considered?

E 6.3   Arnold Company sells motor oil by the case to automobile repair shops and dealerships. Each case of oil costs Arnold $12. The variable selling costs are $1 per case and the fixed costs are $150,000 per period. Each period, Arnold sells approximately 100,000 cases of motor oil at $20 per case. California Classic Cars is requesting an order of 10,000 cases of motor oil in the next period at a price of $15 per case. Since Arnold has no excess capacity, accepting this order means that Arnold can sell only 90,000 cases of motor oil through normal channels. Should Arnold accept this offer? Why or why not?

E 6.4 Montana Outfitters sells three products which appear on the partial income statement shown below. Item B consistently exhibits a net loss. Should Montana delete it from the product line? What about item C? What will happen to the firm costs if Montana eliminates one, or both, of these items? What qualitative factors should the company consider?

	Item A	Item B	Item C
Sales	$10,000	$12,000	$8,000
Cost of sales	6,000	10,000	5,000
Gross margin	$ 4,000	$ 2,000	$3,000
Firm costs*	3,000	3,000	3,000
Net income	$ 1,000	$(1,000)	$ –0–

*Total cost $9,000 divided equally among the products.

E 6.5 Fert-a-lawn Company currently offers three types of lawn care service to its customers: full service, complete service, and partial service. The revenue and costs of each of these services is shown below.

	Full	Complete	Partial
Revenue	$ 60,000	$72,000	$48,000
Cost of service	42,000	43,200	24,000
Gross margin	$ 18,000	$28,800	$24,000
Corporate cost	20,000	20,000	20,000
Net income	$(2,000)	$ 8,800	$ 4,000

The owner wants to discontinue both the full and the partial service and concentrate solely on the complete service line. Is this a good strategy? Why or why not?

E 6.6 Colorado, Inc., manufactures downhill and cross country skis. Although downhill skis are selling very well, sales of cross country skis are declining, and Colorado is considering whether to discontinue manufacturing this product line. A profit report for cross country skis for the most recent period is given below:

Revenue	$85,000
Less variable costs	39,000
Contribution margin	$46,000
Less fixed company costs	58,000
Operating profit	($12,000)

The fixed costs are allocated to the products based on the number of units sold. Sales of downhill skis will not be affected by the discontinuance of cross country skis. Should Colorado, Inc., discontinue the production of cross country skis? Why or why not?

E 6.7 Potter's Wheel manufactures 10,000 units of clay pottery annually. The production cost for 10,000 units is as follows:

Direct materials	$ 20,000
Direct labor	55,000
Unit-variable overhead	45,000
Fixed overhead	70,000
Total	$190,000

A supplier has offered to supply the pottery at a price of $18 per unit. If Potter's Wheel accepts the offer, it will be able to rent some of the facilities it devotes to making the product for an annual rental fee of $15,000. Should Potter's Wheel make or buy the product? Please explain.

E 6.8 Refer to Exercise 6.7. Describe two ways the $15,000 rental fee can be incorporated in the make-or-buy decision. What are some qualitative factors Potter's Wheel should consider?

E 6.9 Damkin Corporation currently produces 5,000 tablecloths per year. The production cost per tablecloth is shown below.

Direct materials	$ 5
Direct labor	2
Unit-variable overhead	3
Fixed overhead	6
Total	$16

A private contractor has offered to supply all the labor needed for production at a cost of $3 per unit. If this offer is accepted, direct labor will be eliminated and variable overhead will be reduced by $2 per unit. Should Damkin accept the contractor's offer? Why or why not? What qualitative factors should be considered?

E 6.10 Xavio Company produces three chemicals, X, Y, and Z through a joint process. The joint production costs are $60,000 per period. At the split-off point, Xavio can sell chemical X for $5 per unit and chemical Y for $6 per unit. Chemical Z requires further processing and cannot be sold at split-off. Chemical Z, after further processing costing $9 per unit, sells for $17 per unit. Alternatively, Xavio can process chemical X further at a cost of $4 per unit and sell it after further processing for $8 per unit. Chemical Y can be processed further at a cost of $2 per unit and sold after further processing for $10 per unit. When, and for what price, should Xavio Company sell its three chemicals? Please explain.

E 6.11 Refer to Exercise 6.10. Are the $60,000 of joint costs relevant to the sell-or-process-further decision? Why or why not? What are some qualitative factors that Xavio should consider?

E 6.12 Wyandot Company manufactures four products from a joint process that costs $350,000 per year. These costs are allocated to the four product lines based on the physical quantities of the products sold. Sales volume, selling prices, and additional processing costs beyond split-off are given below.

	Yearly Volume	Selling Price at Split-Off	Selling Price after Further Processing
Product 1	12,000	$16	$23
Product 2	12,000	8	10
Product 3	24,000	20	21
Product 4	24,000	10	22.50

Additional costs incurred beyond split-off are:

Product 1	$100,000
Product 2	10,000
Product 3	12,000
Product 4	300,000

Which products, if any, should Wyandot sell at the split-off point? Why?

Appendix

E 6.13 Temptations Bakers, Inc., has just completed a linear program to determine the optimal product mix of apple pies and apple cakes. The results are shown below:

Solution	Pies	Cakes	Contribution Margin
1	500	–0–	$1,500
2	–0–	800	1,600
3	300	500	1,900

a. What is the contribution margin per pie?
b. What is the contribution margin per cake?
c. What is the optimal solution? Why?

E 6.14 Tick Tock Corporation produces two clocks, Tick and Tock. Each clock uses the same raw material and the same processing machine. There are only 1,000 units of raw material and 2,500 hours of machine time available per period. The contribution margins, raw material requirements, and machine time requirements of each product are given below.

	Tick	Tock
Contribution margin per unit	$6	$8
Raw material requirement per unit	2 units	3 units
Machine time requirement per unit	1 hour	2 hours

a. What is the objective function?
b. What is the raw material constraint function?
c. What is the machine time constraint function?

E 6.15 Refer to either E6.13 or E6.14. Describe, without using numbers, how you determined the objective function, the constraints, and the optimal solution, if applicable.

PROBLEMS

P 6.1

The Ding-Dong Corporation produced and sold 20,000 cow bells last year. The unit cost of a cow bell is:

Direct material	$0.50
Direct labor	0.75
Unit-variable overhead	0.25
Fixed overhead	0.20
Selling cost (fixed)	0.30
Total	$2.00

The company normally sells cow bells for $2.50 per bell. This year Ding-Dong Corporation again expects to sell 20,000 cow bells; however, in addition, it has received an offer from a fraternal organization that wishes to buy 2,000 cow bells at $1.75 each. The company has the capacity to produce the extra cow bells.

Required:

a. What is the relevant cost of the special order?

b. Should Ding-Dong Corporation accept or reject the special order? Why?

c. Describe the qualitative factors Ding-Dong Corporation must consider.

P 6.2

Quikcalc, Inc., produced 250,000 pocket calculators last year. The company's income statement is shown below.

Sales	$3,000,000
Cost of goods sold	1,750,000
Gross margin	$1,250,000
Selling and administrative cost	750,000
Net income	$ 500,000

Fixed costs included in the total cost of goods sold, and total selling and administrative cost are $500,000 and $250,000, respectively. Quikcalc has the capacity to produce 300,000 pocket calculators per year.

Recently, Quikcalc, Inc., received an offer from Electro Link, a foreign retail firm, to buy 50,000 calculators.

Required:

a. What is the minimum price Quikcalc can accept for the special order and maintain the same net income as last year? Why?

b. If Electro Link increases its order to 100,000 pocket calculators and offers to pay $8 each, should Quikcalc accept the offer? Explain.

c. List five qualitative factors Quikcalc should consider in the decision situation.

P 6.3

TexMex Corporation owns two fast food restaurants featuring Mexican entrees. The company is considering expansion into a third restaurant in the area. Operating performance for TexMex's most recent quarter is:

	Store 1	Store 2
Sales	$670,400	$895,800
Variable cost of sales	268,160	358,320
Contribution margin	$402,240	537,480
Fixed costs	200,000	360,000
Profit	$202,240	$177,480

The new store is expected to generate revenues of $560,000 per quarter. Variable cost of sales for the new store will be at the same percentage as the other two stores, and fixed costs of the new store are expected to be $100,000 per quarter. If TexMex opens the new store, sales in the other two stores are expected to decline by 15 percent and 20 percent, respectively, for store 1 and store 2.

Required:

a. Should TexMex open the third store? Why?

b. Write a memo to the owner of TexMex indicating the best course of action for the company.

P 6.4

Minnot Company makes a product that includes a component part, item XJ7. Presently the company purchases XJ7 from an outside supplier for $25 each. Minnot is considering manufacturing XJ7 itself. Estimated total cost of manufacturing the yearly requirement of 1,000 units of XJ7 is:

Direct materials	$ 6,000
Direct labor	9,000
Unit-variable overhead	4,000
Fixed overhead	16,000
Total	$35,000

The fixed overhead consists of manufacturing overhead that will be assigned to the XJ7 product. This overhead will continue, regardless of the decision made.

Required:
    a. Should Minnot Company make or buy component XJ7? Why?
    b. If the facilities that would be used to produce XJ7 can be rented to another company for $8,000 per year, should Minnot Company make or buy component XJ7? Why?
    c. Describe the other factors that Minnot Company should consider in making this decision.

P 6.5   Utah Enterprises, which produces and sells to wholesalers a very successful line of ski wear, has decided to diversify its product line. It is considering the production of a sunscreen that will be sold in small plastic tubes. The company will sell the sunscreen to wholesalers in boxes of 100 tubes for $10 per box. Due to available capacity, no additional fixed costs will be incurred to manufacture the sunscreen; however, $150,000 of fixed manufacturing overhead will be absorbed by the new product to allocate a fair share of the company's present fixed production costs.

Utah estimates production and sales of sunscreen to be 200,000 boxes during the first year. The estimated cost per box is:

Direct labor	$2.00
Direct material	3.50
Total overhead	2.25
Total cost	$7.75

As an alternative, the company is discussing the possibility of purchasing the plastic tubes from an outside supplier. The purchase price of the empty tubes will be $1.50 per box of 100 tubes. If Utah purchases the plastic tubes, it is estimated that direct labor, direct material, and variable overhead costs will decrease by 30 percent, 50 percent, and 10 percent, respectively.

Required:
    a. What is the relevant cost of the "make" alternative?
    b. What is the relevant cost of the "buy" alternative?
    c. Should Utah make or buy the plastic tubes? Why?
    d. What qualitative factors should the company consider?
    e. If the supplier raises the price of the plastic tubes to $2.50 per box of 100 tubes should Utah Enterprises make or buy the plastic tubes?
    f. If the price of the plastic tubes was $2.50 per box and the company could rent the space needed for production of the plastic tubes to another company for $6,000, should it make or buy the plastic tubes?

P 6.6   Ansome Company manufactures products Alpha and Beta from a joint process. Product Alpha receives $10,000 of allocated total joint costs of $35,000 for the 2,000 units of Alpha produced. Alpha can be sold at the split-off point for $6 per unit or processed further with additional costs of $2,000 and sold for $8 per unit. Product Beta receives the remaining allocated joint cost of $25,000 for the 5,000 units of Beta produced. Beta can be sold at the split-off point for $7 per unit, or it can be processed further with additional costs of $2 per unit and sold for $8 per unit.

Required:
    a. Should Ansome sell Product Alpha at split-off or process it further? Why?
    b. Should the company sell Product Beta at split-off or process it further? Why?
    c. What other factors should Ansome consider?
    d. Explain why the joint costs of $35,000 are irrelevant to this decision.

P 6.7   The human resources manager at MacHalls Company has been told that 500 of the 4,000 production line workers will have to be laid off. The company hopes the layoff is temporary (6 to 12 months), but there are no guarantees. Since he feels that this decision is similar to the decision to delete an existing product line, the manager has asked you to provide input to determine which employees to lay off.

Write a memo to the human resources manager describing your conclusions.

P 6.8   M. C. Commander, the manager of Wansom Company, has been looking over reports concerning the profitability of the products that are produced in Wansom Company's joint manufacturing process. Commander is upset because one of the products is showing a loss. This product generates revenues of $150,000 but after deducting additional processing costs of $85,000 and $90,000 of joint costs (its share when joint costs are allocated to product lines based on the number of units sold), the loss is $25,000. Commander insists that Wansom should drop this product line.

Assume that you are the production manager for this product line. Write a memo to M. C. Commander explaining why you feel the product line should or should not be dropped.

Appendix

P 6.9   Choc-O-Lot is a sole proprietorship that makes and sells chocolate pies and cakes. It takes one hour to produce a pie and two hours to make a cake. The baker works 40 hours a week. Sugar has recently become very expensive and hard to obtain. The owner of Choc-O-Lot has decided to limit the amount of sugar used in a week to 100 cups. Each pie requires four cups of sugar and each cake requires two cups of sugar. The selling prices and the variable costs of the products are shown below:

	Pies	Cakes
Selling price	$6	$10
Unit-variable cost	2	5
Contribution margin	$4	$ 5

Required: *a.* What is the objective function?
b. What is the constraint function for baker hours?
c. What is the constraint function for sugar?
d. What are the possible solutions?
e. What is the optimal production solution?

P 6.10   Wilkens Company manufactures and sells two products. The company can work a total of 300,000 direct labor hours annually. A total of 200,000 hours of machine time is available annually. The unit sales price for product A is $27.50. Product B sells for $75.00 per unit. The variable costs per unit and manufacturing requirements of each product are shown below.

	Product A	Product B
Direct material	$ 3	$ 7
Direct labor	8	12
Unit-variable overhead	6	24
Total variable cost	$17	$43
Direct labor time in hours	1.0	1.5
Machine time in hours	.5	2.0

Required: *a.* What is the objective function?
b. What is the constraint function for direct labor?
c. What is the constraint function for machine time?
d. What are the possible linear programming solutions?
e. What is the optimal production mix?
f. If the direct material cost of each model is reduced by 10 percent, will the optimal production mix change? Explain.

COMPUTER APPLICATIONS

CA 6.1   Wong Fong Corporation owns two Chinese restaurants. It is considering opening a third restaurant in the area. Operating performance for Wong Fong's most recent quarter is given below:

	Store 1	Store 2
Sales	$335,200	$447,900
Variable cost of sales	134,080	179,160
Contribution margin	$201,120	268,740
Fixed costs	100,000	180,000
Store profit	$101,120	$ 88,740
Allocated corporate cost	30,000	30,000
Net profit	$ 71,120	$ 58,740

The new store is expected to generate revenues of $280,000 per quarter. Variable cost of sales for the new store will be at the same percentage as the other two stores, and fixed costs of the new store are expected to be $75,000 per quarter. If the company opens the new store, sales in the other two stores are expected to decline by 20 and 30 percent, respectively, for store 1 and store 2. In addition, corporate costs are expected to increase 15 percent and will be allocated equally to the three stores.

Required: Use a computer spreadsheet. Assume independent situations.
a. Recalculate the income statements assuming the new store opens. Should Wong Fong open the new store?

b. Assume the decline in sales for the other two stores is limited to 10 percent for each store. Recalculate the income statements using this new information. Should Wong Fong open the new store?

c. Assume corporate costs are allocated to the new stores based on the ratio of store profit. Recalculate the income statements using this new information. Should Wong Fong open the new store?

d. Assume that sales in the new store are expected to be 30 percent higher than the original estimates. Recalculate the income statements using this new information. Should Wong Fong open the new store?

e. What additional factors should Wong Fong consider when making this decision?

 CA 6.2

Ogden, Inc., produces and sells to wholesalers a very profitable line of pet products. It is considering the production of matching dog sweaters and leashes. The sweater/leash sets will sell for an average of $40 each. Due to available capacity, no additional fixed costs will be incurred to manufacture the sweater/leash sets; however, $200,000 of fixed manufacturing overhead will be absorbed by the new product to allocate a fair share of the company's present fixed production costs.

Ogden estimates that 100,000 sweater/leash sets will be produced and sold during the first year. The estimated cost per set is:

Direct labor	$ 4.00
Direct material	23.50
Total overhead	8.25
Total cost	$35.75

As an alternative, Ogden is discussing the possibility of purchasing the leashes from an outside supplier. The purchase price of the leashes is expected to be $15. If Ogden purchases the leashes, it is estimated that direct labor, direct material, and unit-variable overhead costs will decrease by 30 percent, 50 percent, and 10 percent, respectively.

Required: Use a computer spreadsheet. Assume independent situations.

a. Calculate the relevant costs of the make and the buy decisions. Should Ogden make or buy the leashes?

b. Assume that Ogden can rent the space required for leash production to a small manufacturing operation for $6,000 per month. Calculate the relevant costs of the make and the buy decisions. Should Ogden make or buy the leashes?

c. Assume that Ogden determines that the direct labor, direct material, and variable overhead costs will decrease by 40 percent, 60 percent, and 15 percent, respectively. Calculate the relevant costs of the make and the buy decisions. Should Ogden make or buy the leashes?

d. Assume that the supplier reduces the purchase price to $12 per leash. Calculate the relevant costs of the make and the buy decisions. Should Ogden make or buy the leashes?

e. What additional factors should Ogden consider?

CASES

C 6.1

The Sommers Company, located in southern Wisconsin, manufactures a variety of industrial valves and pipe fittings that are sold to customers in nearby states. Currently, the company is operating at about 70 percent capacity and is earning a satisfactory profit.

Management has been approached by Glascow Industries Ltd. of Scotland with an offer to buy 120,000 units of a pressure valve. Glascow normally produces its own valves, but a fire in one of its plants has caused a temporary shortage. Glascow needs the 120,000 valves over the next four months to meet commitments to its regular customers. It is prepared to pay $19 for each valve.

Sommers' product cost for the pressure value is:

Direct materials	$ 5.00
Direct labor	6.00
Unit-variable overhead	6.00
Fixed overhead	7.00
Total	$24.00

Additional costs incurred in connection with sales of the pressure valve include sales commissions of 5 percent and freight expense of $1.00 per unit. Sommers normally sells the pressure values at a markup on variable manufacturing cost of 75 percent.

Production management believes that it can handle the Glascow Industries order without disrupting its scheduled production. The order would, however, require additional fixed factory overhead of $12,000 per month in the form of supervision and clerical costs.

If management accepts the order, the company will manufacture 30,000 pressure valves and ship them to Glascow Industries each month for the next four months.

Required:
   a. Identify the relevant costs for this decision.
   b. Should the order be accepted? Explain.
   c. Describe what factors, other than price, Sommers Company's management should consider before accepting the order.

(CMA Adapted)

C 6.2   Refer to the annual report of the company you chose in Chapter 1. Based on your knowledge of this company, which of the decisions discussed in this chapter did the company you chose possibly face during the period? Is there any specific information in the annual report about any decisions made? Speculate on who the other parties might have been. Describe your ideas and findings.

CRITICAL THINKING

CT 6.1   Pins and Needles produces three types of fraternity pins, known as Gamma, Omega, and Lambda. Recently the Gamma and Lambda product lines have not shown net profits. The most recent monthly results for these products are:

	Gamma	Omega	Lambda
Unit sales	1,800	400	1,500
Sales	$ 900	$1,200	$1,500
Cost of goods sold	860	600	1,250
Gross margin	$ 40	$ 600	$ 250
Selling and administrative expense	190	220	250
Net income	$(150)	$ 380	$ –0–

Additional analysis reveals that cost of goods sold for each product line includes a fixed overhead charge of $500. This overhead cannot be eliminated regardless of the decision made. In addition, a $100 per month fixed administrative cost is charged to each product line.

Pins and Needles is analyzing the following four exclusive alternatives:
1. Discontinue the Gamma line, and increase advertising for the Lambda line. This should increase Lambda units' sales by 15 percent. However, selling expense will increase by $50 per month.
2. Discontinue the Gamma and Lambda lines and promote the Omega line. This should increase unit sales of Omega by 10 percent with no substantial increase in cost.
3. Increase promotion of both the Gamma and Lambda lines. The promotion will increase selling costs of each line by $25 per month. Unit sales of Gamma are expected to increase 12 percent due to the promotion, while unit sales of Lambda are expected to increase 8 percent due to the promotion.
4. Do nothing. Leave the Gamma and Lambda lines as is.

Required:
   a. Evaluate each alternative. What action should Pins and Needles choose? Why?
   b. What other factors should Pins and Needles consider?
   c. What long-term plans should Pins and Needles make?

CT 6.2   Readrite produces three grades of computer paper (A, B, and C) from a joint process. Department 1 processes direct materials to manufacture two intermediate products. One of these intermediate products is product C. Product C can be processed further in department 4, or it can be sold for $17 per unit after processing in department 1. The other intermediate product from department 1 is converted into product A and product B in department 2. Product B *must be* processed further in department 3 before it is ready for sale, while product A can be processed further in department 5 or sold for $30 per unit after processing in department 2. The production quantities and selling prices of each of the products are given below. Assume that all departmental costs are discretionary, that is, the costs can be eliminated if the department is not needed.

	Units	Selling Price after Further Processing
Product A	7,000	$35
Product B	7,675	27
Product C	4,600	18

The expected costs of operating each department are:

	Direct Materials	Direct Labor	Manufacturing Overhead
Department 1	$65,000	$35,000	$175,800
Department 2	16,000	2,800	47,500
Department 3	30,000	7,500	54,600
Department 4	4,200	1,500	3,500
Department 5	3,420	5,620	15,810

Required:
a. Determine the point at which Readrite should sell each product.
b. Based on your answer to *a*, what is the expected profit for the company?
c. If some of the departmental costs are fixed, does this change your answer to *a* or *b?* Why or why not?

ETHICAL CHALLENGES

EC 6.1 The Vic Lighter Corporation is located in a small Iowa town and manufactures refrigeration units for over-the-road trailers. The management of Vic Lighter Corporation has recently found a supplier who will sell Vic Lighter the compressor for the refrigeration unit for $300 each. The cost for Vic Lighter to produce the compressor is described below.

Material	$ 85
Labor	165
Variable overhead	55
Fixed overhead	60
Total cost	$365

Up to this point the corporation has manufactured all the components of the refrigeration units and has used this fact as part of their marketing strategy. They have emphasized to their customers that they can count on the quality of their product because they manufacture the product from start to finish in their plant. If Vic Lighter chooses to buy the compressor rather than manufacture it, the company will permanently lay off 200 workers. On the other hand, management has a responsibility to the stockholders of the corporation to operate as efficiently as possible and generate the highest possible return.

Required:
a. Based on the financial information only, should Vic Lighter buy the compressor?
b. What nonquantitative factors are part of the decision?
c. What would be your decision if you were managing Vic Lighter Corporation?

EC 6.2 Nuskin Company manufactures two skin care lotions, Soft as Silk and Intense Care, from a joint process. The joint production costs incurred are $840,000 for a normal production run that generates 360,000 gallons of Soft as Silk and 240,000 gallons of Intense Care. Soft as Silk can be sold at split-off for $4.80 per gallon and Intense Care can be sold at split-off for $7.80 per gallon.

Alternatively, Nuskin can process both products further at a cost of $36,000 for Soft as Silk and $48,000 for Intense Care. After further processing, the products would sell for $5.00 and $8.00, respectively.

Required:
a. Should Soft as Silk be sold at split-off or processed further?
b. Should Intense Care be sold at split-off or processed further?
c. If the additional processing creates pollution that is currently within the limits set by the Environmental Protection Agency, what affect will this have on your decision? Why?

PART THREE

Recording within the Operating Cycles

No communication system, especially one related to accounting information, is complete without understanding what information appears in the system and why. Part Three addresses the accounting cycle the process of recording accounting information in the records of an organization. Chapter 7 addresses the cycle itsself. Chapters 8, 9, and 10 revisit the expenditure, revenue, and conversion operating cycles, respectively, and address the recording process for each in the accounting system.

CHAPTER 7

Recording and Communicating in the Accounting Cycle

Learning Objectives

1. Use the objectivity principle to explain why financial statements reflect historical cost rather than fair market value and replacement cost.
2. Understand the revenue recognition and matching principles and their importance.
3. Define accounts and explain the role of debits and credits in a company's accounting system.
4. Explain the flow of accounting events in the accounting cycle.
5. Demonstrate an understanding of how companies use adjusting entries as an application of the matching principle.
6. Identify how businesses construct financial statements using information contained in the general ledger.
7. Describe how companies perform the end-of-period closing process and explain the need for the process.

From a sports fan's point of view, the Boston Celtics basketball team is one of the most successful in the history of professional sports. Since their inception in 1946, the Celtics have won a total of 16 world championships, more than any other professional athletic team. However, due to the fact that the "Boston Celtics Limited Partnership" is the only publicly owned professional sports team in the United States, there are also approximately 90,000 Celtics partners who care about a great deal more than how the team is performing on the parquet floor of Boston's Fleet Center arena.

In the same way that the sports fan wants to know the vital "stats" of individual players and the team as a whole, the managers, owners, creditors, and even competitors of the Celtics want stats on how the team is performing on the bottom line. Management must develop a formal system for identifying, analyzing, measuring, recording, summarizing, and communicating the information needed to manage the Celtics as a business operation, as well as information needed to assess their performance in generating profits.

In this chapter, we will examine why recording and classifying accounting events are important for generating the information necessary for financial statements. 🚲

IMPORTANCE OF UNDERSTANDING THE FORMAL ACCOUNTING CYCLE

Now that we have discussed the basic tools and techniques involved in planning for operating activities, we will learn how to record and communicate the results of actual operations.

Chapter 2 introduced the important equality, Assets = Liabilities + Owners' equity. We showed the effect of various accounting events on this fundamental accounting equation by introducing a series of increases or decreases demonstrating that every accounting event exhibits a dual nature that maintains the balance of the equation. This approach to the analysis of accounting events helped demonstrate that, for every asset, there is an offsetting claim by either creditors or owners of the business. However, the related discussion in Chapter 2 did not attempt to explain how a company such as the Boston Celtics might keep track of the thousands of transactions that often occur during even a brief period of time.

If you examine the financial statements of the Celtics (found in the Annual Report Booklet) you might wonder, where did all the information come from? How was it gathered? How were the multitude of accounting transactions occurring during the year summarized into the relatively few categories shown in the financial statements?

This chapter discusses in greater detail than Chapter 2 the way we *identify, analyze, measure, record,* and *summarize* accounting events and *communicate* them to *external stakeholders* in the form of periodic financial statements. You will learn how important it is for users of financial information who are attempting to make decisions to have a basic understanding of the formal accounting cycle, especially the fundamental principles and procedures that guide accountants, managers, and others who use accounting information in their daily jobs.

Before we look at this accounting process, it is important to understand several basic accounting principles.

BASIC ACCOUNTING PRINCIPLES

In addition to the basic accounting concepts discussed in Chapter 1 (business entity, going concern, monetary unit, and periodicity), it is important to understand three principles that are fundamental to accounting: (1) objectivity, (2) revenue recognition, and (3) matching.

Why Is the Objectivity Principle Important?

External users of accounting information need assurance that data presented to them are reliable. To help in this regard, the **objectivity principle** requires that information included in published financial statements must be free of bias. This means that measurements included in financial statements could be duplicated by independent parties, if necessary.

Recall that all accounting activity is measured in terms of dollars, or whatever unit of money is appropriate to a particular country (the *monetary unit concept*). How do we *objectively* determine these dollar values so that they are perceived as reliable by independent parties?

Should companies report items on the balance sheet at the dollar amount of their **fair market value,** that is, a sales price that would be agreed upon by willing, unrelated buyers and sellers? Fair market value is probably the most relevant value from the perspective of the majority of financial statement users, but it has one major drawback. It usually cannot be objectively derived. For example, if 10 people were asked to give the fair market value of an office building in any major city in the world, they would probably give 10 different values. Fair market value requires subjective judgment, which renders it unreliable, especially when people preparing financial statements might have an incentive to make "judgments" that paint a favorable picture.

What about using **replacement cost** to report items on the balance sheet? Replacement cost is the cost of producing or otherwise acquiring a similar item. Once again, this often is a subjectively derived value. In addition, in a world of constant technological change, assets are frequently replaced with new and improved versions, thus rendering replacement cost of little value in many situations.

Finally, what about **historical cost?** This is the cash or cash equivalent value that either changed hands, or became obligated when an accounting event occurred. It represents the amount actually paid for an asset, or the amount of money actually borrowed, for example, on a note payable. For revenues and expenses, it represents the cash value of the transaction measured at the date the transaction occurred. The advantage of historical cost is that it can be objectively verified. Thus, accountants in the United States follow the general principle of recording transactions at their historical cost.

Accounting information users should be aware of one significant drawback resulting from the use of historical cost data. If company A, for example, acquired a piece of land 10 years ago at a purchase price of $10,000 and company B acquired an identical piece of land today for $100,000, the balance sheets for the two companies would reflect the different costs, even though the two pieces of land might have the same current fair market value. So long as inflation is not a major factor in the economy, the difference is not that significant. However, in some economies other than the United States where inflation is a significant problem, accountants sometimes use a monetary unit of measure other than historical cost. Brazil, India, Singapore, and Argentina are examples of countries where asset values may be based on current or inflation-adjusted values.[1]

PAUSE & REFLECT	Look at the annual report of the Boston Celtics. Do you see any assets on the balance sheet that might have a current fair market value significantly different from the amount shown? What do you think a National Basketball Association franchise is worth?

What Is the Revenue Recognition Principle?

Revenue is recognized and recorded when it is *earned*. This is known as the **revenue recognition principle.** Revenues result from the performance of a service or the sale of a product. Companies record revenues (recognize them) when they have performed the service or when the sale has occurred, that is, when title has transferred from the seller to the buyer. The recognition of a revenue may or may not coincide with the collection of cash. As we will demonstrate later in this chapter, users of financial information need to be keenly aware of this fact.

Another Important Principle: The Matching Principle

The **matching principle** requires that all expenses incurred attempting to generate revenues be matched with the revenues earned during a given period to determine net income. This "matching" of revenues and related expenses results in a proper measurement and reporting of income on the income statement.

The matching principle dictates that expense recognition follow the basic guidelines established for revenues. Companies recognize and record expenses at the time they derive a benefit from the use of a product or service. For example, companies record supplies expense when they *use* supplies, not when they purchase the supplies, and not necessarily when they make payment for them.

With an awareness of the impact of the objectivity principle, revenue recognition principle, and matching principle, we are ready to look at the process of recording accounting events to understand why the recording process is important to various companies and financial statement users.

THE NEED FOR ACCOUNTS

To help make the process of preparing financial reports more efficient, accountants have developed the use of **accounts,** which they utilize to accumulate the results of accounting events affecting a particular asset, liability, or owners' equity item. Accounts have titles, such as Cash or Accounts Receivable, and there are separate

---

[1] The accounting firm Price Waterhouse publishes an excellent series of information guides called "Doing business in . . ." These guides, which are frequently updated, detail accounting practices in different countries where Price Waterhouse has offices.

columns to reflect recorded increases and decreases, as well as a cumulative balance. All accounts are maintained in a general ledger, which we illustrate later in the chapter.

Businesses record the results of all accounting events in the specific accounts affected. Thus, when interested parties require periodic financial reports, cumulative balances are readily available. For example, when it is necessary to prepare an income statement, the separate revenue and expense account balances necessary to determine income already exist and can easily be organized in an appropriate income statement format.

To understand the use of accounts, we return to the balance sheet equation:

$$\text{Assets} = \text{Liabilities} + \text{Owners' equity}$$

For each item in the balance sheet there will be an account, which, for convenience, can be represented in the form of a "T". We use the **T-account** as an informal representation of each account in the general ledger. Any dollar amount entered on the left side of this account is called a **debit** (abbreviated Dr), and any entry on the right side is called a **credit** (abbreviated Cr).

Debit (Dr)	Credit (Cr)

The balance sheet equation, along with representative T-accounts showing the debit and credit sides, is shown below.

Assets		=	Liabilities		+	Owners' Equity	
Dr	Cr		Dr	Cr		Dr	Cr

Next we must determine what a debit or credit entry signifies for a particular account. Once again, the key to that understanding lies in the balance sheet equation.

We begin by declaring that *for any asset account*, a debit entry will *increase* and a credit entry will *decrease* the balance of the account. This requirement can be added in the balance sheet equation as:

Assets		=	Liabilities		+	Owners' Equity	
Dr	Cr		Dr	Cr		Dr	Cr
+	−						

For example, a $10,000 debit entry to the Cash account would mean the cash balance increased by that amount, whereas a credit to the Cash account would indicate cash decreased (it was spent) for some purpose.

What about liabilities and owners' equity? If assets, which appear on the left side of the balance sheet equation, are increased by debits, what should happen when we move to accounts shown on the right side of the accounting equation? Consistent with the mathematical requirement that the signs of all numbers change (from plus to minus, or minus to plus) when they move from one side of an equation to the other, all liability accounts and owners' equity are increased by means of credits, and are reduced by debits. This additional requirement is depicted in the accounting equation as:

Assets		=	Liabilities		+	Owners' Equity	
Dr	Cr		Dr	Cr		Dr	Cr
+	−		−	+		−	+

Finally, owners' equity is affected by four things: (1) owner investments, (2) dividends, (3) revenues, and (4) expenses. These items affect the balance sheet directly because they affect owners' equity, which appears on the balance sheet. However, it is necessary to record related revenues and expenses in separate accounts because they are needed to prepare an income statement.

The debit and credit rules for revenue and expense accounts are governed by their relationship to owners' equity. Owners' equity increases directly by the amount of any increase in revenues. Therefore, credits increase revenue accounts, just as they increase owners' equity, and debits reduce the balance of revenue accounts. On the other hand, as expenses go up, owners' equity goes down. Thus, there is an inverse relationship between these accounts. Because a debit entry reduces owners' equity, increases in expense accounts are recorded by debits. This final set of rules completes the picture, and is shown below.

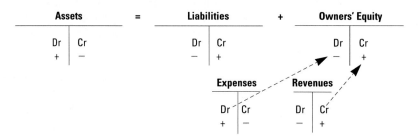

Because of the dual nature of all accounting events, which is directly related to the need to maintain the equality of both sides of the accounting equation, whenever a debit entry is made to any account, there will be a corresponding credit entry made to some other account. Thus, not only will every entry maintain the equality of the balance sheet equation, but also the total of all debits will always equal the total of all credits.

Application of Debit/Credit Rules

To illustrate these ideas more completely, consider an example of a professional hockey team called the Maine Lobsters, Inc., which began operations on January 2, 1997. We will show accounting events for this business, not necessarily in order of occurrence, in a manner designed to illustrate important points that users of financial accounting information need to understand.

Exhibit 7.1 summarizes the effect of the following transactions, with the debit and credit entry for each event designated by the letter corresponding to the event. Refer to this exhibit frequently to understand what effect each event has on the various accounts and on the accounting equation itself.

(*a*). On January 2, 1997, T. O. Clause proudly fulfilled a lifelong dream when he established the Maine Lobsters professional hockey team with an initial investment of $200,000. Clause will operate the Lobsters as a corporation.

The following T-accounts show this entry recorded as a debit to the Cash account and a credit to an owners' equity account called Capital Stock (which represents contributed capital). Notice that the equation will be in balance after this first entry because assets, as well as owners' equity, will increase by $200,000. Notice also that the $200,000 debit entry would be offset by a corresponding $200,000 credit.

Cash	Capital Stock
200,000	200,000

(*b*). On the same day, the Lobsters purchased land and a hockey rink for $300,000 ($100,000 for the land and $200,000 for the hockey rink). Of the total $300,000, Clause paid $140,000 in cash and borrowed the remaining $160,000 from his father.

EXHIBIT | 7.1 | Maine Lobsters, Inc.—Accounting Events Summarized

Assets	=	Liabilities	+	Owners' Equity

Cash

(a) 200,000	140,000 (b)
(g) 70,000	15,000 (d)
(i) 30,000	40,000 (e)
(k) 6,000	3,000 (f)
	4,000 (j)
	10,000 (l)
Bal. 94,000	

Accounts Payable

(j) 4,000	5,000 (c)
	1,000 Bal.

Capital Stock

	200,000 (a)
	200,000 Bal.

Accounts Receivable

(h) 6,000	6,000 (k)
Bal. –0–	

Unearned Ticket Revenue

	30,000 (i)
	30,000 Bal.

Retained Earnings

(l) 10,000	
Bal. 10,000	

Supplies

(c) 5,000	
Bal. 5,000	

Note Payable

	160,000 (b)
	160,000 Bal.

Ticket Revenue

	70,000 (g)
	70,000 Bal.

Prepaid Insurance

(d) 15,000	
Bal. 15,000	

Advertising Revenue

	6,000 (h)
	6,000 Bal.

Land

(b) 100,000	
Bal. 100,000	

Wages Expense

(e) 40,000	
Bal. 40,000	

Hockey Rink

(b) 200,000	
Bal. 200,000	

Utilities Expense

(f) 3,000	
Bal. 3,000	

Assets		=	Liabilities		+	Owners' Equity	
Cash	$ 94,000		Accounts payable	$ 1,000		Capital stock	$200,000
Accounts receivable	–0–		Unearned ticket			Retained earnings	(10,000)
Supplies	5,000		revenue	30,000		Ticket revenue	70,000
Prepaid insurance	15,000		Note payable	160,000		Advertising revenue	6,000
Land	100,000					Wages expense	(40,000)
Hockey rink	200,000					Utilities expense	(3,000)
Total	$414,000	=		$191,000	+		$223,000
						$414,000	

In return for the loan, the Lobsters signed a three-year note payable, requiring the repayment of principal plus interest at the rate of 8 percent per year, with all payments to be made in one lump sum at the end of the three-year period.

This event requires several debit and credit entries to different accounts. First, it is necessary to debit the Land and Hockey Rink accounts for $100,000 and $200,000, respectively. These debits are offset by credits of $140,000 to Cash and $160,000 to Note Payable, as shown in the T accounts:

Land		Cash	
100,000		140,000	

Hockey Rink		Note Payable	
200,000			160,000

PAUSE & REFLECT

What is the balance in each account after events (*a*) and (*b*)? Do total assets equal total liabilities plus owners' equity? Do total debit balances in all accounts equal total credit balances?

During the course of the first year of operations the following events occurred:

(*c*). Supplies totaling $5,000 were bought on account, shown below as a debit to the Supplies account, and a credit to Accounts Payable:

Supplies		Accounts Payable	
5,000			5,000

(*d*). On January 2, 1997, $15,000 was paid for a three-year insurance policy. Since the policy was prepaid (i.e., paid for before any insurance coverage was provided), the company acquired an economic resource—the right to receive the benefit of insurance coverage during the next three-year period. This was recorded by a debit to an asset account called Prepaid Insurance and a credit to Cash:

Prepaid Insurance		Cash	
15,000			15,000

(*e*). Team players were compensated in the amount of $40,000 for their services, based on the number of games actually played. These payments were debited to Wages Expense and credited to Cash:

Wages Expense		Cash	
40,000			40,000

(*f*). Utility bills in the amount of $3,000 were paid for utilities used during the year. Utilities Expense was debited and Cash was credited:

Utilities Expense		Cash	
3,000			3,000

Pause for a minute and think about entries (*c*)–(*f*) as a group. What do they all have in common? Supplies, insurance, wages, and utilities are all normal expenses of running a business, so why did the first two events result in debits to asset accounts?

Remember that expenses are recognized only when benefits are received from using an item. The supplies become an expense when the team uses them, and the prepaid insurance will become an expense as the policy period expires.

Managers and other users of accounting information sometimes make the mistake of equating "cash payments" with "expenses." Events (c)–(f) illustrate an important point. The amount of expense recognized during a given period has *nothing* to do with amounts purchased or with the amount of cash payments made during that period, except in those cases, such as (e) and (f), where payments made equal the dollar amount *used* during the period.

The following events also occurred during the first year of operations:

(g). Although attendance at home games was slow at first due to poor play, the team began to make progress. Total game receipts for games played through December 31, 1997, totaled $70,000 and were recorded as debits to Cash and credits to the Ticket Revenue account as follows:

(h). The Lobsters allowed local advertisers to rent sign space in their building on a monthly basis. They sent invoices to these advertisers on the 15th day of the following month. For example, invoices for January advertising rentals were sent on February 15. Total invoices sent during the year ended December 31, 1997, amounted to $6,000, which resulted in debits to Accounts Receivable, an asset representing the right to collect cash in the future, and credits to Advertising Revenue:

Accounts Receivable		Advertising Revenue	
6,000			6,000

(i). The Lobsters also encouraged fans to buy season tickets *before* the start of the season (which runs from November–April). Receipts from these sales totaled $30,000, recorded by debits to Cash and credits to Unearned Ticket Revenue (a liability account):

Why were events (g) and (h) recorded as revenues, while (i) resulted in a liability? The revenue recognition principle requires that revenues be recognized only when earned. In (i), cash was collected *prior* to the season, so none of it was earned at the time of collection. Instead of generating revenue, these collections created a liability to the fans who had already paid to see games not yet played. Liabilities often involve an obligation to pay money to a creditor at some future date, but they also can involve an obligation to perform a fixed dollar amount of services paid for in advance, as this event illustrates.

Managers and other users of accounting information need to be careful not to confuse *cash collections* and *revenues*. As just explained, the two are not always equal.

(*j*). Of the total Accounts Payable recorded in transaction (*c*), the Lobsters paid off $4,000 during the year, resulting in debits to Accounts Payable and credits to Cash:

Accounts Payable		Cash	
4,000			4,000

(*k*). Collections on the Accounts Receivable balance recorded in transaction (*h*) totaled $6,000 during the year, requiring debits to Cash and credits to Accounts Receivable:

Cash		Accounts Receivable	
6,000			6,000

Neither events (*j*) nor (*k*) had any effect on owners' equity (or the **net worth** of the business). Event (*j*) resulted in a decrease to both an asset account (Cash) and a liability account (Accounts Payable) by the same amount. Event (*k*) resulted in an increase in one asset account (Cash) by the same amount as a decrease in another asset account (Accounts Receivable).

Users of accounting data often make the mistake of thinking that cash collections/payments have some positive/negative effect on net worth. Remember that owners' equity increases at the time revenues are *earned*, *not* when cash is collected. Likewise, the net worth of a business is reduced when expenses are *incurred*, *not* when cash payments are made.

(*l*). The business paid a $10,000 dividend to Mr. Clause at the end of its first year of operations. This is shown below as a debit to Retained Earnings (which reduces owners' equity) and a credit to Cash.

Retained Earnings		Cash	
10,000			10,000

Exhibit 7.1 shows the way in which the entries affected the accounts used to gather and summarize the results of the accounting events for the first year of the Lobsters' operations. At the bottom of Exhibit 7.1 is a list of the account balances that verifies the equality of the accounting equation.

WHAT ARE THE STEPS IN THE ACCOUNTING CYCLE?

The preceding discussion of T-accounts helped illustrate the potential use of accounts to accumulate information needed for financial reports. However, we have yet to discuss the formal process by which companies record accounting information, transfer it to specific accounts, and assemble it in financial statements. The remainder of the

EXHIBIT	7.2	Steps in the Accounting Cycle

Step 1: Identify, analyze, and record accounting events in the general journal.

Step 2: Post general journal entries to the general ledger.

Step 3: Prepare a trial balance at the end of the accounting period to verify that the total of all debit account balances in the general ledger equals the total of all credit account balances.

Step 4: Enter required adjusting entries in the general journal and post them to the general ledger.

Step 5: Prepare an adjusted trial balance.

Step 6: Prepare financial statements using the information in the adjusted trial balance.

Step 7: Enter closing entries in the general journal and post them to the general ledger.

Step 8: Prepare a post-closing trial balance.

chapter focuses on the formal process of recording and communicating accounting information, commonly referred to as the **accounting cycle.** Exhibit 7.2 shows that this cycle consists of eight distinct steps, each of which we will describe in turn.

The first two steps in the cycle mention related sets of records called the *general journal* and the *general ledger*. These records are often referred to as the *books* of the business, a term that has its origin in the past when virtually all journals and ledgers consisted of sheets of paper that were bound together in a book format. Although this is not always true today, especially with computerized accounting systems, accounting records are still generally referred to as the books of the business.

Step 1. Identify, Analyze, and Record Events in the General Journal

Referring back to Exhibit 7.1, notice that the T-accounts do not give a complete picture of the accounting events that occurred. The Cash account shows the cumulative effect of all prior transactions on the cash balance, but a manager looking at the Cash account alone would not see what *caused* cash to go up and down. The same is true for all accounts.

Accountants must identify and analyze accounting events, and then record them in a way that enables users to determine the cause and effect of each individual event. This is the first step in the cycle.

Most accounting events are accompanied by a source document such as those introduced in Chapter 3 that alerts company personnel of the need to record a transaction. For example, preparation of a sales invoice gives evidence that a sale has occurred. The receipt of a bill from a vendor makes the company aware that a purchase has been made. Purchase orders, employee time cards, and receiving reports are additional examples of documents that alert the accountant to record an event. Accounting systems are set up to capture events based on the creation or receipt of these and other source documents, which are analyzed to determine their impact on the accounting equation.

To capture both the cause and effect of the event, the accounts to be debited and credited are initially recorded (or journalized) in a **general journal** as illustrated in Exhibit 7.3 Part (a). This journal is a *chronological* record of accounting events, and includes a place to record the date of the transaction, the account titles to be debited and credited, as well as room for a brief explanation. This explanation generally includes a description of the event being journalized and any calculations involved, as well as the initials of the individual who prepared the journal entry. The preparer's initials are helpful in identifying and assigning responsibility for any errors that may be made in the recording process.

There are two separate columns for the amount of the debit and credit entries, respectively. Notice that, as with the T-accounts, the debit column is to the left of the credit column. We'll discuss the role of the Ref. (reference) column shortly.

Exhibit 7.3 Part (a) shows the journal entry to record the purchase of $250 of supplies on account. Accounts to be debited are always listed first, followed by accounts to be credited. Also, although this is not always the case, names of accounts to be debited are usually listed to the left of the names of accounts to be credited, in

Accountant in Profile, Joe Dilorenzo, Vice President of Finance and Chief Financial Officer for the Boston Celtics

oe loves sports. Beginning in 1971, as a cashier/salesperson for the concession department at the Boston Garden, Joe worked his way through college, earning a bachelor of science degree in accounting in 1977. During the next five years Joe worked his way up the corporate ladder from assistant manager to managing director of the Boston Garden Ticket Office. Hired as the controller in 1982, he became the vice president of finance and CFO for the Boston Celtics in 1986. Joe loves his job.

Joe sees his function primarily as that of financial liaison between executive management and ownership of the Boston Celtics. His primary responsibilities include cash management, forecasting and budgeting, financial and governmental reporting, human resource management, and relations with the thousands of "limited partners," those who are not actively involved in the day-to-day management of the business. His other duties, which he describes as "social responsibilities," include attending all home games, participating in at least one road trip per season with the team, appearing at various charity events, and getting involved with many professional organizations, including the Boston chapter of the Financial Executives Institute, of which he is secretary. Remarking about the highlights of his job, Joe said, "It's the people, the wonderful people I get to associate with; people like Larry Bird, Kevin McHale, Dennis Johnson, and Chris Ford to name but a few." These people, whose pictures adorn his office, are more than just a part of his job, they are part of his life.

Joe Dilorenzo became vice president of finance and CFO for the Boston Celtics in 1986.

keeping with the notion that debits belong on the left and credits on the right side of an account. The entry gives a clear and complete picture of the transaction for future reference, but note that each entry in the journal shows only the effect of the individual transaction. It does not show the resulting *balance* of the Supplies or Accounts Payable accounts needed for the preparation of reports. That is the role of the general ledger.

Step 2. Post General Journal Entries to the General Ledger

As mentioned earlier, the **general ledger** is the place where all accounts are maintained. If prepared manually, a general ledger usually includes a separate page for each account. In a computerized accounting system, each account might be maintained in a separate data file. Refer to Exhibit 7.3, Part (b), which shows what these accounts might look like.

The general ledger includes a column to record the date of the transaction, a column for an explanation, a reference column, debit and credit columns, and a final column to show the cumulative balance in the account. It is easy to see that this account is a more detailed way of presenting what already has been presented in the T-accounts.

Note that the Balance column in Exhibit 7.3 Part (b) does not specify a net debit or credit balance. The normal balance of any account is a positive balance, and is therefore determined by the type of entry—debit or credit—made to increase that account. For all asset and expense accounts, the normal balance is a

EXHIBIT	7.3

Posting Process Illustrated

Part (a)

General Journal					Page 3
Date	Account Titles and Explanation	Ref.	Debit	Credit
1997 Sep. 15	Supplies	109	250	
	Accounts Payable	204		250
	To record purchase of supplies on account.			

Part (b)   **General Ledger**

Account Name: Supplies					Acct. No. 109
Date	Explanation	Ref.	Debit	Credit	Balance
1997 Aug. 12		GJ1	300		300
Aug. 31		GJ2		275	25
Sep. 15		GJ3	250		275

Account Name: Accounts Payable					Acct. No. 204
Date	Explanation	Ref.	Debit	Credit	Balance
1997 Aug. 10		GJ1		500	500
Aug. 20		GJ1	500		–0–
Sep. 15		GJ3		250	250

debit balance, indicating that cumulative debit entries to that account exceed cumulative credit entries. For all liability, revenue, and owners' equity accounts, the normal balance is a credit balance, resulting from cumulative credits in excess of total debits. If the balance is negative, it will be shown in brackets. For example, if the Accounts Receivable account shows a balance of ($600), this indicates that total credits to that account exceed total debits, or in other words, customers have overpaid their accounts. Or, if the Accounts Payable account displays a balance of ($900), this means total debits exceed credits, indicating the company has overpaid liabilities by $900.

There is an identification number assigned to all accounts in the general ledger. Companies prepare a **chart of accounts** showing the name and number of all accounts in the general ledger. To facilitate the preparation of annual reports from the general ledger, accounts are numbered and arranged in the order in which they will appear in the financial statements.

All entries in the general journal must be *posted* to the affected general ledger accounts. Exhibit 7.3 illustrates this **posting process,** which involves recording general journal information (Part a) in the general ledger (Part b). The reference column (Ref.) in the general journal shows the number of the general ledger account to which a particular debit or credit amount was posted, and the general ledger reference indicates the page in the general journal from which the posted amount came. Thus, if an individual is reviewing any account in the general ledger and wants to see what caused a particular increase or decrease in the account, it is easy to find the exact page in the general journal where a complete description of the event is available.

In Exhibit 7.3, the debit to Supplies, initially recorded by the general journal entry in Part (a), is posted to the corresponding Supplies account in the general ledger. This results in a normal (debit) balance of $275, the net result of all debit and credit entries to that account. The credit to Accounts Payable in the general journal is posted to the corresponding account number 204 in the general ledger, resulting in a credit Accounts Payable balance of $250.

After posting every general journal entry for a given period, the general ledger accounts will contain a record of all transactions affecting any given account. Managers who are familiar with this posting process know that it is relatively easy to obtain information regarding the cause of financial account balances included in accounting reports.

Step 3. Prepare a Trial Balance

Assume that all the entries illustrated in Exhibit 7.1 were recorded formally in a general journal and then properly posted to the general ledger to obtain year-end balances for all accounts. Now, the company would have internal records of the cumulative effect of all transactions (shown in the general ledger), as well as a complete picture of the reasons for all general ledger debits and credits (shown in the general journal).

Next, if the company wants to use information contained in the general ledger to prepare financial statements summarizing the results of operations, the first step is to look for errors in the recording and posting of all journal entries. Although it is impossible to ensure against all types of errors, the use of offsetting debits and credits in the recording process makes it easy to check for some purely mechanical errors.

We have already mentioned that total assets must always equal the total of liabilities plus owners' equity. However, if the debit part of a journal entry was posted properly to its general ledger account, but the credit side was not posted or the wrong amount was posted, the whole equation would be out of balance. To help discover this type of error prior to the preparation of financial statements, companies prepare a **trial balance.** This is an internal document, so, unlike financial statements that are prepared for external users in specific formats, there is no requirement that it be prepared in any particular format. However, the trial balance will generally show the account balances in the general ledger in two separate columns—one for debit balances and one for credit balances. Each of these two columns is totaled to check for equality. The trial balance prepared for the data in Exhibit 7.1 would appear as follows:

MAINE LOBSTERS, INC.
Trial Balance
December 31, 1997

	Debits	Credits
Cash	$ 94,000	
Accounts receivable	–0–	
Supplies	5,000	
Prepaid insurance	15,000	
Land	100,000	
Hockey rink	200,000	
Accounts payable		$ 1,000
Unearned ticket revenue		30,000
Note payable		160,000
Capital stock		200,000
Retained earnings	10,000	
Ticket revenue		70,000
Advertising revenue		6,000
Wages expense	40,000	
Utilities expense	3,000	
Total	$467,000	$467,000

Remember that a trial balance only proves equality of debits and credits. It does not guarantee that the correct accounts have been debited and credited, nor does it help locate required journal entries that were never made.

It is possible to prepare financial statements directly from a trial balance. However, before this is done, there is one more very important step to consider.

Step 4. Enter Adjusting Entries in the General Journal and Post Them to the General Ledger

The accounting system is set up to record those events disclosed by the creation or receipt of a source document. However, some revenues earned and expenses incurred during a period may not have been accompanied by a source document and, therefore, might never have been recorded.

Consequently, at the end of each financial period, before preparing financial statements, accountants must *determine whether all revenues earned and expenses incurred during the period have been recorded.* Journal entries recorded as a result of this process are referred to as **adjusting entries,** and fall into three general categories: (1) accruals, (2) deferrals, and (3) estimated allocations.

Accruals   Accruals relate to revenues and expenses that have been earned or incurred, but have *never been recorded* because no source document has been generated or received.

Accrued Revenues   Sometimes a revenue has been *earned but not recorded* because there has been no corresponding cash collection or preparation of an invoice. Failure to record a revenue would understate profits for the year.

Occasionally the earned revenue results from the *passage of time*. For example, assume that a bank made a loan to a customer on December 14, 1997, with required monthly payments of principal and interest that do not begin until January 14, 1998. Even though, as of December 31, 1997, the bank has not collected any cash relative to this loan, it has earned 17 days of interest, which must be recorded as revenue.

Sometimes the revenue has been earned as a result of *activity* that has not yet been recorded, as in the case of legal fees that have been earned but not yet billed to a client.

Let's continue to examine accounting events for the Maine Lobsters, Inc. Exhibit 7.4 shows T-accounts with beginning balances equal to the unadjusted account balances from Exhibit 7.1.

Now, recall that monthly invoices of $500 ($6,000 per year/12 months) for the Lobsters' advertising revenue are not sent out until the 15th of the following month. As a result, $500 of Advertising Revenue for the month of December, although earned, has not yet been recorded at December 31, 1997. Therefore, it is necessary to record the following adjusting entry in the general journal and to post it to the general ledger:

Dec.	31	Accounts Receivable	500	
		Advertising Revenue		500
		Adjusting entry A1.		

Although the Lobsters will not send an invoice for this revenue until January 15, 1998, there is a valid claim against the customer for this amount, which must be reflected on the balance sheet at December 31, 1997.

Exhibit 7.4 shows the result this entry will have when posted. The debit of $500 to Accounts Receivable will increase assets. The credit to Advertising Revenue of $500 will increase net income for the year and, therefore, owners' equity by an equal amount. Therefore, failure to record this entry would understate assets, income, and owners' equity.

Accrued Expenses   Sometimes an expense has been *incurred but not recorded* because no cash has been paid and no invoice received. Failure to record any expense would overstate income for the period.

EXHIBIT | 7.4 | Maine Lobsters, Inc.—Adjusted Account Balances

Assets	=	Liabilities	+	Owners' Equity

Cash

Bal. 94,000	

Accounts Payable

	1,000 Bal.
	900 (A2)
	1,900 Bal.

Capital Stock

	200,000 Bal.

Accounts Receivable

Bal. —0—	
(A1) 500	
Bal. 500	

Unearned Ticket Revenue

(A4) 10,000	30,000 Bal.
	20,000 Bal.

Retained Earnings

	Bal. 10,000

Supplies

Bal. 5,000	4,500 (A6)
Bal. 500	

Note Payable

	160,000 Bal.

Ticket Revenue

	70,000 Bal.
	10,000 (A4)
	80,000 Bal.

Prepaid Insurance

Bal. 15,000	5,000 (A5)
Bal. 10,000	

Interest Payable

	12,800 (A3)
	12,800 Bal.

Advertising Revenue

	6,000 Bal.
	500 (A1)
	6,500 Bal.

Land

Bal. 100,000	

Wages Expense

Bal. 40,000	

Hockey Rink

Bal. 200,000	

Utilities Expense

Bal. 3,000	
(A2) 900	
Bal. 3,900	

Accumulated Depreciation— Hockey Rink

	10,000 (A7)
	10,000 Bal.

Interest Expense

(A3) 12,800	
Bal. 12,800	

Insurance Expense

(A5) 5,000	
Bal. 5,000	

Supplies Expense

(A6) 4,500	
Bal. 4,500	

Depreciation Expense

(A7) 10,000	
Bal. 10,000	

For example, suppose the Lobsters have not yet received their water and electric (utilities) bills for the month of December. They know they have incurred expenses for these items and, based on prior months' bills, are able to estimate fairly accurately the amount of the combined expense at $900. This requires the following journal entry:

Dec.	31	Utilities Expense	900	
		Accounts Payable		900
		Adjusting entry A2.		

Although the $900 does not have to be paid until the bills are received, the liability relates to utilities used during the month of December. Because this liability exists at December 31, 1997, the Lobsters must reflect it on the balance sheet at that date.

The Lobsters also have to record interest expense on their note payable. This is calculated as $160,000 (principal) × .08 (interest) × 1 year (time) = $12,800, and is recorded as follows:

Dec.	31	Interest Expense	12,800	
		Interest Payable		12,800
		Adjusting entry A3.		

Exhibit 7.4 shows that posting these entries to the general ledger increases expense accounts and, therefore, reduces net income for the period. The effect of these entries also will be to increase liabilities and reduce owners' equity. We can see that failure to record any accrued expenses will result in an understatement of expenses, an overstatement of income and owners' equity, and an understatement of liabilities.

Deferrals   **Deferrals** relate to cash and other resources that have been *collected prior to* revenue being earned or cash and other resources that have been *paid prior to* expenses being incurred.

Deferred Revenues   Sometimes revenues are collected before they are earned. Insurance companies often collect policy premiums on or before the date that coverage begins, as in the case of prepaid insurance; publishers of magazines usually are paid by subscribers before mailing the magazines; and lawyers often require clients to pay them before they will begin work on a case.

In these situations, at the time cash is collected, no revenue has been earned. Instead, the collection of the cash creates a *liability* on the part of the insurance company, publisher, or lawyer to perform the service or deliver the product that has been paid for in advance by the customer.

In entry (*i*) in Exhibit 7.1, the Lobsters collected $30,000 in advance for season tickets. At the time of collection, none of this revenue was earned. Therefore, when Cash was debited, a liability account called Unearned Ticket Revenue was credited.

As of December 31, 1997, two of the six months of the season have passed (November and December). Therefore, the season is one-third complete, and the team has earned $10,000 (1/3 × $30,000) of the Unearned Ticket Revenue. This is recognized with the following year-end adjusting entry:

Dec.	31	Unearned Ticket Revenue	10,000	
		Ticket Revenue		10,000
		Adjusting entry A4.		

Revenue on ticket sales is earned when ticket buyers cash in their tickets to view the game.

This entry adds $10,000 to the revenue account, which increases income and owners' equity. It reduces the Unearned Ticket Revenue account to a $20,000 balance, which appears as a liability on the balance sheet.

Failure to adjust an unearned revenue account understates revenues, income, and owners' equity, and overstates liabilities.

Deferred Expenses Expense-related payments are often made before the expense has been incurred. For example, rent is often paid on or before the first day of the rental period, magazine advertising space is often purchased before it appears in the magazine, and supplies are often obtained for future use.

Whenever something is paid for before it is used, the recognition of an expense must be deferred. Therefore, when cash is credited to record the payment, what account should be debited?

Remember from Chapter 2 that an asset is the right to use goods or services that are expected to result in *future* economic benefits. When something is acquired before it is used, the company making the purchase has acquired an asset. Therefore, the debit is made to an asset account, which might be called Prepaid Rent, Prepaid Advertising, or Supplies. This asset account will appear with other assets on the balance sheet.

On January 2, 1997, the Lobsters paid $15,000 for a three-year insurance policy. This was recorded as a debit to Prepaid Insurance and a credit to Cash. At December 31, 1997, one year, or one-third, of this policy has expired. It is necessary to prepare the following journal entry to reflect this insurance expiration ($15,000 × 1/3):

Dec.	31	Insurance Expense	5,000	
		Prepaid Insurance		5,000
		Adjusting entry A5.		

This entry will reduce the Prepaid Insurance account balance to $10,000, representing the 24 months of the policy that are still unexpired, an asset included on the balance sheet at year-end. The $5,000 expired portion is added to the Insurance Expense account and deducted from income and, therefore, owners' equity.

The Lobsters require one more adjusting entry for deferred expenses. In event (c) of Exhibit 7.1, the Lobsters purchased $5,000 worth of supplies. Assume that supplies still on hand at December 31, 1997, amount to $500. The adjusting entry to record supplies used ($5,000 − $500 = $4,500) during the year is:

Dec.	31	Supplies Expense	4,500	
		Supplies		4,500
		Adjusting entry A6.		

The effect of this entry also has been recorded in Exhibit 7.4, and it has the same general effect as entry A5.

Because end-of-period adjusting entries relative to deferred expenses always involve a credit to the asset account that has been used, failure to record the necessary adjustment for any deferred expense overstates an asset. It also understates expenses, thereby overstating income and owners' equity.

PAUSE & REFLECT

None of the accrual or expense adjustments discussed on the preceding pages affected the cash balance. Will adjusting entries ever involve cash? Give a reason for your answer. Adjusting entries always involves a change to either a revenue or expense account. Does this mean adjusting entries will always affect net income? Will adjusting entries always affect some account on the balance sheet? Explain.

Estimated Allocations The accrual and deferral adjustments discussed so far relate to revenues and expenses that have been earned or incurred during a relatively short period of time, generally one year or less. Companies also purchase many long-term assets from which they will derive benefits over a period of years. For example, autos and delivery trucks are typically used by a business for 3 to 10 years, and buildings are often owned and used for 20 to 30 years, or longer.

The matching principle requires that the cost of all these types of assets, called *Plant and Equipment*, which (1) are used by a business and (2) have a finite useful life, be allocated as an expense to the periods in which the benefits associated with their use help generate revenues. This allocation is called depreciation expense, which we introduced in Chapter 2.

Land may be used by a business, but is generally assumed to last forever. Therefore, the use of land results in no expense recognition. However, Plant and Equipment has an estimable determinate life, and so costs to acquire it are expensed over that useful life. Companies can accomplish this allocation of expenses by dividing the cost of the asset by the number of years the company anticipates it will be used. For example, if the Lobsters plan to use their hockey rink on a regular basis for 20 years, they will record $10,000 of expense ($200,000/20 years) at the end of each full year of use. The resulting depreciation expense for the period is recorded as follows:

Dec.	31	Depreciation Expense	10,000	
		Accumulated Depreciation—Hockey Rink		10,000
		Adjusting entry A7.		

Depreciation expense is deducted on the income statement like any other expense.

But what about the Accumulated Depreciation—Hockey Rink account? This type of account, which was briefly referred to in Chapter 2, requires some additional explanation. It is referred to as a **contra-asset.** *Contra* means contrary or opposite, and is appropriate because on the balance sheet accumulated depreciation is subtracted from its related asset account to obtain what is referred to as the **carrying value, book value,** or **undepreciated cost** of the asset. On the Lobsters' balance sheet, the hockey rink will be shown as follows:

Hockey rink (at cost)	$200,000	
Less: Accumulated depreciation	10,000	$190,000

The $190,000 is the carrying value of the rink. Do not confuse carrying value with fair market value. Carrying value merely represents the portion of the original historical cost of the asset that has not yet been depreciated.

When Prepaid Insurance became Insurance Expense (adjusting entry A5), it was necessary to debit the expense account and credit the *asset account* to show that insurance was being used up. Likewise, when supplies were used (adjusting entry A6), the company debited an expense account and credited the related *asset account*. Why then didn't the organization simply credit the Hockey Rink account when depreciation expense was recorded?

To answer this question, one must remember that the information provided on financial statements should be useful for external decision makers. Long-term assets tend to be expensive; for example, the rink represents almost half the cost of the Lobsters' total assets. If a potential investor or creditor is evaluating the ability of a company to repay a loan, he or she will want to know whether the plant and equipment of the company is old or new. If it is old, it is likely to need replacement soon, which can put a severe strain on the company's cash resources, thus inhibiting the ability to repay a loan. The use of an accumulated depreciation account helps people make judgments about how old a particular company is.

By comparing the cost of the hockey rink ($200,000) to the relatively small amount of accumulated depreciation shown on the balance sheet ($10,000), financial statement users will know that the rink is a relatively new asset for the company and that it probably will not have to be replaced for some time. Therefore, by looking at the Accumulated Depreciation account, investors and creditors have one important piece of information that would be lacking if the amount of depreciation were credited directly to the Hockey Rink account.

A final point to remember: In Exhibit 7.4, the Accumulated Depreciation account is listed along with all the asset accounts, even though it *has a credit balance.* This is done to show that this contra-asset account relates to the Hockey Rink account, and it has a credit balance because it *reduces* the carrying value of the hockey rink.

Many companies also have long-term intangible assets, such as patents, copyrights, or franchise arrangements. However, the illustration for the Lobsters does not include such accounts because no such assets exist for them. When allocating the portion of the cost of intangible assets to the periods benefited, we refer to the expense as **Amortization Expense.** The balance sheet for the Boston Celtics includes long-term assets called Property and Equipment, which are being depreciated, and National Basketball Association Franchise, an intangible asset that is being amortized.

Some companies also own natural resources, such as oil wells or various types of mines. Since these do not last forever, it is necessary to reflect a portion of the cost as an expense over a period of time. The allocation process for natural resources results in an expense called **Depletion Expense.**

Conceptually, depreciation expense, amortization expense, and depletion expense are similar. They all include allocation of an asset's cost over a period of use to recognize an expense for the period.

PAUSE & REFLECT

In the annual report of the Boston Celtics, which of the account balances shown on the balance sheet were probably changed as a result of the year-end adjusting process? Which of the revenues and expenses do you think were affected by adjustments?

Step 5. Prepare an Adjusted Trial Balance

Exhibit 7.4 shows all the proper year-end account balances after adjusting entries have been journalized and posted. Some account balances shown in Exhibit 7.4 changed as a result of adjusting journal entries, while others did not. For all accounts, the final balance shown is referred to as the *adjusted balance.* Based on this information, now it is possible to prepare an **adjusted trial balance** to once again check for the equality of debits and credits. This is shown below:

MAINE LOBSTERS, INC.
Adjusted Trial Balance
December 31, 1997

	Debits	Credits
Cash	$ 94,000	
Accounts receivable	500	
Supplies	500	
Prepaid insurance	10,000	
Land	100,000	
Hockey rink	200,000	
Accumulated depreciation—hockey rink		$ 10,000
Accounts payable		1,900
Unearned ticket revenue		20,000
Note payable		160,000
Interest payable		12,800
Capital stock		200,000
Retained earnings	10,000	
Ticket revenue		80,000
Advertising revenue		6,500
Wages expense	40,000	
Utilities expense	3,900	
Interest expense	12,800	
Insurance expense	5,000	
Supplies expense	4,500	
Depreciation expense	10,000	
Total	$491,200	$491,200

Using this adjusted trial balance, it is a relatively easy process to prepare the income statement, statement of stockholders' (owners of corporations) equity, and balance sheet, which follow. Note that the income statement must be prepared first because net income is needed to complete the statement of stockholders' equity. The statement of stockholders' equity must be completed next, because the ending stockholders' equity balance is needed to complete the balance sheet, which is the third statement prepared.

MAINE LOBSTERS, INC.
Income Statement
For the Year Ended December 31, 1997

Revenues:		
Ticket revenue	$80,000	
Advertising revenue	6,500	$86,500
Expenses:		
Wages expense	$40,000	
Utilities expense	3,900	
Interest expense	12,800	
Insurance expense	5,000	
Supplies expense	4,500	
Depreciation expense	10,000	76,200
Net income		$10,300

MAINE LOBSTERS, INC.
Statement of Stockholders' Equity
For the Year Ended December 31, 1997

	Capital Stock	Retained Earnings	Total Stockholders' Equity
Beginning balances	$ –0–	$ –0–	$ –0–
Add: Investments	200,000		200,000
Net income		10,300	10,300
Less: Dividends		(10,000)	(10,000)
Ending balances	$200,000	$ 300	$200,300

MAINE LOBSTERS, INC.
Balance Sheet
As of December 31, 1997

Assets

Current assets:		
Cash		$ 94,000
Accounts receivable		500
Supplies		500
Prepaid insurance		10,000
Total current assets		$105,000
Long-term assets:		
Land		$100,000
Hockey rink	$200,000	
Less accumulated depreciation	10,000	190,000
Total long-term assets		$290,000
Total assets		$395,000

Liabilities

Current liabilities:		
Accounts payable		$ 1,900
Unearned ticket revenue		20,000
Total current liabilities		$ 21,900
Long-term liabilities:		
Note payable		$160,000
Interest payable		12,800
Total long-term liabilities		$172,800
Total liabilities		$194,700

Stockholders' Equity

Capital stock	$200,000	
Retained earnings	300	200,300
Total liabilities and stockholders' equity		$395,000

The statement of cash flows is prepared last. It requires some information that is not included on the adjusted trial balance, because it must show *all* the sources and uses of cash during the year. This information can be obtained by reviewing the journal entries affecting cash to determine the reasons for any increases or decreases. We show the statement of cash flows for the Lobsters below:

MAINE LOBSTERS, INC.
Statement of Cash Flows
For the Year Ended December 31, 1997

Cash flows from operating activities:	
Cash received from ticket sales	$ 100,000
Cash received from advertising sales	6,000
Cash paid for insurance	(15,000)
Cash paid to employees	(40,000)
Cash paid for utilities	(3,000)
Cash paid for supplies	(4,000)
Net cash flow from operating activities	$ 44,000
Cash flows from investing activities:	
Cash paid for land	$(100,000)
Cash paid for hockey rink	(200,000)
Net cash flow from investing activities	$(300,000)
Cash flows from financing activities:	
Cash received from sale of stock	$ 200,000
Cash received from loan	160,000
Cash paid for dividends	(10,000)
Net cash flow from financing activities	$ 350,000
Increase in cash	$ 94,000
Add beginning balance in cash	–0–
Ending balance in cash	$ 94,000

PAUSE & REFLECT

Was the Lobsters' first year successful? Why was the cash flow from operating activities $44,000 while net income was only $10,300? Do you think they will be able to repay their loan when it matures?

Step 7. Enter Closing Entries in the General Journal and Post Them to the General Ledger

After preparing the financial statements, it is time to get ready for the next period. To help explain the importance of this next step, we must first define and explain the difference between real accounts and nominal accounts.

Real Accounts Some accounts in the general ledger carry their balances from one year (period) to the next; others do not. Think about all the accounts on the balance sheet. If the Maine Lobsters, Inc., had $94,000 in cash at the close of business on December 31, 1997, that money would still be there on the first day of the new year—it does not disappear. If they owed $160,000 on the note payable, they would still owe this money when they woke up to begin a new year. The same is true of all accounts on the balance sheet. Accountants refer to these accounts as **real,** or **permanent,** accounts because their account balances carry over from year to year.

Nominal Accounts However, revenue and expense accounts are different. If the balance in the Lobsters' Ticket Revenue account was $60,000 at the end of 1997, what should the balance in that account be when the next year begins? Revenue accounts exist to accumulate revenue information for a given period of time, so they should start each period with a zero balance. The same is true for all expense accounts. Revenue and expense accounts are called **nominal,** or **temporary,** accounts because they relate only to a given period of time, and must be *closed out* before the start of a new period.

If balances in temporary accounts are closed out at the end of each period, what happens to all of this information? It does not just disappear. Another look at Exhibit 7.4 reminds us that revenues cause owners' equity to increase, while expenses cause it to decrease. Although a balance sheet prepared for the Lobsters at December 31, 1997, would show a Retained Earnings balance that reflects the impact of all revenues and expenses that occurred during the year, this information has not yet been formally transferred to the Retained Earnings account in the general ledger. Thus, the **closing process** includes zeroing out all revenue and expense accounts (nominal accounts) and transferring these balances ultimately to Retained Earnings, so that the Retained Earnings account balance in the general ledger equals the year-end figure shown on the balance sheet. This process utilizes an **Income Summary** account, a temporary account used to accumulate all revenue and expense account balances prior to their transfer to Retained Earnings.

Exhibit 7.5 uses T-accounts to show how the closing process would work for the Maine Lobsters, Inc.

Step 1. Debit all revenue accounts (which normally have credit balances) and transfer their credit balances to the Income Summary account:

Ticket Revenue	80,000	
Advertising Revenue	6,500	
Income Summary		86,500
Closing entry C1.		

Step 2. Credit all expense accounts (which normally have debit balances) and transfer their debit balances to the Income Summary account:

Income Summary	76,200	
Wages Expense		40,000
Utilities Expense		3,900
Interest Expense		12,800
Insurance Expense		5,000
Supplies Expense		4,500
Depreciation Expense		10,000
Closing entry C2.		

The combination of steps 1 and 2 accomplishes two things. First, it gives all revenue and expense accounts a zero balance so they are ready for the new period, and, second, it formally records net income for the year in the Income Summary account.

Step 3. Finally, transfer the resulting credit balance in the Income Summary account to the Retained Earnings account by debiting Income Summary (which zeroes out this account) and crediting Retained Earnings to formally increase this account by the amount of income earned during the year:

Income Summary	10,300	
Retained Earnings		10,300
Closing entry C3.		

Notice that, while the net impact of the revenues and expenses was a $10,300 increase in Retained Earnings, the $10,000 dividend payment made at the end of 1997 reduced Retained Earnings, resulting in a net year-end balance of $300.

PAUSE & REFLECT	How would a net loss be transferred to Retained Earnings? What effect would a net loss have on total owners' equity? What would a net loss indicate about the revenues and expenses for that period?

Like other accounting events, all closing entries must be recorded formally in the general journal and then posted to the general ledger accounts affected.

EXHIBIT | 7.5

Closing Process

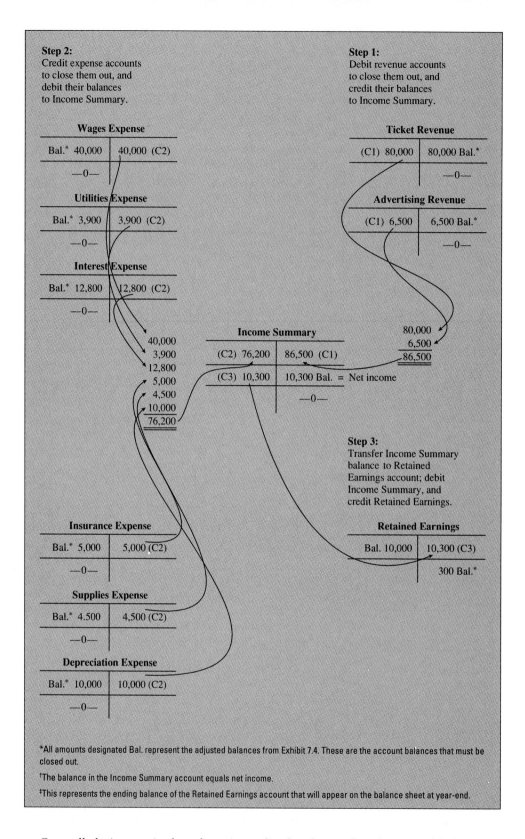

Step 2:
Credit expense accounts to close them out, and debit their balances to Income Summary.

Step 1:
Debit revenue accounts to close them out, and credit their balances to Income Summary.

Wages Expense

Bal.* 40,000	40,000 (C2)
—0—	

Ticket Revenue

	(C1) 80,000	80,000 Bal.*
		—0—

Utilities Expense

Bal.* 3,900	3,900 (C2)
—0—	

Advertising Revenue

	(C1) 6,500	6,500 Bal.*
		—0—

Interest Expense

Bal.* 12,800	12,800 (C2)
—0—	

```
            40,000
             3,900
            12,800
             5,000
             4,500
            10,000
            76,200
```

Income Summary

(C2) 76,200	86,500 (C1)
(C3) 10,300	10,300 Bal. = Net income
	—0—

```
   80,000
    6,500
   86,500
```

Step 3:
Transfer Income Summary balance to Retained Earnings account; debit Income Summary, and credit Retained Earnings.

Insurance Expense

Bal.* 5,000	5,000 (C2)
—0—	

Retained Earnings

	Bal. 10,000	10,300 (C3)
		300 Bal.*

Supplies Expense

Bal.* 4,500	4,500 (C2)
—0—	

Depreciation Expense

Bal.* 10,000	10,000 (C2)
—0—	

*All amounts designated Bal. represent the adjusted balances from Exhibit 7.4. These are the account balances that must be closed out.

†The balance in the Income Summary account equals net income.

‡This represents the ending balance of the Retained Earnings account that will appear on the balance sheet at year-end.

Step 8. Prepare a Post-Closing Trial Balance

Once all closing entries have been journalized and posted to the general ledger, it is possible to prepare a **post-closing trial balance** that will include only those real accounts shown on the balance sheet. (Nominal accounts are generally not listed because all their balances equal zero after completion of the closing process.) For the Maine Lobsters, Inc., the post-closing trial balance would appear as follows:

MAINE LOBSTERS, INC.
Post-Closing Trial Balance
December 31, 1997

	Debits	Credits
Cash	$ 94,000	
Accounts receivable	500	
Supplies	500	
Prepaid insurance	10,000	
Land	100,000	
Hockey rink	200,000	
Accumulated depreciation—hockey rink		$ 10,000
Accounts payable		1,900
Unearned ticket revenue		20,000
Note payable		160,000
Interest payable		12,800
Capital stock		200,000
Retained earnings		300
Total	$405,000	$405,000

This post-closing trial balance serves as one last check on the equality of debits and credits. Now the company has completed the accounting cycle and is ready for the start of a new year.

Closing Entries for Sole Proprietorships and Partnerships

The Maine Lobsters' organization is a corporation. Although closing entries for sole proprietorships and partnerships are similar in nature, users of financial information should understand that some slight modifications are required.

Sole Proprietorships Although corporations maintain separate accounts for contributed capital and retained earnings, sole proprietorships combine the effect of all owners' equity transactions in one account called **Capital.** Thus, investments by owners are added directly to the Capital account, and distributions to owners are deducted from this same account.[2] At the end of each accounting period, all revenues and expenses are closed out to the Income Summary account, just as they are for corporations, but instead of being added to Retained Earnings, they are transferred to the Capital account. This Capital account balance appears on a sole proprietorship's balance sheet as one amount, representing total owners' equity.

Partnerships Partnerships maintain a separate Capital account for each partner, and post individual partner investments and distributions to the appropriate partner's Capital account. When closing the balance of the Income Summary account, they divide up (allocate) the amount of net income according to a partnership agreement, with each partner's share being added to his or her Capital account. Partnership financial statements disclose each partner's Capital account balance, and sum them to obtain total owners' equity reported on the balance sheet.

SUMMARY

Exhibit 7.6 summarizes the formal accounting cycle.

Column (1), Recording, shows that, first, companies analyze source documents as the basis for recording entries in the general journal and posting these entries to the general ledger. At the end of every period, companies prepare a trial balance showing account balances to provide an opportunity to check against some, but not all, common types of errors in the recording process.

---

[2]Distributions to owners are often recorded initially in a separate account referred to as *Owner Withdrawals.* Use of this separate account helps track the dollar amount of owner distributions during a given year. When used, this account is closed out at the end of the accounting period, and the amount of withdrawals made during the year is debited directly to the Capital account. Partnerships also use separate withdrawal accounts to track distributions made to individual partners.

EXHIBIT | 7.6

Summary of Accounting
Cycle

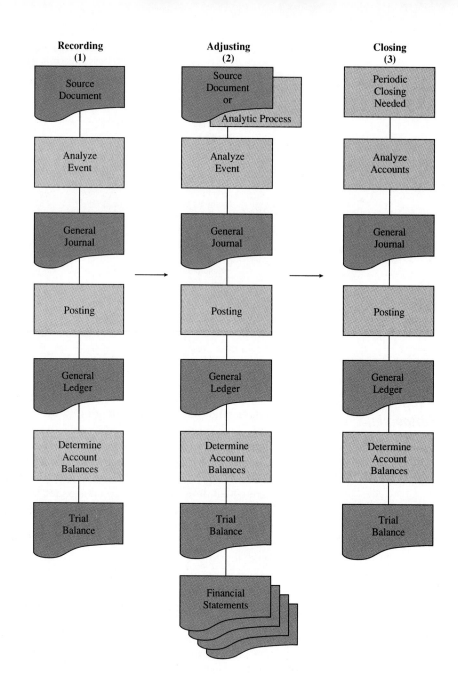

Column (2) summarizes the adjusting process, which has the goal of making sure that all revenues earned and expenses incurred during the period are matched and recorded properly. This process includes the company preparing financial statements from properly adjusted account balances.

Column (3) describes the closing process whereby all temporary (revenue and expense) accounts are closed, and their balances transferred to the appropriate owners' equity account.

- Companies record all accounting transactions at historical cost because this is the most objectively verifiable valuation method available.

- The matching principle requires that revenues earned and expenses incurred to earn those revenues be matched together on the same income statement to properly measure income for a given period.

- Companies record the cumulative balances for all items on the financial statements in accounts. Debit entries increase the balance of asset and expense accounts. Credit entries increase liability and revenue accounts, as well as the Capital Stock and Retained Earnings accounts.

- Accounting events are initially recorded in the general journal, a chronological record of all accounting transactions affecting the business.

- Periodically, it is necessary to post general journal entries to the general ledger to update the cumulative balance of each account.

- Adjusting journal entries are necessary at the end of each period to capture all revenues earned and expenses incurred during the period. These fall into three general categories: accruals, deferrals, and estimated allocations.

- Before preparing financial statements, companies use a trial balance to ascertain that the total of all debit account balances in the general ledger equals the total of all credit account balances.

- Companies prepare financial statements from the cumulative account balances shown in the general ledger.

- After preparing financial statements, companies close out all temporary accounts. Revenue and expense accounts are closed through the Income Summary account to Retained Earnings.

KEY TERMS

account A record of the accumulated results of accounting events affecting particular asset, liability, or owners' equity items

accounting cycle Formal process by which companies record accounting information, transfer it to specific accounts, and assemble it for the preparation of financial statements

accruals Revenues and expenses that have been earned or incurred, but have never been recorded because no source document has been generated or received

adjusted trial balance A summary of the debit and credit account balances prepared after making adjusting entries to check to see that the total amount of debits equals the total amount of credits (that there is an equality) before financial statement preparation

adjusting entries Entries that reflect changes in the amount of accruals, deferrals, and estimated allocations made prior to financial statement preparation

amortization expense The portion of the cost of intangible assets allocated to the periods benefited

capital An owners' equity account in a sole proprietorship or partnership

carrying value The cost of an asset less the amount appearing in its associated contra account. Also referred to as *book value* or *undepreciated cost*

chart of accounts A list of all a company's general ledger accounts by name and number

closing process The process of zeroing out all revenue and expense (nominal) accounts and transferring their balances ultimately to the Retained Earnings account (or to the Capital account in a sole proprietorship or partnership)

contra-asset An account whose balance is deducted from a related asset account to determine the asset's net value

credit (Cr) Any dollar amount entered on the right-hand side of an account

debit (Dr) Any dollar amount entered on the left-hand side of an account

deferrals Revenues collected in advance of being earned and expenses paid in advance of being incurred

depletion expense The portion of the cost of natural resources allocated to the periods benefited

fair market value A sales price that would be agreed upon by willing, unrelated buyers and sellers

general journal A chronological record of the accounting events which shows both the debit and credit side of each accounting event

general ledger The record of all a company's accounts

historical cost The cash or cash equivalent value that either changed hands, or became obligated when an accounting event occurred

Income Summary An account used in the closing entry process to temporarily accumulate all revenue and expense account balances prior to transfer to the Retained Earnings or a capital account

matching principle The requirement that all expenses incurred attempting to generate revenue be matched with the revenues earned during a given period to determine net income

net worth Another way of referring to owners' equity

nominal account A temporary account relating to a given period of time

objectivity principle The accounting principle requiring that information included in published financial statements must be free of bias

post-closing trial balance A trial balance prepared after the closing process as a last check on the equality of debits and credits

posting process Recording the information contained in the general journal to the accounts in the general ledger

real account A permanent account whose balance is carried over from year to year

replacement cost The cost of producing or otherwise acquiring a similar item

revenue recognition principle The requirement that revenues should be recognized and recorded when the service is performed or the sale has occurred

T-account An informal representation of a general ledger account

trial balance An internal document showing a company's account or balances to verify the equality of debits and credits

QUESTIONS

1. Define historical cost and explain why it is used to report accounting data in lieu of using fair market value or replacement cost.

2. What is the matching principle? Why is it necessary?

3. Explain the need for an account.

4. Define the terms *debit* and *credit*.

5. What is a general journal? How does it differ from a general ledger?

6. What is a normal balance of an account? For each of the following accounts, state whether the normal balance is a debit or a credit: asset, liability, Capital Stock, Retained Earnings, revenue, and expense.

7. What does it mean when we say that a trial balance balances? Why should a trial balance always balance?

8. Why are adjusting entries necessary and when are they prepared?

9. Explain the terms *accrual* and *deferral*.

10. The accountant at Taxes R Us forgot to make the adjusting entry to record expired insurance. What affect will that have on the financial statements?

11. The cost of a parcel of land was debited to the Land account and then depreciated. Was this the appropriate treatment? Explain.

12. RAP Industries paid for a one-year insurance policy on January 2, 1997. The entry that was made included a debit to Insurance Expense and a credit to Cash. RAP Industries prepares financial statements once a year on December 31. Was this entry appropriate? Explain.

13. A lawyer received a $50,000 retainer from a client for services to be performed. What type of adjusting entry would result when the lawyer actually performed the services?

14. In January 1998 the accounting department at AMC Corporation received a telephone bill for December 1997. Is an adjusting entry required for the year ended December 31, 1997? If so, what would it be?

15. What are the four primary financial statements and when are they prepared?

16. Is there any special order in which the four financial statements must be prepared? Explain.

17. You are the manager of the local variety store. Describe an internal report that the accounting system might generate that would be of interest to you.

18. What is the difference between a nominal account and a real account? Provide an example of each.

19. If closing entries were not prepared, what problems would be created?

20. Refer to the financial statements for the Boston Celtics in the Annual Report Booklet. List the accounts that would have been closed out at June 30, 1995.

EXERCISES

E 7.1 Various accounts are affected differently by debits and credits. For each account listed below, state whether it is increased or decreased by a debit or credit. The first account is used as an example.

Accounts	Increased By	Decreased By	Normal Balance
a. Cash	debit	credit	debit
b. Salaries Payable			
c. Buildings			
d. Accounts Receivable			
e. Sales			
f. Capital Stock			
g. Prepaid Insurance			
h. Unearned Revenue			
i. Utilities Expense			
j. Accumulated Depreciation			

E 7.2 TLC Corporation began operations with the following transactions. Create and label the T-accounts necessary to record the transactions and enter debit and credit amounts for each event in the T-accounts as appropriate. (Use the letter of the event to identify each amount in the T-accounts.)
a. Sold capital stock for $25,000.
b. Purchased land and a building valued at $35,000 and $65,000, respectively, by paying $10,000 cash and signing a 20-year mortgage for the balance.
c. Purchased office equipment on account, $4,500.
d. Billed a customer for services performed, $2,200.
e. Received a $500 deposit from a customer for services to be performed next month.
f. Made a partial payment on account for the office equipment purchased in *c* above, $1,500.
g. Performed a service and immediately collected $800.
h. Received and immediately paid the telephone bill for the month, $180.
i. Declared and paid a dividend to stockholders, $4,000.
j. Received, but did not pay, the monthly utility bill, $210.

E 7.3 The following transactions occurred during Keester Corporation's first month of operations, June 1996. Journalize the transactions in a general journal, post the transactions to the appropriate T-accounts, and prepare a trial balance.
a. Issued $5,000 of capital stock for cash.
b. Purchased $250 of office supplies on account.
c. Borrowed $1,000 from the bank and signed a note payable for that amount.
d. Billed a client $450 for services rendered.
e. Received and immediately paid the utility bill for the month, $320.
f. Performed a service and immediately collected $200.
g. Paid for the office supplies purchased in transaction *b*.
h. Received $150 from a client who had previously been billed.
i. Recorded, but did not pay, the telephone bill for the month, $180.
j. Declared and paid a $300 dividend to stockholders.
k. Received a $500 deposit from a client for work to be performed next month.

E 7.4 The accounts below are from the general ledger of Daverin Enterprises. For each letter given in the T-accounts, describe the transaction that most likely caused the entry.

Cash	Accounts Receivable
(c) | *(d)*	*(a)* |

Supplies	Land
(b) |	*(e)* |

Building	Accounts Payable
(e) |	| *(b)*

Note Payable	Capital Stock
| *(e)*	| *(c)*

Fee Revenue	Salaries Expense
| *(a)*	*(d)* |

E 7.5 For each of the following entries, describe the event that gave rise to the entry.

a.	Accounts payable	1,300	
	Cash		1,300
b.	Prepaid Rent	4,200	
	Cash		4,200
c.	Office Supplies	1,500	
	Accounts Payable		1,500
d.	Cash	5,000	
	Unearned Revenue		5,000
e.	Accounts Receivable	500	
	Fee Revenue		500
f.	Telephone Expense	200	
	Cash		200

E 7.6 For each of the following entries, describe the event that gave rise to the entry and indicate how each event affected the assets, liabilities, and owners' equity.

a.	Cash	2,400	
	Unearned Revenue		2,400
b.	Supplies	300	
	Accounts Payable		300
c.	Cash	10,000	
	Capital Stock		10,000
d.	Equipment	4,000	
	Notes Payable		3,000
	Cash		1,000
e.	Advertising Expense	600	
	Cash		600
f.	Accounts Receivable	3,800	
	Fee Revenue		3,800

E 7.7 For each of the following situations, (1) prepare the adjusting entry for the month ended October 31 and (2) indicate the effect each adjustment would have on net income.

a. Ace Plumbing had a $20,000 contract with Villas Construction Company to perform plumbing services for a home under construction. Payment was to be received at the end of the job. As of October 31, $8,000 worth of services had been performed.

b. Swifty Bank made a $10,000 loan to a customer on October 1. The terms called for principal and interest of 8 percent to be paid at the end of one year. Swifty prepares monthly financial statements.

c. Decade 31, a real estate company, rents office space to a lawyer for $750 per month. The invoice for October had not been sent as of October 31.

E 7.8   For each of the following situations, (1) prepare the adjusting entry for the month ended May 31 and (2) indicate the effect each adjustment would have on net income.

    a. The May telephone bill for Pa Chime Company arrived in the accounting department on June 8. The invoice totaled $210.

    b. Paperclips, Inc., had an arrangement with a local newspaper to run a full-page advertisement every Sunday. The cost of each ad was $250. The newspaper sends Paperclips a bill on the 15th of the next month. There were four Sundays in the month of May.

    c. Citilimits borrowed $50,000 on October 1. The terms of the note called for repayment of principal and interest of 7 percent one year from the date of the note. Citilimits prepares monthly financial statements.

E 7.9   For each of the following situations, (1) prepare the adjusting entry for the month ended February 28 and (2) indicate the effect each adjustment would have on net income.

    a. On February 1, Ima Loyer received a $10,000 retainer from a client. By the end of February, Ima had earned $3,500 of the retainer.

    b. During January, $24,000 in magazine subscriptions was received by Magazines "R" Us. The subscriptions were for 12 monthly issues of *Summer Sport*, beginning with the month of February. Magazines "R" Us prepares monthly financial statements.

    c. Red Square Insurance Company sells policies that run on a calendar-year basis. They sold $48,000 of insurance policies and collected the cash in early January. Red Square prepares monthly financial statements.

E 7.10   For each of the following situations, (1) prepare the adjusting entry for the month-end July 31 and (2) indicate the effect each adjustment would have on net income.

    a. Outfitters, Inc., purchased a one-year insurance policy on January 2 for $3,600. Outfitters prepares monthly financial statements.

    b. On July 1, Gear and Company had a $390 balance in its Supplies account. During July, $1,450 of additional supplies were purchased. An inventory at July 31 showed $275 of supplies still on the shelves.

    c. Last year, Apparel Enterprises purchased some equipment at a total cost of $45,000. The estimated useful life of the equipment is 15 years. Apparel prepares monthly financial statements.

E 7.11   Prepare the adjusting entry for each of the situations described below.

    a. On May 1, Secret Services, Inc., had a $2,780 debit balance in its Supplies account. During May, $4,250 of additional supplies were purchased. At the end of the month, a count of supplies revealed $2,430 left on hand.

    b. Ski Sports Enterprises, which produces a monthly magazine, received $3,600 in payments from its customers for two-year subscriptions. The subscriptions start with the June issue of this year. The company prepares financial statements annually on December 31.

    c. PJ MAX Industries has the following unadjusted balances on December 31, 1995:

Building	$750,000
Accumulated depreciation—building	112,500

    The building was acquired in early January 1992. It has an estimated useful life of 20 years. The company uses straight-line depreciation and prepares financial statements annually.

E 7.12   Refer to Exercise 7.11. What would be the impact on the financial statements if each of the adjusting entries in situations *a–c* were not recorded?

E 7.13   The following events are among those that occurred during the course of the firm's usual operations for the month of April. The firm adjusts and closes the books monthly. Determine which of the events will normally result in a subsequent adjusting entry. For each event you select, specify the accounts to be debited and credited in the adjustment. Do not attempt to determine the amounts of the adjustments.

    a. Paid insurance premiums of $1,500 in advance.

    b. Made a sale of $750 to a customer on account.

    c. Received cash of $600 from a customer for services to be performed two months later.

    d. Purchased office equipment costing $5,000 on account.

    e. Purchased gasoline costing $225 during the month. It was used for the delivery trucks.

    f. Made a cash sale of $325 to a customer.

    g. Paid $400 rent for the month of April.

    h. Purchased for cash an additional $700 in supplies.

E 7.14 One of the following combinations of effects results from making adjusting entries.
  a. Increases assets, increases revenues, and increases owners' equity.
  b. Decreases assets, increases expenses, and decreases owners' equity.
  c. Increases liabilities, increases expenses, and decreases owners' equity.
  d. Decreases liabilities, increases revenues, and increases owners' equity.

Select one of the items, *a* through *d*, above to match the effect achieved by each of the following adjusting entries.
  1. Salaries earned by employees but unpaid amount to $7,850.
  2. Depreciation expense on equipment is $3,250.
  3. Prepaid insurance expired during the period totals $1,300.
  4. Interest earned, but not yet received, amounts to $800.
  5. Of the revenue received and previously recorded as unearned, $13,675 has been earned this period.
  6. Property taxes accrued, but not yet paid, amount to $6,700.
  7. Supplies used during the period total $2,100.
  8. Interest owed on long-term debt totals $1,500.

E 7.15 Using the annual report you obtained as a Chapter 1 assignment, review the financial statements and notes to the financial statements. List the accounts that were most likely to have been adjusted at the end of the accounting period.

E 7.16 For the following alphabetical list of accounts and their balances, determine: (*a*) net income, (*b*) total assets, (*c*) total liabilities, and (*d*) total stockholders' equity.

Accounts payable	$ 20,000
Accounts receivable	12,500
Accumulated depreciation—buildings	33,700
Buildings	110,000
Capital stock	85,000
Cash	41,000
Depreciation expense	6,400
Insurance expense	2,300
Interest expense	4,800
Interest payable	1,500
Land	75,000
Miscellaneous expense	5,200
Note payable	57,100
Prepaid insurance	7,900
Property taxes expense	3,600
Property taxes payable	900
Rental income earned	97,500
Retained earnings	13,800
Salaries expense	29,400
Salaries payable	1,800
Supplies	6,700
Supplies expense	2,000
Utilities expense	4,500

E 7.17 Fernandez Corporation has closed its revenue and expense accounts to Income Summary. Selected account balances from the firm's general ledger appear below. Determine the net income or loss for the year and the balance in the Retained Earnings account that would appear on the balance sheet. What is total stockholders' equity?

Income Summary		Capital Stock	Retained Earnings
15,670	18,790	22,500	30,430

E 7.18 Given the adjusted trial balance for Spang Editorial Services, Inc., presented below, prepare the income statement and statement of stockholders' equity for the month ended August 31, 1997. Dividends of $2,500 were declared and paid during the month and there were no additional capital stock transactions during the month.

SPANG EDITORIAL SERVICES, INC.
Adjusted Trial Balance
August 31, 1997

	Debits	Credits
Cash	$ 3,100	
Supplies	400	
Prepaid rent	650	
Equipment	5,600	
Accumulated depreciation—equipment		$ 1,200
Furniture	2,700	
Accumulated depreciation—furniture		900
Accounts payable		800
Note payable		3,000
Interest payable		150
Capital stock		6,000
Retained earnings	2,500	
Service fees revenue		4,300
Supplies expense	150	
Rent expense	650	
Interest expense	25	
Depreciation expense	300	
Postage expense	125	
Telephone expense	50	
Utilities expense	100	
Total	$16,350	$16,350

E 7.19 Refer to E7.18. Prepare the balance sheet for Spang Editorial Services, Inc., as of August 31, 1997.

E 7.20 Refer to E7.18. Prepare the closing entries for Spang Editorial Services, Inc., on August 31, 1997.

E 7.21 The adjusted trial balance of Danza Taxi Service, Inc., is presented below. Determine the net income or loss for the month of May and the balance in the Retained Earnings account that would appear on the balance sheet.

DANZA TAXI SERVICE, INC.
Adjusted Trial Balance
May 31, 1996

	Debits	Credits
Cash	$ 1,920	
Prepaid insurance	690	
Automobiles	29,500	
Accumulated depreciation—automobiles		$12,800
Capital stock		15,000
Retained earnings		3,665
Passenger revenue		4,250
Salary expense	2,400	
Fuel expense	485	
Depreciation expense	615	
Repairs and maintenance expense	105	
Total	$35,715	$35,715

E 7.22 Using the annual report you obtained as a Chapter 1 assignment, review the financial statements and notes to the financial statements. List the accounts that would have been closed at the end of the accounting period.

PROBLEMS

P 7.1

Jared Lambert, CPA, opened a practice and completed the following transactions during the first month of operations.

June 1   Lambert deposited $35,000 in a bank account in the name of his business.
     1   Paid $6,000 rent for the next four months.
     2   Obtained a bank loan for $15,000 and signed a note payable.
     5   Purchased $12,500 of equipment on account.
     8   Purchased $1,700 of supplies for cash.
     11   Received $2,200 from customers for services rendered.
     17   Received a $5,000 deposit from a customer for services to be performed in July and August.
     20   Paid for one-half of the equipment purchased on June 5.
     24   Performed services for a client and sent out a bill for $800.
     28   Received and immediately paid the telephone bill for the month, $180.
     30   Paid employees' salaries of $1,300.
     30   Lambert withdrew $2,400 cash for personal expenses.
     30   Paid the bank $2,000 on the note payable plus interest expense of $30 for a total payment of $2,030.

Required: Prepare the entries necessary to record the above events.

P 7.2

Nature's Health Center, Inc., was established in August of the current year. The following transactions were completed during the first month of operations.

Aug. 1   Received $40,000 and issued capital stock.
     1   Paid $10,000 rent for the next five months.
     3   Obtained a bank loan for $30,000 and signed a note payable.
     5   Purchased $35,000 of equipment for cash.
     8   Purchased $2,300 of supplies on account.
     10   Received $1,500 from customers for services rendered.
     12   Received and immediately paid a $225 laundry bill.
     17   Discovered some of the supplies were defective and returned them to the vendor for a $500 credit.
     18   Received a $3,000 deposit from a customer for services to be performed over the next month.
     20   Paid for remaining supplies purchased on August 8.
     25   Performed services for a client and sent out a bill for $600.
     28   Received $4,750 from customers for services rendered.
     31   Paid employees' salaries of $2,200.
     31   Declared and paid a $1,500 dividend to stockholders.
     31   Paid the bank $5,000 on the note payable plus interest expense of $250 for a total payment of $5,250.

Required:
a. Prepare the entries necessary to record the above events.
b. Post the entries to the general ledger and determine the ending balance of each account. Use T-accounts to represent general ledger accounts.
c. Prepare a trial balance.

P 7.3

Adjustment data and the unadjusted trial balance have been gathered by Donahue Express Corporation.

Adjustment Data:

a. Unused supplies on hand, $350.
b. Unexpired rent, $1,350.
c. Depreciation on buildings, $1,300.
d. Depreciation on equipment, $750.
e. Unearned fees still unearned, $900.
f. Salaries earned but not yet paid, $470.
g. Accrued interest on the note, $320.
h. Fees earned but not recorded and not received, $450.

DONAHUE EXPRESS CORPORATION
Unadjusted Trial Balance
March 31, 1996

	Debits	Credits
Cash	$ 7,280	
Accounts receivable	2,150	
Supplies	940	
Prepaid rent	2,400	
Land	52,000	
Buildings	94,000	
Accumulated depreciation—buildings		$ 16,600
Equipment	41,500	
Accumulated depreciation—equipment		13,500
Accounts payable		3,480
Unearned fees		2,970
Note payable		60,000
Capital stock		45,000
Retained earnings		39,150
Fees earned		29,750
Salary expense	9,320	
Telephone expense	260	
Utilities expense	410	
Miscellaneous expense	190	
Total	$210,450	$210,450

Required: Prepare the adjusting entries. In some instances, it will be necessary to establish new accounts.

 P 7.4 The unadjusted trial balance of VQT Delivery Service, Inc., is presented below, together with the information for adjustments.

VQT DELIVERY SERVICE, INC.
Unadjusted Trial Balance
June 30, 1997

	Debits	Credits
Cash	$ 6,340	
Accounts receivable	1,410	
Supplies	890	
Prepaid insurance	1,900	
Land	48,000	
Buildings	82,000	
Accumulated depreciation—buildings		$ 18,960
Equipment	53,000	
Accumulated depreciation—equipment		16,800
Accounts payable		2,160
Unearned delivery fees		2,100
Mortgage payable		58,000
Capital stock		50,000
Retained earnings		21,630
Delivery fees earned		33,460
Salary expense	8,670	
Telephone expense	120	
Utilities expense	350	
Repairs expense	430	
Total	$203,110	$203,110

Adjustment Data:

a. Supplies used, $270.
b. Expired insurance, $600.
c. Depreciation on buildings, $500.
d. Depreciation on equipment, $900.
e. Unearned delivery fees earned this month, $1,300.
f. Salaries earned but not yet paid, $180.
g. Interest on the mortgage, $210.
h. Delivery fees earned but not recorded and not received, $500.

Required:
a. Create T-accounts for the trial balance accounts presented above and enter their balances.
b. Prepare the adjusting entries. In some instances, it will be necessary to establish new accounts for items not shown on the unadjusted trial balance.
c. Post the adjustments to the T-accounts.
d. Prepare an adjusted trial balance.

P 7.5 The adjusted trial balance for Elementary Electric Company as of June 30, 1996, is presented below.

ELEMENTARY ELECTRIC COMPANY
Adjusted Trial Balance
June 30, 1996

	Debits	Credits
Cash	$ 21,700	
Accounts receivable	4,200	
Supplies	1,800	
Prepaid insurance	6,300	
Land	43,500	
Buildings	132,000	
Accumulated depreciation—buildings		$ 25,600
Accounts payable		3,700
Interest payable		10,300
Salaries payable		2,500
Property taxes payable		4,100
Unearned revenue		2,600
Note payable (due in 3 years)		100,000
E. Current, capital		40,000
Service revenue		78,600
Wages expense	14,800	
Utilities expense	4,600	
Property tax expense	3,500	
Insurance expense	6,700	
Supplies expense	5,100	
Depreciation expense	8,800	
Interest expense	13,200	
Miscellaneous expense	1,200	
Total	$267,400	$267,400

Required:
a. Prepare the income statement for the year ended June 30, 1996.
b. Prepare the statement of owner's equity for the year ended June 30, 1996. E. Current withdrew $30,000 cash during the year for personal expenses.
c. Prepare the balance sheet as of June 30, 1996.

P 7.6 See the adjusted trial balance for Yamaguci Equipment Rental Corp. as of December 31, 1997. Dividends declared and paid during the year amounted to $12,000 and there were no capital stock transactions during the year.

YAMAGUCI EQUIPMENT RENTAL CORP.
Adjusted Trial Balance
December 31, 1997

	Debits	Credits
Cash	$ 14,800	
Accounts receivable	3,150	
Supplies	2,100	
Prepaid insurance	8,850	
Land	37,000	
Buildings	175,000	
Accumulated depreciation—buildings		$ 28,250
Accounts payable		2,150
Interest payable		12,000
Salaries payable		3,200
Property taxes payable		4,700
Rent received in advance		1,400
Note payable (due in 5 years)		125,000
Capital stock		40,000
Retained earnings		8,100
Rental revenue		66,950
Wages expense	10,600	
Utilities expense	3,900	
Property tax expense	4,700	
Insurance expense	5,200	
Supplies expense	4,300	
Depreciation expense	9,000	
Interest expense	12,000	
Miscellaneous expense	1,150	
Total	$291,750	$291,750

Required: a. Prepare the income statement for the year ended December 31, 1997.
b. Prepare the statement of stockholders' equity for the year ended December 31, 1997.
c. Prepare the balance sheet as of December 31, 1997.

P 7.7   The following adjusted trial balance was taken from the accounting records of Danbury Enterprises.

DANBURY ENTERPRISES
Adjusted Trial Balance
April 30, 1996

	Debits	Credits
Cash	$ 31,500	
Accounts receivable	12,600	
Supplies	4,300	
Prepaid insurance	700	
Equipment	31,800	
Accumulated depreciation—equipment		$ 3,200
Accounts payable		4,800
Salaries payable		700
Note payable		15,000
Capital stock		45,000
Retained earnings		17,100
Management fees earned		54,000
Appraisal fees earned		8,700
Salaries expense	44,700	
Advertising expense	8,200	
Depreciation expense	2,700	
Supplies expense	4,600	
Interest expense	1,900	
Utilities expense	2,500	
Insurance expense	1,600	
Property tax increase	1,400	
Total	$148,500	$148,500

Required: Prepare the closing entries for Danbury Enterprises on April 30, 1996.

P 7.8 The following adjusted trial balance was taken from the accounting records of Olympia Sports, Inc.

OLYMPIA SPORTS, INC.
Adjusted Trial Balance
September 30, 1997

	Debits	Credits
Cash	$ 26,700	
Accounts receivable	18,500	
Supplies	5,600	
Prepaid insurance	200	
Equipment	41,500	
Accumulated depreciation—equipment		$ 2,600
Accounts payable		2,100
Salaries payable		900
Note payable		12,500
Capital stock		50,000
Retained earnings		13,300
Consulting fees earned		15,000
Service fees earned		70,000
Salaries expense	52,000	
Advertising expense	7,800	
Depreciation expense	3,400	
Supplies expense	5,800	
Interest expense	2,400	
Utilities expense	1,200	
Insurance expense	600	
Property tax expense	700	
Total	$166,400	$166,400

Required:
a. Prepare the closing entries.
b. Post the entries to the general ledger and determine the ending balances in the accounts. Use T-accounts to represent general ledger accounts.
c. Prepare a post-closing trial balance.

P 7.9 M. L. Curly set up his psychology practice on March 1. The following transactions occurred during March.

Mar. 1 M. L. Curly deposited $25,000 in an account in the name of the business.
   2 Paid $5,400 for three months' rent of an office.
   5 Purchased office supplies for cash, $900.
   8 Purchased $4,800 of office furniture on account.
   10 Paid $250 for advertising in the local newspaper.
   12 Completed counseling with a client and sent a bill for $850 for services rendered.
   15 Performed counseling services for a local DJ and immediately collected $350.
   18 Paid the March insurance premium of $300.
   20 Received a $5,000 deposit for counseling services to be performed for the employees of 3S Company beginning next week.
   21 Received a partial payment of $200 from the client billed on March 12.
   25 Paid $1,000 of the amount owed from the purchase of office furniture on March 8.
   27 Withdrew $2,000 for personal living expenses.
   31 Paid the receptionist's salary of $1,200.

Required: *a.* Prepare journal entries for each of the transactions listed above.
            b. Post the entries to the general ledger. Use T-accounts to represent general ledger accounts and determine the ending balance of each account.
            c. Prepare a trial balance.
            d. Using the information below, prepare the necessary adjusting entries and post them to the T-accounts.
               1. One month's rent has expired.
               2. An inventory of supplies showed $250 still on hand.
               3. The office furniture is estimated to have a 10-year useful life.
               4. Of the Unearned Revenue, $400 had been earned by March 31.
               5. The telephone bill for March, for $130, was received on April 3.
               6. A client counseled on March 31 was sent an invoice for $350 on April 2.
            e. Prepare an adjusted trial balance.
            f. Prepare an income statement, statement of owner's equity, balance sheet, and statement of cash flows.
            g. Prepare the closing entries and post them to the T-accounts.
            h. Prepare a post-closing trial balance.

P 7.10   Sun and Fun, Inc., began business on May 1 and during its first month of operations completed the following transactions.

     May 1   Sun and Fun issued capital stock for $30,000.
           2   Paid $4,500 for three months' rent of retail space.
           4   Purchased supplies for cash, $800.
           7   Purchased $6,000 of store fixtures on account.
         10   Paid $450 for advertising in the local newspaper.
         11   Sold $3,700 in services for cash.
         14   Services totaling $2,600 were provided on account.
         15   Paid the May insurance premium of $400.
         19   Received a $500 deposit for services to be performed at the beginning of next month.
         21   Received a partial payment of $200 from the customer of May 14.
         22   Paid $1,500 of the amount owed from the purchase of store fixtures on May 7.
         28   Declared and paid dividends of $1,800.
         31   Paid the salesperson's salary of $1,000.

Required: *a.* Prepare journal entries for each of the transactions listed above.
            b. Post the entries to the general ledger. Use T-accounts to represent general ledger accounts and determine the ending balance of each account.
            c. Prepare a trial balance.
            d. Using the information below, prepare the necessary adjusting entries and post them to the T-accounts.
               1. One month's rent has expired.
               2. An inventory of supplies showed $200 still on hand.
               3. The store fixtures are estimated to have a five-year useful life.
               4. The telephone bill for May, for $180, was received on June 3.
            e. Prepare an adjusted trial balance.
            f. Prepare an income statement, statement of stockholders' equity, balance sheet, and statement of cash flows.
            g. Prepare the closing entries and post them to the T-accounts.
            h. Prepare a post-closing trial balance.

COMPUTER APPLICATIONS

CA 7.1

Companies often make use of computerized spreadsheets to help determine the impact of various adjusting entries before they are formally recorded. Following is a typical spreadsheet layout devised by the Painfree Physical Therapy Center as of June 30, 1997. It enables the company to enter the debit/credit amount of all adjusting entries in the middle set of columns, so that adjusted balances can easily and quickly be determined. By using the spreadsheet, managers can perform calculations to quickly determine the effect of various adjusting entries on account balances.

	Unadjusted Trial Balance		Adjustments		Adjusted Trial Balance	
	Debits	Credits	Debits	Credits	Debits	Credits
Cash	$1,600					
Accounts receivable	1,100					
Supplies	300					
Equipment	3,000					
Accumulated depreciation—equipment		$ 900				
Accounts payable		600				
Unearned revenue		700				
Capital stock		1,500				
Retained earnings		800				
Service revenue		3,300				
Salary expense	1,500					
Utilities expense	100					
Insurance expense	200					
Total	$7,800	$7,800				

Required:

a. Use a computer spreadsheet program to create the above table. For all debit and credit "cells" in the Adjusted Trial Balance columns, insert the formula necessary to determine the account balance that will result from any debit or credit entries made in the set of Adjustments columns.

b. Using your spreadsheet, determine the adjusted account balances that will result, given the following information relative to required adjusting entries.
1. Supplies used during the month amounted to $150.
2. Depreciation on the equipment is $250 for the month.
3. Unearned revenue earned during the month is $300.
4. Revenue earned but unrecorded as of the end of the month totaled $400.

c. How would the adjusted trial balance change if the depreciation for the month was $500 instead of $250?

d. How would the adjusted trial balance change if the accrued revenue was $650 instead of $400?

CA 7.2

Companies often use computerized spreadsheets to predict how income will change as a result of specified changes in various revenues and expenses. Following is an income statement for the month of October 1996 for Computer Rent and Repair, Inc.

COMPUTER RENT AND REPAIR, INC.
Income Statement
For the Month Ended October 31, 1996

Revenues:		
Rental revenue	$27,000	
Repair revenue	12,500	$39,500
Expenses:		
Wages expense	$12,700	
Utilities expense	3,200	
Insurance expense	4,600	
Supplies expense	2,500	
Depreciation expense	5,100	
Miscellaneous expense	1,400	29,500
Net income		$10,000

Required:

a. Construct a computer spreadsheet for the above income statement. Include the appropriate formula in any cell whose balance results from an addition or subtraction calculation.

b. If rental revenue increases 10 percent, what will happen to net income?

c. If wages expense increases 7 percent, utilities expense increases 4 percent, and insurance expense decreases 5 percent, what will happen to net income?

CASES

C 7.1 The partners of Tootsie's Hair Salon have come to you for help in setting up the accounting records for their new business. They anticipate providing hair cuts, styling, and other hair services as well as selling hair products. In addition, they plan to offer nail care and tanning services. Most of their sales will be on a cash basis, but a limited number of customers will be allowed to open charge accounts with the salon. They have located a supplier of hair products who has agreed to let them make purchases on account. Each partner will contribute money to the partnership that will be used to cover initial operating expenses such as rent. Purchases of equipment will be financed by the local bank.

Required: a. Prepare a written report to the partners outlining how a double-entry accounting system will help them in their business.

b. Prepare a list of accounts the general ledger will most likely include.

C 7.2 Upon graduation from high school, Kenny Graham decided to go into business for himself to earn money for his college education. He negotiated a contract to operate a concession in a local park during summers. Kenny was confident the business would be a success because the park contained hiking and jogging trails, a bike pathway, tennis and handball courts, and several ball fields. He had observed that these facilities were used extensively.

He established the business as a sole proprietorship, depositing $2,500 of his savings into a checking account in the company's name, Kool Refreshments. He made a $400 payment to operate the concession for the next four summers under the terms of the contract. Next, he purchased a $3,000 concession stand by paying one-half the price at the time of purchase and promising to pay the remaining one-half 60 days later. The stand can be bolted together on site and dismantled at the end of the season for storage purposes. It is expected to last for four years, at which time it will be discarded. Credit terms were arranged with a local wholesale food supplier, RCA Wholesale Groceries, for the purchase of supplies. The business began operations on June 1, 1997.

The only accounting records he maintained were a checkbook, which included notations showing the reason for each payment, and a file folder for unpaid bills and monthly bank statements. He paid all bills by check and deposited business receipts in the bank regularly, keeping only a small amount of currency and coin on hand for making change.

Kenny noticed many people riding bicycles in the park. On July 1, 1997, believing there might be a market for bike rentals, he arranged a loan of $1,000 from his father, and used the money to purchase several bicycles expected to last through the end of the 2000 season. Kenny plans to donate the bicycles to the local boys club at the end of August 2000. He signed a note payable for the loan and agreed to repay the money, together with interest at 6 percent per year, 14 months later on September 1, 1998.

For the three-month period ending August 31, 1997, receipts from sales of food and drink totaled $16,400, and bicycle rentals generated $1,850. Kenny paid RCA Wholesale Groceries a total of $8,650 for food and drink supplies, and on August 31, 1997, still owed that company $210. He made the final $1,500 payment on the concession stand and also paid $1,700 to part-time workers who helped him during his busy hours in the early evenings and on weekends. Other payments totaled $685 for utilities and $270 for bicycle repairs.

On August 31, the end of the season, Kenny donated his remaining food and drink supplies, which had a cost of $90, to the local youth softball league for their end-of-season picnic.

Required: a. Prepare an analysis of the profitability of Kool Refreshments for the 1997 season. Note: Calculate interest through the end of December 1997 and include it in your analysis.

b. Should Kenny plan to operate the business next season or should he bail out? What issues should he consider in making this decision?

C 7.3 As the accountant for Prime Software Corporation, you are responsible for preparing the financial statements at the end of the fiscal year. However, this year-end there is a problem. You won a free trip to Europe that must be taken at the time you normally prepare the financial statements. You approached your boss asking her to hire a temporary accountant to prepare the financial statements. She agreed to this as long as you write a set of instructions detailing the preparation of financial statements for the temporary accountant to follow.

Required: Assume the temporary accountant has a working knowledge of accounting and that the accounts have already been adjusted. Write the set of instructions for the preparation of the financial statements. Remember, your trip to Europe depends upon it!

C 7.4 In September 1979, the Financial Accounting Standards Board issued *SFAS No. 33*. This statement required companies to report supplemental information regarding replacement cost and changing prices to their stockholders. *SFAS No. 33* was very controversial and was subsequently superseded by *SFAS No. 89*, which encouraged, but no longer required, presentation of this supplemental data.

Required:
a. Go to the library and research this issue using articles written about *SFAS No. 33*. The *Journal of Accountancy*, *CPA Journal*, and *Management Accountant* are good places to start.

b. Using the information you gather, discuss some of the arguments in favor of and against *SFAS No. 33*.

CRITICAL THINKING

CT 7.1 The two companies listed below are similar in nature. Both began operations this year and had a net income of $25,000. However, one of the companies has filed for bankruptcy. Determine which company is bankrupt and why.

COMPANY A Income Statement For the Year Ended December 31, 1997		COMPANY B Income Statement For the Year Ended December 31, 1997	
Revenues	$100,000	Revenues	$100,000
Expenses	75,000	Expenses	75,000
Net income	$ 25,000	Net income	$ 25,000

COMPANY A Balance Sheet December 31, 1997		COMPANY B Balance Sheet December 31, 1997	
Assets		**Assets**	
Cash	$50,000	Cash	$ 7,000
Accounts receivable	7,000	Accounts receivable	50,000
Prepaid expenses	3,000	Prepaid expenses	3,000
Total assets	$60,000	Total assets	$60,000
Liabilities		**Liabilities**	
Accounts payable	$47,000	Accounts payable	$47,000
Owners' Equity		**Owners' Equity**	
Capital	13,000	Capital	13,000
Total liabilities and owners' equity	$60,000	Total liabilities and owners' equity	$60,000

CT 7.2 Your best friend, who knows little about accounting, recently started a landscaping business. During one of your conversations he made the following statements:

> I don't need financial statements prepared by an accountant. All I really need to know is how much money is in my business's bank account so I can pay the bills when they come in. If I need a loan, the bank will demand appraisals of all my property. Why would I need financial statements that list what I paid for the property instead of what it's worth today?

Required: Respond to your friend's statements. Be prepared to present your opinions to the class.

EC 7.1 The owner of Cursor Corp. is upset because a large tract of company-owned land is reported on the balance sheet at its original cost of $50,000, while the owner thinks its true value is 10 times that amount. He fears the low cost figure may hurt the company as it tries to raise capital in the near future. The owner understands that generally accepted accounting principles require assets to be recorded at historical cost. Therefore, he intends to sell the land to his wife for $50,000, and then six months later, have her give it back to the company in exchange for $500,000 of company stock. In this way, the land will be reported on the balance sheet at the higher figure of $500,000.

Required:
  a. Why are assets reported at historical cost, rather than current fair market value?
  b. Is the owner's plan appropriate? Does it raise any ethical questions?

EC 7.2 Just prior to year-end, Ray Jones was hired as the accounting manager for EZ Sports, Inc. When year-end arrived, Ray compiled a list of required adjusting entries and presented them to the owner of the company for approval. The owner quickly agreed to all the expense adjustments, but he told Ray it was not appropriate to record any revenues earned until he had the full payment in hand. "After all" he reasoned, "I may never collect some of that money."

Required:
  a. Is there any way in which the company might benefit from recording only the required year-end expense adjustments?
  b. When should revenue be recorded? Give two examples illustrating situations where revenue might be recorded at year-end, even though it has not been collected.
  c. What is Ray's responsibility in this situation?

CHAPTER 8

Recording and Communicating in the Expenditure Cycle

Learning Objectives

1. Explain the differences among expense, expenditure, and loss, and the distinction between inventoriable and noninventoriable cost.
2. Describe how to record events involving the purchase and use of noninventoriable goods and services in the expenditure cycle.
3. Indicate how to record events involving the purchase of inventory in the expenditure cycle.
4. Explain the difference between the FIFO and LIFO cost flow assumptions.
5. Describe the relationship between operating expenses and cash expenditures.
6. Explain how to communicate the financial effects of the purchase and use of goods and services to external and internal users.

For Wal-Mart Stores, Inc., inventory, at $14.064 billion, was the largest single asset on its 1995 balance sheet and the related cost of goods sold figure of $65.586 billion is the largest expense on the income statement. Wal-Mart uses the LIFO cost flow assumption for its inventory because the company believes this inventory costing method provides a better match of current cost to current revenue. Wal-Mart chose LIFO despite the fact that, if it had used the FIFO cost flow assumption, its income would be higher. In addition, the LIFO-based inventory balance reported on the balance sheet is substantially lower than the cost of replacing the inventory. For example, in 1995 Wal-Mart reported that the replacement cost of its inventory was $351 million higher than the amount of LIFO inventory. If management is trying to increase the wealth of its stockholders, why would Wal-Mart's management use an inventory method that reduces income? Do financial statements effectively communicate the financial position of the company when, for example, the inventory figure on the balance sheet is substantially understated as it was for Wal-Mart?

This chapter examines the important topic of how to account for the events that occur in the expenditure cycle, which include the acquisition and use of goods and services involved in a firm's operations. The significant size of Wal-Mart's inventory and its impact on the company's financial statements is an example of how important expenditure-related events can be for businesses. Companies like Wal-Mart acquire goods and services both externally from vendors and suppliers and internally from its labor force. In turn, these companies create related expenditures as part of these business transactions.

We have discussed how a company acquires goods and services during the expenditure cycle. We have also described how the double entry system captures and summarizes accounting events. Now we will look specifically at how the accounting system records transactions involving the purchase and use of merchandise inventory and noninventoriable goods and services.

We classify goods a merchandising company acquires with the intent of selling them as **merchandise inventory.** When the company sells its merchandise inventory, it has used the asset to produce revenue and must transfer the cost of the inventory into an expense account called Cost of Goods Sold. The way a company accounts for merchandise inventory has a significant impact on a company's earnings and financial position, as the opening vignette illustrates.

Companies also acquire and use other goods and services that support the sale of the firm's goods and services. Such supporting resources are not included in the cost of the merchandise inventory. We refer to them as **noninventoriable goods and services.** Office supplies, insurance, advertising, and payroll are examples of noninventoriable goods and services. Because these items support the day-to-day operations of the firm, they are classified as operating expenses once they are consumed.

Before beginning our discussion of how to account for events in the expenditure cycle, we examine the fundamental relationship between the timing of the cash payments and how the accounting system classifies these payments to support the generation of revenues for the firm. We will use the acquisition and use of noninventoriable goods and services to illustrate these relationships.

UNDERSTANDING FUNDAMENTALS: EXPENDITURES, EXPENSES, AND LOSSES

There are three key accounting terms to consider as we discuss inventory and other related operating items: *expenditure*, *expense*, and *loss*. It is important to know the distinctions among these terms because they are fundamental to understanding and properly interpreting accounting reports.

Expenditures are cash payments made to acquire goods and services, reduce liabilities, and/or reward owners for their interest in the firm. *Expenses* or *losses*, on the other hand result from a particular set of accounting events that might or might not involve cash payments. For example, the purchase of a piece of equipment for cash is an expenditure but is not an expense because an *expense* is a decrease in assets or increase in liabilities and a decrease in owners' equity resulting from the operations of a business. While the purchase of equipment causes an asset, Cash, to decrease, it also results in an increase in another asset, Equipment. Thus, neither the total assets nor liabilities of the firm have changed as a result of this type of transaction.

We defined expenses and learned how to record them, but we have not defined losses. A **loss** is *a decrease in assets or increase in liabilities and a decrease in owners' equity resulting from events that are incidental to the ongoing operations of the firm, with the exception of distributions to the owners.* Note that both expenses and losses cause the company's net assets (Assets – Liabilities) to decrease. However, the distinction between expenses and losses depends upon the nature of the event that causes net assets to decrease. Expenses describe events that reduce a firm's net assets in normal operations. For example, suppose Wal-Mart buys $2,000 of office supplies at the start of the year and uses $1,700 of the supplies during the year. The use of $1,700 of supplies is considered to be an expense because the net assets of the firm decreased during the firm's normal operations. The following entries describe the acquisition and use of the asset Office Supplies.

Office Supplies	2,000	
Cash		2,000
Records the purchase of the office supplies.		

Office Supplies Expense	1,700	
Office Supplies		1,700
Adjusting entry records the use of office supplies		

Losses, however, decrease the firm's net assets as a result of events that are incidental to the firm's operations. For example, if someone stole $200 of the office supplies, the firm's assets are reduced, but not in the normal course of business. Therefore, the theft of the office supplies is considered a loss because the firm was unable to use the $200 of office supplies for their intended purpose. The entry below would reflect the theft of the office supplies in the accounting records. Both expenses and losses are reported on the income statement as reductions of net income.

Loss Due to Theft of Office Supplies	200	
Office Supplies		200
Entry to record the theft of office supplies.		

PAUSE & REFLECT

Since expenses and losses both reduce net income and are both shown on the income statement, why is it important to make a distinction between the two?

ACCOUNTING FOR NONINVENTORIABLE GOODS AND SERVICES

When a business consumes noninventoriable goods and services, it classifies them as operating expenses and matches them with the revenues generated during the period. We divide the discussion of these operating items into two sections. The first section explains how to account for operating expenses acquired externally. The second section describes how to account for the acquisition of services internally, by using the example of labor services which lead to payroll.

External Operating Expenditures and Expenses

We know that the matching principle requires the recognition of expenses when incurred regardless of when the related cash payment occurs. Some operating expenses are recognized when cash is paid, some are recognized after the goods and services are acquired, and some are recognized before the cash payment occurs. We use these relationships to organize our description of how to account for externally acquired, noninventoriable goods and services.

Expense Recognized at the Time of Cash Expenditure   When a cash payment triggers the recognition of an operating expense, the event has no further accounting implications. For example, if a company pays $600 to mail out advertising brochures, the company recognizes the expense incurred at the time it makes the cash expenditure because the post office has rendered its service. The entry below captures this event.

Advertising Expense	600	
Cash		600
Paid postage for mailing brochure.		

Expense Recognized after Goods and Services Are Acquired   Sometimes companies acquire goods and services using cash or credit and utilize those goods and services after they are acquired. An accrual accounting system reflects such events by using asset accounts, such as Office Supplies, Prepaid Rent, Prepaid Advertising, and Prepaid Insurance, to recognize the goods and services acquired. As the company uses goods or services it reflects the reduction in the asset accounts by recognizing related expenses. Operating expenses are usually recognized at the end of the measurement period by a deferral adjusting entry as described in Chapter 7.

Recall that long-term assets such as buildings and machinery support the generation of revenue over several operating periods and that their costs are allocated to operating expense over the life of the asset. Depreciation expense represents the amount of the long-term asset utilized during an accounting period; however, it is considered a noncash operating expense because it is not associated with routine cash expenditure like other operating expenses.

Expense Recognized before the Time of Cash Expenditure The accrual system of accounting recognizes expenses that are incurred but not yet paid. These *accrued expenses* create liabilities. A cash payment is eventually made to remove the liability from the accounting records.

We described how to account for accrued expenses incurred in connection with the use of goods and services in Chapter 7. Now we expand this discussion to account for two other types of accrued expenses—warranties and income taxes.

Warranties Companies offer warranties to assure consumers that the company's products are free of defects and will perform as expected. Warranties not only help convince customers to buy a product, they also provide an incentive for the company to produce a quality product.

The accrual accounting system strives to match warranty expense in the same accounting period that it reflects the revenue from the sale of related goods and services despite the fact that, typically, much warranty work occurs in accounting periods after the sale occurs. For example, warranty work on automobiles with a three-year, 36,000-mile warranty is seldom done in the year of the sale because the automobile is relatively new. The total cost of a warranty on products sold during the period is not known with certainty at the end of an accounting period. Therefore, it is necessary to estimate the amount of the future warranty cost in order to match the warranty expense with the revenue that generated it. These estimates are based on past performance or industry averages.

To illustrate, assume that a Wal-Mart supplier sells VCRs for $235 each and warrants them for two years from the point of sale for parts and labor. During 1996, the company sold 3,000 VCRs and paid $12,000 cash to an independent electronics repair shop for warranty work on VCRs sold during the year. On December 31, 1996, the staff estimates, based on past experience, that the company will spend $15,000 on warranty work on the VCRs sold in 1996 during the remaining warranty period. It is necessary to make an accrual entry on December 31, 1996, to properly match revenue from the sale of the VCRs with the related warranty expense expected from the sales. The entries for the warranty work are below.

Warranty Expense	12,000	
Cash		12,000
Warranty cost incurred on 1996 VCR sales.		

Warranty Expense	15,000	
Estimated Warranty Liability		15,000
Estimate of future warranty cost on 1996 VCR sales.		

When the warranty work is done in the following periods, the expenditures for the warranty work are recognized as a debit to the Estimated Warranty Liability account and a credit to Cash which indicates a decrease in both liabilities and assets. The entry below recognizes $14,000 of warranty work done in 1997.

Estimated Warranty Liability	14,000	
Cash		14,000

Income Taxes Corporations are legal entities whose income is taxed by the U.S. government. The Internal Revenue Services (IRS) has specific rules that corporations must follow to calculate income. Chapter 1 indicated that these rules often differ from how companies determine income using generally accepted accounting principles. For example, interest earned from investments in municipal bonds (a financial instrument issued by a city to borrow money from investors) is included as an addition to income under generally accepted accounting principles but is not included when calculating taxable income. Thus, income for accounting purposes includes the interest, making it higher than income calculated for tax purposes. Therefore, once companies determine the amount of taxes they owe on the accounting income that is subject to tax, it is considered an accrued expense.

Assume that the Wal-Mart supplier illustrated previously, has accounting income of $155,000 and taxable income of $150,000 for its 1995 fiscal year and its average tax rate is 40 percent. The difference between accounting and tax income is due to $5,000 of municipal bond interest the company earned during the period which is not subject to tax. The income tax expense for the period is $60,000 ($150,000 × .40), and the company makes the following journal entry to recognize this operating expense during the fiscal year. The Income Taxes Payable account is eliminated in the following year when the company pays its taxes.

Income Tax Expense	60,000	
Income Taxes Payable		60,000

Most corporations are responsible also for state and local income taxes, which require entries similar to the one described above. Often, corporations make estimated tax payments during the year and reflect these payments by this type of journal entry:

Estimated Tax Expense	2,000	
Cash		2,000

These payments are usually made quarterly and are based on the income earned by the company during the quarter. They are considered estimated payments because the final amount of tax due is based on its actual income determined at the end of its fiscal year.

Internal Operating Expenditures and Expense: Payroll

If you have examined your paycheck from your employer, you have noticed that the amount of take-home pay is less than the full amount you earned due to amounts withheld by the employer. The full amount an employee earns is called **gross pay** and the amounts withheld by the employer are called **deductions. Net pay,** or take-home pay, is the amount remaining after subtracting the deductions from the gross pay. In addition to withholding specified amounts from the employee's paycheck, the company must pay payroll taxes on the employee's wages and salaries.

Mandated and Voluntary Withholding by the Employer for the Employee The employer is required to withhold federal income taxes, as mandated by the Internal Revenue Code, and social security taxes, as dictated by the Federal Insurance Contributions Act **(FICA)** from the employee's gross pay. In addition, in some locations, the employer is also responsible for withholding state and local income taxes. Other deductions for items such as pensions, charitable deductions like the United Way, medical and life insurance, and union dues are voluntary deductions. That is, the employee agrees to have these amounts withheld from his or her gross pay and the employer pays the amounts withheld to the appropriate organization at a later date.

Regardless of the type of deductions, mandatory or voluntary, these deductions become *liabilities to the employer* at the time they are withheld. When a company

A time clock documents the actual time an employee has worked which is used to determine the employee's gross pay. Net pay, or take home pay, is the amount remaining after the employer withholds mandatory and voluntary deductions for payment to other organizations, such as the Internal Revenue Service, Blue Cross & Blue Shield Insurance, or the United Way.

withholds a portion of an employee's wages, the company must pay these deductions to another organization, such as the Internal Revenue Service, Blue Cross & Blue Shield Insurance, or the United Way, *on behalf of the employee.*

PAUSE & REFLECT

Instead of having the employer withhold amounts from employees' paychecks, why not have employers pay their employees their gross pay and then hold employees responsible for making these payments?

Payroll Taxes Paid by the Employer In addition to the deductions just mentioned, the employer must pay a portion of an employee's social security taxes and also must pay unemployment taxes on the salaries and wages of employees. The Federal Insurance Contribution Act requires that employers pay social security taxes equal to the amount withheld from their employees' gross pay. The Federal Unemployment Tax Act **(FUTA)** requires employers to pay payroll-related taxes to support the federal government's administration of unemployment benefits. The State Unemployment Tax Act **(SUTA)** requires employers to pay payroll-related taxes to the state to fund unemployment benefits. We discuss these taxes in more detail in "Of Interest—Payroll Taxes and Employee Income Taxes."

There are many different laws and regulations surrounding payroll that require the use of different tax rates, schedules, and tables. As a result, most payroll departments acquire one of the many computer software packages to facilitate the required recordkeeping.

Accounting for Employee Withholdings

To illustrate how to record employee compensation and related employee withholdings, assume that the employees of a particular Wal-Mart store, earned gross pay of $50,000 during June 1996. The company reflects payroll deductions for FICA, state and federal income taxes, union dues, retirement contributions, and the United Way. Wal-Mart records the net amount due to employees in the Wages Payable account. The following entry reflects the wages expense and liabilities recorded for the month of June.

Wages Expense	50,000	
FICA Taxes Payable		3,825
Federal Income Taxes Payable		7,500
State Income Taxes Payable		750
Union Dues Payable		200
Retirement Contributions Payable		500
United Way Payable		300
Wages Payable		36,925

Note that the gross pay for the period, $50,000, is the debit entry made to Wages Expense while the net pay for the period, $36,925, is the credit entry made to Wages

AYROLL TAXES

The Federal Insurance Contributions Act (FICA) requires most companies to withhold a portion of an employee's earnings to contribute to social security and medicare. The 1996 withholding rate, for example, was 7.65 percent. This rate is a combination of a 6.2 percent rate for social security retirement and disability and 1.45 percent rate for medicare. The 7.65 percent rate is used to withhold FICA taxes on the first $62,700 of an employees' earnings. However, employees who earn above $62,700 will continue to have 1.45 percent of their salary withheld for medicare. Historically, both the rate and the income subject to the tax have increased and there is no reason to believe this trend will not continue.

Unemployment benefits are funded by the Federal Unemployment Tax Act (FUTA) and the State Unemployment Tax Act (SUTA), which are assessed on each employer. The FUTA rate is .8 percent (.008) of each employee's first $7,000 of earnings. The SUTA rate typically is about 5.4 percent of the first $8,000 of an employee's salary but varies based on the type of industry and a company's employment history. For example, construction companies typically pay a higher SUTA rate than retail enterprises because construction companies experience more layoffs than retail firms. However, within an industry classification, the fewer workers a company fires or lays off, the lower the company's SUTA rate. The FUTA and SUTA taxes are deposited quarterly with their respective agencies.

EMPLOYEE'S INCOME TAXES

Federal law and many state and local laws require that the employer withhold certain amounts from the gross earnings of its employees for the payment of the employees' income taxes. The amount withheld depends on the amount of the gross pay, the length of the pay period, and the number of exemptions the employee claims. Each exemption represents a specific dollar amount by which a taxpayer is allowed to reduce his or her taxes. It is also used to determine the amount withheld from an employee's pay for income tax. If you have ever been employed, you have filled out an Employee's Withholding Allowance Certificate, Form W-4, which reports the number of exemptions claimed by the employee to the employer and the Internal Revenue Service. The greater the number of exemptions claimed by the employee, the less that is withheld from the employee's gross pay. The Internal Revenue Service assesses a penalty for under withholding.

At the end of the calendar year, the employer prepares Form W-2 for each employee. Form W-2 indicates the gross pay the employee earned and the amount withheld for social security and income taxes during the period. Each employee is given their W-2, which must be filed with his or her income tax return. The W-2 serves an important internal control function in that, by reporting the amounts withheld to the employees, it holds the company accountable for remitting the proper amounts to the appropriate federal and state agencies.

Payable. In addition to paying the employees their net pay, Wal-Mart also has the obligation to remit the amounts withheld from the employees to the appropriate organizations on behalf of the employees. The employer keeps detailed individual records of the earnings and withholdings of each employee to support the wage-related information reflected in these specific accounts.

Accounting for Employer Taxes

How should employers account for the required FICA, FUTA, and SUTA taxes on their employees' earnings? The employer must recognize related expenses and liabilities for these taxes by recording these items in accounts when the company incurs the payroll taxes.

Companies are assessed FICA taxes that match the amount of taxes withheld from the company's employees. State and federal unemployment taxes (SUTA and FUTA), however, are levied exclusively on the employer to support benefits paid to unemployed workers.

Using the payroll information reflected in the previous entry, the entry to reflect the *payroll taxes assessed against the employer* is given below.

Payroll Tax Expense	6,925	
FICA Taxes Payable		3,825
($50,000 × .0765)		
SUTA Taxes Payable		2,700
($50,000 × .054)		
FUTA Taxes Payable		400
($50,000 × .008)		

While only one expense account, Payroll Tax Expense, is used, separate liability accounts are maintained to reflect various payroll taxes because the company must remit the amounts to different government agencies. The entry below reflects Wal-Mart's payment of payroll taxes.

FICA Taxes Payable	7,650	
SUTA Taxes Payable	2,700	
FUTA Taxes Payable	400	
Cash		10,750

When the company pays the voluntary withholdings, the entries to record the event are similar to those described above. That is, the withholding liability is reduced by the amount of the cash paid.

ACCOUNTING FOR THE ACQUISITION OF MERCHANDISE INVENTORY

We now move from our discussion of noninventoriable items to describe events relating to the acquisition and sale of merchandise inventory. For firms that are in business to sell products, the acquisition and sale of merchandise is the central operating activity of the firm. Therefore, information about the acquisition and sale of inventory is essential. Our discussion of inventory first examines how to account for the cost of acquiring merchandise inventory and then explains how to determine and account for the cost of the products sold.

Merchandise inventory is a substantial investment for merchandising companies, and, when they sell inventory items to customers, companies reflect cost of goods sold, which is typically a sizable expense appearing on the income statement. For example, on its January 31, 1995, balance sheet, Wal-Mart reported the *replacement cost of its inventory* as $14.415 billion, which represented about 44 percent of Wal-Mart's total assets. Wal-Mart's cost of goods sold was $65.586 billion, which was nearly 80 percent of sales. Therefore, proper accounting for inventory is crucial for management decision making, and accurate presentation is required on both the income statement and the balance sheet for external users.

Merchandise inventory is recorded in the accounts of the company at the *cash or cash equivalent* amount at the *time of purchase*. While this rule is straightforward, it brings up two important issues that involve accounting for inventory: (1) what amount to record and (2) how to record purchases in the accounts. We examine each of these issues in the following sections.

What Amount Reflects Inventory Purchases?

The cost of merchandise inventory includes the purchase price of the inventory plus additional costs incurred to obtain the inventory, such as transportation (freight-in) and insurance (insurance-in) charges where appropriate. Exhibit 8.1 illustrates the costs included in merchandise inventory.

Recall that the terms of the sale generally state how the merchandise is shipped, either FOB destination (seller is responsible for freight and insurance charges) or FOB shipping point (buyer is responsible for freight and insurance charges). The cost of shipping paid by the seller is an operating expense called **freight out** and is not included as part of the seller's cost of goods sold. In the case of goods shipped FOB shipping point, the freight and insurance charges

EXHIBIT 8.1

Merchandise Inventory

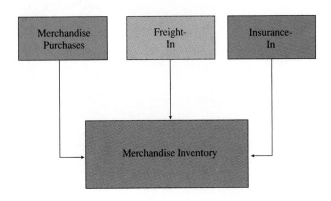

(freight-in and insurance-in, respectively) are included in the buyer's cost of the merchandise inventory purchased.

In addition to freight-in and insurance-in, there are other costs to consider in determining the cost of inventory for the buyer. Sellers of merchandise often offer cash discounts to encourage buyers to pay their bills promptly. Any cash discounts taken by the buyer are known as **purchase discounts.** In addition, in some cases, buyers may either return merchandise or pay less than the original amount due. For the buyer, such returns and allowances are called **purchase returns and allowances.**

Purchase Discounts   The purchasing company could use the **net price method** of recording inventory acquisitions. The net price method assumes that the buyer will take all purchase discounts and, therefore, the cost of merchandise inventory is the *purchase price less any cash discount.* Recall that it is to a company's advantage to take all discounts. If the discount period is allowed to elapse, the additional amount paid is called **purchase discounts lost** and is considered a financing charge to the buyer of the inventory rather than a cost of the inventory. For companies with a policy of taking all cash discounts, the net method indicates the extent of noncompliance with this policy. A zero balance in the Purchase Discounts Lost account means that the company took all purchase discounts available, while a balance in this account means purchase discounts were not taken, which might require further investigation by management.

For example, assume that on April 21, Wal-Mart purchases $20,000 of merchandise from Williams Company on account. The terms of the sale are 3/15, n/30. Using the net method, Wal-Mart records this inventory purchase at $19,400 ($20,000 × .97). Assuming that on or before May 6 (15 days after purchase), Wal-Mart remits payment to Williams Company, and reduces the Cash and Accounts Payable accounts by $19,400. The entries for these two events are as follows:

Inventory	19,400	
Accounts Payable		19,400
Records purchase of inventory using net method.		
Accounts Payable	19,400	
Cash		19,400
Records payment of accounts payable within discount period.		

If, however, Wal-Mart made the payment after the discount period, Accounts Payable is reduced by $19,400 and Cash is reduced by $20,000, the gross price of the

Grocery stores and discount stores typically use a periodic inventory system. This type of recording system reflects the cost of goods sold and inventory only in periodic intervals. The periodic inventory system is popular among stores that sell a high volume and a wide variety of products.

merchandise purchased. The $600 difference between the amount of cash paid, $20,000, and the liability, $19,400, is the purchase discount lost as shown in the entry below.

Accounts Payable	19,400	
Purchase Discounts Lost	600	
Cash		20,000
Records payment of acounts payable after the discount period.		

Because Purchase Discounts Lost is considered a cost of financing the purchase of merchandise inventory, it is included on the income statement as an expense for the period and not as part of the cost of goods sold. It is closed to the Income Summary account with other expenses incurred during the period.

PAUSE & REFLECT   How would a company record discounts if they were recognized on the date of payment and only if they were actually taken? What are the advantages of recording discounts this way?

Purchase Returns and Allowances   When a buyer finds that the merchandise inventory ordered does not meet specifications or is damaged, the buyer has two courses of action—either return the merchandise to the seller or request a purchase allowance, which means keeping the merchandise and asking the seller to reduce the amount due on the purchase. Whether the buyer returns the merchandise or receives an allowance from the seller, the buyer's obligation to the seller and the cost of the inventory are reduced by the same amount.

For example, assume that Wal-Mart purchases $15,000 of merchandise from Sylvan Company on account. Subsequently, Wal-Mart returns $500 of merchandise to Sylvan. When Wal-Mart returns the merchandise, it reduces both the cost of inventory purchased and its accounts payable obligation by $500.

Accounts Payable	500	
Inventory		500

What Is a Perpetual Inventory System?

So far we have described purchases, in general, without regard to the type of inventory system a company uses. There are two types of inventory systems to account for the purchase and sale of inventory—the perpetual inventory system and the periodic inventory system. The perpetual system is used by companies that are capable of keeping a running balance of the cost of goods available for sale and cost of goods sold during an accounting period. Companies such as appliance, clothing, or jewelry stores that have a low volume of sales and an easily identified inventory traditionally use the perpetual inventory system. However, computer technology makes the use of a perpetual inventory system possible for almost any company.

The **periodic inventory system,** on the other hand, is a recording system that reflects the cost of goods sold and inventory on hand only at periodic intervals (e.g., the end of the accounting period).[1] Typically companies, such as grocery stores and discount stores, that sell a high volume of a wide variety of products use a periodic system. In this text, we use the perpetual system to describe the cost flow concepts associated with the purchase and sale of merchandise inventory because it is the more intuitive of the two systems.

---

[1]The periodic inventory system is a residual system because events that affect inventory are recorded in temporary accounts and inventory is adjusted at the end of the period. The cost of goods sold for the period is the difference between the goods available for sale during the time period (Beginning inventory + Purchases during the year) and the amount of ending inventory.

Beginning inventory	$ 10,000
Purchases	150,000
Cost of goods available	$160,000
Ending inventory	15,000
Cost of goods sold	$145,000

In a **perpetual inventory system,** the purchasing company maintains a continual record of the quantity and cost of inventory items purchased and sold. All events that increase inventory quantities or costs, such as purchases, freight in, and insurance, are recorded directly into the Inventory account. Likewise, events that decrease inventory quantity or costs, such as purchase returns and allowances, and cost of goods sold, are recorded as deductions from the Inventory account. To illustrate the perpetual inventory system, we examine a retail company known as Magik Mirrors Company.

On May 15, Magik Mirrors purchases 10 identical mirrors at $200 each (total of $2,000) from Brockway Company on account. The terms of the sale are 2/10, n/30, FOB shipping point. Because Magik Mirrors uses the net price method to record inventory purchases, the mirrors are reflected in Magik's inventory at $1,960, which is the original cost, $2,000, less the $40 cash discount ($2,000 × .02), or $196 per mirror. The journal entry to record the merchandise purchase which reflects the two percent discount available is:

Inventory	1,960	
Accounts Payable		1,960
[($200 × 10) − ($200 ¥ 10 × .02)]		

Magik Mirrors pays the freight carrier $160 and incurs an insurance charge of $50 while the goods are in transit. Both these costs are paid on May 16. The journal entries to record the freight and insurance charges show increases to the cost of inventory.

Inventory	160	
Cash		160
Inventory	50	
Cash		50

On May 20, Magik Mirrors returns three mirrors with a cost of $588 ($196 × 3) to Brockway Company. The entry to record the return of merchandise inventory to the supplier to indicate a decrease in assets and liabilities is:

Accounts Payable	588	
Inventory ($196 × 3 mirrors)		588

On May 25, Magik Mirrors takes advantage of the $28 discount available on the remaining seven mirrors and remits $1,372 ($1,960 − $588), the amount due on the remaining seven mirrors. The journal entry to record the payment for the remaining merchandise inventory is:

Accounts Payable ($1,960 − $588)	1,372	
Cash ($1,400 × .98)		1,372

On May 30, Magik Mirrors sells five mirrors to a customer on account for $3,200. The cost per mirror on the date of sale is $226 [($1,372 + $160 + $50)/7 mirrors]. Two mirrors remain in the inventory at a cost of $452 ($226 × 2). The entries to indicate the sale on account and the cost of the merchandise sold are:

Accounts Receivable	3,200	
Sales		3,200
Cost of Goods Sold	1,130	
Inventory ($226 × 5 mirrors)		1,130

The inventory T-account that summarizes the events is:

Inventory			
5/15	1,960		
5/16	160		
5/16	50		
5/20		588	
5/30		1,130	
Balance	452		

WHY ARE COST FLOW ASSUMPTIONS IMPORTANT?

When a business has a heterogeneous inventory and can identify each inventory item, the date of its purchase, and the price paid for the item, the purchase price of that item is transferred from Inventory to Cost of Goods Sold when the company sells the individual item. This costing system is known as the **specific identification method.** For example, in a car dealership, each item of inventory (car, truck, or van) has an identification code that enables management to monitor the status of each vehicle. The identification code indicates to management the amount the dealership paid for the vehicle and any additional costs incurred to prepare the vehicle for sale. Then the dealership expenses the costs identified with a specific vehicle to cost of goods sold when the vehicle is sold.

In most businesses, specific identification is difficult because, once an item is purchased and stored as inventory, it loses its physical identification. For example, assume that a company buys and sells one type of basketball. Further assume that it purchased basketballs on January 15, February 7, and March 1. On March 7, a customer purchases a basketball. Did this customer purchase a basketball from the group bought on January 15, February 7, or March 1? It is hard to tell because the basketball has lost its identification with a particular purchase date and its specific purchase price because it looks like the other basketballs.

Because these basketballs represent a homogeneous inventory, management must adopt a **cost flow assumption,** that is, a rational and systematic allocation of inventory cost between the Cost of Goods Sold and Inventory accounts based on presumptions made about the order in which the company expenses its inventory cost. One alternative is to average the cost of inventory purchased as the previous example illustrated. However, this method requires more bookkeeping because the cost per unit changes with every purchase made at a different price. (Notice the cost per mirror increased from $196 to $226 in that example.) Most companies use the first-in, first-out (FIFO) and last-in, first-out (LIFO) costing methods which assume an order in which inventory items are sold rather than recalculating inventory cost. To illustrate FIFO and LIFO cost flow assumptions, see the data presented in Exhibit 8.2.

First-In, First-Out (FIFO)

The **first-in, first-out (FIFO)** *cost flow assumption* means that *costs are charged to cost of goods sold in chronological order.* The first inventory costs recorded are the first costs expensed to Cost of Goods Sold and, therefore, the remaining Inventory balance consists of the most recent costs. FIFO approximates the physical flow of the inventory because, generally, companies sell the oldest items first, leaving the most recent purchases in inventory. In periods of rising prices, use of the FIFO cost flow assumption results in the older, lower prices appearing on the income statement as Cost of Goods Sold and the newer, higher prices appearing on the balance sheet as Inventory. We discuss the implications of this cost flow assumption for the users of financial statements later in the chapter.

EXHIBIT	8.2	Inventory Events				
			Inventory			
			Number of Units		Unit	Total
Date		Event	Bought	Sold	Price	Cost
February 1		Beginning inventory	12		$500	$ 6,000
February 3		Sale*		8		
February 6		Purchase	6		510	3,060
February 9		Purchase	5		525	2,625
February 15		Sale*		8		
February 21		Sale*		6		
February 24		Purchase	6		530	3,180
February 26		Purchase	2		540	1,080
February 28		Sale*		3		
Total			31	25		$15,945

*All units sell for $800 each.

In a perpetual inventory system, cost of goods sold is calculated and recorded *at the time a sale is made.* Using the information presented in Exhibit 8.2, we analyze the entries and record purchases and the cost of sales for inventory for the month of February 1996 below. When using a perpetual inventory system, the purchasing company prepares an inventory card for each inventory item (see Exhibit 8.3), which is a supplemental record designed to keep track of the units sold and the inventory on hand for a particular inventory item on a continual basis. Thus, at any point in time, the Inventory balance will reflect all purchases and sales made to date.

EXHIBIT 8.3	FIFO Perpetual Inventory Card		
Date	**Purchases**	**Inventory Sold**	**Inventory Balance**
2/1	Beginning Bal.		12 × $ 500
2/3		8 × $500 = $ 4,000	4 × $ 500
2/6	6 × $510		4 × $ 500 6 × $ 510
2/9	5 × $525		4 × $ 500 6 × $ 510 5 × $ 525
2/15		4 × $500 4 × $510 = $ 4,040	2 × $ 510 5 × $ 525
2/21		2 × $510 4 × $525 = $ 3,120	1 × $ 525
2/24	6 × $530		1 × $ 525 6 × $ 530
2/26	2 × $540		1 × $ 525 6 × $ 530 2 × $ 540
2/28		1 × $525 2 × $530 = $ 1,585	4 × $ 530 2 × $ 540
Total		$12,745	$3,200

Feb. 3 Sold eight units at $800 each. Since the only units available on February 3 come from the beginning inventory of 12 units, cost of goods sold is $4,000 (8 units at $500 each). The journal entries on February 3 are:

Accounts Receivable	6,400	
Sales		6,400
Cost of Goods Sold	4,000	
Inventory		4,000

6 Purchase six units at $510 each. Assuming that all purchase are made on account, the journal entry on February 6 is:

Inventory	3,060	
Accounts Payable		3,060

9 Purchased five units at $525 each. The journal entry is:

Inventory	2,625	
Accounts Payable		2,625

Feb. 15   Sold eight units at $800 each. Since the first costs recorded are the first costs expensed (FIFO assumption), the remaining beginning inventory costs (4 units at $500) are expensed first, followed by the costs recorded on February 6 of which four units are expensed. Cost of goods sold is $4,040 [(4 × $500) + (4 × $510)]. The journal entries on February 15 are:

Accounts Receivable	6,400	
Sales		6,400
Cost of Goods Sold	4,040	
Inventory		4,040

21   Sold six units at $800 each. The oldest costs remaining on February 21 were recorded on February 6 (2 units at $510) and the next oldest were recorded on February 9, of which four units at $525 will be expensed. Cost of goods sold is $3,120 [(2 × $510) + (4 × $525)]. The journal entries on February 21 are:

Accounts Receivable	4,800	
Sales		4,800
Cost of Goods Sold	3,120	
Inventory		3,120

24   Purchased six units at $530 each. The journal entry is:

| Inventory | 3,180 | |
| Accounts Payable | | 3,180 |

26   Purchased two units at $540 each. The journal entry is:

| Inventory | 1,080 | |
| Accounts Payable | | 1,080 |

28   Sold three units at $800 each. The oldest costs remaining on February 28 include one unit from February 9 and six units from February 24. Since three units are sold on February 28, cost of goods sold is $1,585 [(1 × $525) + (2 × $530)]. The journal entries on February 28 are:

Accounts Receivable	2,400	
Sales		2,400
Cost of Goods Sold	1,585	
Inventory		1,585

For the month of February 1996, using the FIFO cost flow assumption for inventory, the total cost of goods sold is $12,745 ($4,000 + $4,040 + $3,120 + $1,585), and the ending balance of the Inventory account in the general ledger is $3,200. The inventory card reflects the dollar amounts to record in Cost of Goods Sold because it keeps a running balance of inventory on hand. The T-accounts for Inventory and Cost of Goods Sold illustrated below summarize the flow of costs from inventory to cost of goods sold.

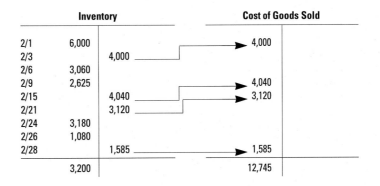

EXHIBIT | 8.4 | LIFO Perpetual Inventory Card

Date	Purchases	Inventory Sold	Inventory Balance
2/1	Beginning Bal.		12 × $ 500
2/3		8 × $500 = $ 4,000	4 × $ 500
2/6	6 × $510		4 × $ 500 6 × $ 510
2/9	5 × $525		4 × $ 500 6 × $ 510 5 × $ 525
2/15		5 × $525 3 × $510 = $ 4,155	4 × $ 500 3 × $ 510
2/21		3 × $510 3 × $500 = $ 3,030	1 × $ 500
2/24	6 × $530		1 × $ 500 6 × $ 530
2/26	2 × $540		1 × $ 500 6 × $ 530 2 × $ 540
2/28		2 × $540 1 × $530 = $ 1,610	1 × $ 500 5 × $ 530
Total		$12,795	$3,150

Last-In, First-Out (LIFO)

In contrast to the FIFO cost flow assumption method of accounting for inventory, the **last-in, first-out (LIFO)** *cost flow assumption* assumes that *costs are charged to cost of goods sold in reverse chronological order.* The last inventory costs recorded are the first costs expensed to Cost of Goods Sold, and the Inventory balance consists of the oldest inventory costs.

Using the information presented in Exhibit 8.2 and the LIFO inventory card shown in Exhibit 8.4, the entries to record purchases and sales of inventory for the month of February 1996 are analyzed below.

Feb. 3 Sold eight units at $800 each. Since the only units available on February 3 come from the beginning inventory, cost of goods sold is $4,000 (8 units at $500 each). The journal entries on February 3 are:

Accounts Receivable	6,400	
Sales		6,400
Cost of Goods Sold	4,000	
Inventory		4,000

6 Purchased six units at $510 each. Assuming that all purchases are made on account, the journal entry on February 6 is:

Inventory	3,060	
Accounts Payable		3,060

9 Purchased five units at $525 each. The journal entry is:

Inventory	2,625	
Accounts Payable		2,625

Feb. 15   Sold eight units at $800 each. Since the last costs recorded are the first costs expensed, the inventory purchased on February 9 is expensed first, followed by the inventory purchased on February 6. Cost of goods sold is $4,155 [(5 × $525) + (3 × $510)]. The journal entries on February 15 are:

Accounts Receivable	6,400	
Sales		6,400
Cost of Goods Sold	4,155	
Inventory		4,155

21   Sold six units at $800 each. The newest costs remaining as of February 21 were recorded on February 6 (3 units at $510) and the next newest are part of beginning inventory, of which three units at $500 will be expensed. Cost of goods sold is $3,030 [(3 × $510) + (3 × $500)]. The journal entries on February 21 are:

Accounts Receivable	4,800	
Sales		4,800
Cost of Goods Sold	3,030	
Inventory		3,030

24   Purchased six units at $530 each. The journal entry is:

Inventory	3,180	
Accounts Payable		3,180

26   Purchased two units at $540 each. The journal entry is:

Inventory	1,080	
Accounts Payable		1,080

28   Sold three units at $800 each. The newest costs available on February 28 were purchased on February 26 and February 24. Since three units are sold on February 28, cost of goods sold is $1,610 [(2 × $540) + (1 × $530)]. The journal entries on February 28 are:

Accounts Receivable	2,400	
Sales		2,400
Cost of Goods Sold	1,610	
Inventory		1,610

For the month of February 1996, total cost of goods sold using the LIFO cost flow assumption is $12,795 ($4,000 + $4,155 + $3,030 + $1,610), and the cost of ending inventory is $3,150. The information on the inventory card reflects the amount to record in the Cost of Goods Sold for each sale by keeping a running balance of the number and cost of goods available for sale at any time. The transactions above are summarized in the T-accounts below.

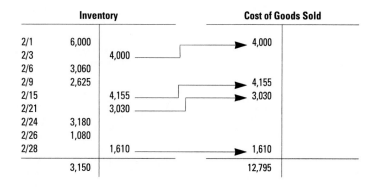

EXHIBIT	8.5	Comparison of FIFO and LIFO		
			FIFO	LIFO
		Sales	$20,000	$20,000
		Less cost of goods sold:		
		February 3	4,000	4,000
		February 15	4,040	4,155
		February 21	3,120	3,030
		February 28	1,585	1,610
		Total cost of goods sold	$12,745	$12,795
		Gross margin	$ 7,255	$ 7,205
		Ending inventory	$ 3,200	$ 3,150

Comparison of Cost Flow Assumptions

Exhibit 8.5 compares gross margins and ending inventories using both the FIFO and LIFO methods. Notice that, since the purchase prices of inventory were rising in this example, the FIFO cost flow assumption results in the lower cost of goods sold amount, the higher gross margin, and the higher ending inventory of the two methods. If the price of acquiring the inventory had decreased during the period, the opposite effects would occur.

PAUSE & REFLECT

If prices remain constant throughout the period, how will cost of goods sold and ending inventory amounts differ between FIFO and LIFO?

While LIFO reflects less income during a period of rising prices, a company may want to adopt a LIFO cost flow assumption because it generates a higher cost of goods sold and, therefore, a lower net income. This results in a smaller income tax expense. To illustrate, use the information in Exhibit 8.5 and assume that operating expenses were $2,000 and the company is subject to a 40 percent average tax rate. The resulting net incomes under FIFO and LIFO are $3,153 and $3,123, respectively, as shown in Exhibit 8.6. Further assume that the cash for all sales is collected and all purchases and expenses are paid in cash during the period. The resulting cash flows under FIFO and LIFO are $5,953 and $5,973, respectively, as shown in Exhibit 8.6.

Exhibit 8.6 illustrates why a company may adopt LIFO in a period of rising prices. While the net income under LIFO is smaller, the cash flows are larger, be-

EXHIBIT	8.6	Comparison of Cash Flows Using FIFO and LIFO		
			FIFO	LIFO
		Gross margin (Exhibit 8.5)	$ 7,255	$ 7,205
		Less operating expenses	2,000	2,000
		Net income before tax	$ 5,255	$ 5,205
		Less income taxes (40%)	2,102	2,082
		Net income	$ 3,153	$ 3,123
		Cash receipts from sales	$20,000	$20,000
		Less cash payments:		
		Purchases made	(9,945)	(9,945)
		Operating expenses	(2,000)	(2,000)
		Income taxes	(2,102)	(2,082)
		Net cash flows	$ 5,953	$ 5,973

cause LIFO saves the company money on income taxes. For example, on July 1, 1988, Quaker Oats, Inc., adopted LIFO, and the effect of this change was to reduce income in the 1989 fiscal year by $16 million. Quaker said it changed from FIFO to LIFO because LIFO provided a better match of current cost to current revenue. Another reason that Quaker switched to LIFO is because LIFO lowered its tax liability and improved the economic position of the firm. In a period of falling prices, a company may want to adopt a FIFO cost flow assumption because FIFO results in the highest cost of goods sold, lowest net income, and smallest income tax expense.

Companies could conceivably switch back and forth between FIFO to LIFO in order to take advantage of changing prices. However, changing inventory methods eliminates the consistency of the financial statements from year to year. As a result, generally accepted accounting principles require the consistent application of cost flow assumptions. A publicly held company that switches cost flow methods must disclose the impact of the change in its financial reports to the public. This disclosure must include a justification of the reason for the change. In addition, the IRS requires that any firm using LIFO for tax purposes also use LIFO for financial statement reporting purposes. In other words, a company cannot use different inventory costing methods in order to report a higher net income to its stockholders and a lower net income to the Internal Revenue Service. The IRS allows the use of FIFO for tax purposes and LIFO for reporting on financial statements. However, it is very unlikely that a firm's management would select this option because, in periods of inflation, a company would report more income and pay more taxes to the IRS but report less income to its stockholders.

REPORTING OPERATING EVENTS

So far in this chapter we have discussed how to record the purchase and use of goods and services that support a firm's operating activities and the purchase and sale of merchandise inventory. Now we discuss how to communicate this information to interested external and internal parties. First, we describe how to report this information on the income statement, balance sheet, and cash flow statements to comply with generally accepted accounting principles. Then, we examine payroll and inventory reports as examples of the type of information companies prepare for their internal users. Finally, we discuss the potential for the distortion of information about the purchase of goods and services due to errors and the application of FIFO and LIFO.

Financial Statements

To facilitate our discussion of how to report the purchases of goods and services on the financial statements, we refer to Exhibit 8.7, which shows the accounts of Magik Mirrors at the start of the accounting period, January 1, 1996, and at the fiscal year-end, December 31, 1996. The company has already made the adjusting entries. Therefore, the account balances on December 31, 1996, summarize the operating events that Magik Mirrors engaged in during the year. The fact that balances exist in the revenue and expense accounts means that Magik has not yet made its closing entries. Magik Mirrors uses the FIFO costing assumption and a perpetual inventory system.

Income Statement   Magik Mirrors uses what we call a *multistep income statement*, illustrated in Exhibit 8.8. This format lists cost of goods sold separately, which, when subtracted from sales, results in the gross margin.

The operating expenses listed below the gross margin represent the noninventoriable goods and services utilized during the period to support the sale of the company's products and services. The income statement summarizes the operating expenses incurred by the company and matches them with the revenue generated in the same time period.

EXHIBIT | 8.7 | **Magik Mirrors Account Balances**

MAGIK MIRRORS COMPANY

Account Balances at

| | 1/1/96 | | 12/31/96 | |
Account Title	Debit	Credit	Debit	Credit
Inventory	$ 56,780		$ 43,745	
Office supplies	9,000		1,250	
Prepaid insurance	1,100		900	
Building	200,000		200,000	
Accumulated depreciation		$ 20,000		$ 30,000
Accounts payable—inventory		67,200		75,500
Accounts payable—noninventory		–0–		16,000
Wages payable		8,000		12,500
Utilities payable		1,300		1,600
Estimated warranty liability		9,200		8,000
FICA payable		3,800		4,200
SUTA payable		2,200		2,000
FUTA payable		–0–		400
Federal income tax withholding payable		4,400		3,900
State income tax withholding payable		900		800
United Way withholding payable		1,250		1,200
Income taxes payable		101,000		119,597
Sales		–0–		1,291,591
Cost of goods sold		–0–	679,785	
Advertising expense		–0–	40,000	
Wages expense			156,000	
Payroll tax expense			15,100	
Utilities expense			21,300	
Office supplies expense			9,400	
Insurance expense			5,700	
Freight out			1,200	
Warranty expense			11,400	
Depreciation expense			10,000	
Income tax expense			119,597	

EXHIBIT | 8.8 | **Partial Income Statement**

MAGIK MIRRORS COMPANY
Partial Income Statement for the Year Ended December 31, 1996

Sales		$1,291,591
Cost of goods sold		679,785
Gross margin		$ 611,806
Operating expenses:		
Advertising expense	$ 40,000	
Wages expense	156,000	
Payroll tax expense	15,100	
Utilities expense	21,300	
Office supplies expense	9,400	
Insurance expense	5,700	
Freight-out	1,200	
Warranty expense	11,400	
Depreciation expense	10,000	
Total operating expenses		270,100
Operating income before taxes		$ 341,706
Income tax expense		119,597
Operating income after taxes		$ 222,109

Exhibit 8.8 lists most of the expenses discussed in the chapter in order to illustrate the relationship of operating expenses to sales. Companies preparing income statements today group their operating expenses into broad categories rather than list the multitude of operating expense accounts they carry in their accounting

EXHIBIT	8.9	Partial Balance Sheet

MAGIK MIRRORS COMPANY
Partial Balance Sheet at December 31, 1996

Current assets:		
Inventory at FIFO cost		$ 43,745
Office supplies		1,250
Prepaid insurance		900
Property, plant, and equipment:		
Building	$200,000	
Less: Accumulated depreciation	30,000	
		170,000
Current liabilities:		
Accounts payable—inventory		75,500
Accounts payable—noninventory		16,000
Wages payable		12,500
Utilities payable		1,600
Estimated warranty liability		8,000
FICA payable		4,200
FUTA payable		400
SUTA payable		2,000
Federal income taxes withholding payable		3,900
State income taxes withholding payable		800
United Way withholding payable		1,200

records. For example, Magik Mirrors might combine Advertising Expense, Freight Out, and Warranty Expense into a Selling Expense classification. The income statements of Walt Disney Company (introduced in Chapter 2), the Boston Celtics (introduced in Chapter 7), and Anheuser-Busch (introduced in Chapter 10) show how each company summarizes its respective operating expenses.

Balance Sheet The assets and liabilities associated with the purchase and use of goods and services by a company are reported on the balance sheet, usually under the current classification. Current assets, such as Office Supplies, Prepaid Rent, and Prepaid Insurance, represent assets the company will utilize in the coming period (year, fiscal year, or operating cycle) to support the sale of the firm's goods and services. Inventory is also a current asset that represents the cost of the products the firm will have available for sale at the beginning of the following accounting period.

Disclosure of the costing method the company uses to account for the inventory, FIFO or LIFO, is required. The cost flow assumption appears in the body of the balance sheet by the inventory classification or in the notes to the financial statements. Current liabilities, such as Wages Payable and Accounts Payable, represent the expenditures the company will make that are associated with the firm's operating activities in the coming year.

In many cases, the market value of the ending inventory is less than the cost of the inventory shown on the balance sheet. When this occurs, the balance sheet reports the market value rather than the cost. The deviation from cost is disclosed as an adjustment to the cost of the inventory on the balance sheet or in the notes to the financial statements.

Exhibit 8.9 is a partial balance sheet for the Magik Mirrors Company that lists many of the asset and liability accounts discussed in this chapter. Note that the costing method used by the company, FIFO, is disclosed as part of the balance sheet presentation. We have presented most of the accounts described earlier in order to illustrate the nature of the accounts; however, as in the case of income statement presentations, companies usually consolidate similar current asset and current liability accounts into one classification. For example, most companies would aggregate the payroll tax liabilities and the withholding accounts into one account, such as Payroll Taxes Payable, because users of the financial statements are not interested in a great level of detail.

EXHIBIT | 8.10 | Partial Statement of Cash Flows

MAGIK MIRRORS COMPANY
Partial Statement of Cash Flows for the Year Ended December 31, 1995

Cash flows from operating activities:		
Cash received from sales		$1,150,000
Cash paid for:		
Merchandise inventory purchased	$658,450	
Advertising	40,000	
Wages	151,500	
Payroll taxes	14,900	
Utilities	21,000	
Office supplies	1,650	
Insurance	5,500	
Freight out	1,200	
Warranties	12,600	
Income taxes	101,000	
Total cash paid		1,007,800
Cash flow from operating activities		$ 142,200

Statement of Cash Flows   While the income statement reflects the firm's income from operations, it does not describe the actual cash flows associated with the firm's operations. Financial statement users want to know not only the expenses incurred in generating revenues, but also the cash flows expended to generate the revenues for the same time period. Identifying a firm's cash flows helps decision makers assess the liquidity of the firm. **Liquidity** refers to the time which is required to convert an asset into cash or use it in operations. The operating section of the cash flow statement, shown in Exhibit 8.10, reflects the cash expenditures associated with operations during the accounting period. This cash flow statement format in Exhibit 8.10, called the *direct method*, identifies the cash expenditures associated with merchandise purchases and, therefore, cost of goods sold and each of the operating expenses on the income statement.

How do we determine the amount of cash expenditures made in connection with cost of goods sold or with any particular operating expense? Answering this question depends on the balance sheet accounts associated with the expenses. With the exception of depreciation expense, operating expenses are either associated with prepaid accounts or liability accounts. For example, Insurance Expense is associated with Prepaid Insurance, while Wages Expense is associated with Wages Payable. Cost of Goods Sold is identified with the Inventory and Accounts Payable—Inventory accounts. When an expense is not associated with a balance sheet account, it is reasonable to assume that the expense was generated by a cash expenditure, which we discuss later in this chapter. We will now describe how to determine the amount of cash expenditures associated with prepaids and expenses, liabilities and expenses, and cost of goods sold.

Prepaids, Expenses, and Cash Expenditures   In order to determine the amount of cash expenditure identified with a particular expense and prepaid account, it is first necessary to determine the maximum expenditure amount by adding the *ending* balance in the prepaid account to the expense for the period. The sum of the ending prepaid account and the expense account represent the maximum cash expenditure possible during the time period for this operating item. Then we subtract the *beginning* balance of the prepaid account from this total because it represents expense recognized in the current time period but paid in a previous time period. To illustrate, Magik Mirrors paid $5,500 for insurance during 1996 as calculated below.

12/31/96 balance—prepaid insurance (Exhibit 8.7)	$ 900	
Insurance expense—1996 (Exhibit 8.7)	5,700	
Maximum possible cash expenditure in 1996		$6,600
Less: 1/1/96 balance—prepaid insurance (Exhibit 8.7)		1,100
Cash paid for insurance in 1996		$5,500

Accrued Liabilities, Expenses, and Cash Expenditures The maximum amount paid in connection with liability and expense accounts is calculated by adding the *beginning* balance of the accrued liability account to the expense for the period. The sum of the beginning balance of the liability account and the expense account represents the maximum amount a firm could pay for this operating item during the year. We then subtract the *ending* liability account from this sum because it represents the portion of the expense that was recognized during the year but not yet paid. Magik Mirrors Company paid $151,500 for wages, as calculated below:

1/1/96 balance—wages payable (Exhibit 8.7)	$ 8,000	
Wages expense for 1996 (Exhibit 8.7)	156,000	
Maximum possible cash paid for wages		$164,000
12/31/96 balance—wages payable (Exhibit 8.7)		12,500
Cash paid for wages in 1996		$151,500

Other Operating Expenses Other operating expenses that are not associated with a balance sheet account, are assumed to equal the cash expenditure for the period. For example, advertising expense has no current asset or liability account associated with it, therefore, we assume that the $40,000 expense was the result of a cash payment.

Depreciation, while an operating expense, results from allocating the cost of plant and equipment over its useful life and is, therefore, not a cash expenditure. Therefore, depreciation expense is considered a noncash expense and does not appear on the cash flow statement using the direct method.

Cost of Goods Sold and Cash Paid for Inventory Determining the amount of cash paid for inventory during the year requires a two-step process. It is necessary to calculate the amount of inventory purchased during the period first, and then to determine the cash paid during the period for inventory. To determine the amount of merchandise inventory purchased during the year, add the *ending* balance in the Inventory account to the cost of goods sold during the period. This represents the cost of goods available for sale during the accounting period. Next, subtract the *beginning* balance of Inventory from the goods available for sale to determine the amount of inventory purchased during the year. The beginning inventory is subtracted from cost of goods available because it was purchased in a prior year. Magik Mirrors purchased $666,750 of inventory during 1996, as calculated below.

12/31/96 balance—inventory (Exhibit 8.7)	$ 43,745	
Cost of goods sold (Exhibit 8.7)	679,785	
Cost of goods available		$723,530
Less: 1/1/96 balance—inventory (Exhibit 8.7)		56,780
Inventory purchased during 1996		$666,750

The amount of cash paid for the inventory purchased is determined by adding the beginning balance in the Accounts Payable—Inventory account to the inventory purchased during the period and then subtracting the ending balance in the Accounts Payable—Inventory account. The sum of the beginning Accounts Payable—Inventory and inventory purchased represents the maximum cash expenditure possible for inventory during the period. Subtract the ending balance of Accounts Payable—Inventory from this sum because it is the amount of inventory purchased during the period that has not been paid for yet. Magik Mirrors paid $658,450 for inventory during 1996, as calculated below.

1/1/96 accounts payable—inventory (Exhibit 8.7)	$ 67,200	
Inventory purchased during 1996 (calculated above)	666,750	
Maximum possible cash expenditure		$733,960
Less: 12/31/96 accounts payable—inventory (Exhibit 8.7)		75,500
Cash paid for merchandise inventory in 1996		$658,450

Interrelationship of the Statements   The income statement, balance sheet, and statement of cash flows generate information that, when used together, provide useful information about the firm's operations. The statements are interrelated. The income statement describes how the company's operations increased or decreased the net assets of the business during the particular reporting period, while the balance sheet depicts the assets available to support operations in the future and the obligations of the firm to its creditors and owners. The statement of cash flows describes the cash expenditures made to acquire the goods and services necessary to support the sales of the company's products and services.

INTERNAL REPORTS

Now we will describe internal reports and their importance to information users inside the entity, especially managers. The number of reports prepared for the company's management regarding the firm's operating expenditures is limited only by the needs of the managers, or any other authorized internal users. While managers use the financial statements prepared for external parties, these statements are usually not timely enough for making the day-to-day decisions about the firm's operations. Internal reports are prepared in more detail, are provided more frequently, and cover a wider variety of operating topics than are on the income statement or balance sheet. We examine payroll and inventory reports as examples.

Payroll Reports

Managers need information about the cost of the firm's human resources because it helps them assess whether the firm is utilizing its human resources efficiently and effectively. Such information also helps identify and remedy problems revealed by the reports. For example, at Wal-Mart, managers of departments within a store, store managers, and corporate management receive reports about the cost of their payroll. Questions about the amounts spent on overtime, sick pay, vacation pay, and holiday pay on individuals and groups are resolved by these reports. Exhibit 8.11 shows reports used by Wal-Mart managers to assess the cost of their human resources. Note that Wal-Mart reports the cost of human resources not only on an individual basis, but it also summarizes information about these costs for zones ("Zone Summary") within the store, for the entire store ("Store Total"), for supervisors responsible for a group of associates ("Supervisor Summary"), and for divisions within the store ("Division Summary").

Inventory Reports

Retail stores such as Wal-Mart make profits based on the amount of shelf space in the store. That is, store managers have a finite amount of space in a store and want products on the store shelves that sell quickly because products that do not sell take up valuable space. Managers responsible for the sale of merchandise want to identify products that are selling well, those that are not, and the amount of the product on hand. Timely inventory reports make managers aware of the status of the inventory and provide input for their inventory decisions. Wal-Mart stores use scanners at their checkout counters to keep track of the type, amount, and cost of inventory sold and available.

Exhibit 8.12 is an example of a sales and purchase recap report prepared by Wal-Mart for its managers. This report is designed for specific store managers and gives information about the inventory a specific store manager is responsible for on a department-by-department basis such as the beginning inventory, inventory purchased during the month, the inventory purchased to date, sales to date, and the ending inventory. This inventory report tells the manager the cost of the inventory, the retail price of the inventory, the markup percentage, and also the markdowns of that price that have occurred during the period.

Note that the report gives the manager data about the current and prior year's inventory (beginning balance) and also the ratio of ending inventory (at retail) to current sales for the department, sales class average, and the company as a whole. This gives managers a basis for assessing what has occurred to date and helps them formulate strategies for future inventory decisions.

EXHIBIT | 8.11 | **Wal-Mart Payroll Reports**

Time and Attendance Reports

Week To Date Hours and Expense Summary

The "Week To Date Hours and Expense Summary" is printed automatically after each Daily Finalize and on Saturday after the Weekly Finalize. This report lists the following information:

- Total hours by day for each associate.
- Total hours by day for the entire store.
- Total hours by week for each associate.
- Total hours by week for the entire store.

EXAMPLE: "Associate Report" section.

RUN ON: 08/05/97 AT 09:22:32
FOR PERIOD ENDING: 08/05/97

WAL-MART STORE, INC.
WEEK TO DATE HOURS AND EXPENSE SUMMARY
FROM 08/01/97 TO 08/07/97

ASSOCIATE REPORT ASSOC. ID NAME	SOC. SEC. #	DIV	ZONE	PAY TYPE	SATURDAY HOURS	SUNDAY HOURS	MONDAY HOURS	WEEKLY HOURS	ADJUSTMENT DOLLARS	TOTAL HOURS	
0002 JONES, DANA	555-55-5555	1	100	Regular Pay	7.00	5.32	0.00	15.52	0.00	34.52	
				Premium Pay	0.00	0.00	0.00	0.00	0.00	0.00	
				TOTAL	7.00	5.32	0.00	15.52	0.00	34.52	
0004 HINES, FRANK	444-44-4444	1	106	Regular Pay	0.00	0.00	0.00	0.00	0.00	00.00	
				Vacation Pay	0.00	0.00	7.00	35.00	0.00	35.00	
				TOTAL	0.00	0.00	7.00	35.00	0.00	35.00	
0005 SMITX, CARI	333-33-3333	1	100	Regular Pay	5.05	0.00	0.00	25.19	0.00	25.13	
			104	Regular Pay	0.00	0.00	7.03	13.71	0.00	13.71	
				TOTAL	5.05	0.00	7.03	38.90	0.00	38.90	
				NON-EXP TOTAL	86.02	56.47	49.00	472.05	20.00	472.05	3780.41
			•••	EXEMPT TOTAL	0.00	0.00	16.00	80.00	0.00	80.00	0.00
				GRAND TOTAL	86.02	56.47	65.00	552.05	20.00	552.05	3780.41

EXAMPLE: "Zone Summary" section.

RUN ON: 08/05/97 AT 09:22:32
FOR PERIOD ENDING: 08/05/97

WAL-MART STORE, INC.
WEEK TO DATE HOURS AND EXPENSE SUMMARY
FROM 08/01/97 TO 08/07/97

ZONE SUMMARY ZONE	PAY TYPE	SATURDAY HOURS	SATURDAY DOLLARS	SUNDAY HOURS	SUNDAY DOLLARS	MONDAY HOURS	MONDAY DOLLARS	WEEKLY HOURS	ADJUSTMENT DOLLARS	TOTAL HOURS	TOTAL DOLLARS	AVERAGE PAY RATE
101	REGULAR	11.00	49.50	5.00	0.00	12.00	74.30	0.00	0.00	69.00	452.90	6.56
	PREMIUM	0.00	0.00	0.00	00.00	0.00	0.00	0.00	0.00	0.00	00.00	
	TOTAL	11.00	49.50	5.00	00.00	12.00	74.30	0.00	0.00	69.00	497.15	7.21
102	REGULAR	18.32	133.14	0.00	0.00	16.12	89.23	0.00	0.00	92.12	573.12	6.22
	PREMIUM	0.00	0.00	5.00	36.70	0.00	0.00	0.00	0.00	5.00	36.70	7.34
	OVERTIME	0.00	0.00	5.00	44.35	0.00	0.00	0.00	0.00	5.00	44.15	8.83
	VACATION	0.00	0.00	0.00	0.00	8.00	8.00	0.00	40.00	40.00	280.00	7.00
103	No Hours Worked											
	GRAND TOTAL	63.50	417.15	42.00	323.41	76.50	490.30	0.00	40.00	393.50	2753.41	7.00

EXAMPLE: "Store Totals" section.

RUN ON: 08/05/97 AT 09:22:32
FOR PERIOD ENDING: 08/05/97

WAL-MART STORE, INC.
WEEK TO DATE HOURS AND EXPENSE SUMMARY
FROM 08/01/97 TO 08/07/97

STORE TOTALS	PAY TYPE	SATURDAY HOURS	SATURDAY DOLLARS	SUNDAY HOURS	SUNDAY DOLLARS	MONDAY HOURS	MONDAY DOLLARS	WEEKLY HOURS	ADJUSTMENT DOLLARS	TOTAL HOURS	TOTAL DOLLARS	AVERAGE PAY RATE
	REGULAR	238.12	1539.94	0.00	1.10	192.42	1346.40	40.00	0.00	912.21	11288.33	12.37
	OVERTIME	0.00	0.00	36.52	253.17	0.00	0.00	0.00	0.00	36.52	253.87	6.95
	PREMIUM	0.00	0.00	22.32	132.57	0.00	0.00	0.00	0.00	22.82	132.57	5.81
	VACATION	0.00	0.00	0.00	1.10	8.00	56.00	0.00	0.00	40.00	320.00	8.00
	SICK PAY	0.00	0.00	0.00	0.10	0.00	0.00	0.00	0.00	6.00	37.90	6.32
	AWARDS	0.00	0.00	0.00	1.10	0.00	0.00	0.00	10.00	0.00	10.00	
	ASST MGR		275.00		273.10		275.00				1925.00	
	TOTAL	238.12	1814.94	58.84	662.24	200.42	1677.40	40.00	10.00	1017.55	13967.67	13.73

EXHIBIT 8.11 *(concluded)*

EXAMPLE: "Supervisor Summary" section

RUN ON: 08/05/92 AT 09:22:32   WAL-MART STORE, INC.
FOR PERIOD ENDING: 08/05/92   WEEK TO DATE HOURS AND EXPENSE SUMMARY
                                              FROM 08/01/92 TO 08/07/92

| SUPERVISOR SUMMARY | SATURDAY | | SUNDAY | | MONDAY | | WEEKLY ADJUSTMENT | | TOTAL | | AVERAGE |
SUPV ZONE PAY TYPE	HOURS	DOLLARS	HOURS	DOLLARS	HOURS	DOLLARS	HOURS	DOLLARS	HOURS	DOLLARS	PAY RATE
101 JOHN FRANK											
101 Dept. No : 1											
REGULAR	11.00	49.50	5.00	22.50	12.00	74.30	0.00	0.00	69.00	458.90	6.65
PREMIUM	0.00	0.00	0.00	00.00	0.00	0.00	0.00	0.00	0.00	00.00	00.0
TOTAL	11.00	49.50	5.00	22.50	12.00	74.30	0.00	0.00	69.00	458.90	6.65
102 CAROL KLINT											
102 Dept No : 2											
REGULAR	18.32	133.14	5.00	36.35	16.12	89.23	0.00	0.00	97.12	604.02	6.32
PREMIUM	0.00	0.00	0.00	00.00	0.00	0.00	0.00	0.00	0.00	00.00	0.00
OVERTIME	0.00	0.00	0.00	00.00	0.00	0.00	0.00	0.00	0.00	00.00	0.00
VACATION	0.00	0.00	0.00	0.00	0.00	0.00	0.00	40.00	40.00	280.00	7.00
103 JIM WEAVER											
103 Dept No : 3											
No Hours Worked											
GRAND TOTAL	63.50	417.15	42.00	323.41	76.50	490.80	0.00	40.00	393.50	2755.41	7.02

WARNING: Please Note:

There are Work Zones with no supervisors assigned. This may cause the Supervisor Summary to be out of balance with the other summaries on this report. The Work Zones are listed below:

    (list of work zones)

To correct this:

1. Choose Associate Scheduling
2. Select Maintenance
3. Choose Supervisor Zone
4. Assign a Supervisor to the zone(s) listed above.

EXAMPLE: "Division Summary" section

RUN ON: 08/05/92 AT 09:22:32   WAL-MART STORE, INC.
FOR PERIOD ENDING: 08/05/92   WEEK TO DATE HOURS AND EXPENSE SUMMARY
                                              FROM 08/01/92 TO 08/07/92

| DIVISION SUMMARY | SATURDAY | | SUNDAY | | MONDAY | | WEEKLY ADJUSTMENT | | TOTAL | | AVERAGE |
DIV PAY TYPE	HOURS	DOLLARS	HOURS	DOLLARS	HOURS	DOLLARS	HOURS	DOLLARS	HOURS	DOLLARS	PAY RATE
01 REGULAR	214.12	1213.74	0.00	0.00	160.42	864.20	0.00	1.00	872.21	10381.13	11.90
OVERTIME	1.00	1.00	36.52	253.87	0.00	0.00	0.00	1.00	36.52	253.87	6.95
PREMIUM	1.00	1.00	22.82	132.57	0.00	0.00	0.00	1.00	22.82	132.57	5.81
HOLIDAY	1.00	1.00	0.00	1.00	0.00	0.00	0.00	1.00	0.00	0 .00	0.00
VACATION	1.00	1.00	0.00	1.00	8.00	56.00	40.00	1.00	40.00	320.00	8.00
SICK PAY	1.00	1.00	0.00	1.00	0.00	0.00	0.00	1.00	6.00	37.90	6.32
AWARDS	0.00	1.00	0.00	1.00	0.00	0.00	0.00	11.00	0.00	0.00	0.00
ASST MGR		275.00		275.00	0.00	275.00			0.00	1925.00	
TOTAL	214.12	1494.74	59.34	665.44	168.42	1195.20	40.00	17.00	977.55	13050.47	6.32
06 No Hours Worked	0.00	1.00	0.00	0.00	0.00	0.00	0.00	1.00	0.00	0.00	0.00
10 REGULAR	24.00	151.20	0.00	0.00	24.00	151.20	0.00	1.00	144.00	907.20	6.30

EXHIBIT | **8.12** | **Wal-Mart Payroll Reports**

		Ordering Merchandise
Sales and Purchase Recap		
EXAMPLE: Purchase Recap		

RUN ON 04/05/94 AT 06:18:16
FOR PERIOD ENDING 03/31/94

WAL-MART STORES INC.
PURCHASE RECAP BY STORES AS OF
03/31/94

REPORT NO. FI253-1 01
PAGE NO. 1

DIVISION 1 COMPARATIVE STORES
FOR STORE NUMBER 01-0255

DEPT	BEG INV RETAIL	INV ADJ RETAIL	--CURRENT PURCHASE-- COST	RETAIL	GROSS	MARKDOWNS CURRENT	PCT	--Y-T-D PURCHASES-- COST	RETAIL	GROSS	MARKDOWNS YTD	PCT	----SALES---- CURRENT	YTD	END INV RETAIL
1TY	203496		212343	253806	16.3	5010	2.0	42375	49768	14.8	8462	1.6	248247	548247	204045
LY	216578		269307	327516	17.7	4133	1.6	43685	51285	14.9	7628	1.5	248695	542263	291266
SC					16.4		3.6			16.4		3.6			
CO					17.0		4.2			17.0		4.2			

END INV/CURRENT SALES RATIO, FOR DEPT = 0.82 SALES CLASS AVG. = 0.68 • COMPANY AVG = 0.89

DEPT	BEG INV RETAIL	INV ADJ RETAIL	COST	RETAIL	GROSS	CURRENT	PCT	COST	RETAIL	GROSS	YTD	PCT	CURRENT	YTD	END INV RETAIL
2TY	476639		158374	194256	18.4	2938	1.3	343185	406328	18.4	5214	1.3	433876	867543	449631
LY	569452		265177	315549	15.9	4543	1.8	501685	581953	16.0	5198	1.3	430186	862457	629737
					17.3		3.9			17.3		3.9			
					17.4		4.2			17.4		4.2			

END INV/CURRENT SALES RATIO, FOR DEPT = 2.05 SALES CLASS AVE = 1.60 • COMPANY AVG = 2.21

While this report can seem confusing, keep in mind that, like all management reports, it was designed for a select group of users who are familiar with the firm's operations. The Wal-Mart managers responsible for a store's inventory are familiar with these terms and their relationships and find this report useful in making purchasing decisions.

FINANCIAL STATEMENTS—IS THERE DISTORTION AND MISINTERPRETATION?

Financial statements reporting the purchase and use of goods and services can be misleading for many reasons. We will first discuss the impact of errors involving noninventoriable goods and services and merchandise inventory on the financial statements. Then we will examine how inventory costing methods affect financial statement users' perceptions of the firm's operating performance and financial condition.

Errors in Accounting for Noninventoriable Goods and Services

The most common error associated with accounting for noninventoriable goods and services is called a *cutoff error*. A **cutoff error** occurs when a firm fails to recognize the appropriate amount of expense in a particular accounting period. This type of error happens when a firm fails to make the appropriate adjusting entry. It results in the overstatement of net income and either the overstatement of the firm's assets or understatement of the firm's liabilities. Cutoff errors are typically associated with accrued interest, accrued wages, and prepaid expenses, such as rent, advertising, and insurance.

To illustrate, assume that a company paid $3,000 for three months rent in advance on December 1, 1996, and failed to make an adjusting entry to recognize $1,000 of rent expense on December 31, 1996, the company's year-end. In addition, the company failed to accrue $2,000 of wages expense at the fiscal year-end. As a result, the expenses for the year are understated by $3,000, and net income is overstated by the same amount. On the balance sheet, the current assets are overstated by $1,000 because the Prepaid Rent account is too high, and current liabilities are $2,000 too low because wages payable was not recorded.

Cutoff errors, if significant, could mislead financial statement users about the financial condition of the company. The overstatement of net income distorts the operating performance of the firm, while the overstatement of current assets and understatement of current liabilities on the balance sheet distort the liquidity and financial position of the firm.

Distortions Created by Inventory Errors

Why are inventory errors significant? Inventory errors can have a dramatic effect on perceived liquidity and operating performance of a firm. They are usually unintentional and, if a company has a good system of internal control, usually detected. Taking a physical count of inventory is one method of checking the accuracy of the accounting records at the end of a reporting period. When a physical count of the inventory does not correspond to the amounts in the accounting records, management must determine whether the difference is due to clerical errors, theft, or spoilage and take the necessary action to correct the cause of the error and the accounting records. Some companies, however, could intentionally overstate the dollar amount of inventory at the end of a reporting period in order to improve the liquidity and operating performance reported on their financial statements.

We will look at how inventory errors affect the financial statements. If, as the result of an error, too little inventory cost is expensed during a period, not only is reported net income too high (because cost of goods sold expense is too low), but also the amount of inventory reported on the balance sheet is overstated. On the other hand, if an error results in too much inventory cost being expensed during the period, both the reported net income and the balance in the Inventory account will be understated.

For example, assume that Magik Mirrors reported the following partial income statement for 1996 and $42,000 in the Inventory account on the balance sheet.

Sales	$520,000
Cost of goods sold	335,000
Gross margin	$185,000
Operating expenses	110,000
Net income	$ 75,000

An examination revealed that ending inventory was overstated by $20,000 because inventory items costing $20,000 were not transferred to the Cost of Goods Sold account, even though the company recorded the related sale during the year. As a result, Cost of Goods Sold was not increased by $20,000, and the Inventory account was not reduced from $42,000 to $22,000. The income statement below shows the correct amount of Cost of Goods Sold and net income. The increase in Cost of Goods Sold results in a decrease in net income of $20,000.

Sales	$520,000
Cost of goods sold	**355,000**
Gross margin	$165,000
Operating expenses	110,000
Net income	**$ 55,000**

Errors involving the ending inventory have a direct effect on the net income of a firm. That is, if ending inventory is overstated, net income is also overstated because cost of goods sold is understated. If ending inventory is understated, as a result of an error, net income is also understated because cost of goods sold is overstated.

PAUSE & REFLECT

If an error in the ending inventory is not detected, what effect will the error have on the financial statements in the next accounting period? What effect will it have after two years?

Accounting Reality versus Economic Reality—Inventory

The use of FIFO and LIFO have the potential for distorting the true financial condition of a company because they both misrepresent a firm's economic condition as a result of the cost flow assumptions each uses. It is important to understand the misleading aspects of these costing methods in order to avoid misinterpreting a firm's financial condition. For example, you may have wondered why a company like Quaker Oats would voluntarily change to an inventory method that reduces its reported net income. You may have assumed that a company would want to report as much income as possible. However, you now know that during periods of rising prices, a company is better off economically using LIFO rather than FIFO, despite the fact that it results in lower reported earnings. We will now take a closer look at how the FIFO and LIFO costing methods affect a company's reporting process.

Although LIFO uses a more realistic measure of income, it creates a reporting problem on the balance sheet. The inventory reported on the balance sheet under a LIFO system becomes seriously undervalued in periods of inflation. Because LIFO assumes that the last costs recorded in are the first costs expensed, the ending inventory balance reflects the first costs recorded. As a result, these first costs become an expense of the period only if a company sells its entire inventory. For example, assume that a company using LIFO has an ending inventory of $5,000 (1,000 units at $5 each) on December 31, 1996, and always maintains 1,000 units in its ending inventory. If, on December 31, 2001, there are 1,000 units in ending inventory, the inventory will have a cost of $5,000 because LIFO assumes that these costs have not been expensed. If these inventory items cost $9 each on December 31, 2001, then the ending inventory of $5,000 is undervalued by $4,000 ($9,000 – $5,000).

To help financial statement readers determine the realistic value of an inventory when using LIFO, companies must disclose the current value of the inventory in the financial statements. For example, Wal-Mart uses LIFO and uses what it calls a *LIFO reserve* to disclose both the current cost to replace the inventory and also the inventory's LIFO cost. Exhibit 8.13 shows the replacement cost of Wal-Mart's inventory as of January 25, 1995 ($14.415 billion), and also the ending inventory based on LIFO ($14.064 billion). By making this disclosure, Wal-Mart and other companies using LIFO keep the financial statement users informed of this balance sheet shortcoming, while receiving a better measure of net income and the tax benefits of using LIFO.

The FIFO costing system reports a company's ending inventory at the most recent cost because it assumes that oldest items in the inventory are sold first. However, as we discussed earlier in the chapter, FIFO generates a larger net income than LIFO in periods of inflation and, consequently, results in a company paying more taxes. In addition, when management's bonuses are based on a percentage of net income, FIFO will generate higher bonuses for management because of higher reported income than the LIFO system would. As a result, FIFO can be viewed as penalizing the firm's stockholders in a period of rising prices because the firm pays too much in taxes and too much in bonuses relative to LIFO.

FIFO's main advantage is that it approximates the physical flow of the goods in the company. This is good not only for the balance sheet, but also for managerial decision making. Managers whose companies use a FIFO cost flow assumption have the most recent cost to use for their inventory decisions.

SUMMARY

This chapter discusses how the accounting system reflects the recording of transactions involving the purchase and use of merchandise inventory and noninventoriable goods and services that support the firm's operations. Accounting for these operating expenditures involves operating expenses that are reported on the income statement and current assets and liabilities that are reported on the balance sheet. Understanding how the accounting system records and reports operating expenditures is important to external and internal users of financial information because it provides insights about a firm's operations, financial condition, and cash flows.

- Expenditures are cash payments, while expenses and losses are accounting terms used to describe a particular set of accounting events.

- Noninventoriable goods and services support the sale of the firms' goods and services. When they are consumed, these goods and services are classified as operating expenses which are matched with the revenues generated during the

| EXHIBIT | 8.13 | LIFO Inventory—Wal-Mart |

CONSOLIDATED BALANCE SHEET
At January 31, 1994, and 1995
(in millions)

	1995	1994
Assets		
Current assets:		
Cash and cash equivalents	$ 45	$ 20
Receivables	700	690
Recoverable costs from sales/leaseback	200	208
Inventories		
At replacement cost	14,415	11,483
Less LIFO reserve	351	469
Inventories at LIFO cost	$14,064	$11,014
Prepaid expenses and other	329	182
Total current assets	$15,338	$12,114
Property, plant, and equipment, at cost:		
Land	3,036	2,741
Buildings and improvements	8,973	6,818
Fixtures and equipment	4,768	3,981
Transportation equipment	313	260
Less accumulated depreciation	$17,090	$13,800
	2,782	2,173
Net property, plant, equipment	$14,308	$11,627
Property under capital leases	2,147	2,059
Less accumulated amortization	581	510
Net property under capital leases	$ 1,566	$ 1,549
Other assets and deferred charges	1,607	1,151
Total assets	$32,819	$26,441
Liabilities and Shareholders' Equity		
Current liabilities:		
Commercial paper	$ 1,795	$ 1,575
Accounts payable	5,907	4,104
Accrued liabilities	1,819	1,473
Accrued federal and state income taxes	365	183
Long-term debt due within one year	23	20
Obligations under capital leases due within one year	64	51
Total current liabilities	$ 9,973	$ 7,406
Long-term debt	7,871	6,156
Long-term obligations under capital leases	1,838	1,804
Deferred income taxes	411	322
Shareholder's equity:		
Preferred stock ($.10 par value; 100 shares authorized, none issued)		
Common stock ($.10 par value; 5,500 shares authorized, 2,297 and 2,299		
issued and outstanding in 1995 and 1994, respectively)	230	230
Capital in excess of par value	539	536
Retained earnings	12,213	9,987
Foreign currency translation adjustment	(256)	—
Total shareholders' equity	$12,726	$10,753
Total liabilities and shareholders' equity	$32,819	$26,441

same accounting period. Expense recognition can be concurrent with, after, or prior to a cash expenditure.

- Payroll generates wages and salary expenses and payroll tax expense. The employer is responsible for paying payroll taxes and also for amounts withheld on behalf of the employees.

- Costs of inventory include the purchase price of the inventory plus the additional costs incurred to acquire the inventory, such as transportation and insurance. Purchase discounts and purchase allowances reduce the cost of the inventory.

- The perpetual inventory system maintains a continuous record of the quantity and cost of each inventory item purchased and sold. All events that change inventory are recorded directly into the Inventory account as they occur.

- When inventory items are homogeneous and cannot be specifically identified, management makes an assumption about the order in which costs are expensed. FIFO and LIFO are cost flow assumptions that provide a rational and systematic way to allocate the cost of inventory between cost of goods sold and ending inventory. In periods of changing prices, cost flow assumptions affect both the income statement and balance sheet.

- The income statement, balance sheet, and cash flow statement generate useful information about the firm's expenditure cycle events. The income statement describes how the firm consumed its net assets during a particular period of time. The balance sheet reports the amount of assets available to support the firm's operation in the coming accounting periods. The statement of cash flows describes the cash expenditures made to support the operation of the firm.

- Internal reports have no set format and are designed to meet the informational needs of management on a timely basis.

- Misleading information about the purchase and use of goods and services happens when errors occur or when FIFO and LIFO distort the economic reality of operating results.

KEY TERMS

cost flow assumption The rational and systematic allocation of inventory cost between the Cost of Goods Sold and Inventory accounts based on presumptions made about the order in which inventory cost is expensed

cutoff error An error that occurs when a firm fails to recognize the appropriate amount of expense in a particular accounting period

deductions Amounts withheld from an employee's gross pay by the employer

expenditure Cash payment made to acquire goods and services, reduce liabilities, or reward owners for their interest in the firm

FICA Social security taxes authorized by the Federal Insurance Contribution Act

FIFO First-in, first-out: a cost flow assumption that presumes inventory purchases (costs) are charged to cost of goods sold in chronological order

freight out The cost of shipping goods paid by the seller; classified as an operating expense

FUTA The Federal Unemployment Tax Act which requires employers to pay payroll-related taxes to support the federal government's administration of unemployment benefits

gross pay The full amount an employee earns

LIFO Last-in, first-out: a cost flow assumption that presumes inventory purchases (costs) are charged to cost of goods sold in reverse chronological order

liquidity The time required to convert an asset into cash or use it in operations

loss A decrease in assets or increase in liabilities and a decrease in owners' equity resulting from events that are incidental to the ongoing operations of the firm, with the exception of distributions to owners

merchandise inventory The goods a company acquires with the intent of selling

net pay The amount of pay remaining after subtracting the deductions from gross pay

net price method A method of recording the acquisition of inventory that assumes the cost of merchandise inventory is the purchase price less any available cash discount

noninventoriable goods and services Goods and services that support the sale of the firm's goods and services but are not included in the merchandise inventory

periodic inventory system A recording system that reflects the cost of goods sold and inventory on hand at the end of the accounting period

perpetual inventory system A recording system that creates a continuous record of the quantity and cost of inventory items purchased and sold

purchase discounts Cash discounts taken by the buyer

Purchase discounts lost An account used by companies using the net price method of inventory to reflect the financing charges paid for not taking available purchase discounts

Purchase returns and allowances A case when the buyer either returns merchandise or pays less than the original amount due

specific identification method An inventory method that transfers the identifiable cost of inventory to the Cost of Goods Sold account when the items that are individually identified are sold

SUTA The State Unemployment Tax Act which requires employers to pay payroll-related taxes to the state to fund unemployment benefits

QUESTIONS

1. What is the distinction between an inventoriable cost and noninventoriable cost? Give an example of each type of cost.

2. Distinguish among expenditure, expense, and loss.

3. What costs are included in Inventory in a merchandising organization?

4. Who pays the freight charges when inventory is shipped FOB destination? When it is shipped FOB shipping point? Why is this distinction important?

5. If goods are shipped FOB destination and are in transit at the end of the period, who owns the inventory? Why?

6. Why are freight charges paid by the seller considered to be an operating expense while freight charges paid by the buyer of merchandise inventory are included in the cost of the inventory?

7. Describe how operating expenses are recognized other than when an operating expenditure takes place.

8. Why is the net rather than the gross price of inventory recorded when using the net method?

9. Describe the payroll taxes assessed on the employer.

10. Describe a perpetual inventory system.

11. If a firm uses a perpetual inventory system, how are the goods available for sale determined?

12. Why is the balance in the Purchase Discounts Lost account not considered to be part of the cost of inventory?

13. What is the distinction between a purchase return and a purchase allowance?

14. When is cost of goods sold determined in a perpetual inventory system? Why?

15. What is meant by the phrase *cost flow assumption* as it relates to inventories?

16. What do the terms *FIFO* and *LIFO* mean? How do they affect cost of goods sold and the ending inventory of a company?

17. Describe the impact of FIFO and LIFO on a firm's financial statements when prices are rising over an accounting period. What is the impact when prices are falling over an accounting period?

18. If the balance of Prepaid Insurance decreases during the period, are cash payments for insurance greater than or less than the insurance expense reported for the period?

19. In periods of changing prices, why does the amount reported for inventory on the balance sheet under LIFO require additional disclosure?

20. In periods of rising prices, why does FIFO distort the income reported by a company?

EXERCISES

E 8.1   For events (*a*) through (*o*), indicate whether the event is classified as an expenditure, expense, or loss as shown in *a*. Answer NA if the event does not fit any of the classifications.

	Expenditure	Expense	Loss
a. Received and paid bill for advertising.	x	x	
b. Paid cash for one year's rent in advance.			
c. Received electricity but won't pay for 30 days.			
d. Fire destroyed $500 of merchandise inventory.			
e. Paid accounts payable.			
f. Paid cash for freight on merchandise sold FOB destination.			
g. Merchandise inventory sold.			
h. Paid cash for warranty work done on the year the merchandise was sold.			
i. Paid for freight on merchandise purchased FOB shipping point.			
j. Purchased merchandise inventory on account.			
k. Paid federal government for income taxes withheld from employees.			
l. Paid cash for warranty work done one year after the sale.			
m. $500 of office supplies were stolen.			
n. Recorded depreciation expense.			
o. Used $630 of office supplies purchased at the start of the year.			

E 8.2 For each of the following, identify whether the cost associated with the event is included in the cost of inventory or is considered a noninventoriable cost as shown in *a*. Answer NA if the event fits neither classification.

	Inventoriable	Noninventoriable
a. Advertising.		x
b. Freight on inventory purchased FOB destination.		
c. Sales commissions.		
d. Insurance on merchandise inventory purchased with terms FOB shipping point.		
e. Purchase discount lost.		
f. Cost of electricity for the warehouse where merchandise inventory is stored.		
g. Freight on inventory sold with terms FOB shipping point.		
h. Insurance on building where inventory sold.		
i. Cost of warranty work.		
j. Cost of insurance on merchandise purchased and in transit.		

E 8.3 On January 1, 1996, the start of its fiscal year, the Beau Beans Company had the account balances listed below. During the year, the company was involved in the operating events described below.

	Debit	Credit
Office supplies	$5,250	
Prepaid insurance	3,000	
Utilities payable		$2,300

Jan. 14   Paid the $2,300 due on the utilities.
March 15   Purchased $3,000 of office supplies on account.
April 1   Paid the amount due on the office supplies.
June 1   Renewed the insurance policy by making a $7,200 cash payment for one year's premium.
Dec. 31   Received December's utility bill for $2,500, which is due January 15, 1997. A count of the office supplies indicates that $2,500 of office supplies are on hand.

Make the entries for operating events listed above and make the appropriate adjusting entries on December 31, 1996.

E 8.4   An abbreviated payroll register for The Smoke Corporation for the week ending August 18, 1995, is shown below.

Employee	Gross Earnings	Federal Income Tax	FICA	Retirement Contribution	Net Pay
Duena Allen	$370.00	$41.50	$28.30	$15.00	$285.20
Martha Cook	352.50	55.00	27.97	14.00	255.53
George Lacy	290.00	37.50	22.19	12.00	218.31

Prepare the journal entry to record:
1. The payroll for the week.
2. Payment of the weekly payroll.
3. The payroll taxes for this time period. (SUTA is 2.5% and FUTA is .8% of gross earnings.)

E 8.5   At the end of the fiscal year on June 30, 1995, Grafton Industries had unpaid accrued wages of $15,000. Assuming a FICA tax rate of 7.65 percent, a FUTA tax rate of .8 percent, and a SUTA tax rate of 3.5 percent, prepare the adjusting entry to record Grafton's payroll tax expense.

E 8.6   During 1995 Donnelly Company sold 57,000 coolers. The beverage coolers have a two-year limited warranty for parts and labor. In 1995 Donnelly spent $2,100 on warranty work on coolers sold in 1994 ($400 on parts and $1,700 on labor) and $9,300 of warranty work on coolers sold in 1995 ($3,000 parts and $6,300 labor). Donnelly expects to spend an additional $4,600 on warranty work on the coolers sold in 1995 in the fiscal years after 1995. Make the entries necessary to account for the warranties in 1995. The estimated warranty liability account had a balance of $2,500 on January 1, 1995.

E 8.7   Determine the amounts in question in the following schedule.

	Company A	Company B	Company C
Beginning inventory	$ 362,800	$ 158,200	?
Merchandise purchased	2,576,400	?	$437,500
Merchandise available for sale	?	$1,490,700	?
Ending inventory	$ 371,900	?	$ 63,900
Cost of goods sold	?	$1,325,900	435,800

E 8.8   Provide the missing data for each of the three cases shown below.

Beginning inventory	$25,000	$ 18,000	?
Goods purchased	62,000	?	$77,000
Cost of goods available for sale	?	?	?
Ending inventory	$21,000	$ 20,000	$13,000
Cost of goods sold	?	152,000	78,000

E 8.9   Using perpetual inventory procedures, journalize the following transactions on the books of Bayer Company. Assume Bayer Company uses the net price method of recording merchandise purchases.

Aug. 8   Bayer Company purchased $6,700 in merchandise from Solder Company; terms 1/10, n/30.
12   One group of items in the August 8 purchase was not up to the purchase specifications. Bayer Company requested and was granted a $300 allowance on the price of those items.
16   Bayer Company paid Solder Company for the purchase and took advantage of the cash discount.

E 8.10   Simpson Company uses the perpetual inventory system. Journalize the entries listed below, assuming Simpson Company uses the net price method of recording merchandise purchases.

April 6   Purchased $5,500 in merchandise from Piper Wholesale; terms 1/15, n/30, FOB shipping point.
9   Paid Morrison Transit $300 freight charges on the purchase of April 6.
12   Return $700 gross price of merchandise from the April 6 purchase to Piper Wholesale because the items were the wrong model.
30   Paid Piper Wholesale the amount due.

E 8.11   For each of the three credit purchases shown below, prepare the journal entry to record (*a*) the purchase of the merchandise, and (*b*) the payment of the obligation. Assume that the first two purchases were paid within the discount period and that the third was paid after the discount period. The purchasing firm uses the net price method of recording and the perpetual inventory system.

Purchase 1   Purchased $6,800 in merchandise from Pittman Company; terms 2/10, n/30.

Purchase 2   Purchased merchandise with a list price of $5,500 from Goodnow Company; terms 1/EOM, n/60.

Purchase 3   Purchased from Boyd Corporation merchandise with a price of $12,000; terms 1/15, n/60.

E 8.12   Mendez and Mendelson, Inc., is in its first year of operating as a wholesale company. During the accounting period just completed, it experienced consistently rising prices on the products it buys and sells. The partial income statement information shown below was developed by its chief accountant using two different cost flow assumptions, FIFO and LIFO.

	Case 1	Case 2
Sales	$500,000	$500,000
Cost of goods sold	325,000	332,000
Gross margin	$175,000	$168,000

Determine which case is FIFO and which is LIFO. State which case would result in the higher inventory value on the balance sheet and indicates why.

E 8.13   Sullivan Industries uses the perpetual inventory system for some of its products. From the information below, prepare the journal entries to record the cost of goods sold under FIFO and LIFO. What is the ending inventory under each cost flow assumption?

			Quantity	Unit Cost
January 1	Beginning inventory		25	$1,200
January 8	Purchase		30	1,400
January 12	Sale		35	—

E 8.14   The following information is taken from the records of the Spencer Company. Spencer uses a perpetual inventory system.

Date	Transaction	Number of Units	Unit Cost
May 1	Beginning inventory	14	$3.50
May 4	Sale	5	
May 12	Purchase	9	3.80
May 16	Sale	3	
May 21	Sale	7	
May 25	Purchase	4	3.95
May 31	Sale	3	

Determine the cost of goods sold for the month using FIFO and LIFO cost flow assumptions. How many units are in ending inventory and what is the cost of ending inventory under each assumption? (The perpetual inventory cards illustrated in Exhibits 8.3 and 8.4 may be helpful in solving this exercise.)

E 8.15   The following information is taken from the records of the Begley Company. Begley uses a perpetual inventory system.

Date	Transaction	Number of Units	Unit Cost
May 1	Beginning inventory	14	$3.95
May 4	Sale	5	
May 12	Purchase	9	3.80
May 16	Sale	3	
May 21	Sale	7	
May 25	Purchase	4	3.50
May 31	Sale	3	

Determine the cost of goods sold for the month using FIFO and LIFO cost flow assumptions. How many units are in ending inventory and what is the cost of ending inventory under each assumption? (The perpetual inventory cards illustrated in Exhibits 8.3 and 8.4 may be helpful in solving this exercise.)

E 8.16   The following information is taken from the records of Turner Company. Turner uses a perpetual inventory system and sells its products for $30 each. Make the entries for the transactions below and determine the cost of goods sold, gross margin, and the ending inventory for the month assuming the FIFO cost flow assumption.

Date	Transaction	Units	Unit Price
Jan. 1	Beginning inventory	10	$12.00
Jan. 3	Purchase	15	13.00
Jan. 4	Sale	15	
Jan. 8	Purchase	15	14.00
Jan. 10	Purchase	10	15.00
Jan. 15	Sale	20	
Jan. 20	Purchase	10	16.00
Jan. 27	Sale	20	
Jan. 31	Purchase	10	17.00

E 8.17   Rework E 8.16 assuming that Turner Company uses the LIFO cost flow assumption.

E 8.18   Singleton Corporation had cost of goods sold of $450,000 during 1996. The beginning and ending balances of the Inventory and Accounts Payable—Merchandise accounts are presented below. How much cash did Singleton Corporation pay to acquire merchandise in 1996?

	1/1/96	12/31/96
Inventory	$37,500	$45,000
Accounts payable—merchandise	89,000	74,000

E 8.19   Given the account balances below determine the cash paid for insurance, office supplies, and wages in 1995.

	1/1/95	12/31/95
Prepaid insurance	$ 4,500	$ 3,900
Office supplies	2,450	3,245
Wages payable	12,000	9,355
Insurance expense		6,675
Office supplies expense		4,449
Wages expense		95,670

E 8.20   For each of the following inventory errors indicate the impact on the financial statement categories listed. Use (+) when the category is too big, (–) when it is too small, and (0) when there is no effect. Assume that the company used a perpetual inventory system. The first one is completed as an example.

1995

	Net Income	Assets	Liabilities	Owner's Equity

a. 12/31/95 inventory is understated.
b. Failed to record credit purchase 1995.
c. 12/31/95 inventory is overstated.
d. Failed to adjust prepaid insurance in 1995.

	Net Income	Assets	Liabilities	Owner's Equity
a.	—	—	0	—

1996

	Net Income	Assets	Liabilities	Owner's Equity

e. 12/31/95 inventory is understated.
f. 12/31/95 inventory is overstated.
g. Failed to accrue salary expense 1995.

PROBLEMS

P 8.1 For each of the events below identify whether it is an inventoriable or noninventoriable cost and whether it is an expenditure, expense, or a loss.

	Inv.	Noninv.	Expenditure	Expense	Loss
a. Paid rent on warehouse.		x	x		
b. Paid freight, terms FOB shipping point, on the inventory.					
c. Inventory purchased on account.					
d. Received utility bill; will pay in 30 days.					
e. Paid for freight on merchandise sold, terms FOB destination.					
f. $1,000 of merchandise inventory in warehouse is now obsolete and cannot be sold.					
g. Paid an account payable.					
h. Paid cash for one-year insurance policy.					
i. Paid cash for warranty work on merchandise sold in prior year.					
j. Paid FICA withholdings.					

P 8.2 The Stark Corporation had the following operating events occur during the month of August 1996. Stark Corporation's fiscal year ends on August 31.

Aug. 1   Paid $3,000 for two months' rent in advance.

     2   Received and paid $1,750 bill for advertising.

     5   Purchased $600 of office supplies on account.

     8   Paid $1,000 on warranty work; 40 percent of the work was done on goods sold in previous accounting periods, and the remainder was on goods sold in the current fiscal year.

     15   Paid $1,200 for life insurance on the company president. This is an annual premium and the first time the company has insured the president.

     21   Received phone bill for $450 and plan to pay it on August 30.

     26   Paid $745 postage to mail advertising brochures to customers.

     30   Paid phone bill.

     31   Adjusting entries.

Additional Information

Account balances August 1:	
Office supplies	$4,000
Estimated warranty liability	1,700
Information for adjusting entries:	
Office supplies on hand August 31, 1996	1,250
Estimate of future warranty cost on merchandise sold during the current fiscal year	4,700

Required: *a.* Make the appropriate entries for the events in August.

       b. Show how the accounts described above are presented on Stark Corporation's income statement and balance sheet.

P 8.3 Gross pay for the employees of Lyle Supply Company for September 1997 is as follows:

Office salaries	$ 28,000
Sales salaries	64,000
Warehouse salaries	56,000
Total salaries	$148,000

Information on withholding and taxes is shown below.

a. Federal income tax withheld, $18,500.

b. FICA taxes withheld on employees, $7,500.

c. State income tax withheld, $4,300.

d. Health insurance premiums withheld, $1,020.

e. Pension contributions withheld, $7,400.

f. SUTA taxes of $2,460, and FUTA taxes of $574 withheld.

Required: *a.* Make the journal entry to record the September payroll.

b. Record the journal entry for the employer's payroll taxes.

c. Make the journal entry to record the employer's monthly payment of payroll tax liabilities.

 P 8.4

Felton Company experienced the following transactions during the month of November 1996. The company sells on terms FOB destination and uses the perpetual inventory system and the net price method.

Nov. 3 Purchased $10,900 in merchandise from Griffith Manufacturing Company; terms 1/15, n/30, FOB shipping point.

8 Made a $12,300 sale to Lunceford Stores on account. The inventory cost $9,000.

11 Paid $250 freight charges to Intercontinental Transit for merchandise from Griffith Manufacturing Company.

15 Bought inventory items totaling $9,850 from Eberwein, Inc.; terms 2/10, n/30, FOB destination.

17 Collected the amount due from the sale to Lunceford Stores on November 8.

19 Paid $175 freight charges to Gray Freight Line on merchandise sold to Lunceford Stores.

20 Returned $400 (gross price) of merchandise to Eberwein, Inc.

23 Sold $8,900 in merchandise to Diana's Gift Shop on account. The inventory cost $6,586.

25 Sent amount due to Eberwein, Inc.

28 Paid Griffith Manufacturing Company amount due for inventory items purchased on November 3.

Required: Record the transactions in general journal form.

P 8.5

Hailie Company had the following transactions during May 1996. The firm records purchases using the net price method and uses a perpetual inventory system.

May 2 Paid accounts payable of $5,100 to Waters Company.

3 Purchased merchandise from Holtman Company, $6,300; terms: 1/10, n/30, FOB destination.

5 Sold $13,800 on account of products that cost $8,970 to Oliver Corporation; terms FOB shipping point.

10 Purchased merchandise from Lambson Company with a price of $7,200; terms n/30, FOB shipping point.

12 Paid Holtman Company for the purchase of May 3.

13 Paid $150 freight and $60 for insurance on shipment from Lambson Company.

15 Returned $1,000 list price of merchandise purchased from Lambson Company because the items were damaged.

16 Purchased merchandise from Allan Company for $3,800; terms: 2/10, n/60, FOB destination.

22 Sold merchandise for $15,100 cash to Parry, Inc., that cost $9,815; terms FOB destination.

23 Paid $130 of freight and $40 of insurance on merchandise shipped to Parry, Inc.

28 Paid Allan Company the amount due on the purchase of May 16.

29 Received payment from the sales to Oliver Corporation of May 5.

Additional Information:

Selected account balances on May 1, 1996:	
Cash	$16,800
Accounts receivable	7,350
Inventory	21,600
Accounts payable	5,100

Required: *a.* Record the transactions in general journal form.

b. Enter the beginning balances shown above as additional information in T-accounts. Post the transactions to the T-accounts and prepare new accounts as necessary.

c. Prepare income statement information showing how to derive the gross margin and show the inventory balance as of May 30.

P 8.6

Data from Pocket Calculators, Inc.'s, perpetual inventory records for the computer component it sells are given below.

	Number of Units	Cost per Unit
Beginning inventory	16,000	$8.25
Purchases:		
March 3	52,000	8.20
June 28	60,000	8.10
September 12	58,000	8.05
November 30	62,000	7.95
Sales:		
March 7	38,000	
July 8	75,000	
October 12	60,000	
December 7	55,000	

The company sold 228,000 components during the year at $20 each. On December 31, the balance sheet date, the replacement cost for the components was $7.90 per unit.

Required:

a. Compute the cost of the ending inventory and the cost of goods sold using both FIFO and LIFO.

b. In your opinion, which of the two methods is a better representation of the balance sheet value for the inventory? Why?

c. Which method do you think is more representative of the firm's income? Why?

d. Which method do you prefer? Why?

P 8.7

JDR Company uses a perpetual inventory system. During the month of February of the current year, the company experienced the following purchases and sales on one item in the stock of goods. The sale price of the product is $900. Assume that all sales and purchases are for cash.

		Number of Units	Unit Cost
February 1	Beginning inventory	8	$500
February 3	Sale	5	
February 9	Purchase	6	575
February 15	Sale	7	
February 24	Purchase	8	580
February 28	Sale	4	

Required:

a. Make the entries for these transactions using FIFO.

b. Make the entries for these transactions using LIFO.

c. What are the cost of goods sold and the cost ending inventory under each of these assumptions? Explain why the two methods generate different amounts.

P 8.8

The Barton Company sells two products, Alpha and Omega. Alpha sells for $700 per unit, and Omega has a price of $1,100. Barton uses the perpetual inventory system and uses the net method of accounting for purchase discounts. On December 31, 1995, Barton had 50 units of Alpha at a cost of $300 each and 20 units of Omega at a cost of $500 each. During the month of December 1995, Barton had the following transactions.

Dec. 1 Purchased 20 units of Alpha from Robson Corporation on account for $310 each; terms 2/10, n/30, FOB destination.

3 Sold six units of Omega to Balfor Corporation on account; terms n/EOM and FOB destination.

4 Paid $57 freight on the shipment to Balfor.

5 Purchased 25 units of Omega from Hamilton Co. on account for $520 each; terms 2/15, n/30, FOB destination.

15 Sold 30 units of Alpha to the Collyer Corporation on account; terms n/30, FOB shipping point.

16 Returned five units of Omega that were defective to Hamilton Co.

20 Paid the amount due to Hamilton Co.

22 Sold 25 units of Omega to Cylex Corp. for cash.

30 Collected amount due from Balfor Corporation from Dec. 3 sale.

31 Paid amount due to Robson Corporation.

Required:

   a. Make the entries for these transactions using the FIFO cost flow assumption.

   b. Make the entries for these transactions using the LIFO cost flow assumption.

   c. What is the amount of gross margin and ending inventory under FIFO?

   d. What is the amount of gross margin and ending inventory under LIFO?

   e. What is the difference in the gross margin, ending inventory, and cash flows between these two methods?

   f. What are the advantages and disadvantages of each method?

P 8.9   Listed below are a partial income statement and a partial balance sheet for the Steinle Company. From this information, calculate the cash paid for merchandise inventory and operating expenses.

STEINLE COMPANY
Partial Income Statement for the Period Ending December 31, 1996

Sales		$956,000
Cost of goods sold		537,000
Gross margin		$419,000
Operating expenses:		
Wages expense	$180,000	
Advertising expense	39,000	
Rent expense	26,000	
Insurance expense	4,000	
Office supplies expense	2,000	
Warranty expense	20,000	
Payroll tax expense	21,000	
Depreciation expense	60,000	352,000
Operating income before income taxes		$ 67,000
Tax expense (30% tax rate)		20,100
Operating income		$ 46,900

STEINLE COMPANY
Partial Comparative Balance Sheet at December 31, 1996 and 1995

	12/31/96	12/31/95
Current assets:		
Inventory	$85,000	$65,000
Prepaid rent	12,000	10,000
Prepaid insurance	700	1,200
Office supplies	900	500
Current liabilities:		
Accounts payable—merchandise	37,000	45,000
Wages payable	13,000	12,000
Estimated warranty liability	3,700	2,000
Income taxes payable	20,100	18,000
Employee income tax withheld	5,500	3,000
FICA payable	2,000	1,500
FUTA payable	800	700
SUTA payable	1,100	1,300

P 8.10   The McAdams Corporation is currently using LIFO to determine its cost of goods sold and ending inventory. However, Jamie McAdams, the company president, has learned that because prices are rising, the company could report higher net income if it switched to FIFO. Mr. McAdams wants you to advise him on whether the company should switch to FIFO. You have the financial information for 1996, described below, at your disposal.

Sales (all cash)	$2,500,000
Operating expenses	1,200,000
Cash paid for operating expenses	900,000
Beginning inventory	250,000
Cost of goods sold (LIFO)	800,000
Cost of goods sold (FIFO)	680,000
Ending inventory (LIFO)	180,000
Ending inventory (FIFO)	300,000
Beginning accounts payable	50,000
Ending accounts payable	60,000

McAdams has a 30 percent income tax rate and paid the income tax in cash.

Required:
a. Calculate the net income using both FIFO and LIFO.
b. Calculate the cash from operations using both FIFO and LIFO.
c. Explain the difference between the cash flows generated by FIFO and those generated by LIFO and advise Mr. McAdams about the proposed switch to FIFO.

COMPUTER APPLICATIONS

CA 8.1 Kirmer Corporation's cost of goods sold in 1996 was $456,700 and its beginning and ending inventory amounts were $56,000 and $36,000, respectively. The Accounts Payable balance had increased $18,000 during the year to $56,000 as of December 31, 1996, the company's fiscal year-end.

Required:
a. Using a spreadsheet application, determine the cash paid for merchandise during the year.
b. What effect would decreasing ending inventory by $5,000 and increasing ending accounts payable by $2,000 have on the firm's cash flow?
c. If ending inventory increased $2,000 and the ending accounts payable decreased $3,000, what effect would the changes have on cash?

CA 8.2 Using a word processing package, write a memo that could be used to summarize and describe any company's inventory. Topics covered should include, but should not be limited to, the firm's costing method, amount of cost of goods sold, and the beginning and ending inventory.

CASES

C 8.1 Go to the library and locate one company that switched from FIFO to LIFO and describe the impact of the change on the financial statements and the justification the company used for the change. What does the company disclose about the LIFO inventory in the years subsequent to the change? (The AICPA publication *Accounting Trends and Techniques* and the Disclosure database are good sources for this information.)

C 8.2 Using the IRS's publication Circular E (you may find it in the library, at a CPA firm, or through the Internal Revenue Service), find the amount of federal income tax and FICA tax that would be withheld from a married person's monthly check in January and December if he or she made the following annual amounts and claimed the specified exemptions.

		January Withholding		December Withholding	
Annual Salary	Personal Exemptions	Income Tax	FICA	Income Tax	FICA
1. 36,000	5				
2. 36,000	1				
3. 60,000	5				
4. 60,000	1				
5. 96,000	5				
6. 96,000	1				

CRITICAL THINKING

CT 8.1 The Hanson Corporation wants to include the cost of operating its warehouse in the cost of inventory. Carol Hanson, the company's controller, argues that the cost of the warehouse is a reasonable and necessary cost of getting the inventory ready for sale and, therefore, should be included in the cost of the inventory. What impact will this decision have on the firm's income statement and balance sheet? Do you think Carol is justified in her actions? Why?

CT 8.2 R. Francis Bell, the controller of Penoke Corporation, has decided to stop making year-end accruals for salaries and wages expense as of December 31, 1996. He says that after the first year the amount of expense reported using the cash basis will be about the same as the amount reported under the accrual basis. Therefore, he argues that the cost of recording year-end accruals exceeds their benefit to financial statement readers. He says he will put a footnote on this year's financial statements to explain his actions. What is your response to Mr. Bell's proposal?

EC 8.1 In 1972 the National Cash Register Company changed from a LIFO to a FIFO inventory method. The change almost completely eliminated a loss that National Cash Register would have reported during 1972 under LIFO. In addition, inflation had reached new highs and was expected to continue into the foreseeable future. Adopting FIFO in this inflationary environment would mean the company would now recognize more income than under LIFO in the coming years. What are the ethical implications of this decision to change inventory costing methods?

EC 8.2 On December 31, 1995, the Alloway Corporation signed an agreement to sell the Murphy Company $600,000 of its products, which cost $443,000. Murphy specified that Alloway was not to ship the merchandise until January 15. Alloway recorded the sale but did not record the reduction of the inventory because it had not left the warehouse. How appropriate is this action? What is the impact of this action on Alloway's financial statements? What are the ethical implications of this action?

CHAPTER 9

Recording and Communicating in the Revenue Cycle

Learning Objectives

1. Understand how to distinguish between revenues and gains.
2. Explain how the accounting system captures information concerning revenues, gains, and related events, including uncollectible accounts.
3. Describe how companies communicate the financial effects of revenues, gains, and related events to their external and internal stakeholders.

The Boeing Company is one of the world's leading manufacturers of commercial aircraft. It is also involved in the defense and space industries and, in 1992, held the distinction of being the United States' largest exporter. Operating revenues for 1994 totaled $21.9 billion. According to its 1994 annual report, Boeing uses several different approaches to record revenues. "Sales under commercial programs . . . are generally recorded as deliveries are made." In the case of some other contracts that "require substantial performance over an extended period before deliveries begin, sales are recorded based upon attainment of scheduled performance milestones." Still other sales are recorded "as costs are incurred."

Revenues appear on every company's income statement. Therefore, financial statement users should understand what they represent, as well as the principles that dictate when companies recognize and report them.

In Chapter 8, we discussed the acquisition and use of goods and services and saw that their use results in expenses that reduce income and net worth. But that's only half of the story. To complete the picture of the earnings process, we must understand that the successful employment of goods and services yields corresponding benefits that increase the income and net worth of a company. These events, reported as either revenues or gains on a company's income statement, increase net assets on the balance sheet and usually result in cash collections reported on the statement of cash flows in current or future periods.

A company's ultimate success depends on its ability to continually generate operating revenues in excess of related expenses, and to convert those revenues into sufficient cash to pay for goods and services consumed during daily business activities. Although gains are nonrecurring in nature, when they do occur, they can be significant. Therefore, it is essential that internal and external stakeholders understand the fundamental issues surrounding the recognition and reporting of both revenues and gains.

In this chapter we discuss the revenue cycle. We define and distinguish between revenues and gains and illustrate how to account for some common revenue and gain events. We show how companies communicate these events to stakeholders. Finally, we discuss potential errors in accounting for revenues and gains.

WHAT ARE REVENUES?

The Financial Accounting Standards Board defines **revenues** as:

> Inflows or other enhancements of assets of an entity or settlements of its liabilities (or a combination of both) from delivering or producing goods, rendering services, or other activities that constitute the entity's ongoing major or central operations.[1]

For instance, revenue events occur when Boeing sells airplanes, when Wal-Mart sells merchandise to customers, and when Federal Express delivers packages.

To gain a more complete understanding of revenues, consider the three major components of the preceding definition.

1.   *Revenues will always increase the net worth of a business.* According to the FASB, revenues represent an enhancement of assets or settlement of liabilities. In other words, they increase assets or reduce liabilities. What does this really mean? Take the basic accounting equation, Assets = Liabilities + Owners' equity, and restate it as:

$$\text{Assets} - \text{Liabilities} = \text{Owners' equity}$$

This restatement helps demonstrate that an increase in assets, a decrease in liabilities, or a combination of both will always increase owners' equity, the residual value or net worth available to the owners of a company.

For example, if a barber accepts $10 to cut a client's hair, each completed haircut represents revenue, which causes cash and owners' equity to increase by $10. Alternatively, if the barber sells $10 gift certificates which are good for one haircut, the sale of a certificate represents unearned revenue. This event creates a $10 liability that is eliminated when the customer redeems the certificate to pay for a haircut. Thus, when one gift certificate is sold, the subsequent process of earning revenue reduces liabilities by $10, which, in turn, increases the value of the left side of the basic accounting equation, and therefore, owners' equity.

PAUSE & REFLECT

Chapter 7 introduced the recording process for revenue transactions. Can you recall one example of a revenue that increased owners' equity by means of (1) an increase in assets, and (2) a decrease in liabilities?

[1]Financial Accounting Standards Board, *Statement of Financial Accounting Concepts, No. 6* (December 1985), par. 78.

When a customer pays for a haircut revenue is earned. If a customer purchases a gift certificate for a haircut, revenue is earned after the customer cashes in the gift certificate.

2.   *Revenues result from an earnings process.* Businesses must *earn* revenues by selling goods or performing services. Although a business's net worth can also increase due to owner investments, this type of increase does not represent revenue because companies do not have to engage in any action to earn the money invested by owners.

3.   *Revenues result from activities that are "ongoing major or central operations."* Whether an activity is major or central depends on the type of enterprise. An automobile manufacturer generates revenue by selling cars, not real estate. A hobby shop produces revenue by selling products, not cars.

To illustrate this point, assume that the Fly-Away Hobby Shop sells remote-control model airplanes. Fly-Away records its sales of model airplanes as revenue, because this is its ongoing major operating activity. However, assume also that Fly-Away sells its old delivery truck for $18,000. If the carrying value of the truck on the date of disposal is $5,700, the net worth of the business will increase by $12,300 ($18,000 – $5,700) as a result of this sale. However, this increase is not the result of a revenue transaction because the sale of the truck is not an ongoing activity for Fly-Away and it is not central to daily operations. Instead, we refer to the profit generated by the disposal of the truck as a *gain*.

WHAT ARE GAINS?

In *Statement of Financial Accounting Concepts No. 6*, the FASB defines **gains** as the increase in net worth resulting from "peripheral or incidental transactions." In other words, businesses have a gain if owners' equity increases as the result of any earnings process not considered as revenue.

An event classified as a gain by one company might be considered revenue for another. For instance, although Fly-Away would report the truck sale on its income statement as a gain, General Motors Company would report the sale of trucks as revenue because selling trucks is one of the primary means by which GM generates income.

RECOGNITION OF REVENUES AND GAINS

Now that we know what revenues and gains are, we move ahead to the topic of revenue and gain recognition. The point of recognition is when revenues and gains increase owners' equity. This point determines the period in which companies report revenues and gains in their financial statements.

When Are Revenues Recognized?

According to the FASB, revenues are recognized *when they have been earned and realized.*[2] But what does this really mean?

SFAC No. 5 declares that revenues are *earned* when an "entity has substantially accomplished what it must do to be entitled to the benefits represented by the

---

[2]Financial Accounting Standards Board, *Statement of Financial Accounting Concepts No. 5* (December 1984), par. 83.

revenues." This generally means that revenues are earned when a company sells a product or renders services to a customer.

Revenues are *realized* when an exchange has taken place that yields cash, a claim to cash, or a claim to some other right that results in increased net worth. Therefore, before a company can recognize a revenue, it must receive something of measurable value and have a reasonable expectation that any noncash assets received, such as accounts receivable, can be converted into a known amount of cash.

To help understand why revenues must be earned and realized before they are considered recognized, consider the following example. If a medical doctor completes an examination of a patient and immediately collects a $100 fee, revenue is recognized because it is both earned and realized. However, if the same doctor donates his time to a free clinic where he performs the same examination at no charge, does he recognize any revenue? The answer is no. Although he performed the same service in both cases, he did not "realize" anything in return in the second case.

The same principle applies to all business situations. When a company sells goods or provides services and immediately collects cash or has a reasonable expectation of collecting a known amount of cash as a result of the event, revenue recognition occurs. If, at the time revenue is earned, serious doubts exist about a customer's ability or willingness to pay, a company will not realize and recognize revenue until it actually receives payment from the customer.

Finally, companies base the *amount* of revenue recognized on the dollar amount of cash received or the cash equivalent value of the increase in net worth resulting from the transaction. *Cash equivalent value* refers to the cash price for which a noncash asset could be sold. For example, if a company accepts a piece of equipment valued at $15,000 in exchange for services rendered, it will record revenue of $15,000 because (1) it has performed all services necessary to earn the revenue, and (2) it has received a noncash asset with a cash equivalent value of $15,000.

When Are Gains Recognized?

Gains, like revenues, are recognized when they are *earned* and *realized*. However, gains are generally not thought of as "earned" in the same sense as revenues. For example, if Boeing purchased a piece of land in 1992 for $10,000, and sold it five years later for $17,000, it would recognize a $7,000 gain in 1997, the year of the sale. Although this gain was "earned" in the sense that Boeing made an intelligent investment that paid off, the company did not have to perform any activity other than waiting for the land to increase in value. When accounting for gains, recognition is based primarily on when they are realized.

HOW ARE REVENUES RECORDED?

We give primary emphasis to the accounting for revenues instead of gains, because revenues, which result from ongoing major activities, are more important than gains when considering the continued success of a company.

In Boeing's 1994 annual report, Note 1 describes its process for recording revenues as follows:

Sales and Other Operating Revenues

Sales under commercial programs and U.S. Government and foreign military fixed-price contracts are generally recorded as deliveries are made. For certain fixed-price contracts that require substantial performance over an extended period before deliveries begin, sales are recorded based upon attainment of scheduled performance milestones. Sales under cost-reimbursement contracts are recorded as costs are incurred. Certain U.S. Government contracts contain profit incentives based upon performance relative to predetermined targets. Incentives based on cost performance are recorded currently, and other incentives and fee awards are recorded when the amounts can be reasonably estimated or are awarded. Income associated with customer financing activities is included in sales and other operating revenues.

The previous discussion of revenue recognition principles helps us understand that Boeing's management is simply declaring that revenues are recorded when they are *earned* and *realized*, and they are attempting to explain how that process takes place. But what entries does the company actually make in its accounting records to reflect various revenue events?

Users of financial reports should become familiar with the variety of accounts commonly used to record revenue transactions because the account titles frequently appear in both internal and external reports prepared by management. Although an exhaustive discussion of all possible methods employed by Boeing and other companies to record revenues is not important for our purposes, financial statement users should have a basic understanding of the recording process and the accounts used to record revenue transactions.

We know that revenue can be recorded (recognized):

1. At the time cash is collected.

2. Before cash is collected.

3. After cash is collected.

Let's discuss and illustrate each of these possibilities separately.

Revenue Recognized at the Same Time Cash Is Collected

When a company performs a service or sells a product and immediately collects cash in return, revenue will be recorded at the same time cash is collected, because the revenue is both earned and realized. For example, if the Fly-Away Hobby Shop sells a model airplane to a customer and immediately collects a cash payment of $500, it should make the following entry to record the revenue from the transaction at the time of the sale:

```
Cash      500
    Sales Revenue                                              500
```

Since the revenue recognition and collection of cash are concurrent, the transaction is complete and the accounting records reflect that fact.

Revenue Recognized before Cash Is Collected

Companies frequently perform a service or sell a product and send the customer a bill that must be paid within some specified time period.

Sales on Account Assume that Fly-Away allows its frequent customers to purchase merchandise on account. If Fly-Away sells one of its top-of-the-line airplanes on account for $1,600 on February 15, 1997, the revenue is considered earned and realized on February 15. At that time, Fly-Away's performance is complete and it has received an asset of measurable value—the legal right to a future collection of a fixed amount of money—in return. The entry to record this event on February 15 is:

```
Accounts Receivable                              1,600
    Sales Revenue                                              1,600
```

When the payment is subsequently received from the customer, it is recorded as:

```
Cash      1,600
    Accounts Receivable                                        1,600
```

Sales Involving Promissory Notes Sometimes, when companies sell a product or perform a service for which they are not immediately paid, they require the customer to sign a **promissory note.** This is an unconditional written promise to pay a fixed sum of money, called the *principal amount of the note*, plus interest on the principal, on or before a specified future date.

For the company making a sale, a signed promissory note has at least three advantages over an accounts receivable balance. First, because it is signed, the customer has already agreed in writing that he or she owes a fixed amount of money. If a subsequent dispute arises regarding payment of the balance, the company to whom the money is owed can present this note as proof of the obligation. Second, promissory notes usually require an interest payment in addition to the principal amount, whereas accounts receivable balances generally do not. Thus, a promissory note allows the company to earn interest on its money due, and the amount of this interest is sometimes significant. Third, promissory notes can more easily be sold to another party prior to their maturity if the holder of the note needs cash immediately.

Because of the popularity of promissory notes, users of accounting information should understand how they work. The date a promissory note is signed is referred to as the **issue date,** and the date by which payment must be made is the **maturity date.** A note is considered short term and will appear on the balance sheet in the current asset section if its duration is less than one year.

Sometimes the life of a note is stated in terms of months, in which case the maturity date is found by starting with the issue date and counting forward to the same day of the appropriate future month. For example, a three-month note dated March 7, will mature on June 7. Often, the maturity of a note is specified in terms of days, such as a 60-day note, or a 90-day note. To determine the maturity date in these cases, it is necessary to count forward, starting with the day immediately following the issue date, *up to and including* the maturity date. For example, a 90-day note issued on May 15, 1997, would mature on August 13, 1997, as shown below:

May 16*–May 31	16 days
June 1–June 30	30 days
July 1–July 31	31 days
August 1–August 13†	13 days
Total	90 days

*Skip the issue date, and begin counting on May 16.

†Include the maturity date in the number of days counted.

To illustrate the recording of revenue when a customer signs and subsequently pays a promissory note, assume that Fly-Away accepts a $3,000, 12 percent, 60-day note signed by a customer on March 3, 1997, in exchange for the sale of merchandise. Fly-Away would make this entry on March 3:

Notes Receivable	3,000.00	
Sales Revenue		3,000.00

The entry to record the customer payment on May 2, the maturity date, is:

Cash	3,059.18	
Notes Receivable		3,000.00
Interest Income		59.18
($3,000 × .12 × 60/365)3		

Observe that although Fly-Away recorded the sales revenue on March 3, it did not recognize the interest income until May 2. The interest is *not* part of the sales price. Rather, it represents a payment for the use of money over a period of time. In effect, by allowing the customer to defer payment for 60 days, Fly-Away made a loan to the customer and it earned interest income over the life of the note.

Revenue Recognized after Cash Is Collected

Companies often collect cash before revenue is earned. For example, customers usually pay for magazine subscriptions at the beginning of the subscription period, insured parties frequently pay for insurance premiums before the start of the policy period, and, in some situations, lawyers and doctors to collect money from clients before performing services.

In these situations, realization, represented by the receipt of cash from the customer, precedes the earnings process, so revenue recognition must wait. Instead, the customer payment creates a legal obligation (or liability) for the business to perform a service or deliver a product in the future.

---

[3]Interest on short-term notes is calculated as: Principal × Annual interest rate × (Number of days to maturity/365). In those cases where the life of the note is defined in terms of months, the Number of months/12 is substituted for the Number of days/365 in the formula.

Assume that Fly-Away collects a $2,400 deposit from a customer on March 1, 1997, for a specially ordered airplane. This deposit, which represents unearned revenue, is recorded as follows:

Cash	2,400	
Customer Deposits		2,400

The Customer Deposits account is a liability. If a balance sheet were prepared by the company on March 1, 1997, this account would be shown in the current liability section. When the specially ordered merchandise arrives and is delivered to the customer, the earnings process will be complete, and the liability will become a revenue, recorded as:

Customer Deposits	2,400	
Sales Revenue		2,400

The liability created by the collection of advance payments from customers may appear in a company's balance sheet under various other names. Some common examples are Advances from Customers, Revenue Received in Advance, Unearned Revenue, or Deferred Revenue. The Boeing Company's balance sheet for the year ended December 31, 1994, shows a liability titled Advances in Excess of Related Costs. As these amounts are earned, that is, as Boeing performs the work for the customer, the company decreases the liability account, recognizes revenue, and reports the revenue on its income statement.

ADDITIONAL REVENUE-RELATED EVENTS

The revenue cycle does not necessarily end once companies recognize and record revenue. For example, if sales are made on account, the company must collect the cash owed by customers. Also, problems of customer dissatisfaction may require attention.

There are three important events related to revenue recognition that affect the amount of income reported for a given time period: sales returns and allowances, sales discounts, and uncollectible accounts. It is important to know what they are and how to account for them in order to understand the impact they have on reported income.

Sales Returns and Allowances

When a product is sold, there is a chance the customer will not be satisfied because, for example, the merchandise may be damaged or, in the case of clothing, the item purchased may be the wrong size. When this occurs, most vendors will either allow the customer to return the merchandise or will negotiate for the customer to keep the merchandise and pay a reduced price. These transactions are referred to as *sales returns* and *sales allowances*, respectively. (We described these transactions from the purchasing company's viewpoint as purchase returns and allowances in Chapter 8.)

To record these events, vendors could simply reverse the entry made at the date of the original sale. This approach might appear logical since returns of merchandise and price allowances are, in a sense, reversals of the original recorded sale. However, companies generally do not follow this practice because reversing the original credit to sales revenue would provide no record of the dollar amount of returns and allowances.

To run a company effectively, managers want to know the portion of merchandise sales that is returned or defective. Changes in this ratio from one year to the next may indicate positive or negative developments that could require attention. Also, there is a cost involved in handling returned merchandise to factor into the prices charged for all merchandise sold. Therefore, rather than debiting the sales revenue account to record returns or price allowances granted, the company reflects these events in its records by debiting a separate account related to sales, titled **Sales Returns and Allowances**. This contra-revenue account represents return by customers and unplanned price allowances granted to customers.

A return reduces revenue.

For instance, assume that on April 15, 1997, Fly-Away sells three airplanes on account to a customer for a total of $1,200. On April 18, because the customer comes in and complains about a troublesome engine in one of the planes, the store manager agrees to a price allowance (reduction in the amount due) of $50. Fly-Away records these events as follows:

Apr.	15	Accounts Receivable	1,200	
		Sales Revenue		1,200
		To record original sale of the airplanes on credit.		
Apr.	18	Sales Returns and Allowances	50	
		Accounts Receivable		50
		To record price allowance.		

The entry to record the subsequent customer payment is:

Cash		1,150	
Accounts Receivable			1,150

The preparer of Fly-Away's income statement would deduct the balance in the Sales Returns and Allowances account ($50) from gross sales ($1,200) to derive the amount of net sales, which equals $1,150. Sometimes the income statement shows this subtraction process, but, generally, companies report one dollar amount representing net sales.

Accountants refer to the Sales Returns and Allowances account as a **contra-revenue account** because it is subtracted from the related Sales Revenue account to determine net sales shown on the income statement. This account is similar in nature to the contra-asset account, Accumulated Depreciation, described in Chapter 7, which is subtracted from the cost of plant and equipment to obtain the net carrying value of plant and equipment presented on the balance sheet.

Sales Discounts

As discussed in Chapter 8, companies often offer customers a cash discount in return for prompt payment of account balances. This sales discount, which is stated as a percentage of the gross sales amount, is available to a customer only when payment is made within a specified discount period. The invoice sent to the customer specifies the discount terms, which might appear as 2/10, n/30. Whereas buyers record such discounts as purchase discounts, sellers record them in the **Sales Discounts** account.

To illustrate the accounting for sales discounts, assume that Fly-Away makes a credit sale of $3,000 to a customer on June 1, 1997. Terms of sale are 3/15, n/45. The journal entry to record the sale is:

Accounts Receivable	3,000	
Sales Revenue		3,000

If the customer makes full payment on June 16 (the last day of the discount period), Fly-Away would subtract a $90 discount ($3,000 × 3%) from the $3,000 sales price to determine the required payment of $2,910. The resulting entry by Fly-Away to record the payment would be:

Cash	2,910	
Sales Discounts	90	
Accounts Receivable		3,000

Sales Discounts is another example of a contra-revenue account that, along with any sales returns and allowances, is subtracted from the gross sales figure to obtain net sales revenue for presentation on the income statement. By using a separate Sales Discounts account, managers can keep track of the cost to the company of receiving prompt payments. This helps determine whether the benefits of offering cash discounts outweigh the costs.

PAUSE & REFLECT | Customers sometimes intentionally make payments after a discount period has lapsed, but still take the discount. If you sold merchandise to a customer who did this repeatedly, what factors would you consider before deciding upon a course of action?

Uncollectible Accounts

When a company makes credit sales, it is an unfortunate fact that some accounts will prove to be uncollectible. Therefore, managers need an accounting system that provides detailed and relevant information regarding the benefits of granting credit (increased sales) versus the cost of granting credit (the amount of losses from uncollectible accounts). An overly restrictive credit policy might result in too many lost sales, while overly generous policies might result in a large proportion of sales that will never be collected.

Granting credit to customers

External users of financial statements do not need the detailed information required by managers to establish credit policies. Instead, they want to know the economic result of credit policies on operations. Thus, when preparing financial statements for external stakeholders, companies should consider these two primary objectives: (1) proper income measurement, and (2) proper asset valuation.

Proper Income Measurement   We know that the matching principle requires the matching of revenues recognized during a given period with all related expenses incurred to earn those revenues. Therefore, it would be inappropriate to record revenue from credit sales in one year and the expense resulting from related uncollectible accounts in the next. The matching requirement creates a problem, because some year-end accounts receivable balances resulting from current year sales will not be identified as uncollectible until the following year.

To solve this problem, at each year-end companies must estimate the portion of the current year's credit sales they anticipate will eventually prove uncollectible and deduct this estimated expense on the current year income statement. This uncollectible accounts expense deduction on the income statement is one example of many reported expenses that are based on estimates. (Remember that depreciation expense is also based on the estimated number of years an asset will be used.) Also, several other year-end adjusting entries discussed in Chapters 7 and 8 were based on estimates regarding anticipated future cash collections or payments related to current period revenues earned and expenses incurred. All these estimates are necessary to properly measure income during any time period.

PAUSE & REFLECT	Uncollectible accounts expense is recognized as an expense on the income statement; however, some accountants maintain that it is really a contra-revenue. What do you think?

Proper Asset Valuation   The estimated uncollectible accounts expense deducted on the income statement has a corresponding impact on the balance sheet. Like any expense, it reduces owners' equity, which, in turn, means that some other balance sheet account must also change in order to maintain the equation Assets = Liabilities + Owners' equity. The affected item on the balance sheet is Accounts Receivable, the asset category that must be reduced to its **net realizable value,** the net dollar amount the company expects to eventually collect after making allowances for estimated uncollectible accounts.

Here are the entries made by companies to record estimated uncollectible accounts expense and reduce reported accounts receivable to their net realizable value.

Entries to Record Uncollectible Accounts   Assume that at December 31, 1997, the end of its fiscal year, Fly-Away has a $30,000 balance in its Accounts Receivable account, of which it estimates that $1,500 will prove uncollectible. The entry to record estimated uncollectible accounts is:

Uncollectible Accounts Expense	1,500	
Allowance for Doubtful Accounts		1,500

The debit to Uncollectible Accounts Expense reduces net income by $1,500. Allowance for Doubtful Accounts is a contra-asset that, when subtracted from the year-end Accounts Receivable balance of $30,000, yields the $28,500 estimated net realizable value of accounts receivable to be reported on the balance sheet. This might be shown in the current asset section of the balance sheet as follows:

Accounts Receivable	$30,000
Less: Allowance for doubtful accounts	1,500
Net accounts receivable	$28,500

Or, more frequently, the balance sheet simply presents the $28,500, identifying it as the net accounts receivable. In notes accompanying their financial statements,

J. C. PENNEY COMPANY, INC.
1994 Annual Report

Receivables (in millions)	1994	1993	1992
Customer receivables serviced	$4,751	$4,410	$4,068
Customer receivables sold	725	725	1,150
Customer receivables owned	4,026	3,685	2,918
Less allowances for doubtful accounts	74	59	69
Customer receivables, net	3,952	3,626	2,849
JCPenney National Bank receivables	729	587	538
Other receivables	478	466	363
Receivables, net	$5,159	$4,679	$3,750

The Company's policy is to write off accounts when the scheduled minimum payment has not been received for six consecutive months, if any portion of the balance is more than 12 months past due, or if it is otherwise determined that the customer is unable to pay. Collection efforts continue subsequent to write-off, and recoveries are applied as a reduction of bad debt losses.

companies often provide schedules showing a breakdown of the net receivables reported on their balance sheets. For example, the 1994 annual report of J. C. Penney Company, Inc., reported the following accounts receivable-related information on its balance sheet:

	Year-End		
	1994	1993	1992
Receivables, net (in millions)	5,159	4,679	3,750

Exhibit 9.1 shows a portion of a note entitled "Summary of Accounting Policies" that was included in J. C. Penney's annual report. Note that the company expected $74 million of their 1994 year-end receivables to be uncollectible.

In subsequent accounting periods, a designated individual or company department monitors customer accounts to identify specific balances that are not going to be paid. For instance, a customer's account balance may be designated as uncollectible if the customer declares bankruptcy or if that particular customer's account remains unpaid after repeated attempts at collection. A company must make appropriate entries to remove these uncollectible balances from the company's accounting records. The note in Exhibit 9.1 identifies the manner in which J. C. Penney determines which accounts to write off. However, J. C. Penney's note does not describe how accounts are written off, or the resulting impact on the financial statements. Financial statement users should understand this process. Let's return to our Fly-Away Hobby Shop example to illustrate how the write-off of Accounts Receivable balances affects a company's financial statements.

Assume that in January of 1998 (the next accounting year), Fly-Away determines that Fred Baron, one of its customers, is unable to pay his $500 Accounts Receivable balance. The entry to remove his account from Fly-Away's accounting records is:

Allowance for Doubtful Accounts	500	
Accounts Receivable		500

Examine the impact of this entry on the net accounts receivable balance.

	Before Write-Off	After Write-Off
Total accounts receivable	$30,000	$29,500
Less: Allowances for doubtful accounts	1,500	1,000
Net accounts receivable	$28,500	$28,500

PAUSE & REFLECT

Using the data in Exhibit 9.1, determine the percentage of "customer receivables owned" that J. C. Penney estimated to be uncollectible at the end of each fiscal year shown. Is this percentage increasing or decreasing? Do you consider this trend a favorable or unfavorable development? Why?

Appropriately, the net accounts receivable balance has not changed. Remember that Fly-Away already reduced the net realizable value of Accounts Receivable at the end of 1997 when the company recorded its uncollectible accounts expense for the year. Thus, to reduce the amount of Accounts Receivable a second time would record the effect of the same expense twice, and in two different periods. Instead, when Fly-Away identifies a specific account as uncollectible, it removes that Account Receivable balance from its records and reduces the Allowance for Doubtful Accounts by the same amount, yielding no change in net accounts receivable.

On rare occasions, companies eventually collect amounts due previously on accounts that have been written off. When this occurs, the company would reverse the entry originally made to record the write-off of the account. Then the company would record the collection of the account in the same manner as the collection of any Accounts Receivable balance due.

Estimating Uncollectible Accounts Expense Two basic methods exist to estimate the amount of uncollectible accounts expense to record at the end of each accounting period. First, companies can base the estimate on the historical relationship between total credit sales and uncollectible accounts. This method emphasizes the relationship between sales revenue and related uncollectible accounts expense, both of which appear on the income statement. Therefore, it is referred to as the **income statement approach** to estimating uncollectible accounts expense. Second, companies can analyze the accounts receivable balances remaining at year-end to estimate what portion will be uncollectible. Because this method places an emphasis on proper presentation of net accounts receivable, which appears on the balance sheet, it is referred to as the **balance sheet approach** to estimating uncollectible accounts expense. We discuss the balance sheet approach below since it is more widely used.

Balance Sheet Approach This method of estimating the uncollectible portion of accounts receivable balances begins with the preparation of an **aging schedule.** This list of a company's accounts receivable balances groups all receivables according to the period of time they have been outstanding. This grouping facilitates analysis, because older receivable balances are generally less likely to be collected.

Based on past experience, as well as an analysis of current business conditions, the company would estimate the percentage of uncollectible accounts in each category. Then it is necessary to multiply these percentages by the dollar amount of receivables in each respective category. The result for each category is summed to obtain the total amount of estimated uncollectible accounts. This figure becomes the basis for the adjusting entry to record uncollectible accounts expense.

To illustrate, assume that a company prepared the following summary of its aged accounts receivable listing at year-end:

	Receivable Amount	Estimated Percentage Uncollectible	Estimated Uncollectible Amount
Not yet due	$25,000	1.5%	$ 375
1–30 days overdue	13,000	5.0	650
31–60 days overdue	11,000	12.5	1,375
61–90 days overdue	5,000	15.0	750
Over 90 days overdue	2,000	25.0	500
	$56,000		$3,650

Based on this analysis, Allowance for Doubtful Accounts should be adjusted to show a year-end balance of $3,650. Assuming that the allowance account has a zero balance immediately before adjustment, the entry is:

Uncollectible Accounts Expense	3,650	
Allowance for Doubtful Accounts		3,650

In the example of the Balance Sheet approach to estimate uncollectible accounts, the goal was to adjust Allowance for Doubtful Accounts to show a credit balance of $3,650. What would the entry have been if Allowance for Doubtful Accounts carried (1) a credit balance of $500, or (2) a debit balance of $850 immediately prior to adjustment? Is it likely that the balance in Allowance for Doubtful Accounts will be zero before each year-end adjustment? Explain.

RECORDING GAINS

Remember that gains result from incidental activities and that they occur less frequently than revenues. Although an income statement without revenues would be highly unusual, it is not unusual for many published financial statements to report no gains at all. This does not mean, however, that gains are unimportant. Gains often represent a significant portion of total reported income.

The most common event resulting in the recognition of a gain is the disposal of an income-producing asset, such as a delivery truck or other depreciable asset, at an amount in excess of its carrying value. We will illustrate how to record this type of event.

Earlier in this chapter, we assumed that Fly-Away sold a truck for $18,000. Assume further that the truck's stated carrying value of $5,700 at the date of disposal resulted from an original cost of $25,000, and $19,300 of accumulated depreciation. Fly-Away would record the $12,300 gain ($18,000 − $5,700), calculated as the difference between the selling price and the carrying value of the truck, with the following entry:

Cash	18,000	
Accumulated Depreciation—Truck	19,300	
Truck		25,000
Gain on Sale of Truck		12,300

It is important for financial statement users to be familiar with this recording process because it helps them understand that the gain on the sale of an asset does *not* represent the amount of cash generated by the sale. Rather, the amount of gain reported is merely the *difference* between the cash or cash equivalent value received and the carrying value of the asset.

Gains appear on the income statement as a separate line item. They are often referred to as *Other Income* or *Nonoperating Income*, because they are not central to the daily operations of the company and because gains are not "earned" as a result of any operating activity.

The $18,000 cash received from Fly-Away's sale will appear on the statement of cash flows under the heading "Cash Flows from Investing Activities." Because gains are incidental and nonrecurring in nature, it would not be appropriate to report the $18,000 under "Cash Flows from Operating Activities."

EXTERNAL REPORTING CONSIDERATIONS

Once a company records information about revenues and gains, it must summarize and report this information to both its internal and external stakeholders so that they can evaluate the company's performance and make operating, investing, and financing decisions. We will describe external reports first, followed by a discussion of internal reporting considerations.

Management prepares reports for external stakeholders, documenting the impact of revenues and gains on the company's income, financial position, and cash flows. Let's look at each of the three relevant financial statements in turn.

Income Statement

Companies generally report income using one of two acceptable income statement formats: multistep and single step. A recent survey of 600 companies indicated that in 1994, 65 percent of them used the multistep approach, while 35 percent employed the single step approach.[4] We briefly examined the multistep approach in Chapter 8. We now examine and contrast both income statement formats.

---

[4]*Accounting Trends and Techniques* (New York: AICPA, 1995), p. 287.

FLY-AWAY HOBBY SHOP
Multistep Income Statement
For the Year Ended December 31, 1997

Net sales		$350,000
Cost of good sold		193,500
Gross margin		$156,500
Operating expenses:		
Selling expenses	$46,300	
General and administrative expenses	39,100	85,400
Operating income		$ 71,100
Other income (expense):		
Gain on sale of plant assets	$12,300	
Interest income	8,500	
Interest expense	(7,600)	13,200
Income before taxes		$ 84,300
Income tax expense		17,600
Net income		$ 66,700

FLY-AWAY HOBBY SHOP
Single-Step Income Statement
For the Year Ended December 31, 1997

Revenues:		
Net sales	$350,000	
Gain on sale of plant assets	12,300	
Interest income	8,500	$370,800
Expenses:		
Cost of good sold	$193,500	
Selling expenses	46,300	
General and administrative expenses	39,100	
Interest expense	7,600	
Income tax expense	17,600	304,100
Net income		$ 66,700

Look at Exhibit 9.2, which illustrates both formats for Fly-Away Hobby Shop, using assumed data for the year ended December 31, 1997. Fly-Away's 1997 income includes sales revenue, as well as other revenues and gains.

Multistep Income Statements   Multistep income statements are so named because they report the calculation of net income in several steps. This format presents net sales first. Fly-Away could report its sales using the following format:

Sales		$377,000
Less: Sales discounts	$13,000	
Sales returns and allowances	14,000	(27,000)
Net sales		$350,000

However, as Fly-Away does, most companies report only one figure, net sales, which might be referred to as *sales, net sales,* or *sales net of returns and allowances.* The Boeing Company uses the term *sales* in its 1994 annual report.

The next item in the multistep format is cost of goods sold, which is deducted from net sales to obtain gross margin, also called *gross profit.* Sales and cost of goods sold are shown first because they generally represent the largest and most important revenue and expense categories, respectively, on the income statement.

This presentation allows investors and creditors to evaluate one aspect of profitability trends for continuing operations by comparing changes in the gross margin from year to year. Also, by calculating gross margin as a percentage of net sales, investors and other financial statement users can identify the amount of gross profit generated by each dollar of net sales. Fly-Away's gross margin equals 45 percent ($156,500/$350,000), which means the company makes $0.45 of gross margin for each $1 of net sales.

Then, operating expenses, often categorized as "selling" and "general and administrative" are subtracted from gross margin to obtain operating income. Selling expenses include expenses such as advertising, salaries and commissions paid to sales personnel, and rent and depreciation expense relative to stores operated by the company. General and administrative expenses include general expenses incurred to run the business, such as officers' salaries, office rent and supplies, and depreciation expense relative to office facilities and equipment.

Gains, as well as losses, are shown in a separate section of the multistep income statement and are often categorized as other items or other nonoperating items. This separate presentation helps emphasize the incidental, nonrecurring nature of gains and losses, which helps investors and creditors, who desire to focus primarily on recurring revenues and expenses when they attempt to predict future performance of the company. For example, a gain on the sale of a building may represent a substantial portion of the current year's income but, once sold, the building is gone. On the other hand, an increase or decrease in sales revenue over several years does help indicate the direction in which company operations are headed.

In Exhibit 9.2, the category labeled Other income (expense) also includes interest income and interest expense. This emphasizes the passive nature of these two items. Although they are recurring, they are not part of Fly-Away's operating activity and, therefore, they appear separately on the income statement. The same is true for Boeing, whose 1994 income statement reported a category titled "Other income, principally interest."

Single-Step Income Statements   Exhibit 9.2 also shows a **single-step income statement,** whose primary benefit is simplicity of presentation. Its name derives from the fact that it reports the calculation of net income in one step—total revenues and gains, minus total expenses and losses.

The multistep and single-step income statements both report the same basic information. The single-step format gives less emphasis to the different natures of various reported items.

One final note: Neither of the income statements illustrated in Exhibit 9.2 shows uncollectible accounts expense. Because this expense is usually small relative to total sales, it does not merit presentation on most income statements. In addition, a company may not want its competitors to have this information. Therefore, uncollectible accounts expense is generally included as part of selling expenses.[5]

Balance Sheet

An awareness of the specific assets and liabilities affected by revenues and gains helps financial statement users understand the important relationship between the income statement and the balance sheet.

Exhibit 9.3 shows comparative balance sheets for Fly-Away Hobby Shop at December 31, 1997, and 1996. As is typically the case, the balance sheet asset accounts that were increased by Fly-Away's recorded revenues and gains are Cash, Notes Receivable, and Accounts Receivable.

Notice that Accounts Receivable is included in the current assets section, net of the balance of Allowance for Uncollectible Accounts. Understanding the relationship between accounts receivable and revenues, investors and creditors often compare changes in the net accounts receivable balance with corresponding changes in net sales to help discover favorable/unfavorable trends. For instance, a 30 percent increase in net accounts receivable from 1996 to 1997, accompanied by a 5 percent decrease in net sales over the same period, would raise questions about whether the company was having difficulty collecting account balances from customers. By the same token, an increase from one year to the next in Allowance for Doubtful Accounts as a percentage of total receivables would also raise concerns about the collectibility of amounts owed to the company at year-end.

Assets are not the only balance sheet accounts affected by revenue transactions. Recall that a liability results when money is collected from customers before it has been earned. Exhibit 9.3 also includes customer deposits in the current liabilities section.

| PAUSE & REFLECT | In its 1994 financial statements, Boeing Company includes a liability called "Advances in excess of related costs." What do you think this represents? |

With an understanding of the impact that revenues and gains have on the income statement and balance sheet, we turn our attention to a discussion of the statement of cash flows.

---

[5]Because uncollectible accounts expense is usually a small amount relative to total sales, investors and creditors are normally not concerned about how it is classified. Although it is generally included as a selling expense, it also could be included as a general and administrative expense on the income statement.

EXHIBIT | 9.3 | Balance Sheet

FLY-AWAY HOBBY SHOP
Comparative Balance Sheets
December 31, 1997 and 1996

	1997	1996
Assets		
Current Assets		
Cash	$ 50,000	$ 65,000
Notes receivable	4,200	4,200
Accounts receivable (net of allowances of $1,500 and $1,200)	28,500	31,000
Inventory	129,200	141,700
Prepaids	20,800	24,300
Total current assets	$232,700	$266,200
Plant and equipment		
Land	$200,000	$200,000
Buildings	375,000	375,000
Equipment	238,300	263,300
Total	$813,300	$838,300
Less accumulated depreciation	113,700	118,000
Plant end equipment, net	$699,600	$720,300
Total assets	$932,300	$986,500
Liabilities		
Current liabilities		
Accounts payable	$ 87,400	$ 94,800
Customer deposits	23,700	33,700
Income taxes payable	14,800	18,300
Total current liabilities	$125,900	$146,800
Long-term liabilities		
Notes payable	$280,000	$380,000
Total liabilities	$405,900	$526,800
Stockholders' Equity		
Common Stock	$250,000	$250,000
Retained earnings	276,400	209,700
Total stockholders' equity	$526,400	$459,700
Total liabilities and stockholders' equity	$932,300	$986,500

Statement of Cash Flows

Exhibit 9.4 is Fly-Away's statement of cash flows for the year ended December 31, 1997. The cash flows from operating activities section shows cash received from customers, which is not equal to the sales figure reported on the income statement. Remember, cash can be collected before, at the same time, or after the related revenue is earned.

The determination of the amount of cash receipts from customers requires understanding the relationship between the income statement and the balance sheet. Many companies have only two kinds of sales—cash and credit. For them, revenue recognition increases one of two balance sheet accounts—Cash or Accounts Receivable. Therefore, companies calculate cash receipts from customers by taking the net sales for the year and adjusting this amount by the increase or decrease in the Accounts Receivable balance from the beginning to the end of the year.[6]

To demonstrate, assume a company's income statement shows net sales of $100,000 for the year ended December 31, 1997. If the comparative balance sheets report no accounts receivable at the beginning or end of the year, the financial statement user can assume that cash receipts from sales for the year are $100,000. However, given the same sales figure, if there were no accounts receivable at December 31, 1996, the end of the prior year, and if $10,000 of accounts receivable exists at December 31, 1997, then the company must have had $10,000 of sales that

---

[6]The discussion of the calculation of cash receipts from customers ignores the impact on Accounts Receivable of any entries made relative to estimated and/or actual uncollectible accounts. Although these entries affect the calculation of cash from customers, they generally represent relatively small adjustments.

EXHIBIT | 9.4 | Statement of Cash Flows

FLY-AWAY HOBBY SHOP
Statement of Cash Flows
For the Year Ended December 31, 1997

Cash flows from operating activities:	
Cash received from customers	$342,500
Cash received for interest	8,500
Cash paid to suppliers	(255,300)
Cash paid for interest	(7,600)
Cash paid for income tax	(21,100)
Net cash flows from operating activities	$ 67,000
Cash flows from investing activities:	
Cash received from sale of equipment	18,000
Cash flows from financing activities:	
Cash paid on note payable	(100,000)
Net decrease in cash	$ (15,000)
Cash balance, beginning of year	65,000
Cash balance, end of year	$ 50,000

are uncollected at December 31, 1997. Given this information, cash receipts from sales for all of 1997 are $90,000 ($100,000 – $10,000).

We can generalize from this example and state that any time the Accounts Receivable balance increases from the beginning to the end of the year, the amount of the increase equals the amount by which net sales for the year exceeds cash receipts for the same year.

The opposite result occurs when the Accounts Receivable balance declines. If a company reports current year sales of $100,000, a beginning Accounts Receivable balance of $10,000, and an ending Accounts Receivable balance of zero, the company must have collected all its current year sales, plus the $10,000 already owed to it when the year began. In this case, total collections for the year are $110,000. Whenever the Accounts Receivable balance declines for the year, the amount of cash collected from customers equals net sales, increased by the amount of the decline in Accounts Receivable for the year.

The calculation of the amount of cash received from customers using the data in Exhibits 9.2 and 9.3, would be:

Accounts receivable (net) at beginning of year	$ 31,000
Accounts receivable (net) at end of year	(28,500)
Net reduction in accounts receivable	$ 2,500
Plus: Net sales for year	350,000
Cash receipts from customers	$352,500

This does not equal the $342,500 that Fly-Away received from customers (see Exhibit 9.4) during 1997 because we have not yet considered the customer deposits shown on the balance sheet in Exhibit 9.3. The calculation of the amount of cash received from customers is further complicated when unearned revenue (customer deposits) has been recorded, as in the case of the Fly-Away Hobby Shop. Exhibit 9.3 shows customer deposits totaling $33,700 at the end of 1996. Assuming that this money was earned during 1997, it is included in the sales figure for the year. However, since the money was collected prior to 1997, it must be subtracted from the 1997 sales to determine actual 1997 collections. But what about customer deposits at the end of 1997? This money has been collected, even though it is not included in current year revenues, so it must be added to the 1997 sales figure. These required adjustments follow:

Cash receipts (per above)	$352,500
Less: Customer deposits at beginning of year	(33,700)
Plus: Customer deposits at end of year	23,700
Cash received from customers (Exhibit 9.4)	$342,500

As these calculations demonstrate, it is important for users of financial statements to understand the integral relationship between income statement and balance sheet accounts.

EXHIBIT	9.5	Internal Report

FLY-AWAY HOBBY SHOP
Quarterly Sales Report by Product
For the Year Ended December 31, 1997

	Jan–Mar	Apr–Jun	Jul–Sep	Oct–Dec	Total
Model Airplane Kits	$24,721	$56,781	$ 68,071	$ 73,596	$223,169
Airplane Parts	8,818	25,110	33,427	27,945	95,300
Remote Control Devices	3,892	9,738	11,580	6,321	31,531
Total Sales	$37,431	$91,629	$113,078	$107,862	$350,000

INTERNAL REPORTING CONSIDERATIONS

As you know, data included in published financial reports are summarized to facilitate analysis by external users. Managers and other employees of a company, the internal users, need more detailed information to make day-to-day operating decisions.

In published financial statements, sales data are generally grouped and shown as one total. Internally, companies might prepare more detailed sales reports showing sales by product category, region, domestic versus foreign, and any other breakdown that is meaningful to decision makers. Internal users also need reports showing sales patterns to facilitate planning future production needs.

Exhibit 9.5 shows a quarterly sales report by product type for the Fly-Away Hobby Shop for the year ended December 31, 1997. It clearly shows that the first quarter was the slowest period of the year. This information helps the owners plan inventory purchases and employee work schedules for 1998.

Additionally, in order to properly control collections from credit sales, the accounting system must provide information regarding the amount of credit sales made to individual customers. In addition to posting the total amount of credit sales to the general ledger accounts Sales and Accounts Receivable, companies also post all individual credit sales to a **subsidiary accounts receivable ledger.** It lists each customer's accounts receivable balance along with all the credit sales made to and the payments received on, account. The aged accounts receivable listing is generally prepared directly from this subsidiary ledger customer account information.

Large companies usually maintain formal subsidiary ledger accounts that require debit and credit postings just like general ledger accounts. On the other hand, smaller companies often have less formal systems. For example, their subsidiary ledger may consist of copies of customer invoices, kept in a file pending receipt of payment. The goal of all companies is to provide whatever information they need to ensure the proper collection of specific account balances due, while keeping costs to a minimum.

Additionally, companies must prepare detailed reports of sales returns and allowances in a timely fashion. A high customer return rate may indicate that company products have unacceptably high defect rates or that there is some other problem requiring immediate corrective action.

Finally, a company cannot exist without revenue. The accounting information system must be structured to respond to the need for coordination among the departments responsible for marketing, sales, production, credit, and the host of other activities necessary to keep the sales effort functioning smoothly.

POTENTIAL ERRORS IN ACCOUNTING FOR REVENUES AND GAINS

When it comes to reporting revenues, companies are often accused of improperly bending the rules. For example, the outside auditors of Kurzweil Applied Intelligence, Inc., accused the company of "irregularities in the company's revenue recognition practices," claiming that Kurzweil had made mistakes in recording revenue for "a significant number of transactions."[7] In another case, auditors accused Sparta

---

[7]As reported in *Accounting Today* 9, no. 4 (February 20–March 12, 1995), p. 10.

Foods, a Minnesota-based company, of reporting revenues for a product before it was actually shipped.[8] These are not isolated cases. Therefore, to complete our understanding of revenues and gains, we must discuss potential reporting errors.

Depending on the circumstances, there may be incentives to either overstate or understate revenues and gains for a given period. Corporate managers may have an incentive to intentionally overstate revenues and/or gains, because the resulting increase in reported income and net worth reflects favorably on shareholder assessment of management performance in running the company. On the other hand, a sole proprietor who does not have to answer to shareholders may have an incentive to understate or omit revenues and gains from a tax return in order to reduce the amount of income taxes owed to the government.

Regardless of motivational factors, most significant errors in recording revenues are due to improper cutoff at the end of the accounting period. The results can be significant, as in the case of Kendall Square Research Corporation, a computer company based in Waltham, Massachusetts.

For the year ended December 26, 1992, Kendall Square originally reported $20.7 in revenues. In a news release by the corporation on March 25, 1994, management announced that 1992 revenues should have been $10.1 million, stating that certain shipments should not have been recognized as revenue during 1992, "because funding requirements or other contingencies were not met." In other words, as of the end of 1992 certain improperly reported revenues had not yet met the revenue recognition requirement. Some, though not all, of these revenues were subsequently reported on the 1993 income statement, which indicates that the error was partially due to timing.

Significant overstatement of revenues may or may not be an indication that a company is having problems. On September 22, 1994, a report indicated that Kendall Square planned to lay off three-fourths of its work force, and "might soon wind up in bankruptcy court." The report went on to state that, "Kendall Square has been foundering since news broke . . . that the company had improperly booked sales."[9]

---

[8]As reported in *Accounting Today* 8, no. 21 (November 21, 1994), p. 12.
[9]Article appearing in the *Boston Globe*, September 22, 1994.

Mistakes in reporting revenues and gains can be the result of honest errors in judgment, or they can be intentional. Regardless, because the consequences of errors can be extremely negative for all stakeholders concerned, companies have an obligation to do everything in their power to minimize their occurrence.

SUMMARY

In Chapter 8 we discussed the recording of events surrounding the purchase and use of goods and services. In this chapter, we expanded the discussion to include the benefits derived from the successful employment of these goods and services. We focused on issues surrounding the recording and reporting of revenues and gains. The revenue cycle of business operations includes revenue-related events that companies reflect in their accounting records. The revenue portion of the earnings process (expenditure is the other significant portion) is important, as summarized in the key concepts below.

- Revenues are the increase in net worth resulting from an earnings process involving activities that are ongoing major or central operations of a company.

- Gains are the increase in net worth resulting from an earnings process involving activities that are peripheral or incidental to operations.

- Revenues and gains are recognized when they have been *earned* and *realized.* They are earned when a business has substantially accomplished all it must do to be entitled to the resulting benefits. They are realized when an exchange has taken place that yields cash, a cash equivalent, or a claim to cash or to some other right that increases net worth.

- If revenue is recorded before cash is collected, either an accounts receivable or notes receivable will result, which must be collected at a later date.

- If cash is collected before revenue is recorded, a liability to perform a future service or provide a product is created. When this obligation is discharged, the revenue is recognized.

- The return of merchandise by customers, unplanned price reductions granted after the date of sale, and cash discounts given to customers are recorded as contra-revenues.

- In order to properly measure income for any given period of time, companies making credit sales require a periodic adjusting entry to record estimated uncollectible accounts expense. This entry also creates a contra-asset account called *Allowance for Doubtful Accounts.* This allowance is subtracted from the gross accounts receivable balance to obtain the net (estimated) collectible amount reported on the balance sheet.

- The gain recorded upon disposal of an asset is the difference between the amount realized and the carrying value of the asset at that date. The carrying value of an asset is the balance remaining when the cost of the asset is reduced by the accumulated depreciation recorded for that asset.

- Information regarding revenues and gains must be reported to external and internal stakeholders. External stakeholders rely on published financial statements prepared in accordance with generally accepted accounting principles for their information. Internal stakeholders use various reports created to suit the special information needs of a particular situation.

KEY TERMS

aging schedule A listing of a company's accounts receivable balances grouped according to the period of time they have been outstanding

balance sheet approach An analysis of outstanding accounts receivable balances to determine what portion will be uncollectible

contra-revenue account An account whose balance is deducted from a related revenue account

gains Increases in net worth of a business resulting from an earnings process involving peripheral or incidental transactions

income statement approach A method of estimating uncollectible accounts expense based on the historical relationship between total credit sales and uncollectible accounts

issue date The date a promissory note is signed

maturity date The date by which a promissory note must be paid

multistep income statements Income statements that classify revenues and expenses by category (e.g., sales, operating expenses, other income and expense) and report the calculation of net income in several distinct steps

net realizable value The net dollar amount the company expects to eventually collect

promissory note An unconditional written promise to pay a fixed sum of money, called *principal*, plus interest on the principal, on or before a certain date.

revenues Inflows or other enhancements of assets of an entity or settlements of its liabilities (or a combination of both) from delivering or producing goods, rendering services, or other activities that constitute the entity's ongoing major or central operations

Sales Discounts A contra revenue representing cash discounts taken by customers when payment is made within a specified discount period

Sales Returns and Allowances A contra revenue representing returns by customers and unplanned price allowances granted to customers

single-step income statement An income statement that reports the calculation of net income in one step, consisting of total revenues and gains less total expenses and losses

subsidiary accounts receivable ledger A list of each customer's accounts receivable balance along with all the credit sales made to and the payments received on, account

QUESTIONS

1. Describe the key characteristics of a revenue, and explain why owner investments are not considered revenues.

2. Explain what is meant by the term *gain*, and distinguish it from revenue.

3. If Sears sells a computer, is this a revenue event? If a college sells a computer it has used for five years, is this a revenue event? Explain.

4. What two conditions must be met for a company to recognize revenue?

5. How are revenues earned? Give two examples of a situation in which a revenue has been earned.

6. How are revenues realized? Give an example of a situation in which a revenue has been realized.

7. Do total assets always increase when revenues are recognized? Explain.

8. Can revenue be recognized prior to the collection of cash? Explain.

9. Distinguish between an account receivable and a note receivable.

10. Determine the maturity date of a 90-day promissory note issued on March 17.

11. Calculate the interest income to be earned on a $6,000, 8 percent, 60-day note receivable.

12. Is revenue ever recognized after the receipt of cash? Explain.

13. Name two contra accounts related to sales revenue. What is the purpose of each account?

14. What are the external reporting objectives in accounting for uncollectible accounts?

15. Where does the account Allowances for Doubtful Accounts appear in a company's financial statements? What purpose does it serve?

16. What is a financial statement effect of writing off a customer's uncollectible account?

17. Describe the balance sheet approach to estimating uncollectible accounts expense. What is the purpose of an aging schedule?

18. In an aging schedule of accounts receivable, why are different percentage rates applied to different aged account groups?

19. Distinguish between a multistep and a single-step income statement. What benefit do you see in using each format?

20. If the Accounts Receivable balance increases during the period, are cash collections from customers equal to, greater than, or less than sales? Assume there is no Unearned Revenue account.

EXERCISES

E 9.1 In each of the following situations, indicate whether the increase in net worth of the business is due to an owner investment, a revenue, or a gain.
   a. The Workout Wear retail store sells athletic clothing. The owner, Paul Stretch, sold a sweatsuit to a customer on account.
   b. Marybeth Sourly operates a lemonade stand at the local high school football games. She bought a 50-pound bag of sugar for the business and paid for it out of her personal checking account.
   c. Samantha Courtland, a real estate attorney, performed legal services for a client, and the client signed a promissory note for the amount of the fee.
   d. The Milky Way dairy farm sold a delivery truck for an amount exceeding the book value of the truck.

E 9.2 In each of the following situations, determine the dollar amount of the revenue to be recognized.
   a. Telebon Corporation received $10,000 from a customer as a deposit on a special order.
   b. Dualcom, Inc., shipped a machine to a customer and billed the customer for the remaining amount owed, $30,000. The customer had made a deposit of $8,000 two weeks prior to the shipment date.
   c. Barbara Kennedy, MD, received $200 in copayments from various patients during the month. She also billed several insurance companies $3,500 for services rendered to these patients. The insurance companies usually pay within 60 days of receipt of the bills.
   d. Richard Shapiro, attorney, received a $50,000 retainer from a client at the beginning of the month. By month-end, he estimates that one-fourth of the retainer has been earned, one-half should remain in Unearned Revenue, and one-fourth should be returned to the client.

E 9.3 In each of the following situations, determine the month in which the business should recognize the revenue.
   a. On June 5, Melanie Gibson, editor, received an advance from a publisher. She performed the work during the period July 8 through July 22. On August 9, Melanie sent the publisher an accounting of her hours.
   b. On February 27, EZ Air placed an advertisement with the *New Jersey Tribune*. The full-page ad ran during the week of March 15–22. *The Tribune* billed EZ Air for the ad on March 7, with payment terms of n/30. Payment was received by the Tribune on April 4.
   c. On November 25, Suntaug Books sold an encyclopedia to Children's Learning Center on account. Payment was due on December 25, but was not received until January 15.
   d. The OK Corral Dude Ranch provides each of its guests with a 7-day real western experience. The ranch requires a 50 percent deposit when a vacation is booked, with the remainder to be paid when the guest first arrives at the ranch. Guests for the week ended June 7 had booked their vacation in April and arrived at the ranch on June 1.

E 9.4 Star Enterprises received a promissory note from one of its customers. The three-month note was dated June 1, and required a payment of $5,000 plus interest at a rate of 8 percent. Determine the maturity date of the note and the amount of interest income that Star should record.

E 9.5 Quilts for Sale, Inc., sold a king-sized quilt to a customer for $1,500. The customer signed a 90-day, 7 percent note dated June 1. What is the maturity date of the note? Give the journal entries to record the receipt of the note and its payment at maturity.

E 9.6 Given the following events, prepare the necessary journal entries.
   a. J. Purisky placed an order for merchandise and made a $2,500 deposit.
   b. The company notified Mr. Purisky that his order was ready for pick-up.
   c. Mr. Purisky picked up his order and paid the balance due, $5,000.

E 9.7 Given the following events, prepare the necessary journal entries.
   a. Kathleen Gilbert, CPA, received $2,000 from a client for services to be performed next month.
   b. Ms. Gilbert performed the services for the client.
   c. An accounting of the work performed was sent to the client.

E 9.8   Journalize the following transactions on the books of Barnum Company.

June 5   Sold $6,500 of merchandise to Bailey Company on account, terms 2/10, n/30. The merchandise had a cost of $4,000.

   8   Bailey requested a reduction in the selling price of the merchandise because of some slight imperfections. Barnum granted a $400 allowance.

   14   Received payment from Bailey for the merchandise purchased on the 5th, less the allowance and the discount.

E 9.9   Journalize the following transactions for the Cappucino Company.

Oct. 8   Sold $8,200 of merchandise to Coffee, Inc., on account, terms 1/15, n/60. The merchandise had a cost of $6,000.

   10   Coffee, Inc., returned some of the merchandise, receiving an $800 credit from Cappucino Company. The merchandise, which originally cost Cappucino $500, was put back into inventory.

   23   Received payment from Coffee, Inc., for the merchandise purchased on the 8th, less the return and any appropriate discount.

E 9.10   Chen Company estimated uncollectible accounts expense for the year ended June 30, 1997 at $4,500. During July 1997, Chen identified the Harper account as uncollectible and wrote off the balance of $375. Give the journal entries to record the above events. What is the effect of each entry on net accounts receivable?

E 9.11   An aging schedule of Boscak Company's accounts receivable at December 31, 1997, reveals the following:

	Amount	Estimated Percent Uncollectible
Not yet due	$153,000	1.0%
1–30 days overdue	61,000	3.5
31–60 days overdue	47,000	5.0
61–90 days overdue	24,000	10.0
More than 90 days overdue	16,000	30.0

Prepare the journal entry to record uncollectible accounts expense, assuming the Allowance for Doubtful Accounts balance is zero just prior to adjustment.

E 9.12   Refer to Exercise 9.11. Explain how Boscak Company would report the recorded amounts for Uncollectible Accounts Expense, Accounts Receivable, and the Allowance for Doubtful Accounts in its financial statements for the year ended December 31, 1997. If the entry to record estimated uncollectible accounts was not made, what would be the impact on net income, total assets, total liabilities, and total stockholders' equity for the year ended December 31, 1997?

E 9.13   A review of the financial statements of Technochronics, Inc., revealed a beginning and ending Allowance for Doubtful Accounts balance of $32,500 and $28,600, respectively. If the uncollectible accounts expense for the period as $17,350, what was the total dollar amount of accounts written off during the period?

E 9.14   Greystone Corporation wrote off $24,700 of accounts receivable during the year ended November 30, 1997. The balance of Allowance for Doubtful Accounts at December 1, 1996, was $34,200, and at November 30, 1997, it was $29,500. Determine the amount of uncollectible accounts expense for the year ended November 30, 1997.

E 9.15   Given the following list of accounts, indicate whether each is an income statement or balance sheet account by placing a checkmark in the appropriate column.

	Income Statement	Balance Sheet
Notes Receivable	_____	_____
Allowance for Doubtful Accounts	_____	_____
Sales Returns and Allowances	_____	_____
Gain on Sale of Plant Assets	_____	_____
Interest Income	_____	_____
Accounts Receivable	_____	_____
Sales Discounts	_____	_____
Uncollectible Accounts Expense	_____	_____
Sales Revenue	_____	_____

E 9.16 Following is an alphabetical list of accounts for the Pappas Company. Using these account balances, prepare a multistep income statement for the year ended July 31, 1997.

Cost of Goods Sold	$ 76,000
Gain on Sale of Land	9,500
General and Administrative Expenses	23,400
Income Tax Expense	5,100
Interest Expense	1,200
Interest Income	2,700
Sales Discounts	3,600
Sales Returns and Allowances	4,300
Sales Revenue	144,900
Selling Expense	28,800

E 9.17 The statement of cash flows for Biotech Corporation, for the year ended June 30, 1997, reported cash received from customers of $4,500,000. Biotech's comparative balance sheets for June 30, 1996, and 1997, reported net accounts receivable balances of $680,000 and $765,000, respectively. Determine the net sales reported by Biotech for the year ended June 30, 1997.

E 9.18 The accountant at Zetec, Inc., gathered the following information:

	12/31/96	12/31/97
Accounts Receivable, net	$ 9,600	$17,200
Unearned Revenue	14,500	23,800

If net sales for the year ended December 31, 1997 were $149,300, determine the amount of cash received from customers during the year.

E 9.19 The Hexagon Company reported $254,700 of cash received from customers on its statement of cash flows for the year ended September 30, 1997. However, the income statement for the same time period reported net sales totaling $231,400. Explain why these two numbers are not equal.

E 9.20 The controller at Bordeaux Corporation told you to record a $500,000 sale of merchandise to Chardonnay Company on December 31, 1996, Bordeaux's year-end. You question the controller, stating that shipment will not be made until January 5, 1997. His response to you is that six days will not make any difference to anyone, and that you should recognize the sale on the 31st. The cost of the merchandise sold is $320,000. Should you record the sale on December 31st? What principle of accounting governs this type of transaction? Assuming the sale is recorded on December 31, 1996, what impact will this have on the financial statements for the years ended December 31, 1996, and 1997?

PROBLEMS

P 9.1 For each of the following situations, determine if the event described is a revenue, a gain, or neither. If it is a revenue or gain, determine the dollar amount to be recognized and the month in which it should be recorded.

a. Synchronized Watch Company sold $45,000 of watches on account to Telltale Time Company on December 4, 1996. Telltale sent checks to Synchronized on December 30, 1996, and January 30, 1997, for $22,500 each.

b. On February 5, 1997, the Colotek Company received $2,800 from a customer in full settlement of its account.

c. During the month of December, Johnny's Mail Order Company received several customer orders, accompanied by checks totaling $4,000. Johnny's deposited the checks and sent out notices to the customers stating that the requested merchandise was on back order and would be shipped sometime in January.

d. The Fox Hunting Lodge requires its guests to pay a 25 percent deposit at the time a reservation is confirmed. During the month of December 1996, the Lodge received $1,750 in deposits for guests who subsequently arrived on January 1, 1997. The guests stayed one week and, upon departing, paid the remaining $5,250.

e. On December 28, 1996, State Express Delivery Services sold one of its delivery trucks for $6,300, at which time the buyer signed a contract requiring payment within 10 days. Payment was received on January 5, 1997. The truck originally cost State Express $18,400 and had been depreciated a total of $13,500.

f. Broadway Bills sold 300 tickets to various broadway shows during the week ended December 21, 1996, for performances during that week. The average ticket price was $57.50.

P 9.2   Gwarz Consulting Service engaged in the following transactions during the last quarter of 1997.

Oct. 3   Accepted a two-month, 8 percent note for $450,000 from FEC Corporation for services rendered.

Nov. 25   Accepted a 60-day, 7.5 percent note for $320,000 from Kernel Electric for services rendered.

Dec. 16   Accepted a 45-day, 8.5 percent note for $500,000 from Saunders & Associates for services rendered.

Required: *a.* Assuming Gwarz's year-end is December 31, determine the amount of interest income to be reported on Gwarz's 1997 income statement.

b. How much revenue, if any, from the above transactions will appear on Gwarz's 1998 income statement?

P 9.3   Wiskup Enterprises operates a chain of retail stores in California specializing in paintings by local artists. During the month of July, the following transactions occurred.

July 3   Sold a $1,200 painting to Leon Associates on account, terms 2/10, n/30. The painting had a cost of $700.

6   Received a $500 deposit from D&W Industries for a painting that was to be reframed. The balance of $500 will be collected at the time of pickup.

10   Sold a painting for $800 cash. The painting had a cost of $450.

12   Received payment from Leon Associates for the painting purchased on July 3rd, less the applicable discount.

15   D&W picked up the reframed painting and paid the balance due.

17   Sold a $1,750 painting to Universal Corporation on account, terms 1/10, n/60. The painting had a cost of $900.

20   Universal requested a reduction in the price of the painting because of a defect in the frame. Wiskup granted a $50 allowance to Universal.

27   Received payment from Universal for the July 17th sale, less the allowance and the discount.

Required: *a.* Prepare journal entries to record the above transactions.

b. Determine the total amount of net revenue reported by Wiskup for the month of July. What is the gross margin for July? Is Wiskup Enterprises a service company or a merchandising company? Explain.

P 9.4   Baskind Consulting & Placement provides personnel services to clients in the Boston area. During the month of November, Baskind engaged in the following transactions.

Nov. 4   Received a $5,000 retainer from Morac & Associates for services to be rendered in January.

8   Sent JM Corporation a bill for $3,400 for services rendered during the week ended November 7, terms 2/10, n/30.

13   Provided services to Dica Company and mailed an invoice for $1,900, terms 1/15, n/60.

17   Received a check from JM Corporation for services billed on November 8, less the applicable discount.

20   Received $4,700 from Natick Industries in full settlement of its account, after the discount period had elapsed.

28   Payment was received from Dica Company for the invoice dated November 13, less the applicable discount.

Required: *a.* Prepare journal entries to record the above transactions.

b. Determine the amount of net revenue reported by Baskind for the month of November.

c. Determine the cash received from customers during the month of November. Would you expect it to be the same as net revenue? Explain.

P 9.5   Scruggs Corporation's general journal included the following selected transactions for the month of May.

May 1	Accounts Receivable		4,000	
	Sales			4,000
	Cost of Goods Sold		2,400	
	Inventory			2,400
3	Cash		2,300	
	Sales			2,300
	Cost of Goods Sold		1,600	
	Inventory			1,600
5	Cash		1,000	
	Customer Deposits			1,000
8	Notes Receivable		5,000	
	Sales			5,000
	Cost of Goods Sold		3,200	
	Inventory			3,200
10	Cash		3,920	
	Sales Discounts		80	
	Accounts Receivable			4,000
14	Sales Returns and Allowances		200	
	Accounts Receivable			200
17	Cash		8,500	
	Customer Deposits		1,000	
	Sales			9,500
	Cost of Goods Sold		6,800	
	Inventory			6,800

Required: *a.* Write a brief description for each of the above transactions.

          b. Calculate the change in total gross margin resulting from all of the above transactions.

P 9.6   Caltech, Inc., sells computer parts to companies throughout the Midwest. Caltech estimates uncollectible accounts expense at 4.5 percent of total outstanding accounts receivable. Selected transactions relating to accounts receivable are presented below.

          a. Identified the Madison Company account as uncollectible and wrote off the $3,200 balance.

          b. Identified the Burr Ridge, Inc., account balance of $1,700 as uncollectible and wrote it off.

          c. Madison Company unexpectedly paid off its account previously written off as uncollectible, $3,200.

Required: *a.* Prepare journal entries for the above transactions.

          b. Determine the impact of each of the above entries on Caltech's net assets.

          c. Assuming a balance of accounts receivable at December 31, Caltech's year-end, was $246,400, and that Allowance for Doubtful Accounts had a zero balance immediately prior to adjusting entries, prepare the year-end entry to record uncollectible accounts expense.

          d. Show how Caltech, Inc., would record its accounts receivable balance on the December 31 balance sheet.

P 9.7   An aging analysis of Nielsson Company's accounts receivable at December 31, 1997, revealed the following:

	Amount	Estimated Percent Uncollectible
Not yet due	$264,400	0.5%
1–30 days overdue	139,100	2.0
31–60 days overdue	72,500	6.0
61–90 days overdue	24,800	9.5
More than 90 days overdue	37,200	25.0

Required: *a.* Assuming the Allowance for Doubtful Accounts had a zero balance at December 31, 1997, prior to adjustment, prepare the adjusting entry to record estimated uncollectible accounts expense. Show how Nielsson would present its accounts receivable balance on its December 31, 1997, balance sheet.

          b. Assuming the allowance for doubtful accounts had a credit balance of $1,750 at December 31, 1997, prior to adjustment, prepare the adjusting entry to record estimated uncollectible accounts expense. Show how Nielsson would present its accounts receivable balance on its December 31, 1997, balance sheet.

          c. Assuming an account is identified as uncollectible on January 2, 1998, what effect will the entry to write off the account have on the net realizable value of accounts receivable?

P 9.8   Selected date for Jinan Industries for the most recent three-year period are shown below in thousands of dollars.

	12/31/97	12/31/96	12/31/95
Net sales	$10,600	$13,300	$15,700
Accounts receivable	1,900	2,000	2,200
Allowance for doubtful accounts	350	200	180

Required: *a.* Determine the annual percentage change in net Sales, Accounts Receivable, and Allowance for Doubtful Accounts. Comment on any apparent trends.

b. Has Jinan Industries' ability to collect from its customers improved or deteriorated over time? Explain.

P 9.9   Following is a random list of selected account balances for the Huertas Company at June 30, 1997.

Selling Expenses	$ 24,500
Accounts Receivable	43,700
Cost of Goods Sold	146,900
Sales Discounts	12,800
Interest Expense	8,100
Sales Revenue	282,600
Gain on Sale of Plant Assets	31,400
Allowance for Doubtful Accounts	5,200
Interest Income	2,700
Sales Returns and Allowances	9,300
General and Administrative Expenses	37,900
Income Tax Expense	29,500

Required: *a.* Prepare a multistep income statement for Huertas Company for the year ended June 30, 1997.

b. Prepare a single-step income statement for Huertas Company for the year ended June 30, 1997.

P 9.10   Cokas Enterprises gathered the following information at the end of each of its three most recent fiscal years:

	12/31/97	12/31/96	12/31/95
Accounts receivable, net	$164,300	$175,400	$167,800
Customer deposits	21,400	19,100	15,200
Net sales for year	942,700	916,500	897,400
Cost of goods sold for year	653,800	640,600	634,900

Required: *a.* Determine the amount of cash received from customers for any accounting period in which sufficient information is given.

b. What additional information is necessary to determine the cash received from customers for all accounting periods shown above?

COMPUTER APPLICATIONS

CA 9.1   Companies often use a computer spreadsheet program to prepare an aging analysis for the purpose of estimating the total amount of year-end accounts receivable that will prove uncollectible. An aging analysis of Seattle Company's accounts receivable at December 31, 1997, revealed the following:

	Amount	Estimated Percent Uncollectible
Not yet due	$367,300	0.5%
1–30 days overdue	251,100	2.0
31–60 days overdue	132,500	3.5
61–90 days overdue	64,800	5.0
91–120 days overdue	40,200	10.0
121–180 days overdue	12,400	23.5
181–270 days overdue	33,600	40.0
271–365 days overdue	8,900	65.0
Over 1 year overdue	4,700	80.0

a. Construct a computer spreadsheet designed to calculate the portion of Seattle Company's accounts receivable deemed uncollectible as of December 31, 1997. What is the net realizable value of accounts receivable at December 31, 1997?

b. Assuming the estimated percentage uncollectible for accounts 91–120 days overdue changes to 15 percent, what effect will this have on the amount of accounts receivable deemed uncollectible?

c. Assuming the estimated percentage uncollectible for accounts 181–270 days overdue changes to 55 percent, what effect will this have on the amount of accounts receivable deemed uncollectible?

CA 9.2   Companies often use computerized spreadsheets to prepare financial statements. Following is an adjusted trial balance for the year ended June 30, 1997, for Vegan Natural, Inc.

VEGAN NATURAL, INC.
Adjusted Trial Balance
June 30, 1997

	Debits	Credits
Cash	$ 27,400	
Accounts receivable	18,500	
Store supplies	1,600	
Prepaid insurance	200	
Store equipment	41,500	
Accumulated depreciation—store equipment		$ 2,600
Accounts payable		2,100
Salaries payable		900
Note payable		12,500
Capital stock		50,000
Retained earnings		23,300
Sales		75,000
Interest income		900
Gain on sale of equipment		1,200
Cost of goods sold	43,000	
Salaries expense	19,700	
Advertising expense	2,800	
Uncollectible accounts expense	1,300	
Depreciation expense	3,400	
Supplies expense	800	
Interest expense	1,400	
Insurance expense	900	
Rent expense	6,000	
Total	$168,500	$168,500

Required: a. Construct a computer spreadsheet for the multistep income statement of Vegan Natural, Inc. Include appropriate formulas necessary to calculate all items presented on the income statement.

b. If sales increase by 10 percent, accompanied by a proportionate increase in cost of goods sold, what will happen to gross margin?

c. If rent expense increases 5 percent, uncollectible accounts expense increases 6 percent, and advertising expense decreases 10 percent, what will happen to operating income?

d. If interest expense decreases 50 percent, what will happen to net income?

CASES

C 9.1 *Statement of Financial Accounting Concepts No. 5* states that revenues are recognized when they have been earned and realized. Define the terms *earned* and *realized*. Identify a situation in which a revenue has been earned but not realized. Identify a situation in which a revenue has been realized but not earned. Be prepared to discuss your examples in class.

C 9.2 As a sales manager for the Pan-Global Shoe Company, you have just returned from a major sales meeting at which several of your largest customers told you they would dramatically increase the dollar amount purchased from your company if you would change credit terms from the current 2/10, n/30 to 3/15, n/60. What issues should you be prepared to discuss when you attempt to convince the company president and credit manager to make the change?

C 9.3 Using the annual report you obtained as a Chapter 1 assignment, review the financial statements and notes to the financial statements. For the most recent fiscal year shown, identify the net sales, the net realizable value of accounts receivable, and the cash received from customers. Did the company have an unearned revenue account? If so, what was it called and what was its balance? Can you identify any gains reported by the company? If so, where were they reported?

CRITICAL THINKING

CT 9.1 Hightech Company offers its customers credit terms of 2/10, n/30. Most customers take advantage of the cash discount, mailing their payments to arrive on the 10th day following the date of the invoice. However, Lowmart Company, Hightech's largest customer, has recently begun sending payments to arrive on the 30th day after invoice, while still taking the 2 percent discount. Hightech's collection department has been in touch with Lowmart regarding the taking of the discount outside the discount period, and Lowmart's response is that they deserve to take the discount whenever payment is made. After all, they are Hightech's biggest customer.

Required: Identify Hightech's possible courses of action as well as the consequences of these actions.

CT 9.2 Xanetics, Inc., recently received a $150,000 special order from Lartech, Inc., for some customized equipment. A 50 percent deposit accompanied the order, with the remaining $75,000 payment to be made at delivery. Xanetics manufactured the equipment and was ready to ship it to Lartech when they were notified that Lartech had declared bankruptcy.

Required: Identify the accounting issues related to the above scenario. Has Xanetics earned a revenue? Has it been realized? Should the company recognize any revenue?

ETHICAL CHALLENGES

EC 9.1 The president of Kuala Company stopped by your office today for a chat. She began by assuring you that, as the controller for Kuala, you have the final say in matters concerning the accounting records. However, she also indicated that unless sales revenue increased by $350,000 before the end of next week, the fiscal year-end of the company, the bank would call in the company's loan, and Kuala might have to declare bankruptcy. She has asked you to review the current orders in house to determine if this goal will be met.

After performing your analysis, you note that sales revenue should increase $250,000 by the end of next week. You contact the president, who says that's not good enough. She then tells you to ship $100,000 of merchandise to Aussie Company and record the sale on the last day of the fiscal year. You know that Aussie Company is owned by a close personal friend of the president and that the company will just return the merchandise after the end of the fiscal year.

Required:
a. Identify the accounting and ethical issues in the above scenario.
b. If you were the controller for Kuala Company, how would you attempt to resolve this issue?

EC 9.2 Assume you are the controller for the Hercules Roofing and Siding Company, Inc., which sells roofing and vinyl siding materials, as well as storm doors and windows. You have noticed that business for your most recently completed fiscal year was off by 20 percent compared to the prior year, and that credit customers have been unusually slow in making payments on their account balances. You are fairly certain that many of these customers will never be able to pay.

When you proposed that the company should increase its Allowance for Doubtful Accounts to twice the amount shown at the end of the year, the president of Hercules nearly exploded, stating that he was afraid of losing his job because of the drop in current year income. He added that the entry to record uncollectible accounts was only an estimate, and that he believed there was no reason for any increase over the prior year balance.

Required:
a. Why would the president of the company care whether the balance in Allowance for Doubtful Accounts is larger or smaller than at the prior year-end?
b. What responsibility do you have if the president insists on an entry that you believe understates the estimated uncollectible accounts?

CHAPTER 10

Recording and Communicating in the Conversion Cycle

Learning Objectives

1. Explain why cost accumulation is important during the conversion cycle.
2. Indicate how companies analyze and record material- and labor-related events during the conversion cycle.
3. Describe how companies analyze and record manufacturing overhead events during the conversion cycle.
4. Describe how companies analyze and record cost of goods manufactured and cost of goods sold during the conversion cycle.
5. Explain how companies communicate conversion cycle events to users.

Appendix:

6. Explain the differences among job order costing, process costing, and backflush costing.

Anheuser-Busch Companies, Inc., is the world's largest brewer of beer and ranks in the top 55 companies in the Fortune 500. In 1994, Busch sold 88.5 million barrels of beer, representing approximately 45 percent of total brewing industry sales. Busch brands are exported to 60 foreign countries, and Anheuser-Busch European Trade Ltd. continues to perform very well marketing Busch products in more than 20 European countries. In 1993, the company purchased a 17.7 percent interest in Mexico's largest brewer, Grupo Modelo, and a 5 percent interest in Tsingtao Brewery, China's largest brewer. In 1995, Anheuser-Busch purchased an 80 percent interest in a joint venture Budweiser-Wuhan International Brewing Company, Ltd., which owns a brewery in Wúhan, the fifth largest city in China.

Anheuser-Busch Companies, Inc., is much more than beer. In 1913, August A. Busch, realizing that prohibition would be enacted, began to diversify his company. In 1919, he changed the company's name from Anheuser-Busch Brewing Association to Anheuser-Busch, Incorporated, to reflect anticipated changes. Today, Anheuser-Busch is a multinational diversified company with three primary business segments—beer and beer-related, food products, and entertainment.

Agricultural Resources, Inc., a subsidiary of Busch, provides high-quality raw materials to Busch and operates three malt plants, two rice mills, two rice research

centers, a barley research center, 12 barley elevators, and a hops farm, among other things. Anheuser-Busch Recycling Corporation operates six processing facilities recycling more than 635 million pounds of aluminum beverage cans—the equivalent of 100 percent of Anheuser-Busch's annual aluminum cans sold.

Busch Entertainment Corporation operates theme parks including Busch Gardens and Sea World.

In Chapter 8 we examined how a company analyzes its expenditure cycle events and in Chapter 9 we studied how a company analyzes its revenue cycle events. Anheuser-Busch is a good example of a diversified company with significant activities devoted to its manufacturing processes (conversion activities). This chapter explores how a manufacturing firm like Busch analyzes events that occur during the conversion cycle.

We know from Chapter 3 that the conversion cycle consists of scheduling production, obtaining raw materials, using labor and other resources to produce finished goods from raw materials, and storing finished goods. This chapter's focus is on the purchase and use of raw materials, the use of labor, and the application of overhead to production using an activity-based costing system. The chapter focuses on a manufacturing company's inventory accounting system, which is different from the merchandising company's system we presented in Chapter 8. In addition, we will look briefly at the sale of finished goods, which is similar, but not identical to, the types of sales events examined in Chapter 9.

WHY IS COST ACCUMULATION IMPORTANT?

As you know, a manufacturing company buys raw materials and then uses labor and other resources to convert these raw materials into finished products that are sold to other parties. Cost accumulation is important in a manufacturing company for four primary reasons: (1) to determine the cost of products, (2) to determine if the selling prices for products were appropriate to achieve the company's goals, (3) to determine if the mix of products produced and sold was appropriate to achieve the company's goals, and (4) to determine the cost of goods sold for the period.

Recall that, in the long run, a company must set its selling prices to cover the company's costs and provide a return to the owners. Therefore, cost accumulation is necessary to determine the costs of products in order to set selling prices. In addition, a manufacturing company should produce and sell the mix of products that provides it with the largest profit, therefore the company must know which products are most profitable. Finally, a manufacturing company must report the cost of goods sold on its income statement for the accounting period. In order to do this the company must be able to distinguish between product and nonproduct costs. We look at this issue later—now we examine the activities in the manufacturing process (conversion cycle).

WHAT ARE CONVERSION CYCLE ACTIVITIES?

The conversion cycle differs in the types of activities undertaken and the length of time required for conversion depending on the types of products manufactured. For example, the conversion cycle at Ford Motor Company is different than that at Anheuser-Busch, Inc., because the products of the two companies are different. However, the basic conversion cycle activities are the same—raw materials are converted into finished products using labor and other manufacturing resources. Next examine the conversion process at Anheuser-Busch.

This brewing process is one of the three primary operations that make up Anheuser-Busch's conversion cycle

The conversion cycle at Anheuser-Busch consists of three primary operations: (1) brewhouse, (2) fermenting and lagering, and (3) packaging. In the brewhouse operation, barley malt and rice are ground in mills and then mixed separately with water. The rice mix is boiled and combined with malt to produce enzymes that break down the grains into fermentable sugars. This mash, and the mash from the barley malt, are strained and combined to produce an amber liquid called *wort*. Wort is boiled in brew kettles and hops are added to give it flavor. After boiling, the hops are removed and the wort is cooled.

In the fermenting and lagering process, yeast is added to the cooled wort, and this mixture is allowed to "rest" for approximately six days. During this process, the yeast converts the sugars to carbon dioxide and alcohol and the wort becomes beer. The beer is then put into lager tanks where kraeusen (a mixture of freshly yeasted wort) is added and a second fermentation process begins. During the second fermentation, lasting up to 21 days, a layer of beechwood chips is spread on the tank's bottom, which is known as *beechwood aging*.

The packaging process consists of four activities: (1) bottle rinsing, (2) bottle filling, (3) bottle inspecting, and (4) pasteurization. First, the bottles (or cans) are rinsed and sterilized. Then they are filled on several different assembly lines. The speeds of the assembly lines vary. For example, one line is able to fill 1,885, 12-ounce cans per minute, while another fills 1,030, 12-ounce bottles per minute! After the bottles and cans are filled they are inspected to ensure that they have been filled properly. Then they enter the pasteurization process, which partially sterilizes the beer and allows it to be stored without refrigeration.

Now that you understand the conversion cycle activities at Anheuser-Busch, we turn to the accounting issues involved in this process.

WHAT IS THE DIFFERENCE BETWEEN PRODUCT AND NONPRODUCT COSTS?

For a manufacturing firm like Anheuser-Busch, a **product cost** is a cost incurred in connection with the production of products for resale. A **nonproduct cost** is a cost incurred to sell the products or to administrate the business, that is, a cost that supports the production process. The distinction between product costs and nonproduct costs is important because *product costs are assets until the products are sold.* On the other hand, nonproduct costs may be assets or expenses, depending on whether

EXHIBIT 10.1

Product versus Nonproduct
Costs

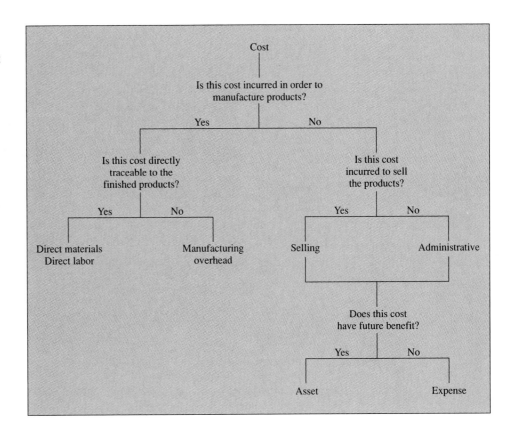

they provide future benefits. For example, the cost of the brewhouse is a product cost, while the cost of Anheuser-Busch's office building is a nonproduct cost. In both cases, the costs are assets that are expensed (depreciated) throughout the life of the asset. However, in the case of the brewhouse the depreciation expense does not appear on the income statement. Rather, it is part of the cost of manufacturing the products and, therefore, is part of cost of goods sold. Similarly, when office employees earn wages, the company incurs a wage expense. However, the wages of manufacturing employees increase the cost of production. The manufacturing employees' wages become an expense when the products are sold.

Exhibit 10.1 illustrates the classification of product and nonproduct costs. Notice that product costs are either traceable to the finished products as direct materials or direct labor, or not traceable, in which case they appear as manufacturing overhead. Nonproduct costs are either selling or administrative costs.

Since a manufacturing firm incurs many different product costs throughout the production process, accurate accounting for these costs is important in order to determine cost of goods sold correctly. For this reason, many manufacturing firms have an extensive inventory accounting system, which we discuss next.

WHAT ARE THE MANUFACTURING INVENTORIES?

As we discussed in Chapter 2, a manufacturing firm typically maintains three types of inventory accounts: (1) Raw Materials Inventory, (2) Work-in-Process Inventory, and (3) Finished Goods Inventory. These reflect, respectively, the costs for raw materials purchases and related freight and insurance costs; the costs of products started but not completed during the period—products that are in the conversion process; and the costs of all completed goods on hand, but not sold.

These three accounts, called *control accounts*, actually reflect a summary of individual costs for many items. For example, the Raw Materials Inventory account of Anheuser-Busch represents the costs of all raw materials stored for use in production, such as, barley malt, hops, and rice. The Work-in-Process Inventory account represents the

EXHIBIT | 10.2

Cost Flows and Product Flows in the Conversion Cycle

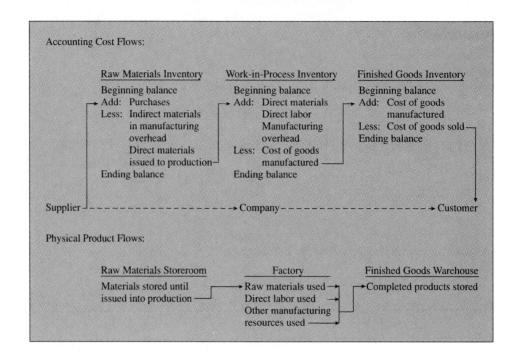

costs of all products, such as O'Doul's, Budlight, Budweiser, and Michelob, that are still in the production process; and the Finished Goods Inventory account represents the cost of these same products that are finished, but not sold.

Exhibit 10.2 illustrates the cost flows through the various manufacturing inventories during the conversion cycle and the related product flows from suppliers to customers. Notice that the cost flows mirror the physical product flows. As raw materials are physically moved from the storeroom to the factory where they are issued into production, their cost is transferred from Raw Materials Inventory to Work-in-Process Inventory. As products are finished and physically transferred from the factory to the finished goods warehouse, their cost is transferred from Work-in-Process Inventory to Finished Goods Inventory.[1] Note also that the product costs become expenses (Cost of Goods Sold) when the products are sold.

In order to keep track of the items making up the control accounts, companies like Anheuser-Busch maintain subsidiary ledgers, which we introduced in Chapter 9. For example, as Exhibit 10.3 illustrates, Anheuser-Busch might maintain one subsidiary ledger for barley malt, another for rice, and a third subsidiary ledger for hops. The total of all the ending balances in the individual raw materials subsidiary ledgers equals the total of the Raw Materials Inventory control account. The same is true for each of the other inventory control accounts, which we discuss below as we analyze conversion cycle events.

HOW DO COMPANIES ANALYZE AND RECORD MATERIAL AND LABOR EVENTS?

Now that you understand the cost and product flow of conversion activities in manufacturing firms, we will examine the analysis and recording of the conversion cycle events in a company's accounting system. We look first at the analysis and recording of material and labor costs; then we turn our attention to analyzing and recording manufacturing overhead.

The recording of conversion cycle costs is important to understand, not so much because you might actually do this in your career, but, rather, because it allows you to see the source of financial information provided by companies to their internal

---

[1]It is not necessary that the accounting records exactly mirror the physical production flows. In some cases, products are constantly moved, but the costs are transferred periodically. For purposes of this chapter, the timing is not important.

EXHIBIT 10.3 | Work-in-Process Control and Subsidiary Ledgers

Control Account

Raw Materials Inventory

Beginning balance	8,000		
Purchases	100,000	80,000	Issued into production
Ending balance	28,000		

Subsidiary Ledgers (see Note below)

	Barley Malt		Rice		Hops	
Beginning balances	5,000	50,000	2,500	25,000	500	5,000
Purchases	60,000		30,000		10,000	
Ending balances	15,000		7,500		5,500	

Note: The total of ending balances in the subsidiary ledgers for barley malt, rice, and hops ($15,000 + $7,500 + $5,500) equals the ending balance in the Raw Materials Inventory control account ($28,000).

and external users. If you understand where and why the financial data appear, you will have a better idea about the nature of the company's activities and what the reported numbers mean in a manufacturing company's financial statements.

Analysis and Recording of Raw Materials

As indicated in Chapter 8, when companies purchase raw materials, the cost of acquiring them (net of any discounts), along with any related freight or insurance charges are recorded as inventory—in this case as Raw Materials Inventory. For example, assume Anheuser-Busch purchases $100,000 of barley malt, rice, and hops on account for use in the production of O'Doul's. In addition, Anheuser-Busch pays cash for the related freight and insurance charges of $2,500. The entry to record this purchase is:

Raw Materials Inventory	102,500	
Accounts Payable		100,000
Cash		2,500

The raw materials purchases costs remain in Raw Materials Inventory until the production department requisitions these materials into production. When that happens, the raw materials must be classified either as direct or indirect materials.[2] The cost of direct materials used is transferred to Work-in-Process Inventory when the items are requisitioned into production. Since indirect materials are not traced directly to production, their costs are assigned to manufacturing overhead when they are requisitioned.[3] If Anheuser-Busch treats barley malt and rice as direct materials and treats hops as an indirect material, the entry to transfer $150,000 of barley, $25,000 of rice, and $5,000 of hops into production is:

Work-in-Process Inventory	175,000	
Manufacturing Overhead	5,000	
Raw Materials Inventory		180,000

Once raw materials are issued into production, the company uses labor and manufacturing overhead to convert these materials into finished goods. We look at the labor component of the conversion process next.

---

[2]Recall that direct materials are traceable to the product and must be of sufficient cost to warrant tracing them. On the other hand, indirect materials either cannot be physically traced to the product or the cost incurred to trace them exceeds the benefit derived from tracing.

[3]Some companies prefer to reflect the costs of indirect materials as manufacturing overhead at the time of purchase. In these cases, the cost of indirect materials purchases is not recorded as inventory and instead the company uses the inventory, *Direct Materials Inventory.*

Analysis and Recording of Labor

The cost of labor is the sum of the employee's gross wages plus the cost of employee fringe benefits. In addition, other employee-related costs, such as employee taxes and the cost of on-the-job training provided to employees, are considered to be labor costs.

Like raw materials, labor must be classified as direct or indirect.[4] As labor is used in the production process, its total cost, including fringe benefits and other employee-related costs, is recorded in the Work-in-Process Inventory account for direct labor and in the Manufacturing Overhead account for indirect labor.[5]

For example, assume that on Friday, January 25, employees of Anheuser-Busch submit their time cards for the hours worked that week. Further assume that there are two groups of labor. One group, direct labor, worked 6,000 hours at $12 per hour, for a total of $72,000 direct labor cost. The other group, indirect labor, earned a salary of $3,000 for the week. We show the related journal entry to record the payment of the manufacturing payroll, ignoring withholdings,[6] below.

As is the case for indirect materials, indirect labor is not traced to specific products, therefore, its cost is assigned to manufacturing overhead.[7]

Work-in-Process Inventory	72,000	
Manufacturing Overhead	3,000	
Wages Payable		75,000

HOW DO COMPANIES ANALYZE AND RECORD MANUFACTURING OVERHEAD EVENTS?

Manufacturing overhead is a temporary account used to reflect the indirect product manufacturing costs of the period. It includes the total of all **indirect product costs,** that is, product costs that are not traced directly to the product, but are incurred to manufacture products. In addition to indirect materials and indirect labor, the category includes many other costs incurred in the manufacturing process that are not directly traceable to specific products. These costs include items such as supplies used to maintain the production equipment, utilities used in the manufacturing process, and property taxes paid on the production facilities. To keep track of these various costs, companies maintain one or more *temporary* accounts known collectively as Manufacturing Overhead. Next look at how companies use these accounts during the conversion cycle.

---

[4]Recall that the cost of direct labor is the cost of those employees who manufacture the product, while the cost of indirect labor is the cost associated with other manufacturing employees who support the production process.

[5]The treatment of fringe benefits differs among companies. Some companies treat all fringe benefits as manufacturing overhead, while others account for fringe benefit costs the same way as the related labor cost.

[6]We examined payroll withholdings and payroll taxes in Chapter 8 and do not repeat that information here.

[7]Some companies charge all labor cost, both direct and indirect, to manufacturing overhead because the cost of direct labor is relatively small when compared to other production costs. And, often, the direct labor personnel also perform "indirect labor" activities. In addition, as manufacturing processes have become more automated, the amount of direct labor has decreased significantly because machines have replaced direct laborers.

Analyzing and Recording Actual Manufacturing Overhead Costs

As companies incur manufacturing overhead costs (rent, supplies, depreciation, etc.) during the period, the manufacturing overhead accounts are increased (debited) and the related cash, payable, or other relevant accounts are credited for the *actual* cost incurred. **Actual manufacturing overhead,** then, is the amount of overhead incurred during the period, recorded as debits to Manufacturing Overhead when the cost is incurred.

For example, assume that Anheuser-Busch incurs the following manufacturing overhead costs, in addition to indirect materials and indirect labor, during January 1996:

Production utilities	$ 5,600
Rent on production facilities	12,000
Depreciation on production equipment	20,000
Insurance on production facilities	3,000
Total manufacturing overhead	$40,600

Anheuser-Busch would make the following journal entry in its accounting records to reflect these costs, assuming that the insurance is prepaid and that the utilities and rent are paid in cash.

Manufacturing Overhead[8]	40,600	
Cash ($5,600 + $12,000)		17,600
Accumulated Depreciation		20,000
Prepaid Insurance		3,000

Notice that the manufacturing overhead costs incurred are recorded in the Manufacturing Overhead account rather than in the Work-in-Process Inventory account because they are indirect costs. The debit side of the Manufacturing Overhead account reflects the actual costs incurred for overhead items. Then, it is necessary to somehow "assign" overhead costs to the products themselves. The process of assigning manufacturing overhead to work-in-process inventory is called *applying manufacturing overhead,* which we discuss next.

Analyzing and Recording Applied Manufacturing Overhead

Applied manufacturing overhead is the amount of manufacturing overhead applied to work-in-process during the period, recorded as credits to Manufacturing Overhead for each cost pool based on the actual amount of the cost driver used (described subsequently). There are two basic ways to apply manufacturing overhead to work in process. First, the company can wait until the end of the period, or until specific points throughout the period, to transfer the balance in the Manufacturing Overhead account to Work-in-Process Inventory. This accomplishes the task of applying manufacturing overhead to work-in-process and closes the temporary Manufacturing Overhead account. However, it has one major weakness—its timing.

Think about the costs that we call *manufacturing overhead.* If companies assign all manufacturing costs only at the end of the accounting period, products completed and sold prior to transferring these costs to the Work-in-Process Inventory account would not reflect manufacturing overhead. Therefore, they would be undercosted. Also, products represented in the Work-in-Process Inventory account at the end of the period when the overhead is transferred to the account would be overcosted relative to products sold during the period because they would receive all of the overhead costs from the period.

To eliminate such cost distortions, most companies apply overhead to Work-in-Process Inventory throughout the period by using a **predetermined overhead rate.** A predetermined overhead rate is the estimated amount of overhead per cost driver. Recall from Chapter 4 that cost drivers measure activity and are assumed to cause costs to change. The predetermined overhead rate is used to apply manufacturing overhead to production throughout the accounting period as the cost driver is used.

---

[8]We use one Manufacturing Overhead account here for simplicity. Generally, companies use more than one overhead account.

The entry to apply $56,700 of manufacturing overhead to the Work-in-Process Inventory account is shown below. Since this entry applies overhead to production, it is not dependent on the actual incurrence of an overhead cost and can be done whenever it is convenient to do so during the accounting period.

Work-in-Process Inventory	56,700	
Manufacturing Overhead		56,700

The application of overhead is the responsibility of the accounting department, which relies heavily on the purchasing, production, and human resources departments for information about cost drivers and estimated overhead costs. Chapter 4 presented a discussion of the process of using regression analysis to determine the best cost driver for a given cost. Once the cost driver is chosen, the regression output also can be used to determine the overhead rate. We now discuss this application process.

Applying Overhead Using Activity-Based Costing

An activity-based costing system uses more than one predetermined overhead rate to assign overhead costs to production. This ensures that the amount of overhead assigned is representative of the resources consumed.

When companies use an activity-based costing (ABC) system, they first assign estimated manufacturing overhead costs to cost pools. A **cost pool** is a group of costs that change in response to the same cost driver. Cost drivers measure activity in the conversion cycle and are assumed to cause conversion cycle costs to change. For example, cost drivers could be the number of direct labor hours to measure the activity, assembling products; the number of production runs to measure the activity, setting up machines; the number of square feet to measure the activity, using facilities; or the number of design hours to measure the activity, developing products. Decision makers chose cost drivers to represent the activities being performed. The amount of resources consumed by activities represented by the same cost driver are combined in the same cost pool. Then, in order to compute the predetermined overhead rate, it is necessary to divide the estimated amount of manufacturing overhead in each cost pool by the estimated amount of the cost driver for that cost pool for the coming period. We illustrate the steps in the ABC overhead application process next.

The ABC Overhead Application Process The process of applying manufacturing overhead to production in an ABC system is accomplished in a six-step process. The first five steps occur *prior to the start* of the period, while the last step occurs *throughout* the period.

1. Identify and classify production activities by level.

2. Determine the appropriate cost driver for each activity.

3. Estimate the amount of overhead related to each cost driver.

4. Estimate the amounts of cost drivers to use.

5. Determine the predetermined overhead rate for each cost driver.

6. Apply manufacturing overhead to Work-in-Process Inventory using the predetermined overhead rate.

Identify and Classify Production Activities by Level Activities are typically classified into one of four different levels depending on the purpose of the activity. The activity levels help identify why the activities are undertaken. This understanding helps identify value-added and nonvalue-added activities (discussed in Chapter 5 and further described in Chapter 13). In addition, companies use these levels to help identify appropriate cost drivers. The four levels are:

Facility-sustaining level. Those activities that maintain the productive capacity of the company, such as insuring the building or paying property taxes on the production facilities.

- *Product-sustaining level.* Those activities that maintain a product line, such as developing a particular product line or pretesting a product line.
- *Batch-related level.* Those activities performed each time a batch (group) of a particular product is produced or batches are ordered, such as setting up production machinery or moving products in the factory from one production station to another.
- *Unit-related level.* Those activities performed each time a unit is produced, such as using machines to drill holes or inspecting each unit.

Not all companies have activities in each level. In some firms, for example, most activities are unit related. On the other hand, many companies have several activities in each level. For example, a clothing manufacturer would have mostly unit-related activities because the production process is labor intensive. Conversely, a pharmaceutical drug manufacturer would have product-sustaining activities connected with developing new drugs and batch-related activities related to producing batches of drugs.

In addition, many companies do not apply facility-sustaining overhead to production for internal reporting purposes. However, for external reporting, FASB requires **full-absorption costing,** a costing system in which *all* production costs are applied to the products manufactured during the period.

Determine the Appropriate Cost Driver for Each Activity Exhibit 10.4 shows examples of activities for each of the four activity levels and examples of appropriate related cost drivers. Because cost drivers are measures used for the activities being performed, they must relate as closely as possible to the activities examined. For example, designing products is a product-sustaining activity because it is done to develop products for consumers. Therefore, an appropriate cost driver to use for this activity might be the number of design hours required to develop a product. In another case, owning buildings (production facilities) is a facility-sustaining activity because it maintains the company's ability to produce products. Therefore, the number of square feet used is an appropriate cost driver because it measures the size of the facilities. Finally, cutting or drilling products is a unit-related activity because it must be done on each individual unit produced. The number of machine hours is an appropriate cost driver if the cutting or drilling is done by machines.

EXHIBIT 10.4	Activity-Based Costing Overview		
Activity Level	**Types of Activities**	**Types of Costs**	**Examples of Cost Drivers**
Facility sustaining	Owning buildings	Depreciation	Number of square feet
	Occupying buildings	Property taxes	Number of square feet
	Using buildings	Utilities	BTUs of heat produced
	Maintaining buildings	Insurance	Number of square feet
Product sustaining	Testing products	Testing costs*	Number of tests required
	Designing products	Design costs*	Number of hours of design time
	Maintaining parts inventory	Carrying costs	Number of parts required
	Using specialized machinery	Depreciation	Number of specialized processes required
Batch related	Ordering parts	Ordering costs	Number of orders placed
	Setting up machines	Setup costs*	Number of setups required
	Handling materials	Moving costs*	Number of moves required
	Requisitioning parts	Requisition cost	Number of requisitions made
Unit related	Cutting/drilling units	Power costs	Number of machine hours
	Assembling units	Indirect labor	Number of labor hours
	Painting units	Indirect materials	Direct materials cost
	Inspecting units	Rework costs*	Number of units reworked

*Includes the salaries and wages of those individuals involved in the activity.

Estimate the Amount of Overhead Related to Each Cost Driver There may be more than one cost pool for each activity level depending on the number of cost drivers for the level's activities. For example, designing products and maintaining a parts inventory are both product-sustaining activities, but designing products is related to the number of design hours required while maintaining a parts inventory is related to the number of different parts required.

Costs cannot be combined into a cost pool unless they are represented by the same cost driver. Therefore, at the facility-sustaining level, depreciation, property taxes, utilities, insurance, and repair costs may be combined into one cost pool since their related activities may be represented by the cost driver, number of square feet. On the other hand, at the product-sustaining level, the costs of designing (for example, engineering salaries and the cost of the blueprints) and maintaining parts inventory (for example, inventory control salaries and shelving costs) cannot be combined because they are represented by different cost drivers—the number of design hours and the number of different parts, respectively.

The number of cost pools in a given company varies with the complexity of the operations. Some companies, such as General Motors, have many cost pools for each level, while others, such as a clothing manufacturer, may have only one, or perhaps no, cost pools for a given level.

Once companies have identified their cost pools, they estimate the costs using a cost estimation technique, such as linear regression. For example, the accountant would estimate the costs associated with owning and using the building based on the level of these costs in the past and the expected level of operations for the coming period. Thus, if there is an anticipated increase of 10 percent in property taxes during the current year and all other facility-sustaining costs remain the same, the accountant would estimate facility-sustaining overhead at 110 percent of last period's property tax cost plus last period's other facility-sustaining costs.

Often steps 2 and 3 of applying overhead are accomplished simultaneously because the cost driver is used to estimate the cost and the best cost driver for a given cost is determined in the estimation process. For example, using regression analysis, the accountant discovers that the number of machine hours is the best cost driver for unit-related overhead costs because that regression has the highest *R*-squared and lowest relative standard error of the *X* coefficient.[9]

PAUSE & REFLECT Look at Exhibit 10.4. Why is the number of square feet an appropriate cost driver for facility-sustaining costs? What other costs might be included in this cost pool?

Estimate the Amounts of Cost Drivers to Use Estimating the quantities of cost drivers to use requires input from those who are in charge of the related activities. To estimate the number of design hours expected for the coming period, for example, individuals in the product design department must forecast their time requirements based on past experience and anticipated future products and developments. Normally this occurs as part of the planning and budgeting process.

Determine the Predetermined Overhead Rate for Each Cost Driver Calculating the predetermined overhead rate for each cost driver involves dividing the estimated total manufacturing overhead amount for the cost pool by the estimated amount of the appropriate cost driver. The predetermined overhead rate is used throughout the period as the estimate of manufacturing overhead per "unit"[10] of cost driver. The number of predetermined overhead rates, then, depends on the number of cost pools used.

---

[9]Chapter 4 indicated that the *R*-squared measures the strength of the relationship between the cost and the cost driver, while the standard error of the *X* coefficient measures the probability that the variable cost per cost driver is zero.

[10]*Unit*, as used here, is a generic term; it does not refer to the number of units produced.

When determining how many cost pools to use and, therefore, how many overhead rates to calculate, the accountant must weigh the benefits of more accurate costing against the costs incurred to provide additional information.

Apply Manufacturing Overhead to Work-in-Process Inventory Using the Predetermined Overhead Rates   Throughout the conversion cycle, the accounting department applies manufacturing overhead to the Work-in-Process Inventory account as the cost driver is used. This is done by multiplying the predetermined overhead rate by the *actual amount of the cost driver used* and then adding this amount to the Work-in-Process Inventory account.

Assume that a company has determined that the predetermined, unit-related overhead is $25 per machine hour. At the end of the week, the production department reports that it used 800 machine hours. The accounting department then applies $20,000 ($25 × 800) of unit-related overhead to the Work-in-Process Inventory account using the entry shown below. This entry reflects the production department's estimated usage of unit-related manufacturing overhead resources for the week.

Work-in-Process Inventory	20,000	
Manufacturing Overhead		20,000

ABC Overhead Application Process Illustrated   We use the following simplified example to illustrate the application of manufacturing overhead to production using activity-based costing. See Exhibit 10.5, which shows the activities, the estimated costs, and the appropriate cost drivers for the coming period in connection with the production of O'Doul's.

Step 1: Identify levels and activities. There are two facility-sustaining activities (owning and using the building), two product-sustaining activities (developing and testing the products), two batch-related activities (setting up machines and inspecting production runs), and one unit-related activity (using machines) given for this example.

Step 2: Choose Cost Drivers. Using the list of appropriate cost drivers in Exhibit 10.5, take a minute to analyze why each cost driver is appropriate. For example, the number of design hours is an appropriate cost driver for the costs of developing products because the costs are expected to change when the number of design hours changes. On the other hand, the number of design hours is not an appropriate cost driver for testing products because product testing costs are more closely associated with the number of tests conducted.

PAUSE & REFLECT	Examine Exhibit 10.5. Why is the number of production runs an appropriate cost driver for the costs of both setting up machines and inspecting production? Is there another cost driver that would be more appropriate?

EXHIBIT	10.5	Activity-Based Costing Analysis

Activity Level	Type of Activity	Estimated Cost	Appropriate Cost Driver
Facility sustaining	Owning building	$100,000	Number of square feet
	Using building	400,000	Number of square feet
Product sustaining	Developing products	150,000	Number of design hours
	Testing products	50,000	Number of tests required
Batch related	Setting up machines	170,000	Number of production runs
	Inspecting production	70,000	Number of production runs
Unit related	Using machines	80,000	Number of machine hours required

Step 3: Estimate Costs. The activities identified in step 1 result in five cost pools, with five respective cost drivers shown below. Remember that activities must have the same cost driver before they can be combined into cost pools. For example, since owning the building and using the building are both related to the size of the building, these costs are combined into one cost pool using the number of square feet as the cost driver. We outline the costs associated with each of the five cost pools below.

- *Building costs, $500,000.* This cost pool includes insurance, depreciation, and property taxes on the building.

- *Product development costs, $150,000.* This cost pool includes engineering salaries and design costs, as well as engineering change costs.[11]

- *Product testing costs, $50,000.* This cost pool includes the quality inspectors' salaries and testing costs incurred to develop the product line.

- *Setup and inspection costs, $240,000.* This cost pool includes the costs to change the production line from cans to bottles or from product to product and the cost to inspect each batch of production for quality.

- *Machine usage costs, $80,000.* This cost pool includes the costs associated with using the machinery, such as utility costs, repair and maintenance costs, and the cost of owning the machines (depreciation, property taxes, and insurance).

Step 4: Estimate Cost Driver Usage. Assume that a budgeting analysis of O'Doul's and the other Anheuser-Busch products reveals that the production facilities occupy 200,000 square feet, the engineering department estimates using 1,000 hours for product development, the quality testing department expects to conduct 10 tests, 120 production runs are planned, and the machinery is expected to operate 4,000 hours during the coming period.

Step 5: Calculate Predetermined Overhead Rates. To calculate the predetermined overhead rates, divide the amount of each estimated cost pool by its estimated cost driver. Using the numbers presented in steps 3 and 4, we calculate the predetermined overhead rates for each cost driver as follows:

- Building costs: $\dfrac{\$500,000}{200,000 \text{ square feet}} = \$2.50$ per square foot

- Development costs: $\dfrac{\$150,000}{1,000 \text{ development hours}} = \$150$ per development hour

- Product testing costs: $\dfrac{\$50,000}{10 \text{ quality tests}} = \$5,000$ per test

- Setup and inspection costs: $\dfrac{\$240,000}{120 \text{ production runs}} = \$2,000$ per production run

- Machine usage costs: $\dfrac{\$80,000}{4,000 \text{ machine hours}} = \$20$ per machine hour

Step 6: Apply overhead.[12] Assume that *during* the period, the production of O'Doul's *actually required* the following resources:

- 20,000 square feet of building space.

- 250 hours of development time.

---

[11]Research and development costs are treated as selling and administrative expenses for external reporting purposes as required by the FASB. However, these costs may be treated as manufacturing overhead for internal reporting. At the end of the reporting period, an adjusting entry is made to remove these costs from Manufacturing Overhead and to assign them to Selling and Administrative Expense for external reporting purposes.

[12]Note that this step occurs throughout the period—we are summarizing the entries over the entire period.

- 1 quality test.
- 12 production runs.
- 400 machine hours.

Using the predetermined overhead rates calculated in step 5, manufacturing overhead is *applied* to the production of O'Doul's as follows:

Building costs:	20,000 square feet x $2.50	=	$ 50,000
Development costs:	250 development hours x $150	=	37,500
Product testing costs:	1 quality test x $5,000	=	5,000
Setup and inspection costs:	12 production runs x $2,000	=	24,000
Machine usage costs:	400 machine hours x $20	=	8,000
Total manufacturing overhead applied in the period		=	$124,500

The accounting department would reflect the application of these costs to the Work-in-Process Inventory account by making the following summary entry:

Work-in-Process Inventory—O'Doul's	124,500	
Manufacturing Overhead—Building		50,000
Manufacturing Overhead—Development		37,500
Manufacturing Overhead—Testing		5,000
Manufacturing Overhead—Setup and inspection		24,000
Manufacturing Overhead—Machining		8,000

This entry is a summary entry that reflects all the entries made during the year. The actual number of entries made depends on the accounting system and when the necessary information becomes available. For example, machining overhead would be applied whenever the production department reports the number of machine hours used. Development overhead would be applied whenever the engineering department reports the number of hours worked, probably weekly. On the other hand, building overhead might be applied monthly because it is convenient and efficient for the accounting department to do this as part of the monthly reporting process.

Over- or Underapplied Manufacturing Overhead

A company records both actual and applied overhead in the same manufacturing overhead account for each individual cost pool.

- *Actual overhead* (debit to manufacturing overhead) is the actual amount of overhead incurred for the various overhead items consumed during the entire production process.

- *Applied overhead* (credit to manufacturing overhead) is the estimated consumption of overhead resources based on the *actual usage* of the various cost drivers.

Rarely does the amount of actual overhead equal the amount of applied overhead, so the individual manufacturing overhead accounts show balances at the end of the accounting period. If there is a debit balance in the account, the actual manufacturing overhead for the period is greater than the applied manufacturing overhead. In this case, overhead is said to be **underapplied** for that overhead cost pool. This implies that the amount of overhead applied to Work-in-Process Inventory throughout the period was not as much as the actual amount of manufacturing overhead cost incurred to produce the products. Therefore, the cost of the products manufactured during the period is understated.

Conversely, a credit balance in the manufacturing overhead account would indicate that the amount of applied overhead was greater than the actual overhead, and, therefore, that overhead is **overapplied** for that cost pool. That is, the amount of overhead applied to Work-in-Process Inventory was greater than the actual amount of overhead for that cost pool. Thus, the cost of the products manufactured during the period is overstated.

In either case, the balance in the manufacturing overhead account must be closed because it is a temporary account. If the balance is "small," it is closed to Cost of Goods Sold because the amount of over- or understating is not large enough to warrant tracing it to partially completed products (Work-in-Process

Inventory), completed products (Finished Goods Inventory), and products sold (Cost of Goods Sold). However, if the balance is "large," it is closed to Cost of Goods Sold, Work-in-Process Inventory and Finished Goods Inventory based on the balances in these accounts because the over- or understating of the cost of products is considered to be significant.

For example, assume that Anheuser-Busch applied building overhead to production at $2.50 per square foot and it used 200,000 square feet of manufacturing space during the period. The actual building overhead, in total, incurred during the period consisted of insurance, $80,000; depreciation, $200,000; property taxes, $60,000; maintenance, $45,500; and security, $108,000 (total amount of $493,500). The total applied building overhead for the period was $500,000 ($2.50 × 200,000). The Manufacturing Overhead—Building account shown here reflects these facts.

Manufacturing Overhead—Building

Actual Overhead		Applied Overhead	
Total	493,500	500,000	
		6,500	Balance before closing entry

In this case, building overhead is overapplied because the amount of overhead applied to Work-in-Process Inventory is greater than the actual amount of overhead incurred during the period by $6,500. If management considers this amount small (it is only 1 percent of the total actual cost [$6,500/$493,500]), it is closed to the Cost of Goods Sold account as shown below:

Manufacturing Overhead—Building	6,500	
Cost of Goods Sold		6,500

We show the effect of this entry on the Manufacturing Overhead—Building account below.

Manufacturing Overhead—Building

Total	493,500	500,000	
		6,500	Balance before closing entry
Closing entry	6,500		
–0–		–0–	

Now consider the case when management determines that the amount of over- or underapplied overhead is large. Assume that at the end of the reporting period, total *actual* machine setup and inspection overhead is $290,000, and *applied* setup and inspection overhead is $200,000. In this case, the amount of setup and inspection overhead is underapplied by $90,000. If management considers this amount large (it is 31 percent of total actual cost [$90,000/$290,000]), it would allocate the balance among the Work-in-Process Inventory, Finished Goods Inventory, and Cost of Goods Sold accounts based on the ratio of their respective ending balances. If the balances in these accounts are $825,000, $475,000, and $1,100,000 (total $2,400,000), respectively, this entry would reflect the transfer.

Work-in-Process Inventory		
(825,000/2,400,000 x 90,000)	30,938	
Finished Goods Inventory		
(475,000/2,400,000 x 90,000)	17,812	
Cost of Goods Sold		
(1,100,000/2,400,000 x 90,000)	41,250	
Manufacturing Overhead—		
Setup and Inspection		90,000

PAUSE & REFLECT   Without the above allocation of overhead, the current assets on the balance sheet would be understated by $48,750. What other financial statement differences would exist? Why?

Now that you understand how to analyze and record direct materials, direct labor, and manufacturing overhead, we examine how to analyze and record the cost of finished products.

RECORDING COST OF GOODS MANUFACTURED AND COST OF GOODS SOLD

As the production process is completed, it is necessary to transfer the cost of manufacturing the products, called **cost of goods manufactured,** from Work-in-Process Inventory to Finished Goods Inventory. Cost of goods manufactured includes costs of direct materials, direct labor, and applied manufacturing overhead. Assume that during the period, the cost of O'Doul's manufactured is $842,000. The following summary entry reflects the transfer of costs from Work-in-Process Inventory to Finished Goods Inventory when the product is completed.

Finished Goods Inventory	842,000	
Work-in-Process Inventory		842,000

Now, the final step in the accounting process requires that Anheuser-Busch transfer the cost of finished goods to Cost of Goods Sold when the items are sold using a cost flow assumption such as FIFO or LIFO. If, during the period, $1,233,000 of O'Doul's is sold to distributors for $2,152,500 on account, the summation entry to record the sale is given below.

Cost of Goods Sold	1,233,000	
Finished Goods Inventory		1,233,000
Accounts Receivable	2,152,500	
Sales		2,152,500

COMMUNICATING RESULTS OF EVENTS IN THE CONVERSION CYCLE

The results of conversion cycle activities must be communicated to interested users in a timely manner. These users include external users such as creditors and stockholders who want to evaluate manufacturing companies as possible investment opportunities. In addition, internal users need the same type of conversion cycle activity information to evaluate the effectiveness and efficiency of operations. We discuss conversion cycle reporting next.

EXHIBIT	10.6	Cost of Goods Manufactured Report

ANHEUSER-BUSCH
Cost of Goods Manufactured Report—O'Doul's
For the Period Ending December 31, 1995

Beginning balance, raw materials	$ 148,650
Add purchases of raw materials	662,600
Raw materials available for use	$ 811,250
Less ending balance of raw materials	119,280
Raw materials issued into production	$ 691,970
Less indirect materials used	25,300
Direct materials issued	$ 666,670
Direct labor used	102,350
Manufacturing overhead applied	800,410
Beginning balance work-in-process inventory	106,440
Cost of goods in production	$1,675,870
Less ending balance work-in-process inventory	50,820
Cost of goods manufactured	$1,625,050

For external and internal users, the income statement reflects cost of goods sold during the period and the balance sheet shows the ending balances in the related manufacturing inventory accounts. In addition, many firms prepare what they call a **cost of goods manufactured report,** which is used internally to show the changes that occurred in the Raw Materials Inventory and Work-in-Process Inventory accounts during the period.

What Does the Cost of Goods Manufactured Report Tell Readers?

The cost of goods manufactured report allows comparison of the cost of manufacturing products during the period with the budgeted production costs as part of the evaluation process. It includes the costs for direct materials, direct labor, and manufacturing overhead, and shows the summary of the events during the period that affected the Raw Materials and Work-in-Process Inventory accounts.

Exhibit 10.6 shows a cost of goods manufactured report for Anheuser-Busch based on the following information. Production cost flows during the period to manufacture O'Doul's were:

Purchases of raw materials	$662,600
Indirect materials used	25,300
Direct labor used	102,350
Manufacturing overhead applied	800,410

Further assume that Anheuser-Busch had the following balances in the inventory records related to O'Doul's:

Raw material inventory, beginning	$148,650
Raw material inventory, ending	119,280
Work-in-process inventory, beginning	106,440
Work-in-process inventory, ending	50,820

Notice that the report illustrates the cost flow for the period through the Raw Materials and Work-in-Process Inventory accounts. Raw Materials Inventory increases by the amount of purchases of raw materials ($662,600) to determine the amount of raw materials available for use. This amount then decreases by the amount of raw materials on hand at the end of the period (ending balance of $119,280) to show the amount of raw materials issued into production. These materials are separated into indirect ($25,300) and direct materials ($666,670) as shown in Exhibit 10.6.

Also note that the beginning Work-in-Process Inventory ($106,440) increases by the costs added to production for direct materials, direct labor, and applied manufacturing overhead ($666,670, $102,350, and $800,410, respectively) and decreases by the ending balance of Work-in-Process Inventory ($50,820) to derive the cost of goods manufactured ($1,625,050).

What Does the Income Statement Tell Readers?

We now look at the effects of these production-related accounts on the income statement. The income statement includes the cost of goods sold section, which reflects the period's events affecting the Finished Goods Inventory account. Finished goods' beginning and ending inventory balances, plus the information in the cost of goods manufactured report are combined to reflect the cost of goods sold that appears on the income statement. In addition, it is necessary to close the amount of under- or overapplied overhead to Cost of Goods Sold *prior to* calculating the ending balance of Cost of Goods Sold. This tells users the *actual cost* of the goods sold during the period. Continuing with our previous example, assume that Anheuser-Busch's manufacturing overhead is overapplied by $23,500 during the year. The records related to O'Doul's also reveal the following information.

Finished goods inventory, beginning	$115,400
Finished goods inventory, ending	114,700

Based on this information and the information about the cost of goods manufactured shown in Exhibit 10.6, we calculate the cost of goods sold as follows:

Finished goods, beginning	$ 115,400
Add cost of goods manufactured	1,625,050
Cost of goods available for sale	$1,740,450
Less ending finished goods	114,700
Unadjusted cost of goods sold	$1,625,750
Less overapplied overhead	23,500
Cost of goods sold	$1,602,250

Exhibit 10.7 shows the actual income statement of Anheuser-Busch. Notice that Anheuser-Busch reports the marketing, distribution, and administrative expenses separately from cost of goods sold because these costs are nonproduct costs. Also notice that cost of goods sold does not match the amount just determined because Anheuser-Busch's cost of goods sold also includes other retail items sold, such as Michelob and BudLight, which are not included in our O'Doul's calculations. The notes to Anheuser-Busch's financial statements reveal that the beer and beer-related segment showed an operating income of $1,786.5 million in 1994, while the food products and entertainment segments reported operating income of $43.8 million and 68.8 million, respectively. (See Anheuser-Busch Annual Report.)

What Does the Balance Sheet Tell Readers?

On the balance sheet, manufacturing inventories appear in the current asset section because Anheuser-Busch expects to use them within one year of the operating cycle. We show the actual balance sheet of Anheuser-Busch in Exhibit 10.8. Notice that the inventories are a significant part of assets, accounting for 34 percent of the current assets. Also note that Anheuser-Busch reports its manufacturing inventories separately on its balance sheet while many companies show this information in the notes to the financial statements. The notes to the financial statements also reveal that Anheuser-Busch's inventories are determined using LIFO for brewing inventories and FIFO for food product inventories.

EXHIBIT **10.7** Income Statement—Anheuser-Busch

Consolidated Statement of Income
Anheuser-Busch Companies, Inc., and Subsidiaries

(In millions, except per share data)

Year Ended December 31,	1994	1993	1992
Sales	$13,733.5	$13,185.1	$13,062.3
Less federal and state excise taxes	1,679.7	1,679.8	1,668.6
Net sales	12,053.8	11,505.3	11,393.7
Cost of products and services	7,784.4	7,419.7	7,309.1
Gross profit	4,269.4	4,085.6	4,084.6
Marketing, distribution and administrative expenses	2,370.3	2,308.7	2,308.9
Restructuring charge	—	565.0	—
Operating income	1,899.1	1,211.9	1,775.7
Other income and expenses:			
Interest expense	(221.4)	(207.8)	(199.6)
Interest capitalized	22.1	36.7	47.7
Interest income	3.3	5.2	7.1
Other income/(expense), net	4.0	4.4	(15.7)
Income before income taxes	1,707.1	1,050.4	1,615.2
Provision for income taxes:			
Current	588.6	562.4	561.9
Deferred	86.4	(139.5)	59.1
Revaluation of deferred tax liability (FAS 109)	—	33.0	—
	675.0	455.9	621.0
Net income, before cumulative effect of accounting changes	1,032.1	594.5	994.2
Cumulative effect of changes in the method of accounting for postretirement benefits (FAS 106) and income taxes (FAS 109), net of tax benefit of $186.4 million	—	—	(76.7)
NET INCOME	$ 1,032.1	$ 594.5	$ 917.5
PRIMARY EARNINGS PER SHARE:			
Net income, before cumulative effect	$ 3.91	$ 2.17	$ 3.48
Cumulative effect of accounting changes	—	—	(.26)
Net income	$ 3.91	$ 2.17	$ 3.22
FULLY DILUTED EARNINGS PER SHARE:			
Net income, before cumulative effect	$ 3.88	$ 2.17	$ 3.46
Cumulative effect of accounting changes	—	—	(.26)
Net income	$ 3.88	$ 2.17	$ 3.20

Source: Anheuser-Busch 1994 Annual Report, p. 45.

EXHIBIT 10.8   Balance Sheet—Anheuser-Busch

Consolidated Balance Sheet

Anheuser-Busch Companies, Inc., and Subsidiaries

ASSETS (In millions)

December 31,	1994	1993
CURRENT ASSETS:		
Cash and marketable securities	$ 156.4	$ 127.4
Accounts and notes receivable, less allowance for doubtful accounts of $7.7 in 1994 and $6.7 in 1993	784.6	751.1
Inventories		
Raw materials and supplies	421.5	385.5
Work in process	87.8	99.4
Finished goods	115.5	141.8
Total inventories	624.8	626.7
Other current assets	295.8	290.0
Total current assets	1,861.6	1,795.2
INVESTMENTS AND OTHER ASSETS	1,636.1	1,588.0
PLANT AND EQUIPMENT, NET	7,547.7	7,497.1
Total Assets	**$11,045.4**	**$10,880.3**

LIABILITIES AND SHAREHOLDERS EQUITY		
CURRENT LIABILITIES:		
Accounts payable	$ 850.9	$ 812.5
Accrued salaries, wages and benefits	288.5	243.9
Accrued taxes, other than income taxes	107.8	121.7
Restructuring accrual	52.6	189.2
Other current liabilities	369.2	448.3
Total current liabilities	1,669.0	1,815.6
POSTRETIREMENT BENEFITS	624.3	607.1
LONG-TERM DEBT	3,078.4	3,031.7
DEFERRED INCOME TAXES	1,258.2	1,170.4
COMMON STOCK AND OTHER SHAREHOLDERS EQUITY:		
Common stock, $1.00 par value, authorized 800,000,000 shares	343.8	342.5
Capital in excess of par value	856.8	808.7
Retained earnings	6,656.7	6,023.4
Foreign currency translation adjustment	(21.8)	(33.0)
	7,835.5	7,141.6
Treasury stock, at cost	(3,042.6)	(2,479.6)
ESOP debt guarantee offset	(377.4)	(406.5)
	4,415.5	4,255.5
COMMITMENTS AND CONTINGENCIES	—	—
Total Liabilities and Equity	**$11,045.4**	**$10,880.3**

Source: Anheuser-Busch Annual Report, p. 44.

SUMMARY

A manufacturing company maintains three inventory accounts to reflect the events occurring during the conversion cycle. Increases in the Raw Materials Inventory account occur when companies purchase raw materials, and decreases occur when companies issue direct and indirect materials into production. The increases to the Work-in-Process Inventory account reflect the cost of direct materials issued into production, direct labor used in production, and manufacturing overhead *applied* to production. Decreases to Work-in-Process Inventory reflect the cost of goods manufactured during the period. Finally, increases in Finished Goods Inventory are due to the cost of goods manufactured, and decreases reflect the cost of goods sold during the period.

- Companies record *actual* manufacturing overhead costs in the manufacturing overhead account throughout the period as the costs are incurred. Manufacturing overhead is *applied* to Work-in-Process Inventory throughout the period using predetermined overhead rates determined through activity-based costing.

- It is necessary to transfer the difference between the actual overhead cost and the applied overhead cost out of Manufacturing Overhead at the end of the period. If actual overhead is greater than applied overhead, overhead is underapplied. On the other hand, if actual overhead is less than applied overhead, overhead is overapplied.

- If the amount of over- or underapplied overhead is small, it is transferred to Cost of Goods Sold at the end of the reporting period. If the over- or underapplied overhead is large, it is allocated among Work-in-Process Inventory, Finished Goods Inventory, and Cost of Goods Sold in relationship to the respective ending balances of these accounts.

- The cost of goods manufactured report reflects the sequence of events affecting the Raw Materials and Work-in-Process Inventory accounts during the period.

KEY TERMS

actual manufacturing overhead The amount of overhead incurred during the period, recorded as debits to Manufacturing Overhead for each cost pool when the cost is incurred

applied manufacturing overhead The amount of manufacturing overhead applied to work-in-process during the period, recorded as credits to Manufacturing Overhead for each cost pool based on the actual amount of the cost driver used

backflush costing (Appendix) A product costing system used to reflect the assumption that raw materials purchased, direct labor used, and manufacturing overhead applied will be expensed during the period

cost of goods manufactured The cost of manufacturing products during the period, including direct materials, direct labor, and applied manufacturing overhead

cost of goods manufactured report The report that shows management the changes in the Raw Materials and Work-in-Process Inventory accounts during the period

cost pool A group of costs that change in response to the same cost driver

full-absorption costing A costing system in which all production costs are applied to the products manufactured during the period

indirect product costs Product costs that are not directly traced to the product

job order costing system (Appendix) A product costing system that accumulates production costs based on individual jobs or batches

manufacturing overhead A temporary account used to reflect the indirect product manufacturing costs of the period

nonproduct cost A cost incurred to sell products or to administrate the business

overapplied overhead The excess of applied overhead over the actual overhead for the accounting period

predetermined overhead rate The estimated amount of overhead per cost driver to

process costing system (Appendix)
A product costing system that accumulates production costs by departments because products are not individually identifiable; as

product cost A cost incurred in connection with the production of products for resale in a manufacturing company

Raw and In-Process Inventory (Appendix)
A current asset account used in a backflush costing system to represent the cost of unused raw materials (including freight and insurance), work-in-process, and finished goods

underapplied overhead The excess of actual overhead over the applied overhead for the accounting period

APPENDIX 1

MANUFACTURING COSTING SYSTEMS

As we discussed in this chapter, the inventory accounts of a manufacturing company are control accounts that reflect the total costs of many individual items. For example, the Raw Materials Inventory Control account reflects the total costs of all the various raw materials purchased during the period, and the Finished Goods Inventory account reflects the total cost of the various finished products of the company. In this appendix, we examine the Work-in-Process Inventory control account.

In order to reflect the accumulated production costs during the conversion cycle, companies typically use either a job order or process costing system. The choice depends on the type of production activities in the company A job order costing system is ideal for companies that produce a variety of *different products simultaneously*, while a process costing system is ideal for companies that produce *homogeneous products continuously*. We look at each of these costing systems, in turn. Then, we examine a relatively new costing system called *backflush costing*, which is popular in just-in-time inventory companies.

Job Order Costing Systems

A job order costing system accumulates production costs based on individual jobs or batches. It is used primarily by companies with jobs that are separate and distinct from one another. Job order costing systems are commonly used in industries such as printing, where each printing order is different from any other printing order; in custom-cabinet making, where each set of cabinets is made to customer specification; in aircraft manufacturing, where each airplane is distinct from any other airplane; and in construction, where each project (house, bridge, office building, or mall, for example) is unique.

A job order costing system reflects each job order as its own production unit with its own accumulated production costs recorded on a job cost sheet. In this system, the Work-in-Process Inventory control account reflects the total costs of all jobs in process.

Exhibit 10.9 illustrates a job cost sheet that we discuss in the following example. Assume that the College of Business at Fairmont University orders 10,000 brochures to be printed for distribution to high schools in the area. When the printing department receives the order, it issues a job cost sheet and assigns the College of Business a job number, Job No. 2001, in this case. As the printing department prints the brochures, it reflects on the job cost sheet, the costs of the raw materials used by engraving (one plate at $100) and printing (no. 35 ink at $160 and no. 5 paper at $300); the costs of direct labor used by engraving (three hours at $12 = $36) and printing (6 hours at $15 = $90); and the overhead assigned to the job by the accounting department ($189). Therefore, total cost of Job No. 2001 is $875. Note that Job No. 2001 did not include any binding department costs because the brochures did not require binding services.

Process Costing Systems

A **process costing system** accumulates production costs by departments because products are not individually identifiable. In contrast to industries that use job order costing systems, industries that commonly use process costing systems manufacture homogeneous products in an assembly-line process. Companies that produce automobiles, chemicals, beverages, processed food products, and pharmaceuticals typically use process costing systems.

EXHIBIT 10.9

Job Cost Sheet

Fairmount Print Shop

Customer College of Business   Job No. 2001

Date Received 3/1/96   Due Date 3/15/96

Description: 10,000 Recruiting Brochures

Engraving Department

Materials	Labor	Total		
1 plate @ $100	3 hours @ $12	Materials	$	100
		Labor		36

Printing Department

Materials	Labor	Total		
#35 Ink 4 @ $40	6 hours @ $15	Materials	$	460
#5 Paper 20 @ $15		Labor		90

Binding Department

Materials	Labor	Total		
NA	NA	Materials	$	0
		Labor		0

| Overhead | | | $ | 189 |

| | | TOTAL | $ | 875 |

In a process cost system, production costs are accumulated in subsidiary ledgers representing work-in-process inventory for each production department. The costs accumulated in one department are transferred to subsequent departments in the production process so that the costs accumulated in the final production department reflect all the costs incurred to produce the products. The total of all the individual department subsidiary accounts is reflected in the Work-in-Process Inventory ontrol account.

For example, assume that Anheuser-Busch requires three production processes—brewing, fermenting, and packaging—and that the costs are accumulated in these three processing departments. Exhibit 10.10 illustrates the flow of costs through these three departments. The brewhouse process uses direct materials (barley malt and rice), direct labor (brewers), and applied manufacturing overhead. These costs are transferred to the fermenting department, which also requires applied manufacturing overhead. The total of both departments' costs are transferred to packaging, which also requires direct materials (cans, bottles, etc.), direct labor (assembly-line workers), and applied manufacturing overhead. Finally, the total production costs from all three departments are transferred to finished goods to reflect the cost of the beverages produced during the period.

Backflush Costing Systems

Many manufacturing companies, particularly those that adopt the just-in-time philosophy, use a product costing system known as **backflush costing.** This system reflects the assumption that the amount of raw materials purchased, direct labor used, and manufacturing overhead applied in the Cost of Goods Sold account for the period will be expensed during the period. Then, at the end of the period, if any inventory remains on hand, it is necessary to make an entry to adjust the Cost of Goods Sold account to reflect the cost of the remaining inventory. The cost of the ending inventory, whether it is raw materials, work-in-process, or finished goods,[13] is recorded in a current asset account called **Raw and In-Process Inventory.** This

---

[13]Typically, in such companies, the cost of finished goods on hand at the end of the accounting period is very small.

EXHIBIT 10.10

Process Costing Work-in-Process Inventory Accounts

Work-in-Process—Brewhouse

Beginning balance	Costs transferred to fermenting
Direct materials	
Direct labor	
Applied manufacturing overhead	
Ending balance	

Work-in-Process—Fermenting

Beginning balance	Costs transferred to packaging
Costs transferred from brewhouse	
Applied manufacturing overhead	
Ending balance	

Work-in-Process—Packaging

Beginning balance	Costs transferred to Finished Goods— O'Doul's
Costs transferred from fermenting	
Direct materials	
Direct labor	
Applied manufacturing overhead	
Ending balance	

Finished Goods—O'Doul's

Beginning balance	Costs transferred to Cost of Goods Sold
Costs transferred from packaging	
Ending balance	

eliminates the need for separate Raw Materials, Work-in-Process, and Finished Goods Inventory accounts, so it saves record-keeping time and cost.

For example, assume that Anheuser-Busch adopts a backflush costing system and during the period incurs the following costs in connection with the production of O'Doul's:

Raw materials purchased	$240,000
Direct labor used	345,000
Manufacturing overhead applied	860,000

During the period, the following summary journal entries are made in connection with these costs. Notice that all costs are recorded as Cost of Goods Sold on the assumption that they will be transferred to in the income statement during the period:

Cost of Goods Sold	240,000	
Accounts Payable		240,000
To record the purchase of inventory.		
Cost of Goods Sold	345,000	
Wages Payable		345,000
To record the labor used in production.		
Cost of Goods Sold	860,000	
Manufacturing Overhead		860,000
To record the overhead applied to production.		

EXHIBIT 10.11

Comparison of Traditional
and Backflush Costing

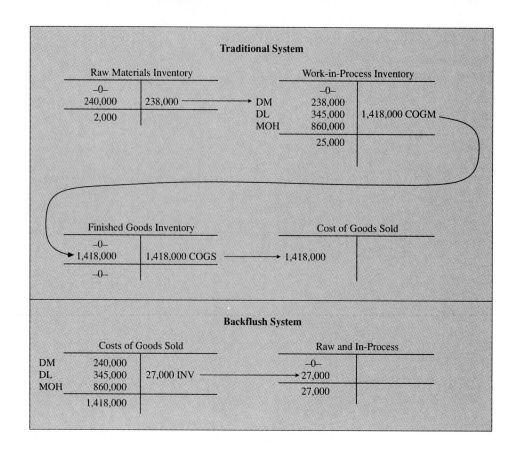

Assume that at the end of the period, the cost of O'Doul's still in process is $25,000 and there is $2,000 of raw materials stored. This means that $27,000 of costs assigned to Cost of Goods Sold for the period must be "backflushed" into inventory. That is, $27,000 must be added to the Raw and In-Process Inventory account and subtracted from the Cost of Goods Sold account. This requires the following entry:

Raw and In-Process Inventory	27,000	
Cost of Goods Sold		27,000

Exhibit 10.11 compares, in T-account form, the traditional product costing system to the backflush system. Notice that even in this simple example, the backflush costing system allows the elimination of many journal entries. Also note that the total ending inventories and Cost of Goods Sold are the same in the backflush and traditional systems.

QUESTIONS

1. Explain why cost accumulation is important in the conversion cycle.

2. What is the difference between product and nonproduct costs? Why is the distinction important?

3. Explain the purpose of each of the three inventory accounts used in a manufacturing company such as Ford Motor Company.

4. Why (when) do companies increase and decrease the Raw Materials Inventory account?

5. If the Raw Materials Inventory account decreased during the period, were purchases greater than or less than the amount of materials issued into production? Why?

6. Why (when) is the Work-in-Process Inventory account increased and decreased?

7. If Work-in-Process Inventory increases during the period, was cost of goods manufactured greater than or less than the total product costs transferred into Work in Process during the period? Why?

8. Why (when) is the Finished Goods Inventory account increased and decreased?

9. If the Finished Goods account decreases during the period, is cost of goods manufactured greater than or less than cost of goods sold? Why?

10. Explain the difference between direct and indirect materials and give examples of each for a manufacturing company such as Levi Strauss.

11. Explain the difference between direct and indirect labor and give examples of each for a manufacturing company such as Boeing.

12. What is the difference between actual and applied manufacturing overhead? Why are they important to product costing?

13. Explain the process of applying manufacturing overhead to Work-in-Process Inventory.

14. There are four levels of production activities. What are they and why are they important?

15. Explain the concept of a cost driver and how to determine an appropriate cost driver for a given activity.

16. Explain the concept of cost pool and how to determine cost pools.

17. How do companies use the predetermined overhead rate to assign overhead to work-in-process?

18. Explain the difference between over- and underapplied manufacturing overhead. What is the implication of each type of manufacturing overhead on: (1) product costs and (2) net income for the period?

19. At the end of the period, Jefferson Company had a large debit balance in its Manufacturing Overhead account for a particular cost driver. Explain how Jefferson would allocate this balance at the end of the period. Why?

20. At the end of the period, Jackson Company had a small credit balance in its Manufacturing Overhead account for a particular cost driver. How would Jackson allocate this balance at the end of the period? Why?

Appendix

21. Explain how to accumulate costs in a job order costing system and why this is important in certain companies. Other than the examples given in the chapter, name two types of companies that are likely to use this system.

22. In a process costing system, how are costs accumulated and why is this important in certain types of companies? Other than the example given in the chapter, name two types of companies that are likely to use this system.

23. Explain the pattern of cost flows in a backflush costing system and the advantages of such a system.

EXERCISES

E 10.1 The following costs are for Bob McFadden, Inc., a manufacturer of labels used in the packaging of a variety of products. Classify the costs as one of the following four options by placing the number of the correct answer in the space provided.

1. Direct materials cost.
2. Direct labor cost.
3. Manufacturing overhead cost.
4. Selling and administrative cost.

_____ *a.* Ink used in printing labels.
_____ *b.* Salary of the corporate controller.
_____ *c.* Depreciation on the factory building.
_____ *d.* Rent on finished goods warehouse.
_____ *e.* Paper for labels.
_____ *f.* Wages paid to machine operator.
_____ *g.* Insurance on manufacturing facilities.
_____ *h.* Income tax expense.
_____ *i.* Cost of electricity to operate factory machinery.
_____ *j.* Boxes used to ship finished labels.
_____ *k.* Advertising.
_____ *l.* Salespersons' commissions.
_____ *m.* Vacation pay for factory employees.
_____ *n.* Property taxes on corporate office building.
_____ *o.* Salary of production foreman.

E 10.2   Bestline, Inc., is a manufacturing firm that makes table tennis paddles. Each paddle consists of a handle, a wooden paddle, and a rubber backing for each side of the wooden paddle. As the paddles progress through the assembly process, workers attach the handles, and glue the rubber backing into place. Classify the following costs as one of the following two options by placing the number of the correct answer in the space provided.

     1. Product cost.
     2. Nonproduct cost.

_____   *a.* Cost of handles for the paddles.
_____   *b.* Wages of assembly workers.
_____   *c.* Rent on production facilities.
_____   *d.* Wages of sales personnel.
_____   *e.* Utilities for the production facilities.
_____   *f.* Cost of rubber backing for the paddles.
_____   *g.* Cost of wooden paddles.
_____   *h.* Production supervisor's salary.
_____   *i.* Cost of glue.
_____   *j.* Cost of shipping crates.
_____   *k.* Office workers' salaries.
_____   *l.* Depreciation on the delivery trucks.
_____   *m.* Depreciation on the factory equipment.
_____   *n.* Rent on finished goods warehouse.
_____   *o.* Rent on raw materials warehouse.

E 10.3   Packard Company had inventories at the beginning and end of 1996 as follows:

	January 1, 1996	December 31, 1996
Raw materials inventory	$35,000	$45,000
Work-in-process inventory	76,000	60,000
Finished goods inventory	30,000	65,000

During 1996, Packard purchased raw materials of $300,000, incurred direct labor costs of $100,000, and applied manufacturing overhead of $230,000 to production. Prepare T-accounts to show the flow of costs through the company's inventory accounts during 1996.

E 10.4   Barkley, Inc., incurred the following costs during 1997:

Direct material	$316,000
Direct labor	680,000
Manufacturing overhead	360,000

During 1997, cost of goods manufactured totaled $840,000, and goods costing $824,000 were sold. Inventory balances at January 1, 1997, were as follows:

Raw materials	$420,000
Work-in-process	36,000
Finished goods	60,000

Prepare T-accounts to show the flow of costs through the company's inventory accounts during 1997.

E 10.5   Prepare the journal entries for the transactions of Chernak Company shown below.

April 8   Purchased $3,100 in raw materials; terms 1/10, n/30, FOB shipping point.
     11   $1,080 direct materials were requisitioned from the raw materials warehouse.
     15   Filled indirect material requisition, $500.
     17   $180 in direct materials requisitioned on April 11 were not used in production and were returned to the warehouse.

E 10.6   Given the following information, prepare the journal entries for Armbruster Manufacturing to record the monthly payroll at March 31, 1996.

President	$10,000
Factory supervisor	3,000
Machinist	2,000

E 10.7   Bogolub Company incurred the following manufacturing overhead costs during the month of June 1996. Prepare the journal entry to record the costs.

Depreciation, building	$3,800
Wages earned but not yet paid, janitor	800
Electricity used and paid, factory	380
Rent on equipment previously paid	70

E 10.8   Oller Company, a basketball manufacturer, applies unit-related manufacturing overhead on the basis of machine hours. The following unit-related overhead data was accumulated by the accounting department.

	Estimated	Actual
Machine hours	300,000	225,000
Overhead costs	$360,000	$340,000

  a. Calculate the predetermined overhead rate.
  b. Calculate the amount of overhead applied to Work-in-Process Inventory.
  c. Calculate the amount of over- or underapplied overhead.

E 10.9   Caruso Company manufactures air conditioners and applies batch-related overhead to production using an estimated overhead rate of $500 per production run. In March 1997, the company actually produced 3,560 air conditioners in four production runs. Actual batch-related overhead for the month of March was $2,100.
  a. Compute the amount of overhead applied to production in March.
  b. Compute the under- or overapplied overhead at the end of March.
  c. Prepare the journal entry to close the under- or overapplied overhead assuming the difference is considered small.

E 10.10   Harwick Manufacturing produces three different models of water softeners: the standard model, the super model, and the deluxe model. The models differ in the features offered and the warranties given to customers. The deluxe model has the most features and the best warranty. Harwick applies product-sustaining overhead to each product based on the number of hours of engineering time. It estimates that Harwick will require a total of 800 engineering hours in the coming period and that product-sustaining overhead costs will be $225,000.

At the end of the period, it was discovered that the standard model required 200 engineering hours, the super model used 250 engineering hours, and the deluxe model required 450 engineering hours. The actual product-sustaining overhead for the period was $240,000.
  a. Compute the predetermined overhead rate for product-sustaining overhead.
  b. Determine the amount of overhead applied to each product line during the year.
  c. Compute the amount of over- or underapplied overhead for the period.

E 10.11   Artex, a clothing manufacturer, incurs the following types of costs. Classify the costs *(a-g)* as one of the following four options (1–4) by placing the number of the correct answer in the space provided.
              1. Facility sustaining.
              2. Product sustaining.
              3. Batch related.
              4. Unit related.
  _____ *a.* Designing clothing.
  _____ *b.* Occupying the factory.
  _____ *c.* Using specialized cutting equipment.
  _____ *d.* Inspecting production.
  _____ *e.* Setting up sewing machines.
  _____ *f.* Maintaining materials inventory.
  _____ *g.* Using sewing machines.

E 10.12   Refer to E 10.11. For each of the activities, prepare a list of the types of overhead costs that would be included in the cost pool. The first one has been done for you.

Activity	Costs
Designing clothing	Indirect materials, indirect labor, cost of patterns, cost of mannequins, cost of cloth

E 10.13 Refer to E 10.11 and E 10.12. For each of the activities, determine an appropriate cost driver. The first one has been done for you.

Activity	Cost Driver
Designing clothing	Number of designs done

E 10.14 Jackson Ice Cream has identified the following operating activities for its company, the estimated overhead costs associated with each activity, an appropriate cost driver for each activity, and the estimated usage of the cost driver for the coming period. Using this information, determine the appropriate overhead rates.

Activity	Costs	Cost Driver	Estimated Usage
Occupying facilities	$800,000	Square feet	100,000
Testing quality	50,000	Production runs	100
Carrying inventory	125,000	Pounds of material	1,500
Setting up machines	60,000	Production runs	100
Packing containers	400,000	Units made	200,000
Using machines	200,000	Machine hours	100,000

E 10.15 Refer to E 10.14. For each activity, determine the type of costs included in the overhead cost pool. The first one has been done for you.

Activity	Costs
Occupying facilities	Depreciation, cost of security personnel, property taxes, utilities such as light and heat, maintenance

E 10.16 Refer to E 10.14 and E 10.15. Determine whether any of the activities can be combined in one cost pool. Why or why not?

E 10.17 Using the following information, determine the cost of goods manufactured and cost of goods sold for Roche Company during August 1998 assuming that over- or underapplied manufacturing overhead is closed to Cost of Goods Sold at the end of the period.

Raw materials inventory, August 1, 1998	$11,000
Raw materials inventory, August 31, 1998	?
Work-in-process inventory, August 1, 1998	4,000
Work-in-process inventory, August 31, 1998	12,000
Finished goods inventory, August 1, 1998	6,000
Finished goods inventory, August 31, 1998	21,000
Direct materials used	20,000
Direct labor used	30,000
Raw materials purchased	65,000
Indirect materials used	6,000
Indirect labor used	5,000
Manufacturing overhead, other	29,000
Administrative salaries	15,000
Sales salaries and commissions	10,000
Depreciation on sales and office equipment	14,000
Manufacturing overhead, applied	65,000

E 10.18 Refer to E 10.17. Is the overhead over- or underapplied? Why? If this amount is considered large, what would be the journal entry prepared at the end of the period to close the Manufacturing Overhead account?

Appendix:

E.10.19 During 1996, Pelle Company purchased raw materials of $600,000, incurred direct labor of $200,000, and applied manufacturing overhead of $460,000 to production. At the end of the period, a count of inventory revealed that $2,000 of raw materials, $4,000 of work in process, and $1,000 of finished goods remained on hand. Prepare the journal entries to record these events in a backflush costing system.

E 10.20   Backman, Inc., which uses a backflush costing system, incurred the following costs during 1996:

Direct materials	$ 632,000
Direct labor	1,240,000
Manufacturing overhead, applied	720,000
Selling and administrative costs	980,000

At the beginning of 1996, Backman's manufacturing inventories were $4,000 in total. A count of inventory at the end of 1996 showed inventory of $5,000 on hand. What was the cost of goods sold for 1996?

PROBLEMS

P 10.1   For each of the three cases below, determine the missing amounts indicated by question marks.

	Case 1	Case 2	Case 3
Sales	$95,000	?	?
Finished goods inventory, beginning	9,000	$ 34,000	$ 19,480
Work-in-process inventory, beginning	8,000	18,000	?
Direct materials	19,000	86,000	134,650
Direct labor	30,000	38,000	76,420
Manufacturing overhead applied	26,000	?	157,830
Work-in-process inventory, ending	?	34,000	28,845
Cost of goods manufactured	66,000	146,000	350,175
Finished goods inventory, ending	32,000	?	?
Cost of goods sold	?	132,000	352,095
Gross margin	?	36,000	177,715
Operating expenses	19,000	28,000	?
Net income (loss)	33,000	?	(39,707)

P 10.2   The following events occurred during the month at the Adams Company, manufacturers of golf clubs. Prepare the appropriate journal entries.
1. Purchased $55,000 of raw materials and $45,000 of indirect materials, both on account.
2. Sold 10,000 shares of capital stock for $50,000.
3. Direct materials of $48,000 were issued into production.
4. Indirect materials of $36,000 were issued into production.
5. Collected $12,000 on accounts receivable.
6. Paid $11,500 in wages to employees: $7,200 was direct labor and $4,300 was indirect labor. (Ignore payroll taxes.)
7. Paid the electricity bill for the factory when received, $3,200.
8. Manufacturing overhead of $27,200 was applied to production.
9. Paid selling and administrative costs of $17,000.
10. Paid $12,500 in wages to employees: $8,200 was direct labor and $4,300 was indirect labor. (Ignore payroll taxes.)
11. Manufacturing overhead of $35,400 was applied to production.
12. Completed jobs costing $175,000.
13. Sold jobs costing $300,000 for $450,000. The proceeds of the sale were $200,000 in cash with the balance to be paid next month.
14. Paid selling and administrative expenses of $30,000.

P 10.3   Refer to the transactions in P 10.2.

Additional Information:
1. Depreciation expense for the month was $12,500 on the factory building and $5,000 on the manufacturing equipment.
2. Depreciation expense for the month was $3,000 on selling and administrative items.
3. Overhead is closed to cost of goods sold after the adjusting entries are made.
4. Income tax expense is 40 percent of net income before tax.

5. Beginning account balances are presented in the following trial balance.

TRIAL BALANCE

Cash	$ 82,300	
Accounts receivable	20,000	
Raw materials inventory	21,000	
Work-in-process inventory	100,000	
Finished goods inventory	165,000	
Manufacturing equipment	300,000	
Accumulated depreciation—manufacturing equipment		$ 188,000
Factory building	1,100,000	
Accumulated depreciation—factory building		612,000
Selling and administrative equipment	20,000	
Accumulated depreciation—selling and administrative equipment		5,000
Accounts payable		34,000
Taxes payable		22,000
Long-term notes payable		500,000
Common stock		250,000
Retained earnings		197,300
	$1,808,300	$1,808,300

Required:
a. Use the trial balance given above to determine the beginning balance of the accounts.
b. Post the journal entries prepared in P 10.2 to the appropriate accounts.
c. Prepare a trial balance.
d. Prepare the adjusting entries as needed and post to the appropriate accounts.
e. Prepare an adjusted trial balance.
f. Prepare the closing entries needed and post these to the appropriate accounts.
g. Prepare a post-closing trial balance.
h. Prepare a schedule of cost of goods manufactured and sold for the month.

P 10.4 An analysis of the direct material inventory of Thomas Company reveals the following activity.

	Units	Total Cost
Beginning balance	5,000	$ 9,000
Purchases:		
January 5	6,000	12,600
January 10	4,000	9,000
January 20	7,500	16,500
January 30	3,000	6,450
Issued to production:		
January 7	7,000	
January 15	5,000	
January 25	9,000	

In addition, Thomas incurred direct labor costs of $50,000 and overhead costs of $75,000 during the month. The beginning and ending balances of Work-in-Process inventory were, respectively, $6,000 and $3,000.

Required: Determine the cost of goods manufactured using each of the following cost flow assumptions for raw materials inventory.
a. FIFO.
b. LIFO.

P 10.5   The following information was obtained from the account records of Foster Company.

Raw materials inventory, beginning	$ 45,000
Raw materials inventory, ending	37,500
Work-in-process inventory, beginning	–0–
Work-in-process inventory, ending	25,000
Finished goods inventory, beginning	22,500
Finished goods inventory, ending	25,000
Raw materials purchased	375,000
Indirect materials used	27,500
Direct labor	245,000
Indirect labor	80,000
Depreciation, factory	67,500
Depreciation, factory machinery	35,000
Utilities, factory and machinery	40,000
Insurance, factory and machinery	25,000
Selling and administrative expenses	140,000
Property taxes, factory	50,000
Manufacturing overhead, applied	294,000
Sales	1,058,000

Required:
a. Determine the over- or underapplied overhead for the period.
b. Prepare a cost of goods manufactured report.
c. Prepare a schedule of cost of goods sold assuming the under- or overapplied overhead is small.
d. Determine the gross margin for the period.
e. Determine the net income for the period.

P. 10.6   Refer to the cost of goods manufactured report and cost of goods sold schedule prepared in P 10.5.

Required:
a. Assume that one-quarter of the recorded direct materials costs were actually indirect materials. Explain the impact that this error had on the amount of over- or underapplied overhead for the period.
b. Assume that one-half of the indirect labor costs incurred were actually direct labor costs. Explain the impact that correcting this error would have on the cost of goods manufactured and cost of goods sold.
c. Discuss the effect on cost of goods manufactured and net income if the insurance was classified as a selling and administrative expense.

P 10.7   Woods Company manufactures bookcases. Unit-related manufacturing overhead is applied based on the number of direct labor hours worked. Estimated unit-related manufacturing overhead for the year is $60,000. Employees are expended to work 40,000 direct labor hours during the year. Batch-related overhead is applied on the basis of the number of production runs. Estimated batch-related manufacturing overhead for the coming year is $400,000. There are 1,000 production runs planned for the year. The following events occurred during the month of April.
1. Purchased 70,000 board feet of lumber @ $.27 per board foot
2. Requisitioned 50,000 board feet of lumber into production.
3. Indirect materials in the amount of $2,500 were placed into production.
4. Twelve production runs producing 1,200 bookcases and requiring a total of 6,100 hours of direct labor at $4.25 per direct labor hour were completed during the month. Overhead is applied to production at this time.
5. Indirect labor costs incurred totaled $3,000.
6. Utility bill for the factory received and paid, $550.
7. Depreciation on the factory for April, $6,000.
8. A bill for advertising was received, but not paid, in the amount of $120.
9. Other manufacturing overhead totaling $5,000 was incurred.
10. Bookcases with a cost of $47,000 were completed during the month and transferred to the finished goods warehouse.
11. Bookcases costing $53,000 were sold for $100,000.

Additional Information:

Balance at April 1:

Raw materials inventory	$20,000
Work-in-process inventory	50,000
Finished goods inventory	40,000

Required:
  a. Calculate the predetermined overhead rates.
  b. Trace the flow of costs through the inventory accounts for the events described above.
  c. Determine the over- or underapplied overhead, in total, for the period.

P 10.8   The following incomplete ledger accounts were obtained from the records of Arnold Company, which applies unit-related manufacturing overhead to production at the rate of 150 percent of direct labor costs.

Raw Materials Inventory

460,000	1,100,000
960,000	
?	

Work-in-Process Inventory

300,000	1,720,000
1,020,000	
?	
?	
860,000	

Finished Goods Inventory

?	2,100,000
?	
380,000	

Manufacturing Overhead

640,000	680,000

Cost of Goods Sold

?	

Sales

	3,300,000

Required:
  a. Determine the missing amounts indicated by question marks in the above ledger accounts.
  b. Determine the amount of over- or underapplied overhead.

P 10.9   The following information was provided by Graham Manufacturing for the month of August 1996.

	Beginning Balance	Ending Balance
Raw materials inventory	$ 80,000	$ 60,000
Work-in-process inventory	100,000	120,000
Finished goods inventory	140,000	110,000

Additional Information:

Direct materials purchased	$450,000
Direct labor costs incurred	$300,000
Machine hours worked	33,000
Actual unit-related manufacturing overhead	$315,000
Applied unit-related manufacturing overhead	$10 per machine hour

Required: Calculate the following amounts.
  a. Direct materials used in production.
  b. Applied manufacturing overhead.
  c. Cost of goods manufactured.
  d. Over- or underapplied manufacturing overhead.
  e. Cost of goods sold.

P 10.10   The following *annual budgeted* information is available for Clarkson Company, which manufactures folding tables, chairs, and footstools.

Activity	Cost	Cost Driver	Estimated Usage
Setting up machines	$ 90,000	Number of production runs	150
Processing orders	150,000	Number of orders	300
Handling materials	60,000	Pounds of materials	12,000
Using machines	180,000	Number of machine hours	20,000
Managing quality	150,000	Number of inspections	60
Packing and shipping	120,000	Number of units shipped	30,000
Using building	600,000	Square feet occupied	300,000
Total cost	$1,350,000		

During the *current month*, the following cost drivers were used:

	Tables	Chairs	Footstools
Number of production runs	2	4	8
Number of orders	8	8	4
Pounds of materials	400	200	200
Number of machine hours	500	300	300
Number of inspections	2	2	4
Number of units	1,000	500	300
Square feet occupied	60,000	40,000	100,000

Required: *a.* Classify each of the activities as facility sustaining, product sustaining, batch related, or unit related.
b. Determine the types of costs included in each activity.
c. Calculate the overhead rate for each cost driver.
d. Determine the overhead allocated to each product line.
e. Determine the overhead cost per unit.

Appendix:

P 10.11   Ideal Bike Company produces bicycles and uses a process costing system with two departments—painting and assembly. In the painting department, the bicycle frame is painted and allowed to dry before being transferred to the assembly department. In the assembly department, seats, handle bars, brakes, and decals are added to the bicycle frames transferred from the painting department. The beginning balances of its inventory accounts are shown below:

Raw materials	$15,000
Work in process (control)	31,400
Finished goods	8,500

Ideal's subsidiary ledger shows that the beginning balance in the Work-in-Process inventory—Painting Department was $14,000. During fiscal 1996, the following relevant events occurred:
1. Purchased $350,000 of raw materials from suppliers on account.
2. Issued $190,000 of direct materials to the painting department.
3. Issued $140,000 of direct materials to the assembly department.
4. Issued $5,000 of indirect materials into production.
5. Used $475,000 of direct labor
6. Used $720,000 of direct labor in the assembly department.
7. Indirect labor incurred during the period was $500,000.
8. Manufacturing overhead applied to the painting department was $380,000.
9. Manufacturing overhead applied to the assembly department was $1,080,000.
10. Other, actual manufacturing overhead costs incurred were $950,000.
11. Production costs of $1,048,500 were transferred from the painting to the assembly department during the period.
12. Production costs of $2,990,700 were transferred from the assembly department to finished goods during the period.
13. Cost of goods sold, before closing overhead, was $2,993,200.
14. Any over- or underapplied overhead is closed to Cost of Goods Sold at the end of the period.
15. Sales for the period were $3,741,500.

Required: *a.* Determine the ending balances in each of the manufacturing inventory accounts using a separate work-in-process inventory account for each department.
b. Determine the over- or underapplied overhead for the period.
c. Determine the cost of goods sold for the period.
d. Determine the gross margin for the period.

COMPUTER APPLICATIONS

CA 10.1   The following *annual budgeted* information is available for Dickerson Company, which manufactures picnic tables, lawn chairs, and table umbrellas.

Activity	Cost	Cost Driver	Estimated Usage
Setting up machines	$ 180,000	Number of production runs	225
Processing orders	300,000	Number of orders	450
Handling materials	120,000	Pounds of materials	18,000
Using machines	360,000	Number of machine hours	30,000
Managing quality	300,000	Number of inspections	90
Packing and shipping	240,000	Number of units shipped	45,000
Using building	1,200,000	Square feet occupied	450,000
Total cost	$2,700,000		

During the *current month*, the following cost drivers were used:

	Tables	Chairs	Umbrellas
Number of production runs	4	8	16
Number of orders	16	16	8
Pounds of materials	800	400	400
Number of machine hours	1,000	600	600
Number of inspections	4	4	8
Number of units	2,000	1,000	600
Square feet occupied	120,000	80,000	250,000

Required: *Use a computer spreadsheet.*
a. Calculate the overhead rate for each cost driver.
b. Determine the overhead allocated to each product line.
c. Determine the overhead cost per unit.
d. Assuming that in the next month, all production activities are doubled, determine the overhead allocated to each product line by multiplying each cost driver used by 2.
e. Refer to *d* above. Determine the overhead cost per unit.

CA 10.2   Prepare a computer spreadsheet that can be used to trace the product cost flows through the accounts assuming that the companies recorded the purchase of indirect materials in Manufacturing Overhead rather than Raw Materials Inventory. Then, determine the missing amounts in each of the cases that follow.

	Case 1	Case 2
Raw materials, beginning	$ 8,000	$ 2,000
Raw materials, ending	?	1,500
Work in process, beginning	6,500	3,000
Work in process, ending	4,500	3,600
Finished goods, beginning	4,000	2,000
Finished goods, ending	?	2,400
Direct materials used	448,000	35,000
Direct labor incurred	250,000	?
Applied manufacturing overhead	600,000	?
Actual manufacturing overhead	?	20,000
Purchases of direct materials	450,000	?
Overapplied overhead	5,000	1,000
Cost of goods manufactured	?	103,400
Cost of goods sold	1,295,000	?

CASES

C 10.1   Freelance Enterprises recently completed their first fiscal year and developed the following income statement. M. Simone, the manager, can't understand why they are showing a net loss when the number of units sold exceeded expectations. Analyze the following income statement and other information given and write a memo to M. Simone explaining your findings.

FREELANCE ENTERPRISES
Income Statement
For the Year Ending September 30, 1996

Sales (120,000 units)		$1,800,000
Less operating expenses:		
Administrative salaries	$110,000	
Advertising expense	54,000	
Batch-related overhead applied	185,500	
Depreciation on office equipment	34,500	
Depreciation on factory	108,000	
Direct labor salaries	200,000	
Heat, light, and power for offices	20,000	
Heat, light, and power for factory	48,000	
Insurance expense for offices	18,000	
Insurance expense for factory	36,000	
Purchases of raw materials	800,000	
Product-sustaining overhead applied	250,000	
Sales salaries	180,000	
Selling expense	12,000	
Transportation out expense	30,000	
Unit-related overhead applied	100,000	
Total expenses		2,185,500
Net loss		$ 385,500

Additional Information:

1. The ending balances of Raw Materials, Work-in-Process, and Finished Goods inventories were $200,000, $381,750, and $76,350, respectively.
2. There were no indirect materials used in production.
3. Facility-sustaining overhead consists of depreciation on factory; heat, light, and power for factory; and insurance for factory.
4. There was no over- or underapplied overhead at any level.

Appendix:

C 10.2   Lewis Company is a manufacturing firm. An examination of its records reveals the following:

Beginning balance of inventory accounts:	
Raw materials	$10,000
Work-in-process	5,200
Finished goods	16,500

Job status:

Job No. 201 has been started and Job No. 200 has been finished at the beginning of the period.

Job No. 202 and Job No. 203 are started during the period.

Job No. 201 and Job No. 202 are finished during the period.

Job No. 200 and Job No. 201 are sold during the period.

Relevant facts and events:

1. Unit-related overhead is applied to production at $40 per machine hour.
2. Direct labor workers are paid $6 per hour.
3. Purchases of materials were $20,000.
4. Indirect materials issued into production were $2,500.

5. Direct materials issued into production were:

Job No. 201	$ 1,000
Job No. 202	10,000
Job No. 203	9,000

6. Direct labor used in production was:

Job No. 201	200 hours
Job No. 202	300 hours
Job No. 203	450 hours

7. Indirect labor used in production was $2,000.
8. Machine hours used in production were:

Job No. 201	50 hours
Job No. 202	75 hours
Job No. 203	30 hours

9. Miscellaneous manufacturing costs were $2,500.
10. Job Nos. 201 and 202 priced at cost plus 75 percent and are sold on account.
11. Miscellaneous selling and administrative expenses were $8,600 for the period.
12. Under- or overapplied overhead is closed to Cost of Goods Sold.

Required:
a. Prepare a cost of goods manufactured report.
b. Prepare an income statement.
c. Determine the balances in the manufacturing inventory accounts that would appear on the balance sheet at the end of the period.

CRITICAL THINKING

CT 10.1. Refer to P 10.10. The manager of Clarkson Company likes the old way of allocating overhead based on the number of direct labor hours used. Additional information is available as follows:

Direct labor hours expected during the year	4,000
Direct labor hours used during the month:	
For table production	200
For chair production	100
For footstool production	60

Required:
a. Determine the manufacturing overhead rate based on direct labor hours.
b. Determine the overhead cost for each product.
c. Explain why direct labor hours is, or is not, an inappropriate overhead allocation basis for this company.

CT 10.2 Commander Company manufactures three types of computer games: Dragons, Wizards, and Knights. It allocates overhead to the games based on the number of direct labor hours worked on each product. The results of the most recent period are given below.

	Dragons	Wizards	Knights
Units produced and sold	9,000	8,000	7,000
Selling price	$ 45.00	$30.00	$25.00
Less:			
Direct material per unit	5.50	4.25	3.00
Direct labor cost per unit	9.00	2.00	3.00
Manufacturing overhead per unit	27.00	6.00	9.00
Gross margin	$ 3.50	$17.75	$10.00
Less:			
Selling cost per unit	2.25	1.50	1.25
Administrative cost per unit	3.75	3.00	2.75
Net income per unit	$(2.50)	$13.25	$ 6.00

Don, the manager of Commander Company, is concerned that Dragons seems to be a net loser and he is considering whether to drop this game. He has asked you to analyze the situation and make a recommendation. Your analysis reveals that Commander Company has three different levels of overhead—facility sustaining, batch related, and unit related—and that the appropriate overhead rates are $6.00 per square foot, $1,000 per production run, and $4 per unit, respectively. Resource usage during the past period is given below. In addition, you discover that administrative costs are fixed while selling costs are variable per unit.

	Dragons	Wizards	Knights
Square feet occupied	10,000	12,500	15,000
Production runs	9	12	12

Required: *a.* Determine whether Commander Company should drop any game.
   b. Write a memo to Don with your recommendation.

ETHICAL CHALLENGES

EC 10.1   During the period, the following errors were made in the accounting records of Wynet Company.
1. Sales salaries of $400,000 were recorded as direct labor.
2. Depreciation on the offices of $350,000 was recorded as facility-sustaining manufacturing overhead.

The manager of Wynet Company, S. Shurley, doesn't want to correct these errors since the financial statements have already been prepared and sent to stockholders. Shurley argues,

> The errors will correct themselves next year, because the products will be sold, and, therefore, the cost of goods sold next year will be higher. So, over the two-year period, the combined net income will be the same as if the errors had never been made. There is no sense alarming our stockholders for no reason. Furthermore, year-end bonuses have already been paid. If we change our net income number now, we might force our employees to pay back some of their year-end bonuses. We simply can't do that.

Required: Analyze S. Shurley's argument. What would you do if you were in Shurley's position? Why?

EC 10.2   Refer to P 10.10 and CT 10.1. Assume that each product is manufactured in a different department under the supervision of a different manager. Discuss the issues that may arise when choosing one method of applying overhead to production over another method.

Controlling within the Cycles

Part Four presents important information for an organization's decision makers about the evaluation and control of business operations. Accounting information is a useful tool for performing these evaluation and control functions. Chapter 11 addresses the evaluation and control methods surrounding the important area of cash in a business. Information presented in previous chapters comes together in Chapter 12, where the topic turns to the analysis and control of the expenditure and revenue cycles. Financial statement analysis tells interested parties, both inside and outside the organization, how the entity is really "doing."

Chapter 13 addresses the area of production analysis and control. This chapter also introduces recent ideas regarding quality costs and other measures of production and operating efficiency.

CHAPTER 11

Cash: Management and Control

Learning Objectives

1. Explain how companies manage cash by investing excess cash on a short-term basis and raising additional cash through short-term borrowing.
2. Identify the process of and reasons for factoring accounts receivable and discounting notes receivable.
3. Describe cash-related internal controls businesses use.

For Toys 'R' Us, an international toy retailer, the busiest time of year is during the months of November and December. After that time operating activity is relatively slow for six or seven months until the company starts to build inventory for the next busy season.

Most businesses experience increases in cash inflows at certain times of the year. Such inflows of cash may not always coincide with rises in outflows. For example, these opposing flows of cash are exaggerated in seasonal businesses like ski resorts or toy manufacturers.

Toys 'R' Us gains operating efficiency by "managing" its cash in order to use it where and when it is most productive. During the off season, the toy store chain has no need to carry large inventories. So, rather than immediately replacing its sold inventory, the company invests its "idle" cash to provide some return to the company. Toys 'R' Us chooses investments for its idle cash that allow easy conversion back to cash in order to pay vendors when the company starts to build inventory again.

In order to effectively manage its cash in such a cyclical business, Toys 'R' Us must always know what its cash balance is. In addition, it must be able to accurately forecast cash flows so the company knows its expected sources and uses of cash for the coming periods.

CASH: THE ESSENTIAL INGREDIENT

We find businesses that are profitable, yet go bankrupt for lack of cash, while other businesses never show a profit but have enough cash to stay in business. Regardless of how profitable a business is, it has to have cash to survive. In order to have the right amounts of cash at the right times, businesses must manage and safeguard their cash.

We begin this chapter by discussing why businesses keep cash on hand and how they manage their cash in order to have the right amounts available when needed. In terms of cash management, we will describe what businesses do with temporary excess cash and how businesses can obtain cash when they have a temporary shortage of cash. Then, we discuss some of the internal controls businesses use to protect the cash they receive and to ensure proper cash disbursements. Later in the chapter, we discuss the importance of businesses knowing how to determine the correct balance in their cash accounts.

CASH MANAGEMENT: WHO NEEDS IT?

Generally, businesses need to hold cash as a medium of exchange in transactions, but cash held in this way does not earn a return. For our purposes here, a return is an increase in the value of something owned. (Chapter 14 explains the concept of a return in more detail.)

Management constantly faces a trade-off between not having enough cash to make necessary transactions and, at the same time, having cash on hand that generates little or no return. Cash held in checking accounts may pay interest if the company maintains minimum balances. Such interest payments provide the company with a return on the amount held by the bank. However, such interest rates are usually low.

Therefore, businesses are much better off if they place excess cash in investments that yield a better return than interest-bearing checking accounts, as long as the investments also provide ready conversion back to cash. It is possible to convert these types of investments to cash whenever the business needs additional cash.

Why Keep Any Cash?

Typically, businesses keep a minimum of cash on hand and in their checking accounts to pay vendors and employees. Even if the business uses checks for its payments, banks usually require that the company have an amount of cash in the bank account at least as large as the total amount of checks written. Businesses also are likely to hold some additional cash as a precaution, or cushion, against unforeseen events.

The amount needed as a precaution varies greatly from one type of business to another because there are unpredictable cash flows in some businesses due to factors such as their markets and/or their competition. Businesses with more reliable and certain cash inflows and outflows require lower amounts of precautionary holdings.

For example, retail stores typically have enough sales transactions each month or quarter so that they can predict the average amount of sales and, therefore, cash flow. However, because businesses that have a few large transactions, like small real estate offices, find it harder to predict their cash position at any point in time they should hold more cash in their checking accounts as a precaution against periods of slow sales.

Cash balances allow firms to take advantage of unforeseen short-term profit-making opportunities. However, there is a cost to a firm of holding cash. If profit-making opportunities do not arise during the time the business holds the cash, there is no opportunity for the business to generate a return on its cash by investing the cash.

Consider a small manufacturer that makes custom furniture. Suppose a customer requests a large special order and offers a substantially higher than normal price. If the manufacturer has the cash to buy the wood and other materials to make the special order, then it can accept the order and take advantage of the price to make extra profit. However, if the business does not have enough cash on hand to make the unplanned production, it may have to borrow the money to complete the special order.

Money is being added to the economy every day. It is essential that a company have the right amount of cash to transact with people, governments and other businesses.

Suppose, instead, that the furniture manufacturer keeps extra cash in case it receives such special orders, and that the orders never come. In such situations, the manufacturer has not only missed the special orders, but also has earned no return on the cash set aside for that purpose. Thus, management always faces the trade-off between having certain amounts of cash on hand versus investing that cash to earn a return.

Forecasting Cash Flows

The timing of cash receipts and cash payments is crucial to the survival of any organization. Many small businesses have failed, not due to inferior products or services, but because of poor cash management regarding forecasting the timing of cash receipts and payments. Businesses and other organizations should analyze the timing of the receipt of most of their cash as well as the timing of their peak cash outflow points. Such analyses allow businesses to determine both when their cash balances are likely to be more than sufficient and when they might not be adequate to meet operating requirements. Planning cash receipts and disbursements is part of the normal budgeting process. At the end of the period, management analyzes its actual cash inflows and outflows to determine whether the plans were met. We discuss cash analysis in detail in Chapter 24.

PAUSE & REFLECT When making decisions regarding cash, the relevant amounts are the present balance and future inflows and outflows. What are some factors that will affect future cash flows? What information might be used to improve forecasts of future cash flows?

What to Do with Excess (Idle) Cash?

Cash that a business does not need at certain points in time is considered excess, or **idle,** cash, which the business can invest to earn a return. By investing idle cash temporarily, the company can earn return that and increases its net income in order to remain in a position to pay its current liabilities as they become due.

Short-term investments of cash in other liquid assets are known as **temporary investments** because they are invested for period of less than one year—sometimes for as little as a few days. Financial institutions invest their excess cash as loans to individuals, businesses, and other banks.

Most businesses that do not have the magnitude of excess cash found in financial institutions place their excess operating cash in temporary investments such as Treasury bills, certificates of deposit, or money market funds. These investments can improve overall profitability by using otherwise idle cash.

Treasury Bills By buying **Treasury bills,** often called *T-bills*, businesses are essentially making loans to the U.S. government. T-bills are short-term securities issued and backed by the U.S. government, so they are virtually risk-free. Treasury bills typically mature in 3 to 12 months from the date of issue, and their interest rates (the amount of interest they pay) are typically 2 to 4 percentage points below the **prime rate,** which is the interest rate that banks charge their best customers for making loans to them.

As a short-term place to "park" cash, Treasury bills offer the advantages of being risk-free and easy to convert to cash because they mature, that is, the U.S. government repays the loan, in a very short time. In addition, T-bills can be bought and sold on organized exchanges. The disadvantage of Treasury bills is their low rate of interest compared to other investments.

Certificates of Deposit **Certificates of deposit,** called *CDs*, are guaranteed savings deposits placed in banks or savings and loan institutions which are insured by the Federal Deposit Insurance Corporation (FDIC) or the Federal Savings and Loan Insurance Corporation (FSLIC). The company investing cash in certificates of deposit can withdraw it at anytime if necessary. However, there is a substantial penalty for early withdrawal.

Maturity periods for certificates of deposit typically range from three months to five years. Interest rates for CDs are also lower than the prime rate because the CD rate is the amount of money that the bank must pay to borrow funds from depositors, while banks loan money to their customers at the prime rate. Thus, banks make a profit by loaning money at a higher (prime) interest rate than they pay to borrow the money they eventually loan (on certificates).

The advantages of certificates of deposit are that they are insured, or guaranteed, up to certain limits and they pay higher interest rates than Treasury bills. The primary disadvantage of certificates of deposit is that those with longer terms (a year or longer) essentially lock in the investment because of the penalty for early withdrawal. As an investor, it is costly to take early withdrawals, even though it might be possible to invest the amount of cash received in other investments that would yield higher interest rates.

Money Market Accounts **Money market accounts** are similar to checking accounts except that the banks where they are held pay interest on the amount of funds deposited, allow a limited number of withdrawals, and require that the investors maintain a minimum balance in the accounts. The interest rates paid vary widely among institutions, although they typically pay more than the rates paid on personal checking accounts, but less than CD or Treasury rates. Money market accounts are extremely liquid investments because they typically offer a prespecified number of cash withdrawals during each month with no penalty.

Money market accounts are good temporary investments because the amounts invested in these accounts are almost always available. However, the limited number of withdrawals allowed, and relatively low interest rates paid are considered disadvantages.

In summary, when businesses have excess cash that they don't need immediately, they can invest, with fairly low risk, in short-term securities like Treasury bills, certificates of deposit, or money market funds and earn interest while the money remains relatively liquid. We summarize their respective advantages and disadvantages in Exhibit 11.1.

Businesses also have to address the potential problem of having too little cash, which can result from unusual demands on cash, such as unforeseen expenses or cash shortages due to slow sales or collections. Next we discuss what businesses can do about this problem.

EXHIBIT	11.1	Advantages and Disadvantages of Types of Short-Term Investments	
Investment Type	**Advantages**		**Disadvantages**
Treasury bills	Short maturity means good availability; low risk since they are backed by the U.S. government		Low return
Certificates of deposit	Pay higher interest rates than T-bills; federally insured		Longer terms reduce availability; high penalty for early withdrawal
Money market accounts	Withdrawals at any time		Limited number of withdrawals; return lower than T-bills

What Happens When There Is a Shortage of Cash?

When a company is faced with a temporary cash shortage, it must obtain funds from outside sources. Here we discuss some of these sources: financial institutions loans; suppliers who issue notes payable; companies that issue commercial paper; companies that factor accounts receivable; and companies that discount notes receivable. Of course, the cost of borrowing these funds for the borrowing company, or interest, is related to obtaining cash in all cases. Interest can be paid either at maturity when the loan is repaid or at origination when the money is initially borrowed.

Obtaining Short-Term Loans from Financial Institutions   It is possible for businesses to obtain short-term loans from banks and other financial institutions when they need immediate cash. The terms of these loans depend on the length of the borrowing period and the financial institution's perception regarding the company as a credit risk. These loans usually require formal applications, including financial statements of the borrowers, and frequently cover periods ranging from 30 days to one year. One form of these loans is a **note payable,** which is a short-term promise to pay cash supported by a written promissory note. An **interest bearing note** has an explicitly stated interest rate where the amount due at maturity is equal to the face amount of the note plus interest on the note.

Assume that on June 1, 1996, Toys 'R' Us signs a 60-day, $500,000 note payable with a major New York bank. The interest rate charged by the bank for the use of its money is 12 percent. For this particular loan, Toys 'R' Us, the **maker of the note** (party borrowing money using a promissory note), is promising to pay the bank, the **payee of the note** (party lending money using a promissory note), $500,000, the amount of *principal (face value* of the note), *plus* the interest of 12 percent on the amount borrowed for 60 days.

Using the formula to calculate interest on the note, the interest cost for a $500,000, 60-day, 12 percent interest loan is $9,863 ($500,000 × .12 × 60/365). Since the loan is a 60-day note signed on June 1, its due date is July 31. Therefore, on July 31, Toys 'R' Us must pay the financial institution $509,863 ($500,000 principal + $9,863 interest).

Financial institutions' loans to businesses and other organizations also can be structured as a **line of credit,** which, in effect, is a preapproved loan up to a maximum prespecified amount. The amount of the approved line of credit depends on the total needs of the business and the creditworthiness of the business entity as determined by the lending financial institution. Using a line of credit, the business can borrow the amount of cash it needs at any time, up to the amount of the credit limit and any other written terms, and repay the amounts due on the line according to the terms agreed upon.

For example, Toys 'R' Us may establish a $1 million line of credit with the bank, which means that Toys 'R' Us can borrow up to the $1 million limit at any time by simply notifying the bank of the amount that it needs. Toys 'R' Us can repay the borrowed sums as soon as possible as long as the borrowing time period does not exceed the terms of the line of credit agreement. Thus, Toys 'R' Us keeps its interest

DI stands for electronic data interchange. It allows two (or more) businesses to exchange information in a structured format between their computer applications. About half of all transactions between mid- to large-sized corporations in the United States use EDI. Smaller companies use it too because their customers insist that they do.

EDI is becoming a viable way to do business because computer message standards are becoming well-developed and because there is software capable of translating messages received by a computer from another company's computer. Such software is now available for almost every type of computer. Since computers are now able to talk to each other, there is no need for paper to record transactions.

For example, a customer company's computer can determine what inventory items the customer needs by reviewing data about current inventory levels of products. Thus, a customer's computer can draw together information about quantities needed, due dates required, and identification numbers of the inventory items. The computer can place this information into a standard-formatted electronic purchase order and send the purchase order to the supplier's electronic mail box. Upon receipt of the order, the supplier's computer can retrieve the message, send an electronic acknowledgment back to the customer's computer, and begin to go through the procedures required to fill the order within minutes after the customer initiated the order. Then the customer can use an electronic

message to authorize his or her bank to transfer the cash into the supplier's bank account. All these steps can theoretically happen without human intervention and without errors.

When surveying EDI users and potential users about the amount of savings EDI generated per document, the answer was that it saved an average of $3.21. When asked about the reduction in error rates, users said that the average amount of error reduction was 5.5 percent. The survey also asked respondents to compare "total cycle time, from the beginning to end, of the most representative process in your functional area" before and after implementing EDI. The average cycle time dropped from 8.1 to 4.3 days, a savings of almost 100 percent.

EDI has the potential to improve business practices in many areas including sales where the salesperson will no longer be the conduit for sales information and can spend more time consulting, selling, and merchandising. EDI also can lead to changes in a company's credit policies. There will be less ambiguity about when the credit period starts (invoice date, shipment date, or receipt of goods). In addition, companies can substantially shorten discount periods, which were 30 days, when the buyer can pay in as little as 5 days.

EDI directly affects many aspects of doing business and will certainly affect all business aspects indirectly. It is not merely a technology, but a new way to do business.

Adapted from Hill and Swanson, "The Impact of EDI on Credit and Sales," *Business Credit,* January 1995, pp. 24–28.

costs low by borrowing as small an amount as possible for as short a period as possible. Terms of lines of credit often require that the borrower keep a minimum balance at all times in a checking account with a bank to ensure a continuing relationship between the bank and the company.

The disadvantage of a line of credit is that the interest rates typically charged may be higher than other financing alternatives that might be available. The higher rates are due to the fact that the loans are not backed by specific assets that the financial institution could take if the loans were not repaid. The lender charges higher interest rates to compensate for the potential risk of losing the money it loans.

Obtaining Notes Payable from Suppliers   Businesses also can obtain short-term loans from their suppliers. A supplier may require a note payable at the time of purchase, or it can require that the borrower sign a note payable at a later date to settle the borrower's account payable due to the supplier. The company and the supplier often negotiate the terms of these notes that may be affected by the mutual dependency in their relationship. When a business and its supplier have a close relationship, that is, when they operate almost like partners, the terms of the loan usually are much more favorable than the business might be able to obtain from borrowing elsewhere. When the relationship is not close, or if the business cannot obtain financing elsewhere and needs the supplier's products, the business would have to pay higher interest rates to suppliers.

Loans from suppliers may be interest-bearing or noninterest-bearing.

A **noninterest-bearing note** has only a face value but not an interest rate specified on the face of the note. Instead, the supplier actually gives the business less money or goods/services than the amount shown on the note's face value. The difference between the amount of money or services the business receives and the face value of the note is considered to be the interest charge.

For example, assume Toys 'R' Us receives $720,000 of merchandise from Learning Time Toys by signing a 60-day, noninterest-bearing note with a face value of $734,000. In 60 days, Toys 'R' Us must pay Learning Time, $734,000, although it received only $720,000 of merchandise at the time it signed the note. The difference between the value of the merchandise received and the face value of the note, $14,000 ($734,000 – $720,000) is the interest charge for the 60-day period. We calculate the annual interest rate for this noninterest-bearing note as show below:

$$\frac{\text{Face value} - \text{Amount received}}{\text{Face value}} \times \frac{365 \text{ days}}{\text{Length of the loan in days}} = \text{Interest rate}$$

$$\frac{\$14,000}{\$720,000} \times \frac{365}{60} = 11.83\%$$

The $14,000 difference between the merchandise that Toys 'R' Us received and the $734,000 it has to repay after 60 days is equivalent to paying an annual interest rate of 11.83 percent.

Issuing Commercial Paper   **Commercial paper** is a short-term note payable issued in large amounts, typically $100,000 or more, by big companies with very good credit ratings. The maturity of commercial paper is usually 270 days or less, and interest rates are typically slightly below the prime rate. Only nationally recognized companies are able to market their commercial paper because the dealers who manage commercial paper transactions between buyers of the paper and the companies that borrow using commercial paper will not associate with a borrower that is in an uncertain financial position. The risk of default on commercial paper issues is low because borrowers that issue commercial paper typically arrange a line of credit to repay these loans in case the companies are unable to repay the loans at maturity.

Usually pension funds and other large institutional investors purchase commercial paper as investments. These companies earn moderately high interest rates on commercial paper with fairly low risk and maintain liquidity because there is a ready market to sell the commercial paper when they need cash. The borrower of cash—the company issuing commercial paper—benefits from the ability to obtain large amounts of money for short periods of time without having to make costly financing arrangements.

Factoring Accounts Receivable   **Factoring accounts receivable** involves businesses which sell some or all of their accounts receivable for a fee in order to raise cash. The amount of factored receivables depends on the amount of cash the selling company needs. As Exhibit 11.2 shows, after creating accounts receivable through making credit sales, a business might sell its accounts receivable to a third party, called a **factor.** The factor usually assumes the responsibility for collecting the receivables from the customers when the accounts become due. The company selling the receivables would receive immediate cash from the factor, less a fee that the factor charges for its service. The fee compensates the purchaser of receivables for the risk it assumes regarding uncollectible accounts receivable. By selling its accounts receivable, a company obtains cash immediately rather than waiting for the customers to pay. However, the required fees that the company must pay to the factor can be high which can make this option unattractive.

To illustrate, assume that Matherly's, a small specialty toy manufacturer, sells goods on credit to many of its long-time customers and factors some of its accounts receivable every month. Further assume that a local finance company acts as a factor

EXHIBIT | 11.2

Typical Factoring Arrangement

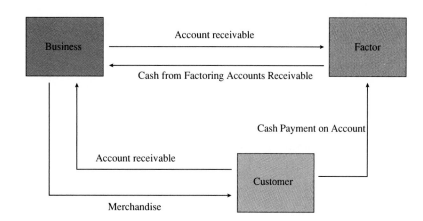

and charges a 15 percent fee for the accounts receivable that it buys. Monthly, Matherly's factors $50,000 of its accounts receivable, and the factor withholds a 10 percent "reserve" for sales returns and allowances during the entire credit term. The factor returns any remainder of the reserve to Matherly's if the amount of sales returns and allowances is less than the amount reserved. Returns and allowances that exceed the reserve are the responsibility of the factor.

Matherly's offers credit terms of net 60 to its customers. The amount of cash immediately available to Matherly's each month is show below.

Amount of accounts receivable factored	$50,000
Less 10% reserve for 60-day period ($50,000 × .10)	(5,000)
Less 15% factoring fee ($50,000 × .15 × 60/365)	(1,233)
Amount of cash immediately available to Matherly's	$43,767

As this illustration shows, the total cost of factoring to the selling company is high. Matherly's receives only $43,767 on its accounts receivable of $50,000, or less than 88 percent of the initial value of its outstanding accounts. Matherly's also may receive a portion of the $5,000 reserve at the end of the 60-day period if returns and allowances related to the factored accounts receivable do not consume the 10 percent reserve.

Discounting Notes Receivable   Businesses can also sell the notes receivable to banks or other third parties who provide the business with immediate cash. These are called **discounted notes receivable** because the amount of the proceeds received by the business selling the note is the difference between the maturity value of the note and the amount of the discount, which is essentially interest. See the calculation below:

$$\begin{array}{ccccc} \text{Discount} = & \text{Maturity} & \times & \text{Discounting} & \times & \text{Discount} \\ \text{amount} & \text{value} & & \text{rate} & & \text{period} \end{array}$$

The **discounting rate** determined by the bank or third party is the rate of interest the purchaser of the note wants to earn. The **discount period** is the time from the date of discount until the note matures.

When a note is discounted, it is transferred either *with* or *without recourse.* When a note is discounted **with recourse,** the company transferring the note is obligated to pay the note if the issuing party fails to do so. **Without recourse** means that the company transferring the note has no further obligation with regard to the note if the maker fails to pay the note when it matures.

Consider this example. Assume that Matherly's sells toys to a chain of specialty toy retailers in resort cities on the lower east coast of the United States. On November 1, 1996, the chain exchanges its $3,000 balance in accounts receivable for a $3,000, 12 percent, 90-day note that matures on January 30, 1997. On December 1, Matherly's needs cash and takes the note to the bank to be discounted. The bank is willing to accept the note at the discount rate of 14 percent. The note receivable's maturity value at January 30 as:

$$\begin{array}{ccc} \text{Maturity} = & \text{Face} & + \text{Interest to} \\ \text{value} & \text{value} & \text{maturity} \end{array}$$

$$\$3,088.77 = \$3,000 + (\$3,000 \times .12 \times 90/365)$$

The amount of proceeds that Matherly's receives on December 1 are determined as:

Discount rate charged by the bank: 14%

Discount period from the date the note is discounted,
December 1, to its maturity date January 30:   60 days

Discount amount ($3,088.77 \times .14 \times 60/365$): $71.08

Cash proceeds to Matherly's ($3,088.77 – $71.08): $3,017.69

Thus, Matherly's is giving up $71.08 of the maturity value of the note in order to have immediate cash of $3,017.69.

We've now completed our discussion of the sources of cash available to meet short-term cash needs as well as the places where businesses can temporarily invest excess cash. Since cash is easily moved and because it is difficult to prove cash ownership, the business must have good control procedures to secure cash. Next we describe controls that businesses use to safeguard cash in their possession and to ensure its proper disbursement.

PAUSE & REFLECT   **If a company discounts a note without recourse, is the discounting rate likely to be higher or lower than a note discounted with recourse?**

INTERNAL CONTROLS TO PROTECT CASH

Security over cash is critical because possession implies ownership. It is impossible to determine who owns cash by simply looking, and there is no realistic way of tracking ownership of cash outside the banking system. Thus, controls over cash receipts and disbursements are an important part of a company's internal control system.

Recall from Chapter 3 that internal control systems can use five general types of procedures: (1) requiring proper authorization for transactions, (2) separating incompatible duties, (3) maintaining adequate documents and records, (4) physically controlling assets and documents, and (5) providing independent checks on performances. All of these are important control procedures over cash receipts and disbursements.

Cash is necessary for virtually everything a business does, including paying for goods, paying employee's wages, and repaying debt. A business can operate for a short time by borrowing cash, but, ultimately, operating activities must yield cash in order for the business to continue. Next we describe cash controls associated with the revenue cycle in which there is an exchange of goods and services for cash. Later we describe controls found in the expenditure cycle in which firms disburse cash to pay for goods and services.

Controls over Cash Receipts

Activities in the revenue cycle are the principal source of cash receipts, although the sources we discussed earlier in the chapter also provide occasional cash receipts. The procedures to protect cash receipts include: physically safeguarding the cash, separating duties of those with custody of cash from those who keep the accounting records, assigning duties so that cash is deposited and recorded as soon as possible after receipt, and having independent checks on cash balances and cash handling procedures.

Many of the sales transactions at retailers like Toys 'R' Us are cash sales. The cash register used to hold cash and checks is an example of physically protecting the asset,

Receipts ensure that the transaction is recorded, so that the records can be compared with the cash on hand.

cash. For each sales transaction, one copy of a sales slip is given to the customer. Sales slips (or sales receipts) provide two control procedures: adequate documentation of the transaction and an opportunity for an independent check by the customer.

You have probably seen stores in places like malls with signs at the cash register that say "If you are not offered a receipt, your purchase is free." This is done because there is rarely adequate supervision of the clerks to ensure that all cash received by clerks is placed in the register. Such a policy allows owners and managers who cannot observe whether the money is put in the cash register to safeguard the cash received. In order for the clerk to give the customer a receipt, the transaction must get recorded in the register. Someone independent from such transactions can compare the amount of money in the register at the end of a shift with the recorded sales. This serves as a check to ensure that receipts (cash, checks, and charge slips) equal the amount of sales. Another good control is to deposit the receipts each day from the register into the bank to secure the cash. This results in keeping only a minimum amount of cash in the register, which is the amount of cash "at risk."

Cash received from credit sales or in advance of sales requires different controls. These cash receipts arrive in the company's mail room, along with part of the customer invoice known as a **remittance advice,** which indicates the amount paid, or remitted, by the customer. The mail clerk should separate the checks or cash immediately from the remittance advice and make a list of both the cash received and who sent it. A person who does not have access to the accounting system should deposit the cash into the bank as soon as possible. The cash receipts should be recorded by someone who does not have access to the cash itself. This segregation of duties is a control which makes it unlikely that one person acting alone can divert the company's cash without being detected because it prevents access to both the cash itself and the accounting records related to the cash received.

A means of both protecting cash receipts and speeding the availability of cash receipts is through use of a **lockbox collection system.** Large businesses with customers that are geographically dispersed, like major oil companies and retailers whose customers make credit purchases with the business's credit card, use lockbox systems to collect cash receipts from customers.

In a lockbox system, the business establishes bank accounts at various locations around the area where their customers live. Then, the customers mail their payments to the post office ("locked box") of the business's bank nearest to them. Each day the bank collects the cash receipts, deposits the cash into the business's account, and sends the business a listing of the customer receipts. This provides good cash control because it segregates the duties of cash handling and depositing from the business personnel's other duties. And it makes the cash available to the business quicker than it would be if customers mailed payments to the company itself.

Controls over Cash Disbursements

The expenditure cycle includes making cash disbursements. As a business receives goods and services, it usually either pays in cash or promises to pay later by purchasing on credit. The main concern with cash disbursements is that all expenditures should be made *only* for items the business has approved. Control procedures over cash disbursements include: (1) separating the responsibilities of check writing, check signing, check mailing, and keeping the accounting records, and (2) ensuring that payments are properly authorized.

The segregation of the various duties in paying obligations serves the same role that it does elsewhere in the control system—that is, it makes it difficult for one person to divert company assets. The strongest control over cash disbursements is to have a company policy requiring proper authorization for payments. Often different purchase amounts require different levels of authorization. Small purchases often are authorized by various persons throughout an organization, while purchases of major investments, such as purchases by Southwest Airlines of $3 billion worth of jets from Boeing, would require recommendation of the CEO (chief executive officer) and approval by the company's board of directors.

Controls over cash are important, and the segregation of incompatible duties is a very effective control for both receipts and disbursements. Physical protection is particularly important for cash receipts, while for cash disbursements it is important to be sure that they are properly authorized. Now we'll describe an important way of determining whether the Cash account reflects the correct amount of the company's cash.

PAUSE & REFLECT

In small businesses, proper segregation of duties for cash handling is often impossible. What other procedures could be used instead of segregation of duties to ensure adequate internal control?

What Is the Cash Balance?

Most businesses use a double-entry accounting system and depend on a system of internal controls to help ensure that transactions are properly recorded on their books. However, it is a good idea to periodically compare any business's records against the records of outside parties as an additional check on accuracy, especially regarding the important area of cash. This might require comparing the company's balance of a customer's account receivable with the customer or verifying the amounts of accounts payable due to vendors with the amounts due according to the vendors themselves.

Several procedures in accounting systems can do this. For example, monthly statements of accounts sent to customers who can independently verify balances are a good check on the accuracy of the recorded accounts receivable balance at a certain point in time.

In order to verify the balance in the Cash account, businesses periodically compare the amount that they have recorded in their accounts with the balance recorded by the bank responsible for handling their checking accounts.

Maybe the Bank Knows Banks record in their customers' accounts the results of every transaction that involves checks and cash deposits, along with other cash-related events originated by the banks, such as service charges. **Service charges** are fees that banks charge customers for the benefit of providing customers with the bank accounts. Service charges vary widely in amount, depending on the type of account as well as the financial institution. In addition to service charges, a bank also would record interest that the business has earned on its cash due to the bank's use of the business's money for the period. However, not all checking accounts are interest-bearing, particularly those with small average balances.

Another item that a bank knows about before the business with an account at the bank does is the amount of **nonsufficient funds (NSF) checks.** When the business deposits a customer's check, the amount of the check is credited to the business's bank account. If the customer's check amount exceeds the balance in the customer's bank account, that is, if there are not sufficient funds in the customer's account, the check is returned to the business's bank by the customer's bank with the NSF designation. The business's bank then deducts the check amount from the business's account and notifies the business of the NSF check. In addition, the bank normally charges an NSF fee to the business because of the work required to correct the account balance and return the check to the depositor.

Bank statements are reports sent by banks to their customers showing all the transactions in each customer's cash account for the period (typically a month), including: (1) the beginning and ending balance of the account according to the bank's books, (2) the total amount deposited to the account during the period, together with a detailed listing of the individual deposits, (3) the total amount withdrawn from the account during the period, along with the amounts of individual checks and other withdrawals, and (4) any additional charges against or credits to the account according to the bank, such as service charges or interest earned.

The amount shown on the bank statement for service charges is deducted from the bank's balance, and the amount shown as interest earned on the bank statement is added to the business's bank balance. If any NSF checks reach the bank shortly before the bank statements are mailed to the business customers, they will be included along with the bank statement. Both the NSF check and the NSF fee are deducted from the bank's balance.

The bank knows about all of these types of events and transactions and has recorded their effects when determining the customer's cash balance. However, the customer may not be aware of all of these items that will appear on the bank statement.

Maybe the Bank Does Not Know   The bank will not know the actual cash balance of its customers' accounts at any point in time because businesses often record payments and deposits in their records before the bank becomes aware of them. Thus, some items affecting the business's cash balance of which the business is aware become known later by the bank, for example, outstanding checks and deposits in transit.

Outstanding checks are written and mailed by the business and deducted in the business's Cash account, but the bank has not processed them yet. Therefore, the *amount of outstanding checks is not deducted from the business's bank balance* at the end of the bank statement period.

Deposits in transit are deposits that the business has recorded in its cash records and sent to the bank or put in the night depository. However, *the bank has not received and recorded the amounts of deposits in transit.*

It Takes Two to Reconcile!   Usually, at the time the bank issues the bank statement, neither the bank nor its business customer has updated its records to reflect all information required for a correct cash balance at any point in time. Thus, it is necessary to reconcile the business's and bank's books at the end of each period. This provides an opportunity to calculate the correct cash balance that should be reflected in the business's account at that time.

Because the amount recorded as cash in the business's records is rarely the same as the amount recorded in the bank's records, businesses (or other bank customers) must periodically prepare a **bank reconciliation.** This control procedure requires that the company periodically adjust the recorded cash amounts in its records to reflect any differences between its cash balance and the cash balance according to the bank.

A bank reconciliation is an important internal control procedure because it allows for the detection of errors, either on the business's books or in the business's account at the bank. The bank reconciliation process helps ensure that all checks and deposits are recorded properly in the business records.

Internal Control Considerations As part of good control over cash, companies should have their bank reconciliations done on a regular basis by an employee who is involved in neither the receipt nor the deposit of cash, nor the approval or payment of cash payments for liabilities. This segregation of duties serves as an effective check on the persons writing the checks or making deposits at the bank because the person doing the bank reconciliation would detect any irregularities.

During the reconciliation process, the person performing the reconciliation would look for checks for unauthorized purposes, such as unauthorized checks to employees, or checks to pay obligations that were not debts of the business. Reconciliations performed by a employee who is independent of cash transactions also can help detect whether the amounts deposited differ from the amounts that should have been deposited. If the proper amount was not deposited, an independent person would report any differences he or she finds because this person would not have been involved in misappropriation.

What Does the Reconciliation Do? Reconciling the business's cash balance with the balance recorded by the bank highlights any differences due to timing of withdrawals, deposits, and other account increases and decreases. It, therefore, allows unrecorded items to be reflected in the records of the business and the bank and for errors to be corrected.

A good approach to reconciling timing differences is, first, to ask the question Who has not yet recorded the item? If the answer is the bank, it is necessary to adjust the bank's balance by the amount of the item. If the answer is the business, it is necessary to adjust the business's balance by the amount of the appropriate item. The next decision to make is to indicate whether the item(s) will increase or decrease the cash balance. After highlighting and recording these timing differences, the responsible company employee can look for any errors or irregularities that may exist.

There are a variety of approaches to preparing a bank reconciliation. We show the two-column approach where *both the cash balance according to the bank and the cash balance according to the books are reconciled to an adjusted "correct" balance.* If the reconciliation is done correctly, and if there are no errors in either the business's or the bank's books, the adjusted bank and the adjusted book balances will equal after reconciliation.

Reconciliation Illustrated Before doing a bank reconciliation, consider how banks report customers' accounts on monthly bank statements. From the bank's perspective, the customer's cash deposits, which are an asset to the company (the bank's customer), represent a liability to the bank. When a business or other customer deposits cash and checks in its bank account, or when the customer earns interest on cash deposited, there is an increase in the balance of the customer's account. Increases in customers' bank accounts are reflected as increased liabilities on the bank's records. Thus, increases in the customer's account are reported on the bank statement as credits. Conversely, banks reflect decreases in the customer's account due to checks written, cash withdrawals, or service charges as debits in their records.

The following example illustrates the bank reconciliation shown in Exhibit 11.3. Exhibit 11.4 shows the February 12, 1997 bank statement that Learning Time Toys receives from its bank on February 14, 1997.

By comparing the list of individual deposits and checks recorded in Learning Time's account by the bank, the employee responsible for the business's reconciliation noted the following things:

- Three (outstanding) checks totaling $3,320.51 have not cleared the bank.

- A deposit (in transit) of $389.74 made on the last night of the accounting period has not been recorded by the bank.

- The ending balance in the Cash account per the business's records is $7,598.28.

The actual cash amount (balance per bank) reconciles to a balance of $6,639.63, which is the correct balance for the Cash account in the general ledger on February 12. Thus, it should be the amount included in the company's periodic financial statements

EXHIBIT | 11.3 | Bank Reconciliation

LEARNING TIME TOYS
Bank Reconciliation
February 14, 1997

Balance per bank		$9,520.40
Add: Deposits in transit	$ 389.74	
Error	50.00	
Deduct: Outstanding checks	3,320.51	
Adjusted balance per bank		$6,639.63
Balance per books		$7,598.28
Add: interest earned		90.85
Deduct:		
Service charge	$ 25.50	
NSF check	500.00	
NSF fee	15.00	
Error	9.00	
Error	500.00	
Adjusted balance per books		$6,639.63

if the accounting period ended on that date. Notice, however, that the current balance recorded in the Cash account (balance per books) is $7,598.28. Therefore, Learning Time will need to adjust its book cash balance by making journal entries to reflect the correct cash balance.

Any item added to or deducted from the balance per the books in the reconciliation requires a journal entry. In this case, Learning Time should add the $90.85 in interest earned to its cash balance and deduct the $25.50 service charge, the $500 NSF check, and the associated $15 fee, which are found on the bank statement (Exhibit 11.4).

The check for $500 from Stonehouse Development Center was originally recorded as an increase in cash and a decrease in accounts receivable. However, since the check is not good, Learning Time must reverse this original entry to indicate

EXHIBIT | 11.4

Bank Statement

Coastal National Bank
Richmond, Virginia 20096

Statement of Account

Statement period	*Account number*	*Account description*
1/12/97 thru 2/12/97	9217321-9	checking

SUMMARY

Learning Time Toys
7293 West 10th Avenue
Richmond, Virginia 20098

9,050.83 begin
112,626.60 credits
112,157.03 debits
9,520.40 ending

DATE	AMOUNT	DESCRIPTION
1/13	15,256.20	deposit
1/17	20,941.88	deposit
1/21	22,119.13	deposit
1/23	17,876.62	deposit
1/28	19,010.09	deposit
2/4	500.00	NSF check
2/4	15.00	NSF fee
2/8	17,331.83	deposit
2/12	90.85	int.
2/12	25.50	ser. chg.

CK.	AMOUNT	DAY	CK.	AMOUNT	DAY	CK.	AMOUNT	DAY
9852	20,983.00	13	9853	18,350.32	18	9854	2,851.19	20
9855	28,132.27	22	9856	3,311.91	27	9859	3,008.20	31
9860	988.43	03	9861	16,707.76	05	9863	17,783.45	09

EXHIBIT | 11.5 | Errors Found in Learning Time's Bank Reconciliation

Error	Effect and Proper Correction
1. A check properly written for $76.76 to pay an account payable was recorded by the business as $67.76.	Learning Time's Cash and Accounts Payable accounts are overstated by $9 ($76.76 – $67.76). The company must reduce Cash and Accounts Payable by $9.
2. A check written for $500 for rent was never recorded in the business's books.	Learning Time's Cash is overstated and its Rent Expense (or Prepaid Rent) accounts are understated by $500. It must record the $500 decrease in Cash along with the debit to either Rent Expense or Prepaid Rent, depending on the circumstances.
3. The bank charged the business $50 for a check written by another business with a checking account number similar to Learning Time's.	Learning Time's books are correct. The bank needs to add $50.00 to Learning Time's account.

that it received no cash and, therefore, should reflect no increase in its Cash account. This reversal of the original entry accomplishes two things: (1) it results in the correct cash balance being reflected in Learning Time's Cash account records, and (2) since Stonehouse still owes the business $500, its account at Learning Time now reflects this. In addition, there will be a charge to Stonehouse for the NSF fee, so Stonehouse now owes the Learning Time Toys an additional $15, for a total of $515.

The final reconciling items Learning Time must address are errors. Errors can be made by either, or both, the bank and the company. If the bank made an error, Learning Time should notify the bank and request an immediate correction. If Learning Time made an error, it should make an entry correct its records immediately.

During its bank reconciliation, Learning Time Toys discovered the errors shown in Exhibit 11.5. The first two errors were made by the business and require journal entries to correct the balance in its Cash account. The last error was made by the bank. Learning Time should notify the bank as soon as it discovers the bank's error so that the bank can correct the error.

As we've seen, cash is an essential part of doing business. The controls and procedures for cash are extensive and expensive. So how can businesses reduce the cost of protecting cash? The next section describes a way of protecting cash and reducing the cost of the procedures for making cash disbursements.

PAUSE & REFLECT

In virtually every bank reconciliation there will be outstanding checks and deposits in transit. What are some of the reasons the bank has not recorded these items? Do any of these reasons indicate internal control weaknesses in the business? If so, what control weaknesses do they indicate?

Making "Small" Cash Disbursements

The cash disbursement system described previously in this chapter is an excellent internal control mechanism, but it is expensive to operate because every transaction requires high-level authorization and control. To make "small" cash disbursements at lower processing costs, businesses use what we call *imprest cash accounts*.

Imprest Cash Accounts Routine transactions that involve relatively small amounts of cash should not need authorization by upper-level management. One way of providing cost-effective controls over these kinds of transactions is by using imprest cash accounts. **Imprest cash accounts** are established for fixed amounts, and commonly are used either to pay small amounts or routine cash payments such as payroll. The person responsible for these accounts usually is a lower-level department manager.

What we mean by *small* amounts is determined by the specific organization. Typically, a large business sets a dollar limit beyond which the purchasing department must be involved in approving transactions. If purchasing department involvement is required, it processes purchase orders, determines the lowest possible price for purchases, and, for expensive items, conducts a competitive bidding process with vendors to obtain reasonable price bid comparisons.

For "small" purchases, maybe those that amount to from $200 to $500 in many cases, the expense of following the formal purchasing procedures is greater than the potential savings it offers. Therefore, businesses establish an authorized amount of funds to include in the imprest cash accounts to pay for these small transactions. This does not require the level of approval and administrative costs that larger purchases require.

Once the business approves and makes the purchase, the vendor sends the invoice, which is compared with the receipt of goods or services at the time of the purchase to ensure that the details of the goods sent match the goods received. If the amounts and terms of the invoice agree with the goods received, the company approves the invoice for payment from the imprest cash fund.

The imprest fund contains enough cash to pay for transactions that are expected to occur over a specified time period, such as a month or a quarter. Someone within the department other than the person who authorizes disbursements usually maintains the fund records. At the end of the period, or when the fund runs low, the person in charge of the imprest account submits copies of the receipts and other documentation for purchases made during the period. Then the treasurer or controller issues a check to reimburse the account for the total amount of the purchases. This restores the fund to its original preapproved total. Now we will consider the petty cash fund as an example of an imprest cash fund.

Petty Cash Funds Many companies find it useful to keep a small amount of cash on hand for immediate small cash disbursements. A **petty cash fund** is an imprest account (fund) maintained for the immediate use of small amounts of cash. The fund is initially started by writing a check for cash on the business's bank account. The check is cashed, and the money is placed in a locked box and kept on the premises. The person responsible for the petty cash fund is often an office manager or someone with similar adminstrative responsibility. This person should not be involved with any other cash receipts or payments. This helps ensure that the fund is used only for the intended purpose and that other cash is not used for unauthorized purposes. In this case, such a segregation of duties makes it difficult to substitute cash from one source for cash from another source. For example, cash from the petty cash fund could not be substituted for the cash on hand for sales transactions because different individuals would be responsible for each cash source.

Whenever authorized employees or managers need small amounts of cash immediately, they receive cash from the petty cash fund. For example, assume that the toy manufacturer, Matherly's, ran out of paper for the office copier and needed more copier paper immediately. The office clerk receives $40 from the petty cash fund and when the clerk returns with the paper, he or she must give the office manager in charge of the petty cash fund the receipt for $33.94 from the paper purchase and the change from the $40. The receipt is placed in the petty cash box, along with the $6.06 in change. At all times, the total of the receipts plus the remaining cash should equal the beginning (authorized) amount in the petty cash fund.

When the cash balance in the Petty Cash account becomes low or when an accounting period ends, it is necessary to replenish the petty cash fund. At that time, the person in charge would remove the receipts from the cash box and record the related transactions in the business's books as debits to the appropriate expense accounts for which the payments were made. The difference between the beginning petty cash balance and the remaining amount of petty cash itself would be credited at that time to the Cash account. Then a check written on the company's Cash account is cashed and the cash is used to replenish the petty cash fund to its original balance.

Whether we generate cash through operations or borrow it, making sure that cash is safeguarded and used only for authorized uses is important. Bank reconciliations and maintenance of a petty cash fund are efficient and relatively low cost ways to protect cash.

SUMMARY

The importance of cash cannot be overemphasized. Virtually all business transactions require cash. But since cash itself doesn't provide a return, having too much on hand is not a good business practice. Businesses need to invest as much of their excess cash as possible and provide good, cost-effective controls over the cash they hold.

- Cash management involves planning the amount of cash needed for necessary operations and placing excess cash in investments to yield a return. Such investments include Treasury bills, certificates of deposit, or money market funds, which readily convert back to cash.

- Companies can obtain needed short-term funds by borrowing from outside sources, including financial institutions and suppliers, issuing notes and commercial paper, factoring accounts receivable, and discounting notes receivable.

- Controls to safeguard cash include performing bank reconciliations on a regular basis to determine the correct cash balance in the accounts at a point in time and to detect errors either in the business's Cash account or in its account at the bank.

- One way to reduce the cost of controls over cash is by using imprest cash accounts. They provide cost-effective controls over routine transactions involving relatively small cash amounts that do not need upper-level management authorization.

KEY TERMS

bank reconciliation A control procedure performed periodically by a company to adjust the recorded cash amounts and to reflect any differences between its cash balance and the cash balance according to the bank's

bank statements Reports sent by banks to their customers showing all transactions in the customer's cash account during the period

certificates of deposit (CDs) Guaranteed savings deposits placed in banks or savings and loan institutions

commercial paper Short-term notes payable issued in large amounts typically by big companies with very good credit ratings

deposits in transit Deposits in the bank and recorded on the company's books that have not been recorded by the bank

discount period The period of time from the date of discount until the note matures

discounted notes receivable Notes receivable that a business sells to a bank or other third party; the proceeds equal maturity value less the amount of discount (interest)

discounting rate The rate determined by the bank or third party purchasing the note. It is the rate the purchaser wants to earn

factor A third party that pays cash to a company for some or all of the company's accounts receivable

factoring accounts receivable The process involved when a company sells some or all of its accounts receivable to a third party for a fee in order to obtain immediate cash

idle cash Excess cash. Cash held which exceeds the company's immediate needs

imprest cash accounts Cash accounts established in fixed amounts to pay small, routine cash amounts

interest-bearing note A note with an explicitly stated interest rate where the amount due at maturity is equal to the face amount of the note plus interest on the note

line of credit A preapproved loan that allows the borrower to request money when needed up to the total preapproved amount of the line

lockbox collection system A company's cash collection system which requires that customers mail payments to a post office ("locked box") near a business's bank

maker of a note The party borrowing money using a promissory note

money market accounts Accounts that pay interest on the amount of funds deposited, allow a limited number of withdrawals, and require a mimimum balance

noninterest-bearing note A note that has only a face value but not an interest rate specified on the face of the note

nonsufficient funds checks (NSF) Checks written for amounts that are greater than the balance of the bank account on which they are written

note payable A short-term promise to pay cash supported by a written promissory note

outstanding check Checks written, mailed, and deducted from a business's Cash account, but not processed by the bank

payee of a note The party lending money using a promissory note

petty cash fund An imprest account, or fund, maintained for the immediate use of small amounts of cash

prime rate The interest rate banks charge to their best customers

remittance advice A document returned (remitted) to the company by a customer with his or her payment on account to ensure proper credit to the account

service charges Fees charged by banks for the benefit of providing customers with the bank accounts

temporary investments Short-term investments of cash in other liquid assets

Treasury bills Short-term securities issued and backed by the U.S. government

with recourse The party (company) transferring a note is obligated to pay if the issuing party fails to do so

without recourse The party (company) transferring a note has no further obligation if the issuing party fails to pay

QUESTIONS

1. Explain why it is necessary for a business to keep cash.
2. What is the opportunity cost of holding cash?
3. What are the advantages and disadvantages of purchasing Treasury bills as a temporary investment rather than keeping cash in a checking account?
4. What are the advantages and disadvantages of purchasing certificates of deposit rather than Treasury bills as a temporary investment?
5. What are the advantages and disadvantages of putting cash in a money market account rather than a checking account?
6. What are the advantages and disadvantages of using financial institution loans as a means of short-term credit?
7. What are the advantages and disadvantages of using supplier-generated notes payable rather than borrowing from a financial institution as a means of short-term credit?
8. What is a noninterest-bearing note payable? Is it really interest-free? Why or why not?
9. What are the advantages and disadvantages of using commercial paper rather than borrowing from a financial institution as a means of short-term credit?
10. Describe the process of factoring accounts receivable.
11. Why would a company want to factor its accounts receivable?
12. Describe the process of discounting notes receivable.
13. Why would a company want to discount its notes receivable?
14. What is meant by the term *with recourse?* From the seller's point of view, is with recourse or without recourse preferable? Why?
15. What are the five general procedures for protecting cash?
16. What is a lockbox system and why do companies use these systems?
17. What are the purposes of a bank reconciliation?
18. Who should have the responsibility for preparing the bank reconciliation? Why?
19. What is meant by outstanding checks and deposits in transit?
20. What is an NSF check?
21. In general, how do you decide how to treat a particular reconciliation item?
22. Explain why companies maintain imprest cash accounts.
23. Explain how an imprest petty cash fund operates.

EXERCISES

E 11.1   Barlow Company needs funds temporarily. Management is deciding whether to give up discounts from one of its three largest suppliers or to borrow from its bank at 15 percent for three months. The suppliers terms are given below:

Anderson Company	1/10, n/30
Colby Enterprises	2/15, n/60
Dexter, Inc.	3/10, n/90

Which is the best source of temporary funds for Barlow Company? Why?

E 11.2   Williams uses a central collection system to process its cash receipts from customers. Currently, it takes an average of six days for mailed checks to be received, three days for them to be processed, and two days for the checks to clear the bank. A lockbox system, which would cost $4,000 per month, would reduce the mail and processing time to four days. The average daily collections are $150,000 and the money market rate of interest is 6 percent. Should Williams adopt the lockbox system? Explain.   *(CMA Adapted)*

E 11.3   Tyrone Company must borrow money in order to pay a supplier's invoice within the discount period. The invoice amount is $66,000 and the terms are 2/15, n/45. The company is able to borrow money for 30 days at 12 percent interest, but it must maintain a balance in its cash account of 10 percent of the loan amount as a compensating balance. Should Tyrone borrow the money and if so, how much must it borrow? Why?

E 11.4   Sae Won Company can issue $500,000 of commercial paper for six months and receive cash of $450,000. The transaction costs will be $6,500. What is the effective annual interest cost of issuing the commercial paper?

E 11.5   What is the opportunity cost of not accepting credit terms of 3/15, n/60, if the company can earn 8 percent in its money market account?

E 11.6   Describe the internal control that is lacking in the following situation. The cashier has been pocketing money from cash sales.

E 11.7   How would you prevent the following situation from occurring? The office manager, who is authorized to sign checks in the absence of the president, has been stealing money from the petty cash fund she controls.

E 11.8   Describe the internal control that is lacking in the following situation: The company allows the cashier to make small payments for various miscellaneous items with cash from the cash register. He is required to make note of the amount and reasons for payments so that the accountant can record the expense.

E 11.9   Jefferson, Inc., has a $1,000 invoice that is due in 60 days. If Jefferson pays the invoice in 10 days, it can take advantage of a 2 percent cash discount offered by the supplier. Alternatively, Jefferson can invest the money in a money market account paying 6 percent annual interest. Should Jefferson, Inc., pay the invoice within 10 days? Why or why not?

E 11.10   On June 1, 1997, William Cosby gave a $150,000, 90-day, 7 percent note to Poindexter Corporation for a stage set the company manufactures. July 1, 1997, Poindexter Company took the note to its bank and discounted the note without recourse.

a. What are the proceeds of the note if the bank discounts the note using a 12 percent rate?

b. Is Poindexter responsible for the note if William Cosby fails to pay the note at its maturity date? Why or why not?

E 11.11   Barker Company often factors its accounts receivable. The finance company requires an 8 percent reserve and charges a 1.5 percent fee on the amount of the receivable factored. The *remaining amount* to be advanced is further reduced by an annual factoring charge of 16 percent. What amount will Barker Company receive if it factors $110,000 of accounts receivable that are due in 60 days?

(CMA Adapted)

E 11.12   At the end of November, Hutchinson Company had a general ledger cash balance of $7,810. The bank statement on November 30 showed a balance of $8,315. What is the amount of deposits in transit, assuming the only other reconciling items consist of a service charge of $7 and outstanding checks of $825?

E 11.13   Colby Industries' bank statement had a balance of $12,978 on April 30. Its general ledger Cash account showed a balance of $12,845 on that date. What is the amount of its outstanding checks if the only other reconciling items are service charges of $12, a nonsufficient funds check of $65, and deposits in transit of $480?

E 11.14   Hays Company has the information shown below available on May 31. Prepare the bank reconciliation for May.
  a. Cash balance in the general ledger, $9,170.
  b. Ending balance on the bank statement, $9,400.
  c. A deposit of $685 made after the close of banking hours on May 31.
  d. Checks issued by the company but not yet cleared through the bank, $920.
  e. A $5 charge on the bank statement for servicing the account in May.

E 11.15   Barnard Sporting Goods established a petty cash fund of $150 on March 1. During the month, payments were made, and signed petty cash vouchers were obtained, for the following items.

Postage expense	$33.50
Office supplies	23.70
Repairs expense	15.85
Freight in	38.65
Miscellaneous expense	14.30

How much cash should be in the petty cash fund on March 31?

PROBLEMS

P 11.1   Dillon Company needs cash on a short-term basis. It has three options available to it:
  1. Factor accounts receivable of $500,000 that are due in 30 days. The factor charges a 5 percent reserve and the factoring fee is 20 percent.
  2. Discount a 60-day, $500,000 note receivable that is due in 30 days with no recourse. The note has a stated rate of interest of 10 percent, and the bank charges a 15 percent discounting rate.
  3. Borrow $500,000 for 30 days at 18 percent interest.

Required: a. Determine the amount of cash generated from each option.
  b. Which option is most desirable?
  c. Would your answer change if the note was discounted with recourse? Why or why not?

P 11.2   Your company has just factored accounts receivable of $97,500 for $80,000 *with recourse*. Should this transaction be shown as a *sale of receivables* or *short-term borrowing?* Why?

P 11.3   The Wallenburg Corporation has decided to factor $40,000 of its accounts receivable due in 30 days to Allegeny Credit Company. The terms of the factoring agreement call for a 5 percent reserve for sales returns and allowances to be established and a factoring fee of 13 percent.

Required: a. How much cash will Wallenburg get immediately when they factor these accounts receivable?
  b. Is there any chance that Wallenburg will get any more cash from these accounts receivable later? Explain your answer.
  c. If Wallenburg's customers do not pay, what recourse does Allegeny Credit Company have against Wallenburg? Explain, please.

P 11.4   The Lopez Corporation received a $60,000 60-day, 8 percent note receivable in payment for one of its machines from the Tai Company on March 31, 1995. On April 15, 1995, Lopez discounted Tai's note with recourse at its bank. The bank used a 10 percent discounting rate.

Required: a. How much cash did Lopez receive as a result of discounting the note?
  b. Is Lopez responsible for the note if Tai does not pay the note when it is due?
  c. If Lopez wants to discount this note without recourse, will the interest rate charged by the bank be higher or lower than 10 percent? Why?

P 11.5   Mica Company maintains a petty cash fund of $500. During May the following payments were made from the fund.

May 2 $12.50 freight charge on merchandise purchased for resale.
5    $30.00 to students to distribute advertising circulars in shopping center parking lots.
8    $22.80 for flowers for an employee's funeral.
10    $25.00 for cleaning oil paintings in office reception room.
11    $58.30 for office supplies.
16    $50.00 for postage stamps.
19    $18.80 to salesperson for entertaining customers.
20    $66.90 for office supplies.
23    $23.60 freight charge on merchandise purchased for resale.

Since the fund always has a sizable balance at the end of the month, it is to be reduced for $500 to $350.

Required: *a.* Determine the amount of the check written to replenish the fund for the new balance of $350 assuming that the petty cash fund was in balance at the end of the period.
b. What would happen if only $190 in cash was in the fund at the end of the month?

P 11.6   Sabetha Company keeps a petty cash fund of $500. During February, the following payments were made from the fund.
- $18.50 to repair broken window.
- $85.75 for office supplies.
- $125.00 for travel advance for salesperson.
- $21.50 for flowers for conference room.
- $16.35 for advertising.
- $75.00 for charity.
- $26.40 for postage.
- $68.80 for office supplies.

Cash on hand on February 28 was $62.70.

Required: *a.* Determine the amount of the check written to replenish the fund.
b. Does the petty cash fund balance prior to the check being written to replenish it?

P 11.7   Information related to the Cash account of Seacraft Limited for July is given below.
a. The ending balance per books is $12,874.63.
b. The bank statement balance on July 31 is $13,257.27.
c. The following checks are outstanding on July 31: check 742 for $132.68; 758 for $356.44; 762 for $87.32; and 765 for $563.70.
d. Cash receipts deposited in the bank on the evening of July 31 totaled $718.53.
e. A credit memo for $1,242 included in the bank statement is for the collection of noninterest-bearing note by the bank for Seacraft Limited. The note receivable was for $1,250, and the bank charged a fee of $8 for the service.
f. A debit memo for $248.27 included in the bank statement is for an NSF check from Everett Jones.
g. A check for $843.10 written by another company was erroneously charged to Seacraft's account by the bank.
h. Included among the checks paid by the bank is check 735 for $153.60, which had been stolen. The check was paid by the bank after Seascraft had issued a stop payment order to the bank.
i. A deposit of $815.63 on July 23 was properly recorded by the bank, although it was erroneously recorded in the books as $851.63. These were collections on accounts receivable.

Required: 1. Prepare a bank reconciliation for July.
2. Determine the amount of cash to be shown on the July 31 balance sheet.

P 11.8 The following information was obtained from the books of Mason Products for the month of March.

Cash Receipts (CR)			Cash Payments (CP)		
Date	Amount		Date	Check No.	Amount
March 4	$ 228.00		March 3	415	$ 375.00
March 8	187.00		March 9	416	80.00
March 14	392.00		March 13	417	160.00
March 20	256.00		March 18	418	235.00
March 25	243.00		March 21	419	95.00
March 31	319.00		March 28	420	540.00
	$1,625.00		March 29	421	105.00
			March 31	422	330.00
					$1,920.00

Cash

2-28 Balance	2,387.00		3-31 CP	1,920.00
3-31 CR	1,625.00			
3-31 Balance	?			

The bank statement for March is presented below.

Sentinel National Bank 1443 Woodlawn Avenue			
In account with:	Mason Products 1804 Oak Street		
Date	Checks and Other Debit Items	Deposits	Balance
March 1	Balance forwarded		2,316.00
March 1		356.00	2,672.00
March 4	285.00	228.00	2,615.00
March 8	375.00	187.00	2,427.00
March 14	80.00 160.00	392.00	2,579.00
March 19	235.00		2,344.00
March 20		256.00	2,600.00
March 25	95.00 170.00 NSF	243.00	2,578.00
March 27	150.00 15.00 SC		2,413.00
CM = Credit Memo NSF = Nonsufficient Funds Check		DM = Debit Memo SC = Service Charge	

Additional Information:

1. The reconciliation on February 28 included the following two items:

   Outstanding check 412 $285

   Deposit in transit $356

2. The service charge includes a $5 fee for the nonsufficient funds check.
3. The nonsufficient funds check was from Mark Edgerston and was included in Mason Products deposit on March 27.
4. Check 421 issued on March 29 for office supplies was for $150. The bookkeeper made a transposition error in recording the check in the cash payments journal.

Required: *a.* Prepare the bank reconciliation for March.

b. Determine the cash balance that should appear on the March 31 balance sheet.

P 11.9 The ending cash balance for Darby Foods on September 30, 1995, was $16,427.18. Appropriate portions of the cash receipts and cash payments records are illustrated below.

Cash Receipts		Cash Payments	
Date	**Amount**	**Date**	**Amount**
Oct. 4	$ 1,876.07	Oct. 1	$ 1,278.62
Oct. 8	1,457.26	Oct. 4	2,010.70
Oct. 12	1,582.80	Oct. 6	878.91
Oct. 18	1,718.53	Oct. 8	1,716.12
Oct. 21	1,685.73	Oct. 14	1,051.17
Oct. 26	1,345.68	Oct. 17	426.18
Oct. 31	$ 1,415.72	Oct. 20	795.33
	$11,081.79	Oct. 22	47.83
		Oct. 25	621.42
		Oct. 26	344.81
		Oct. 28	591.10
		Oct. 31	$ 1,320.62
			$11,082.81

The bank statement for October is presented below.

First State Bank 175 North Main				
In account with:		Darby Foods 428 South Baltimore		
Date Oct. 1	Checks and Other Debit Items Balance forwarded		Deposits	Balance $15,865.34
Oct. 1	135.12 1,278.62		1,322.18	15,773.78
Oct. 5	541.62		1,876.07	17,108.23
Oct. 9	878.91 1,716.12	82.58	1,457.26	15,887.88
Oct. 13	2,010.70 321.18 NSF		1,582.80	15,138.80
Oct. 19	426.18		1,718.53	16,431.15
Oct. 22	795.33 1,051.17		1,685.73	16,270.38
Oct. 27	621.42 47.83		1,345.68	16,946.81
Oct. 31	344.81 35.75 SC			16,566.25

Additional Information:

1. The NSF check was from the collection on account of B. Ogilvel and was included in the Darby Foods deposit of October 26.
2. The service charge of $35.75 includes a $25 fee for the NSF check.
3. During the September reconciliation, a deposit in transit of $1,322.18 and outstanding checks of $135.12 and $541.62 were discovered.
4. A check for $82.58, which was outstanding at September 30, cleared the bank on October 9.

Required:
  a. Prepare the October 31 bank reconciliation.
  b. Determine the amount of cash to be shown on the October 31 balance sheet.

P 11.10 Companies often factor accounts receivable and discount notes as a means of obtaining cash. Answer each of the following questions concerning factoring and discounting.
  a. What is the difference between factoring and discounting?
  b. Which is riskier to the company, factoring or discounting?
  c. Which is typically more costly to the company, factoring or discounting?
  d. If a company regularly factors its accounts receivable, what are the long-term cost savings to the company? Why?

CA 11.1 O'Brien Company normally factors $200,000 of its n/30, accounts receivable each month. The finance company requires a 10 percent reserve and charges a 2 percent fee on the amount of the receivable. The *remaining amount* is also reduced by the annual finance charge of 15 percent.

Required: Use a computer spreadsheet. Assume independent situations.
  a. How much cash will O'Brien receive from factoring accounts receivable?
  b. If the reserve percentage is increased by 2 percent, how much cash will the company receive from factoring?
  c. If the fee is decreased by 1 percent, how much cash will O'Brien receive from factoring?
  d. If the finance charge is increased to 18 percent, how much cash will O'Brien receive from factoring?

CA 11.2 Walson Company received a $100,000, 90-day, 9 percent interest note receivable in payment of an overdue accounts receivable from a customer on January 1, 1995. On January 15, Walson discounted this note with recourse at its bank. The bank charges a 12 percent discounting rate.

Required: Use a computer spreadsheet. Assume independent situations.
  a. How much cash will Walson receive from discounting the note?
  b. If Walson waits until January 31 to discount the note, how much cash will it receive?
  c. If the discounting rate is increased to 15 percent, how much cash will Walson receive?
  d. If Walson discounts this note without recourse, will the discounting rate be higher or lower than 12 percent? Why?

CASES

C 11.1 During 1997, the following events occurred in your firm:

June 1 Jack Reynolds, a customer who has owed the firm $50,000 since January 15, gives the firm a $50,000, 120-day note payable to pay off his account.
Oct 1 The firm discounts Jack Reynold's note receivable with recourse at a 15 percent discount rate.

Required: Determine how these transactions should be reflected on the October 31 financial statements. Prepare an argument defending your reasoning.

C 11.2 You are currently the only bookkeeper at a small business. You are going on vacation, so the firm will hire a temporary person to replace you while you are away. Unfortunately, you are leaving today and the new person cannot start work until tomorrow. Prepare an instruction sheet that can be given to the temporary person so that he or she can perform the monthly bank reconciliation.

CRITICAL THINKING

CT 11.1 Jean Locks works part-time in the afternoons in the office of a manufacturing firm. In addition to Jean, there are 10 full-time office employees and an office manager. The company requires approval before paying its accounts payable. Jean receives the approved accounts payable and writes the checks and makes entries in the check register simultaneously on a semiautomated accounting machine.

The company operates two checking accounts, a general account for all accounts payable payments and a payroll account maintained on the imprest basis. A voucher is prepared and a check written on the general account in the amount of the net pay for the weekly payroll and deposited in the payroll checking account. Jean obtains the payroll bank statement and cancelled checks weekly and reconciles the account.

The firm has approximately 300 hourly workers who are paid each Friday for the workweek ending the previous Tuesday. On Wednesdays, Jean helps two of her co-workers collect the time cards and compute the individual employees' pay. She and another of the office employees write the payroll checks on the accounting machines on Thursdays. The financial vice president processes the payroll checks through a check-signing machine, although he sometimes gives Jean the key and she runs the checks through. Each Friday afternoon, she delivers the checks to the department supervisors who distribute them to the employees.

The company does not have a centralized personnel office. Each department head hires new employees for his or her department and completes the necessary paperwork, which is then forwarded to the central office where Jean works. The new employee's personnel records are filed in the central office, the individual's name is added to the master list of employees, and time cards are prepared from that list. When an employee leaves, the central office is notified by the department head, the employee's file is moved to the inactive group, and his or her name is removed from the master list of employees.

Required: Discuss the weaknesses of internal control for the payroll procedures and specify some steps that the company should take to strengthen the internal control system.

CT 11.2 SofCenter Co. is a computer software retail and development firm that began operations in 1996. The customer base is comprised of small, service businesses, and 90 percent of SofCenter's sales are on credit. The company has recently experienced major growth in the sales of its new product, Compueaze, a user-oriented software program for small-business planning and scheduling. Management has projected the monthly cash needs for the expansion of Compueaze and realizes that it needs to better manage its cash.

The company has hired a new cash manager, Erica Johansen. As part of her review of cash management, she has decided to look at the current accounts payable policy and procedures. Up to now, the accounts payable clerk has been following the directive to pay all invoices 30 days after receipt. Consequently, Johansen has noticed that the company does not take the cash discounts offered under its vendor's trade credit terms. Data about SofCenter's current major vendors, including average monthly purchases and credit terms, are listed below.

Allied	$ 50,000	n/30
Compdisc	150,000	2/10, n/30
Compuworks	500,000	5/10, n/120
Software Ideas	300,000	3/10, n/45

Johansen plans to use accounts payable as a discretionary form of short-term financing. She is considering recommending the discontinuance of the current accounts payable policy of paying all invoices 30 days after they are received. Johansen believes that SofCenter should take vendor discounts within the allotted discount period or pay invoices on the last day of the credit period.

Required:
a. Calculate the annual interest cost of not taking the discounts for each of SofCenter's vendors.
b. SofCenter's cash reserves are minimal, and the cost of alternative short-term financing is 18 percent annually. Determine which invoices SofCenter should pay within the discount period and which invoices it should pay on the last day of the credit period.
c. If there is no trade discount offered by a vendor, does this imply that there is no cost of trade credit? Why or why not? *CMA Adapted*

ETHICAL CHALLENGES

EC 11.1 The Ott Corporation has annual sales of $5,000,000, of which $3,000,000 are credit sales. Ott's current credit policy is to extend credit only to its best customers by giving them 30 days to pay from the date of purchase. The average monthly balance in Ott's accounts receivable account is $265,000.

The credit manager of Ott Corporation, Mary Pergorin, is considering extending credit to more customers and feels that credit sales will increase 15 percent. Her analysis, however, indicates that this credit group will not pay their balance for 60 days and will have a higher default rate than the current group of creditors. Ms. Pergorin has suggested factoring this group of accounts receivables and has found that Baker Credit Company is willing to factor these receivables if it receives a 5 percent reserve and a 12 percent factoring fee.

Required:
a. What effect will the new credit sales have on the cash flow of Ott Corporation if the new accounts receivable are not factored?
b. How much will Ott receive each month from the factor, assuming the increase in sales occurs equally throughout the year?
c. Should Ott factor these receivables?
d. What are the ethical issues involved when a company loosens its credit policy in order to increase sales, but is unsure of the collectibility of the additional sales?

EC 11.2   Your employer, C. J. Auto Accessories, sells automative accessories in a retail environment. The company employs five in-store salespeople currently and operates two cash registers. You have mentioned to the manager that this is a violation of good internal control since five people have access to the same two cash registers. Your employer, however, is reluctant to change this system because he feels that employees should be trusted.

Required: *a.* Discuss this situation from both C. J. Auto Accessories' and the employees' points of view.

                  b. What should C. J. do?

                  c. If it decides to change its policy, how would you go about making the change?

CHAPTER 12

Revenue and Expenditure Cycles: Analysis and Control

Learning Objectives

1. Discuss ways in which managers can evaluate operating activities.
2. Identify what type of information results from vertical and horizontal analyses.
3. Identify the type of information obtained from ratio analysis and what it tells the user of accounting information.

Kroger, one of the largest retail grocers in the United States, and its competitors in the $400 billion grocery industry are constantly faced with the need to improve operating efficiency. The difference between the price at which grocers sell individual items and the cost of those items—the contribution margin—is smaller for the grocery business than almost any other business. Consequently, grocery stores sell many other nongrocery items, such as flowers and magazines, which provide higher contribution margins. Among the things Kroger has done to increase its profitability is to offer prepared foods for busy customers including *Chef's Express,* which is a line of restaurant-quality dinners and entree items.

One means that Kroger uses to increase its margins and to control costs is electronic labor scheduling. By tracking sales information, Kroger is able to forecast daily activity by store and, in response, to create a daily work schedule for each store. This not only reduces costs but also increases the number of customers that can be served per hour and shortens the time customers spend in line. In order to monitor the effects of these actions, Kroger constantly uses the information in its financial statements to assess operating decisions and to plan for future decisions.

HOW CAN COMPANIES USE FINANCIAL STATEMENTS TO ANALYZE OPERATIONS?

 While the operating activities of other types of businesses may not be as visible as those in the grocery industry, all businesses operate by buying and selling goods and/or services. How do these businesses know how well they are performing their operating activities? Decision makers use the information in financial statements—a company's balance sheet, statement of cash flows, and income statement[1]—to evaluate ongoing operating decisions such as how much inventory to buy, to whom to extend credit, and how to price products.

Whether a company has a complex operation, like Kroger, or a simple one, like a small shoe repair business, it needs to analyze how well it has performed operating activities. Managers and other decision makers can use the performance information to evaluate previous plans and decisions and to plan for future operations.

We begin the chapter by describing, in a general way, how companies use three approaches to financial statement analysis. Then we focus on using the information derived from this analysis to evaluate specific operating decisions.

Why Evaluate Operations?

One of the most important tasks of managers is to determine and assess whether the business is better or worse off than in previous periods. How can they do this? One way of analyzing a business's performance is by using sources of information such as industry reports to compare the performance of a company with others in the industry. However, these reports are often only broad assessments, such as the company's share of industrywide sales for a certain type of product or the seasonal fluctuations in industry sales. Therefore, companies have found that an effective alternative way to evaluate specific aspects of their operations is to analyze the data contained in their financial statements.

Financial statements contain information that produces measurable criteria to determine whether a company's goals and objectives were met. Managers can use this information to better understand the impact of events that occurred and decisions that were made during the period as well as to plan operating decisions in future cycles.

Suppose, for example, that a business had planned for cost of goods sold to equal 55 percent of sales. Analysis and comparisons using the period's financial statements reveal that the actual cost of goods sold was 60 percent of sales. Or, suppose that it had projected collections on credit sales to occur within 45 days of the date of sale and finds that the average collection period was 3 days longer than planned. Also, what if managers find that credit purchases were paid in 24 days when it had planned for a 30-day time period? Analysis of the company's financial statements highlights these differences, as well as others, to indicate the operational areas where actual results differ from planned results.

Such differences show managers and other planners where to focus their efforts when evaluating actual operating results. This first step of the evaluation process addresses the impact of events and decisions on actual operations. After this, what happens? It is up to managers and others to determine:

- The causes of the significant differences noted.

- What was better than expected.

- What may have gone wrong.

- Who may have been responsible.

- How to address and fix the problems and plan better for the future.

---

[1]The statement of cash flows and the statement of retained earnings are also required financial statements for reporting purposes. However, here we use information only from the balance sheet and income statement.

Returning to the example of the company with cost of sales at 60 percent of sales instead of the planned 55 percent, management could look at sales to see whether the sales prices of the goods were lower than planned. Or they could investigate to see if the company paid more than the planned amount for the goods it sold. If management finds that too much was paid for purchases, then it must look for the cause. If the goods were purchased from the lowest priced source available, then management might consider raising sales prices to attain the 55 percent cost of sales desired. On the other hand, if the company had not purchased from the lowest priced source, it could consider switching to that source if the other important factors like quality meet the company's standards.

There may be other explanations for higher costs of sales. Perhaps the vendor from whom they planned to buy went out of business, leaving only higher priced vendors. Or perhaps freight costs were higher than planned due to a new labor contract with the shipping company. Or perhaps the company paid more to get quicker shipment in order to fill unexpected demand. Each of these possibilities would have different implications for how management should respond to an unexpectedly high cost of sales.

Actual events can differ from planned events in ways that initially may imply mistakes or mismanagement. However, management needs to examine the underlying facts of each situation to determine the real cause. For example, higher costs incurred due to a rush order to satisfy an important customer might be acceptable in the long run even though such costs vary from planned results in the short run.

Management can also compare the results of the current period's analysis with those of prior periods and with the plans outlined at the beginning of the period in the master budget (more on this later in the text). Comparisons with prior periods can show trends such as increasing sales or expenses. Comparisons to budgeted amounts indicate to management how actual events compare to those expected at the beginning of the period.

Good or Bad News?   It is impossible to know whether comparisons, as reflected by numbers or ratios, indicate good or bad news without having a standard for comparison. A number or ratio by itself does not reveal much to an analyst or financial statement reader. For example, if the average cost of sales ratio for the industry in the previous example rose to 65 percent, then the company is still maintaining a cost of sales ratio below the industry average.

Experience with a company over time helps to identify important basic relationships, such as the cost of goods sold relative to sales and the amount of inventory relative to cost of goods sold. It is possible to use these basic relationships to help develop internal financial statement standards by analyzing the business's actual financial statements over a number of years. This allows management to plan for a particular level of sales for the coming period, and, based on past relationships, it can also help predict the related amounts of cost of goods sold and inventory that should correspond to those sales.

Alternatively, if management decides that previously existing relationships among items like sales, inventory, and cost of goods sold were unsatisfactory, planning for future operations would include the types and amounts of desired changes in these

EXHIBIT	12.1	Sources of External Standards

Dun & Bradstreet	Published annually as *Key Business Ratios,* it contains 14 different ratios for more than 70 lines of business activities.
Annual Statement Studies	Robert Morris Associates, a national association of bank loan and credit officers, publishes these yearly. They contain 11 ratios for more than 150 lines of business, as well as some percentage distributions for items on the income statement and balance sheet.
Quarterly Financial Report for Manufacturing Corporations	Published jointly by the Federal Trade Commission and the Securities and Exchange Commission. This provides a "representative" balance sheet and income statement developed from financial data provided by individual companies grouped by various sizes within industry classifications.
Trade Associations	Many trade associations compile and publish ratios and other financial data relating to their particular industry. For example, the National Retail Furniture Association and the National Hardware Association provide financial statement analysis data to their members.

relationships as specific objectives. For example, when a company adopts just-in-time inventory policies, the past relationship between cost of goods sold and inventory will not apply because of decreased inventory levels in a just-in-time system. Therefore, the company would base its future plans on managing inventories on a just-in-time basis.

In addition to using these types of internal standards, management can look to external sources to make meaningful comparisons regarding company operations. Exhibit 12.1 shows some sources of external standards usually available in university and public libraries. These external sources usually include composite pictures of the financial performance and financial position of businesses within particular industries. Managers use such statistics to evaluate their individual businesses by comparing their company's performance to the averages within the same industry for the same time period. Generally, such external sources of industry information provide both an average result and a range of possible results regarding particular relationships for businesses in the same or similar kinds of business. We discuss external sources in greater detail in Chapter 25.

PAUSE & REFLECT

Why are external standards so important to financial statement analysis? How can financial statements be analyzed if there are no external standards available?

THREE ANALYSIS APPROACHES

In general, the three major approaches to financial statement analysis to assess a company's short-term liquidity, results of operations, and long-term profitability are (1) horizontal analysis, (2) vertical analysis, and (3) ratio analysis. In order to show how and why managers perform each of these analyses, we use the Natural Frozen Foods Company's comparative balance sheets and income statements presented in Exhibits 12.2 and 12.3.

PAUSE & REFLECT

Though we usually talk about financial statements being prepared in order to communicate information, how might the fact that this information becomes public and, therefore, available to a company's competitors impact this reporting process?

EXHIBIT | 12.2 | Statements of Financial Position

NATURAL FROZEN FOODS COMPANY
Comparative Balance Sheets
As of December 31, 1997, and 1996

	1997	1996
Assets		
Current assets:		
Cash	$ 9,500	$ 3,600
Temporary investments	13,000	11,000
Accounts receivable, net	123,000	141,000
Inventories	157,000	136,000
Supplies	15,000	12,000
Prepaid expenses	2,500	2,400
Total current assets	$320,000	$306,000
Investments:		
Land held for sale	$ 7,000	$ 8,500
Investment in ABC stock	2,000	3,000
Total investments	$ 9,000	$ 11,500
Property, plant, and equipment:		
Land	$ 50,000	$ 50,000
Building	400,000	400,000
Less: Accumulated depreciation—	(120,000)	(100,000)
Equipment	100,000	100,000
Less: Accumulated depreciation—	(60,000)	(40,000)
Total property, plant, and equipment	$370,000	$410,000
Intangibles:		
Patents, net	$ 14,000	$ 18,000
Copyrights, net	6,000	6,500
Total intangibles	$ 20,000	$ 24,500
Total assets	$719,000	$752,000
Liabilities and Owners' Equity		
Current liabilities:		
Accounts payable	$ 10,000	$ 20,000
Notes payable	45,000	60,000
Income taxes payable	1,000	3,000
Interest payable	6,500	7,000
Salaries payable	2,000	2,500
Accrued expenses	31,500	27,000
Total current liabilities	$ 96,000	$119,500
Long-term liabilities:		
Notes payable	$109,000	$155,500
Mortgage payable	74,000	80,000
Total long-term liabilities	$183,000	$235,500
Owners' equity:		
Capital stock	$ 99,000	$ 89,000
Additional paid-in capital	124,000	104,000
Retained earnings	217,000	204,000
Owners' Total equity	$440,000	$397,000
Total liabilities and owners' equity	$719,000	$752,000

Horizontal Analysis

Horizontal analysis is a system of financial statement analysis that shows a comparison of each item on a financial statement with that same item on statements from previous periods. That is, it compares one item to itself over time on both an absolute basis (dollar amount) and percentage basis to indicate the amount of change that occurred over time. In order to determine the percentage change, it is necessary to divide the amount of change in dollars by the amount of the item in the base year, which is generally the earliest period shown on the statements. The general formula to find the amount by which an item has changed on a percentage basis is:

$$\text{Percentage of change for an item} = \frac{\text{Amount of the item in comparison year} - \text{Amount of the item in base year}}{\text{Amount of the item in base year}}$$

EXHIBIT | 12.3 | Multistep Income Statements

NATURAL FROZEN FOODS COMPANY
Comparative Income Statements
For the Years Ended December 31, 1997, and 1996

	1997	1996
Sales	$850,000	$630,000
Less: Sales discounts	(50,000)	(30,000)
Net sales	$800,000	$600,000
Cost of goods sold	600,000	450,000
Gross margin	$200,000	$150,000
Selling expenses:		
Depreciation expense	(40,000)	(40,000)
Salaries expense	(86,000)	(64,500)
Administrative expenses:		
Amortization expense	(4,500)	(4,500)
Salaries expense	(48,000)	(20,000)
Income from operations	$ 21,500	$ 21,000
Other revenues and expenses:		
Interest expense	(1,500)	(3,000)
Income before taxes	$ 20,000	$ 18,000
Income tax expense (35%)	(7,000)	(6,300)
Net income	$ 13,000	$ 11,700

Horizontal analysis is helpful for discovering trends in financial statement relationships in order to predict short-term results for financial statement items. Longer range forecasts require more sophisticated statistical techniques like regression analysis. Trends suggest both how items, for example, sales and cost of goods sold, are growing and how fast. While trends may not predict the future perfectly, understanding their implications can provide useful insights into future operations.

See the horizontal analyses of Natural Frozen Foods Company, a frozen food distributor, in Exhibits 12.4 and 12.5 for the balance sheet and income statement, respectively. Note that some accounts, such as Cash, Income Taxes Payable (both in Exhibit 12.4), Sales Discounts, and Administrative Salaries Expense (Exhibit 12.5), changed more than 60 percent from the base year to the current year. Such large changes should certainly prompt management to seek explanations regarding their causes. Increases in sales are generally good news and may have been planned. The increase in sales discounts may indicate that Natural Frozen Foods' customers are paying their accounts more promptly.

Other accounts, such as Prepaid Expenses, and Mortgage Payable, changed very little from the base year. Management should evaluate these changes internally against its goals and objectives for the period. If management had expected little change, they are not likely to investigate further. On the other hand, if management had planned a 25 percent decrease in inventories from 1996 to 1997 and the horizontal analysis indicates that inventories increased 15.4 percent (Exhibit 12.4) there should be an investigation regarding why the planned decrease did not occur.

Horizontal analysis focuses on changes in financial statement items from period to period, which may indicate changes in underlying operating activities or changes in the business environment. For example, competitors may have changed the business environment by bringing out new products or lowering prices on old ones. Noting these changes and comparing the amounts to those planned will prompt management to find explanations for unexpected changes.

EXHIBIT | 12.4 | Balance Sheet: Horizontal Analysis

NATURAL FROZEN FOODS COMPANY
Horizontal Analysis
As of December 31, 1997, and 1996

	1997	1996	Difference Amount	Difference Percent
Assets				
Current assets:				
Cash	$ 9,500	$ 3,600	$ 5,900	163.9
Temporary investments	13,000	11,000	2,000	18.2
Accounts receivable, net	123,000	141,000	(18,000)	(12.8)
Inventories	157,000	136,000	21,000	15.4
Supplies	15,000	12,000	3,000	25.0
Prepaid expenses	2,500	2,400	100	4.2
Total current assets	$320,000	$306,000	24,000	7.8
Investments:				
Land held for sale	$ 7,000	$ 8,500	(1,500)	(17.6)
Investment in ABC stock	2,000	3,000	(1,000)	(33.3)
Total investments	$ 9,000	$ 11,500	(2,500)	(21.7)
Property, plant, and equipment:				
Land	$ 50,000	$ 50,000	-0-	0.0
Building	400,000	400,000	-0-	0.0
Less: Accumulated depreciation	(120,000)	(100,000)	20,000	20.0
Equipment	100,000	100,000	-0-	0.0
Less: Accumulated depreciation	(60,000)	(40,000)	20,000	50.0
Total property, plant, and equipment	$370,000	$410,000	(40,000)	(9.8)
Intangibles:				
Patents, net	$ 14,000	$ 18,000	(4,000)	(22.2)
Copyrights, net	6,000	6,500	(500)	(7.7)
Total intangibles	$ 20,000	$ 24,500	(4,500)	(18.4)
Total assets	$719,000	$752,000	(33,000)	(4.4)
Liabilities and Owners' Equity				
Current liabilities:				
Accounts payable	$ 10,000	$ 20,000	(10,000)	(50.0)
Notes payable	45,000	60,000	(15,000)	(25.0)
Income taxes payable	1,000	3,000	(2,000)	(66.7)
Interest payable	6,500	7,000	(500)	(7.1)
Salaries payable	2,000	2,500	(500)	(20.0)
Accrued expenses	31,500	27,000	4,500	16.7
Total current liabilities	$ 96,000	$119,500	23,500	19.7
Long-term liabilities:				
Notes payable	$109,000	$155,500	(46,500)	(29.9)
Mortgage payable	74,000	80,000	(6,000)	(7.5)
Total long-term liabilities	$183,000	$235,500	(52,500)	(22.3)
Owners' equity:				
Capital stock	$ 99,000	$ 89,000	10,000	11.2
Additional paid-in capital	124,000	104,000	20,000	19.2
Retained earnings	217,000	204,000	13,000	6.4
Total owners' equity	$440,000	$397,000	43,000	10.8
Total liability and owners' equity	$719,000	$752,000	(33,000)	(4.4)

Vertical Analysis

Vertical analysis is a system of financial statement analysis that shows the relative size of selected items to a base item within one statement for the same period. This type of analysis would show the relationship of all the other items to some base item, or a reference point, *within* that particular statement.

Vertical analysis indicates the relative importance of various items on the financial statements. Rather than comparing the dollar amounts of items, users of vertical analysis rely on percentages so that there is an evaluation of the relative size of

EXHIBIT | 12.5 | Income Statement: Horizontal Analysis

NATURAL FROZEN FOODS COMPANY
Horizontal Analysis
For the Years Ended December 31, 1997, and 1996

	1997	1996	Difference Amount	Difference Percent
Sales	$850,000	$630,000	$220,000	34.9
Less: Sales discounts	(50,000)	(30,000)	20,000	66.7
Net sales	$800,000	$600,000	200,000	33.3
Cost of goods sold	600,000	450,000	150,000	33.3
Gross margin	$200,000	$150,000	50,000	33.3
Selling expenses:				
Depreciation expense	(40,000)	(40,000)	-0-	0.0
Salaries expense	(86,000)	(64,500)	21,500	33.3
Administrative expenses:				
Amortization expense	(4,500)	(4,500)	-0-	0.0
Salaries expense	(48,000)	(20,000)	28,000	140.0
Income from operations	$ 21,500	$ 21,000	(500)	(2.4)
Other revenues and expenses:				
Interest expense	(1,500)	(3,000)	(1,500)	(50.0)
Income before taxes	$ 20,000	$ 18,000	2,000	11.1
Income tax expense (35%)	(7,000)	(6,300)	700	11.1
Net income	$ 13,000	$ 11,700	1,300	11.1

items, for example, salaries expense as a percentage of sales. The percentages of the "base" item are expressed by dividing the amount of the base item into the amount of each of the other items. The general formula for the vertical analysis of an item is

$$\text{Percentage of base} = \frac{\text{Individual amount}}{\text{Amount of base item}}$$

Percentages avoid distortion caused by comparing businesses of different sizes. Whether sales are $10,000 and cost of goods sold is $3,000, or sales are $1,000,000 and cost of goods is $300,000, cost of goods sold is 30 percent of sales. That allows useful comparisons between two different companies or between a company and the average percentages calculated for the company's industry.

Vertical analyses of income statements use sales as the base item because of the importance of sales to operations and because interpreting expense items relative to sales is a logical way to analyze items on the income statement. Thus, all items appearing below sales on the income statement will be less than 100 percent, and it is possible to add the percentages of those items in meaningful way.

Vertical analyses of the balance sheet use total assets as the base item because total assets is the largest item. This means that the percentages calculated for the other assets (liabilities and equities), when added, equal the amount of total assets (100%).

Exhibits 12.6 and 12.7 present vertical analyses of the balance sheets and income statements of Natural Frozen Foods using sales and total assets, respectively, as the base items.

For the balance sheet (Exhibit 12.6), vertical analysis shows the relative importance of asset, liability, and owners' equity accounts. Analysts and other financial statement users can compare these percentages with the percentages planned to evaluate a period's performance. For example, if Natural Frozen Foods had a goal for inventories as a percentage of total assets to decrease to 15 percent in 1997, management may want to investigate why the results of vertical analysis indicate that the actual percentage was 21.8 percent.

EXHIBIT | 12.6 | Balance Sheet: Vertical Analysis

NATURAL FROZEN FOODS COMPANY
Vertical Analysis
As of December 31, 1997, and 1996

	1997	Percent	1996	Percent
Assets				
Current assets:				
Cash	$ 9,500	1.3	$ 3,600	0.5
Temporary investments	13,000	1.8	11,000	1.5
Accounts receivable, net	123,000	17.1	141,000	18.8
Inventories	157,000	21.8	136,000	18.1
Supplies	15,000	2.1	12,000	1.6
Prepaid expenses	2,500	0.3	2,400	0.3
Total current assets	$320,000	44.5	$306,000	40.7
Investments:				
Land held for sale	$ 7,000	1.0	$ 8,500	1.1
Investment in ABC stock	2,000	0.3	3,000	0.4
Total investments	$ 9,000	1.3	$ 11,500	1.5
Property, plant, and equipment:				
Land	$ 50,000	7.0	$ 50,000	6.6
Building	400,000	55.6	400,000	53.2
Less: Accumulated depreciation	(120,000)	16.7	(100,000)	13.3
Equipment	100,000	13.9	100,000	13.3
Less: Accumulated depreciation	(60,000)	8.3	(40,000)	5.3
Total property, plant, and equipment	$370,000	51.5	$410,000	54.5
Intangibles:				
Patents, net	$ 14,000	1.9	$ 18,000	2.4
Copyrights, net	6,000	0.8	6,500	0.9
Total intangibles	$ 20,000	2.8	$ 24,500	3.3
Total assets	$719,000	100.0	$752,000	100.0
Liabilities and Owners' Equity				
Current liabilities:				
Accounts payable	$ 10,000	1.4	$ 20,000	2.7
Notes payable	45,000	6.3	60,000	8.0
Income taxes payable	1,000	0.1	3,000	0.4
Interest payable	6,500	.9	7,000	0.9
Salaries payable	2,000	0.3	2,500	0.3
Accrued expenses	31,500	4.4	27,000	3.6
Total current liabilities	$ 96,000	13.4	$119,500	15.9
Long-term liabilities:				
Notes payable	$109,000	15.2	$155,500	20.7
Mortgage payable	74,000	10.3	80,000	10.6
Total long-term liabilities	$183,000	25.5	$235,500	31.3
Owners' equity:				
Capital stock	$ 99,000	13.8	$ 89,000	11.8
Additional paid-in capital	124,000	17.2	104,000	13.8
Retained earnings	217,000	30.2	204,000	27.1
Total owners' equity	$440,000	61.2	$397,000	52.8
Total liability and owners' equity	$719,000	100.0	$752,000	100.0

Using the data from Natural Frozen Food's income statement in 1997 (Exhibit 12.7), income from operations was 2.5 percent of sales; subtracting interest expense and income tax expense, which were .2 and .8 percent of sales, respectively, yields net income of 1.5 percent of sales.

Vertical analysis used along with horizontal analysis reveals trends in financial data relationships. Together these analyses can show whether the relative importance of items has changed over time. Using percentages for comparisons within a firm at two points (horizontal analysis) in time removes the effect of changes in the base in vertical analysis. Some items are expected to increase as the level of sales

| EXHIBIT | 12.7 | Income Statement: Vertical Analysis |

NATURAL FROZEN FOODS COMPANY
Vertical Analysis
For the Years Ended December 31, 1997, and 1996

	1997	Percent	1996	Percent
Sales	$850,000	100.0	$630,000	100.0
Less: Sales discounts	(50,000)	5.9	(30,000)	4.8
Net sales	800,000	94.1	600,000	95.2
Cost of goods sold	600,000	70.6	450,000	71.4
Gross margin	$200,000	23.5	$150,000	23.8
Selling expenses:				
Depreciation expense	(40,000)	4.7	(40,000)	6.3
Salaries expense	(86,000)	10.1	(64,500)	10.2
Administrative expenses:				
Amortization expense	(4,500)	0.5	(4,500)	0.7
Salaries expense	(48,000)	5.6	(20,000)	3.2
Income from operations	$ 21,500	2.5	$ 21,000	3.3
Other revenue and expenses:				
Interest expense	(1,500)	0.2	(3,000)	0.5
Income before taxes	$ 20,000	2.4	$ 18,000	2.9
Income tax expense (35%)	(7,000)	0.8	(6,300)	1.0
Net income	$ 13,000	1.5	$ 11,700	1.9

increases, for example, cost of goods sold. So, dollar changes for such items would be harder to interpret if the change in the level of sales were not taken into account by using percentages. For example, Natural Frozen Food's depreciation expense of $40,000 may appear to have changed (6.3 percent of sales in 1996 and 4.7 percent in 1997) when, in fact, it did not. Note that whether vertical and horizontal analyses are used together or separately, interpreting the results requires careful reflection about changes and their implications.

The 1996 and 1997 vertical analyses for Natural Frozen Foods (Exhibits 12.6 and 12.7) indicate that the mix of operating assets and liabilities has remained constant over the two-year period. By comparing the vertical analysis for each year across years (a horizontal analysis), we can see changes in the importance of items over time. If Natural Frozen Foods had not anticipated any changes, this comparison would indicate that the actual results were expected. On the other hand, if Natural Frozen Foods expected changes in items, such as the proportion of inventory to total assets, or discounts as a percentage of sales, then it should investigate why those changes did not occur.

Certain accounts should be related because they reflect related transactions. For example, Cost of Goods Sold and Sales are related because the cost of goods sold exists because of sales. Therefore, we would expect changes in sales to result in similar changes in cost of goods sold. Credit Sales and Accounts Receivable are linked, too. Vertical and horizontal analysis are limited in their ability to capture these interrelationships among accounts because they do not focus on such detail regarding the specific relationships. Vertical analysis captures information about broader relationships, such as the relationship of Inventory or Accounts Receivable to total assets, rather than specific relationships based on the underlying activities. Horizontal analysis focuses on changes in single items over time rather than related accounts. It is possible to develop ratios comprised of balances from related accounts so that the financial statement analysis focuses on relationships that reflect underlying business activities.

In the next section, we examine how to use ratios to answer questions about operating activities in the revenue and the expenditure cycles. We will describe evaluation of the activities in the conversion cycle in Chapter 13.

EXHIBIT | 12.8 | Operating Ratios

Inventory turnover	$$\frac{\text{Cost of goods sold}}{\text{Average inventory}}$$	The average number of times during the period that the company completed the purchasing cycle
Average selling period	$$\frac{365 \text{ days}}{\text{Inventory turnover}}$$	The average number of days in the purchasing cycle this period
Payables turnover	$$\frac{\text{Total cash expenses}}{\text{Average current liabilities (except principal on bank loans)}}$$	The average number of times during the period that the company completed the payment cycle
Payment period	$$\frac{365 \text{ days}}{\text{Payables turnover}}$$	The average number of days in the payment cycle this period
Accounts receivable turnover	$$\frac{\text{Net credit sales}}{\text{Average (net) accounts receivable}}$$	The average number of times during the period that the company completed the collection cycle
Average collection period	$$\frac{365 \text{ days}}{\text{Receivables turnover}}$$	The average number of days in the collection cycle this period
Gross margin ratio	$$\frac{\text{Gross margin}}{\text{Net sales}}$$	Proportion of the sales revenue remaining after deducting cost of goods sold
Return on sales	$$\frac{\text{Net income from continuing operations}}{\text{Net sales}}$$	Proportion of the sales revenue remaining after deducting all operating expenses
Current ratio	$$\frac{\text{Current assets}}{\text{Current liabilities}}$$	The company's ability to meet its current obligation with current assets
Quick ratio	$$\frac{\text{Cash + Temporary Investments + Accounts receivable}}{\text{Current liabilities}}$$	The company's ability to meet its current obligation with quick assets (current assets considered most liquid)

Ratio Analysis

Ratio analysis involves creating ratios that use two or more accounts on the same statement or accounts related by the transactions they represent from two different statements. The analysis uses these relationships to assess whether amounts in one account (or group of accounts, e.g., current assets) are at the level they should be given the amounts of the other account(s). Ratio analysis focuses specifically on interrelationships of accounts to answer questions like: Is inventory at the level we expect given the amount of cost of goods sold for the period? Or, is accounts receivable at the level we expect based on this period's sales? Unlike horizontal analysis, which focuses on one account over time, or vertical analysis, which uses only one financial statement, ratio analysis may use accounts from the same statement for related items on two different statements of the same accounting period.

This section examines the financial ratios that enable management to analyze the operations of the company.[2] See Exhibit 12.8 for the financial ratios commonly used to analyze operating activities of businesses.

Some ratios measure the relationships between accounts across a period, for example, income statement ratios, because they summarize the effects of transactions throughout the period. However, balance sheet accounts reflect balances at only one point in time. Therefore, when ratios reflect both income statement and balance sheet items, we use averages for the balance sheet items based on two or more points in time. Using averages reflects changes in the balance sheet items through time, which makes the ratio more meaningful.

The potential explanations for results of ratio analysis are usually limited to the types of transactions underlying the relationship. For example, the relationship between credit sales and accounts receivable is not affected by purchases. So ratio analysis involves specific numerator and denominator effects, rather than a wide variety of causes that would be found in horizontal analysis. Next we discuss and illustrate how to use ratio analysis for evaluation based on the information provided for Natural Frozen Foods Company.

---

[2]We present other ratios for other assessments, such as creditworthiness, later in the investing and financing sections of the book.

Ratios help point out problems in operations. It is up to management to answer questions like Were the wrong products purchased? Were they properly cared for after the purchase?

USING RATIOS TO EVALUATE EXPENDITURE CYCLE DECISIONS

Recall that in the expenditure cycle, managers make two general types of decisions: (1) what and how much to purchase and (2) when to pay for the purchases. These are important operating decisions, and it is critical that management knows how well these decisions are being made. We illustrate how to apply ratio analysis to evaluate such expenditure decisions.

Purchasing Decisions

The principal objective of inventory management is to have enough inventory on hand to meet demand, either from customers or production, without holding unnecessary inventory and risking spoilage or obsolescence. In the short term, inventory order costs are the costs incurred to place one additional order for inventory, thus, the greater the number of orders during the period, the larger the short-term ordering cost. Also, short-term carrying costs are the costs of carrying one additional unit in inventory for the period; therefore, the greater the number of units carried in inventory, the larger the short-term carrying cost. As you know, managers try to balance the costs of ordering inventory at frequent intervals against the cost of carrying too much inventory.

In large organizations, inventory management is the responsibility of the purchasing department. Purchasing-related analyses are also relevant in small companies where the owner makes the purchases and needs to know whether he or she is purchasing too much or too little inventory.

One way that managers assess whether they are achieving the right balance between order costs and excess inventory is to analyze the inventory turnover ratio. The **inventory turnover** indicates how many times during the period the company completed the purchasing cycle, or the sequence of events from acquiring inventory through the sale of inventory, for the period. We calculate the inventory turnover ratio as follows:

$$\text{Inventory turnover} = \frac{\text{Cost of goods sold}}{\text{Average inventory}}$$

Using the average inventory better represents the amount of inventory on hand during the period over which cost of goods sold was measured.[3] The lower the amount of average inventory relative to the cost of goods sold, the higher the inventory turnover ratio. A higher turnover rate means that inventory turns over more

---

[3]We typically use an average of beginning and ending balances of balance sheet items (beginning balance plus ending balance divided by 2) in ratios that include both balance sheet and income statement accounts.

times, or sells quicker. Usually a high inventory turnover indicates that inventory is marketable and that the company does not hold excessive amounts of inventory. The higher the turnover rate, the smaller the investment in inventory relative to cost of goods sold. However, rates that are too high may indicate lost sales because items were not available when customers wanted them. Using the data found in Exhibits 12.2 and 12.3, we calculate the inventory turnover for Natural Frozen Foods Company for 1997 below.[4]

$$\frac{\$600,000}{(\$157,000 + \$136,000)/2} = 4.10$$

This indicates that inventory turned over 4.10 times during the period. To evaluate purchasing decisions by using this number, managers begin by comparing the current inventory turnover ratio to past ratios, to the budgeted inventory turnover for the current period, and to industry standards. This gives them information to assess whether inventory is selling at an adequate rate compared to the past, at the expected rate for the current period, and at a rate comparable to the competition.

If the inventory turnover is significantly lower than expected, it may indicate that product demand was overestimated and, thus, that the product is not selling as quickly as expected. This would create higher carrying costs due to a larger than expected amount of inventory. On the other hand, an inventory turnover that is higher than expected may indicate that inventory levels are too low to meet demand and, thus, that the company has not maintained sufficient inventory and could be experiencing lost sales.

PAUSE & REFLECT	Suppose a company decides to maintain inventory at the same dollar amount during periods of inflation. What effect will this have on the inventory turnover ratio? What other things might be affected by this decision?

Also, inventory turnover may differ from standards or expectations because inventory may have been misappropriated, which would result in a lower level of inventory than planned. To safeguard against misappropriated inventory, management should undertake a physical count of the inventory in all locations each period. This physical count helps ensure that the amount of inventory on hand agrees with the amount in the accounting records. In addition, the purchasing department manager should ensure that responsible individuals check purchase invoices and receiving reports to see that proper amounts ordered are received and that accounting procedures are being followed to safeguard inventory assets.

Another way to express how fast inventory is turning over, or selling, is to calculate the average number of days in the selling period. We use the **average selling period ratio** to represent the number of days it takes to sell the average amount of inventory. That indicates that the number of days per turnover is the average selling period for inventory. We calculate the average selling period ratio by dividing the number of days in the period by the inventory turnover ratio, as shown below.

$$\text{Average selling period} = \frac{365 \text{ days}}{\text{Inventory turnover}}$$

We show the formula using 365 days assuming that the period is one year. For shorter periods, such as months or quarters, we would change the number of days used, for example, to 30 and 90 days, respectively.

---

[4]We use the beginning and ending balances as the period's average balance of inventory because monthly data are not available.

Calculating the average selling period is another way of assessing whether management is maintaining the proper level of inventory. An extremely long selling period compared to the industry average may indicate that management has overestimated demand for its products or that it has overinvested in inventory. A selling period that is shorter than others in the same industry may indicate a company that is not maintaining an adequate inventory to meet customer demand, which could result in lost sales.

The average selling period and the inventory turnover ratio are reciprocal measures of purchasing activity. Thus, a lower turnover means a longer selling period and higher turnover means a shorter selling period.

We show the calculation for the average selling period of Natural Frozen Foods Company for 1997 below.

$$\frac{365}{4.10} = 89.02 \text{ days}$$

This means that it takes the company approximately 89.02 days to sell the average amount of inventory.

Management can evaluate this ratio by comparing it to the company's selling policies that are based, in part, on the shelf life of the inventory. For instance, if Natural Frozen Foods was a grocery store, a selling period of 89 days is too long since some of a grocer's inventory is perishable. On the other hand, a large appliance dealer may be very content with a selling period of 89 days since appliances are considered durable goods whose shelf life is virtually indefinite. As it does with ratios, management also should evaluate the average selling period against past trends, industry averages, and its budget-based ratio. If Natural Frozen Foods planned that its goods should be in inventory only 45 days, then the 89-day period is too long. It should determine whether it is carrying too much inventory to justify the carrying costs of those items.

Businesses with diverse inventories, such as grocers, should calculate inventory turnover on various inventory groups rather than on inventory as a whole. This gives the business a better understanding of how particular classes of inventory items are moving and provides additional information concerning spoilage and obsolescence.

PAUSE & REFLECT   If a business has a selling period of 25 days, what action, if any, should be taken? Why?

Payment Decisions

In the expenditure cycle, decisions regarding the timing of payment for purchases are important also. As you know, good management of payables dictates that managers delay payments as long as possible, while still taking advantage of all discounts offered and always meeting payment deadlines.

One way managers can assess how well they are managing payments for operating expenses is by comparing the total discounts taken with the amounts anticipated. Another way to evaluate whether payments for operating expenses are made on time involves comparing the current operating liabilities to cash expenses, which is known as the *payables turnover ratio*. **Payables turnover** is the ratio of cash expenses, or expenses that require a cash payment, for example, salaries or cost of goods sold, to the average current liabilities, excluding the principal portions of bank loans. Generally, it is found by:

$$\text{Payables turnover} = \frac{\text{Total cash expenses}}{\text{Average current liabilities}}$$
$$\text{(except principal portions of bank loans)}$$

Cash expenses are found by considering all the expenses on the income statement, except those that do not require cash payments. For example, depreciation of equipment does not affect the operating cash flows of any period because the cash flows associated with a piece of equipment are the purchase of the equipment, repairs to the equipment, and the disposal value of the equipment—not depreciation expense. Therefore, we exclude depreciation expense from the numerator when calculating the payables turnover ratio. Bank loans, usually in the form of notes payable, are excluded from the denominator of average current liabilities because they are financing activities rather than operating activities.

Although the principal amounts of bank loans are eliminated from current operating liabilities because they are a financing activity, interest expense is included. Once the decision is made to borrow money, the payment of the interest must be generated from operations. Thus, interest expense is considered to be an operating expense, while the principal amounts of related loans are not.

The cash expenses (Exhibit 12.3) of Natural Frozen Foods Company are the cost of goods sold, salaries expense, interest expense, and income tax expense. Natural Frozen Foods' operating liabilities (Exhibit 12.2) include all current liabilities except for notes payable. Using this information, we calculate Natural Frozen Foods' payables turnover for 1997 below.[5,6]

$$\text{Payables turnover} = \frac{\$742.5}{(\$51 + \$59.5)/2} = 13.44$$

This means that payables turned over 13.44 times during the year. In other words, the payment cycle, that is, the events from the purchase of the goods to the receipt of the vendor's invoice for payment, was completed 13.44 times during the past year, or more than once per month, on average.

Evaluating payables management involves comparing the payables turnover ratio to the turnovers planned for the current period, as well as to the past company payables turnover and to industry standards. The higher the accounts payable turnover, the shorter the payment period for current operating expenses. However, a high payable turnover may indicate that the business is not taking advantage of credit opportunities because it may be paying sooner than the credit period allowed by vendors, or the business could be making cash purchases when no-interest credit is available. On the other hand, a low accounts payable turnover ratio may indicate that the business is not paying its obligations when they are due, which may affect its credit standing or that the company is missing purchase discounts dates, and therefore, that the effective interest rate on payables is much higher than necessary.

Another means of assessing how effectively a business is managing its payables is to consider the **payment period ratio.** The payment period for cash expenses measures the average number of days required to pay the average amount of current operating liabilities. It is calculated by dividing the number of days in a period by the payables turnover ratio, as follows:

$$\text{Payment period} = \frac{365 \text{ days}}{\text{Payables turnover}}$$

Management can compare the actual payment period with the anticipated length of the payment period for liabilities according to company policy and the credit requirements of suppliers. Then, management will know if it needs to take corrective

---

[5]Natural Frozen Foods' $742,500 in cash expenses for 1997 include: Cost of Goods Sold, $600,000; Salaries Expense, $86,000; Salaries Expense, $48,000; Interest Expense, $1,500; and Income Tax Expense, $7,000.

[6]Natural Frozen Foods' current liabilities (except Notes Payable, which are bank loans) include:

	1997	1996
Accounts payable	$10,000	$20,000
Income taxes payable	1,000	3,000
Interest payable	6,500	7,000
Salaries payable	2,000	2,500
Accrued expenses	31,500	27,000
Total	$51,000	$59,500

action. Most businesses in a given industry have similar payment schedules, which allow comparisons between the average collection period of a particular company and the average payment period of companies in the same industry. If the company's payment period is longer relative to others in the industry, it may indicate that the business is unable or unwilling to pay its obligations on time. If the payment period is shorter than that of others in the industry, it may indicate that the business is not applying good cash management techniques because it is paying its obligations prior to their due dates. Management also can evaluate the payment period ratio in conjunction with the current and quick ratios (discussed later) to assess the impact of the company's short-term cash outflows.

The payment period of Natural Frozen Foods Company for 1997 is:

$$\frac{365}{13.44} = 27.16 \text{ days}$$

This means its takes, on average, 27.16 days for Natural Frozen Foods Company to pay the average amount of payables. If the suppliers of Natural Frozen Foods Company's goods and services require payment within 30 days, the payment period indicates that bills are being paid promptly. However, if its suppliers do not require payment for 60 days, Natural Frozen Foods Company may want to lengthen its payment period in order to have longer use of its cash in operations since there is no additional cost to do so.

PAUSE & REFLECT

If a business has analyzed their most recent financial statements and found that its payment period is 60 days, and its vendors require payment in 30 days, what action, if any, should it take? What additional information is needed? Why?

Purchasing the right amount of goods and paying for them at the right time are critical operating decisions. The payables turnover and the payment period ratios are two effective indicators of how financial statement analysis can help evaluate management decisions. Next we focus on using statement analysis to evaluate decisions in the revenue cycle.

EVALUATING DECISIONS IN THE REVENUE CYCLE

As we discussed in Chapter 3, managers make two general types of decisions in the revenue cycle: (1) credit decisions involving whom to sell to and when to collect, and (2) pricing decisions. Below are discussions of ratio analysis applied to evaluation of credit and pricing decisions as well as illustrations using the data from the Natural Frozen Foods Company.

Evaluating Credit Decisions

Good management of credit sales results in the maximum amount of cash being collected from credit sales. In order to do this, managers must balance the benefits of having more credit sales with the related risk of having more uncollectible sales. Extending credit works as long as the increase in cost (uncollectible accounts) does not exceed the increase in benefit (sales).

Often competition directly affects credit policies and collection terms. If a company that offers its customers credit terms of 3/15, n/30 has a major competitor who offers credit terms of 3/15, n/60, this may force the company to change its credit policies or lose customers to the competition. The crucial question is: Which alternative will make the business better off—not extending the due date on accounts receivable or following the competitor's lead?

There are several ways to determine whether managers are setting and following appropriate credit policies. One way is to note the amount of sales discounts taken and the amount of uncollectible accounts expenses for the period. Managers also can determine the **accounts receivable turnover** which indicates whether the amount of accounts receivable is appropriate for the company's sales level. The accounts receivable turnover is the ratio of net credit sales to the average balance in the accounts receivable account, less the allowance for uncollectible accounts:

$$\text{Accounts receivable turnover} = \frac{\text{Net credit sales}}{\text{Average (net) accounts receivable}}$$

Since credit sales, not cash sales, lead to accounts receivable and potential collection problems, we use net credit sales in the calculation. Recall that to determine net credit sales, you subtract sales returns and sales discounts from gross credit sales. If you cannot determine separate credit sales data, substitute total sales based on the assumption that most sales are on account. Likewise managers use net accounts receivable in order to evaluate the relationship between "collectible" accounts and sales.

The lower the amount of receivables relative to sales, the greater the accounts receivable turnover. For a given amount of sales, a higher turnover rate means that receivables are collected quicker. The higher the turnover rate, the smaller is the investment in accounts receivable relative to sales.

We calculate the accounts receivable turnover of Natural Frozen Foods for 1997 below using data from Exhibits 12.2 and 12.3.

$$\frac{\$800,000}{(\$123,000 + \$141,000)/2} = 6.06$$

The 6.06 turnover means that the process of selling products and collecting the amounts due from customers occurred 6.06 times in 1997.

As part of the evaluation of credit decisions, the analyst would compare the accounts receivable turnover ratio to past turnovers, budgeted turnover rate, and industry standards. This gives management information concerning how well the credit and collection policies of the company are working. An accounts receivable turnover that varies significantly from what was expected may be an indication that either credit granting policies need attention and/or collection policies are not working as planned. Another common means of assessing credit policies is through the examination of the aging of accounts receivable.

An accounts receivable turnover that is too low could occur because the accounting system is not working as intended. For example, if payments made by customers are not recorded properly as deductions from accounts receivable, the amount of accounts receivable will be overstated, causing the accounts receivable turnover to be understated. To guard against this type of accounting irregularity, companies independently verify the balances of accounts receivable with the customers themselves as part of their internal control procedures. That is, a random sample of customers receive verifications (confirmations) from the company in order to independently check the accuracy of the recording process. The verifications require that the customer notify the company if the amount shown due in their account differs from the amount in the customer's records. This allows any discrepancies to be investigated, if necessary.

The **average collection period ratio** for accounts receivable measures the average number of days it takes to collect the average balance in accounts receivable. The collection period provides feedback similar to the accounts receivable turnover ratio because it indicates whether sales are generating enough cash to meet the company's current obligations in a timely fashion. The formula for the average collection period is:

$$\text{Average collection period} = \frac{365 \text{ days}}{\text{Receivables turnover}}$$

It is determined by dividing the number of days in the year by the receivables turnover ratio calculated previously.

Decision makers can evaluate the average based on the ratios established as part of the credit policies set by management for the collection period in order to determine if the policy is appropriate. Perhaps the collection period is longer than planned which may mean that the company extended credit too easily. Or perhaps the company is missing sales because its credit policies are too restrictive. Management can then decide if the present collection period is in line with its goals for credit collection. However, the length of the collection period itself does not indicate whether credit policies are good or bad.

It is important to evaluate the length of the collection period in conjunction with the current and quick ratios (discussed later) to assess the adequacy of future short-term cash inflows.

We show the average collection period of Natural Frozen Foods Company for 1997 below.

$$\frac{365}{6.06} = 60.23 \text{ days}$$

This means that it takes, on average, 60.23 days to collect the average amount of accounts receivable. While this may indicate a problem in the collection and credit department, analysts must evaluate this against past trends and industry averages. If credit terms are 2/10, n/60, a collection period of 60.2 days is on target, though it suggests that many customers choose to forgo the discount. However, if terms are 2/10, n/30, management may need to evaluate its credit and collection policies more closely. For example, if Natural Frozen Foods Company's management normally extends credit for 30 days, a collection period of 60.2 days may indicate that credit and/or collection policies are too lax or that a few very large accounts are slow in remitting payment. On the other hand, if management normally extends credit for 60 days, a collection period of 60.2 days may indicate either that the credit and collection policies are working well or that the credit and/or collection policies are too restrictive and Natural Frozen Foods may miss potential credit customers. Periodic comparison of the amount of time in the collection period with management's credit and collection policies enables corrective action on a timely basis. In addition, management may want to compare its collection period to those of its competitors.

PAUSE & REFLECT	If a business has credit terms of 2/10, n/60 and its collection period is 45 days, what action, if any, should be taken? Why?

Pricing Decisions

The other important type of decision in the revenue cycle is product pricing. While the prices at which a business sells its products are often limited by market conditions, pricing and profitability are closely linked. Evaluating pricing decisions can lead to changes in marketing strategies or to the discontinuation of product lines.

We evaluate pricing decisions indirectly by using profitability ratios. These ratios measure a business's ability to generate a return from sales activities by the extent to which sales less expenses are generating profits. We examine two important profitability ratios—gross margin and return on sales—below.

The **gross margin ratio** is the ratio of gross margin to net sales. It measures, in percentage terms, that portion of sales revenue available after deducting the cost of goods sold.

$$\text{Gross margin ratio} = \frac{\text{Gross margin}}{\text{Net sales}}$$

We show the gross margin of Natural Frozen Foods Company for 1997 using data from Exhibit 12.3:

$$\frac{\$200,000}{\$800,000} = 25\%$$

This means that, for every dollar in net sales, Natural Frozen Foods Company is generating $0.25 in gross margin. Or, for every dollar in net sales, the cost of the goods sold is $0.75. The gross margin percentage must be large enough to ensure that selling prices can cover operating expenses and provide a satisfactory income. As is the case of all statement analysis calculations, management should compare the

Evaluating profitability requires management to look beyond overall results and look at the effect of specific events like sales, or the sales of specific stores or product lines.

current period's gross margin percentage against prior periods' percentages and industry standards to determine the implications of any noted variances.

The **return on sales ratio** is the ratio of income from operations to net sales. It measures that portion of sales revenue remaining after deducting all operating expenses. This is an indication of the business's overall profitability.

Most companies calculate return on sales using income from continuing operations, that is, income before interest and taxes, rather than net income. Income from operations reflects the ability of the company to generate income independently from the financing of the business and income tax expense.

$$\text{Return on sales ratio} = \frac{\text{Income from operations}}{\text{Net sales}}$$

The return on sales ratio for Natural Frozen Foods Company in 1997 using data from Exhibit 12.3 is:

$$\frac{\$21,500}{\$800,000} = 2.7\%$$

This means that for every dollar in net sales, Natural Frozen Foods Company has generated 2.7 cents in income, excluding interest and taxes. Thus, the operating costs of Natural Frozen Foods Company, excluding interest and taxes, are 97.3 percent of net sales. The company should compare this ratio to past returns on sales and to the returns planned for this year.

A low return on sales could result from pricing products too low or from expenses that are higher than they should be. Comparisons between Natural Frozen Foods' return on sales ratio and the industry average should reveal how Natural Frozen Food's profitability compares. Explanation for any difference in profitability might be found by comparing industry prices, sales volume, and expenses with those of Natural Frozen Foods.

Managers can also evaluate the amount of time which elapses between the purchase of inventory and the subsequent collection of cash from customers. We discuss this measure of the business's operating efficiency next.

The Operating Cycle: Cash to Cash

The **operating cycle** for a business is the time it takes to sell inventory on account and receive the related cash from customers. The total of the selling period plus the collection period is an approximation of the business's operating cycle.[7] During normal operations, the operating cycle begins with sales, converting inventory into accounts receivable. The subsequent collection of accounts receivable reflects the

---

[7]We could calculate the operating cycle as selling period plus collection period less payment period. This is somewhat misleading because it assumes that the payment cycle overlaps the cash inflow cycle. For many companies, sales and collections must be made *before* obligations can be paid.

inancial ratios based on cash flows can be a useful complement to ratios based on accrual accounting numbers. Financial reporting standards require companies to prepare a statement of cash flows. Each of the ratios described here uses cash flows from operations as a component. Cash flows from operations is the portion of the statement of cash flows that summarizes the cash effects of operating activities—those associated with the production and delivery of goods and services. The cash flow ratios described here are *sufficiency ratios,* which measure the adequacy of cash flows for meeting company needs, and *efficiency ratios,* which measure how well the company generates cash flows.

We calculate the cash flow adequacy ratio as follows.

$$\text{Cash flow adequacy ratio} = \frac{\text{Cash from operations}}{\text{Long-term debt payments} + \text{Purchases of assets} + \text{Dividends paid}}$$

The cash flow adequacy ratio measures whether a company's cash from operations is sufficient to cover its primary cash requirements. A company's average cash flow adequacy ratio evaluated for a number of years must be at least 1.

Another measure of the sufficiency of a company's cash flows is the *debt coverage ratio,* which is found as follows.

$$\text{Debt coverage ratio} = \frac{\text{Total debt}}{\text{Cash from operations}}$$

The debt coverage ratio estimates, at the current level of cash flows, how long it will take to retire all debt. Then, managers can use this ratio to gauge the effect on cash flows of the company's debt burden.

A third cash flow ratio that may be useful in evaluating operations is the *cash flow to sales ratio.* The cash flow to sales ratio measures company efficiency in a manner that is similar to the accrual-based return on sales. We calculate it as follows.

$$\text{Cash flow to sales ratio} = \frac{\text{Cash from operations}}{\text{Net sales}}$$

A recent study of the Fortune 500 compared cash flow ratios for companies in three industries: electronics, food, and chemical. The results show that chemical companies had the highest average cash flows from sales over the three years studied, 12 percent, while electronics and food showed 9 percent and 6 percent, respectively.

Analyzing cash flows is not a substitute for analyzing accrual accounting amounts. However, cash flow information can provide managers with useful data about the sufficiency and efficiency of their cash flow from operations. And, such information also can provide an additional basis for comparing their company's performance with other companies.

Adapted from Don E. Giacomino, David E. Mielke "Cash Flows: Another Approach to Ratio Analysis," *Journal of Accountancy,* March 1993, pp. 55–58.

conversion of inventory into cash, which the company uses to pay off liabilities as they come due. While this conversion process constitutes normal operations, there also must be a sufficiently large quantity of cash, receivables, inventory, and sales. Creditors cannot be expected to wait for payment while the purchaser produces, sells, and collects on its products. Liquidity analysis must, therefore, be concerned with the adequacy of resources to meet current obligations. Comparing the operating cycle with the average payment period is one way to assess the business's ability to meet its current obligations as they become due.

By looking at the trend in the operating cycle, managers are able to analyze the relative strengths and weaknesses in the company's liquidity position. For example, a trend toward a shorter collection period may indicate that the business is improving its collection policies. A trend toward a longer collection period may indicate financial difficulty.

Natural Frozen Foods' approximate operating cycle is shown below.

Selling period (average selling period ratio)	89.02 days
Collection period (average collection period ratio)	60.23 days
	149.25 days

This means that it takes approximately 149.25 days for Natural Frozen Foods Company to sell inventory and collect the related cash from customers. Since Natural Frozen Foods Company pays its operating payables in approximately 27 days, it must rely on other assets to meet its current obligations. The company cannot purchase merchandise that will take 149 days to become cash and pay off the liabilities associated with converting that inventory to cash in 27 days unless it has some additional assets on their way to becoming cash.

EVALUATING CASH POSITION

Solvency: Converting Other Assets to Cash

In Chapter 11, we discussed ways to invest excess cash as well as the various sources of short-term borrowing available to companies. Now we are going to describe how to use financial ratios to evaluate a company's cash position.

Businesses rarely have enough cash on hand at any one time to pay off all of their short-term obligations. Nor is it necessary for them to maintain a cash balance that would allow them to do so. Generally, businesses depend on the timing of their cash inflows in connection with the timing of their cash outflows to ensure that they have the ability to pay their obligations when they become due.

Quick assets are current assets that are most liquid, that is, they can be converted to cash quickly and easily. Quick assets are cash, accounts and notes receivable, and marketable securities (temporary investments). Remember that a business can convert its accounts receivable to cash by factoring or assigning them, and it can discount notes receivable for cash, as described in Chapter 11. Inventory is a current asset that is not considered a quick asset because it usually cannot be converted to cash quickly.

The timing of cash inflows and outflows is crucial to operations management. A business's ability to pay its short-term financial obligations is known as **solvency.** Managers use **solvency ratios** to evaluate the company's ability to meet its short-term obligations and, thus, to measure the viability of the business in the short term. Here we explain two solvency ratios: current and quick. Current and quick ratio management involves maintaining adequate amounts of current and quick assets to meet current liabilities.

Current Ratio   Since current obligations are expected to be paid from the cash generated from current assets, one measure of the adequacy of a company's current assets to meet its current obligations is the **current ratio.** It is determined by comparing total current assets with total current liabilities. We calculate the current ratio as:

$$\text{Current ratio} = \frac{\text{Current assets}}{\text{Current liabilities}}$$

Management uses the current ratio to gain insight about the ability of the company to meet its current obligations as they become due. In general, for most businesses, a current ratio greater than 1 is expected because a current ratio of less than 1 indicates that current liabilities exceed current assets. For most major industries, the average current ratio is between 1.5 and 2. It does not vary as much across industries as other ratios, such as inventory turnover, which can range from just over 3 in the tobacco industry to over 12 in the printing and publishing industry.[8] If a business does not have a current ratio that exceeds 1, it may indicate that anticipated cash inflows from current assets may not be sufficient to meet required future cash outflows as represented by current liabilities.

In order to ensure that a business has enough cash to make payments as scheduled, lending institutions often require borrowers to maintain a certain current ratio as a condition of any loan. Therefore, it is important for management to be aware of events that might have a negative impact on the current ratio. Since stockholders often use the current ratios of companies for comparison purposes, management should try to keep its current ratio within the range considered appropriate for its industry.

A high current ratio does not always indicate that management is doing a good job. If a business has a high current ratio, it may result from holding more current assets than it should. A well-run business holds only enough current assets to operate

---

[8]United States Department of Commerce, *Quarterly Financial Report for Manufacturing, Mining and Trade Corporations*, Fourth Quarter.

effectively, since current assets like cash, accounts receivable, and prepaid items provide no return.

We show the current ratio of Natural Frozen Foods Company for 1997 using data from Exhibit 12.2.

$$\frac{\$320,000}{\$96,000} = 3.33$$

This means that for every dollar of current liabilities, Natural Frozen Foods has $3.33 of current assets available. The current ratio for 1996 was 2.56 ($306,000/$119,500), so the amount of current assets relative to current liabilities has increased since 1996. Analysts at Natural Frozen Foods should compare the current ratio to previous years' and to industry averages to determine if it is adequate. Current ratios of 3.33 and 2.56 for 1997 and 1996, respectively, indicate that Natural Frozen Foods is in a solid short-term liquidity position and should have no problem meeting its near-term obligations.

Quick Ratio Another measure of a company's ability to meet its current debt obligations is the **quick ratio,** also known as the *acid-test ratio.* It is the ratio of quick assets to current liabilities. Quick (liquid) assets are cash and cash equivalents, which are one step removed from cash—the next step in the normal cycle of cash equivalent items in their conversion to cash. Inventories are two steps removed from cash because they are sold on account (step one) and before the cash is collected (step two). The quick ratio is:

$$\text{Quick ratio} = \frac{\text{Cash} + \text{Temporary investments} + \text{Accounts receivable}}{\text{Current liabilities}}$$

The quick ratio is a more reliable test of solvency than the current ratio because it eliminates a potentially large current asset, inventory, from consideration. Office supplies and prepaid items also are removed from the analysis because they are purchased for use, rather than for conversion into cash.

Analysts would evaluate the quick ratio in much the same way as the current ratio. Natural Frozen Foods' 1997 quick ratio using data from Exhibit 12.2 is:[11]

$$\frac{\$145,500}{\$96,000} = 1.52$$

This means that for every dollar of current liabilities, Natural Frozen Foods Company has $1.52 of quick assets. As with the current ratio, to determine the adequacy of the ratio, the user must compare it against past ratios and external standards. The quick ratio for 1996 was 1.30 ($155,600/$119,500). These ratios indicate that Natural Frozen Foods is in good position to meet its current obligations, and, given the increase in its quick ratio from 1.30 to 1.52 between 1996 and 1997, its short-term liquidity position is improving.

Like the current ratio, the quick ratio is often used as a benchmark for solvency. Lenders may require the company to maintain a certain quick ratio before they will lend the company money. Stockholders may be concerned when the quick ratio falls outside industry guidelines.

Evaluating Solvency Comparing a company's current and quick ratios measures the quality of a business's current assets. If a business has a big difference between its current and quick ratios, its current assets may not be available to pay current obligations. If the difference is due to inventory, analysts should look to the inventory turnover ratio to see if the business is holding excess inventory.

---

[11]Natural Frozen Foods' quick assets of $145,500 include: Cash, $9,500; Temporary investments, $13,000; and Accounts receivable (net) $123,000.

The current and quick ratios also provide management with valuable information about the relationship of payables to current and quick assets. If management notices any significant unexplained changes in any of these ratios, further analysis is warranted. For example, if the current ratio dropped dramatically in the current period while the level of current assets remained constant, it may indicate that the company's obligations are not being paid in a timely manner. On the other hand, a sudden rise in the current ratio when current assets remain constant may indicate that management is not taking advantage of the credit terms offered by suppliers. As an additional control, management should send accounts payable verifications (confirmations) to suppliers. These verifications include the amount the company has recorded as its obligation to the supplier. If the amount the supplier has recorded differs from the amount on the verification, they are instructed to notify the company in order to resolve the difference. This helps ensure that the accounting records accurately reflect the amount of the business's actual obligations. Also, it is a good idea to randomly analyze vouchers and payment authorizations as a test of whether the company is following proper accounting procedures for recording obligations and making payments.

SUMMARY

Analysis of financial statement information is important in evaluating activities in the revenue and expenditure cycles. By making appropriate comparisons of the current period's information with the previous periods' results and external information sources about other companies in the industry, management can plan future operations by building on the things that were done right and correcting operating decisions that hurt financial performance. To evaluate operating activities, management uses the information contained in the company's primary financial statements to perform horizontal, vertical, and ratio analysis. In this chapter, we show how to use these types of analyses to evaluate the decisions found in the revenue and expenditure cycles of business operations.

- Evaluation requires use of some sort of standard as a basis for comparison. These standards can be either internal, for example, the budget or prior periods' financial statements, or external, for example, from sources like *Annual Statement Studies* published by Robert Morris and Associates, which provide industry data to make comparisons.

- Horizontal analysis involves comparing an item on the current period's statement, such as sales or accounts receivable, with the same item on previous periods' statements, either in absolute terms or as a percentage of the item in some base year.

- Vertical analysis focuses on the relative importance of items within a given statement. All items are expressed as a percentage of a base item, for example, sales on the income statement. Combining vertical and horizontal analysis allows comparisons of the relative importance of items over time.

- Ratios capture the relationships between accounts that are related logically in the activities of businesses, for example, sales and accounts receivable. Management and investors can use ratios to evaluate operating performance.

- Companies analyze purchasing decisions involving the quantities and type of items purchased with the inventory turnover and the average selling period ratio. The period of time that items remain in inventory is reflected in these ratios, which, in turn, allows assessment of whether purchasing decisions reflect demand for the product.

- Management uses the accounts receivable turnover and average collection period ratios to evaluate credit-granting decisions in the revenue cycle. Such decisions indicate the rate at which companies collect their accounts receivable balances.

- Pricing decisions are evaluated indirectly by using two profitability ratios: gross margin and return on sales. By assessing overall profitability as well as profitability of specific products, management can decide whether prices are set at reasonable levels.

- One of the major considerations of management is whether they have sufficient cash or cash equivalents to meet their current debt obligations. The current and quick ratios measure management's ability to meet short-term obligations. The length of the operating cycle is also a measure of the flow of cash through a business as a result of selling and collecting from customers.

KEY TERMS

accounts receivable turnover The ratio of net credit sales to the average (net) accounts receivable

average collection period ratio The average number of days it takes to collect the average balance in accounts receivable; determined by dividing the number of days in the period by the accounts receivable turnover

average selling period ratio The number of days it takes to sell the average amount of inventory determined by dividing the number of days in the period by the inventory turnover

current ratio The ratio of total current assets to total current liabilities, which measures the ability of the company to meet its current obligations

gross margin ratio The ratio of gross margin to net sales; the portion of sales revenue available after deducting the cost of goods sold

horizonal analysis Comparison of each item on a financial statement with that same item on statements from previous periods

inventory turnover The ratio of cost of goods sold to the average balance in the Inventory account

operating cycle The time it takes to sell inventory on account and receive the related cash from customers

payables turnover The ratio of cash expenses (expenses that require a cash payment) to the average amount of current liabilities, excluding principal portions of bank loans

payment period ratio The average number of days required to pay the average amount of current operating liabilities determined by dividing the number of days in the period by the payables turnover

ratio analysis The realtionship between two or more accounts on the same statement or accounts from two different statements related by the transactions they represent

quick assets Current assets that are most liquid, that, they can be converted to cash quickly and easily

quick ratio (Also known as the *acid-test ratio*.) It is the ratio of quick assets to current liabilities, which is a strict measure a company's ability to meet current obligations

ratio analysis The relationship between two or more accounts on the same statement or accounts from two different statements related by the transactions they represent

return on sales ratio The ratio of income from operations to net sales; the portion of sales revenue remaining after deducting all operating expenses

solvency A business's ability to pay its short-term financial obligations

solvency ratios Ratios that measure a company's ability to meet its short-term obligations to maintain adequate amounts of assets to pay liabilities.

vertical analysis Analysis of the relative size of items to a base item within one statement for the same period

QUESTIONS

1. Why is it important for managers to evaluate operations?
2. How does management use internal standards to measure performance?
3. How does management use external standards to evaluate performance?
4. Name four sources of external standards and where to find them.
5. Explain the purpose of each of three general approaches of financial statement analysis.
6. Explain the purpose of ratio analysis.
7. What information is determined by calculating an inventory turnover?
8. How does the inventory turnover relate to the selling period?

9. What would an inventory turnover ratio of 7.2 mean? Why?

10. What information is determined by calculating an accounts receivable turnover?

11. How does the accounts receivable turnover relate to the collection period?

12. Explain what an accounts receivable turnover of 5.0 indicates. Is it adequate? Why or why not?

13. If the selling period is 40 days, is this enough information to judge the activity of the inventory? Why or why not?

14. What information is determined by calculating a payables turnover?

15. Explain why depreciation expense and bank notes payable are omitted from the payables turnover calculation.

16. Why is interest expense included as an operating expense, while notes payable are excluded as an operating liability in the payables turnover ratio?

17. If the payables turnover is 6, is this enough information to judge the speed with which obligations are paid? Why or why not?

18. How are the current and quick ratios different?

19. If you know a company has a current ratio of 2 to 1, is this enough information to judge its solvency position? Why or why not?

20. Explain what is meant when it is stated that a company has a quick ratio of 1.75.

21. How are the gross margin ratio and return on sales ratio related?

22. How are the collection and selling periods used to estimate the operating cycle?

EXERCISES

E 12.1   Georgia Peach Company predicts that cost of goods sold next year will be $365,000. In the past average inventory has been $37,000. What are the expected inventory turnover and number of days in the selling period for Georgia Peach Company?

E 12.2   Pittsburg Painting has sales of $950,000 in 1997 when its average accounts receivable balance was $140,000. During 1997, sales returns and allowances were $7,500, and sales discounts were $19,000. What was the accounts receivable turnover and collection period?

E 12.3   Florida Tanning Enterprises expects sales next year of $4,000,000. It expects to maintain an average accounts receivable balance of $60,500 throughout the year. What are the expected accounts receivable turnover and number of days in the collection period for Florida Tanning Enterprises?

E 12.4   Hawaii Tropical Fruit Mix, Inc., has an accounts receivable turnover of 5.75 and an inventory turnover of 6.40. What is the estimated length of the operating cycle in days for Hawaii, Inc.?

E 12.5   Honolulu Leis Incorporated has sales of $1.6 million in 1996, of which 20 percent was cash sales. During this same period, the sales discounts given to customers were $38,000, and the accounts receivable balance decreased from $102,000 to $82,000. What was Honolulu Leis' accounts receivable turnover and collection period?

E 12.6   The summarized data below were obtained from the accounting records of Falmera Company at the end of its fiscal year, September 30, 1997.

	1997	1996
Cash	$ 24,180	$ 27,240
Accounts receivable	119,500	120,160
Inventory	143,390	101,690
All noncurrent assets	348,780	353,580
Accounts payable	95,340	89,590
Bank note payable, due in 90 days	48,000	26,000
Note payable, due in 8 years	27,500	27,500
Sales	940,240	838,240
Cost of goods sold	689,590	641,780
Operating expenses (including depreciation of $5,160 in both years and uncollectible accounts expense of $1,280 in 1996 and $1,190 in 1997)	28,510	25,330

Compute the following for 1997:
a. Accounts receivable turnover and average collection period.
b. Inventory turnover and average selling period.
c. Payables turnover and average payment period.
d. Approximate length of the operating cycle.

E 12.7 Refer to E 12.6. Compute the current and quick ratios for both years. Comment on the solvency of the company.

E 12.8 Refer to E 12.6. Compute the return on sales and gross margin percentage for both years. Is the company profitable?

E 12.9 The current assets for 1995 and 1996 together with sales and cost of goods sold for 1996 are presented below for Anders Windows Company. Compute the approximate length of the operating cycle.

	1996	1995
Cash	$ 12,500	$11,050
Accounts receivable	21,800	23,200
Inventory	32,700	29,600
Unexpired insurance	400	1,000
Totals	$ 67,400	$64,850
Sales credit	$368,510	
Cost of goods sold	257,680	
Gross margin	$110,830	

E 12.10 Refer to E 12.9. Assume that current liabilities are $32,700 for 1996 and $35,900 for 1995. What are the current and quick ratios for 1996 and 1995? Comment on the cash position of the company.

E 12.11 D's Hardware Company currently has $256,700 of current assets and $163,890 of current liabilities. Fifty percent of the current assets are liquid. What are D's Company's current and quick ratios?

E 12.12 Kowa Corporation shows a current ratio of 3.56 to 1, a quick ratio of 1.99 to 1, and an operating cycle of 45 days. Comment on Kowa Corporation's ability to meet its current obligations.

E 12.13 Brevit, MacKenzie and Company's financial statements contain the information shown below. Compute the approximate length of the operating cycle for 1996 and 1997.

	1997	1996	1995
Accounts receivable	$ 92,120	$ 86,580	$ 84,940
Inventory	110,710	104,250	101,410
Sales	908,390	843,920	—
Cost of goods sold	610,890	578,430	—

E 12.14 Refer to E12.13. Complete a horizontal analysis for 1997.

E 12.15 Make the appropriate computations for each of the following situations:
a. The firm's average collection period is 40, and its sales are $276,300. What is its average accounts receivable balance?
b. If a company maintains an average inventory of $60,000, which it plans to turn over every 45 days, what will be the amount of its cost of goods sold?
c. A business is attempting to forecast the average balance of current liabilities associated with operations. It expects to have a 40-day payment period. Sales are expected to be $500,000 with a gross margin of 60 percent. Operating expenses exclusive of noncash items are estimated at $105,000.

E 12.16 The Malcom Corporation currently has a 37 percent gross margin ratio on sales of 15,000 units at $17 each. Malcom anticipates a 10 percent increase in the cost of its merchandise. How much will Malcom have to increase its selling price to maintain the same gross margin ratio?

E 12.17 Quigley Corporation has a return on sales of 3 percent on sales of 25,000 units at $12 per unit. Due to competition, Quigley must reduce its selling price $1 per unit. If Quigley wants to maintain a 3 percent return on sales, how much will expenses need to decline?

E 12.18   Last year, 1996, the Bora Bora Export Company sold 150,000 units of its product for $22 per unit. The cost of goods sold averages 57 percent of sales. What are Bora Bora's gross margin percentage and gross margin in dollars for 1996? Bora Bora expects cost of its product to increase 8 percent next year and will increase its selling price 10 percent in response to this price increase. Sales in 1997 are expected to be 140,000 units. What is the expected gross margin percentage for 1997?

E 12.19   A firm has a current ratio of 2.66. Its current liabilities are $80,800. Its liquid assets are 25 percent of its current assets. What is the quick ratio?

E 12.20   A firm has an accounts receivable turnover of 6. Its average accounts receivable is $72,000. Cost of goods sold is 56 percent of sales and its inventory turnover is 5. What is the average amount of inventory?

E 12.21   A firm has a gross margin ratio of 40 percent and a return on sales of 8 percent. Its cost of goods sold for the year were $7,580,400. What was the operating income for the year?

PROBLEMS

P 12.1   The following information has been gathered from the financial records of Tawny Enterprises.

	1997	1996
Cash	$ 250,140	$ 231,860
Temporary investments	-0-	520,370
Accounts receivable	2,925,540	2,589,950
Inventories	3,480,210	3,684,970
Long-term assets	4,219,750	2,494,730
Accounts payable	1,054,950	1,142,630
Other current liabilities	685,160	571,320
Long-term liabilities	2,000,000	2,500,000
Sales	22,838,400	23,804,700
Cost of goods sold	18,910,190	20,543,450
Operating expenses	2,968,995	2,332,870

Required: Compute the following items for 1997:
   a. Current ratio.
   b. Quick ratio.
   c. Accounts receivable turnover.
   d. Number of days in the collection period.
   e. Inventory turnover.
   f. Number of days in the selling period.
   g. Estimated length of the operating cycle.

P 12.2   Refer to P 12.1 Complete a vertical and horizontal analysis of Tawny Enterprises for 1997.

P 12.3   Anderson Mercantile is planning to expand its operations during the coming year. Its present financial position and the results of its operation for the year are shown below in summary form. These statements are representative of its operations for the past few years.

ANDERSON MERCANTILE
Statement of Financial Position
As of December 31, 1996

Cash	$11,600	Accounts payable	$27,200
Accounts receivable	21,400		
Inventory	19,800	Owners' equity	203,600
Long-term assets	178,000		
	$230,800		$230,800

ANDERSON MERCANTILE
Income Statement
For the Year Ending December 31, 1996

Sales		$260,000
Less expenses:		
Cost of goods sold	$161,200	
Depreciation	1,500	
Other expenses	74,400	237,100
Net income		$ 22,900

A planned expansion during 1997 will result in the following:

1. Cash increase of $3,400.
2. Accounts receivable increase of $3,000.
3. Inventory increase of $6,500.
4. Long-term asset increase, net of depreciation of $10,400.
5. Accounts payable increase of $3,300.
6. Sales increase of 30 percent.
7. Cost of goods sold increase to 68 percent of sales.
8. Depreciation increase to $1,800.
9. Other expenses increase to $76,800.

Required:
a. Compute the following items for 1996 and 1997 as projected:
   1. Current ratio.
   2. Quick ratio.
   3. Accounts receivable turnover.
   4. Number of days in the collection period.
   5. Inventory turnover.
   6. Number of days in the selling period.
   7. Estimated length of the operating cycle.
b. Do you recommend the expansion: Why or why not?

P 12.4   Financial statements for Dylan Company are presented below.

DYLAN COMPANY
Comparative Balance Sheets
As of December 31, 1997, and 1996

	1997	1996
Cash	$ 12,000	$ 10,000
Accounts receivable	34,000	30,000
Allowance for uncollectible accounts	(1,000)	(1,000)
Inventory	27,000	24,000
Plant and equipment	188,000	165,000
Accumulated depreciation	(70,000)	(64,000)
Total assets	$190,000	$164,000
Accounts payable	$22,950	$37,300
Wages payable	3,575	2,000
Taxes payable	4,675	2,385
Bonds payable	10,000	-0-
Common stock	30,000	30,000
Retained earnings	118,800	92,315
Total liabilities and owners' equities	$190,000	$164,000

DYLAN COMPANY
Income Statement
For the Year Ended December 31, 1997

Sales		$300,000
Cost of goods sold		135,000
Gross margin		$165,000
Operating expenses:		
Selling expense	$39,000	
Rent expense	45,000	
Depreciation expense	11,000	
Bad debt expense	500	
Interest expense	15,000	110,500
Income from operations		$ 54,500
Gain on sale of equipment		500
Income before taxes		$ 55,000
Income tax expense		18,700
Net income		$ 36,300

Required:
a. Calculate the appropriate ratios for 1997.
b. Complete a vertical analysis for 1997.
c. Complete a horizontal analysis of the balance sheet for 1997.
d. Explain the information generated by these analyses.

P 12.5   The condensed financial statements of Belleville Company for 1995 and 1996 are shown below.

BELLEVILLE COMPANY
Income Statement
For the Years Ended December 31, 1996, and 1995

	1996	1995
Sales	$280,000	$260,000
Cost of goods sold:		
Inventory, January 1	$ 22,700	$ 20,500
Purchases	166,000	153,000
Goods available for sale	$188,700	$173,500
Inventory, December 31	23,500	22,700
Cost of goods sold	$165,200	$150,800
Gross margin	$114,800	$109,200
Operating expenses*	84,000	83,200
Net income before taxes	$ 30,800	$ 26,000
Income taxes	5,600	3,900
Net income	$ 25,200	$ 22,100

*Includes depreciation expense of $5,000.

BELLEVILLE COMPANY
Statement of Financial Position
As of December 31, 1996 and 1995

	1996	1995
Cash	$ 9,800	$ 8,400
Accounts receivable	18,200	17,600
Inventory	25,300	22,700
Property, plant, and equipment, net	58,700	49,300
Total assets	$112,000	$98,000
Current liabilities	$ 24,200	$19,500
Long-term liabilities	12,000	12,000
Owners' equity	75,800	66,500
Total liabilities and owners' equity	$112,000	$98,000

Other Information:

Ending balances, December 31, 1994
   Accounts receivable $17,200
   Inventory   20,500

Required: *a.* Compute the following items for each year:
1. Current ratio.
2. Quick ratio.
3. Average collection period.
4. Average selling period.
5. Gross margin ratio.
6. Return on sales.

b. What information is generated by your analyses?

P 12.6   Financial statements for Merchalis Retail Store are presented below.

MERCHALIS RETAIL STORE
Income Statement
For the Year Ended September 30, 1997

Revenue:	
Sales	$485,000
Expenses:	
Cost of goods sold	331,000
Salaries	87,000
Rent	16,000
Depreciation	7,000
Other operating expenses	20,000
Net income	$24,000

MERCHALIS RETAIL STORE
Statement of Financial Position
As of September 30, 1997, and 1996

	1997	1996
Assets		
Current assets:		
Cash	$ 23,000	$ 16,000
Accounts receivable	36,000	28,000
Inventory	120,000	135,000
Prepaid rent	4,000	-0-
	$183,000	$179,000
Long-term assets:		
Furniture and fixtures	$148,000	$148,000
Accumulated depreciation	(88,500)	(81,500)
	$ 59,500	$ 66,500
Total assets	$242,500	$245,500
Liabilities and Owner's Equity		
Current liabilities:		
Accounts payable	$ 28,000	$ 25,000
Salaries payable	5,000	5,500
Accrued liabilities for operating expense	7,500	4,000
Notes payable	35,000	-0-
	$ 75,700	$ 34,500
Long-term liabilities:		
Notes payable	$ -0-	$ 35,000
Owner's equity:		
Merchalis, capital	$167,000	$176,000
Total liabilities and owner's equity	$242,500	$245,500

Required:
a. Calculate the appropriate ratios for 1997.
b. Complete a vertical analysis for 1997.
c. What information is generated by your analyses?

P 12.7 Refer to the financial statements of Disney Company.

Required:
a. Compute all the appropriate ratios to evaluate operations.
b. Perform a vertical analysis on the current balance sheet accounts and the operating section of the income statement.
c. Perform a horizontal analysis on the current balance sheet accounts and the operating section of the income statement.
d. What information is generated by your analyses?

P 12.8 Refer to the financial statements of Anheuser-Busch, Inc.

Required:
a. Compute all the appropriate ratios to evaluate operations.
b. Perform a vertical analysis on the current balance sheet accounts and the operating section of the income statement.
c. Perform a horizontal analysis on the current balance sheet accounts and the operating section of the income statement.
d. What information is generated by your analyses?

P 12.9 Bonaville Products presently has a current ratio of 2.3 to 1 and a quick ratio of 1.7 to 1. For each of the following transactions, specify the effect of the transaction on the respective ratios. Use *I* for increase, *D* for decrease, and *NC* for no change. Consider each transaction separately.

	Current Ratio	Quick Ratio
a. Collect an accounts receivable.	_____	_____
b. Pay an accounts payable.	_____	_____
c. Purchase inventory on account.	_____	_____
d. Receive, but do not pay, utility bill.	_____	_____
e. Borrow money from the bank for 90 days.	_____	_____
f. Pay insurance for six months in advance.	_____	_____
g. Borrow money from the bank for five years.	_____	_____
h. Issue capital stock for cash.	_____	_____
i. Purchase equipment for cash.	_____	_____
j. Purchase temporary investments.	_____	_____

P 12.10   Backwards Corporation has a current ratio of 2.6 and a quick ratio of 1.0. Its accounts receivable turnover is 4.2, its inventory turnover is 3.1, and its payables turnover is 6.4. Cash expenses, excluding cost of goods sold, were $504,000. Cost of goods sold is $1,736,000. Cash sales were $1,230,000, and credit sales were $966,000.

Required: *a.* Assuming that there was no change in the balance of accounts receivable during the period, what is the ending accounts receivable balance?

b. Assuming that there was no change in the balance of inventory during the period, what is the ending inventory balance?

c. Assuming that there was no change in the balance of current liabilities during the period and that Backwards Corporation had no notes payable during the period, what is the ending balance of current liabilities?

d. Assuming that the only current assets of Backwards Corporation are accounts receivable, inventory, and cash, what is the ending balance of cash?

e. What is the estimated length of the operating cycle?

COMPUTER APPLICATIONS

CA 12.1   The following information was taken from the accounting records of Callum Company.

CALLUM COMPANY
Balance Sheet
As of December 31, 1997, and 1996, and 1995

	1997	1996	1995
Current assets:			
Cash	$ 35,000	$ 31,000	$ 26,000
Temporary investments	12,000	8,000	10,000
Accounts receivable, net	180,000	176,000	169,000
Inventories	225,000	219,000	216,000
Total current assets	$452,000	$434,000	$421,000
Property, plant, and equipment:			
Land	$ 50,000	$ 50,000	$ 50,000
Buildings, net of depreciation	141,000	149,000	157,000
Equipment, net of depreciation	32,000	47,000	52,000
Total property, plant, and equipment	$223,000	$246,000	$259,000
Total assets	$675,000	$680,000	$680,000
Accounts payable	$ 96,000	$ 77,000	$ 80,000
Notes payable, current	40,000	60,000	60,000
Other current liabilities	32,000	41,000	39,000
Total current liabilities	$168,000	$178,000	$179,000
Long-term liabilities	75,000	75,000	75,000
Owners' equity	432,000	427,000	426,000
Total liabilities and owners' equity	$675,000	$680,000	$680,000

CALLUM COMPANY
Income Statement
For the Period Ending December 31, 1997, 1996, and 1995

	1997	1996	1995
Sales	$1,920,000	$2,085,000	$1,880,000
Cost of goods sold	1,152,000	1,209,000	1,110,000
Gross margin	$ 768,000	$ 876,000	$ 770,000
Operating expenses*	688,000	771,000	678,000
Net income	$ 80,000	$ 105,000	$ 92,000

*Includes depreciation of $23,000 each year.

Required: Use a computer spreadsheet.
a. Complete a vertical analysis for 1996 and 1997.
b. Complete a horizontal analysis for 1996 and 1997.

CA 12.2   Design a spreadsheet that will illustrate the following effects on the accounts receivable and inventory turnover ratios of each of the following events:
- *a.* Increase in sales.
- *b.* Decrease in average accounts receivable
- *c.* Decrease in cost of goods sold.
- *d.* Increase in average inventory.

CASES

C 12.1   Using the company financial statements you obtained in Case 1.1, determine the industry your company is in. Calculate all the appropriate ratios and compare them to the industry averages shown in Dun & Bradstreet or Robert Morris Associates' publications of industry statistics. Describe the liquidity and profitability of the company selected.

C 12.2   Refer to the accounting records of Callum Company shown in CA 12.1.

Required:
- *a.* Compute the appropriate ratios for 1996 and 1997.
- *b.* Comment on your results. Are there any trends evident?
- *c.* Is the company profitable?
- *d.* Does the company show adequate liquidity?

CRITICAL THINKING

CT 12.1   Go to the library or other source of financial statement data such as *Disclosure* or *Compustat*. Obtain five years of data on a company you are interested in learning more about.

Required:
- *a.* Calculate the appropriate ratios for each year.
- *b.* Are there any trends? Explain.
- *c.* Does the company appear to have an adequate cash position? Why or why not?
- *d.* Does the company appear to be profitable? Why or why not?
- *e.* Would you recommend investing in this company? Why or why not?

CT 12.2   Find a company that has failed or declared bankruptcy within the past five years. Obtain the financial statements for the five years prior to the failure or bankruptcy from *Disclosure*, *Compustat*, or *Lexis*.

Required:
- *a.* Calculate the appropriate ratios for each year.
- *b.* Comment on your results. Did any of the ratios indicate the impending trouble for the company?

ETHICAL CHALLENGES

ET 12.1   Brown & Son is a retail stereo outlet store. Sales last year were $1.2 million with a gross margin of 30 percent. The average inventory balance was $120,000. J. B., one of the owners, is concerned because his suppliers expect an inventory turnover of at least 10. M. H., the new salesperson, guarantees J. B. that he can obtain an inventory turnover of at least 10 in the next year. He makes a deal with J. B. that he will work for only a 1 percent commission, but if the inventory turnover is at least 10 at the end of the year, he will receive a $50,000 bonus.

The following year sales are again $1.2 million with a gross margin of 30 percent. The average industry balance is also the same, except that on December 28, M. H. returns $80,000 of merchandise to the supplier for credit.

On December 31, M. H. collects his bonus check and quits.

Required: Explain what happened to J. B.

ET 12.2   You are a new loan officer at a large bank. Taylor Company, which is experiencing cash flow problems, has applied for a $150,000, 90-day bank loan. Taylor Company's current ratio is 1.1 to 1. Your bank requires a minimum current ratio of 2.5 to 1 before making short-term loans. However, you feel that without this loan, Taylor Company may go bankrupt within the next year.

Required: Write a letter to Kim Taylor, the president of Taylor Company, explaining why you will or will not loan her the money.

CHAPTER 13

Conversion Cycle: Analysis and Control

Learning Objectives

1. Describe how to use variances to evaluate the efficiency of the conversion cycle.
2. Explain how to use variances to evaluate the use of direct materials and direct labor.
3. Explain how managers use variances to evaluate overhead costs.
4. Describe how companies determine which variances require additional investigation.
5. Explain how companies use performance measures other than variance analysis to evaluate quality and processes.

Has Hewlett-Packard been one of the best managed companies in America? Many analysts seem to think so. Its sales expanded $4 billion in 1993, and another $4 billion in 1994! In 1993, Hewlett-Packard (HP) sold its ten millionth HP LaserJet Printer. How was Hewlett-Packard able to maintain this phenomenal growth in an industry where technology changes rapidly and where what is selling today may be obsolete tomorrow?

The secret to HP's success lies in its ability to periodically reinvent itself by finding new markets for its products. In addition, HP has strong employee loyalty, refusing to resort to mass layoffs in an effort to cut costs. Rather, HP cut overhead by consolidating its personal computer operations and trimming its work force through early retirement and voluntary departures.[1]

Another reason for Hewlett-Packard's success is the HP philosophy. The original founders of HP, William Hewlett and David Packard, believed in empowering employees long before employee empowerment was a corporate buzzword. They believed that getting people to work together in teams and giving them both the responsibility for, and the rewards of, a job well done were the secrets to long-term success. This philosophy still exists at HP. Division managers

---

[1]Robert Ristelheuber, "HP: America's New Best Managed Company," *Electronic Business Buyer*, June 1994, pp. 36–41.

430

of HP know exactly what their costs are and where they come from. "Companies like IBM and DEC haven't figured out how to do that," says Jim McDonnell, marketing manager for the network server division of Hewlett-Packard.[2]

Hewlett-Packard's accomplishments stem from its ability to respond to customers and control its costs. Clearly, it has come a long way from the business begun by Hewlett and Packard in a Palo Alto garage in 1939 when the Silicon Valley was only a stretch of orchards known as Santa Clara County. From their initial $538 investment, they built a company that today provides quality high-tech products in five primary areas—computer products, electronic test equipment, medical electronic equipment, analytical instruments, and electronic components. ⚙️🚲

Companies like Hewlett-Packard are able to control costs because they monitor their operations. Part of this monitoring process involves the comparison of the budgets developed in the planning phase of operations to the results of operations carried out in the performing phase to determine whether the company achieved its financial goals and objectives during the period.

Chapter 12 discussed how to analyze the revenue and expenditure cycles of a business. In this chapter, we examine how companies evaluate and control the conversion cycle. Manufacturing companies need to evaluate the effectiveness, efficiency, quality, and processes of the conversion cycle. **Effectiveness** is a condition relating to whether the goals of the company were achieved during the period, while **efficiency** is a condition relating to whether the goals were achieved using the best combination of the company's resources. **Quality** is the degree of excellence in the products and services provided to customers, and **processes** are the methods used to achieve the company's goals during the period. Managers compare budgeted and actual output to measure effectiveness and use a technique known as *variance analysis* to measure efficiency. Other performance measures discussed later in the chapter show how to evaluate quality and processes.

EFFECTIVENESS AND EFFICIENCY MEASURES

Effectiveness is measured by comparing the *actual outputs* of the company to the *expected outputs*. If the company achieved or exceeded its planned outputs, it is said to be effective. Effectiveness is a measure of the performance of the entire company, which we address in greater detail in Chapters 22 to 25. Efficiency is measured by comparing the *actual inputs* of the company to the *expected inputs*. To measure efficiency we need to calculate variances.

What Are Variances?

Variances are the differences between budgeted and actual financial amounts of inputs. **Variance analysis** is the inquiry into these variances to determine their causes. It is part of management's process of evaluating operations. Variance analysis answers questions such as: Were the company's expenditures too high for materials this period? Did it use too much direct labor? Did it spend more money on overhead than planned? Companies do not have the resources available to investigate the cause of every variance. Thus, they adopt a philosophy known as **management-by-exception** whereby they investigate only unusual or unexpected outcomes. For purposes of our analysis here, it is necessary to understand the role of standard costs in budgeting and performance evaluation.

---

[2]Alan Deutschman, "How H-P Continues to Grow and Grow," *Fortune*, April 2, 1994, p. 98.

What Are Standard Costs?

A **standard cost** is a predetermined cost estimate of a particular operating input. Chapter 10 indicated that the operating inputs in the conversion cycle are direct materials, direct labor, and manufacturing overhead. Companies prepare budgets based on the standard costs of the operating inputs. Chapter 5 indicated that standards, or estimates, can be set at either the normal or ideal level. Regardless of the standard that companies use, we determine the estimated costs of an input by multiplying the predetermined amount, or the **standard quantity,** of the input (direct labor hours, for example) by the predetermined cost, or the **standard price,** of the input (direct labor wage rate per hour, for example) to determine the standard cost per unit of output for the particular input (direct labor).

Service and merchandising companies also use standard costs. For example, an accounting firm estimates the number of staff hours and the wage rate per staff hour to conduct an audit, a physician estimates the number of tests a patient needs and the cost of each test, and a lawyer estimates the number of hours needed to prepare a legal case and the cost of the legal assistants used. Merchandising companies routinely estimate the amount of merchandise needed and the cost of each item so that they can determine the quantity of inventory to carry.

The focus here is on manufacturing companies that determine standard costs in order to predict and control the cost of a finished product. Assume that Hewlett-Packard developed the standard costs of inputs to produce the computer whose elements are shown in Exhibit 13.1. Thus, Hewlett-Packard plans for direct materials (motherboards) to cost $200 (1 board × $200 per board) per computer and for direct labor to cost $9 (1/2 hour × $18 per hour) per computer. These standards are based on past information concerning costs and available information about future costs obtained from the purchasing and human resources department. These departments, in turn, obtain information from sources such as suppliers, labor unions, and inflation reports that may indicate future inflation levels.

COMPARISON OF ACTUAL RESULTS TO THE MASTER BUDGET

The first step in the analysis and control of the conversion cycle is to compare the budgeted costs of production inputs to the actual costs incurred to reveal whether production required too much or too little input. However, the master budget set for a certain level of production is inappropriate to use if the actual production level was different from the planned level. When this occurs, the actual use of production inputs would be either more or less than the quantities planned in the master budget. If direct materials costs increase as production increases, as we would expect, knowing that the quantity of direct material used was greater than the amount planned does not tell us whether the company used direct materials efficiently. As Exhibit 13.2 illustrates, Hewlett-Packard's master budget is based on the *budgeted production of 15,000 computers for 1996*. For simplicity, we have combined all the various manufacturing overhead cost pools into the four activity levels for overhead application—unit-related, batch-related, product-sustaining, and facility-sustaining levels. Exhibit 13.2 indicates that, in this case, Hewlett-Packard's master budget includes $5,235,000 for all production inputs during the period.

EXHIBIT	13.1	Hewlett-Packard Standards	
Production Inputs		**Elements: Input Specifications**	
Direct materials		1 motherboard × $200 per motherboard	
Direct labor		1/2 hour per computer × $18 per hour	
Manufacturing overhead:			
Unit related		3 machine hours per computer × $12 per hour	
Batch related		$700 per production run	
Product sustaining		$30,000 per design	
Facility sustaining		$150 per square foot occupied	

EXHIBIT 13.2 | Master Budget: Total Manufacturing Cost

Production Inputs Needed for 15,000 Computers	Costs
Direct materials (15,000 computers × 1 motherboard × $200 per board)	$3,000,000
Direct labor (15,000 computers × 1/2 hour per computer × $18 per hour)	135,000
Manufacturing overhead:	
Unit related (15,000 computers × 3 machine hours per computer × $12 per hour)	540,000
Batch related (300 production runs planned × $700 per production run)	210,000
Product sustaining (20 designs × $30,000 per design)	600,000
Facility sustaining (5,000 square feet × $150 per square foot occupied)	750,000
Total manufacturing cost	$5,235,000

Exhibit 13.3 shows that the actual amounts of production inputs used by Hewlett-Packard *to produce 16,000 computers* during the period were $5,803,200. What does this tell the managers who are interested in analyzing this production process? We show a comparison of each individual cost category below:

Production Inputs	(1) Master Budget (Exhibit 13.2)	(2) Actual Results (Exhibit 13.3)	(2) – (1) Variance
Direct materials	$3,000,000	$3,420,000	$420,000
Direct labor	135,000	148,200	13,200
Manufacturing overhead:			
Unit related	540,000	620,000	80,000
Batch related	210,000	285,000	75,000
Product sustaining	600,000	590,000	(10,000)
Facility sustaining	750,000	740,000	(10,000)
Total manufacturing inputs	$5,235,000	$5,803,200	$568,200

How should management interpret the variances shown here? The comparison clearly shows that actual costs were $568,200 more than budgeted costs. Does this imply that the production and purchasing managers were negligent? For example, since actual direct material costs were $420,000 more than the budgeted costs, does this mean that the purchasing manager is buying motherboards that are too expensive? The actual cost of direct labor was $13,200 more than the budgeted costs. Does this suggest that the production workers are inefficient and take too long to produce each computer? Unfortunately, these questions cannot be answered by comparing the master budget to the actual results because *the level of actual production achieved (16,000 computers) during the period is different from the planned production level (15,000)*. Since such a comparison would not be between equivalent levels of production, analysis of master budget versus actual results would be like comparing apples to oranges. The solution to this problem is to prepare a flexible budget, which we discuss next.

EXHIBIT 13.3 | Actual Amounts Used in Production

Production Inputs Used for 16,000 Computers	Actual Costs
Direct materials (18,000 motherboards purchased at $190 each, 16,500 used)	$3,420,000
Direct labor (7,800 hours worked at $19 per hour)	148,200
Manufacturing overhead:	
Unit related (50,000 machine hours used)	620,000
Batch related (300 production runs used)	285,000
Product sustaining (18 designs used)	590,000
Facility sustaining (5,000 square feet occupied)	740,000
Total manufacturing cost	$5,803,200

COMPARISON OF ACTUAL RESULTS TO THE FLEXIBLE BUDGET

A **flexible budget** is a budget prepared to reflect the actual production level of the period. It enables users to interpret results based on the actual costs versus planned costs at the same level of production and is prepared at the end of the production period. The preparer of the flexible budget uses the standard cost of production inputs and the actual production output achieved during the period to determine the flexible budget. This, in effect, "adjusts" the planned quantities and costs of master budget inputs to the expected quantities and costs based on the actual production level. A flexible budget is appropriate for *evaluation* because it is based on the *actual output* for the period, whereas the master budget is appropriate for *planning* because it is based on the *expected output* for the period.

To prepare a flexible budget, it is necessary to determine *what amount of inputs should have been used given the actual level of production achieved* so that it is possible to compare the budgeted and the actual results at the same production level. Computation of the flexible budget cost requires multiplying the standard cost of an input and the actual output quantity, which gives us the budgeted cost for that level of output. At that point, both the budgeted and actual results are based on the same level of production, which is 16,000 computers in this case.

Using the standard costs for Hewlett-Packard from Exhibit 13.1, we develop the flexible budget illustrated in Exhibit 13.4. Notice that the flexible budget amount shown for direct materials is $3,200,000 (16,000 computers × 1 motherboard × $200 standard cost per motherboard), whereas the master budget amount of direct materials is only $3,000,000 (15,000 computers × 1 motherboard × $200 standard cost per motherboard). The difference between the flexible and master budget amounts of direct materials is due to the difference between the planned and actual levels of production. Now it is possible to compare the flexible budget to the actual results.

Production Inputs	(1) Flexible Budget (Exhibit 13.4)	(2) Actual Results (Exhibit 13.3)	(2) − (1) Variance
Direct materials	$3,200,000	$3,420,000	$220,000
Direct labor	144,000	148,200	4,200
Manufacturing overhead:			
Unit related	576,000	620,000	44,000
Batch related	210,000	285,000	75,000
Product sustaining	600,000	590,000	(10,000)
Facility sustaining	750,000	740,000	(10,000)
Total manufacturing	$5,480,000	$5,803,200	$323,200

Based on the actual production of 16,000 computers during the period, this analysis indicates that the following variances regarding the quantities of inputs actually used occurred:

- $220,000 more direct materials.

- $4,200 more direct labor.

- $44,000 more unit-related manufacturing overhead.

EXHIBIT 13.4	Flexible Budget
Production Inputs Needed for 16,000 Computers	**Costs**
Direct materials (16,000 computers × 1 motherboard × $200 per board)	$3,200,000
Direct labor (16,000 computers × 1/2 hour per computer × $18 per hour)	144,000
Manufacturing overhead:	
Unit related (16,000 computers × 3 machine hours per computer × $12 per hour)	576,000
Batch related (300 production runs planned × $700 per production run)	210,000
Product sustaining (20 designs × $30,000 per design)	600,000
Facility sustaining (5,000 square feet × $50 per square foot occupied)	750,000
Total manufacturing cost	$5,480,000

- $75,000 more batch-related manufacturing overhead.
- $10,000 less product-sustaining manufacturing overhead.
- $10,000 less facility-sustaining overhead.

Notice that the amount of batch-related, product-sustaining, and facility-sustaining overhead is the same on the master budget as on the flexible budget because these *costs do not vary with the level of production.*

What caused the difference between budgeted and actual results? For example, did the company buy more expensive materials or use more materials than they should have? Did the workers work more hours or was the pay for the laborers more per hour? And who is responsible for these differences? Did the purchasing department spend too much on direct materials, or did the production department waste the materials? Did the human resources department authorize unexpected raises for direct laborers, or did the production manager use labor inefficiently?

To begin to answer these questions and to evaluate the decisions made by management during the period, it is necessary to conduct a variance analysis, which we discuss next.

PAUSE & REFLECT	What might happen if companies evaluated their department managers using the master budget rather than a flexible budget? Why?

DIRECT LABOR VARIANCE ANALYSIS

We will continue to use the Hewlett-Packard information in Exhibits 13.3 and 13.4 to illustrate the direct labor and direct material variances.

As the analysis in Exhibit 13.4 indicates, there is a $4,200 difference between the actual and flexible budget results for direct labor. An examination of direct labor indicates the possible causes for this difference. Either the price (wage rate) incurred per hour of direct labor was different from the rate planned, or the quantity (number of hours) of direct labor used was different from the amount planned, or both. To analyze these possibilities, we calculate a direct labor price variance and a direct labor usage variance.

Direct Labor Price Variance

The **direct labor price variance** is the difference between the actual wage rate per hour and the standard wage rate per hour times the actual number of hours worked. This isolates the wage difference and applies it to the actual quantity of labor used. This variance indicates whether the wage rate incurred per hour of direct labor was greater or less than expected. Since the wage rate earned by employees is assumed to be controllable by the human resources and/or the production departments, responsibility for the direct labor price variance lies with one or both of these groups.

To calculate the direct labor price variance, use the following formula:

$$
\begin{array}{ll}
\text{Actual price} \times \text{Actual quantity of hours worked} & = \quad AP \times AQ \\
- \text{Standard price} \times \text{Actual quantity of hours worked} & = \; - SP \times AQ \\
\hline
= \text{Direct labor price variance} & = \quad DLPV
\end{array}
$$

What does this actually signify? Since the number of actual hours worked in each of these calculations is the same, we simplify the analysis as follows:

$$
\begin{array}{l}
\dfrac{\text{Direct labor}}{\text{price variance}} = (\text{Actual price} - \text{Standard price}) \times \dfrac{\text{Actual quantity of}}{\text{hours worked}} \\[2ex]
DPLV = [(AP - SP)\,AQ]
\end{array}
$$

In other words, the direct labor price variance is the difference between the actual price and the standard price of direct labor per hour, times the actual number of hours worked during the period.

If the actual price (*AP*) is greater than the standard price (*SP*), the direct labor price variance is a positive number that indicates that the direct labor price variance is unfavorable (*U*). This means that the actual price per hour exceeded the standard price allowed per hour. If the actual price is less than the standard price, the direct labor price variance is a negative number, indicating that the direct labor price variance is favorable (*F*).

The terms *favorable* and *unfavorable* should not be construed to mean good and bad, respectively. As stated earlier, management investigates the causes of any significant favorable or unfavorable variance to determine its underlying cause. Only then can it determine whether the variance is good or bad. For example, the actual wage rate may be lower than the standard wage rate which would create a favorable variance. But, if employees are unhappy due to their low wages, they may not be productive which would be an unfavorable result.

PAUSE & REFLECT	When, and why, might an unfavorable direct labor rate variance be considered a favorable result?

Refer to the information in Exhibit 13.3 and Exhibit 13.4 to calculate the direct labor price variance for Hewlett-Packard. The variance is:

Actual wage rate (Exhibit 13.3)	$ 19
Standard wage rate (Exhibit 13.4)	$ −18
Difference in wage rate	$1
Actual hours worked (Exhibit 13.3)	× 7,800
DLPV	$7,800*U*

This variance is unfavorable because Hewlett-Packard paid its workers $1 more per hour than the standard amount allowed for direct labor. Remember, this is not necessarily bad or good at this point. Perhaps the labor union demanded and won a wage dispute and, therefore, the increase in direct labor cost was unavoidable. On the other hand, the production manager may have used more experienced, higher-paid workers rather than less experienced, lower-paid workers. Management would need to investigate and determine the exact cause of this variance. Once the cause is known, management can take steps to correct operations, if a problem exists, or to correct the standard, if needed. For example, if Hewlett-Packard discovers that the direct labor wage rate is permanently increased due to a labor dispute, the company would adjust the standard wage rate per hour to reflect this fact. On the other hand, if the mix of workers used to produce computers included too many high-paid workers, the production manager would adjust the mix for the next period's production.

Direct Labor Usage Variance

A **direct labor usage variance** is the difference between the actual number of hours worked and the standard number of hours allowed for the actual production, times the standard wage rate per hour. Companies calculate this variance to determine if the actual quantity of direct labor used during the period was greater or less than the standard quantity established by the flexible budget.

The direct labor usage variance indicates whether workers are producing products in the amount of time allowed. Since the quantity of direct labor used, or number of hours worked, is assumed to be controllable by the production department, the responsibility for controlling the direct labor usage variance lies with this department. To calculate the direct labor usage variance, management would use the following formula:

Actual quantity of hours used × Standard price	=	$AQ \times SP$
− Standard quantity of hours budgeted × Standard price	=	$- SQb \times SP$
= Direct labor usage variance	=	$DLUV$

Simplifying this expression, we determine the direct labor usage variance (DLUV) as follows:

$$\text{Direct labor usage variance} = \left(\begin{array}{l} \text{Actual quantity of hours used} \\ - \text{Standard quantity of hours budgeted} \end{array} \right) \times \text{Standard price}$$

$$\text{DLUV} = [(AQ - SQb)\ SP]$$

where

SQb = Standard quantity allowed on the flexible budget

Thus, the direct labor usage variance is the difference between the actual number of hours worked and the number of hours that *should have been worked* to produce the actual amount of output during the period, multiplied by the standard price per hour for direct labor.

If the actual number of hours worked is greater than the standard number of hours allowed, the direct labor usage variance is a positive number, which indicates that the direct labor usage variance is unfavorable (*U*). This implies that the actual number of hours exceeded the standard number of hours that *should have been used* for the actual amount of production. If the number of actual hours worked is less than the number of standard hours allowed, then the direct labor usage variance is a negative, or favorable (*F*), number.

PAUSE & REFLECT

If management uses ideal standards, would you expect the direct labor usage variance to be favorable or unfavorable? Why? How would management interpret the analysis in these cases?

Using the information in Exhibits 13.3 and 13.4, the direct labor usage variance for Hewlett-Packard is:

Actual hours worked (Exhibit 13.3)	7,800
Standard hours allowed (Exhibit 13.4)	−8,000 (16,000 × 1/2 hour)
Difference in hours	200
Standard wage rate per hour (Exhibit 13.3)	× $18
	$3,600*F*

This is a favorable variance because the flexible budget allowed 8,000 hours to produce 16,000 computers (1/2 hour per computer), but Hewlett-Packard only required 7,800 hours. What are some possible causes for this variance? Perhaps, as discussed previously, the production manager used more experienced workers who were able to produce the computers faster. On the other hand, workers may have been motivated by a wage increase and, therefore, may have worked more efficiently. Again, an investigation is necessary to pinpoint the exact cause of this variance. For example, assume that Hewlett-Packard discovers that the production manager did change the mix of workers in an effort to increase efficiency. Since the unfavorable price variance ($7,800*U*) outweighs the favorable usage variance ($3,600*F*), the change may not have been worthwhile and, therefore, would be corrected next period.

DIRECT MATERIALS VARIANCE ANALYSIS

There is a $220,000 difference between actual and flexible budget direct materials costs (Exhibit 13.4). An examination of direct materials costs indicates the possible causes for this difference. Perhaps the price incurred to purchase the direct materials was different from the price planned, and/or the quantity of direct materials used was different from the amount planned, and/or the quantity of direct materials purchased was different from the quantity of direct materials used in production. To analyze these possible causes, companies calculate a direct materials price variance, a direct materials usage variance, and a direct materials inventory variance.

Direct Materials Price Variance

A **direct materials price variance** is the difference between the actual price paid to purchase direct materials and the standard price allowed, times the actual quantity of direct materials purchased. It shows whether the price incurred per unit of direct materials input was greater or less than the price expected. A direct materials price variance is based on the number of units, for example, pounds, board feet, or liters, of input *purchased*. Since the price incurred for direct materials is assumed to be controllable by the purchasing department, that department is responsible for the direct materials price variance. The formula for the direct materials price variance is:

Actual price × Actual quantity purchased	=	$AP \times AQp$
− Standard price × Actual quantity purchased	=	$- SP \times AQp$
= Direct materials price variance	=	$DMPV$

Since the actual quantity purchased is the same in both expressions, this formula may be simplified as: $(AP - SP) \times AQp = DMPV$, where AQp is the actual quantity of materials purchased.

Like the direct labor price variance, if the actual price paid for direct materials is greater than the standard price allowed, the direct materials price variance is a positive number, or an unfavorable (U) variance. If the actual price is less than the standard price, the direct materials price variance is a negative number, indicating a favorable (F) variance. An unfavorable price variance indicates that the purchasing department is paying more than it planned for direct materials, while the opposite is true for a favorable variance. Since these changes may be due to suppliers changing prices or to the company changing suppliers, it is important to monitor the price variance in order to control the cost of direct materials and, perhaps, their quality. In addition, an unfavorable price variance may be caused by production needing materials on a rush basis, causing the purchasing manager to pay more than normal.

PAUSE & REFLECT When, and why, might a favorable direct material price variance be considered to be an unfavorable result?

Refer to Exhibits 13.3 and 13.4 for the Hewlett-Packard information used to calculate the direct materials price variance shown below:

Actual price per board (Exhibit 13.3)	$ 190
Standard price per board (Exhibit 13.4)	$ − 200
Difference in price	$ 10
Actual quantity of motherboards purchased (Exhibit 13.3)	× 18,000
DMPV	$180,000F

The direct materials price variance is favorable because Hewlett-Packard paid $10 less per motherboard than planned. Why did this happen? Maybe, the purchasing manager obtained a good deal from a supplier. On the other hand, maybe the purchasing manager bought inferior materials that were less expensive to obtain. While the first scenario would be considered positive, the second may cause production problems if computers have to be reworked due to the poor quality of the motherboards. In addition, if the boards fail in the customer's possession, Hewlett-Packard may have to incur significant additional costs to satisfy the customer.

Direct Materials Usage Variance

A **direct materials usage variance** is the difference between the actual quantity of direct materials used in production and the standard quantity of direct materials allowed for the actual amount of production achieved, times the standard price of the direct materials. It is calculated to determine whether the actual quantity of direct materials used during the period was greater or less than the amount budgeted.

The direct materials usage variance compares the actual quantity of material *used* and the quantity of material that *should have been used* given the actual level of production, that is, the flexible budget amount. Since the quantity of direct materials used is assumed to be controllable by the production department, production is responsible for controlling the direct materials usage variance. To calculate the direct materials usage variance, companies use the following formula:

$$
\begin{array}{ll}
\text{Actual quantity used} \times \text{Standard price} & = \quad AQu \times Sp \\
\underline{-\text{ Standard quantity budgeted} \times \text{Standard price}} & = \underline{- SQb \times SP} \\
= \text{Direct materials usage variance} & = \quad DMUV
\end{array}
$$

Because the standard price is the same, this formula may be simplified as: $(AQu - SQb) \times SP = DMUV$.

If the actual quantity of materials used is greater than the standard quantity of materials that should have been used, the direct materials usage variance is a positive number, indicating an unfavorable variance. On the other hand, if the actual quantity used is less than the standard quantity, a negative number, or a favorable variance, results. That is, if the production department wastes direct materials, an unfavorable variance results; however, management must investigate to ensure that this is the case before concluding that any waste was due to inefficiencies in the production department. Through investigation it might be discovered that the waste was due to the poor quality of direct materials purchased.

Using the information in Exhibits 13.3 and 13.4, Hewlett-Packard's direct materials usage variance is:

Actual quantity of motherboards used (Exhibit 13.3)	16,500	
Standard quantity of motherboards allowed for the actual output (Exhibit 13.4)	− 16,000	(16,000 × 1)
Difference in quantity	500	
Standard price per board (Exhibit 13.4)	× $200	
DMUV	$100,000U	

This unfavorable variance indicates that Hewlett-Packard used 500 more motherboards in production than the budget allowed for the computers produced. Why? Perhaps, as discussed earlier, the purchasing manager bought inferior motherboards, resulting in more waste during the production process. Or, maybe a machine was out of alignment causing some motherboards to be damaged during production. Or, perhaps employees are stealing motherboards and, therefore, it only appears that more boards were used in production. Hewlett-Packard would have to investigate further to find out exactly what happened.

Direct Materials Inventory Variance

Companies that operate in a JIT environment also need to monitor their inventory levels because one of the goals of JIT is to reduce inventory levels so that materials arrive just as they are needed in the production process. In a JIT system, the quantity of direct materials purchased should equal the quantity of direct materials used. Companies can determine if this objective is met by calculating a direct materials inventory variance.

A **direct materials inventory variance** is the difference between the actual quantity of direct materials purchased and the actual quantity used in production, times the standard price of direct materials. It is calculated as follows:

$$
\begin{array}{ll}
\text{Actual quantity purchased} \times \text{Standard price} & = \quad AQp \times SP \\
\underline{-\text{ Actual quantity used} \times \text{Standard price}} & = \underline{- AQu \times SP} \\
= \text{Direct materials inventory variance} & = \quad DMIV
\end{array}
$$

We can simplify this formula as: $(AQp - AQu) \times SP = DMIV$.

If the result of this calculation is a positive number, indicating that more material was purchased than used, the variance is unfavorable. Conversely, a negative result means that less material was purchased than used, requiring a reduction in inventory, or a favorable variance.

Using Exhibits 13.3 and 13.4, Hewlett-Packard's direct materials inventory variance is:

Actual quantity of motherboards purchased (Exhibit 13.3)	18,000
Actual quantity of motherboards used (Exhibit 13.3)	16,500
Difference in quantity	1,500
Standard price (Exhibit 13.4)	$\times$ $200
DMIV	$300,000 *U*

Since Hewlett-Packard purchased 18,000 motherboards and used only 16,500, its direct materials inventory increased, resulting in an unfavorable variance. Clearly, this is not appropriate for a JIT company. However, Hewlett-Packard would need to determine why inventory increased. The unfavorable variance alerts management that inventory levels are increasing and, therefore, that the company is tying up more resources than it planned in the company's inventory. It is up to management to determine why this happened. Perhaps inventory levels increased because the purchasing manager had to purchase a large quantity of motherboards in order to obtain the reduced price (remember the direct materials price variance was favorable). Or, perhaps, suppliers informed the purchasing manager that a price increase would occur early in the following year, so the manager purchased a larger quantity than normal in order to defer the increased cost.

PAUSE & REFLECT | **What does a zero direct materials inventory variance indicate? Why?**

In summary, the difference between the actual cost and the flexible budget cost of direct labor is due to the price paid laborers (*DLPV*), or the amount of direct labor used (*DLUV*), or both. The difference between the actual cost and the flexible budget cost of direct materials is due to the price paid for direct materials (*DMPV*), the quantity used (*DMUV*), or the change in inventory level (*DMIV*), or some combination of the above.[3] Now that you understand how to calculate and analyze direct labor and direct material variances, we turn to a more complex topic—overhead analysis.

ABC OVERHEAD VARIANCE ANALYSIS

Activity-based costing (ABC) overhead variance analysis is more complex than direct labor or direct materials variance analysis for two primary reasons. First, since overhead, by its nature, cannot be physically traced, it is more difficult to develop standard costs for these items. Second, it is more difficult to assign responsibility for overhead items since they involve many different departments. Despite these difficulties, overhead variance analysis is very important to companies because overhead represents a significant portion of the total cost of production. We examine the basics of overhead analysis next.

Chapter 10 illustrated that overhead is applied to production based on the quantity of the cost driver used. Therefore, the possible reasons for actual overhead to differ from planned amounts are:

1. The overhead costs are more (or less) than expected.

2. Production used more (or less) of the cost driver than expected.

The first point means that the company incurred more (or less) overhead cost than it had expected due to such things as spending more (or less) on overhead items such as machine oil or using more (or less) machine oil. Since indirect materials and other overhead items are not physically traced to production, we do not calculate a separate usage variance for these items. Instead, we analyze expenditures made for these items by calculating overhead price variances.

---

[3]Dr. Horace W. Harrell suggests that a finished goods inventory variance and a sales completion variance may be determined also. For more information, see Horace W. Harrell, "Materials Variance Analysis and JIT: A New Approach," *Management Accounting*, May 1992, pp. 33–38.

The second point implies that the company used more (or less) of the cost driver than it should have. An overhead usage variance results if production uses more (or less) amounts of the cost driver than was expected. We discuss these overhead variances next.

Overhead Price Variance

An **overhead price variance** is the difference between the actual amount of overhead incurred for the period and the amount of overhead applied to production during the period. Recall that the amount of overhead applied to production is equal to the actual amounts of the cost driver used multiplied by the predetermined overhead rate for that cost driver. The overhead price variance is calculated for each *individual overhead cost pool*, so the number of overhead price variances depends on the complexity of the company's operations.

To calculate the overhead price variance (OPV) for a particular cost pool, companies would use the following formula:

OPV = Actual overhead incurred for the cost pool – (Actual cost driver used
× Predetermined overhead rate for the cost pool)

If the actual amount of overhead incurred during the period is greater than the amount of overhead applied to production, the overhead price variance is positive, or unfavorable (U). If the actual amount of overhead incurred during the period is less than the amount of overhead applied to production, the overhead price variance is negative, or favorable (F). As you know, the amount of overhead applied to production is an estimate of what overhead should be, so analyzing the price variance is an important first step in controlling overhead spending.

Again, the responsibility for the variance depends on what caused the variance to arise. For each significant variance calculated, management must determine the underlying cause before assigning responsibility. Recall that a particular overhead cost pool is composed of many types of costs, and any one, or all, of these costs may cause the variance.

Using the actual overhead cost and cost driver information from Exhibit 13.3 multiplied by the respective predetermined overhead rates from Exhibit 13.4, Hewlett-Packard's overhead price variances would be:

Unit-Related Overhead:
$$\$620,000 - [50,000 \times \$12] = \$20,000U$$

Batch-Related Overhead:
$$\$285,000 - [300 \times \$700] = \$75,000U$$

Product-Sustaining Overhead:
$$\$590,000 - [18 \times \$30,000] = \$50,000U$$

Facility-Sustaining Overhead:
$$\$740,000 - [5,000 \times \$150] = \$10,000\,F$$

Take a moment to make sure you understand these calculations and where the numbers originated. This analysis indicates that the actual unit-related, batch-related, and product-sustaining overhead costs exceeded the amounts applied. In other words, these overhead cost pools were *underapplied—too little overhead was added to production during the period.* On the other hand, the actual facility-sustaining overhead cost was less than expected, so it was *overapplied—too much overhead was added to production during the period.* (This is the same type of calculation made in Chapter 10 when we discussed the application of manufacturing overhead to production.)

What does this mean? The analysis indicates that unit-related, batch-related, and product-sustaining overhead were more than expected based on the actual amounts of cost drivers used during the period. Management, however, must determine whether this is due to spending too much money on overhead items or whether it results from using too much of the overhead items. For example, the unfavorable unit-related overhead variance might be due to *spending too much* for indirect materials such as machine oil, or it might be due to *consuming too many* indirect materials. Investigation is necessary to determine whether spending, consumption, or both, are responsible for this difference. On the other hand, the favorable facility-sustaining overhead might be due to a decrease in the property tax rate, for example. Since these variances arise from very different types of activities, it is important to investigate those that are deemed significant.

PAUSE & REFLECT   How would Hewlett-Packard determine if an overhead price variance was due to spending or consumption?

Overhead Usage Variance

An **overhead usage variance** is the difference between the overhead applied to production during the period and the flexible budget amount of overhead for the period. It shows whether the amount of overhead applied was greater (or less) than the amount budgeted.

Recall that unit-related overhead requires using a flexible budget amount because it is expected to change with the level of production. Conversely, batch-related, product-sustaining, and facility-sustaining overhead costs are independent of the level of production. Therefore, for these costs, the master budget and the flexible budget numbers are the same.

The overhead usage variance indicates whether the amount of cost driver used during the period was greater or less than the amount budgeted. However, additional analysis is necessary to determine if the usage is good or bad.

Unit-Related Overhead Usage Variance   To calculate the unit-related overhead usage variance (UOUV), use the following formula:

UOUV = (Actual cost driver used × Predetermined unit-related overhead rate)
  − (Standard amount of cost driver required for the actual production
    × Predetermined unit-related overhead rate)

Since the predetermined overhead rate is the same in both calculations, the expression can be shortened to:

UOUV = (Actual cost driver used − Standard cost driver allowed)
  × Predetermined unit-related overhead rate

Take a moment to look at this presentation of the overhead usage variance. Is this different from the usage variance for direct labor or direct materials? Not really, because, in all cases, we are comparing the actual inputs (cost drivers, in this case) to the inputs allowed on the flexible budget. The quantity of the cost driver is multiplied by the standard price of the input, or, in this case, the predetermined overhead rate (the standard cost of overhead per cost driver). Therefore, if we let Q = Quantity of cost driver and SP = Overhead rate, the equation just presented is shortened to the following notation:

$$(AQ - SQb) \times SP$$

where,

SQb = Standard quantity of cost driver budgeted for the actual amount of production as shown on the flexible budget

Batch-Related, Product-Sustaining, and Facility-Sustaining Overhead Usage Variances

For batch-related, product-sustaining, and facility-sustaining overhead, the company would calculate the overhead usage variance (OUV) as:

OUV = (Actual cost driver used × Predetermined overhead rate for the cost pool) – Flexible (master) budget level of overhead cost for the cost pool

In all cases, if the amount of overhead applied to production is greater than the amount of overhead appearing in the flexible budget, the overhead usage variance is a positive, or unfavorable, number. If the amount of overhead applied to production is less than the amount of overhead budgeted, the result is a negative, or favorable, number.

As with the overhead price variance, the underlying cause of any significant overhead usage variance must be discovered before assigning responsibility for the variance to any particular department or individual.

Using the information contained in Exhibits 13.3 and 13.4, the overhead usage variances for Hewlett-Packard are:

Unit-Related Overhead Usage Variance:

$$[50,000 - (16,000 \times 3)] \times \$12 = \$24,000U$$

Batch-Related Overhead Usage Variance:

$$300 \times \$700 - \$210,000 = 0$$

Product-Sustaining Overhead Usage Variance:

$$18 \times \$30,000 - \$600,000 = \$60,000F$$

Facility-Sustaining Overhead Usage Variance:

$$5,000 \times \$150 - \$750,000 = 0$$

Take a moment to make sure you understand these calculations and where the numbers originated. This analysis indicates that Hewlett-Packard applied more unit-related overhead than the amount it budgeted and less product-sustaining overhead than the amount budgeted. The $24,000 unfavorable unit-related usage variance is due to working more machine hours than planned (50,000 versus 48,000). The $60,000 favorable product-sustaining usage variance is due to using two fewer designs than planned (18 versus 20).

It is hard to determine, at this point, if these results are good or bad. For example, did production workers use more machine hours than allowed by the standards because the motherboards were defective and several computers had to be reworked? Or did they use more machine hours because machine operators were inefficient? There were fewer designs used than the number planned during the period. Is this good? Did the engineering department work more efficiently and, therefore, need fewer design modifications, or did they simply run out of time and not complete the necessary designs? These questions can be answered only after conducting a variance investigation.

PAUSE & REFLECT   How is an overhead variance analysis useful for controlling overhead?

EXHIBIT | 13.5

General Variance Diagram

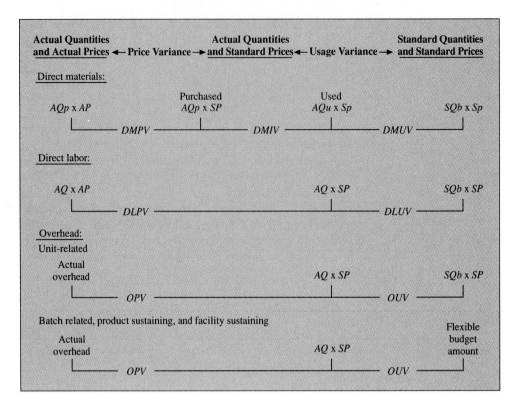

Direct materials:

Actual Quantities and Actual Prices	← Price Variance →	Actual Quantities and Standard Prices	← Usage Variance →	Standard Quantities and Standard Prices

$AQp \times AP$ — DMPV — Purchased $AQp \times SP$ — DMIV — Used $AQu \times Sp$ — DMUV — $SQb \times Sp$

Direct labor:

$AQ \times AP$ — DLPV — $AQ \times SP$ — DLUV — $SQb \times SP$

Overhead:
Unit-related

Actual overhead — OPV — $AQ \times SP$ — OUV — $SQb \times SP$

Batch related, product sustaining, and facility sustaining

Actual overhead — OPV — $AQ \times SP$ — OUV — Flexible budget amount

PUTTING IT ALL TOGETHER—THE VARIANCE DIAGRAM

Accountants typically analyze direct labor, direct materials, and manufacturing overhead at the same time to ensure that they consider all the relevant facts. A useful tool for completing this analysis is called a *variance diagram*, depicted in Exhibit 13.5. Notice that it shows actual quantities and prices in the far-left column and the budgeted (standard) quantities and prices in the far right column. The middle column represents the actual input at the standard price. The difference between the far-left and the middle column, then, is the price variance, while the difference between the middle and the far right column is the usage variance. For materials, the inventory variance is the difference between the amounts purchased and used (two middle columns).

Exhibit 13.6 shows the variance analysis diagram for H-P. Notice that using this diagram decreases the number of calculations required. It shows that the total price variance was $37,200 favorable (see the total inputs section), meaning that Hewlett-Packard *spent* $37,200 less on all actual manufacturing inputs than the amount budgeted. The variance diagram also indicates a total usage variance of $60,400 unfavorable, implying that H-P *used* $60,400 more actual manufacturing inputs than the amount budgeted. The total of the price, inventory, and usage variances is $323,200 unfavorable ($5,803,200 – $5,480,000), which is the difference between the actual results and flexible budget. Now that the company knows the source of the differences, it must determine which differences warrant further investigation.

INVESTIGATION OF VARIANCES

Knowing that variances have arisen in operations is only the first step in evaluating and controlling the conversion cycle. Next, management must determine the cause of the variances so that it can decide whether it needs to make changes in operating activities or the budgeting process, or both.

Often companies award bonuses based on the variances, so understanding the causes of variances is important to the individual responsible as well as to the company. Many variances are caused by standards that may be inappropriate, such as an out-of-date standard. Therefore, if the standard is unsuitable, it is inappropriate to reward or punish the individuals assigned responsibility for controlling the variance. On the other hand, if operations are exceeding or not meeting expectations, rewards

EXHIBIT | 13.6

Hewlett-Packard
Variance Diagram

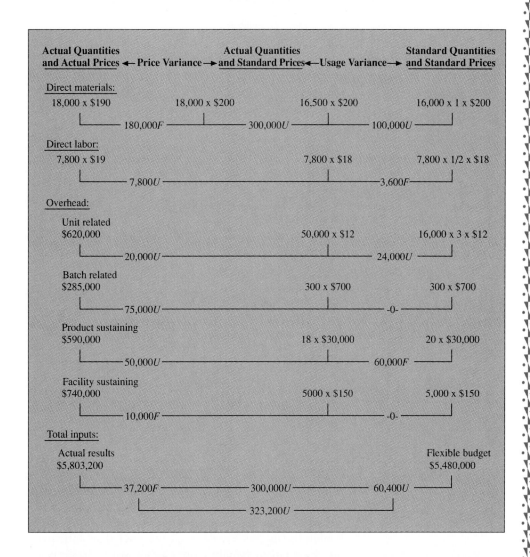

Exhibit 13.6 Hewlett-Packard Variance Diagram

| EXHIBIT | 13.7 | Hewlett-Packard Variance Report |

HEWLETT-PACKARD
Variance Analysis Report

Input	Actual	Flexible Budget	Total Variance	Price	Inventory	Usage
Direct materials	$3,420,000	$3,200,000	$220,000U	$180,000F	$300,000U	$100,000U
Direct labor	148,200	144,000	4,200U	7,800U		3,600F
Overhead:						
Unit related	620,000	576,000	44,000U	20,000U		24,000U
Batch related	285,000	210,000	75,000U	75,000U		-0-
Product sustaining	590,000	600,000	10,000F	50,000U		60,000F
Facility sustaining	740,000	750,000	10,000F	10,000F		-0-
Total	$5,803,200	$5,480,000	$323,200U	$ 37,200F	$300,000U	$ 60,400U

or negative consequences, respectively, may be warranted. In either case, if the variance is significant, further management action may be necessary.

Management usually examines variances by reviewing a variance report like the one shown in Exhibit 13.7. This report shows all the variances calculated previously. In this particular report, all variances, regardless of significance, are reported to management. Notice that this variance report indicates the actual costs incurred for each input, the amount of each input on the flexible budget, and the resulting variances. In this way, management can see exactly where the difference between budgeted and actual results occurred. For example, it shows that the difference between the actual amount incurred and the flexible budget amount for direct materials was $220,000 unfavorable. That is, the company spent $220,000 more on motherboards than anticipated. Why did this happen? The variance report indicates that the company bought the motherboards at a lesser price than anticipated (favorable price variance), but the company bought more motherboards than it needed for production (unfavorable inventory variance) and it used more motherboards in production than anticipated (unfavorable usage variance). If management concludes that these variances are significant (discussed below), it would investigate to determine the cause(s). Also notice that the total of the variances is the same as the difference between the total actual costs incurred and the total flexible budget. Therefore, the variances indicate the areas, but not the causes, of the differences between actual and budgeted production costs.

Most companies use **management-by-exception variance reports,** which show only the significant variances because the number of variances calculated is large. In order for the accounting department to prepare a management-by-exception variance report, the company must adopt criteria to determine which variances warrant further investigation. There are a variety of criteria adopted by companies to make this determination, such as the size of the variance, trends in variances, or the cost of investigating the variance.

Size of the Variance

The absolute size of the variance is one consideration when determining which variances to investigate. Large variances, either favorable or unfavorable, are more likely to require additional attention than small variances because they indicate a larger difference between the actual and expected results. However, the relative size of the variance in relation to the standard cost is often a better measure of the importance of the variance because the variance should be evaluated in relation to the costs. For example, a $50,000 unfavorable direct materials price variance, which is 2 percent of the standard direct materials cost, may not be as important as a $5,000 direct labor variance, which is 25 percent of the standard direct labor cost. All other things equal, large relative variances are investigated before small relative variances. Often, companies require investigation of all variances that exceed a predetermined percentage of standard cost or exceed a predetermined absolute amount.

For example, assume that Hewlett-Packard investigates all variances that exceed $50,000 during the period because they believe that $50,000 is a significant difference. In this case, H-P's accounting department would report the following variances for further analysis:

Direct materials price variance	$180,000 favorable
Direct materials inventory variance	$300,000 unfavorable
Direct materials usage variance	$100,000 unfavorable
Batch-related overhead price variance	$ 75,000 unfavorable
Product-sustaining overhead usage variance	$ 60,000 favorable

On the other hand, if H-P investigates all variances that exceed 5 percent of the standard cost of the input, the accounting department would have reported the following variances to management for further analysis:

Direct materials inventory variance ($300,000/$3,200,000)	9.4%
Direct labor price variance ($7,800/$144,000)	5.4%
Batch-related overhead price variance ($75,000/$210,000)	35.7%
Product-sustaining overhead price variance ($50,000/$600,000)	8.3%
Product-sustaining overhead usage variance ($60,000/$600,000)	10.0%

Notice that different variances are significant when using the relative, rather than the absolute, size of the variance as a criterion. Using the size of the variance implies that slight deviations from standards are allowed, but significant deviations are unacceptable. Thus, by using the size criterion, management does not waste time investigating variances that are not significant when compared to the standard cost of the input.

Trends in Variances

Another consideration in deciding which variances to investigate is the presence of trends in variances. A variance that has steadily increased in amount through time or that is consistently either favorable or unfavorable may warrant more attention than a variance that is unfavorable one period and favorable another. Companies sometimes require investigation of all variances that are consistent in direction regardless of whether they pass a size test. Often a trend indicates a standard that is in error rather than a cost that is out of control. For example, assume that Hewlett-Packard set an ideal standard of producing one computer using 15 minutes of direct labor time. However, no matter how efficient the production workers are, they cannot produce a computer every 15 minutes. Using this standard will cause unfavorable direct labor usage variances but may not indicate inefficiency in production.

Other trends would indicate cost or quality problems. For example, assume that H-P's direct materials price variances were $150,000 favorable last year, $144,000 favorable two years ago, and $165,900 favorable three years ago. During this same time period, the direct labor price variances were $8,000 favorable, $7,000 unfavorable, and $5,000 favorable. Management may chose to investigate the direct materials price variance before, or rather than, the direct labor price variance due to the consistently favorable results. Such consistent favorable price variances may indicate that the company is purchasing less expensive motherboards that may cause management to have concerns about quality. This decision may be made without regard to the size of the variance.

Costs of Investigating Variances

Management also must consider the costs of investigating variances. In general, variances that can be investigated without incurring large costs are more likely to be investigated than variances requiring more costly investigation procedures. The cost to investigate a variance includes the time spent by the manager and other employees, the disruption of normal operating activities, and the costs incurred to detect the problem if one exists. A company may choose to investigate all variances whose investigation costs do not exceed a predetermined amount or whose investigation costs do not exceed a predetermined percentage of the variance amount.

For example, assume that Hewlett-Packard can investigate a direct materials price variance by comparing vendor invoices to the budgeted amount of purchases. This procedure is not very costly because the accounting system includes this information. On the other hand, assume that, in order to investigate a direct materials usage variance, it is necessary to disassemble the machinery that controls the material, and that this requires shutting down the production line. The costs incurred to investigate this usage variance would be much higher. Management must decide whether the cost of investigating the usage variance is greater or less than the benefit derived from fixing the problem, if one exists.

OTHER PERFORMANCE MEASURES

To obtain information about overall operating efficiency, management often uses other measures of performance in addition to variance analysis. There are two other common performance measurement areas—quality and processes. Both of these are commonly investigated in companies that have adopted the JIT philosophy because JIT requires minimal defects (high quality) and maximum process efficiency.

Quality Measurements

Companies today are very concerned about quality control because quality is one way a company can differentiate itself from its competition. This concern for quality grew in the 1980s as foreign competition increased. For example, Texas Instruments started a corporate program called Total Quality Thrust, which tracks expenditures made for quality control. Xerox, which also advocates quality, was the 1989 Malcolm Baldrige Award winner for quality. In 1989, IBM started a quality control program called Market Driven Quality. The purpose of this program is to establish a system of quality measurement.[4] Although quality control measurements tend to be more subjective than variances, they are equally important. To understand their importance, we take a brief look at quality issues.

In the 1970s, it was commonly thought that a company could determine the optimal number of its quality defects. That is, companies believed that there was a level of quality such that the costs of preventing and appraising quality were equal to the costs of having defects, which are known as *failure costs*. Exhibit 13.8 illustrates this

---

[4]Lawrence P. Carr and Thomas Tyson, "Planning Quality Cost Expenditures," *Management Accounting*, October 1992, pp. 52–56.

Optimal Defect Level

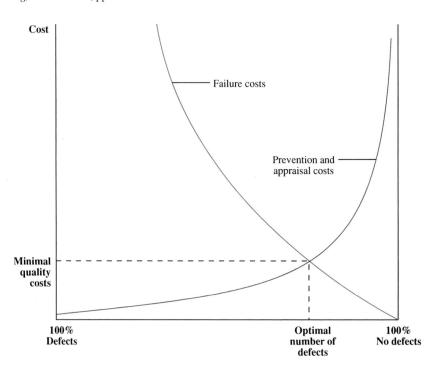

concept graphically. Notice that prevention and appraisals costs increase as the level of defects decreases (upward sloping line), while failure costs decrease as the level of defects decreases (downward sloping line). The company accepts the level of quality where the costs of preventing and appraising quality and the cost of failure intersect because, at that point, total quality costs are minimized. Thus, in the 1970s, companies commonly had measures of the "optimal" number of defects. The number of defects exceeding optimal was subject to investigation.

In the 1980s, companies began to take a closer look at quality costs. Researchers examined the cost of quality closer and identified four types of quality costs:

Prevention cost. The cost incurred to prevent defects from occurring in the production process, such as the cost incurred to institute quality circles (small groups of employees who meet to discuss how to improve quality).

Appraisal cost. The cost incurred to detect defects in the production process, such as the cost incurred to test products for quality defects.

Internal failure cost. The cost incurred to correct defects in the products before they are shipped to the customer, such as the cost of rework on defective products.

External failure cost. The cost incurred to correct defects in the products after they are shipped to the customer, such as the cost of warranty claims.

Both prevention and appraisal costs are voluntary. That is, the company intentionally spends money on these items in an attempt to increase quality. In fact, prevention costs are often incurred prior to production, while appraisal costs are incurred during production. On the other hand, internal and external failure costs are involuntary. That is, the company incurs these costs to correct defects that occurred in the production process. The company does not voluntarily undertake these activities, such as reworking or replacing defective products.

As researchers studied failure costs, they discovered that external failure costs were miscalculated because it is hard for companies to measure the biggest external failure cost. Think about external failure cost for a moment. If a customer receives defective products, even if the defect is corrected, is this customer likely to continue to do business with the company? The answer is probably not, which creates an additional external failure cost—customer ill will. And, ill will includes the cost of losing customers, as well as the damage done to the company's reputation as a result of such losses. In addition, if quality failures result in litigation, the cost to the company increases even more. When these costs are added to the other external failure costs, the result (shown in Exhibit 13.9) indicates that the optimal quality level of the company becomes zero defects. Notice that the total quality cost intersection has moved much further to the right, compared to Exhibit 13.8, as additional external failure costs are considered. Thus, the company is better off spending more money on prevention and appraisal costs in an effort to reduce or eliminate internal and external failure costs.

In order to control quality, companies monitor prevention, appraisal, and internal and external failure costs. Exhibit 13.10 shows costs that are typically included in each of these categories. For example, prevention costs, which are voluntary and occur prior to production, include supporting suppliers so that defects in raw materials do not occur. Appraisal costs, which are also voluntary costs, occur during production and include testing both work-in-process and finished goods inventories. The goal of the company is to reduce total quality costs by increasing prevention and appraisal costs. Thus, the company might implement quality control circles in an attempt to reduce product liability claims. The company's quality control report would indicate both the amount of money spent on various quality control measures, such as quality circles and product liability claims, and the percentage of total quality costs represented by each measure. The goal is for the prevention and appraisal cost percentages to increase while the internal and external failure percentages decrease and total quality costs decrease.

EXHIBIT | **13.9**

Optimal Defect Level with Customer III Will

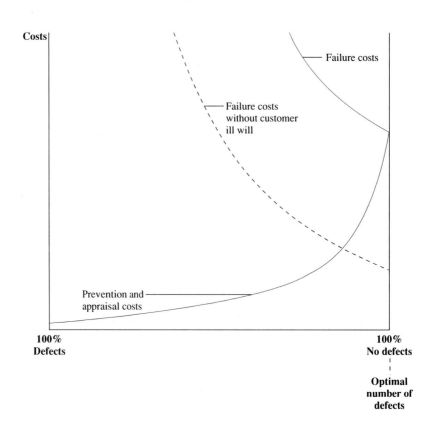

EXHIBIT | **13.10** | **Quality Costs**

Type of Cost	Why Incurred	Time of Occurrence	Examples
Prevention	Voluntary	Before production	Quality circles
			Product design
			Supplier support
			Raw materials testing
Appraisal	Voluntary	During production	Work-in-process testing
			Finished goods testing
			Test equipment costs
			Inspection personnel costs
Internal failure	Involuntary	After production	Rework
			Scrap
			Disposal of defective products
			Downtime
External failure	Involuntary	After sale	Recall costs
			Product liability claims
			Warranty costs
			Customer ill will

Many companies have significantly reduced their costs by increasing their voluntary quality costs. For example, Xerox initiated a quality control program where teams of employees were empowered to find and correct problems in its billing process. This program cost Xerox $7,000, but it saved the company $112,000![5]

Process Measurements

In addition to quality, a company's reputation is also based on its on-time deliveries and other types of processes, such as response time to customer complaints and its payment period on accounts payable. On-time delivery is important because a

[5]David M. Buehlmann and Donald Stover, "How Xerox Solves Quality Problems," *Management Accounting*, September 1993, pp. 33–36.

Quality control is a preventative measure companies take to ensure the production of quality products and ultimately reduce costs.

PAUSE & REFLECT   Is there an upper limit to what a company can spend on prevention and appraisal costs? Why or why not?

company that is chronically slow in delivering customer orders also may suffer customer ill will. To increase the efficiency with which orders are filled, companies monitor throughput and delivery times.

Throughput Time   **Throughput time,** as used in a manufacturing company, is the amount of time required to convert raw materials into a finished product. Throughput time indicates how long it takes to manufacture a product and how long raw materials remain in inventory. The faster the throughput time, the quicker the production process. In addition, faster throughput times lead to smaller raw materials and work-in-process inventories because raw materials and work in process are not sitting idle waiting for production machinery to become available. Throughput time has several important components as follows:

Throughput time = Storing time + Waiting time + Processing time + Inspecting time

- *Storing time* is the time that elapses between when the raw material is received from the supplier and when it is issued into production.
- *Waiting time* is the time the raw materials and work-in-process inventories are idle during the production process.
- *Processing time* is the time in which the raw materials are converted into a finished product.
- *Inspecting time* is the time when the raw materials, work-in-process, or finished goods inventories are inspected while not being processed.

Throughput Time and Nonvalue-Added Activities   Companies that have adopted JIT and ABC use throughput time to control nonvalue-added activities in the conversion cycle. Here, we expand the definition presented in Chapter 5 of a **nonvalue-added** activity to indicate that it is any activity that adds cost but that is not valued by the customer *or* required by law. A **value-added activity** is any activity that is valued by the customer or required by law. For example, filing reports with the Department of Occupational Safety and Health regarding the conditions in which production workers operate is a value-added activity because, even though the activity does not add value for the customer, it is required by law.

PAUSE & REFLECT   Is filing an income tax return a value-added activity? Why or why not?

Many value-added activities as well as many nonvalue-added activities occur outside of the conversion cycle and, therefore, do not directly impact throughput time. Regardless of when they occur, the goal of management is to reduce or eliminate nonvalue-added activities. Reduction of nonvalue-added activities is a long-term project. The reductions must be done without affecting the quality of products or services. For example, it is not possible to eliminate inspecting time until inspecting time becomes part of processing time.

When referring to the components of throughput time, you should understand that storing raw materials is an activity that adds cost to the product (insurance, depreciation, utilities, etc.); however, storing is not required by law nor does the customer value it. Therefore, storing is a nonvalue-added activity. Waiting time also is a nonvalue-added activity. It adds cost to the product (insurance, spoilage, etc.), but it does not add value to the product and is not required by law. Inspecting also is a nonvalue-added activity because customers do not value inspecting as a separate process; they simply want a defect-free product. And, inspecting is not generally required by law.

We can see that storing time, waiting time, and inspecting time are all nonvalue-added activities involved in throughput time. Therefore, management's goal is to reduce these activities in order to decrease total throughput time. To monitor their process toward this goal, companies often compute the percentage of value-added activities, as shown below:

$$\text{Percentage of value-added activities} = \frac{\text{Time spent on value-added activities}}{\text{Throughput time}}$$

As this ratio approaches 1, nonvalue-added activities are decreasing and value-added activities are increasing as a percentage of total processing time. For example, assume that Hewlett-Packard reports the following times on average (in days) for January and February:

Activity	Number of Days January	February
Storing time	3.2	2.4
Waiting time	.5	.3
Inspecting time	1.1	1.0
Moving time	.6	.1
Processing time	15.1	15.1
Total time	20.5	18.9

Based on this information, H-P's throughput time decreased from 20.5 days to 18.9 days, while its percentage of value-added activities increased from 73.7 percent (15.1/20.5) to 80 percent (15.1/18.9). This indicates that Hewlett-Packard is eliminating its nonvalue-added activities and decreasing total throughput time, which means that its production process is becoming more value-added.

Delivery Time   In addition to the time spent manufacturing products, another measure of process efficiency is delivery time. **Delivery time** is the time that elapses between when the customer places an order and when the customer receives that order.[6] The faster the delivery time, the quicker the customer-response

---

[6]From the customer's point of view, this is called *lead time*, which was discussed in Chapter 5.

time. In addition, faster delivery times lead to smaller finished goods inventories because finished goods do not need to be held in anticipation of orders. Delivery time is calculated as:

$$\text{Delivery time} = \text{Wait time before processing} + \text{Throughput time} + \text{Travel time to the customer}$$

Again, the goal is to reduce delivery time while maintaining a high-quality product. Using the throughput times calculated previously, and assuming that the wait time before processing is 3 days in January and 2 days in February and that the travel time to the customer is 2 days in both months, the delivery times for January and February are 25.5 (20.5 + 3 + 2) and 22.9 (18.9 + 2 + 2) days, respectively. Again, H-P's delivery times are decreasing, which indicates that its response time to customer orders is decreasing.

Many companies have achieved dramatic improvements in their production processes. For example, Oregon Cutting System reduced changeover time from 6.5 hours to 1 minute and 40 seconds, reduced setup time from 3 hours to 4.5 minutes, and achieved a 90 percent improvement in shipping productivity by reorganizing its conversion cycle processes![7] Southwire Company implemented a program of reporting scrap and reduced its scrap costs dramatically by reducing wire breaks by 50 percent.[8] Such dramatic improvements are possible because production processes are arranged for maximum efficiency; high-quality raw materials are received on time, every time; and a defect-free product is produced the first time.

SUMMARY

Variance analysis is one tool used to analyze whether management's goals and objectives set forth in the planning phase have been met by the operating results of the performing phase. Since management cannot investigate every variance, companies adopt a philosophy known as *management-by-exception*, to investigate only significant variances. In addition to variance analysis, other common performance measurements include quality and process measurements.

- A favorable variance occurs when the standard amount (price or usage) is less than the actual amount. An unfavorable variance occurs when the actual amount (price or usage) is greater than the standard amount. Favorable and unfavorable do not denote good or bad.

- The difference between the budgeted and actual amounts of direct labor is attributable to the difference in the price paid (*DLPV*) and the quantity used (*DPUV*) of direct labor.

- The difference between the budgeted and actual amounts of direct materials is attributable to the difference in the price paid (*DMPV*), the quantity stored (*DMIV*), and the quantity used (*DMUV*) of direct materials.

- The overhead price variance indicates whether more or less overhead cost was incurred during the period than was applied to production. The overhead usage variance indicates whether more or less overhead cost was applied to production than was budgeted during the period.

- The cost of quality has four components: prevention, appraisal, internal failure, and external failure. Quality costs are minimized when the company adopts a zero defect policy because external failure costs are very large.

- Companies use process measures, such as throughput time and delivery time, to monitor the time it takes to manufacture and deliver products to customers.

[7]Jack C. Bailes and Ilene K. Kleinsorge, "Cutting Waste with JIG," *Management Accounting*, May 1992, pp. 28–32.

[8]Gilda M. Agacer, Donald W. Baker, and Les Miles, "Implementing the Quality Process at Southwire Company," *Management Accounting*, November 1994, pp. 59–62.

appraisal cost The cost incurred to detect defects in the production process

delivery time The time that elapses between when the customer places an order and when the customer receives that order

direct labor price variance The difference between the actual wage rate per hour and the standard wage rate per hour, times the actual number of hours worked

direct labor usage variance The difference between the actual number of hours worked and the standard number of hours allowed for the actual production, times the standard wage rate per hour

direct materials inventory variance The difference between the actual quantity of direct materials purchased and the actual quantity used in production, times the standard price of direct materials

direct materials price variance The difference between the actual price paid for direct materials and the standard price allowed, times the actual quantity of direct materials purchased

direct materials usage variance The difference between the actual quantity of direct materials used in production and the standard quantity allowed for the actual production, times the standard price of direct materials

effectiveness A condition relating to whether the goals of the company were achieved during the period

efficiency A condition relating to whether the goals of the company were achieved with the best combination of the company's resources

external failure cost The cost incurred to correct defects after the product is shipped to the customer

flexible budget A budget prepared to reflect the actual production level of the period

internal failure cost The cost incurred to correct defects before the product reaches the customer

management-by-exception A philosophy in which only unusual or unexpected outcomes are investigated

management-by-exception variance report A variance report which shows only the significant variances

nonvalue-added activity Any activity that adds cost to the product but is not valued by customers or required by law

overhead price variance The difference between the actual overhead costs incurred during the period and the overhead costs applied to production during the period

overhead usage variance The difference between the amount of overhead applied to production during the period and the flexible budget amount of overhead for the period

prevention cost The cost incurred to prevent defects from occurring in the production process

processes The methods used to achieve the company's goals during the period

quality The degree of excellence in the company's products and services

standard cost A predetermined cost estimate of a particular operating input; calculated as the standard price times the standard quantity

standard price The predetermined cost of an input

standard quantity The predetermined amount of an input expected per unit of output

throughput time The amount of time required to convert raw materials into a finished product

value-added activity Any activity that adds value to the product for the customer or that is required by law

variance The difference between the budgeted and actual financial amounts of an input

variance analysis Inquiry into variances to determine their causes as part of management's process of evaluating operations

1. What is a standard cost of an input and how do managers and employees use it in planning and evaluation?

2. Why is the comparison of the master budget to the actual results misleading?

3. What is a flexible budget and how is it different from the master budget?

4. Why is a master budget used primarily for planning while a flexible budget is used primarily for evaluation and control?

5. Explain the concept of variance analysis. Illustrate your point by including an example.

6. Is a favorable variance "good" and an unfavorable variance "bad"? Why or why not?

7. What are the two direct labor variances and what is the purpose of each?

8. What departments are normally held responsible for the direct labor price and direct labor usage variances? Why?

9. If the actual rate paid for direct labor is less than the standard rate, is the resulting variance favorable or unfavorable? Why?

10. Does the direct labor price variance plus the direct labor usage variance equal the difference between the actual amount of direct labor incurred and the flexible budget cost of direct labor? Why or why not?

11. What are the two direct materials variances and what is the purpose of each?

12. What departments are normally held responsible for the direct materials price and direct materials usage variances? Why?

13. If the actual quantity of material used in production is less than the amount allowed in the flexible budget, is the resulting variance favorable or unfavorable? Why?

14. Does the direct materials price variance plus the direct materials usage variance equal the difference between the actual direct materials cost and the flexible budget direct materials cost? Why or why not?

15. Explain how to calculate and interpret the overhead price variance. Illustrate your points by including an example.

16. Explain how to calculate and interpret the overhead usage variance for unit-related overhead. Illustrate your points by including an example.

17. Why are the master budget and flexible budget amounts of batch-related, product-sustaining, and facility-sustaining overhead the same?

18. Explain how to interpret the overhead usage variance for batch-related, product-sustaining, and facility-sustaining overhead. Illustrate your points by including an example.

19. Explain why internal and external failure costs can be reduced by increasing appraisal and prevention costs.

20. Explain how throughput time measures efficiency in processing.

EXERCISES

E 13.1   T. Berry Travel is a travel agency that books cruises and tours for its clients. A travel agent spends an average of two hours discussing the options and booking a cruise for a client. The travel agent is paid $12.50 per hour. Compute the standard direct labor cost of booking a cruise. How would management use this cost?

E 13.2   Charlotte's Apparel Company sells women's professional wear. Charlotte orders a classic navy suit in batches of 12. Each order costs $1,200 plus freight of $36. Compute the standard cost of a classic navy suit. How would management use this cost?

E 13.3   The Framemaker manufactures oak picture frames. An 8 x 10 frame requires 3 1/2 feet of oak molding. In addition, each frame requires a piece of glass and a back. Oak molding costs $5.00 per foot, glass costs $.50 per 8 x 10 frame, and a back costs $.25. Compute the standard direct materials cost of an 8 x 10 oak frame. What information is provided to management by this computation?

E 13.4   Acme Chemical Company manufactures industrial chemicals. Each batch of the chemical Azon consists of 12 kilograms of compound W and 9.8 liters of solution X. After combining and heating these two elements, 5 kilograms of compound H is added. The standard purchase price of compounds W and H are $1.50 and $2.75 per kilogram, respectively. The standard price of solution X is $1.95 per liter. Compute the standard materials cost of one batch of Azon. What information is provided to management by this computation?

E 13.5   Refer to E 13.4. To produce each batch of the chemical Azon requires 75 minutes of direct labor time. Direct labor wages are $15 per hour. Compute the standard labor cost of one batch of Azon. Why would management be interested in this information?

E 13.6 Hawkeye Company manufactures bookcases. Direct materials standards are 10 board feet of lumber per bookcase at a cost of $3.00 per board foot. During the month of February, Hawkeye purchased 18,000 board feet of lumber at a total cost of $55,800. Production during February used 20,000 board feet of lumber to make 1,900 bookcases. Compute the direct materials price, usage, and inventory variances. What are some possible causes for these variances?

E 13.7 Klinger Company's direct materials costs for the month of April are shown below. Compute, and give some possible causes for, the direct materials price, inventory, and usage variances.

Actual quantity purchased	4,800 pounds
Actual quantity used in production	4,900 pounds
Actual price per pound purchased	$13
Standard price per pound	$12.50
Standard quantity allowed for actual production	5,000

13.8 Radar, Inc.'s direct labor cost information for the month of November is given below. Compute, and give some possible explanations for, the direct labor price and usage variances.

Actual direct labor hours	40,000
Standard direct labor hours allowed for the actual production	42,000
Actual direct labor rate per hour	$16.25
Standard direct labor rate per hour	$16.20

E 13.9 Based on the standards set by Burns Company, 5,500 direct labor hours should have been used in production this period at a cost of $20 per hour. The actual results indicate that 5,600 hours were used at a total cost of $106,400. Compute, and give some possible explanations for, the direct labor price and usage variances.

E 13.10 Refer to E 13.9. Burns Company applies its unit-related overhead based on the number of direct labor hours worked. The predetermined overhead rate is $5 per direct labor hour. Actual unit-related overhead was $30,000. Compute the overhead price and usage variances. Why did these variances occur?

E 13.11 During 1995, Albertson Company incurred $106,000 of unit-related overhead. Albertson applies unit-related overhead to production based on the number of machine hours worked at the rate of $2 per hour. During 1995, 50,000 machine hours were worked, and 47,500 units were produced. The overhead usage variance for 1995 was $5,000U. What was the overhead price variance?

E 13.12 Refer to E 13.11. What were the standard number of machine hours allowed per unit?

E 13.13 Campi Company prepared its master budget based on using 5,000 design hours. Product-related overhead is applied to production at $2,000 per design hour. At the end of the year, actual product-related overhead was $10 million and 5,100 design hours were used. Compute the price and usage variances. Why did these variances occur?

E 13.14 On January 1, 1995, Gaff Enterprises estimated that its batch-related overhead for the coming year would be $920,000 based on an anticipated 400 production runs. During the period, 395 production runs were completed. At the end of the period, batch-related overhead totaled $900,000. Compute the overhead price and usage variances. Why did these variances occur?

E 13.15 Victor Company applies facility-sustaining overhead to production based on the number of square feet occupied at the rate of $15 per square foot. During 1996 it used 200,000 square feet and $3.2 million of facility-sustaining overhead to produce 1 million baseball bats. The overhead usage variance for the period was $0. Compute the overhead price variance and the flexible budget amount of facility-related overhead.

E 13.16 McCune Company had the following direct materials and direct labor variances for the month of June.

Direct materials price variance	$10,000 favorable
Direct materials usage variance	2,000 unfavorable
Direct labor price variance	15,000 unfavorable
Direct labor usage variance	8,000 favorable

The standard direct materials and direct labor costs for the month of June were $400,000 and $500,000, respectively. McCune investigates all variances that are 2 percent or more of the applicable standard cost. Which variances should be investigated? Why?

E 13.17　In the past your company has investigated all variances that exceeded a predetermined dollar amount. Write a memo to your supervisor explaining why relative rather than absolute size of a variance is a better criterion for determining which variances to investigate. Provide examples to illustrate your point.

E 13.18　Kaplan Company collected the following data for the past four months concerning its manufacturing operations:

	Average per Month (in days)			
	Month 1	**Month 2**	**Month 3**	**Month 4**
Move time	.6	.45	.6	.6
Order wait time before processing	3.15	3.0	2.85	2.7
Processing time	24.0	26.25	28.50	30.75
Inspection time	.9	1.05	1.05	.9
Wait time during processing	6.5	7.5	8.7	10.0

What is the throughput time and percentage of value-added time for each month? Is the company improving its process efficiency? Why or why not?

E 13.19　Refer to E 13.18. If travel time to the customer is two days, what is the delivery time? Is the company improving its customer response time? Why or why not?

E 13.20　Refer to E 13.18. Assume that the production process is improved such that the wait time during processing is eliminated. What is the throughput time and percentage of value-added time each month?

PROBLEMS

P 13.1　Randolph Company manufactures a product with the following standard material costs:

> Material A　　20 pounds at $2.60 per pound
>
> Material B　　50 pounds at $3.00 per pound

During the month of May, 18,000 pounds of material A were purchased at a cost of $2.76 per pound, of which 9,500 pounds were used in production. During the period, 25,000 pounds of material B were purchased at a cost of $2.98 per pound; 27,000 pounds were used in production. The actual production for the month of May was 500 units.

Required:　
a. Compute the direct materials price variance for each material.
b. Compute the direct materials usage variance for each material.
c. Compute the direct materials inventory variance for each material.
d. Interpret each of these variances and determine who is responsible for them.

P 13.2　Vickery produces a product that requires two different types of labor: assembly and finishing. The standard and actual cost data for the month of October are as follows:

	Standard Cost per Unit	Actual Hours	Actual Cost
Assembly	24 hours at $8 per hour	5,100	$38,250
Finishing	18 hours at $10 per hour	3,450	33,810

A total of 200 units of finished product were produced during October.

Required:　
a. Compute the direct labor price variance for each type of labor.
b. Compute the direct labor usage variance for each type of labor.
c. Interpret each variance and determine who is responsible for them.

P 13.3 Parker Company uses a standard costing system. Information on its overhead costs follows:

Actual overhead:

Unit related	$500,000
Batch related	23,000
Product sustaining	528,000
Facility sustaining	900,000
Actual production	49,000 units
Actual machine hours	99,800 hours
Actual number of diagnostic tests	510 tests
Actual number of moves required	230 moves
Actual square feet used	575,000 square feet

Flexible budget:

Unit-related overhead	2 machine hours at $5 per hour
Batch-related overhead	200 moves at $110 per move
Product-sustaining overhead	500 tests at $1,050 per test
Facility-sustaining overhead	575,000 square feet at $1.50 per square foot

Required: a. Compute the overhead price variances.
b. Compute the overhead usage variances.
c. Interpret the variances computed in *a* and *b*.

P 13.4 Mills Manufacturing manufactures ready-mix cement with the following standard costs:

Direct materials	3 pounds at $2.00 per pound
Direct labor	2 hours at $14.00 per hour
Unit-related overhead	$1.50 per machine hour, 2.5 machine hours required per unit
Batch-related overhead	$250 per purchase order, 100 purchase orders planned
Facility-sustaining overhead	$1 per square feet, 50,000 square feet required for the production of 4,000 units

Actual results for the month of September were:

Square feet occupied	50,500
Units produced	4,100
Machine hours used	10,200
Purchase orders processed	110
Material purchased	15,000 pounds at a total cost of $29,250
Material used	12,500 pounds
Labor used	8,400 hours at a total cost of $115,000
Unit-related overhead	$15,000
Batch-related overhead	$27,000
Facility-sustaining overhead	$49,000

Required: a. Calculate the following variances for the month of September.
- Direct materials price variance.
- Direct materials usage variance.
- Direct materials inventory variance.
- Direct labor price variance.
- Direct labor usage variance.
- Overhead price variances.
- Overhead usage variances.

b. Interpret each of the variances calculated.

P 13.5 Classify each of the following costs as appraisal (A), prevention (P), internal failure (I), or external failure (E) and determine which costs the company should attempt to eliminate. Give a justification for your answer.

a. Systems development.
b. Testing of incoming materials.
c. Setups for testing.
d. Cost of field service.
e. Warranty repairs.
f. Scrap.
g. Spoilage.
h. Quality circles.
i. Technical support provided to suppliers.
j. Quality data gathering and analysis.
k. Maintenance of test equipment.
l. Downtime.
m. Disposal of defective products.
n. Product recalls.
o. Liability claims.
p. Quality engineering.
q. Product design.
r. Rework.
s. Retesting of reworked products.
t. Customer ill will.
u. Final product testing.
v. Depreciation of test equipment.
w. Returns and allowances due to poor quality.
x. Increased overhead due to rework.
y. Depreciation on computerized manufacturing equipment.
z. Supplies used in testing.

P 13.6   Havenstein Corporation manufactures futons with the following standard costs per unit

Direct materials	80 yards at $2.00 per yard
Direct labor	20 hours at $20 per hour
Unit-related overhead	$1.50 per direct labor hour
Product-sustaining overhead	$500 per setup, 1,200 setups planned
Facility-sustaining overhead	$15 per square foot, 59,900 square feet
	allocated to production

The actual results for the year were:

Direct materials	120,000 yards purchased at a total cost of
	$264,000; 118,000 yards used
Direct labor	32,000 hours worked at a total cost of $604,800
Unit-related overhead	$44,000
Facility-sustaining overhead	$904,000
Product-sustaining overhead	$512,000
Production	1,500 units
Setups	1,100
Square feet used	59,900

Required: *a.* Compute the following variances:
  • Direct materials price variance.   • Direct labor usage variance.
  • Direct materials usage variance.   • Overhead price variances.
  • Direct materials inventory variance.   • Overhead usage variances.
  • Direct labor price variance.

b. Interpret each of the variances and determine who is responsible for them.

c. Assume that Havenstein investigates all variances that exceed 2 percent of the standard cost. Which variances, if any, should be investigated? Why?

P 13.7   The following direct materials variance report was presented to the controller of Aztec Manufacturing.

AZTEC MANUFACTURING
Direct Materials Variance Report
For the Year Ended December 31, 1995

Month	Price Variance	Usage Variance
January	$ 400*U*	$ 2,500*U*
February	2,450*U*	3,750*U*
March	50*F*	4,850*U*
April	1,000*F*	6,400*U*
May	1,600*U*	10,050*F*
June	1,950*U*	8,500*U*
July	2,100*U*	14,250*U*
August	2,550*U*	19,000*F*
September	2,400*U*	18,500*U*
October	2,850*U*	21,000*U*
November	2,100*U*	13,000*F*
December	2,150*F*	12,600*F*

Total standard direct materials cost for 1995 was $250,000.

Required: *a.* Determine which variances by month and by type should be investigated using each of the following criteria.
  1. All variances greater than or equal to $10,000 should be investigated.
  2. All variances greater than or equal to 6 percent of standard direct materials cost should be investigated.

b. If materials variances are investigated based on trends, which variances by month and by types should be investigated? Why?

P 13.8   The following information is available from Capone Company.

Direct materials price variance	$9,000*U*
Direct materials usage variance	6,000*U*
Direct labor price variance	1,300*U*
Direct labor usage variance	3,000*U*

During the period, 4,500 pounds of direct materials costing $99,000 were purchased and used, 3,250 direct labor hours were worked at a total cost of $40,300, and 2,000 finished units were produced.

Required: *a.* Compute the actual cost per pound of materials purchased and used.
   b. Compute the actual cost per direct labor hour.
   c. Compute the standard cost per pound of materials used.
   d. Compute the standard cost per direct labor hour.
   e. Compute the standard number of pounds of materials per unit of finished product.
   f. Compute the standard number of direct labor hours per unit of finished product.

P 13.9 The following information is available from Davidson Enterprises.
- Unit-related overhead is applied to production at the rate of 150 percent of direct materials cost. Standard direct materials cost per unit is $38.40.
- Product-sustaining overhead is applied to production at the rate of $1,000 per part. Davidson expects to maintain a parts inventory of 1,200 parts.
- Total overhead in the flexible budget is $4,272,000.
- Total actual overhead is $4,470,000.
- Total overhead applied to production is $4,200,000.
- Batch-related overhead applied to production is $420,000 ($1,050 per requisition).
- The actual cost of direct materials used in the period is $800,000.
- Actual facility-sustaining overhead is $1,480,000.
- The batch-related overhead usage variance is $0.
- The unit-related overhead price variance is $40,000U.
- The product-sustaining overhead price variance is $100,000U.
- The facility-sustaining overhead price variance is $20,000F and the usage variance is $0.

Required: Determine each of the following:
   a. Actual unit-related overhead for the period.
   b. Actual number of units produced in the period.
   c. Actual batch-related overhead for the period.
   d. Batch-related overhead price variance.
   e. Product-sustaining usage variance.
   f. Actual product-sustaining overhead for the period.
   g. Applied facility-sustaining overhead for the period.
   h. Facility-sustaining overhead applied to production during the period.

P 13.10 Your company has never calculated variances because it had no reason to be concerned about costs in the past. However, due to increased competition in the industry, your boss is considering whether the company should adopt some type of variance analysis system. Write a memo to your boss describing the benefits derived from variance analysis and the information provided by each of the following variances.
  1. Direct materials price variance.
  2. Direct materials usage variance.
  3. Direct materials inventory variance.
  4. Direct labor price variance.
  5. Direct labor usage variance.
  6. Overhead price variance.
  7. Overhead usage variance—unit-related overhead.
  8. Overhead usage variance—batch related, product sustaining, or facility sustaining.

COMPUTER APPLICATIONS

CA 13.1 Carlton Manufacturing has begun tracking its process times. Data gathered for the past six months are shown below. These data show the average number of days required by various process activities.

Activities	Months					
	1	2	3	4	5	6
Order delay time	6.5	7.0	6.3	6.2	6.0	5.4
Work-in-process delay time	9.0	8.0	6.5	6.0	5.5	5.0
Moving time	1.0	1.0	1.0	0.5	0.5	0.3
Processing time	10.1	10.1	10.1	9.1	9.1	9.1
Inspection time	0.5	0.5	0.5	0.1	0.1	0.1
Travel time	2.5	2.4	2.3	2.2	2.1	2.0

Required: *a.* Determine throughput time each month.
b. Determine the percentage of value-added time each month.
c. Determine delivery time each month.
d. Is the company improving? Why or why not?

 CA 13.2 Tykes Bykes has the following standard costs for its direct materials and direct labor in the production of tricycles.

Direct materials	3 wheels at $0.50 each
	1 metal frame at $2.50 each
	1 handlebar set at $1.00 per set
Direct labor	3/4 of an hour at $8.00 per hour

Actual results for each month of the first quarter are shown below:

	January	February	March
Tricycles produced	10,600	11,100	10,800
Wheels purchased	35,000	35,000	35,000
Wheel cost	$21,000	$21,000	$22,750
Wheels used	31,950	33,300	32,500
Frames purchased	11,000	12,000	10,500
Frame cost	$33,000	$29,400	$26,250
Frames used	10,600	11,500	10,800
Handlebars purchased	10,000	12,500	13,500
Handlebar cost	$11,000	$12,500	$14,850
Handlebars used	11,000	11,900	13,500
Direct labor hours used	8,500	8,300	8,000
Direct labor cost	$65,000	$70,550	$68,850

Required: *a.* Determine the direct materials price variance for each month.
b. Determine the direct materials inventory variance for each month.
c. Determine the direct materials usage variance for each month.
d. Determine the direct labor price variance for each month.
e. Determine the direct labor usage variance for each month.

CA 13.3 Sherman Company has begun tracking its quality costs. It gathered data for the past three months (January through March) concerning its estimated quality costs in each category. These data are shown below.

	January	February	March
Appraisal costs	$ 5,000	$12,000	$17,000
Prevention costs	6,500	13,000	13,000
Internal failure costs	45,000	40,000	25,000
External failure costs	85,000	55,000	35,000

Required *a.* Determine the total quality costs for each month.
b. Determine the total voluntary quality costs for each month.
c. Determine the percentage of voluntary quality costs for each month.
d. Do you feel the company is improving quality? Why or why not?

CASES

C 13.1 Funtime Company manufactures video game machines and uses a standard costs system. The standard costs for video game machines are as follows:

	Standard Quantity	Cost per Unit	Total Cost
Direct materials:			
Housing unit	1	$20	$ 20
Printed circuit boards	2	15	30
Reading heads	4	10	40
Direct labor:			
Assembly	2	8	16
PCB group	1	9	9
RH group	1.5	10	15
Unit-related overhead	4.5	2	9
Total			$139

Funtime's accountant prepared the following usage report:

	Quantity	Cost
Housing units	2,200	$ 44,000
Printed circuit boards	4,700	75,200
Reading heads	9,200	101,200
Assembly labor	3,900	31,200
PCB labor	2,400	23,760
RH labor	3,500	38,500
Unit-related overhead		18,800
Total		$332,660

Production for the month of May was 2,200 units. Facility-sustaining overhead was budgeted at $600,000 for the year. Actual facility-sustaining overhead costs for the month of May were $49,000 and the facility-sustaining overhead usage variance was zero. There was no batch-related or product-sustaining overhead incurred.

Required: Compute the following variances:
   a. Direct materials price variance.
   b. Direct materials usage variance.
   c. Direct labor price variance.
   d. Direct labor usage variance.
   e. Overhead price variances.
   f. Overhead usage variances.

(CMA Adapted)

C 13.2   Coldking Company is a small producer of fruit-flavored frozen desserts. For many years, Coldking's products have had strong regional sales on the basis of brand name recognition; however, other companies have begun marketing similar products in the area, and price competition has become increasingly important. Jane Wakefield, the company's controller, is planning to implement a standard cost system for Coldking and has gathered considerable information from her co-workers on the production and material requirements of Coldking's products. Wakefield believes that the use of standard costing will allow Coldking to improve cost control and make better pricing decisions.

Coldking's most popular product is raspberry sherbet. The sherbet is produced in 10-gallon batches, and each batch requires six quarts of good raspberries. The fresh raspberries are sorted by hand (requiring three minutes) before entering the production process. Because of imperfections in the raspberries and normal spoilage, one quart of berries is discarded for every four quarts of acceptable berries. The acceptable raspberries are then blended with the other ingredients. Blending requires 12 minutes of direct labor time. After blending, the sherbet is packaged in quart containers. Wakefield has gathered the following pricing information:
   1. Coldking purchases raspberries at a cost of $.80 per quart. All other ingredients cost a total of $.45 per gallon.
   2. Direct labor is paid at the rate of $9.00 per hour.
   3. The total cost of materials and labor required to package the sherbet is $.38 per quart.

Required: Develop the standard cost for the direct cost components of a 10-gallon batch of raspberry sherbet.

(CMA Adapted)

CRITICAL THINKING

CT 13.1   Refer to Case 13.2. As part of the implementation of the standard cost system at Coldking, Jane Wakefield plans to begin tracking the time spent to manufacture the sherbet.

Required: Write a memo to Jane to describe how to calculate throughput time and what benefits she can derive from tracking throughput time.

CT 13.2   You have recently been hired by a fast growing company in a very competitive industry. Your boss is very interested in achieving quality and would like to be recognized for that quality. Since you are in college, your boss recognizes that you have excellent research skills. Therefore, he has asked you to investigate something he heard recently at a convention called ISO 9000. When you have completed your investigation, he would like a memo discussing ISO 9000 and how your company can become certified.

EC 13.1   Mark-Wright, Inc. (MWI), is a specialty frozen food processor located in the Midwest. Since its founding in 1982, MWI has enjoyed a loyal clientele that is willing to pay premium prices for the high-quality frozen foods it prepares from specialized recipes. In the last two years, the company has experienced rapid sales growth in its operating region and has had many inquires about supplying its products on a national basis. To meet this growth, MWI expanded its processing capabilities, which resulted in increased production and distribution costs. Furthermore, MWI has been encountering pricing pressure from competitors outside its normal marketing region.

As MWI desires to continue its expansion, Jim Condon, CEO, has engaged a consulting firm to assist MWI in determining its best course of action. The consulting firm concluded that, while premium pricing is sustainable in some areas, if sales growth is to be achieved, MWI must make some price concessions. Also, in order to maintain profit margins, costs must be reduced and controlled. The consulting firm recommended the institution of a standard cost system that also would facilitate a flexible budgeting system to better accommodate the changes in demand that can be expected when serving an expanding market area.

Condon met with his management team and explained the recommendations of the consulting firm. Condon then assigned the task of establishing standard costs to his management team. After discussing the situation with their respective staffs, the management team met to review the matter.

Jane Morgan, purchasing manager, advised that meeting expanded production would necessitate obtaining basic food supplies from other than traditional MWI sources. This would entail increased raw material and shipping costs and could result in lower-quality supplies. Consequently, the increased costs would need to be made up by the processing department if current cost levels were to be maintained or reduced.

Stan Walters, processing manager, countered that the need to accelerate processing cycles to increase production, coupled with the possibility of receiving lower-grade supplies, can be expected to result in a slip in quality and a greater product rejection rate. Under these circumstances, per unit labor utilization cannot be maintained or reduced, and forecasting future unit labor content becomes very difficult.

Tom Lopez, production engineer, advised that if the equipment is not properly maintained and thoroughly cleaned at prescribed intervals, it can be anticipated that the quality and unique taste of the frozen food products will be affected. Jack Reid, vice president of sales, states that if quality cannot be maintained, MWI cannot expect to increase sales to the levels projected.

When Condon was apprised of the problems encountered by his management team, he advised them that if agreement could not be reached on appropriate standards, he would arrange to have them set by the consulting firm and everyone would have to live with the results.

Required: *a.* Discuss the major advantages of using standards to control behavior.
              b. Identify those who should participate in setting the standards and describe the benefits of their participation in the standard-setting process.
              c. What could be the consequences if Jim Condon has the standards set by the outside consulting firm?

(CMA Adapted)

EC 13.2   Master Teaching is a rapidly expanding company that mass-produces instruction materials for teachers. The owner of Master Teaching, Byron White, has made an effort to provide quality products at fair prices with delivery as promised. White is concerned because it is increasingly difficult to oversee the daily operations of Master Teaching.

White has recently transferred control over departmental operations to each departmental manager. However, the quality control department still reports directly to White. A materials manager was hired to purchase all raw materials and to oversee the materials handling functions. A production manager was hired to oversee production, including hiring practices.

White wants to implement standard costs for materials and labor control.

Required: Write a memo to Bryon White discussing each of the following:
              a. Who should be involved in setting the standards and why.
              b. The factors to consider when setting the standards.
              c. Who will be assigned responsibility for the standards.

PART FIVE

Planning and Decision Making

In part 5, the planning section, the processes and procedures firms use for planning investing and financing activities are discussed. These chapters discuss how operating leverage, various types of available financing, and various capital budgeting techniques are used in planning and decision making.

CHAPTER 14

The Time Value of Money: A Tool for Decision Making

Learning Objectives

1. Explain the cyclical relationship of financing, investing, and operating decisions.

2. Describe the distinction between return of and return on investment and the difference between rate of return and expected rate of return.

3. Explain the risk-return relationship.

4. Describe the difference between simple and compound interest and how interest relates to the time value of money.

5. Illustrate how to use the future value of the amount of $1 and the present value of $1 to solve problems that involve lump-sum cash flows at different points in time.

6. Demonstrate how to use the future value of an annuity and the present value of an annuity to solve problems that involve annuity cash flow.

Want to retire with a million dollars? Would you like your five-year-old child to have $50,000 when he or she is ready for college? Reputable investment companies like Fidelity Investments and the Vanguard Group offer tax-deferred investments that make these goals a reality with relatively small investments. Investment companies like these achieve their investment goals because they understand the risk-return relationship, the time value of money, and the way to utilize the power of compound interest.

In prior chapters, we focused on examining how businesses operate, how decision makers use accounting information for planning business operations, how the accounting system captures the operating information surrounding business events, and how internal and external stakeholders use accounting information to evaluate a firm's operations. The remaining chapters of the text explore how businesses obtain and invest financial resources. We examine the financing and investing activities of a business enterprise, learn how management uses accounting information to plan for these types of activities, how the accounting system captures these events, and how internal and external stakeholders use accounting information to evaluate the firm's financing and investing decisions.

Exhibit 14.1 depicts the interdependent and cyclical nature of financing, investing, and operating decisions. When starting a business enterprise, the person(s) responsible for obtaining the necessary funds must determine not only the amount of funds needed, but also the source of the financing. The firm can acquire funds through debt financing (creditors) or equity financing (owner contributions).

Next the decision makers must determine how to invest the funds obtained. In general, the firm invests in either current assets or long-term assets. Current assets, such as inventory and office supplies, are necessary to sell the firm's products or to render its services. Investments in long-term assets, such as buildings and equipment, provide the infrastructure necessary to support the daily operating activities of the firm.

Using the resources at its disposal, management next makes the various operating decisions that will generate an operating profit if management utilizes the resources effectively.

Operating profits generated are used for three primary purposes: (1) to pay the interest on borrowed funds, (2) to reward the owners in the form of dividends (or in the form of withdrawals in proprietorships and partnerships), and (3) to reinvest funds in the firm to maintain the existing operational capacity and finance additional long-term investments in the firm.

The operating cycle starts again when the funds from profits retained in the company are reinvested in the firm. If additional investments are needed, the firm will again borrow from creditors or solicit contributions from new or existing owners. The amount and sources of funds needed for new investments depend on management's operating plans and the long-term assets needed to successfully implement the plans.

EXHIBIT 14.1

Operating and Decision Cycle

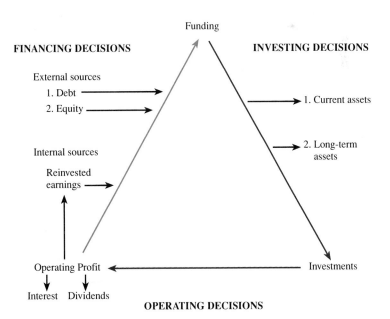

THE FAR SIDE   By GARY LARSON

Einstein discovers that time is actually money.

Before going any further, however, it is imperative that you understand the fundamental concepts underlying financing and investing decisions. In this chapter we expand the definitions of return and risk and introduce the concept of the time value of money. These essential tools for making financing and investing decisions are as important as hammers, saws, and tape measures are to a carpenter building a house. With these tools, you can make informed financing and investing decisions for a business enterprise. In addition, they are also useful for making personal financial decisions, such as determining how much to save for your retirement or children's college education and the best way to finance the purchase of a car or a house or to start a business after graduation.

RETURN OF AND RETURN ON INVESTMENT: WHAT IS THE DIFFERENCE?

The concept of *return* is associated with investing decisions involving the acquisition of assets, such as certificates of deposit, government bonds, and new equipment. As discussed in Chapter 1, there are two types of return: return of investment and return on investment. When assessing investment alternatives, investors expect to receive a return of investment. That is, investors only make investments that they believe will return their initial investment. For example, if you invest $1,000 in a savings account for one year, you expect, at a minimum, to receive $1,000 at the end of the year. The $1,000 you receive at the end of the year is your return of investment.

Return on investment is money received in excess of the initial investment. If the $1,000 in the savings account generates $1,050 at the end of one year, there is a *return of* the initial $1,000 investment, and a *return on* the investment of interest of $50.

The Importance of Time

Return on investment is not adequate to differentiate among investments because it does not consider the length of time that investments are held or the amount of the initial investment. For example, investments X and Y shown in Exhibit 14.2 generate a return on investment of $300 and $400, respectively. How would you choose between the two investments based on the dollar amount of the return? You might select investment Y because its return is $100 greater than investment X. However, this does not consider the length of time investments X and Y were held. If the $1,300 accumulated by investment X on January 1, 1996, is reinvested and held as long as investment Y (until July 1, 1996), it could generate an additional return that equals or exceeds the $100 difference between the two investments.

EXHIBIT	14.2	Return on Investment

Investment X		Investment Y	
January 1, 1995 Invest	$1,000	January 1, 1995 Invest	$1,000
January 1, 1996 Receive	1,300	**July 1, 1996** Receive	1,400
RETURN ON INVESTMENT on January 1, 1996	$ 300	RETURN ON INVESTMENT on July 1, 1996	$ 400

The Importance of the Amount of the Initial Investment

Even when investments are held for the same period of time, the amounts of the initial investment can distort comparisons. Consider investments X, Y, and Z in Exhibit 14.3. One might choose to make investment Z because it has the largest dollar amount of return on investment of the three investments. However, this choice does not take into account the differences in the size of the initial investments—$1,000, $2,000, and $3,000, respectively.

What we need to analyze the investments realistically is a common-size measure of performance, that is, a measure that allows us to compare and rank the performance of investments regardless of the size of the initial investment.

Rate of Return

The **rate of return** (a percentage) measures the performance of investments on a common-size basis and eliminates any distortion caused by the size of the initial investment. Exhibit 14.3 uses the rate of return formula, shown below, to determine the rate of return for investments X, Y, and Z. We calculate rate of return as follows:

$$\text{Rate of return} = \frac{\text{Dollar amount of return on investment}}{\text{Dollar amount of initial investment}}$$

In these cases, the 10 percent rate of return on investment X is greater than those on investments Y (8 percent) and Z (6 percent).

The rate of return on investments is usually expressed as an annual (one-year) rate even if the life of the investment is greater or less than one year. The return percentage in Exhibit 14.3 is based on a one-year time period and is called an *annual rate of return.*

Investments can have a negative rate of return when they do not recover the initial investment, that is, when there is a failure to get a return of investment. For example, if an investment returns only $800 of the $1,000 initially invested, the $200 difference is described as a 20 percent negative rate of return [($800–$1,000)/$1,000].

In the example in Exhibit 14.3, we measured the performance of the investments by calculating the rates of return on investment *after* the returns were generated by the investments. However, most investments are made before investors know what their actual rates of return will be. How can potential investors measure the performance of investments before knowing the actual rate of return the investments will generate?

EXHIBIT	14.3	Rate of Return

	Investments		
	X	Y	Z
January 1, 1995 Invest	$1,000	$2,000	$3,000
January 1, 1996 Receive	1,100	2,160	3,180
Return on investment	$ 100	$ 160	$ 180
Calculation of Rate of Return:			
Rate of return calculation	$ 100	$ 160	$ 180
	$1,000	$2,000	$3,000
Annual rate of return	10%	8%	6%

EXHIBIT	14.4	Expected Outcomes and Probabilities			
		Possible Outcomes	Possible Returns	Rate of Return if Event Occurs	Probability of Outcome
		Mother lode	$1,000,000	1,000%	.01
		College lode	150,000	150	.20
		Baby lode	50,000	50	.40
		No lode	−100,000	−100	.39

Expected rate of return (*ERR*) = (.01 × 1,000%) + (.2 × 150%) + (.4 × 50%) + (.39 × −100%) = 21%

Expected Rate of Return

Unfortunately, individuals make investment decisions without the benefit of clairvoyance and, as a result, they must predict rates of return on investments they are considering. The predicted return rate is known as the **expected rate of return,** a summary measure of an investment's performance, stated as a percentage, based on the possible rates of return and the likelihood of those rates of return occurring. The expected rate of return is a useful measure for choosing among investment alternatives.

To ascertain an investment's expected rate of return, it is necessary to: (1) forecast the investment's possible rates of return, (2) establish a probability that each forecasted rate of return will occur, and (3) multiply each forecasted return by its respective probability and sum the resulting products.

To illustrate, assume that an investor has the opportunity to buy a gold mine for $100,000. Exhibit 14.4 lists the four possible outcomes to expect in terms of dollars and rates of return on the investment. The exhibit also shows the probability of the four outcomes occurring. The investor believes that there is 1 chance in 100 (.01), or a 1 percent chance, of the miners hitting the "mother lode" and getting a 1,000 percent rate of return ($1,000,000/$100,000). At the other extreme, there are 39 chances in 100 (.39), or a 39 percent chance, of finding "no lode" and a negative 100 percent rate of return (−$100,000/$100,000). The expected rate of return for this gold mining investment is 21 percent, as calculated in Exhibit 14.4.

The gold mine's 21 percent expected rate of return does not mean that the gold mine will earn a 21 percent rate of return. Instead, it summarizes the gold mine's possible rates of return.

Do not confuse the expected rate of return with the actual rate of return of an investment. An investor estimates the expected rate of return before making the investment, while the actual rate of return on an investment is calculated after the outcome of the investment is revealed at some future date. For example, if the miners do hit the "college lode," the actual return of the investment is 150 percent rather than the 21 percent expected rate of return.

The concepts of return of investment, return on investment, rate of return, and expected rate of return are fundamental when making any investment decision. However, investors do not automatically select the investment alternative that generates the highest expected rate of return. Before selecting an investment, it is necessary to appraise not only the expected return but also the risk of the investments under consideration.

WHAT IS THE RISK OF INVESTMENT?

Recall that *risk* is the exposure to the chance that an unfavorable outcome will occur at some future point in time. Typically, people take risks because some monetary or psychic reward is possible. For example, people go to Las Vegas and gamble even though they know that casinos are profitable because most people lose money. However, there are many people who are willing to put their money at risk in the hope of beating the odds and winning. The likelihood of losing money is offset by the belief that it is possible to beat the odds and by the enjoyment of actually taking the risk itself.

Attitudes toward Risk

The amount of risk people are willing to assume depends on their attitudes toward risk and the decision under consideration. People who enjoy risky situations are called *risk seekers*, whereas those who avoid risk are called *risk avoiders*. However, the decision under consideration may change the decision maker's normal attitude toward risk. For example, in terms of taking physical risks, a mountain climber is a risk seeker; however, the climber might be a risk avoider when making investment decisions that affect his or her ability to finance the next climbing expedition.

Risk is associated with the uncertainty of an unfavorable outcome actually occurring. To illustrate, assume that an alternative to the previous gold mine investment is buying a $100,000 one-year U.S. government security that yields a 10 percent rate of return. Because the U.S. government has never defaulted on its debt, there is little doubt that the government will return the initial investment of $100,000 and pay an actual return on investment of $10,000 ($100,000 × .10). This investment, therefore, has very little risk because there is very little chance of an unfavorable outcome occurring.

Investing in the gold mine could generate an actual rate of return that is much greater than the government security. However, the gold mine investment is risky because there is a significant chance of losing the entire investment. In this case, the choice the investor makes depends on how willing he or she is to risk the $100,000 investment for a possible return.

Measuring Risk

The risk of any investment is related to the possibility of earning less than the expected rate of return and is impounded in the expected rate of return figure. Impounding means that the expected rate of return captures the effects of both the positive and the less desirable outcomes of an investment in one summary measure of return. For example, the gold mine investment's 21 percent expected rate of return is based upon possible returns that range from a 1,000 percent rate of return and a negative 100 percent rate of return.

There are several ways to measure the risk of an investment. The **relative risk ratio** is a rather simple common-size risk measure that reflects the risk of an investment as a percentage of the expected return lost if the worst-case outcome occurs.[1] The amount of risk depends on the difference between the worst possible outcome and the expected rate of return. Because the relative risk ratio is a common-size measure, it is possible to rank respective risks of two or more investments from high to low.

$$\text{Relative risk ratio} = \frac{\substack{\text{Expected rate} \\ \text{of return}} - \substack{\text{Lowest possible} \\ \text{rate of return}}}{\text{Expected rate of return}}$$

To illustrate how to use the relative risk ratio, assume that an investor is considering investment alternatives A and B presented in Exhibit 14.5. Both investment A and investment B cost $100,000 and have two possible outcomes. The two outcomes of each investment have the same .5 probability, or a 50 percent chance of occurring.

Exhibit 14.5 Panels A and B show two methods for calculations of the expected rates of return for investments A and B. The first method uses rates of return described earlier. The second is based on an investments' **expected return,** which is also a summary measure of an investment's performance, stated in dollars, based on the possible returns on investment in dollars and the likelihood of those returns occurring. Both methods indicate that investments A and B have the same 10.5 percent expected rate of return. However, the investments do not have the same risk.

---

[1]This measure assumes that there is a normal distribution of possible returns. Therefore, the expected rate of return is the midpoint of the range of returns, and the relative risk ratio measures the difference between this midpoint and the worst possible outcome in the range of outcomes. When the outcomes are not distributed normally around the mean, the relative risk ratio is not an appropriate measure of risk. Other measures of risk, in such cases, would require the use of statistics.

Exhibit 14.5 Panels C and D show calculations of the relative risk ratios using both the expected rates of return and the expected returns. The relative risk ratios provide a means of quantifying a difference in the risk of the two investments.

To determine the relative risk ratio using rates of return, subtract the worst possible rate of return from the expected rate of return. This yields the amount of the expected rate of return lost if the worst outcome occurs. For example, for investment A, the amount of the expected rate of return lost is .5 percent, which is the difference between investment A's expected rate of return, 10.5 percent, and the worst possible rate of return, 10 percent ($10,000/$100,000). Dividing this difference (.5%) by the expected rate of return (10.5%) yields the percentage of the expected return that is lost if the worst outcome occurs. For investment A this percentage, or relative risk ratio, is 4.76 percent.

Determining the relative risk ratio using expected returns follows similar procedures but dollar values rather than percentages are used. For example, the expected return for investment A is $10,500 and its worst return expected is $10,000. When the $500 difference between these two returns is divided by the expected return, the relative risk ratio is 4.76 percent. In either case, the common-size measure provides a basis for comparing the risk of the investment alternatives. The larger the relative risk ratio, the higher an investment's risk.

EXHIBIT	14.5	Expected Rate of Return and Relative Risk Ratio

	Investment A	Investment B
Amount invested	$100,000	$100,000
Possible outcomes and (probabilities)	10,000 (.5)	20,000 (.5)
	11,000 (.5)	1,000 (.5)

Expected Rates of Return

Panel A: Calculated Using Rates of Return

Investment A

$$\frac{\$10,000}{\$100,000}(.5) + \frac{\$11,000}{\$100,000}(.5) = 10\%(.5) + 11\%(.5) = 10.5\%$$

Investment B:

$$\frac{\$20,000}{\$100,000}(.5) + \frac{\$1,000}{\$100,000}(.5) = 20\%(.5) + 1\%(.5) = 10.5\%$$

Panel B: Calculated Using Expected Returns

$$\text{Expected rate of return} = \frac{\text{Expected return on investment}}{\text{Amount of initial investment}}$$

Investment A: $10,500/$100,000 = 10.5%

Investment B: $10,500/$100,000 = 10.5%

Relative Risk Ratios

Panel C: Calculated Using Rates of Return

Investment A: $\dfrac{10.5\% - 10\%}{10.5\%} = 4.76\%$

Investment B: $\dfrac{10.5\% - 1\%}{10.5\%} = 90.48\%$

Panel D: Calculated Using Expected Returns

Investment A: $\dfrac{\$10,500 - \$10,000}{\$10,500} = 4.76\%$

Investment B: $\dfrac{\$10,500 - \$1,000}{\$10,500} = 90.48\%$

*Expected returns:
   Investment A: $10,000 (.5) + $11,000 (.5) = $10,500
   Investment B: $20,000 (.5) + $1,000 (.50) = $10,500

Investment A loses only 4.76 percent of the expected return if the worst outcome occurs. Investment B, however, is riskier because if the worst outcome actually occurs, 90.48 percent of the expected return is lost.

The relative risk ratio quantifies the risk of an investment and helps investors determine if the risk of the investment is justified given its potential return.

THE RISK-RETURN RELATIONSHIP

Risk and return are directly related; that is, the greater the risk, the greater the return the investor expects. When choosing among investment alternatives, investors want the investment with the highest return, but they must also consider the riskiness of the investment. Typically, investors select investments with the highest expected return for a given level of risk. For example, investment A in Exhibit 14.5 is more desirable than investment B because it has the same expected rate of return as investment B (10.5 percent), with lower risk (4.76 percent versus 90.48 percent).

To consider investment B as a legitimate alternative, the investor would need a greater expected return before assuming the greater investment risk. This increase in the expected rate of return is called a **risk premium.**

Assume that an investor wants investment B to yield an expected rate of return of 16.5 percent in order to consider it to be a reasonable investment. The additional 6 percent desired (16.5 percent versus 10.5 percent) is the risk premium placed on this investment and compensates the investor for assuming the additional potential risk of the investment. The expected rate of return including the risk premium is called the **risk-adjusted expected rate of return.**

Changes in an investor's risk-adjusted rate of return affect the amount the investor will pay for an investment. Also, the amount of the investment varies inversely with the change in risk-adjusted rate of return. That is, when the risk-adjusted expected rate of return increases an investor pays less for the investment in order to achieve the revised expected (risk-adjusted) rate of return.

To illustrate why this occurs, assume that an investor revises her assessment of an investment's risk but not the outcomes or probabilities of those outcomes occurring. For example, in order to get a 16.5 percent risk-adjusted expected rate of return on investment B, the investor will revise the price she is willing to pay for investment B from $100,000 to $63,636 (calculated below) using the expected rate of return formula. If the seller of investment B accepts $63,636 rather than $100,000, then the investor's initial investment of $63,636 will have a risk-adjusted expected rate of return of 16.5 percent.

$$\text{Expected rate of return} = \frac{\text{(Probability)(Outcome)} + \text{(Prob)(Out)} + \ldots + \text{(Prob)(Out)}}{\text{Amount invested in B}}$$

$$.165 = \frac{(.5)(\$20,000) + (.5)(\$1,000)}{\text{Amount invested in B}}$$

$$.165 \times \text{Amount invested in B} = \$10,500$$

$$\text{Amount invested in B} = \$63,636$$

Now, both investment A and investment B are equally desirable to the investor because the amount of investment B reflects the risk premium the investor demanded. That is, the investor is compensated for the additional risk by the reduction in the price of investment B from $100,000 to $63,636.

PAUSE & REFLECT   If you were a risk seeker, would you have demanded a risk premium for investment B?

This example illustrates the direct relationship between risk and return. Investors who are risk avoiders and assume greater risk want a greater expected rate of return on their investments. Keep in mind that the notions of risk and return are based on investors' beliefs about the likelihood of future events. Therefore, the assessment of risk, return, and the resulting valuation of investments is the result of the subjective assessments and the ability of the buyer and seller of the investment to agree on a price.

Risk Factors Considered in Determining Expected Return

All investors expect some return on their investment, even if an investment has no risk. The determination of the expected return on any investment begins with an assumption called the **risk-free rate of return,** or the rate of return that a virtually riskless investment produces. Risk premiums for risk factors associated with particular investments are added to the risk-free rate to determine the risk-adjusted expected rate of return of an investment. There are three primary risk factors to consider that generate risk premiums—inflation risk, business risk, and liquidity risk.

Inflation Risk   Inflation causes the purchasing power of the monetary unit to decline. For example, suppose $1 would buy a loaf of bread as of January 1, 1995, and at the end of the year the same loaf of bread cost $1.05. The purchasing power of the dollar declined by 5 percent ($.05/$1.00 = .05 or 5%) during 1995 because it would take $1.05 instead of $1 to buy the same loaf of bread at the end of the period. **Inflation risk,** then, is the chance of a decline in purchasing power of the monetary units during the time money is invested. It is factored into every investment decision to allow for the chance of inflation during the investment period. If an investor expects inflation to continue at the same rate into the foreseeable future, he or she must add a constant percentage as the inflation risk premium to the expected return for any investment being considered.

Business Risk   **Business risk** is the risk associated with the ability of a particular company to continue in business. A business fails when its revenues do not cover its operating expenses or when cash flows are insufficient to pay the interest or principal on the business's debt. The business risk factor reflects the likelihood of a company ceasing normal operations. For example, a company in financial difficulty has to pay a higher rate of interest on its debt than a financially sound company because its financial difficulty increases the chance that the business may not be able to continue its operations.

A bank's prime interest rate is the interest rate charged to a bank's most financially sound customers. The rate of interest on borrowed funds increases as the chance of business failure increases. For example, an airline company such as America West, which filed for bankruptcy protection in 1993, has higher business risk than Southwest Airlines, which is not faced with similar financial difficulties.

Liquidity Risk   Investments that are quickly converted into cash are considered to be liquid. **Liquidity risk** is the chance that an investment cannot be readily converted into cash and generates a risk premium to compensate investors for the inability to convert their investment into cash quickly. For example, a holder of 100 shares of General Motors stock could quickly sell the shares on the New York Stock Exchange; therefore, such an investment is considered to be liquid. On the other hand, if an investor purchased 100 shares of Richards' Auto Parts, Inc. stock, which is not traded on any organized stock exchange, a quick conversion of the stock to cash would be difficult. If the investor needs cash immediately, he might have to reduce the price of the stock substantially in order to attract a buyer. On the other hand, he could borrow money until he finds a buyer who would be willing to pay the higher price. Then the investor would repay the principal and interest on the loan from the proceeds of the sale of the stock. In either case, to compensate for liquidity risk, an investor would have a higher expected rate of return for investing in Richards' Auto Parts stock than in a company with more readily convertible stock.

To illustrate how risk factors work, assume that an investor is considering the purchase of Richards' Auto Parts stock. Assume that the investor expects a 4 percent inflation rate and that estimates for the business risk and liquidity risk premiums for

Richards' stock are 3 percent and 1 percent, respectively. If the risk-free rate of return is 3 percent, the risk-adjusted expected rate of return for Richards' stock is 11 percent, as shown below:

Risk-free rate of return	3%
Inflation risk premium	4
Business risk premium	3
Liquidity risk premium	1
Risk-adjusted expected rate of return	11%

Thus, to compensate for the respective risks anticipated, the investor needs an 11 percent expected rate of return to make the Richards' investment worthwhile.

PAUSE & REFLECT   For many years, rates charged by banks for long-term loans such as home mortgages were lower than rates charged for short-term loans, such as car loans. In the mid-1970s this relationship reversed, and long-term loans were charged a higher interest rate than short-term loans. Why did this relationship change?

Investors' Perception of Return and Risk

We are now aware that, in order to earn a higher rate of return, investors must assume more risk. All investors want to obtain the greatest return possible on their invested funds but must temper their investment decision by the amount of risk they are willing to assume. On an individual basis, investment decisions are subject to the investor's willingness to accept risk.

A company's management team makes similar return-risk assessments as it invests the resources of the firm. However, its investment decisions cannot be based exclusively on the team members' personal attitudes toward risk. The risk that management assumes must be consistent with the risk preferences of the firm's owners because managers act on the owners' behalf.

Perception of Return and Risk on Borrowed Funds

Businesses use borrowed funds in the expectation of earning a greater return on the funds they invest than it costs to borrow the funds (interest). Therefore, businesses want to minimize the interest on the borrowed funds. In order to do so, these businesses must convince their creditors (lenders) that the investments made with the borrowed funds will generate a return sufficient to pay the interest and principal on the loan. The lower the probability that a firm will default on the payment of interest or principal on a loan, the lower the rate of interest creditors will charge for borrowed funds. A lower interest rate improves the chance of increasing the rate of return on the business owners' investment. The business, in such situations, would earn more on its borrowed funds, with the excess return going to the owners.

Borrowing money, soliciting contributions from owners, and investing these funds all involve evaluating dollar amounts at different points in time. Understanding the relationship of money and time is critical to all investing and financing decisions.

TIME VALUE OF MONEY

The expectation that investments generate returns over time implies that a dollar today, given that it can generate a return on investment over time, is worth more than a dollar one year from today. This concept is known as the *time value of money*.

The **time value of money** is the tool used to solve problems involving the comparison of cash flows that occur at different points in time. While you may not be directly responsible for calculating the impact of the time value of money on a business decision, it is important to understand what such calculations mean, as well as when specialists might be required to provide you or your firm with such information.

The time value of money allows individuals and businesses to determine the cash equivalent today of cash flows that will occur at some point in time in the future. The interest rates assumed determine the size of the cash equivalent given for a particular period of time.

For example, if an investor could receive 10 percent interest on his investments, $100 on January 1, 1996, is the cash equivalent of $110 on January 1, 1997. Thus, any amount less than $110 on January 1, 1997, is not as valuable as $100 on January 1, 1996. It follows that any amount greater than $110 on January 1, 1997, is more valuable than the $100 on January 1, 1996, because the most the $100, 10 percent investment could generate on January 1, 1997, is $110. Thus, assuming a 10 percent return, the following relationships hold.

1/1/96		1/1/97
$100	is cash equivalent of	$110
100	is worth more than	108
100	is worth less than	112

Our illustration describes the concept of cash equivalents and the role that interest rates play in determining cash equivalents. However, before going any further, it is necessary to understand the two alternative methods for calculating interest on an investment.

Simple and Compound Interest

As you know, interest is the cost of borrowing money and can be calculated on either a simple or compound basis. **Simple interest** is interest calculated only on the amount borrowed. The amount of interest depends on the amount loaned or borrowed (principal), the annual interest rate, and the amount of time the principal is used. Recall that the formula for calculating interest is:

$$\text{Principal} \times \text{Rate} \times \text{Time} = \text{Interest}$$

For example, assume that you borrow $1,000 for two years at 10 percent simple interest. The amount of each year's interest is computed using the original $1,000. The calculation of simple interest below for the two-year period is:

Year 1	$1,000 $\times$ .10 $\times$ 1 =	$ 100
Year 2	$1,000 $\times$ .10 $\times$ 1 =	$ 100
Total Simple Interest		$ 200
Add: Principal		1,000
Total amount due on note		$1,200

The total amount you owe on the note on its maturity date is $1,200, or $1,000 of principal plus $200 of interest.

Compound interest is interest that is based on a principal amount that includes interest from previous time periods. Like simple interest, compound interest is interest calculated on the principal in the first interest period. However, at the start of the second interest period, the interest from the first period is added to the principal and becomes part of the principal on which interest is calculated for the second period. The process of adding interest to the principal is called **compounding** and is repeated at the start of each subsequent interest period. In other words, compound interest is *interest paid on interest.*

To illustrate, assume that you borrow $1,000 for two years at a 10 percent interest rate that is compounded annually. The total amount of interest due at the end of two years is $210, as shown below.

Year 1	$1,000 $\times$ .10 $\times$ 1 =	$100
Year 2	$1,100* $\times$ .10 $\times$ 1 =	$110
Total Compound Interest		$210

*$1000 principal + $100 interest from year 1 = $1,100.

The difference between the amount of compound and simple interest is the $10 interest charged on year 1's interest of $100. Note that the first year's interest of $100 becomes part of the principal on which the second year's interest of $110 is calculated [($1,000 + $100 interest) × .10 × 1 = $110]. The computation of the total amount you would owe on the note on its maturity date, $1,210, is:

Total interest	$ 210
Add: Principal	1,000
Total amount due on note	$1,210

This illustration shows how to compound interest annually; however, it is possible to compound interest more frequently. By increasing the frequency of the compounding, more interest accumulates on the note.

To illustrate, suppose the 10 percent interest on the $1,000 note is compounded semiannually. Thus, the interest on the note is added to the principal every six months. Consequently, the total amount of interest on the note for two years is $215.51, as shown below.

Year 1:
1st six months	$1,000 × .10 × 1/2	=	$ 50.00
2nd six months	$1,050 × .10 × 1/2	=	$ 52.50

Year 2:
3rd six months	$1,102.50 × .10 × 1/2	=	$ 55.13
4th six months	$1,157.63 × .10 × 1/2	=	$ 57.88
Total compound interest			$ 215.51
Add: Principal			1,000.00
Total amount due on note			$1,215.51

The $215.51 of interest for two years is $5.51 more than the interest earned when the interest was compounded annually. After six months, $50 of interest is added to principal and, as a result, interest for the first year is $2.50 higher than the $100 interest earned when compounding the 10 percent rate annually. Therefore, as the frequency of compounding increases, the total amount of interest increases. Interest can be compounded quarterly, monthly, daily, hourly, or even continuously.

Based on the concept of compounding, there are four basic tools used to determine cash equivalents of cash flows that occur at different points in time. These four tools are: (1) the future value of the amount of $1, (2) the present value of the amount of $1, (3) the future value of an annuity, and (4) the present value of an annuity.

Future Value of the Amount of $1

We have shown how to calculate the total amount due on a note at some point in the future. The combination of principal and interest on the principal at some specified date in the future (due date) is the note's **future value.** By using the formula for the *future value of the amount of $1* (shown and defined below) it is possible to quickly calculate future values. *Table 1 at the end of the text is based on the output of this formula.*

The future value of the amount of $1 or, in notation, a_{ni}, is

$$a_{ni} = (\$1 + r/c)^n$$

Where

> r = Annual rate of interest
>
> c = Number of compoundings in one year
>
> n = Number of compoundings over the entire time period
>
> i = Interest of each compounding period (r/c)

The **future value of the amount of $1** is the amount that $1 becomes at a future date, if invested at a specified annual interest rate (r) and compounded a certain number of times per year (c) over the investment period. The future value factor for the amount of $1 invested at 10 percent for two years, compounded annually is

$a_{2,10\%} = (\$1+.10/1)^2 = \$1.21$. We find the future value factor, 1.21, in Table 1 by locating the intersection of the $n = 2$ row and the 10 percent interest column.[2] Therefore, the future value of a two-year, \$1,000 loan at 10 percent interest compounded annually is \$1,210 (\$1,000 × 1.21).

If interest is compounded semiannually, what is the future value factor of the amount of \$1 at 10 percent? Using the formula $a_{4,5\%} = (\$1+.10/2)^4$, the future value factor is 1.2155. The 4 in $a_{4,5\%}$ indicates the number of semiannual compoundings in the two-year period and 5 percent represents the interest (r/c) during each semiannual compounding period. In Table 1, locate the intersection of the $n = 4$ row and the 5 percent interest column to find the 1.2155 factor. Therefore, the future value of a two-year, \$1,000 note at 10 percent interest compounded semiannually is \$1,215.50 (\$1,000 × 1.2155).

The future value of the amount of \$1 is a means of determining the amount of money in the future that is equivalent to an amount today. For example, assume that a customer owes a company \$1,000 and wants to delay the payment for two years. How much will the company accept two years from today in lieu of collecting \$1,000 today from the customer?

If the company earns a 10 percent rate of interest compounded semiannually on its investments, the customer must pay \$1,215.50 two years from today, which is the cash equivalent of \$1,000 today, as shown below:

Present value	×	$a_{4,5\%}$	=	Future value
\$1,000	×	1.2155	=	Future value
		\$1,215.50	=	Future value

Investment companies like Fidelity Investments and the Vanguard Group use the future value of the amount of \$1 to determine retirement amounts. For example, suppose an individual wants to invest \$5,000 in a Fidelity Investment retirement plan for her daughter on the child's fifth birthday. The investor would want to know how much her daughter will have in her retirement account on her 65th birthday. If the representative of Fidelity Investment assumes a 10 percent rate of return, compounded annually, the daughter's account will have a balance of \$1,522,300 upon her retirement, as shown below.

Present value	×	$a_{60,10\%}$	=	Future value
\$5,000	×	304.46	=	Future value
		\$1,522,300	=	Future value

Present Value of the Amount of \$1

The cash equivalent today of some specified amount of cash at a specified date in the future is called the **present value** of that future amount. It is equivalent to the future amount less the interest that has accumulated over the intervening time period. For example, the present value of \$110 one year from today is \$100 if the interest rate is 10 percent compounded annually [\$110 – (\$100 × .10 × 1)].

Present value problems can be solved using the future value of the amount of \$1. For example, what amount must be invested today to accumulate \$1,215.50 two years from today if the money can be invested at a 10 percent interest rate that is compounded semiannually? The answer to this question is presented below.

$$\text{Present value} \times a_{4,5\%} = \$1,215.50$$
$$\text{Present value} = \$1,215.50 \times \frac{1}{a_{4,5\%}}$$
$$= \$1,215.50 \times \frac{1}{1.2155}$$
$$= \$1,215.50 \times .8227$$
$$\text{Present value} = \$1,000$$

---

[2]All the table values are dollars even though they are not labeled.

A more direct way to determine the dollar equivalent today of some amount in the future is to use the **present value of the amount of $1** formula presented below. The present value of the amount of $1 represents the amount of money that, if invested today at some compounded interest rate for a specified time period, will equal $1 at the end of that time period. *Table 2 at the end of this book is based on the output of this formula.*

The present value of the amount of $1, or, in notation, $p_{n,i}$, is

$$p_{n,i} = \frac{1}{a_{n,i}}$$

or

$$p_{n,i} = \frac{1}{(\$1 + r/c)^n}$$

Where

r = Annual rate of return

c = Number of compoundings in one year

n = Number of compoundings over the entire time period

i = Interest of each compounding period (r/c)

The present value of the amount of $1 is the reciprocal of the future value of the amount of $1. The present value of $1 two years from today is $0.8227. That is, $0.8227 invested today at 10 percent interest compounded semiannually will become $1 in two years. The factor, .8227, is found by looking in Table 2 and locating the intersection of the n = 4 row and the 5 percent interest column. If $0.8227 is the present value of $1, then the present value of $10,000 is $8,227 ($10,000 × .8227). Likewise, by using the formula for the present value of the amount of $1, we can determine that the present value of $10,000 is $8, 227.

Like future values, the size of the present value is affected by the number of compoundings. However, present values *decrease* as the number of compoundings increase. For example, what is the present value of $10,000 at 10 percent for two years compounded quarterly?

We determine the present value factor, .8207, by looking in Table 2 and finding the intersection of the n = 8 row and the 2.5 percent interest column (or by using the formula). If the present value of $1 is .8207, then the present value of $10,000 is $8,207, as shown below.

Future value	×	$p_{8,2.5\%}$	=	Present value
$10,000	×	.8207	=	Present value
		$8,207	=	Present value

Note that increasing the number of compoundings each year decreases the dollars needed today to achieve the same future value.

Investment companies use the present value of the amount of $1 to resolve problems similar to the prior example involving the $5,000 investment on the daughter's fifth birthday. Now, however, assume that the investor wants to know how much she has to invest on her daughter's 5th birthday so that her daughter will have $50,000 for college on her 18th birthday. If the Fidelity representative assumes that the investment will earn 10 percent interest compounded annually, he will tell the investor to invest $14,485, as shown below.

Future value	×	$p_{13,10\%}$	=	Present value
$50,000	×	.2897	=	Present value
		$14,485	=	Present value

Finding Unknown Rates or Time Periods

All present or future value problems involve four elements: (1) the interest rate for each compounding period, r/c; (2) the number of compounding periods, n; (3) the present value amount and (4) the future value amount. When examining the relationship of present and future values, it is necessary to use these four elements to determine either unknown future or present values. These four elements are also useful when calculating unknown interest rates or the length of time periods for investments. Solving for these unknowns is important when we discuss capital budgeting in Chapter 16.

To illustrate, assume that $1,000 is invested today for two years and the interest is compounded semiannually. What annual interest rate is necessary to accumulate $1,215.50? To answer this question, we must determine the factor for the present value of the amount of $1 as illustrated below.

$$
\begin{aligned}
\text{Future value} \times p_{4,i} &= \text{Present value} \\
\$1,215.50 \times p_{4,i} &= \$1,000 \\
p_{4,i} &= \$1,000/\$1,215.50 \\
p_{4,i} &= .8227
\end{aligned}
$$

This factor, .8227, is the present value of $1 for four periods at some unknown interest rate. Determining the interest for each compounding period (r/c) involves performing three steps.

1. Using the present value of amount of $1 table (Table 2), locate four compounding periods on the left side of the table.

2. Starting at row 4, move right along the row until the present value factor of .8227 is located.

3. At the table value .8227, move up the column to the interest rate at the top of the column, 5 percent.

The 5 percent interest rate, however, is not the annual interest rate. Rather, 5 percent is the interest rate for each compounding period. Since interest is compounded semiannually, we multiply 5 percent, the interest rate for the compounding period (i), by 2, the number of compoundings during one year (c) to find the annual interest rate of 10 percent. Similarly, we can solve this problem using the future value of $1 as:

$$
\begin{aligned}
\text{Present value} \times a_{4,i} &= \text{Future value} \\
\$1,000 \times a_{4,i} &= \$1,215.50 \\
a_{4,i} &= \$1,215.50/\$1,000 \\
a_{4,i} &= 1.2155
\end{aligned}
$$

This factor, 1.2155, is the future value of $1 for four periods at some unknown interest rate. To determine the interest rate, use Table 1 and locate the four compounding periods. Then move right across this row to locate the future value factor of 1.2155. Move up the column to the interest rate, 5 percent. Remember to multiply the 5 percent semiannual rate by 2 compounding periods per year to determine the annual interest rate of 10 percent.

We follow similar procedures if the number of compounding periods (n) is unknown. For example, assume that $1,000 is invested today at 10 percent interest compounded semiannually. How long will it take for this investment to result in $1,215.50? To answer this question, we determine the present value of the amount of $1 as illustrated below.

$$
\begin{aligned}
\text{Future value} \times p_{n,5\%} &= \text{Present value} \\
\$1,215.50 \times p_{n,5\%} &= \$1,000 \\
p_{n,5\%} &= \$1,000/\$1,215.50 \\
p_{n,5\%} &= .8227
\end{aligned}
$$

In this case, after we determine the table value, we will use a similar three-step approach to determine the number of compounding periods.

1. Using the present value of $1 table (Table 2), locate the 5 percent interest rate (10%/2 compoundings) at the top of the table.

2. Moving down the 5 percent column, locate the present value factor of .8227.

3. At the .8227 present value factor, move to the left to find the number of compounding periods, four.

We have arrived at the number of compounding periods, but not the length of time of the investment period. To determine the time period in years, divide n, the number of compoundings in the life of the investment, by c, the number of compoundings in one year. In this case, there are four semiannual compounding periods, so it would take two years ($n/c = 4/2 = 2$ years) to achieve this goal. Similarly, this problem can be solved using the future value of $1 as illustrated previously.

ANNUITIES

An **annuity** is a series of equal cash payments made at equal intervals. Car or house payments are examples of annuities.

Understanding the future or present value of annuities is very helpful in making financing and investment decisions. For example, suppose a consultant completed a project for a client and sent a bill for $15,000. The client offers to pay the bill by making payments of $5,000 a year for the next three years. Because the consultant understands the time value of money, she rejects this offer. However, if she extends this client credit, how does the consultant determine the amount of the yearly payments that would be the equivalent of $15,000 cash today? We will examine future and present value of annuities in order to answer this type of question.

Future Value of an Annuity

The **future value of an annuity** is the amount of money that accumulates at some future date as a result of making equal payments over equal intervals of time and earning a specified interest rate over that time period. The amount of money that accumulates is a function of *the size of the payments, the frequency of the payments,* and *the interest rate used over the life of the annuity.* Businesses and individuals use the future value of annuities to determine the amount to save on a regular basis to buy new assets or retire debt at some future date.

Exhibit 14.6 illustrates the future value of an ordinary annuity. Notice that the three $1,000 payments plus the compound interest accumulate to a future value of $3,310. An ordinary annuity assumes that the final payment is made on the future value date; consequently, *there is one less interest period than the number of payments.*

EXHIBIT 14.6

Future Value of an Ordinary Annuity

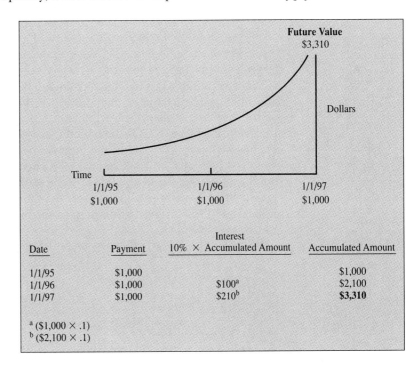

Date	Payment	Interest 10% × Accumulated Amount	Accumulated Amount
1/1/95	$1,000		$1,000
1/1/96	$1,000	$100[a]	$2,100
1/1/97	$1,000	$210[b]	**$3,310**

[a] ($1,000 × .1)
[b] ($2,100 × .1)

$A_{n,i}$ is the symbol for the future value of an ordinary annuity, and the annuity factor represents the future value of a $1 annuity, given some annual interest rate and a specified number of payments.[3] The values in Table 3 at the end of the book are the factors produced by the formula for the future value of an ordinary annuity. The left side represents the total number of annuity payments (n). The interest rates across the top represent the interest rates earned during the time period between each annuity payment. This interest rate (i) is determined by dividing the annual interest rate (r) by the number of compoundings during the year (c), that is, $i = r/c$. The formula assumes that interest is compounded every time a payment is made; therefore, the number of compoundings in a year is equal to the number of payments made in one year. The intersection of the row and column represents the factor produced by the formula for the future value of an ordinary annuity.

To illustrate, let's find the future value of a three-payment, $1,000, annual annuity, that earns 10 percent interest. First, it is necessary to find the appropriate factor by locating the number of payments ($n = 3$) on the left side of Table 3 and the interest rate ($i = r/c = 10\%/1$) at the top of the column. At the intersection of the appropriate row (3) and column (10%) is the factor 3.310. The 3.310 factor represents the amount that three annual payments of $1 would accumulate to when the third payment was made. Thus, solving for the unknown in the equation below gives the future value of a three-payment, $1,000, annual annuity.

$$\text{Annuity} \times A_{3,10\%} = \text{Future value}$$
$$\$1,000 \times 3.310 = \text{Future value}$$
$$\$3,310 = \text{Future value}$$

Performing this calculation results in the same solution as the year-by-year calculations of the future value used in Exhibit 14.6, but it is much faster.

Present Value of an Annuity

The **present value of an annuity** is the amount of money that, if invested at some interest rate today, will generate a set number of equal periodic payments that are made over equal time intervals. Exhibit 14.7 shows the cash flows and interest of the present value of an annuity.

Note that the first $1,000 payment occurs one period after the present value date and that the number of payments (three), equals the number of interest periods (three). If the present value of $2,486.90 earns 10 percent interest compounded annually, then the present value amount can generate three $1,000 payments. Each $1,000 payment consists of 10 percent interest earned on the present value amount at the beginning of the period and the return of a portion of the present value (principal). Every payment reduces the present value amount until the last payment brings the present value balance to zero.

The data presented in Exhibit 14.7 describes a personal application of the present value of an annuity. Suppose that after graduating you want to borrow some money to furnish your new apartment. After setting up a budget, you conclude that you can afford annual payments of $1,000 for the next three years. If the interest rate available for the loan is 10 percent, the maximum amount you can borrow is $2,486.90, which you will repay in three annual payments of $1,000. Each payment you make pays the interest on the loan and part of the loan's principal (see Exhibit 14.7).

Your first payment of $1,000 covers the 10 percent interest of $248.69 incurred on the $2,486.90 borrowed at the start of the previous year. The remaining $751.31

---

[3]Future value of an ordinary annuity or, in notation, $A_{n,i}$:

$$A_{n,i} = \frac{(\$1 + r/c)^n - \$1}{r/c}$$

Where

   r = Annual rate of interest
   c = Number of compoundings in one year
   n = Number of payments
   i = Interest rate for annuity period (r/c)

EXHIBIT | 14.7

Present Value of
an Ordinary Annuity

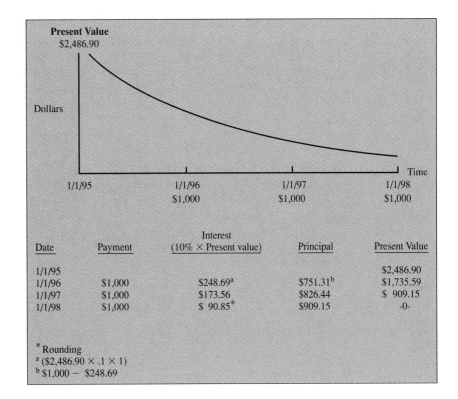

Date	Payment	Interest (10% × Present value)	Principal	Present Value
1/1/95				$2,486.90
1/1/96	$1,000	$248.69[a]	$751.31[b]	$1,735.59
1/1/97	$1,000	$173.56	$826.44	$ 909.15
1/1/98	$1,000	$ 90.85[*]	$909.15	-0-

[*] Rounding
[a] ($2,486.90 × .1 × 1)
[b] $1,000 − $248.69

reduces the principal of the loan. The amount due after the first payment is $1,735.59. Each subsequent $1,000 payment follows the same pattern until the loan is repaid on January 1, 1998.

The formula for the present value of an ordinary annuity, like the future value of an annuity, uses a $1 annuity and a specified interest rate to calculate a present value factor for an ordinary annuity, $P_{n,i}$.[4] The values in Table 4 at the end of the book are the factors generated by the formula. As in Table 3, the left side of Table 4 represents the total number of payments (n), while the interest rates at the top of the columns are the rates earned during each annuity period (i). Like the future value of an annuity, we assume that the interest is compounded every time a payment occurs. Therefore, the interest rate for the period (i) is determined by dividing the annual interest rate (r) by the number of payments during one year (c) or $i = r/c$.

Using Table 4 to determine the annuity factor in the example described in Exhibit 14.7, locate the intersection of the $n = 3$ row (the number of payments) and the $i = 10$ percent interest column ($i = r/c = 10\%/1$). Using the equation presented below and the factor from Table 4, it is possible to calculate the present value of the $1,000, three-payment, annual annuity.

$$
\begin{aligned}
\text{Annuity} \quad \times \quad P_{3,10\%} \quad &= \quad \text{Present value} \\
\$1,000 \quad \times \quad 2.4869 \quad &= \quad \text{Present value} \\
\$2,486.90 \quad &= \quad \text{Present value}
\end{aligned}
$$

The $2,486.90 is the cash equivalent today of three $1,000 payments made one year apart, starting one year from today assuming a 10 percent interest rate.

---

[4]Present value of an ordinary annuity or, in notation, $P_{n,i}$:

$$P_{n,i} = \frac{\$1 - \$1/(\$1 + r/c)^n}{r/c}$$

Where

r = Annual rate of interest
c = Number of compoundings in one year
n = Number of payments
i = Interest rate for annuity period (r/c)

Annuities and Compound Interest

The annuity problems illustrated to this point assumed that the number of payments per year corresponds to the number of times the interest is compounded. However, in order to determine the appropriate interest rate to use to calculate annuities, it is necessary to divide the annual interest rate (r) by the number of payments during one year (c). To illustrate an annuity with more than one compounding in a year, let's use the future value of an annuity problem we discussed earlier.

Suppose that instead of investing $1,000 in each of the next three years, you decided to invest $500 every six months. Find the future value of an ordinary annuity factor for a six-payment, 10 percent annuity in Table 3. The factor is located at the intersection of the $n = 6$ row and the 5 percent (10%/2) percent column. See the solution to this annuity problem in Exhibit 14.8. Note that the process for determining the future value of this semiannual annuity is the same as that for determining an annual annuity, except the payments are more frequent and the interest compounds with each payment.

Solving Annuity Problems

Annuity problems may seem rather straightforward at this point, but they can become confusing rather quickly. Take, for instance, the problem presented at the start of the annuity section about payment of $15,000 of consulting fees over three years. It is clear that the consultant, in this case, should reject the first offer of three annual payments of $5,000 in lieu of the $15,000 fee. However, how is it possible to determine the amount of three future payments that would be acceptable in lieu of $15,000 today?

We will look at a four-step process for solving such annuity problems and then apply this process to a variety of business situations.

Step 1. Determine Whether the Problem Is an Annuity Does the problem involve payments of the same amount made over equal periods of time using a constant interest rate? If the answer is yes, it is an annuity problem. In this case, you want to know the size of the three equal payments made one year apart. Also, one interest rate is assumed, although it is not stated at this point, so it is an annuity problem. If it is not an annuity problem, it is either a future or present value of the amount of $1 problem like those discussed earlier.

Step 2. Determine Whether the Annuity Is Present or Future Value Deciding whether the problem involves the future or present value of an annuity is essential, but often difficult. For example, you might conclude that, because the unknown annuity payments occur in the future, this is a future value problem. However, the problem of determining the size of the payments for the $15,000 fee is a present value problem, as we demonstrate below.

EXHIBIT	14.8	Future Value of Three-Year, Semiannual, $500 Ordinary Annuity

Annuity $\times$ $A_{6,5\%}$ = Future value
$500 $\times$ 6.8019   = Future value
$3,400.95 = Future value

Date	Payment	Interest (5% × Future value)	Future Value
1/1/95	$500		$ 500.00
7/1/95	500	$ 25.00*	1,025.00
1/1/96	500	51.25	1,576.25
7/1/96	500	78.81	2,155.06
1/1/97	500	107.75	2,762.81
7/1/98	500	138.14	3,400.95

*($500 × .05) = $25.

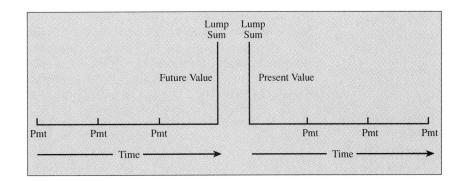

EXHIBIT | 14.9

**Lump Sums and
Payment Periods**

Determining whether we are dealing with the future or present value of an annuity depends on the relationship of the annuity payments to the *lump sum*. Every annuity, whether present or future value, has a large sum of money or an asset with a specified monetary value as one of its features. *With the future value of an annuity,* the lump sum *or future value occurs* after *the annuity payments are made. However, in the case of the present value of an annuity, the lump sum or present value* precedes *the annuity payments.*

Exhibit 14.9 illustrates the relationship between the timing of the annuity payments and the lump sums for both future and present value problems. By identifying the relationship of the timing of the annuity payments to the annuity's lump sum, we can determine the type of annuity. The $15,000 service fee charged is the lump sum, and the payments come after the lump sum; therefore, this is a present value of an annuity problem.

Step 3. Identify the Missing Annuity Element   All annuities involve four fundamental elements: (1) a specified number of payments, *n;* (2) equal cash payments; (3) an interest rate for each annuity period, *i* (*r/c*); and (4) a lump sum of money (either a present or future value). If three of the four elements are known, it is possible to determine the remaining element.

In the case of the $15,000 fee, only two of the four elements are known—the present value ($15,000) and the number of payments (3). To find the amount of the annuity, an interest rate, *i*, is necessary. Assume that the consultant wants a 9 percent return on her money.

Step 4. Solve for the Missing Element   At this point, it is necessary to calculate the value of the missing element. If, in Step 2, we determined that the annuity is a future value of an ordinary annuity, then we use Equation (14.1) below and Table 3 to solve the problem. On the other hand, if the annuity is a present value of an ordinary annuity, then we use Equation (14.2) below and Table 4.

$$\text{Annuity} \times A_{n,i} = \text{Future value of annuity} \tag{14.1}$$
$$\text{Annuity} \times P_{n,i} = \text{Present value of annuity} \tag{14.2}$$

The answer is now at hand—the interest rate is 9 percent, the number of payments is 3, and the amount of the present value is $15,000. Because this is a present value of an annuity problem, the amount of the annuity is found by using Equation (14.2).

$$
\begin{aligned}
\text{Annuity} \times P_{3,9\%} &= \text{Present value of annuity} \\
\text{Annuity} \times 2.5313 &= \$15,000 \\
\text{Annuity} &= \$5,925.81
\end{aligned}
$$

This analysis indicates that the consultant would accept three, $5,925.81 annual payments because they are the equivalent of $15,000 today, assuming a 9 percent interest rate. Another way to think of this is that the consultant is lending her client the value of her service for three years. If the client makes three $5,925.81 payments, this will ensure the recovery of the $15,000 fee and also generate a 9 percent rate of return on the "loan."

BUSINESS APPLICATIONS OF THE TIME VALUE OF MONEY

It is important to be able to apply the time value of money to business in a variety of ways. Using the time value of money is an important tool that captures the economic substance of business events so that information provided to decision makers does not mislead them. The following examples illustrate how accountants use the time value of money to facilitate business decisions.

Asset Valuation

Suppose that the Burger King Corporation purchases a plot of land on July 1, 1996, for a new restaurant location. It agrees to pay for the land with four semiannual payments of $10,000 each beginning January 1, 1997. If Burger King typically borrows money at a 12 percent annual rate, what is the cost of the land?

Some people might argue that the cost of the land is $40,000, or the sum of the four $10,000 payments. However, this clearly disregards the time value of money and overstates the cost of the land. Given the facts of the problem, the four-step process shows how to derive the land's cost.

Step 1. Is the problem an annuity?

Yes, because there are four equal payments over four semiannual periods.

Step 2. Is the annuity a present or future value?

The cost of acquiring the land today is the lump sum in this case. Because the payments occur after the acquisition date, it is a present value problem.

Step 3. What is the missing annuity element?

There are four payments ($n=4$). The interest rate is 6 percent ($i=6\%$) because the semiannual payments create semiannual compounding (r/c or 12%/2). The annuity payments are $10,000 each; therefore, the missing element is the present value.

Step 4. Solve for the missing element.

Annuity	×	$P_{4,6\%}$	=	Present value
$10,000	×	3.4651	=	Present value
		$34,651	=	Present value

Therefore, the actual cost of the land is $34,651. The difference between this amount and the sum of the payments ($40,000) is the amount of interest paid on the loan over the life of the loan ($40,000 − $34,651 = $5,349).

What is the effect on the cost of the land if the annual interest rate were 8 percent instead of 12 percent? Table 4 shows that the value for $P_{4,4\%}$ is 3.6299. Therefore, the cost of the land would increase to $36,299 if the interest rate were 8 rather than 12 percent. Note that the lower the interest rate, the higher the cost of the asset because *a lower interest rate causes present values to increase.*

Financial Planning

An understanding of the time value of money helps individuals or businesses meet financial goals. Suppose that you approached a representative of the Vanguard Group about establishing a retirement plan that would generate $1 million when you retire at age 65. You want to make 40 yearly payments into the retirement plan starting on your 26th birthday. The Vanguard Group representative believes that its retirement account can earn a 10 percent rate of return on your investment. How much do you have to pay each year to achieve this goal? We will use the four-step method to solve this problem.

preadsheet packages such as Lotus 123 quickly and easily calculate present and future values, unknown interest rates, required payment periods, and payment amounts. Lotus 123 refers to these calculations as functions. To activate a function, the @ character is used, followed by the function name and the required data items. A few examples follow:

@PMT
(principal,interest,term)

Calculates the amount of a loan payment given the principle amount borrowed, the interest rate, and the term of the loan.

@PV
(payments,interest,term)

Calculates the present value of a stream of equal periodic payments discounted at a given interest rate for a specified period time.

@FV
(payments,interest,term)

Calculates the future value of a stream of equal periodic payments compounded at a given interest rate for a specified period of time.

Step 1. This is an annuity because the payments are the same size and are made yearly.

Step 2. This is a future value of an annuity problem because the lump sum, $1 million, occurs after the annuity payments.

Step 3. The future value is $1 million, the interest rate is 10 percent, and there are 40 payments. The amount of the annuity is the missing element.

Step 4. Annuity $\times$ $A_{40,10\%}$ = Future value
Annuity $\times$ 442.593 = $1,000,000
Annuity = $2,259.41

Based on the available information, if you make 40 payments of $2,259.41 starting on your 26th birthday and the retirement fund earns 10 percent interest, you will have $1 million when you retire at age 65.

SUMMARY

Business enterprises are in a continuous cycle of generating and investing money. The invested funds must produce a satisfactory financial reward for the people or institutions who fund the enterprise. People invest believing that they will receive a return *of* investment and an adequate return *on* investment.

Risk is impounded in the expected return of an investment. Investments are exposed to three types of risk: inflation risk, business risk, and liquidity risk. Each type of risk is factored into the risk assessment of any investment. Management must consider the relationship of return and risk, both when trying to invest funds at its disposal and also when trying to acquire funds from owners and creditors.

Considering the time value of money is essential for long-term investing and financing decisions. The future value of a dollar is the amount that a dollar will become if invested today for a specific period of time at a specific rate of interest. The present value of a dollar is the amount today that is equivalent to a dollar at some specified future time when invested at a specified rate of interest. Present and future values also can be calculated for annuities.

- The rate of return is a common-size measure of the return on an investment and presumes the return of and a return on the investment. The expected rate of return of an investment is a summary measure of possible rates of return the investment might generate that investors use to evaluate alternative investments.

- The risk of an investment is the chance it will result in an unfavorable outcome. The relative risk ratio is a common-size measure used to evaluate the risk of prospective investments.

- A person's willingness to make risky investments depends on whether he or she is a risk seeker or a risk avoider. Risk avoiders want an additional return called a *risk premium* for accepting any additional risk.

- A firm's management invests the firm's resources in an attempt to maximize the return of the firm at a level of risk that is acceptable to the firm's owners. However, when borrowing funds, management tries to minimize the risk of the firm in order to lower the cost of using borrowed funds.

- The time value of money is a tool that uses compound interest to determine the cash equivalents for single or multiple cash flows that occur at different points in time.

KEY TERMS

annuity A series of equal cash payments made at equal intervals

business risk The risk associated with the ability of a particular company to continue in business

compound interest Interest that is based on a principal amount that includes interest from previous time periods

compounding The process of adding interest to principal for purposes of interest calculation

expected rate of return A summary measure of an investment's performance, stated as a percentage, based on the possible rates of return and on the likelihood of those rates of return occurring

expected return A summary measure of an investment's performance, stated in dollars, based on the possible returns on investment in dollars and on the likelihood of those returns occurring

future value The combination of principal and the interest on the principal at some specified date in the future

future value of amount of $1 The amount that $1 becomes at a future date, if invested at a specified annual interest rate and compounded a certain number of times per year over the investment period

future value of an annuity The amount of money that accumulates at some future date as a result of making equal payments over equal intervals of time and earning a specified rate of interest over that time period

inflation risk The chance of a decline in the purchasing power of the monetary units during the time money is invested

liquidity risk The chance that an investment cannot be readily converted to cash

present value The cash equivalent today of some specified amount of cash at a specified date in the future

present value of the amount of $1 The amount that, if invested today at some compound interest rate for a specified period of time, will equal $1 at end of that time period

present value of an annuity The amount of money that, if invested at some rate of interest today, will generate a set number of equal periodic payments that are made over equal time intervals

rate of return A percentage measurement of the performance of investments on a common-size basis

relative risk ratio A common-size measure of an investment's risk based on the percentage of expected return lost if the worst-case outcome occurs

risk-adjusted expected rate of return An expected rate of return including the risk premium

risk-free rate of return The rate of return that a virtually riskless investment produces

risk premium An increase in the rate of return expected by an investor for assuming greater investment risk

simple interest Interest calculated only on the amount borrowed

time value of money A tool used to solve problems involving the comparison of cash flows that occur at different points in time

QUESTIONS

1. Discuss how management uses the operating profit of an enterprise.

2. What are the different sources used by a business to raise money for its operations?

3. What is the distinction between return *of* investment and return *on* investment?

4. How does *rate* of return on an investment differ from return on investment? What are the advantages of using a rate of return on investment when choosing among alternative investments?

5. Explain in your own words the concept of annualized rate of return.

6. Under what conditions does a negative rate of return occur?

7. Define risk. How does a person's attitude toward risk affect his or her decision-making process?

8. Contrast expected rate of return on an investment with the actual rate of return on investment.

9. What is the purpose of the relative risk ratio?

10. Describe the relationship between risk and return and give an example of the relationship.

11. What is a risk premium? Describe the three factors that generate risk premiums and give an example of each.

12. How is the price of an investment related to its risk-adjusted rate of return?

13. Contrast the perspective of return and risk of a person borrowing funds with that of a person lending funds.

14. Explain what is meant by the time value of money.

15. How does simple interest differ from compound interest?

16. Describe the four elements of the future value of the amount of $1.

17. How does the future value of an amount of $1 differ from the present value of an amount of $1? How are they similar?

18. What are the characteristics of an annuity?

19. What is the difference between the future and present value of an annuity?

20. Describe the four-step process for solving annuity problems.

EXERCISES

E 14.1   Each of the three investments below cost $20,000. Calculate the expected rate of return on these investments. Each outcome described below will occur at the end of one year.

	Possible Outcome	Probability
Investment A	$2,000	.3
	1,500	.4
	1,000	.3
Investment B	$2,500	.1
	1,750	.4
	1,250	.3
	1,000	.2
Investment C	$3,000	.4
	2,000	.3
	500	.3

E 14.2   Calculate the relative risk ratio for each of the investments in E 14.1. Which of the investments would you prefer? Why?

E 14.3   Brad Brenneman wants a risk-adjusted expected rate of return of 12 percent on his investments. What price would Brad be willing to pay for investment P if he predicts the following outcomes and probabilities of those outcomes occurring one year from today?

	Possible Outcome	Probability
Investment P	$5,500	.3
	7,200	.4
	9,500	.3

E 14.4   How much will an investment of $2,000 be worth at the end of five years if it earns:
a. 8 percent simple interest?
b. 8 percent interest compounded annually?
c. 8 percent interest compounded semiannually?
d. 8 percent interest compounded quarterly?

E 14.5   What is the present value of $2,000 five years from today if interest is:
a. 8 percent compounded annually?
b. 8 percent compounded semiannually?
c. 8 percent compounded quarterly?

E 14.6   What will be the maturity value of $6,000 deposited in a three-year certificate of deposit that earns 6 percent interest compounded semiannually?

E 14.7   Jon Steffens, a recent accounting graduate, has just accepted a staff accounting position with a firm and will receive a salary of $30,000. The firm guarantees that Jon will receive a 5 to 7 percent raise each year for the next five years depending on his performance. What will Jon's salary be in five years if he gets a 5 percent raise each year? What would his salary be in five years if the annual raise is 7 percent?

E 14.8   Mike Parker is 30 years old today and wants to return to school by the time he is 35 to pursue his Ph.D. in taxation. He wants to have $20,000 set aside by the time he is 35 to help defray the cost of the program. How much must he invest today, his 30th birthday, to achieve his goal if he can generate a 10 percent return that is compounded semiannually on the invested funds?

E 14.9   Eileen Meyer is going to put $5,000 in a savings account that pays 8 percent interest and is compounded annually to fund her new baby's college education. How much will be in the education fund 18 years from today when her child starts college?

E 14.10   If $50,000 were invested five years ago and has accumulated to $66,910, what rate of interest was earned if the interest was compounded annually?

E 14.11   If $3,000 was invested at 8 percent and has grown to $4,118.40, how many years has the money been invested if interest was compounded quarterly?

E 14.12   Answer each of the following independent questions.
a. If $2,000 is invested today at 8 percent compounded semiannually, how long will it take to accumulate $2,960.40?
b. If $5,000 is invested today and will accumulate to $13,266.50 in 10 years, what annual interest rate compounded semiannually will generate this amount?

E 14.13   How long will it take to double an investment of $2,000 if the investment can generate a 10 percent return that is compounded semiannually?

E 14.14   Determine the future value of the following annuities, if each annuity can earn 10 percent interest and assuming that the first payment is made on January 1, 1996.
a. Six annual payments of $6,000 each.
b. 12 semiannual payments of $3,000 each.
c. 24 quarterly payments of $1,500 each.

E 14.15   Determine the present value of the following annuities as of today, January 1, 1996, if the annuity earns an 8 percent interest rate.
a. Five annual payments of $10,000 starting January 1, 1997.
b. 20 quarterly payments of $2,500 starting April 1, 1996.
c. 10 semiannual payments of $5,000 starting July 1, 1996.

E 14.16   Fast Action Garage Door, Inc., has just purchased a piece of equipment for $25,000. The company paid $5,000 down and is going to borrow the remaining $20,000. The First National Bank will loan money at 12 percent interest. What will the payments be if:
a. The payments are monthly over the next two years?
b. The payments are quarterly over the next two years?
c. The payments are semiannual over the next two years?
d. Set up an annuity table for your answer to *c* to prove your answer.

E 14.17   Eric Burke is going to make three annual payments of $3,000 each into a savings account starting today, March 1, 1996.
a. How much will Mr. Burke have in his savings account on March 1, 1998, if he can get 9 percent interest?
b. Set up an annuity table to prove your answer.

E 14.18   White Travel Agency has just borrowed $30,000 to purchase office furniture for its agents and is going to make 10 yearly payments of $5,309.55 beginning one year from today. What is the annual interest rate White is paying?

E 14.19   Tiffany Bea is going to make semiannual payments of $4,296.27 until she has accumulated $100,000. If she can earn 12 percent interest on her investment, how long will it take her to accumulate $100,000?

E 14.20   Riley County wants to raise $30,000,000 to finance the construction of a new hospital. The hospital board wants to make semiannual payments to repay the loan over the next 15 years. What will be the amount of the payments assuming the interest rates presented below?
  a. 10%
  b. 8%
  c. 6%

PROBLEMS

P 14.1   An investor has two investment alternatives:

Investment A $100,000		Investment B $80,000	
Probability	Return	Probability	Return
.5	$10,000	.4	$12,000
.3	15,000	.3	16,000
.2	20,000	.2	20,000
		.1	(800)

Required: *a.* Which investment has the greatest expected rate of return?
  b. Calculate the relative risk ratio for each investment and determine which has the greatest risk.
  c. Which investment would you choose?
  d. What is the basis of your choice?
  e. Is there any circumstance that would change your choice?

P 14.2   An investment analysis has determined the returns and the probabilities of the return for investments A and B shown below.

Investment A		Investment B	
Probability	Return	Probability	Return
.3	$15,000	.4	$20,000
.4	20,000	.3	30,000
.2	25,000	.3	5,000
.1	(10,000)		

Required: *a.* Determine the price of investment A if its expected rate of return was 10 percent.
  b. Determine the price of investment B if its expected rate of return was 7 percent.
  c. Given the prices determined for the investments, calculate the relative risk ratio for each investment.
  d. Explain the relationship between expected return and price.

P 14.3   Cambridge Corporation just sold inventory with a cost of $20,000. In exchange for the inventory, Cambridge received $5,000 cash and a note promising to pay $30,000 in five years (there is no interest rate specified on the note).

Required: *a.* How much did Cambridge make on this sale if it usually loans money at 10 percent interest compounded annually?
  b. How much did Cambridge make on this sale if it usually loans money at 12 percent interest compounded annually?
  c. How much did Cambridge make on this sale if it usually loans money at 8 percent interest compounded annually?
  d. Explain how the interest rate assumed affects the income of the company.

P 14.4   John Carper has just received $250,000 from winning the lottery. He has decided to spend $100,000 immediately and to invest the remaining $150,000 for five years.

Required: a. If he can get a 8 percent rate of return that is compounded quarterly, how much will he have at the end of five years?

b. If he can get a 12 percent rate of return that is compounded quarterly, how much will he have at the end of five years?

c. If he can get a 4 percent rate of return that is compounded quarterly, how much will he have at the end of five years?

P 14.5   Craig Peterson has been married for 15 years and decided he wants to surprise his wife with a special present on their 20th anniversary. Starting today, June 1, 1996, he is going to put $1,200 in a savings account every six months that has a 6 percent annual interest rate.

Required: a. If his last payment is five years from today, how much will he have for the anniversary present?

b. If he can earn 8 percent annually, how will this affect the amount he will accumulate?

P 14.6   Miledon Gofast can afford car payments of $300 per month for three years. The interest rate on car loans is 12 percent.

Required: a. How much can he spend for a car?

b. How much can he spend for a car if he could make payments of $900 every three months with an interest rate of 10 percent?

c. How would your answer to *a* change if Miledon could make a $1,500 down payment?

P 14.7   Ron Gfeller has signed a contract to buy a tract of land on March 1, 1996. The contract calls for Ron to make three annual payments of $3,500 starting March 1, 1997, and a final payment of $5,000 on March 1, 2000. Ron can borrow money at 7 percent interest.

Required: a. What price did Ron pay for the land?

b. What is the price of the land if the interest rate is 5 percent?

c. Explain why the land's cost calculated in *a* and *b* above differs when the cash flows are the same.

P 14.8   Chris Jay Company just acquired office furniture that had a list price of $40,000. The furniture store said that it would finance the entire price at 0 percent interest by letting the company make four semiannual payments of $10,000 starting six months from the date of purchase.

Required: a. If Chris Jay Company can borrow money at 10 percent, what is the cost of the office furniture?

b. What is the cost of the office furniture if Chris Jay Company usually borrows money at 8 percent?

c. What is the cost of the office furniture if Chris Jay agrees to make four quarterly payments of $10,000 each if it usually borrows money at 8 percent?

P 14.9   Perry Corporation has identified two buildings that are suitable for its new office. For building A, Perry will have to pay $24,500 a year for 10 years while building B will cost $20,000 a year for 15 years. The interest rate on both loans is 9 percent.

Required: a. Which building is less expensive?

b. Which building is less expensive if the interest rate was 5 percent?

c. Which building is less expensive if building A had payments of $20,000 for 20 years and the interest rate was 9 percent?

P 14.10   Alan G. Houlick has acquired a new piece of equipment with a price of $550,000 and is considering two financing alternatives. If Acme National Bank makes the loan, Houlick will make 10 annual payments of $89,509.49 to repay the debt. If Last National Bank makes the loan, the payments will be $52,068.04 every six months for the next seven years.

Required: a. What is the interest rate charged by Acme National Bank?

b. What is the interest rate charged by Last National Bank?

c. What other factors should Houlick take into consideration when deciding which bank to use?

P 14.11   Pete M. Mitchel has a customer whom he has just billed for $6,000 for services rendered. The customer wants to pay for this bill by making quarterly payments over the next three years.

Required: a. Determine the amount of the customer's quarterly payments if Pete wants an 8 percent annual return on the loan.

b. Determine the amount of the customer's quarterly payments if Pete wants a 12 percent annual return on the loan.

c. Assume Pete wants an 8 percent return but the customer wants to make semiannual payments over the next three years. Determine the amount of the payment that Pete would find acceptable in this situation.

P 14.12   Buzz Stark wants to have $700,000 in his retirement account when he retires on his 65th birthday. He is 26 today and will make annual payments once he starts paying into the retirement fund.

Required: How much will Buzz have to pay annually to achieve his goal if he can get an 8 percent annual rate of interest and he starts payments at:
a. Age 26
b. Age 36
c. Age 46

P 14.13   Buzz Stark is confident he can achieve his goal of accumulating $700,000 by his 65th birthday as described in P 14.12. He wants to know how much cash the $700,000 will provide after he retires at age 65.

Required: How much cash will Buzz receive if he can earn 10 percent and if he wants:
a. To receive 30 semiannual payments starting six months after his 65th birthday?
b. To receive 20 annual payments starting at age 66?
c. To receive only interest on the $700,000 annually starting at age 66?
d. How much of Buzz's $700,000 will remain at the end of plans *a* and *b*?
e. How much of Buzz's $700,000 will remain after 20 years of plan *c*?

P 14.14   John Rich is 33 years old today and wants to retire at age 60. On his 60th birthday he wants to start receiving $65,000 a year for 30 years. John will start making payments today and will make his last payment on his 59th birthday.

Required: How much must he make in annual payments from age 33 to 59 to achieve his retirement goal if he can earn:
a. 6 percent interest over the entire time period?
b. 8 percent interest over the entire time period?

P 14.15   Janet Tapehorn was given the assignment of finding suitable office space for her company. She found a great office in an upscale office park that requires a two-year lease. There are two options to pay for this lease. The first is to pay $44,000 on the first day of the lease, and the second is to make monthly payments of $2,000 for two years starting one month from today. She must decide which of the two payment methods is the most economical for her company. Janet knows the firm usually borrows money at 12 percent interest.

Required: Which payment plan should Janet select? Why?

COMPUTER APPLICATIONS

CA 14.1   Organza Florist needs to buy a new delivery van. The automobile dealership has a van they will sell for $25,800. Organza has obtained bank financing for five years at 12 percent interest.

Required: Use a computer spreadsheet package.
a. What is the amount of each monthly payment?
b. Prepare a monthly payment schedule that indicates the amount of interest and principal paid each month over the term of the loan.

CA 14.2   Zerfelt Company plans to buy a new computer in five years. It can save $100 each month toward the computer purchase.

Required: Use a computer spreadsheet package. Assume independent situations.
a. How much will Zerfelt have available at the end of five years if it can earn 6 percent?
b. How much will Zerfelt have available at the end of five years if it can earn 8 percent?
c. How much will Zerfelt have available at the end of five years if it can earn 6 percent and it increases its monthly payment by $50?
d. If Zerfelt delays its computer purchase for an additional two years, how much will Zerfelt have available at the end of seven years if it can earn 6 percent?

CASES

C 14.1 Banner Corporation, a small manufacturing firm, wants to establish a pension fund for its 10 employees who range from 28 to 51 years of age. Banner wants each employee who retires with the firm at age 65 to receive an annual pension on the retirement date that is 70 percent of the employee's annual wages at retirement. What factors must Banner Corporation take into consideration in order to determine how much the firm must contribute to the pension fund each year in order to meet the terms of their retirement plan?

C 14.2 Pat Crick wants to buy a new Chrysler New Yorker and has been negotiating with two dealerships on identical cars with sticker prices of $24,890. The first dealer is offering to finance the car at 0 percent interest for the next 30 months, or $829.67 ($24,890/30 months) per month. The second dealer has offered to sell Pat the car for $20,500 and Pat will finance the price with a bank loan over the next 30 months at a 12 percent annual rate of interest. How much will Pat pay the bank each month? Which of the two deals is better for Pat if 12 percent is the going car loan interest rate? Why would Chrysler Corporation be willing to loan money at 0 percent interest?

CRITICAL THINKING

CT 14.1 Managers are hired by the company's owners. What factors do managers consider when assessing the owners' risk preferences? What effect do the owners' risk preferences have on management's financing and investing decisions?

CT 14.2 On September 1, 1994, the Little Broadway Players signed a note to raise cash to buy a theater. The terms of the note call for seven annual payments of $5,000 and an interest rate of 9 percent. However, because the Players are just starting this enterprise, the bank has agreed to defer the first of the seven payments until September 1, 1997. How much cash will the bank loan the Little Broadway Players given the terms of this note?

ETHICAL CHALLENGES

EC 14.1 Many furniture stores advertise that they will finance purchases made during a particular time period at 0 percent interest. Is this type of promotion deceptive and unethical? Justify your position.

EC 14.2 Lincoln Savings and Loan of California, while under the direction of Charles Keating, sold investments to its customers, promised them very high rates of return, and assured them these were safe investments. When these investments failed, the investors lost their entire investment. Keating defended the sale of these investments saying he did not intend to harm anyone and that reasonable investors should have realized that investments with high rates of return are risky. What responsibility does a bank or savings and loan have to monitor the investment decisions of its customers?

CHAPTER 15

Planning for Equity and Debt Financing

Learning Objectives

1. Explain the risks and rewards of equity financing, describe the characteristics of equity instruments, and identify the sources of equity financing.
2. Explain why companies use debt rather than equity financing.
3. Describe the characteristics of the three basic types of long-term debt instruments, explain how the market interest rate affects the proceeds generated by these debt instruments, and identify sources of debt financing.

Kmart Corporation's balance sheet reports that, as of January 25, 1995, its owners financed $6,032 million of the firm's $17,029 million in assets (about 35%) while the creditors financed $10,997 million (about 65%) of the assets. The bal-  ance sheet and accompanying notes also describe whether the liabilities are due in the near or long term, the type of financial instruments used to raise funds, the amounts raised by issuing these financial instruments, and the amount of earnings retained to finance the firm.

While these facts are important and answer many questions, they also raise a variety of other questions. Why would a company choose to finance its activities by borrowing money? What are the risks and rewards of both equity and debt financing? What are the characteristics of the financial instruments used in equity and debt financing? What are the potential sources of equity and debt financing?

Many types of businesses, including Kmart, must address the type of financing questions presented in the opening vignette. Understanding financing alternatives and their risks and rewards helps management design the financial structure best suited for its firm. Creditors and investors are interested in the answers to these questions because it helps them evaluate whether to lend or invest funds in a business enterprise.

In order for businesses to make the investments necessary to begin and carry out operations, they can acquire funds from three possible sources: (1) owners' contributions, (2) earnings generated by the firm's operating activities, and (3) debt. The balance sheet reflects information about the source of funding that a firm's management has decided to use to finance the business entity.

We classify the three sources of funds into two financing categories—equity and debt. **Equity financing** is a means for firms to obtain funds in exchange for an ownership interest in the firm. Firms raise equity funds (1) when owners acquire a financial interest in the firm and (2) when management elects to reinvest the firm's earnings in the firm. **Debt financing** arises when a company obtains funds (cash) in exchange for a liability to repay the borrowed funds.

While we discuss the nature of equity and debt, in general, the focus of this chapter is on equity and long-term debt financing. The discussion of short-term debt, which usually relates to financing a firm's operating activities, appeared in Chapter 11.

The risks and rewards of equity financing, the characteristics of the financial instruments used to acquire equity financing, and the sources of equity financing are important areas addressed next.

USING THE OWNERS' MONEY

Regardless of the legal form of business entity—sole proprietorship, partnership, or corporation—owner financing comes from acquiring an ownership interest in the firm or reinvesting the firm's earnings. The first source includes the contribution of assets to the firm by investors in exchange for an ownership interest in the business entity. Initial contributions provide the funds necessary to begin the firm's operations, while subsequent contributions are used for expansion. The second source of owner financing is reinvested earnings. The net income of a firm represents the increase in the net assets of the firm as a result of its operations. The net income, or earnings, belongs to the owners and is either distributed to them as dividends or

If Calvin owned stock he could raise money by selling his shares instead of his parents' car. (CALVIN AND HOBBES © Watterson. Dist. by UNIVERSAL PRESS SYNDICATE. Reprinted with permission. All rights reserved.)

reinvested in the firm. When the earnings are reinvested in the business entity, the owners are keeping the funds in the entity and, thereby, increasing their interest in the firm.

Rewards and Risks of Equity Financing

What are the rewards and risks of equity financing, and which equity financing instruments do corporations and security markets use?

Before a business can begin, the owners of the firm commit their resources to the enterprise in the expectation that the business will produce a satisfactory return on their initial investment. Ownership is attractive because the return the business generates on owners' investment is limited only by the performance of the firm. In addition to realizing financial rewards, many owners enjoy the psychological reward of knowing they own a business enterprise.

Owners of a business entity face the risk of not receiving a satisfactory return on their invested funds or of losing some or all of their investment. The owners' risk is directly related to the firm's ability to sell goods and services, cover operating expenses, and generate sufficient net income to provide a satisfactory return on their investment. Obviously, firms that consistently provide a satisfactory return on the owners' investment have less risk than those whose earnings and return are more erratic.

Recall from Chapter 1 that sole proprietorships and partnerships have higher risk than corporations because of their unlimited liability. That is, owners of these two types of entities can lose not only what they have invested in the firm, but they also place at risk their personal assets if the creditors' claims are not satisfied by the assets of the firm. Many sole proprietors and partners, however, are owner/managers who find that their financial and psychic rewards exceed the benefits of incorporating and reducing the risk of unlimited liability. For corporations, the risk to the owners is limited to the amounts they have invested in the business enterprise.

When a firm uses debt to finance its operations, the risk to the owners increases. Owners have a residual interest in the firm and, therefore, must satisfy the terms of any debt agreements *before* benefiting from the firm's operations. In general, the greater the debt the firm incurs, the greater the risk to the owners. However, by using debt financing, as we will describe later in the chapter, owners create the potential for generating a rate of return on their equity that is greater than the rate of return that equity financing alone can generate.

How Is Equity Financing Used?

Contributions by owners are usually used to acquire long-term assets such as buildings, equipment, land, patents, and franchises that provide the infrastructure for the firm's operations. Owner contributions also are used to retire long-term debt and, therefore, to reduce the risk of the firm. The earnings reinvested in the firm are used to support the daily operations, acquire long-term assets, or retire long-term debt, based on recommendations by management.

Indicators of Ownership Interest

Sole proprietorships and partnerships do not need tradeable financial instruments to prove the ownership interest of those who make contributions to their type of firms. In these cases, the number of owners is limited. In addition, joining or leaving a partnership is not a simple process—adding new partners requires the approval of all existing partners. Therefore, the ability of an existing partner to transfer his or her ownership interest to another person is limited.

Corporations that have a large number of owners must issue shares of capital stock to indicate an owner's interest in the corporation. The shares of stock of a corporation allow the owners to increase or decrease their interest in the organization without the consent of the other owners. The next section discusses the characteristics of the financial instruments used by corporations for equity financing.

EQUITY INSTRUMENTS

In general, corporations issue two classes of stock: common and preferred. The difference between common and preferred stock lies in their respective ownership rights.

Common Stock

If a corporation has only one class of stock, it is called *common stock*. **Common stock** represents the basic ownership unit of the corporation, and, unless specifically noted in the corporation's charter and bylaws, it confers all the rights of ownership.

We know that common stockholders have the right to vote on significant events that affect the corporation. Common stockholders elect members of the board of directors who, in turn, hire the corporation's professional managers. Common stockholders normally have other rights that include: the right to dividends, the right to the residual assets upon liquidation of the corporation, the right to dispose of the shares by sale or gift, and the preemptive right.

The **preemptive right** gives common stockholders the right to maintain their percentage interest in the corporation when it issues new shares of common stock. For example, suppose a common stockholder owns 10 percent of the shares of the corporation and the corporation is going to issue 200,000 new shares of common stock. The preemptive right requires that the corporation offer the current stockholder the right to buy 20,000 (200,000 × .10) shares of the new issue in order to maintain his or her 10 percent interest in the company. Today, most stockholders of large corporations do not have the preemptive right but it is common in smaller corporations.

Common stock represents *the residual* ownership interest in the corporation because the common stockholders, upon liquidation of the corporation, receive benefits *only* after the corporation satisfies all creditors' and other owners' claims. Thus, the common stockholders receive the remainder, or residual, interest in the corporation.

Some corporations, like Nike for example, have more than one class of common stock (Class A common stock and Class B common stock). The difference between the classes of stock usually involves the voting rights associated with each class of stock and is described in the corporation's charter and bylaws. Exhibit 15.1 shows the portion of a note to Nike's balance sheet that describes its Class A and Class B common stock. Note that the voting rights of Nike's Class B common stockholders are limited.

EXHIBIT	15.1	Description of Nike's Common Stock		
Shareholders' equity (Note 8):				
Common Stock at stated value:				
Class A convertible—26,679 and 26,691 shares outstanding			159	159
Class B—46,521 and 49,161 shares outstanding			2,704	2,720
Capital in excess of stated value			108,284	108,451
Foreign currency translation adjustment			(15,123)	(7,790)
Retained earnings			1,644,925	1,539,279
Total shareholders' equity			1,740,949	1,642,819

Note 8—Common Stock:
The authorized number of shares of Class A Common Stock no par value and Class B Common Stock no par value are 60,000,000 and 150,000,000, respectively. [Each share of Class A Common Stock is convertible into one share of Class B Common Stock. Voting rights of Class B Common Stock are limited in certain circumstances with respect to the election of directors.]

Preferred Stock

Preferred stock represents an ownership interest in a corporation with special privileges or preferences as to liquidation and dividends. Upon liquidation of the corporation, the preferred stockholders are paid before the common stockholders. In addition, preferred stockholders are entitled to receive dividends before common stockholders receive dividends. *Thus, the preference conferred on preferred stockholders is in reference to common stockholders, rather than to creditors.*

In exchange for these preferences, preferred stockholders usually give up the right to vote, and the dividends they receive are usually limited to a set amount per share of stock. Preferred stock dividends are stated in either predetermined dollar amounts or as a percentage of *par value* (defined and discussed later in the chapter). For example, stock that is termed $5.50 preferred would receive a dividend of $5.50 per share before common stockholders would receive any dividends. If a preferred stock has a $100 par value and a 10 percent dividend rate, each preferred stockholder would receive a $10 dividend ($100 par × .10) for every share held.

Companies often issue one or more of five basic types of preferred stock: (1) cumulative preferred stock, (2) participating preferred stock, (3) callable preferred stock, (4) redeemable preferred stock, and (5) covertible preferred stock. Each feature is designed to make the preferred stock more attractive to investors and can be used individually or in combination.

Cumulative preferred stock accumulates unpaid dividends over time. When cumulative preferred stock dividends are not paid when stipulated they are called **dividends in arrears.** If a corporation does not pay dividends in a given year, the next time dividends are paid, all the preferred dividends skipped in prior years plus the preferred dividend due for the current year must be paid before the common stockholders can receive any dividends. This provides preferred stockholders some assurance that preferred dividends, if missed in one year, will be paid in a subsequent year.

To illustrate, assume that a corporation does not pay its normal stated amount of preferred stock dividend of $100,000 in 1996. In 1997, if the corporation pays dividends of $250,000, the preferred stockholders will receive $200,000 ($100,000 for 1996 and $100,000 for 1997), and the common stockholders will receive the residual $50,000.

Participating preferred stock allows preferred stockholders the right to receive an amount in excess of the stated dividend rate or amount. *After* common stockholders have received a dividend rate or amount equal to that paid to preferred stockholders, any dividend remaining is shared between preferred and common stockholders. For example, if a $500,000 dividend is available to the stockholders, the basic preferred dividend is $100,000, and the common stockholders' equivalent share is $200,000, the remaining $200,000 [$500,000 – ($100,000 + $200,000)] is divided between the preferred and common stockholders. The amount of the residual dividends that each class of stockholders receives depends on the terms of the participation outlined in the corporation's charter.

Callable preferred stock gives the corporation the right to repurchase the preferred stock at a stipulated price. If the corporation decides it wants to reduce the number of shares of preferred stock or eliminate all preferred stockholders, it can "call" or buy back some or all of the preferred stock. When the corporation "calls" the preferred stock, the preferred stockholders must relinquish their shares. The corporation must compensate the preferred stockholders for the shares relinquished. Normally, call prices are listed on the preferred stock at a certain dollar amount, such as "callable at $108 per share."

PAUSE & REFLECT	When would a corporation consider calling its preferred stock?

Redeemable preferred stock is similar to callable preferred stock except it gives the stockholder the option to turn in (redeem) the stock for cash at the stockholder's option. If the stockholder no longer wishes to hold preferred stock, he or she can "redeem" or sell the stock to the corporation for a predetermined price per share. Of course preferred stockholders also could sell the stock in the secondary market at any time. The redemption price assures the preferred stockholder of a guaranteed minimum price for the stock.

Convertible preferred stock is preferred stock that gives stockholders the right to convert (exchange) preferred shares for other forms of capital, as stated in the corporate charter, at the option of the preferred stockholder. Preferred stock is normally convertible into common stock, although occasionally it is convertible into debt instruments. When preferred stock is convertible into common stock, the conversion is normally stated as a number of shares, such as "convertible into four shares of common stock." This attractive feature gives the shareholder the option to own preferred stock or convert it into another equity instrument at a later date if the other instrument becomes more valuable than the preferred stock.

Kmart, for example, has two classes of preferred stock—Series A and Series C. Both classes of stock are cumulative and convertible, and the Series A preferred stock has a participation feature. Exhibit 15.2 shows the stockholders' equity section of Kmart's January 25, 1995, balance sheet and the footnote disclosure that describes Kmart's preferred stock.

EXHIBIT	15.2	Description of Kmart's Preferred Stock

Shareholders' Equity:

Preferred stock, 10,000,000 shares authorized:		
Series A, 5,750,000 shares authorized and issued at January 26, 1994	—	986
Series C, 790,287 shares authorized; shares issued 658,315 and		
784,938, respectively	132	157
Common stock, 1,500,000,000 shares authorized; shares issued		
464,549,561 and 416,546,780 respectively	465	417
Capital in excess of par value	1,505	538
Performance restricted stock deferred compensation	—	(3)
Retained earnings	4,074	4,237
Treasury shares	(86)	(109)
Foreign currency translation adjustment	(58)	(130)
Total shareholders' equity	6,032	6,093

Shareholders' Equity

In October 1992, Kmart Corporation issued 784,938 shares of Series B convertible preferred stock in exchange for all the outstanding stock of Borders, Inc. As of July 8, 1994, all outstanding shares of Series B convertible preferred stock were exchanged for 784,938 shares of Series C convertible preferred stock. The Series C convertible preferred stock has substantially the same terms as the Series B convertible preferred stock, i.e. each share of Series C convertible preferred stock is convertible by the holders at any time into 6.49 shares of common stock, subject to adjustment in certain events, and is redeemable for Kmart Corporation after November 1, 1999 at a redemption rate based on the then-current market price of the common stock.

Ten million shares of no par value preferred stock with voting and cumulative dividend rights are authorized; 658,315 are issued as Series C convertible preferred stock and 9,341,685 are unissued. Of the unissued, 500,000 have been designated Series A junior participating preferred stock.

HOW MANY SHARES ARE THERE?

When referring to the number of shares of stock in a corporation, the number of shares can refer to the number authorized, issued, or outstanding. Each term describes a different aspect of a corporation's stock.

Shares Authorized

When a company files its articles of incorporation with the state's secretary of state, it specifies the number of shares it wants to have the ability to sell. The number of **authorized shares** is the total number of shares the state has approved for a corporation to sell. The corporation can issue more than the number of authorized shares only by obtaining permission from the incorporating state. The number of shares authorized is usually set high enough so additional authorization from the state is unnecessary.

Shares Issued

A corporation raises money to fund its investments by selling its stock to individuals, groups, or businesses that want to have an ownership interest in the corporation. When the corporation sells its stock initially, it has "issued" its shares. The number of **issued shares** refers to the number of authorized shares a corporation has sold to stockholders. After the corporation issues stock, shareholders are free to buy and sell the issued shares. Secondary markets such as the New York Stock Exchange and NASDAQ exist to facilitate the stockholders' desire to trade these securities. The number of shares issued is unaffected when the corporation's stock is traded in secondary markets because investors are merely trading existing shares of stock. The number of shares issued changes *only* when the corporation sells more of its authorized shares or buys back some of its issued shares.

Shares Outstanding

The number of **outstanding shares** is the number of shares issued and held outside the corporation. Because a corporation is a legal entity, it can buy its own stock in the secondary market. Typically, a corporation buys its owns shares in anticipation of reissuing the stock at a higher price and, therefore, raising additional capital. In many cases, corporations purchase their stock to give to their executives as compensation. **Treasury stock** is the amount of a corporation's repurchased stock that it intends to reissue at a later date. When a corporation buys treasury stock, it is liquidating the stockholders' interest in the corporation by giving them cash in exchange for their ownership interest. *When a corporation buys treasury stock, it is not buying an asset; rather, it is reducing its stockholders' equity.*

The number of shares outstanding is the number of shares issued less the number of shares of treasury stock held by the corporation. If the corporation has no treasury shares, the number of shares outstanding and the number issued are the same.

In most states, the number of shares a company is allowed to repurchase is limited to 20 percent of the number of shares issued in order to protect corporate creditors. Because corporations have limited liability, creditors of a corporation only have claim to the assets of the corporation. If the corporation could buy all of its stock back, the stockholders would receive their interest in the corporation (cash payment for the repurchased stock) before the creditors, and the assets remaining might not be sufficient to satisfy the claims of the creditors upon liquidation.

PAUSE & REFLECT | If a corporation could buy back all its issued stock, who would own the corporation?

CAPITAL STOCK VALUES

Capital stock has several "values" depending on the context in which it appears. The first two values, par value and no-par value, are established to comply with the legal requirements of issuing stock, while the third value, market value, represents the economic value of capital stock.

Par Value

Par value is an arbitrary value assigned to shares of capital stock which is approved by the state in which the business is incorporated. The par value is specified in the corporation's charter and is printed on the stock certificates. In most states, the par value is the minimum price the stock can sell for when it is sold initially. Kmart's par value is $1 per share.

Since the par value of common stock is a purely arbitrary amount, and because a high par value might impair the firm's ability to sell its shares, most par values of common stock are quite low.

The **legal capital** of the corporation is the portion of stockholders' equity required by state law to be retained for the protection of the corporation's creditors. In many states it is calculated by multiplying the par value times the number of shares of stock issued. The corporation cannot pay dividends that cause its total assets to

EXHIBIT | **15.3**

No-Par Stock Certificate

drop below the sum of its legal capital and the total liabilities of the corporation, thus providing some protection for the creditors of the corporation.

The amount of proceeds received from stock issuance in excess of the par value of the stock when it is issued is called **paid-in capital in excess of par** or **contributed capital in excess of par**. This classification makes the distinction between monies received that satisfy legal capital requirements (par values) and the amounts that are in excess of the legal minimum.

No-Par Value

No-par stock does not have a minimum price assigned to each share of stock. Its initial purpose was to overcome two problems associated with par value shares: (1) the possible need to issue stock below par value, and (2) the confusion that existed about par values and any relationship they might have to the market value of the stock.

No-par, stated value stock is stock that has a minimum price or stated value established by the corporation's board of directors but no par value specified in the charter. In effect, a stated value stock makes a no-par stock function the same way as par value stock. This type of stock allows creditors to have the assurance that a minimum amount of capital is available in the corporation to protect their interest. The advantage of stated value stock is that the board of directors decides whether to establish a stated value on the no-par stock. This creates more flexibility for the corporation than when a stock has its par value established in its articles of incorporation.

Market Value

The market value of a share of stock is the price agreed to by an unrelated willing buyer and seller. For stocks traded in organized secondary markets, the market values of stock are readily available from listings in financial news sources such as *The Wall Street Journal* and *Barron's*. For stocks that are not traded on organized exchanges, individuals who are making trades determine market values. Unlike par values, which are determined prior to the issuance of the stock and cannot be changed without approval by the incorporating state, the market value of stock is constantly changing based on willing buyers' and sellers' estimates of the value of the corporation.

The market price a corporation receives in the initial issue market determines the amount of cash the corporation receives from investors to finance its operations.

The New York Stock Exchange is a marketplace for the sale and purchase of stock. The market value of stock is agreed to by the willing buyer and the willing seller.

Corporations continue to monitor the market value of their stock in the secondary market after the initial sale of the stock. Increasing or decreasing market values reflect the investors' perceptions of the corporation's financial condition and future profit potential. Rising stock prices reflect increasing investor confidence, while declining prices indicate an erosion of their confidence. The market price of stock in the secondary market gives the corporation's management an idea of the amount of cash it could raise if additional shares of stock were issued.

DIVIDENDS

Dividends are a distribution of the assets of the corporation to the owners of the corporation. Typically these distributions are made from the earnings of the firm, although there are also liquidating dividends, which are dividends in excess of the earnings accumulated by the firm or a return of the stockholders' investments.

Dividends usually are distributed in the form of cash; however, corporations routinely issue stock dividends, and can issue property dividends. A **cash dividend** is a cash distribution in the form of a check that is sent to each stockholder as of a certain date.

When a corporation issues a **stock dividend,** it distributes additional shares of the corporation's stock to existing stockholders. Stock dividends have no effect on the assets of the firm because each stockholder is receiving more shares of stock rather than corporate assets. Although each investor has more shares as a result of a stock dividend, his or her percentage interest in the corporation does not change.

For example, if Kmart issues a 10 percent stock dividend on the number of shares issued, a stockholder who owns 100 shares of stock will receive 10 new shares (100 shares × .10). However, because the number of shares every Kmart stockholder owns will increase by 10 percent, no single stockholder will have a greater interest in the firm than he or she did before the stock dividend.

PAUSE & REFLECT   **What is the benefit to the stockholder of receiving a stock dividend? Why would a corporation issue a stock dividend?**

Property dividends typically involve the distribution of specific noncash assets, such as inventory or investments in other corporation's securities, to stockholders. They usually are paid in corporations with just a few stockholders. Property dividends

EXHIBIT | **15.4**

Dividend Dates

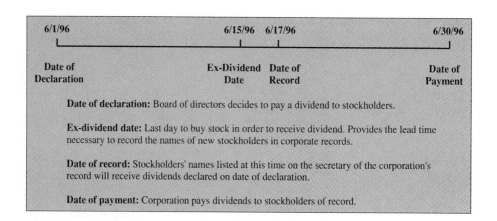

Date of declaration: Board of directors decides to pay a dividend to stockholders.

Ex-dividend date: Last day to buy stock in order to receive dividend. Provides the lead time necessary to record the names of new stockholders in corporate records.

Date of record: Stockholders' names listed at this time on the secretary of the corporation's record will receive dividends declared on date of declaration.

Date of payment: Corporation pays dividends to stockholders of record.

are not as popular with stockholders as cash dividends due to the difficulty of receiving and disposing of the corporation's property.

Four dates related to dividends are important to remember: (1) the date of declaration, (2) the date of record, (3) the ex-dividend date, and (4) the date of payment. Exhibit 15.4 shows the sequence of these dates, which we next describe in detail.

Date of Declaration

The **date of declaration** is the date on which the board of directors announces its decision to pay a dividend. The board of directors usually declares dividends after the company has generated sufficient earnings and has cash on hand to provide stockholders with a return on their investment. On the date of declaration, the board of directors sets the amount of the dividend and the date to distribute it. For cash and property dividends, once the board declares the dividend, the corporation incurs the obligation to pay the dividend on the date of payment, which gives rise to a related liability. However, because stock dividends involve the distribution of shares of stock rather than the firm's assets, no liability is incurred on the date of declaration for stock dividends.

Date of Record

The **date of record** is the date on which the secretary of the corporation examines the stock ownership transfer book to determine who is officially registered as a stockholder of the corporation and, therefore, eligible to receive the corporation's dividends. Those persons listed in the ownership book on this date will receive the dividend. *Stockholders can sell their stock after this date but before the date of payment and still receive the declared dividend.* The date of record is set at the time the board of directors decides to declare the dividend.

Ex-Dividend Date

The **ex-dividend date** occurs two or three days prior to the date of record and is the last date when an individual can buy the stock of the corporation and still receive the corporation's declared dividend. Setting the ex-dividend date depends on how long it takes for the corporate secretary to record a change in the ownership of the stock.

Date of Payment

The **date of payment** is the date on which the company formally pays the dividends to stockholders of record. Normally, no more than 90 days elapse from the date of declaration until the date of distribution. Once the corporation has distributed the dividend, it has met its dividend obligation created on the date of declaration.

STOCK SPLITS

A **stock split** occurs when a corporation calls in its old shares of stock and issues a larger number of new shares of stock in their place. Each stockholder retains the same percentage interest in the company after the stock split. When stock splits, the par or stated value of the stock also changes to reflect the number of new shares on the market.

Assume that a company has 400,000 shares of common stock issued and outstanding with a par value of $9 per share and that its board of directors approves a three-for-one stock split. To implement the split, the company will call all the old $9 par value common stock and replace it with 1,200,000 (400,000 × 3) shares of $3 par value common stock. Notice that the stock split increases (triples) the number of shares issued and decreases the par value ($9) to one-third of its original amount ($3). However, the total par value of the shares issued ($3,600,000) remains the same.

After a stock split, each stockholder owns a greater number of shares, each share has a proportionately lower par value, and the total legal capital for the corporation remains the same as it was prior to the stock split. Thus, each shareholder's percentage ownership of the company has remained unchanged. A stock split does not increase an individual stockholder's interest in the corporation nor does it cause a distribution of any monies to the stockholders.

Companies undertake stock splits for a variety of reasons. The most common reason is to lower the market price of the company's stock to allow the price to be affordable to a wider group of potential investors. Because stockbrokers prefer to sell stocks in **round lots,** that is, 100 shares of stock sold together, as a company becomes successful and its stock prices increase, it becomes more difficult for small investors to afford round lots. Therefore, to make purchasing its shares more affordable, a corporation splits its stock to reduce the market price per share of stock.

While investors own the same amount of the company in terms of the percentage of shares after the split as before the split, their personal financial condition may improve as a result of the stock split. For example, in September of 1994 Harley-Davidson, Inc., had a 2-for-1 stock split. The number of shares issued doubled and the market price of the stock went from $54 per share before the split to $28 per share after the split. Therefore, a stockholder with 100 shares of Harley-Davidson before the split, which was worth $5,400, owned 200 shares worth $5,600 (200 shares × $28) after the split. This increase in the total market value of the stock occurs because stockholders consider the split a positive signal from the company. That is, the stockholders believe that the company split the stock anticipating an increase in the firm's future profitability and, therefore, an increase in stock prices.

WHERE DO CORPORATIONS FIND EQUITY FINANCING?

We know that, regardless of their size, corporations raise equity capital by issuing common and preferred stock. Smaller corporations usually raise equity capital (cash) by selling stock directly to those persons who have an interest in the business.

For existing business entities that are changing from a sole proprietorship or partnership to a corporation, the owners exchange their interest in their sole proprietorship or partnership for common stock of the corporation. While this exchange process raises no cash, the owners are, in effect, providing equity financing for the new business entity by contributing their interest in the old entity.

For large businesses, the initial issue of capital stock is usually sold by investment bankers who act as an agent for the corporation and charge a fee for their service. Corporations hire investment bankers to sell their securities because of the investment banker's knowledge of the securities market and ability to find buyers for the stock. The New York Stock Exchange, the American Stock Exchange, the NASDAQ Exchange, and the regional stock exchanges are markets for these initial issues of capital stock.

Exhibit 15.5 shows a *Wall Street Journal* ad that describes the stock offering of Finlay Enterprises, Inc., and the brokerage firms that are going to be selling the stock. These ads are called *tombstones* and, in addition to disclosing the name of the company and the names of the investment firms selling the stock, they describe the type of stock (common stock with a $.01 par value), the number of shares being offered (2,615,000), and the price of the stock ($14).

Cash raised from the issuance of common and preferred stock provides the equity financing necessary to start a business enterprise or provides needed funds for subsequent expansion. However, many firms that can raise sufficient cash through equity financing choose to use debt to finance operations. Why is this true?

EXHIBIT | 15.5

Stock Offering

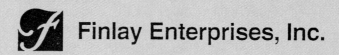

2,615,000 Shares

Finlay Enterprises, Inc.

Common Stock
(par value $.01 per share)

Price $14 Per Share

Upon request, a copy of the Prospectus describing these securities and the business of the Company may be obtained within any State from any Underwriter who may legally distribute it within such State. The securities are offered only by means of the Prospectus, and this announcement is neither an offer to sell nor a solicitation of an offer to buy.

Goldman, Sachs & Co.

Donaldson, Lufkin & Jenrette
Securities Corporation

Robertson, Stephens & Company

Bear, Stearns & Co. Inc.	CS First Boston	Dean Witter Reynolds Inc.
A.G. Edwards & Sons, Inc.	Wasserstein Perella Securities, Inc.	Advest, Inc.
Sanford C. Bernstein & Co., Inc.	J. C. Bradford & Co.	Dain Bosworth Incorporated
J. J. B. Hilliard, W. L. Lyons, Inc.	Edward D. Jones & Co.	McDonald & Company Securities, Inc.
Parker/Hunter Incorporated	Rauscher Pierce Refsnes, Inc.	Scott & Stringfellow, Inc.
Sutro & Co. Incorporated	Tucker Anthony Incorporated	Wheat First Butcher Singer

April 20, 1995

WHY BORROW?

At first glance, the answer to the question, "Why borrow?," may seem quite simple due to our personal experiences with debt. Individually, we borrow when we want to purchase a product or service but do not have enough money on hand to buy it. The desire to acquire goods or services immediately, rather than waiting until there is enough money saved to make the purchase, justifies the cost of using the borrowed funds. In business, however, the decision to borrow is centered around the risks and rewards of debt financing.

Debt financing occurs when a firm incurs a liability in the process of acquiring goods or services. Typically, liabilities require the repayment of an amount of cash that is greater than the amount of the original obligation. From the borrower's point of view, this excess amount is interest expense and represents the cost of using borrowed funds. From the lender's point of view, this additional amount is interest revenue and is the return on the investment necessary to justify lending the money to the firm.

The risk of debt financing is called **financial risk** and is the chance that a firm will default on its debt. A firm defaults if it is unable to meet (make) either the interest or principal payments that come due on the debt. When this occurs, the lender has the legal right to require the debtor to liquidate (sell) its assets to raise the cash necessary to pay the debt.

For example, assume that in 1992 a company borrowed $100,000 from the bank and signed a note agreeing to repay the money in 10 years and to pay 10 percent interest on the $100,000 each year over the life of the note. Suppose that the company made the yearly interest payments of $10,000 for 1993, 1994, and 1995, but, in 1996, cannot pay the annual interest. At this point, the company has failed to comply with the terms of the note and is in default on the debt. Then, the bank can, by law, demand payment of the entire note. If the company does not have sufficient cash, this would force the sale of enough of its assets to collect the original amount of the note plus the interest due. The sale of the company's assets might impair its ability to continue its normal operations and could result in the demise of the firm.

Consider, however, the reward for using debt financing. When companies generate a return on their borrowed funds that is greater than the cost to them of using the borrowed funds, the companies benefit. Any excess return on the borrowed funds belongs to the owners and, therefore, increases their return on investment. When this occurs, we say that the owners used financial leverage to increase the rate of return on their investment.

Financial Leverage

Financial leverage is a financing strategy designed to increase the rate of return on owners' investment by generating a greater return on borrowed funds than the cost of using the funds. To illustrate the concept, suppose that two firms, NODEBT and LEVER, each have $100,000 in assets and receive a 20 percent return on these assets before deducting interest and taxes. The only difference between these firms is how the assets of NODEBT and LEVER are financed.

NODEBT finances 100 percent of its $100,000 in assets by using only its owners' money, whereas LEVER has borrowed $60,000 at 10 percent annual interest creating a $60,000 liability and uses $40,000 of its owners' money, as shown below.

			Financing Method		
Firm	ASSETS	=	Liabilities	+	Owners' Equity
NODEBT	$100,000	=	$ 0	+	$100,000
LEVER	$100,000	=	$60,000	+	$ 40,000

We show the effects of the different financing arrangements in Exhibit 15.6. Note that both companies generate $20,000 income before interest and taxes as a result of the 20 percent return on the $100,000 of assets. LEVER's net income, however, is further reduced by the $6,000 of interest expense ($60,000 × .10) charged for the use

EXHIBIT 15.6 Financial Leverage		
	NODEBT	**LEVER**
Income before interest and taxes ($100,000 × 20%)	$ 20,000	$20,000
Interest expense	0	6,000
Income before taxes	20,000	14,000
Tax expense (40%)	8,000	5,600
Net income	$ 12,000	$ 8,400
Rate of return on owners' equity (ROE)	$ 12,000 / $100,000 = 12%	$ 8,400 / $40,000 = 21%
After-Tax Cost of Debt:		
Interest on $60,000 debt at 10%		$ 6,000
Tax without interest	$ 8,000	
Tax with interest	5,600	
Tax saving from interest		2,400
After-tax cost of debt		$ 3,600
After-tax rate of interest	$ 3,600 / $ 60,000 = 6%	

oody's Investors Service, Inc., provides bond ratings for investors that describe the relative investment qualities (risk) of both initial issue bonds and bonds in the secondary market.

Moody's rates the investment quality of bonds using the nine symbols shown below. Each symbol represents a group in which the quality characteristics are broadly the same. The symbols indicated the rank of the bonds from the highest investment quality, Aaa, to the lowest investment quality, C.

Aaa Aa A   Baa Ba B   Caa Ca C

Aaa Bonds that are rated Aaa are judged to be of the best quality. They carry the smallest degree of investment risk and are generally referred to as "gilt edged." Interest payments are protected by a large or by an expectionally stable margin and the principal is secure.

Baa Bonds that are rated Baa are considered as medium-grade obligations (i.e., they are neither highly protected nor poorly secured). Interest payments and principal security appear adequate for the present but certain protective elements may be lacking or may be characteristically unreliable over any great length of time.

Caa Bonds that are rated Ca are of poor standing. Such issues may be in default or there may be present elements of danger with respect to principal or interest.

C Bonds that are rated C are the lowest rated class of bonds, and issues so rated can be regarded as having extremely poor prospects of ever attaining any real investment standing.

Source: *Moody's Bond Record,* Moody's Investors Service.

---

of the borrowed funds. Both firms are subject to a tax rate of 40 percent, but LEVER will pay $2,400 less in taxes than NODEBT because the $6,000 of interest expense is tax deductible. This means that the after-tax cost to LEVER of borrowing the funds is $3,600 ($6,000 − $2,400), or 6 percent [($6,000 − $2,400)/$60,000]. While NODEBT's net income, $12,000, is greater than LEVER's net income of $8,400, LEVER's owners have less money invested in the company than NODEBT's owners.

The rate of return on owners' equity, (ROE), discussed in greater detail in Chapter 25, measures the performance of the firm in terms of the owners' investment, as shown below.

$$ROE = \frac{\text{Net income}}{\text{Owners' equity}}$$

It might appear that because NODEBT's net income is higher ($12,000) than LEVER's ($8,400), NODEBT has the more desirable financing structure. However, the only way to compare their performance is by using a common-size measure such as the rate of return on owners' equity. LEVER's rate of return on owners' equity, 21 percent ($8,400/$40,000), is greater than NODEBT's ROE of 12 percent ($12,000/$100,000).

PAUSE & REFLECT

Suppose that you had a choice of investing $1,000 with NODEBT or $1,000 with LEVER. Which would you prefer? Why?

LEVER's return on its assets, $20,000 ($100,000 × .20), is the same dollar amount as NODEBT's return. However, by financing $60,000 of the assets with borrowed funds, LEVER has *levered* its ROE from 12 percent to 21 percent.

Exhibit 15.7 shows that the 21 percent return is possible because LEVER is using the lender's funds to generate enough money ($12,000) to meet the interest obligation on the debt ($6,000) and to supplement the owners' return with the $3,600 remaining after subtracting taxes of $2,400. The additional $3,600 LEVER is making on the borrowed funds is added to the return of $4,800 generated by the owners' $40,000 investment to arrive at LEVER's net income of $8,400.

Debt to Equity: A Measure of Financial Leverage

Debt financing can reward business owners with high rates of return, but it also increases their exposure to the risks of default. The **debt-to-equity ratio** measures the relationship between the amount of debt and the amount of owners' equity used to finance the firm. A debt-to-equity ratio of 1 means that equal amounts of debt

EXHIBIT 15.7	LEVER's Return			
		Owners' Funds	Borrowed Funds	Total
Assets		$40,000	$60,000	$100,000
Rate of return (20%)		.2	.2	.2
Return on assets		8,000	12,000	20,000
Interest on debt		0	6,000	6,000
Income before taxes		8,000	6,000	14,000
Tax (40% of income)		3,200	2,400	5,600
Income after tax		$ 4,800	$ 3,600	$ 8,400

$$\text{Rate of return on owners' equity} = \frac{\$4,800 + \$3,600}{\$40,000} = 21\%$$

and owners' equity finance the firm. The larger the debt-to-equity ratio, the greater the amount of debt used to finance the firm and, therefore, the greater the financial risk. As a firm's debt increases, it needs more earnings to cover the interest incurred on its debt and, as a result, the financial risk of the firm increases. The formula for the debt-to-equity ratio presented below reflects Kmart's financial structure as of January 25, 1995.

$$\text{Debt to equity} = \frac{\text{Total debt}}{\text{Stockholders' equity}} = \frac{\$10,997,000,000}{\$6,032,000,000} = 1.823$$

Financial Leverage and Risk

The financial risk of a firm depends not only on the amount of its financial leverage, but also on the volatility of its sales, that is, the tendency of its sales to increase and decrease dramatically from one time period to the next. In general, when a firm has a high debt-to-equity ratio and its sales are volatile, it has greater financial risk. The financial risk increases because a decline in sales will substantially reduce the firm's ROE or might cause the firm to default on its debt obligations. However, some firms, such as power companies, have and can operate with high debt-to-equity ratios because their sales are stable.

How Is Debt Financing Used?

Debt not only serves to finance a firm's day-to-day operations, but also it is a means to acquire the assets that provide the infrastructure that supports operations, as we mentioned previously. In general, short-term, or current, liabilities, such as accounts payable, salaries payable, and notes payable, finance the daily operations of the firm.

Firms use long-term liabilities to finance the acquisition of long-term assets such as buildings, equipment, land, and patents that support their operations. The cash flows these assets generate over their useful lives make it possible to meet the obligations of the long-term debt used to finance their acquisition. In this next section, we discuss the basic characteristics of financial instruments used in long-term debt financing.

LONG-TERM DEBT INSTRUMENTS

When long-term debt is issued, both the borrower and lender are careful to formalize the terms of the debt. In corporations, the board of directors must approve the issuance of long-term debt. Lenders may place certain restrictions on the borrowing company called **covenants,** which they document in the debt agreement to protect the lenders' interest. For example, a lender may limit the amount of additional long-term debt the company can issue in order to provide the lender some assurance that the company's debt will not become too large and impair the firm's ability to service its present debt commitments.

As you know, notes are the written promises of the firms that borrow funds. Each note describes the cash flows the borrower, or maker, of the note is willing to pay in return for the use of the lender's, or note holder's funds.

The face value of the note indicates the amount that the note's maker will ultimately pay the note's holder. The face rate on the note determines the amount of cash interest the maker will pay the holder of the note. The amount of cash raised from the issuance of the debt is called the **proceeds** of the note. The *actual* interest rate charged for the use of the proceeds of the note is called the **market** or **effective interest rate.** *The effective rate may or may not be the face rate of interest printed on the note.* The effective interest rate is negotiated by the borrower and the lender. The borrower wants the use of the funds at the lowest possible cost, while the lender wants the highest possible return for the risk assumed.

For example, suppose Kmart wants to borrow $500,000 for a long-term project and is willing to pay 8 percent interest. Citibank is interested in making the loan but wants a 9 percent rate on the loan. If Citibank agrees to Kmart's terms, the market rate of interest would be 8 percent, but if Kmart agrees to Citibank's terms, the market rate of interest would be 9 percent. If both parties compromise and agree to 8.5 percent, then 8.5 percent would be the market rate of interest.

When companies plan to use long-term debt financing, they typically select one of three basic types of notes. These notes are classified based on their promised cash flows and are described below.

Periodic Payment Notes

A **periodic payment note** is a debt instrument that contains a promise to make a series of equal payments consisting of both interest and principal at equal time intervals over a specified time period. Assume Kmart borrowed $60,000 on July 1, 1994, signed a note with a $60,000 face value, and agreed to repay the money over the next two years at an annual face rate of 12 percent by making 24 monthly payments. The amount of the monthly payments, $2,824.41, is determined by using the present value of an annuity formula as shown below.

$$\text{Annuity} \times P_{24,1\%} = \text{Present value}$$
$$\text{Annuity} \times 21.2434 = \$60,000$$
$$\text{Annuity} = \$2,824.41$$

The periodic payment note is typically called an *installment note*. A monthly car payment is an example of an installment note. Each payment that is made consists of the interest for the last installment period; the remainder is repayment of the principal. Exhibit 15.8 illustrates Kmart's periodic note schedule for the first two months of the $60,000 loan period.

The first payment of $2,824.41 pays the $600 interest that has accumulated on the $60,000 debt for the first installment period of one month ($60,000 × .12 × 1/12). The remainder of the payment reduces the amount of the principal by $2,224.41. The second payment repeats the process, except the amount of interest, $577.76 ($57,775.59 × .12 × 1/12), is less because a portion of the principal was paid in the first month's payment. Notice that the monthly payments are the same for each of the 24 months, but, for each month, the amount of interest will get smaller because the principal on which the borrower pays interest is reduced with each consecutive payment.

EXHIBIT	15.8	Periodic Payment Note Schedule			
		(1)	**(2)**	**(3)**	**(4)**
Date		Payment	Interest (1% × Loan Balance)	Principal	Loan Balance
7/1/94					$60,000.00
8/1/94		$2,824.41	$600*	$2,224.41	57,775.59
9/1/94		2,824.41	577.76†	2,246.65	55,528.94

*$60,000 × .12 × 1/12 = $60,000 × .01 = $600.

†$57,775.59 × .12 × 1/12 = $577.76.

Lump-Sum Payment Notes

A **lump-sum payment note** is a debt instrument that contains a promise to pay a specific amount of money at the end of a specific period of time. Lump-sum payment notes are often called *noninterest-bearing notes* because the note only specifies a face value and a due date. Thus, the note does not have a face interest rate, but specifies only the amount the borrower promises to pay back at a future date.

The amount a lender is willing to give in exchange for this type of market note depends on the interest rate the borrower and lender agree upon. Once the borrower and lender agree upon the market rate, the proceeds of the note are calculated using the present value of the amount of $1 (see Table 2 at the end of the book).

Assume Kmart issues a $60,000, noninterest-bearing note on July 1, 1996, due on June 30, 1998, to the Bank of America. Kmart, as maker of the note, is promising to pay $60,000 in two years on June 30, 1998, in exchange for some amount of cash on July 1, 1996. Clearly, the loan officer at Bank of America would not give Kmart $60,000 in exchange for the promise to return the $60,000 at the end of two years. The amount of cash loaned by the Bank of America is the present value of the $60,000 at some market rate of interest.

Assuming that the two parties decide on a 12 percent market rate that is compounded semiannually, the proceeds of the note are calculated below.

$$\text{Future value} \times p_{4,6\%} = \text{Present value}$$
$$\$60,000 \times .7921 = \text{Present value}$$
$$\$47,526 = \text{Present value}$$

This means Bank of America will loan Kmart, the maker of the note, $47,526 if Kmart promises to pay the Bank of America, the holder of the note, $60,000 in two years on July 1, 1998. If Kmart complies with the terms of the note, Bank of America will earn a 12 percent return, while Kmart will incur a 12 percent interest expense.

The excess of the face value of a note over its cash preceeds is called a **discount on a note.** The discount itself represents the difference, in dollars, between the *face rate of interest*, which is zero because it is a noninterest-bearing note, and the *market rate of interest* (12%) over the life of the note. In this case, the discount is $12,474 ($60,000 – $47,526) and is the amount of interest on the note for two years. The amortization table in Exhibit 15.9 shows how to allocate the discount over the life of the note. The **carrying value of a note** is the face value minus the discount ($60,000 – $12,474 on 7/1/96) or $47,526 in this case.

The amortization table indicates that in the first year of the note's life (7/1/96 to 7/1/97) the interest incurred by the borrower is $5,874.21 ($2,851.56 + $3,022.65). Notice that although interest has been incurred, Kmart has paid no cash to the lender, Bank of America. Kmart pays the interest on the note, represented by the discount $12,474, when it pays the $60,000 face value on 7/1/98. Thus Kmart has had the use

EXHIBIT	15.9	Lump-Sum Note Schedule		
Date	(1) Cash Payment	(2) Interest (.06 × Carrying value)	(3) Remaining Discount	(4) Carrying Value
7/1/96			$12,474.00	$47,526.00
1/1/97		$2,851.56*	9,622.44†	50,377.56‡
7/1/97		3,022.65	6,599.79	53,400.21
1/1/98		3,204.01	3,395.78	56,604.22
7/1/98		3,395.78	–0–	60,000.00
7/1/88	$60,000			–0–

*$47,526 × .12 × 1/2 = $2,851.56.

†$12,474 – $2,851.56 = $9,622.44.

‡$60,000 – $9,622.44 = $50,377.56, or $47,526 + $2,851.56 = $50,377.56.

of $47,526 for two years and, by paying $60,000 at the end of two years, is returning the $47,526 borrowed from the Bank of America plus $12,474 of interest.

This type of note can be confusing because the borrower does not receive the $60,000 face value when the note is issued. Care must be taken not to confuse the *face value* with the *proceeds* of the note. Remember, the note merely specifies the cash flows promised by the note's maker. The cash proceeds of the note depend on the market rate of interest used to find the present value of the promised cash flows. In this case, the $47,526 of proceeds are the present value of the $60,000 promised by the maker of the note assuming a 12 percent annual market rate that is compounded semiannually.

Periodic Payment and Lump-Sum Notes

A **periodic payment and lump-sum note** is a debt instrument that combines periodic payments and a final lump-sum payment. It has a face rate of interest and a face value that indicates that the maker promises to make periodic cash interest payments *and* a lump-sum payment on the date the note matures. To determine the periodic cash payments, multiply the face rate of interest by the face value of the note. For example, suppose that on July 1, 1996, Kmart makes a $60,000, two-year note that has a face interest rate of 8 percent that is paid semiannually. The note is the maker's written promise to pay $2,400 ($60,000 × .08 × 1/2) every six months for two years, in addition to $60,000 at the end of the two years.

The amount of proceeds that Kmart receives for the note depends on the market rate of interest. The face rate and face values are used to determine the cash flows promised by Kmart. We will examine how the proceeds of a note are affected when (1) the market rate is greater than the face rate, (2) the market rate is less than the face rate, and (3) the market rate is equal to the face rate.

Market Rate Greater Than Face Rate   When the market rate of interest is *greater* than the face rate of interest, the proceeds of the note are *less* than the face value of the note. Under these circumstances, the note is issued at a *discount* to make the note yield the market interest rate. To illustrate, assume that Kmart, the maker of the $60,000 note described above, takes the note to the Bank of America. The banker thinks that, due to Kmart's level of risk, it needs a 12 percent interest rate before it can lend money. To make the 8 percent face rate note yield the desired 12 percent market rate, the bank determines the proceeds of the note by finding the present value of the cash flows specified on the note *using the 12 percent market rate*. The result, calculated in Exhibit 15.10, shows that Bank of America will loan Kmart $55,842.24, or the present value of the semiannual and lump-sum components of the note, which is $4,157.76 less than the $60,000 face value of the note.

The note promises to make two types of future cash payments, and the two present value calculations determine the value of each of these cash flows today. Therefore, the value of the note is the sum of the present value of a $2,400 annuity and the present value of a $60,000 lump-sum payment. The $4,157.76 discount represents the additional interest that Kmart will incur over the life of the note because the market rate, 12 percent, is greater than the face rate, 8 percent. Kmart receives $55,842.24 instead of $60,000, but will have to pay $60,000 at the end of the note's life.

Since the amount of the discount is actually additional interest that Kmart will pay over the life of the note, the 8 percent note has effectively become a 12 percent note. The amortization table in Exhibit 15.11 illustrates how to determine the amount of interest for each period.

EXHIBIT 15.10 | Market Rate Greater Than Face Rate

Cash Flows Promised by the Note

Cash flow 1   Four, $2,400 semiannual payments

Cash flow 2 $60,000 lump-sum payment, two years from today

Present Value of Promised Cash Flows

Cash flow 1:

$$\text{Present value of annuity} = \text{Annuity} \times P_{4,6\%}$$
$$= \$2,400 \times 3.4651$$
$$= \$8,316.24$$

Cash flow 2:

$$\text{Present value of lump sum} = \text{Future value} \times p_{4,6\%}{}^{*}$$
$$= \$60,000 \times .7921$$
$$= \$47,526$$

Present value of cash flow 1	$ 8,316.24
Present value of cash flow 2	47,526.00
Present value of note	$55,842.24

*Because the annuity is semiannual and the interest is compounded semiannually, the present value of the amount of $1 is also compounded semiannually.

Notice that the cash interest (column 1) is not the same as the amount of effective interest (column 2). Remember that the cash interest is based on the face interest rate applied to the face value, while the effective interest is the market rate of interest of the note times the carrying value of the note (column 5). Kmart can use $55,842.24 of the Bank of America's money for six months at a cost of $3,350.53 calculated as follows:

$$\text{Effective interest} = \text{Principal} \times \text{Rate} \times \text{Time}$$
$$\$3,350.53 = \$55,842.24 \times .12 \times 1/2$$

The amount that the effective interest exceeds the cash interest for the time period is the **amortized discount** (column 3). Remember that the difference between the proceeds of $55,842.24 and the $60,000 face value is paid at the maturity date. The discount represents the additional interest Kmart is paying because the market interest rate is 12 percent and not the 8 percent face rate.

The amortization process allocates a portion of the total discount amount to each six-month period. For example, the $950.53 of amortized discount on January 1, 1995,

EXHIBIT 15.11 | Discount Amortization Schedule

Date	(1) Cash Interest (.04 × Face value)	(2) Effective Interest (.06 × Carrying value)	(3) Amortized Discound	(4) Remaining Discount	(5) Carrying Value
7/1/96				$4,157.76	$55,842.24
1/1/97	$ 2,400*	$3,350.53†	$ 950.53‡	3,207.23§	56,792.77‖
7/1/97	2,400	3,407.57	1,007.57	2,199.66	57,800.34
1/1/98	2,400	3,468.02	1,068.02	1,131.64	58,868.36
7/1/98	2,400	3,531.64	1,131.64	–0–	60,000.00
7/1/98	$60,000 payment of face value				

*$60,000 face value × .08 face rate ×1/2 = $2,400.

†$55,842.24 carrying value ×.12 market rate × 1/2 = $3,350.53.

‡$3,350.53 − $2,400 = $950.53.

§$4,157.76 − $950.53 = $3,207.23.

‖$60,000 − $3,207.23 = $56,792.77, or $55,842.24 + $950.53 = $56,792.77.

EXHIBIT | 15.12 | Market Rate Less Than Face Rate

Present Value of Promised Cash Flows

Cash flow 1:

$$\text{Present value of annuity} = \text{Annuity} \times P_{4,3\%}$$
$$= \$2,400 \times 3.7171$$
$$= \$8,921.04$$

Cash flow 2:

$$\text{Present value of lump sum} = \text{Future value} \times p_{4,3\%}{}^*$$
$$= \$60,000 \times .8885$$
$$= \$53,310$$

Present value of cash flow 1	$ 8,921.04
Present value of cash flow 2	53,310.00
Present value of note	$62,231.04

*Because the annuity is semiannual and the interest is compounded semiannually, the present value of the amount of $1 is also compounded semiannually.

is the amount of the discount allocated to the first six-month time period. The discount is reduced over the life of the note and becomes zero when the note reaches maturity.

Market Rate Less Than Face Rate   When the market rate of interest is *less* than the face rate of interest on the note, the proceeds of the note are *greater* than the face value of the note. This means that the note is issued at a *premium* in order to make the note yield the market rate of interest, which is less than the face rate of interest. A **premium on a note,** then, is the amount that the cash proceeds of a note exceed its face value which occurs because the market rate of interest is less than the face rate of interest.

To illustrate, assume that Kmart takes the same $60,000 note to the Bank of America when the market rate of interest is 6 percent. In this case, Kmart will not pay 8 percent when the 6 percent rate is available. To determine the proceeds of this note the lender finds the present value of the two promised cash flows using the 6 percent market rate, illustrated in Exhibit 15.12. In this case, the Bank of America will loan Kmart $62,231.04, which is $2,231.04 greater than the face value of the note.

The premium of $2,231.04 will reduce the amount of Kmart's interest over the life of the note. Kmart will get the use of $62,231.04 instead of $60,000, but will only pay the $60,000 face value at maturity. Because the premium of $2,231.04 is not repaid, it, in effect, reduces the interest cost from 8 percent to 6 percent on the note. The amortization table in Exhibit 15.13 illustrates how to determine the amount of interest for each period.

EXHIBIT | 15.13 | Premium Amortization Schedule

Date	(1) Cash Interest (.04 × Face value)	(2) Effective Interest (.03 × Carrying value)	(3) Amortized Premium	(4) Remaining Premium	(5) Carrying Value
7/1/96				$2,231.04	$62,231.04
1/1/97	$ 2,400*	$1,866.93†	$533.07‡	1,697.97§	61,697.97‖
7/1/97	2,400	1,850.94	549.06	1,148.91	61,148.91
1/1/98	2,400	1,834.47	565.53	583.38	60,583.38
7/1/98	2,400	1,816.62	583.38	–0–	60,000.00
7/1/98	60,000 payment of face value				

*$60,000 face value × .08 face rate × 1/2 = $2,400.

†$62,231.04 carrying value × .06 market rate × 1/2 = $1,866.93.

‡$2,400 – $1,866.93 = $533.07.

§$2,231.04 – $533.07 = $1,697.97.

‖$60,000 + $1,697.97 = $61,697.97, or $62,231.04 – $533.07 = $61,697.97.

EXHIBIT | 15.14 | Market Rate Equal to Face Rate

Present Value of Promised Cash Flows

Cash flow 1:

$$\text{Present value of annuity} = \text{Annuity} \times P_{4,4\%}$$
$$= \$2{,}400 \times 3.6299$$
$$= \$8{,}712$$

Cash flow 2:

$$\text{Present value of lump sum} = \text{Future value} \times p_{4,4\%}{}^*$$
$$= \$60{,}000 \times .8548$$
$$= \$51{,}288$$

Present value of cash flow 1	$ 8,712.00
Present value of cash flow 2	51,288.00
Present value of note	$60,000.00

*Because the annuity is semiannual and the interest is compounded semiannually, the present value of the amount of $1 is compounded semiannually.

As in the case of the discount, the amount of cash interest actually paid differs from the effective interest. The cash interest, or cash flow, promised by Kmart to the Bank of America is calculated by multiplying the face rate times the face value (column 1). The effective interest, $1,866.93 (column 2), is the actual cost of using the lender's money for the first six months of the note's life, as shown below:

$$\text{Interest} = \text{Principal} \times \text{Rate} \times \text{Time}$$
$$\$1{,}866.93 = \$62{,}231.04 \times .06 \times 1/2$$

The cost of using $62,231.04 of the Bank of America's money for the first six months is $1,866.93, and the amount that the cash interest, $2,400, exceeds the effective interest for the time period is the **amortized premium**, $533.07. The amortized amount represents the difference between the face rate (8%) and the effective interest rate (6%). The premium is allocated over the life of the note and becomes zero at the maturity date of the note.

Market Rate Equal to Face Rate When the market rate of interest is the *same* as the face rate, the proceeds of the note are the *same* as the face value of the note. To illustrate, assume that Kmart took the same $60,000 note to the Bank of America when the market rate is 8 percent. Exhibit 15.14 shows that the Bank of America will loan Kmart $60,000, the same amount as the face value of the note.

No premium or discount exists because the face rate and the market rate of interest are the same and, therefore, the present value of the note's promised cash flows is equal to the note's face value. The amortization table in Exhibit 15.15 illustrates that the amount of cash interest is the same as the effective interest. Note that the carrying value does not change because the proceeds of the note are the same as the amount due at the maturity date.

To this point we have discussed the characteristics of debt financing. Now we will examine the sources of debt financing available to companies.

EXHIBIT	15.15	Amortization Schedule When Market Rate Equals Face Rate

Date	(1) Cash Interest (.04 × Face value)	(2) Effective Interest (.04 × Carrying value)	(3) Amortized Discount/ Premium	(4) Discount/ Premium	(5) Carrying Value
7/1/96					$60,000
1/1/97	$ 2,400*	$2,400*			60,000
7/1/97	2,400	2,400			60,000
1/1/98	2,400	2,400			60,000
7/1/98	2,400	2,400			60,000
7/1/98	60,000 payment of face value				

*$60,000 face value × .08 face (and market) rate × 1/2 = $2,400.

SOURCES OF LONG-TERM DEBT FINANCING

Long-term debt financing is available from a variety of sources that are classified as nonpublic and public. The nonpublic sources include individuals and institutions, such as banks, savings and loans, and insurance companies. The public source of debt financing is the bond market.

Nonpublic Sources of Debt Financing

Nonpublic debt financing occurs when a firm enters into an agreement with a person or institution to borrow funds. For most businesses, nonpublic debt financing is the most common source of long-term debt. While firms sometimes approach individuals to borrow funds, banks and savings and loans are the most common nonpublic sources of debt financing because they are in business specifically to lend money and want to make loans to qualified companies and individuals. Insurance companies are also a source of long-term debt financing because they need to invest to generate a return on the premiums they receive from their policyholders.

Firms may use any of the three types of notes described earlier—periodic payment notes, lump-sum payment notes, and periodic payment and lump-sum notes—to acquire financing. The form of the note depends on the cash flows the firm feels are appropriate and on the agreement reached between the borrower and creditor. In addition to describing the face value of the note, the face rate of interest, if any, and its time period, the note may include covenants that protect the claims of the holder of the note.

Collateral   A typical means of protecting creditors' claims is to require the borrower to use some asset(s) as **collateral** for the note. Collateral is an asset or group of assets specifically named in a debt agreement to which the creditor has claim if the borrower fails to comply with the terms of the note. For example, for most car loans, the car that is acquired is collateral for the note. If the car buyer fails to make the installment payments, the lending institution can repossess the car and sell it to satisfy the debt. In most cases, the firm borrowing the money cannot dispose of the collateral unless it reaches an agreement with the lending institution about paying off the loan or providing another asset as collateral. A **mortgage** is a long-term note that is secured with real estate, such as land or buildings, as collateral.

Leases   In recent years, extensive use has been made of leasing as another way for a firm to secure the use of an asset. A **lease** is an agreement to convey the use of a tangible asset from one party to another in return for rental payments. The agreement usually covers a specified period of time. It is, in effect, a contract whereby the owner (the lessor) agrees to rent an asset to another party (the lessee) in return for rental payments. There are a wide variety of lease agreements but, in general, they fall into two classifications: operating leases and capital leases.

Typically, an **operating lease** is a rental agreement for a period of time that is substantially shorter than the economic life of the leased asset. However, when a lessee (user) company acquires such a substantial interest in the leased property that the lessee company, for all practical purposes, owns the asset, there is recognition of the acquisition of an asset and a related liability in the lessee's records. This type of lease is called a **capital lease.**

A lease classified as a capital lease recognizes the substance of the economic event over the legal form of the transaction. The economic substance of the lease transaction, the lessee's control of the asset for its useful life, takes precedence over legal requirements (the formal transfer of the title from the seller to the buyer) used to determine when the transfer of ownership occurs.

When a firm enters into a capital lease, it recognizes the leased property as an asset and reflects the related liability incurred in its records. The amount of the asset is the present value of the lease payments, using the firm's market rate of interest. Kmart's January 25, 1995, balance sheet reports capital lease obligations of $1,777,000,000.

To illustrate, let's assume that Kmart signs a five-year lease on equipment that has an estimated useful life of five years. Kmart agrees to pay $5,000 today and $5,548.16 per year, for five years, starting one year from today. Kmart has entered into a capital lease, because, in economic substance, it has purchased the equipment, since the lease term is the same as the life of the equipment.

On the date it signs the lease, Kmart records a long-term liability of $20,000, which is the present value of the $5,548.16, five-payment annuity at Kmart's market rate of interest, 12 percent. Kmart also recognizes and records a leased asset in the amount of $25,000, which is the present value of the lease payments, $20,000, plus the initial $5,000 payment. The liability is a periodic payment note, described earlier in the chapter.

$$\text{Present value of note} = \text{Annuity} \times P_{5,12\%}$$
$$= \$5,548.16 \times 3.6048$$
$$= \$20,000$$

Present value of lease payments	$20,000
Down payment	5,000
Cost of the leased asset	$25,000

Public Sources of Debt Financing: Bonds

Bonds are long-term debt instruments issued by corporations to raise money from the public. Bonds usually take the form of periodic payment and lump-sum notes. However, rather than being in the form of one note, a bond issue typically consists of a group of $1,000 face value notes (bonds) with a specified face interest rate, often paid semiannually, which mature in 10 or more years.

For example, a $5,000,000, 10-year bond issue with a 10 percent face interest rate that is paid semiannually consists of 5,000 bonds, each with a $1,000 face value. Each $1,000 bond has a 10-year life and a 10 percent face rate paid semiannually printed on a note called a **bond certificate.**

As with any note, the 5,000 bond certificates are the corporation's promise to pay the bondholders the cash flows indicated on the bond certificate. In this example, a person holding one bond would receive $50 ($1,000 × .1 × 1/2) every six months for 10 years and $1,000 at the end of 10 years. In total, the corporation promises to pay $250,000 ($5,000,000 × .1 × 1/2) cash interest every six months and $5,000,000 at the end of 10 years. The amount of cash the corporation can borrow by issuing bonds, like any other note payable, is based on the present value of the promised cash flows using the corporation's market interest rate.

Corporations issue bonds because individual financial institutions are unwilling or unable to accept the risk of making very large long-term loans to one corporation. However, because individual bonds are relatively small investing units, many investors can lend funds to the corporation. This enhances the company's ability to borrow large amounts of funds. Individual investors, banks, insurance companies, and other corporations can lend the corporation money by acquiring as many bonds as they deem prudent.

The bond contract is called a **bond indenture.** This contract specifies the amount of the bond issue, the life of the bond, the face value of each bond, and the face interest rate of the bond issue. The bond indenture also may have covenants that place restrictions on the issuing corporation. Many covenants limit the amount of long-term debt a corporation can have.

Normally, the corporation's board of directors must give formal approval before the company can issue bonds. In cases where the bonds are publicly traded on organized bond exchanges, the Securities and Exchange Commission also must approve the bond issue. Once the corporation obtains all of the necessary approvals, it can offer the bonds to the public.

The sale of a bond issue is usually handled by an underwriter at an investment banking firm. The investment banking firm can buy the entire bond issue from the corporation and then resell the bonds to the public. However, if the investment banking firm does not want to underwrite (buy) the entire bond issue, it can sell the bonds and take a percentage of the proceeds of the bond issue as a commission before remitting the cash to the corporation. In some cases, the company issuing bonds sells them directly to specific financial institutions or individuals without using an underwriter. This is called a private (direct) placement of a bond issue.

Regardless of whether a bond issue is underwritten, sold on a commission basis, or privately placed, the corporation obtains the use of money from a bond sale just as if it borrowed money from a bank in a traditional lending process. However, because the lender is the public, and because investment bankers must convince a variety of potential lenders to loan the corporation money, *the process of borrowing the money by issuing bonds takes on the form of a sale. The buyers are acquiring, and the corporation is selling, the right to a set of future cash flows promised in each bond.*

Selling the bond issue and transferring the proceeds of the sale to the corporation takes place in an initial issue market. After the bonds are sold in the initial issue market, they are bought either from another individual, through bond brokers, or in a bond market like the New York Bond Exchange. The buying and selling of the bonds after they are initially issued takes place in what is called the *secondary bond market*. This secondary market allows bondholders to sell their bonds and receive cash from their investment without waiting for the bonds to mature.

Bond prices in the secondary market are quoted as a percent of the face value of the bond. For example, a $1,000 bond with a price of 98 1/2 is selling for .985 of its $1,000 face value, or $985. A bond quoted at a price of 101 3/4 is selling for $1,017.50 or 1.0175 times its $1,000 face value.

Bond Provisions   Although the contractual arrangements of bonds vary greatly, we describe bond issues in terms of how their provisions relate to ownership, repayment, and security. Each bond may have several of the following provisions.

Ownership Provisions   **Registered bonds** are numbered and made payable in the name of the bondholder. The issuing company or its appointed agent maintains a list, called the *bond register*, of the individual who owns the bonds. If the bond changes ownership, it is endorsed on the back and sent to the registrar for recording and reissue, and the issuing company is notified of that change. Interest on these bonds is generally paid by a check made payable to the registered owner on the interest date.

Bearer bonds are made payable to the bearer or person who has physical possession of the bond. Interest is paid by means of coupons attached to the bond. Each coupon is dated and has a dollar value shown on it. The number of coupons and the amount on each coupon depends on the face rate of interest on the bond and the frequency of interest payments during the year. For example, a 10-year, $1,000 bearer bond with a 10 percent face rate that is paid semiannually has 20, $50 coupons attached to it ($1,000 × .1 × 1/2). On the date printed on the coupon, the coupon is detached from the bond and deposited in a bank in the same way as a check is deposited. Bearer bonds are sometimes referred to as *coupon bonds* due to their interest payment procedures.

While bearer bonds still exist in the secondary market, the 1984 Tax Reform Act prohibited any further issuance of bearer bonds due to the difficulty the IRS had in identifying the interest income received by the bearers.

Repayment Provisions   **Callable bonds** give the firm issuing the bonds the right to buy them back before the maturity date at a specified price. Corporations use the call feature when they want to ensure the retirement of all or part of their bond issue. The call feature specifies the dates on which the debtor company may call, or buy back, a bond. If a bond has a call feature, the bond indenture must also state the price, usually expressed as a percentage of the face value, that the firm will pay for the bonds on those dates. For example, if a $1,000 bond has a call price of 105, the issuing company can buy the bond back at $1,050, or 105 percent of the bond's face value ($1,000 × 1.05). Calling the bonds in for redemption is *at the option of the debtor company*, and the bond owner must surrender the securities for the call price. The call price is always greater than the face value of the bond.

Convertible bonds allow bondholders to exchange their bonds for common or preferred stock. The bond indenture describes both the time at which the conversion may take place and the number of shares of stock that the bondholder can obtain. The privilege of converting the bonds into other specific securities rests with the bondholder. Once the bonds are converted to common or preferred stock, the bonds no longer exist, and the company is no longer responsible for the cash flows promised by the bond.

Bondholders only convert bonds into common stock if the stock has the potential of generating a greater return than the bond. For example, suppose a $1,000, 12 percent bond has a 50-to-1 conversion ratio, that is, when the bond is converted, the bondholder will receive 50 shares of common stock for each bond converted. If the price of the common stock is $10, the bondholder is unlikely to convert the bond, because the value of the stock received upon conversion will only be $500 ($10 × 50). However, if the common stock price rises to $40 per share, the bondholder would probably convert the bond because the value of the converted stock, $2,000, is far greater than the value of the bond.

A **serial bond** is a bond issue that has specified portions of the bond issue coming due periodically over the life of the bond issue. For example, a $20 million, 20-year bond that has $5 million of its face value maturing every 5 years over its 20-year life is a serial bond.

Security Provisions **Secured bonds** have some part of the issuing corporation's assets serving as security for the loan. Quite often these bonds are secured by a mortgage on the corporation's real estate (buildings or land), in which case they may properly be called **mortgage bonds.** The object of the security feature is to assure bondholders that there are specific assets to which they have first claim in the event that the bond indenture is violated.

Unsecured bonds do not have any specific assets pledged as security against their repayment. Rather, their security rests on the general creditworthiness of the issuing company. Bondholders of unsecured bonds are general creditors of the firm just like the accounts payable creditors. Unsecured bonds are usually called **debenture bonds.** Most bond issues are of this type.

Subordinated bonds are unsecured bonds whose rights to repayment are ranked after, or subordinated to, some other person or group of creditors. Subordinated bonds are unsecured debts that are usually the last obligation the firm pays in the event the firm is liquidated. Their claims do, however, continue to rank ahead of the owners' claims.

| **PAUSE & REFLECT** | If risk and interest rates are directly related, which bond would have a lower interest rate—a debenture or a secured bond? |

Exhibit 15.16 shows the liability section of Kmart's January 25, 1995, balance sheet and a portion of the note to the financial statement that describes the long-term debt of the company. Note the variety of debt instruments used to finance operations and their differing due dates and interest rates.

| **PAUSE & REFLECT** | What type of long-term debt instruments does Kmart use? Is Kmart publicly or privately financed? |

EXHIBIT	15.16	Kmart's Long-Term Debt Disclosure (in $ millions)		

	January 25 1994	January 26 1995
Current liabilities:		
Long-term debt due within one year	$ 236	$ 390
Notes payable	638	918
Accounts payable—trade	2,910	2,763
Accrued payrolls and other liabilities	1,313	1,347
Taxes other than income taxes	272	271
Income taxes	257	35
Total current liabilities	5,626	5,724
Capital lease obligations	1,777	1,720
Long-term debt	**2,011**	**2,227**
Other long-term liabilities (includes store restructuring obligations)	1,583	1,740
Long-term debt:		
Kmart Corporation's long-term debt, net of unamortized discount, is comprised of the following:		
8 3/8% debentures due 2017	—	$ 300
12 1/8% notes due 1995	$ 150	150
8 1/8% notes due 2006	199	199
8 1/4% notes due 2022	99	99
12 1/2% debentures due 2005	100	100
8 3/8% debentures due 2022	100	99
7 3/4% debentures due 2012	198	198
7.95% debentures due 2023	299	299
Medium-term notes due 1995 through 2020 (8.36% weighted average interest rate)	680	745
Mortgages	315	330
Other	107	98
Total	2,247	2,617
Portion due within one year	236	390
Long-term debt	$2,011	$2,227

SUMMARY

Equity and debt are the financing alternatives available to business enterprises. Both have risks and rewards that financial managers must weigh when considering their financing decisions.

Equity financing is provided by owners who accept the risks of ownership in exchange for its financial and psychological rewards.

Debt financing is provided by creditors and creates the risk that the firm's inability to meet interest and principal obligations will result in foreclosure on the firm's assets. Financial leverage created by debt financing creates the potential for boosting the owners' return on investment. Accounting provides vital information to internal and external decision makers about prior financing decisions and the financing alternatives available to the firm in the future.

- Equity financing comprises the contributions of assets to the firm by investors in exchange for an ownership interest and also results when the owners elect to reinvest the firm's earnings.

- The owners' risk is the chance of not getting a satisfactory return on their invested funds or having the potential loss of some or all of their investment.

- Common stock represents the residual ownership in the corporation, while preferred stock represents an ownership interest with special privileges as to dividends and liquidation.

- Treasury stock is the corporation's stock it repurchases for the purpose of either reissuing it to key employees as compensation or selling at a higher price in the market at a later date.

- The market price of stock is the cash price investors are willing to pay for an ownership interest in a corporation.

- Corporations reward their stockholders by distributing to them cash, property, and stock dividends. The board of directors declares dividends on the date of declaration; dividends are distributed on the date of payment to the stockholders who were registered owners on the date of record.

- A stock split occurs when a corporation calls in all its old shares of stock and issues a larger number of new shares. The purpose of a stock split is to reduce the price per share to make the round lots of shares more affordable in the secondary market.

- Financial leverage provides a reward for debt financing. It increases the rate of return on owners' equity by generating a greater return on borrowed funds than the cost of using the borrowed funds. One measure of a firm's financial leverage is its debt-to-equity ratio.

- The three basic notes used as debt instruments are the periodic payment note, the lump-sum note, and the periodic payment and lump-sum note. Each of these notes is the creditor's promise to make a particular set of payments. The present value of the cash flows using the market rate of interest determines the cash proceeds or cash equivalent of these notes.

- Debt financing is acquired from nonpublic and public sources. Nonpublic sources are banks, insurance companies, leasing companies, and individuals. Bonds are the debt instruments used to acquire debt financing from the public.

KEY TERMS

amortized discount The amount that effective interest exceeds cash interest for the time period

amortized premium The amount that cash interest exceeds effective interest for the time period

authorized shares The total number of shares the state has approved for a corporation to sell

bearer bond Bonds that are payable to bearer or person who has physical possession of the bond

bond A long-term debt instrument issued by corporations to raise money from the public

bond certificate The note given to bondholders

bond indenture The bond contract

callable bond A bond that gives the firm issuing the bond the right to buy them back before the maturity date at a specified price

callable preferred stock Preferred stock that gives the issuing corporation the right to repurchase the preferred stock at a stipulated price

capital lease A lease in which a company acquires such a substantial interest in the leased property that, the lessee company, for all practical purposes, owns the asset

carrying value of a note The face value of a note plus its remaining premium or minus its remaining discount

cash dividend A cash distribution in the form of a check drawn on the corporation's bank account that is sent to each stockholder as of a certain date

collateral An asset or group of assets specifically named in a debt agreement to which the creditor has claim if the borrower fails to comply with the terms of the note

common stock The basic ownership unit of a corporation

convertible bond A bond feature that allows bondholders to exchange their bonds for common or preferred stock

convertible preferred stock Preferred stock that gives the stockholder the right to convert (exchange) the preferred shares for other forms of capital, as stated in the corporate charter, at the option of the preferred stockholder

covenants Restrictions that lenders place on the borrowing company to protect the lender's interest

cumulative preferred stock Preferred stock that accumulates unpaid dividends over time

date of declaration The date on which the board of directors announces its decision to pay a dividend

date of payment The date on which the corporation formally pays dividends to stockholders of record

date of record Date on which the secretary of the corporation examines the stock ownership transfer book to determine who is officially registered as a stockholder of the corporation and, therefore, eligible to receive the corporation's dividends

debenture bonds Unsecured bonds— bonds with no specific assets pledged as collateral

debt financing A means for a firm to obtain funds (cash) in exchange for a liability to repay the borrowed funds

debt-to-equity ratio A measure of the relationship between the amount of debt and the amount of owners' equity used to finance the firm

discount on a note The excess of the face value of a note over its cash proceeds

dividends in arrears The amount of cumulative preferred stock dividends not paid in full when stipulated

equity financing A means for a firm to obtain funds in exchange for an ownership interest in the firm

ex-dividend date The last date when an individual can buy the stock of the corporation and still receive the corporation's declared dividend

financial leverage A financing strategy designed to increase the rate of return on owners' investment by generating a greater return on borrowed funds than the cost of using the funds

financial risk The chance that a firm will default on its debt

issued shares The number of authorized shares a corporation has sold to stockholders

lease An agreement to convey the use of a tangible asset from one party to another in return for rental payments

legal capital The portion of stockholders' equity required by state law to be retained for the protection of the corporation's creditors

lump-sum payment note A debt instrument that contains a promise to pay a specific amount of money at the end of a specified period of time

market or effective interest rate The actual interest rate charged on a note's proceeds

mortgage A long-term note secured with real estate, such as land or buildings, as collateral

mortgage bond A bond that is secured with real estate

no-par stock Stock that does not have a minimum price assigned to each share of stock

no-par, stated value stock Stock with a minimum issue price or stated value established by the corporation's board of directors but no par value specified in the charter

operating lease A rental agreement for a period of time substantially shorter than the economic life of the leased asset

outstanding shares The number of shares issued and held outside the corporation

paid-in or contributed capital in excess of par The amount of proceeds received from stock issuance in excess of a stock's par value when it is issued

par value An arbitrary value assigned to shares of capital stock which is approved by the state in which the business is incorporated

participating preferred stock Preferred stock that allows preferred stockholders the right to receive an amount in execss of the stated dividend rate or amount

periodic payment and lump-sum note A debt instrument that combines periodic payments and a final lump-sum payment

periodic payment note A debt instrument that contains a promise to make a series of equal payments consisting of both interest and principal at equal time intervals over a specified time period

preemptive right A right of common stockholders that allows them to maintain their percentage interest in the corporation when it issues new shares of common stock

preferred stock An ownership interest in a corporation with special privileges or preferences as to liquidation and dividends

premium on a note The amount that the cash proceeds of a note exceed its face value

proceeds The amount of cash raised from issuance of a note

property dividend The distribution of specific noncash assets to the stockholders of a corporation

redeemable preferred stock Preferred stock that allows a stockholder to turn in (redeem) the preferred stock for cash at the stockholder's option

registered bonds Bonds that are numbered and made payable in the name of the bond-holder

round lot 100 shares of stock sold together

secured bond A bond that has some part of the issuing corporation's assets serving as security for the loan

serial bond A bond issue that has specified portions of the bond issue coming due periodically over the life of the bond issue

stock dividend The distribution of additional shares of the corporation's stock to existing stockholders

stock split The corporation's recall of its old shares of stock and issuance of a larger number of new shares in their place

subordinated bonds Unsecured bonds whose rights to repayment are ranked after, or subordinated to, some other person or group of creditors

treasury stock The amount of a corporation's repurchased stock that it intends to reissue at a later date

unsecured bonds Bonds that do not have any specific assets pledged as security against their repayment

QUESTIONS

1. Describe the three general sources of financing available to a firm and indicate what is most significant about each.

2. What are the rewards and risks of equity financing?

3. Firms raise equity financing from contributions and reinvested earnings. How do firms use the funds from these sources?

4. What factors are important when determining the amount of earnings to reinvest and the amount of earnings to distribute to the owners of the firm?

5. Compare and contrast the following:
   a. Common stock versus preferred stock.
   b. Cumulative versus participating preferred stock.
   c. Callable versus redeemable preferred stock.
   d. Treasury stock versus issued stock.

6. Distinguish among authorized shares, issued shares, and outstanding shares of stock.

7. What is the distinction between the par value and market value of a stock? Why is the Paid-in Capital in Excess of Par account used when accounting for the issuance of stock?

8. What are the four key dividend dates? Why is each important?

9. How does a stock dividend differ from a cash dividend?

10. What is the distinction between stock splits and stock dividends?

11. What is financial leverage?

12. Describe the risks and rewards of financial leverage.

13. What does a firm's debt-to-equity ratio reflect?

14. Distinguish between the market rate of interest and the face rate of interest on a note.

15. Distinguish among a periodic payment note, a lump-sum note, and a periodic payment and lump-sum note.

16. What is a discount on a note? What is a premium on a note?

17. Compare and contrast the important features of an operating and a capital lease.

18. What distinguishes a bond from other types of debt instruments?

19. Describe how a corporation raises money by issuing bonds.

20. Compare and contrast the following:
   a. Debenture bond versus mortgage bond.
   b. Call feature versus convertible feature.
   c. Registered bond versus bearer bond.

EXERCISES

E 15.1   Phoenix, Inc., is authorized to issue 500,000 shares of its $5 par value common stock and 200,000 shares of $100 par value preferred stock. Phoenix sold 1,000 shares of common stock at $27.50 and 300 shares of its preferred stock at $105 per share. How much capital did Phoenix generate by this sale? What is Phoenix's legal capital?

E 15.2   Fusco Corporation issued 2,100 shares of its $1 par value common stock for $48 per share and 500 shares of its $20 par value preferred stock for $21 per share. What is Fusco's legal capital? What is the amount of capital received in excess of the par value of common and preferred stock? Why is a distinction made between legal capital and total capital?

E 15.3   Washington, Inc., is authorized to issue 500,000 shares of no-par common stock and 300,000 shares of $25 par value preferred stock. During its first year of operation, the company issued 200,000 shares of common stock for $3,400,000 and 50,000 shares of its preferred stock for $1,400,000. The firm had net income of $335,000 for the year and paid dividends of $50,000 during the year. What is the total amount of the firm's stockholders' equity? How much of the firm is financed by contributions by its owners and how much by its operations?

E 15.4   The board of directors of Alexander Company is going to pay a dividend of $32,000 to its common stockholders. Describe what will happen on each of the dates below in relation to this $32,000 dividend.
a. Date of declaration.
b. Ex-dividend date.
c. Date of record.
d. Date of payment.

E 15.5   Jacinta Products has 10,000 shares of 6 percent, $20 par value cumulative preferred stock issued and outstanding. Jacinta has 50,000 shares of $1 par value common stock issued and outstanding. If Jacinta declares a $75,000 dividend, how much of the dividend will the preferred and common stockholders receive if the preferred stock is not in arrears? If Jacinta declares a $235,000 dividend and the preferred stock is two years in arrears, how much of the dividends will the preferred and common stockholders receive?

E 15.6   When the board of directors of Daniels Industries declared a dividend of $600,000, the corporation had 50,000 shares of 8 percent, $50 par value cumulative preferred stock outstanding. There were 200,000 shares of $5 par value common stock outstanding at the time Daniels declared dividends. Determine the dividends the preferred and common stockholders will receive if the preferred stock is one year in arrears.

E 15.7   The board of directors of Columbus Manufacturing, Inc., declared a dividend in 1996, but did not declare dividends in 1995 or 1994. The corporation has 100,000 shares of $1 par common stock authorized and 60,000 shares issued and outstanding. It also has 50,000 shares of 5 percent, $10 par preferred stock authorized, of which 35,000 shares are issued and 30,000 shares are outstanding. The preferred stock is cumulative and two years in arrears. Compute the amount of dividends for common and preferred stockholders if the dividend declared is $45,000. How much will preferred and common stockholders receive if the company declares dividends of $120,000?

E 15.8   Calculate the distribution of dividends in E 15.7 assuming that the preferred stock is noncumulative.

E 15.9   Milo Corporation has 1,000,000 shares of $2 par common stock authorized of which 250,000 shares were issued for $1,250,000 and are currently selling for $10 in the stock exchange. Milo Corporation is considering a two-for-one stock split. What will be the impact of the stock split on Milo Corporation?

E 15.10   Dundee Sales has 150,000 shares of $5 stated value common stock issued and outstanding. The stock has a fair market value of $16 per share on October 14 when the board of directors declared a 10 percent stock dividend to holders of record on October 20. The new shares are to be issued on November 1. Explain the impact of the stock dividend.

E 15.11   Arthur Co. has $500,000 in assets and no liabilities, while Andersen, Inc., has $500,000 in assets and a $300,000 note payable at 10 percent annual interest. Assume that both companies are subject to a tax rate of 30 percent. What is the return on owners' equity for each company if each firm can generate a 20 percent return on its assets? Which company would be a more desirable investment? Why?

E 15.12   The Adocat Corporation had its controller, Donna New, prepare the income statement below:

ADOCAT CORPORATION
Income Statement

Sales	$9,800,000
Cost of goods sold	4,000,000
Gross margin	$5,800,000
Operating expenses	4,000,000
Earnings before interest and taxes	$1,800,000
Interest expense	600,000
Earnings before taxes	$1,200,000
Tax expense (30%)	360,000
Net income	$ 840,000

Adocat Corporation has assets of $15,000,000 and debt of $6,000,000 that carries a 10 percent interest rate. From Donna's information, calculate the rate of return on assets and rate of return on stockholders' equity for Adocat Corporation. What is your assessment of Adocat's financial risk? Justify your position.

E 15.13   The Antinaro Corporation has assets of $6,500,000, debt of $2,300,000, earnings before taxes of $600,000, and a tax rate of 30 percent. Interest on the corporation's debt is $184,000 for the current year. Calculate Antinaro's rate of return on assets, debt-to-equity ratio, and rate of return on stockholders' equity. What is your assessment of Antinaro's financial risk? Justify your position.

E 15.14   On April 1, 1995, Clifford Products borrowed $50,000 at 10 percent on a four-year installment loan. Annual payments starting on April 1, 1996, are $15,774. How much of the first $15,774 is principal and how much is interest? How much of the second $15,774 payment is principal and how much is interest?

E 15.15   On June 1, 1996, John Truillo received a $6,000 noninterest-bearing note from his brother-in-law, Thomas, who has agreed to pay $6,000 at the end of two years. Assume that the market rate of interest is 8 percent on the date the note is made. If the interest is compounded annually, what are the proceeds of the note that Thomas will receive? Prepare an amortization schedule for the life of the note.

E 15.16   Swanson Company issued $600,000 of a 10-year, 9 percent interest note on July 1, 1995, when the market interest rate was 8 percent. The face rate of interest is paid annually. Determine the amount of cash Swanson will receive from the note. Make an amortization table for the note for the first two years of the note's life.

E 15.17   Mid-States Supply has been authorized by its board of directors to issue $5,000,000 in 15-year 12 percent bonds. The bonds are dated May 1, 1995, and interest is payable semiannually on November 1 and May 1.

   On May 1, 1995, the bonds were sold to yield the 12 percent market rate of interest. How much cash did Mid-States Supply raise by issuing the bonds? How much cash would Mid-States Supply raise if the market rate of interest was 10 percent? 14 percent?

E 15.18   Determine the cash received from a $2,000,000 bond issue if the bonds were issued at each of the following prices.
   a. 97 1/2
   b. 101 7/8
   c. 103 1/4
   d. 89 3/8

E 15.19   On December 1, 1995, the Arapaho Corporation issued bonds with a face value of $1,400,000. The bonds mature in 10 years and pay 8 percent interest semiannually. The market rate of interest the bonds were issued at was 10 percent. Prepare an amortization schedule for the first two years of the bond's life.

E 15.20   On September 1, 1996, Semiconductor Industries signed a capital lease for machinery with a fair market value of $25,548.16 for a five-year period. The company made the first of six $5,548.16 annual payments on September 1, 1996. The interest rate is 12 percent. What is the amount of the liability generated by this capital lease? Prepare a schedule showing the first two years' lease payments.

PROBLEMS

P 15.1 List and describe the risks and rewards of equity and debt financing in the following format.

	Risks	Rewards
Debt		
Equity		

P 15.2 Beltway Fabrication Corporation has the following stocks issued and outstanding when the board of directors declared a $225,000 dividend.

Preferred stock: 20,000 shares issued and 18,000 shares outstanding, 8%, $25 par value

Common stock: 100,000 shares issued and outstanding, $10 par value

Determine the amount of dividends each class of stock will receive given the following assumptions.
a. Preferred stock is noncumulative.
b. Preferred stock is cumulative (two years in arrears).
c. Preferred stock is cumulative (one year in arrears).

P 15.3 Kelly Burke is the controller for the TSZ Corporation and has prepared the income statement below:

TSZ CORPORATION
Income Statement

Sales	$6,400,000
Cost of goods sold	3,100,000
Gross margin	$3,300,000
Operating expenses	2,000,000
Earnings before interest and taxes	$1,300,000
Interest expense	270,000
Earnings before taxes	$1,030,000
Tax expense (40%)	412,000
Net income	$ 618,000

Additional information: Total assets $8,662,000, total liabilities $4,500,000.

Required: Calculate the following for TSZ Corporation:
a. Rate of return on assets.
b. Rate of return on equity.
c. Debt-to-equity ratio.
d. Explain the risks of TSZ Corporation using financial leverage.

P 15.4 On August 1, 1996, Brighton Manufacturing arranged to purchase a $50,000 piece of equipment by making a 20 percent down payment and signing a three-year installment loan contract with interest at 12 percent per year for the balance. The loan is to be repaid in semiannual installments starting on February 1, 1997. What is the amount of the payments on the installment note? Prepare a repayment schedule for the first two payments of the loan.

P 15.5 Reynolds Manufacturing acquired a delivery truck on July 1, 1995, that had a list price of $22,000 by paying $2,000 down and signing a two-year $20,000 noninterest-bearing note. The market rate of interest on the date the company acquired the truck was 12 percent.

Required: a. What price did Reynolds pay for the truck?
b. How much interest will Reynolds pay over the life of the note?
c. Set up an amortization schedule for the life of the note.

P 15.6 Determine the amount of cash a company would receive from the following long-term notes:
a. $100,000, 8 percent note, interest payable annually, due in eight years, market rate 9 percent.
b. $500,000, 10 percent note, interest payable semiannually, due in 10 years, market rate 6 percent.
c. $250,000, 12 percent note, interest payable quarterly, due in six years, market interest rate 12 percent.

P 15.7   Sara Stubler is the controller for a construction company and is responsible for buying a new truck that has a sticker price of $18,000. The dealer has offered to finance the truck at 0% interest for 36 months, that is, require payments of $500 per month ($18,000/36 months) for 36 months. The construction company usually borrows funds at 12 percent.

Required: *a.* What cost will Sara assign to the truck and the note if she accepts this offer?

b. If the price of the truck is negotiable, at what price would Sara elect to borrow the money at 12 percent to buy the truck?

P 15.8   Stacey Perry Service recently purchased equipment for $70,000 and leased it to Marcus Machine and Foundry on April 1, 1996. The equipment has an estimated useful life of five years, and Marcus signed a lease to use the equipment for five years.

During the period of the lease, Marcus is responsible for all repairs and maintenance of the leased property. Marcus will make five annual lease payments of $16,510 starting April 1, 1996. The interest rate is 9 percent.

Required: *a.* What makes this lease qualify as a capital lease?

b. What is the value of the equipment and the amount of the liability generated by this transaction?

c. Prepare a lease payment schedule for Marcus Machine and Foundry for the first three lease payments.

P 15.9   Wheat Corporation issued $10,000,000 of bonds on September 1, 1995. The bonds have a face interest rate of 8 percent that is paid semiannually on March 1 and September 1. The bonds mature in 10 years.

For each of the independent situations below, calculate the price of the bond and set up an amortization table for the first year of the bond's life.

Situation 1: The market rate of interest is 6 percent.

Situation 2: The market rate of interest is 10 percent.

Situation 3: The market rate of interest is 8 percent.

P 15.10   Appleseed Corporation has a $5,000,000 bond issue that has a carrying value of $4,932,125 as of September 1, 1997. For each of the scenarios below, describe what happens and the impact that each scenario would have on Appleseed's financial structure. Consider each scenario an independent event.

a. Appleseed Corporation's bonds have a call price of 102 and, on September 1, 1997, the corporation exercised the call feature on the entire bond issue.

b. Appleseed Corporation's bonds have a 50-to-1 common stock conversion feature; that is, one bond is convertible into 50 shares of Wheat Corporation's common stock. On September 1, 1997, the bondholders converted 25 percent of the bonds into common stock.

COMPUTER APPLICATIONS

CA 15.1   Donahoe Company needs to borrow $500,000 to finance an addition to its manufacturing facilities. It has obtained an installment note at 12 percent interest for 20 years. Payments will be made annually beginning one year from today.

Required: Use a computer spreadsheet package.

a. What is the amount of each yearly payment?

b. Prepare a payment schedule that indicates the amount of each payment, how much of each payment is interest, how much of each payment is principal, and the remaining balance on the loan.

CA 15.2   Winifred Corporation needs to buy a new computer system. Compuland has agreed to sell them a computer system and accept a $60,000, ten-year, noninterest-bearing note payable. The market rate of interest is currently 10 percent.

Required: Use a computer spreadsheet package.

a. What is the value of the computer, that is, what is the present value of the noninterest-bearing note?

b. Prepare a schedule that indicates the interest cost associated with the loan each year.

CA 15.3 Rick Lakey Enterprises plans to issue $750,000 of 15-year, 10 percent interest bonds. The bonds pay interest semiannually. The market rate of interest at the time of issue is 8 percent.

Required: Use a computer spreadsheet package.
  a. How much cash will Rick Lakey receive when they issue the bonds (ignore issue costs)?
  b. Prepare a schedule that indicates over the life of the bonds, the amount of the semiannual payments, the interest cost for each semiannual period, and the carrying value at the end of each period.

CASES

C 15.1 In the summer of 1992, the airline industry entered into a price war and airline ticket sales jumped dramatically as the price of tickets dropped. Despite the increase in the sale of tickets, most airlines claimed this pricing strategy hurt their short-term financial position. Keeping pace with these price cuts forced Braniff into bankruptcy. How could increasing sales cause financial hardships in the airline industry? What role did the firm's leverage play in this scenario? (Resource material can be found in the disclosure database located in the library. Examine the financial statements of several airlines for the fiscal years ending in 1991.)

C 15.2 Sun Valley Enterprises needs to acquire a new piece of equipment that costs $100,000 and is expected to be useful for approximately five years. There are two alternatives for financing the acquisition of the equipment.

Alternative 1. Lease the equipment for five years as a capital lease. There would be five lease payments of $24,769 each, the first of which would be paid on the date the equipment was acquired.

Alternative 2. Purchase the equipment outright for $100,000 from the proceeds of a $100,000, five-year, 8 percent, note payable. The loan would require annual interest payments of $8,000 and repayment of the principal at the end of five years.

Which of these two financing alternatives would be best for Sun Valley Enterprises? Why?

CRITICAL THINKING

CT 15.1 The chief financial officer of Nafta Company wants to finance the acquisition of a new, $1,300,000 manufacturing facility in Canada. Nafta already has $1,300,000 of debt and a debt-to-equity ratio of 1.3 to 1. What will Nafta's debt-to-equity ratio be if it incurs this debt? Write a memo to Nafta's CFO outlining the factors he should consider before taking this action.

CT 15.2 Each of the following $1,000,000 debt instruments is subject to a 10 percent market rate of interest. Which of the following is the most expensive debt to use?
  a. $1,000,000 noninterest-bearing, 10-year note
  b. $1,000,000 bond with an 8 percent face rate that is paid annually; the bond is due in 10 years.
  c. $1,000,000 note payable, with a 10-year life, and a 12 percent face rate of interest that is paid annually.

ETHICAL CHALLENGES

EC 15.1 In 1995, the President of CB Corporation expects that the firm will generate a severe loss in 1996. He has told the members of the board of directors and other key stockholders that the corporation will buy their shares of common stock before the stock takes a dramatic drop. He says that he believes the earnings will improve in 1997 and that he will offer these treasury shares to these key stockholders before the stock price goes up again. He says he views this as compensation for their loyal service to the corporation. What is your opinion of this offer?

EC 15.2 Bob Pool is the president of Pooling Company, a sole proprietorship. Bob wants to incorporate because he recognizes the advantages of limited liability and the ability to raise additional funds by issuing stock. He has proposed issuing a special class of common stock that is convertible into long-term debt, but to no more than 10 wealthy stockholders. This select group of common stockholders could convert their stock into a debt instrument that would have precedence over any other debt in the event of the company's liquidation. Comment on Mr. Pool's convertible common stock.

CHAPTER 16

Planning for Investing Activities

Learning Objectives

1. Describe the capital budgeting process.
2. Explain the net present value method of discounted cash flow analysis.
3. Describe the time-adjusted rate of return method of discounted cash flow analysis.
4. Explain the impact of taxes on the net present value method.
5. Describe how judgment and uncertainty impact the capital budgeting process.

In its 1995 cash flow statement, IBM reported that it had invested $4.744 billion in cash for plant, rental machines, and other property during fiscal 1995. IBM's management continually faces investment decisions involving long-lived assets that make it possible for a company to conduct its daily operations. How does IBM decide whether to buy a new office building, keep or buy new manufacturing equipment, or lease or buy a new warehouse? Clearly, the company's management wants to acquire only those long-term investments that increase the wealth of the firm. How do IBM's managers decide whether an investment in plant and equipment will generate a return sufficient to merit its acquisition?

In the business environment, the purpose of any investment is to produce a return that is satisfactory for the investor. IBM's December 31, 1995, balance sheet reports that its total investment in plant, rental machines, and other property amounts to $16.579 billion. IBM's management invested in these assets with the expectation of generating a return on investment that would be large enough to satisfy its stockholders.

Capital budgeting is the process managers use for analysis and selection of the long-term investments of a business. Because the amounts spent on long-term investments, such as buildings, equipment, and even other businesses, are usually quite large and, therefore, affect the long-term profitability of the firm, they require systematic and careful consideration.

The capital budgeting process requires cooperative input from functional departments throughout the organization. For example, without the marketing department's forecast of demand for the firm's services or products, it would be difficult for a firm to assess its potential need for plant expansion. Without the production department's recommendations for the timely acquisition of machines to cut costs and improve product quality, it might be difficult to maintain efficiency. The finance department fulfills an important capital budgeting function by monitoring the cost and sources of funds needed to pay for selected projects. Finally, the accounting department collects, organizes, analyzes, and distributes the information necessary to facilitate capital budgeting decisions.

In this chapter we examine the capital budgeting process, which includes defining the tools used to evaluate the viability of potential long-term investments.

THE CAPITAL BUDGETING PROCESS

While the capital budgeting process itself is unique to each firm or enterprise, its four basic processes apply in all situations. Notice that the capital budgeting process follows the planning, performing, and evaluating cycle.

1. Identifying long-term investment opportunities.

2. Selecting the appropriate investments.

3. Financing the selected investments.

4. Evaluating the investments.

We address each of these in turn.

Identifying Long-Term Investment Opportunities

The capital budgeting process usually involves the acquisition of operational investments. These assets provide the infrastructure of the business enterprise, that is, the facilities and equipment necessary for firms to conduct their basic business activities. For example, a new car dealership needs a showroom and a car lot in order to sell cars. IBM needs equipment to produce its computers and patents to protect the company from duplication of its products by other firms. Physicians need offices and medical equipment to provide quality health care services to their patients.

In order to identify investment opportunities, managers must recognize what is included in the cost of a firm's long-term investments. In addition, they must understand both their motives for making these investments and the organizational and other mechanisms that identify the need for operational investments.

What Expenditures Are Included in the Cost of a Firm's Long-Term Operational Investments? There are many expenditures that you might not normally think of as being part of an investment that are included in its cost. In addition to the purchase price of an asset, the related sales tax, freight charges, brokerage fees, and installation costs all become part of an investment's (asset's) cost when they are reasonable and necessary to get the asset ready for its intended use. For example, if IBM pays $300,000 for an electronic scanner, $500 for freight charges, and $10,000 for installation, the cost of the scanner would be $310,500 because all of these expenditures are reasonable and necessary to get the scanner ready for its intended use.

Why Make the Investment?   There are three significant reasons that companies make capital investments. The first is the need to replace worn out or unproductive operating assets, such as buildings, machinery, and equipment. The critical factor in deciding to replace assets is knowing what constitutes a worn out or unproductive asset. This decision must come from operating personnel who are familiar with the capabilities of the old assets and their proposed replacements.

Another reason to make a capital expenditure is to expand the business's operating capacity. This decision is stimulated by increased demand for existing products and services or the demand for new products or services. Usually, the marketing department identifies these opportunities. Once the marketing department quantifies the production necessary to meet the increased demand, they inform the firm's production managers. The production managers use the marketing department's projections to determine the specifications of the asset(s) that can meet the increased demand.

Finally, capital expenditures are made to comply with mandates of the government. In order to comply with environmental or safety regulations, companies are often required to make capital expenditures that alter their normal operating activities. For example, power companies that use coal-fired generating plants are required to install costly scrubbers to reduce the pollutants emitted from their power plants that cause acid rain, smog, or other environmental hazards.

What Mechanisms Identify the Need for Capital Expenditures?   An organization's strategic planning document, which covers a 5- to 10-year time period, is one means of identifying long-term investment opportunities. Such documents reflect top management's vision of how the organization will grow and change during the period of the plan. Long-term plans identify and include the required capital expenditures associated with changes anticipated by management, for example, replacement of existing equipment or plant expansions.

Suppose IBM created a five-year plan in 1996 that called for the expansion of its manufacturing facilities in 2001. The plan would outline management's assumptions about both the demand for IBM computers and the profitability of the company for the specified period. While the goals in the five-year plan are subject to change as each year passes, this document helps management focus its efforts on the basic company goals. The planning document is rolled forward each year when management reassesses its long-term commitments in relation to the company's yearly performance.

Long-term planning documents are not the only means of identifying investment opportunities. Because businesses exist in a dynamic environment, management must be able to identify and evaluate business opportunities whenever they occur, even if they are unexpected. For example, if IBM becomes aware of a new copier on the market that could reduce the company's copying cost by 20 percent, the company should begin the capital budgeting process to determine if it should replace its existing copiers, even though replacement might not have been planned until some time in the future.

Selecting Appropriate Investments

Once management identifies a potential capital expenditure, it evaluates the investment to assess whether it is capable of generating a satisfactory rate of return for the firm. Any return that is greater than or equal to the firm's cost of capital is considered a satisfactory return.

Cost of Capital   A firm's **cost of capital** is the weighted-average cost of a firm's debt and equity financing. It represents the amount of return that the assets of the firm must generate in order to satisfy *both* creditors and owners. Recall that the cost of debt financing is the rate of interest the creditors receive for the use of their money, and the cost of equity financing is the rate of return the owners receive for the use of

IBM may decide to purchase these new copiers, if they determine that the new copier's efficiency will outweigh the cost involved to replace existing copiers.

their money. Owners expect the firm to provide a return on their investment, and, if they are not satisfied, they can dispose of their holdings in the firm or vote to replace the management of the firm. Calculating the amount of return that owners expect is unique to each firm.

Calculating a firm's cost of capital is complicated, and the following example simplifies the process in order to illustrate the concept. Assume that Benchmark Corporation is financed by using $1,000,000 of debt and $3,000,000 of stockholders' equity. If the debt has an interest rate of 12 percent, and the stockholders demand a 16 percent rate of return, what is the cost of capital? Exhibit 16.1 shows that Benchmark's cost of capital is 15 percent. This amount is the weighted average of the returns demanded by the creditors and owners and represents the minimum rate of return that the firm's assets must generate to keep *both* creditors and stockholders satisfied.

Ignoring the complicating factor of income taxes, assume that Benchmark's earnings before interest for the year are $560,000, or a 14 percent rate of return on the $4,000,000 of the firm's assets. Exhibit 16.2 shows that, while the creditors of the firm would receive their required amount of interest (12%), the remaining income ($440,000) is not sufficient to generate the 16 percent rate of return demanded by the stockholders. Instead, it generates only an 14.67 percent rate of return.

However, when the rate of return on assets (Earnings before interest/Total assets), discussed in Chapter 25, meets or exceeds the cost of capital, both creditors and

EXHIBIT	16.1	Benchmark Corporation—Cost of Capital

Capital Structure

Assets	=	Liabilities	+	Stockholders' Equity
$4,000,000	=	$1,000,000	+	$3,000,000

Source of Financing	Amount Financed	Cost of Financing
Liabilities	$1,000,000	12%
Stockholders' equity	3,000,000	16
Total amount financed	$4,000,000	

$$\text{Ratio of debt to total financing} = \frac{\$1,000,000}{\$4,000,000} = .25$$

$$\text{Ratio of stockholders' equity (SE) to total financing} = \frac{\$3,000,000}{\$4,000,000} = .75$$

Cost of Capital (CC)

$CC = (\text{Cost of debt})(\text{Debt ratio}) + (\text{Cost of } SE)(SE \text{ ratio})$
$CC = (12\%)(.25) + (16\%)(.75)$
$CC = 15\%$

EXHIBIT | 16.2 | Return on Assets Less Than Cost of Capital

Income available for distribution	$560,000
Less: Interest to creditors	(120,000)
Residual distribution for stockholders	$440,000

$$\text{Return for creditors} = \frac{\text{Interest}}{\text{Debt}} = \frac{\$120,000}{\$1,000,000} = 12\%$$

$$\text{Return for stockholders} = \frac{\text{Income}}{\text{Stockholders' equity}} = \frac{\$440,000}{\$3,000,000} = 14.67\%$$

EXHIBIT | 16.3 | Return on Assets Greater Than Cost of Capital

Income available for distribution	$640,000
Less: Interest to creditors	(120,000)
Residual distribution for stockholders	$520,000

$$\text{Return for creditors} = \frac{\text{Interest}}{\text{Debt}} = \frac{\$120,000}{\$1,000,000} = 12\%$$

$$\text{Return for stockholders} = \frac{\text{Income}}{\text{Stockholders' equity}} = \frac{\$520,000}{\$3,000,000} = 17.33\%$$

stockholders are satisfied. Exhibit 16.3 illustrates how a 16 percent return on Benchmark's assets ($640,000/$4,000,000) would satisfy both creditors and stockholders.

Because the assets produced a 16 percent rate of return, which is greater than the 15 percent cost of capital (Exhibit 16.1), the creditors' interest demands (12%) were met, and the stockholders' demands for a 16 percent return were exceeded (17.33%).

This illustrates the importance of a firm's cost of capital in management's decisions regarding acceptable investments in the capital budgeting process. The cost of capital is also called a *hurdle rate*. Unless management's analysis indicates that the expected rate of return on a long-term asset meets or exceeds the hurdle rate, the investment in the asset would not be able to satisfy both the creditors' and owners' desire for a satisfactory return.

Cash Flow Analysis   In order to estimate the rate of return of a potential investment, decision makers must be able to estimate the future cash inflows and outflows attributable to the investment if it is acquired. These cash flows represent the future costs and benefits of acquiring the asset. Management must be able to estimate cash flows with as much care and precision as possible because the accuracy of the estimates directly affects the quality of the investment decision.

Financing Selected Investments

The decision about how to finance capital expenditures comes only after management has made a decision to acquire them. The firm has a choice of using debt or equity financing, and the firm's finance department must consider how the financing decision will affect the financial leverage of the firm.

Once financial management makes the financing decision, the implications of this decision are introduced into the capital expenditure and financing budgets. The **capital expenditure budget** presents information regarding the amount and timing of the capital expenditures planned for the designated time period. The **financing budget** outlines the amounts and sources of funds needed to finance the firm's investments for the designated time period.

The components of an organizational budget illustrated in Exhibit 16.4 show how the capital expenditure and financing budgets interface with the overall budgeting process. The investing and financing budgets at the end of a fiscal period affect the

EXHIBIT | **16.4**

Components of an Organizational Budget

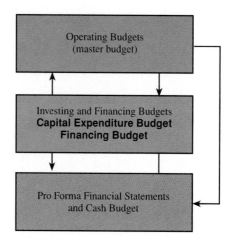

operating budgets being developed for the coming period. Once the operating budgets are developed, specific decisions about what to buy and how to finance these acquisitions are built into the investing and financing budgets. Finally, all of these budget data appear in the pro forma financial statements and cash budget of the firm.

Evaluating Investments

Evaluating capital expenditures occurs in two phases. In the **acquisition phase,** the first phase of evaluation, the managerial accountant is responsible for monitoring costs incurred in conjunction with the asset's acquisition. The purpose of this phase is to control the cost of the project by identifying how the actual acquisition expenditures deviate from budgeted acquisition expenditures in a timely manner and to hold accountable those responsible for the deviations.

The second evaluation phase, called the **postaudit,** involves comparing the cash flow projections made in preacquisition analysis with actual cash flows generated by the asset. The postaudit evaluates the accuracy of the original cash flow projections and methods and assumptions used. It is a starting point for finding ways of improving future cash flow estimates.

Accountants play a vital role in the entire capital budgeting process. They are responsible for gathering the estimated projections and actual data, preparing timely reports on their findings, and distributing these findings to those involved in planning for, acquiring, and operating the capital assets. The accountants' reports assist decision makers in the capital acquisition process and also are useful for gaining insights into how to improve the capital budgeting process itself.

DISCOUNTED CASH FLOW ANALYSIS

Discounted cash flow analysis is a method to evaluate investments that uses the time value of money to assess whether the investment's expected rate of return is greater than the firm's cost of capital. If the expected rate of return is greater than the firm's cost of capital, the firm should acquire the asset.

Discounting cash flows refers to the practice of finding the present value of expected future cash flows. The rate of return used to determine present values is also called the *discount rate.*

Net Present Value Method

The **net present value** method of discounted cash flow analysis requires that decision makers find the present value of an investment's estimated future cash flows by using the firm's cost of capital as the discount rate. If the cost of the asset is less than the present value of the future cash flows, the investment's return is greater than the firm's cost of capital, making it a favorable investment.

The net present value (NPV) method includes the following four steps:

1. Identify the timing and amount of all cash inflows and outflows associated with the potential investment over its anticipated life.

2. Calculate the present value of the future cash flows using the firm's cost of capital as the discount rate.

3. Compute the net present value by subtracting the initial cash outflows necessary to acquire the asset from the present value of the future cash flows.

4. Decide to make or reject the investment in the capital asset. If the net present value is zero or positive, the proposed investment is acceptable. If the NPV is negative, the company should reject the project.

The following example illustrates the net present value method. Assume that IBM is considering the acquisition of a new chip press that would cost $75,925 and have a useful life of four years. The chip press will save IBM $25,000 per year over its life. If IBM's cost of capital is 10 percent, should it acquire the chip press?

Exhibit 16.5 illustrates the four steps in the NPV method of analysis used to resolve this capital budgeting decision. Notice that the current cash outflow would be $75,925 to acquire the chip press and that the related inflows over the next four years for IBM are expected to be $25,000 per year.

EXHIBIT	16.5	Net Present Value Method—IBM Chip Press

Step 1. Identify the Cash Flows.

		Time (years)			
	0	**1**	**2**	**3**	**4**
Cash to acquire	($75,925)				
Cash inflows		$25,000	$25,000	$25,000	$25,000

Step 2. Find Present Value of Future Cash Flows.

$$\text{Present value of annuity} = \text{Annuity} \times P_{4,10\%}$$
$$= \$25,000 \times 3.170$$
$$= \$79,250$$

Step 3. Compute NPV.

Present value of cash flows (see step 2)	$79,250
Initial cost of chip press	(75,925)
Net present value	$ 3,325

Step 4. Accept or Reject Asset Acquisition.
Accept because the NPV is positive; therefore, the rate of return on the chip press is greater than the firm's cost of capital.

The decision, in this case, is to acquire the new chip press because its NPV is positive, $3,325 (step 3). This indicates that if the cash flows occur as projected, the new chip press will have a greater return than IBM's 10 percent cost of capital, or the firm's hurdle rate of return. While the net present value method reveals that the rate of return on the chip press is greater than the cost of capital, it does *not* reveal what the expected rate of return is.

What NPV Tells Us Why does a positive NPV indicate that the rate of return is greater than the cost of capital? The answer lies in understanding step 2 of the analysis illustrated in Exhibit 16.5. The present value of the future cash flows represents the maximum price that IBM would pay for the chip press because it is based on the minimum rate of return, 10 percent, that IBM would accept. Stated another way, if IBM invested $79,250 in an asset and received $25,000 each year for four years, it would recover its original investment and receive a 10 percent return on its investment. Exhibit 16.6 illustrates how the cash flows expected (column 2) would provide both a 10 percent return *on* a $79,250 investment (column 3) and the return *of* the $79,250 initial investment (column 4).

EXHIBIT	16.6	Proof of 10 Percent Return		
(1) Time (years)	(2) Cash Inflow	(3) 10 Percent Return on Investment	(4) Return of Investment	(5) Investment
0				$79,250.00
1	$25,000	$7,925.00	$17,075.00	62,175.00
2	25,000	6,217.50	18,782.50	43,392.50
3	25,000	4,339.25	20,660.75	22,731.75
4	25,000	2,268.25*	22,731.75	–0–

*Difference due to rounding.

The maximum price that IBM would pay for the machine is $79,250 given the projected cash flows and IBM's desired minimum rate of return of 10 percent (IBM's cost of capital). If IBM pays an amount *greater* than $79,250, and the $25,000 cash flows occur as projected, the investment in the new equipment would yield a rate of return that is *less* than the required 10 percent.

If IBM pays any amount *less* than $79,250, and the $25,000 cash flows occur as expected, the new equipment will yield a rate of return *greater* than 10 percent. The positive NPV of $3,325 means that IBM is paying less than the amount required to generate a 10 percent return and, therefore, will receive a rate of return higher than 10 percent. Thus, if an investment of $79,250 that produces $25,000 cash at the end of each year for the next four years yields a 10 percent return, then IBM's investment of $75,925 that generates the same cash flows must earn more than a 10 percent return on the investment. How much more than 10 percent is determined by using the time-adjusted rate of return, discussed in the next section.

What NPV Does Not Represent A project's NPV *does not* represent the amount of profit or loss that the asset will realize. For example, if the estimated cash flows for IBM's chip press were $23,000 per year, the present value of the cash flows would be $72,910 ($23,000 × 3.170), and the project would have a negative net present value of $(3,015), or $72,910 – $75,925 (price of the chip press). This does not mean that IBM would lose $3,015. Rather, it means that the maximum price IBM should pay for a chip press to produce four annual $23,000 cash flows yielding a 10 percent return would be $72,910. Before IBM could earn a 10 percent rate of return, the seller would have to lower the price of the machine by $3,015. If the seller is unwilling to lower the price by at least $3,015, then IBM should not buy the equipment.

Time-Adjusted Rate of Return Method

The **time-adjusted rate of return (TARR**—also known as *internal rate of return*) is another discounted cash flow method used to determine whether a firm should acquire a long-term asset. It requires using the cost of the potential investment as the present value of the projected cash flows in order to determine the rate of return of the proposed investment. (In contrast, the NPV method discounts the future cash flows by using the cost of capital to determine the present value of the projected cash flows.) However, the time-adjusted rate of return calculates the rate of return on the investment given the future cash flows and then compares the TARR to the cost of capital to see if it is higher or lower than the hurdle rate. The TARR method has three steps:

1. Identify the timing and amount of all cash inflows and outflows associated with the investment over its life.

2. Determine the time-adjusted rate of return.

3. Decide to make or reject the investment in the asset under consideration. Make the investment if its time-adjusted rate of return is greater than the cost of capital; otherwise, reject the investment.

EXHIBIT 16.7 | Time-Adjusted Rate of Return

Step 1. Identify the Cash Flows.

		Time (years)			
	0	**1**	**2**	**3**	**4**
Cash outflows	($75,925)				
Cash inflows		$25,000	$25,000	$25,000	$25,000

Step 2. Calculate the Time-Adjusted Rate of Return.

$$\text{Annuity} \times P_{4,?\%} = \text{Cost of the investment}$$
$$\$25,000 \times P_{4,?\%} = \$75,925$$
$$P_{4,?\%} = \$75,925/\$25,000$$
$$P_{4,?\%} = 3.037$$
$$?\% = 12\%$$

Step 3. Accept or Reject the Acquisition.

Acquire the chip press because the time-adjusted rate of return is greater than the cost of capital.

$$TARR\ 12\% > CC\ 10\%$$

Exhibit 16.7 shows the time-adjusted rate of return for IBM's new chip press. In this illustration, the cash flows in step 1 are the same as those featured in the net present value method shown in Exhibit 16.5. We use the present value of an ordinary annuity to calculate the time-adjusted rate of return. The cost of the new machine, $75,925, is the present value of the four-payment, $25,000 annuity. That is, the machine is expected to generate four $25,000 payments, but the rate of return that generates this cash flow is still unknown.

Calculating the rate of return is possible because it is the only unknown element in the present value of an ordinary annuity formula. Dividing the annuity ($25,000) into the price of the press ($75,925) produces the present value factor of an ordinary annuity, 3.037. The rate is found in Table 4 at the end of the book by locating four payments on the left side of the table and then moving across the row until finding the 3.037 factor under the 12 percent column. Thus, the machine's time-adjusted rate of return is 12 percent.

The decision to acquire the new equipment is very straightforward. IBM should acquire the new machine because it is expected to generate a 12 percent rate of return, which is greater than its 10 percent cost of capital.

The Effect of Uneven Cash Flows on Net Present Value

The discounted cash flow methods just illustrated used equal cash flows each period. In reality, cash flows generated by operating assets are seldom constant over time. We now illustrate how to use the net present value method when cash flows are uneven. Exhibit 16.8 shows, in step 1, a new set of cash flows that the chip press is expected to generate if it is acquired. As you can see, there are now both cash inflows

EXHIBIT 16.8 | Uneven Cash Flows

Step 1. Identify the Cash Flows.

		Time (years)			
	0	**1**	**2**	**3**	**4**
Cash to acquire	$(75,925)				
Operating cash flows:					
Cash inflows		$45,000	$49,000	$47,000	$46,000
Cash outflows		(15,000)	(23,000)	(23,000)	(26,000)
Net cash flows	$(75,925)	$30,000	$26,000	$24,000	$20,000

EXHIBIT | 16.9 | Net Present Value of Uneven Cash Flows

Step 2. Find Present Value of Future Cash Flows.

Time (years)	Net Cash Flow (from Exhibit 16.8)	×	10 Percent PV Factor	=	Present Value
1	$30,000	×	.9091	=	$27,273
2	$26,000	×	.8264	=	$21,486
3	$24,000	×	.7513	=	$18,031
4	$20,000	×	.6830	=	$13,660
Present value of future cash flows				=	$80,450

Step 3. Compute NPV.

Present value of future cash flows	$80,450
Initial cost of the asset	75,925
Net present value	$ 4,525

Step 4. Accept or Reject Asset Acquisition.
Acquire the chip press because NPV is positive; therefore, the return earned on the asset is greater than the cost of capital.

and cash outflows. The difference between the inflows and outflows in each year is called the *net cash flow*. In this case, the net cash flows decrease in each year of the asset's four-year life.

To calculate the net present value of the cash flows, it is necessary to find the present value of each of the future cash flows using the present value of the amount of $1. Exhibit 16.9 shows step 2, discounting each year's cash flows using the 10 percent cost of capital. The sum of each of these discounted cash flows is the present value of all the future cash flows and represents the maximum price the firm should pay for the new machine. The remaining steps of the net present value method show that the net present value of $4,525 is positive, and that the initial cost of the asset is less than the maximum price of $80,450 IBM could pay. Therefore, IBM should buy the chip press.

PAUSE & REFLECT

In both the even and uneven cash flow scenarios, the cash flows for the four-year period totaled $100,000. Why is the present value of the future cash flows in step 2 larger for the uneven cash flow example, $80,450, than for the even cash flow example, $79,250?

Advantages and Disadvantages of the Discounted Cash Flow Methods

The major advantage of the time-adjusted rate of return method is that once it is calculated, the decision about whether to make a capital expenditure is rather straightforward. If the cost of capital is lower than the time-adjusted rate of return on the project, the project should be accepted. If the cost of capital is greater than the TARR, the project should be rejected.

The disadvantage of TARR is the time-consuming trial-and-error process required when dealing with uneven cash flows. In contrast, the net present value method is easier to compute because its requirements include only the firm's cost of capital, the projected cash flows, and the initial cost of the project.

The major advantage of the net present value method is that it can be adjusted for risk, while the time-adjusted rate of return cannot. The further into the future cash flows are projected, the riskier they become because the cash flows are more uncertain. The net present value method adjusts for this risk by incorporating higher discount rates for later cash flows. The TARR cannot adjust for this risk because it is based on the assumption that the asset produces only one rate of return over its entire life.

For example, assume IBM is considering the acquisition of a building that it expects to hold seven years. Exhibit 16.10 lists the cash flows along with the discount

EXHIBIT	16.10	Risk-Adjusted Cash Flows		
		Time (years)	Net Cash Inflow	Discount Rate
		1	$20,000	12%
		2	30,000	12
		3	35,000	12
		4	43,000	13
		5	45,000	13
		6	40,000	15
		7	39,000	15

rates that IBM is going to use to assess the acquisition. Note that in years four and five, the discount rate is 13 percent and in years six and seven the rate is 15 percent. These higher discount rates reflect IBM's desire to adjust for the risk associated with the greater uncertainty in projecting cash flow for these later periods.

Assumptions Underlying Discounted Cash Flow Analysis

There are three common assumptions underlying discounted cash flow analysis:

1. **All cash flows are known with certainty.** Although cash flow projections are really estimates and, therefore, are subject to uncertainty, we are willing to accept this assumption. The net present value method can adjust for the risk of uncertainty without increasing the complexity of the model.

2. **Cash flows are assumed to occur at the end of the time period.** Although cash flows occur throughout the year, any distortion caused by this assumption is not sufficient to significantly affect the decision.

3. **Cash inflows are immediately reinvested in another project that earns a return for the company.** This assumption does not take into consideration the fact that cash flows might be distributed to stockholders or creditors. The NPV method assumes that the cash flows are reinvested at a rate equal to the cost of capital. The time-adjusted rate of return model assumes that the return is reinvested at the project's rate of return.

These assumptions, while not always realistic, provide the structure that makes net present value and time-adjusted rate of return effective capital budgeting tools, if the decision maker considers these limitations.

The Source of Cash Flows

The discounted cash flow methods incorporate cash flows into the models because the acquisition and operation of capital assets produce cash flows. What is not always obvious about this process is the source of these cash flows. The following description reviews the typical cash inflows and outflows used in capital budgeting projects.

The initial cash outflows are the expenditures made to acquire the asset in addition to other acquisition costs such as freight charges, sales tax, and installation costs. Another possible related cash outflow that could occur is an increase in working capital. Working capital, or the excess of current assets over current liabilities, increases when a project requires more cash on hand, supplies, and inventories. When acquiring a new manufacturing facility, for example, a company might need additional cash and inventory to operate the facility on a day-to-day basis.

Cash inflows occur during the investment's life because the investment generates revenues, decreases operating expenses, or both. For capital budgeting purposes, a decrease in operating expenses is considered to be a cash inflow because it increases the cash flows of the firm. At the end of the investment's life, cash inflows occur when the amount of working capital necessary to operate the facility is reduced and the investment is sold for salvage.

In discounted cash flow analysis, the cash flows can be either certain and precise or quite uncertain and imprecise. For example, there is little uncertainty about the amount of cash outflow necessary to acquire the asset. However, the amount of cash inflow from the sale of the asset at the end of its useful life is much more uncertain.

Managers should make their cash flow projections with the best information possible, including information obtained from postaudit evaluations that help evaluate cash flow projections and find ways to improve the process of projecting cash flows.

Income Taxes and Cash Flows

Income taxes can significantly affect capital budgeting decisions because they change both the amount of cash inflows and cash outflows used in the capital budgeting process. Understanding how income taxes affect discounted cash flow techniques is essential to the proper use of these methods.

Because income taxes are paid based on the amount of income a business generates, they typically represent cash outflows. Proposed capital expenditures will affect the firm's income and, therefore, the tax liability of the firm.

After-Tax Cash Flows After-tax cash flows are the estimated cash flows associated with a potential investment *after* considering the impact of income taxes. Determining the after-tax cash flows is the first step in the discounted cash flow analysis used by for-profit businesses.

Exhibit 16.11 presents the Benchmark Corporation's accrual basis and cash basis income statements in sections A and B, respectively. These statements show how capital expenditures impact the income statements, the company's taxes, and the firm's cash flows.

Assume that the tax rate for Benchmark is 40 percent, that it collects all revenues, and that all expenses, except depreciation, are paid with cash. Benchmark's accrual basis accounting income (net income) is $36,000 (section A) and includes depreciation expense of $10,000. The company's cash basis income is $46,000 (section B) because depreciation expense is not included since it is a noncash expense.

After-Tax Cash Inflows Capital expenditures can generate taxable cash inflows and, consequently, an increase in the amount of income taxes due. An after-tax cash inflow is the difference between the taxable cash inflow and the amount of tax paid on it.

Exhibit 16.12 shows how Benchmark's cash basis income statement, shown in section B, is affected by two independent situations: (1) when cash sales increase [column 2] and (2) when cash operating expenses decrease [column 3]. Note that the

EXHIBIT	16.11	Benchmark Corporation Income Statements: Accrual and Cash Basis

BENCHMARK CORPORATION
Income Statement

A. Accrual Basis

Sales	$100,000
Operating expenses	(30,000)
Depreciation expense	(10,000)
Income before taxes	$ 60,000
Tax expense*	(24,000)
Net income	$ 36,000

B. Cash Basis

Sales	$100,000
Operating expenses	(30,000)
Depreciation expense	–0–
Cash before taxes	$ 70,000
Tax paid*	(24,000)
Net income	$ 46,000

*40% × Accrual basis income.

EXHIBIT | 16.12 | Tax Effects on Increased Cash Flows

BENCHMARK CORPORATION
Income Statement

| | (1) | Increases in Cash Due to | |
		(2) Increase in Cash Sales	(3) Decrease in Cash Operating Expenses
A. Accrual Basis			
Sales	$100,000	$110,000	$100,000
Operating expenses	(30,000)	(30,000)	(20,000)
Depreciation expense	(10,000)	(10,000)	(10,000)
Income before taxes	$ 60,000	$ 70,000	$ 70,000
Tax expense*	(24,000)	(28,000)	(28,000)
Net income	$ 36,000	$ 42,000	$ 42,000
B. Cash Basis			
Sales	$100,000	$110,000	$100,000
Operating expenses	(30,000)	(30,000)	(20,000)
Depreciation expense	–0–	–0–	–0–
Cash before taxes	$ 70,000	$ 80,000	$ 80,000
Tax paid	(24,000)	(28,000)	(28,000)
Cash from operations	$ 46,000	$ 52,000	$ 52,000

*40% × Accrual basis income ($60,000 × .4) in column *1* and ($70,000 × .4) in columns *2* and *3*.

$10,000 increase in income before taxes (section A), created by both situations *2* and *3*, increases the income tax paid by $4,000 (from $24,000 [$60,000 × .4] in column *1* to $28,000 [$70,000 × .4]) in the scenarios described in columns *2* and *3*. Therefore, when cash inflows increase by $10,000 in columns *2* and *3* of section B, cash outflows will increase by $4,000 due to the increase in taxes paid, and the after-tax cash inflow is $6,000 ($10,000 – $4,000). This is reflected in the $6,000 increase in the cash basis income from operations shown in columns *2* and *3* in section B.

Use the formula below as a shorter method to determine the after-tax cash inflows.

$$\text{After-tax cash inflow} = \text{Taxable cash inflows} \times (1 - \text{Tax rate})$$
$$= \$10,000 \times (1 - .4)$$
$$= \$6,000$$

The (1 – Tax rate) portion of the formula represents the portion of $1 of pretax cash inflow, or $0.60, that would remain after paying the 40 percent tax due on $1. Therefore, if this relationship is true for $1, then 60 percent of any dollar amount of taxable cash inflows will yield the after-tax cash flow.

After-Tax Cash Outflows Cash outflows associated with capital expenditures after acquisition normally include cash expenditures made to operate or maintain the asset. After-tax cash payments are smaller than pretax cash payments because pretax cash payments reduce the income subject to tax, and, therefore, the firm's tax liability.

To illustrate the impact of deductible cash outflows on taxes, assume that Benchmark Corporation's cash operating expenses increased by $10,000 from $30,000 to $40,000 as illustrated in Exhibit 16.13. As a result, the income before taxes decreases by $10,000, and taxes decrease by $4,000, from $24,000 to $20,000 (shown in section A). Note in section B of Exhibit 16.13 that while the cash before taxes decreased $10,000, from $70,000 to $60,000, the cash from operations decreased by only $6,000, from $46,000 to $40,000. The decrease in cash is only $6,000 because the $10,000 increase in cash operating expenses reduced taxable income and, therefore, created a tax savings of $4,000.

EXHIBIT | 16.13 | Tax Effects on Decreased Cash Flows

BENCHMARK CORPORATION
Income Statement

	(1)	(2) Increase in Cash Operating Expenses
A. Accrual Basis		
Sales	$100,000	$100,000
Operating expenses	(30,000)	(40,000)
Depreciation expense	(10,000)	(10,000)
Income before taxes	$ 60,000	$ 50,000
Tax expense*	(24,000)	(20,000)
Net income	$ 36,000	$ 30,000
B. Cash Basis		
Sales	$100,000	$100,000
Operating expenses	(30,000)	(40,000)
Depreciation expense	–0–	–0–
Cash before taxes	$ 70,000	$ 60,000
Tax paid	(24,000)	(20,000)
Cash from operations	$ 46,000	$ 40,000

*40% × Accrual basis income ($60,000 × .4) in column *1* and ($50,000 × .4) in column *2*.

As indicated previously for cash inflows, the use of a formula is a shorter way to determine the after-tax cash outflows of a deductible cash expenditure.

$$\text{After-tax cash outflow} = \text{Deductible cash outflow} \times (1 - \text{Tax rate})$$
$$= \$10,000 \times (1 - .4)$$
$$= \$6,000$$

Here the (1 – Tax rate) represents the after-tax cost of spending $1. When multiplied by the deductible cash outflows, it yields the after-tax cash outflows.

Noncash Expenses

Depreciation, like all noncash expenses, does not directly decrease cash, but it reduces income subject to tax and, therefore, the related amount of income taxes due on income. Therefore, depreciation provides a **tax shield** because it reduces the potential amount of a firm's tax liability by reducing its taxable income without affecting its pretax cash flows. Tax shields keep firms from being taxed on the recovery of the cost of their investments.

To illustrate, assume that a company invests $5,000 in an asset that will last only one year and, at the end of the year, the use of the asset will have contributed $6,000 to the company's revenue. The $6,000 is a combination of a $5,000 return *of* investment and a $1,000 return *on* the investment. Only $1,000 of the $6,000 cash inflow is subject to tax because it is the amount of income generated by the $5,000 investment.

Now, assume that the $5,000 asset has a five-year life and, by its use, creates cash inflows of $1,200 in each of these five years. If the company depreciates the cost of the asset equally over five years, the return on investment each year would be:

	Years					
	1	2	3	4	5	Total
Cash flows	$1,200	$1,200	$1,200	$1,200	$1,200	$6,000
Depreciation	(1,000)	(1,000)	(1,000)	(1,000)	(1,000)	(5,000)
Return on investment	$ 200	$ 200	$ 200	$ 200	$ 200	$1,000

EXHIBIT 16.14 Tax Effect of Depreciation

BENCHMARK CORPORATION
Income Statement

	(1) With Depreciation	(2) No Depreciation
A. Accrual Basis		
Sales	$100,000	$100,000
Operating expenses	(30,000)	(30,000)
Depreciation expense	(10,000)	–0–
Income before taxes	$ 60,000	$ 70,000
Tax expense*	(24,000)	(28,000)
Net income	$ 36,000	$ 42,000
B. Cash Basis		
Sales	$100,000	$100,000
Operating expenses	(30,000)	(30,000)
Depreciation expense	–0–	–0–
Cash before taxes	$ 70,000	$ 70,000
Tax paid	(24,000)	(28,000)
Cash from operations	$ 46,000	$ 42,000

*40% of Accrual basis income ($60,000 × .40) in column *1* and ($70,000 × .4) in column *2*.

Just as in the case of the one-year investment, the firm is not taxed each period on the return *of* the investment ($1,000), only on the return *on* the investment ($200). Thus, the amount of yearly depreciation effectively shields $1,000 of the yearly cash inflows of $1,200 from taxes because it represents the return *of* the initial investment. Note that the total amount of cash inflows, $6,000, less the sum of the depreciation, $5,000, yields the same $1,000 return *on* investment as the one-year investment in the previous example.

PAUSE & REFLECT   Why are the cash flows generated from the rental of land not shielded from taxation?

Depreciation's tax shield creates a tax savings and, therefore, indirectly increases the amount of net cash flow for firms. In Exhibit 16.14, section A, column (2), we illustrate depreciation's tax shield by eliminating the $10,000 of depreciation from Benchmark's income statement. With no depreciation, income before taxes increases by $10,000 from $60,000 to $70,000 and the related amount of taxes increases by $4,000 from $24,000 to $28,000, because more income is subject to tax. As a result, even though Benchmark's net income increases by $6,000 (Section A) by eliminating depreciation, its cash from operations actually decreases by $4,000 from $46,000 to $42,000, as shown in section B. Therefore, while depreciation reduces accounting income, it shields Benchmark from $4,000 in taxes.

Use the following formula to determine the amount of cash saved as a result of noncash expenses. Note that the tax rate is applied directly to the amount of depreciation.

$$\text{Cash saved as a result of noncash expense} = \text{Depreciation (or other noncash expense)} \times \text{Tax rate}$$

$$= \$10,000 \times .4$$

$$= \$4,000$$

When projecting the amount of cash flows for a project, the tax savings generated by depreciation are a critical part of the process. The only uncertainty involved in projecting these cash savings is whether the tax rates will remain the same over the life of the asset.

In Chapter 20, we describe various depreciation methods used to allocate the cost of the asset over its useful life. For financial reporting purposes, companies select the method that best matches depreciation expense with the benefits the asset generates over the asset's life. However, when determining taxable income, companies use accelerated depreciation methods approved by the Internal Revenue Service. These tax depreciation methods allow more (accelerated) depreciation in the first years of an asset's life and, therefore, create larger tax shields earlier in the asset's life and smaller tax shields later in the asset's life. These accelerated tax shields allow firms to take advantage of the time value of money. That is, the firm would prefer to get more of the tax savings from depreciation earlier rather than later in the asset's life.

Gains and Losses on Disposal

In capital budgeting decisions, the disposal of assets occurs when organizations either replace old assets or sell the assets for salvage at the end of their useful life. When a firm disposes of such assets, there are usually two sources of cash flows: (1) the proceeds of the sale, and (2) the change in the amount of taxes due when the asset is sold for a gain or a loss.

We have referred to *book value* as the original cost of an asset less the accumulated depreciation taken to a particular point in time. The book value represents the undepreciated portion of the asset's original cost rather than the market value of the asset, or the amount for which the company could sell the asset on the market.

A gain on disposal occurs if the proceeds from the sale of an asset exceed its book value at the date of disposal. A loss on disposal occurs if the proceeds from the sale of an asset are less than its book value at the date of the sale.

To illustrate the cash flows surrounding the disposal of an asset, we will describe both a gain and a loss on disposal. Assume that Benchmark Corporation has a piece of equipment that originally cost $10,000 and that at the point of sale the equipment has a book value of $2,000. Recall that Benchmark's tax is 40 percent.

Gain and Its Tax Effects   If the equipment is sold for $3,000 cash, there would be a gain on disposal of $1,000.

Cash proceeds from the sale	$3,000
Less: Book value of equipment	2,000
Gain on disposal	$1,000

Although $3,000 cash is received from the sale, the actual cash flow from the disposal is $2,600 due to the effect of Benchmark's 40 percent tax rate.

Cash proceeds from the sale	$3,000
Less: Taxes paid on gain ($1,000 × .4)	400
Net cash proceeds from disposal	$2,600

The gain from the transaction increases income by $1,000 and, therefore, increases taxes by $400. As a result, the $400 in taxes paid on the gain ($1,000 × .4) reduces the $3,000 proceeds of the sale, leaving $2,600 as the net cash proceeds (inflow to Benchmark).

Loss and Its Tax Effects   If the equipment is sold for $1,500 cash, there would be a loss on disposal of $500.

Cash proceeds from the sale	$1,500
Less: Book value of equipment	2,000
Loss on disposal	$ (500)

Although only $1,500 is received from the sale, the cash inflow from the transaction actually is $1,700. The sale of the equipment generates $1,500 in cash, while the loss reduces Benchmark's income by $500 and, therefore, reduces its taxes by $200 ($500 × .40).

Cash proceeds from the sale	$1,500
Add: Taxes saved on loss ($500 × .4)	200
Net cash proceeds from disposal	$1,700

General Formulas The formulas below describe how the cash flows from the disposal of assets are affected by the gains and losses associated with the disposal.

Net-of-tax cash flows from asset sold with a gain =
Proceeds from disposal − (Gain on disposal × Tax rate)

Net-of-tax cash flows from asset sold with a loss =
Proceeds from disposal + (Loss on disposal × Tax rate)

Together, the proceeds of the sale and the related tax effects from the gain or loss on the disposal make up the cash flow to consider in the capital budgeting process.

CAPITAL BUDGETING: A COMPREHENSIVE ILLUSTRATION

This comprehensive illustration is designed to review most of the capital budgeting topics covered to this point. In the illustration assume that IBM is considering the acquisition of a new $450,000 computerized conveyer system on January 1, 1998, for its warehouse and will use the net present value method to assess the potential investment. The following facts are related to this capital budgeting decision.

- The conveyer system will increase the speed and accuracy of IBM's delivery system and has a useful life of seven years.

- The greater efficiency in filling orders will increase revenues by $80,000 each year of the conveyer's life, but it requires a one-time $50,000 increase in the amount of inventory in order to avoid running out of stock.

- Automating the warehouse will reduce labor cost by $15,000 each year and cause utility cost to increase $10,000 each year.

- The conveyer system will be depreciated equally over the next five years resulting in annual depreciation expense of $90,000.

- The book value of the old equipment is $60,000; its market value is $40,000.

- The conveyer system can be sold at the end of year 7 (1/1/2005) for $80,000.

- IBM has a 12 percent cost of capital.

Exhibit 16.15 provides the after-tax cash flows anticipated as a result of the acquisition. Determining the cash flows net of their tax effects is the first step in net present value analysis.

- The initial cash outflows on 1/1/98 consist of the cost of the conveyer system ($450,000) and the additional inventory required to operate the system efficiently ($50,000).

- If the conveyor system is purchased, IBM can sell the six forklifts used currently. The forklifts have a total book value of $60,000, and they can be immediately sold for a total of $40,000. The $20,000 loss creates a tax savings of $8,000 (see cash inflows, 1/1/98).

- The proceeds of the sale plus the tax savings from the loss will reduce the initial cash outflows of the conveyer system by $48,000.

- The net operating cash inflows that result from the acquisition of the conveyer amount to $51,000 after taxes (see after-tax cash inflows 1/1/99–1/1/05).

EXHIBIT	**16.15**	**Identification of After-Tax Cash Flows**

1/1/98

Cash outflows:

Cost of conveyer (no tax effect)		$(450,000)
Investment in working capital (no tax effect)		(50,000)

Cash inflows:

Proceeds from sale of old equipment	$40,000	
Add: Tax savings from loss*	8,000	
Net cash inflow from sale of old equipment		48,000

1/1/99–1/1/05

Net operating cash inflows:

Increase in sales	$80,000	
Decrease in labor costs	15,000	
Increase in utility costs	(10,000)	
Net cash inflows from operations—Pretax	$85,000	

After-tax cash inflows = $85,000 \times (1 - .4) = $51,000

1/1/99–1/1/03

Annual depreciation $450,000 \div 5 = $90,000

$$\begin{aligned} \text{Tax savings on depreciation tax shield} &= \text{Depreciation} \times \text{Tax rate} \\ &= \$90,000 \quad \times \ .4 \\ &= \$36,000 \end{aligned}$$

1/1/05

Cash inflows:

Release of working capital (no tax effect)		$50,000
Proceeds from sale of the conveyer	$80,000	
Less: Additional tax on gain[†]	32,000	
Net cash inflow from sale of new conveyer		48,000

*Proceeds from sale of equipment	$ 40,000	
Less: Book value of equipment	(60,000)	
Loss on disposal	$(20,000)	
Tax savings on loss = $20,000 \times .4 = $8,000		

[†]Proceeds from sale of conveyer	$ 80,000	
Less: Book value of conveyer	–0–	
Gain on disposal	$ 80,000	
Additional tax on gain = $80,000 \times .4 = $32,000		

- The depreciation creates a tax shield that produces a tax savings of $36,000 per year (see 1/1/99–1/1/03).

- At the end of the conveyer's useful life, IBM will reduce its amount of inventory and sell the conveyer. Because the conveyer is fully depreciated in 2003, its book value is zero and, as a result, the gain on the sale of the conveyer will equal the $80,000 in proceeds from the sale. The gain on the sale is subject to $32,000 tax, which reduces the cash proceeds to $48,000 ($80,000 proceeds from sale – $32,000 tax on gain). (See 1/1/05.)

Exhibit 16.16 shows the cash flows for each year of the useful life of the conveyer and, using a 12 percent cost of capital as the discount rate, calculates the net present value of the equipment. Take a moment to be sure you understand these calculations.

The conveyer produces a negative net present value of ($45,152) as shown in step 3. If IBM acquires the conveyer and the cash flows remain as projected, the rate of return on the conveyer system will be less than IBM's cost of capital or minimum acceptable rate of return. Threfore, IBM should not purchase the conveyor system.

Calculating the net present value of the conveyer system yielded a measure that helps management decide whether to acquire this capital asset. However, the apparent mathematical precision of this process should not obscure the fact that it is based on human judgment. The impact and importance of good judgment on the capital budgeting process is the focus of the rest of this chapter.

EXHIBIT 16.16 Net Present Value Computation

Step 1. Identification of Cash Flows (see Exhibit 16.15).

Time (years)

	1/1/98	1/1/99	1/1/00	1/1/01	1/1/02	1/1/03	1/1/04	1/1/05
a	$(450,000)							
b	(50,000)							
c	48,000							
d		$51,000	$51,000	$51,000	$51,000	$51,000	$51,000	$ 51,000
e		36,000	36,000	36,000	36,000	36,000		
f								50,000
g								48,000
Total	($452,000)	$87,000	$87,000	$87,000	$87,000	$87,000	$51,000	$149,000

where:

a = Cost of conveyer
b = Investment in working capital—inventory
c = After-tax proceeds from sale of old equipment
d = After-tax operating cash inflows
e = Tax savings on depreciation tax shield
f = Release of working capital
g = Net cash inflow from sale of the conveyer

Step 2. Calculate Present Value of Future Cash Flows.

Time	Cash Flow (step 1)	×	$P_{n,12\%}$	=	Present Value
1/1/99	$ 87,000	×	.8929	=	$ 77,682
1/1/00	87,000	×	.7972	=	69,356
1/1/01	87,000	×	.7118	=	61,927
1/1/02	87,000	×	.6355	=	55,289
1/1/03	87,000	×	.5674	=	49,364
1/1/04	51,000	×	.5066	=	25,837
1/1/05	149,000	×	.4523	=	67,393
Present value of future cash flows				=	$406,848

Step 3. Compute the Net Present Value.

Present value of future cash flows	$406,848
Less: Initial cost of acquisition (step 1)	(452,000)
Net present value	$ (45,152)

Step 4. Make Decision about Acquisition of Capital Investment.

Investment decisions: Reject proposal to acquire the conveyer because NPV is negative.

CONFLICTING SIGNALS: A PERFORMANCE EVALUATION PROBLEM

Discounted cash flow analysis and accrual accounting are based on different assumptions. Discounted cash flow analysis considers only the amount and timing of cash flows, whereas accrual accounting measures the economic consequences of business transactions, whether or not cash was a part of the transaction. When a decision maker does not understand the differences in these two systems, the potential for suboptimal capital budgeting decisions exists.

For example, Shannon Jackson, the eastern division manager of Benchmark Corporation, is opposed to the acquisition of a new plant for which she will be responsible, even though it has a positive net present value. She bases her opposition on the fact that the projected accounting income of the plant during its four-year life shows that the plant would have a net loss in each of its first two years. The negative income in these first two years will have a significant impact on the division's income, and Shannon's performance is evaluated based on the division's accounting earnings. Her yearly bonus is 5 percent of the division's accounting income.

Exhibit 16.17 depicts the effects of the apparent conflict between NPV and accrual basis accounting income. Assume that the cost of capital for Benchmark Corporation is 12 percent. You can see that the NPV of the new plant is a positive $35,794, which

EXHIBIT 16.17 — Conflict between NPV and Accrual Basis Accounting Income: BenchmarkCorp.

	Time (years)				
	0	**1**	**2**	**3**	**4**
Cash flows:					
Plant cost	$(200,000)				
Cash revenues		$10,000	$40,000	$140,000	$150,000

Cash flow	$\times$	$p_{n,12\%}$	=	Present value
$10,000	$\times$	.8929	=	$ 8,929
$40,000	$\times$	.7972	=	31,888
$140,000	$\times$	.7118	=	99,652
$150,000	$\times$	.6355	=	95,325
Present value of future cash flows			=	$235,794
Less: Plant cost				(200,000)
Net present value				$ 35,794

	Time (years)			
	1	**2**	**3**	**4**
Accrual Income				
Revenues	$ 10,000	$ 40,000	$140,000	$150,000
Depreciation	(50,000)	(50,000)	(50,000)	(50,000)
Net income (Loss)	$(40,000)	$(10,000)	$ 90,000	$100,000

indicates that the plant would be a favorable investment for Benchmark Corporation. The projected accrual income for the plant indicates that, for the first two years of its life, the plant will generate losses of $(40,000) and $(10,000), respectively.

The evaluation system encourages Ms. Jackson to oppose the acquisition of this plant, despite the fact it is a good decision for the company. If the Benchmark Corporation acquires the plant, Ms. Jackson will be penalized by losing a potential bonus in years 1 and 2.

Managerial accounting systems need evaluation mechanisms that reward managers for decisions that increase the wealth of the firm. For Benchmark Corporation, the evaluation system clearly allows for conflicts based on its bonus reward structure. This, of course, can lead to decisions that are not in the company's best interest.

CAPITAL BUDGETING AND THE NEED FOR INFORMED SPECULATION

Capital budgeting relies upon the use of many technical tools to facilitate the decision-making process. What is often lost in the process of applying these tools is the realization that informed speculation is a necessary component of the capital budgeting process. What do we mean by *informed speculation?*

Because making capital budgeting decisions requires the personal judgment of decision makers, forecasting can be affected by personal perceptions of the decision maker.

PAUSE & REFLECT

Suppose the person responsible for forecasting cash flows took a very conservative approach and the resulting net present value on a $500,000 project was a negative $110. Should the project be rejected? Would your answer be the same if the cash flows were based on very optimistic assumptions?

Managers should keep the subjective aspects of the capital budgeting process in mind when evaluating the output of their computations. People who review the input and output of accounting systems should recognize the subjective nature of the capital budgeting process and provide the support necessary to facilitate this dynamic process. Sensitivity analysis is one way to deal with the uncertainty inherent in the capital budgeting process.

Sensitivity Analysis

Sensitivity analysis, which we described in Chapter 4, reflects the results of changing a key assumption in a decision model. Capital budgeting uses a sensitivity analysis to evaluate how a change in estimated cash flows or discount rates might affect the capital budgeting decision.

To illustrate, assume that IBM has a 10 percent cost of capital and is considering the two $100,000 investments A, and B, shown in Exhibit 16.18. IBM's accountants have suggested that the cash flow estimates may vary downward by as much as 10 percent. The exhibit illustrates how a 10 percent fluctuation might affect the investment decision.

For investment A, the possible fluctuation in cash flows from $32,000 per year (line 2) to $28,800 (line 3) would not affect the decision to acquire the investment because both possible cash flows have positive net present values of $21,305 and $9,175, respectively.

Investment B, on the other hand, has a small NPV, $2,352, and a 10 percent drop in the projected cash flows from $27,000 to $24,300 and would result in a negative

EXHIBIT	16.18	Sensitivity Analysis

Investment A

Price	$100,000
Estimated annual cash inflows for five years	32,000
Estimated cash flows reduced 10% ($32,000 × .9)	28,800

$$\text{Present value of future cash flows} = \text{Annuity} \times P_{5,10\%}$$
$$= \$32,000 \times 3.7908$$
$$= \$121,305$$

$$\text{Present value of future of reduced cash flows} = \text{Annuity} \times P_{5,10\%}$$
$$= \$28,800 \times 3.7908$$
$$= \$109,175$$

	Forecasted Cash Flows	
	$32,000	$28,800
Present value of future cash flow	$121,305	$109,175
Initial cost of investment A	(100,000)	(100,000)
Net present value	$ 21,305	$ 9,175

Investment B

Price	$100,000
Estimated annual cash inflows for five years	27,000
Estimated cash flows reduced 10% ($27,000 × .9)	24,300

$$\text{Present value of future cash flows} = \text{Annuity} \times P_{5,10\%}$$
$$= \$27,000 \times 3.7908$$
$$= \$102,352$$

$$\text{Present value of future of reduced cash flows} = \text{Annuity} \times P_{5,10\%}$$
$$= \$24,300 \times 3.7908$$
$$= \$92,116$$

	Forecasted Cash Flows	
	$27,000	$24,300
Present value of future cash flow	$102,352	$ 92,116
Initial cost of investment B	(100,000)	(100,000)
Net present value	$2,352	$ (7,884)

preadsheets are an ideal way to quickly and easily calculate net present values and to use sensitivity analysis in capital budgeting. To calculate net present value in Lotus, the function @NPV(interest, range) is used. However, Lotus assumes that the initial payment is made at the *end of the first period.*

For example, to use Lotus for the comprehensive example illustrated in the chapter, simply enter the cash flow amounts in a column, enter the interest rate, and enter the net present value function. Assuming cash flows are entered in column A, rows 1–8 and the required interest rate is entered in column A, row 9, then the output appears in column A, row 10 with the following

command: @NPV(a9,a1.a8). The resulting amount, $(40,309) is returned in column A, row 10. Notice that this in NOT the same answer shown in Exhibit 16.16 due to the assumption that the first cash flow occurs at the end of the first period.

To use the @NPV funcation assuming that the initial cash outflow is at the beginning of the period, simply eliminate it from the cash flows entered and subtract it from the resulting value. For example, enter the following in Column A, row 10: @NPV(a9,a2.a8)+a1. The result, $(45,146) is returned in column a, row 10 (the difference is due to rounding). Sensitivity analysis is completed by simply changing the cash flows and/or the interest rate. The result will change automatically!

NPV of $(7,884), leading to the suggestion that IBM should reject the investment. The closer the NPV is to zero and the greater the uncertainty about the cash flows, the greater the chance of making an incorrect investment decision. Sensitivity analysis helps clarify this type of risk.

Qualitative Factors

In addition to the uncertainty about future cash flows, managers must also consider qualitative factors that affect capital expenditure decisions. For example, suppose a firm is considering the construction of a new parking garage, and discounted cash flow analysis indicates that the parking garage will yield a return well above the firm's cost of capital. However, the construction of the parking garage would require the destruction of an important historic landmark. The decision to build the garage must take into consideration this qualitative factor as well as the financial considerations.

In some cases, the nature of the investment may deter its acquisition despite a positive net present value. For example, a chemical company might reject the acquisition of a commercial fishing operation even though the computations of net present value indicate that it would exceed the firm's cost of capital. Management might reject this investment opportunity because it has no expertise in the fishing business.

SUMMARY

Capital budgeting is an important process used for analysis and selection of a firm's long-term investments. It requires input from many functional areas in the firm in order to be effective.

- Capital budgeting is the process used to select the long-term investment of a business and involves identifying the firm's long-term investment needs, determining the investment alternatives that can satisfy its needs, deciding which investments to acquire, and evaluating the performance of the investments after acquisition.

- Investments are made to replace worn or obsolete assets, expand the firm's operating capacity, or comply with government mandates.

- The cost of capital is the minimum acceptable return for a firm's assets and serves as a hurdle rate for screening potential investments.

- Firms use discounted cash flow analysis as a tool to evaluate whether potential investments meet the firm's cost of capital. Decision makers who use discounted cash flow analysis should consider the uncertainty about future cash flows and the qualitative aspects of the capital expenditure decision under consideration.

- Decision makers use net present value (NPV) and time-adjusted rate of return (TARR) cash flow analysis methods to assess whether an investment will generate a return that is greater than a firm's cost of capital.

- NPV uses the *cost of capital* to discount the projected cash flows of an investment and to determine the maximum price a firm should pay for an asset and still generate a satisfactory return. If the cost of the investment exceeds this price, the investment should be rejected.

- TARR uses the *cost of the potential investment* as the present value of the projected cash flows and derives the rate of return on the project given the projected cash flows. The investment is accepted or rejected based on whether the rate of return exceeds the firm's cost of capital.

- The two phases of evaluating capital expenditures are: (1) determination of whether the actual cost to acquire the assets was consistent with cost projections, which occurs during the process of acquiring the asset, and (2) the postaudit phase, which takes place after acquisition to determine if the initial projections were reasonable and to review the methods and assumptions used.

- Discounted cash flow analysis is based on assumptions that (1) all cash flows are known with certainty, (2) cash flows occur at the end of the time period, and (3) cash inflows are immediately reinvested in another project that earns a return at the same rate for the company.

- Income taxes reduce cash revenues and expense, and depreciation provides tax shields from taxes. The tax effect of gains and losses reduces and increases, respectively, the proceeds from the disposal of assets.

- Capital budgeting and management incentives based on accrual accounting can result in suboptimal decisions.

- Sensitivity analysis is a means of evaluating how capital budgeting decisions would change if the assumptions about estimated cash flows change.

KEY TERMS

acquisition phase The first capital expenditure evaluation phase in which the management accountant monitors costs incurred in conjunction with the asset's acquisition

after-tax cash flows The estimated cash flows associated with a potential investment after considering the impact of income taxes

capital budgeting The process used for analysis and selection of the long-term investments of a business

capital expenditure budget A budget that describes the amount and timing of the capital expenditures planned for the designated time period

cost of capital The weighted-average cost of a firm's debt and equity financing

discounted cash flow analysis A method to evaluate investments that uses the time value of money to assess whether the investment's expected rate of return is greater than a firm's cost of capital

financing budget A budget that outlines the amounts and sources of funds needed to finance the firm's investments for the designated time period

net present value A discounted cash flow analysis requires that decision makers find the present value of an investment's estimated future cash flows by using the firm's cost of capital as the discount rate

postaudit The second evaluation phase of the capital budgeting process, which involves comparing cash flow projections made in the preacquisition analysis with actual cash flows generated by the asset

tax shield A noncash expense that reduces the potential amount of a firm's tax liability by reducing its taxable income without affecting its pretax cash flows

time-adjusted rate of return (internal rate of return) A discounted cash flow method that requires using the cost of a potential investment as the present value of the projected cash flows in order to determine the rate of return on the proposed investment

1. What is the purpose of capital budgeting, and why is it important?
2. How are long-term investments identified in a business?
3. List and briefly describe the four basic processes of the capital budgeting process.
4. What is a firm's cost of capital, and what role does it play in the capital budgeting process?
5. What does a positive net present value tell the person making a capital budgeting decision?
6. Describe the four steps used in the net present value method.
7. What is the decision rule used to accept or reject a potential investment when using the net present value method? Why does it work?
8. What does the time-adjusted rate of return tell the person making the capital budgeting decision?
9. There are three steps used in the time-adjusted rate of return method. Why is each important?
10. Compare and contrast the time-adjusted rate of return method and the net present value method.
11. What are the advantages and disadvantages of both the net present value method and the time-adjusted rate of return method?
12. Why can't the TARR be adjusted for changing levels of risk?
13. Identify and explain the three key assumptions underlying discounted cash flow analysis.
14. Why do we continue to use capital budgeting techniques that are based on assumptions that do not always reflect business reality?
15. How do income taxes impact the cash flows of capital budgeting decisions?
16. How does a noncash expense create a tax shield?
17. What causes gains and losses from the disposal of assets?
18. Describe how taxes impact the cash flows generated by the disposal of assets.
19. Why is sensitivity analysis useful in capital budgeting?
20. What constitutes a qualitative factor in a capital budgeting problem?

EXERCISES

E 16.1   Locket Corporation's capital structure consists of $1,345,000 of assets and liabilities of $900,000. Kevin Locket, the corporation's CEO and largest shareholder, says that the debt has an average interest rate of 9 percent and the stockholders want a 14 percent return. What is Locket Corporation's cost of capital?

E 16.2   Charlotte Company is considering purchasing a new machine with a cost of $6,000, no salvage value, and a useful life of five years. The machine is expected to generate $1,900 in cash inflows during each year of the machine's five-year life. Charlotte Company's cost of capital is 15 percent. Disregarding taxes, what is the maximum price Charlotte should pay for this machine? Why? Compute the net present value of the machine. Should Charlotte Company acquire the machine? Why?

E 16.3   Edwards, Inc., is considering the acquisition of a computerized bailingswatcher that costs $93,200. The bailingswatcher has an expected life of 10 years and is expected to reduce production costs by $17,867 a year. Edwards' cost of capital is 12 percent. Disregarding the impact of taxes, compute the time-adjusted rate of return of the bailingswatcher. Should Edwards acquire the bailingswatcher? Why?

E 16.4   Laura Wyndom is the chief financial officer of 56th Street Enterprises. She is considering the acquisition of a farthing processor with a cost of $524,000 and an installation cost of $10,200. Her analysis suggests that the farthing processor will produce $122,986 a year for the next eight years. Disregarding the impact of taxes, what is the farthing processor's time-adjusted rate of return? Should Laura buy the farthing processor if the firm's cost of capital is 14 percent?

E 16.5   The Riley Company is considering replacing its manual accounting system with a computerized accounting system. As of January 1, 1997, the software package and related equipment will cost the company $100,000 and are expected to have a useful life of five years. Riley's analyst has forecast that efficiencies created by the new system will reduce the cost of operating the accounting system by the amounts described below:

1997	$20,000
1998	30,000
1999	50,000
2000	25,000
2001	25,000

Disregarding taxes and assuming that Riley's cost of capital is 12 percent, what is the maximum price Riley should pay for this accounting system? What is the net present value of the software package? Should Riley Company buy the software package? Why?

E 16.6   Rizwan Company is contemplating the acquisition of a new copier on December 15, 1997. The copier costs $21,950, has an estimated life of six years, and is expected to save paper and time, as well as reduce repair cost. The cash Rizwan expects to save as a result of buying the copier over the next six years is shown below.

1997	$7000
1998	6,000
1999	5,000
2000	4,000
2001	3,000
2002	2,000

Disregarding taxes, what is the maximum price Rizwan should pay for the copier if its cost of capital is 15 percent? Calculate the net present value of the new copier. Should Rizwan Company buy the copier? Why?

E 16.7   Clark Company's sales for the year were $500,000 and operating expenses were $200,000. Included in the operating expenses was $50,000 of depreciation expense. If Clark Company's tax rate is 40 percent, calculate the after-tax cash flows of sales, operating expenses, and depreciation. Given the information above, what is Clark's after-tax cash flows?

E 16.8   In January of 1996, Applegate Company bought a new delivery van for $15,000 that it expects to use for four years. The new van will increase delivery revenue each year by $8,000. The projected gas and repair expense and accelerated depreciation expense for each of the next four years appears below:

	Gas and Repair Expense	Accelerated Tax Depreciation
1996	$2,000	$5,000
1997	2,500	4,000
1998	3,000	3,000
1999	3,500	3,000

If Applegate's tax rate is 30 percent, what is the tax shield created by the depreciation for each year? What are the after-tax cash flows for each year?

E 16.9   Rogers Construction Company purchased a new road grader on July 1, 1993, for $95,000. On April 22, 1997, Rogers sold the grader. On the date of the sale, the accumulated depreciation on the grader was $44,700. Rogers' tax rate on the date of the sale was 30 percent. What is the book value of the grader on April 22, 1997? If the grader sold for $60,000 cash, what is the after-tax cash inflow from the sale of the grader? If the grader sold for $42,000 cash, what is the after-tax cash inflow from the sale of the grader?

E 16.10   On November 12, 1996, Ringneck Corporation sold a pickup truck for $3,000 and gave a 486 computer to a local Boy Scout troop. The truck originally cost $12,000 and had accumulated depreciation of $10,255 when it was sold. The computer originally cost $2,500 and had accumulated depreciation of $1,975 when it was donated to the local scout troop. If Ringneck's tax rate is 30 percent, what is the cash flow generated by these two transactions?

E 16.11   As of January 1, 1997, Roberts Company wants to acquire a new machine costing $91,000. The machine has an estimated useful life of seven years and no salvage value. Roberts' tax rate is 30 percent and the annual depreciation on the machine is $13,000. The expected pretax cash flows are described below:

	Pretax Cash Revenues	Pretax Cash Expenses
1997	$34,000	$11,000
1998	36,000	12,000
1999	40,000	15,000
2000	33,000	10,000
2001	30,000	9,000
2002	29,000	9,000
2003	25,000	8,000

If Roberts Company has a 12 percent cost of capital, what is the maximum price Roberts should pay for the machine? Why? Calculate the net present value of this project. Should Roberts buy the machine? Why?

E 16.12   In 1997, Shifferdecker Corporation is considering investing in a new five-year project that will require an initial cash outlay of $330,000. When the project is undertaken, Shifferdecker will sell old equipment with an initial cost of $400,000 and accumulated depreciation of $250,000 for $50,000 cash. Shifferdecker's management anticipates that the new project will generate $140,000 of cash revenue and require $44,000 of cash expenses in each of the five years. Depreciation associated with the project is $40,000 each year. Shifferdecker has a 14 percent cost of capital and a 30 percent tax rate. Calculate the project's net present value. Should Shifferdecker undertake the project? Why?

E 16.13   Kung Chen Corporation is trying to decide whether or not to make the following two investments. The first is a piece of equipment that costs $20,000 but will save the company $4,500 after taxes in each year of its 10-year life. The second is a patent that costs $30,000 but will generate $4,700 in after-tax cash flows over its 17-year life. Kung Chen Corporation's cost of capital is 14 percent. Calculate the net present value of each investment. Should the company acquire one, both, or neither investment?

E 16.14   In 1995, Erin Imports generated the data below about investments A and B which the company is considering. Erin's cost of capital is 12 percent, and its tax rate is 30 percent.

	Investment A	Investment B
Initial cost	$52,000	$75,000
Annual depreciation	13,000	12,500
Net pretax cash inflows:		
1996	19,000	29,000
1997	21,000	28,000
1998	17,000	30,000
1999	18,000	25,000
2000		27,000
2001		26,000

What is the net present value of each investment? Would you recommend that Erin purchase one, both, or neither investment? Why?

E 16.15   Late in 1996, the Marta Ott Corporation has projected the pretax cash flows shown below for a nadleprocter that cost $235,000. If Ott's tax rate is 40 percent and its cost of capital is 14 percent, calculate the net present value for this piece of equipment. Should Ott invest in the nadleprocter? Why or why not?

	Pretax Cash Inflows	Pretax Cash Outflows	Accelerated Tax Depreciation
1997	$110,000	$175,000	$90,000
1998	200,000	160,000	80,000
1999	300,000	140,000	65,000
2000	325,000	120,000	
2001	360,000	110,000	

Would your answer be the same if the depreciation was $47,000 each year for five years and the pretax cash flows remained the same? Why?

E 16.16   In 1997, Med-Tech Company is considering the acquisition of a new $520,000 diagnostic machine and has projected the after-tax cash flows related to the machine. Chris Kohlrus, Med-Tech's manager, has decided to use multiple cost of capital figures to calculate the net present value of this potential investment. The cash flows and cost of capital figures are presented below. Calculate the net present value of the investment. Should Med-Tech buy the diagnostic equipment? Why or why not?

	Cost of Capital	Years	After-Tax Cash Flows
1998-2000	12%	1998	$125,000
2001-2003	14	1999	130,000
2004-2005	15	2000	133,000
		2001	145,000
		2002	155,000
		2003	122,000
		2004	120,000
		2005	110,000

E 16.17   Mark Hammond, manager for the Trego Company has projected the after-tax cash flows shown below for a $87,000 machine he wants to buy in December of 1996. The cash flows represent a worst-case scenario for the machine. Jeff Suttle, another Trego Company manager, feels however, that the projected cash flows are much too conservative and that they should be higher by as much as 5 percent each year. Trego's cost of capital is 14 percent.

	After-Tax Cash Flows
1997	$21,100
1998	22,700
1999	23,000
2000	22,500
2001	23,000
2002	22,400

Calculate the net present value of the machine based on the given projections. Should Trego buy the machine?

E 16.18   The Sublette Corporation is trying to decide whether to acquire a new manufacturing facility. Three after-tax cash flows have been projected for the $1,000,000 facility's 10-year life. Sublette has a 15 percent cost of capital.

	Projection 1	Projection 2	Projection 3
After-tax cash flows	$195,000/year	$199,250/year	$205,000/year

Calculate the net present value of each cash flow projection. Should Sublette buy the manufacturing facility? Under what circumstances and why?

E 16.19   In 1996, the Alaska Company is considering whether to replace its old deicer with a more efficient deicer that costs $25,000. The old deicer has a book value of $6,000 and can be sold for $7,000. The new deicer will save $7,000 of operating cash flow before taxes in each of the next five years. Alaska will take $5,000 of depreciation in each of the next five years, has a 30 percent tax rate, and an 18 percent cost of capital. Calculate the NPV of this potential investment. Should Alaska buy the new deicer?

E 16.20   Federated Company is a small company that employs 15 people in a town with a population of about 20,000. Phil Irwin, Federated's plant manager, is considering the acquisition of a new machine that will cost $950,000. The machine will replace five long-time employees and is expected to generate savings of $211,400 in after-tax cash flows for the next 10 years. Federated's cost of capital is 18 percent. Based on the net present value of the machine, should Federated buy the machine? Are there qualitative factors that Mr. Irwin should consider in his decision? Why?

PROBLEMS

P 16.1 The following cash savings are expected to occur if the city of Joplin, Missouri, buys a new street sweeper at the start of 1998 that costs $146,456. The city of Joplin pays no taxes and has a cost of capital of 10 percent.

1998	$42,000
1999	39,000
2000	41,000
2001	44,000
2002	43,000
2003	38,000

Required: a. What is the maximum price Joplin should pay for the sweeper?
b. Calculate the net present value of the street sweeper.
c. Should the city of Joplin acquire the street sweeper? Explain your answer.

P 16.2 Treemont, Inc., is considering replacing an existing chipper-shredder machine with a new chipper-shredder. The existing chipper-shredder originally cost $90,000 and has a book value of $46,000 today. The existing chipper-shredder machine is depreciated at a rate of $9,000 per year, has a remaining useful life of four years, and no salvage value. The old chipper-shredder costs $74,000 per year to operate and can be sold today for $40,000.

Model Z45 chipper-shredder costs $80,000 and is expected to have a four-year life and no salvage value. The Z45 model will be depreciated at $20,000 per year and costs $52,000 to operate.

Treemont's cost of capital is 15 percent and its tax rate is 30 percent.

Required: a. Calculate the net present value of the Z45 chipper.
b. Should Treemont replace its existing machine? Explain your answer.

P 16.3 ADPL Corp. manufactures screws and nails. ADPL is considering replacing a machine that produces concrete nails and has received a proposal from a vendor for the new machine. ADPL Corp. has a 15 percent cost of capital and a 30 percent tax rate.

The vendor will sell the company a new machine for $620,000 and buy the old machine, which has a $10,000 book value, for $40,000. The new machine is expected to generate $190,000 of pretax cash inflows, and the company can recognize $124,000 of depreciation expense each year of its five-year life.

Required: a. Calculate the net present value of the new machine.
b. Should ADPL buy the new machine? Explain your answer.

P 16.4 At the end of 1997 Window Company is planning to buy a new machine for $40,000. The new machine has a useful life of seven years and is expected to have no salvage value. The pretax cash flows and the depreciation for tax purposes are described below. Window's tax rate is 30 percent and its cost of capital is 16 percent.

	Pretax Cash Flow	Tax Depreciation
1997	$10,500	$10,000
1998	12,500	8,000
1999	11,000	7,000
2000	10,000	4,000
2001	9,500	3,000
2002	8,500	2,000
2003	8,000	1,000

Required: a. Calculate the net present value for the new equipment.
b. Should Window buy the new machine? Why?

P 16.5   As of April 1996, the Tom Robinson Guide Service is considering the acquisition of a new fishing boat that costs $80,000. If the new boat is purchased, an old boat with a book value of $5,000 will be sold for $2,000. The new boat is expected to have a useful life of six years and have no salvage value. The pretax cash flows and depreciation are shown below. The Guide Service has a cost of capital of 15 percent and a tax rate of 30 percent.

	Pretax Cash Inflow	Pretax Cash Outflow	Depreciation
1996	$45,000	$20,000	$24,000
1997	56,000	30,000	21,000
1998	49,000	25,000	15,000
1999	45,000	23,000	8,000
2000	41,000	20,000	7,000
2001	39,000	21,000	5,000

Required: *a.* Calculate the net present value for the new boat.
               b. Should Tom Robinson Guide Service buy the new boat? Explain your answer.

P 16.6   The Charlie Sparks Company wants to replace a machine that has a zero book value and a market value of $3,400 in January of 1998. The new machine Charlie Sparks is considering has a cost of $50,000 and an estimated useful life of five years. The new machine will create cost savings of $14,500 per year. The machine will require an additional investment in working capital of $3,000, which would be recovered at the end of the machine's life. Depreciation on the new machine would be $10,000 per year. Charlie Sparks has a 30 percent tax rate and a 12 percent cost of capital.

Required: *a.* Calculate the net present value of the new machine.
               b. Should the Charlie Sparks Company buy the machine? Explain your answer.

P 16.7   Sherman Company is examining a proposal to acquire a new production facility in December 1997. If the new facility is acquired, Sherman will sell one of its plants. The new facility would cost $10,800,000 and would have an expected life of 15 years. The old plant has a book value of $1,200,000 and can be sold for $1,550,000. The tax law will permit the new plant to be depreciated over 10 years at $1,080,000 a year. At the end of the facility's life, the projected cost of dismantling and disposing of the facility is $300,000.

Due to the length of the new facility's life, Sherman wants to use 12 percent as the cost of capital for the first 10 years and 15 percent for the last 5 years. Sherman's tax rate is 30 percent. The estimated pretax cash flows for the new facility are listed below.

	Estimated Pretax Cash Flows
1998-2000	$(200,000)
2001-2005	1,180,000
2006-2007	860,000
2008-2012	975,000

Required: *a.* Develop a schedule of projected after-tax cash flows for the new facility.
               b. Calculate the net present value of the new facility.
               c. Should Sherman buy the new facility? Why or why not?

P 16.8   The Ellis Cake Company is considering a new, more efficient machine to replace its existing snack cake machine. While the new machine won't produce more snack cakes, it will reduce the cost of producing the snack cakes. The snack cakes are sold in a twin pack at $1 per pack, and management expects to sell 400,000 packs in each of the next six years.

The old machine originally cost $80,000 and currently has a book value of $48,000 and a remaining useful life of six years. The new machine will cost $220,000 and would have a useful life of six years. The following information is available to help resolve this capital budgeting question.

	Old Machine	New Machine
Expected Annual Cash		
Operating expenses:		
Variable cost per pack	$ .48	$ .29
Fixed operating expenses	14,000	13,000
Noncash Expenses		
Annual depreciation	8,000	35,000
Market value of machine:		
Today	32,000	220,000
In six years	–0–	20,000

Ellis' tax rate is 30 percent and its cost of capital is 12 percent.

Required: *a.* Calculate the net present value for the new machine.

b. Should Ellis buy the new machine? Why?

P 16.9 In December 1996, the Sheridan Company is trying to decide whether to buy one, both, or neither of the investments shown below. Sheridan's cost of capital is 16 percent and its tax rate is 30 percent. Neither investment has a salvage value.

	Investment A	Investment B
Price	$430,000	$430,000
Annual depreciation	86,000	86,000
Projected pretax cash flows:		
1997	134,600	127,400
1998	163,100	141,700
1999	191,700	156,000
2000	220,300	170,200
2001	248,900	184,600

Required: *a.* Compute the net present value for both investments.

b. Assume that the cash flows could vary up and down by as much as 10 percent. How would fluctuation affect the investment decision?

c. Given the potential fluctuations, which investment would you consider acceptable? Explain your decision.

P 16.10 Alma Advertising manufactures promotional gifts. In January 1997, Alma developed a promotional gift for hardware stores, and its sales force has generated orders for this product for the next three years. To produce this product, Alma had to buy two new machines and lease more building space. Each new machine cost $200,000 and installation costs were $65,000 each. To test-run both machines cost a total of $40,000. The additional space was leased for $25,000 per year for three years starting in January of 1997.

The entire cost of the equipment will be depreciated over the next three years for tax purposes. Despite the zero book value at the end of the third year, the equipment can be sold for $50,000. The company expects to increase its inventory by $60,000 in the first year; this excess inventory will be disposed of in the last year of the equipment's life.

The company projects the following estimates of the revenue and cash expenses for this product.

	1997	1998	1999
Sales revenues	$500,000	$800,000	$400,000
Variable operating expenses	175,000	350,000	155,000
Depreciation	190,000	190,000	190,000
Rent expense	25,000	25,000	25,000

Required: *a.* Prepare a schedule showing the after-tax cash flows for this project if Alma's tax rate is 30 percent.

b. Calculate the net present value for this project if Alma's cost of capital is 20 percent.

c. Comment on whether Alma should have taken the orders for this new promotional product.

CA 16.1

Rutherford Company wants to determine whether it should invest in a piece of equipment that costs $1 million and is expected to last 10 years. At the end of the 10-year period, the equipment will be scrapped and has no salvage value. Rutherford has a 12 percent cost of capital. The expected after-tax net cash flows of the machine (including the tax shield) are shown below:

Year	After-Tax Cash Flow
1	$225,000
2	200,000
3	250,000
4	250,000
5	(300,000)
6	250,000
7	250,000
8	225,000
9	125,000
10	50,000

Required: Use a computer spreadsheet package.

a. What is the net present value of this equipment assuming the cash flows begin one year from today?

b. What is the net present value of this equipment assuming cash flows begin today?

c. Should Rutherford invest in the equipment? Why or why not?

CA 16.2

Barnes & Son, Inc., wants to buy a new printing press. The cost of the press is $300,000 and it is expected to last for 10 years, after which it will be scrapped with no salvage value. Barnes & Son has an 8 percent cost of capital. The pretax net cash inflows are shown below. Barnes & Son is subject to a 40 percent tax rate.

Year	Pretax Cash Flow
1	$ 80,000
2	90,000
3	100,000
4	110,000
5	100,000
6	90,000
7	75,000
8	60,000
9	50,000
10	25,000

Required: Use a computer spreadsheet package.

a. What is the net present value of the printing press assuming the cash flows begin one year from today?

b. What is the net present value of this equipment assuming cash flows begin today?

c. Should Barnes & Son invest in the new printing press? Why or why not?

CRITICAL THINKING

CT 16.1

Milford Company is going to buy one of the two machines described below. Each machine meets the specifications for a particular task in the company. Milford's tax rate is 30 percent, and its cost of capital is 15 percent. Which machine should Milford buy and why?

Machine A: Costs $45,000 to acquire and $6,000 cash a year to operate in each year of its 10-year life. Annual depreciation is $4,500, and the machine has no salvage value.

Machine B: Costs $25,000 to acquire and $12,300 a year to operate in each year of its 10-year life. Annual depreciation is $2,500, and the machine has no salvage value.

CT 16.2

Your supervisor has just completed a discounted cash flow analysis on a 15-year, $10,000,000 project. She is very excited that the net present value was positive and is getting ready to report her findings to senior management and to strongly recommend that the company undertake the project.

Upon reviewing the computations, you discover that the net present value on this $10,000,000 project was a positive $148. What factors about the analysis would you suggest that your supervisor consider before she makes her report strongly recommending this project?

CASES

C 16.1   As of January 10, 1996, you have just completed a discounted cash flow analysis on a $25,000 investment. You calculated that the net present value of the after-tax cash flows shown below is $6,357 using the company's cost of capital of 15 percent. You reported your findings to your supervisor and recommended that the company make the investment.

To your surprise, the supervisor rejected the acquisition. He said that it is company policy not to invest in any project in which the cash flows do not recover the initial investment in three years. He points out that of the $25,000 expended, only $19,000 would be recovered in three years.

	After-Tax Cash Flow
1996	$ 2,000
1997	5,000
1998	12,000
1999	10,000
2000	10,000
2001	9,000
2002	8,000
Present value of cash flow at 15% cost of capital	$31,357
Cost of investment	25,000
Net present value	$ 6,357

Write a memo explaining why the company should make this investment and why the company should scrap its three-year payback rule.

C 16.2   Graham Products, Inc., manufactures a product it sells for $20. Graham sells all the 12,000 units it is capable of producing at the current time, and a marketing study indicates that it could sell 7,000 more units. To increase its capacity, Graham must buy a machine that has the capacity to produce 30,000 units of its product.

The existing equipment can produce the product at a variable cost of $8 per unit. Today it has a book value of $40,000 and a market value of $30,000. It has a remaining life of five years but no salvage value. The depreciation on the old equipment is $8,000 per year.

The new equipment could produce 30,000 units at a variable cost of $6 per unit. The new equipment would cost $250,000 and has a five-year life, which would be depreciated at a rate of $50,000 per year. If the new machine is purchased, fixed operating costs will decrease by $10,000 per year.

If Graham's cost of capital is 18 percent and its tax rate is 30 percent, should Graham buy the new machine? Why or why not?

ETHICAL CHALLENGES

EC 16.1   Wal-Mart recently ran into opposition when it tried to open Wal-Mart stores in certain New England and Pennsylvania towns. Wal-Mart's capital budgeting process has determined that these locations would be profitable for the corporation. However, these communities have successfully fought to keep Wal-Mart from opening new stores. The communities argue that a Wal-Mart store will destroy the downtown business of the community and hurt the town's quality of life. Despite being rebuffed by the citizens of these towns, Wal-Mart has continued its efforts to locate stores in these communities. Should Wal-Mart continue or stop its efforts to open stores in these communities? Why or why not?

EC 16.2   The Bolloville Corporation has the opportunity to manufacture a new chemical but will have to buy a new machine that costs $350,000 to produce the chemical. The net present value of the new machine is $2,500. However, you have learned that in calculating the net present value, the cost of disposing of the waste product that the EPA has labeled mildly hazardous was excluded. Bolloville disputes the EPA's claim that the waste product is toxic. Therefore, Bolloville's management decided it could avoid the disposal cost by dumping the waste with other trash. Should Bolloville buy the new machine? Why or why not?

CHAPTER 17

Planning Investments in Human Resources

Learning Objectives

1. Explain the impact of employee-related costs on operating decisions.
2. Identify the sources of employee-related costs other than salaries and wages.
3. Identify the types of pension plans and explain their implications for employee compensation.
4. Describe deferred compensation and explain the motivations for employers and employees to choose deferred compensation.
5. Explain the role of monetary compensation as well as other forms of compensation in motivating employee performance.

Have you ever thought about what products computer software companies actually sell? While their products may be referred to as computer code on disks, the actual products are the result of very careful work by talented, creative people. The 1994 annual report of software giant Microsoft Corporation explains that "[o]ur products are intellectual in nature, and people are our most important asset."[1]

Not surprisingly, one of the biggest cost categories for computer software products is the labor of the people who design and write computer codes. In 1994 Microsoft Corporation spent $610 million on research and development, much of which was paid to "programmers, developers, code sizzlers and code cowboys."[2]

In addition to receiving direct pay, Microsoft employees have other forms of compensation. They have a stock purchase plan that allows them to buy Microsoft stock at prices below market value, in addition to a savings plan that allows them to save up to 15 percent of their salary before income taxes are deducted. Some Microsoft employees receive certificates allowing them to purchase Microsoft stock for a specified time period at a lower price than they

[1] Microsoft Corporation, 1994 annual report.
[2] Ibid.

563

would have to pay if they bought the stock from a current stockholder. At the end of 1994, employees and directors owned the equivalent of 47 percent of Microsoft stock.

Most companies carefully consider the costs of labor, including its associated costs such as employee training and health insurance benefits, when making their investment decisions. Microsoft is a good example of such a company.

IMPACT OF COMPENSATION ISSUES ON BUSINESS DECISIONS

When managers make investment decisions, they weigh a number of alternatives. Often the choice involves either investing in long-lived assets to produce products or increasing the labor force to do the job. That is, management can substitute labor for capital investment in the production process. Labor-related costs are important considerations when managers decide whether to invest in people or in machines and equipment that can often do the same job. In this chapter, we describe the implications of many labor-related costs on business decisions.

What labor-related costs must managers consider when planning investment decisions? What are a company's compensation alternatives, including bonuses, and the implications of these compensation alternatives for motivating employees? We discuss each of these issues, in turn.

Human Resources: The Unrecorded Investment

It is reasonable for companies to expect their employees to contribute future economic benefits to the company's operations in the same way that other assets, which are reflected in accounting records, do. Why, then, aren't the future economic benefits of employees recorded and communicated in the same way as other assets?

There are two important differences between people and other assets that make recording human assets inappropriate. One difference is the difficulty in measuring the value of employees' potential contributions. The other more important difference is the idea that a company cannot own its employees in the same way that it owns its other assets. Employees can leave a company anytime they want, though sometimes the company and its employees have a contract that penalizes employees if they break the contract by leaving. In contrast to its labor, a company's other assets require that management decide when to sell or dispose of them. Thus, the future benefits of employees are neither sufficiently measurable or certain, which are both necessary conditions to qualify as an asset.

Although companies do not record their investment in human resources as an asset, they must recognize the costs associated with employees as expenses when determining periodic income. Employment costs affect the operations of companies as well as their financing and investing decisions.

Impact of Compensation on Operating Decisions

Employee compensation directly affects operating decisions in two important ways. One involves the decision about whether to have existing employees work overtime or to hire additional employees when there is increased workload demand. The other employee-related operating decision concerns whether to use full-time or part-time employees.

The decision about whether to have employees work overtime should be viewed in terms of the economics of the situation. Part of compensation costs for companies is fixed, such as the weekly or monthly salaries for employees or the health and life insurance benefits they receive. Other employee costs are variable, such as hourly wages and wage-related expenses like FICA and unemployment taxes. The higher the fixed portion of employee compensation, the better it is to have employees work overtime instead of hiring additional employees.

How Much Do You Need to Save for Retirement?

ost of you are many years from retirement. But, if you are going to have enough money to live comfortably in your retirement years, you need to start saving well before you retire. As an example of the timing and amount of savings necessary, assume that you will retire when you are 65 years old and will live another 20 years after that. In addition, you want to have $2,000 each month during retirement. If you can earn only 3 percent on your investments during retirement (a conservative estimate), then you will need $360,622 at the date you retire to provide you with the $2,000 a month you need. (This example ignores other sources of retirment income like Social Security.) The table below shows the **amount that you would need to save**

each month until retirement, under various assumptions of return and the age at which you start your savings. The return rates are those you earn on your savings before retirement.

As you see, the sooner that you start saving, the more the compounding of interest will help you save the amount you need. You also can see the importance of getting a good return on your savings.

(In our example, we ignore the likely decline in purchasing power of future dollars, an important consideration in long-term planning. Remember, if the inflation rate in the U.S. economy is 3 percent, then a gallon of gas that costs $1.25 today will cost about $4.08 in 40 years when today's 25-year-olds retire.)

Age When You Start Saving (years)	Return on Savings Prior to Retirement				
	3 Percent	4 Percent	6 Percent	8 Percent	10 Percent
25	$ 389	$ 305	$ 181	$ 103	$ 57
30	486	394	253	157	94
35	618	519	359	241	159
40	808	701	520	379	271
45	1,098	983	780	612	474
50	1,588	1,465	1,240	1,042	870
55	$2,580	$2,449	$2,200	$1,971	$1,760

In making the decision about having employees work overtime, employers also should consider the nature of their business cycle. Does it require temporary seasonal overtime? Will overtime last for a long period and lead to employee burnout, which could cause the company to lose employees? Employee turnover, regardless of its cause, requires that companies hire new employees who often require expensive training and other costs to start up and/or catch up to the levels of expertise required.

PAUSE & REFLECT

Public accounting firms face the dilemma of whether to have their employees work overtime because a major portion of their business occurs in the first three months of the year. Should the firms have their employees work overtime to handle the intense schedule and risk having to deal with higher turnover and higher training costs? Or should accounting firms hire temporary employees during the busy parts of the year?

Compensation expense also affects the employer's decision about hiring part-time employees. One advantage of hiring part-time employees is that they do not require payment of the same benefits that full-time employees require. However, can part-time employees do the same job as full-time employees? Are there other costs related to employing part-time employees that may be higher than they would be if the company used full-time employees?

Recently, a form of organization has evolved that serves as a compromise between the need to hire part-time or full-time employees—the professional employer organization (PEO).[3] PEOs are essentially employee leasing firms that hire some or all of

---

[3]Stuart Schear, "Would You Live Better without Your Employees?" *Business & Health*, April 1995, pp. 55–62.

a company's employees, including the CEO, and then "lease" them back to the company for an administrative fee. As the employer, the PEO administers the payroll and ensures compliance with federal and state laws. By including employees from a number of companies, PEOs can provide employee benefits at lower costs than small businesses can individually. This offers full-time labor at a lower cost.

Impact of Compensation on Investment Decisions

Sometimes companies face the choice of either investing in equipment and machines to produce products and provide services or hiring people who can perform the same function. Both long-lived assets and employees have initial costs. Equipment has relatively large acquisition costs, which often include financing, and hiring people often involves initial training costs as well as the costs of finding the employees, such as advertising available positions and interviewing prospective candidates. In addition, there are inefficiencies, and therefore significant costs, associated with new employees' learning processes. In 1993, employers in the United States spent about 1.47 percent of total payroll costs on formal training and development, which was about $30 billion for the year!

After acquiring machines and equipment, companies must invest in related repair and maintenance costs, as well as labor costs for operators to run them. But by far, the major cost of purchasing such investments is the initial acquisition cost. Alternatively, the costs of having people, rather than machines, do the job continue as long as the company employs these workers. Those costs include not only what the employees are paid, but also the cost of the benefits they receive as part of their employment.

Consider, for example, a very important recent development that companies sometimes consider as part their investment strategy—automation. Automation reduces operator labor, a major cost of production. This has led to significant changes in companies' investment decisions, particularly for manufacturing companies. Now companies are shifting from investing in labor to investing in sophisticated, high-tech equipment that either replaces employees (robotics) or requires that employees have a higher level of technical training. This, of course, causes companies to pay higher wages for more well-trained technical employees. Between 1990 and 1994, employment in the manufacturing sector dropped by 5.6 percent in the United States, while jobs in the service sector increased 4.1 percent.

We move from this discussion of how compensation-related costs affect businesses' decisions about investing in people or machines to discuss some of the employee benefits that employers incur when they employ people.

LABOR COSTS ARE NOT THE SAME AS PAYMENTS TO EMPLOYEES

As we discussed in Chapter 8, there are employee-related costs other than wages or salaries. These **fringe benefits** include items such as payroll taxes, including social security taxes (FICA); health and life insurance; and retirement pay (pensions). In 1993, employee benefits, including payroll taxes and holidays and vacations totaled 41.3 percent of total payroll costs.[4]

Some payroll-related costs, such as payroll taxes and insurance payments, are easy to match with current revenues earned during the period to derive net income. However, matching the cost of other benefits, such as retirement benefits, is a more complicated and important issue affecting income measurement.

The Real Costs of Employees

Whether employees are accountants, production workers, or upper-level managers of the corporation, the costs of benefits paid by employers are part of the price of obtaining the skills and talent of employees. Other costs, such as the cost of maintaining a pleasant work environment, are also required to attract good employees.

Now we look more closely at three important employee benefits: health and life insurance, paid leave from work, and postretirement benefits.

---

[4]M. P. Patterson, "1994 KPMG Retirement Benefits Survey," *Journal of Compensation and Benefits* 10 (March/April 1995), pp. 5–11.

Employees' Health and Life Insurance   In general, most businesses buy insurance policies in order to manage business risks. The insurance policies spread the risk of the costs of certain events, like a fire or flood, over a large group of people or businesses, for example, building owners. The intent of insurance is to provide coverage for the cost of required repairs and recovery due to an unforeseen event and, at the same time, ensure that the costs for every member of the group equal the insurance payments made by the group.[5] So when a company insures a building it owns, it is insuring against events that could directly affect its economic well-being. If a warehouse burns or sustains water damage due to flooding, the company loses the use of the warehouse and the inventory it contains. The company, therefore, has a direct economic interest in insuring the warehouse. In contrast, health and life insurance policies for employees do not cover company assets. Rather, such insurance policies are insuring the company's employees' health and lives.

Companies that provide insurance for their employees incur substantial costs. The average cost of health premiums per employee was $2,851 in 1993, a 10.5 percent increase from the year before.

Why do companies pay for health and life insurance for their employees and subsidize insurance payments for the employees' families? The best answer is that, by offering these forms of compensation in addition to wages or salaries, companies can attract better employees at lower salaries. If companies offered employees salaries and wages that were high enough to allow employees to buy their own health and life insurance, it would cost companies more than it does to offer lower wages or salaries and to buy health and life insurance policies directly.[6] It is less expensive for companies to buy employee health and life insurance because they can do so at group insurance rates, which are significantly lower than the rates available to individuals. Therefore, the cost of paying lower salaries *plus* the cost of group insurance is less than the alternative of paying salaries that would have to be high enough to cover costs of more expensive individual insurance policies.

Group insurance spreads the cost of claims among group members. Group health plans insure everyone in the group, including some individuals who frequently require insurance benefits as well as others who would not ordinarily buy insurance at all because they face below-average risks of ill health. This provides insurance companies with access to the diverse population they need to be able to offer lower group rates.

Health and life insurance-related issues do not pose any difficult accounting problems. Companies usually pay premiums to insurers once a month or once per quarter. Employers include the cost of these premiums in their accounting records as part of the salary or wage expense for the period. Manufacturing companies include the portion of insurance costs pertaining to employees' involvement in production as part of overhead (or direct labor) and allocate these costs to products through appropriate cost drivers.

Paid Leave   Most businesses pay their employees for certain times when employees are away from work, such as when they are sick or take a vacation. As with insurance benefits, the employer offers these types of fringe benefits based on the belief that they help the company attract better employees and provide incentives for employees to be more productive when they are at work.

Sometimes an employee earns the right to paid vacation or sick leave in one accounting period and does not take the leave time until a later accounting period. This raises the following accounting question: When should the company recognize the expense of vacation time and sick leave in determining net income?

---

[5]We ignore the profits to the insurance companies, which are the difference between the amounts they collect in premiums and the accounts they pay in claims to the insured.

[6]The employee's portion of health insurance premiums for group health insurance is often paid before calculating his or her income tax, so the employee does not pay income tax on those earnings.

Pensions are an important means of ensuring that retirement income provides adequate comfort and financial security.

Generally, companies recognize the cost for vacation leave as an expense in the period when the employee has both (1) performed whatever service is necessary to earn the time and (2) earned the right to the paid leave, that is, the leave does not depend on any future event.[7]

Whenever the right to receive any benefit is irrevocable and does not depend on the occurrence of any future event, that right is said to be **vested.** For example, if an employee earns the right to two weeks of paid vacation after one year of employment, the company would record no expense for vacation time during the employee's first year. However, in the employee's second year, the right to take the vacation is vested because this employee has performed necessary services and earned the right to paid leave, which does not depend on any future event. During the second year, the company would record the amount expected to be paid to the employee during vacation as an expense, whether the employee actually takes the vacation or not.

PAUSE & REFLECT

If an employee's right to vacation or sick leave is vested and the employee voluntarily quits the job, how does he or she receive that vested compensation? Would your answer be different if the employee was fired from the job for violating the company rules?

We now turn to a discussion of the major postretirement benefits that firms offer to employees after they retire. This includes pension and health care benefits.

Postretirement Benefits   Employees consider benefits received after they retire as an important part of their benefit package. Postretirement benefits include all benefits that employees receive after their years of employment, for example, pension and health care expenses. We focus on pensions because they involve large amounts of company resources and influence business decisions regarding hiring and making other investments.

---

[7]These guidelines apply to all kinds of paid leaves: sick, personal-time, vacation leaves, and so on.

EXHIBIT | **17.1**

Pension Plan Events

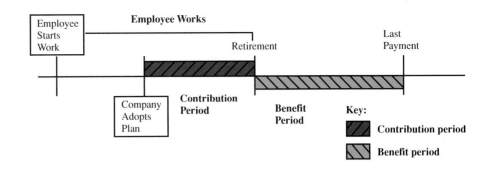

Employee Pension Plans. One way employees could pay for their retirement would be for them to save money they earn while they are employed. The money to be saved would be taxed before it is saved. A common alternative to saving earnings "as they go" is for employers to offer pensions as part of their compensation to employees.

Employee pension plans involve payments made by companies to their retired employees on a regular (usually monthly) basis. Consider the significance of pension plans. In 1994, 89 percent of employers with 200 or more employees offered pension plans as part of their employee benefits package. Such postretirement benefits are important because they amount to huge sums of money and, therefore, are a major expense for companies. In 1995, U.S. companies were expected to pay $106 billion in postretirement benefits to former employees from an estimated 1.1 million private pension plans. The assets of these plans exceeded $4 trillion, which was about one-fifth of total U.S. assets.[8] Because of the magnitude of this type of investment for companies, it is important to understand how employees earn and receive payment for these benefits as well as how employers record and finance them.

Agreements regarding pension arrangements are described in a **pension plan,** which is a contract between the employee and the employer that sets out the responsibilities that each party assumes. Pension contracts describe who will pay for the pension benefits that the employee will receive, how the money contributed to the pension plan will be invested between the time it is paid and the time of the employee's retirement, and how and when the benefits will be paid to the employees.

Exhibit 17.1 shows the timing of significant pension-related events for an employee who is employed when the pension plan is adopted by the employing company. We can see that, typically, the employee works a number of years, retires, and receives benefits, which end upon the employee's death (last payment). The period of employment is the period when a company and/or its employees contribute to the plan. Then after retirement, the employee receives the related compensation benefits that have accumulated.

Funding Pension Plans Generally, pension plans involve three important groups: employees, employers, and pension plan trustees. Exhibit 17.2 shows the relationships among these three parties. The employee provides labor to the employer and receives as compensation, among other things, the right to receive pension benefits during retirement. The employee, and usually the employer, make contributions to the pension plan trustee, which is a separate entity with its own accounting system and financial statements. After retirement, the employee receives benefits from the trustee.

Pension funding, or the act of making contributions to a pension plan, includes setting aside contributions and investing these funds to accumulate pension benefits to pay the employee during retirement. Usually the employer sends funds, whether

[8]D. Kieso and J. Weygandt, *Intermediate Accounting,* 8th ed. (New York: John Wiley & Sons, 1995), p. 1057.

EXHIBIT | **17.2**

Pension Plan Parties

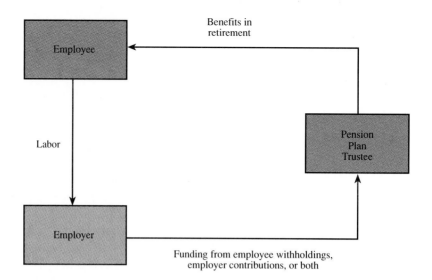

paid by the employer, paid by withholdings from the employee's pay, or both, to the pension trustee. The trustee has the responsibility to safeguard and invest contributed funds to earn a return on the amounts invested.

Types of Pension Plans Exhibit 17.3 shows the four basic types of pension plans. **Noncontributory pension plans** are funded solely by employers, with no contributions from employees. For **contributory pension plans,** the employee contributes some or all of the funding for the plan. Both contributory and noncontributory plans are further categorized into defined contribution and defined benefit plans. **Defined contribution pension plans** set out the amounts to be contributed to the plan, but do not specify the benefits to be paid to the employee during retirement. **Defined benefit pension plans** indicate amounts that the employee will receive during retirement according to a benefit formula that is usually based on the employee's salary and the number of years worked. For defined benefit plans, there are no specific provisions regarding the amounts of funding or when such amounts should be remitted to the plan trustee.

To explain the differences among these types of pension plans, assume that a company has one employee who is 58 years old and will retire at age 62. This employee is expected to live another 20 years after retirement.

A defined contribution pension plan would specify the amount to be funded in each of the remaining four years that the employee will work. A common way to determine the amount of contributions is to base it on a percentage of the employee's salary each year. For example, a plan that specifies that the contribution must be 15 percent of an annual salary of $46,000 results in an annual contribution of $6,900. If the defined contribution plan is contributory, the employee usually makes the contributions that he or she provides through payroll withholding, and the employer remits the amounts withheld, in addition to any amounts the employer contributes, to the pension trustee. If the plan is a noncontributory plan, the employer makes all of the funding contributions.

What will the employee actually receive from the company during retirement? In a defined contribution plan, the benefits to be received are not known until retirement. Once the contributions are set, two factors influence how much the employee will receive: (1) how long he or she worked and made contributions and (2) the return that the trustee of the pension plan earns on the funds it receives.

In our example, assume that the trustee earns 6 percent on the funds received from the employer, regardless of whether the plan is contributory or noncontributory. After four years, the employee would have $30,185 available for retirement,

EXHIBIT | 17.3 | Basic Pension Plans

	Defined Contribution Plan	Defined Benefit Plan
Noncontributory Plan	Funded by employer	Funded by employer
	Contributions rather than benefits are specified in the plan	Benefits rather than contributions are specified in the plan
	Expense recognized by the firm equals the firm's contribution for the period.	Expense recognized by the firm is determined under the rules of FASB Statement 87.
Contributory Plan	Funded by employee or both employee and employer	Funded by employer or both employee and employer
	Contributions rather than benefits are specified in the plan	Benefits rather than contributions are specified in the plan
	Expense recognized by the firm equals the firm's contribution for the period.	Expense recognized by the firm is determined under the rules of FASB Statement 87.

which is the future value of an annuity with payments of $6,900 for four years at 6 percent. At that point, the trustee determines the amount of the retirement benefits based on the estimates of life expectancy of the employee.

The fund trustee usually settles the retirement obligation by using an **annuity contract** that generates payment to the employee of an agreed-upon amount each period for the rest of his or her life. The amount of the annuity paid to the employee under this contract is based on an interest rate comparable to what the employee might earn if he or she received the money at retirement. The trustee does not know how long the retired employee will live, but, if it acts as the trustee for a large number of retirees, it pays for average life expectancies of all retirees.

If the plan in our example were a defined benefit plan, the amount that the employee would receive each month during retirement would be specified by the plan's benefit formula. The amount of benefits is often based on the highest or average amount of the five highest years' salaries for the employee.

Assume that the plan stated that the employee would receive 60 percent of the average of his or her five highest years' salaries. If the average was $52,000, the employee would receive $31,200 ($52,000 × 60%) during each year of retirement. So, in the case of the defined benefit plan, we can answer the question of how much the employee will receive during retirement. Once the trustee estimates the amount needed for pension benefits, it is possible to estimate the amount that has to be available at retirement.

Accounting for Pension Plans Accounting for the cost of pension benefits reflects the differences between the defined benefit and defined contribution plans. Proper accounting requires matching the cost of employees' work during an accounting period with the revenue they helped to generate that period. This matching requires recognizing as expense in the current period amounts that will not be paid to employees until retirement. In many cases, retirement and other benefit payments can be as much as 20 to 40 years in the future.

Accounting for a defined contribution plan is simple. For defined contribution plans, the company recognizes an expense amount that equals the funding contribution it makes in each period. Defined benefit plans involve a very complex process of determining each period's pension expense. This process is carried out by highly trained pension actuaries and accountants.

Other Retirement Benefits   Pensions are not the only benefits that employees earn while they are employed but receive after retirement. Employees also can receive health and group life insurance in addition to other benefits. These forms of postretirement benefits are likely to grow in importance in the future, and many of the accounting issues surrounding them are similar to those found regarding pensions.

Because fringe benefits such as health insurance and pensions are part of the cost of employees, employers must consider these costs when they are making hiring decisions. In addition to the cost of hiring people, companies must consider the timing of when they pay employees. Next, we discuss ways that employees can work now and receive their pay later—possibly many years later.

DEFERRED COMPENSATION: EFFECT ON LABOR COSTS

Sometimes the business and the employee both benefit from **deferred compensation,** which is a means of payment to employees that allows them to work now and receive compensation for that work sometime in the future. The timing of the actual payment to the employee depends on the terms of the contract between the employer and employee.

In a system of deferred compensation, the employer receives the benefits of the employee's labor *plus* the advantage of the time value of the money due to deferring compensation to later periods. So what is the advantage for the employee? In a deferred compensation pay scheme, the employee usually receives higher pay and often receives possible income tax benefits.

In the United States, individuals pay tax on their **taxable income,** which is income as determined by the set of rules found in the *Federal Income Tax Code.* These rules prescribe what is considered taxable revenue for an individual as well as the expenditures, or deductions, that reduce taxable revenue. Income taxes in the United States are slightly progressive. That is, as shown in Exhibit 17.4, as an individual's income goes up, he or she pays a higher proportion of income as income tax. For example, the

EXHIBIT | **17.4**

Progressive Income Taxes

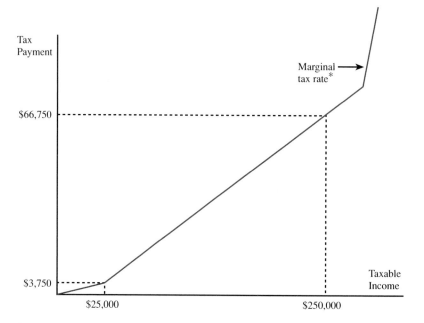

*The portion of each additional dollar of income that is paid in income taxes.
Income taxes rise faster than taxable income increases in the progressive tax structure found in the United States and many other countries.

tax code could specify that taxable incomes up to $25,000 have a tax rate of 15 percent, taxable income from $25,001 to $250,000 would be taxed at a higher rate of 28 percent, and incomes exceeding $250,000 would be taxed at an even higher rate. In this example, a taxpayer who had taxable income of $25,000 would pay $3,750 ($25,000 × 15%). A taxpayer with $250,000 of taxable income would pay the $3,750 for the first $25,000 of taxable income and $63,000 for the portion of his or her taxable income between $25,000 and $250,000 [($250,000 − $25,000) × 28% = $63,000], or a total income tax of $66,750.

Employees benefit from deferring taxable income to future periods when they plan to have lower income. Or employees can also benefit simply by spreading out the income over a longer period of time. Then, in each year, the amount received as income is lower, which requires a lower tax rate.

Compensation requirements have an important effect on the decisions made by employers and are a very important facet of operating a business. In order to determine how many employees to hire and whether to hire full- or part-time workers, management must decide how best to compensate its employees depending on the nature of the jobs it expects them to do.

Alternatives to Paying Employees Now

There are a number of ways that the employer and the employee can move the employee's taxable income into future periods.

Employment Contracts   One way to move compensation pay into the future is simply to sign an employment contract in which both the employer and employee mutually agree that some or all of the money earned in the current period will be paid in future periods in certain amounts, and at certain times, as stated in the contract. This type of employment contract applies to the way that many professional athletes are paid. Athletes sign contracts with owners that determine what they will earn and when their earnings will be paid. This deferred compensation benefits both the players and the owners.

We do not know the nature of the contract that Larry Bird signed when he was playing for the Boston Celtics, but it is likely that it contained deferred compensation. Let's assume that 1990 was Larry Bird's last year as a player and that his compensation included $1.5 million of deferred compensation to be paid in the years after he retired, in equal payments over 20 years, or $75,000 a year. For the Celtics, the deferred compensation is an expense that has not been paid. To record the amount of this deferred compensation, the Celtics find the present value of the annuity of $75,000 for 20 years at an interest rate that reflects what they would have to pay to borrow the money. The present value of a $75,000 annuity for 20 years at an assumed rate of 8 percent is $736,365 ($75,000 × 9.8182). They would record this expense and related liability at less than half the $1.5 million agreed to because of the time value of money.

In the same way that selling inventory bought on credit in the current period is an expense (Cost of Goods Sold) and a liability (Accounts Payable) for a company, receiving the services of employees before paying them is also a liability. Look at the financial statements of the Boston Celtics (introduced in Chapter 7) to see how they reflect deferred compensation.

Employee Stock Option Plans   Another way that the employees can work now and move the related wage payments into the future is by means of **employee stock option plans.** Employee stock option plans offer employees stock options as compensation, thereby allowing company ownership to be spread among employees. As you know, when a company issues a stock option certificate, the option gives the holder the right to purchase a share of the company's stock within some specified time at some specified price.

The employee benefits from a stock option plan because these options typically offer the stock at less than its market price. When the employee exercises the options,

EXHIBIT | 17.5

Option Alternatives: To Hold
or Not to Hold?

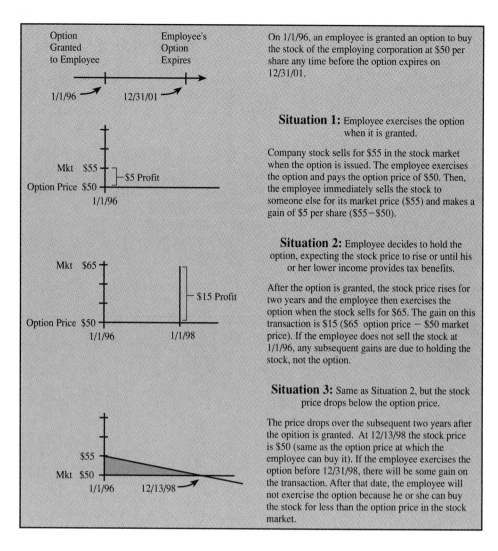

On 1/1/96, an employee is granted an option to buy the stock of the employing corporation at $50 per share any time before the option expires on 12/31/01.

Situation 1: Employee exercises the option when it is granted.

Company stock sells for $55 in the stock market when the option is issued. The employee exercises the option and pays the option price of $50. Then, the employee immediately sells the stock to someone else for its market price ($55) and makes a gain of $5 per share ($55−$50).

Situation 2: Employee decides to hold the option, expecting the stock price to rise or until his or her lower income provides tax benefits.

After the option is granted, the stock price rises for two years and the employee then exercises the option when the stock sells for $65. The gain on this transaction is $15 ($65 option price − $50 market price). If the employee does not sell the stock at 1/1/96, any subsequent gains are due to holding the stock, not the option.

Situation 3: Same as Situation 2, but the stock price drops below the option price.

The price drops over the subsequent two years after the opition is granted. At 12/13/98 the stock price is $50 (same as the option price at which the employee can buy it). If the employee exercises the option before 12/31/98, there will be some gain on the transaction. After that date, the employee will not exercise the option because he or she can buy the stock for less than the option price in the stock market.

he or she exchanges the option and cash in the amount of the option price for a share of common stock. Exhibit 17.5 shows the types of alternatives an employee might face when granted a stock option. For example in situation 2, the employee, granted the option on January 1, 1996, holds it until January 1, 1998, when the market price of the stock is $65. On January 1, 1998, the employee exercises the option and pays the $50 option price per share. Then, the employee can sell the stock immediately at the $65 market price per share. The $15 per share difference between the exercise price ($50) and the market price ($65) is a gain for the employee.

For example, assume Microsoft issued 10 options to each of its employees and each option offered a share of Microsoft common stock at the option price of $56. If Microsoft's common stock was being traded at that time for $60 per share, employees could exercise their options and immediately sell the stock in the stock market for $60 per share, making $4 per share ($60 market price – $56 option price). On the date of the grant, which is the date that Microsoft gives options to its employees, the company would record compensation expense in the amount of $40 ($4 × 10 options) times the number of employees.

In this case, Microsoft would record the compensation expense when the options are granted even if the employee does not exercise the options immediately. Subsequently, if 400 employees immediately exercise their options, Microsoft would record this event by showing the receipt of option prices of $224,000 (400 × 10 options × $56) from its employees in addition to reflecting the related issuance of the common stock.

Employees may defer exercising options if there are other ways to profit from them. If the employee expects the market value of the company's stock to go up, one way to potentially profit from the option is to keep it. Then, for example, if the market price of Microsoft stock does, in fact, rise, the difference between the amount the employee has to pay for the stock (the option price stated in the stock option agreement or contract) and the market value of the stock is even greater, which leads to a higher profit for the employee. On the other hand, if the market price of Microsoft's stock goes down, the employee is still okay as long as the market price of the stock is above the option price of $56. Even if the market price drops below the option price before the employee exercises the options, there is no loss to the employee because he or she did not pay for the option. Employees would rationally choose not to pay the option price for the stock when the market price drops below the option price because they could buy the same stock for less than the option price in the stock market.

If the employee expects his or her income to be lower in the future, for example, after retirement, there are tax benefits from not exercising the option until after retirement. The employee's income in retirement will be lower and, therefore, so will the related marginal income tax rate. This means that not exercising options until retirement can result in tax savings.

Another way for an employee to profit from stock options is by selling the options themselves. Since the option is the right to buy stock at a fixed (sometimes bargain) price, it also has a market price. Therefore, the employee can sell the option in the market rather than exercising it or keeping it.

If employees do not sell or exercise their stock options, the value of their stock options can increase due to changes in the market value of the options.[9] These increases, which lead to gains, can amount to substantial sums. For example, the CEO of First Hospital Corp. of America, Thomas F. Frist, Jr., earned $129.9 million in stock option gains in 1992.

In 1989, PepsiCo began a stock option plan that covers 100 percent of its workers. As an example, one worker under the plan was a local market manager for KFC Corporation[10] (which PepsiCo owns). He received options on company stock equal to 10 percent of his previous year's earnings. During the period from 1989 to 1993, the market price of those options doubled.

Another very significant benefit for employers of firms that offer employee stock option plans is that the plans create a sense of ownership among employees and, thus, can serve to align the interests of executives and employees. Referring to PepsiCo's stock option plan, the market manager for KFC said, "I think like I am an owner of the company."[11] (See discussion of goal congruence in the subsequent section on employee motivation.)

Employee Stock Option Compensation Controversy

The proper means of accounting for options is a matter of great controversy. The controversy pivots around the value of what is given to the employee and how to measure the related expense to be recognized in the company's accounting records.

For many years, the GAAP rule for accounting for employee stock option compensation has been to measure the difference between the option price and the market value of the stock *when the option is granted to the employee*. For an employee receiving an option exercisable on the date of grant at an option price of $25 per share, the amount of compensation expense recognized by the company would depend on the market price of the stock at that date. Assume that the market price was higher than the option price, say $32, in this case. The employer firm would recognize the difference, $7 ($32–$25), multiplied by the number of options granted under

---

[9]The market value of stock options is linked to the market value of the stock to which the options apply and the variability of that stock's market price.

[10]KFC Corporation's former name was Kentucky Fried Chicken.

[11]"More Workers Are Getting a Stake—For Now," *Business Week*, April 12, 1993.

the employee stock option plan as compensation expense in the current period's income statement. On the other hand, if the stock's market price was less than the option price when the company granted the option, for example, if it was $23, there would be *no* compensation expense recognized at any time for the options granted during the period.

During the early 1990s, many investors were upset when they discovered that some top executives in major corporations were receiving millions of dollars worth of stock options that were not being treated as an expense of those corporations. In response, the FASB considered ways of recording compensation expense for employee stock option plans based on the market value of the options themselves at the date of grant. This meant that anytime corporations issue stock options to their employees, the corporation would recognize compensation expense equal to the estimated market value of the options. While this might give investors a better idea of the amount of compensation paid to executives, many accountants opposed this approach because of the subjectivity involved in determining the value of stock options. In addition, some corporations, such as start-up companies in high-tech industries, opposed recognizing compensation expense based on the market value of the options because they use option-based compensation to attract talented individuals to employment. This allows start-up companies to use most of their available cash to fund operations until they develop and begin to sell their products. If they have to recognize compensation expense in determining their net income in the short run, the lower, and perhaps even negative, income may adversely affect their ability to borrow and raise capital by offering new stock issues. In 1996, the FASB issued a statement that requires companies to disclose the market value of employee stock options they grant in the notes that accompany the financial statements. Thus, the value of the options is not included in the statements themselves.

The issues surrounding options and other forms of compensation are complicated. And when the potential tax benefits to the employees are also considered, we can expect there to be a continual debate about accounting for options given as employee compensation. Because the use of options can result in the alignment of the interests of stockholders and managers as well as the interests of managers and other employees, options are likely to remain a major source of compensation in many industries.

Employers can move payment of employees' compensation into future periods with deferred compensation contracts and employee stock option plans. But what about motivating employees to perform well? Next we discuss some of the issues associated with using compensation to motivate employees to perform.

WHAT ABOUT EMPLOYEE MOTIVATION AND PERFORMANCE-BASED LABOR COSTS?

Does paying someone more money induce them to work harder? Not always. Sometimes nonmonetary compensation, such as recognition, can better induce an employee to exert more effort on the job. In addition, there are ways other than wages and salaries to compensate employee performance, such as offering sales commissions. In the case of sales commissions, employers believe that when a salesperson is paid a percentage of the total value of the goods or services he or she sells in a period, the salesperson will sell more goods. (See discussion below.)

Some people work because they like to work or because they would be bored otherwise, but the principal reason people work is for monetary compensation. Employers pay employees for providing their skills and efforts to complete a job. Below we look at how the form and amount of compensation affect the decisions of both employers and employees.

The Economics of Employee Motivation

Compensation is one way to motivate employees to provide effort and to work skillfully and carefully. Generally, employers offer the employee a mutually agreeable wage to do the job. When the work is completed, the employee gets paid. But there are a number of ways to compensate employees—hourly wages, salaries, bonus plans, or some form of deferred compensation.

In industries like textiles, it is easy to measure a worker's productivity.

In order to explore which of these forms of compensation might be satisfactory to an employer, consider two critical aspects of the workplace: (1) whether employers can determine the amount of effort that an employee expends and (2) whether there is uncertainty about how good business will be, and if so, what the amount of uncertainty is.

It is relatively easy for employers in businesses like clothing manufacturing to determine how hard an employee has worked because it is possible for them to identify the quantity of items produced. In such situations, an employee's pay can be directly linked to the number of pieces of clothing that the employee produced in a period. Paying employees according to the *number of items produced in a period* is called **piece-rate pay.** However, for other types of jobs, it is much harder for the employer to witness or assure the effort of employees. For example, it would be hard for a sales manager of a traveling salesperson to tell whether the salesperson actually called on all the customers that he said he did. And it is also difficult for the sales manager to tell how hard the salesperson tried to make the sale. So in industries that use a traveling sales force, it is very common to pay employees on a **commission basis.** That is, salespeople are often paid a percentage of the *dollar amount of goods that they sell in a period*, in part because the employer cannot tell how hard they worked.

In order to motivate employees in situations where it is hard to determine their effort, employers link pay to something that both parties can agree upon. This might include, for example, the amount of sales. It also should relate to something that the employee wants at the same time. When the goals of the employer and employee are aligned, as we discussed in previous sections, it is called **goal congruence.** Employee stock option plans, which link the employee's compensation to employer's goals, can benefit both the employee and the employer. Therefore, this is a good example of a way to compensate employees that produces goal congruence.

Motivating Employees to Accept Risk

In the workplace, there is a reasonable amount of uncertainty about the prospects for the business itself. Chapter 14 indicated that uncertainty about how future events will unfold creates risk. If we assume that most people prefer less risky situations to those with more risk, it follows that employees prefer as little uncertainty about their future compensation as possible.

Now think about the kinds of risks that the employer faces. There can be business difficulties because products do not sell; because there are problems with suppliers that drive up the cost of sales, which the business cannot pass on to customers; or because of competitors or government regulation, which can damage the market in which the business sells its products. Since risk is inherent in business, what can an employer do?

If the employer bears all the risk and the employee gets paid regardless of how the business succeeds, what incentive is there for the employee to work hard? The worker might put a lot of effort into work because of a belief that it is his or her obligation as an employee and because it is the right thing to do. However, if the employee shares some of the risk that the employer faces, then this employee will work harder and will tend to make the choices that are in the best interest of the business.

If employers assume that employees are not sufficiently motivated by their work ethic, they might use compensation to induce employees to accept some of the risk the employers face. For example, employers can motivate employees by offering higher pay and, at the same time, linking that pay to specific desired outcomes. **Bonuses** are forms of compensation that are contingent on the occurrence of some specified future event, such as the amount of sales in the period exceeding some pre-set target level or the amount of expenses remaining below some benchmark level. If the goals of the employer include cost containment for certain expenses, then offering a bonus plan that pays the bonus when costs are below a certain target level (a specific desired outcome) shifts some of the risk to the employees. The risk comes from the possibility that the expense may be higher than the target amount set, whether it is the employee's fault or not. In such a case, the employee would not receive the bonus.

Such bonus plans offer employees higher potential pay in return for accepting risk, and accepting risk can motivate the employee to make decisions that are more in line with those the employer wants.

Stock options are also a way to get employees to accept business risk. As we said earlier, new high-tech businesses like those in the Silicon Valley of northern California use stock options as a way to compensate employees because risk is a major facet of their business. The high-tech industry often experiences fast changes and unpredictable directions. A new product that has taken years to develop that has a large investment in research and development can become obsolete almost instantly. Consequently, in these industries, stock options are often a large part of employee compensation. This provides incentives to employees to make the business successful so that the firm's stock is more valuable, causing their compensation to increase.

Motivating Teams

In manufacturing businesses, management increasingly is adopting goals such as faster throughput time, zero defect rates, and continuous improvement. These goals call for cooperative behavior. However, many individually based compensation schemes do not encourage cooperation among employees. Thus, in many business settings, the organization's goals are better met by compensation schemes that promote cooperation among teams of employees. For example, in a manufacturing plant where the goals are to minimize throughput time (discussed in Chapter 13), management can use a bonus scheme that rewards all members of a team when they meet a target throughput time to encourage the type of cooperation necessary to meet this and other goals.

Other situations also benefit from group compensation schemes. In companies where customer service is a major part of the business strategy, paying bonuses to a group of employees based on some overall measure, such as the number of items returned or the number of customer complaints, motivates employees to cooperate in ensuring that the goal of customer service is met.

Bonuses as Compensation

As discussed above, companies use bonuses to pay employees, either in addition to salaries and wages or instead of those forms of compensation. Companies pay bonuses based on both individual and group performance depending on the objective of management.

Calculation of Bonuses Bonuses that are contingent on sales levels or expense levels are simple to calculate, as this formula shows:

$$\text{Bonus base} \times \text{Bonus rate} = \text{Bonus}$$

Assume that a production plant manager has a bonus base that equals the amount by which wage expense for the plant is under $1,200,000 during the period. The bonus rate is 15 percent of the base. If the actual wage expense for the plant during the period is $1,110,000, the bonus base is $90,000 ($1,200,000 − $1,110,000), and the plant manager would earn a bonus of $13,500 ($90,000 × 15%).

When employee bonuses are based on a company's net income and are also used to determine net income, finding the amount paid as bonuses can be a little more difficult. For example, if a key executive has an employment contract stating that she or he will receive a bonus of 10 percent of net income, how do we find the bonus when the amount of the bonus also affects net income?

Since the bonus base is the amount of income before the bonus less the bonus to be paid, substitute that amount in the previous equation for calculating bonuses. Use the following formula:

$$(\text{Income before bonus} - \text{Bonus}) \times \text{Bonus rate} = \text{Bonus}^{12}$$

Assume that the company's income before the bonus was $11 million. Find the bonus by inserting the known amounts into the formula:

$$(\$11,000,000 - \text{Bonus}) \times 10\% = \text{Bonus}$$

So,

$$.1(\$11,000,000) - .1\text{Bonus} = \text{Bonus}$$

Adding .1Bonus to both sides, gives us

$$1.1\text{Bonus} = 1,100,000$$

or

$$\text{Bonus} = \$1,000,000$$

Accounting for bonuses is not different from accounting for compensation in the form of wages or salaries. Bonus compensation still has related withholding and payroll taxes that the business must recognize. Bonuses, like employee stock options, align the interest of employees with those of executives and owners.

Unions: Labor's Voice

Labor unions arose to counter the management practices that developed during the Industrial Revolution of the 19th century. These practices included low pay; poor, and sometimes dangerous, working conditions; and no employee benefits. Labor demands for improvements led to very adversarial positions by managers and labor. In the United States, the labor movement gained support from New Deal laws such as the Wagner Act passed in 1935 which established workers' rights to organize. It also required employers to accept collective bargaining. Labor unions brought bargaining power to employees during discussions with employers for compensation and other job-related conditions.

In earlier periods, the focus of discussions between management and labor was on employee working conditions and the amount of base pay that employees received. However, since the 1980s, U.S. labor unions' negotiations with employers have focused on job security and the quality of the benefits packages that employees receive. In 1993, only 11.2 percent of private-sector workers belonged to unions, which was down from 16.3 percent 10 years earlier.[13]

As services and automation have more recently made their way into the economy, labor unions and management have started to see that a less adversarial stance can benefit both groups. Unions and management benefit from working together so that employees take on broader job descriptions. This gives the employer flexibility to meet changing business demands and, in exchange, the employee receives

---

[12]If the bonus paid by the company is used to determine the company's income taxes, then the effect of taxes should also be considered in determining the bonus. We ignore the additional complication of tax effects.

[13]See Howard Banks and Janet Novack, "What's Ahead for Business?" *Forbes*, January 16, 1995, p. 37.

job security. In addition, negotiations have led to other benefits, such as additional training for employees, on-site day care, and leave time to care for newborns or aging sick parents.

In many businesses, employees are not unionized, yet they receive many of the same benefits that employees in unionized companies receive. This occurs because employers in nonunionized companies offer comparable benefits to unionized companies in an effort to keep employees from organizing.

Regardless of whether employees belong to a union or not, they represent investments made by businesses whose costs differ substantially from those of other long-lived assets. Understanding the costs associated with hiring employees is essential to making good investment decisions for businesses.

PAUSE & REFLECT

Without unions to represent them, how can individual employees manifest enough influence to persuade an employer to provide necessary compensation and working conditions? What alternatives are available to these employees?

SUMMARY

The costs associated with employee compensation are critical elements for making many business decisions. The amounts and timing of these costs are important to both the employer and the employee.

- Businesses often face the choice between hiring employees or acquiring equipment to replace some of the production capabilities of employees. Factors such as the fixed portion of labor costs and the flexibility of the business in hiring part-time employees influence this choice.

- Pensions and other postretirement employee benefits are growing in importance as means of employee compensation. Defined benefit pension plans specify the formula by which pension payments will be made to the employee during retirement, but not the amounts or timing of the funding during the period of employment. In contrast, defined contribution plans specify the funding of the plan during an employee's employment period, but not the benefits to be received after retirement. Either of these types of plans can be funded by both employer and the employee or only the employer.

- Fringe benefits such as health and life insurance often attract employees more than base salaries/wages. These costs can add significantly to the cost of labor.

- Deferred compensation defers payment for the current work of employees but includes the expense of their labors in the current period. Employers benefit from deferring compensation by having the use of the money until compensation is paid. The employee has the advantage of higher wages under deferred compensation plans as well as the tax benefits he or she can realize as a result of receiving compensation payment later when the employee is paying a lower income tax rate.

- Employers can use compensation methods to motivate employees to contribute more effort on the job and encourage them to accept some risks of the business, and, therefore, act in the interests of the employer.

KEY TERMS

annuity contract A contract often used by fund trustees to settle the retirement obligation, which generates payment to the employee of an agreed-upon amount each period for the rest of his or her life

bonuses Forms of compensation that are contingent on the occurrence of some specified future event

commission basis A means of making payments to employees in which employees receive pay based on a percentage of the dollar amount that they sell in a period

contributory pension plans Pension plans to which the employee contributes some or all of the funding for the plan

deferred compensation A means of payment to employees that allows them to work now and receive compensation for that work sometime in the future

defined benefit pension plans Pension plans that indicate the amounts the employee will receive during retirement according to a benefit formula that is usually based on the employee's salary and the number of years worked

defined contribution pension plans Pension plans that set out the amounts to be contributed to the plan, but do not specify the benefits to be paid to the employee during retirement

employee stock option plans Compensation plans in which corporations offer employees stock options as compensation, which spreads ownership among employees

fringe benefits Employee-related costs other than wages or salaries, including payroll taxes, health and life insurance, and retirement pay

goal congruence Alignment of goals between employers and employees

noncontributory pension plans Pension plans funded solely by the employers, with no contributions from employees

pension funding The act of making contributions to a pension plan, including setting aside contributions and investing funds to accumulate pension benefits

pension plan A contract between the employee and the employer that sets out the responsibilities that each party assumes regarding pension benefits

piece-rate pay A compensation method that pays employees according to the number of the items they produced in a period

taxable income Income determined in accordance with the set of rules found in the *Federal Income Tax Code*

vested The condition that exists when an employee's right to receive any benefit is irrevocable and does not depend on the occurrence of any future event

QUESTIONS

1. Describe the difficulties in measuring the value of employees.
2. Explain why the work force of a company is not recorded as an asset on the company's balance sheet.
3. What costs are associated with maintaining a qualified work force?
4. Describe the costs associated with the decision to have employees work overtime.
5. Describe the costs associated with hiring a qualified work force.
6. Explain the difficulties associated with matching the cost of fringe benefits to revenue generated during a particular accounting period.
7. Explain how fire insurance on a company's buildings differs from accident insurance on its work force.
8. Why is it less expensive for a company to supply health insurance for its work force than to pay the employees more and require them to purchase their own insurance?
9. Discuss the reasons that many companies require their employees to take vacation time.
10. If an employee earns $500 per week during 1996 and $600 per week during 1997, what cost is recorded for a two-week vacation earned in 1996, but taken in 1997? Why?
11. Explain why an employee might want to defer some part of his or her compensation into the future.
12. Explain why an employer might want to defer some part of an employee's compensation into the future.
13. Explain how an employee stock option works.
14. If an employee has a stock option for $50 and the market price of the stock falls to $40, has the employee lost $10? Why or why not?
15. Explain how to calculate a bonus based on net income after the bonus. (Include an example.)
16. What is meant by *funding* a pension?
17. What is the difference between defined benefit and defined contribution pension plans?
18. How do contributory pension plans differ from noncontributory pension plans?
19. Explain the difference between piece-rate pay and commissions.
20. What is the importance of the concept of goal congruence? Explain by providing one or two examples.

E 17.1   Pallet Company employs a work force of 1,000 employees. Of these employees, 850 are paid $12 per hour with time and a half for overtime. Overtime is paid for working more than 8 hours per day or more than 40 hours per week. The remaining 150 employees are salaried workers who are paid $600 per week regardless of the number of hours worked. During the current week, all employees averaged 45 hours. Compute the cost of payroll for the week, ignoring payroll taxes. If the hourly employees are willing to accept the same salary as the other employees, at what level of workweek (in hours) should management consider switching the hourly employees to salaries?

E 17.2   Refer to E 17.1. Assume that FICA is 7.35 percent, federal unemployment taxes are 0.5 percent, and state unemployment taxes are 3.5 percent. Compute the cost of payroll taxes for the week.

E 17.3   Wong and Chevez, CPAs, hires accounting staff throughout the year, but has only three starting dates so that employees begin their careers in groups. The three starting dates are January 1, June 1, and September 1. Approximately one-third of the staff began work on each of these dates. Wong and Chevez employ 150 staff accountants, 30 of whom were hired in the current year. The average salary is $3,000 per month for those hired this year and $6,000 for those previously employed. Each employee earns two weeks of vacation for each year worked. Wong and Chevez uses a December 31 year-end. Compute the vacation expense for the current year.

E 17.4   BBC Company recently hired a new CEO at a salary of $1 million per year payable annually and an additional $1 million per year to be paid in 15 years. If BBC can earn 8 percent on its investments, what is the cost of the deferred compensation contract?

E 17.5   Refer to E 17.4. If BBC can earn 12 percent on its investments, is the cost of the deferred compensation contract more or less than a deferred compensation contract based on 8 percent? Why? Show a mathematical proof for your answer.

E 17.6   Allegeny Enterprises has a stock option plan that is available for its 5,000 employees regardless of rank. The plan offers employees one share of common stock at $40 for each year they work. The market price of the stock is $50 per share on March 31, $45 per share on June 30, $65 per share on September 30, and $48 per share on December 31. What is the annual cost of the stock option?

E 17.7   Refer to E 17.6. Assume you are an employee of Allegeny. If the stock option allows stock to be purchased for $40 per share, would you exercise your options? Why or why not?

E 17.8   Spurlock, Inc., has a stock option plan that allows its 10,000 employees to purchase two shares of its $1 par value common stock for $25 per share. The market price of the stock is $28 on the date the options are granted. Two weeks after the options are granted, the market price of the stock falls to $20 per share. What is the cost of the stock option compensation? Explain.

E 17.9   Refer to E17.8. Assume you are an employee of Spurlock who failed to exercise your stock options. Since you could have bought two shares at $25 and sold them for $28, have you lost $6? Or, have you lost $16, since the value of the two shares is now only $40? Explain.

E 17.10   Skinner Company rewards its managers for outstanding performance by issuing year-end bonuses based on net sales for the division. The bonus rate is 5 percent of net sales for the period. During 1996, Sherri Curkland, the manager of the Northeast Division, received a bonus of $100,000. What was the amount of net sales in the Northeast Division for 1996?

E 17.11   Drucker Can Company recently adopted a bonus plan for its divisional managers. The bonus is 10 percent of the division's net income after the bonus. The net income, stated in dollars, before the bonus of the four divisions is shown below. Compute the amount of bonus cost of Drucker Can Company.

European Division	$657,000
Central-American Division	540,000
Canadian Division	832,500
American Division	986,400

E 17.12   Wilson Basketball Company currently pays members of its work force a fixed salary of $8,000 per week. Management is considering instituting a piece-rate pay system where employees would be paid $0.50 per unit produced. What is the level of production where management would be indifferent between these two compensation plans? Explain.

E 17.13   Refer to E 17.12. If the level of production exceeds the indifference point, which compensation plan will management prefer? Why?

E 17.14   Refer to E 17.13. Assume you are an employee of Wilson Basketball Company. Which compensation plan do you prefer? Why?

PROBLEMS

P 17.1   Turn to the annual report of Disney Company referred to in Chapter 2. Write out answers to each of the following questions.
a. Does the corporation report employees as assets? If so, what does the corporation disclose?
b. Does the corporation report pension liabilities? If so, what does the corporation disclose?
c. Does the corporation report stock options? If so, what does the corporation disclose?
d. Can you tell if the corporation is using a defined benefit plan or a defined contribution plan? If so, how do you know?
e. Can you tell if the corporation has a contributory or noncontributory pension plan? If so, how do you know?
f. What other information is disclosed with regard to employees?

P 17.2   Turn to the annual report of the Boston Celtics referred to in Chapter 7. Prepare responses to each of the following questions.
a. Does the company report employees as assets? If so, what does the company disclose?
b. Does the company report pension liabilities? If so, what does the company disclose?
c. Does the company report stock options? If so, what does the company disclose?
d. Can you tell if the company is using a defined benefit plan or a defined contribution plan? If so, how do you know?
e. Can you tell if the company has a contributory or noncontributory pension plan? If so, how do you know?
f. What other information is disclosed with regard to employees?

P 17.3   Turn to the annual report of Anheuser-Busch referred to in Chapter 10. Prepare responses to each of the following questions.
a. Does the corporation report employees as assets? If so, what does the corporation disclose?
b. Does the corporation report pension liabilities? If so, what does the corporation disclose?
c. Does the corporation report stock options? If so, what does the corporation disclose?
d. Can you tell if the corporation is using a defined benefit plan or a defined contribution plan? If so, how do you know?
e. Can you tell if the corporation has a contributory or noncontributory pension plan? If so, how do you know?
f. What other information is disclosed with regard to employees?

P 17.4   In 1994, accounting for stock options was a controversial issue. Look up the following article from *Management Accounting*, March 1994, and prepare a one-page written summary of the article, including additional questions about accounting for stock options that are unanswered by the article.

Murray S. Akresh and Janet Fuersich, "Stock Options: Accounting, Valuation, and Management Issues," *Management Accounting*, March 1994, pp. 51–53.

P 17.5   Pension fund managers are responsible for investing pension funds in order to earn an adequate return. How should pension fund managers' performance be evaluated? Look up the following article from *Management Accounting*, January 1994, and prepare a one-page written summary of the article, including your ideas about how employees' views of pension fund management might differ from that of a controller.

Myron D. Stolte, "Pension Fund Management: A Controller's Perspective," *Management Accounting*, January 1994, pp. 49–55.

P 17.6   In 1987, accounting for pensions was a controversial issue. Look up the following article from the *Journal of Accountancy*, January 1987, and prepare a one-page written summary of the article, including your views on how the new disclosures will help financial statement users.

Paul B. W. Miller, "The New Pension Accounting (Part 1)," *Journal of Accountancy*, January 1987, pp. 98–108.

P 17.7 The human resources department typically relies on the accounting department for information concerning employees. Many companies are designing human resource information systems. Look up the following article in *Management Accounting,* January 1994, and prepare a one-page written summary of the article, including your views on the costs and benefits of human resource accounting systems from management's perspective.

William E. Berry, "The Human Resource Information System," *Management Accounting,* January 1994, pp. 56–57.

P 17.8 Many factors influence how much money you will need during retirement, such as, how much you can earn on your investments and how long you live. Retirement income can be treated as an annuity that you receive each month during retirement. Assume that you want the total amount necessary to pay for your retirement on the date you retire and that you have no other sources of retirement income. Calculate the amount you will need at the date of your retirement under each of the following independent situations.

 a. You will live 18 years, need a monthly income during retirement of $3,000, and earn 6 percent during retirement.

 b. Same facts as *a* except you will earn only 4 percent.

 c. You will live 32 years, need a monthly income during retirement of $2,500, and earn 7 percent during retirement.

 d. Same facts as *c* except you will need a monthly income during retirement of $4,500.

 e. Retirement benefits are often settled at retirement by the retiring employee's or pension fund's purchase of an annuity contract from an insurance company that promises to pay a certain amount for the rest of the retiree's life. What do insurance companies do when the retiree receiving annuity payments lives longer than the insurance company expected? What is the impact of this on the insurance company?

P17.9 Pathway Computers has one employee and it is considering establishing a defined contribution pension plan and acting as its own fund trustee. At the inception of the plan, the employee will be 56 years old and will retire at 64 years old. The life expectancy of the employee is 84 years old. Provide the analysis described below.

 a. Draw a time line similar to Exhibit 17.1 and show the number of years in the contribution and benefit periods.

 b. If the employee wants to receive $44,000 at the end each year during retirement, how much money must Pathway accumulate by the date the employee retires (assume that the employee's interest rate during retirement is 4%)?

 c. What amount should the annual funding payments be, if Pathway earns 6% on its investments during the contribution period which are made at the end of each year?

 d. What will be the after-tax cash flows associated with the plan in its second year following adoption, if Pathway pays 35% income tax on the earnings of the plan and the plan's investments earn the expected 6%?

P17.10 Assume that you are an employee who receives a salary of $80,000 each year. You are five years from retirement and your employer has offered you a choice between the following two ways of receiving additional compensation:

 i. A deferred compensation plan where you would receive a lump sum payment on the first day of your retirement

 ii. An employee stock option plan where you would receive 5,000 options on the corporation's $1 par common stock exercisable at an option price of $22

Your current income tax rate is 35% on every dollar earned, but after you retire you will not receive the $80,000 salary and your tax rate will drop to 15%.

 a. If the current market price of the stock is $78 per share, what is the lowest lump sum payment of the deferred compensation plan you would prefer over the alternative of exercising the options now?

 b. What is the lowest lump sum payment of the deferred compensation plan you would prefer if the options could not be exercised until the same date that the lump sum payment could be received?

 c. What are the sources of risk for the two options in part *a*? In part *b*?

CA 17.1

Wellington Car Dealership plans to offer its sales personnel a commission based on the dollar amount of sales each person makes during the period. It is considering the following three programs:
1. A 6 percent commission based on total sales in dollars for the period.
2. A 5 percent commission based on sales in dollars of luxury cars during the period plus a 1 percent commission based on sales in dollars of economy cars during the period.
3. A 2 percent commission based on sales in dollars of luxury cars during the period plus a 4 percent commission based on sales in dollars of economy cars during the period.

The average selling price of a luxury car is $35,000 while the average selling price of an economy car is $15,000.

Unit sales for each of the five salespersons is given below:

	Fred	Kathy	Jo	Gary	Ismael
Luxury	100	150	225	120	180
Economy	200	150	75	180	120

Required: Use a computer spreadsheet program
   a. Compute the commission due to each employee if compensation program 1 is implemented.
   b. Compute the commission due to each employee if compensation program 2 is implemented.
   c. Compute the commission due to each employee if compensation program 3 is implemented.
   d. Compute the commission due to each employee under compensation plan 1 if the rate is changed to 5 percent.
   e. Compute the commission due to each employee under compensation plan 2 if the rate of luxury cars is changed to 6 percent and the rate on economy cars is changed to 2 percent.
   f. Compute the commission due to each employee under compensation plan 3 if the rate of luxury cars is changed to 3 percent and the rate on economy cars is changed to 6 percent.
   g. Which plan is best? Why?

CA 17.2

(Requires prior study of Chapter 4.)

Abernathy Manufacturers sells folding chairs for $12 each. The variable cost to make and sell a chair is $7 and fixed costs average $500,000 per period. Abernathy is subject to a 45 percent tax rate and desires a $55,000 net income after taxes. Abernathy plans to begin a bonus plan whereby employees will share a bonus equal to 5 percent of net income before taxes.

Required: Use a computer spreadsheet package. Assume independent situations.
   a. How many units must be sold to achieve the desired net income after tax if the bonus plan is implemented?
   b. How many units must be sold to achieve the desired net income after tax if the bonus rate is increased to 6 percent?
   c. How many units must be sold to achieve the desired net income after tax if the tax rate is reduced to 30 percent?
   d. How many units must be sold to achieve a net income of $100,000 after tax?

CASES

C 17.1

Turn to the annual report of the company you chose in Chapter 1, C 1.1. Prepare responses to each of the following questions.
   a. Does the company report employees as assets? If so, what does the company disclose?
   b. Does the company report pension liabilities? If so, what does the company disclose?
   c. Does the company report stock options? If so, what does the company disclose?
   d. Can you tell if the company is using a defined benefit plan or a defined contribution plan? If so, how do you know?
   e. Can you tell if the company has a contributory or noncontributory pension plan? If so, how do you know?
   f. What other information is disclosed with regard to employees?

C 17.2 Companies often base their bonuses on net income after bonus and after taxes. In such cases, they use the following formula: Bonus = (Net income – Bonus – Taxes) × Bonus rate. Assume that the bonus rate is 10 percent and the tax rate is 40 percent.

Required:
a. If net income before bonus and taxes is $1 million, what is the bonus?
b. If the bonus is based on net income before bonus, but after taxes, what is the bonus? Please explain.

CRITICAL THINKING

CT 17.1 Abraham Maslow developed a motivational theory commonly known as needs theory or the hierarchy of needs. F. Herzberg developed a motivational theory commonly known as hygiene theory. These psychological theories, among others, are often called *content theories* because they focus on the "things" that motivate people. You should familiarize yourself with each of these theories—an introductory psychology book might be a good place to start. Alternatively, you can read the following:

A. Maslow, "A Dynamic Theory of Human Motivation," *Psychological Review* 50 (1943), pp. 370-73.

F. Herzberg, B. Mausner, and B. Snyderman, *The Motivation to Work*, 2nd ed. (New York: John Wiley & Sons, 1959).

Required:
a. Compare and contrast these theories.
b. What do each of theories indicate about the usefulness of money (raises for employees) to motivate performance?

CT 17.2 V. Vroom developed a motivational theory known as expectancy theory. His, and other theories advanced by researchers such as L.W. Porter and J.S. Adams, are commonly called *process theories* because they attempt to explain the process of motivation. You should familiarize yourself with Vroom's theory—an introductory psychology book might be a good place to start. Alternatively, you can read the following:

V.H. Vroom, *Work and Motivation* (New York: John Wiley & Sons, 1964).

Required:
a. Explain Vroom's theory.
b. What does his theory indicate about the usefulness of money (raises for employees) to motivate performance?

ETHICAL CHALLENGES

EC 17.1 In 1993, Leslie Fay, a dress manufacturer, was featured in an article in *The Wall Street Journal* which stated that Leslie Fay had backdated invoices in order to record revenue in the quarter *prior* to the sale. Further investigation revealed that the CEO and CFO were paid bonuses if the net income reached $16 million, but they received no bonus if net income was less than $16 million. Read the following article:

"Loose Threads, Dressmaker Leslie Fay Is an Old-Style Firm That's in a Modern Fix," *The Wall Street Journal*, February 23, 1993, p. A20.

Required:
a. Explain how backdating invoices affected reported profits.
b. In your opinion, did the bonus system contribute to the fraud? Why or why not?
c. In your opinion, did the organization of the company contribute to the fraud? Why or why not?
d. What should have been done to prevent this from occurring?

EC 17.2 In the early 1990s, corporate downsizing was commonplace. The benefits of downsizing to a company include decreased compensation cost, but, in some cases, morale is also negatively affected. In 1994, Robert B. Reich, then U.S. Secretary of Labor, commented that perhaps employees should be treated as assets to be nurtured, rather than costs to be expensed. Explain in one or two pages your views supporting or refuting this idea.

PART SIX

Recording within the Financing and Investing Cycles

Part 6, the recording section, examines financing and investing events and how these events are recorded. Financing events are examined first to facilitate accounting for investing events such as the purchases of stocks and bonds. In this area the student learns how to account for long-term debt and owners' contributions, as well as operational and nonoperational investments.

CHAPTER 18

Recording and Communicating Long-Term Debt Financing Activities

Learning Objectives

1. Explain how and why to record and communicate activities concerning long-term periodic payment notes.
2. Describe how and why to record and communicate events pertaining to long-term lump-sum (noninterest-bearing) notes.
3. Illustrate how and why to record and communicate bond activities.
4. Explain how and why to record and communicate operating and capital leases.

The Archer Daniels Midland Company (ADM) is in the business of procuring, storing, processing, and merchandising agricultural products and calls itself the "supermarket to the world." In addition to offering a variety of agricultural products and services, ADM meets the expectations of its investors in another important way. The company has the technology to produce products to provide an individual with a proper level of protein for as little as $0.125 per day.[1] This allows ADM to provide products that can meet the nutritional needs of starving people around the world and at the same time, be profitable and generate excellent returns for its investors. ADM enhances its returns by using financial leverage and has financed as much as 23 percent of its assets with long-term debt.

[1]Archer Daniels Midland, Annual Report, 1992.

Companies like Archer Daniels Midland use long-term debt to finance their operational infrastructure to generate higher returns for their stockholders. Such companies use financial leverage to do this and, therefore, are willing to accept the risks inherent in this type of financing. (See ADM's financial statements in the annual report booklet.)

Long-lived assets typically require sizable expenditures and are not converted into cash quickly. Companies financing such assets with long-term debt plan to repay the debt with the cash flows generated by the long-term investments over their lives. For example, in 1995, ADM raised $17.626 million by issuing long-term debt and may have used this to finance some of the $558 million it spent to acquire property, plant, and equipment that year.

In this chapter we describe how to account for long-term debt financing events and how the accounting system provides useful information related to these events for both internal and external decision makers. Chapter 15 introduced the three basic types of notes businesses use to acquire funds or other assets. Now we will discuss how the accounting system reflects information about these three types of long-term notes payable—periodic payment, lump-sum payment, and periodic payment and lump-sum notes—in the company records. In addition, the chapter describes how these notes payable appear in the financial statements of a firm. The chapter also addresses how to account for and report lease transactions, a special type of debt financing.

ACCOUNTING FOR LONG-TERM NOTES PAYABLE

Each type of long-term note payable promises a specific type of cash flow in exchange for cash or other assets. Recall from Chapter 15 that the periodic payment (installment) note includes a promise to make cash payments at equal intervals over a specified period of time. The lump-sum payment (noninterest-bearing) note is a promise to pay a specific cash amount—the note's face value—at a particular point in the future, the note's maturity date. The periodic payment and lump-sum note consists of a promise to make both periodic cash interest payments based on the face value of the note and a lump-sum payment of cash at a specific future date. The following discussion explains how the accounting system captures and reports information about each type of note.

Periodic Payment Long-Term Notes Payable

Accounting for installment notes requires timely recognition of the interest expense on the notes and proper classification of the note itself as either a long-term or short-term liability. The following example illustrates how to account for an installment note.

Assume that on February 1, 1994, Banner Corporation arranged to purchase a $50,000 piece of equipment by making a 20 percent down payment ($10,000) and signing a three-year installment note with a 12 percent interest annual rate on the $40,000 balance. The loan document calls for six semiannual installments of $8,135 starting August 1, 1994. Exhibit 18.1 shows how to determine the amount of the payment, in panel A, and the repayment schedule for the note, in panel B.

The repayment schedule shows the portion of each payment that covers the interest on the loan (column 2) and the portion that reduces the principal of the note (column 3). The difference between the amount of the payment made (column 1) and the interest expense for a particular period (column 2) is the amount by which the payment reduces the principal of the note.

Exhibit 18.2 shows the entries recorded in conjunction with the note over its life. The cost of the equipment is the sum of the face value of the note, N/P, ($40,000) and the cash down payment ($10,000). The entry to record the first payment on August 1, 1994, mirrors the information in the repayment schedule. That is, interest expense of $2,400 is recorded, and $5,735 of principal is reduced with the required semiannual payment of $8,135.

Banner Corporation closes its books on December 31. In order to comply with the matching principle, Banner makes an adjusting entry at closing to record five

EXHIBIT 18.1 | Installment Note—Banner Corporation

A. Determining the Installment Payment

$$\text{Annuity} \times P_{6,6\%} = \text{Present value of annuity}$$
$$\text{Annuity} \times 4.9173 = \$40,000$$
$$\text{Annuity} = \$\ 8,135$$

B. Repayment Schedule

Date	(1) Payment	(2) Interest (6% × Loan balance)*	(3) Principal (1) – (2)	(4) Loan Balance
2/1/94				$40,000
8/1/94	$8,135	$2,400	$5,735	34,265
2/1/95	8,135	2,056	6,079	28,186
8/1/95	8,135	1,691	6,444	21,742
2/1/96	8,135	1,305	6,830	14,912
8/1/96	8,135	895	7,240	7,672
2/1/97	8,135	463*	7,672	–0–

*Rounded.

EXHIBIT 18.2 | Entries for Installment Note—Banner Corporation

	1994	1995	1996	1997
February 1 Entries				
Equipment	50,000			
Cash		10,000		
Installment N/P		40,000		
Interest Expense		342.75	217.90	79.40
Interest Payable		→1,713.25	→1,087.10	→ 383.60
Installment N/P		6,079.00	6,830.00	7,672.00
Cash		8,135	8,135	8,135
August 1 Entries				
Interest Expense	2,400	1,691	895	
Installment N/P	5,735	6,444	7,240	
Cash	8,135	8,135	8,135	
December 31 Entries				
Interest Expense	1,713.25	1,087.10	383.60	
Interest Payable	1,713.25 ⌐	1,087.10 ⌐	383.60 ⌐	

months' interest (August through December) on the note (see Exhibit 18.3). The adjusting entry identifies the interest expense associated with the year in which it was incurred. At the same time, it reflects the obligation of the firm to pay the interest at year-end. As of December 31, 1994, the amount of accrued interest for the five months since August 1, 1994, is $1,713.25 [Unpaid loan balance ($34,265) × Annual interest rate (12%) × Percentage of year since the last payment (5/12)].

Then, on the next payment date, February 1, 1995, Banner would debit the Interest Payable account for $1,713.25, and record January 1995's interest expense of $342.75. The interest expense for the month of January in 1995 is the difference between the $2,056 of interest for the entire six-month period ending January 31, 1995, and the $1,713.25 of interest accrued for August through December 1994.

Even though the second payment occurs on February 1, 1995, the company allocates the interest expense of $2,056 (footnote 2) for the six-month period between two accounting periods—$1,713.25 [(footnote 3) in Exhibit 18.3)] accrued for the five months in 1994 and $342.75 [(footnote 4) in Exhibit 18.3)] for the final month's interest expense in January 1995, the next accounting period.

The time line in Exhibit 18.3 shows how the interest expense incurred during the first year of this note's life is allocated between 1994 and 1995.

Exhibit 18.4 shows how this installment note impacts Banner's financial statements for 1994. The income statement for 1994 shows the interest expense incurred

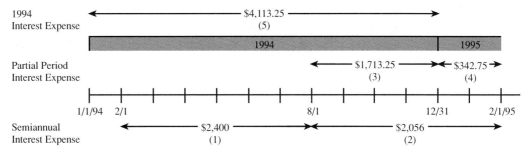

EXHIBIT 18.3

Interest Expense Allocation—Banner Corporation

(1) Interest expense from 2/1/94 to 8/1/94
(2) Interest expense from 8/1/94 to 2/1/95
(3) Interest expense from 8/1/94 to 12/31/94, or ($2,056 × 5/6)
(4) Interest expense from 1/1/95 to 2/1/95, or ($2,056 × 1/6)
(5) Interest expense incurred in 1994, from 2/1/94 to 12/31/94, or $2,400 (1) + $1,713.25 (3)

during the year, which amounts to $4,113.25 ($2,400 + $1,713.25). The balance sheet shows the amount of interest accrued as of December 31, 1994, $1,713.25, as a current liability. As of December 31, 1994, Banner still owes $34,265 (See Exhibit 18.1) on the installment note. The portion of the installment note's principal due in 1995, $12,523 ($6,079 + $6,444 in Exhibit 18.1), is reported as a current liability. Banner classifies the remaining principal of the installment note, $21,742, as a long-term liability because it is due after 1995.

The issuance of the note does not affect the cash flow statement for 1994 because the company received equipment rather than cash from the transaction. However, the company would report $2,400 of the first $8,135 payment as cash paid for interest in the operating section of the statement of cash flows, while the remaining $5,735 would appear as a reduction of the balance of the installment note payable in the financing section of the cash flow statement.[2]

Lump-Sum Payment Long-Term Notes Payable

Lump-sum payment, or noninterest-bearing notes, do not have a face interest rate on the note. Instead, the note's face value is the amount that the maker of the note pays on the note's maturity date.

As we discussed in Chapter 15, the value of this type of note depends on the market rate of interest of the firm at the time the note is issued. The accountant's job is to ensure that the market rate used to value the note is appropriate and to record the transaction so that the assets, liabilities, and interest on the note are presented fairly on the company's financial statements.

---

[2]There is also an investing cash outflow of $10,000 shown on the cash flow statement.

EXHIBIT 18.4 | **Banner Corporation's Financial Statements for Installment Note**

	1994	1995	1996	1997
Income Statement				
Interest expense	$ 4,113.25	$ 3,120.85	$ 1,496.50	$ 79.40
Balance Sheet				
Current liabilities:				
Interest payable	1,713.25	1,087.10	383.60	
Installment N/P	12,523.00	14,070.00	7,672.00	
Long-term liabilities:				
Installment N/P	21,742.00	7,672.00	–0–	
Cash Flow Statement				
Operating section:				
Cash interest	2,400	3,747	1,394	463
Financing section:				
Cash paid on note	5,735	12,503	14,876	7,672

To illustrate, assume that Banner Corporation issued a four-year, $1,000,000 non-interest-bearing note on April 1, 1996, to acquire a piece of equipment when the market rate of interest was 12 percent. Zach Kohlrus, Banner's controller, calculated the value of the transaction and set up the amortization table illustrated in Exhibit 18.5.

Based on Mr. Kohlrus' calculations in panel A of Exhibit 18.5, the present value of the note on April 1, 1996, is $635,500. Because Banner was able to exchange the note for the equipment, the assumption here is that the value of the equipment is the same as the note. In other words, Banner could have gone to a bank with this note and borrowed $635,500 in cash and then purchased the equipment. The entry to record the acquisition of the equipment on April 1, 1996, should have been:

Equipment	635,500	
Discount on Note Payable	364,500	
Note Payable		1,000,000

The Discount on Note Payable account represents the difference between the market rate of interest, 12 percent, and the face rate of interest, 0 percent. In this case, it represents all of the interest that Banner will recognize over the life of the note. The discount account is a **contra liability** account because its debit balance offsets, and therefore reduces, a specific related liability account. In this case, the discount offsets the face value of the Note Payable account to reflect the note's carrying value, or amount of the liability reported on the firm's balance sheet. For example, on the date of the note's issuance, the carrying value or liability incurred by Banner was the $1,000,000 note payable less the $364,500 discount on the note payable, or $635,500.

The amortization table shown in panel B of Exhibit 18.5 shows the amount of interest expense, or effective interest, recognized each year in the life of the note (column 2). The interest for the first year of this note, April 1, 1996, to April 1, 1997, is $76,260. Entries to reflect interest in the accounting records show a credit to the Discount on Note Payable account and a debit to Interest Expense. As the company

EXHIBIT	18.5	Noninterest-Bearing Note—Banner Corporation

A. Determination of the Present Value of the Note

$$\text{Present value} = \text{Future value} \times p_{4,12\%}$$
$$= \$1,000,000 \times .6355$$
$$= \$635,500$$

B. Amortization of Discount

Date	(1) Cash Payment	(2) Effective Interest ($.12 \times$ Carrying value)	(3) Remaining Discount	(4) Carrying Value
4/1/96			$364,500.00	$ 635,500.00
4/1/97		$ 76,260.00	288,240.00	711,760.00
4/1/98		85,411.20	202,828.80	797,171.20
4/1/99		95,660.54	107,168.26	892,831.74
4/1/00		107,168.26*	–0–	1,000,000.00
4/1/00	$1,000,000			–0–

*Rounded.

EXHIBIT 18.6 · Entries for Noninterest-Bearing Note—Banner Corporation

	1996	1997	1998	1999	2000
April 1 Entries					
Equipment	635,500				
Discount on N/P	364,500				
N/P	1,000,000				
N/P					1,000,000
Cash					1,000,000
December 31 Entries					
Interest Expense*	57,195	83,123.40	93,098.21	104,291.37	26,792.08
Discount on N/P	57,195	83,123.40	93,098.21	104,291.37	26,792.08

*Interest expense calculations: (Use amounts from Exhibit 18.5, column 2):
1996: $76,260 × 9/12 = $57,195
1997: ($76,260 × 1/4) + ($85,411.20 × 9/12) = $83,123.40
1998: ($85,411.20 × 1/4) + ($95,660.54 × 9/12) = $93,098.21
1999: ($95,660.54 × 1/4) + ($107,168.30 × 9/12) = $104,291.37
2000: $107,168.30 × 1/4 = $26,792.08

reduces the Discount on Note Payable account, the carrying value of the note increases. The entry to record the interest for 1996 (April through December) is:

Interest Expense	57,195*	
Discount on Note Payable		57,195

*$76,260 × 9/12 of a year.

Exhibit 18.6 illustrates the entries that Banner would make in its accounting records over the life of the note. In 1997, the interest is $83,123.40, which consists of one-fourth of the note's interest in its first year ($76,260 × 1/4), plus three-fourths, or nine months, of the note's second year of interest ($85,411.20 × 9/12). Banner will amortize the discount on the note until the company makes the final payment of the $1,000,000 face value on April 1, 2000.

Exhibit 18.7 shows Banner's financial statement presentation of the note during its term. The interest reported on the income statement each year is recorded as part of Banner's adjusting entries on December 31. The carrying value of the note for 1996 is $692,695 and $775,818.40 for 1997. The note's carrying value increases each

EXHIBIT 18.7 · Financial Statements for Noninterest-Bearing Note—Banner Corporation

	1996	1997	1998	1999	2000
Income Statement					
Interest expense	$ 57,195	$ 83,123.40	$ 93,098.21	$ 104,291.35	$ 26,792.08
Balance Sheet					
Current liabilities:					
N/P				1,000,000.00	
Less: Discount on N/P				26,792.08	
Carrying value				$ 973,207.92	
Long-term liabilities:					
N/P	1,000,000	1,000,000.00	1,000,000.00		
Less: Discount on N/P	307,305	224,181.60	131,083.39		
Carrying value	$ 692,695	$ 775,818.40	$ 868,916.61		
Cash Flow Statement					
Financing section:					
Cash paid on note					1,000,000

year because of the amortization of the Discount on Note Payable account each time the company records interest. On December 31, 1999, the carrying value of the note becomes a current liability because Banner will pay the note in full in the year 2000.

As in the case of the installment note, the interest expense amounts and carrying values on the note's amortization schedule do not correspond to the amounts reported on Banner's income statement and balance sheet because the note's yearly cycle does not correspond to Banner's fiscal year. Because this is a noninterest-bearing note, the only cash flow reported during the life of the note is the cash payment of the face value of the note, $1,000,000, in the financing section of Banner's cash flow statement for the year 2000.

Periodic Payment and Lump-Sum Long-Term Notes Payable—Bonds

We use bonds as our example for the accounting treatment for periodic payment and lump-sum notes. Chapter 15 indicated that bonds are a form of long-term debt designed to raise funds from public rather than private sources. A bond issue typically consists of a specific number of $1,000 face value notes. The amount of cash interest stipulated by the face rate of interest printed on each bond is usually paid on a semiannual or annual basis.

To illustrate how to account for periodic payment and lump-sum notes, assume the Banner Corporation is planning a $15,000,000 capital expenditure and has the authorization from its board of directors to issue $10,000,000 of 10-year bonds on March 1, 1995, to finance part of the project. Thus, Banner will issue 10,000 bonds, each with a face value of $1,000. The bonds have a 10 percent face rate that is paid semiannually on September 1 and March 1. Banner Corporation has a December 31 fiscal year-end.

Market Rate Equal to the Face Rate   If the market rate of interest for Banner Corporation is 10 percent when it issues the bonds, the proceeds of the sale of the bonds will be $10,000,000, as panel A in Exhibit 18.8 shows. Because the market and face rate are the same, the bond issue has no discount or premium, and the interest expense equals the amount of cash interest paid, as shown in panel B of Exhibit 18.8.

The entries for the issuance of the bonds on March 1, 1995, and the first interest payment on September 1, 1995, are:

3/1/95	Cash	10,000,000	
	Bonds Payable		10,000,000
9/1/95	Interest Expense	500,000	
	Cash		500,000

Exhibit 18.9 presents the entries Banner will make in its accounting records for the first two years of the bond issue's life. Banner's adjusting entries on December 31 recognize the interest expense incurred from September 1 to December 31 and also the obligation to pay $333,333 of cash interest as of that date (interest payable). On March 1 of the following year, when the company pays the cash interest due, it recognizes interest expense for the first two months of 1996 and removes the liability for the interest recognized at fiscal year-end 1995 from the company's records. Because the bond was issued at its face value, the exhibit's entries are the same for each date over the life of the bond.

Exhibit 18.10 shows how to report the bonds on Banner's financial statements. The yearly interest expense is the balance in the Interest Expense account after recording the adjusting entries on December 31. The carrying value of the bond on the balance sheet of Banner Corporation is $10,000,000 for each year of its life. Banner classifies the bond as a long-term liability until 2004 when it becomes a current liability because it matures on March 1, 2005.

The cash reported on the cash flow statement is the same for each year of the bond's life except for the first and last years. In 1995, the cash flow statement shows

EXHIBIT | 18.8 | Bonds Issued at Face Value—Banner Corporation

A. Present Value of Cash Flows

Cash Flow 1:

$$\text{Present value of annuity} = \text{Annuity} \times P_{20,5\%}$$
$$= \$500,000 \times 12.4622$$
$$= \$6,231,100$$

Cash Flow 2:

$$\text{Present value of lump sum} = \text{Future value} \times p_{20,5\%}$$
$$= \$10,000,000 \times .3769$$
$$= \$3,769,000$$

Present value of cash flow 1	$ 6,231,100
Present value of cash flow 2	3,769,000
Present value of note	$10,000,100*

B. Amortization Table

Date	Cash Interest $(.05 \times FV)^\dagger$	Effective Interest $(.05 \times CV)^\ddagger$	Premium or Discount Amortized	Premium/ Discount	Carrying Value
3/1/95					$10,000,000
9/1/95	$500,000	$500,000	—	—	10,000,000
3/1/96	500,000	500,000	—	—	10,000,000
9/1/96	500,000	500,000	—	—	10,000,000
3/1/97	500,000	500,000	—	—	10,000,000

*This amount should equal $10,000,000; the present value factor is limited to four decimal places, and results in the $100 rounding difference shown here.
†FV is the face value of the note.
‡CV is the carrying value of the note.

EXHIBIT | 18.9 | Entries for Bonds Issued at Face Value—Banner Corporation

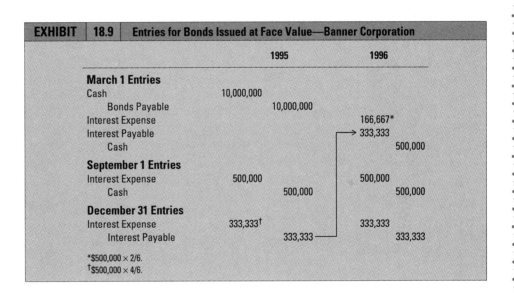

	1995	1996
March 1 Entries		
Cash	10,000,000	
Bonds Payable		10,000,000
Interest Expense		166,667*
Interest Payable		333,333
Cash		500,000
September 1 Entries		
Interest Expense	500,000	500,000
Cash	500,000	500,000
December 31 Entries		
Interest Expense	333,333†	333,333
Interest Payable	333,333	333,333

*$500,000 × 2/6.
†$500,000 × 4/6.

the receipt of the $10,000,000 from the sale of the bonds in the financing section and $500,000 of cash interest Banner paid in the operating section of the cash flow statement. During the next eight years, Banner reports only the $1,000,000 of cash interest paid in the operating section of the cash flow statement. In 2005, the year the bond matures, the cash flow statement reports the payment of $500,000 of cash interest in the operating section and the $10,000,000 payment of the face value to retire the bonds in its financing section of the cash flow statement.

	1995	1996
Income Statement		
Interest expense	$ 833,333*	$1,000,000†
Balance Sheet		
Long-term liabilities:		
Bonds payable	10,000,000	10,000,000
Cash Flow Statement		
Operating section:		
Cash interest paid	(500,000)	(1,000,000)
Financing section:		
Cash received from bond	10,000,000	

*$500,000 + $333,333 = $833,333.
†$166,667 + $500,000 + $333,333 = $1,000,000.

Market Rate Greater Than Face Rate When the market rate of interest is greater than the face rate of the bond issue, the proceeds from the issuance of the bond are smaller than the face value of the bonds. That is, the bond is issued at a discount. Assume that Banner Corporation issued the 10 percent face rate bonds when the market rate of interest was 12 percent. Then the bonds' proceeds are $8,852,950, as panel A of Exhibit 18.11 illustrates. Panel B shows the bond amortization table for the first two years of the bond issue's life. The entry to reflect the issuance of the bonds in Banner's records on March 1, 1995, is:

3/1/95	Cash	8,852,950	
	Discount on Bonds Payable	1,147,050	
	Bonds Payable		10,000,000

Exhibit 18.12 presents the entries for the first two fiscal years of the bonds' life—1995 and 1996. Banner has borrowed $8,852,950 but must repay the $10,000,000 face value on the maturity date. Therefore, the $1,147,050 difference represents the discount on bonds payable (B/P), or the amount of additional interest that Banner Corporation incurs to make this 10 percent bond yield 12 percent interest. Because the discount represents the difference between the face rate of interest and the market rate of interest over the life of the bond issue, the company will amortize the discount over the life of the bond.

On the first payment date, September 1, 1995, Banner Corporation pays $500,000 cash interest, as promised in the bond indenture (Exhibit 18.11, panel B, column 1). However, the actual interest expense for the six-month period is $531,177 (Exhibit 18.11, panel B, column 2), or $8,852,950 (amount borrowed) × 12 percent × 6/12 (six months of the year). The $31,177 difference between the cash interest paid ($500,000) and the effective interest ($531,177) is the amount by which the company will reduce or amortize the discount account. It represents the difference between the face rate of interest (10 percent) and the effective rate of interest (12 percent). The entry for the first payment is shown in the first September 1 entry in Exhibit 18.12.

The adjusting entries of December 31 in Exhibit 18.12 reflect the recognition of the interest expense incurred from September 1 to December 31 and also the obligation to pay $333,333 of cash interest as of that date. The interest expense, $355,365 ($533,048 × 4/6), is greater than the $333,333 entry made to the Interest Payable account. The $22,032 difference is the amount of the discount amortized for this four-month period ($33,048 × 4/6). On March 1, 1996, when the company pays the amount of cash interest due, it recognizes the interest expense of $177,683 ($533,048 × 2/6) for the first two months of the next fiscal year and amortizes the $11,016

EXHIBIT | 18.11 | Bonds Issued at a Discount—Banner Corporation

A. Present Value of Bond's Cash Flows

Cash Flow 1:

$$\text{Present value of annuity} = \text{Annuity} \times P_{20,6\%}$$
$$= \$500,000 \times 11.4699$$
$$= \$5,734,950$$

Cash Flow 2:

$$\text{Present value of lump sum} = \text{Future value} \times p_{20,6\%}$$
$$= \$10,000,000 \times .3118$$
$$= \$3,118,000$$

Present value of cash flow 1	$5,734,950
Present value of cash flow 2	3,118,000
Present value of note	$8,852,950

B. Bond Amortization Table

Date	(1) Cash Interest $(.05 \times FV)$*	(2) Effective[†] Interest $(.06 \times CV)$[‡]	(3) Discount Amortized	(4) Discount	(5) Bond Carrying Value
3/1/95				$1,147,050	$8,852,950
9/1/95	$500,000	$531,177	$31,177	1,115,873	8,884,127
3/1/96	500,000	533,048	33,048	1,082,825	8,917,175
9/1/96	500,000	535,031	35,031	1,047,794	8,952,206
3/1/97	500,000	537,132	37,132	1,010,662	8,989,338

*FV is the bond's face value.
[†]Rounded.
[‡]CV is the bond's carrying value.

EXHIBIT | 18.12 | Entries for Bonds Issued at a Discount—Banner Corporation

	1995	1996
March 1 Entries		
Cash	8,852,950	
Discount on B/P	1,147,050	
Bonds Payable	10,000,000	
Interest Expense		177,683[a]
Interest Payable		333,333
Discount on B/P		11,016[b]
Cash		500,000
September 1 Entries		
Interest Expense	531,177	535,031
Discount on B/P	31,177	35,031
Cash	500,000	500,000
December 31 Entries		
Interest Expense	355,365[c]	358,088[d]
Discount on B/P	22,032[e]	24,755[f]
Interest Payable	333,333[g]	333,333

See Exhibit 18.11 for quantities used.

[a]$533,048 (3/1/96, Col. 2) × 2/6.
[b]$ 33,048 (3/1/96, Col. 3) × 2/6.
[c]$533,048 (3/1/96, Col. 2) × 4/6.
[d]$537,132 (3/1/97, Col. 2) × 4/6.
[e]$ 33,048 (3/1/96, Col. 3) × 4/6.
[f]$ 37,132 (3/1/97, Col. 3) × 4/6.
[g]$500,000 (3/1/96, Col. 1) × 4/6.

discount for the two-month period ($33,048 × 2/6). Banner also removes the related liability (interest payable) recognized on December 31, 1995, from its records. This adjusting process continues throughout the life of the bond because the fiscal year does not correspond to the timing of the cash flows promised in the bond indenture.

	1995	1996
Income Statement		
Interest expense	$ 886,542*	$ 1,070,802†
Balance Sheet		
Long-term liabilities:		
Bonds payable	10,000,000	10,000,000
Less: Discount	1,093,841	1,023,039
	$ 8,906,159	$ 8,976,961
Cash Flow Statement		
Operating section:		
Cash interest paid	(500,000)	(1,000,000)
Financing section:		
Cash received from bond	8,852,950	

*$531,177 + $355,365 from Exhibit 18.12.
†$177,683 + $535,031 + $358,088 from Exhibit 18.12.

PAUSE & REFLECT

If the amounts Banner records in the December 31 adjusting entries in the Interest Expense and Discount accounts change each year, why does the amount of interest payable remain the same?

Exhibit 18.13 shows how to report a bond issued at a discount on Banner's financial statements for the first two years of the bond's life. The interest expense of $886,542 in 1995 and $1,070,802 in 1996 is the balance in the Interest Expense account after recording the adjusting entries on December 31. The company reports the bonds on the balance sheet as a long-term liability and the accrued interest as a current liability.

The contra liability account, Discount on Bonds Payable, is subtracted from the Bonds Payable account to show the bond issue's carrying value on the balance sheet date. As each year passes, the carrying value of the bond becomes larger because the discount gets smaller as it is amortized. On the maturity date of the bonds, the Discount on Bonds Payable account is fully amortized and the amount of Banner's liability for the bonds equals the face value of the bonds.

In 1995, Banner's cash flow statement reflects the receipt of the bond proceeds, $8,852,950, in the financing section and $500,000 of cash interest paid in the operating section. However, from this point on, the amount of cash flows reported on the cash flow statement is the same as those for the bonds issued at their face value. That is, Banner will report $1,000,000 of cash interest paid in the operating section of the cash flow statement each year until the year the bond matures. In that year, the cash flow statement will report the payment of cash interest of $500,000 in the operating section and the repayment of the $10,000,000 face value of the bond in the financing section.

PAUSE & REFLECT

How much interest expense did ADM incur in 1995? How much cash interest was paid in 1995? Explain the reason for the difference in these two numbers.

Market Rate Less Than Face Rate   When the market rate is less than the face rate of interest on a bond, the proceeds from a bond issue exceed the face value of the bond issue, and the bonds are issued at a premium. If Banner Corporation's 10 percent bonds were issued when the market rate was 8 percent, the proceeds of the sale of the bonds would yield $11,359,150 as shown in panel A of Exhibit 18.14.

Exhibit 18.14, panel B, presents the first two years of the bonds' amortization schedule. Semiannual payments dictate that it is necessary to compound the 8 percent market rate of interest semiannually. The $1,359,150 premium on bonds

EXHIBIT | 18.14 | Bonds Issued at a Premium—Banner Corporation

A. Present Value of Bonds' Cash Flows

Cash Flow 1:

$$\text{Present value of annuity} = \text{Annuity} \times P_{20,4\%}$$
$$= \$500,000 \times 13.5903$$
$$= \$6,795,150$$

Cash Flow 2:

$$\text{Present value of lump sum} = \text{Future value} \times p_{20,4\%}$$
$$= \$10,000,000 \times .4564$$
$$= \$4,564,000$$

Present value of cash flow 1	$ 6,795,150
Present value of cash flow 2	4,564,000
Present value of note	$11,359,150

B. Bond Amortization Table

Date	(1) Cash Interest $(.05 \times FV)$*	(2) Effective† Interest $(.04 \times CV)$‡	(3) Premium Amortized	(4) Premium	(5) Bond Carrying Value
3/1/95				$1,359,150	$11,359,150
9/1/95	$500,000	$454,366	$45,634	1,313,516	11,313,516
3/1/96	500,000	452,541	47,459	1,266,057	11,266,057
9/1/96	500,000	450,642	49,358	1,216,699	11,216,699
3/1/97	500,000	448,667	51,333	1,165,366	11,165,366

*FV is the bond's face value.
†Rounded.
‡CV is the bond's carrying value.

payable is the amount of proceeds generated in excess of the bonds' face value. Banner does not have to pay this amount back to the holders of the bonds; rather, the premium reduces the amount of interest due on the note over its life. This, in effect, makes the bond yield the 8 percent effective rate of interest rather than the 10 percent face interest rate. Using this information, the journal entry to record the issuance of the bond on March 1, 1995, is:

Cash	11,359,150	
Premium on Bonds Payable		1,359,150
Bonds Payable		10,000,000

Exhibit 18.15 illustrates Banner's journal entries for the first two fiscal years of this bond. On the first payment date, September 1, 1995, Banner Corporation recognizes interest of $454,366 (column 2, Exhibit 18.14) but pays $500,000 cash interest (column 1, Exhibit 18.14) as promised in the bond indenture. The interest expense for this six-month period, $454, 366, is incurred because Banner has borrowed $11,359,150 for six months. The difference between the amount of cash paid for interest and the effective interest, $45,634 (column 3, Exhibit 18.14), is the amount by which Banner will reduce (amortize) the Premium on Bonds Payable account. It represents the difference between the 10 percent face rate of interest and the 8 percent effective rate of interest. Exhibit 18.15 shows the journal entry to record this first payment on September 1, 1995.

The adjusting entries on December 31 shown in Exhibit 18.15 recognize the interest expense incurred on the bond from September 1 to December 31 and also the obligation to pay $333,333 of cash interest as of that date. For example, the interest expense on December 31, 1995, $301,694 ($452,541 × 4/6) is less than the $333,333 shown in the Interest Payable account. The $31,639 difference is the premium amortized for this four-month period ($47,459 × 4/6). On March 1, 1996, when the company pays $500,000 of cash interest due, it recognizes the interest expense of $150,847 ($452,541 × 2/6) for the first two months of 1996, amortizes the

EXHIBIT | 18.15 | Entries for Bonds Issued at a Premium—Banner Corporation

	1995	1996
March 1 Entries		
Cash	11,359,150	
Premium on B/P	1,359,150	
Bonds Payable	10,000,000	
Interest Expense		150,847[a]
Interest Payable		333,333
Premium on B/P		15,820[b]
Cash		500,000
September 1 Entries		
Interest Expense	454,366	450,642
Premium on B/P	45,634	49,358
Cash	500,000	500,000
December 31 Entries		
Interest Expense	301,694[c]	299,111[d]
Premium on B/P	31,639[e]	34,222[f]
Interest Payable	333,333[g]	333,333

[a]$452,541 (3/1/96, col 2) × 2/6.
[b]$ 47,459 (3/1/96, col 3) × 2/6.
[c]$452,541 (3/1/96, col 2) × 4/6.
[d]$448,667 (3/1/97, col 2) × 4/6.
[e]$ 47,459 (3/1/96, col 3) × 4/6.
[f]$ 51,333 (3/1/97, col 3) × 4/6.
[g]$500,000 (3/1/96, col 1) × 4/6.

	1995	1996
Income Statement		
Interest expense	$ 756,060*	$ 900,600[†]
Balance Sheet		
Current liabilities:		
Interest payable	333,333	333,333
Long-term liabilities:		
Bonds payable	10,000,000	10,000,000
Add: Premium on B/P	1,281,877	1,182,477
	$11,281,877	$11,182,477
Cash Flow Statement		
Operating section:		
Cash interest paid	(500,000)	(1,000,000)
Financing section:		
Cash received from bond	11,359,150	

*$454,366 + $301,694 from Exhibit 18.15.
[†]$150,847 + $450,642 + $299,111 from Exhibit 18.15.

$15,820 ($47,459 × 2/6) premium for the two-month period, and removes the amount of interest payable of $333,333 recognized on December 31, 1995, from Banner's records.

Exhibit 18.16 shows the impact of this bond issue on Banner's financial statements for 1995 and 1996. The interest expense on Banner's income statement of $756,060 in 1995 and $900,600 in 1996 reflects balances in the Interest Expense account after adjusting entries. The carrying value of the bond, that is, the amount reflected in the Bonds Payable account *plus* the balance in the Premium on Bonds Payable account on December 31 appears on the balance sheet as a long-term liability. As each year passes, the carrying value becomes smaller as the premium account is amortized. On the maturity date, the premium account is amortized fully, and the carrying value of the bonds is its $10,000,000 face value.

In 1995, the cash flow statement shows the receipt of the proceeds for the issuance of the bonds, $11,359,150 in the financing section and $500,000 of cash interest paid in the operating section. From this point on, the bond's cash flows reported on the statement of cash flows for the remainder of the bond's life are the same as those shown in the previous examples.

PAUSE & REFLECT

How many bond issues does ADM have outstanding in 1995? How many were issued at a premium and how many at a discount? What amount of cash did ADM raise from long-term debt, and how much cash did the company pay to reduce long-term debt in 1995?

Periodic and Lump-Sum Notes Payable—Private

Frequently companies use periodic payment and lump-sum types of notes to acquire debt financing from nonpublic sources. When this occurs, determining the amount received for the note, the accounting entries, and the financial statement presentation for the long-term notes is the same as the procedures described for bonds. However, instead of using bonds payable as the account title, companies would use note payable.

EARLY RETIREMENT OF BONDS

Bonds contain provisions that allow a company to retire the debt before it matures. Retirement usually occurs in one of three ways: (1) buying the bonds in the secondary bond market, (2) using the bond's call feature, and (3) converting bonds into stock. In this section we describe how to account for each of these events.

Buying Bonds in the Secondary Market

Firms can retire debt by buying their bonds in the secondary bond market where the bonds are traded among investors. Recall from Chapter 15 that the prices of bonds in the secondary market are quoted as a percent of the bond's face value, such as 101 1/2 (1.015 × Face value) or 89 3/4 (.8975 × Face value). These prices change as the market interest rates on the bonds change.

Some investors buy bonds so they can lock in a specific return for a long period of time. Other short-term investors buy bonds anticipating a decline in interest rates that would drive bond prices up, therefore, generating a profit when they sell the bonds.

The corporation that issues bonds is free to participate in the secondary bond market. If the market rate of interest on the bonds increases, bond prices decline. This presents an opportunity for the corporation to retire its debt early at a lower price.

Brokers facilitate investor trading in the secondary market for bonds.

EXHIBIT | 18.17 | Purchase of Bond in Secondary Market

Carrying Value of Bonds 9/1/96

Bonds payable	$10,000,000
Add: Premium on bonds payable	1,216,699
Carrying value of bonds (Exhibit 18.14, panel B)	$11,216,699

Gain on the Retirement of the Bond

Carrying value of the bond	11,216,699
Price paid for bonds*	8,962,500
Gain on retirement of bond	$ 2,254,199

*$10,000,000 × .89625, where the price of a bond, 89 5/8, is expressed as a
   percent of the face value of the bond.

Suppose that after Banner Corporation issued its bonds at a premium that yields 8 percent (Exhibit 18.14), the market interest rate for the company increased. By September 1, 1996, the market price of the bond was 89 5/8. Assume that, at this point, Banner Corporation's management decides to buy the entire bond issue and retire it.

When the purchase price exceeds the bond's carrying value, the company recognizes a loss because it is paying more than the liability due on that date. However, when the purchase price is less than the carrying value of the bond, it recognizes a gain because the liability is being paid off for an amount less than the debt due on that date.[3]

Exhibit 18.17 shows that the gain on the bond retirement of $2,254,199 is the difference between the carrying value of the bond ($11,216,699) and its market price, $8,962,500. The entry below reflects the bond's retirement on September 1, 1996.

9/1/96	Bonds Payable	10,000,000	
	Premium on Bonds Payable	1,216,699	
	Cash		8,962,500
	Gain on Retirement of Bonds		2,254,199

Notice that this entry removes both the bond and the related premium from the accounting records.

Using the Bond's Calling Feature

Chapter 15 introduced the idea that many bonds have a call feature in their indenture that enables the company to retire the bonds before their maturity date by paying the bondholders a specified call price. For example, if a bond issue has a call price of 106, the company can buy a $1,000 bond for $1,060, or 106 percent of the $1,000 face value ($1,000 × 1.06). When a bond is called, the bondholder must surrender the bond to the company for the call price. Typically a company cannot call a bond in the first three to five years of its life, and, after that time period, it can call the bond only on the bond's interest payment dates.

When a company calls a bond, it is paying off its debt obligation prior to the maturity date. The carrying value of the bond when it is called usually differs from the call price. If the call price is greater than the carrying value, the company would record a loss on the redemption of the bonds, and, if the call price is less than the carrying value, it would record a gain. The following example describes how to account for called bonds.

Assume the Banner Corporation can call its bonds after two years at a call price of 101. If Banner issued the bonds at a discount, as shown in Exhibit 18.11, and the entire bond issue was called on March 1, 1997, the company would make the entry below.

3/1/97	Bonds Payable	10,000,000	
	Loss on Retirement of Debt	1,110,662	
	Discount on Bonds Payable		1,010,662
	Cash		10,100,000

[3]Both gains and losses on early debt retirement are considered extraordinary items which we discuss in Chapter 22.

Because the price paid to retire the debt, $10,100,000, is greater than the carrying value of the debt, $8,989,338, when it is called on March 1, 1997 (Exhibit 18-11, panel B), the company would record a $1,110,662 loss. Remember that the carrying value is a combination of two accounts, Bonds Payable and Discount on Bonds Payable, and the entry must eliminate both of these accounts when the company calls the bonds.

Converting Bonds into Stock

As indicated in Chapter 15, convertible bonds allow the bondholders to convert their bonds into stock *at the bondholder's option.* The conversion feature is attractive because it gives the bondholder the assurance of a stable return from the interest on the bond over its life. The conversion feature also provides bondholders with the potential for a higher return if the underlying stock of the company becomes more valuable than the bond. When bondholders convert their bonds into common stock, they are exchanging creditors' equity in the firm for owners' equity in the firm. This is called, therefore, an **interequity transaction,** or an exchange of one type of equity in the firm for another. As a result, the debt of the firm is retired without a cash expenditure by the corporation.

Bondholders will only convert their bonds into stock when the value of the stock they will receive upon conversion exceeds the value of the bond. *Remember that the decision to convert rests with the bondholders and not with the corporation.* Therefore, it is unusual for all of a company's bondholders to convert all of a corporation's bonds at one point in time.

When conversion of bonds occurs between the bond's interest dates, the company accrues the interest to the date of conversion, but the converting bondholder forfeits the cash interest due at that date. As a result, most bonds are converted at or soon after their interest date.

The entries for the issuance of a convertible bond and its bond interest are the same as those for nonconvertible bonds. However, the conversion feature usually brings a greater initial selling price for convertible bonds than bonds without a conversion feature. The person buying the bond is receiving not only a bond, but also the option to acquire the stock of the corporation. This makes the bond a more attractive investment. The increased flexibility for the investor reduces the risk of the bond and, therefore, lowers the market rate of interest, which increases the price of the bond.

To illustrate how to account for the conversion of bond, assume that Banner Corporation issued bonds at a premium (Exhibit 18.14), that the bonds had a call price of 101, and that they were convertible to common stock on a 50:1 basis. This means that every bondholder can convert each bond held into 50 shares of Banner Corporation, no-par common stock. When Banner issued the bonds, its common stock was selling for $10 per share.

Assume that on September 1, 1996, the price of the Banner Corporation stock is $24 per share and 1,000 of the 10,000 bonds originally issued at a premium are converted into common stock. Bondholders who have converted are taking advantage of the fact that the value of the stock, $1,200 ($24 × 50 shares per bond) is well above $1,135.92, ($11,359,150 ÷ 10,000 bonds) the initial price paid for one bond. The entry to record this event must remove the carrying value of the 1,000 converted bonds and increase the amount of common stock reflected in Banner's records. Exhibit 18.18 shows how to determine the amount of the bonds' carrying value ($11,216,699) that is removed upon the bonds' conversion.

Recording the Conversion of Bonds   The book value method of recording the conversion of bonds merely transfers the carrying (book) value of the 1,000 converted bonds $1,121,670 (Exhibit 18.18), into the Common Stock account.

9/1/96	Bonds Payable	1,000,000	
	Premium on Bonds Payable	121,670	
	Common Stock (50,000 no-par shares)		1,121,670

EXHIBIT | 18.18 | Carrying Value of Bonds Prior to Conversion

Carrying Value of Entire Bond Issue 9/1/96

Face value	$10,000,000
Premium on bonds payable	1,216,699
Carrying value of bonds 9/1/96 (Exhibit 18.14)	$11,216,699

Carrying Value of One-Tenth (1,000 of 10,000) of Bond Issue on 9/1/96

$11,216,699 × .1 = $1,121,670 (rounded here for calculation purposes)

or

Bonds payable	$10,000,000	×	.1	=	$1,000,000
Premium on bonds payable	1,216,669	×	.1	=	121,670
Carrying value	$11,216,669	×	.1	=	$1,121,670

Note that there is no cash involved in the conversion process and that the entry transfers debtors' equity into owners' equity as a result of this interequity transaction.

In our example, Banner Corporation's convertible bonds have a call price of 101. Corporations can use the call feature of a bond to force convertible bondholders to convert their bonds. For example, if Banner Corporation's common stock reaches $24 a share, the value of the 50 shares of stock associated with the bond is $1,200. Banner Corporation could notify the bondholders that it intends to call the bonds, which means each bondholder would receive $1,010 in cash for their bonds on the next interest date. Then the bondholders have a choice of either converting their bonds into stock worth $1,200 or taking $1,010 in cash. Given the choice, most rational bondholders would convert their bonds into stock and, as a result, the corporation is able to reduce its debt through the conversion process rather than paying cash.

PAUSE & REFLECT

What is the size, term, face interest rate, and conversion rate of the convertible long-term debt issued by Anheuser-Busch? (See the Annual Report booklet.)

ACCOUNTING FOR LEASES

We described the features of operating and capital leases in Chapter 15. This section describes how to account for capital leases, a type of long-term debt financing. Leases are a source of long-term debt whose features cause their accounting treatment to differ from the basic types of notes just discussed.

Reflecting Operating Leases in the Accounting Records

Operating leases typically are rental agreements for a period of time that is substantially shorter than the economic life of the asset. In addition, the lessor in an operating lease expects to retain title to the asset. Any payments made by the lessee to the lessor for the use of the asset are considered rent expense, and the lessee records them as such.

For example, suppose Banner Corporation signs a three-year lease agreeing to pay $250 each month for the use of a Honda Accord as a salesperson's vehicle. Banner would debit the Rent Expense account when it makes each rental payment but would record no liability at any time during the life of the lease.

Rent Expense—Selling	250	
Cash		250

Reflecting Capital Leases in the Accounting Records

A capital lease is a rental agreement that confers such a substantial interest in the leased asset to the lessee that, in economic substance, the lessee owns the asset. When the lessee signs a capital lease, the lessee records an asset for the leased property and a related liability for the lease obligation in its accounting records. *The amount of the lease obligation for the lessee is equal to the present value of the future lease*

EXHIBIT | 18.19 | Capitalization of Lease Payments—Banner Corporation

A. Determining the Installment Payment

$$\text{Present value of annuity} = \text{Annuity} \times P_{4,9\%}$$
$$= \$8,642.78 \times 3.2397$$
$$= \$28,000$$

B. Lease Payment Schedule

Date	Payment	Interest (9% × Loan balance)	Principal	Loan Balance
1/1/96				$28,000.00
12/31/96	$8,642.78	$2,520.00	$6,122.78	21,877.22
12/31/97	8,642.78	1,968.95	6,673.83	15,203.39
12/31/98	8,642.78	1,368.31	7,274.47	7,928.92
12/31/99	8,642.78	713.86*	7,928.92	–0–

*Rounded.

payments, while the value of the asset on the lessee's records is the amount of the lease obligation plus any cash payments made when the lease is signed. The lessee records subsequent lease payments like those made for an installment note.

Assume that Banner Corporation signed a four-year lease on January 1, 1996, for a copier that has a four-year life. The terms of the lease call for Banner to pay $4,000 immediately and to make four payments of $8,642.78 each year starting December 31, 1996. Banner is responsible for all maintenance and repairs to the copier after the first two years and has the option to buy the copier at the end of the third year for its market price at the time. Banner's market rate of interest is 9 percent. This leasing agreement is clearly a capital lease because Banner Corporation has, in effect, purchased the machine.

This capital lease creates a leased asset of $32,000, which is equal to the $4,000 cash paid and the $28,000 lease liability incurred to acquire the asset. The $28,000 lease liability is the present value of the four $8,642.78 lease payments (shown in Exhibit 18.19 panel A) using Banner's 9 percent borrowing rate. The lease liability takes the form of an installment note because each lease payment covers the amount of interest expense due and also reduces a portion of the principal. The entry to record the lease is:

Copier	32,000	
Cash		4,000
Lease Payment Obligation		28,000

Exhibit 18.19 panel B presents the lease payment schedule. The entries for the lease payments are the same as those made for installment notes. The entry shown below for the first lease payment reflects the interest expense of $2,520 and the reduction of the lease liability of $6,122.78 at December 31, 1996.

Interest Expense	2,520.00	
Lease Payment Obligation	6,122.78	
Cash		8,642.78

The liability account, Lease Payment Obligation, decreases each year as payments are made. The company classifies it as a long-term liability for 1996 and 1997 and as a current liability for 1998. Banner would report the associated cash flows of a lease on its cash flow statement in the same way it would for the cash flows of an installment note. Since Banner records a tangible, operating asset on the books at the time of signing the lease, it records depreciation expense on the leased asset at the end of the fiscal year.

A capital lease requires the recognition of a liability on the financial statements. Some firms may want to avoid this because the liability increases the firm's debt-to-equity ratio and could have an adverse effect on the interest rates available to the firm. For this reason, firms signing lease agreements may structure the lease to qualify as an

Note 4—Long-Term Debt and Financing Arrangements

	1992	1991
	(In thousands)	
8.875% Debentures $300 million face amount, due in 2011	$ 298,078	$ 298,040
8.125% Debentures $300 million face amount, due in 2012	297,805	
8.375% Debentures $300 million face amount, due in 2017	293,826	
7% Debentures $250 million face amount, due in 2011	122,356	121,202
Zero Coupon Debt $400 million face amount, due in 2002; $100 million retired in 1992	107,810	183,062
10.25% Debentures $100 million face amount, due in 2006	98,516	98,467
6% Bonds Deutsche Mark 150 million face amount, due in 1997	98,171	82,559
Industrial Revenue Bonds at various rates from 5.90% to 13.25% and due in varying amounts to 2012	80,639	80,265
Lease obligations (see Note 5)	43,902	49,074
Other	151,649	204,374
Total long-term debt	1,592,752	1,117,042
Less current maturities	(30,261)	(136,770)
	$1,562,491	$ 980,272

Unamortized original issue discounts on the 7% Debentures and Zero Coupon Debt issues are being amortized at 15.35% and 13.80%, respectively. Accelerated amortization of the discounts for tax purposes has the effect of lowering the actual rate of interest to be paid over the remaining lives of the issues to approximately 11.16% and 6.29%, respectively.

The aggregate maturities of long-term debt for the five years after June 30, 1992 are $30 million, $32 million, $25 million, $16 million, and $117 million, respectively.

Note 5—Leases

The Company leases certain processing plants and transportation equipment under capital and operating leases. At June 30, 1992, and 1991, property, plant, and equipment includes approximately $17 million for leases capitalized.

Future minimum rental commitments for all capital leases and noncancellable operating leases are as follows:

	Capital Leases		Operating Leases	
	Agricultural Processing	Transportation	Agricultural Processing	Transportation
	(In thousands)			
1993	$10,145	$ 2,670	$15,442	$13,839
1994	9,676	2,670	12,901	12,042
1995	7,740	2,670	11,490	10,817
1996	3,492	2,671	1,334	9,952
1997	2,294	2,671	732	6,790
Thereafter	2,489	8,860	8,123	10,341
Total mimimum lease payments	35,836	22,212	$50,022	$63,781
Less amounts representing interest	(8,398)	(5,748)		
Present value of net mimimum lease payments	$27,438	$16,464		

Lease commitments expire on various dates through 2026. Certain leases require payment of property taxes, insurance and maintenance costs in addition to the rental, and contain provisions under which the Company indemnifies the lessors against certain losses.

Tariff rates which the Company would otherwise pay would ordinarily exceed the rent obligations for transportation equipment. Railroad car leases are included in the total commitment to lessors without deduction for mileage credits.

Rent expense for 1992, 1991, and 1990 was $59 million, $61 million, and $74 million, respectively.

---

operating lease, thus getting the advantage of the leased assets without recording an asset or a liability. If significant, however, the company must disclose the terms of the operating lease in footnotes to the financial statements.

PAUSE & REFLECT

Exhibit 18.20 shows Notes 4 and 5 from ADM's 1992 financial statement. Using this information describe what ADM is leasing and how much debt ADM has incurred as a result of capital leases. How much rental expense has ADM incurred in 1992 as a result of operating leases?

INFORMATION PROVIDED FOR DECISION MAKERS

External and internal decision makers who are interested in a firm's long-term debt find the information described in this chapter quite useful. External decision makers want to know the amount, type, and cost of a firm's long-term debt, as well as its related cash flows. A firm's financial statements and footnotes to the statements provide external decision makers with useful information about the uses of a firm's long-term debt and its ability to service its debt. Financial statements also provide a means of comparing the financial structure of two companies.

Internal decision makers are in a position to influence the amount and type of the firm's long-term debt. They use information on the financial statements and also etting up a bond payment schedule on a spreadsheet requires a little planning, but the result is well worth the effort because the computer will do all the tedious calculations. For example, let's set up a bond payment schedule for a 20-year bond issue with a $1,000,000 face value that pays 13 percent interest semiannually. Assume the bond was issued when the market rate of interest was 12 percent, therefore, the company received $1,075,231 for the bonds. Set up the spreadsheet with the following column headings in rows 1 and 2:

Period	Cash Interest	Effective Interest	Premium Amortized	Carrying Value

Then enter the current carrying value, $1,075,231 in column e, row 3. Use the fill command then enter the number of periods

from 1 to 40 in column a, starting with row 4. Next, you must decide how the cell amounts can be calculated using other cell amounts and the appropriate interest rates. In cell b4, enter: **+1000000*.13*1/2** to calculate the semiannual cash interest amount. Then use the copy command to copy this cell to the other 39 periods. In cell c4, enter: **+e3*.12*1/2** to calculate the semiannual interest expense amount. In cell d4, enter: **+b4–c4** to calculate the amount of premium amortized each semiannual period. In cell e4, enter: **+e3–d4** to calculate the new carrying value. Now use the copy command to copy cells c4, d4, and e4 to the remaining periods. Finally, format the cells for dollars with the desired number of decimal places. Remember, if you round to even dollars you may have a small rounding error at the end.

internal reports that impact their decisions about specific long-term notes. Their goal is to balance the risk and reward of using long-term debt and to incur the smallest cost possible for the use of the funds obtained by issuing debt.

In addition to balancing the risk and reward of long-term debt financing, internal decision makers must understand the amount and timing of cash flows associated with their debt financing decisions. Financial managers have reports prepared that describe the cash flows mandated by their debt financing decisions and the cash flows expected from the firm's operation. These internal reports help identify any potential solvency problems in meeting the firm's debt obligations. This in turn reduces the chance of the firm defaulting on its long-term debt.

SUMMARY

Long-term debt is a means of raising large amounts of cash typically used to acquire a firm's operational investments. Each of the three types of notes used to raise these funds receives a slightly different accounting treatment because the cash flows specified by the notes differ according to the form of the note. The resources acquired depend upon how the market rates affect the cash flows promised by the notes.

A firm's accounting records reflect the long-term obligation created by these notes as well as the cost of using long-term debt financing.

- Each type of long-term note used to obtain funds or resources—periodic payment, lump-sum payment, and periodic payment and lump-sum notes—is recorded and reported in a manner consistent with its respective cash flow characteristics and the matching principle.

- A periodic payment note has a portion of the note reported as a current liability and a portion reported as a long-term liability.

- The discount on a lump-sum or noninterest-bearing note represents the interest over the entire life of the note and is reported as a contra liability on the balance sheet.

- Premiums and discounts on bonds represent the difference between the face rate of interest and the market rate of interest on the bond. Amortization of premiums results in interest expense reported on the income statement that *is less than* the amount of cash interest reported on the cash flow statement. Amortization of discounts causes effective interest reported on the income statement to be *greater* than the amount of cash interest reported on the cash flow statement.

Early retirement of bonds occurs when bonds are purchased in the secondary market, or when they are called, or converted. Gains and losses are recorded when the carrying value of the bonds differs from the market price of the bonds at the time of retirement.

KEY TERMS

contra liability An account that has a debit balance that reduces the amount of a specific related liability account to show its carrying value

interequity transaction A transaction that reflects the exchange of one type of equity in a firm for another

QUESTIONS

1. Why does management finance a company's operational infrastructure with long-term debt?
2. What two accounts are debited when a company makes a payment on an installment loan? Why?
3. When is an adjusting entry recorded for an installment note? Why is it necessary?
4. When is an installment note classified as both a current liability and a long-term liability?
5. Describe what the Discount on Note Payable on a noninterest-bearing note represents.
6. Describe how the Discount on Note Payable on a noninterest-bearing note is reported on the balance sheet.
7. How does the entry to record the issuance of a bond at a premium differ from a bond issued at a discount? Why?
8. How should a company report a premium on bonds payable on its balance sheet? A discount on bonds payable?
9. What constitutes the carrying value of a noninterest-bearing note? A bond?
10. Explain why and how the premiums and discounts on bond accounts affect interest expense.
11. How does the adjusting entry for a noninterest-bearing note differ from a periodic payment and lump-sum note (bond)? Why are they different?
12. What impact does amortization have on the carrying value of bonds issued at a premium? At a discount?
13. Describe the difference in cash flows between two identical bonds when one is issued at a discount and the other is issued at a premium.
14. If a company repurchases its bonds in the secondary market, under what circumstances would the company record a gain?
15. How is the price paid to call a bond determined?
16. Describe what happens to a company's balance sheet when a convertible bond is converted to common stock.
17. When a bond is converted into common stock, it is called an *interequity transaction*. What does this mean?
18. Compare and contrast accounting for a called bond and a converted bond.
19. What are the differences between the entries to record an operating and a capital lease? Why do these differences exist?
20. Describe the difference between how an operating lease and a capital lease are reported on the income statement, the balance sheet, and the statement of cash flows for the lessor.

EXERCISES

E 18.1   The schedules below describe three notes.
   a. Which schedule describes a periodic payment and lump-sum note?
   b. Which schedule describes a lump-sum payment note?
   c. Which schedule describes a periodic payment note?
   d. What is the interest rate on each of the notes?
   e. Assuming each note was issued for cash, show the entry to record the issuance of each of the notes.

Schedule 1

Date	Cash Payment	Interest Expense	Principal	Loan Balance
2/1/94				$40,000
8/1/94	$8,135	$2,400	$5,735	34,265
2/1/95	8,135	2,056	6,079	28,186
8/1/95	8,135	1,691	6,444	21,742
2/1/96	8,135	1,305	6,830	14,912
8/1/96	8,135	895	7,240	7,672
2/1/97	8,135	463	7,672	–0–

Schedule 2

Date	Cash Payment	Interest Expense	Discount	Carrying Value
4/1/92			$364,500.00	$ 635,500.00
4/1/93		$ 76,260.00	288,240.00	711,760.00
4/1/94		85,411.20	202,828.80	797,171.20
4/1/95		95,660.54	107,168.26	892,831.74
4/1/96		107,168.26	–0–	1,000,000.00
4/1/96	$1,000,000			–0–

Schedule 3

Date	Cash Interest	Interest Expense	No Discount or Premium	Carrying Value
3/1/95				$10,000,000
9/1/95	$500,000	$500,000		10,000,000
3/1/96	500,000	500,000		10,000,000
9/1/96	500,000	500,000		10,000,000
3/1/97	500,000	500,000		10,000,000

E 18.2   Presented below is a partial schedule for a note payable of the Buckingham News Service.

Date	Cash Payment			
3/1/95				$25,000
6/1/95	$1,529	$500	$1,029	23,971
9/1/95	1,529	479	1,050	22,921
12/1/95	1,529	458	1,071	21,850
3/1/96	1,529	437	1,092	20,758
6/1/96	1,529	415	1,114	19,644

a. Is this a periodic payment, a lump-sum payment, or a periodic payment and lump-sum note?
b. What is the note's market interest rate?
c. If the note was used to pay for a truck, make the entry for the acquisition of the truck.
d. Make the entry for the 6/1/95 payment.

E 18.3   Using the data in E 18.2 and assuming that Buckingham has a June 30 fiscal year-end, make the appropriate adjusting entry for June 30, 1995. Describe how Buckingham News Service would report this note on its balance sheet, income statement, and statement of cash flows.

E 18.4   On April 1, 1996, Clifford Products borrowed $50,000 cash at 10 percent on a four-year installment note. Annual payments starting on April 1, 1997, are $15,774. Prepare an installment loan repayment schedule for the first year of the note. Make the entries for the first year of the note assuming that Clifford has a December 31 fiscal year-end.

E 18.5   The payment schedule below is for a $75,000 note the Michelle Dugan Corporation issued for cash on August 1, 1996. If Dugan Corporation has a December 31 fiscal year-end, make the entries for the issuance of the note and through December 31, 1997.

Date	Cash Payment	Interest Expense	Principal	Loan Balance
8/1/96				$75,000.00
2/1/97	$14,776.29	$3,750.00	$11,026.29	63,973.71
8/1/97	14,776.29	3,198.69	11,577.60	52,396.11
2/1/98	14,776.29	2,619.81	12,156.48	40,239.63

E 18.6   Using the information in E 18.5, show how the Michelle Dugan Corporation's installment note is reported on its income statement, balance sheet, and statement of cash flows for 1996 and 1997.

E 18.7   On April 1, 1996, Jeff Suttle, the chief financial officer of the Quinter Corporation, raised $995,880 by issuing a 10-year, $2,150,000, noninterest-bearing note. The amortization table for the note is presented below. Make the entries for the note from April 1, 1996, to December 31, 1997.

Date	Cash Payment	Interest Expense	Discount	Carrying Value
4/1/96			$1,154,120	$ 995,880
4/1/97		$79,670	1,074,450	1,075,550
4/1/98		86,044	988,406	1,161,594

E 18.8   Using the information in E 18.7, show how Quinter Corporation's income statement and balance sheet report the impact of this note on December 31, 1996, and December 31, 1997.

E 18.9   Solar Furnace Company purchased equipment from Reyes Pipe and Fittings on January 1, 1996, by issuing a five-year noninterest-bearing note with a face value of $300,000. If Solar Furnace has a December 31 fiscal year-end, prepare the journal entries for the acquisition of the equipment and the first two years of the note. Assuming that Solar's market rate of interest is 10 percent, how much interest will Solar report on its 1996 income statement? How would Solar report the note on its balance sheet? How does the note affect Solar's statement of cash flows in 1996?

E 18.10   On February 1, 1996, Dible Corporation purchased a piece of equipment with a list price of $30,000 and signed a two-year noninterest-bearing note. Given the amortization schedule below for the note and the fact that Dible has a December 31 fiscal year-end, make the entries necessary for the life of the note.

Date	Cash Payment	Interest (.08 × Carrying value)	Discount	Carrying Value
4/1/96			$4,281.00	$25,719.00
2/1/97		$2,057.52	2,223.43	27,776.57
2/1/98		2,223.43	-0-	30,000.00
2/1/98	$30,000			-0-

E 18.11   Using the information in E 18.10, show how much interest Dible Corporation will report on its income statement in 1996, 1997, and 1998. How would Dible report the note on the balance sheets in 1996 and 1997? What are the cash flows reported on the cash flow statements for 1996 and 1997?

E 18.12   Busar Company borrowed $50,000 cash and signed a $50,000, 9 percent, 5-year note payable dated September 1, 1996. Interest on the note is payable semiannually on March 1 and September 1 each year. Bursar closes its books annually on June 30. Prepare the entries for the issuance of the note and for events related to the note during the first year of the note's life. How is the note reported on Busar's balance sheet and income statement for June 30, 1997?

E 18.13   Royce Purinton, the chief financial officer of Aries Corporation, issued for cash a $70,000, 9 percent, three-year note payable on April 1, 1996, that pays interest annually. Aries Corporation has a December 31 fiscal year-end. Make the entries for the first year of the note's life if the market rate is 8 percent.

E 18.14   The Hanson Corporation issued $55,000,000 of bonds on May 1, 1996, and prepared the amortization schedule shown below. Given this information, make the entries for the first year of the bond issue's life if the Hanson Corporation has a December 31 fiscal year-end. Show how Hanson reports the bond issue on its income statement and balance sheet in 1996.

Date	Cash Interest	Interest Expense	Discount Amortized	Discount	Carrying Value
5/1/96				$6,308,775	$48,691,225
11/1/96	$2,750,000	$2,921,424	$171,474	6,137,301	48,862,699
5/1/97	2,750,000	2,931,762	181,762	5,955,539	49,044,461

E 18.15   Morgan Corporation has issued $1,500,000 of 10-year, 8 percent bonds on September 1, 1997, that pay interest semiannually on March 1 and September 1 each year. The bonds will yield a 6 percent effective rate of interest. Prepare the journal entries for the first year of the bonds' life if Morgan Corporation has a December 31 fiscal year-end.

E 18.16   Travis Corporation is authorized to issue 3,000 10-year, 9 percent bonds. Each bond has a $1,000 face value, is convertible into 50 shares of Travis' no-par common stock, and has a call price of 105. Travis issued the bonds on March 1, 1995, at a discount and prepared the amortization schedule shown below. On March 1, 1996, the market price of Travis' stock had risen to $30 per share, and bondholders had turned in 1,000 bonds for conversion to stock. Make the entry for the conversion of the bonds on March 1, 1996.

Date	Cash Interest	Effective Interest	Discount Amortized	Bond Discount	Carrying Value
3/1/95				$516,163	$2,483,837
9/1/95	$135,000	$149,030	$14,030	502,133	2,497,867
3/1/96	135,000	149,872	14,872	487,261	2,512,739
9/1/96	135,000	150,764	15,764	471,497	2,528,503
3/1/97	135,000	151,710	16,710	454,787	2,545,213

E 18.17   Using the information in E 18.6, make the entry for Travis Corporation assuming it called the entire bond issue on September 1, 1996.

E 18.18   Given the amortization table shown in E 18.16, assume that the market price of Travis' bond had dropped to 90 3/4 on March 1, 1996, and Travis purchased 2,000 of the bonds in the secondary market. Make the entry for Travis' purchase of the bonds. After the bonds are purchased, what is the entry to record the interest on the bond issue on September 1, 1996?

E 18.19   On September 1, 1995, a capital lease was signed by Clyde Industries in which it agreed to lease machinery with a fair market value of $26,585 for a five-year period, which is the machine's useful life. Annual payments of $6,585 are to be made at the beginning of each year, and Clyde's interest rate was 12 percent. Given the lease payment schedule below, make the entries for the lease payments for the first two years of the lease if Clyde has a December 31 fiscal year-end.

Date	Lease Payment	Interest	Principal	Lease Obligation
9/1/95				$26,585
9/1/95	$6,585			20,000
9/1/96	6,585	$2,400	$4,185	15,815
9/1/97	6,585	1,898	4,687	11,128

E 18.20   On May 1, 1996, Smoke Corporation signed a lease for a delivery truck that called for seven lease payments of $2,500. Smoke Corporation could borrow funds at a 12 pecent rate of interest when the lease was signed. The first lease payment is made when the lease is signed, and the remaining payments are made every six months. If this is considered an operating lease and Smoke Corporation has a December 31 fiscal year-end, make the entries for the first year of the lease.

E 18.21   The Beans Corporation signed a three-year capital lease for a copier on June 1, 1995. The lease calls for four annual payments of $1,800. The first payment was made when the lease is signed. Make the entries for the first two lease payments if Beans Corporation's interest rate for the lease is 10 percent and it has a December 31 fiscal year-end. How would Beans report the lease on its 12/31/95 balance sheet and income statement?

PROBLEMS

P 18.1

Kahil Products has the following transactions during 1996.

May 1   Borrowed $14,000 on a three-year, 10 percent installment note with quarterly payments.

June 15   Signed a four-year operating lease for additional equipment. Semiannual lease payments are $1,500 and the first payment was made when the lease was signed.

Aug. 1   Made the first quarterly installment payment on the May 1 installment loan.

Sept. 1   Issued a $20,000 noninterest-bearing note that is due in two years in exchange for a piece of equipment. Kahil's market rate of interest is 10 percent.

Nov. 1   Paid the second quarterly installment on the May 1 loan.

Dec. 15   Made the semiannual lease payment.

Required:
a. Prepare the journal entries for the events described at Kahil.
b. Make the necessary adjusting entries on December 31, the company's fiscal year-end.
c. Show how Kahil reports the notes on its balance sheet.
d. How much interest is reported on Kahil's income statement in 1996?
e. Does the cash paid for interest in 1996 differ from the amount reported on its income statement? Explain.
f. How much cash was paid to reduce principal on the notes?

P 18.2

The Tom Wenke Corporation made the following transactions in 1996 when its market rate of interest was 10 percent. Wenke has a December 31 fiscal year-end.

Apr. 1   Purchased $50,000 of office equipment from Office World by paying $5,000 down and signing a three-year note with a face interest rate of 10 percent that is paid annually.

July 1   Purchased a piece of equipment with a list price of $15,000 and signed a two-year noninterest-bearing note for that amount.

Required:
a. Make the entries to record the transactions above.
b. Make the appropriate adjusting entries for the notes.
c. Show how the notes are reported on the balance sheet.
d. How much interest was reported on the income statement?
e. Does the cash paid for interest differ from the amount reported on the income statement? Explain.
f. How much cash was paid to reduce the principal of the notes?

P 18.3

Carla Bailey Corporation has an 8 percent market interest rate and a December 31 fiscal year-end. During 1996 the following notes were issued to acquire equipment:

Mar. 1   Issued a $50,000, two-year, noninterest-bearing note for a conveyor system.

May 1   Issued a $50,000, two-year, 8 percent installment note for two trucks. The payments are due semiannually on November 1 and May 1.

June 1   Issued a $50,000, two-year, 6 percent note for a fabrication machine. The face interest is paid semiannually on December 1 and June 1.

Required:
a. Make the entries for the issuance of each of these notes.
b. Make the entries for the notes through December 31, 1996.
c. Show how the notes are reported on the December 31, 1996, balance sheet.
d. What is the interest expense reported on the December 31, 1996, income statement?
e. How much cash interest was paid in 1996 and does this differ from the interest expense recognized in 1996? Explain.

P 18.4

Fairfax Industries' board of directors authorized the issue of $6,000,000, of 20-year, 10 percent bonds. The bonds are dated October 1, 1996, and interest is paid semiannually on April 1 and October 1. Fairfax closes its books on June 30 each year. The bonds were issued on October 1, 1996, when the market rate of interest was 12 percent.

Required:
a. How many individual bonds make up the bond issue?
b. Prepare the journal entries for the issuance of the bonds and the first year of the bonds' life.
c. Describe how the bonds are reported on Fairfax's income statement, balance sheet, and statement of cash flows on June 30, 1997.

P 18.5   On May 1, 1995, Mid-States Supply issued $5,000,000 in 15-year, 12 percent bonds that pay interest annually on May 1. The bonds were issued on May 1, 1995, when the market interest rate was 10 percent. Mid-States' fiscal year ends December 31.

Required   a. Prepare the journal entries for the first two years of the bond issue's life.
  b. Show how Mid-States Supply reports the events involving their bond issue on its income statement, balance sheet, and statement of cash flows for December 31, 1995, and December 31, 1996.

P 18.6   Hodges Corporation has a market interest rate of 10 percent and is authorized to issue $25,000,000 in 10-year bonds on March 1, 1996. The face interest rate on the bonds will be paid semiannually.

Required: a. Make the entries for the bond issue and for the first year of the bond's life if the face interest rate is 8 percent.
  b. Make the entries for the bond issue and for the first year of the bond's life if the face interest rate is 12 percent.
  c. Given the two possible face rates above, which one generates the most cash? Which one is the least expensive for Hodges Corporation?

 P 18.7   Parker Metals is authorized to issue $20,000,000 in 10-year, 6 percent bonds on September 1, 1997. The bonds pay interest annually on September 1, and Parker's fiscal year-end is on December 31.

1997
Sept. 1   Issued the bonds when the market rate of interest was 8 percent.
Dec. 31   Record the adjusting entry for the bond interest.

1998
Sept. 1   Made the first interest payment.

Required: a. Prepare the journal entries for the events above.
  b. Determine the amount of interest expense incurred in 1997.
  c. How much cash was paid in interest in 1997? How does this relate to your answer in *b* and why?
  d. Show how to report the liabilities associated with the bonds on the 1997 balance sheet.

P 18.8   On June 1, 1996, Wildcat Corporation issued 5,000 10-year bonds with a $1,000 face value. The bonds have a face rate of 10 percent and pay interest semiannually on December 1 and June 1. The bonds have a 50:1 conversion feature, that is, the bondholders can exchange one bond for 50 shares of Wildcat's no-par common stock.

On June 1, 1998, bondholder Arlo Artichoke converted 10 of his bonds. The carrying value of all the bonds on Wildcat's books at the time of conversion was $5,080,000.

Required: a. Prepare the entry for Wildcat Corporation to record the conversion of the 10 bonds.
  b. Why would an investor want to convert the bonds?
  c. Why would the Wildcat put a conversion feature on the bonds?
  d. What is the carrying value of the remaining bonds after the conversion?

P 18.9   Using the same facts as in P 18.8, assume that on June 1, 1998, Wildcat purchased 100 of its bonds in the bond market when the price was 98.

Required: a. Prepare the necessary journal entry for the purchase of the bonds.
  b. Why would Wildcat take such an action?
  c. What is the carrying value of the remaining bonds after the purchase?

P 18.10   Assume the Wildcat bonds in P 18.8 were issued with a call feature of 105 and that on June 1, 1998, Wildcat called 200 bonds when the market price of the bonds was 108.

Required: a. Make the journal entry to record the calling of the bonds on June 1, 1998.
  b. Why would a company have a call feature on a bond?
  c. What is the carrying value of the remaining bonds after the bonds are called?

P 18.11 On March 1, 1996, the Cole/Jess Corporation issued $30,000,000 of 10-year, 8 percent, convertible bonds. The bonds have a call price of 105, and interest is paid semiannually on September 1 and March 1. Each $1,000 bond is convertible into 60 shares of Cole/Jess's no-par common stock. The bond was issued to yield an effective rate of interest of 6 percent. Cole/Jess Corporation has a December 31 fiscal year-end.

Required:
a. Make the entry to record the issuance of the bonds.
b. Set up an amortization table for the first four interest payments of the bond issue.

Treat each of the following as independent events.

c. Show the entry if 1,000 bonds are converted on March 1, 1997, when the stock is selling for $30 per share. Explain why the bondholders would convert these bonds.
d. Show the entry Cole/Jess would make if the company calls 1,000 bonds on March 1, 1997. Why would Cole/Jess call its bonds?
e. Make the entry if Cole/Jess buys 1,000 bonds in the secondary bond market for 98 3/4 on March 1, 1997.

The following requirements assume that c, d, and e have all occurred.

f. Make the entry to record the interest on the remaining bonds on September 1, 1997, and December 31, 1997.
g. How would the remaining bonds be reported on Cole/Jess's 12/31/97 balance sheet?

P 18.12 Lazari Leasing Service recently purchased equipment for $70,000 and leased it to Baker Machine and Foundry on April 1, 1996. The equipment has an estimated useful life of five years. Baker has leased the equipment for five years with an option to purchase it for $1 at the end of the fifth year. During the period of the lease, Baker is responsible for all repairs and maintenance of the leased property. Baker will make five annual lease payments of $16,510; the first is due on the date of the lease. Baker's interest rate is 9 percent and it closes its books annually on December 31.

Required:
a. Is this a capital or operating lease?
b. Make Baker's April 1, 1996, entry for the lease.
c. Prepare the appropriate adjusting entries at December 31, 1996.
d. Describe how Baker would report information regarding this lease on its income statement and balance sheet for 1996.
e. Record the second annual lease payment on April 1, 1997.

COMPUTER APPLICATIONS

CA 18.1 Bradley Logdston Electronics plans to issue $1 million of 10 percent, 20-year bonds. The market rate of interest at the time of issue is 8 percent. The bonds are issued on June 30 and pay interest semiannually. Bradley Logdston Electronics has a December 31 year-end.

Required: Use a computer spreadsheet.
a. Determine the amount of cash Logdston will receive when the company issues the bonds, assuming they are issued on an interest payment date.
b. Prepare a bond amortization schedule that indicates the amounts of cash, interest expense, amortization, and bond carrying value on each interest payment date.

CA 18.2 Refer to CA 18.1. Assume that the market rate of interest at the time of issue is 12 percent.

Required: Use a computer spreadsheet.
a. Determine the amount of cash Logdston will receive when the bonds are issued assuming they are issued on an interest payment date.
b. Prepare a bond amortization schedule that indicates the amounts of cash, interest expense, amortization, and bond carrying value on each interest payment date.

CRITICAL THINKING

CT 18.1 Zaicek's Furniture World is offering "interest-free financing for three full years—just divide the price of the furniture by 36 months to determine the monthly payment." Khouri Company purchased $27,000 of office furniture under this plan on November 15, 1996.

Required:
    a. Make the entry to record Khouri's purchase if the company usually borrows money at 12 percent.
    b. Make the entry for the first $750 payment on December 15, 1996.
    c. Make the adjusting entry on December 31, Khouri's fiscal year-end.
    d. Make the entry for the second payment on January 15, 1997.
    e. How is this note reported on Khouri's December 31, 1996, balance sheet? Why?

CT 18.2 Bob Holtfretter, the promotions manager of Waterbed Bonanza Company, is interested in running a "24 months, no interest sale." He wants to offer customers the opportunity to buy waterbeds and to finance the purchase by merely dividing the price of the waterbed by 24 to determine the customer's monthly payment. However, he realizes that the "sale price" must somehow include the 12 percent interest usually charged to finance credit purchases. He has asked you to show him how to determine the "sale price" of a waterbed that normally sells for $1,000.

CT 18.3 Farthington Corporation wants to raise $10,000,000 by issuing zero-coupon (noninterest-bearing) bonds that are due in 10 years. How many $1,000 zero-coupon bonds must they issue if Farthington's market rate is 8 percent? How would Farthington record the issuance of these bonds?

CASES

C 18.1 Note 4 of Archer Daniels Midland Company's annual report describes a variety of debentures issued by the company. For the debentures described, determine the amount of cash interest paid on the bonds. Is the interest expense on these debenture bonds greater or less than the cash interest paid? Describe ADM's zero-coupon (noninterest-bearing) debt.

C 18.2 Note 5 of Archer Daniels Midland Company's annual report for 1995 describes the leasing activity of the company. Compare Note 5 of the 1995 statement with Note 5 of ADM's 1992 financial statements as shown in Exhibit 18.20 and describe the change in ADM leasing arrangements. What is management's incentive to structure leases so they qualify as operating rather than capital leases?

C 18.3 Using the annual report of a company of your choice, describe the firm's long-term notes (bonds, etc.). You should describe: (1) the type of debt instruments used, (2) the cost of using debt financing, (3) the existence of capital leases, and (4) how the long-term notes are reported on the annual report.

ETHICAL CHALLENGES

EC 18.1 When the Advent Corporation issues long-term notes for noncash assets, it uses a face interest rate on the note that is 2 percent less than the company's market interest rate at the time and records the notes at their face values. The corporation's chief financial officer argues that, because the notes are not issued to a bank for cash, they are secured with the assets of the company and, therefore, have less risk than if they were borrowing cash from the bank to buy these assets. Do you agree or disagree with this reasoning? Why or why not? What is the company's incentive for following this course of action? What is the impact of this policy on Advent's income statement and balance sheet?

EC 18.2 The Defender Corporation has a considerable amount of long-term installment notes. The company controller, Ron Jury, has made it a company policy to report the entire amount of these installment notes as long-term liabilities. Ron argues that because the notes are all for long periods of time they constitute long-term debt. Do you agree or disagree with Mr. Jury's policy? Why or why not? What is the incentive for Defender Corporation to follow this policy?

CHAPTER 19

Recording and Communicating Equity Financing Activities

Learning Objectives

1. Describe how and why to record and communicate equity fiancing activities for sole proprietorships and partnerships.
2. Explain how and why corporations record contributed capital.
3. Illustrate how and why to determine corporate earnings and losses and how the firm's earnings are distributed to its owners.
4. Describe how and why corporations account for treasury stock and stock splits.
5. Describe how and why corporations communicate stockholders' equity activities.

E. I. du Pont de Nemours and Company (Du Pont) is the largest chemical company in the United States and one of the largest in the world. It employs more than 124,000 people worldwide.[1] The company was founded in 1802 as a manufacturer of gunpowder. Today, Du Pont describes itself as a customer-focused chemical and energy company. It produces a multitude of products such as Conoco petroleum products, Teflon and Silverstone nonstick coatings for cookware, Kevlar fibers for military helmets and bulletproof vests, and herbicides.

Today, any person interested in becoming an owner of this diversified, multinational corporation can do so by acquiring its preferred or common stock. How do corporations like Du Pont account for their owners' interest in the enterprise, and why is it necessary? Does the system used to account for an owner's interest in a business enterprise depend on the form of ownership? Why is accounting information concerning the owners' equity of a firm of interest to a firm's creditors?

---

[1] E. I. du Pont de Nemours and Company, Annual Report, 1995.

Each form of business ownership, whether sole proprietorship, partnership, or corporation, has unique features. The accounting system records and communicates what is unique about a business's equity financing. It is important to understand the differences related to equity for each type of organization.

It is also important to look beyond the recording process to understand the nature of changes in a business's owners' equity and what events the accounting entries represent. Therefore, understanding both how and why companies make these entries and communicate resulting information is essential for owners as well as other financial statement users.

The first section of this chapter describes how to account for equity financing events pertaining to sole proprietorships and partnerships—the types of organizations that are not separate legal entities from the owner(s). Accounting for these two types of ownership structures is quite similar because the organizations are easy to form and have unlimited liability.

We follow the discussion of sole proprietorships and partnerships by examining the equity events of corporations, which we introduced in Chapter 15. Accounting for corporate ownership reflects the complicating factor that corporations are separate legal entities from their owners, which provides limited liability for the owners.

NONCORPORATE FORMS OF BUSINESS

For sole proprietorships and partnerships, the amount of each owner's contribution and personal share of the firm's undistributed earnings are combined in one account. Use of one account reflects the fact that these organizations have economic rather than legal distinctions between the business and the owners. Combining contributed capital and retained earnings in each owner's capital account is done because, unlike corporations, the creditors of sole proprietorships and partnerships can lay claim to the personal assets of each owner if the business's assets are insufficient to meet its creditors' claims.

SOLE PROPRIETORSHIP

Accounting for a sole proprietorship requires only one permanent balance sheet equity account, called the *owner's capital account*. The account title includes the owner's name and the designation capital. For example, when Eleuthere Irenee du Pont de Nemours founded Du Pont in 1802, he could have used the owner's equity account, E. I. du Pont, Capital.

To illustrate, assume that Mr. Du Pont started his business, E. I. du Pont de Nemours and Company (Du Pont), by depositing $15,000 cash in the bank in the name of his new company and contributing a building he owned on the Brandywine River in Delaware with a fair market value of $75,000. The entry to record the establishment of the business would be:

Cash	15,000	
Building	75,000	
E. I. du Pont, Capital		90,000

Observe that the entry reflects the impact of the event on the business entity's assets and equity rather than on the owner's personal financial condition. If, during the course of the accounting period, Mr. Du Pont made additional contributions to the business, each contribution would be recorded in the same way as the initial contribution.

The amount in the owner's capital account changes at the end of an accounting period as revenue and expense accounts are closed to Income Summary, which, in turn, is closed to the owner's capital account. The closing entries illustrated below assume that Du Pont made a profit of $24,300 (Revenues $329,000 – Expenses $304,700) during its first year of operation.

Revenues	329,000	
Income Summary		329,000
Income Summary	304,700	
Expenses		304,700
Income Summary	24,300	
E. I. du Pont, Capital		24,300

The closing entries represent the magnitude of the change in the owner's interest in the business due to the firm's operating performance. The capital account, after closing, includes the original investment plus net income. In this case, the net income generated by the firm provided a $24,300 return for the year on Mr. Du Pont's initial investment and increased his financial interest in the business.

Drawing Account for a Sole Proprietorship

The proprietor controls withdrawal of assets from the business for personal use and could record the withdrawal by reducing the capital account directly. However, by using a separate capital account reserved exclusively for withdrawals, the proprietor can quickly identify the amount and timing of each withdrawal from the business.

Traditionally, a contra equity account called the **drawing account** is used in proprietorships and partnerships to summarize the dollar amount of assets withdrawn from the business entity for personal use. The drawing account title includes the owner's name, such as E. I. du Pont, and the label, Drawings or Withdrawals. When the proprietor takes assets, most commonly cash, from the business for personal use the drawing account is debited. If Mr. Du Pont withdrew $1,000 cash for his own use, the following entry would have been made.

E. I. du Pont, Drawings	1,000	
Cash		1,000

The owner's decision to withdraw assets is at his or her discretion and can occur at any time. The drawing account balance reflects the running total of the amount the owner has withdrawn over a specific time period, usually one year. If Mr. Du Pont made withdrawals totaling $20,600 during the period, at the end of the period, the balance in the drawing account would be closed to Mr. Du Pont's capital account. The balance in the capital account after closing represents the original investment, plus net income, less the amount withdrawn.

E. I. du Pont, Capital	20,600	
E. I. du Pont, Drawing		20,600

Withdrawals by the proprietor are not an expense of the business. Even though an owner who also manages the business may make regular withdrawals that resemble payment of a salary, these withdrawals are a distribution of the return on the owner's investment. However, if the withdrawal exceeds the amount of income generated by the firm, the distribution constitutes a return of the owner's investment.

Statement of Changes in Owner's Equity for a Sole Proprietorship

The statement of changes in owner's equity reflects the changes in the owner's capital account from one accounting period to the next. Exhibit 19.1 illustrates how today's statement of changes in owner's equity would reflect Mr. Du Pont's equity transactions in 1802.

The statement first states the owner's capital balance at the beginning of the period, then shows any additional investment made and the increase (decrease) due to the period's net income (net loss). Finally, the statement presents the

The Dream Works is a partnership of Steven Spielberg, Jeffrey Katzenberg, and David Geffen.

EXHIBIT	19.1	Statement of Changes in Owners' Equity

E. I. DU PONT DE NEMOURS GUNPOWDER
Statement of Changes in Owner's Equity
For the Year Ended December 31, 1802

E. I. du Pont de Nemours, capital, 1/1/1802		$ 90,000
Add: Additional owner investment	$ 5,000	
Net income	24,300	29,300
Subtotal		$119,300
Less: Drawings		(20,600)
E. I. du Pont de Nemours, capital, 12/31/1802		$ 98,700

amount of drawings deducted in determining the ending balance in the capital account, which becomes the owner's equity section of the current period's balance sheet.

PARTNERSHIPS

Accounting for partnership equity is similar to accounting for the equity of sole proprietorships. However, a partnership requires a separate capital and drawing account for each partner in order to determine each owner's interest in the firm. The respective capital accounts summarize the increases and decreases for each individual partner's ownership interest in the business. For example, if Larry Moritz and Pamela Curry form a partnership, and Moritz contributes $10,000 in cash while Curry contributes $8,000, the entry to record the transaction is:

Cash	18,000	
Moritz, Capital		10,000
Curry, Capital		8,000

When partners contribute assets other than cash, the noncash assets are recorded at their *fair market value at the time of contribution*. All the partners must agree upon the valuation of these noncash assets.

Occasionally, a partnership may take over an entire established business and assume its liabilities. For example, assume that Glenda Reynard has operated a business but she wants to move to a new location. She discovers that Kurt Taylor owns a building that is ideal for her operations, and they decide to form a partnership. Ms. Reynard has assets with fair market values as follows: cash, $5,000; accounts receivable, $8,000; and inventory of $12,000. She also has accounts payable of $9,000, which the partnership will assume. Mr. Taylor originally paid $60,000 for his building and $10,000 for the land, but today the fair market values of the building and land are $70,000 and $10,000, respectively. There is a $50,000 mortgage on the building, which the partnership will assume. We illustrate the entries to record the formation of the partnership below.

Cash	5,000	
Accounts Receivable	8,000	
Inventory	12,000	
Accounts Payable		9,000
Reynard, Capital		16,000
Building	70,000	
Land	10,000	
Mortgage Payable		50,000
Taylor, Capital		30,000

In each instance, the incoming partner was credited with the difference between the amount of assets contributed and the liabilities assumed by the partnership. The original cost of the assets to the individuals is of no consequence to the partnership because the market value of the noncash assets represents the economic substance of the contribution event. For example, the $70,000 fair market value of the building became part of the partnership organization rather than its original cost of $60,000.

Closing Entries for Partnerships

When the revenue and expense accounts are closed to Income Summary, the income or loss generated by the partnership during the period is allocated to the partners, resulting in an increase or decrease to the capital accounts accordingly. For example, if Glenda Reynard and Kurt Taylor agreed to divide income and loss equally and the partnership generated $32,000 of income, the allocation of the income between the two partners is recorded with the following entry.

Income Summary	32,000	
Reynard, Capital		16,000
Taylor, Capital		16,000

Statement of Changes in Partners' Capital

The **statement of changes in partners' capital** presents the changes in the individual partner's capital balances that result from additional contributions, the firm's income or loss, and the partners' withdrawals from the firm over a specific period of time. The balance sheet reflects ending balances in the capital accounts.

A statement of changes in partners' capital, as illustrated in Exhibit 19.2, reflects the results of these events. Additional investments made to the partnership by any partner during the time period appear as additions to the partner's capital account.

EXHIBIT	19.2	Statement of Changes in Partners' Capital

THE BAYLOR COMPANY
Statement of Changes in Partners' Capital
For the Year Ended December 31, 1997

	Reynard	Taylor	Total
Capital balance, 1/1/97	$16,000	$30,000	$46,000
Add: Net income	16,000	16,000	32,000
Contributions	4,000	–0–	4,000
Subtotal	$36,000	$46,000	$82,000
Less: Drawings	(17,000)	(13,000)	(30,000)
Capital balance, 12/31/97	$19,000	$33,000	$52,000

Division of Income for Partnerships

In the absence of an agreement to the contrary, the law provides that partners share profits and losses equally. However, partners typically do not do this because each partner's involvement with the firm varies. For example, a partner who contributes $10,000 to a firm and is not involved with its operations would not receive the same share of the profits as a person who contributes $50,000 and manages the firm's activities on a daily basis. Therefore, the division of the partnership's earnings and losses usually reflects the nature of each partner's involvement.

A firm's partnership agreement should describe in detail how the partners agree to divide the profits and losses of the firm, which can change whenever they deem it appropriate.

These are the commonly used methods for division of earnings:

1. Fixed ratios.

2. Ratio of capital account balances.

3. Salary allowances and some determination of distribution of any remainder.

4. Interest allowance on capital balances and some determination of distribution of any remainder.

5. Combination of methods 3 and 4.

It is important to note that partnership losses, unless otherwise specified, are divided using the same method by which profits are allocated. When using methods 3, 4, or 5 to allocate a partnership's net loss, it is possible for a partner's capital account to increase. We illustrate this paradox later.

Fixed Ratios   Reynard and Taylor (discussed previously) used the fixed ratio method to divide partnership profit or loss equally since the ratio in their situation was fixed at one-to-one. The partners can establish any ratios (or fraction) they desire.

Suppose that Margie and Greg Klocke and Ellie and Pat Beans form a partnership called the Doane Company to offer accounting services. They agree to distribute income or loss on a fixed ratio of 4:2:1:1, respectively. Since 4 + 2 + 1 + 1 = 8, Margie will get 4/8 or 1/2 of the total, Greg 2/8 or 1/4, and Ellie and Pat 1/8 each. If Doane generates $48,000 of net income, using the fixed ratio method of dividing profits will increase Margie's capital account by $24,000, Greg's capital account by $12,000, and Ellie's and Pat's capital accounts by $6,000 each.

Margie	1/2 × $48,000 =	$24,000
Greg	1/4 × $48,000 =	12,000
Ellie	1/8 × $48,000 =	6,000
Pat	1/8 × $48,000 =	6,000
Total		$48,000

This entry closes the Income Summary account to the owners' capital accounts:

Income Summary	48,000	
Margie Klocke, Capital		24,000
Greg Klocke, Capital		12,000
Ellie Beans, Capital		6,000
Pat Beans, Capital		6,000

Ratio of Capital Account Balances   Sometimes the amount of net income is closely related to the amount invested by the individual partner in the partnership entity. Consequently, a method of allocating earnings based on the relationship of the amounts of the partners' investments offers a fair approach to distribute the firm's income. However, because of withdrawals and additional investments made during the accounting period, the capital balances may change. In such circumstances, partners must agree on which capital balances to use as a basis for earnings allocation—beginning, ending, or some average for the period.

Assume that the partners agree to divide income based on the beginning capital balances and that each of them had the capital balances shown below at the beginning of the current period:

Margie Klocke, Capital	$ 15,000
Greg Klocke, Capital	10,000
Ellie Beans, Capital	45,000
Pat Beans, Capital	30,000
Total	$100,000

The distribution is computed by developing a ratio of each capital balance to the total of the capital balances, and then multiplying the amount of the profits by that ratio.

The ratio of Margie's capital to total capital is $15,000/$100,000, or 15 percent of the total capital balances. Greg's ratio ($10,000/$100,000) converts to 10 percent, Ellie's to 45 percent, and Pat's to 30 percent. If the partnership's income for the period was $48,000, the division of earnings would be:

Margie	.15 × $48,000 =	$ 7,200
Greg	.10 × $48,000 =	4,800
Ellie	.45 × $48,000 =	21,600
Pat	.30 × $48,000 =	14,400
Total		$48,000

The closing entry reflects a debit to Income Summary for $48,000 and a credit to each partner's capital for the respective amounts of income allocated. Unlike the fixed ratio division method discussed earlier, ratios based on the capital balances will change as the balances in the individual partners' capital accounts and the amount of total owners' equity change.

Salary Allowances If a partner spends all or part of his or her time on partnership business while others are not as involved in operations, the partners may agree to recognize the value of these services. A **salary allowance** is a method of allocating partnership earnings based on the amount of time respective partners spend operating the business enterprise. It is particularly important to realize that the salary allowance is not considered an expense of the business and is not shown as an expense on the income statement.

Suppose Margie and Greg run the accounting service on a full-time basis while Ellie and Pat provide tax expertise only for selected clients. In these circumstances, it is agreed that Margie and Greg are to receive salary allowances, with any additional amounts of profit or loss divided according to the agreement. To illustrate, assume that Margie gets a salary allowance of $15,000 and Greg receives one of $10,000, with any remainder divided equally among the four partners.

Assume again that Doane Company generated net income of $48,000. See Exhibit 19.3 for the computations showing the allocation of net income with these salary allowances. After allocating the salary allowances of $25,000, the $23,000 remainder is divided into four $5,750 parts and allocated to each partner. The closing entry would increase Margie's capital account by $20,750, Greg's capital account by $15,750, while Ellie and Pat's capital accounts increase by $5,750 each.

EXHIBIT 19.3	Distribution of Net Income with Salary Allowances					
Item	Margie	Greg	Ellie	Pat	Amount Distributed	Amount Remaining
Net income						$48,000
Salary allowances	$15,000	$10,000	$ –0–	$ –0–	$25,000	23,000
Remainder	5,750	5,750	5,750	5,750	23,000	–0–
Totals	$20,750	$15,750	$5,750	$5,750	$48,000	–0–

EXHIBIT | 19.4 | Distribution of Net Income with a Negative Remainder

Item	Margie	Greg	Ellie	Pat	Amount Distributed	Amount Remaining
Net income						$21,000
Salary allowances	$15,000	$10,000	$ –0–	$ –0–	$25,000	(4,000)
Remainder	(1,000)	(1,000)	(1,000)	(1,000)	(4,000)	–0–
Totals	$14,000	$9,000	($1,000)	($1,000)	$21,000	–0–

When Margie's salary allowance is $15,000 and Greg's is $10,000, any amount of net income less than $25,000 will result in a negative remainder. The amount of the remainder, whether positive or negative, is always distributed according to the terms of the partnership agreement. For example, if the net income amounted to $21,000, the negative remainder of $4,000 would be divided among all four partners. As Exhibit 19.4 shows, after the $25,000 salary allowance is awarded, each partner's capital is reduced by $1,000, or their equal shares of the negative residual. The journal entry shown below reflects the calculations shown in Exhibit 19.4.

Income Summary	21,000	
Ellie Beans, Capital	1,000	
Pat Beans, Capital	1,000	
Margie Klocke, Capital		14,000
Greg Klocke, Capital		9,000

Notice that the increase in Margie's capital account is the result of a $15,000 salary allowance minus her $1,000 share of the negative remainder. Greg's capital account increased because he was allocated $10,000 for the salary allowance minus his $1,000 share of the negative remainder. Since neither Ellie or Pat has a salary allowance, each of them receives only her/his share of the negative remainder and, therefore, their capital accounts are reduced by $1,000. It may seem unusual to decrease a partner's capital account when the firm made a profit, but the practice follows the terms of the partnership agreement.

PAUSE & REFLECT

Why would partners knowingly construct a partnership agreement that would result in a decrease in their capital accounts when the firm generated profit? If a partnership suffers a loss, is it possible for one or more of the partner's capital accounts to increase after the loss is allocated? Explain.

Interest Allowance on Capital Balances   The **interest allowance** method uses an interest rate multiplied by each partners' capital balance to allocate partnership earnings. This method of allocating income is an incentive designed to reward partners who invest and maintain capital in the business. Just as in the case of the salary allowance, the interest on capital balances is merely one step in the method of computing the distribution of earnings and is not an expense of the firm.

The partnership agreement must specify the interest rate, the capital balance (beginning, ending, or average) that the rate applied to, and the basis for allocating any residual income or losses. Assume that the partners have agreed to apply a 10 percent rate to the average capital balances for the period, and that the average capital balances are:

Margie Klocke, Capital	$13,000
Greg Klocke, Capital	9,000
Ellie Beans, Capital	40,000
Pat Beans, Capital	28,000
Total	$90,000

EXHIBIT 19.5 Distribution of Net Income with Interest Allowances

Item	4 : Margie	2 : Greg	1 : Ellie	1 : Pat	Amount Distributed	Amount Remaining
Net income						$48,000
Interest allowances	$ 1,300	$ 900	$ 4,000	$2,800	$ 9,000	39,000
Remainder	19,500	9,750	4,875	4,875	39,000	–0–
Totals	$20,800	$10,650	$ 8,875	$7,675	$48,000	–0–

The interest allowance of $9,000 (10% of $90,000), is:

Margie	$13,000 × .10 =	$1,300
Greg	$9,000 × .10 =	900
Ellie	$40,000 × .10 =	4,000
Pat	$28,000 × .10 =	2,800
	Total allocation	$9,000

Further assume that Margie, Greg, Ellie, and Pat agree to divide any remainder after interest allowances in a ratio of 4:2:1:1. Exhibit 19.5 shows the distribution among the partners, again assuming a net income of $48,000.

Once the initial $9,000 allowance for interest is allocated, Margie receives an additional $19,500 (4/8 of $39,000), Greg receives $9,750 (2/8 of $39,000), while Ellie and Pat each receive $4,875 (1/8 of $39,000). The closing entry credits each partner's capital account for the amounts shown in the totals line in Exhibit 19.5.

Given the capital balances and the 10 percent rate in this example, any loss or an income figure less than the $9,000 amount of interest allowance will result in a negative remainder that must be allocated among the partners. The process is similar to that shown in Exhibit 19.4.

Combination of Salary and Interest Allowance   Some partnership agreements provide both salary and interest allowances as well as an agreement for dividing the remainder. For example, assume that Margie receives a salary allowance of $10,000, that Greg receives one for $5,000, and that all the partners are allowed 10 percent on their average capital balances. Exhibit 19.6 shows the resulting distribution if profits were $48,000 and any remainder after salary and interest allowance was to be divided equally. Margie's, Greg's, Ellie's, and Pat's capital accounts will increase by $17,300, $11,900, $10,000, and $8,800, respectively, as a result of this partnership agreement.

Admission of a New Partner

Admitting a new partner dissolves the old partnership and creates a new partnership. Because partnerships have unlimited liability and mutual agency, the admission of a new partner requires the approval of the existing partners. When this occurs, the partners may also rewrite certain aspects of the partnership agreement, such as the basis for distribution of earnings. This is done to clarify the rights and responsibilities of the new and existing partners after the formation of the new partnership.

EXHIBIT 19.6 Distribution of Net Income with Salary and Interest Allowances

Item	Margie	Greg	Ellie	Pat	Amount Distributed	Amount Remaining
Net income						$48,000
Salary allowances	$10,000	$ 5,000			$15,000	33,000
Interest allowances	1,300	900	$ 4,000	$ 2,800	9,000	24,000
Remainder	6,000	6,000	6,000	6,000	24,000	–0–
Totals	$17,300	$11,900	$10,000	$ 8,800	$48,000	–0–

A new partner is admitted in one of two ways: (1) by purchasing all or part of the interest of an existing partner by payment to the existing partner, or (2) by investing directly in the partnership organization.

Purchase of an Existing Interest   An existing partner can sell all or a portion of his or her interest in the firm directly to a new partner, subject to the approval of the other partners. Because the payment goes to the existing partner, the new partner would receive either all or only a portion of the selling partner's capital. Total partnership equity would remain the same. To illustrate, assume that Bob Hays and Linda Hernandez are partners, and each has a capital balance of $40,000. If Bob Hays agrees to sell one-half of his interest, $20,000, to Mohamad Nemazi for $30,000, and Linda Hernandez agrees to admit Mr. Nemazi, the entry to reflect this event is:

Bob Hays, Capital	20,000	
Mohamad Nemazi, Capital		20,000

While Hays and Nemazi have agreed on a price, $30,000, the price does not correspond to the $20,000 amount in Nemazi's capital account. This transaction does not change the amount of assets of the firm because Mr. Hays, not the partnership, receives the $30,000 cash. As a result, Linda Hernandez's capital account remains the same. Only Bob Hays' capital account reflects a reduction of $20,000, the same amount by which Mr. Nemazi's capital account is increased upon his admission.

PAUSE & REFLECT	**Why would Mr. Nemazi pay $30,000 for only $20,000 interest in the firm? Under what circumstances would Mr. Hays sell $20,000 of his interest for less that $20,000?**

Direct Investment in the Firm   When the new partner's admission to the partnership involves the investment of money or other assets in the firm, the payment increases the amount of the firm's total assets as well as its total owners' equity. The new partner's interest in the firm is either the same, smaller, or larger than the amount of the assets contributed.

For example, assume that Bob Hays and Linda Hernandez, with their capital balances at $40,000 each, agree to admit Mohamad Nemazi to a one-third interest if he invests $40,000 cash in the partnership. The entry to record Nemazi's admission into the firm is:

Cash	40,000	
Mohamad Nemazi, Capital		40,000

The total capital after admission of Nemazi is $120,000. Nemazi's one-third interest ($120,000/3) is $40,000.

Such an arrangement presumes that Hays and Hernandez are content to allow Nemazi to have a capital balance equal to the amount of his investment. However, if the partnership has enjoyed above-average earnings, the existing partners may require that a new partner pay a price greater than the amount credited to his or her capital account. The excess of the cash payment over the amount of the new partner's capital account is viewed as a bonus to the existing partners. We discuss the accounting treatment to reflect this event in the next section.

Bonus to Existing Partners   To illustrate how to account for the bonus to existing partners, again assume that Hays and Hernandez are partners and that each has a $40,000 capital balance. Nemazi agrees to pay $49,000 in exchange for a one-third interest in the partnership. To compute the one-third amount to be credited to Nemazi's account, add the amount of the original owners' equity of $80,000 to the

$49,000 contributed by Nemazi for a total equity of the new partnership of $129,000. Nemazi's one-third interest in the $129,000 is $43,000 ($129,000/3). The difference of $6,000 between Nemazi's contribution of $49,000 and the $43,000 credited to his capital account represents the bonus to Hays and Hernandez. The bonus belongs to both Hays and Hernandez and is divided between them and reflected in their capital accounts in accordance with their original agreement on division of earnings. If Hays and Hernandez had agreed to divide profits and losses equally, then each of their capital accounts is credited for $3,000, as shown.

Cash	49,000	
Mohamad Nemazi, Capital		43,000
Bob Hays, Capital		3,000
Linda Hernandez, Capital		3,000

Bonus to a New Partner   If the incoming partner has a needed skill or has an established business with above-average earnings, existing partners may offer the new partner a bonus to enter into the partnership. Assume that the existing partners, Hays and Hernandez, each had capital balances of $40,000 and share profits and losses equally. They decide to admit Nemazi to a one-third interest for only $31,000 in cash because he has unique technical abilities that can improve the quality and sales of their product. With the $31,000 contribution, owners' equity is $111,000—the original equity of $80,000 of Hays and Hernandez plus the $31,000 contribution from Nemazi. Nemazi's one-third equity in the new firm is $37,000, or one-third of the total capital of $111,000. The difference between his $31,000 payment and the $37,000 credited to his capital account comes from a reduction in the amounts of the original partners' capital accounts. This $6,000 is not a loss for the partnership. Rather, it represents a bonus that Hays and Hernandez are willing to give Nemazi to convince him to join the partnership. The partners would expect to make up the bonus amount via the earnings that Nemazi is expected to generate. Since Hays and Hernandez share profits equally, each reduces his/her capital accounts by $3,000 in order to increase Nemazi's capital account to $37,000 to reflect Nemazi's one-third interest in the company.

Cash	31,000	
Bob Hays, Capital	3,000	
Linda Hernandez, Capital	3,000	
Mohamad Nemazi, Capital		37,000

After posting the entry, the three capital accounts will total $111,000. Whether the bonus is allowed to the existing partners or to the incoming partner, the new total of the capital accounts must equal the original capital balances plus the amount of the new partner's contribution.

Revaluation of Assets before Admission of a New Partner

It is not unusual for a firm to revalue its assets before admitting a new partner. This usually occurs when the partnership structure has not changed for an extended period of time or when the value of the partnership's assets has changed substantially since the last change in the partnership structure. If the existing partnership assets have a fair market value in excess of their recorded book values, the increase in value represents a gain and is distributed to the original partners' capital accounts based on the terms of their profit and loss agreement. By distributing the gain before the new partner is admitted, the old partners benefit from the appreciation of the assets. If the market value of the assets is less than the book value of the assets, it is necessary to reduce the assets to their market values and distribute the loss to the original partners' capital accounts in accordance with their partnership agreement.

Assume that Hays and Hernandez's partnership has an accounts receivable balance of $6,000 and inventory carried at $8,000. A careful analysis indicates that the receivables are really worth only $5,000 and that the inventory has a fair market value of \$12,000. Further assume that Hays and Hernandez share gains and losses equally. Before a new partner is admitted, they should adjust the value of the assets and their capital accounts as reflected in the following entry.

Inventory	4,000	
Accounts Receivable		1,000
Bob Hays, Capital		1,500
Linda Hernandez, Capital		1,500

This records the net increase in assets of \$3,000 (a \$4,000 increase in inventory and a \$1,000 reduction in receivables) and divides that gain between the two partners in accordance with their profit-and-loss ratio.

PAUSE & REFLECT

Assume that the fair market value of the partnership's assets was less than the book value. Would the existing partners or the new partner benefit from the failure to revalue the assets to their fair market value before the admission of a new partner? Why?

Withdrawal of a Partner

When a partner withdraws from a partnership, his or her interest is purchased directly by one or more of the remaining partners, by an outsider seeking admission to the partnership, or by the partnership itself. As we illustrated in the case with the admission of a partner, the assets of the firm are often revalued prior to the withdrawal of a partner. The sale of a withdrawing partner's interest to existing partners or to an incoming partner requires only the transfer of the retiring partner's capital account balances to an existing or new partner's capital account.

When the partnership uses its assets to pay for a withdrawing partner's interest, the amount may equal, exceed, or be less than the balance in the partner's capital account. When the partner receives the same amount as the balance in his or her capital account, the other partners' capital accounts are not affected. To illustrate, if Bob Hays decides to leave the Hayes, Hernandez, and Nemazi partnership and receives \$45,000, the exact amount of his capital account balance, the entry to record this event is:

Bob Hays, Capital	45,000	
Cash		45,000

When a partner receives more than the amount reflected in his or her capital account, the difference reduces the remaining partners' capital accounts in accordance with the terms of the partnership agreement. To illustrate, if Bob Hays receives \$50,000 in cash for his \$45,000 partnership interest, he receives a bonus of \$5,000. If Hernandez and Nemazi share profits and losses equally, the entry to record Hays' withdrawal is:

Bob Hays, Capital	45,000	
Linda Hernandez Capital	2,500	
Mohamad Nemazi, Capital	2,500	
Cash		50,000

PAUSE & REFLECT

Why would existing partners pay a departing partner more than his or her capital account? Why would a withdrawing partner accept an amount less than the balance in his or her capital balance? In the second case, how would the accounting system reflect the difference between the amount of cash paid and the partner's capital balance?

CORPORATIONS

Now we turn to the corporate ownership structure and its related ownership accounts. For corporations, unlike sole proprietorships and partnerships, the accounting system makes a distinction between the two principal sources of ownership funds: (1) the contributions made by the stockholders in exchange for an ownership interest; and (2) the reinvested earnings of the firm. The capital contributed by the stockholders (owners) is recorded in the appropriate capital stock and related accounts, while the net income, net losses, and dividends are recorded in the Retained Earnings account.

Why does corporate accounting segregate the contributions made by stockholders from the undistributed earnings of the firm? Because corporations are separate legal entities, corporate stockholders have limited liability; therefore, creditors can only satisfy their claims with the corporation's assets. As a result, creditors need to know whether a distribution of corporate assets is a return on investment or a return of investment that may impair their claim. The distinction between contributions and reinvested earnings allows creditors to determine if distributions to the stockholders are made from the corporation's earnings (a return on investment) or whether they are a return of the stockholders' investment.

HOW TO ACCOUNT FOR CAPITAL CONTRIBUTED TO THE CORPORATION

One of the strengths of the corporate form of business is its ability to raise large sums of money. It has such ability because its ownership structure allows a large number of people to acquire an ownership interest in the corporation for a relatively small amount of money. Investment in corporations is possible without putting the investor's personal assets (other than the amount invested) at risk if the corporation fails. Cash and other resources given by stockholders and others to the corporation are classified as contributed capital. We will now describe how to record the issuance of stock by a corporation by using Du Pont as an example.

Accounting for Par Value Stock

As discussed in Chapter 15, the par value of stock represents the minimum issue price of the stock. When accounting for par value stock, *the amount of the par value is credited to the capital stock account regardless of the amount paid for the shares.* The total par value of the stock issued provides financial statement users with information about the amount of the corporation's legal capital.

Stock Issued above Par Du Pont is authorized by its charter to issue 900 million shares of $.60 par value common stock. Therefore, if an investor pays Du Pont $70 per share for 1,000 shares of its common stock, the Common Stock account is credited for $600 (1,000 shares × .60 par value per share). The remaining $69,400 ($70,000 – $600) is credited to an account called Paid-in Capital in Excess of Par, which represents the amount by which the market price of the stock exceeds the legal minimum price. The entry for this equity financing event is:

Cash	70,000	
Common Stock (1,000 shares × $.60)		600
Paid-in Capital in Excess of Par—Common Stock		69,400

Accounting for No-Par Stock

Since no-par stock does not have a minimum legal issue price for each share, the amount credited to the capital stock account is the amount received for the shares. To illustrate the difference in accounting for no-par-value stock and par value stock, we will account for the issuance of 1,000 shares of Du Pont's no-par-value common stock for $70 each. The entry below reflects this event.

Cash	70,000	
Common Stock		70,000

Notice that in both the par value and no-par cases, the $70,000 received by the corporation is credited to capital stock accounts. In the case of no-par stock, however, there is no Paid-in Capital in Excess of Par account because the shares do not have par values.

Accounting for No-Par Stated Value Stock

When a corporation is authorized to issue no-par stated value stock, the amount credited to the capital stock account is the amount of the stated value, regardless of the amount of money received at the time of the sale of stock. Entries for the issuance of no-par stated value stock are the same as par value stock, except that the Paid-in Capital in Excess of Stated Value account is used instead of the Paid-in Capital in Excess of Par account.

Noncash Stock Issue

Often corporations issue shares of stock, either in exchange for assets other than cash or in payment for services rendered. This raises the question of how to determine the dollar value of such a transaction.

When the transaction does not involve cash, the fair market value of the stock issued or of the goods or services received, whichever is more readily determinable, provides the cash equivalent amount. To illustrate, suppose that Du Pont issued 2,000 shares of its $.60 par common stock in exchange for equipment having a fair market value of $150,000. The entry to reflect this event is:

Equipment	150,000	
Common Stock (2,000 × .60)		1,200
Paid-in Capital in Excess of Par—Common Stock		148,000

If Du Pont could not determine the fair market value of the equipment, it would record the transaction using the fair market value of the shares of stock issued. Occasionally, neither the fair market values of the asset or stock are determinable. When this occurs, the corporation records the transaction using either an appraised value of the asset or an amount set by the board of directors.

PAUSE & REFLECT   What is a company's incentive to overvalue a noncash stock transaction? Is there an incentive to undervalue a noncash stock transaction?

Donated Capital

Corporations often receive assets without issuing common or preferred stock. For example, in 1995 Cessna Corporation received a $21 million financial package that included cash, land, buildings, and tax abatements from Independence, Kansas, in exchange for locating a large manufacturing plant there that would employ 1,000 people. As a result of this situation, Cessna would record only the tangible assets it receives as donated capital, as follows:

Cash	5,000,000	
Land	500,000	
Building	6,000,000	
Donated Capital		11,500,000

The **Donated Capital** account reflects the dollar value of the assets given to a corporation that increases the contributed capital of the corporation's stockholders' equity but does not change the number of shares or shareholders.

ACCOUNTING FOR CORPORATE EARNINGS

The cash and assets a corporation accumulates by the issuance of stock and receipt of donations are invested in the corporation with the expectation of generating a return. The net income from corporate operations represents the return for the corporation's stockholders. The accumulation and disposition of these corporate earnings is accounted for independently from the contributions of its owners. Corporate management can elect to distribute the corporate earnings to the owners in the form of dividends, to reinvest the earnings, or to provide some combination of the two events. The following section describes how corporations account for their earnings.

Retained Earnings

Retained earnings, or the amount of a corporation's earnings since its inception less all dividends distributed, appears on the balance sheet as a part of the corporation's stockholders' equity. The account normally has a credit balance because the amount of net income usually exceeds the combined amount of net losses and dividends that would reduce the balance in the account. A credit balance in the Retained Earnings account represents the amount of earnings reinvested in the corporation rather than distributed to the stockholders as dividends.

When the cumulative total of net losses plus dividends declared exceeds the cumulative total of net income, the Retained Earnings account will have a debit balance, which is referred to as a **deficit in retained earnings.** A deficit balance indicates that some portion of the stockholders' contributed capital was lost in the firm's attempt to generate income. Exhibit 19.7 shows the accumulated deficit in the shareowner's deficit section of the balance sheet of Kroger Company.

How Does Net Income and Net Loss Change Retained Earnings? When a company generates net income, the firm has increased its net assets and the stockholders' interest in the firm as a result of its ongoing operations. To illustrate this and the other equity events that impact the Retained Earnings account, we will use the Givarz Corporation. We show closing entries for Givarz Corporation as of December 31, 1995, below.

a.	Sales	950,000	
	Gain on Sale of Equipment	25,000	
	Income Summary		975,000
b.	Income Summary	625,000	
	Cost of Goods Sold		300,000
	Operating Expenses		250,000
	Loss on Sale of Land		75,000
c.	Income Summary	350,000	
	Retained Earnings		350,000

EXHIBIT | 19.7 | Kroger Company, Retained Earnings Deficit

Consolidated Balance Sheet
(in thousands of dollars)

	December 31, 1994	January 1, 1994
Assets		
Current assets		
Cash and temporary cash investments	$ 27,223	$ 121,253
Receivables	270,811	287,925
Inventories:		
FIFO cost	2,053,207	2,001,376
Less LIFO reserve	(438,184)	(422,097)
	1,615,023	1,579,279
Property held for sale	39,631	37,721
Prepaid and other current assets	199,437	199,652
Total current assets	2,152,125	2,225,830
Property, plant and equipment, net	2,252,663	1,981,308
Investment and other assets	302,886	273,326
Total assets	$4,707,674	$4,480,464
Liabilities		
Current liabilities:		
Current portion of long-term debt	$ 7,926	$ 63,053
Current portion of obligations under capital leases	8,467	7,962
Accounts payable	1,425,612	1,357,532
Other current liabilities	952,963	822,284
Total current liabilities	2,394,968	2,250,831
Long-term debt	3,726,343	3,975,362
Obligations under capital leases	162,851	159,651
Deferred income taxes	172,690	182,891
Other long-term liabilities	404,506	371,371
Total Liabilities	6,861,358	6,940,106
Shareowners' Deficit		
Common capital stock, par $1		
Authorized: 350,000,000 shares		
Issued: 1994—120,573,148 shares, 1993—118,549,173 shares	338,568	308,534
Accumulated deficit	(2,248,736)	(2,490,932)
Common stock in treasury, at cost:		
1994—9,576,231 shares, 1993—10,901,846 shares	(243,516)	(277,244)
Total shareowners' deficit	(2,153,684)	(2,459,642)
Total liabilities and shareowners' deficit	$4,707,674	$4,480,464

The accompanying notes are an integral part of the consolidated financial statements.

Income Summary			Retained Earnings		
	(a)	975,000			500,000
(b) 625,000				(c)	350,000
	Balance	350,000		Balance	850,000
(c) 350,000					

When the expenses and losses exceed the amount of revenues and gains, the Income Summary Account will have debit balance, which, when transferred to the Retained Earnings account, represents a decrease in the shareholders' interest in the firm's assets resulting from the firm's ongoing operations.

How Do Dividends Change Retained Earnings? Chapter 15 indicates that there are four important dates associated with the payment of corporate dividends:

- Date of declaration
- Ex-dividend date
- Date of record
- Date of payment

Accounting entries are made only on the date of declaration and the date of payment.

On the *date of declaration*, the board of directors announces the amount of the dividend, the date on which investors must officially own the stock (the *date of record*) in order to receive the declared dividends, and the date when the dividend will be paid (the *date of payment*.) Stockholders must acquire the stock two or three days before the date of record on the *ex-dividend date* to ensure that their ownership is duly recorded by the corporation on the date of record.

A typical dividend announcement might read as follows: "At the regular meeting of the board of directors of Givarz Corporation, on June 1, 1995, a quarterly dividend of $.50 per share was declared payable on June 25, 1995, to the stockholders of record on June 15, 1995." Notice that the announcement specified the important dates as well as the amount of the dividend per share. If more than one class of stock is outstanding, the announcement would specify the dividend per share for each class of stock.

The Dividends account is closed to Retained Earnings at the end of an accounting period. For example, assume that Givarz Corporation had 150,000 shares of $1 par common stock outstanding and its board of directors declared a $.50 per share dividend on June 1 to stockholders of record on June 15, payable on June 25. Givarz would record the following entries for the declaration and payment of this $75,000 dividend (150,000 shares of common stock × $.50 per share).

Date of Declaration:

June 1	Retained Earnings	75,000	
	Dividends Payable		75,000

Ex-Dividend Date

June 12	No entry necessary. If stock is purchased after this date, the investor buying the stock will not receive the dividend.

Date of Record:

June 15	No entry necessary. Those stockholders whose names appear in the stock transfer records on this date will receive the dividend.

Date of Distribution:

June 25	Dividends Payable	75,000	
	Cash		75,000

Once the declaration is made, the corporation incurs and records a liability in the amount of the dividends declared. Since the earnings of the corporation for each accounting period are accumulated in the Retained Earnings account through the closing entries, the distribution of those earnings reduces Retained Earnings. The retained earnings account after these events are posted, is shown as follows.

Retained Earnings

		500,000	Beginning balance
Dividends 6/30	75,000		
		425,000	
		350,000	Net income 12/31
		775,000	Ending balance

A corporation with preferred and common stock must determine the amount of dividends that owners of each class of stock will receive when it declares the dividends. Keep in mind that the amount of dividends that each class of stockholders receives does not necessitate changing the entries to record the events.

Stock Dividends

If a company's board of directors declares a dividend that is settled by issuing the corporation's own stock rather than cash, it has declared a stock dividend. As indicated in Chapter 15, stock dividends are issued to satisfy stockholders without distributing cash that may be needed in the business.

"Small" Stock Dividends   If the additional number of shares to be issued in settlement of the stock dividend is small, usually 20 to 25 percent or less of the shares outstanding, the amount debited to Retained Earnings as a dividend is the *fair market value* of the stock multiplied by the number of new shares issued. If Givarz Corporation, with 150,000 shares of $1 par value common stock outstanding, declared a 10 percent stock dividend, it would issue an additional 15,000 shares of stock. The amount of the debit to Retained Earnings would depend on the fair market value of the stock on the date of declaration. The amount credited to the **Stock Dividends Distributable** account on the date of declaration is the par value of the shares the corporation will issue on the date of payment. Any excess of the market price over par value is credited to Paid-in Capital in Excess of Par. If the fair market value on the date of declaration is $32 per share, the company would make the following entry.

Retained Earnings ($32 × 15,000 shares)	480,000	
Stock Dividends Distributable ($1 par × 15,000)		15,000
Paid-in Capital in Excess of Par—Common		465,000

Stock Dividends Distributable is not a liability account because a stock dividend does not involve the distribution of the firm's assets. Rather, it is a contributed capital account because the company will issue the new shares of common stock on the date of payment. The entry below shows how to record the distribution of the additional shares.

Stock Dividends Distributable	15,000	
Common Stock		15,000

"Large" Stock Dividends   A large stock dividend, one that is greater than 25 percent of the number of shares issued, *requires the use of the par value rather than the market value of the stock to value the transaction.* Using par value as opposed to market value is done for two reasons. First, the issuance of such a large number of additional shares usually reduces the market value of the stock and makes it difficult to determine the appropriate market price. Second, the total market value of such a large number of shares might reduce retained earnings to such an extent that it could impair the future dividend-paying ability of the firm.

To illustrate, assume that Givarz Corporation declared a 50 percent stock dividend; $75,000 of retained earnings would be transferred to common stock—that is, 75,000 new shares of common stock (150,000 shares of common stock ×.5) times the $1 par value common stock. The company would record the same sequence of entries it used for stock dividends without including the Paid-in Capital in Excess of Par account.

Stock dividends are called *interequity transactions* because the amount of the dividend is taken from one stockholders' equity account, Retained Earnings, and transferred into the Common Stock and/or Paid-in Capital in Excess of Par accounts of the contributed capital section of stockholders' equity.

EXHIBIT | 19.8 | Balance Sheet Presentation of Treasury Stock

GIVARZ CORPORATION
Partial Balance Sheet
Date

Stockholders' Equity

Common stock, $5 par value, 50,000 shares authorized,	
35,000 shares issued, 34,900 shares outstanding	$ 175,000
Paid-in capital in excess of par—common	593,000
Total paid-in capital	$ 768,000
Retained earnings	438,000
Total stockholders' equity before treasury stock	$1,206,000
Less: Treasury stock (100 shares)	(3,500)
Total stockholders' equity	$1,202,500

HOW TO ACCOUNT FOR ADDITIONAL EQUITY EVENTS

The following section discusses two equity events that are common to corporations. Treasury stock transactions and stock splits both affect stockholders' equity but do not fit into either the contributed capital or retained earnings categories discussed thus far.

Treasury Stock

Recall from Chapter 15 that treasury stock is a company's own stock reacquired with the intent of reissuing it a later date. It should not be confused with a corporation's authorized but unissued shares or with investments in the stock of other companies.

Regardless of the reasons for a corporation to buy its own stock, treasury stock is not an asset to the corporation. Rather, treasury stock represents the amount paid to liquidate one or more stockholders' interest in the corporation. The debit balance of the Treasury Stock account is reported as a contra equity account that reduces total Stockholders' Equity on a company's balance sheet.

Although transactions involving treasury stock affect stockholders' equity, these transactions cannot result in a gain or loss on the income statement because treasury stock is not an asset of the company. Since the company purchases its shares of stock with the intent of reissuing them at a later date, the shares are still considered issued but are no longer outstanding. There are no dividends paid on treasury shares.

Purchase of Treasury Stock   When a firm purchases its own shares in the open market, the company debits the Treasury Stock account for the cost of those shares. For example, if Givarz Corporation purchased 100 shares of its own $5 par common stock for cash at $35 per share, the entry is:

Treasury Stock	3,500	
Cash		3,500

Exhibit 19.8 shows how to report treasury stock on Givarz Corporation's balance sheet. Observe that the presentation of information about treasury stock contains the number of shares of treasury stock (100) and that the difference between the number of shares issued (35,000) and outstanding (34,900) is the number of treasury shares. Also note that the entire cost of the treasury shares is subtracted from total stockholders' equity.

Reissue of Treasury Stock   Assume that sometime after the purchase of those 100 shares of treasury stock, Givarz Corporation sells 50 shares at $38 per share. Since treasury stock is a stockholders' equity account and is not an asset, the difference between the sales price ($38) and the purchase price ($35) is recorded in a contributed capital account rather than being recognized as a gain.

Cash (50 shares × $38)	1,900	
Treasury Stock (50 shares × $35)		1,750
Paid-in Capital from Treasury Stock Transactions		150

reverse stock split reduces the shares outstanding of a corporation. In some cases this is done to increase the price of the stock in the secondary market by reducing the number of shares of a company in the market. Management can also use a reverse stock split to take over a company. The Metropolitan Maintenance Co. used a 1 for 3,000 reverse stock

split for such a takeover. The company issued one share of stock for every 3,000 shares held and cash was paid to those shareholders who did not have 3,000 shares. It was no coincidence that the only people with more than 3,000 shares were two of Metropolitan's top officers. (*Forbes,* November 19, 1984, p. 54)

On the balance sheet, the Paid-in Capital from Treasury Stock Transactions account is included with the other Paid-in Capital accounts.

When treasury stock is reissued at a price below its initial cost, then the difference between the market price and the initial cost is debited to the Paid-in Capital from Treasury Stock Transactions account. If the Paid-in Capital from Treasury Stock Transactions account has no balance, or if the balance is insufficient to offset the entire amount of the difference between the cost and the smaller reissue price, then it is necessary to subtract the remainder of the difference from Retained Earnings. For example, if the remaining 50 shares of Givarz Corporation's treasury stock were sold for $27 per share, the entry to record this transaction would be:

Cash (50 shares × $27)	1,350	
Paid-in Capital from Treasury Stock Transactions	150	
Retained Earnings	250	
Treasury Stock (50 shares × $35)		1,750

By reducing Retained Earnings rather than a contributed capital account, the corporation reduces its dividend-paying ability rather than the initial contributions of the owners. By maintaining the corporation's initial contributed capital and, instead, reducing the amount of stockholders' equity available for distribution as dividends, creditors' interest in the firm is protected.

If the Paid-in Capital from Treasury Stock Transactions account does not have a balance, Givarz would debit Retained Earnings for the entire $400 difference between the cost ($1,750) and the reissue price ($1,350).

Stock Splits

Chapter 15 indicated that a stock split occurs when a corporation calls in all the shares issued, reduces the par value of the shares, and issues a larger number of new shares in their place. For example, if Du Pont's board of directors approved a two-for-one split, it would call in the old $.60 par value shares and replace them with twice as many $.30 par value shares.

Although a stock split, like a stock dividend, does not change the total amount of stockholders' equity, there is a difference in accounting for these two events. Recall that a stock split does not change the balance in any stockholders' equity account; it merely changes the par value of the stock and increases the number of shares authorized, issued, and outstanding.

A stock dividend reduces retained earnings and increases the contributed capital of the firm by increasing the stock accounts and, possibly, the paid-in capital accounts. It is important to remember that stock splits and stock dividends do not result in either a reduction of assets or an increase in liabilities.

HOW ARE CORPORATE EQUITY EVENTS REPORTED?

Reporting on the status of a corporation's stockholders' equity is more involved than reporting on the same type of transactions for a sole proprietorship or partnership because a corporation has a wider variety of accounts. The information is relatively easy to organize if we keep in mind the two distinct parts of a corporation's stockholders' equity: (1) contributed capital and (2) retained earnings.

EXHIBIT | 19.9 | Retained Earnings and Stockholders' Equity

BRX, INC.
Statement of Retained Earnings
For the Year Ended December 31, 1996

Retained earnings 1/1/96		$1,575,000
Add: Net income		190,000
Less: Preferred stock dividends	$85,000	
Common stock dividends	35,000	(120,000)
Retained earnings 12/31/96		$1,645,000

BRX, INC.
Stockholders' Equity Section of Balance Sheet
December 31, 1996

Preferred stock: 10%, $50 par value, 50,000 shares authorized,	
17,000 shares issued and outstanding	$ 850,000
Paid-in capital in excess of par—preferred stock	83,000
Total paid-in capital—preferred stock	$ 933,000
Common stock: no par, 200,000 shares authorized,	
132,000 shares issued and 125,000 shares outstanding	990,000
Paid-in capital from treasury stock transactions	15,000
Donated capital—land	250,000
Total contributed capital	$2,188,000
Retained earnings	1,645,000
Total stockholders' equity before treasury stock	$3,833,000
Less: Treasury stock—common stock, 7,000 shares	70,000
Total stockholders' equity	$3,763,000

To illustrate how to report the equity events of a corporation, we assume that BRX, Inc., is authorized to issue 50,000 shares of preferred and 200,000 shares of common stock. The preferred stock has a $50 par value, and the common stock is no par.

On January 1, 1996, BRX, Inc., has a balance in its Retained Earnings account of $1,575,000. Using this information, Exhibit 19.9 shows the statement of retained earnings and the stockholders' equity section of BRX, Inc.'s balance sheet for 1996.

The financial statement presentation made here shows a summary of how to report most of these types of corporate equity events described in this chapter to financial statement users. We will examine what each of these statements reports.

Statement of Retained Earnings

We know that the statement of retained earnings shows the effects of operating performance and dividend policy on the stockholders' interest in the corporation. For BRX, Inc., the statement in Exhibit 19.9 reveals that, of the $190,000 of net income generated by the corporation, there was a distribution of dividends of $85,000 to the preferred stockholders and $35,000 to the common stockholders, with $70,000 of net income reinvested in the firm.

This information allows stockholders and other interested parties to evaluate corporate management's policy on reinvesting the earnings of the firm. Is corporate management's dividend policy appropriate, or should the corporation reinvest more or less of the firm's earnings? The ending balance on the statement of retained earnings, $1,645,000, is the amount of retained earnings reported in the stockholders' equity section of BRX, Inc.'s balance sheet.

Stockholders' Equity

The contributed capital section of BRX, Inc.'s stockholders' equity section reports the dollar amount of resources contributed to the corporation. Typically an ownership interest was given in exchange for the contribution, but contributed capital also can include donations.

BRX, Inc.'s stockholders' equity section in Exhibit 19.9 reports that it has issued 17,000 of the 50,000 shares of the authorized preferred stock and, in exchange, received $933,000 in assets. The $933,000 is a combination of the par value of the

17,000 shares issued, $850,000, and the Paid-in Capital in Excess of Par, $83,000. In addition, BRX, Inc., raised $990,000 by issuing 132,000 shares of its 200,000 authorized shares. However, only 125,000 shares of common stock are outstanding because 7,000 shares of common stock were acquired by BRX as treasury stock.

The $15,000 of Paid-in Capital from Treasury Stock Transactions means that BRX increased its assets by selling treasury stock for a price greater than the price paid to reacquire it. The Donated Capital—Land account reflects the market value of the land that BRX received in exchange for locating a manufacturing plant in a particular city. Total Contributed Capital summarizes the dollar amount of the assets raised by BRX, Inc., in exchange for an ownership interest or other considerations.

The contributed capital and the retained earnings sections of stockholders' equity reflect the amount and source of stockholders' equity. Treasury stock, however, reduces the sum of Total Contributed Capital and Retained Earnings because it represents the portion of total stockholders' equity that was liquidated with the repurchase of issued stock. While BRX, Inc., paid $70,000 to liquidate an owner's interest in the corporation, it expects to reissue the treasury stock at a later date. However, until the company reissues the treasury stock, it will reflect the price paid as a contra equity account in the stockholders' equity section of the balance sheet.

Internal users, of course, have all of the information available to external users. In addition, management would receive periodic reports from the company's stock agent outlining stock-related activity during the period.

SUMMARY

This chapter discusses how the accounting system captures and reports the changes in the ownership interest of a business enterprise. The accounting treatment reflects the respective characteristics of the sole proprietorship, partnership, and corporate forms of ownership. Sole proprietorships and partnerships use simple capital accounts to show their owners' interest because the organizations are not separate legal entities from the owners. The accounting treatment of a corporation's owners' equity reflects that it is a separate legal entity and that its owners have limited liability.

- Accounting for sole proprietorships and partnerships requires a permanent balance sheet account called the *owner's capital account.* A withdrawal by an owner represents a reduction in an owner's capital account and is not an expense of the business entity.

- A statement of changes in owner's capital and the statement of changes in partners' capital summarize and reflect the changes in the owners' capital accounts during the year.

- In absence of a partnership agreement, profits and losses are divided equally among partners. However, partnerships typically do not share the profits and losses equally because each partner's involvement with the firm varies. The fixed ratio, ratio of capital balances, salary allowance, and interest allowance methods are means used for allocating partnership income and loss.

- Before a new partner is admitted or when a partner withdraws from a partnership, the firm often adjusts the asset values to their market values and allocates the difference to the partners' capital accounts based on the specified profit and loss ratio.

- A new partner can buy an interest in the firm from a partner or make a direct investment in the firm in exchange for an ownership interest. In either case, the existing partners must approve the admission of the new partner.

- The stockholders' equity section of a corporation's balance sheet is divided into contributed capital and retained earnings sections. This allows creditors to determine whether any dividends paid are a distribution of earnings or a return of stockholders' contributions, which would place the owners' claims ahead of the creditors.

- Par value represents the minimum issue price of corporate stock, and any amount paid in excess of the par value is accounted for in the Paid-in Capital in Excess of Par account.

- Stock that is issued for noncash assets is valued at the fair market value of the asset or the stock, whichever is more reasonably determinable.

- Retained earnings typically represent the amount of earnings reinvested in the corporation. When the Retained Earnings account has a debit balance, it is referred to as a *deficit of retained earnings.*

- Dividends are usually either cash or stock dividends. Cash dividends reduce the assets of the firm as well as the amount of retained earnings. Stock dividends do not change the amount of total stockholders' equity because they increase contributed capital and reduce retained earnings. For this reason, stock dividends are called *interequity transactions.*

- The Treasury Stock account is considered a contra equity account and is reported as a reduction of total stockholders' equity. When a company reissues treasury stock, the difference between the initial cost paid to acquire the stock and the reissue price will either increase or decrease stockholders' equity.

- Stock splits reduce the par value of stock and increase the number of authorized, issued, and outstanding shares of stock. However, stock splits do not change the amount of contributed capital or retained earnings in stockholders' equity.

- The status of a corporation's stockholders' equity is reported in two sections of the balance sheet. Contributed capital reflects the type and amount of stock and the assets received from the issue of stock and donations. The retained earnings section of the balance sheet describes the stockholders' claims to the firm's reinvested earnings.

KEY TERMS

deficit of retained earnings A negative or debit balance in the Retained Earnings account created when the cumulative total of net losses plus dividends declared exceeds the cumulative total of net income

Donated Capital An account that reflects the dollar value of the assets given to a corporation that increases the contributed capital of the corporation's stockholders' equity but does not change the number of shares or shareholders

drawing account A contra equity account used in proprietorship and partnership accounting to summarize the dollar amount of assets withdrawn from the business entity for personal use

interest allowance A method of allocating partnership earnings using an interest rate multiplied by each partner's capital balance

salary allowance A method of allocating partnership earnings based on the amounts of time respective partners spend operating the business enterprise

statement of changes in partners' capital A financial statement that presents the changes in the individual partners' capital balances that result from additional contributions, the firm's income or loss, and the partners' withdrawals from the firm over a specific period of time

Stock Dividends Distributable The account credited on the date of declaration of a stock dividend to show the par value of the shares the corporation will issue on the date of payment

1. What accounting treatments are common to accounting for both sole proprietorships and partnerships?

2. What is the purpose of a drawing account in accounting for a sole proprietorship and a partnership? Why is the drawing account not an expense item used to determine net income?

3. What is the difference between the owners' equity sections of the balance sheets of sole proprietorships and partnerships?

4. Suppose two individuals formed a partnership and one partner contributes most of the capital but does little of the day-to-day work, while the other partner spends most of her time running the business. What basis for sharing the profits of the partnership would you recommend for the partners? Why?

5. If the agreement to divide profits and losses includes a salary allowance and an allowance for interest on capital balances, should these be included as expenses on the income statement? Explain.

6. Is it possible for a partnership to generate a profit and have one or more of the partners' capital accounts get smaller after the distribution of the income? Please explain.

7. When the partnership agreement calls for salary and interest allowances but the partnership operates at a loss, how should the partnership compute the division of the loss?

8. If an outside party buys the interest of a partner with the consent of all partners, when is the price paid for the partnership included in the entry to record the admission of the new partner? Why?

9. If a partner withdraws from a partnership and is paid with partnership assets more or less than the balance in his or her partnership account, how is the difference accounted for in the partnership's accounting records?

10. How does a sole proprietor or a partner determine how much of his or her earnings have been reinvested in the business since the firm has started? How does a stockholder determine the earnings his or her corporation has reinvested?

11. Why is the par value rather than the market value recorded in a stock account?

12. How do journal entries reflect the market value of par value stock when the stock is first issued?

13. What distinguishes par value from no-par stock in the stockholders' equity section of balance sheet?

14. Explain the basis for determining the issue price of shares of stock when the stock is exchanged for noncash asset.

15. What event does the Donated Capital account represent?

16. What is the purpose of the Retained Earnings account, and what business events cause it to change during the year?

17. Why would a company buy treasury stock? How is it reported on a firm's financial statements?

18. What does the Paid-in Capital on the Sale of Treasury Stock account represent? How is it reported on a firm's financial statements?

19. Explain the difference between a 100 percent stock dividend and a two-for-one stock split.

20. What does a deficit in Retained Earnings represent?

E 19.1

Michael Brown started his business in January 1996 with a contribution of $50,000 cash and a building he had recently purchased for $75,000. In August 1996, he withdrew $12,000 from the business's Cash account for his personal use. On December 31, 1996, his business had revenues of $200,000 and expenses of $132,000. Make the journal entries to record:

a. His initial contributions.
b. His cash withdrawal.
c. The closing entries at December 31.

What is the ending balance in his capital account?

E 19.2 Melvin Squires and Kenny Deitz were both operating advertising agencies as sole proprietors when they decided to merge their businesses and form a partnership. Listed below are the balance sheets for both sole proprietorships before the merger as well as the current market value of the respective assets of the two businesses. Make the entry required to establish the partnership, given this information.

SQUIRES'S ADVERTISING AGENCY

	Cost	Market
Cash	$10,000	
Accounts receivable	40,000	$35,000
Office equipment	50,000	44,000
Accounts payable	40,000	
Squires's capital	60,000	

DEITZ'S ADVERTISING AGENCY

	Cost	Market
Cash	$ 5,000	
Accounts receivable	15,000	$ 12,500
Building	90,000	124,000
Accounts payable	20,000	
Deitz's capital	90,000	

E 19.3 Marvin Ayers and Janet Simpson have just completed their first year of business as a partnership. Their agreement is to divide profits and losses equally. The revenue and expense accounts have been closed, and the accounting records contain the accounts and balances shown below. Using these data, make the entries to complete the closing process.

	Debit	Credit
Income summary		$ 56,000
Ayers, capital		127,000
Ayers, withdrawals	$21,000	
Simpson, capital		148,000
Simpson, withdrawals	24,000	

E 19.4 The partnership of Kelly, Peters, and Thompson specifies a division of profits in a ratio of their respective capital balances at the start of the period. These balances are as follows:

Kelly	$39,200
Peters	44,800
Thompson	28,800

Prepare the journal entry to close the Income Summary account if that account has (1) a credit balance of $50,000 and (2) a debit balance of $10,000.

E 19.5 Supply the missing figure for each of the partners below.

Partner One
Partner One's capital at the beginning of the year	$_____
Partner One's capital at the end of the year	92,670
Partner One's share of income for year	38,900
Partner One's drawings during the year	26,600

Partner Two
Partner Two's capital at the beginning of the year	$85,380
Partner Two's capital at the end of the year	97,410
Partner Two's share of income for year	_____
Partner Two's drawings during the year	22,690

Partner Three
Partner Three's capital at the beginning of the year	$98,620
Partner Three's capital at the end of the year	89,110
Partner Three's share of income for year	19,240
Partner Three's drawings during the year	_____

E 19.6   Blakely, Connert, and Norley are in partnership and have agreed to share profits and losses in a ratio of 5:3:2, respectively. Determine the increase or decrease in their individual capital accounts if the partnership has (1) a net income of $53,000 and (2) a net loss of $16,500.

E 19.7   In their partnership agreement, Martin, Resler, and Watson agreed that Martin should receive a salary allowance of $15,000 per year and that Watson should receive a salary allowance of $6,000. Any remainder is divided equally among the three partners. Prepare the journal entry to divide the following: (1) net income of $39,000, (2) net income of $14,000, and (3) net loss of $24,000.

E 19.8   French, Imel, and Langley have agreed to divide profits and losses as follows: 8 percent interest on beginning capital balances and the remainder divided equally. The beginning capital balances are: French $60,000, Imel $30,000, and Langley $40,000. Determine the increase or decrease in each partner's capital account if: (1) net income is $36,000, (2) net income is $10,000, and (3) net loss is $5,800.

E 19.9   When Tolbert and Adams formed their partnership, it was agreed that Tolbert would operate the business, although Adams supplied most of the financing. In view of these facts, Tolbert is to receive a salary allowance of $25,000 per year, each partner is to receive a 5 percent interest allowance on their beginning capital balances, and any remainder is to be divided equally.

At the beginning of the year, Tolbert's capital balance was $140,000 and Adams' was $300,000. Determine the amount of profit or loss allocated to each partner given the following income and loss figures: (1) net income is $75,000, (2) net income is $23,000, and (3) net loss is $40,000.

E 19.10   Daran Lemon, who is a partner in Tiad Company, has decided to sell his ownership interest in the firm. The balance in his capital account is $90,000. With the consent of the other partners, he sells two-thirds of his interest to Rob Thummel, an incoming partner, for $71,000 and the remaining one-third to Jeff Placek, an existing partner, for $32,000. If no partnership assets were used to buy Mr. Lemon out, prepare the journal entry to record this transfer of ownership interest.

E 19.11   Edwards and Livingston, each of whom has a partnership capital balance of $65,000, admit Blake to a one-third interest in the firm upon Blake's payment of $75,000 to the partnership. If Edwards and Livingston share profits and losses equally, record the entry to reflect the admission of Blake to the partnership.

E 19.12   The firm of Wembly and Crane decided to admit Forslund to the partnership. Forslund paid $60,000 cash for a one-third interest in the firm. At the time, Wembly has a capital balance of $55,000, and Crane had a balance of $50,000. They shared profits and losses equally. Record the entry to reflect the admission of Forslund to the partnership.

E 19.13   Diane Salcheck was invited to join an existing partnership. She paid $130,000 to the firm for a one-fourth interest. At that time the other two existing partners' capital balances were: Carmichael $168,000 and Martin $194,000. Carmichael and Martin shared profits in a ratio of 3:2 respectively. Prepare the journal entry to record the admission of Salcheck to the partnership.

E 19.14   Erik Olson and Valarie Boyd decided to accept Scott Norton into their partnership because he has an established reputation as an excellent salesperson in the community. He was admitted with a one-third interest for $42,000 cash. Olson and Boyd had capital balances of $47,000 and $46,000, respectively, and shared profits equally. Show the journal entry required to reflect the admission of Norton to the firm.

E 19.15   The partnership of Pollard and Blackburn needs additional financial resources, and they have asked Rick Cummins to join their company. Immediately prior to Cummins' admission, they reviewed their accounting records, and all parties agreed to the following changes: revalue inventory, which was maintained on a LIFO basis, upward by $18,000 and increase the allowance for doubtful accounts by $1,500. Pollard and Blackburn share profits and losses on a 2:1 basis, respectively.

Prepare the entry to revalue the partnership assets before the admission of Cummins to the partnership. Why is revaluation necessary?

E 19.16   Jeff Lippond has a capital balance of $72,000 in a partnership. The other two partners in the business have capital balances as follows: Keith Anderson $88,000 and Marie Chavey $81,000. Profits and losses are shared equally. Prepare the journal entry to record Lippond's withdrawal from the firm under each of the following circumstances.

a. He sold one-half of his interest to each of the other two partners for $44,000 (not the firm's cash).

b. He was paid $88,000 cash from the partnership assets.

c. He was paid $69,000 cash from the partnership assets.

E 19.17   Corcurun, Inc., is authorized to issue 500,000 shares of $1 par common stock and 200,000 shares of $100 par preferred stock. Prepare the journal entries to record the sale of 1,000 shares of common stock at $27.50 and 150 shares of preferred stock at $110 per share.

E 19.18   Ithicao Corporation issued 100 shares of its no-par common stock for $48 per share and 500 shares of its $20 par value preferred stock for $22.50 per share. Prepare the journal entry to record the sale of the stock.

E 19.19   March Company's no-par common stock has a stated value of $3 per share. Journalize the entries for the following sales of March's stock:

a. 1,300 shares at $3.50 per share.

b. 1,800 shares for a total of $5,940.

E 19.20   Baker-Roil, Inc., is authorized to issue 500,000 shares of no-par common stock and 300,000 shares of $25 par value preferred stock. During its first year of operations, the company issued 200,000 shares of common stock for a total amount of $3,400,000 and 50,000 shares of preferred stock for a total of $1,400,000. The firm has net income of $335,000 for the year, but declared no dividends.

Prepare the stockholders' equity section of the balance sheet as it would appear after this first year's operations.

E 19.21   Minotaur Products issued 3,000 shares of its $1 par, common stock in exchange for some machinery. Prepare the journal entry for each of the following situations.

a. The machinery has a fair market value of $17,000.

b. The machinery has a list price of $26,000, but the stock sold earlier in the day for $6 per share.

E 19.22   Make the entries for the following events of the David Baumgartner Corporation.

a. Sold 1,000 shares of a $50 preferred stock for $59,000.

b. Received a tract of land valued at $70,000 in exchange for promising to open a new plant in Moscow, Idaho.

c. Declared a two-for-one stock split on its $1 par value common stock. There are 600,000 shares of common stock authorized and 200,000 issued and outstanding.

E 19.23   On February 23, 1995, Domini, Inc., purchased 1,400 shares of its own $2 par common stock for $16 per share and held it as treasury stock. Three hundred of the treasury shares were reissued on June 10 for a total price of $5,700. On August 18, an additional 200 shares were reissued at $14 per share.

a. Prepare the entries to record the acquisition and reissue of the treasury stock.

b. If Domini has 300,000 shares of common stock authorized and 50,000 shares of common issued before the treasury stock was purchased, how many shares of common stock are authorized, issued, and outstanding after these transactions? What reasons would Domini possibly have for the acquisition?

E 19.24   On July 1, 1996, Jay Heckman Corporation purchased 1,000 shares of its $1 par common stock for $15 per share.

• On July 18, 1996, it sold 300 of the treasury shares for $16 per share.

• On August 1, 1996, it sold 400 more shares for $13.50 per share.

• On December 1, 1996, Heckman sold the remaining 300 shares for $20 per share.

Make the entries for these treasury stock transactions.

E 19.25   On May 18, 1996, the board of directors of Belex Company declared a $32,000 dividend for its common stockholders. The date of payment for the dividend is June 10, 1996, to stockholders of record on May 28, 1996.

Record all the appropriate journal entries.

E 19.26   Daryl Loyd Corporation decided to pay a dividend of $1.20 per share. The corporation has 1,500,000 shares authorized, 600,000 shares issued, and 575,000 shares outstanding on the date of declaration. Make the entries necessary for the dividend on the following dates.

June 15, 1997	Date of declaration
July 13, 1997	Ex-dividend date
July 15, 1997	Date of record
August 1, 1997	Date of payment

E 19.27   Halburt Sales, Inc., has 1,000,000 shares of $1 par common stock authorized and 150,000 shares issued and outstanding. The stock had a fair market value of $16 per share on October 15, 1996, when the board of directors declared a 10 percent stock dividend to holders of record on October 27, 1996. The new shares were distributed on November 1, 1996.

Make the journal entries to record the declaration and distribution of the stock dividend. How are the par value per share, total stockholders' equity, and number of shares authorized, issued, and outstanding affected by the stock dividend?

E 19.28   Using the information in E 19.27, how would your answer differ if Halburt Sales, Inc., had declared a 50 percent stock dividend?

PROBLEMS

P 19.1   Bart Shoemaker has owned and operated his own business, Computer Haven, for several years. On May 8, 1996, in order to expand his operations, he borrowed $50,000 using his personal residence as security for the loan. He placed $45,000 from the proceeds of the loan in his business account. At the start of 1996 his capital account had a credit balance of $172,800. A partial listing of accounts and related balances from the firm's general ledger on December 31, 1996, is shown below.

Sales	$621,600
Service revenue	15,900
Rental revenue	71,700
Cost of goods sold	416,300
Selling expense	108,600
Administrative expense	89,100
Shoemaker, drawings	41,400

Required: a. Journalize the closing entries for December 31, 1996.
b. Prepare a statement of changes in owner's equity for 1996.

P 19.2   Barry Hoagland holds a patent on a new electronic device. Although the patent has an estimated fair market value of $62,000, he is unable to obtain sufficient financing to start his own manufacturing plant. He contacts James Carrol, who owns a building and equipment appropriate for manufacturing the new device.

The building is carried on Mr. Carrol's records as having an original cost of $115,000 less accumulated depreciation of $48,000, and the equipment has an original cost of $92,000 less accumulated depreciation of $37,000. Currently, the fair market value of the building is $84,000, and that of the equipment is $61,000.

Barry Hoagland contributes his patent and James Carrol his building and equipment to form a partnership. They are joined in the new partnership by Marian Sill, who invests $43,000 in cash.

Required: Prepare the journal entries to record the contribution of each of the partners to the partnership.

P 19.3 Klein, Jefferson, and Maxwell agreed to divide partnership profits and losses as follows:
1. Annual salary allowance of $8,000 to Jefferson and $11,000 to Maxwell.
2. Interest allowance of 10 percent on beginning capital balances.
3. Remainder divided by Klein, Jefferson, and Maxwell in a ratio of 7:5:3, respectively.
The beginning capital balances are: Klein $95,000, Jefferson $27,000, and Maxwell $38,000.

Required: Determine the amount of net income or loss that is allocated to each of the partners if:
a. Net income is $50,000.
b. Net loss is $10,000.
c. Net income is $20,000.

P 19.4 The owners' capital balances and profit-sharing percentages of the B/D Company are shown below.

	Capital Balance	Profit Ratio
Barton	$66,000	20%
Burnett	74,000	30
Dobenin	48,000	30
Dubois	52,000	20

Barton decides to withdraw from the firm and is paid from the partnership's assets.

Required: Prepare the journal entry to record Barton's withdrawal assuming a payment from partnership cash of:
a. $66,000
b. $82,000
c. $58,000

P 19.5 Prior to completing the closing procedures on December 31, 1995, the accounting records of Fairbanks Company contained the following accounts and balances.

	Debit	Credit
Income summary		$ 10,000
Potter, capital		120,000
Potter, withdrawals	$22,000	
Sampson, capital		90,000
Sampson, withdrawals	28,000	

The profit and loss agreement provides the following: salary allowance of $14,000 to Sampson; 10 percent interest allowance on each partner's beginning capital balance; and the remainder divided in a ratio of 3:2, Potter to Sampson, respectively.

Required: *a.* Prepare the journal entries to complete the closing process.
b. Prepare a statement of changes in partners' capital for the year ended December 31, 1995.

P 19.6 The partnership agreement of Lavel and Martini Company specifies a division of profits in a ratio of 3:2, Lavel and Martini, respectively. Prior to admitting Grayson to a one-fourth interest in the firm, the partnership hired an independent appraiser to determine the value of the partnership's assets.

The inventory is overvalued by $10,000 because it contains some obsolete items. The fair market value of the building is $35,000 greater than book value, and the equipment's fair market value is $7,000 greater than its book value. Immediately before the revaluation of assets and admission of Grayson, the partners' capital balances were $87,000 for Lavel and $93,000 for Martini.

Required: *a.* Journalize the entry to record the revaluation of the assets.
b. Prepare the journal entry to record the admission of Grayson assuming payments of:
(1) $76,000
(2) $68,000

P 19.7   Abby, Bertha, and Charlie form a partnership called the Trois Company. Abby contributes inventory having a fair market value of $30,000; Bertha contributes a building currently appraised at a fair market value of $50,000; and Charlie invests $20,000 in cash. They agree to divide profits and losses as follows: Abby receives a salary allowance of $10,000 because she operates the business full-time. Each partner receives a 10 percent interest allowance on the beginning balance of their respective capital accounts, and the residual is divided equally.

During the first period of operations, Abby withdrew $8,000, Bertha also withdrew $8,000, and Charlie did not withdraw anything.

Required: *a.* Prepare the journal entries to record:
(1) The individual contributions by the partners.
(2) The remaining closing entries, presuming that the Income Summary account has a credit balance of $32,000.
b. Prepare a statement of changes in partners' capital.

Immediately after the first year of operation, Darrell buys out Bertha's interest directly from her for $60,000. At this time, the three new partners, Abby, Charlie, and Darrell, agree that they will divide all future profits and losses in a ratio of 3:1:2—Abby, Charlie, and Darrell, respectively. At the end of that year's operations, profits amounted to $42,000, and withdrawals were: Abby, $11,000; Charlie, $6,000; and Darrell, $9,000.

Required: *c.* Record the transfer of Bertha's share of the partnership.
d. Make the closing entries starting with closing the balance in the Income Summary account.

After the books are closed on that second year of operations, Emmett asks to buy into the partnership. All parties agree that he should pay $50,000 for a one-fourth interest. It is further agreed that all profits after Emmett's admission will be divided in the ratio of 2:1:2:2—Abby, Charlie, Darrell, and Emmett, respectively. Profits for the third year of operations are $49,000 and withdrawals are: Abby, $12,000; Charlie, $11,000; Darrell, $11,000; and Emmett, $8,000.

Required: *e.* Record the admission of Emmett to the partnership.
f. Complete the closing entries starting with the Income Summary Account.

At the start of the fourth year of operations, Abby decides to withdraw from the firm. All parties agree that she should receive $70,000 for her interest, and she is paid $10,000 cash at the time of the withdrawal and given a six-month, 10 percent note payable by the partnership for the $60,000 balance.

Required: *g.* Record Abby's withdrawal from the firm.
h. Determine the balance in each of the remaining partner's capital accounts.

P 19.8   The charter of the BBM Corporation authorizes the issue of 150,000 shares of no-par common stock and 50,000 shares of 7 percent, $10 par, cumulative preferred stock. Events affecting the Stockholders' Equity account during the first years of operations are listed below.
1. 25,000 shares of common stock were sold for $15 per share.
2. 10,000 shares of preferred stock were sold at $22 per share.
3. A building with a fair market value of $280,000 was acquired for a cash payment of $75,000 and the 13,000 shares of common stock.
4. 40,000 shares of common stock were issued for cash of $640,000.
5. A dividend of $1 per share of common and $.70 per share for preferred stock was declared.

Required: *a.* Record the transactions described above.
b. Prepare the stockholders' equity section of the balance sheet for the end of the year assuming that BBM generated $114,000 of income.

P 19.9   Overhill Corporation is authorized to issue 50,000 shares of $50 par, 10 percent preferred stock and 200,000 shares of $.50 par value common stock. The following transactions summarize the events affecting its capital stock accounts during its first year of operations.
1. The company issued 150,000 shares of common stock for cash of $30 per share.
2. 30,000 shares of preferred stock were sold for cash of $53 per share.
3. Overhill repurchased and held as treasury stock 5,000 shares of its own common stock at $31 per share.
4. 3,000 shares of the treasury stock were reissued at $33 per share.

Required: *a.* Make the entries to record these events.
b. Prepare the stockholders' equity section of Overhill's balance sheet assuming Retained Earnings has a credit balance of $276,000.

P 19.10   The stockholders' equity section of Railet Company's balance sheet appeared as follows on August 15, 1996.

Common stock, $2 par value; 100,000 shares authorized, 70,000 shares issued and outstanding	$140,000
Paid-in capital in excess of par	170,000
Total contributed capital	$310,000
Retained earnings	206,000
Total stockholders' equity	$516,000

On August 15, 1996, the board of directors declared a 10 percent stock dividend. The date of distribution was September 25, 1996, to the stockholders of record on September 1, 1996. The stock was selling for $10.50 per share on the date of declaration.

On November 30, Railet Company repurchased and held as treasury stock 2,000 shares of its common stock at $11 per share.

On December 15, 1996, the company received land with a fair market value of $40,000 in exchange for a promise to locate a new distribution facility in Moberly, Missouri.

Railet generated $200,000 of net income in 1996.

Required: a. Make the entries to record these equity events.
   b. Prepare the stockholders' equity section to reflect these events.

P 19.11   On December 31, 1995, the stockholders' equity section of Kanark Products' balance sheet was as follows:

Preferred stock, 6%, $10 par, 50,000 shares authorized, 30,000 issued and outstanding	$ 300,000
Paid-in capital in excess of par—preferred	7,500
Common stock, no par, 100,000 authorized, 70,000 issued and outstanding	875,000
Total contributed capital	$1,182,500
Retained earnings	478,300
Total stockholders' equity	$1,660,800

During 1995, the following transactions affecting stockholders' equity took place.

Feb. 17   Sold 10,000 shares of common stock for $12.75 per share.
June 1   Declared a $.65 per share dividend on common stock and $.30 per share dividend on preferred stock. Dividends are payable on June 25 to stockholders of record on June 10.
   25   Paid the dividend declared on June 1.
July 15   Received a tract of land valued at $67,000 in consideration for locating a manufacturing plant in Ridings Cove, Virginia.
Aug. 12   Purchased and held in treasury stock 5,000 shares of common stock for $13 per share.
Sept. 18   Sold 1,000 shares of treasury stock at $13.50 per share.
Oct. 18   Sold 1,000 shares of treasury stock for $14 per share.
Nov. 1   Declared a 10 percent common stock dividend. New shares are distributable on November 20 to shareholders of record on November 14.
   20   Distributed the common stock dividend.
Dec. 1   Declared a $.70 per share dividend on common stock and a $.30 per share dividend on preferred stock. Dividends are payable on December 28 to stockholders of record on December 10.
   28   Paid the dividend declared December 1.
   31   Closed the $210,000 credit balance in the Income Summary account.

Required: a. Give the journal entries to record these events.
   b. Prepare the stockholders' equity section of Kanark Products' balance sheet.

CA 19.1

L&E Consulting has four partners—Leroy, Ellis, Whitney, and Jamia. During the last accounting period its net income was $50,000. The partners are currently debating how the firm's net income should be divided among the partners. The partners are considering the following four alternatives:
1. Divide net income in the ratios of the partners' average capital balances during the year.
2. Give a $10,000 salary allowance to Leroy and a $5,000 salary allowance to Ellis and divide the remainder equally among all the partners.
3. Give each partner an interest allowance equal to 5 percent of his or her average capital balance during the year and divide the remainder equally among the partners.
4. Divide the net income among Leroy, Ellis, Whitney, and Jamia—25 percent, 10 percent, 35 percent, and 30 percent, respectively.

The average capital balances for Leroy, Ellis, Whitney, and Jamia during the past year were $20,000, $10,000, $30,000, and $40,000, respectively.

Required:
Use a computer spreadsheet package.
a. Determine each partner's share of net income using alternative 1.
b. Determine each partner's share of net income using alternative 2.
c. Determine each partner's share of net income using alternative 3.
d. Determine each partner's share of net income using alternative 4.
e. Repeat requirements *a* through *d* assuming that net income was only $10,000 for the past year.

CA 19.2

Zerotech Corporation currently has 500,000 shares of $10 par value common stock outstanding. The market value of the stock is currently $45 per share.

Required:
Use a computer spreadsheet package. Assume independent situations.
a. Determine the amounts to be used in the journal entry to record a 5 percent stock dividend.
b. Determine the amounts to be used in the journal entry to record a 15 percent stock dividend.
c. Determine the amounts to be used in the journal entry to record a 30 percent stock dividend.
d. Determine the amounts to be used in the journal entry to record a 50 percent stock dividend.
e. Repeat requirements *a* through *d* assuming that the par value of the stock is only $5 per share.
f. Repeat requirements *a* through *d* assuming that the par value of the stock is only $1 per share.

CASES

C 19.1

Lori Rock has operated her own business as a sole proprietorship for several years. Although the business is quite profitable, she believes profits would increase significantly if she expanded her operations by increasing the quantity of inventory, hiring an additional employee, and doing some remodeling in the production area. This would require a minimum investment of $40,000.

The company uses FIFO inventory costing and, with the exception of the equipment that the firm owns, the assets' values on the books are reasonably close to their fair market values. The equipment has a net book value of $18,500 and a fair market value of $22,000. Lori Rock's capital balance is $90,000.

Fred Neuman is willing to contribute $45,000 for a one-third interest in the firm providing he is allowed a 10 percent allowance on his average capital balance and the remaining profits are split on a 2:1, Rock to Neuman basis. Since he is not very knowledgeable about Rock's business, he wants her to continue to manage the business.

Rock was offered a job by a larger firm at $30,000 per year, but she has a strong preference to continue her own business if she can acquire the additional capital necessary for the expansion.

Required: Prepare a brief report to Lori Rock outlining your assessment of Mr. Neuman's proposal. You should discuss the following:

   a. What impact would the admission of Mr. Neuman as a partner have on her capital account?

   b. What sort of income must the firm generate to reach Ms. Rock's goal of $30,000?

   c. Whether you recommend the proposal. If not, what counterproposal should Ms. Rock make?

C 19.2   Kim Owens, your long-time friend, owns 1,000 shares of $5 par value common stock in Electronics, Inc. There are 100,000 shares of common stock authorized, and all shares are issued and outstanding.

    Recently, the company was authorized to issue 20,000 shares of $50 par value preferred stock. These shares have a dividend rate of 6 percent based on par, and they are cumulative. The company expects to sell 5,000 shares of the preferred stock in the near future to finance the acquisition of more production facilities.

    Kim has studied the firm's annual reports in an effort to determine the effects the new stock issue will have on her dividends. She is confused because her $5 par value common stock has a market value of $50 per share. She has received a $4 dividend per share in recent years. The company has consistently maintained a policy of paying out 70 percent of its after-tax net income as dividends, a policy management expects to continue into the foreseeable future. Aside from being confused about the difference between par value and market value, Kim is concerned that the company will not make enough net income to maintain her $4 per share dividend.

Required: *a.* Explain the difference between par value and market value to Kim in memo form.

   b. Show Kim how to compute the minimum amount of after-tax net income the company must earn in order for her to receive a $4 per share dividend if the 5,000 shares of preferred stock are sold.

CRITICAL THINKING

CT 19.1   Mitch Holtus and Stan Weber are partners in a company called Sports Voice. Ron Paradise has approached the partners about joining the firm, and he wants to buy a 25 percent interest in the firm. Sports Voice has $100,000 in liabilities, and its assets are undervalued by $22,000.

    Mr. Holtus has a capital balance of $80,000; Mr. Weber's capital balance is $92,000; they share profits and losses equally. How much money will Mr. Paradise have to contribute to the firm to obtain a 25 percent interest if the existing partnership does not revalue the assets?

CT 19.2   The Upchurch Corporation was authorized to issue 1,000,000 shares of $1 par common stock and 100,000 shares of $100 par, 10 percent preferred stock. To date Upchurch has issued 300,000 shares of common stock and no preferred stock.

    Upchurch is contemplating the acquisition of a new piece of equipment and wants to issue stock to raise the $100,000 cash to finance its acquisition. The company is trying to decide whether to issue 5,000 shares of common stock or 900 shares of preferred stock.

Required: *a.* Describe how the issue of each type of stock would affect the stockholders' equity of Upchurch Corporation.

   b. If Upchurch generates about $1,800,000 of net income each year and the new machine can generate an additional $20,000 of after-tax income, how will the earnings of the common stockholders be affected if:

    (1) Common stock is issued.

    (2) Preferred stock is issued.

ETHICAL CHALLENGES

EC 19.1 John McKain and Willard Davis are partners in a struggling business that is badly in need of cash. Arlo Waters has expressed an interest in buying a one-third interest in the partnership. McKain and Davis know that the market value of the firm's assets is substantially lower than their book value. Mr. Davis suggests that they not tell Mr. Waters about this situation and not revalue the assets.

What are the financial and ethical ramifications of not revaluing the assets before Arlo Waters is admitted to the partnership?

EC 19.2 Grant Corporation's management expects the firm to have some financial difficulties in the next year. In fact, they expect their common stock, which is currently selling at $53 per share, to drop to about $25 per share as a result of these difficulties. One member of management suggests that the corporation buy the stock of selected stockholders now to spare them this loss of value. Discuss the ethics of this proposal.

CHAPTER 20

Recording and Communicating Operational Investment Activities

Learning Objectives

1. Explain the issues involved in determining the cost of operational investments.
2. Explain the nature of depreciation and related issues regarding the use of plant assets.
3. Determine the financial impact of plant asset disposals.
4. Describe the characteristics of natural resources and the process of depletion.
5. Discuss the characteristics of intangible assets and the process of amortization.
6. Explain how to communicate events involving operational investments to external and internal users.

Union Pacific Corporation is a transportation company with a rich heritage. In 1994, the company proudly celebrated the 125th anniversary of its participation in the driving of the golden spike that marked completion of a "transcontinental railroad that changed the course of this nation's future."[1]

But Union Pacific is more than a transportation company. It also has operated businesses involved in natural gas production and continues to develop software used by customers to help coordinate transportation operations.

On its December 31, 1993, balance sheet, Union Pacific reported total assets of approximately $15 billion. Of this amount, $11.4 billion, or 76 percent, represented plant assets and natural resources, and another $1.6 billion, or 11 percent of total assets, was classified as "Intangible and Other Assets." Over the 10-year period leading up to and including 1993, the company spent an average of $1.2 billion per year on capital investments, and 1993 expenses resulting from the cost of these assets totaled $949 million, or 16 percent of total operating expenses.

---

[1]"From the Chairman," Union Pacific's 1993 annual report.

The successful utilization of plant assets, natural resources, and intangible assets has been vital to the continuing success of Union Pacific and many other companies. Therefore, it is important to understand the accounting principles related to the recording and reporting of these assets.

In this chapter we discuss **operational investments,** which are long-term investments made to acquire the facilities necessary to conduct basic business activities. Operational investments fall into three major categories, which we will discuss in turn:

- plant assets,
- natural resources, and
- intangible assets.

The benefits derived from investments in plant assets, natural resources, and intangible assets represent an important factor in the successful operation of most companies. Because of the importance of operational investments, it is vital that we understand not only what these assets represent, but also how companies record and report their acquisition, use, and disposal.

PLANT ASSETS

Plant assets, often referred to as *property, plant, and equipment*, are tangible assets acquired by a company primarily for use in the business over a time span covering more than one accounting period. This category includes land, buildings, and equipment employed to help create and deliver goods and services to customers. It represents the basic infrastructure of the business, without which successful business operations would be impossible.

Determining whether to categorize any tangible, long-term asset as a plant asset depends on its intended use. For example, if a company acquires a parcel of land as the site for a new factory building, it is a plant asset because of its intended use as a place to manufacture the company's product. However, if the company acquires the same piece of land because it plans to hold the land vacant for several years and then sell it at a profit, it is not a plant asset because the company will not use the land to create any of the goods or services it provides. In this second case, the company would report the land as a long-term investment.

There are three stages to consider when describing the accounting process for plant assets:

1. Acquisition

2. Use

3. Disposal

Users of financial statements should understand the recording process at each stage in order to meaningfully analyze the activities involved in plant asset purchase, use, and disposal.

ACQUISITION OF PLANT ASSETS

To understand why certain expenditures are added to or excluded from the acquisition cost of a plant asset, one must understand the difference between capital and revenue expenditures. A **capital expenditure** creates the expectation of future benefits that apply beyond the current accounting period. Because companies use plant assets for more than one accounting period, an expenditure to acquire any plant asset is a capital expenditure, which companies **capitalize,** or add to the cost of the plant asset rather than expensing it immediately. On the other hand, a **revenue expenditure** provides benefits exclusively during the current accounting period.

Revenue expenditures include the costs of annual repairs and maintenance, as well as real estate taxes, utility bills, and most other day-to-day operating costs. Because revenue expenditures provide current benefits, companies generally expense them when incurred.

The capital expenditures added to the cost of any particular purchased plant asset include all normal, reasonable, and necessary expenditures to acquire the asset and prepare it for its intended future use. As discussed in Chapter 16, the cost of a building normally includes its purchase price, as well as related legal fees and any broker's commissions paid. These are all considered normal, necessary costs of acquiring real estate. If the building is constructed rather than purchased, all normal costs incurred during the period of construction must be accumulated and added to the cost of the building.

The accounting for construction costs helps illustrate the difference between capital and revenue expenditures. Remember that assets represent economic resources with expected future benefits, and that assets become expenses as they are used up to generate current benefits. During construction of a building, *all* normal, necessary costs incurred provide future benefits and, therefore, are capital expenditures added to the cost of the building. These costs include labor and materials directly associated with construction, permits, architect's fees, and taxes paid. They also include indirect costs, such as wages paid to security personnel, insurance payments, and interest costs on money borrowed during construction. However, once a company begins to use the completed building, it derives current benefits from the asset's use; therefore, expenditures for normal repairs and maintenance to maintain these current benefits are revenue expenditures, which the company reflects as expenses as they are incurred.

The cost of land, like that of a building, includes its purchase price and any related legal and broker's fees paid. When purchasing land, frequently the buyer also pays for a survey and title search, title insurance, and various other fees that are necessary to transfer ownership. The buyer adds all of these expenditures to the cost of the land. If it is necessary to level out uneven sections of the land or to remove existing structures on the land before using it for its intended purpose, the buyer would include all of these expenditures as part of the cost of the land.

PAUSE & REFLECT

When insurance and interest costs are incurred during the course of a long-term construction project, they are added to the cost of the asset. If insurance and interest costs continue after the asset is completed and placed in service, should a company continue to add these expenditures to the cost of the asset? If not, how should they be treated?

Often a buyer pays one price to purchase land and a building together. When this occurs, the buyer must allocate the total purchase price between the two, because buildings and equipment are depreciable assets, whereas land is not. Allocation frequently occurs based on the relative dollar amount of separate appraisals completed for each asset. Or, to save money, small businesses may use real estate tax bills showing values assigned to the land and building by local tax assessors.

To illustrate how this allocation works, assume a company paid $380,000 for a building sitting on one acre of land. An appraisal paid for by the purchasing company immediately prior to the transaction indicated that the land and building were worth $100,000 and $300,000, respectively. The company would allocate the total purchase price based on the following two-step calculation:

1. Calculate the percentage of the total appraised values applicable to each asset:

	Appraised Value	Percentage of Total Appraised Value
Land	$100,000	$100,000/$400,000 = 25%
Building	300,000	$300,000/$400,000 = 75%
Total	$400,000	

If a company purchases this car, any service required prior to use would be capitalized.

2. Use the percentages calculated in step 1 to allocate the purchase price between the acquired assets:

	Percentage of Total Appraised Value	×	Total Purchase Price	=	Portion of Total Purchase Price Allocated to Each Asset
Land	25%	×	$380,000	=	$ 95,000
Building	75%	×	$380,000	=	285,000
Total	100%				$380,000

As a result of the allocation, the recorded cost of the land is $95,000, and the cost of the building is $285,000. These two amounts sum to the total purchase price of $380,000.

PAUSE & REFLECT

When land and buildings are purchased together for one price, a company might look for a justification to assign the smallest possible portion of the purchase price to the land. Why would it do this?

The cost of equipment normally includes the purchase price, freight charges, sales taxes paid, and installation costs. Any other normal, necessary costs, such as assembly and testing before use, are added to the cost of the equipment, and any discounts allowed, such as those for prompt payment, are deducted from the cost.

An interesting issue may arise when purchasing used equipment. What if a company paid $6,000 to purchase a used automobile with a remaining useful life of four years, and the company also paid $250 for a necessary tune-up before placing the auto in service? Assuming that the tune-up is a necessary, normal cost of readying the asset for use, the company would capitalize the cost of the tune-up as part of the total cost of the auto. However, if the company pays an additional $250 for a second tune-up one year later to maintain the car in good working order, the second payment is not added to the cost of the auto. Rather, this cost would be charged to repairs and maintenance expense for that time period. In the first case, the tune-up was a capital expenditure because it helped *prepare* a newly acquired asset for use during future accounting periods. In the second case, the tune-up was a revenue expenditure because it simply *maintained* a working asset in good condition for use in the current accounting period.

Finally, many companies choose not to capitalize certain capital expenditures on the grounds that the dollar amount involved is insignificant. For example, if a company purchases a screwdriver for $5, even though the screwdriver may last for many years and is, therefore, theoretically a plant asset, the company will probably charge the $5 to an expense account. This is an application of the accounting concept of **materiality** which relates to whether an item's dollar amount or its inherent nature is significant enough to influence a financial statement user. When a company prepares financial statements in accordance with generally accepted accounting principles, the goal is to prepare statements that are free of material errors. However, accountants have much latitude regarding the recording and reporting of immaterial items because, by definition, these items will not affect decisions made by users of the financial statements.[2] Therefore, most companies have capitalization policies stating that any expenditure less than some specified dollar amount will be expensed regardless of whether it is capital in nature or not.

Now that we understand the factors affecting their recorded acquisition cost, let's examine how to account for the use of plant assets.

USE OF PLANT ASSETS

After placing a plant asset in service, a company begins to receive benefits from its use and must recognize the cost of these benefits as an expense over the useful life of the asset. Proper determination of net income requires the recording of expenses in the period when benefits are received.

We know from our previous discussion in Chapter 7 that the expense associated with using plant assets is called *depreciation*, and that companies record it as follows:

| Depreciation Expense | XXX | |
| Accumulated Depreciation | | XXX |

There is a separate accumulated depreciation account maintained for each asset or group of assets. Each separate accumulated depreciation account serves as a contra asset account and appears on the balance sheet as a deduction from the asset (or a group of assets) to which it relates. Whereas the depreciation expense account is closed out to income summary and owners' equity at the end of each period, accumulated depreciation is a permanent account, just like its related asset account. Its balance carries over and "accumulates" from one year to the next. Therefore, if a piece of equipment costing $10,000 was depreciated $1,000 per year for three full years, at the end of year three it would appear on the balance sheet as:

| Equipment (at cost) | $10,000 | |
| Less: Accumulated depreciation | (3,000) | $7,000 |

Recall that the $7,000 figure is variously referred to as the *carrying value, book value*, or *remaining undepreciated cost of the equipment*.

Many individuals operate under the mistaken impression that accountants use depreciation to reflect the decline in value of an asset. It is important to emphasize that depreciation is actually a process whereby accountants systematically allocate the net cost of a plant asset to the various periods receiving benefits from the use of that asset to obtain a proper matching of revenue and related expense. *It is not an attempt to measure declining value.* Thus, the carrying value of any plant asset shown on the balance sheet represents the remaining undepreciated cost of the asset—not its fair market value. In fact, at the same time that companies record depreciation on buildings they own, many of those buildings are increasing in value due to inflation and other factors.

---

[2]Further discussion of the concept of materiality is beyond the scope of this text. However, students may find it interesting to look at the report of independent accountants (the auditor's report) included in companies' annual reports to shareholders. In the auditor's report, the use of the word *material* is in accordance with the discussion in this text. Accountants do not generally attempt to prepare financial statements that are free of all errors. The goal is to prepare statements that are free of material errors and omissions.

Because of the impact of inflation, it is possible that a 20-year-old building that originally cost $100,000 might be fully depreciated on a company's balance sheet, even though it is currently worth $1,000,000. What problems does this cause for the user of financial statements? What problems would be created if businesses were required to report the current values of all of their plant assets?

Factors Affecting Depreciation Calculations

Before calculating depreciation for any given plant asset, it is necessary to know the following:

- Cost of the asset.
- Useful life of the asset.
- Salvage value of the asset.
- Method of depreciation.

We have already discussed those expenditures included in the cost of plant assets, but the useful life, salvage value, and method of depreciation require further explanation.

Useful Life   Useful life is the period of time over which a business expects to obtain economic benefits from the use of a plant asset or any other operational investment. Of necessity, it is an estimate based on information available to management at the date that a company places an asset in service.

With the exception of land, the useful life of operational investments is limited due to two factors: (1) physical wear and tear resulting from use of the asset or the passage of time, and (2) obsolescence.

Obsolescence results from changing technology, tastes, and/or preferences. For example, businesses generally replace computers because improved hardware is available, not because the computers no longer function for their originally intended purpose. Or, even though an automobile could be used for 7 to 10 years, a company may have a policy of buying a new automobile every three years simply because of a preference for newer automobiles.

Useful life can be expressed as a period of time or defined as the total number of units of output expected over the useful life of the asset, such as the estimated total miles an automobile will be driven.

Salvage Value   The expected fair market value of a plant asset at the end of its useful life is referred to as the **salvage value** or **residual value** of the asset. The portion of a plant asset's total cost that will be depreciated over its useful life, which is called its **depreciable cost,** is calculated as:

$$\text{Cost} - \text{Salvage value} = \text{Depreciable cost}$$

As in the case of useful life, the salvage value is based on an estimate made at the time an asset is placed in service.

Students often wonder about the accuracy of a depreciation expense figure calculated using an "estimated" useful life and salvage value. How can a company possibly know what a piece of equipment will be worth at the end of its useful life? Even more difficult, imagine estimating what a building will be worth at the end of an estimated useful life of 30 years! One should always remember that accounting is not an exact science. The matching principle requires that there be an honest attempt to record expenses in the period when related benefits are derived. A company could wait and record depreciation only after an asset is sold, at which time both its useful life and salvage value would be known with certainty. However, that would violate the matching principle and would result in improper determination of income during every period of the asset's life.

Depreciation is just one of many examples demonstrating that amounts reported in financial statements are frequently based on estimates involving individual judgment.

Method of Depreciation

Three common methods exist for calculating the amount of depreciation reported in financial statements:

- Straight-line method.
- Units-of-production method.
- Accelerated methods.

We discuss each method in turn in the following pages.

Straight-Line Depreciation   The **straight-line depreciation** method reflects the calculation of annual depreciation by allocating the depreciable cost of the asset to depreciation expense equally over its useful life. We calculate straight-line depreciation as follows:

$$\text{Annual depreciation expense} = \frac{\text{Cost} - \text{Salvage value}}{\text{Estimated number of years in useful life}}$$

For example, assume a delivery truck purchased by CDL Company for a total cost of $22,000 has an anticipated useful life of five years and a salvage value estimated at $2,000. The company would calculate annual straight-line depreciation expense for the truck as:

$$\frac{\$22,000 - \$2,000}{5 \text{ years}} = \$4,000/\text{year}$$

Exhibit 20.1 panel A shows annual straight-line depreciation expense (column *1*), as well as the resulting accumulated depreciation (column *2*), and asset carrying value (column *3*) at the end of each year of the truck's useful life. Notice that the annual depreciation expense shown in column *1*, which is deducted in calculating income each year, is a constant figure, while the amount of accumulated depreciation shown in column *2* increases by the amount of depreciation expense taken each year. The balance of accumulated depreciation at the end of each year is subtracted from the asset's original cost to obtain the year-end carrying value shown in column *3* to be reported in the plant asset section of the company's balance sheet.

Straight-line depreciation is based on the assumption that benefits derived from an asset are constant during each year of its use. This justifies recording the same dollar amount of expense annually. When this assumption is not valid, companies may employ one of the other methods of depreciation.

Units-of-Production Depreciation   The **units-of-production** method is a way of calculating annual depreciation expense based on actual usage rather than the passage of time. Instead of defining the useful life of an asset in terms of years, this depreciation method expresses an asset's useful life in terms of total expected units of output. For example, a company might expect a piece of manufacturing equipment to last for a total of 20,000 hours of operating use. Or the company may assign an automobile a useful life of 100,000 miles. Thus, the depreciable cost of the asset is divided by the expected total units of output to determine the depreciation rate per unit of output. This rate is used to calculate annual depreciation based on the actual output for the period.

EXHIBIT	20.1	Comparison of Various Depreciation Methods

Assumptions

Asset description	Delivery truck
Cost of asset	$22,000
Useful life	5 years
Salvage value	$2,000

Panel A. Straight-Line Depreciation

Year	(1) Annual Depreciation Expense*	(2) Accumulated Depreciation as of Year-End	(3) Carrying Value as of Year-End
1	$4,000	$ 4,000	$18,000
2	4,000	8,000	14,000
3	4,000	12,000	10,000
4	4,000	16,000	6,000
5	4,000	20,000	2,000

Panel B. Units-of-Production Depreciation

Year	(1) Annual Depreciation Expense†	(2) Accumulated Depreciation as of Year-End	(3) Carrying Value as of Year-End
1	$.20 × 14,000‡ = $2,800	$ 2,800	$19,200
2	.20 × 23,000 = 4,600	7,400	14,600
3	.20 × 18,700 = 3,740	11,140	10,860
4	.20 × 21,300 = 4,260	15,400	6,600
5	.20 × <u>23,000</u> = 4,600	20,000	2,000
	<u>100,000</u> miles		

Panel C. Double-Declining-Balance (DDB) Depreciation
(rounded to nearest whole dollar)

Year	(1) Annual Depreciation Expense§	(2) Accumulated Depreciation as of Year-End	(3) Carrying Value as of Year-End
1	$22,000 × .4 = $8,800	$ 8,800	$13,200
2	13,200 × .4 = 5,280	14,080	7,920
3	7,920 × .4 = 3,168	17,248	4,752
4	4,752 × .4 = 1,901	19,149	2,851
5	851‖	20,000	2,000

*Annual depreciation expense = ($22,000 − $2,000)/5 years.

†Annual depreciation calculated in two steps:

 Step 1: ($22,000 − $2,000)/100,000 miles = $.20/mile

 Step 2: $.20/mile × Actual miles driven each year

‡The mileage figures shown for each year are assumed.

§Annual depreciation expense calculated as follows:

 Step 1: Straight-line rate = 20%
 Double-declining-balance rate = 2 × 20% = 40%

 Step 2: Depreciation for each year is equal to:
 Carrying value at beginning of year × .4

‖In year 5, the depreciation calculation yields the following: $2,851 × .4 = $1,140. However, if this amount is used, total depreciation taken over the useful life of the asset will exceed the $20,000 of total depreciation allowed. This is a common problem of DDB depreciation. When this happens, companies simply record the final year's depreciation as the amount that will bring total accumulated depreciation to the amount desired ($20,000, in this case).

The units-of-production method of depreciation involves calculating depreciation expense in two steps:

Step 1: $\dfrac{\text{Cost} - \text{Salvage value}}{\substack{\text{Estimated total output} \\ \text{over life of asset}}}$ = Depreciation per unit of output

Step 2: $\substack{\text{Depreciation per} \\ \text{unit of output} \\ \text{(from step 1)}}$ × $\substack{\text{Actual output} \\ \text{for current year}}$ = $\substack{\text{Depreciation expense} \\ \text{for current year}}$

If the CDL Company from the prior example expects its delivery truck to have a useful life of 100,000 miles, and it was actually driven 14,000 miles in its first year of use, depreciation expense for year 1 calculated using the units-of-production method is:

1. $\dfrac{\$22,000 - \$2,000}{100,000 \text{ miles}}$ = \$.20 depreciation per mile of use

2. \$.20/mile × 14,000 miles = \$2,800 depreciation for year

Exhibit 20.1 panel B shows the calculation of depreciation expense for each year of the truck's use, based on the following assumptions:

Year	Actual Miles Driven
1	14,000
2	23,000
3	18,700
4	21,300
5	23,000

The advantage of the units-of-production method of depreciation is that it allows a company to record varying amounts of depreciation expense each year, as illustrated in Exhibit 20.1 panel B, to properly match the amount of expense recognized with actual rates of usage. In our example, the rate of asset use and the corresponding benefit derived from that use are measured in terms of miles driven each year.

Accelerated Depreciation   Even when the use of a plant asset is expected to be at a constant rate over its useful life, many accountants believe that benefits derived from the use of a new asset are greater than the benefits from the use of the same asset as it ages. For example, a new computer functions at "state-of-the-art" efficiency, but, after just a few years, the computer may no longer provide the same relative degree of benefit to the company. Also, a brand new automobile benefits a company by providing not only transportation, but also a certain image of success. As the automobile ages it still provides adequate transportation, but it no longer carries the same prestige and "image" value that it conveyed when new. Additionally, as it gets older, it is much more likely to need repairs to keep it running properly.

If benefits derived from the use of an asset tend to decline over time, then the matching principle justifies using one of various **accelerated depreciation** methods designed to recognize relatively greater expense in early years of asset use and progressively less expense as time passes.

Declining-balance depreciation is a type of accelerated depreciation which reflects depreciation expense for each year based on a constant percentage of a declining balance equal to the remaining undepreciated cost of the asset at the start of each year. The asset's undepreciated cost is its original cost less the total of any depreciation taken in prior years. The multiplication of a constant rate by this declining balance yields the greatest amount of depreciation in the asset's first year of use, and a declining amount in each subsequent year; thus, the depreciation expense recorded each year declines along with the declining benefits of asset use.

To "accelerate" the amount of depreciation expense taken each year, companies multiply the asset's beginning-of-year undepreciated cost by a constant percentage that exceeds the rate applicable for straight-line depreciation.

In the case of the delivery truck purchased by CDL Company, the amount of annual straight-line depreciation resulted from dividing the depreciable cost of the asset by five years (the asset's useful life), which is the same as multiplying by 1/5th, or 20 percent. Using the declining-balance method, the company would compute annual depreciation expense by multiplying the truck's undepreciated cost at the start of each year by some multiple of this rate. **Double-declining balance depreciation** (DDB) is specific type of declining-balance depreciation that reflects annual depreciation expense using a constant percentage equal to twice the straight-line rate of depreciation. For example, the double-declining-balance method would use a depreciation rate of 40 percent per year (2 × 200%), in this case.[3]

The complete set of steps to calculate double-declining-balance depreciation follows:

Step 1: Determine the straight-line rate of depreciation for the asset and double it.

Step 2: Calculate depreciation for the first year by multiplying the rate determined in step 1 by the *original* cost of the asset. (Note: Do not reduce the cost by the salvage value of the asset.[4])

Step 3: Determine depreciation for the second and all subsequent years by multiplying the rate from step 1 by the undepreciated cost (original cost – accumulated depreciation) of the asset as of the beginning of the year until the asset's salvage value remains.

Exhibit 20.1 panel C illustrates this calculation for each year of the useful life of CDL Company's delivery truck.

Although the depreciation expense in the early years of an asset's life are larger, accelerated depreciation does not increase the total amount of depreciation taken over the life of the asset, which is always limited to depreciable cost (cost – salvage value) of the asset. Notice in Exhibit 20.1 that total depreciation recorded under each of the three methods equals $20,000 ($22,000 original cost – $2,000 salvage value).

Because of this requirement, it is generally necessary to modify DDB depreciation taken during the last portion of an asset's useful life. In Exhibit 20.1 panel C, depreciation calculated for year 5 under the DDB formula requires us to multiply $2,851 (the remaining undepreciated cost of the truck at the beginning of the year) by 40 percent, which would result in year 5 depreciation equal to $1,140. However, this amount would cause total accumulated depreciation to exceed $20,000, so we must limit the amount of depreciation expense in year 5 to $851, the amount that will bring total accumulated depreciation to $20,000. It is usually necessary to adjust the amount of double-declining-balance depreciation expense taken in the final portion of an asset's life so that total accumulated depreciation taken over the life of the asset equals the estimated net depreciable cost of the asset.

Partial-Year Depreciation   What if a company with a December 31 year-end purchases or disposes of a plant asset on April 5, 1997? If it uses the units-of-production depreciation method, the timing of the disposal is not an issue, because depreciation for any period is based on actual output or use for that period. But, if the company uses either straight-line or accelerated depreciation, which define useful life in terms of years, the fact that the asset was not used for a full 12-month period in 1997 will require a modification in the amount of depreciation expense recorded for that year.

---

[3] In addition to 200 percent declining-balance depreciation, 150 percent declining-balance depreciation is also possible, as are various other percentages, each of which uses a stated multiple of the straight-line rate of depreciation, ranging up to 200 percent.

[4] The curious student may wonder why we do not use the asset's depreciable cost ($20,000) as we did for the other depreciation methods. Although the depreciable cost represents the total amount of depreciation to take over the life of the asset, if we take 40 percent of $20,000 in year 1, 40 percent of the remainder in year 2, and so on, the depreciation calculated for each of the five years will sum to less than $20,000. Use of the asset's original cost helps solve this problem.

There are several ways to deal with this issue. Companies making numerous plant asset purchases and disposals spread out evenly during the course of the fiscal year frequently use the **midyear convention** which reflects depreciation expense for each asset as if it were purchased or disposed of exactly halfway through the company's fiscal year. This avoids the expense of tracking the exact date that the business places each asset in service, and, so long as acquisitions/disposals of assets occur uniformly, it yields an annual depreciation expense that is not significantly different from the result that would have been obtained by tracking each asset individually.

Other companies record depreciation based on the actual number of months an asset was in service during the year. When following this approach, businesses that acquire assets on or before the 15th of each month record depreciation expense for these assets as if they were in service for the entire month. They treat assets acquired after the 15th of any month as being placed in service at the start of the next month. Similarly, assets disposed of after the 15th of any month get a full month's depreciation, while those disposed of on or before the 15th receive no depreciation for the month.

To illustrate, if CDL Company has a December 31 year-end, purchased its delivery truck in April 1997, and expects to dispose of it five years later in April 2002, straight-line depreciation for each fiscal year of use would be:[5]

Year Ended	Number of Months Used	Depreciation Expense*			
12/31/97	9	9/12	× $4,000	=	$ 3,000
12/31/98	12	12/12	× 4,000	=	4,000
12/31/99	12	12/12	× 4,000	=	4,000
12/31/00	12	12/12	× 4,000	=	4,000
12/31/01	12	12/12	× 4,000	=	4,000
12/31/02	3	3/12	× 4,000	=	1,000
			Total		$20,000

*Full year of depreciation = ($22,000 − $2,000)/5 = $4,000

Selection of Depreciation Method   Each depreciation method discussed is acceptable for financial statement reporting purposes. Companies should select the one that, in their view, most closely matches benefits received with expenses recognized in all periods. However, when choosing which method of depreciation to use for tax reporting purposes, other issues come into play.

Depreciation for Tax Purposes   It is important to begin a discussion of tax depreciation with an understanding of these points:

- A primary objective of financial statement reporting is to properly measure and communicate income earned during a given time period. The major objective of taxing authorities is to collect necessary taxes in a manner designed to promote certain desirable social, political, or economic consequences. The goal of company managers and accountants is to legally minimize the company's tax liability.

- There is no requirement that the amount of depreciation expense reported to shareholders in a company's annual financial report equal the amount of depreciation deducted on that company's annual tax returns. In fact, because the tax statutes passed by legislatures of some states have established depreciation

---

[5]Although not illustrated in the text, declining-balance depreciation can also be calculated based on the number of months an asset is actually used during a fiscal year.

rules that are different from those required by the federal government, some companies use one method of depreciation for their annual report to shareholders, another for a required state tax return, and still another for the return filed each year with the Internal Revenue Service.

How Businesses Benefit from Tax Depreciation   As we already know, depreciation expense is different from most other expenses. Wages, electricity, advertising, and most other expenses usually require cash payments. However, depreciation expense does not.

As explained in Chapter 16, although a business makes no cash payment when recording depreciation, this expense still reduces taxable income and thus serves as a "tax shield" that reduces income taxes paid by the business. *Therefore, instead of requiring a current cash outflow, depreciation generally puts money back in the hands of the company.*

If the federal government desires to stimulate the economy, one effective approach it uses is to give companies more generous tax depreciation deductions. For example, in the early 1980s, when the United States was in a recession, Congress, at the urging of President Reagan, enacted laws establishing the accelerated cost recovery system (ACRS). These laws included the following changes, all designed to increase the amount of depreciation allowable:

- The period of time over which tax laws allowed assets to be depreciated was reduced, thus accelerating the rate of depreciation allowed.

- For all assets, companies generally were instructed to use a salvage value equal to zero, thus increasing the total amount of depreciation expense allowed over the life of an asset.

- Companies were allowed to deduct a full year of depreciation expense for any newly acquired plant asset, regardless of the timing of asset acquisition and placement in service.

Our current tax depreciation system is referred to as the **modified accelerated cost recovery system (MACRS).** It is much less stimulative in nature than its predecessor, ACRS because it lengthens the depreciable lives for many assets and is more restrictive regarding the use of accelerated depreciation.

The MACRS classifies assets according to the period of time over which the Internal Revenue Code requires those assets to be depreciated. For example, the IRS considers automobiles, trucks, computers, and typewriters to be five-year property, which companies must generally depreciate over five years. The normal depreciation period allowed for office desks and files is 7 years, and for residential buildings the period is 27.5 years. All assets other than real property (real estate) are depreciated using the midyear convention discussed earlier in the chapter, and real property requires the use of a midmonth convention whereby the asset is assumed to be placed in service halfway through the first month of its use. For example, if a company places a building in service on any day in February of 1997, there will be 10.5 months of depreciation included on the company's 1997 tax return.

Exhibit 20.2 shows the method of depreciation allowed for selected categories of assets. The truck purchased by CDL Company is five-year property, so it can be depreciated using 200 percent declining-balance depreciation.

Using the prescribed method of depreciation, companies can determine annual depreciation expense by using the methods described in this chapter, or they can use IRS tables designed to simplify the calculations, such as those shown in Exhibit 20.3. Although this exhibit only shows tables for three-, five-, and seven-year property,

EXHIBIT	20.2	Method of Depreciation Allowable under MACRS

Type of Property	Depreciation Method Allowable*
3-, 5-, 7-, and 10-year	200% declining balance
15- and 20-year	150% declining balance
Residential and nonresidential real estate	Straight-line depreciation (accelerated depreciation not allowed)

*Depreciation method shown represents the most accelerated form allowed. Straight-line depreciation and units-of-production depreciation are also allowed for the categories shown.

EXHIBIT	20.3	Tax Depreciation Tables for Three-, Five-, and Seven-Year Property*

Year	Three-Year Property	Five-Year Property	Seven-Year Property
1	33.33%	20.00%	14.29%
2	44.45	32.00	24.49
3	14.81	19.20	17.49
4	7.41	11.52	12.49
5		11.52	8.93
6		5.76	8.92
7			8.93
8			4.46

*Table based on 200 percent declining-balance depreciation, using the midyear convention and switching to straight-line depreciation during the last half of asset life. Depreciation for each year is calculated by multiplying appropriate percentage by the original cost of the asset.

similar tables exist for all types of property shown in Exhibit 20.2. Companies use these tables to calculate annual depreciation expense by multiplying the original cost of an asset by the appropriate percentage shown for each year.

Exhibit 20.4 illustrates the calculation of depreciation expense for the delivery truck purchased by CDL Company. The left-hand side of this table shows the calculation of 200 percent declining-balance depreciation using the standard technique described in this chapter. Note that only one-half year of depreciation is allowed in the first year because of the midyear convention, and that the company switches to straight-line depreciation in the last half of the asset's life.[6] The right side of the table shows calculation of the same annual depreciation expense by multiplying the original cost of the truck ($22,000) by the IRS provided percentages shown in Exhibit 20.3. These calculations yield amounts identical to the standard calculations, but this table is much easier to use.

Other Issues Relative to the Use of Plant Assets

Revision of Estimates   The original useful life and salvage value assigned to any plant asset for financial reporting purposes are simply estimates. Due to the principle of materiality, companies do not worry if these projections are marginally inaccurate, as is normally the case. But what happens if a company originally assigns a useful life of seven years to a computer and, one year after the date of purchase, realizes that it will have to replace the computer after a total of three years? When it becomes clear that there were significant mistakes of judgment in estimating the useful life and/or salvage value of any asset, companies usually do the following: *Depreciate the remaining undepreciated cost of the asset over the asset's revised remaining useful life using the appropriate depreciation method and, when deemed necessary, a revised salvage value.*

---

[6]The MACRS provides for a switch to straight-line depreciation when that method results in a larger expense than accelerated depreciation. When making the switch, the company calculates depreciation for each remaining year by dividing the remaining undepreciated cost of the asset by its remaining useful life.

To illustrate, assume that on January 1, 1997, a company purchases and begins to use office equipment costing $12,000, with an expected useful life of 10 years and a salvage value of $2,000. Assuming the business uses the straight-line method of depreciation for the asset, accumulated depreciation at December 31, 1999, would be $3,000 [($12,000 – $2,000)/10 × 3 years]. The remaining undepreciated cost of the asset at that time would be $9,000 ($12,000 – $3,000). If, during the following year, the company realizes that the equipment will last only four more years, after which its estimated salvage value will be $3,000, then depreciation expense for each of the remaining four years of the asset's useful life would be:

$$\frac{\text{Remaining undepreciated cost of asset} - \text{Revised salvage value}}{\text{Remaining useful life}} = \frac{\text{Depreciation}}{\text{expense}}$$

$$\frac{\$9,000 - \$3,000}{4 \text{ years}} = \$1,500 \text{ year}$$

This change in depreciation is prospective. That means it will only affect the current and future year financial statements.

Continued Use of Fully Depreciated Asset   The fact that an asset is fully depreciated does not mean that a company must stop using it. However, since total costs associated with the use of any asset cannot exceed the total cost of the asset (reduced by its salvage value), the company must stop recording annual depreciation expense.

PAUSE & REFLECT	How do fully depreciated assets appear on the balance sheet? Should companies report them or not? Why?

Extraordinary Repairs and Betterments   After placing a plant asset in service, businesses record expenditures to maintain the asset in normal operating condition as expenses in the period incurred. However, some expenditures relating to the continued use of the asset may be capital in nature. These are classified as either extraordinary repairs or betterments. **Extraordinary repairs** are capital expenditures which extend the remaining useful life of an operational asset and **betterments** represent capital expenditures to improve the asset's performance capabilities.

When making such capital expenditures for a plant asset already in use, the company would add the amount of the expenditure to the depreciable cost of the asset and then depreciate it over the asset's remaining useful life. For example, $30,000 spent to add a new room onto an existing building with a remaining useful life of

15 years will increase straight-line depreciation expense by $2,000 ($30,000/15 years) per year for each of the last 15 years of the building's life, assuming the improvement does not change the building's expected salvage value.

We have discussed the acquisition and use of operational investments. Now we look at their disposal.

DISPOSAL OF PLANT ASSETS

Eventually, it is necessary to dispose of depreciable assets, either because they have worn out or because management has determined that disposal is an economically desirable course of action. The asset may be discarded, sold, or exchanged for other assets. Whatever the method, the entries made to record disposals must generally accomplish the following:

- Record partial-year depreciation expense up to the date of disposal.
- Remove both the cost of the asset and its related accumulated depreciation from the accounting records.
- Record any gain or loss, calculated as the difference between the carrying value of the disposed asset and the fair market value of any assets received in return.

Discard Plant Assets

Sometimes an asset with little or no value will be disposed of, with nothing at all received in return. When this happens, it is necessary to record a loss equal to the carrying value of the asset at the date of disposal. For example, discarding equipment that cost $5,000, with $4,200 of accumulated depreciation at the date of disposal, results in a loss of $800 (its carrying value), recorded as follows:

Loss on Disposal of Equipment	800	
Accumulated Depreciation—Equipment	4,200	
Equipment		5,000

Any amount paid to discard the asset would be added to the amount of the recorded loss.

Sell Plant Assets

Plant assets may be sold for an amount equal to, less than, or greater than their carrying value. Terms of sale might require a cash payment of the selling price or an agreement in the form of a promissory note obligating the purchaser to make specified future cash payments. We discussed the recording of losses and gains on disposals of assets in Chapters 8 and 9. To review and summarize the accounting for various possibilities, assume that a company sells the following piece of equipment:

Cost of asset	$8,000
Accumulated depreciation through date of sale	(6,000)
Carrying value at date of sale	$2,000

The following accounting entries illustrate the three different possibilities:

Sales Price Equal to Carrying Value

Cash (Assumed Sales Price)	2,000	
Accumulated Depreciation—Equipment	6,000	
Equipment		8,000

Sales Price Greater Than Carrying Value

Cash (Assumed Sales Price)	2,700	
Accumulated Depreciation—Equipment	6,000	
Equipment		8,000
Gain on Sale of Equipment		700

Sales Price Less Than Carrying Value

Cash (Assumed Sales Price)	1,600	
Loss on Sale of Equipment	400	
Accumulated Depreciation—Equipment	6,000	
Equipment		8,000

Each of the above entries assumed the receipt of cash at the date of sale. In those cases where the buyer signs a promissory note at the date of sale, the selling company would debit Notes Receivable instead of Cash.

Exchange Plant Assets

Companies occasionally exchange plant assets for other noncash assets. Sometimes these exchanges involve partial cash payments; other times they do not. For example, a business might trade in an old automobile as part of the purchase price of a new vehicle, making a cash payment for the remaining amount owed. Or a business might make an even trade of two different pieces of equipment or two different parcels of land, with no cash changing hands.

The exchanged assets can be dissimilar or similar in nature. An exchange of a building in return for a stock investment held by another company represents an exchange of dissimilar assets. We define similar productive assets as those *"that are of the same general type, that perform the same function or that are employed in the same line of business."*[7] A trade-in of an old automobile as part of the purchase price of a new one involves the exchange of similar assets.

Exchanges of Dissimilar Assets   When a business disposes of a plant asset via an exchange of dissimilar assets, it calculates and records a gain or loss on the transaction as the difference between the carrying value of the asset given up and whichever of the following two values it can determine more objectively:

- Fair market value of the asset received in the exchange.

- Fair market value of the asset given up in the exchange.

Whichever value the company uses to calculate the gain or loss becomes the recorded "cost" of the newly acquired asset.

To illustrate, assume the Union Pacific Corporation exchanges the following building for 10,000 shares of stock held by another company as an investment.

Cost of building	$100,000
Accumulated depreciation at date of exchange	(75,000)
Carrying value at date of exchange	$ 25,000

Assume further that the fair market value of the building on the date of the exchange is difficult to determine, but that the stock received is selling for $4 per share. The entry to record the transaction is:

Investment in Stock (10,000 × $4)	40,000	
Accumulated Depreciation—Building	75,000	
Building		100,000
Gain on Exchange		15,000

The entry to record any exchange of dissimilar assets follows essentially the same rules governing the sale of an asset for cash. Accountants view the exchange of one asset for a fundamentally different type of asset, whether it be cash or a noncash asset, as the completion of an earnings process requiring the recognition of gain or loss.

Exchanges of Similar Assets   The accounting treatment applicable to exchanges of similar assets represents an exception to the general rule requiring recognition of gains and losses. The exception stems from the fact that accounting authorities do not view the exchange of similar assets as the culmination of an earnings process. If two stores, for example, exchange items from their inventory to enable one of the stores to sell a particular product to a customer, the earnings process is complete only upon final sale to the customer, not when the stores exchange the merchandise.

---

[7]The discussion of the accounting for exchanges of similar and dissimilar assets is based on principles enunciated in *Accounting Principles Board Opinion No. 29*, paragraph 3.

Likewise, if the Boston Celtics and the Los Angeles Lakers exchange player contracts, neither has "earned" anything as either of the teams would have if it sold a player's contract to another franchise for a fixed sum of money.

Because we do not view exchanges of similar assets as completed earnings processes, accountants rely on the principle of conservatism when they record these events. Thus, accountants do not record any gain determined by comparison of the fair market value and carrying value of the asset given up, yet they do record any loss on the exchange.

To illustrate, assume that company A, which is headquartered in Oregon, plans to close down a factory building it owns in Michigan and move this operation to California. The 10-year-old building has a carrying value of $100,000 (original cost of $500,000 less accumulated depreciation of $400,000) and has a current market value of $800,000. Company B owns a one-year-old building just outside of San Francisco with a carrying value of $950,000 (cost of $1,000,000 less accumulated depreciation of $50,000). This building has a current market value of $800,000. Companies A and B swap buildings.

Company B has a $150,000 loss calculated as the difference between the fair market value of the company's building ($800,000) and its carrying value on the date of the exchange ($950,000). Company B makes the following entry to record this loss:

Loss on Exchange	150,000	
Building (Acquired in Exchange)	800,000	
Accumulated Depreciation—Building (Given up in Exchange)	50,000	
Building (Given up in Exchange)		1,000,000

On the other hand, the same transaction results in a gain of $700,000 for company A, calculated as the difference between the $800,000 fair market value of its building and its $100,000 carrying value, which it does *not* record. Instead, it removes the carrying value of the old building from its books and *assigns this same carrying value, not the fair market value,* to the cost of the new building acquired in the exchange. The entry is:

Building (Acquired in Exchange)	100,000	
Accumulated Depreciation—Building (Given up in Exchange)	400,000	
Building (Given up in Exchange)		500,000

The fact that this new building has the same carrying value that the old building had on company A's books ensures that company A will eventually recognize the implied gain from the disposal of the old building, plus or minus any additional gain or loss from changes in the value of the new building, when and if the company sells the new building for cash.[8] That is, if company A turned around and immediately sold this newly acquired building for its current value of $800,000, the earnings process would finally be complete, and the company would recognize the full $700,000 gain that would have been recorded if its original building had been sold for cash rather than exchanged for the new building.

PAUSE & REFLECT

In the previous example, company A did not record the implied gain of $700,000. Accountants often say that this unrecorded gain will be recognized through use of the asset. Does this make sense? How much depreciation will company A record over the life of the newly acquired building? Would this amount have been different if the company recognized the $700,000 gain at the date of the exchange and added the recognized gain to the recorded value of the new asset?

[8]When similar assets are exchanged, it is rare that both assets have exactly equal values. When the values of exchanged assets are different, some cash also will probably change hands at the date of the exchange. If cash (or a promissory note) is received as part of an exchange of similar assets, the company receiving the cash must immediately record the portion of any gain attributable to this cash receipt. A description of the calculation of this recognized gain is beyond the scope of this text.

Trade-Ins   A trade-in of an old asset as part of the purchase price of a new, similar asset is by far the most commonly encountered example of an exchange involving similar assets. Cars and trucks are often traded in partial payment for a new vehicle, as are computers and many other categories of equipment. Most trade-ins involve giving up an old, used asset plus an additional amount of cash in exchange for the new asset.

Gain or loss on disposal of the old asset (the one traded in) is measured as the difference between the carrying value of the old asset and the trade-in allowance assigned to it in the exchange transaction. As with any other exchange involving similar assets, losses are recognized, but not gains.

When assigning a value to the new asset acquired as a result of the trade-in transaction, the new asset's carrying value is increased by the amount of any cash given up.

Illustration of Accounting for Trade-Ins   To illustrate the accounting for trade-ins, assume a company approaches a computer dealer offering to trade-in an old computer system as part of the purchase price of a new one. The old computer system cost $25,000 and at the trade-in date has $15,000 of accumulated depreciation, yielding a carrying value of $10,000.

Loss on Exchange   If the negotiated price for the new computer system is $28,000, and the dealer grants a trade-in allowance of $8,000 on the old computer system, the company will recognize a $2,000 loss on the trade-in of the old computer system, and it will have to make an additional $20,000 payment to acquire the new computer system. The $2,000 loss results from the difference between the trade-in allowance and the carrying value of the old computer system ($8,000 – $10,000). The cash payment is calculated as the difference between the purchase price of the new computer system and the trade-in allowance on the old one ($28,000 – $8,000). The transaction is recorded as follows:

Computer System (New)	28,000	
Loss on Exchange	2,000	
Accumulated Depreciation—Computer System (Old)	15,000	
Computer System (Old)		25,000
Cash		20,000

Gain on Exchange   Recall that gains on the exchange of similar assets are not recognized. If the negotiated price of the new computer system is $28,000, but the dealer grants a trade-in allowance of $12,000 on the old computer system, the company will have a $2,000 gain on the trade-in, which it will not record. This gain results from the difference between the $12,000 trade-in allowance and the $10,000 carrying value of the old computer system. The company will have to pay $16,000 in cash, calculated as the difference between the purchase price of the new computer system and the trade-in allowance ($28,000 – $12,000).

The new computer system will be assigned a cost of $26,000. This amount can be calculated in either of two ways: (1) reduce the $28,000 purchase price of the new computer system by the $2,000 of unrecognized gain, or (2) add the $10,000 carrying value of the old computer system to the $16,000 cash given in the exchange. The $2,000 reduction in the value assigned to the new computer system is necessary to offset the $2,000 of unrecognized gain.

The resulting entry is:

Computer System (New)	26,000	
Accumulated Depreciation—Computer System (Old)	15,000	
Computer System (Old)		25,000
Cash		16,000

Tax Issues Relative to Exchanges   When businesses exchange dissimilar assets, they include all resulting gains and losses when calculating the amount of income reported to the Internal Revenue Service. However, when companies exchange similar productive assets, they *do not include the gain or loss* resulting from the exchange on their tax returns. These procedures represent one of the primary reasons why

companies, when they want to dispose of assets that have appreciated in value, sometimes consider an exchange for a similar asset the company needs, rather than a cash sale of the asset.

To illustrate the potential tax benefit from an exchange of similar assets, assume that company A in the foregoing illustration sold its building in Michigan for $800,000. Assuming the carrying value of the building for financial accounting and tax purposes was the same, the company would have had a taxable gain of $700,000 (selling price of $800,000 less the asset's $100,000 carrying value). Assuming a tax rate of 30 percent, the company would have paid $210,000 in taxes as a result of this gain, leaving it with $590,000 cash (selling price of $800,000 less taxes of $210,000), not enough to purchase the $800,000 building in California. The exchange of assets enabled company A to accomplish two things: (1) defer the payment of $210,000 of taxes and (2) obtain the California building that the company needed for its operations.

NATURAL RESOURCES

Natural resources are nonrenewable assets such as coal mines and oil rights. A company's investment in natural resources is determined according to the same general rules established for assigning costs to plant assets; typically the cost includes the purchase price of the asset and related legal fees, as well as items such as surveying and various development costs.

As with plant assets, the benefits associated with natural resources dissipate with use. Once coal or oil reserves are exhausted, they cannot be renewed. Therefore, the cost of these assets also must be allocated as an expense over the periods they benefit. This process is called **depletion,** and, because benefits from natural resources usually correlate with usage rather than the passage of time, it is generally calculated using the units-of-production method.

To illustrate, assume that a company paid $1,400,000 for a mine estimated to contain 2,000,000 tons of ore. The residual value of the land after extraction of all the ore is estimated at $100,000. The depletion charge per ton of extracted ore is:

$$\frac{\$1,400,000 - \$100,000}{2,000,000 \text{ tons}} = \$.65/\text{ton}$$

If this company mines 300,000 tons of ore during a given accounting period, total depletion will be $195,000 ($.65 × 300,000 tons), recorded as follows:

Depletion—Mine	195,000	
Accumulated Depletion—Mine		195,000

The company does not expense the recorded depletion immediately. Instead, it adds the amount of depletion to the cost of the company's inventory of extracted ore. Therefore, as long as the ore remains on hand, the depletion is a cost of the inventory reported on the balance sheet. When the company sells the ore, the depletion, along with all other costs of the ore, becomes part of cost of goods sold reported as an expense on the company's income statement.

PAUSE & REFLECT

When depreciation was recorded earlier in the chapter, it resulted in an expense on the income statement. The amount of depletion on the mine in the preceding example was added to the cost of inventory. Why was one expensed while the other became part of the cost of an asset? Can you think of any situations where depreciation would be added to the cost of inventory rather than being immediately expensed?

INTANGIBLE ASSETS

As introduced in Chapter 2, intangible assets, unlike plant assets and natural resources, have no tangible or visible physical presence. However, they convey to their owner a legal right or benefit that is often vital to successful operations. Therefore, intangible assets usually represent some of the most important and valuable assets owned by a company. Let's look at some examples.

Patents

A **patent** is an intangible asset giving its owner the exclusive legal right to the commercial benefits of a specified product or process. For instance, the manufacturer of the pain reliever Tylenol introduced a new Extended Relief Tylenol for which it obtained a patent to ensure the exclusive right to produce and sell this product.

In the United States, the U.S. Patent Office issues patents that last for a period of 17 years. However, even though they exist for 17 years, the economically useful life of patents may be much shorter if technological developments render the patented product or process obsolete.

The determination of a patent's cost raises an interesting question. Virtually all accountants agree that the normal and necessary expenditures made to buy an existing patent from another entity, as well as legal costs directly incurred to obtain a patent, should be added to the cost of the patent. But what about costs involved when a company spends money on research and development (R&D) to create a process or product that it hopes will lead to a patent?

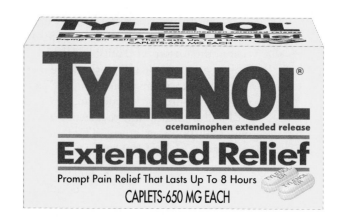

One could argue that all R&D costs, whether successful or not, should be accumulated and added to the cost of any patents obtained as a result. Since patents, like any asset, do not generate expenses until the periods when they are used, this approach would postpone the expensing of R&D costs. Such expense postponement would tend to increase a company's current reported income. On the other hand, since it is questionable whether money spent on R&D will ever provide any future benefits, one could argue that these expenditures should be expensed immediately as incurred. This more conservative approach would yield more current expenses and, therefore, less current income.

Generally accepted accounting principles, taking the more conservative view, require that companies expense most research and development costs in the period incurred.[9] As a result, companies that develop their own products often own extremely valuable patents that they do not report or report at very low costs on their balance sheets.

Copyrights

A **copyright** is an intangible asset which gives its owner an exclusive legal right for the reproduction and sale of a literary or artistic work. Copyrights last for the life of the creator plus 50 years. However, their economically useful life is almost always substantially less and, therefore, not significant for financial statement users.

Because the fee to initially establish a copyright is minimal, businesses usually write this cost off as an expense. However, when a company purchases a copyright from the original owner, the expenditure is often substantial, therefore, the company must capitalize the cost as an intangible asset. For example, the Academy Award winning movie, *Forest Gump*, is a copyright owned by Paramont Pictures.

Franchises

A **franchise** is an intangible asset representing the exclusive right to operate or sell a brand name product in a specified territory. A franchise is granted by one entity, called the franchisor, to another party, called the franchisee. Burger King and McDonald's are examples. If the franchisee pays an up-front fee for this right, it has an intangible asset to report on the balance sheet.

PAUSE & REFLECT

How much would you be willing to pay for a franchise giving you the exclusive right to provide cable TV service in your home town? How much do you think it would be worth to be the only individual able to open a Burger King where you live?

---

[9]*SFAS No. 2*, issued in October 1974, established this requirement.

Leaseholds and Leasehold Improvements

A **leasehold,** is an intangible asset conveyed by a lease to use equipment, land, and/or buildings for a specified period of time. Periodic payments made on operating leases are generally expensed when paid.[10]

Some leases require a down payment at the inception of the lease. For example, a car lease might require payments of $399 per month, plus an initial $2,000 down payment. If the amount of the down payment is material, companies will capitalize it by debiting an intangible asset account called Leasehold. This asset has a useful life equal to the term of the lease.

Additionally, the amount paid to a lessee to purchase the rights to a lease creates an intangible asset, also referred to as a *leasehold*, with a useful life that equals the remaining life of the lease. To illustrate, assume that Bob Smith has a lease to rent 3,000 square feet of prime space in a mall at an attractive rate for the next five years. Bob has been in business for years and now wants to retire. A company that operates fast food restaurants immediately approaches Bob and offers to purchase the rights to this lease for $10,000 because there is no other space available in the mall. If Bob sells the lease, the restaurant company will record a $10,000 leasehold with a useful life of five years.

Any amounts paid by a lessee to make physical improvements constituting an integral part of leased property are recorded as an intangible asset referred to as a **leasehold improvement.** Accountants consider this asset to be intangible because, although the improvement represents tangible property, the lessee possesses only the legal right to *use* the improvement during the remaining life of the lease.

Goodwill

Goodwill is an intangible asset representing the value assigned to a purchased company's ability to generate an above average return on invested capital. This may result from a combination of many factors, including efficient management, good labor relations, superior product quality, and brand name recognition. Companies record goodwill only if they pay an identifiable amount of money to acquire it. Thus, businesses generally record goodwill only when they pay for it as part of the purchase price to acquire another company. The amount of goodwill recorded in connection with the purchase of another company is the difference between the total price paid to purchase the company and the value of the purchased company's underlying net assets (all identifiable assets minus liabilities).

To illustrate, assume the Progressive Grocery Corporation wants to purchase the Healthy-Deli Company, a small delicatessen supply firm, and is willing to pay $250,000. The Healthy-Deli has net identifiable assets (excluding goodwill) with an appraised value of $210,000. If the offer is accepted, Progressive will record $40,000 of goodwill on its books, calculated as:

Total purchase price	$250,000
Less: Appraised value of Healthy-Deli's net identifiable assets	210,000
Amount of goodwill	$ 40,000

Users of financial statements should understand that unless a company purchases another company, goodwill is not recorded. Therefore, internally generated goodwill is a valuable asset that goes unreported on balance sheets.

PAUSE & REFLECT

Goodwill is often "purchased" as part of the price paid to acquire another business. What attributes must goodwill possess before it can be sold? Hint: If a doctor wants to sell a medical practice and retire, can the doctor sell the goodwill associated with his/her name? Why or why not?

---

[10]As discussed in Chapter 18, there are two types of leases—operating leases and capital leases. The majority are operating leases whose required periodic payments are expensed when made.

Use of Intangible Assets

As they do for plant assets and natural resources, companies must expense the cost of intangible assets over the periods they benefit. This process, called **amortization,** is calculated as follows:[11]

1. Use the straight-line method.[12]

2. Amortize the full cost of the asset without reduction for any salvage value, because intangibles generally have no significant economic value once their useful life is complete.

3. Utilize a useful life that does not exceed 40 years. Accountants base this number on the assumption that it is impossible to predict economic usefulness past a certain point in the future. Thus, even though a copyright has a legal life in excess of 40 years, its useful life for calculating amortization is the lesser of: (*a*) the period of time its owner expects it to yield economic benefits, or (*b*) 40 years.

To illustrate, assume Purinton Corporation paid $3,000,000 for a patent on a device that reduces acid rain pollutants produced during certain manufacturing operations. Although 15 years of the patent's legal life remain, the company believes that new technology will render the patent obsolete after 10 years. Amortization expense for the year is $300,000 ($3,000,000/10 years), recorded as:

Amortization Expense—Patent	300,000	
Patent		300,000

Note that, unlike depreciation and depletion, there is no accumulated amortization account. Instead, companies typically deduct the amount of amortization directly from the Patent, or other intangible asset, account.

We have now seen how to account for operational investments. In the final portion of the chapter, we turn our attention to reporting issues related to these types of investments.

REPORTING OPERATIONAL INVESTMENTS

Operational investment activities result in assets, expenses, and cash flows. These activities are communicated to both internal and external stakeholders.

Internal Reporting

Every company operates differently and, therefore, has its own unique system of accounting for plant assets. However, with regard to the recording and communicating of operational investments, every good system of internal control must provide adequate documents and records. For each plant asset, managers want to know the original cost, any additional capital expenditures made, and accumulated depreciation taken to date for both financial statement and tax return purposes.

Therefore, in addition to the general ledger which keeps track of the *total* for each category of plant assets, companies maintain a detailed subsidiary ledger that includes a separate record for each individual asset. In the absence of such a subsidiary ledger, companies might continue to depreciate fully depreciated assets and would not know the amount of gain or loss to record on the disposal of any specific asset.

To help safeguard their plant assets, some companies even place a unique identification number on each individual asset. This helps companies perform periodic checks to verify the physical location and proper utilization of plant assets. Also,

---

[11]*APB Opinion No. 17*, issued in August 1970, spells out the rules for amortization of intangible assets.

[12]Although generally used, the straight-line method is not required. For some intangibles, such as copyrights, the units-of-production method is also common.

periodic comparison of these ID numbers with assets actually on hand helps keep records accurate and also deters theft.

Companies must also maintain similar records for all natural resources and intangible assets.

External Reporting

When analyzing a company's financial statements, one of the first things external stakeholders should determine is the method of depreciation used. In accordance with requirements for full disclosure of all relevant data, companies usually give this information (as well as related information regarding any material amount of depletion of natural resources and amortization of intangible assets) in one of the first notes attached to the financial statements.

A note in the 1993 annual report of Union Pacific, entitled "Significant Accounting Policies," included the following excerpts:

Property and Depreciation

Properties are carried at cost. Provisions for depreciation are computed principally on the straight-line method based on estimated service lives of depreciable property.

Exploration and Production

Depletion and amortization of producing properties, including depreciation of well and support equipment and amortization of related lease costs, are determined by using a unit-of-production method.

Intangible Assets

Amortization is generally recorded over 40 years on a straight-line basis.

The method of depreciation, useful lives, and salvage values selected can have a significant impact on the amount of operating income for the year. All else equal, straight-line depreciation results in a higher reported income, and accelerated depreciation in a lower income. A change to longer useful lives and higher salvage values reduces depreciation expense, while shorter lives and lower salvage values increase it.

For instance, in a note included in its 1995 annual report, Royal Caribbean Cruises, Ltd., one of the world's largest cruise lines, disclosed:

Property and Equipment

Depreciation of property and equipment . . . is computed using the straight-line method over useful lives of primarily 30 years for vessels and three to ten years for other property and equipment. The Company revised its depreciation policy to recognize extended estimated service lives from 25 to 30 years and higher residual values on certain of its vessels effective January 1, 1994. The change in vessel depreciation reduced depreciation expense and increased net income by approximately $10.0 million, or $0.16 per share, during 1994.

When comparing reported income of two competitor companies, one should remember that the utilization of different depreciation methods distorts the comparison process. When comparing two consecutive income statements for the same company, look for disclosure of any changes in depreciation policy that will affect the amount of income reported from one year to the next. Unless otherwise stated in the notes, the consistency principle requires the use of the same method and policies from one year to the next.

Financial statement users also need to remember that the MACRS generally allows companies to deduct an amount of depreciation expense on their tax returns that exceeds the amount deducted in their annual reports to shareholders. Because depreciation expense reduces taxes, companies benefit from this excess tax depreciation. However, recall that total depreciation taken over the life of an asset is the same regardless of the method used. As a result, the excess tax depreciation initially allowed under the MACRS is eventually offset by lower depreciation taken toward the end of an asset's life and, therefore, the MACRS only serves to postpone taxes that companies will have to pay later on. Companies report this "deferred tax" as a liability on their balance sheets.[13] At December 31, 1993, the long-term liability section of Union Pacific's balance sheet included the following:

| | Millions of Dollars | |
	1993	1992
Deferred income taxes	$2,676	$2,376

According to note number 7 in Union Pacific's annual report, $2.459 billion of the 1993 deferred tax liability (92 percent of the total) resulted from "excess tax over book depreciation."

Balance Sheet: Reporting Operational Investments

The December 31, 1993, balance sheet of Union Pacific (with 1992 figures included for comparative purposes) reported operational investments under two headings:

| | Millions of Dollars | |
	1993	1992
Properties:		
Cost	$17,860	$16,385
Accumulated depreciation, and amortization	(6,419)	(5,785)
Net	11,441	10,600
Other:		
Intangibles and other assets—net	1,553	1,513

The category entitled Properties included a reference to note 6, which showed the following additional detail:

6. Properties

Major property accounts are as follows:

Millions of Dollars	1993	1992
Railroad:		
Road and others	$ 7,935	$ 7,282
Equipment	4,575	4,328
Total Railroad	12,510	11,610
Natural resources	4,144	3,785
Trucking	621	555
Waste management	464	350
Other	121	85
Total	$17,860	$16,385

---

[13]Depreciation is one of several factors contributing to the postponement of taxes. The subject of deferred taxes is discussed in more detail in Chapter 23.

Accumulated depreciation, depletion and amortization are as follows:

Millions of Dollars	1993	1992
Railroad:		
Road and others	$ 1,990	$ 1,693
Equipment	1,769	1,730
Total Railroad	3,759	3,423
Natural resources	2,364	2,124
Trucking	165	138
Waste management	101	82
Other	30	18
Total	$ 6,419	$ 5,785

Note that companies often use the terms *depreciation* and *amortization* interchangeably. This practice is common and should not be misunderstood by informed users.

Income Statement: Gains and Losses from Operational Investments

We already know that companies report gains and losses as "nonoperating" items on the income statement. If any individual gain or loss is material, the income statement may show it as a separate line item. However, income statements usually lump all gains and losses together with various other categories of nonoperating income and include them as one line item. The comparative income statement in Union Pacific's 1993 annual report, on a line immediately following the calculation of Operating Income, showed:

	Millions of Dollars		
	1993	1992	1991
Other Income—Net (note 13)	$ 89	$146	$122

Reference to note 13 revealed:

13. Other Income—Net

Other Income—Net includes the following:

Millions of Dollars	1993	1992	1991
Rental income	$33	$ 38	$ 45
Net gain on property dispositions	18	36	51
Interest on tax settlements	—	55	15
Interest and other—Net	38	17	11
Total	$89	$146	$122

The $18 million net gain on property dispositions reported in 1993 represented 3.4 percent of Union Pacific's total of $530 million reported net income for 1993.

Statement of Cash Flows: Acquisition and Disposal of Operational Investments

The Investing Activities section of the statement of cash flows reports the amount of cash used and provided by the acquisition and disposal of operational investments. Investing activities often represent a significant portion of a company's total cash flows. For instance, the statement of cash flows in Union Pacific's 1993 annual report showed:

	Millions of Dollars		
	1993	1992	1991
Capital investments and exploratory expenditures	$(1,574)	$(1,567)	$(1,231)
Investments and acquisitions	(75)	(71)	—
Proceeds from sale of assets and other investing activities	96	291	94
Cash used for investing activities	(1,553)	(1,347)	(1,137)

The dollar amounts shown for capital investments and exploratory expenditures represented the largest single item on Union Pacific's statement of cash flows for each of the three years shown.

Errors in Reporting

Whether a company reports an expenditure as a capital or a revenue expenditure is an important and sometimes controversial decision. Publicly owned corporations, which are required to issue annual reports to shareholders, are mindful of the stock market's reaction to published earnings reports. Because of the potential market reaction, companies may have a predisposition to improperly capitalize expenditures as a means of postponing expenses and thereby increasing reported profits. On the other hand, privately held businesses owned by a small group of closely related individuals frequently do not have to make their earnings a matter of public record. When earnings are confidential, a business may prefer to treat all expenditures as current expenses in order to reduce the amount of taxable income reported to the Internal Revenue Service. This is especially true in the case of sole proprietorships and partnerships where the owners are personally responsible for payment of the taxes on the business's income.

PAUSE & REFLECT

Assume the CORE Company just spent $100,000 to put a new roof on its building. Is this a capital or revenue expenditure? What arguments exist for each point of view? Assuming straight-line depreciation is used, that the building has a remaining useful life of 10 years, and that the new roof will not change the salvage value of the building, by how much will current year income change if the expenditure is expensed rather than capitalized?

SUMMARY

Operational investments represent some of the most significant long-term uses of a company's capital. This chapter presented information about plant assets, natural resources, and intangible assets, and introduced some of the fundamental principles that determine how accountants record the acquisition, use, and disposal of these assets. Finally, we discussed and illustrated the manner in which companies report information regarding operational investments to stakeholders.

- Operational investments are capital expenditures made to acquire the facilities necessary for the conduct of basic business activities. They include investments in plant assets, natural resources, and intangible assets.

- Plant assets are investments in property, plant, and equipment used for business operations over a time span covering more than one accounting period.

- The cost of a plant asset includes all the normal, reasonable, and necessary expenditures to acquire the asset and make it ready for its intended use.

- Depreciation is the process of systematically allocating the net cost of a plant asset to the various periods benefiting from the use of that asset. For financial statement reporting, depreciation can be calculated using the (1) straight-line method, (2) units-of-production method, or (3) accelerated method.

- For federal tax purposes, depreciation is calculated using the modified accelerated cost recovery system (MACRS). When preparing tax returns, businesses benefit from depreciation deductions because they reduce taxes without requiring any current cash outlay.

- The gain or loss on the disposal of plant assets is the difference between the carrying value of the asset (Cost – Accumulated depreciation) and the fair market value of any assets received in return. When a business sells assets for cash or exchanges dissimilar noncash assets, it records and reports all resulting gains and losses. For financial reporting purposes, when there is an exchange of similar assets, companies record losses but not gains. For tax purposes, no gains or losses are reported upon the exchange of similar assets.

- Natural resources are a company's investment in nonrenewable assets such as coal mines and oil rights. The expense resulting from the cost of these assets is called *depletion*, and is usually calculated using the units-of-production method.

- Intangible assets have no physical presence that can be seen or touched. They convey a legal right or benefit to their owner. Examples include patents, copyrights, franchises, leaseholds, and goodwill. The cost of intangible assets is amortized, generally by the straight-line method, over the expected useful life of the assets or 40 years, whichever is shorter.

- Information regarding operational investments must be reported to internal and external stakeholders. Internal stakeholders require detailed information about individual assets. External stakeholders prefer summarized data about events pertaining to the acquisition, use, and disposal of operational investments. Companies report this information on their balance sheet, income statement, and statement of cash flows, and frequently include additional detail in attached notes.

KEY TERMS

accelerated depreciation A method of depreciation that recognizes relatively greater expense in early years of asset use and progressively less expense as time passes

amortization The process of allocating the cost of intangible assets to an expense over the periods they benefit

betterments Capital expenditures that improve an asset's performance capabilities

capital expenditure An expenditure that creates the expectation of future benefits that apply beyond the current accounting period

capitalize To add an expenditure to the cost of an asset, rather than expensing it immediately

copyright An intangible asset which gives its owner the exclusive legal right for the reproduction and sale of a literary or artistic work

declining-balance depreciation A type of accelerated depreciation which reflects depreciation expense for each year based on a constant percentage of a declining balance equal to the remaining undepreciated cost of the asset at the start of each year

depreciable cost The portion of a plant asset's total cost that will be depreciated over its useful life

depletion The process of allocating the cost of natural resources to an expense over the periods they benefit

double-declining-balance depreciation A specific type of declining-balance depreciation that reflects annual depreciation expense using a constant percentage equal to twice the straight-line rate of depreciation

extraordinary repairs Expenditures that extend the remaining useful life of an operational investment

franchise An intangible asset representing the exclusive right to operate or sell a brand name product in a specified territory

goodwill An intangible asset representing the value assigned to a purchased company's ability to generate an above average return on invested capital

leasehold An intangible asset conveyed by a lease to use equipment, land, and /or buildings for a specified period of time

leasehold improvement An intangible asset representing the amounts paid by a lessee to make physical improvements that are an integral part of leased property

MACRS (Modified accelerated cost recovery system) The system of laws that currently govern the calculation of depreciation for federal tax purposes

materiality An accounting concept which relates to whether an item's dollar amount or its inherent nature is significant enough to influence a financial statement user

midyear convention The convention which reflects depreciation expense for each asset as if it were purchased or disposed of exactly halfway through the company's fiscal year

natural resources Nonrenewable assets such as coal mines or oil rights

operational investments Long-term investments made to acquire the facilities necessary for the conduct of basic business activities

patent An intangible asset giving its owner the exclusive legal right to the commercial benefits of a specified product or process

plant assets Tangible assets acquired primarily for use in a business over a time span covering more than one accounting period

revenue expenditure An expenditure that provides benefits exclusively during the current accounting period

salvage value The expected fair market value of a plant asset at the end of its useful life. Also referred to as *residual value*

straight-line depreciation A method of calculating annual depreciation by allocating the depreciable cost of the asset to depreciation expense over its useful life

units-of-production depreciation A method of calculating annual depreciation based on actual usage rather than the passage of time

useful life The period of time over which a business expects to obtain economic benefits from the use of an operational investment

QUESTIONS

1. What three characteristics define a plant asset?

2. What factors do companies consider in determining the cost of plant assets?

3. Distinguish between *capital* and *revenue* expenditures and give an example of each.

4. Should the cost of paving a parking lot be treated as a capital expenditure or a revenue expenditure? Why?

5. Exec Temp's purchasing agent was presented with an offer he couldn't refuse and purchased 5,000 number 2 lead pencils for $500. The pencils will last the company at least five years. How should Exec Temp record this transaction and why?

6. What special problem exists when a company purchases several assets for one lump sum of money? How is it solved?

7. Is the following statement true or false? Depreciation is the opposite of appreciation and represents the asset's decline in value. Explain your answer.

8. What four factors affect the calculation of depreciation? Which factors are merely estimates involving individual judgment?

9. Why is land not depreciated? Are there any other plant assets whose costs are not allocated over their useful life?

10. What is meant by the term *depreciable cost* and how is it determined?

11. Identify the various methods of depreciation mentioned in the chapter. In your opinion, which method is the easiest to calculate? Which method do you think is most likely to be used by the majority of companies in preparing their financial statements? Why?

12. Explain how the choice of a depreciation method might affect financial statements of a company.

13. What is the *midyear convention* and why do companies use it?

14. Explain the term *MACRS*. When is it used, by whom, and for what purpose?

15. Identify the two factors involved in determining the amount of gain or loss on the sale of a plant asset.

16. Give an example of a dissimilar asset exchange as well as a similar asset exchange. Is a gain or loss always recorded for both types of transactions? Explain.

17. What are natural resources? Where do they appear on the financial statements? Are they depreciated?

18. Explain the term *intangible asset* and provide three examples. What is the maximum possible useful life for each of your examples? Where do intangible assets appear on the financial statements?

19. How do companies reflect plant assets on their financial statements? What specific disclosures are required?

20. Spartan Auto Parts purchased a delivery truck and immediately expensed the $23,500 cost. Do you agree with this treatment? Why or why not? What effect will this transaction have on the financial statements?

EXERCISES

E 20.1 For each of the situations described below, indicate whether it is a capital or revenue expenditure.
 a. Purchased land and a building at a cost of $550,000 by paying $110,000 down and signing a two-year note payable for the remainder.
 b. Spent $195 on a tune-up for a truck used in making deliveries.
 c. The owner of a restaurant paid a plumber $320 to install a new dishwasher in the kitchen.
 d. Paid $1,000 in sales tax on a new delivery van when registering the van at the Registry of Motor Vehicles.
 e. A new machine was damaged during installation. The uninsured cost to repair the machine was $750.

E 20.2 For each of the situations described below, what account would be debited to record the expenditure?
 a. Constructed a warehouse for storing merchandise.
 b. Purchased 300 reams of 8 1/2-by-11-inch paper for the fax machine.
 c. Purchased a parcel of land in a nearby town because of rumors that a new mall would be built on adjoining land. Management expects to sell the land in three years at a substantial profit.
 d. Bought 20 used desks and 30 used chairs to be utilized at corporate headquarters in the accounting office.
 e. Paid for a new battery installed in the delivery truck.

E 20.3 Professional Cleaning Systems (PCS) purchased a new van to expand its business. The invoice price of the van was $23,400, with additional costs of $350 for dealer prep and $275 in destination charges. PCS also had the dealer install special roof racks at a cost of $1,430 and paid $1,200 in sales tax, $85 in registration fees, and $50 for the title. The annual insurance bill totaled $1,960, and PCS opted for an extended warranty package costing $935. Within one month's time, PCS spent $230 for gasoline. Determine the dollar amount that PCS should debit to the Vehicles account.

E 20.4 Vicor Communications purchased land, a building, and several pieces of equipment for $2,400,000. An appraisal of the purchased items estimated the value of the land at $662,500, the building at $1,590,000, and the equipment at $397,500. Determine the portion of the total purchase price applicable to each asset.

E 20.5 Gibbs Electronics recently acquired a new machine at a cost of $54,000. The machine has an estimated useful life of eight years or 24,000 production hours, and salvage value is estimated at $6,000. During the first two years of the asset's life, 2,700 and 3,100 production hours, respectively, were logged by the machine. Calculate the depreciation charge for the first two years of the asset's life using the (*a*) straight-line method, (*b*) units-of-production method, and (*c*) double-declining-balance method.

E 20.6 Delano Industries purchased a copier with a cost of $37,000 and a salvage value estimated at $5,000. It was expected that the copier would last four years, over which time it would produce 6,400,000 copies. The copier actually produced 1,500,000 copies in year 1, 1,800,000 copies in year 2, 1,700,000 copies in year 3, and 1,400,000 copies in year 4. Calculate the depreciation expense and carrying value of the asset at year-end for each of the four years using the following methods: (*a*) straight-line method, (*b*) units-of-production method, and (*c*) double-declining-balance method.

E 20.7   In each of the following situations, determine the age of each asset in either years or units, whichever is appropriate.

    a. Equipment appears on the balance sheet at a cost of $28,500 with accumulated depreciation of $14,100. The salvage value was estimated at $5,000, life was estimated at five years, and the straight-line method of depreciation is used.

    b. The cost of the truck is $21,800 with $17,100 of accumulated depreciation. Salvage value was estimated at $2,800, and the truck would most likely be driven for 100,000 miles. The company uses the units-of-production method of depreciation.

    c. Machinery was purchased for $64,500 and, at present, has accumulated depreciation of $23,220. The useful life was estimated at 10 years, with a salvage value of $9,500. The double-declining-balance method of depreciation is used.

E 20.8   Coral Computer Company purchased several cash registers on April 2, 1997, at a total cost of $4,350. Estimated useful life of the registers is five years, and their total expected salvage value is $600. Coral uses the straight-line method of depreciation and has a December 31 year-end. Determine the amount of depreciation expense in 1997 assuming, alternatively, that (*a*) depreciation is calculated to the nearest month, and (*b*) Coral uses the midyear convention.

E 20.9   Westbrook Industries purchased a computer for $35,000 on January 2, 1998. Its useful life is estimated at five years, with a salvage value of $2,500. Westbrook uses straight-line depreciation for its own books and follows the MACRS for tax purposes, taking advantage of the most accelerated method allowed. Westbrook's year-end is December 31. Compute the book and tax depreciation for the first three years of the computer's life. Use Exhibits 20.2 and 20.3 as a reference.

E 20.10   Eagle Limited purchased a building 12 years ago at a price of $650,000. At that time, useful life was estimated at 25 years with a $75,000 salvage value, and straight-line depreciation was used. After recording depreciation for the 12th year, Eagle decided that for future years it would revise its original estimate of the building's useful life from 25 to 39 years and salvage value from $75,000 to $50,000. Calculate the depreciation expense that Eagle should record for each of the remaining years of the building's life.

E 20.11   Kumulani Interiors owns a computer that it purchased two years ago at a total cost of $9,250. At that time it was estimated that the company would use the computer for six years and then sell it for $850. Recently Kumulani upgraded the computer at a cost of $4,500. This upgrade did not extend the life of the computer, nor did it change the estimated salvage value. Prepare journal entries to record the cost of the upgrade and the depreciation expense for the third year assuming that Kumulani uses straight-line depreciation.

E 20.12   Mammoth Corporation owns a delivery van with an original cost of $18,400 and accumulated depreciation of $13,750. Determine the amount of gain or loss on the sale of the van under each of the following situations:

    a. Van is sold for $5,300 cash.

    b. Van is sold for $4,180 cash.

    c. Van is sold for $1,500 cash plus a six-month $3,150 note receivable with a stated 10 percent interest rate.

E 20.13   Spectrum Products closes its books on October 31 and prepares depreciation adjustments annually. On July 27, 1998, Spectrum sold some equipment with an original cost of $26,250 for $8,500. The equipment was purchased on November 4, 1993, and was depreciated using the straight-line method and had an estimated useful life of eight years and a salvage value of $650. Prepare the entries to update the depreciation and record the sale of the equipment.

E 20.14   On July 1, 1997, Federated Supply Company exchanged a warehouse and some land for 50,000 shares of Geico Corporation stock. The stock was selling for $12 per share, and a recent appraisal of the land and warehouse set their total value at $650,000. The warehouse and land originally cost $450,000 and $225,000, respectively. Accumulated depreciation on the warehouse was $320,000. Prepare the entry to record the exchange. What value did you assign to the stock acquired in the transaction? Why?

E 20.15 Willow & Company exchanged a building it owned in Wichita for a building in Kansas City owned by Candid Corporation. The buildings were both valued at $575,000, so there was no cash transferred between the companies. Just prior to the exchange, Willow's accounts showed the cost of the original building as $425,000, with accumulated depreciation of $260,000. Candid's Kansas City building was on its books with a cost of $750,000 and accumulated depreciation of $160,000. Determine the gain or loss that each company should recognize. What dollar amount should each company assign to the building it acquired?

E 20.16 Adventure World is trading in its old computer system for a new model. The old computer system is on the books at a cost of $270,000 with accumulated depreciation of $185,000. The new model has a list price of $450,000, but the manufacturer has agreed to reduce this amount by $75,000 in return for Adventure's old computer system. Prepare the journal entry to record the acquisition of the new computer system.

E 20.17 Harah Minerals owns oil reserves in Texas. The reserves were originally purchased for $14,900,000 and were estimated to contain 3,500,000 barrels of oil. The salvage value of the property was established at $200,000. Production for the current period amounted to 850,000 barrels, all of which are still on hand. Determine the depletion cost per barrel and prepare the journal entry to record the depletion for the current period. How would your entry have changed if one-half the barrels of oil had been sold as of the end of the period?

E 20.18 Rega Forest paid $65,000 for the right to operate a Copy Master store in her hometown for the next eight years. Copy Master specializes in printing and copying jobs, both large and small. Prepare journal entries to record the purchase of the franchise and the amortization expense for the first full year.

E 20.19 Refer to the financial statements of the Boston Celtics introduced in Chapter 7. For the most recent fiscal year shown, find the total plant assets, intangible assets, and natural resources, if any. Calculate the percentage of total assets represented by each category above. Compare these percentages to those mentioned in the opening vignette for Union Pacific. Were you surprised by the results? Explain.

E 20.20 Frontier Express recently repaved its parking lot at a total cost of $50,000. The estimated useful life of the parking lot is five years with zero salvage value, and Frontier uses the straight-line method of depreciation for all plant assets. Assuming Frontier treats this as a revenue expenditure, what effect will it have on income? Assuming Frontier treats it as a capital expenditure, what effect will it have on income?

PROBLEMS

P 20.1 Riviera Industries recently completed several transactions relating to plant assets. For each transaction described, determine the dollar amount to be capitalized as well as the account title to be used.

    a. Riviera purchased a parcel of land on which it will construct a manufacturing facility. The purchase price of $135,000 included survey fees of $2,500, a title document costing $1,300, and brokers' fees of $6,500. Riviera also incurred $8,600 in blasting costs to prepare the land for construction of the building.

    b. Riviera constructed the manufacturing facility referred to in *a* above. Materials and labor costs amounted to $278,000, the architect's fee was $18,500, and the necessary permits totaled $3,600. Insurance carried during the construction was $2,300, and interest on the construction loan amounted to $14,200.

    c. Riviera purchased the machinery and office furniture of a company that was going out of business. The total package price was $90,000. Appraisers valued the machinery at $83,000 and the office furniture at $17,000.

    d. Riviera paid the following bills relating to the use of its plant assets: (1) Annual real estate taxes, $14,250; (2) annual insurance premiums, $8,380; (3) annual mortgage payments, $124,800, of which $61,700 was interest; and (4) painting of the outside of the buildings, $7,200.

    e. Riviera purchased a new computer system for $437,000 and paid $3,600 for a three-year service contract. The company also paid $650 to send one of its employees to computer training school to learn how to use the new computer.

P 20.2 Dickinson Corporation purchased a computer system at a total cost of $375,000. As the accountant for the company, you estimated a useful life of four years or 40,000 hours of operation, with a salvage value of $55,000. The president of the company wants to know what impact this capital expenditure will have on income over the next four years. (Assume the computer is used 7,000 hours the first year and that its usage increases 20 percent in each succeeding year.)

Required: *a.* Prepare a schedule showing the depreciation expense and year-end carrying value of the asset for each of the next four years under each of the following methods of depreciation:
   (1) Straight-line method.
   (2) Units-of-production method.
   (3) Double-declining-balance method.
b. Which method produces the highest income in year 1? Which produces the lowest income in year 1?

P 20.3 Langer Travel, whose year-end is December 31, purchased $36,500 worth of office furniture on January 7, 1997. The company uses straight-line depreciation for financial statement purposes based on an estimated useful life of five years and a salvage value of $3,500. Langer's tax return preparer follows the MACRS rules for income tax purposes using the most accelerated method allowed.

Required: *a.* Calculate depreciation expense for financial statement purposes for each year of the asset's life.
b. Calculate depreciation expense for tax purposes for each year of the asset's life. Use Exhibits 20.2 and 20.3 as a reference.
c. Why is it appropriate to use two different methods of depreciation for the same asset?

P 20.4 Almeda, Inc., whose year-end is December 31, purchased a delivery truck on May 2, 1997. The invoice price was $43,600 and included dealer prep and destination charges of $875. Almeda also paid sales tax of $2,200, registration fees of $95, and a $100 fee to obtain a title. On May 5, 1997, the company installed air conditioning in the truck at a cost of $1,850. On January 10, 2000, the company installed a new transmission in the truck at a cost of $3,700, and paid $425 for a tune-up of the engine. Almeda uses straight-line depreciation and the midyear convention. The estimated useful life of the truck is eight years with a $6,000 salvage value.

Required: *a.* Determine the dollar amount that should be capitalized to the Truck account in May 1997.
b. Calculate the depreciation expense to be recorded for 1997.
c. Should Almeda account for the expenditures made in January 2000 as capital or revenue expenditures?
d. If the useful life of the truck was extended two years by the installation of the new transmission, calculate the depreciation expense for 2000, assuming that the salvage value did not change.

P 20.5 CATCO Laboratories owns various types of equipment used in its research labs. The company, whose year-end is June 30, uses straight-line depreciation calculated to the nearest whole month. On June 30, 1997, the accounting records showed the following:

Equipment	Cost	Salvage Value	Estimated Life	Accumulated Depreciation
Microscope	$ 5,300	$ 800	5 years	$2,025
Autoclave	12,800	1,500	7 years	5,670
Refrigerator	7,500	900	10 years	2,420

The following events took place in fiscal 1998:
Aug. 29   The microscope was stolen, and CATCO received a check from the insurance company for $3,000.
Nov. 5   The autoclave was sold for $7,300 cash.
Dec. 17   The refrigerator was sold for $2,300 cash plus a one-year, $2,000 note receivable with a stated interest rate of 12 percent.

Required: *a.* Update the depreciation expense through the date of disposal for each piece of equipment.
b. Prepare the journal entry to record the disposal of each piece of equipment.

P 20.6   Peoples Medical Center owns a CAT scan machine that it wants to dispose of. The original cost of the machine was $245,000, and depreciation of $192,500 has been recorded to date. The purchasing manager is contemplating the following alternatives to dispose of the machine. (Treat each alternative independently.)

1. Mainland Medical Supply is willing to take the old machine and give Peoples a $45,000 trade-in allowance towards the purchase of a new CAT scan machine with a list price of $310,000. The balance of the price must be paid in cash.
2. Cornell Medical Supply is willing to give Peoples a $65,000 trade-in allowance on a new CAT scan machine with a list price of $325,000, the balance to be paid in cash.
3. Century Medical Center is willing to make an even exchange. Century will exchange a parcel of land worth $50,000 for Peoples' CAT scan machine.
4. Saxony Medical Center is willing to give Peoples an ambulance worth $65,000 for Peoples' CAT scan machine plus $10,000 cash.

Required: *a.* Prepare Peoples' required journal entry to record each of the above alternatives for financial statement purposes.
　　　　　 b. Was the gain/loss recognized for each of the above alternatives? If not, why not?

P 20.7   Donovan Touring Company owns a luxury motorcoach it uses in long distance tours. The motorcoach originally cost the company $285,000, and depreciation taken to date amounts to $227,000.

Donovan's president is considering several alternative methods of disposing of the motorcoach and is concerned about the financial statement impact. The alternative methods of disposal available are as follows. (Treat each alternative independently.)

1. The motorcoach will be sold for $65,000 cash.
2. The motorcoach will be exchanged for a stock investment in Recreation, Ltd. The value of the stock is estimated at $67,500.
3. The motorcoach will be traded in on a new model valued at $325,000. A trade-in allowance of $55,000 will be granted by the manufacturer with the balance paid in cash.
4. The motorcoach will be traded in on a new model valued at $370,000. A trade-in allowance of $73,000 will be granted by the manufacturer with a cash down payment of $50,000 and the balance on a two-year note payable.

Required: *a.* Determine the amount of gain or loss to be recognized in each of the above alternatives.
　　　　　 b. Calculate the net increase/decrease in total assets for each of the above alternatives.

P 20.8   American National Corporation owns a coal mine, an oil field, and a tract of timberland. Information regarding these assets follows:

1. The coal mine was purchased several years ago at a total cost of $865,000. The mine was estimated to contain 200,000 tons of ore and to have a $35,000 salvage value. During the current year, 49,000 tons of ore were mined.
2. The oil field was acquired in exchange for stock and was initially valued at $12,600,000. It was estimated to contain 500,000 barrels of oil and to have a salvage value of $100,000. During the current year, 115,000 barrels of oil were extracted.
3. The timberland was obtained through a land swap and was initially recorded at $1,350,000. The number of board feet of timber estimated to be available amounted to 120,000, and the salvage value of the land was estimated at $150,000. During the current year, 17,000 board feet of timber were cut.

Required: *a.* Assuming American uses the units-of-production method of depletion, determine the depletion rate per ton, barrel, and board foot.
　　　　　 b. Compute the amount of depletion for each of the assets for the current year.
　　　　　 c. Will the depletion charge appear on the financial statements as depletion expense? If not, where would it most likely appear?

P 20.9   Chandler Recording Company acquired the following assets during 1998:

1. The patent to manufacture a revolutionary compact disc. The purchase price was $2,300,000, and there are 16 years remaining in the legal life of the patent.
2. The copyright to an album by the newest country western group, Best of the West. The total amount spent to obtain the copyright was $480,000. The album is expected to be produced for three years, but royalties from the album are expected to continue for 10 years.

3. The copyright to a music video by the hottest new female vocalist, Flamingo. Chandler paid $1,000,000 to Flamingo for this right, which is expected to be produced for two years. However, royalties from the video are expected to continue for six years.

Required: *a.* Assuming Chandler uses the straight-line method of amortization, determine the amortization expense for 1999 for each of the assets above.

        b. Give the journal entry to record the 1999 amortization expense for the patent.

P 20.10   In each of the following situations, determine if the appropriate action was taken. If not, describe the financial statement impact of the error.

        a. Recorded the $50,000 purchase of land acquired for investment purposes as a debit to the Land account.

        b. A $450 tune-up to the delivery truck was capitalized to the Truck account.

        c. Land to be used as the site for a new warehouse was purchased for $250,000 plus a broker's commission of $12,500. The Land account was debited for $250,000, and the $12,500 broker's commission was recorded as commission expense.

        d. The $650 cost to install a new water heater was charged to plumbing repairs expense.

        e. A patent was purchased for $475,000 and recorded in the Equipment account.

        f. Depletion relating to the extraction of 200,000 barrels of oil was not recorded since the oil is still sitting in inventory and has not been sold.

COMPUTER APPLICATIONS

CA 20.1   Calcutta Corporation purchased five new assets at the beginning of its accounting period. The cost, salvage value, and estimated useful lives of these assets appear below:

Asset	Cost	Salvage Value	Useful Life
1	$45,000	$3,500	7 years
2	14,400	0	3 years
3	25,200	1,200	6 years
4	28,900	1,900	6 years
5	38,200	2,500	5 years

Required: Use a computer spreadsheet package.

        a. Your spreadsheet package's financial functions should include a function to calculate depreciation. Use this function to calculate the straight-line depreciation on each asset for the first year.

        b. Repeat requirement *a* using the double-declining-balance method.

CA 20.2   Cierno Company purchased an asset for $125,000. It has an expected useful life of 10 years and no salvage value. Cierno uses the double-declining-balance depreciation method.

Required: Use a computer spreadsheet package.

        a. Prepare a schedule that indicates the depreciation expense, ending balance of accumulated depreciation, and ending book value of each year of the asset's life. (Do not be alarmed if you still have a book value at the end of 10 years.)

        b. Because double-declining-balance does not balance to zero, particularly when the cost of the asset is high and the salvage value is low, companies often switch to straight-line depreciation some time during the life of the asset. Determine when Cierno should switch to the straight-line method and prepare a schedule as indicated in requirement *a.*

CASES

C 20.1   Using the annual report you obtained as a Chapter 1 assignment, review the financial statements and accompanying notes. For the most recent fiscal year shown, identify the types and amounts of plant assets, natural resources, and intangible assets, if any, as well as any related accumulated depreciation or depletion accounts.

        How much depreciation, depletion, or amortization expense did the company report? Which method of depreciation, depletion, or amortization did the company use?

C 20.2   Review the financial statements and accompanying notes of three companies in the same industry. Which depreciation method does each company use? Would you expect them to be the same? Explain.

  For each company, calculate total property, plant, and equipment as a percentage of total assets. Can you explain the similarities or the differences in this percentage among the three companies? Are your results consistent with your expectations? Why or why not?

C 20.3   (This is a continuation of Case C 7.4.) In December 1986, the Financial Accounting Standards Board issued *SFAS No. 89*. This statement superseded *SFAS No. 33* and its subsequent amendments, and, although it encouraged the disclosure of supplementary current cost/constant purchasing power information, it no longer required it.

Required: *a.* Obtain a copy of *SFAS No. 89*, and read paragraphs 1 through 4.
  b. Prepare a report on the dissenting opinions given by three board members. Be prepared to discuss your findings in class.

CRITICAL THINKING

CT 20.1   International Communications recently exchanged a warehouse it owned in Boston, Massachusetts, for a warehouse owned by Austin Tea Company in Austin, Texas. The market value of the Boston warehouse was $730,000 and the market value of the Austin warehouse was $850,000. To make the deal work, International paid Austin Tea $120,000 cash. Prior to the exchange, International's original warehouse was on its books at a cost of $275,000, with accumulated depreciation of $92,000.

Required: *a.* Record the exchange on the books of International Communications assuming the gain is recognized.
  b. Record the exchange on the books of International Communications assuming the gain is not recognized.
  c. Prepare separate depreciation schedules for alternatives *a* and *b* above, using straight-line depreciation, a zero salvage value, and a useful life of five years.
  d. Accountants sometimes claim that any unrecorded gain resulting from an exchange of similar assets is recognized over the useful life of the acquired asset. Does your answer to requirement *c* give any justification for this belief?

CT 20.2   For one lump-sum payment of $2,500,000, Treton Industries recently purchased a parcel of land with a building on it, as well as some equipment located in the building. What special problem exists with lump-sum purchases? How would you determine the dollar value to assign to each of the three individual assets in Treton's accounting records?

  Do the following individuals have any incentive to over/understate the value of any one of the three assets acquired? Explain.
  a. Treton's president, who receives an annual bonus equal to 5 percent of net income.
  b. The owners of the company.

ETHICAL CHALLENGES

EC 20.1   The president of your company paid you a visit today. He believes that the financial statements misrepresent the financial condition of the company and you, as the accountant, have the job to rectify these mistakes. As an example, he pointed out that the land and buildings have a carrying value on the books of $350,000 but were recently appraised for insurance purposes at $900,000. In addition, he knows for a fact that the company has generated large amounts of goodwill over the years as the result of its dependable service to customers. Yet there is no goodwill listed in the asset section of the balance sheet.

  He has asked you to estimate the amount of goodwill and record it on the books. He also wants you to increase the value of all plant assets to their appraised values. He stresses the importance of these changes to the company's ability to obtain a much needed bank loan next week.

Required: *a.* Identify the accounting and ethical issues in the above scenario.
  b. As the accountant for the company, what would you do?

EC 20.2   Southwest Manufacturers is having one of its worst years ever. Profits are plummeting, and the controller has approached you, the plant asset accountant, with a proposal. She wants you to reduce depreciation expense by increasing the salvage values on all plant assets and lengthening their useful lives. In this way, she says, the company can end up reporting current year income that is not much lower than in prior years. If need be, the company can change back to the original salvage values and useful lives in future accounting periods. She states that, "No one gets hurt and, anyway, no one will even notice the change."

Required: *a.* Identify the accounting and ethical issues in the above scenario.

               b. As the plant asset accountant, what would you do?

CHAPTER 21

Recording and Communicating Nonoperational Investment Activities

Learning Objectives

1. Explain why investments are classified as trading securities and how to account for and communicate transactions involving these investments.

2. Describe why investments are classified as available-for-sale securities and how to record and communicate transactions involving these investments.

3. Explain the importance of investments classified as held-to-maturity securities and how to account for and communicate transactions involving these investments.

4. Describe how to account for investments that give a corporation significant influence or control over another corporation.

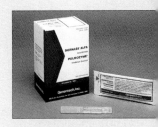

Genentech, Inc., is a biotechnology company founded in 1976 in San Francisco, California. It describes itself as a company that discovers, develops, manufactures, and markets human pharmaceuticals internationally. In his letter to stockholders in the 1994 annual report, G. Kirk Raab, Genentech's president and chief executive officer, said the company's goal is "to apply excellent science toward innovative products that substantially help people with serious medical conditions, while increasing returns for our stockholders."[1]

Genentech's business is creating, producing, and selling pharmaceuticals. Yet the company invests a significant portion of its financial resources in assets that are not directly involved in the research and development of new products or in the marketing and production of their existing products. Genentech's 1995 balance sheet reports that 48 percent of its assets consist of short-term (30 percent) and long-term (18 percent) investments in debt and equity securities. These investments generated $60,562,000 of interest revenue, which represented 6.6 percent of total revenues and 41 percent of the firm's net income in 1995.

Why do companies make such nonoperating investments, and how do they account for the events involving the acquisition and disposal of these

[1]Genentech, Inc. *Annual Report*, 1994.

nonoperating investments? How does the accounting system present information about the cost, type, market value, and earnings of these investments to internal and external parties who have an interest in the firm? And, most important, why are these types of investments significant? 🚲

 Genentech's management teams are responsible for deciding which projects to move to the marketplace and for generating profitable growth. In choosing among alternative projects, President Raab says the company tries to balance the risk and return of the projects as a portfolio manager would.[2]

> Some projects have potential for high return, but at a higher risk than we might otherwise consider. Others may have lower potential for return, but also lower risk. Of course we make a priority of those with low relative risk and high potential for return. The result is a balanced mix offering good opportunity for significant return with reasonable risk.

WHY INVEST?

For Genentech, Inc., and other companies, investing in debt and equity securities allows them to generate returns on funds that they plan to use at a later date. Firms use these funds to meet short-term objectives like buying inventory or to accomplish long-term objectives such as developing new products or increasing the firm's productive capacity. Management is responsible for generating a satisfactory return on investments and also for making sure that funds are available when needed.

For example, excess cash accumulates at certain points in a firm's operating cycle. Often, investing excess cash in debt and equity securities generates a greater return for the firm than it would have by allowing the cash to remain in a checking account until the time to buy more inventory. An alternative use for any excess cash is to buy more inventory. However, this requires that the company incur additional storage costs, thereby losing the return on the funds tied up in the inventory.

Cash generated from the firm's profits is either distributed to the shareholders as dividends or reinvested in the firm. Many firms reinvest some of this cash in debt and equity securities on a long-term basis. These long-term investments allow firms to finance the expansion of existing capacity or to develop new products without incurring more debt or issuing more stock. Then, when firms need the funds for a new project, they can sell their long-term investments.

This chapter begins with a discussion of what constitutes debt and equity investments and the three classifications used to group these securities for reporting in the financial statements. Following this, we discuss how to account for the acquisition and disposal of debt and equity securities within these accounting classifications. Next we explain how to account for investments in the stock of another company that give the investing company a significant influence or control over the investee company. The chapter concludes with a discussion of how to summarize events involving debt and equity securities in both external and internal reports.

WHAT ARE DEBT AND EQUITY INVESTMENTS?

In prior chapters, we discussed the nature of debt and equity securities and described how to account for them *from the perspective of the issuing company.* This chapter addresses the nature of debt and equity securities *from the perspective of the buyer of these securities.*

Today most investments made in debt and equity securities fall into one of these three classifications:

• **Trading securities.** Companies purchase these debt and equity securities with the intent of selling them after holding them for a short period of time. Therefore, the balance sheet reflects a company's trading securities as current assets.

---

[2]Genentech, Inc. *Annual Report*, 1994.

- **Available-for-sale (AFS) securities.** Companies purchase certain debt and equity securities in order to maintain a portfolio of securities that management can sell, as needed, to raise cash for particular projects. Such investments typically appear on the balance sheet as long-term assets, but individual debt and equity securities that qualify are classified as current assets.

- **Held-to-maturity securities.** Firms purchase these debt securities with the intent of holding them until they mature. They are considered long-term assets and appear in the investments section of the balance sheet. However, if these securities are due to mature within the next accounting period, they are classified as current assets.

Each classification requires a distinct accounting treatment that reflects the nature of the particular investment, as the next three sections of the chapter show.

TRADING SECURITIES

Trading securities have little associated risk because companies can readily convert them into cash and typically hold them for no more than a few months. The bulk of such temporary investments are made in U.S. government securities, prime commercial paper, and other types of debt securities, and, much less often, in equity securities of other companies. Exhibit 21.1 shows some of the investment alternatives available and their usual maturity lengths.

Trading Securities: Debt Instruments

Trading securities that are debt instruments usually consist of the types of noninterest-bearing notes and interest-bearing notes described earlier in Chapter 15.

Noninterest-Bearing Notes: Trading Securities   Recall that noninterest-bearing notes do not have a face interest rate. The purchaser of the note pays an amount that is less than the note's face value based on the present value of the promised future cash flows at the market interest rate. Upon maturity, the investor receives the full amount of the face value of the note.

The amount of interest earned on noninterest-bearing notes is the difference between the note's purchase price and its face value upon maturity. However, if the investor sells the note before its maturity date, the difference between the purchase price and the proceeds from the sale is considered a gain or loss on the sale of the security.

When a firm buys a noninterest-bearing note, the purchase price reflects the market value of the note, rather than the note's face value. For example, if Genentech

EXHIBIT	21.1	Trading Security Alternatives

Type of Security	Approximate Maturities*
Debt Securities	
Noninterest-bearing notes	
U.S. Treasury bills	3 to 12 months
Prime commercial paper	Various, up to 270 days
Interest-bearing notes	
U.S. Treasury notes	1 to 5 years
U.S. Treasury bonds	Various, usually over 5 years
Bonds of corporations	Various, up to 30 years
Equity Securities	
Common and preferred stock of other corporations	No maturity

*Maturity from issue date. It is possible to obtain shorter maturity lengths by trading securities in the open market.

purchased U.S. Treasury bills with a maturity, or face, value of $10,000 for $9,500, the company would make the following entry to record the purchase.

Trading Securities—U.S. Treasury Bills	9,500	
Cash		9,500

The purchaser of a noninterest-bearing note does not use a discount account to show the difference between the face value and the sales price of the debt security, as the company would if it issued the note.

When the Treasury bills mature, the entry made to reflect this event will show the amount of interest earned as the difference between the $9,500 cost and the $10,000 maturity value.

Cash	10,000	
Trading Securities—U.S. Treasury Bills		9,500
Interest Revenue		500

If the company sells Treasury bills before their maturity dates, it reflects the difference between the proceeds of the sale and the cost of the Treasury bills as either a gain or a loss. For example, if Genentech sells the Treasury bills for $9,600 before they mature, it would make the following entry to record the event.

Cash	9,600	
Trading Securities—U.S. Treasury Bills		9,500
Gain on Sale of U.S. Treasury Bills		100

PAUSE & REFLECT

If a noninterest-bearing note earns interest from the date it is purchased, why wouldn't part of the gain on the sale of the noninterest-bearing note, which is a trading security, be recognized as interest revenue?

Interest-Bearing Notes Companies also record their investments in interest-bearing debt securities, such as U.S. Treasury notes, at the cost of those securities rather than the amount of their face value. These securities may be issued at a premium or a discount, depending upon whether the market interest rate at the time of the investment is greater or less than the face interest rate.

Assume that Genentech, Inc., purchased U.S. Treasury notes with a face value of $15,000 at a total cost of $14,850. Further assume that the face interest rate is 10 percent and that it is paid semiannually. Therefore, the investment pays $750 of cash interest every six months ($15,000 × .10 × 1/2). The entries shown below illustrate how Genentech would reflect the acquisition of the securities and the subsequent receipt of one semiannual interest payment in its records.

Trading Securities—U.S. Treasury Notes	14,850	
Cash		14,850
Cash	750	
Interest Revenue		750

Note that Genentech does not record the $150 discount ($15,000 − $14,850) on the U.S. Treasury note separately. In addition, Genentech does not amortize the discount when it receives the cash interest payment because the company does not intend to hold the note to maturity. Therefore, Genentech will not record the effective interest rate of the note. At the end of an accounting period, Genentech would accrue only the amount of cash interest on its interest-bearing notes held as trading securities.

If interest-bearing debt securities are sold on an interest payment date, the difference between the amount of the proceeds from the sale and the cost of the investment determines the gain or loss on the transaction. For example, if the proceeds from the sale of the U.S. Treasury note were $14,900 on any given interest payment date, the entry would reflect a $50 gain on that transaction as shown below.

Cash	14,900	
Trading Securities—U.S. Treasury Notes		14,850
Gain on Sale of U.S. Treasury Notes		50

Determining the Cost of Debt Securities Recall that bond prices are quoted on the market on the basis of 100. In addition to the basic price of the debt security, two other factors may affect the amount of cash paid for the debt instrument: (1) the broker's commission or fee and (2) the accrued interest. The amount of any commission or fee paid to a broker when purchasing securities is included in the cost of the investment because it is a reasonable and necessary cost of acquiring the asset. However, interest accrued on the note is *paid to the seller of the note* and is not included in the cost of the security. The purchasing company excludes the accrued interest from the cost of the investment because it will receive the accrued interest as part of the cash interest at the next interest payment date.

Assume that Genentech purchases Quintico Manufacturing bonds with a face value of $10,000 on May 1 through a security broker. The bonds have a 12 percent face rate that is paid semiannually on March 1 and September 1. The price of the bonds is 101, and the broker's fee is $90.

We show the computation of the cost of the bonds and the total cash paid below.

Basic price of the bonds ($10,000 × 1.01)	$10,100
Broker's fee	90
Cost of bonds	$10,190
Accrued interest (10,000 × .12 × 2/12)	200
Total cash paid	$10,390

Genentech must pay the seller the interest from the last interest date to the time of the purchase (March and April) because Quintico Manufacturing will pay the cash interest for the entire six months to whomever holds the bonds on the next interest date. Therefore, if Genentech does not pay the interest, the seller would not receive the interest due for the two months it held the bonds, and Genentech would receive six months' interest even though it held the bonds for only four months. We show the entry to record this transaction below.

Trading Securities—Quintico Mfg. Bonds	10,190	
Interest Receivable	200	
Cash		10,390

When Genentech receives the semiannual interest payment of $600 on September 1, it will record the event as follows.

Cash ($10,000 × .12 × 1/2)	600	
Interest Receivable		200
Interest Revenue		400

Of the $600 Genentech receives, $200 relates to the interest paid to the seller when Genentech purchased the bonds; the remaining $400 is the amount of cash interest earned on the bond.

Sale of Interest-Bearing Debt Securities between Interest Dates When an interest-bearing note such as a bond is sold between its interest dates, the cash proceeds of the note consist of the sale price of the note, less the brokerage fees, plus the accrued interest on the note from the last interest date to the date of the sale. We calculate the gain or loss on the sale of an interest-bearing debt security by comparing the cost of the debt security with the net sales price of the debt instrument. The net sales price is the quoted sale price of the security less the brokerage fee. It does not include the accrued interest.

Continuing with the example of Genentech's investment in Quintico Manufacturing's bonds, assume that it sold those bonds on October 1. The quoted sales price is 102 plus accrued interest of $100 for one month, and the broker's fee is $85.

Basic price of security ($10,000 × 1.02)	$10,200
Less: Broker's fees	85
Net sales price	$10,115
Plus accrued interest ($10,000 × .12 × 1/12)	100
Cash received	$10,215

The following entry reflects this transaction.

Cash	10,215	
Loss on Sale of Bonds	75	
Trading Securities—Quintico Mfg. Bonds		10,190
Interest Revenue		100

In this case, the loss on the sale is the difference between the *net sales price* of the bonds ($10,115) and the *book value* of the bonds ($10,190).

Trading Securities: Equity Instruments

Companies invest in equity securities because they expect to generate a return on their short-term investment from dividends and the appreciation of the purchased stock. However, equity investments in other companies' capital stock normally present a greater risk of price change than do investments in debt securities. Although the prices of debt securities change in response to changes in interest rates and economic conditions, they are not subject to the rapid increases and decreases in prices experienced by equity securities.

PAUSE & REFLECT   **Why do equity investments have a greater risk of price change than debt securities?**

When a company buys the stock of other companies, the cost of the securities includes the brokerage fees paid to acquire the stock. For example, assume Genentech purchased 1,000 shares of American Electric Power (AEP) common stock at $19 per share and paid $570 in brokerage fees. The cost per share of AEP common stock is $19.57 ($19,570/1,000 shares), and the entry to record this transaction is:

Trading Securities—AEP Common Stock	19,570	
Cash		19,570

Income from Equity Investments   Investors in stock receive earnings from their investments in the form of dividends declared by the investee company. These investors record their receipt of cash dividends when they are received. For example, if AEP declared and paid a quarterly dividend of $.50 per share, the entry below would record the event on Genentech's books.

Cash (1,000 shares × $.50)	500	
Dividend Revenue		500

Gains and Losses from the Sale of Equity Investments   Companies compute gains and losses realized through the sale of equity investments on the basis of the cost of the securities held compared to the net proceeds from the sale. The sale of an equity trading security is recorded by a debit to Cash and a credit to the specific trading security—equity account. If the net proceeds from the sales exceed the carrying cost of the equity security, there is a gain on the sale of trading securities; if the net proceeds are less than the carrying cost, a loss on the sale of trading securities results.

For example, assume that Genentech sells 100 shares of AEP stock for $2,500 less broker's fees of $60. The net proceeds, $2,440 ($2,500 − $60), less the cost of the

AEP stock, $1,957 ($19.57 × 100 shares), generate a gain of $483 that Genentech records as shown in the following entry.

Cash	2,440	
Gain on Sale of Trading Securities—AEP		483
Trading Securities—AEP Common Stock		1,957

What Are Trading Securities Really Worth?

Both debt and equity trading securities change in value over time, and the fair value of a firm's portfolio of trading securities is of interest to many financial statement users. Recall that fair value, or fair market value, is the amount at which a debt or equity security could be exchanged in a current transaction between willing parties.[3] Therefore, we use a method of investment valuation called **mark to market** to show the fair value of the entire portfolio of trading securities on the balance sheet without altering the cost of the individual securities. That is, a company reflects its investment portfolio at the equivalent market value at the time it issues its financial statements.

Mark-to-market accounting for investments in debt and equity securities helps financial statement users get a more realistic assessment of the value of a company's investments. It also helps both internal and external financial statement users evaluate the effectiveness of a company's investment policies.

We use market values rather than historical cost to account for investments in financial instruments because it is possible to verify the market value of these securities. Financial publications such as *The Wall Street Journal* and *Barron's* report on the activities of the financial markets and give financial statements users reasonable assurance that the "market values," of a company's investments are objectively and fairly determined.

When the fair value of all the trading securities held at the balance sheet date differs from the total cost of those securities, the reporting company creates a **market adjustment account.** This balance sheet account reflects adjustments made to the total cost of the trading securities to show the total fair value of the securities.

For example, on December 31, 1995, Genentech, Inc., had trading securities with a total cost of $135,325,000 and a total fair market value of $135,311,000 (see note to Genentech, Inc., financial statements in the annual report booklet). In order to report the fair value on the balance sheet, Genentech would create a market adjustment account to reflect the difference between the cost and fair value of its trading securities at that date. Genentech credits the market adjustment account and subtracts the $14,000 amount from the total cost figure on the balance sheet to reflect the $135,311,000 fair value of the trading security portfolio. The offsetting debit is made to the **Unrealized Loss** account. This represents a decrease in the fair value of the portfolio of trading securities that has not yet been recognized in the accounts (therefore, it is "unrealized") because Genentech has not actually sold the securities.

The entry below shows how Genentech, Inc., records the difference between the cost and market value of its portfolio of trading securities.

Unrealized Loss	14,000	
Market Adjustment—Trading Securities (TS)		14,000

When the fair value of the trading securities is more than the cost of the securities, the market adjustment account would have a debit balance and the company would record a corresponding **Unrealized Gain** in its accounting records. This balance sheet account would reflect the amount of increase in the fair value of the portfolio of trading securities that has not been recognized because there has been no sale of the securities.

The *unrealized gains and unrealized losses are closed to the Income Summary account in the closing process and reported on the income statement.* The trading securities are

---

[3]From "Accounting for Certain Debt and Equity Securities," *Statement of Financial Accounting Standards No. 115.*

reported in the current assets section of the balance sheet at their fair value using either format shown below.

Trading securities at fair value (net)	$135,311,000

or

Trading securities	$135,325,000
Less: Market adjustment—TS	14,000
Trading securities at fair value	$135,311,000

Because the market adjustment account reflects the market adjustment required to show the fair value of the entire portfolio of trading securities, it is not affected by the purchase and sale of individual debt and equity securities during the year. Rather, by the end of the next accounting period, most, if not all, of the securities held as trading securities at the previous balance sheet date probably have been sold and replaced with a new portfolio of debt and equity securities. Nevertheless, at the end of each accounting period, it is necessary to adjust the balance in the market adjustment account to reflect the difference between total cost and total fair value of the trading securities.

Suppose that on December 31, 1996, Genentech, Inc., has a portfolio of trading securities that cost $75,603,000 with a fair value of $75,605,000. The market adjustment account has not been closed and still has the $14,000 credit balance that was established at the prior year's balance sheet date. Therefore, in order to adjust the portfolio of trading securities from cost to its fair value on the December 31, 1996, balance sheet date, the market adjustment account needs to have a $2,000 debit balance. This is accomplished with the following entry.

Market Adjustment—TS	16,000	
Unrealized Gain		16,000

Market Adjustment—TS

			12/31/95	Balance	14,000
12/31/96	Adjustment to achieve desired balance	16,000			
12/31/96	Desired balance	2,000			

The related unrealized gain on the trading securities would be reported on the income statement for 1996, and the trading securities for 1996 would be reported in the current asset section of the balance sheet at their fair value in either form shown below.

Trading securities at fair value (net)	$75,605,000

or

Trading securities	$75,603,000
Add: Market adjustment—TS	2,000
Trading securities at fair value	$75,605,000

PAUSE & REFLECT

If Genentech's fair value is $2,000 more than its cost in 1996, why isn't the unrealized gain recorded in the entry and reported on the income statement as a $2,000 gain rather than the $16,000 gain described above? What entry would be necessary if the fair value of Genentech's trading securities was $75,600,000 on December 31, 1997?

AVAILABLE-FOR-SALE SECURITIES

Management expects to sell available-for-sale (AFS) debt and equity securities, but not in the near future. For this reason, these investments usually consist of corporate and government bonds and common and preferred stock. Because management expects to sell these securities, the portfolio of available-for-sale securities is reported at the fair value of the securities on the balance sheet, in the investments classification. However, individual debt and equity securities that qualify are classified as current assets.

Accounting for the purchase and sale of individual equity securities classified as available-for-sale securities is the same as trading securities except they are labeled AFS. However, accounting for available-for-sale debt securities and the process of adjusting the portfolio of available-for-sale debt and equity securities from mark to market differs from trading securities.

Available-for-Sale Securities: Debt

Available-for-sale debt securities usually consist of bonds, and the process of recording their acquisition is the same as that described for debt trading securities. However, because firms buying available-for-sale bonds do not intend to sell these bonds in the near future, they are interested in the effective interest rate of these debt instruments. Therefore, *firms amortize the premiums and discounts on these bonds and maintain each debt security on an amortized cost basis.*

When a company purchases bonds as an investment, the price paid for the bonds is determined by finding the present value of the remaining cash flows of the bond using the market interest rate. The bond is purchased at a premium if the market rate of interest is less than the face rate of interest and at a discount if the market rate is greater than the face interest rate.

For example, suppose that on July 1, 1995, Genentech, Inc., purchased 20, $1,000 bonds of the Chappuy Corporation that are due in five years and have a face interest rate of 12 percent. Interest is paid on June 30 and December 31 of each year. Genentech purchased the bonds for $21,544 when the market interest rate was 10 percent. The entry to record the acquisition of the bond appears below.

Available-for-Sale—Chappuy Bonds	21,544	
Cash		21,544

Exhibit 21.2 shows how to determine the market price of the bonds (panel A) and presents the premium amortization table for the first year of the bonds' life (panel B). The company records the bond at its cost in the available-for-sale investment account. Typically, companies do not use a separate premium or discount account when reflecting investments in debt instruments.

PAUSE & REFLECT

Would the amortization schedule in Exhibit 21.2 be the same as the amortization schedule for the company that issued the bonds? Explain.

EXHIBIT	21.2	Investment in AFS Bonds

A. Market Price Determination

Cash flow 1:

$$\text{Annuity} \times P_{10,5\%} = \text{Present value of annuity}$$
$$\$1,200 \times 7.7217 = \$9,266$$

Cash flow 2:

$$\text{Future value} \times p_{10,5\%} = \text{Present value}$$
$$\$20,000 \times .6139 = \$12,278$$

Present value of cash flow 1	$ 9,266
Present value of cash flow 2	12,278
Price of bond	$21,544

B. Premium Amortization Schedule

Date	Cash Interest ($.06 \times$ FV*)	Effective Interest ($.05 \times$ CV*)	Amortized Premium	Premium	Carrying Value
7/1/95				$1,544	$21,544
12/31/95	$1,200	$1,077	$123	1,421	21,421
6/30/96	1,200	1,071	129	1,292	21,292

*FV is the face value of the bond, and CV is the carrying value of the bond.

The entry for the first interest payment presented here shows that the premium is amortized by decreasing the carrying value of the Available-for-Sale—Chappuy Bond account and that the company recognizes the effective interest for the six-month period. When the bonds mature in five years, the Available-for-Sale—Chappuy Bonds account will equal the face value of the bonds, or $20,000.

Cash	1,200	
Available-for-Sale—Chappuy Bonds		123
Interest Revenue		1,077

When a company purchases bonds between interest dates, the purchaser must pay the seller of the bond the amount of cash interest accrued from the last interest date. The accounting treatment for this is the same as that illustrated earlier in determining the cost of trading securities debt instruments. At the date of purchase, the purchaser would record any accrued interest as interest receivable and *not* as part of the cost of the bond.

Companies acquire long-term investments as a means of funding capital expenditures to enhance the productivity of the firm's operations. Companies sell their available-for-sale bonds when they need cash to fund these types of capital expenditures. The entry to record the sale of available-for-sale bonds is the same as the entry made for trading securities except that *the cost of the bond is the amount of its amortized cost on the date of the sale rather than its original cost.* For example, suppose that Genentech, Inc., sold five of its 20 Chappuy bonds on June 30, 1996, at 108 1/2. The amortized cost of five of the bonds on the sale date is $5,323 ($21,292 × 1/4). The entry to record the sale is:

Cash ($5,000 × 1.085)	5,425	
Available-for-Sale—Chappuy Bonds		5,323
Gain on Sale of Investment in Bonds		102

PAUSE & REFLECT	Companies invest in bonds in the expectation of generating a return on their investment. How can an investor lose money on a bond?

What Are Available-for-Sale Securities Really Worth?

Companies report available-for-sale debt and equity securities on fair value basis. As in the case of presenting trading securities, companies use a market adjustment account to reflect the adjustment of the total cost of the available-for-sale portfolio to its fair value. In order to indicate the required balance in the market adjustment account, it is necessary to compare the total cost of the available-for-sale portfolio to the fair value of the portfolio. An adjusting entry changes the existing market adjustment account balance to the desired balance. Accounting for the fair value of available-for-sale securities differs from trading securities in how it reports unrealized gains and losses.

For trading securities, the unrealized gains and losses are shown in the income statements as other gains or losses. However, for available-for-sale securities, an **Unrealized Gain or Loss account** *reflects the adjustments made to total stockholders' equity* to correspond to the balance in the market adjustment account for available-for-sale securities on the balance sheet. The adjustment is *not* considered a gain or loss and, therefore, is not part of periodic income.

On December 31, 1995, Genentech, Inc., reported (see the notes to Genentech's financial statement) that it held available-for-sale securities at an amortized cost of $305,304,000 that had a fair value of $359,577,000. The entry to record the required adjustment of $54,273,000 (cost of $305,304,000 to market value of $359,577,000) is:

Market Adjustment—AFS	54,273,000	
Unrealized Gain or Loss		54,273,000

The debit balance in the market adjustment account is added to the cost of the available-for-sale portfolio and reported in the investments section of the balance sheet in either of these ways:

Available-for-sale securities at fair value (net)	$359,577,000	

or

Available-for-sale securities	$305,304,000
Add: Market adjustment—AFS	54,273,000
Available-for-sale securities at fair value	$359,577,000

Genentech, Inc., calls the unrealized gain or loss account Net Unrealized Gain on Securities Available-for-Sale and reports a $54,273,000 addition to stockholders' equity.

If, at December 31, 1996, the fair value of the portfolio of available-for-sale securities was $388,900,000 and the cost of the portfolio remained at $305,304,000, the following entry would be made.

Market Adjustment—AFS	29,323,000	
Unrealized Gain or Loss		29,323,000

The difference between the fair value and cost of the portfolio is $83,596,000 ($388,900,000 – $305,304,000). However, the existing balances in both the Market Adjustment—AFS and the Unrealized Gain and Loss accounts are $54,273,000 (see the December 31, 1995, journal entry). Therefore, the December 31, 1996, entry changes the Market Adjustment—AFS account to its desired balance of $83,596,000 ($83,596,000 – $54,273,000) and increases the Unrealized Gain and Loss account to the same amount.

We show the balance sheet presentation for the available-for-sale portfolio in the investments section of the 1996 balance sheet below. The $83,596,000 balance in the Unrealized Gain and Loss account would be reported as an addition to Genentech's stockholders' equity in the same way it was on the 1995 balance sheet.

Available-for-sale securities at fair value (net)	$388,900,000	

or

Available-for-sale securities	305,304,000
Add: Market adjustment—AFS	83,596,000
Available-for-sale securities at fair value	$388,900,000

HELD-TO-MATURITY SECURITIES

Held-to-maturity securities consist of only debt securities, usually bonds, that a firm buys with the intent to hold until they mature. The purchaser amortizes any premium or discount on individual debt instruments to generate the effective interest earned during an accounting period, as is the practice with available-for-sale securities. Therefore, the entries to acquire and hold held-to-maturity securities are the same as those for available-for-sale debt securities.

However, companies do not report held-to-maturity securities on the balance sheet at their fair value. Rather, they appear at their amortized cost because they will not be sold before their maturity dates. Typically, these securities appear in the investments section of the balance sheet. However, when individual held-to-maturity securities mature within the next fiscal year, companies classify them as current assets. For example, in the Investment Securities note, Genentech, Inc., reports that in 1994 it had $724,345,000 of held-to-maturity securities. Of this amount,

$559,916,000 would mature within one year and, therefore, are classified as current assets while the remaining $164,429,000 were classified as long-term investments. In 1995, all $456,137,000 of held-to-maturity securities mature within one year.

ACQUIRING A SIGNIFICANT INFLUENCE IN OR CONTROL OF ANOTHER CORPORATION

Whether an investing firm can or does exercise a significant influence or control over an investee firm's operations usually depends on the percentage of voting stock it owns of the investee firm. In general, we assume that when a company owns less than 20 percent of another firm's voting stock, it does not have the ability to significantly influence or control the invested company, although it could. When a company does not have a significant influence in an investee company, it accounts for the stock investment as either trading or available-for-sale securities depending on management's intent for the holding the investments. Ownership of between 20 and 50 percent of a company's stock, in absence of evidence of the contrary, is presumed to give the investor the ability to exercise a significant influence over the investee company. Ownership of more than 50 percent of another corporation's stock gives the investing corporation control of the investee corporation.

Accounting for an Investment that Creates a Significant Influence over Another Company

When a company has a significant influence over another company due to stock ownership (20 to 50 percent), the investee company is viewed as an extension of the investor's operations. In these cases the investor company uses the *equity method* to account for these investments.

The **equity method** of accounting for an investment reflects increases and decreases in the investment account of the investor company in *proportion to the changes in the investee's stockholders' equity* (net assets of the investee company). Consequently, the investor records its proportionate share of the investee's net income as an increase in the value of its investment account. The investor also records the dividends it received as a decrease in the investment account. The equity method violates the historical cost principle but is used because it better reflects the investor's changing financial interest in the investee corporation's net assets.

Assume that Genentech, Inc., purchases 35 percent of the voting stock of Cell Research Corporation (CRC) for a total of $400,000. CRC's net income for the period in which Genentech acquires CRC's stock is $50,000, and CRC paid dividends of $30,000. Since Genentech, Inc., owns 35 percent of CRC's voting stock, its proportionate share of the net income is $17,500 ($50,000 × .35), and it receives dividends of $10,500 ($30,000 × .35). The entries to record the purchase of the stock and the recognition of Genentech's proportionate share of CRC's net income and dividends follow.

Investment in CRC Stock	400,000	
Cash		400,000
Investment in CRC Stock	17,500	
Investment Income		17,500
Cash	10,500	
Investment in CRC Stock		10,500

Genentech records its share of CRC's net income in the Investment in CRC account based on its percentage of ownership in CRC. Thus, Genentech's investment account reflects the increase in CRC's stockholders' equity account generated by net income and a decrease in CRC's stockholders' equity account because of CRC's declared dividends.

The increase in CRC stockholders' equity is $20,000 ($50,000 net income less $30,000 of dividends) and Genentech's Investment in CRC has increased by the 35 percent share of the increase in CRC's stockholders' equity ($20,000 × .35) or $7,000. If, at a subsequent date, Genentech decides to sell some or all of its stock in

CRC, the gain or loss on the sale will be determined by comparing the net proceeds from the sale to the carrying value of the stock in the investment account at the time of the sale.

Accounting for an Investment that Creates Effective Control of Another Company

When the investment of one company in the voting stock of another company, exceeds 50 percent, the investing company has effective control of the firm. The controlling company is known as the **parent company,** and the investee firm is called the **subsidiary company.** The investment account on the parent company's books is maintained using the equity method just described. When this type of extensive financial interrelationship exists, the legal distinction between the parent and subsidiary is usually ignored for reporting purposes, and financial statements for the companies are prepared as *if* the two companies were one economic unit.

For example, PepsiCo, Inc., owns Pizza Hut, Frito-Lay, KFC, and Taco Bell and prepares *consolidated financial statements* to reflect the combined financial statements of the subsidiary companies and the parent company. Therefore, PepsiCo's income statement reflects the sales and expense associated with PepsiCo's soft drinks as well as the sales and expenses associated with pizza, chips, chicken, and tacos. The consolidated balance sheet reports the assets (cash, inventory, plant and equipment, etc.) and liabilities (accounts payable to bonds payable) of all the companies controlled by PepsiCo.

Most large corporations today have subsidiaries, which require accounting procedures to reflect the consolidation. In essence, the accounting procedures transfer the relevant balance sheet and income statement balances to the parent company in order to consolidate, or bring together, the information from two or more companies.

HOW DO COMPANIES REPORT THEIR INVESTMENTS?

Information about a company's investment in debt and equity securities is important to both external and internal users of financial information. External users, such as investors and creditors, are interested in the liquidity of the investments, the return they generate, and the reason why the investments are being made. Such users obtain most of their information from the firm's general purpose financial statements.

Internal users, such as cash flow managers, members of the finance department, and strategic planners who are responsible for financing and investing decisions, need reports designed specifically to meet their respective needs. These users are interested in the timing of the cash flows, whether the return on investments reflects the risk assumed, and whether the investments are compatible with the company's short- and long-term goals.

The balance sheet, income statement, and cash flow statements provide information to external users about the firm's short-term and long-term nonoperational investments. In the next section, we summarize the investment-related information on each of these statements.

External Reporting—The Financial Statements

Balance Sheet   The balance sheet classification of a firm's investments in debt and equity securities includes current and long-term investments. Trading securities are reported at their fair value as current assets. The held-to-maturity and available-for-sale debt securities that mature in the coming fiscal year, as well as individual available-for-sale equity securities that qualify, are also classified as current assets and are reported as current assets. For example, Genentech, Inc.'s December 31, 1995, balance sheet reports that the company had $603,296,000 of short-term investments. The Investment Securities note tells the financial statement user that these investments consist of $456,137,000 of held-to-maturity securities that will mature in the next fiscal year, $4,328,000 of accrued interest, available-for-sale securities maturing within one year of $7,520,000, and trading securities with a fair value of $135,311,000. While the company could list each of these classifications separately as current assets, most companies choose to aggregate this information and, as Genentech, Inc., does, present the detailed information about the short-term investments in a note to the statement.

The investments section, which is located immediately after the current assets section of the balance sheet, reports the long-term investments of a firm. It shows the fair value of available-for-sale investments, the amortized cost of the held-to-maturity investments, and also the carrying value of the investments that have a significant influence in another company. Each of these classifications could be reported separately. Available-for-sale securities would reflect the fair value of the debt and equity securities in the company's portfolio, while held-to-maturity securities would reflect investments at their amortized cost. Genentech, however, aggregates the available-for-sale and held-to-maturity classifications on the balance sheet but reports the amount of available-for-sale and held-to-maturity securities in the Investment Securities note. For example, the 1994 balance sheet reports long-term marketable securities of $201,726,000, which the note says consists of $164,429,000 of held-to-maturity securities, available-for-sale securities with a market value of $35,660,000, and accrued interest of $1,637,000. In 1995, the note reveals that there are no held-to-maturity securities included in the $356,475,000 of long-term marketable securities reported on the balance sheet. The total consists of $4,418,000 of accrued interest and the $352,057,000 market value of the available-for-sale securities.

The amounts associated with investments using the equity method represent neither the cost nor the market value of the stock. Rather, the balance in these accounts represents the investor firm's dollar amount of its interest in the stockholders' equity of the investee corporation.

In contrast, as the fair value of a company's investment in available-for-sale securities changes, its stockholders' equity will increase or decrease depending on whether the fair value of the portfolio is greater or less than its cost. When the fair value is greater (less) than the securities' cost, stockholders' equity increases (decreases) by the difference.

Exhibit 21.3 summarizes these various investment categories and indicates how companies classify and value each of them on the balance sheet, and their impact on the income statement.

Cash Flow Statement   The investing section of the cash flow statement reflects the amounts of cash paid and received as a result of a company's investing activity. For example, Genentech, Inc.'s cash flow statement points out that, in 1995, the company purchased $682,396,000 of held-to-maturity securities and also spent $353,118,000 to

EXHIBIT | **21.3** | **Summary of Investments on Financial Statements**

Classification of Investment	Balance Sheet	Income Statement
Trading Securities:		
All debt and equity securities	Current assets reported at fair value	Dividends and interest and unrealized holding gains and losses included in income
Available-for-Sale		
Debt securities maturing in next fiscal year	Current assets reported at fair value	Dividends and interest included in income
All other debt and equity securities	Investments reported at fair value	Dividends and interest included in income
	Unrealized holding gains and losses for both current and long-term assets are reported as a separate item of stockholders' equity	
Held-to-Maturity		
Debt securities maturing in next fiscal year	Current asset reported at amortized cost	Interest revenue included in income
All other debt securities	Investments reported at amortized cost	Interest revenue included in income
Significant Influence in Another Corporation		
Ownership of 20 to 50% of common stock of another company	Investments reported at cost adjusted for investee's income, losses, and dividends (equity method)	Proportionate share of investee's income or loss included in investor's income
Control of Subsidiary		
Ownership of more than 50% of common stock of subsidiary company	Assets, liabilities, and stockholders' equity of parent and subsidiary are combined	Revenues, expenses, gains and losses of parent and subsidiary are combined

buy available-for-sale securities. Also, during 1995, it received $924,345,000 in cash from held-to-maturity securities that matured and received cash proceeds of $101,591,000 from the sale of available-for-sale securities. Presenting the specific cash inflows and outflows associated with particular investments helps external users evaluate how the firm's investing activities affect a firm's cash flows.

Internal Reporting

The content of internal reports depends upon the needs of the decision maker. While external reports aggregate and classify data, internal reports help financial managers make decisions about specific securities as well as portfolios of securities.

The accounting system reflects information about the cost of each security purchased and its performance. Portfolio managers need this information to decide whether to keep or sell particular securities. Accounting information helps assess whether portfolios of securities are performing as expected.

For example, a manager who is responsible for investing idle cash needs to know whether short-term debt instruments mature when cash is needed at some point in the future and whether the return the cash is generating is satisfactory. Accounting information also helps decision makers identify the securities that have performed well or poorly in the past.

For managers who are responsible for making long-term investments, the accounting information helps them assess whether the risk they have assumed is justified by the returns being generated by the investment. These managers must also consider whether funds invested in debt and equity securities would generate a better return if they invested in operating assets that increase or improve the operating capacity of the firm.

SUMMARY

Investment criteria rest on the timing of the firm's needs for cash and the risk of loss associated with the related investment. Trading securities are usually short-term, low-risk government or corporate noninterest-bearing or interest-bearing notes. Generally, short-term investments are made in debt securities rather than in the common stock of other companies because of the risk of rapid price changes of equity securities. The portfolio of a firm's trading securities is reported at its fair market value.

Companies make long-term investments because of the opportunity to enhance the investing firm's overall net income directly through interest and dividends, or indirectly through exerting significant influence or control over the investee's operations. The circumstances surrounding the type of securities purchased and the existence of influence or control over the investee's operations determine how a company reports these investments.

- Firms invest in debt and equity securities in order to manage their short-term cash flows, provide funds to finance future long-term operational projects, or to influence or control another corporation.

- The classifications, trading securities, available-for-sale securities, and held-to-maturity securities, identify investments in debt securities and equity securities that are less than 20 percent of a corporation's voting stock.

- Trading securities are considered current assets and are reported at their fair value.

- Available-for-sale securities, except for those individual securities that qualify as current assets, are classified as long-term assets. Both current and long-term AFS securities are reported at their fair value.

- An investor company uses the equity method if it owns enough of an investee company's common stock (usually 20 to 50 percent) to have a significant influence on the company. When using the equity method, the investor increases its investment account based on increases in the stockholders' equity of the investee company due to the recognition of income. Also, the investor's investment account would decrease when the investee declares dividends. The equity method violates the historical cost principle in an effort to reflect the investor's interest in the investee's stockholders' equity.

- An investor company prepares consolidated financial statements when it owns a controlling interest in an investee company (50 percent or more of the investee's common stock). Consolidation includes reporting the income statements, balance sheets, and cash flow statements of two separate legal entities as one economic entity.

KEY TERMS

available-for-sale securities Debt and equity securities bought with the intent of maintaining a portfolio of securities that management can sell, as needed, to raise cash for particular projects

consolidated financial statements The combined financial statements of an inventory company, which owns more than 50 percent of another company, and the invested company, which reported operating results, financial position, and cash flows as if the companies were one economic entity

equity method The accounting method used by an investor company that exercises a significant influence over an investee company's operations which reflects increases and decreases in the investment account of the investor company in proportion to the investee's stockholders' equity

held-to-maturity securities Debt securities the firm buys with the intent of holding them until they mature

mark to market A method of showing the fair value of the entire portfolio of trading securities and available-for-sale securities on the balance sheet without altering the cost of the individual securities

market adjustment account A balance sheet account that reflects adjustments made to the total cost of trading securities and available-for-sale securities to show the fair value of the securities' portfolio

parent company The investor company that owns more than 50 percent of another corporation's voting stock

subsidiary company An investee company that has more than 50 percent of its voting stock owned by another company

trading securities Debt and equity securities bought with the intent of selling the securities after holding them for a short period of time

Unrealized Gain An increase in the fair value of the portfolio of trading securities that has not yet been realized by the sale of the securities

Unrealized Gain or Loss account A balance sheet account that reflects the adjustments made to total stockholders' equity to correspond to the balance in the market adjustment account for available-for-sale securities

Unrealized Loss A decrease in the fair value of the portfolio of trading securities that has not yet been realized by the sale of the securities

QUESTIONS

1. Why do firms make short-term investments in debt and equity securities?

2. Why do firms make long-term investments in debt and equity securities?

3. What constitutes a trading security?

4. What is the distinction between available-for-sale securities and held-to-maturity securities?

5. When and why do companies use the equity method to account for an investment?

6. What items are included in or excluded from the cost of an investment in debt securities?

7. Why are discounts and premiums on trading debt securities not amortized?

8. When a noninterest-bearing note that is a trading security matures, the amount of cash received is greater than the cost of the investment. How does the accounting system reflect this difference?

9. Why are the fair values of trading securities and available-for-sale securities reported on the financial statements?

10. Why are held-to-maturity securities not shown at their fair value?

11. What is the distinction between realized gains and losses and unrealized gains and losses on trading securities?

12. Why are discounts and premiums on available-for-sale debt securities amortized when discounts and premiums on trading securities are not amortized?

13. When premiums and discounts are amortized on long-term investments in bonds, which of these makes interest income greater than the amount of cash interest received? Why?

14. Explain what impact the investor's ability or inability to exercise significant influence or control over the investee's operations has on how to account for long-term investments in equity securities.

15. Can a company that owns a large number of debt securities of another company have the same level of influence as a company that holds 20 percent or more of a company's stock? Why?

16. What is the role of the Unrealized Gains and Loss account for available-for-sale securities?

17. Explain how the sale of individual trading or available-for-sale securities affects the market adjustment account.

18. What are consolidated financial statements and why do companies prepare them?

19. What information about investments in debt and equity securities appears on the cash flow statement?

20. How do internal reports about the investments in debt and equity securities differ from their presentation on external financial statements?

EXERCISES

E 21.1 Match the following terms with the descriptions below.
  a. Equity method.
  b. Trading security investments.
  c. Consolidated financial statements.
  d. Available-for-sale investments.
  e. Equity security investments.
  f. Held-to-maturity investments.
  g. Debt security investments.
  h. Mark to market.

  _____ 1. Investments in the stock of another company.
  _____ 2. The financial statements that reflect the control of one corporation over another.
  _____ 3. Used when one company has a significant influence over another company.
  _____ 4. Debt and equity securities that will be sold in the near term.
  _____ 5. Reporting the fair value of a company's portfolio of investments.
  _____ 6. Investments in debt securities held until they mature.
  _____ 7. Debt and equity securities of another company that could be sold but which management does not expect to sell in the near future.
  _____ 8. Securities that describe a creditorship relationship between the holder of a note and the maker of the note.

E 21.2 Match the following balance sheet classification with the type of security.
  a. Current assets.
  b. Investments.
  c. Included in consolidated balance sheet.

  _____ 1. Investment in 30 percent of another company's common stock.
  _____ 2. Trading Securities—Equity.
  _____ 3. Available-for-sale securities.
  _____ 4. Investment in 60 percent of another company's common stock.
  _____ 5. Held-to-maturity securities.
  _____ 6. Held-to-maturity securities that mature in the next year.

E 21.3 On February 1, the Boone Corporation purchased for $49,200, a U.S. Treasury bill with a $50,000 face value that was due in two months. Boone collected the $50,000 when the Treasury bills matured on April 1. Make the entries for Boone's Treasury bill transactions.

E 21.4 Jefferson Company purchases a $30,000 face value U.S. Treasury bill issued on a discounted basis, for $28,400 and paid brokerage fees of $100. Four months later when it needed the cash, Jefferson Company sold the investment for $29,300. Prepare the journal entries to record the purchase and sale of this trading security.

21.5 Wilson Manufacturing Corporation purchased interest-bearing U.S. Treasury notes with a face value of $30,000 on August 1, 1995, as a trading security. The purchase price of $28,750 included $400 in accrued interest.

On December 1, 1995, Wilson received a check for $1,200 for 6 months' interest. On February 28, 1996, the investment was sold for $29,100 including accrued interest of $600. Assuming that Wilson has a December 31 fiscal year-end, journalize all transactions related to Wilson's investment in U.S. Treasury notes.

E 21.6 Columbia, Inc., paid $20,560 to purchase $20,000 face value 9 percent bonds issued by Kavco Products as a temporary investment on May 31. The purchase price includes brokerage fees and interest accrued on the bonds since March 1, the most recent interest payment date. Kavco pays interest on March 1 and September 1 each year. Columbia sold the investment on September 30. The proceeds from the sale, including accrued interest, amounted to $20,700. Prepare all journal entries required for Columbia's investment in the bonds.

E 21.7 Burr Industries' accounting records are maintained on a calendar-year basis. On May 15, the firm purchased 1,500 shares of English Company's common stock at $42 per share plus brokerage fees of $350. Burr Industries expected to hold the shares for less than 3 months. On July 1, Burr Industries received a cash dividend of $1.50 per share from the stock. The shares were sold on August 4 at $42.50 per share. Brokerage fees on the sale were $370. Prepare all journal entries required in relation to Burr Industries' investment in the stock of English Company.

E 21.8　On February 15, 1996, the Burtscher Corporation purchased 300 shares of AVCO Corporation's common stock for $26 per share plus $200 in brokerage fees. Burtscher expects to sell the stock within the 3 months. On April 2, Burtscher received a $.20 per share dividend. On May 8, it sold 100 of the shares for $27.50 per share less brokerage fees of $80. On June 1, it sold the remaining shares for $26, less brokerage fees of $120. Make the entries necessary for these transactions.

E 21.9　Salem Enterprises had the following trading securities on December 31, 1996. The current market value amount represents the fair value of the securities on December 31, 1996. Make the entry to adjust these trading securities to their market value assuming that the market adjustment account does not have a balance as of the end of the fiscal year. Show how the firm's trading debt securities are reported on its balance sheet. Why are these securities shown at their fair value?

	Historical Cost	Current Market Value
U.S. Treasury bills	$13,170	$13,540
U.S. Treasury notes	31,360	31,450
Adams Company bonds	24,875	24,750
Quincy Corporation bonds	57,250	57,260

E 21.10　Hamilton Company occasionally buys and sells shares of stock in various other companies as a part of its cash management program. The total cost and fair value of its trading securities at the end of 1995 and 1996 are shown below. For each year, prepare the necessary entries to adjust the portfolio from cost to market, and show how Hamilton's trading securities would appear in the balance sheet for each year. At the start of 1995, Hamilton had no balance in its market adjustment account.

	Cost	Market Value
1995	$43,200	$42,870
1996	36,950	38,600

E 21.11　Using the data in E 21.10, make the mark-to-market entries necessary and show the balance sheet presentation assuming that these are available-for-sale securities.

E 21.12　On December 31, 1996, Dible Corporation had trading securities that cost $150,000 and had a market value of $159,000. Included in Dible Corporation's investments are 20 shares of Adams Products Company stock acquired at a total cost of $1,128. Those 20 shares had a market value of $1,250 at the end of 1996. Early in 1997, the investment in Adams Products was sold. The net proceeds from that sale were $1,083. Prepare the journal entry to record the sale of Adams Products stock by Dible Corporation.

E 21.13　The Pfeifer Corporation had the following portfolio of trading securities on its fiscal year-end, December 31, 1996.

	Cost	Market
100 shares InFel common stock	$5,200	$5,375
200 shares ABCO preferred stock	3,500	3,450
3, $1,000 Gyro Corporation bonds	2,980	3,120

Make the entry to record Pfeifer's mark-to-market adjustment on December 31, 1996, and show how Pfeifer's portfolio of trading securities are reported on its balance sheet. On January 15, 1997, Pfeifer sold 50 of the ABCO shares at $18 per share. Make the entry to record the sale of the ABCO shares.

E 21.14　On August 1, 1996, Rhoden Company purchased bonds with a face value of $5,000 and a face interest rate of 10 percent that was paid August 1 and February 1. The bonds were initially issued by the Shearer Corporation in 1992 and had a 10-year life. Rhoden purchased the bonds to yield an effective rate of interest of 8 percent and considered them to be available-for-sale security. What price did Rhoden pay for the Shearer bonds? Given that Rhoden Corporation has a December 31 fiscal year-end, make the entries for the Shearer bonds on Rhoden's books from August 1 to the first interest date of February 1, 1997. If the bonds were the only available-for-sale securities Rhoden owned and had a market price of 101 3/4 on December 31, 1996, show how Rhoden would report these bonds on its December 31, 1996, balance sheet.

E 21.15   Mason Manufacturing purchased bonds of Dixon Products on May 1, 1995, that had a face value of $20,000 and a face rate of interest of 8 percent that is paid annually. The bonds mature on May 1, 1998, and Mason is going to hold the bonds to maturity. Make the entry to record the bonds for the period from May 1, 1995, to May 1, 1996, if the bonds were purchased to yield an effective rate of interest of 9 percent. Show how Mason's balance sheet would report the bonds on December 31, 1995, if the bonds had a market value of 102.

E 21.16   On July 10, 1995, Alamo Distributors purchased 5,000 shares of Austin Manufacturing common stock at 33 1/4 plus brokerage fees of $600. This investment represents 5 percent of the common stock of Austin. Alamo also purchased 1,000 shares of Dallas Corporation common stock for 23 1/4 plus brokerage fees of $100 on September 1, 1995. On November 15, Alamo sold 500 shares of Austin for $35 3/8 less brokerage fees of $80. The market price of Austin's and Dallas's common stock on December 31, 1995, Alamo's fiscal year-end, was 32 7/8 and 25, respectively.

   Prepare the entry to record Alamo's purchase and sale of these available-for-sale equity securities. Make the mark-to-market adjusting entry on December 31 assuming the market adjustment account has a zero balance.

E 21.17   Given the information in E 21.16, show the balance sheet presentation of Alamo Corporation's available-for-sale equity securities on December 31, 1995.

E 21.18   Colony Corporation has an investment in the common stock of Plymouth Company. The investment is accounted for on the equity basis because Colony owns 40 percent of Plymouth's common stock and exercises significant influence over its investee. On August 1, 1995, Colony received a dividend check for $15,000 from Plymouth. After closing its books on September 30, 1995, Plymouth reports a total net income of $200,000 to its investors. Prepare the journal entries to be made on Colony Corporation's books on August 1, 1995, and on September 30, 1995. How would Colony report its investment in Plymouth on its balance sheet?

E 21.19   On July 1, 1996, Stradal Corporation purchased 25 percent of Squyers Corporation's voting common stock for $525,000 plus a commission of $10,000. During the year Squyers declared and paid $8,000 of dividends and reported that for its fiscal year ending on December 31, 1996, it had incurred a loss of $40,000. What is the ending balance in Stradal's Investment in Squyers Corporation account? Show how Stradal will report its investment on its balance sheet. What impact will Stradal's investment in Squyers Corporation have on its income statement in 1996?

E 21.20   Tucker Corporation owns the following securities at December 31, 1996.

	Cost	Market
Harris Corporation common stock	$41,225	$42,126
U.S. Treasury bills	19,850	19,950
Lang Corporation preferred stock	5,760	5,554
Wagner Corporation bonds	34,950	35,180
ATT bonds	9,950	9,865
Superscope common stock	6,775	5,605
Crick Corporation common stock	40,350	41,349

If Tucker classifies its securities as described below, show how Tucker will report these securities on its December 31, 1996, balance sheet.

Trading securities:
  U.S. Treasury bills
  Lang preferred stock

Available-for-sale securities:
  Superscope common stock
  Crick Corporation common stock
  ATT bonds
  Harris Corporation common stock

Held-to-maturity securities:
  Wagner Corporation bonds

PROBLEMS

P 21.1
On February 1, 1997, Jackson Corporation purchased bonds of Washington Foundry, Inc., as trading securities for 103 1/4 plus a brokerage fee of $1,000. The bonds have a face value of $50,000 and a face interest rate of 10 percent that is paid on April 1 and October 1, and mature 20 years from the date of purchase.

Required:
a. How much cash did Jackson Corporation pay to acquire the bonds?
b. Prepare the journal entries to record:
  (1) The acquisition of the bonds.
  (2) The receipt of the cash interest on October 1, 1997.
  (3) The adjusting entry for the December 31 fiscal year-end.
c. What is the cost of the investment of the bonds on December 31, 1997?

P 21.2
On September 1, 1996, Bartlet Corporation purchased bonds of Menno Products as an available-for-sale investment. The bonds had a face value of $100,000, bear a 12 percent face interest rate that is paid on March 1 and September 1, and mature on September 1, 1998. No brokerage fees were involved.

Required:
a. What price did Bartlet Corporation pay for these bonds if the bonds will yield 10 percent?
b. Prepare the journal entries to record:
  (1) The acquisition of the bonds.
  (2) The accrual of the interest on the bonds on December 31, 1996.
  (3) The receipt of the interest on March 1, 1997.
c. What is the cost of the bonds as of Bartlet's fiscal year-end?

P 21.3
Cilin, Inc., owns 100,000 shares of Victor Enterprise's common stock, which represents 40 percent of Victor's outstanding shares. Cilin accounts for the long-term investment using the equity method. On December 31, 1996, the balance in the investment account was $800,000, and the market value per share was 8 1/4.

In 1997, Victor Enterprise paid dividends totaling $187,500 and reported net income of $400,000. Market value per share on December 31, 1997, was 8 7/8.

Victor Enterprises reported a net loss of $100,000 in 1998. Dividends of $50,000 were declared and paid during the year. Market value per share of Victor's common stock was 9 3/8 on December 31, 1998.

Required:
a. Prepare the journal entries for Cilin, Inc., for 1997 and 1998.
b. Describe how the investment is reported on Cilin's balance sheet on December 31, 1997, and December 31, 1998.

P 21.4
Sakett Industries owns 40,000 shares of common stock in Able Company. This represents a 10 percent interest in Able's outstanding shares that Sakett considers an available-for-sale security. The balance in the investment account on December 31, 1995, was $1,400,000. Market value per share of Able Company was 36 1/4 on that date. The Able Company stock is Sakett's only available-for-sale security.

During 1996, Able Company paid dividends to common stockholders totaling $150,000, and its net income for the year was $660,000. Market value of the stock on December 31, 1996, was 38 1/2.

On January 1, 1997, Sakett Industries sold 20,000 shares of the Able Company stock for $38 per share less a $10,000 brokerage fee. In 1997, Able Company paid dividends to the common stockholders totaling $120,000, and the firm had a total loss for the year of $90,000. The market value of the stock on December 31, 1997, was 35 3/4 per share.

Required:
a. Prepare the journal entries for Sakett Industries' records for 1996 and 1997.
b. Give Sakett's balance sheet presentation of these securities for 1995, 1996, and 1997.

P 21.5 In the month of March, Far West Company had the following transactions in its trading securities classification.

March 5 Sold U.S. Treasury notes for $103,000 including accrued interest. The notes are carried at a cost of $101,800. Unrecorded interest of $1,600 had accrued on the notes up to the date of sale.

10 Purchased $25,000 face value of State Power Company's bonds for 101 1/2 plus accrued interest of $800 and brokerage fees of $150.

17 Purchased U.S. Treasury bills with a face value of $30,000 for $29,550.

22 Received interest of $1,500 on U.S. Treasury notes. No interest was accrued when the notes were purchased.

28 Sold the U.S. Treasury bill purchased on March 17. The sales price was $29,635.

Required: Prepare the necessary journal entries to record the March transactions.

P 21.6 During August, Commonwealth Company had the following transactions related to its trading securities.

Aug. 3 Received a check for $1,800 for interest on the investment in Independence Company bonds. Of the total received, $500 is accrued interest that had been paid for when the bonds were purchased. Brokerage fees of $80 were already deducted from the check.

6 Purchased U.S. Treasury notes with a face value of $50,000 for $50,200 plus brokerage fees of $360 and accrued interest of $1,750.

11 Received dividends of $450 on an investment in common stock of United Gas and Oil Corporation.

14 Sold 600 shares of Tory Company stock for $13,820 less brokerage fees of $140. The stock is carried in the accounts at a cost of $13,385.

18 Sold U.S. Treasury certificates with a face value of $20,000, which were purchased at a total cost of $19,250 for net proceeds of $19,600.

20 Purchased 250 shares of Colony Corporation stock for $88 per share plus brokerage fees of $200.

24 Sold Freedom Corporation bonds, which are carried at a cost of $32,650. The cash received of $32,900 included accrued interest to the date of sale of $730 less brokerage fees of $1,200.

31 Received $2,000 for 6 months' interest on U.S. Treasury notes purchased on August 6.

Required: Prepare the necessary journal entries to record August's transactions.

P 21.7 The Ray-Beam Corporation has calculated the total cost and the market values of its investments below.

	Cost	Market Value
Trading securities	$ 124,300	$ 124,600
Available-for-sale securities	1,256,000	1,259,000
Held-to-maturity securities	532,540	529,000

Before the year-end adjustment was made, the market adjustment account for trading securities has a debit balance of $900, while the market adjustment account for available-for-sale securities has a credit balance of $2,000. The held-to-maturity securities has $20,000 of bonds that will mature in the next year.

Required: a. Make the adjusting entries for Ray-Beam's investments.

b. Prepare the balance sheet presentation of these investments.

P 21.8 At the end of 1995, Marchall-Gorem & Company's asset accounts included the following.

Available-for-sale investments	$216,890
Less: Market adjustment account	4,525
	$212,365

During 1996, the firm sold securities that cost $45,400 for $46,250. It also purchased additional securities costing a total of $61,300. The market value of the available-for-sales securities at December 31, 1996, totaled $255,850. Securities costing $23,670 were sold in 1997. Proceeds from that sale totaled $23,450. No additional transactions occurred in 1997. The market value of all securities held at the end of 1997 amounted to $234,770.

Required:
a. Prepare the journal entries to record the sales and acquisitions of securities each year.
b. Prepare the adjusting entry at the end of each year to value the securities at their fair value.
c. Show how the available-for-sale investments are presented on Marchall-Gorem & Company's balance sheet on December 31, 1996, and 1997.

P 21.9 The following accounts and balances appeared in the asset section of Lincoln Company's balance sheet at the end of 1996.

Investments:	
Available-for-sale securities	$93,760
Less: Market adjustment	2,140
Investments at market	$91,620

During 1997, Lincoln sold securities that cost $26,890 for $28,120. It also purchased additional securities so that at the end of the year it held available-for-sale securities costing $103,400 whose market value was $100,980.

More available-for-sale securities were purchased in 1998, and the company sold some of its investments that cost $48,720, for $46,950. The available-for-sale securities held at the end of 1998 had a cost of $86,390 and a market value of $89,100. On December 30, 1998 Lincoln purchased a held-to-maturity bond for $5,220.

Required:
a. Prepare the journal entries to record the sale and purchase of the securities for 1997.
b. Prepare the adjusting entry necessary to value the securities at their fair values for 1997.
c. Show the balance sheet presentation for 1997.
d. Prepare the journal entries to record the sale and purchase of the securities for 1998.
e. Prepare the adjusting entry necessary to value the securities at their face value for 1998.
f. Show the balance sheet presentation for 1998.

P 21.10 Madison Company's cash management policy is to invest idle cash in trading securities and to sell those securities as the company approaches its peak season when it needs funds. On December 31, 1995, the end of the fiscal year, Madison's had the following information related to its trading securities.

U.S. Treasury bills, maturing on March 12, 1996, face value $10,000 (market value $9,850)	$9,815
Clay Corporation 8% bonds, face value of $30,000 (market value $29,400)	28,860
Interest receivable on Clay Corporation bonds	600
Revere, Inc., common stock, 200 shares (market value $8,625)	8,485
Union Products Company common stock, 200 shares (market value $7,350)	7,570

The market adjustment account had a credit balance of $380 before the mark-to-market adjusting entry was made in 1995.

During 1996, Madison Company had the following transactions related to its trading securities.

March 12 The U.S. Treasury bills matured and were converted to cash.
   18 Purchased 300 shares of Hancock Corporation stock at $27 per share plus brokerage fees of $85.
April 1 Collected six months' interest on Clay Corporation bonds.
May 3 Sold 200 shares of Union Products Company stock at $34.75 per share. Total brokerage fees on the sale were $65.
June 30 Purchased $30,000 face value of Washington Company 9 percent bonds for $30,650, including brokerage fees of $175 and accrued interest of $225. The bonds pay interest on June 1 and December 1. (They are accounted for on cost basis.)
July 8 Purchased $40,000 in U.S. Treasury bills at a total cost of $39,920.
Aug. 27 Sold 200 shares of Revere, Inc., stock for net proceeds of $8,690.
Sept. 17 The U.S. Treasury bills purchased on July 8 matured and were converted to cash.
Oct. 1 Collected six months' interest on Clay Corporation bonds and sold the bonds for 99 1/4.
   17 Purchased 400 shares of Monroe, Inc., common stock at $47 per share plus brokerage fees of $170.
Dec. 1 Collected six months' interest on Washington Company bonds.

On December 31, 1996, the market value of Hancock Company common stock was $25.50 per share, and the Monroe, Inc., common stock was $48.25 per share. The Clay Corporation bonds had a fair value of $29,500 and the Washington Company bonds had a fair value of $30,530.

Required: *a.* Make the entry to record the mark-to-market adjustment for 1995.

b. Record the entries for the transactions in 1996.

c. Prepare the necessary adjusting entries for December 31, 1996.

d. Show how to report the trading securities on the December 31, 1995, and 1996, balance sheets.

P 21.11   On June 1, 1997, Eau Claire Corporation purchased 100 Wildcat Corporation bonds that had a total face value of $100,000. The bonds had a face rate of 10 percent and paid interest semi-annually on December 1 and June 1 and were issued to yield an 8 percent market rate of interest. The bonds had a 10-year life when Wildcat issued them on June 1, 1994. Eau Claire Corporation intends to hold the bonds to maturity and has a December 31 fiscal year-end.

Required: *a.* Make the entry to record the acquisition of the bonds.

b. Make the entry to record the receipt of the cash interest on December 1, 1997.

c. Make the entry(ies) necessary on December 31, 1997, assuming that the market price of the bonds is 101 3/4 and Eau Claire only owns the Wildcat bonds.

d. Show how the bonds are reported on Eau Claire's balance sheet.

e. Give the entry to record the receipt of the cash interest on June 1, 1998.

f. Assume that Eau Claire sold 10 of the Wildcat bonds for 102 on June 1, 1998.

COMPUTER APPLICATIONS

CA 21.1   Carlos Company purchased a $1 million bond issue on the interest payment date when the market rate of interest was 8 percent. The bonds pay interest semiannually at the rate of 10 percent. There are 15 years remaining in the 20-year life of the bonds.

Required: Use a computer spreadsheet package.

a. Determine how much Carlos paid to obtain these bonds.

b. Assuming that Carlos intends to hold these bonds until maturity, prepare a schedule that indicates the amounts needed for journal entries on each semiannual interest payment date.

CA 21.2   Vreotek Enterprises plans to purchase a $500,000 bond issue on the interest payment date when the market rate of interest is 12 percent. The bonds in question pay interest semiannually at an 8 percent rate. The bonds mature in eight years.

Required: Use a computer spreadsheet package.

a. Determine how much Vrotek must pay to obtain the bond issue.

b. Assume that Vrotek plans to hold the bonds until maturity. Prepare a schedule that shows the amount of cash received, the change in the investment account, the interest revenue, and the carrying value of the bonds on each interest payment date.

CASES

C 21.1   Carly Marken, president of Peregrine, Inc., is conducting the annual stockholders' meeting. After she completes her remarks on the company's objectives for the coming year, which include introducing a new product line, she asks you, the financial vice president, to answer stockholders' questions on the financial statements contained in the firm's annual report. Kelly Harper, who owns a substantial number of shares of common stock, makes the following statement:

> I'm not going to quote a bunch of numbers, but I see the company has a lot of money tied up in short-term investments and there is some kind of market adjustment account that lowers them to market. Does that mean we have lost money on those investments? Besides that, the income statement shows we have interest income, losses on the sale of investments, and some kind of unrealized gain. How can the company have an unrealized gain when the market value of these investments is less than their cost? Anyway, why don't you just put all of those gains and losses and the investment income together in one amount and be done with it? Furthermore, if the company has so much extra cash that you can play around investing it, I'd just as soon you increase the dividends and give that cash to the stockholders.

Required: Answer the specific questions Kelly Harper has raised and respond to her comment about the extra cash.

C 21.2 Using the financial statements of Disney Corporation, find the following information about Disney's short-term and long-term investments.

    a. What is the cost and fair value of Disney's trading securities?

    b. What is the cost and fair value of their available-for-sale securities?

    c. What is the dollar value of the bonds held to maturity?

    d. How much cash was generated by the sale of investments? How much cash was paid to acquire investments?

    e. Does Disney have a significant influence on another company?

    f. Does Disney have a controlling interest in other corporations?

CRITICAL THINKING

CT 21.1 It is possible for a corporation to report an unrealized gain on trading securities on its income statement when the market value of its portfolio of trading securities is less than its cost. How could this occur? Is it possible to have an unrealized loss or gain on the income statement if a corporation does not have any trading securities at the end of a fiscal year? Explain.

CT 21.2 Accounting principles require companies to report the unrealized gains and losses associated with their portfolio of trading securities on the income statement, but not the unrealized gains and losses from available-for-sale securities. Why do you think these unrealized gains and losses are reported differently?

ETHICAL CHALLENGES

EC 21.1 Ataway Corporation has a practice of moving its investments from the long-term to the short-term investment classification whenever their current ratio becomes too low. Once the current ratio becomes high enough, they reclassify the short-term investment back to the long-term classification.

Required: Comment on this practice. What are the implications for financial statement readers?

E 21.2 The management of Fry Corporation is very concerned because it anticipates that 1997's income is going to be its lowest in five years. Darla Fry, the corporation's president, has suggested a unique solution to this problem. She realizes that the company holds a large number of bonds purchased in 1988 that are classified as held-to-maturity securities. Because the interest rates have decreased dramatically since the bonds were purchased, their market value greatly exceeds their cost. She suggests that the company reclassify the bonds as trading securities. In this way, the bonds will be adjusted to their market value and the unrealized gain will appear on the income statement and boost this year's earnings. Once the current crisis is over, she suggests the bonds be reclassified as held to maturity. Ms. Fry defends this action because she says that the increase in the bonds' value is hidden from the investors. She contends that this action will actually show a more realistic picture of the company's financial position.

Required: Comment on the advisability of Ms. Fry's proposal.

PART SEVEN

Firm Performance: Evaluation and Control

Part 7, the evaluation section, teaches the student how internal and external stakeholders use accounting information to evaluate the firm's performance. The evaluation is based on the profitability, financial position, and cash flows of the firm. This brings closure to the business activities of the firm as well as the accounting process. The final part of the evaluation section is comprehensive financial statement analysis.

CHAPTER 22

Firm Performance: Profitability

Learning Objectives

1. Explain the importance of the components of earnings (income from continuing operations) to users.
2. Describe what is important about the components of nonowner changes in equity and cumulative accounting adjustments.
3. Explain how companies determine earnings per share and what information it provides to users.
4. Identify the elements of the statement of retained earnings.
5. Describe the limitations of the income statement.
6. Explain why companies use product line (divisional) income reports and current cost income reports internally.

Harley-Davidson is the only American-based motorcycle manufacturer and is a leading supplier of heavyweight (750cc or larger) motorcycles to the global market. In 1993, Harley-Davidson celebrated its 90th anniversary, posted record sales and earnings, and declared its first quarterly cash dividend for shareholders. In 1994, it generated a record net income of $104,272,000.[1] Its 1994 sales from motorcycles and related products were $1.2 billion while net sales from other transportation vehicles were $383 million.[2] Clearly motorcycles remain Harley-Davidson's primary product line. The key to Harley-Davidson's success lies in its commitment to its recognized stakeholders—customers, dealers, suppliers, shareholders, employees, government, and society. In fact, 96 percent of current Harley-Davidson customers claim that they intend to buy another Harley product. With demand for Harley-Davidson motorcycles exceeding the supply, the temptation to overproduce exists, but Harley-Davidson remains committed to quality. According to Tom Gelbt, vice president of continuous improvement, "We will not compromise quality for quantity."[3] That philosophy underlies Harley-Davidson's commitment to its stakeholders as

---

[1]Harley-Davidson, Inc., Form 10-K, 1994, p. 35.
[2]Harley-Davidson, Inc., Form 10-K, 1994, p. 50.
[3]Harley-Davidson, Inc., Annual Report, 1993, p. 14.

exemplified by its employee education programs, total quality management, and involvement in the Make-A-Wish Foundation. Harley-Davidson's commitment to quality has also resulted in increased sales and earnings, allowing the company to once again reign as the "king of motorcycles."

Throughout this text, we have talked about business events that affect a company's profitability and are reported on the income statement. In this chapter, we look at the income statement in its entirety, exploring issues such as what information the income statement and its related notes actually provide to users, and what income statement limitations users should consider. We also examine the statement of retained earnings, which provides the link between the income statement and the balance sheet. Finally, we introduce other important sources of information available to management concerning a firm's profit-making activities.

We will refer to the financial statements and related notes of Harley-Davidson, included in the annual report booklet, throughout our discussion.

WHAT IS THE PURPOSE OF THE INCOME STATEMENT?

The purpose of the income statement is to reflect the earnings (income) generated by the company during the accounting period. It is vital for both internal and external users to comprehend the components of reported earnings.

The FASB's conceptual framework states that the three objectives of financial reporting are to provide information that is: (1) useful for making investment and credit decisions, (2) useful for assessing cash flow prospects, and (3) relevant to evaluating enterprise resources, claims to those resources, and changes in the resources.[4]

The income statement fulfills these three objectives by disclosing information about the earnings of the company during the fiscal year, which current and potential investors and creditors use to assess the future earnings potential of the firm. Such assessment of earnings also provides information that allows external users to evaluate the amounts, timing, and uncertainty of future cash flows from dividends or interest. The income statement also provides important information about changes in the company's resources (assets) and claims to those resources (equities) due to the operating activities of the company. Investors and creditors use this type of past operating performance information to predict the future performance of the company.

The income statement is the most widely quoted of the financial statements, yet it is relatively new compared to the balance sheet. The income statement did not become popular until corporations became widespread in the late 1800s. The corporate form of business made income reporting necessary because corporations are a separate legal entities and, therefore, generate taxable profits. In addition, the income statement, which reports the earnings performance of an entity for a period of time, was (and is) vitally important to both absentee owners and to creditors for evaluating the company. Finally, the existence and publication of periodic income statements made it easier for owners to buy and sell their stock because interested parties could assess the current operating performance of the company as part of the negotiation process.

HOW DOES GAAP AFFECT THE INCOME STATEMENT?

Generally accepted accounting principles (GAAP) require that externally reported income statements comply with the comprehensive concept of income. **Comprehensive income,** commonly called *net income,* reported externally should reflect *all* changes in owners' equity during the period except those resulting from investments by, or distributions to, owners and those resulting from errors made in

---

[4]Financial Accounting Standards Board, *Statements of Financial Accounting Concepts No. 1,* paragraphs 34, 37, and 40, 1986.

previous periods. (We present a discussion of the latter items in the section on the statement of retained earnings later in this chapter.) The elements of comprehensive income are illustrated below:[5]

+	Revenues
–	Expenses
+	Gains
–	Losses
=	**Earnings (income from continuing operations)**
+/–	Other nonowner changes in equity
+/–	Cumulative accounting adjustments
=	**Comprehensive income (net income)**

As you can see, comprehensive (net) income often is not the same as earnings. **Earnings** are income from continuing operations and include revenues minus expenses plus gains and minus losses. Earnings are recurring, whereas, the events included in comprehensive income are not necessarily recurring. Rather, they are reported as part of comprehensive income so that financial statement users have a complete picture of both the operating and nonowner activities that caused changes in owners' equity during the period.

Comprehensive income is important because it reflects *both* the recurring and nonrecurring aspects of the firm's earnings. This gives financial statement users a better idea of how to predict future earnings and cash flows as well as how to evaluate management's actions for the current period. We discuss this issue in more detail as we explore the components of earnings and comprehensive income next.

Exhibit 22.1 shows the income statement for Alvarez Enterprises, which we will use as our road map for this chapter. We discuss the income statement in three sections:

[5]Financial Accounting Standards Board, *Statement of Financial Accounting Concepts No. 5*, paragraph 44, 1986.

EXHIBIT | 22.1 | Multistep Income Statement

ALVAREZ ENTERPRISES
Income Statement
For the Year Ended December 31, 1996
(in thousands except per share data)

Sales	$2,458,160
Cost of goods sold	1,752,817
Gross margin	**$ 705,343**
Selling and administrative expenses	424,136
Income from operations	**$ 281,207**
Other revenues and gains:	
Interest income	613
Dividend revenue	201
Other expenses and losses:	
Interest expense	450
Loss on sale of investment	100
Income from continuing operations before taxes	**$ 281,471**
Income tax expense	126,662
Income from continuing operations	**$ 154,809**
Discontinued operations:	
Income from operations of division, net of applicable taxes	120
Loss on disposal of division, net of applicable taxes	1,450
Income before extraordinary items and cumulative effect of accounting change	**$ 153,479**
Extraordinary loss from flood, net of applicable taxes	1,100
Cumulative effect of change in depreciation method, net of applicable taxes	880
Net income	**$ 151,499**
Earnings per share:	
Income from continuing operations	$7.14
Income before extraordinary items and cumulative effect of accounting change	7.08
Extraordinary loss	−.05
Cumulative effect of accounting change	−.04
Net income	6.99
Diluted earnings per share:	
Income from continuing operations	$6.70
Income before extraordinary items and cumulative effect of accounting change	6.65
Extraordinary loss	−.05
Cumulative effect of accounting change	−.04
Net income	6.56

(1) earnings; (2) other nonowner changes in equity, which are discontinued operations and extraordinary items; and (3) cumulative accounting adjustments, which are changes in accounting principles. Following this discussion we look at the reporting of earnings per share.

What Is Reported as Earnings?

The earnings of the firm include its revenues minus expenses plus gains and minus losses. The business activities that result in income from continuing operations are assumed to be recurring. Revenue and expense events clearly are recurring events because they take place daily, and many gains and losses can occur often enough to be considered recurring events. Other gains and losses, such as those regarding discontinued operations, are not recurring events.

As discussed in Chapter 9, the income statement is shown in either a multistep or single-step format. Exhibit 22.1 is an example of a multistep income statement that shows subdivided earnings (income) based on the types of company activities reported. For example, cost of goods sold ($1,752,817) is subtracted from sales ($2,458,160), which results in gross margin ($705,343). Selling and administrative expenses ($424,136) are subtracted from gross margin, which results in income from operations ($281,207).

Then, other revenues and gains ($613 and $201) are added and other expenses and losses ($450 and $100) are subtracted to calculate income from continuing operations

EXHIBIT | 22.2 | Single-Step Income Statement

ALVAREZ ENTERPRISES
Income Statement—Single Step
For the Year Ended December 31, 1996
(in thousands)

Sales	$2,458,160	
Interest income	613	
Dividend revenue	201	
Total revenue		**$2,458,974**
Less expenses:		
Cost of goods sold	$1,752,817	
Selling and administrative expense	424,136	
Interest expense	450	
Loss on sale of investment	100	
Income tax expense	126,662	
Total expenses		2,304,165
Income from continuing operations		$ 154,809
Discontinued operations:		
Income from operations of division, net of applicable taxes		120
Loss on disposal of division, net of applicable taxes		1,450
Income before extraordinary items and cumulative effect of accounting change		$ 153,479
Extraordinary loss from flood, net of applicable taxes		1,100
Cumulative effect of change in depreciation method, net of applicable taxes		880
Net income		$ 151,499

Earnings per share:	
Income from continuing operations	$7.14
Income before extraordinary items and cumulative effect of accounting change	7.08
Extraordinary loss	−.05
Cumulative effect of accounting change	−.04
Net income	6.99
Diluted earnings per share:	
Income from continuing operations	$6.70
Income before extraordinary items and cumulative effect of accounting change	6.65
Extraordinary loss	−.05
Cumulative effect of accounting change	−.04
Net income	6.56

before taxes ($281,471). After taxes are subtracted, the resulting amount is called *income from continuing operations* ($154,809).

On the other hand, to calculate income from continuing operations using a single-step format, it is necessary only to add all revenues and gains and then subtract all expenses and losses, as Exhibit 22.2 shows. In this case, the total revenue ($2,458,974) is decreased by the total expenses ($2,304,165) to determine income from continuing operations ($154,809).

Regardless of the format of the income statement, the notes to the financial statements are required because they provide valuable information for income statement users. For example, looking at the income statement of Harley-Davidson, we cannot tell how the company determined its cost of goods sold or what depreciation method it used. However, this information is available in the notes to the financial statements. Note number 1 to the Harley-Davidson statements indicates that it determines its cost of goods sold using LIFO for some inventories and FIFO for others and calculates depreciation using the straight-line method.

PAUSE & REFLECT

Examine the income statement of Harley-Davidson. Would you consider it to be a single-step or a multistep income statement? Why? Is there any information concerning recurring operations that you would like to know but is not reported? Explain.

Nonowner changes in equity resulting from discontinued operations and extraordinary items appear net of taxes after income from continuing operations, which is the basis for a company's income tax calculation. See Exhibit 22.1 which shows income from continuing operations before these items on the income statement. We discuss discontinued operations and extraordinary items in turn.

Discontinued Operations   **Discontinued operations** are the result of a company selling or disposing of a segment of its business. The results of these types of events are presented separately on the income statement because they are unique and infrequent and, thus, not a regular part of ongoing operations. However, discontinued operations do have ramifications on the future earnings potential and cash flows of the company and, therefore, provide useful information to income statement users.

When a segment of a business is discontinued, two items are reported, either on the income statement itself or in the notes to the financial statements. The first is the income or loss generated based on the operations of the segment from the beginning of the accounting period through the disposal date.[6] The second item reported is the gain or loss resulting from the disposal of the segment's net assets. Separating these items allows income statement readers to assess management's actions concerning the current and future aspects of disposing of the segment.

To illustrate how discontinued operations appear on the income statement, assume that during 1996, Alvarez Enterprises disposed of a segment of its operations that had income of $218,182 before taxes. Assuming a 45 percent tax rate, the income from operations, net of tax, reported on the income statement, is $120,000, as shown below:

Income from operations of division	$218,182
Less applicable taxes (45%)	98,182
Income from operations of division, net	$120,000

The loss incurred by Alvarez to dispose of the segment was $2,636,364 before taxes. The amount of the loss from disposing of the segment, net of tax, reported on the income statement is $1,450,000, as shown below:

Loss from disposal	$(2,636,364)
Less tax savings (45%)	1,186,364
Loss from disposal of division, net	$(1,450,000)

Take a moment to locate these items in Exhibit 22.1.

Typically, companies report a single line item, called *discontinued operations*, on the face of the income statement and provide additional information concerning the disposal in the notes, as mentioned earlier. For example, in 1993, American Express reported a loss from discontinued operations, net of tax, of $127 million on the face of the income statement. The notes to the financial statements reveal that the loss resulted from the disposal of Shearson-Lehman Brothers (SLB) and The Boston Company (TBC). Exhibit 22.3 shows additional detailed information provided in the notes concerning the American Express disposal. The company reported both the amount of the income or loss generated by the segment prior to disposal ($24 million and $63 million, respectively, for SLB and TBC) and the gain or loss generated by the disposal ($165 million gain on disposal of TBC and $630 million loss on disposal of SLB) are both reported.

Extraordinary Items   **Extraordinary items** are events that occurred during the accounting period that are *both unusual and infrequent*. Extraordinary events are often the result of a major casualty, such as assets that are expropriated by a foreign

---

[6]Additional accounting issues arise when the measurement date (date that management formally commits to dispose of the segment) and the disposal date (date the segment is formally sold) differ. We limit our discussion here to the broad accounting issues only.

| EXHIBIT | 22.3 | Discontinued Operations |

Components of income (loss):	
Income (loss) from Lehman's continuing core business	$376
TBC operations	**24**
SLB operations	**63**
Gain on sale of TBC	**165**
Loss on sale of SLB	**(630)**
Noncore business reserves	(100)
Income (loss) before accounting changes	$(102)
Preferred dividends	(25)
Discontinued operations	$(127)

Source: American Express, Annual Report, 1993.

government, losses sustained from a disaster, or material gains and losses from early extinguishment of debt.

It is not always easy to determine if a particular event is an extraordinary item. For example, a Florida company's loss due to a hurricane is not an extraordinary item because hurricanes in that region are not unusual. On the other hand, a Tennessee company's loss due to a hurricane would be an extraordinary item because hurricanes are rare in that region of the United States.

Extraordinary items appear net of taxes, the details of which are often found in the notes. To illustrate extraordinary items, assume that Alvarez Enterprises suffered an uninsured loss from a flood during 1996. The total loss was $2,000,000; however, the amount shown on the income statement (see Exhibit 22.1) is only $1,100,000 due to the tax savings resulting from the loss, as calculated below:

Loss due to flood	$(2,000,000)
Less tax savings (45%)	900,000
Extraordinary loss, net	$(1,000,000)

Now turn to the Harley-Davidson financial statements and notice that the company reported an extraordinary item, loss on debt repurchases, net of tax of $(388,000) for fiscal 1992.[7] This event also has an impact on future income because Harley-Davidson's interest expense will be lower, thus, increasing its net income.

What Are Cumulative Accounting Adjustments?

Cumulative accounting adjustments are modifications made to the accounting records that result from changes in accounting principles. These events occur when the company *switches from one generally accepted accounting method to another* (for example, from straight-line to double-declining-balance depreciation), or *when the company adopts a new accounting standard.*[8] For example, in 1992, the FASB passed *Statement of Financial Accounting Standards (SFAS) No. 106*, which changed the way that companies could account for their postretirement benefits (health care and insurance benefits provided to retirees and/or their families). Thus, in 1992 and 1993, many companies, including Harley-Davidson, reported a cumulative effect of accounting change as they adopted *SFAS No. 106*. Since cumulative effects of accounting changes are not recurring, they are shown separately on the income statement, net of tax.

---

[7]The notes to the 1992 annual report of Harley-Davidson revealed that "in May, 1992, the Company redeemed the remaining $7.8 million of subordinated notes outstanding, which resulted in an extraordinary charge of approximately $0.4 million, net of tax" (rounded). The FASB requires that companies report material gains or losses on extinquishment of debt as extraordinary items without regard to whether the event is unusual and infrequent.

[8]Special rules apply if a company switches its method of accounting for inventories to/from FIFO to/from LIFO. If a company changes to FIFO from LIFO, it must restate its income for any years shown on the comparative financial statements. However, if a company switches from FIFO to LIFO, this restatement is not required because it is impractical to ascertain the LIFO inventory numbers due to LIFO layers.

Regardless of management's reasons for making an accounting principle change, the statements presented for the current accounting period will not be prepared on the same basis as previous financial statements. This results in a lack of consistency between statements for consecutive reporting periods, which could mislead financial statement users. Therefore, it is necessary to disclose the reasons for the inconsistent presentation of events. The cumulative effect of the accounting change is shown because it is not feasible to go back and restate all previous years' financial statements to make them comparable to the current period's statements.

For example, assume that Alvarez Enterprises has assets with a 10-year useful life and no salvage value that were originally purchased in 1994 for $10 million. During 1994 and 1995, these assets were depreciated using the straight-line method. In 1996, management decided to switch to the double-declining-balance depreciation method. The difference in the depreciation expense for 1994 and 1995, respectively, using straight-line versus double-declining-balance is shown below.

	1994	1995
Double-declining-balance depreciation	$2,000,000	$1,600,000
Straight-line depreciation (former method)	1,000,000	1,000,000
Excess over straight-line	$1,000,000	$ 600,000

Thus, if the company had used double-declining-balance depreciation in 1994 and 1995, the reported net income before taxes would have been $1,000,000 and $600,000 lower, respectively, for each year. But the increased expense, which would have created lower income, also would have reduced the amount of income tax expense. Assuming a 45 percent marginal income tax rate, the tax savings resulting from the increased amount of depreciation expense are shown below:

	1994	1995
Increased depreciation expense	$1,000,000	$600,000
Marginal tax rate	.45	.45
Tax savings	$ 450,000	$270,000

Therefore, the 1996 cumulative effect of this accounting change, net of taxes, is an increase in expenses and, therefore, a reduction in income, of $880,000 ($1,000,000 + $600,000 – $450,000 – $270,000). The $880,000 of net reduction is shown on the face of the income statement (see Exhibit 22.1). The company would report the details of this calculation as well as management's reasons for making the change from one depreciation method to the other in the notes to the financial statements.

Now turn to the Harley-Davidson financial statements. In 1993, Harley-Davidson adopted *SFAS No. 106*, which resulted in a cumulative effect of an accounting change of $(32,124,000). Note no. 9 of the statements presents information about how the company calculated this amount.

Now that you understand the components of comprehensive income, we look at how to report that income on a per share basis.

WHAT DOES EARNINGS PER SHARE REPRESENT?

Fundamentally, **earnings per share** is a common-size measure of a company's earnings performance that allows financial statement users to compare the *operating performance* of large and small corporations on a share-for-share basis.

Earnings per share is the most frequently quoted measure of firm performance in the financial press, and it is a required disclosure on the face of the income statement. It reflects the amount of the company's earnings belonging to each shareholder on a per share basis. Earnings per share is *not* the amount that each stockholder will receive as dividends because, as you know, companies typically do not pay out all their earnings in dividends.

Calculating Earnings per Share

In its basic form, earnings per share is the current period's net income reported on a per share basis, or the net income of the current period available to common shareholders divided by the weighted-average number of common shares outstanding. It is calculated as shown below:

$$\frac{\text{Net income} - \text{Preferred stock dividends}}{\text{Weighted-average number of common shares outstanding}}$$

Take a closer look at this formula. First, it is necessary to reduce net income by the amount of preferred stock dividends because preferred stockholders have a pre-specified first claim on the earnings of the firm if any of those earnings are paid out as dividends. The remaining amount is known as *earnings available to common stockholders*. Second, the company uses the weighted-average number of common shares outstanding to measure the average number of shares held outside the company during the entire accounting period. It reflects an adjustment made for issuances and re-purchases of shares during the period.

For example, suppose that, on January 1, 1996, Alvarez Enterprises had 20 million common shares outstanding. On May 31, 1996, it issued an additional 3,000,000 shares and on October 1, 1996, it repurchased 600,000 shares to hold as treasury stock through the end of the year. Using this information, we calculate the weighted-average number of shares outstanding below:

Time Period, 1996	Shares	Partial-Year Ratio	Weight
Jan. 1–May 31	20,000,000	5/12	8,333,333
June 1–Oct. 1	23,000,000	4/12	7,666,667
Oct. 2–Dec. 31	22,400,000	3/12	5,600,000
Weighted-average number of shares outstanding			21,600,000

Assuming that net income is $151,499,000 (see Exhibit 22.1) and that preferred dividends are $600,000, the earnings per share is:

$$\frac{\$151,499,000 - \$600,000}{21,600,000} = \$6.99$$

This indicates to financial statements users that stockholders earned, on average, $6.99 per share held. Take a moment to examine Exhibit 22.1 and locate the earnings per share of $6.99.

Calculating Diluted Earnings per Share

How do securities that can be converted into common stock, such as convertible preferred stock and convertible bonds, affect earnings per share? What about stock options? Because earnings per share is often used as an indication of future earnings, it is necessary to show the amount of dilution, or decrease, in earnings per share that *would* occur as a result of activities like conversions and the exercise of stock options referred to as **diluted earnings per share.**

For example, assume that Alvarez offers its employees stock options as additional compensation. Further suppose that if these stock options were exercised, the weighted-average number of shares outstanding would be 23,000,000 (versus the 21,600,000 calculated previously). Using this information, the diluted earnings per share would be:

$$\frac{\$151,499,000 - \$600,000}{23,000,000} = \$6.56$$

Take a moment to locate the amount of diluted earnings per share in Exhibit 22.1 and notice that it is lower than the amount of earnings per share because the existing stockholders' interests will be diluted if the options are exercised.

Diluted earnings per share also appear on the income statement with the details regarding the calculation disclosed in the notes to the financial statements.[9]

---

[9]The detailed calculation of diluted earnings per share is beyond the scope of this text.

PAUSE & REFLECT

Turn to Harley-Davidson's 1994 annual report. What are the 1994 and 1993 earnings per share and diluted earnings per share? How are these amounts determined (see notes)?

Other Earnings per Share Disclosures

Companies must show the per share effects of extraordinary items and accounting changes so that users can assess, on a per share basis, the effects of these items on net income. For example, the income statement of Alvarez Enterprises (see Exhibit 22.1) indicates that earnings per share from continuing operations was $7.14 [($154,809,000 − $600,000)/21,600,000] and that income before extraordinary items and cumulative effect of accounting change on a per share basis was $7.08 [($153,479,000 − $600,000)/21,600,000]. The per share effects of the extraordinary loss and cumulative effect of accounting change were −$0.05 (−$1,100,000/21,600,000) and −$0.04 (−880,000/21,600,000), respectively.

Exhibit 22.1 indicates that diluted earnings per share from continuing operations was $6.70 [($154,809,000 − $600,000)/23,000,000], and that income before extraordinary items and cumulative effect of accounting change on a diluted per share basis was $6.65 [($153,479,000 − $600,000)/23,000,000].

PAUSE & REFLECT

On the Alvarez income statement, how were the amounts shown as per share effects of extraordinary items and as the cumulative effect of an accounting change on a diluted per share basis determined? Does Harley-Davidson disclose additional per share amounts?

WHAT IS THE PURPOSE OF THE STATEMENT OF RETAINED EARNINGS?

For corporations, the statement of retained earnings indicates the changes that occurred in the Retained Earnings account during the period. These changes arise from three sources: (1) net income or loss, (2) cash or stock dividends declared, and (3) prior period adjustments. Previously, we discussed how the balance of Retained Earnings increases or decreases during the closing process to reflect the net income or net loss of the period. In Chapter 19 we examined the effect of cash and stock dividends on retained earnings. Here we will discuss prior period adjustments.

A **prior period adjustment** is a correction of a previously undetected error that affected the net income or loss of a previous accounting period. The correction is made to beginning Retained Earnings because net income or loss is closed to Retained Earnings. Therefore, the beginning balance of Retained Earnings would be incorrect if an error affecting net income had occurred in a previous accounting period. When the error is discovered in the current year, companies report the impact of the error on Retained Earnings as an adjustment, net of tax.

For example, assume that Alvarez discovered in 1996 that rent of $30,000 was incorrectly recorded as prepaid rent rather than rent expense in 1995. Thus, Alvarez's 1995 income and assets were overstated. If the entry had been made correctly, 1995 expenses would have been greater, and prepaid rent would have been smaller by $30,000 each, as shown below.

	Prepaid Rent	Rent Expense
Amounts actually recorded	$ 30,000	$ –0–
Amounts that should have been recorded	–0–	30,000
Correction needed	$(30,000)	$30,000

However, if the rent expense had been recorded, the tax expense would have been smaller due to the smaller net income, so the 1995 tax expense and taxes payable were overstated by $13,500 each ($30,000 × .45). For example, assuming that the reported 1995 net income before tax was $250,000, then the tax expense would have been $112,500 ($250,000 × .45). But the correct 1995 net income before tax would be only $220,000, resulting in a tax expense of only $99,000 ($220,000 × .45). Note the difference between the two tax expense amounts in the following prior period adjustment.

Harley-Davidson's EPS reflects earnings from Harley-Davidson motorcycles as well as Holiday Rambler vehicles.

	Net Income Before Tax	Tax Expense
Amounts actually recorded	$250,000	$112,500
Amounts that should have been recorded	220,000	99,000
Correction needed	$ (30,000)	$(13,500)

Since both the Rent Expense and Tax Expense accounts were closed into Retained Earnings at the end of 1995, the 1996 beginning balance of Retained Earnings must be reduced by $16,500 ($30,000 – 13,500) as a result of the information shown below.

Error	Correction to Retained Earnings
1994 rent expense understated	Decrease $30,000
1994 tax expense overstated	Increase $13,500

PAUSE & REFLECT

The accountant would make the correcting entries for the prior period adjustment regarding the $30,000 rent error at Alvarez. What is the effect of these entries on assets, liabilities, and owners' equity?

Exhibit 22.4 is an example of a statement of retained earnings. Notice that the beginning Retained Earnings balance is corrected for the $30,000 error, net of 45 percent tax, which is a prior period adjustment. Then, the balance is increased by the amount of net income generated during 1996 and decreased by the dividends declared in 1996.[10]

WHAT ARE THE LIMITATIONS OF THE INCOME STATEMENT?

No discussion of the income statement is meaningful without reference to its potential reporting limitations. Because the income statement of a publicly held company is based on historical cost, and, for manufacturing firms, full-absorption costing, it is subject to certain limitations. These include financial capital maintenance, cost allocations, and full-absorption costing distortion. Understanding these limitations is necessary in order to use the income statement properly for evaluation purposes.

---

[10]When companies present comparative financial statements and the error occurred in any period shown, the previous financial statements are restated and a prior period adjustment is not required. In such a case, a note to the financial statements is necessary to call attention to the restatement of the previous financial statements.

EXHIBIT | 22.4 | Statement of Retained Earnings

ALVAREZ ENTERPRISES
Statement of Retained Earnings
For the Year Ended December 31, 1996

Retained earnings, December 31, 1995		$322,345,000
Correction of error, net of tax		(16,500)
Adjusted balance of retained earnings		$322,328,500
Add net income		151,499,000
		$473,827,500
Less dividends declared:		
Preferred stock	$600,000	
Common stock	500,000	1,100,000
Retained earnings, December 31, 1996		$472,727,500

Financial Capital Maintenance

We have discussed the concepts of return of and return on investment throughout the second part of this text. Investment itself pertains to the amount of capital invested in assets, and determining the return on investment depends on how capital is defined. **Financial capital** is the capital of the company measured in dollars, while **physical capital** is the company's capital measured in units of operating capacity.

The **financial capital maintenance** concept results from using historical costs. A company receives a return on investment if the *financial* (money) amount of the net assets at the end of the accounting period exceeds the financial amount of net assets at the beginning of the period, excluding the effects of owners' transactions.[11] That is, a company earns a return on investment only if the *dollar amount* of its net assets increase during the period.

Physical Capital Maintenance

In contrast, the **physical capital maintenance** concept means that the company receives a return on investment if the *physical productive capacity* of the company increases during the period, excluding any transactions with owners. This means that owners receive a return on investment only after maintaining or increasing the company's *operating capacity*, or its ability to provide goods and services.

Physical capital maintenance requires restatement of assets and liabilities at their current cost in order to be able to recognize holding gains and losses (explained below) when incurred. In contrast, holding gains and losses using financial capital maintenance are normally recognized only when assets are sold or when liabilities are eliminated.

A **holding gain or loss** is the amount of gain or loss in the value of an asset due to the passage of time, in contrast to any value added by the company. For example, assume that a company buys a building on January 1, 1996, for $400,000. During the year, it does not remodel or change the building in any way. On December 31, the building is appraised at $485,000. In this case, the company has a holding gain of $85,000 ($485,000 − $400,000). If the company uses the financial capital maintenance concept, this holding gain is not recognized in the accounting reports unless and until the building is sold. However, if the physical capital maintenance concept is used, the holding gain is recognized during 1996 because the value of the building has increased. This holding gain has implications for the future earnings of the firm: therefore, it is important information for income statement users.

As the above simplified example illustrates, the limitation of financial capital maintenance is that it mixes holding gains and losses with operating gains and losses because holding gains are not recognized when incurred. Therefore, it is more difficult for external users to assess future earnings and operating cash flows of the company. In addition, the idea of financial capital maintenance may lead managers and other users to think that the firm is generating large profits from operations when, in fact, changing prices, rather than operations, are causing increasing reported profits.

---

[11]Financial Accounting Standards Board, *Statement of Financial Accounting Concepts No. 5*, paragraph 47, 1986.

Cost Allocations

Another income statement limitation that external users need to understand concerns cost allocations. Depreciation (depletion and amortization) expense does *not* measure the economic deterioration of assets—it is merely the allocation of the cost of the asset over its expected useful life. As you learned in Chapter 20, there are a variety of methods available to allocate the cost of depreciable assets to the income statement. Therefore, readers of financial statements must look to the notes accompanying the financial statements to determine which depreciation method a company uses in order to compare companies.

Some accounting theorists think that all cost allocations are arbitrary and should be eliminated.[12] They feel that the number of alternatives available to companies makes the financial statements incomparable. We take the position that alternatives are necessary because cost allocation, by its very nature, is an estimate. Since companies use assets in different ways, alternatives are necessary to allow companies to describe and best reflect their operations. Therefore, knowing how management chooses to estimate its cost allocation is as important as knowing the actual amount of the estimate. However, financial statement users must be aware that different companies use different allocation methods and should take this into account when reading financial statements and other information. Cost allocation information is normally disclosed only in the notes to the financial statements, so users should investigate note information when comparing companies.

Full-Absorption Costing Distortion

As discussed in Chapter 10, full-absorption costing, the required costing method for manufacturing companies, assigns all production costs, such as direct materials, direct labor, variable manufacturing overhead, and fixed manufacturing overhead, to the units produced during the period. The cost of goods sold, then, is the amount of beginning finished goods inventory plus the cost of goods manufactured minus the amount of ending finished goods inventory.

When a manufacturing company prepares an income statement for external users, it often calculates cost of goods manufactured and cost of goods sold by applying overhead to production based on the number of units produced. We know from Chapters 10 and 13, however, that much overhead cost does not vary with the number of units produced. Therefore, distortions in income can result when overhead costs are treated as though they vary with the level of production.

To illustrate this issue, consider a very simple situation where two companies (company A and company B), in their first year of operations (1996), have only two types of overhead—unit related and facility sustaining. These companies are identical except that company A produced 15,000 units while company B produced 30,000 units during 1996.

Exhibit 22.5 shows the number of units produced and sold (panel A), the costs incurred during the period (panel B), and the resulting income statement (panel C) for company A. Using absorption costing, the cost of goods sold includes an amount of facility-sustaining overhead per unit, $50 ($750,000/15,000 units), in this case.

Full absorption costing implies that facility-sustaining overhead varies with the number of units produced rather than with a facility-related cost driver. What problems can result from this? A company can increase its income simply by increasing the *number of units produced* during the period, even if the number of units sold remains the same!

---

[12]Arthur L. Thomas, "Arbitrary and Incorrigible Allocations: A Comment," *Accounting Review* 53, no. 1 (1978), pp. 263–69.

EXHIBIT	22.5	Full-Costing Example: Company A

A. Physical Unit Information

Units produced	15,000
Units sold	12,000

B. Selling Price and Cost Information

Selling price per unit	$ 100.00
Direct materials per unit	4.25
Direct labor per unit	1.75
Unit-related overhead per unit	6.50
Variable selling cost per unit	2.00
Facility-sustaining overhead per year	$750,000
Fixed administrative cost per year	175,000

C. Results of Operations

COMPANY A
Income Statement
For the Year Ended December 31, 1996

Sales		$1,200,000
Less cost of goods sold:		
Beginning inventory	$ –0–	
Add cost of goods manufactured*	937,500	
Cost of goods available	$937,500	
Less ending inventory†	187,500	750,000
Gross margin		**$ 450,000**
Less other expenses:		
Selling expenses	$ 24,000	
Administrative expenses	175,000	199,000
Net income		**$ 251,000**

*Cost of goods manufactured:	
Direct materials ($4.25 × 15,000)	$ 63,750
Direct labor ($1.75 × 15,000)	26,250
Unit-related overhead ($6.50 × 15,000)	97,500
Facility-sustaining overhead	750,000
Total cost of goods manufactured	$937,500

†Cost of ending inventory:	
Direct materials ($4.25 × 3,000)	$ 12,750
Direct labor ($1.75 × 3,000)	5,250
Unit-related overhead ($6.50 × 3,000)	19,500
Facility-sustaining overhead ($750,000/15,000 × 3,000)	150,000
Total cost of ending inventory	$187,500

Now look at Exhibit 22.6, which shows the number of units produced and sold (panel A), the costs incurred during the period (panel B), and the resulting income statement (panel C) for company B. Notice that although the sales ($1,200,000), selling expenses ($24,000), and administrative expenses ($175,000) are the same as company A's (compare Exhibit 22.5 to Exhibit 22.6), the gross margin and net income are each $300,000 greater due solely to an increase in production of 15,000 units! For company B, cost of goods sold includes an amount of facility sustaining overhead per unit of $25 ($750,000/30,000).

This $300,000 difference in income is due to the facility-sustaining overhead cost per unit, which can be found by looking at the facility-sustaining overhead component included in the cost of ending inventory. Company A, which has only 3,000 units in ending inventory, shows a facility-sustaining overhead cost included in the cost of ending inventory of $150,000 ($750,000/15,000 × 3,000). Company B, however, which has 18,000 units in ending inventory, has a facility-sustaining overhead cost included in the cost of ending inventory of $450,000 ($750,000/30,000 × 18,000).

This simplified example illustrates that users must evaluate the change in cost of goods sold in relation to the change in inventory levels to judge whether the gross

EXHIBIT | 22.6 | **Full-Costing Example: Company B's Production Doubled**

A. Physical Unit Information

Units produced	30,000
Units sold	12,000

B. Selling Price and Cost Information

Selling price per unit	$100.00
Direct materials per unit	4.25
Direct labor per unit	1.75
Unit-related overhead per unit	6.50
Variable selling cost per unit	2.00
Facility-sustaining overhead per year	$750,000
Fixed administrative cost per year	175,000

C. Results of Operations

COMPANY B
Income Statement
For the Year Ended December 31, 1996

Sales		$1,200,000
Less cost of goods sold:		
Beginning inventory	$ –0–	
Add cost of goods manufactured*	1,125,000	
Cost of goods available	$1,125,000	
Less ending inventory†	675,000	450,000
Gross margin		**$ 750,000**
Less other expenses:		
Selling expenses	$ 24,000	
Administrative expenses	175,000	199,000
Net income		**$ 551,000**

*Cost of goods manufactured:

Direct materials ($4.25 × 30,000)	$127,500
Direct labor ($1.75 × 30,000)	52,500
Unit-related overhead ($6.50 × 30,000)	195,000
Facility-sustaining overhead	750,000
Total cost of goods manufactured	$1,125,000

†Cost of ending inventory:

Direct materials ($4.25 × 18,000)	$ 76,500
Direct labor ($1.75 × 18,000)	31,500
Unit-related overhead ($6.50 × 18,000)	117,000
Facility-sustaining overhead ($750,000/30,000 × 18,000)	450,000
Total cost of ending inventory	$675,000

margin and ending inventory are larger than expected based on the past performance of the company. If the gross margin and ending inventory are larger than expected, this may indicate that the number of units produced far exceeded the number of units sold. Since inventories are costly to hold, a manager of a company that produces more than the amount sold may not be utilizing the company resources in an efficient and effective manner. This would be important for financial statement users to know because it has implications for the future earnings and cash flows of the company.

Now that we have looked at the limitations of the income statement, we turn to the topic of internal reporting of earnings. As you will notice in this section, many of the reporting methods used internally are a result of the limitations of general purpose income statements prepared for external users.

INCOME REPORTS FOR INTERNAL USERS

Two internal reports used frequently by internal financial statement users in profitability reporting are product line, or divisional, income reports and current cost income reports.

Product line (divisional) income reports are specific purpose reports designed to provide more detailed information than general purpose income statements

EXHIBIT 22.7 — Product Line Income Report—Divisional Basis

ALVAREZ ENTERPRISES
Product Line Income Report
For the Year Ended December 31, 1996
(in thousands)

	Division 1	Division 2	Division 3	Company Total
Sales	$933,262	$822,929	$701,969	$2,458,160
Less unit variable costs:				
Direct materials	233,316	92,500	126,354	452,170
Direct labor	135,614	138,750	88,448	362,812
Unit-related overhead	39,372	180,381	26,534	246,287
Variable selling	58,329	40,980	39,452	138,761
Contribution margin	**$466,631**	**$370,318**	**$421,181**	**$1,258,130**
Less other variable costs:				
Batch-related overhead	31,109	18,501	52,648	102,258
Product-sustaining overhead	62,217	18,531	157,942	238,690
Product margin	**$373,305**	**$333,286**	**$210,591**	**$ 917,182**
Less other controllable costs:				
Advertising	8,500	7,500	5,200	21,200
Market analysis	1,225	1,100	750	3,075
Segment margin	**$363,580**	**$324,686**	**$204,641**	**$ 892,907**
Less other fixed costs:				
Facility-sustaining overhead				350,600
Other corporate expenses				261,100
Income from operations				**$ 281,207**

regarding the results of operations for a product line or company division. A **current cost income report** uses the current costs of assets, rather than the historical cost, to reflect net income. It is designed to overcome the limitations of financial capital maintenance. We discuss these, in turn, next.

Product Line (Divisional) Income Reports

Internally, product line or divisional managers are often evaluated and rewarded based on the income of their product lines or divisions. The goal of a good reward and control system is to assign responsibility for those items for which the manager has control (recall our related discussion in Chapter 13). These income reports, then, are prepared to eliminate costs assigned to the product or division that the manager cannot control as well as to overcome the problems associated with full absorption costing just discussed.

Exhibit 22.7 illustrates Alvarez Enterprises' income report on a divisional basis. Notice that there are many divisions of earnings, such as contribution margin (sales less variable costs), product margin (contribution margin less batch-related and product-sustaining overhead), and segment margin (product margin less facility-sustaining and other costs that are *controllable* by the manager).

As Exhibit 22.7 shows, the segment margins of the three divisions are $363,580, $324,686, and $204,641, respectively. Also notice that other fixed costs are deducted from the *total* segment margin of the company, and not from the segment margins of the respective product lines or divisions. In this case, facility-sustaining overhead and other corporate expenses are not allocated to the divisions because their respective managers cannot control these costs. Therefore, the income from operations of the company is *not the sum of the segment margins*. Rather, it is the sum of the segment margins less the costs that were not assigned to the divisions.

Finally, notice that these internal income reports do not use the comprehensive income concept used for external parties because they do not reflect discontinued operations, extraordinary items, and cumulative accounting adjustments, which are assumed to be beyond the control of product line or division managers.

Current Cost Income Reports

During times of inflation (deflation) or when the costs of specific items are rising (falling), it is often necessary to prepare income reports that are not based on historical cost in order to reflect changing prices. The reason for doing this is that changing prices cause holding gains and losses and, therefore, affect the physical capital maintenance of the company. There are two primary methods of preparing the current cost reports.

The first method, which results in general price-level-adjusted financial statements, uses published indexes of inflation such as the gross national product (GNP) deflator or the consumer price index (CPI) to adjust the income statement numbers for inflation. There are two problems to consider when using this method, however. The first problem is determining which index to use. For example, the CPI measures inflation by using a representative market basket of consumer goods. This is clearly inappropriate for manufacturing firms because their inventories are raw materials, not consumer goods. The second problem is that an index assumes that inflation (deflation) is uniform across the economy. Clearly, this is not true. For example, in the 1970s when inflation averaged over 8 percent, the price of hand-held calculators dropped because inflation was not the same in the electronics industry as in other industries. Due to such problems in preparing meaningful income reports, we will not use the indexing method to adjust income.

The second primary method for dealing with price changes is to report the current costs of expenses and the resulting holding gains. Typically, this requires an adjustment to cost of goods sold and other allocated costs, such as depreciation, which are based on historical cost. In addition, holdings gains are often subdivided into **realized holding gains,** which result from the use or sale of assets during the period, and **unrealized holding gains,** which result from assets being held during the period.

To illustrate the current cost income report, we will use the following simplified example of company C for 1997.

Historical Cost Income Report

Sales (6,000 units at $100)		$600,000
Cost of goods sold		140,000
Gross margin		$460,000
Less operating expenses:		
Depreciation	$ 50,000	
Other	260,000	310,000
Income from operations		$150,000

Additional investigation reveals that straight-line depreciation is used, the assets have a 10-year life remaining, and the replacement cost of the depreciable assets is $620,000. Cost of goods sold is calculated using FIFO and the following purchase schedule:

• 4,000 units purchased at $20 per unit.

• 3,000 units purchased at $30 per unit.

• 3,000 units purchased at $40 per unit.

The replacement cost of the inventory is $45 per unit at the end of the period. Using this information, we derive the current cost income statement presented in Exhibit 22.8.

Notice that income is subdivided into components based on various business activities involved. The difference between income from operations and realized income is the amount of the holding gains realized on assets sold or used during the period. In this case, realized holding gains resulted from inventory sold (current cost of goods sold [$270,000] less historical cost of goods sold [$140,000]) and equipment used (current cost of depreciation [$62,000] less historical cost of depreciation [$50,000]).

EXHIBIT | 22.8 | Current Cost Income Report

COMPANY C
Current Cost Income Report
For the Year Ended December 31, 1997

Sales (6,000 × $100)		$600,000
Less cost of goods sold*		270,000
Gross margin		$330,000
Less operating expenses:		
Depreciation expense[†]		62,000
Other		260,000
Income from operations		**$ 8,000**
Realized holding gains:		
Inventory sold ($270,000 − $140,000)		130,000
Equipment used ($62,000 − $50,000)		12,000
Realized income		**$150,000**
Unrealized holding gains:		
Inventory held ($180,000 − $150,000)[‡]		30,000
Equipment held ($558,000 − $450,000)[§]		108,000
Current cost net income		**$288,000**

*Cost of goods sold = 6,000 × $45 = $270,000.
[†]Depreciation expense = $620,000 × 1/10 = $62,000.
[‡]Unrealized holding gain in inventory:

Current cost of ending inventory (4,000 × $45)		$180,000
Historical cost of purchases (4,000 × $20) +		
(3,000 × $30)+ (3,000 × $40) =	$290,000	
Less historical cost of goods sold	140,000	
Historical cost of ending inventory		150,000
		$ 30,000

[§]Unrealized holding gain on equipment:

Current cost book value ($620,000 − $62,000)	= $558,000	
Historical cost book value ($500,000 − $50,000)	= 450,000	
	$108,000	

The difference between realized income and current cost net income is due to the unrealized holding gains on assets that the company still has at the end of the period. In this case, the difference results from unrealized holding gains from inventory held (current cost of ending inventory [$180,000] less historical cost of ending inventory [$150,000]) and equipment (current cost book value [$558,000] less historical cost book value [$450,000]).

Using this format, management can clearly see the difference between profits generated from sales and profits generated from holding assets. In addition, the gains realized versus those not realized is clear. For example, the gross margin, adjusted for the changes in price that occurred during the year, is only $330,000 as compared to the gross margin shown in the historical cost income report of $460,000. Reporting only the historical cost gross margin might lead management to believe that the company's operations are more profitable than they actually are when, in fact, changing prices account for $130,000 of the historical cost gross margin. Since this inventory must be replaced if the company is to remain in business, the current cost gross margin is more relevant for statement users' purposes because it reflects the current cost to replace the inventory rather than the historical cost of the inventory. In addition, since fixed assets eventually must be replaced, their current (replacement) cost should be allocated to the time periods over which they are used to reflect the cost of using them.

However, current cost income reports are more costly to prepare because assets must be appraised or current selling prices must be ascertained in order to determine their current costs. In addition, many companies find it difficult to determine the current costs of their assets, such as work-in-process inventories and obsolete (but functional) equipment, because they are not readily marketable. For these reasons, companies often choose to produce current cost reports only in times of significantly changing prices or only on a limited (regional or divisional) basis.

SUMMARY

The income statement is vitally important to both external and internal users in order to evaluate a company's operating activities. It is important for users to understand the actual components of income presented as well as the limitations of the income statement itself. Internally, these limitations are often corrected by preparing more detailed income reports.

- Comprehensive income is reported to external users to provide them with a complete picture of the recurring operating activities of the company during the period as well as other nonowner changes in equity that occurred during the period.

- Discontinued operations, extraordinary items, and cumulative accounting adjustments are shown on the income statement after income from continuing operations. These items appear net of tax because income tax expense is based on income from continuing operations.

- Earnings per share is shown on the income statement as a common-size measure of company performance. Companies often report diluted earnings per share, which indicates the decrease in earnings per share if additional shares were outstanding.

- The statement of retained earnings indicates the changes that occurred in the Retained Earnings account during the period due to net income or loss, cash and stock dividends, and prior period adjustments.

- Using the financial capital maintenance concept, holding gains are not recognized until assets are sold. Under the physical capital maintenance concept, holding gains are recognized when incurred, which requires the presentation of current costs, rather than historical costs, on the income statement.

- Using full-absorption costing, income increases with increases in production because fixed production costs are assigned to inventory and, therefore, some fixed costs remain on the balance sheet until the inventory is sold.

- Internally, product line and current cost income reports are often used to overcome the limitations of general purpose income statements designed for external users.

KEY TERMS

comprehensive (net) income Income that reflects all changes in owners' equity during the period except those resulting from investments by, or distributions to, owners and those resulting from errors made in previous periods

cumulative accounting adjustments Modifications made to the accounting records that result from changes in accounting principles which occur when a company switches from one generally accepted method of accounting to another or when a company adopts a new accounting principle

current cost income report An internal report that uses the current costs of assets, rather than the historical cost, to reflect net income

diluted earnings per share Earnings per share that reflect the amount of decrease in earnings per share that would occur as a result of activities like conversions and the exercise of stock options

discontinued operations The result of a company selling or disposing of a segment of its business

earnings Income from continuing operations; it includes revenues minus expenses plus gains and minus losses

earnings per share A common-size measure of a company's earnings performance; the reported net income of the company less preferred dividends for the period divided by the weighted-average number of common shares outstanding

extraordinary items Events that occurred during the accounting period that are *both* unusual and infrequent

financial capital The capital of the company measured in dollars

financial capital maintenance A return on investment resulting from the financial amount of net assets at the end of the period exceeding that at the beginning of the period, excluding the effects of owners' transactions resulting from using historical costs

holding gain or loss The gain or loss in the value of an asset due to the passage of time, in contrast to any value added by the company

physical capital The capital of the company measured in units of operating capacity

physical capital maintenance A return on investment resulting from an increase in a company's physical productive capacity during the period, excluding transactions with owners

prior period adjustment A correction of a previously undetected error that affected the net income or loss from a previous accounting period

product line (divisional) income report Specific purpose internal reports designed to provide more detailed information than general purpose income statements regarding the results of operations for a product line or company division

realized holding gain A holding gain that results from the use or sale of assets during the period

unrealized holding gain A holding gain that results from assets being held during the period

QUESTIONS

1. Explain the difference between earnings and comprehensive income. Why is this important?

2. What are the two types of nonowner changes in equity? Why are they important?

3. Explain cumulative accounting adjustments. Why are they important?

4. Explain the difference between a single-step and a multistep income statement. Which one do you prefer? Why?

5. Why are discontinued operations, extraordinary items, and cumulative accounting changes shown net of tax on the income statement?

6. Why is the income (loss) from discontinued operations shown separately from the gain (loss) on disposal of a segment? Where is this information usually found? Why?

7. Is a Georgia company's loss from a tornado an extraordinary item? Why or why not?

8. When a company changes its method of accounting for inventories from FIFO to LIFO, does it restate the prior years' financial statements? Why or why not?

9. What is earnings per share and how can it be diluted?

10. What is a prior period adjustment, and why is it important?

11. Why is a prior period adjustment shown net of taxes?

12. Assume a company with a 45 percent tax rate forgot to record $100,000 of expenses in 1995. How would this error be shown on the 1996 retained earnings statement?

13. Explain the difference between financial and physical capital maintenance. Why is this difference an important issue?

14. Explain how holding gains and losses occur. Do you think holding gains and losses should be shown separately from operating gains and losses? Why or why not?

15. If a company sells inventory that originally cost $50,000 for $120,000 at a time when the replacement cost of the inventory is $75,000, what is the cost of goods sold using the physical capital maintenance concept? Explain.

16. Explain how a company can increase net income by increasing production even though sales remain the same.

17. Explain the advantages of a product line income report for internal users. Do you think this information would be useful for external users? Why or why not?

18. Explain how a current cost income report differs from an income statement prepared for external users. Why is the information on a current cost income report useful internally? Do you think this information would be useful for external users? Why or why not?

19. What is the difference between a realized and an unrealized holding gain on a current cost income report? Why is this difference important?

20. Why are current cost reports more costly to prepare? Do you think that the accounting profession would be reluctant or eager to have current cost reports prepared for external users?

E 22.1   The accounts below are from the Mo Scharifi Company. Show how this information is presented on a single-step income statement and explain the benefits of this format.

Cost of goods sold	$110,000
Sales	405,000
Selling expenses	45,000
Administrative expenses	35,000
Sales salaries	85,000
Depreciation expense	20,000
Loss on sale of equipment	8,000
Sales returns	10,000

E 22.2   Refer to E 22.1. Show how this information is presented on a multistep income statement and explain the benefits of this format.

E 22.3   The Finley Graves Corporation has the following information available on December 31, 1996. The tax rate is 40 percent. Show how this information is presented to external users in a multistep format.

Interest expense	$ 36,000
Sales salaries	228,000
Rental revenue	8,000
Accounts receivable	101,000
Administrative salaries	300,000
Sales	2,483,000
Depreciation (40% selling, 60% administrative)	130,000
Dividends paid	48,000
Cost of goods sold	841,000
Sales returns and allowances	45,000
Loss due to meteor damage	700,000
Gain on sale of equipment	79,000

E 22.4   Assays' Sporting Goods decided to sell its children's toys division during 1995. The following relevant information is available. Use this information to determine the income (loss) from operations of the division and the income (loss) upon disposal of the division.

Loss from operating activities of toy division	$900,000
Gain on sale of toy division	600,000
Effective tax rate	40%

E 22.5   Refer to E 22.4. How does your answer change if the toy division showed a profit from operating activities of $900,000 and if Assays experiences a loss on disposal of $540,000? Show your calculations.

E 22.6   The Specialty Stores Corporation segregated the following item because of its unusual nature. They have calculated the income before taxes and this extraordinary item but want you to advise them on how to present this information to external users. Determine the extraordinary loss, net of tax, calculate the net income for the year, and explain in a brief memo to the owners how to present this information on the income statement.

Earnings before taxes and extraordinary items	$950,000
Tax rate	30%
Extraordinary loss due to earthquake in Kansas	$250,000

E 22.7   Tauscher Corporation repurchased $1,000,000 of its 12 percent interest, subordinated debenture bonds during 1997 and experienced an extraordinary gain on the repurchase of $300,000. Tauscher's income tax rate is 45 percent. What is the extraordinary gain (loss) shown on the income statement for 1997? Show your calculations.

E 22.8   Tracey Green, Inc., had operating income of $1,900,000 in 1996. The following transactions occurred in 1996, but were not considered when calculating operating income. Green's income tax rate is 40 percent. Use this information to determine income from continuing operations and net income.
1. The corporation, which is located in South Dakota, suffered an uninsured earthquake loss of $230,000.
2. Sale of investment in bonds resulted in a $40,000 gain.

E 22.9   Horton Hatcheries Company had operating income of $635,000 in 1997. Its income tax rate is 35 percent. Use the information below to determine income from continuing operations and net income.
1. The corporation sold one of its buildings at a $89,000 loss.
2. The corporation disposed of its dairy division at a loss of $197,000 before taxes. The division suffered a $200,000 operating loss during the year.

E 22.10   Ridder Corporation is going to change from the double-declining-balance method of depreciation to straight-line depreciation in 1996. The differences in the two depreciation methods for the years affected are presented below. The tax rate is 30 percent. Determine the cumulative accounting change. What information should Ridder disclose in the notes to its financial statements?

	Declining Balance	Straight Line
1992	$400,000	$200,000
1993	360,000	200,000
1994	324,000	200,000
1995	291,600	200,000
1996	262,440	200,000

E 22.11   Jeters Company has $10,000,000 of equipment with a $500,000 salvage value and a 10-year life. The equipment was purchased four years ago and has been depreciated using straight-line depreciation. Jeters plans to switch to the double-declining-balance depreciation method this year. The income tax rate is 45 percent. Determine the cumulative accounting change. What information should Jeters disclose in the notes to its financial statements?

E 22.12   Brown Company has 500,000 shares of common stock issued and 250,000 shares of common stock outstanding. Determine the earnings per share for 1996 if its net income is $100,000.

E 22.13   Daran Lemon Corporation has 50,000 shares of common stock outstanding and 10,000 shares of $100 par value, 6 percent preferred stock outstanding. Determine the earnings per share for 1996 if net income is $150,000.

E 22.14   Brenda Knoeber Enterprises had 200,000 shares of common stock outstanding on January 1, 1995, and issued an additional 50,000 shares on March 1, 1995. Determine the earnings per share for 1995 if net income was $225,000.

E 22.15   Jennifer Lima Company had 200,000 shares of common stock outstanding on January 1, 1995, and repurchased 60,000 shares of common stock on March 31, 1995. Determine the earnings per share for 1995 if net income was $350,000.

E 22.16   In 1995, Kirmer Corporation failed to record depreciation expense of $30,000. The accountant discovered this error in 1996. Kirmer Corporation is subject to a 40 percent income tax rate. What is the effect of this error on the 1996 statement of retained earnings? What other accounts must be corrected in Kirmer's accounting records? Explain.

E 22.17   In 1995, Hsu-Lin Company, which is subject to a 35 percent tax rate, recognized interest revenue of $15,000. On January 16, 1996, the accountant discovered that the correct amount of interest revenue for 1995 was $25,000. What is the effect of this error on the 1996 statement of retained earnings? What other accounts must Kirmer correct in Hsu-Lin's accounting records? Explain.

E 22.18   Teema Roberts Clothing Store made the following purchases of merchandise inventory during 1995.

Purchase 1	$60,000
Purchase 2	50,000
Purchase 3	75,000
Purchase 4	80,000

During 1995, Teema sold all its merchandise inventory except purchase 4 for 200 percent of cost. The current cost of the merchandise inventory at the end of the year is shown below:

Purchase 1	$66,000
Purchase 2	55,000
Purchase 3	81,000
Purchase 4	84,000

Determine the gross margin that would be shown on a current cost income report.

E 22.19   Refer to E 22.18. Determine the realized and unrealized holding gains that would be shown on a current cost income report.

E 22.20   On January 1, 1996, Kylie Roberts Company purchased equipment costing $500,000, which it will depreciate over the equipment's five-year useful life using straight-line depreciation with no salvage value. At the end of 1996, the replacement cost of this equipment was $600,000. Determine the realized and unrealized holding gains on this equipment that would be shown on a current cost income report.

PROBLEMS

P 22.1   John Rich Equipment Corporation provided the following relevant information for its fiscal year ending September 30, 1995.

Sales	$2,280,000
Cost of goods sold	1,231,600
Sales returns	41,000
Depreciation on sales equipment	6,500
Sales commissions	103,000
Sales salaries	62,300
Administrative salaries	98,200
Depreciation on office equipment	8,500
Bond interest expense	22,000
Selling expenses	168,900
Administrative expense	134,600
Gain on disposal of marine products division	280,000
Marine products division operating income	100,000
Dividend income	4,000
Entertainment expense	23,100
Dividends declared on preferred stock	14,000

On October 1, 1994, John Rich Equipment's Retained Earnings balance was $238,790. The tax rate for John Rich Equipment Corporation is 30 percent. There are 85,000 shares of common stock outstanding. In addition, in 1995, the company discovered that a $10,000 piece of equipment with a five-year useful life was expensed when purchased on October 2, 1994. John Rich Company uses straight-line depreciation.

Required:
  a. Prepare a multistep income statement for fiscal 1995.
  b. Calculate the earnings per share for 1995.
  c. Prepare a statement of retained earnings for fiscal 1995.

P 22.2   The income statement below was prepared by Bob's Bookkeeping Service for the Acme Corporation.

ACME CORPORATION
Income State
At December 31,1996

Sales	$1,250,000
Interest income	5,000
Less: Sales returns	9,000
Net sales	$1,246,000
Cost of goods sold	740,000
Gross margin	$ 506,000
Gain on sale of equipment	40,000
Total revenue inflows	$ 546,000
Administrative expenses	120,000
Selling expenses	45,000
Loss on sale of land	10,000
Operating income	$ 371,000
Interest expense	9,000
Extraordinary loss on building, net	20,000
Income from continuing operations	$ 342,000
Tax expense	102,600
Net income	$ 239,400

Required:
  a. Make a list of all the errors found on this income statement and briefly describe what is wrong.
  b. Prepare a correct multistep income statement for Acme Corporation.

P 22.3   Refer to the income statement of Entergy Corporation in the annual report booklet.

Required: *a.* What was the income from operations during the year?
   b. What was the income from continuing operations during the year?
   c. What was the net income?
   d. Did they discontinue any operations during the year? If so, what were they?
   e. Did they experience any extraordinary events during the year? If so, what were they?
   f. Did they have a cumulative accounting change during the year? If so, what was the change?
   g. What were the earnings per share for the year?
   h. Based on the income statement, would you advise someone to invest in Entergy? Why or why not?

P 22.4   Refer to the income statement of Southwestern Public Service Company in the annual report booklet.

Required: *a.* What was the income from operations during the year?
   b. What was the income from continuing operations during the year?
   c. What was the net income?
   d. Did they discontinue any operations during the year? If so, what were they?
   e. Did they experience any extraordinary events during the year? If so, what were they?
   f. Did they have a cumulative accounting change during the year? If so, what was the change?
   g. What were the earnings per share for the year?
   h. Based on the income statement, would you advise someone to invest in Southwestern Public Service Company? Why or why not?

P 22.5   Refer to the consolidated statement of common shareholders' equity of Southwestern Public Service Company in the annual report booklet.

Required: *a.* How is this statement different from a statement of retained earnings?
   b. Did the company declare any dividends during the year? If so, what were they?
   c. Did the company report any prior period adjustments? If so, what were they?

P 22.6   The income statement of Ashenfelter Company prepared on a historical cost basis is shown below, along with additional information related to the statement.

ASHENFELTER COMPANY
Income Statement
For the Year Ended December 31,1995

Sales		$1,600,000
Cost of goods sold:		
Inventory, January 1	$ 500,000	
Purchases	1,040,000	
Goods available	$1,540,000	
Inventory, December 31	600,000	940,000
Gross margin		$ 660,000
Selling and administrative expense		340,000
Depreciation expense		20,000
Income before income taxes		$ 300,000
Income taxes		135,000
Net income		$ 165,000

Additional Information:

1. Cost of goods sold on a current cost basis at different dates during the year was $1,520,000. The current cost of inventory on December 31 was $1,000,000.
2. The current cost of equipment at the end of 1995 excluding accumulated depreciation was $360,000. Equipment has a useful life of 15 years and is depreciated using the straight-line method. Its net book value on January 1, 1995, was $300,000.
3. Current cost of land used in the business is $1,800,000; its historical cost is $900,000.
4. The current cost and historical cost of all assets were the same on January 1, 1995.
5. The current cost of selling and administrative expense as well as the current cost of income tax expense are the same as their historical costs.

Required: *a.* Determine the gross margin using current cost for 1995.
   b. Determine the realized holding gains using current cost for 1995.
   c. Determine the unrealized holding gains using current cost for 1995.

> *d.* Determine the current cost net income for 1995.
>
> *e.* Interpret your results.

P 22.7 In the early 1980s, the FASB issued *SFAS No. 33*, which required certain companies to prepare current cost financial statements as additional disclosures. Go to the library and research *SFAS No. 33*. Determine why this statement was issued and why it is no longer in effect. Prepare a brief written summary of your findings.

P 22.8 College Publishers produces three textbooks for various college campuses—*Introductory Marketing*, *Introductory Management*, and *Introductory Accounting*. Each book sells for $60. The manager of College Publishers is concerned that *Introductory Marketing* appears to be losing money. The most recent income report is shown below:

	Marketing	Management	Accounting	Total
Sales	$400,000	$500,000	$900,000	$1,800,000
Less expenses:				
Printing	160,000	200,000	360,000	720,000
Commissions	40,000	50,000	90,000	180,000
Warehousing	48,000	48,000	48,000	144,000
Salaries	34,000	34,000	34,000	102,000
Depreciation 1	36,000	36,000	36,000	108,000
Depreciation 2	24,000	24,000	24,000	72,000
Miscellaneous	34,000	34,000	34,000	102,000
Advertising	8,000	8,000	8,000	24,000
Shipping	48,000	60,000	108,000	216,000
Net income (loss)	$(32,000)	$ 6,000	$158,000	$ 132,000

An analysis of the records reveals that printing, commissions, and shipping costs are traced directly to the product lines, while the remaining costs are allocated equally to the three product lines. Further analysis reveals the following:

1. The warehouse consists of 60,000 square feet of which 30,000 square feet are used for accounting books, 16,000 are used for management, and the remaining square feet are used to house marketing texts.

2. Depreciation 1 is depreciation on production equipment. During the past year the production equipment operated a total of 2,500 hours, of which 1,250 hours were used to produce accounting texts, 750 hours were used for management texts, and 500 hours were used to produce marketing texts.

3. Depreciation 2, salaries, advertising, and miscellaneous costs, cannot be traced to any particular product line.

Required:
a. Prepare a product line income report.

b. Should College Publishers drop the marketing text? Why or why not?

P 22.9 Refer to P 22.8. Assume that management decides to drop the marketing text.

Required:
a. Determine the net income of the company.

b. Determine the product margins of the accounting and management texts.

c. Analyze your results.

P 22.10 Vinson Products produces specialty alarm clocks that it sells to novelty stores throughout the mid-Atlantic. It uses FIFO costing to determine cost of goods sold. During the current period, the following results were obtained:

Sales	650,000 clocks at $40
Beginning finished goods inventory	10,000 clocks at $20
Cost of goods manufactured	700,000 clocks at $28
Variable selling cost	650 clocks at $9
Fixed selling and administrative cost	$645,000
Cost of goods manufactured consists of:	
Direct materials	$5
Direct labor	2
Unit-related overhead	8
Other nonvariable overhead	13
	$28

Other nonvariable overhead consists of depreciation on machinery and buildings, insurance, and other items that do not vary with the number of clocks produced during the period. The unit cost is calculated by dividing the total nonvariable overhead for the period by the number of clocks produced in the period as shown below:

$$\frac{\$9,100,000}{700,000} = \$13 \text{ per clock}$$

Required:
   a. Determine the net income for the period using full absorption costing.
   b. Determine the net income for the period by producing a product line income report and treating nonvariable overhead as a current period expense. Assume that last period's variable costs were the same as this period's.
   c. Compare the net incomes you calculated in *a* and *b* above. Which net income is a more accurate presentation of current period earnings? Why?

COMPUTER APPLICATIONS

CA 22.1   The following list of items (accounts) was obtained from the 1993 annual report of Braun's Fashions Corporation.

Depreciation and amortization	$ 2,052,707
Interest expense	210,678
Merchandise, buying, and occupancy expenses	56,406,679
Provision for income taxes	1,615,931
Selling, publicity, and administrative expenses	18,379,253
Net sales	81,301,766

The following additional information is available:
1. The beginning balance of Retained Earnings was a deficit of $(14,536,277).
2. Braun's has 3,664,625 common shares outstanding.
3. No dividends were declared during the period.

Required: Use a computer spreadsheet.
   a. Determine the net income for fiscal 1993.
   b. Determine the ending balance of Retained Earnings.
   c. Determine the earnings per share.
   d. Assume that in 1994, net sales were 25 percent greater, merchandise and taxes remained at the same percentage rate, and all other expenses remained at the same dollar amount. What would be the amount of net income for 1994?
   e. Refer to part *d.* What would be the amount of the ending Retained Earnings balance in 1994?

CA 22.2   Use a computer spreadsheet program to determine earnings per share in each of the following independent situations. Assume a calendar year-end in each situation.
   a. Net income is $500,000. There are 250,000 shares of common stock and 50,000 shares of $10 par, 8 percent preferred stock outstanding.
   b. Net income is $600,000. There were 200,000 shares of common stock outstanding on January 1. On March 31, 100,000 additional shares were issued. On September 1, 50,000 additional shares were issued.
   c. Net income is $250,000. There were 300,000 shares of common stock outstanding on January 1. On July 31, 50,000 shares of common stock were repurchased and held as treasury stock.
   d. Net income is $425,000. There were 200,000 shares of common stock and 100,000 shares of $100 par, 6 percent preferred stock outstanding on January 1. On May 1 60,000 shares of common stock were issued. On October 31, 10,000 shares of preferred stock were issued.

CASES

C 22.1   Use the annual report you obtained in Chapter 1 (C 1.2) to answer the following questions:
   a. What was the income from operations during the year?
   b. What was the income from continuing operations during the year?
   c. What was the net income for the year?
   d. Did they discontinue any operations during the year? If so, what were they?
   e. Did they experience any extraordinary events during the year? If so, what were they?

f. Did they have a cumulative accounting change during the year? If so, what was the change?

g. What were the earnings per share for the year?

h. Did the company declare any dividends during the year? If so, what were they?

i. Did the company report any prior period adjustments? If so, what were they?

j. Based on this information would you advise someone to invest in this company? Why or why not?

C 22.2 By consulting NEXIS, Disclosure, or a similar annual report database determine the following:

a. How many companies reported discontinued operations during the period?

b. Of the companies that reported discontinued operations, did they report gains or losses?

c. How many companies reported extraordinary items during the period?

d. Of the companies that reported extraordinary items, did they report gains or losses?

e. How many companies reported cumulative accounting changes?

f. Of the companies that reported cumulative accounting changes, what were the two most common changes reported?

g. Of the companies that reported cumulative accounting changes, did the changes result in gains or losses?

h. How many companies reported a loss per share?

i. How many companies declared both common and preferred stock dividends during the period?

j. How many companies reported prior period adjustments during the period?

CRITICAL THINKING

CT 22.1 In the first year of operations, Jamison Company experienced a $500,000 net loss even though it sold 250,000 units. Management was very concerned about this outcome, so they hired an efficiency expert to turn their operations around. The efficiency expert guaranteed Jamison a profitable second year. The expert stressed, "I agree to work for you for one year at no salary. At the end of the year, if your net income is not at least $500,000, you pay me nothing. If your income is $500,000 or more, you pay me $500,000."

Jamison's income statement for the first year of operations is shown below:

Sales (250,000 units at $16)		$4,000,000
Cost of goods sold:		
Beginning inventory	$ -0-	
Cost of goods manufactured	3,750,000	
Cost of goods available	$3,750,000	
Ending inventory	-0-	3,750,000
Gross margin		$ 250,000
Selling and administrative expenses		750,000
Net income		$ (500,000)

Cost of goods manufactured is composed of the following:

Direct materials	$ 750,000
Direct labor	500,000
Unit-related overhead	1,000,000
Other nonunit related overhead	1,500,000
	$3,750,000

In the second year of operations, the same number of units were sold, but the company produced 750,000. The selling price and costs remained constant, which resulted in the following income statement:

Sales (250,000 unites at $16)		$4,000,000
Cost of goods sold:		
Beginning inventory	$ -0-	
Cost of goods manufactured	8,250,000	
Cost of goods available	$8,250,000	
Ending inventory	5,500,000	2,750,000
Gross margin		$1,250,000
Selling and administrative expenses		750,000
Net income before bonus		$ 500,000
Bonus		500,000
Net income		$ -0-

Write a memo to the managers of Jamison Company explaining, in detail, what happened to operations in the second year.

CT 22.2 Michael Loritz, the manager of Loritz Toy Store, has asked you to evaluate his operations and recommend a marketing strategy. Lately, his suppliers have been raising their prices, but since he has plenty of inventory in stock and is using FIFO costing, he has not raised his selling prices, thereby maintaining a constant gross margin percentage. He is concerned, however, about future operations and wonders if he should slowly begin to raise his prices to offset future price increases.

The following information has been provided to you by Mr. Loritz.

	This Year	Last Year
Sales	$800,000	$700,000
Cost of goods sold	600,000	525,000
Gross margin	$200,000	$175,000
Other operating expenses	120,000	110,000
Net income	$ 80,000	$ 65,000
Beginning inventory, at cost	$400,000	$150,000
Purchases, at cost	950,000	775,000
Ending inventory, at cost	750,000	400,000
Cost of goods sold, current cost	690,000	577,500
Ending inventory, current cost	900,000	460,000

Other operating expenses are cash expenses.

Required:
a. Compute the current cost net income for both years.
b. Write a memo to Michael Loritz explaining your findings and recommending a marketing strategy for next year.

ETHICAL CHALLENGES

EC 22.1 *The Wall Street Journal* on November 3, 1994, reported the following headline: "Managing Profits: GE Deftly Damps Fluctuations in Earnings by Timing Write-Offs and Other Moves."

Required: Read this article and write a one-page ethical evaluation of its topic.

EC 22.2 Earnings management is a common practice. Some argue that it is unethical, if not illegal, while others argue that earnings management is necessary to avoid large fluctuations in income that could confuse stockholders. Perform library research on this subject and write a two- to three-page paper supporting or refuting the practice of earnings management.

CHAPTER 23

Firm Performance: Financial Position

Learning Objectives

1. Explain the purpose of properly classifying asset, liability, and equity items on the balance sheet.
2. Describe the financial disclosures required beyond the balance sheet itself.

At June 30, 1995, Quaker Oats had over $4.8 billion in assets. Those assets were located around the world, as were the holders of the 168 million shares of Quaker's common stock. Quaker's assets represent the company's resources available to generate future profits. The company's liabilities and owners' equity represent the claims on those assets and profits.

By carefully examining Quaker's balance sheet, readers can combine the information presented with other available information to predict how the company will perform over the next few years. For example, the balance sheet and related notes show that Quaker's products included a broad line of dog foods with brands such as Kibbles `n Bits. In 1995, Quaker sold all of its dog food lines to Heinz Foods. Financial analysts saw this sale as good for both parties because the dog food industry was "over capacity." Sales of pet foods industry-wide had declined, and it appeared that the industry was not growing any longer. Careful study of Quaker's balance sheet and related disclosures might have shown that it was operating more profitably in other areas like breakfast foods and sports drinks. Selling the pet foods division allowed Quaker to concentrate on its other more profitable areas.

The balance sheet, along with its related disclosures, provides a great deal of information about the resources a company has and where it might use future operating profits. Understanding the nature of those resources helps to predict how profitable the company might be, how easily the company can pay its debts, and how likely stockholders are to receive dividends.

The balance sheet—the statement of financial position—reports the amount and type of assets the firm controls and the claims the owners and creditors have on those assets on the last day of a reporting period. This financial statement is an important means of communication with parties outside the business.

In this chapter, the emphasis is on the external reporting rules embodied in generally accepted accounting principles as they apply to a company's reporting practices. While we have described these rules throughout the book, here we provide a comprehensive overview of the balance sheet and expand upon previous discussions of the reporting rules for balance sheet items. In addition, we discuss other disclosures required to communicate transactions and events of the business to external stakeholders.

WHAT DOES FINANCIAL POSITION TELL US?

We know that a company's financial position is the summary of the relationship between its assets and the claims of its creditors, owners, and other suppliers of goods and services to those assets at a certain point in time. The concept of financial position conveys information about the nature of the company's resources and obligations, its ability to meet its obligations, and its prospects for future profitability. Measuring financial position differs from measuring profitability, as discussed in Chapter 22, because firms measure financial position at a point in time, while they measure profit over a period of time.

How does financial position reveal future profit potential? Assets reported as part of financial position are the economic resources that the company has available in the future to operate and generate future profits. Information about the quantities and types of assets a company has communicates the profit potential of the company. In addition, information about the claims on those assets by owners, creditors, and others reveals how the firm might use its future profits. Possible uses could include providing a return to creditors in the form of interest, repaying amounts borrowed from creditors, or, for owners, either taking a return in the form of dividends or reinvesting in additional assets.

In earlier chapters, we explained that the principal role of financial statements is to communicate economic information about the company to outside parties like creditors and investors. Management and other insiders, too, use financial statements, but, in addition, they use many other sources of information about the company. Some of these other sources are internal reports, which differ from published financial statements in two important ways: (1) they are more detailed and contain proprietary information that companies would prefer that competitors not know, and (2) they are not constrained by GAAP rules that apply to asset valuation and cost allocation methods used in determining product costs.

The simplest balance sheet consists of the same number reported twice—once for total assets and once for total liabilities and owners' equity. So a company with $100 million in assets, $65 million in liabilities, and $35 million in owners' equity would report a balance sheet with $100 million for both total assets and the total of liabilities and owners' equity. That type of balance sheet, however, does not reveal meaningful information about a company's financial position. At the other extreme, consider a balance sheet that lists every permanent account found in a company's general ledger. For most major manufacturers like Quaker Oats, this could involve more than 2,000 accounts, which would make such a detailed type of presentation cumbersome for the readers of the statement. However, the users of financial statements who take the time to analyze such detailed content on the balance sheet could learn more company information than management is required, or might prefer, to reveal. A properly classified balance sheet fits somewhere between these two extremes. It aggregates related accounts into line items such as those shown on the balance sheet of Quaker Oats in Exhibit 23.1.

This chapter begins by describing the way that companies organize assets, liabilities, and equity accounts on the balance sheet, and also includes other disclosures required by GAAP. Then, we discuss other types of information included in the annual reports of corporations. The chapter concludes with a discussion of the different approaches to asset valuation that companies use on their balance sheets.

WHAT DOES "CURRENT" TELL THE FINANCIAL STATEMENT READER ABOUT AN ITEM?

Amounts appearing on a balance sheet are intended to provide statement users with enough information to make good assessments of the firm's financial position without revealing more about the operations of the business than the company believes it should. One important assessment that external stakeholders make, particularly creditors, is the status of a company's short-term solvency. That is, how likely is the company to pay its obligations for the next year? Classifying assets and liabilities as current and noncurrent helps to answer that question.

A firm reflects its short-term liquidity and solvency on the balance sheet by the relationship of its current assets to its current liabilities. Recall that *liquidity* refers to the time required for a firm to convert its assets to cash, and *solvency* is simply the ability to meet obligations when they are due.

You already know that current assets include cash and other assets a firm expects to convert into cash, sell, or use in one year or in the business's operating cycle, whichever is longer. Also recall that the operating cycle is the length of time it takes to: (1) invest cash in the acquisition or production of inventory, (2) sell the inventory, and (3) collect the cash from the sale.

Current liabilities are obligations that will become due in one year or within the operating cycle and will be paid with current assets or replaced with another current liability. Note that this definition includes not only the element of time, but also the means by which the firm will liquidate the debt. If a liability is due within one year and management intends to pay for it with noncurrent assets or refinance it with some form of long-term debt, the liability would be considered long term. Thus, obligations due within one year may be classified as long term, depending on the means management intends to liquidate the debt.

The calculation of current and quick ratios (explained in Chapter 12) is affected if current assets and current liabilities are not classified properly. For example, the classification of marketable securities as either long- or short-term depends on whether management intends to sell the securities within the coming fiscal year. It is a violation of GAAP for management of a firm to reclassify marketable securities held as long-term investments as trading securities if it does not intend to sell the securities in the coming fiscal year. Such a reclassification would mislead statement readers because it would increase the firm's current assets, and, therefore, falsely make the firm appear to be more liquid than it actually is.

The decision to classify a liability as either short term or long term also affects how investors and creditors perceive the solvency of the firm. Classification of liabilities may seem straightforward, but managers must exercise care when doing this. For example, firms often sign a one-year note knowing that at the end of the year they will pay all of the accrued interest, but only part of the note's principal and will then refinance the unpaid balance with another one-year note. To illustrate, assume that on June 30, 1997, Quaker Oats gives a one-year, $500 million, 10 percent note to the Minneapolis National Bank. Both Quaker Oats and the bank are aware that

Consolidated Balance Sheets

June 30	1995	1994	1993
Assets			
Current Assets			
Cash and cash equivalents	$ 101.8	$ 140.4	$ 61.0
Trade accounts receivable — net of allowances	546.8	509.4	478.9
Inventories			
Finished goods	267.4	266.5	241.5
Grains and raw materials	94.4	78.8	73.1
Packaging materials and supplies	44.2	40.2	39.4
Total inventories	406.0	385.5	354.0
Other current assets	262.0	218.3	173.7
Total Current Assets	1,316.6	1,253.6	1,067.6
Property, Plant and Equipment			
Land	25.0	30.6	28.7
Buildings and improvements	376.0	455.0	441.5
Machinery and equipment	1,442.7	1,640.3	1,589.0
Property, plant and equipment	1,843.7	2,125.9	2,059.2
Less accumulated depreciation	730.3	911.7	831.0
Property — Net	1,113.4	1,214.2	1,228.2
Intangible Assets — Net of Amortization	2,311.1	493.4	431.3
Other Assets	85.8	82.1	88.8
Total Assets	$4,826.9	$3,043.3	$2,815.9

EXHIBIT	23.1	Concluded

Dollars in Millions

June 30	1995	1994	1993
Liabilities and Shareholders' Equity			
Current Liabilities			
Short-term debt	$ 510.1	$ 211.3	$ 128.0
Current portion of long-term debt	38.8	45.4	48.9
Trade accounts payable	423.8	406.3	391.6
Accrued payroll, pension and bonus	123.8	158.9	161.3
Accrued advertising and merchandising	165.0	149.6	130.6
Income taxes payable	180.1	40.6	33.7
Other accrued liabilities	371.3	247.0	211.0
Total Current Liabilities	1,812.9	1,259.1	1,105.1
Long-term Debt	1,103.1	759.5	632.6
Other Liabilities	530.0	481.4	426.2
Deferred Income Taxes	233.3	82.2	89.5
Preferred Stock, Series B, no par value, authorized 1,750,000 shares; issued 1,282,051 of $5.46 cumulative convertible shares (liquidating preference of $78 per share)	100.0	100.0	100.0
Deferred Compensation	(74.9)	(80.8)	(85.9)
Treasury Preferred Stock, at cost, 81,194 shares, 47,817 shares and 34,447 shares, respectively	(6.3)	(3.9)	(2.7)
Common Shareholders' Equity			
Common stock, $5 par value, authorized 400 million, 200 million and 200 million shares, respectively	840.0	420.0	420.0
Reinvested earnings	1,499.3	1,273.6	1,190.1
Cumulative translation adjustment	(61.4)	(75.4)	(65.4)
Deferred compensation	(132.2)	(143.5)	(154.0)
Treasury common stock, at cost	(1,016.9)	(1,028.9)	(839.6)
Total Common Shareholders' Equity	1,128.8	445.8	551.1
Total Liabilities and Shareholders' Equity	$ 4,826.9	$ 3,043.3	$ 2,815.9

Quaker Oats does not intend to pay off the entire note at the end of one year. Instead, Quaker Oats intends to pay $175 million of the $500 million due, and the bank expects to accept another one-year note. The $175 million will cover the $50 million accrued interest payable ($500 million at 10 percent) and will reduce the principal of the note to $375 million ($500 million – $125 million).

Should management classify all or part of this note as a short- or long-term liability on Quaker Oats' June 30, 1997, balance sheet? If Quaker Oats can perform as intended, then it would classify $125 million of the note as short term and $375 million as long term on the June 30, 1997, balance sheet. This classification is based on the substance of the transaction, not on its form. That is, the transaction's form indicates that the company will repay this debt within one year, which would imply that Quaker should classify the debt as short term. However, management's intention to repay the debt in more than one year using a series of one-year notes overrides the consideration of the form of the note and determines the substance of the transaction. Therefore, Quaker should classify the note as long term. If there is a doubt about Quaker Oats' ability to refinance the note, management should classify the entire note as a current liability.

PAUSE & REFLECT	If a company uses a portion of long-term assets during a year, why is the portion of the asset that will be consumed during the coming year not classified as a current asset?

Proper classification of current items also affects the assessment of short-term solvency ratios, such as the current and quick ratios. Assume that before Quaker Oats borrowed the $500 million by issuing the note, total current assets were $1,257 million and current liabilities were $1,209 million. Thus, before the loan, the current ratio was 1.04 ($1,257/$1,209).

If management classifies $125 million as a current liability and $375 million of the note as a long-term liability, current liabilities would then total $1,334 ($1,209 + $125) million. Thus, the current ratio would increase to 1.32 due to both the $500 million received in cash, which increases current assets to $1,757 million, and the $125 million in additional current liabilities ($1,757/$1,334). However, if the company classified the entire note as current, total current liabilities would be $1,709 million, and the current ratio would decrease slightly from its initial position to 1.03 ($1,757/$1,709). Thus, the proper classification of the note is an effective means to communicate management's intent regarding conversion of assets or debt payment to outsiders who are assessing the short-term cash flows of the firm.

Management's decision to classify assets and liabilities as long term or short term is subjective. Keep in mind that a firm's management realizes that reporting more assets as current and classifying liabilities as long term rather than short term enhances the appearance of the firm's liquidity and solvency. Thus, statement readers must consider the implications of such management decisions regarding the classification of current assets and liabilities as they study a firm's balance sheet.

Classifying assets and liabilities as current and noncurrent is one way to classify assets. We describe other classifications that communicate information to external stakeholders next.

IS THERE INFORMATION TO BE GAINED FROM BALANCE SHEET CLASSIFICATIONS?

Those who use financial statements as their source of information about companies want to know more than the firm's liquidity and short-term solvency. They also want to know useful information about the nature of the firm's assets and its capital structure. One way accountants provide this information is by summarizing the accounts and recommending appropriate account classifications. See Exhibit 23.2 for the most common currently used balance sheet classifications.

EXHIBIT | 23.2 | Balance Sheet Classifications

Assets	=	Liabilities	+	Stockholders' Equity
Current assets		Current liabilities		Contributed capital
Investments		Long-term debt		Donated capital*
Property, plant, and equipment		Other long-term liabilities		
Intangible assets				Retained earnings
Other assets				Valuation capital*

*These terms are discussed more completely later in the chapter.

Firms are not required to use these specific classifications and may use alternatives to make the balance sheet more descriptive, as noted previously when discussing management's classification of assets and liabilities. Next we describe each of the major asset classifications and the related additional disclosures.

ASSETS

Current Assets

Asset classifications are listed on properly classified balance sheets in order of their liquidity, which is how quickly the firm will convert them to cash or consume them as part of operations. Assets found within the current asset classification are listed in the order of their liquidity, too. They include cash, short-term investments in marketable securities, accounts and notes receivable, inventory, and prepayments.

Cash Companies carry cash on the balance sheet at its stated value, assuming it is readily available to meet any current obligation. Petty cash funds are included in cash because they are available to meet current operating needs of the business.

PAUSE & REFLECT

When a check marked NSF (not sufficient funds) is returned by the bank to the company that deposited it, should the company classify the check as cash? If not cash, where should it classify this check? Do returned NSF checks belong on the balance sheet at all?

Companies should not classify as cash any cash which is restricted for a particular use. For example, some banks require that a company borrowing from the bank maintain a compensating balance in a checking account at the bank. A **compensating balance** is a minimum cash balance that the company (depositor) must maintain either to continue to earn interest on the amount deposited in the bank account or to avoid certain fees from the bank such as service charges. Compensating balances may also be required by banks in order to maintain lines of credit or similar short-term lending arrangements.

Assume Quaker Oats Company has a checking account with Minneapolis National Bank and has a $10 million line of credit from the bank. As part of the agreement, the bank requires Quaker to maintain a minimum of $500,000 in its checking account as a compensating balance. Therefore, if at the end of the year, the cash in the checking account was $830,000, only $330,000 would be classified as cash on the balance sheet. This reflects the restriction on the $500,000, which Quaker must keep as a compensating balance. Quaker, instead, classifies the $500,000 properly as a long-term investment rather than cash.

Marketable Securities Short-term investments in marketable securities is the second item under the current assets classification. As we discussed in Chapter 11, these securities are temporary investments that companies intend to convert to cash when needed. Because they are trading or available-for-sale securities, the securities appear on the balance sheet at their market value. This helps the reader understand the amount of cash that the company would realize if it sold the securities immediately.

EXHIBIT | 23.3

Quaker Oats Company's 1995 Trade Receivables Footnote

Note 4

Trade Accounts Receivable Allowances

Dollars in Millions	1995	1994	1993
Balance at beginning of year	$ 17.5	$15.0	$16.6
Provision for doubtful accounts	11.2	7.5	5.7
Provision for discounts and allowances	19.4	16.6	13.8
Write-offs of doubtful accounts—net of recoveries	(6.1)	(5.2)	(4.4)
Discounts and allowances taken	(15.6)	(13.9)	(13.9)
Effect of acquisitions and divestitures	1.4	—	—
Effect of exchange rate changes	(1.0)	(2.5)	(2.8)
Balance at end of year	$ 26.8	$17.5	$15.0

Accounts and Notes Receivable Accounts and notes receivable appear after marketable securities on the balance sheet. Companies show accounts receivable at their net realizable value, which represents the amount of accounts receivable currently due that the firm estimates is collectible. When the company reports only the net accounts receivables on the balance sheet, it would disclose the amount of the allowance for doubtful accounts in the notes to the financial statements. If accounts and notes receivable arise from persons who acquired goods and services, companies label them as trade receivables. Companies must disclose the total amount of trade receivables as a separate item either on the balance sheet or in the notes.

Exhibit 23.3 contains the note to Quaker Oats' 1995 financial statements that presents information about Quaker's trade accounts receivable. The provision for doubtful accounts is the amount of Quaker's allowance for uncollectible accounts. The company also discloses the provision for the amount of sales discounts and allowances that it expects in the future for items sold before the end of 1995. By showing the amount of accounts written off and discounts and allowances taken in 1995, Quaker provides statement readers with all the information needed to explain the changes in the two provision accounts.

Exhibit 23.3 also includes the effects of exchange rate fluctuations for receivables generated by transactions conducted in currencies other than U.S. dollars. For example, if the U.S. currency (dollars) strengthens against the German mark, a transaction denominated in German marks will require fewer U.S. dollars to settle. Since accounts receivable on Quaker Oats' financial statements are reported in dollars, receivables recorded in a foreign currency against which the dollar is strengthening such as German marks have a lower dollar value, which is what happened to Quaker in each of the three years shown. A weakening U.S. dollar would result in higher receivables on the balance sheet.

Inventory Inventory follows the receivables in the current asset section of the balance sheet. The balance sheet or related notes must disclose the inventory method used to determine the cost of the inventory (for example, FIFO or LIFO). In addition, the firm must disclose whether it reports the inventory amount at its cost or its market value whichever is lower at the end of the period. If a company has an inventory of raw materials or goods in process, it can show these amounts separately, although frequently the amounts are included with the inventory of merchandise available for sale.

As part of the accompanying notes to the financial statements, a company's annual report includes a **summary of significant accounting policies.** This summary includes descriptions of the accounting principles and methods the company has chosen to use, such as the method of computing inventory values, depreciation methods, and any other accounting methods about which the company has a choice among alternatives. Below is the excerpt from the June 30, 1995, summary of significant accounting policies of Quaker Oats that describes its inventory reporting policies:

Inventories. Inventories are valued at the lower of cost-or-market using various cost methods, and include the cost of raw materials, labor, and overhead. The percentage of year-end inventories valued using each of the methods was as follows:

June 30	1995	1994	1993
Last-in, first-out (LIFO)	46%	60%	53%
Average quarterly cost	47	30	35
First-in, first-out (FIFO)	7	10	12

If the LIFO method of valuing inventories was not used, total inventories would have been $10.5 million, $19.6 million and $17.2 million higher than reported at June 30, 1995, 1994 and 1993, respectively.

This note shows that Quaker, like many large companies, uses more than one method of accounting for inventories. As shown on its balance sheet in Exhibit 23.1, Quaker Oats had $406 million of inventory at June 30, 1995, reported in three categories: finished goods, grains and raw materials, and packaging materials and supplies. It is likely that Quaker uses the inventory method it finds most appropriate for each category depending on the ease of application and the effects on tax and financial income determination. Recall that LIFO usually produces inventory values that are significantly lower than the current market value, and income determined under LIFO is typically lower than income determined under other methods.

Prepaid Expenses Prepaid expenses are classified as current assets because they support the operating activities of the firm and are usually consumed during the operating cycle. They appear as current assets because they require the payment of cash during the next year. Furthermore, prepayments made for items such as insurance and rent are considered current because, if the contract for either item is cancelled, the firm would receive a cash refund.

Investments

Following the current assets section on the balance sheet is the investments section. The investment classification on the balance sheet describes the type and extent of the company's long-term, nonoperational investments. Acquiring long-term, nonoperational investments, such as stock or bonds of other companies, is an alternative to investing in operational assets such as production plants or equipment. Sometimes investing in nonoperating assets is a better management strategy because investing in operating assets might increase the firm's productive capacity beyond the demand for the products and services the firm provides. We previously described various long-term investments available to the firm, why companies acquire them, and how companies record them. For the financial statement users, a relatively detailed description of a company's long-term investments is often included in the notes to the financial statements.

Property, Plant, and Equipment

Property, plant, and equipment follows the investments section and shows the tangible operational investments that support the infrastructure of the firm. This balance sheet classification typically has the largest dollar amounts of any of the asset classifications and represents the largest and most diverse group of assets. The classifications found most typically in property, plant, and equipment are land, buildings, and equipment.

Land in the property, plant, and equipment section represents the land acquired to provide a site for the firm's operational activities. The buildings classification summarizes the cost of the various structures used by the firm to conduct its operations. Some firms subdivide this classification into more specific classifications such as manufacturing plants, office buildings, or retail outlets if such distinctions are deemed useful to the financial statement users. Buildings are depreciable assets and,

EXHIBIT | 23.4

Quaker Oats Company's 1995
Lease Disclosure Footnote

Note 13

Lease and Other Commitments

Certain equipment and operating properties are rented under non-cancelable operating leases. Total rental expense under operating leases was $35.2 million, $33.1 million and $34.3 million in fiscal 1995, 1994 and 1993, respectively. The following is a schedule of future minimum annual rentals on non-cancelable operating leases, primarily for sales offices, distribution centers and corporate headquarters, in effect as of June 30, 1995.

Dollars in Millions	1996	1997	1998	1999	2000	Later	Total
Total payments	$24.5	$22.6	$20.5	$19.3	$18.4	$72.0	$177.3

The Company enters into executory contracts to promote various products. As of June 30, 1995, future commitments under these contracts amounted to $57.9 million.

therefore, companies show buildings at their book values, that is, net of their accumulated depreciation. This is accomplished either by showing the original cost of the buildings less the accumulated depreciation or by showing the net book value and then separately disclosing the related amount of accumulated depreciation in the notes.

Exhibit 23.1 shows the total of Quaker Oats' plant, property and equipment at June 30, 1995, as $1,113 million. At that time, Quaker Oats operated 53 manufacturing plants in 18 states and 12 foreign countries, and it owned or leased distribution centers, warehouses, and sales offices in 22 states and 24 foreign countries.[1]

Leased Assets   As discussed in Chapter 15, leasing assets is an alternative to buying them. Recall that assets leased under capital leases appear on the leasee's balance sheet as property, plant, and equipment. There are other types of lease agreements—operating leases—that are simply rental agreements whose obligation is not recorded in a company's accounting records. For capital leases, the economic substance of the lease agreement implies that the asset was purchased instead of leased thus, overriding the legal form of the lease itself.

Quaker appropriately includes its capital leases as part of property, plant and equipment. Exhibit 23.4 shows that Quaker had significant commitments under its operating leases and it does not reflect the amount of its property under its capital leases and the fixed payments under those agreements because they were not large enough to warrant reporting separately.

Natural Resources   Quaker Oats had no significant investment in natural resources, which, as you know, are nonrenewable resources such as mineral, timber, or oil rights. If they had such an investment, Quaker would report it in the property, plant, and equipment classification on a classified balance sheet. Recall that as natural resources are consumed, the original cost of the asset is depleted. The original cost of the natural resource usually is maintained on the balance sheet, and the depletion taken to date is reported as a contra asset, accumulated depletion or a company can show the net book value of the natural resource on the balance sheet and report accumulated depletion in the notes. Companies reveal the rate of depletion and how they determine its amount in the summary of significant accounting policies.

Intangible Assets   Intangible assets are operational investments that a firm has acquired and appear following property, plant, and equipment on a company's balance sheet. Intangibles have no physical substance, but are expected to generate some economic benefit for the firm in the future. Companies report intangible assets on the balance sheet at the original cost less the amortization taken on the assets up to that point in time.

---

[1]Quaker Oats Company, Annual Report, 1995.

PAUSE & REFLECT

Accounts receivable's only physical substance usually is the invoice sent to the customer. Why, then, are accounts receivable not classified as intangible assets? What other unique characteristic do most intangibles have?

Other Assets

Firms use the last asset classification, other assets, for unusual items that do not fit in the previous asset classifications. The items found in this classification vary in practice and include items such as noncurrent receivables and special funds. Many accountants consider other assets to be too general a description and, therefore, recommend that items found in this classification be placed in another more specific asset classification.

Deferred charges (deferrals) frequently are found in the other asset classification. Such charges are long-term prepayments that companies amortize over various lengths of time, depending on how long management believes the firm will benefit from the expenditures. For example, organization costs—the money spent for starting a business, including licenses and attorney fees—is an example of a deferred charge typically found in the other asset classification. Organizational costs are amortized on a straight-line basis over a minimum of 5 to a maximum of 40 years depending on management's view of the period they benefit.[2]

Now we have described the major classifications of assets found on most balance sheets. The "other side" of the balance sheet generally reflects the means by which a company has chosen to finance its assets. This portion of the balance sheet includes a company's obligations to creditors and other outside parties as well as its investments from owners. In the next section, we discuss the major classifications found in the liabilities section of the balance sheet.

LIABILITIES: DEBT AND OTHER OBLIGATIONS

There are three basic classifications of liabilities on the balance sheet: current liabilities, long-term debt, and other long-term liabilities. The latter two classifications differ from each other in that long-term debt refers to obligations to creditors from borrowing, and long-term liabilities include obligations that arise from other means than borrowing, such as obligations under capital leases and pension obligations.

Current Liabilities

Current liabilities are listed first in the liabilities section of the balance sheet. They result from one of four events: (1) the receipt of loan proceeds by the firm, (2) the receipt of goods and services when using credit as a means of payment for them, (3) the receipt of prepayments for goods and services promised to be provided by the firm during the next year, and (4) the reclassification of the portion of long-term debt that becomes due within the coming fiscal year.

The acquisition of goods and services on credit creates the most common type of current liability. Accounts payable, notes payable, wages and salaries payable, interest payable, and even taxes payable all reflect short-term obligations to pay for goods or services acquired by the firm. When the firm receives payments in advance, it is required to either perform the prepaid service or to provide the goods promised or return the cash advanced. The accounts associated with this type of obligation include unearned rent, unearned subscription revenue, and deposits made by customers to hold merchandise for future delivery. The balance sheet for Quaker Oats (Exhibit 23.1) shows current liabilities, as of June 30, 1995, of $1,812.9 million, $38.8 million of which was the current portion of long-term debt.

As discussed earlier, firms must classify any portion of a long-term debt that comes due within the time frame established for current liabilities as current. The exception to this rule occurs regarding those liabilities the firms expect either to pay with a noncurrent asset or refinance with another long-term debt agreement. Installment notes, lease obligations, bonds, and mortgage notes can appear as both a current liability and a long-term liability if part of the debt meets the current liability

---

[2] The maximum of 40 years is determined by GAAP.

criteria. If the entire amount of the debt meets the current liability criteria, it is properly classified, in total, as a current liability. As part of its 1995 note for short-term debt, Quaker explained that it refinanced part of its short-term debt and, therefore, classified that debt as long-term in its 1993 balance sheet which was included for comparative purposes.

> The consolidated balance sheet as of June 30, 1993 included the reclassification of $50.0 million of short-term debt to long-term debt, reflecting the Company's intent and ability to refinance this debt on a long-term basis.

Long-Term Debt

Long-term liabilities are not expected to come due within one year or the operating cycle, whichever is longer. However, as we discussed earlier, the classification, long-term liabilities, also can include those liabilities that will come due within the next fiscal year. In the latter case, the company expects to pay for these liabilities with noncurrent assets, or the company expects to refinance them with another long-term debt instrument. Chapters 15 and 18 discussed the different types of long-term debt instruments and their accounting treatments.

Most long-term debt instruments specify the terms promised by the borrower as well as the restrictions imposed for the benefit of the lender. Companies disclose these details in the notes to the financial statements.

A long-term note payable reflects a firm's debt agreement with an individual or institution. A long-term note commonly found on the balance sheet is the mortgage note payable, which shows the amount of borrowing secured with the real estate of the borrower.

Bonds payable differ from long-term notes payable in that the firm typically is borrowing the needed funds from the public and not from a specific individual or institution. Recall that firms amortize any premium or discount as a way of adjusting interest on the income statement to reflect the market rate of interest at the time the company issued the bond. The unamortized premium or discount is shown either as an adjustment to the bond's face value on the balance sheet or in the notes to the statements where the bonds appear at their carrying value.

The amount of information about a bond issue presented on the face of the balance sheet is limited. Companies often show detailed information about bond issues, such as the life of the bond, its effective interest rate, and whether it was secured, in the notes to the financial statements. The notes to the financial statements also include a description of any other features of the bonds, such as conversion rates, call price, and the restrictions the bond indebtedness places on the corporation.

Exhibit 23.5 shows the detailed information about the long-term debt of Quaker Oats at June 30, 1995, and the two previous year-ends. The three debt issues listed first represent funds borrowed to buy stock, which Quaker will distribute as part of its employee stock ownership plan. The term *senior* used to describe the ESOP notes means that those notes have preference over another unsecured debt in the event of a company's liquidation. The order of preference begins with secured debt, followed by the senior unsecured debt, and then the other unsecured debt. Recall that all debtholders have preference over stockholders.

Since the noninterest-bearing installment note does not have an explicit interest rate, Quaker Oats explained the payments and interest rates of that debt as follows:

> The non-interest bearing installment note for $55.5 million has an unamortized discount of $50.4 million, $51.0 million and $51.5 million as of June, 30, 1995, 1994 and 1993, respectively, based on an imputed interest rate of 13 percent.

Other Long-Term Liabilities

Companies classify long-term obligations other than amounts explicitly borrowed, such as pension and lease obligations, as other long-term liabilities. Recall from Chapter 18 that, for capital leases, firms report the present value of the future lease payments as a long-term liability. Firms disclose other lease terms, including minimum payments for the next five years, in the notes to the financial statements. This disclosure helps statement users predict how these lease agreements will affect the firm's future cash flows.

Companies also include the liability under their pension plans as an other long-term liability. Chapter 17 indicated that defined benefit pension plans require companies to base the pension benefits paid to employees on factors including estimates of the time employees will work and their expected life. This makes accounting for these plans very complicated, including the calculation of the amount that companies should record as pension liability. Though we have not dealt with the details of these calculations, nor have we shown the complexity of determining other postretirement benefit obligations, you should know that these obligations are reported under this liability classification.

Deferred income tax liability is another long-term liability reported on most corporate balance sheets as an other long-term liability. However, due to the complexities surrounding this account, discussion of this account was delayed to this point. The brief discussion that follows presents basic information to provide a fundamental understanding of why this account exists. A more detailed discussion of this topic is found in more advanced accounting textbooks.

The deferred income tax liabilities (and assets) result from differences between computing income using generally accepted accounting principles and computing taxable income using tax laws. Remember that accounting principles are designed to measure and reflect business events on an objective basis, whereas tax laws are designed to raise money for the government and encourage, or discourage, particular types of business transactions. Because firms must comply with both accounting principles and tax laws, the resulting tax calculations can differ from the financial accounting treatment of a particular business event. Such differences create a deferred income tax amount that appears on the balance sheet.

To illustrate how a deferred tax liability arises, assume that Quaker Oats Company has a tax rate of 34 percent and signs a sales contract on December 15, 1997, for $100,000, which is considered revenue for financial accounting purposes. However, because the receipt of payment for the contract is delayed until July 15, 1998, for tax purposes this is not considered taxable until Quaker receives the cash. Note that both Quaker and the IRS consider this as revenue, but they differ about the time period in which to recognize it.

To comply with GAAP, Quaker recognizes the $1 million as revenue and reflects the related tax expense of $340,000 ($1 million × 34%) for the fiscal year ended June 30, 1998. When it recognizes the tax expense, there is also a related Deferred Income Tax Liability account, which indicates that the taxes are due from Quaker.

EXHIBIT | 23.5

Quaker Oats Company's
1995 Long-term Debt
Footnote

Note 6

Long-term Debt

Dollars in Millions	1995	1994	1993
7.76% Senior ESOP Notes due through 2002	$ 74.9	$ 80.8	$ 85.9
8.0% Senior ESOP Notes due through 2002	125.7	133.9	140.3
8.75% ESOP installment loan due through 1996	2.9	5.5	7.9
7.4%-7.9% Series A Medium-term Notes due through 2000	56.7	71.8	86.8
8.15%-9.34% Series B Medium-term Notes due through 2020	216.4	229.6	248.0
6.5%-7.48% Series C Medium-term Notes due through 2024	200.0	200.0	—
6.45%-7.77% Series D Medium-term Notes due through 2025	212.0	—	—
6.63% deutsche mark swap due 1998	20.2	17.5	16.3
5.7%-10.75% Industrial Revenue Bonds due through 2010, tax-exempt	34.4	34.4	35.6
Non-interest bearing installment note due 2014	5.1	4.5	4.0
Short-term debt to be refinanced	188.0	—	50.0
Other	5.6	26.9	6.7
Subtotal	1,141.9	804.9	681.5
Less: Current portion of long-term debt	38.8	45.4	48.9
Long-term debt	$ 1,103.1	$759.5	$632.6

All maturity dates presented refer to fiscal years.

Aggregate required payments of maturities of long-term debt for the next five fiscal years are as follows:

Dollars in Millions	1996	1997	1998	1999	2000
Required payments	$ 38.8	$ 53.9	$ 131.5	$ 50.9	$ 113.7

During fiscal 1994, the Company issued $200.0 million of Series C Medium-term Notes bearing interest rates ranging from 6.5 percent to 7.48 percent per annum with maturities from 10 to 30 years. The debt was issued under a $600.0 million shelf registration filed with the SEC in January 1990. In April 1995, the Company filed a prospectus supplement with the SEC for the issuance of an additional $400.0 million of medium-term notes under the 1990 shelf registration. As of June 30, 1995, the Company has issued $212.0 million of Series D Medium-term Notes bearing interest ranging from 6.45 percent to 7.77 percent per annum with maturities from three to 30 years. The Company intends to issue the remaining $188.0 million of medium-term notes by December 31, 1995. As a result, the consolidated balance sheet as of June 30, 1995 included the reclassification of $188.0 million of short-term debt to long-term debt.

The consolidated balance sheet as of June 30, 1993 included the reclassification of $50.0 million of short-term debt to long-term debt, reflecting the Company's intent and ability to refinance this debt on a long-term basis.

EXHIBIT | 23.6

Quaker Oats Company's 1995
Deferred Tax Footnote

Deferred tax assets and deferred tax liabilities were as follows:

Dollars in Millions	1995		1994		1993	
	Assets	**Liabilities**	Assets	Liabilities	Assets	Liabilities
Depreciation and amortization	$ 59.7	$ 395.2	$ 21.1	$ 219.3	$ 14.5	$ 211.0
Postretirement benefits	97.2	—	94.1	—	85.9	—
Other benefit plans	54.9	15.6	52.4	11.5	42.0	13.5
Accrued expenses including restructuring charges	155.1	17.7	112.9	21.7	59.1	4.1
Loss carryforwards	8.7	—	24.3	—	20.8	—
Other	15.2	48.5	18.1	33.5	21.8	34.6
Subtotal	390.8	477.0	322.9	286.0	244.1	263.2
Valuation allowance	(18.7)	—	(28.1)	—	(18.1)	—
Total	$ 372.1	$ 477.0	$ 294.8	$ 286.0	$ 226.0	$ 263.2

Quaker will actually have to pay the related taxes when the IRS recognizes the $1 million as taxable income in 1998. In this case, Quaker would report a deferred tax liability of $340,000 as a liability on its 1998 balance sheet.[3]

There are numerous differences between tax law and GAAP that cause taxable income and accounting income to differ. The important differences result from recognizing certain revenues and expenses for tax purposes at different times than they are recognized for financial accounting purposes, which creates deferred income tax assets and liabilities. Exhibit 23.6 shows Quaker Oats' deferred assets and liabilities in 1995 and a list of accounting events that produced them. Postretirement benefits gave rise to deferred assets because the financial expense preceded the deductibility for tax purposes. On the other hand, the tax deductions for depreciation and amortization were greater than the related financial expenses of the period. This means that taxable income was lower than financial income and that Quaker has an obligation, or a liability, for the difference.

PAUSE & REFLECT

Since long-term obligations do not require payment within the next year, why is it necessary to distinguish between long-term debt and other long-term obligations? In what important ways are they different? What useful information can a statement reader glean from the distinction?

Off-Balance-Sheet Financing

Some financial reporting rules for liabilities, such as capital lease obligations, allow the substance of the transaction to override its form, so companies are obligated to record the amounts of the related debt and reflect them in their financial statements. These reporting rules arose in response to managers' attempts to borrow money in ways that would avoid having to record such borrowings on the balance sheet (known as **off-balance-sheet financing**).

When a manager leases an asset under a long-term noncancellable lease, he or she is obligated to reflect the lease payments on the financial statements as if the company had borrowed the money and bought the asset. Without such obligations created by GAAP rules, the noncancellable lease obligation would not be reported on the company's balance sheet.

When balance sheets omit reflecting the sources of off-balance-sheet financing, such as long-term leases classified as operating leases (even though there are substantial obligations to make future lease payments), it affects how balance sheet readers perceive the risk and financial health of the business. Not recording such liabilities affects indicators of financial risk such as the current ratio and the debt-to-equity ratio, by making them appear better than if the obligation were recorded.

Understanding the nature of current liabilities, long-term debt, and other long-term liabilities helps financial statement readers assess the nature of the obligations that the company faces. Next we describe the classifications in the stockholders' equity section.

---

[3]As of December 1996, Quaker Oats switched from a June 30 fiscal year end to a December 31 year end. The 1995 Balance Sheet discussed in this chapter had a June 30 year-end.

EXHIBIT | 23.7

Quaker Oats Company's 1995 Capital Stock Footnote

Note 7

Capital Stock

In fiscal 1995, shareholders of record received an additional share of common stock for each share held, pursuant to a two-for-one stock split-up approved by the Board of Directors. Per share data and average number of common shares outstanding have been retroactively restated. As a result of the increase in issued shares, common stock has been increased and reinvested earnings has been decreased by $420.0 million. In November 1994, shareholders approved an increase in authorized shares from 200 million to 400 million.

During fiscal 1995, 0.6 million shares of the Company's outstanding common stock were repurchased for $22.5 million under a 10 million share repurchase program announced in August 1993.

The Company is authorized to issue 10 million shares of preferred stock in series, with terms fixed by resolution of the Board of Directors. One million shares of Series A Junior Participating Preferred Stock have been reserved for issuance in connection with the Shareholder Rights Plan (see Note 10).

An additional 1,750,000 shares of Series B ESOP Convertible Preferred Stock (Series B Stock) have been reserved for issuance in connection with the Company's ESOP. As of June 30, 1995, 1,282,051 shares of the Series B Stock had been issued and are each convertible into 2.1576 shares of the Company's common stock. The Series B Stock will be issued only for the ESOP and will not be traded on the open market.

The Company is also authorized to issue one million shares of redeemable preference stock, none of which had been issued as of June 30, 1995.

STOCKHOLDERS' EQUITY

Here we review some important points about stockholders' equity. Dividing the stockholder's equity section into contributed capital (often called *paid-in capital*) and retained earnings reflects the resources provided by the owners and the claims generated by retaining the corporation's profits, respectively. Retained earnings is also called the *undistributed earnings of the corporation*.

Contributed Capital

Chapter 18 discussed the equity financing events that create the accounts found in the contributed capital section of stockholders' equity on the balance sheet. The following discussion focuses on how the balance sheet reports these events. (Refer to the stockholder's equity section of Quaker Oats' balance sheet in Exhibit 23.1 to find the parts of the equity section we discuss.)

Quaker has chosen to separate the preferred stock section of equity from the common stockholders' equity. This presentation reflects the idea that the nature of preferred stock is like debt because preferred stockholders cannot vote in shareholder meetings. In addition, as you know, the preferred stock dividends usually are set at a fixed amount, and preferred stock has preference over common stock regarding the receipt of dividends and in liquidation. On more traditional balance sheets, preferred stock typically appears as the first item in the contributed capital section because of its preference.

In the case of Quaker, its preferred stock was no par, consequently, they had to disclose the liquidation value of their preferred stock ($78 per share). This amount represents the minimum amount that Quaker would pay for each share of preferred stock before the common stockholders could receive any distribution in the event of a liquidation.

In the notes to the financial statements Quaker disclosed that it split its common stock two-for-one in 1995, as shown in Exhibit 23.7. Thus, the earnings per share data for previous years as well as the average number of shares outstanding for those years are adjusted for the effect of the split. In addition, Quaker disclosed a plan, begun in 1993, to repurchase 10 million shares of its outstanding common stock. This type of disclosure is important because investors can adjust their expectations for earnings per share and ownership share.

Donated Capital

Donated capital is a type of contributed capital shown in the contributed capital section. Corporations use this classification when they receive assets but give no ownership interest in exchange. For example, it is not uncommon for a city to give a corporation land or buildings in exchange for its locating a production plant or corporate headquarters in that city. When this occurs, the company would record the asset at its fair market value and would increase the donated capital account by the same amount; the city receives no ownership interest in the corporation.

Valuation Capital

Appearing between the contributed capital and retained earnings sections of the stockholders' equity section if it is a credit balance or after retained earnings if it is a debit balance is a valuation capital section. The most common source of valuation capital comes from fluctuations in market value for investments in securities classified as available-for-sale (discussed in Chapter 21). Recall that available-for-sale securities are those that management does not intend to sell in the next year. Usually management has purchased these types of securities in order to have control over or influence on another corporation rather than for short-term returns. Since the principal reason corporations hold these securities is not for short-term returns, fluctuations in their market value might distort current income. Therefore, by requiring that companies show these fluctuations as part of stockholders' equity, GAAP ensures that the corporation can show the market value of its investments without affecting the current period's reported income.

Retained Earnings

Recall that retained earnings represents the earnings that have been reinvested in the firm and have not been distributed to the stockholders. Corporations may restrict retained earnings, which limits the dividend-paying ability of the corporation. Any restriction on retained earnings means that the corporation may not pay the entire amount of retained earnings as dividends.

A restriction is often placed on retained earnings when a corporation issues bonds and the bonds' covenants restrict the dividend-paying ability of the corporation to protect the bondholders. When corporations purchase treasury stock, they may restrict retained earnings by the amount paid for the treasury stock. Because the purchase of treasury stock represents the amount paid to former stockholders, both common and preferred, the purchase liquidates an owner's interest. Therefore, creditors of the company want to limit the dividend-paying ability of the corporation to protect them from further distribution of the firm's assets to stockholders. As the corporation sells treasury stock, it removes any related restrictions. When the retained earnings of the firm are restricted, corporations disclose the amount of and reason for the restriction in a note.

Treasury Stock

Treasury stock is shown after retained earnings in the stockholders' equity section of the balance sheet. Note that treasury stock is not a reduction in the amount of retained earnings; rather, it reflects a reduction in the total amount of stockholders' equity. Because corporations assume that they will reissue treasury shares, they treat treasury stock as a temporary reduction in stockholders' equity, which they eliminate when they reissue the shares.

Notice in Exhibit 23.1 that Quaker Oats had treasury stock for both preferred and common stock. They chose to report each type of treasury stock separately with the related type of stock rather than as a total at the bottom of the stockholders' equity section. Quaker held these shares to distribute as part of its employee stock ownership plan. The debt that Quaker issued to obtain the money to buy these shares of treasury stock appears as part of the long-term debt shown in Exhibit 23.5.

Investors use environmental accounting and research how a company disposes of its product before making an investment.

PAUSE & REFLECT

Corporations often buy their outstanding shares of stock as treasury stock to issue as part of stock option plans. Why should they buy their outstanding stock rather than simply issuing authorized but unissued stock?

THERE IS MORE TO ANNUAL REPORTS THAN FINANCIAL STATEMENTS

Corporations usually issue financial statements to outside parties, particularly stockholders and potential investors, as part of the annual report. An annual report, as you have seen, includes not only the financial statements, but also reflects other disclosures that management wants to communicate, along with some supplementary required disclosures. This section discusses other important items found in corporate annual reports.

Reconsider here the essential components of a company's annual report. Included in the annual reports distributed by corporations are topics that the management wants to present to stakeholders, including descriptions of new products or markets, as well as management's views of the business's outlook. Annual reports also include the report that external auditors issue on the financial statements as well as other disclosures about the business.

Management's View of the Business

Most major corporations are run by professional managers whose actual ownership may be only a small portion of the company's outstanding stock. The annual report is the principal way that managers communicate their assessment and perception of the company.

Much of the information that managers want to communicate appears in the management's **letter to stockholders.** This written report gives an overview of the items other than financial statements in the annual report and highlights important aspects of financial performance. Exhibit 23.8 shows selected parts of the letter from Quaker Oats' Chairman William D. Smithburg and President Philip A. Marineau. Quaker chose to use this letter to describe the major investment changes in 1995.

Business Segment Information

In addition to financial statements, annual reports provide details about the performance of the company. One important disclosure for large corporations includes **segment data.** Large corporations usually are involved in several lines of business that often are spread around the globe. Companies must disclose segment activities as part of the annual report in certain circumstances. Anytime that a segment, which can be an identifiable geographic region or an identifiable product line, accounts for 10 percent or more of total company sales or assets, related segment data must appear as part of the annual report. By revealing this information, stakeholders can assess major parts of the business. Using 10 percent as the threshold for disclosure, the

Dear Quaker Shareholders,

In fiscal 1995, we upgraded Quaker's portfolio to bring you greater future value.

We added brands with high-growth potential like Snapple, and divested lower-growth, lower-margin businesses, like pet foods. We expanded the international reach of our Gatorade and grain-based food businesses. At the same time, we streamlined our internal structure to focus every resource in the Company on profitable growth.

Granted, it is a bold step to make all these moves in one year. But our promise of greater value is significant. Going forward, we plan to achieve annual earnings growth of at least 10 percent after inflation.

This year, we built the framework for a new era of growth . . .

. . . Why all this change in one year? It became clear that delivering significant earnings growth with the mix of mature products in our existing portfolio would be increasingly difficult. So, we changed our portfolio through a series of acquisitions and divestitures, and now feel we have the potential for substantial growth, well into the future.

We expect to obtain this growth by bringing high-quality, value-added brands to consumers, and by delivering reliable service and greater profit opportunities to our customers. When we do these things efficiently, we produce superior returns. That is why our energy and resources are directed to growing our strong consumer brands. It is also why we acquired *Snapple* beverages.

Snapple adds another excellent consumer brand. We bring *Snapple* beverages both the resources for greater growth and the discipline needed for economic-value creation. With *Snapple*, Quaker now competes in three of the fastest growing beverage categories: iced teas, fruit juice drinks and sports beverages. Domestic and international expansion of our beverages has the potential for double-digit sales and profit growth for years to come.

But beverages are not our only growth engine. Quaker's grain-based products achieved strong sales growth this year as well. With consumers' increasing interest in adding more complex carbohydrates to their diets, we are confident that the long-term growth potential of our grain-based businesses remains exceptional. In the United States, our cereal, snack, rice and pasta businesses are excellent value drivers. In Latin America and the Asia/Pacific region, we have been expanding our traditional and new grain-based products. These two areas have growing populations, an emerging middle class and, most importantly, a hunger—and thirst—for high-quality, brand-name products. With the acquisitions and divestitures of this year, we now have stronger brand portfolio than ever, well-positioned in more growing categories. Combined, our brands give us excellent opportunities for profitable growth.

To finance these growth opportunities, in fiscal 1995 we increased our debt. It peaked at about $3 billion. However, after-tax proceeds from our divestitures totalling over $1.2 billion let us reduce total debt to under $1.7 billion by fiscal year end.

Concurrent with the development of our portfolio, we made substantial changes inside the Company. We removed layers of management to become even more responsive to our consumers and trade customers. We reduced the number of people, warehouses and other overhead expenses needed to support our business. The cost of this restructuring totaled $76.5 million pretax, or $.35 per share.

Overall, earnings grew to $5.97 per share because of substantial gains from the divestitures of our worldwide pet foods, U.S. bean and chili, Mexican chocolate and Dutch honey businesses. These gains totaled $1.2 billion, or $5.20 per share. Fiscal 1995 sales reached a record $6.4 billion. However, mid-year acquisitions and divestitures make comparisons to the prior year less meaningful. The reported numbers do not reflect the relative weakness in operating returns experienced in some of our businesses. Higher advertising and merchandising spending, lower volume in our hot cereals business (related to warmer weather and private-label competition) and higher raw material and manufacturing costs all lowered our returns. We have taken aggressive steps to address these issues. We are establishing more stringent business controls and believe our new alignment of key decision makers will get the Company back on a profitable growth track.

The profitable growth potential of our new portfolio is obscured by the combination of special charges, lost income from divested businesses, higher interest expense and investment in existing businesses. We are confident that future growth will be above average, once we pass through this period of transition.

amount of data is limited and also assures interested parties that the information disclosed concerns parts of the business that are big enough so that significant effects on a segment will also have an effect on the firm.

Exhibits 23.9 and 23.10 show the two types of segment data for Quaker Oats in 1995. The geographic disclosure (Exhibit 23.9) shows that Quaker Oats had most of its 1995 sales in the United States and Canada. Exhibit 23.10 shows the three product categories within the U.S. grain-based products segment. Hot cereals had a 10 percent drop in sales, which was attributed to warm weather and competition from generic brands. Ready-to-eat cereals showed modest growth, while grain-based snacks was the fastest growing product category in the segment. Disclosures like these help investors assess the prospects of future sales and earnings associated with specific product categories. Elsewhere in its 1995 annual report, Quaker reported that Gatorade had $1.3 billion in sales, and was distributed in 35 countries.

Periodic Reports— More Timely Reporting

Because investors and stockholders want to know how the business is faring more often than once a year, companies often issue quarterly financial statements. Issuing statements at three-month intervals provides stockholders and investors with timely information to use in decision making. Exhibit 23.11 shows Quaker Oats' 1995 quarterly reports, which it included as part of the annual report. Unlike some businesses, Quaker's business activity is fairly constant across the four quarters. While Quaker's business activity was fairly constant, its net income varied across the four quarters of 1995 due to the effect of a change in accounting principles begun in the third quarter. Quaker also includes the amount of quarterly cash dividends it declared each quarter ($.285 per share each quarter) and the market price range—high and low—of the common stock during each quarter.

Contingent Liabilities

Some events, such as lawsuits or claims by customers for defective products, may affect the business negatively. However, in some cases, the actual events that create the specific losses have not occurred at the end of the reporting period, such as a judgment in a lawsuit that is filed but not settled. Outside stakeholders would like to know about these potential events, and companies are required to disclose them under certain conditions. These potential losses are called **contingent liabilities,** which *represent events that could create negative financial results for a company at some future point.* Companies must actually record losses when the related event is considered probable *and* when the company can estimate its monetary effect on the financial statements.

Even when corporations cannot estimate the impact of the events or whether the likelihood of such events is less than probable, they must disclose the existence of contingent liabilities as part of the notes that accompany the financial statements. Exhibit 23.12 shows the note that Quaker Oats included in its 1995 annual report to disclose contingent liabilities. Quaker disclosed a lawsuit concerning its use of the phrase "thirst aid" in advertisements before December 1990. Quaker appealed a judgment against it and lost the appeal and filed another. Quaker appears to believe that a loss is probable and that it can be reasonably estimated because in 1995 they recorded a loss of $29 million even though the judgment is still on appeal.

The Auditor's Report

One other important disclosure included in annual reports is the auditor's report. Recall that CPAs provide an opinion about the fairness of the financial statements using GAAP as the criteria. There are four kinds of reports issued (given) by external auditors: unqualified, qualified, and adverse opinions, and a disclaimer of opinion. When an auditor issues an **unqualified opinion,** it means that the financial statements are fair representations of the business's financial position and reported income and that, in the auditor's opinion, the company has applied GAAP appropriately. A **qualified opinion** indicates that either the auditors found parts of the

EXHIBIT 23.9 Quaker Oats Company's 1995 Geographical Segment Disclosure

The Quaker Oats Company and Subsidiaries

Dollars in Millions

Geographic Segment Information	Year Ended June 30	1995	1994	1993	1992	1991
	Identifiable Assets					
	U.S. and Canadian Grocery Products	**$3,917.5**	$1,999.4	$1,877.3	$1,997.9	$2,228.7
	Europe	**255.0**	576.5	562.9	687.5	533.5
	Latin America and Pacific	**369.9**	209.4	182.4	154.4	122.5
	International Grocery Products	**624.9**	785.9	745.3	841.9	656.0
	Total Operating Businesses	**4,542.4**	2,785.3	2,622.6	2,839.8	2,884.7
	Corporate(a)	**284.5**	258.0	193.3	200.1	175.8
	Total Assets	**$4,826.9**	$3,043.3	$2,815.9	$3,039.9	$3,060.5
	Capital Expenditures					
	U.S. and Canadian Grocery Products	**$ 193.1**	$ 123.9	$ 107.2	$ 110.7	$ 167.0
	International Grocery Products	**69.6**	51.2	65.1	65.7	73.6
	Total Operating Businesses	**262.7**	175.1	172.3	176.4	240.6
	Corporate	**12.8**	—	—	—	—
	Total Capital Expenditures	**$ 275.5**	$ 175.1	$ 172.3	$ 176.4	$ 240.6
	Depreciation and Amortization					
	U.S. and Canadian Grocery Products	**$ 155.3**	$ 131.6	$ 117.6	$ 116.6	$ 112.9
	International Grocery Products	**35.0**	38.5	38.2	38.2	36.4
	Total Operating Businesses	**190.3**	170.1	155.8	154.8	149.3
	Corporate	**1.1**	1.1	1.1	1.1	1.0
	Total Depreciation and Amortization	**$ 191.4**	$ 171.2	$ 156.9	$ 155.9	$ 150.3

(a)Includes corporate cash and cash equivalents, certain other current assets, property and miscellaneous other assets.

U.S. Grain-Based Products

	Sales	Volume	Category Growth
Hot Cereals	-10%	-10%	-2%
Ready-to-Eat Cereals	+4%	+3%	+1%
Granola Bars	+11%	+10%	+20%
Rice Cakes	+27%	+29%	+18%

Hot Cereals *Quaker* oatmeal—in instant, quick and long-cook form—is the leading competitor in the hot cereal category. Instant *Quaker* Oatmeal is the leading brand in the instant category and the number-three selling product in the overall cereal category, rivaling many ready-to-eat cereals as the breakfast of choice. *Quaker Oats* offer consumers a product that is 100-percent natural and low-fat while providing no sodium and good fiber, making it an important part of a healthy diet. Warm winter weather and private-label competition dampened sales in fiscal 1995.

Ready-to-Eat Cereals Quaker's ready-to-eat products compete on a brand-by-brand basis, with sales substantially driven by three top selling products—*Cap'n Crunch*, *Quaker Toasted Oatmeal* and *Life* cereals. In addition, Quaker markets *Quaker 100% Natural*, *Quaker Oatmeal Squares* and a growing variety of value-priced bagged cereals. In fiscal 1995, *Quaker* ready-to-eat cereals continued a long trend of significant sales growth. Though a number-four market position is usually not acceptable by Quaker standards, the size of the ready-to-eat cereal market and the profitability of individual leading brands allow the Company to generate attractive returns from this business.

Grain-Based Snacks Quaker is a leading competitor in the fast-growing rice cake and granola bar categories. With outstanding flavor variety and healthy nutritional profiles, *Quaker* rice cakes and *Quaker Chewy* granola bars offer consumers a more wholesome alternative to salty, fatty and highly sugared snacks. In fiscal 1995, low-fat flavor innovation in *Chewy* granola bars helped increase product popularity with health-conscious consumers. Effective marketing support and new varieties have kept *Quaker* rice cakes well ahead of the competition.

EXHIBIT | 23.11

Note 19

Quarterly Financial Data (Unaudited)

Dollars in Millions (Except Per Share Data)

1995	First Quarter *(a)*	Second Quarter	Third Quarter *(b)*	Fourth Quarter *(c)*
Net sales	$1,636.4	$1,507.9	$1,633.5	$1,587.4
Cost of goods sold	825.2	791.2	871.0	894.1
Gross profit	$ 811.2	$ 716.7	$ 762.5	$ 693.3
Income before cumulative effect of accounting change	$ 61.4	$ 34.4	$ 366.1	$ 344.2
Net income	$ 57.3	$ 34.4	$ 366.1	$ 344.2
Per common share:				
Income before cumulative effect of accounting change	$ 0.45	$ 0.25	$ 2.73	$ 2.57
Net income	$ 0.42	$ 0.25	$ 2.73	$ 2.57
Cash dividends declared	$ 0.285	$ 0.285	$ 0.285	$ 0.285
Market price range:				
High	$ 42½	$ 38¾	$ 36½	$ 37½
Low	$ 35³⁄₁₆	$ 29¾	$ 30¼	$ 32⅛

(a) Includes an $18.4 million pretax provision ($11.0 million after-tax or $.08 per share) for estimated litigation costs. First quarter per share data have been restated to reflect the fiscal 1995 two-for-one stock split-up.
(b) Includes a $513.0 million pretax gain ($322.2 million after-tax or $2.41 per share) for the sale of the North American pet food business and a $4.9 million pretax gain ($2.8 million after-tax or $.02 per share) for the sale of the Dutch honey business.
(c) Includes a $487.2 million pretax gain ($272.6 million after-tax or $2.04 per share) for the sale of the European pet food business; a $74.5 million pretax gain ($43.9 million after-tax or $.33 per share) for the sale of the Mexican chocolate business; a $91.2 million pretax gain ($53.1 million after-tax or $.40 per share) for the sale of the U.S. bean and chili businesses; a $76.5 million pretax charge ($46.1 million after-tax or $.35 per share) for cost-reduction and realignment activities; and an additional $10.6 million pretax provision ($6.2 million after-tax or $.05 per share's for estimated litigation costs.

company's financial statements are not in accordance with GAAP, or that the auditor's ability to examine the underlying records used to develop the financial statements was limited. Qualified opinions mean that, overall, the statements are fair representations of the business's financial position and reported income, but that certain parts of the statements, as indicated by the auditor as a portion of his or her report, are not disclosed as specified by GAAP.

CPAs rarely issue the other two kinds of audit reports. An **adverse opinion** indicates that the external auditor believes that the financial statements are not fair representations of the company's financial position or income. The financial statements are management's representations, and an adverse opinion means that the CPA finds that management's financial statements do not comply with GAAP and, therefore, are not fair representations of the company's financial position or performance. A **disclaimer of opinion** means that the auditor was not able to gather sufficient evidence to support an opinion or that the auditor was not sufficiently independent of the company to issue an opinion.

The auditor's report is an important part of the annual report because it provides assurance that the financial statements meet the reporting standards represented by GAAP. When CPAs state that financial statements considered as a whole are materially correct, they believe that if any remaining errors were considered together, such

EXHIBIT 23.12

Quaker Oats Company's Contingent Liabilities Disclosure

Note 18

Litigation

On December 18, 1990, Judge Prentice H. Marshall of the United States District Court for the Northern District of Illinois entered judgment against the Company in favor of Sands, Taylor & Wood Co., holding that the use of the words "thirst aid" in advertising *Gatorade* thirst quencher infringed the Plaintiff's rights in the trademark THIRST-AID. On July 9, 1991, Judge Marshall entered a judgment of $42.6 million, composed of $31.4 million in principal, prejudgment interest of $10.6 million, and fees, expenses and costs of $0.6 million. The order enjoined use of the phrase "THIRST-AID" in connection with the advertising or sale of *Gatorade* thirst quencher in the United States. The Company appealed the judgment. On September 2, 1992, the Court of Appeals for the Seventh Circuit affirmed the finding of infringement, but found that the monetary award was an inequitable "windfall" to the Plaintiff, and it therefore remanded the case to the District Court. On June 7, 1993, Judge Marshall issued a judgment on remand of $26.5 million, composed of $20.7 million in principal, prejudgment interest of $5.4 million, and fees, expenses and costs of $0.4 million. The Company appealed this judgment.

On September 13, 1994, the Court of Appeals affirmed the lower court's award of a reasonable royalty and prejudgment interest, but again remanded the case to allow the District Court to explain the enhancement of the royalty award. On April 11, 1995, Judge Marshall affirmed his prior ruling and the Company filed another appeal. Management, with advice from outside legal counsel, has determined that the Court of Appeals' opinion appears to indicate a range of exposure between $18 million and $30 million. The Company recorded a provision of $29.0 million for this litigation in fiscal 1995.

The Company is not a party to any other pending legal proceedings or environmental clean-up actions that it believes will have a material adverse effect on its financial position or results of operations.

errors would not change the outcome of decisions (such as whether to buy or sell the company's stock or whether to lend the company money) made by an "informed" reader of the statements.

Exhibit 23.13 shows that the auditors found Quaker's 1995 financial statements to "present fairly." Note that they remind readers of the report that the statements are the representations of management. Also note that the auditor's report states that the examination was done on a test basis, which means that there was no audit, or verification of every transaction. Auditors attempt to gain sufficient evidence to support their opinion that the statements are materially correct. They do not attempt to correct every error because they rely upon the principle of materiality.

We have discussed many of the rules that guide how balance sheet information is reported to external parties and what additional disclosures are necessary to complete the picture of the firm's financial position. There is no need to limit internal users to the same data reported on statements issued to external parties. In the next section we describe some of the data included on balance sheets for internal users.

EXHIBIT | **23.13**

Quaker Oats
Company's 1995
Auditor's Report

Report of Independent Public Accountants

To the Shareholders of The Quaker Oats Company:

We have audited the accompanying consolidated balance sheets of The Quaker Oats Company (a New Jersey corporation) and subsidiaries as of June 30, 1995, 1994 and 1993, and the related consolidated statements of income, common shareholders' equity and cash flows for the years then ended. These financial statements are the responsibility of the Company's management. Our responsibility is to express an opinion on these financial statements based on our audits.

We conducted our audits in accordance with generally accepted auditing standards. Those standards require that we plan and perform the audit to obtain reasonable assurance about whether the financial statements are free of material misstatement. An audit includes examining, on a test basis, evidence supporting the amounts and disclosures in the financial statements. An audit also includes assessing the accounting principles used and significant estimates made by management, as well as evaluating the overall financial statement presentation. We believe that our audits provide a reasonable basis for our opinion.

In our opinion, the financial statements referred to above present fairly, in all material respects, the financial position of The Quaker Oats Company and subsidiaries as of June 30, 1995, 1994 and 1993, and the results of their operations and their cash flows for the years then ended in conformity with generally accepted accounting principles.

As indicated in Note 12, effective July 1, 1992, the Company changed their accounting for postretirement benefits other than pensions and effective July 1, 1994, the Company changed their accounting for postemployment benefits. As indicated in Note 16, effective July 1, 1992, the Company changed their accounting for income taxes.

Arthur Andersen LLP

Chicago, Illinois,
August 1, 1995

> The statement may contain errors, but in the auditors' opinion, none are material in size.

> Audits are conducted by examining only some of the underlying transactions using a sampling approach.

> Auditors do not claim that the financial statements on which they issue an unqualified opinion are correct only that they make a fair presentation.

BALANCE SHEETS USED FOR INTERNAL REPORTING

Balance sheets issued to external parties are limited in their usefulness for internal decision makers because of their use of historical cost asset valuation. The assets of most companies are at least a few years old, and many include buildings that are 30 and 40 years old. The use of historical cost valuation understates firms' investments because the assets are shown at these old prices. This means that the firms appear to have much lower investments in assets than they actually have.

Reporting assets at their historical cost is required by GAAP, but internal users do not face this same restriction when formulating their reports. An alternative to using historical cost valuation is using current replacement cost. Current cost valuation of assets means that long-lived assets' values are adjusted to their replacement cost at the balance sheet date. Companies can obtain current cost data by obtaining catalogues that report average recent prices for certain types of equipment or by having their assets appraised by independent appraisers.

To explain the decision-making usefulness of current cost valuation, consider the steel industry during the middle of this century. Steel manufacturers had large investments in buildings and equipment like blast furnaces. When the return earned by these companies was measured using historical cost, they appeared to be earning sufficient return. However, the return that they were earning was not sufficient to replace the equipment as technology changed and their equipment became obsolete. If the equipment had been valued at its replacement cost, which was higher than its historical cost, then the denominator of the return calculation (Return on assets = Net income/Average total assets) would have been larger, and the calculated return would have been lower. The lower return on assets based on replacement costs would have indicated that higher prices were necessary to earn the return they thought they were getting, and that replacement of the equipment with more efficient equipment would have been a good decision.

Current cost valuation presents two problems that led GAAP to adopt historical cost valuation. First, obtaining current cost data can be costly, and the benefits of collecting that data need to exceed its cost. The other problem with current cost data is that the data are subjective. Different appraisers rarely appraise an asset at exactly the same value, and if a published value is used to value the asset, the condition of the asset is probably not the same as the assumed condition of the asset with the published price.

The subjectivity inherent in replacement cost valuation allows a range of potential values, any of which can be justified as the asset's replacement value. When managers report to outside parties, they may bias the information to influence someone to invest or lend by choosing from the set of possible valuations the one that makes the company appear better. In contrast, the subjectivity of the replacement cost is less of a problem for internal users because they want to use it to make better decisions and have no motivation to bias the information through their choice of replacement values.

As you can see, there is much more important information to consider when reviewing a company's financial statements than the statements themselves. Readers must be careful to assess not only the financial statements but also the other related informative disclosures as well.

SUMMARY

A company's assets, along with the claims to those assets by owners and creditors, represent its financial position, which the balance sheet presents. Classifying assets, liabilities, and equity accounts allows readers to assess the nature of the significant items in each category. Understanding the meaning of balance sheet classifications facilitates the communication process between managers and external stakeholders.

- Proper classification of assets and liabilities as current and noncurrent facilitates assessment of a firm's solvency and liquidity. Management intends to convert assets classified as current to cash within a year. Companies expect to liquidate liabilities classified as current with current assets or to refinance them with current liabilities within a year.

- Proper classification of assets allows statement readers to assess the nature of a firm's assets. This allows financial statement readers to determine the firm's prospects for profitability and future cash flows.

- Proper classification of liabilities allows the financial statement reader to assess some of the uses of future profits and cash flows. Specifically, the level of current assets relative to current liabilities shows the firm's short-term solvency. Long-term obligations require the use of current assets or additional long-term assets sometime in the future.

- Corporate annual reports include financial statements as well as other disclosures, such as the management letter and the auditor's report, that help external stakeholders interpret those statements.

adverse opinion The report issued by the external auditor that indicates that the financial statements are not fair representations of the company's financial position or income

compensating balance A minimum cash balance that the depositor (company) must maintain either to continue to earn interest on the amount deposited in the bank account or to avoid certain fees, such as service charges

contingent liabilities Events that could create negative financial results for a company; required to be recorded when the event is probable *and* estimable in terms of its monetary effects

deferred charges (deferrals) Long-term prepayments frequently found in the "other assets" classification that companies amortize over various lengths of time, depending on how long the company will benefit from the expenditures

disclaimer of opinion The report issued by an external auditor that indicates that the auditor was not able to gather sufficient evidence to support an opinion or that the auditor was not sufficiently independent of the company to issue an opinion

letter to stockholders Management's written report that presents an overview of the items in the annual report other than financial statements and highlights important aspects of financial performance

off-balance-sheet financing Borrowing money in ways that would avoid having to record the obligation on the balance sheet

qualified opinion The report issued by independent auditors stating that parts of the financial statements are not in accordance with GAAP or that the auditor's ability to examine the underlying records used to develop the financial statements was limited

segment data Part of the annual report that discloses financial information for product lines or identifiable geographic regions that account for 10 percent or more of total company sales or assets

summary of significant accounting policies Part of the accompanying notes to the financial statements that describe the accounting principles and methods the company has chosen to use

unqualified opinion The report issued by independent auditors stating that the financial statements are fair representations of the business's financial position and reported income and that the company has applied GAAP appropriately

1. What is meant by the term *financial position*, and what is the purpose of the statement of financial position?

2. How is financial position related to profit potential?

3. What is a current asset? Give three examples for a manufacturing firm.

4. What is a current liability? Give three examples for a service firm.

5. Explain the effects on the current ratio if long-term liabilities are mistakenly classified as current liabilities.

6. Explain why a long-term note is classified as current if the fiscal year ends during the last year of the note's life.

7. In what order are current assets listed on the balance sheet? Why is this order important?

8. What does the term *valued* mean as it relates to the accounts shown on the balance sheet?

9. Why is a prepaid insurance policy with a three-year life often listed as a current asset?

10. Explain how each of the following current assets is valued on the balance sheet: (1) accounts receivable, (2) inventory, and (3) prepaid insurance.

11. How can a reader of the financial statements determine how the company's current assets are valued?

12. How are investments valued on the balance sheet? Why?

13. How are property, plant, and equipment accounts valued on the balance sheet? Why?

14. How are intangible assets valued on the balance sheet? Why?

15. What is an other asset? Give two examples.

16. In what order are current liabilities listed on the balance sheet? Why is this order important?

17. How are current liabilities valued on the balance sheet? Why?

18. How are long-term liabilities such as bonds payable valued on the balance sheet? Why?

19. What are other long-term liabilities? Give two examples.

20. What is the order of the items included in the stockholders' equity section on the balance sheet? Why is this order important?

21. What is donated capital? How is it different from contributed capital?

22. What is the difference among an unqualified opinion, a qualified opinion, an adverse opinion, and a disclaimer of opinion?

EXERCISES

E 23.1　For each of the following accounts, determine its classification on the balance sheet using the following classifications. Put the letters in the space provided.

CA　　Current assets
INV　　Investments
PPE　　Property, plant, and equipment
INT　　Intangibles
OA　　Other assets
CL　　Current liabilities
LTL　　Long-term liabilities
OL　　Other liabilities
CC　　Contributed capital
RE　　Retained earnings
OOE　　Other owners' equity

_____　1. Common Stock
_____　2. Wages Payable
_____　3. Building
_____　4. Land Held for Speculation
_____　5. Cash
_____　6. Bonds Payable
_____　7. Accumulated Depreciation
_____　8. Accounts Payable
_____　9. Treasury Stock
_____　10. Marketable Securities

E 23.2　For each of the following accounts, determine its classification on the balance sheet using the following classifications. Put the letters in the space provided.

CA　　Current assets
INV　　Investments
PPE　　Property, plant, and equipment
INT　　Intangibles
OA　　Other assets
CL　　Current liabilities
LTL　　Long-term liabilities
OL　　Other liabilities
CC　　Contributed capital
RE　　Retained earnings
OOE　　Other owners' equity

_____　1. Deferred Income Tax Payable
_____　2. Mining Property
_____　3. Bonds Payable Due Next Year
_____　4. Goodwill
_____　5. Donated Land
_____　6. Common Stock Subscribed
_____　7. Allowance for Uncollectible Accounts
_____　8. Mortgage Payable
_____　9. Accumulated Depletion
_____　10. Discount on Bonds Payable

Use the following information for Exercises 23.3 through 23.9. Rameriz Manufacturing Company has just completed its first year of operations. It has the following accounts in the general ledger. The bookkeeper is unsure which accounts to show on the balance sheet and which accounts to report on the income statement.

Accounts Receivable
Accounts Payable
Accumulated Depreciation, Building
Accumulated Depreciation, Machinery
Additional Paid-In Capital
Allowance for Uncollectible Accounts
Bonds Payable
Building
Cash
Common Stock
Copyright
Cost of Goods Sold
Deferred Income Tax Payable
Discount on Bonds Payable
Dividends Payable
Finished Goods
Income Tax Expense
Income Taxes Payable
Insurance Expense
Interest Expense
Land
Land Held for Speculation
Machinery
Marketable Securities (trading)
Notes Payable, Due in 90 Days
Petty Cash
Preferred Stock
Prepaid Insurance
Prepaid Rent
Purchases Discounts
Raw Materials Inventory
Rent Expense
Retained Earnings
Sales
Sales Returns and Allowances
Sales Discounts
Selling and Administrative Expenses
Supplies
Wages Payable
Work-in-Process Inventory

E 23.3   Prepare a list of all the accounts that will *not* appear on the balance sheet.

E 23.4   Determine the accounts that will appear in the current asset section of the balance sheet and the order in which they should be listed.

E 23.5   Determine the accounts that will appear in the long-term assets section of the balance sheet and the order in which they should be listed.

E 23.6   Determine the accounts that will appear in the current liability section of the balance sheet and the order in which they should be listed.

E 23.7   Determine the accounts that will appear in the long-term liability section of the balance sheet and the order in which they should be listed.

E 23.8   Determine the accounts that will appear in the shareholders' equity section of the balance sheet and the order in which they should be listed.

E 23.9   Determine the account(s) that will appear in the statement of shareholders' equity.

E 23.10   Smyth Company has provided you with the following information concerning its stockholders' equity.

Common stock, $1 par value, 1,000,000 shares authorized, 800,000 shares issued, 750,000 shares outstanding. The average additional paid-in capital was $25 per share when the shares were issued.

Preferred stock, $100 par value, 500,000 shares authorized, 400,000 shares issued and outstanding. There is no additional paid-in capital on preferred shares. The preferred stock pays a 6 percent dividend and is cumulative.

The beginning balance of retained earnings was $1,545,000. Dividends were declared during the year. The common stock dividend was $1.50 per share. The net income for the period was $8,590,500. Treasury stock was purchased during the year for $20 per share.

Prepare the stockholders' equity section of the balance sheet for Smyth Company.

E 23.11   Turn to the annual report of Disney Company. Describe management's responsibilities as they relate to communication of financial results.

E 23.12   Turn to the annual report of Disney Company. What type of audit report was issued? Why?

E 23.13   Compare and contrast the four types of audit opinions.

E 23.14   Using Lexis/Nexis or a similar database, find a company that received a qualified opinion. What was the cause of the qualification? How was the audit report written to reflect the qualification?

E 23.15   Describe the role of the auditor in communicating financial information to external users.

PROBLEMS

P 23.1 The following list of accounts was provided by Donnelly Transportation Corporation, which has a September 30 fiscal year-end. Using these accounts, prepare a balance sheet for Donnelly Transportation Corporation for fiscal 1996.

Accounts payable	$ 221,200
Accounts receivable	261,300
Accumulated depreciation, barges	124,900
Accumulated depreciation, buildings	123,600
Accumulated depreciation, tugboats	1,660,100
Allowance for uncollectible accounts	9,500
Barges	291,000
Buildings	265,000
Common stock	500,000
Cash	89,300
Installment note payable, long term	675,400
Interest payable	36,300
Investment in BR, Inc., common stock	72,000
Land	115,700
Mortgage payable	86,300
Trade notes payable	175,000
Payroll taxes payable	14,900
Prepaid insurance	36,500
Retained earnings	?
Salaries and wages payable	26,800
Supplies	17,800
Temporary investments (trading securities)	121,500
Tugboats	2,785,400

P 23.2 Presented below is a list of accounts taken from the general ledger of Barstow Electric Company. Prepare a balance sheet for the fiscal year ending December 31, 1996. Ignore income taxes.

Cash	$ 254,000
Sales	16,000,000
Marketable securities (trading)	306,000
Cost of goods sold	9,600,000
Investment in Ford Motor Company bonds	538,000
Investment in General Motors Company common stock	654,000
Notes payable, due in 120 days	180,000
Accounts payable	950,000
Selling and administrative expenses	5,800,000
Interest revenue	64,560
Land	620,000
Buildings	2,080,000
Dividends payable	300,000
Dividend revenue	61,440
Accrued liabilities	192,000
Accounts receivable	870,000
Accumulated depreciation, buildings	304,000
Allowance for uncollectible accounts	50,000
Interest expense	422,000
Inventory	1,194,000
Gain on sale of equipment	160,000
Prior period adjustment of underreported expenses (net of tax of $84,000)	196,000
Long-term notes payable	1,800,000
Discount on notes payable	20,000
Equipment	1,200,000
Bonds payable	2,200,000
Premium on bonds payable	45,000
Accumulated depreciation, equipment	80,000
Copyrights and patents	675,000
Treasury stock	382,000
Retained earnings (January 1,1996)	404,000
Preferred stock	800,000
Common stock	1,180,000
Additional paid-in capital	160,000
Prepaid assets	120,000

P 23.3 Refer to the annual report of Archer Daniels Midland and answer the following questions.

    a. What is the total amount of the current assets, and what type of assets are classified as current?

    b. What is the total amount of the long-term assets, and what type of assets are classified as long term?

    c. What is the total amount of the current liabilities, and what type of liabilities are classified as current?

    d. What is the total amount of the long-term liabilities, and what type of liabilities are classified as long term?

    e. How did this company value its inventories?

    f. What depreciation method did this company use?

    g. Did this company report any items as "other assets" or "other liabilities"? If so, what are they?

    h. Is this company's financial position better or worse than last period? Why or why not?

    i. Is this company a good investment? Why or why not?

P 23.4 Refer to the annual report of Disney Company and answer the following questions.

    a. What is the total amount of the current assets, and what type of assets are classified as current?

    b. What is the total amount of the long-term assets, and what type of assets are classified as long term?

    c. What is the total amount of the current liabilities, and what type of liabilities are classified as current?

    d. What is the total amount of the long-term liabilities, and what type of liabilities are classified as long term?

    e. How did this company value its inventories?

    f. What depreciation method did this company use?

    g. Did this company report any items as "other assets" or "other liabilities"? If so, what are they?

    h. Is this company's financial position better or worse than last period? Why or why not?

    i. Is this company a good investment? Why or why not?

P 23.5 Refer to the annual report of the Celtics and answer the following questions.

    a. What is the total amount of the current assets, and what type of assets are classified as current?

    b. What is the total amount of the long-term assets, and what type of assets are classified as long term?

    c. What is the total amount of the current liabilities, and what type of liabilities are classified as current?

    d. What is the total amount of the long-term liabilities, and what type of liabilities are classified as long term?

    e. How did this company value its inventories?

    f. What depreciation method did this company use?

    g. Did this company report any items as "other assets" or "other liabilities"? If so, what are they?

    h. Is this company's financial position better or worse than last period? Why or why not?

    i. Is this company a good investment? Why or why not?

P 23.6 Refer to the annual report of Anheuser-Busch and answer the following questions.

    a. What is the total amount of the current assets, and what type of assets are classified as current?

    b. What is the total amount of the long-term assets, and what type of assets are classified as long term?

    c. What is the total amount of the current liabilities, and what type of liabilities are classified as current?

    d. What is the total amount of the long-term liabilities, and what type of liabilities are classified as long term?

    e. How did this company value its inventories?

    f. What depreciation method did this company use?

    g. Did this company report any items as "other assets" or "other liabilities"? If so, what are they?

    h. Is this company's financial position better or worse than last period? Why or why not?

    i. Is this company a good investment? Why or why not?

P 23.7   Refer to the annual report of Harley-Davidson and answer the following questions.

a. What is the total amount of the current assets, and what type of assets are classified as current?

b. What is the total amount of the long-term assets, and what type of assets are classified as long term?

c. What is the total amount of the current liabilities, and what type of liabilities are classified as current?

d. What is the total amount of the long-term liabilities, and what type of liabilities are classified as long term?

e. How did this company value its inventories?

f. What depreciation method did this company use?

g. Did this company report any items as "other assets" or "other liabilities"? If so, what are they?

h. Is this company's financial position better or worse than last period? Why or why not?

i. Is this company a good investment? Why or why not?

P 23.8   Assume you have recently been hired to provide investment advice to the manager of Claussen Company. The company has excess cash that it needs to invest. The manager, Jenny Lyn, is concerned that she does not understand how to read financial statements. Write a memo to Jenny Lyn describing how to read and interpret a balance sheet.

P 23.9   Refer to P 23.8. Write a memo to Jenny Lyn describing how to read and interpret an auditor's report.

P 23.10   Using *Disclosure* or a similar database find a company that was issued a qualified audit opinion and determine why the qualification was necessary.

COMPUTER APPLICATIONS

CA 23.1   The following list of accounts was taken from the 1996 annual report of Braun's Fashions Corporation.

Accounts payable	$ 4,669,902
Accounts receivable	664,065
Accrued liabilities	1,639,292
Accrued rent obligation—long term	861,421
Accrued store closing costs	1,134,714
Accumulated depreciation and amortization	8,783,914
Additional paid-in capital	25,032,637
Cash	261,394
Common stock	37,688
Construction in progress	904,560
Deferred tax asset	478,200
Furniture and fixtures	4,727,134
Leasehold improvements	10,633,116
Leasehold interests, net	953,645
Long-term debt	2,200,000
Merchandise inventory	13,134,317
Other assets	65,005
Other equipment	1,432,871
Prepaid expenses	493,148
Retained deficit	10,612,113

Required: Use a computer spreadsheet program.

a. Arrange the accounts in proper balance sheet order and show the equality of assets with liabilities and stockholders' equity. Hint: If you are unfamiliar with some of the accounts, use the balance sheet equation as an aid.

b. Determine the total dollar amount of current assets.

c. Determine the total dollar amount of long-term assets.

d. Determine the total dollar amount of current liabilities.

e. Determine the total dollar amount of long-term liabilities.

f. Determine the total dollar amount of stockholders' equity.

g. Repeat requirements *a* through *f* above assuming that all accounts increase by 15 percent.

CA 23.2 The following list of accounts was adopted from the 1994 annual report of Dillard Department Stores, Inc. Amounts are shown in thousands.

Accumulated depreciation	$ 911,996
Additional paid-in capital	622,634
Buildings and leasehold improvements	1,162,120
Buildings under capital leases	29,416
Buildings under construction	13,977
Capital lease obligations	31,621
Cash and cash equivalents	51,244
Commercial paper—current	145,276
Common stock, class A	1,090
Common stock, class B	40
Current portion of capital lease obligation	2,242
Current portion of long-term debt	65,061
Deferred income taxes	282,648
Federal and state income taxes	54,011
Furniture, fixtures, and equipment	1,583,380
Investments and other assets	52,110
Land and land improvements	44,573
Long-term debt	1,238,293
Merchandise inventories	1,299,944
Other current assets	8,976
Preferred stock	440
Retained earnings	1,457,443
Trade accounts receivable, net	1,096,530
Trade and other accounts payable	529,475

Required: Use a computer spreadsheet program.

a. Prepare a classified balance sheet and prove that total assets equal total liabilities plus total stockholders' equity. Hint: If you are unfamiliar with some of the accounts, use the balance sheet equation as an aid.

b. Determine the balance in Retained Earnings if total assets decrease by 5 percent, total liabilities remain the same, and stockholders' equity other than Retained Earnings remains the same.

CASES

C 23.1 Refer to the annual report of the company you selected in Chapter 1, (C 1.1) and answer the following questions.

a. What is the total of the current assets, and what type of assets are classified as current?

b. What is the total of the long-term assets, and what type of assets are classified as long term?

c. What is the total of the current liabilities, and what type of liabilities are classified as current?

d. What is the total of the long-term liabilities, and what type of liabilities are classified as long term?

e. How did this company value its inventories?

f. What depreciation method did this company use?

g. Did this company report any items as "other assets" or "other liabilities"? If so, what are they?

h. Is this company's financial position better or worse than last period? Why?

i. Is this company a good investment? Why?

C 23.2 The balance sheet of Zimmerman shown below for fiscal 1994 contains several errors. Identify each of the errors and determine how to correct them.

THE ZIMMERMAN COMPANY
Statement of Finances
For the Period Ending December 31, 1994

Debits

Current assets:	
Cash	$ 12,000
Accounts receivable, net	29,000
Prepaid rent	6,000
Total current assets	$ 47,000
Long-term assets:	
Land	50,000
Patents, net	45,000
Inventory	75,000
Buildings	280,000
Investment in Durk bonds	59,000
Discount on bonds payable	20,000
Silver mine	261,000
Total long-term assets	$790,000
Total assets	$837,000

Credits

Current liabilities:	
Accounts payable	$ 35,000
Note payable, due June 1, 2001	50,000
Income tax payable	28,000
Total current liabilities	$113,000
Long-term liabilities:	
Accumulated depreciation, buildings	32,000
Mortgage payable	65,000
Accumulated depletion	26,000
Bonds payable	250,000
Total long-term liabilities	$373,000
Owners' equity:	
Common stock	200,000
Additional paid-in capital	125,000
Retained earnings	51,000
Treasury stock	25,000
Total owners' equity	$401,000
Total liabilities and owners' equity	$887,000

CRITICAL THINKING

CT 23.1 Throughout this textbook you have seen examples regarding the relationships among the income statement, statement of retained earnings, and balance sheet. Write a paper describing, in detail, how these three statements are related.

CT 23.2 Historical cost is a basic concept of accounting. Describe the concept of historical cost, and evaluate each of the items found on a typical balance sheet to determine if it is reported at historical cost.

ETHICAL CHALLENGES

EC 23.1   Assume you are an auditor and have significant doubts about whether your client is a going concern. According to the auditing standards, you must issue an adverse opinion. If you issue this adverse opinion and the company pulls through, the management will probably sue. However, if you do not issue an adverse opinion and the company fails, the creditors and stockholders will probably sue. What will you do in this situation?

EC 23.2   Assume you are an auditor and are concerned about how a client is reporting its marketable securities. You know that under certain circumstances marketable securities must be marked to market. In addition, you realize that if the marketable securities are classified as trading securities, any unrealized gains are shown on the income statement while unrealized gains on available-for-sale securities are disclosed in the owners' equity section of the balance sheet. Your client has recently reclassified a large amount of marketable securities from available-for-sale to trading securities. This reclassification increased its current ratio from 1.9 to 2.3. The company has a large loan outstanding that requires a current ratio of 2.0. How will you determine if the securities are correctly classified? How will the various stakeholders be affected by your decision?

CHAPTER 24

Firm Performance: Cash Flows

Learning Objectives

1. Describe the information companies provide users through the statement of cash flows.
2. Discuss how companies determine and analyze cash flows from operating activities.
3. Explain how companies determine and analyze cash flows from financing and investing activities.
4. Discuss how companies analyze budgeted versus actual cash flows.

Southwestern Public Service Company and Entergy Corporation are public utilities operating in the Southwest and south central United States. Southwestern Public Service Company's strategy is to achieve growth through acquisition of new service areas, sales into other markets, economic development of areas in which it operates, and growth in related businesses. Cash construction expenditures were $94.7 million in 1995. During 1995 the company internally generated almost all of its cash requirements.[1]

Entergy Corporation's strategy is building shareholder value by improving its core business and expanding business by investing in related businesses. It strives to decrease costs, increase revenues, and reinvest its cash.

Both businesses provide annual financial statements to shareholders that include a statement of cash flows; however, Entergy prepares its statement of cash flows differently than Southwestern Public Service does.[2] Is the difference in reporting format significant to users of financial statements? While individual users may prefer one format to another, effective cash flow analysis is possible in either case.

---

[1]Southwestern Public Service Company, Annual Report, 1995, p. 50.

[2]The financial statements and related footnotes from the annual report of Southwestern Public Service Company and Entergy Corporation are included in the annual report booklet that accompanies this text. We refer to these reports throughout the chapter.

In previous chapters, we examined the income statement, the statement of retained earnings, and the balance sheet. In this chapter, we examine the fourth financial statement required by the FASB—the statement of cash flows.

The statement of cash flows provides the link between the accrual-based income statement and the balance sheet. Users need to comprehend the components of the elements included on the cash flow statement so that they can make informed decisions regarding the liquidity and solvency of the reporting company.

GAAP AND THE STATEMENT OF CASH FLOWS

The statement of cash flows is designed to supplement the accrual-based earnings information provided in the income statement, statement of retained earnings, and balance sheet.

Comparatively speaking, the statement of cash flows is a new statement. Prior to its adoption in 1987, companies prepared a statement of changes in financial position. That statement was designed to show the sources and uses of working capital[3] provided to, or used by, a company during the period of time covered by the income statement. Due to the variety of methods used to prepare the statement of changes in financial position and the resulting confusion that existed among statement users, the Financial Accounting Standards Board (FASB) determined that a statement that showed cash flows is more useful.[4]

The following classic example shows how cash flow information is more useful than working capital information. In 1975, when W. T. Grant Company declared bankruptcy, it was the nation's 17th largest retailer competing with companies such as Kmart and J. C. Penney. It achieved this growth by expanding its product line into durable goods, marketing its products to lower-income consumers, and offering easy financing through a credit card system. Most customers were allowed 36 months to pay the balances they owed Grant with a $1 minimum payment per month. Thus, W. T. Grant showed large amounts of both inventory and accounts receivable on its financial statements.

In the 10 years prior to Grant's bankruptcy declaration, the company showed positive net income and working capital (current assets minus current liabilities). As Exhibit 24.1 shows, beginning in 1973, its net income and working capital position began to deteriorate. However, the cash flows of the company began to decline much earlier (in 1969), falling off sharply in 1972. This was due to the large amount of uncollectible receivables on the books of W. T. Grant. Eventually, credit was denied Grant; the company was unable to pay its debts, and it ceased to be a going concern.

If W. T. Grant had presented and relied upon the information included in a statement of cash flows instead of a statement of changes in financial position, its management, stockholders, and creditors would have been warned of its impending doom much sooner and, perhaps, Grant could have been saved.[5]

What is the Purpose of the Statement of Cash Flows?

The statement of cash flows has four primary purposes. According to the FASB, the statement of cash flows is useful to:

1. **Assess the entity's ability to generate positive future net cash flows.**
   Operating activities must provide sufficient net cash flows to support the firm's future operations. The relationship between sales and the operating cash flows from year to year provides insights into the firm's ability to sustain positive net cash flows.

---

[3]*Working capital* was defined a variety of ways. Some firms used cash, some cash plus liquid assets, and others used current assets minus current liabilities.

[4]*Statement of Financial Accounting Standards (SFAS) No. 95*, 1987, requires companies to use statement of cash flows for reporting purposes.

[5]For more information on this case, see James A. Largay III and Clyde P. Stickney, Jr., *W. T. Grant: A Study in Bankruptcy*, 1979.

EXHIBIT | **24.1**

**Cash versus Working
Capital Flows**

**W. T. Grant Company Net Income, Cash Flow from Operations, and Working
Capital from Operations for the Years Ending January 31, 1966 to 1975**

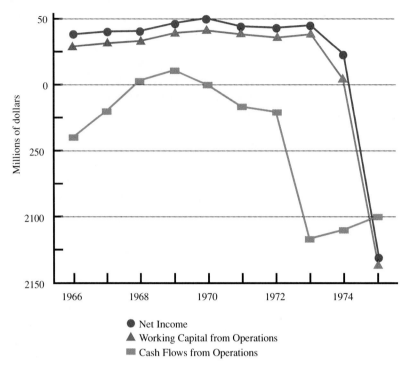

Adapted from: "Reporting Funds, Flows, Liquidity, and Financial Flexibility," *FASB Discussion Memorandum,*
(Stamford, CT: FASB), 1980, p. 36.

2. **Assess the entity's ability to meet its obligations and pay dividends, and its
need for external financing.** The statement of cash flows provides a clear picture
of the sources and uses of a company's cash flows. It indicates whether the firm
has the ability to generate the cash needed to meet its obligations to its creditors
and owners.

3. **Assess the reasons for differences between income and associated cash
receipts and payments.** The statement of cash flows provides information that
highlights the specific reasons for the difference between accounting income and
cash flow from operations.

4. **Assess both the cash and noncash aspects of the entity's investing and
financing transactions during the period.** The statement of cash flows
specifically identifies and discloses significant noncash investing and financing
activities undertaken by the firm to provide complete information about the
events that have future cash flow implications.

*Why Are the Sections
of the Statement of
Cash Flows
Important?*

The statement of cash flows is divided into three distinct sections—operating, investing, and financing. These sections represent the basic and significant functions of any
business enterprise and the amounts of cash flowing in and out of the enterprise as a
result of the business activities in each of these functional areas. In addition, the information contained in these sections achieves the four purposes of the statement of
cash flows presented previously. Exhibit 24.2 shows the basic functions of business
and how they are classified on the statement of cash flows. We look at each of the
cash flow sections in turn.

EXHIBIT	24.2	Cash Inflows and Outflows

Business Activities	Inflows	Outflows
Operating activities	Collections from customers Collections of interest Collections of dividends	Payments to suppliers of goods and services Payments to employees Payments for interest Payments for taxes
Investing activities	Proceeds from sales of long-term assets Collections of loans made to other entities	Purchases of long-term assets Loans made to other entities
Financing activities	Proceeds from issuance of debt Proceeds from issuance of stock Donations of cash to the company	Payment of long-term debt Purchase of treasury stock Payment of cash dividends

Operating Activities   As Exhibit 24.2 illustrates, operating activities involve transactions that result from the earnings process of the company. Cash inflows from operating activities are primarily from customers, but cash also increases due to interest and dividends received by the company. Cash outflows from operating activities result from payments made for operating expenses, including the purchase of inventory.

Notice that cash received from dividends is an operating activity, but cash paid for dividends is a financing activity. Dividends received are earned income from investments, while dividends paid are not expenses of the business; that is, they are not incurred in an attempt to generate revenues. Rather, dividends paid reflect the company's decision about when and how to distribute its earnings.

The presentation of the operating section of the statement of cash flows allows readers to (1) assess the entity's ability to generate positive future cash flows and (2) assess the reasons for differences between a company's accounting income and its associated cash receipts and payments.

Investing Activities   Investing activities usually involve acquiring and disposing of property, plant, and equipment; other long-term investments; and short-term or temporary investments that are not considered cash equivalents. Exhibit 24.2 shows that disposing of these assets results in cash inflows, while purchasing them results in cash outflows.

Analyzing the investing activities section of the statement of cash flows allows users to assess the entity's ability to meet its obligations and pay dividends, as well as its need for external financing. Since the company needs assets to operate, and because long-term assets are normally financed with long-term debt or equity, analyzing the investing activities of the company provides users with insight into both the future investing and the future financing needs of the company.

Financing Activities   Financing activities involve borrowing from and repaying creditors, raising funds from owners, and distributing funds to owners that are either a return on, or a return of, investment. Exhibit 24.2 shows that issuing debt and issuing stock both result in cash inflows, while repayment of debt and equity result in cash outflows.

Analyzing financing activities of the statement of cash flows also allows users to assess the entity's ability to meet its obligations and pay dividends, as well as to determine its need for external financing. For example, if a company issues long-term debt in the current period, it must repay this debt in future periods.

Noncash Financing and Investing Activities   In addition to the types of cash flow events shown in Exhibit 24.2, companies also present noncash investing and financing events either on the statement of cash flows or in the notes to the financial statements. For example, if Southwestern Public Service Company or Entergy Corporation issues 100,000 shares of its common stock in exchange for a building, this would be reported as a noncash investing/financing event.

It is necessary to show financial statement users the noncash means of financing that the company uses to acquire its assets because of their *future* cash flow impact. In the example of the utility companies issuing stock, such activities may have cash flow implications because of the related dividends that the company may pay in the future.

Now that you understand the purpose of the statement of cash flows, we focus attention on the determination and analysis of cash flows. Externally, cash flows are evaluated by analyzing the statement of cash flows in conjunction with the income statement, statement of retained earnings, and balance sheet. Internally, management uses cash flow statement information plus additional information it has available concerning the amounts and timing of cash flows. We examine the external analysis of cash flows next. Then, we address the internal analysis of cash flows.

DETERMINATION AND ANALYSIS OF OPERATING CASH FLOWS

The events represented in the *operating activities section* of the statement of cash flows may be presented in either the direct or indirect format. The **direct format** shows the actual cash inflows and outflows of operating activities. The **indirect format** shows the differences between accrual-based net income and cash flows from operations. Regardless of the format used, the amount of net cash flows from operating activities is the same.

Exhibit 24.3 is an example of the direct format for the statement of cash flows while Exhibit 24.4 is an example of the indirect format. The corresponding income statement, statement of retained earnings, and balance sheet are illustrated in Exhibits 24.5, 24.6, and 24.7, respectively.

Take a moment to examine Exhibits 24.3 to 24.7. Notice that the amount shown as net income on the income statement in Exhibit 24.5 is also shown as an increase to retained earnings on the statement of retained earnings in Exhibit 24.6. The amounts shown as the beginning and ending balances of retained earnings on the statement of retained earnings are also shown on the comparative balance sheets in Exhibit 24.7. How does the statement of cash flows fit with the other three financial statements? It indicates the difference between accrual-based net income and cash flows from operations, and it shows the change in the Cash account on the balance sheet due to operating, investing, and financing activities.

As Exhibit 24.3 illustrates, one advantage of the direct format is that it clearly shows the amounts of cash received by or paid for operating activities. However, one disadvantage is that the FASB requires companies to disclose, either on the statement or in the notes, a reconciliation of accrual-based net income to the amount of cash flows from operations to achieve the fourth purpose of the statement of cash flows. This reconciliation (shown on the bottom of Exhibit 24.3) is essentially the same information shown in the indirect format for the statement of cash flows in Exhibit 24.4.

Although the FASB suggests the use of the direct format for presenting cash flows from operations, *Accounting Trends and Techniques*, 1994, reports that 97.5 percent of companies use the indirect format. We examine the direct and indirect formats of reporting operating cash flows in more detail next.

| EXHIBIT | 24.3 | A&E Corporation Statement of Cash Flows—Direct Format |

A&E CORPORATION
Statement of Cash Flows
For the Year Ended September 30, 1995
(In thousands)

Net cash flows from operating activities:

Cash received from customers	$ 201,000
Cash received from renters	1,500
Cash paid for inventory	(116,250)
Cash paid for insurance	(5,400)
Cash paid for wages	(9,600)
Cash paid for miscellaneous expenses	(8,400)
Cash paid for income taxes	(12,150)
Cash paid for interest	(1,920)
Net cash flows from operating activities	$ 48,780

Net cash flows from investing activities:

Cash received from sale of trading securities	$ 3,900
Cash received from sale of equipment	1,600
Cash paid for building	(51,300)
Cash paid for equipment	(12,100)
Net cash flows from investing activities	$ (57,900)

Net cash flows from financing activities:

Cash received from short-term note payable	$ 300
Cash received from bond issue	28,200
Cash paid for treasury stock	(25,000)
Cash paid for dividends	(10,000)
Net cash flows from financing activities	$ (6,500)

Net change in cash during 1995	$ (15,620)
Add beginning balance of cash	84,500
Ending balance of cash	$ 68,880

Other investing and financing activities not requiring cash:

Purchase of building with preferred stock	$ 24,300

Reconciliation of net income to cash flows from operations:

Net income	$ 27,300
Adjustments to reconcile net income to net cash flows from operations:	
Depreciation expense—buildings	11,700
Depreciation expense—equipment	6,300
Amortization expense—patent	2,100
Gain on sale of investment	(1,800)
Loss on sale of equipment	4,500
Amortization of discount on note	30
Increase in accounts receivable, net	(16,200)
Increase in inventory	(1,200)
Decrease in prepaid insurance	600
Increase in accounts payable	16,350
Increase in rent received in advance	300
Decrease in wages payable	(600)
Decrease in interest payable	(150)
Decrease in taxes payable	(450)
Net cash flow from operating activities	$ 48,780

Determination of Operating Cash Flows: Direct Format

As Exhibit 24.3 illustrates, the direct format indicates the amounts of cash received from customers and the other sources of operating cash, such as dividends and interest. In addition, it shows how much cash the company paid for interest, taxes, and other operating activities. Throughout the text, we have shown calculations of cash flows using the direct format. We briefly review this process of determining operating cash flows next.

EXHIBIT 24.4 A&E Corporation Statement of Cash Flows—Indirect Format

A&E CORPORATION
Statement of Cash Flows
For the Year Ended September 30, 1995
(In thousands)

Net cash flows from operating activities:	
Net income	$ 27,300
Adjustments to reconcile net income to net cash flows from operations:	
Depreciation expense—buildings	11,700
Depreciation expense—equipment	6,300
Amortization expense—patent	2,100
Gain on sale of investment	(1,800)
Loss on sale of equipment	4,500
Amortization of discount on note	30
Increase in accounts receivable, net	(16,200)
Increase in inventory	(1,200)
Decrease in prepaid insurance	600
Increase in accounts payable	16,350
Increase in rent received in advance	300
Decrease in wages payable	(600)
Decrease in interest payable	(150)
Decrease in taxes payable	(450)
Net cash flow from operating activities	$ 48,780
Net cash flows from investing activities:	
Cash received from sale of trading securities	$ 3,900
Cash received from sale of equipment	1,600
Cash paid for building	(51,300)
Cash paid for equipment	(12,100)
Net cash flows from investing activities	$(57,900)
Net cash flows from financing activities:	
Cash received from short-term note payable	$ 300
Cash received from bond issue	28,200
Cash paid for treasury stock	(25,000)
Cash paid for dividends	(10,000)
Net cash flows from financing activities	$ (6,500)
Net change in cash during 1995	$ (15,620)
Add beginning balance of cash	84,500
Ending balance of cash	$ 68,880
Other investing and financing activities not requiring cash:	
Purchase of building with preferred stock	$ 24,300

(Note: During this discussion, some pause and reflect questions request that you determine the cash flow amounts shown on the statement of cash flows. Other pause and reflect questions request that you relate what you have learned to Southwestern Public Service Company's statement of cash flows.)

To determine the cash flows for a particular operating item on the income statement, it is necessary to relate that item to a balance sheet account because the income-generating activities of the company also cause changes in the balance sheet accounts of the company. Companies use the beginning and ending balances of a given balance sheet account, along with the related revenue or expense amount from the income statement, to determine the related cash flow for the period.

For example, if a company's beginning balance of Utilities Payable was $5,000, its ending balance was $6,000, and its Utilities Expense for the period as shown on the

EXHIBIT | 24.5 | A&E Corporation Cash Income Statement

A&E CORPORATION
Income Statement
For the Year Ended September 30, 1995
(In thousands)

Sales		$219,000
Cost of goods sold		131,400
Gross margin		$ 87,600
Operating expenses:		
Wages	$ 9,000	
Insurance	6,000	
Uncollectible accounts	1,800	
Miscellaneous expense	8,400	
Depreciation—buildings	11,700	
Depreciation—equipment	6,300	
Amortization—patent	2,100	45,300
Operating income		$ 42,300
Other revenues and gains:		
Rent revenue	$ 1,200	
Gain on sale of trading securities	1,800	3,000
Other expenses and losses:		
Interest expense	1,800	
Loss on sale of equipment	4,500	6,300
Income from continuing operations before taxes		$ 39,000
Income tax expense		11,700
Net income		$ 27,300

EXHIBIT | 24.6 | A&E Corporation's Statement of Retained Earnings

A&E CORPORATION
Statement of Retained Earnings
For the Year Ended September 30, 1995
(In thousands)

Retained earnings, September 30, 1994	$170,770
Add net income	27,300
	$198,070
Less dividends declared	9,900
Retained earnings, September 30, 1995	$188,170

income statement was $28,000, then the amount of cash paid for utilities during the period was $27,000 as shown below:

Beginning balance, utilities payable	$ 5,000
Add utility expense	28,000
Less cash paid for utilities	?
Ending balance, utilities payable	$ 6,000

Why Don't Revenues Equal Cash Inflows? Remember that a company's revenues shown on its income statement might differ from its cash inflows from operations for two reasons: (1) the revenue is earned before the cash is collected or (2) the cash is collected before the revenue is earned.

EXHIBIT | 24.7 | A&E Corporation Balance Sheet

A&E CORPORATION
Balance Sheets
As of September 30, 1995, and 1994
(In thousands)

	1995	1994
Assets		
Cash	$ 68,880	$ 84,500
Trading securities	1,500	3,600
Accounts receivable, net	44,820	28,620
Inventories	40,200	39,000
Prepaid insurance	900	1,500
Building	300,900	225,300
Accumulated depreciation, building	(91,800)	(80,100)
Equipment	103,800	101,700
Accumulated depreciation, equipment	(33,300)	(30,900)
Patent, net	23,400	25,500
Total assets	$459,300	$398,720
Liabilities and Owners' Equity		
Liabilities		
Accounts payable	$ 48,450	$ 32,100
Notes payable	600	300
Rent received in advance	1,200	900
Interest payable	450	600
Taxes payable	850	1,300
Wages payable	1,500	2,100
Dividends payable	200	300
Notes payable, due 1-1-98	1,500	1,500
Discount on notes payable	(120)	(150)
Bonds payable	27,000	–0–
Premium on bonds payable	1,200	–0–
Total liabilities	$ 82,830	$ 38,950
Owners' equity		
Common stock	$ 46,000	$ 46,000
Additional paid-in capital, common stock	65,100	65,100
Preferred stock	73,000	60,000
Additional paid-in capital, preferred stock	29,200	17,900
Retained earnings	188,170	170,770
Treasury stock (cost)	(25,000)	–0–
Total owners' equity	$376,470	$359,770
Total liabilities and owners' equity	$459,300	$398,720

For example, A&E Corporation allows its customers to charge purchases on account (accounts receivable) and it accepts rent payments in advance from customers (rent received in advance), as noted on its balance sheets in Exhibit 24.7. Thus, we would expect the cash inflows from customers to be different from the amount of revenues earned during the period because revenues would be recognized before the cash is actually received, when customers charge on account, and after cash is received when customers pay in advance.

The accounts receivables on the balance sheets are shown net of related allowance for doubtful accounts, so the ending balance of A&E's Accounts Receivable account is calculated as follows:

> Beginning balance of Accounts Receivable, net
> + Sales on account
> – Uncollectible accounts expense
> – Cash collections from customers
> = Ending balance of Accounts Receivable, net

These wind turbines will provide 35 megawatts of power to the Lower Colorado River Authority and the City of Austin which will result in revenues and cash received from customers.

Using the information in Exhibits 24.5 and 24.7, the cash collections from customers shown in Exhibit 24.3 are determined as follows:

$$
\begin{array}{rl}
 & \$\ 28{,}620{,}000 \\
+ & 219{,}000{,}000 \\
- & 1{,}800{,}000 \\
- & \text{Cash collections from customers} \\
\hline
= & \$\ 44{,}820{,}000
\end{array}
$$

Therefore, cash collections from customers equal $201,000,000. Take a moment to locate these items on the appropriate exhibits.

Companies follow this type of approach to determine the amount of cash received from other operating sources such as dividends, interest, and rent. For example, A&E Corporation's cash received from renters ($1,500,000 as shown in Exhibit 24.3) is determined as:

$$
\begin{array}{l}
 \text{Beginning balance of Rent Received in Advance} \\
+ \text{ Cash received from renters} \\
- \text{ Rent revenue} \\
\hline
= \text{ Ending balance of Rent Received in Advance}
\end{array}
$$

$$
\begin{array}{rl}
 & \$\ 900{,}000 \\
+ & \text{Cash received from renters} \\
- & 1{,}200{,}000 \\
\hline
= & \$1{,}200{,}000
\end{array}
$$

PAUSE & REFLECT	Refer to the financial statements of Southwestern Public Service company. Did it report cash inflow from operating activities? If so, how much cash inflow did it receive and from what sources?

Why Don't Expenses Equal Cash Outflows? Recall that a company's expenses differ from the actual amounts of cash paid for expense items for two reasons: (1) the expenses are incurred before the cash is paid or (2) the expenses are incurred after the cash is paid.

For example, A&E purchases its inventory on account (accounts payable), which it records as an asset (inventory) until it is sold. Therefore, to determine the amount of cash paid for inventory, it is necessary to analyze the changes in *two accounts*—Inventory and Accounts Payable. The Inventory account's ending balance is:

> Beginning balance
> + Net purchases of inventory on account
> − Cost of goods sold
> _____
> = Ending balance

Using the information contained in the income statement and balance sheets in Exhibits 24.5 and 24.7, we know:

> $ 39,000,000
> + Net purchases of inventory on account
> − 131,400,000
> _____
> = $ 40,200,000

Thus, the net purchases of inventory on account equals $132,600,000.

Next, we look at the Accounts Payable account, and determine that:

> Beginning balance
> + Net purchases of inventory on account
> − Cash paid for Inventory purchases
> _____
> = Ending balance

> $ 32,100,000
> + $132,600,000 (from above)
> − Cash paid for inventory purchases
> _____
> = $ 48,450,000

Therefore, cash paid for inventory purchases equals $116,250,000.

Take a moment to locate these amounts on the appropriate exhibits. Notice that although the amount of net purchases is not shown, we were able to determine it based on the changes in the Inventory account.

Companies follow a similar approach to determine the amounts of cash paid for other operating expenses such as wages, interest, and taxes. For example, A&E Corporation's cash paid to employees for wages ($9,600,000 as shown in Exhibit 24.3) is determined as follows:

> Beginning balance of Wages Payable
> + Wages expense
> − Cash paid for wages
> _____
> = Ending balance of Wages Payable

> $2,100,000
> + 9,000,000
> − Cash paid for wages
> _____
> = $1,500,000

PAUSE & REFLECT

Using the information from A&E Corporation's income statement and balance sheets in Exhibits 24.5 and 24.7 show that cash paid for insurance, miscellaneous expense, income taxes, and interest are the amounts reflected on the statement of cash flows.

PAUSE & REFLECT

Refer to the financial statements of Southwestern Public Service Corporation. Did the company report any cash outflow for operating activities? If so, what are the amounts and sources of this cash outflow?

Analysis of Cash Flows from Operating Activities: Direct Format

When companies present operating cash flows using the direct format, external users can analyze operating cash flows to determine if cash inflows are large enough to cover cash outflows. Users can also assess whether the company is collecting revenue and paying current obligations in a timely fashion. Although the exact timing of cash flows is unknown to external users, they can get a general idea of the timing by examining the amounts of cash inflows and outflows compared to the total amounts due.

For example, A&E Corporation collected 81 percent of the amount due from accounts receivable customers as shown (in thousands) below:

$$\frac{\text{Cash collected from customers}}{\text{Beginning accounts receivable + Sales}} = \frac{\$201,000}{\$28,620 + \$219,000} = 81\%$$

A&E also paid 71 percent of the total amount due to inventory suppliers as indicated by the following calculation (in thousands):

$$\frac{\text{Cash paid to suppliers}}{\text{Beginning accounts payable + Purchases}} = \frac{\$116,250}{\$32,100 + \$132,600} = 71\%$$

Determination of Operating Cash Flows: Indirect Format

As Exhibit 24.4 illustrates, the indirect format for the statement of cash flows presents the amount of cash generated from operations by adjusting the net income for items that cause cash from operations to differ from accrual-based net income. To present cash flows in the indirect format, also called the *reconciliation format*, companies begin with the amount of accrual-based net income and apply a series of adjustments to convert net income to cash from operations.

The four adjustments made to net income to determine cash flows from operations using the indirect format are:

- Adjustments for noncash income statement items.

- Adjustments for gains and losses.

- Adjustments for changes in noncash current operating assets.

- Adjustments for changes in current operating liabilities.

(Note: Throughout our discussion of the indirect format, pause and reflect questions will request that you determine some of the adjustments required. Other pause and reflect questions request that you relate what you learn to Entergy Corporation's statement of cash flows.)

Adjustments for Noncash Income Statement Items Noncash income statement items increase or decrease income but do not affect operating cash flows. Therefore, for any noncash expenses that reduce income but do not reduce operating cash flows, it is necessary to add them back to net income in order to convert net income to cash from operations. For any noncash revenues that increase net income but do not increase operating cash flows, it is necessary to deduct them from net income to convert the net income to cash from operations.

We discuss three common noncash adjustments next: (1) depreciation, depletion, and amortization; (2) interest expense adjustments due to premiums or discounts; and (3) interest income adjustments due to premiums or discounts. All of these items affect the amount of accrual-based net income but do not require the use or receipt of cash.

Depreciation, Depletion, and Amortization Items such as depreciation of plant assets, depletion of natural resources, and amortization of intangibles, are added back to net income to derive cash flows because they do not require an outlay of cash. Therefore, these types of items do not reduce operating cash flows.

For example, Exhibit 24.5 indicates that A&E Corporation's depreciation expense for buildings was $11,700,000, which is added back to net income to determine cash flows from operations, as shown in Exhibit 24.4.

Interest Expense Adjustments   The portion of interest expense related to amortization of discounts on notes and bonds payable is also added back to net income to determine cash flows from operations. The expense is different from the actual amount of cash outflow, thus requiring a net income adjustment. This type of adjustment is necessary when a company pays interest on a discounted note because the amount of interest expense is greater than the actual amount of cash paid.

For example, A&E Corporation's income statement in Exhibit 24.5 shows that interest expense for the period is $1,800,000 while its balance sheets in Exhibit 24.7 show that the Discount on Notes Payable account decreased by $30,000. Therefore, the actual cash flow impact of interest for the period was $1,770,000 ($1,800,000 − $30,000). The $1,800,000 was deducted from accrual-based net income, although the actual cash outflow was only $1,770,000 for this note.[6] Therefore, A&E must add back the $30,000 difference to net income to determine operating cash flows, as shown in Exhibit 24.4.

Interest Income Adjustments   For creditors, the amount of interest income due to the amortization of discounts on notes receivables and investments in bonds is subtracted from accrual-based net income because the amount of cash received by the company is less than the interest income it earned during the period. Conversely, the amount of interest income due to the amortization of premiums on notes receivables and investments in bonds is added to net income because the amount of cash received is greater than the interest income earned during the period. (Note that A&E did not require any adjustments for interest income during the period.)

Adjustments for Gains and Losses   The events that generate gains and losses may affect the cash flows of the firm, but these events are either investing or financing events and are reported as such on the statement of cash flows. Therefore, it is important to remove the impact of gains and losses from accrual-based net income when converting income to cash from operations using the indirect format. Since gains increase reported net income, they must be subtracted as a net income adjustment to determine cash flows from operations. On the other hand, losses decrease reported net income and, therefore, must be added as a net income adjustment to determine cash flows from operations.

For example, as shown in Exhibit 24.5, A&E has an $1,800,000 gain from the sale of temporary investments and a loss of $4,500,000 from the sale of equipment. On the statement of cash flows, the gain is subtracted from net income because it increased net income but did not provide operating cash flows, while the loss is added to net income because it decreased income but did not use operating cash flows (see Exhibit 24.4).

---

[6]As shown in Exhibit 24.3, the actual amount of cash paid for interest was $1,920,000 rather than $1,770,000 due to a decrease of $150,000 in A&E's Interest Payable account: Beginning balance, $600,000; plus interest expense, $1,800,000; minus discount amortized, $30,000; minus cash paid for interest, $1,920,000; equals ending balance of interest payable, $450,000.

Adjustments for Changes in Noncash Current Operating Assets   The indirect format uses the *changes* in noncash current operating asset accounts to adjust accrual-based net income. **Noncash current operating assets** are noncash accounts that represent operating activities. Note that not all current asset accounts fall into this category. For example, trading securities, which are not cash equivalents, and nontrade notes receivables reflect investing events and, therefore, the cash flows associated with these events appear in the investing activities section of the statement of cash flows.

An *increase* in a noncash current operating asset during the period indicates one of two things: (1) *the revenue associated with the account was greater than the amount of cash inflow* or (2) *the expense associated with the account was less than the cash outflow.* Since the related revenues and expenses are reflected in net income at the end of the period, *the increase in a noncash current operating asset must be deducted from accrual-based net income to derive the amount of cash flows from operations.*

To illustrate the process of adjusting for an increase in a noncash current operating asset, examine the indirect cash flow statement and balance sheets of A&E Corporation in Exhibits 24.4 and 24.7. Notice that $16,200,000 is subtracted from net income to determine net cash flows from operations and that accounts receivable, net, increased by $16,200,000 ($44,820,000 – $28,620,000). This adjustment is necessary because net income increased by the amount of sales ($219,000,000) and decreased by the amount of uncollectible accounts expense ($1,800,000) while net cash flows increased only by the amount of cash received from customers ($201,000,000) we calculated previously. Therefore, the increase in net income was $16,200,000 *greater than* the increase in net cash flows from operations, so this increase must be subtracted from accrual-based net income to derive net cash flows from operations.

Adjustment for Changes in Current Operating Liabilities   As in the case of current assets, the indirect format adjusts accrual-based net income for *changes* in current operating liabilities to derive cash flows from operating activities. **Current operating liabilities** are accounts representing operating obligations. Nontrade notes payable, bank loans payable, and dividends payable are generally excluded from this category because they represent financing events and appear in the financing section of the cash flow statement.

When a current operating liability increases during the period, it indicates one of two things: (1) *the revenue associated with the account was less than the cash inflow* or (2) *the expense associated with the account was greater than the cash outflow.* Since the related revenues and expenses are reflected in net income at the end of the period, *the amount of the increase in a current operating liability must be added to net income to determine cash flows from operations.*

PAUSE & REFLECT	If a current operating liability decreases during the period, what does this indicate about the relationship between net income and cash flows from operations? How should net income be adjusted in these circumstances?

To illustrate the process of adjusting for an increase in a current operating liability, look at the indirect cash flow statement (Exhibit 24.4) and the balance sheets (Exhibit 24.7) of A&E Corporation. Notice that $300,000 of rent received in advance is added to net income to determine cash flows from operating activities and that the Rent Received in Advance account on the balance sheets increased by $300,000 ($1,200,000 – $900,000).

This adjustment is necessary because rent revenue ($1,200,000) as shown on the income statement (Exhibit 24.5) is less than the cash received from renters ($1,500,000) determined previously. Thus, net income increased by $300,000 *less than* the increase in net cash flows from operations and, therefore, net income must be increased by the $300,000 to derive net cash flows from operations using the indirect format.

PAUSE & REFLECT	Using the information on A&E's balance sheets, show how the change in the Accounts Payable, Interest Payable, and Wages Payable accounts should be shown on the statement of cash flows using the indirect format. With regard to the Wages Payable account, is this adjustment appropriate given the previous determination of cash paid for wages? Explain.

PAUSE & REFLECT	Refer to Entergy Corporation's financial statements. How many current operating liabilities increased during the period? How were these increases reflected in the statement of cash flows? How many current operating liabilities decreased during the period? How were these decreases reflected in the statement of cash flows? Why?

Exhibit 24.8 summarizes the adjustment process when using the indirect format for the operating section of the statement of cash flows.

EXHIBIT	24.8	Net Income Adjustments

Change in Account	Adjustment to Net Income	Reasoning
Increase in current asset	Subtract the amount of the increase	Revenue > Cash inflows, or Expense < Cash outflow
Decrease in current asset	Add the amount of the decrease	Revenue < Cash inflows, or Expense > Cash outflow
Increase in current liability	Add the amount of the increase	Expense > Cash outflow, or Revenue < Cash inflow
Decrease in current liability	Subtract the amount of the decrease	Expense < Cash outflow, or Revenue > Cash inflow

Analysis of Cash Flows from Operating Activities: Indirect Format

When companies present cash flows from operations using the indirect format, external users can evaluate how much cash is generated by operations by calculating the ratio of cash flows from operations to net income. However, it is difficult for users to analyze actual cash inflows and outflows.

For example, A&E Corporation's cash flows from operations to net income ratio is:

$$\frac{\$48,780,000}{\$27,300,000} = 1.79$$

This indicates that A&E's cash flows from operations are 1.79 times larger than its net income. It is possible to use this ratio to compare A&E to other companies in the same industry. (We discuss ratio analysis and industry evaluation in more detail in Chapter 25.)

PAUSE & REFLECT

Given the analytical limitations of the indirect format, why do you think more companies use this format?

DETERMINATION AND ANALYSIS OF CASH FLOWS FROM INVESTING ACTIVITIES

Cash flows from investing activities are associated with the company's long-term assets and its current nonoperating assets, such as nontrade notes receivable and trading securities.

Determination of Cash Flows from Investing Activities

The cash flows from the investing activities section of the statement of cash flows reflects the amount of cash received from sales of long-term and current nonoperating assets and the amount of cash paid to purchase these assets.

For example, A&E Corporation reports on its statement of cash flows that it paid $51,300,000 for a building during 1995, but the balance sheet shows an increase in the Building account of $75,600,000 ($300,900,000 – $225,300,000). How can this be?

Look at the bottom of the statement of cash flows in Exhibit 24.3 or 24.4 and notice that under the heading "Other investing and financing activities not requiring cash" A&E reports the purchase of a building with preferred stock for $24,300,000. Therefore, the total purchase price of the building(s) was $75,600,000 ($51,300,000 cash + $24,300,000 stock) as reflected in the change in the amount of the Building account.

As another example, notice that A&E Corporation reports $3,900,000 received from the sale of trading securities, yet the balance sheet reports the decrease in this account of only $2,100,000 ($3,600,000 – $1,500,000). The $1,800,000 gain on sale of trading securities shown on the income statement indicates that the asset was sold for more than its book value. The total of the gain recognized plus the book value of the trading securities is the actual amount of cash received ($1,800,000 + $1,500,000 = $3,900,000) as a result of this transaction.

PAUSE & REFLECT

The cash flow statement of A&E Corporation (Exhibit 24.3 or 24.4) indicates $1,600,000 was received from the sale of equipment and $12,100,000 was paid for the purchase of equipment. Why are these events separated on the cash flow statement? Are these amounts appropriate given the other information on the balance sheets and income statement concerning equipment? Explain. (Hint: Look at the change in the Accumulated Depreciation—Equipment account to help determine the book value of equipment sold during the period.)

Analysis of Cash Flows from Investing Activities

External users evaluate investing cash flows to determine if a company is making adequate investments in long-term assets and other investments. Users compare the investing cash flows of a particular company, both over time and with other companies in the same or similar industries.

For example, A&E Corporation shows a net cash outflow from investing activities of $57,900,000, indicating that it purchased more assets than it sold. This trend is common, but investors should be aware that long-term assets can be costly to maintain, so the amount and timing of the purchase and sale of investments is crucial.

PAUSE & REFLECT

Turn to Southwestern Public Service Company's and Entergy Corporation's cash flow statements. What types of investing activities do they report?

DETERMINATION AND ANALYSIS OF FINANCING CASH FLOWS

Cash flows from financing activities are associated with long-term liabilities; current nonoperating liabilities, such as nontrade notes payable and dividends payable; and the owners' equity of the company. Financing activities include the issuance and repayment of notes and bonds, the sale and repurchase of stock, and the distribution of the company's earnings. Financing activities *do not include* the change in owners' equity caused by the company's net income. That change is accounted for by cash flows from operations.

Determination of Financing Cash Flows: Nonowner

The amounts shown on the statement of cash flows represent the cash flows that occurred as a result of increases or decreases in the long-term and current nonoperating liabilities (excluding dividends payable, which relates to owner financing) during the period.

For example, A&E Corporation reports $300,000 cash received from a short-term note payable, and the balance sheets show that the Notes Payable account increased $300,000 ($600,000 – $300,000). A&E also reported a receipt of $28,200,000 from a bond issue, but the balance sheets indicate that the Bonds Payable account increased only $27,000,000. Recall, however, that bonds are often issued for more or less than their face value. Further investigation of the balance sheets reveals that the Premium on Bonds Payable account increased $1,200,000 during 1995. Therefore, the total cash receipts related to bonds equals the increases in the Bonds Payable and Premium on Bonds Payable accounts ($27,000,000 + $1,200,000 = $28,200,000).

Determination of Financing Cash Flows: Owner

The amounts on the statement of cash flows show the cash flows that resulted from changes in the owners' equity and Dividends Payable account during the period.

For example, A&E Corporation reports $25,000,000 cash paid for treasury stock (Exhibit 24.3), which corresponds to the $25,000,000 increase reported in the Treasury Stock account on its balance sheets (Exhibit 24.7). Finally, A&E Corporation's statement of cash flows indicates that $10,000,000 was paid to stockholders for dividends during the period. This amount is reflected by the dividends declared during the period ($9,900,000) as shown on the statement of retained earnings in Exhibit 24.6 and the decrease in the Dividends Payable account of $100,000 ($300,000 – $200,000 in Exhibit 24.7).

PAUSE & REFLECT

Turn to the cash flow statements of Southwestern Public Service Company and Entergy Corporation. What types of financing activities are reported on their respective statements of cash flows?

Analysis of Cash Flows from Financing Activities

External users evaluate financing cash flows to determine if the company is obtaining adequate amounts of cash to enable it to invest in long-term assets. Financial statement users compare the financing cash flows of a particular company, both over time and against other companies, in the same or similar industries.

For example, A&E Corporation shows a net cash outflow from financing activities of $6,500,000 (Exhibit 24.3) indicating that it paid off more obligations than it incurred or that its owner-related transactions resulted in cash outflow. Users must determine whether these actions were appropriate given the current economic climate. For example, A&E Corporation issued bonds at a premium, indicating that market interest rates are lower than the face rate on the bonds. Users may question whether the company should have issued the bonds. A&E also repurchased stock during the period. If this was done to make the stock available for stock options, users might infer that this indicates the company's long-term commitment to its employees.

DETERMINATION AND ANALYSIS OF OTHER INVESTING AND FINANCING ACTIVITIES

Cash flows associated with the operating, investing, and financing activities of the firm are the only required disclosures on the face of the statement of cash flows. Other significant noncash investing and financing events that are important to readers of the cash flow statement are reported either on the statement itself or in the notes to the financial statements. Typical noncash events reported are:

- Acquisition of assets by issuing debt or equity securities.
- Exchanges of assets.
- Conversion of debt or preferred stock to common stock.
- Issuance of common or preferred stock to retire debt.

It is important for readers to analyze these events because of their future cash flow implications. If a company acquires assets by issuing debt, for example, it will need cash in the future to make the required periodic payments of interest and principle. Or, if a company retires debt by issuing stock, it is relieved from the periodic payments on the debt, but may face future dividend payments.

Take a moment to locate A&E Corporation's disclosure of its other investing and financing activities on the statement of cash flows.

PAUSE & REFLECT   Examine the annual reports of Southwestern Public Service Company and Entergy Corporation. Did they report any "other financing and investing activities" during the year?

CASH FLOW ANALYSIS: INTERNAL USERS

Internal financial statement users have additional information concerning cash flows that, for reasons of privacy, is not available to external users. For example, internal users have information concerning the timing of cash receipts from customers and cash payments to suppliers, which they would not want competitors to know. In addition, insiders have knowledge about the cash flows generated by different divisions within the company. Finally, managers know the level of cash flows expected at the beginning of the period and can compare it to the actual level of cash flows to determine whether or where problems might exist. We discuss this analysis next.

Comparison of Budgeted and Actual Cash Flows

Companies often analyze the difference between budgeted and actual amounts of cash receipts and disbursements. If there are significant differences, management must investigate to determine their cause(s).

However, for some cash outflows, the master budget must be transformed into a flexible budget to reflect expected costs for the actual level of sales for the period. (Recall the discussion of the flexible budget in Chapter 13.) For example, if more sales were made during the period than the company budgeted, it should expect more purchases to be made that would require more cash outflows for purchases.

Typically, cash inflows from customers and cash outflows for inventory purchases are the largest operating cash flows and, therefore, are subject to more detailed analysis.

Actual versus Budgeted Cash Inflows from Customers

The difference between actual and budgeted cash inflows from customers is due to one or more of three factors: (1) the timing and amounts of customers' payments were different from those expected, (2) the selling prices for products were different from those expected, which changed the total dollar amount of sales, and (3) the volume of sales was different from the volume expected, which changed the total dollar amount of sales. See Of Interest . . . Cash Flow Variances for more details.

Actual versus Budgeted Cash Outflows to Inventory Suppliers

The difference between actual and budgeted cash payments to suppliers is also due to one or more of three factors: (1) the timing and amounts of payments were different from those expected, (2) the purchase price was different from that expected, which changed the total dollar amount of purchases, and (3) the volume of purchases was different from the volume expected for the actual amount of products sold, which changed the total dollar amount of purchases. See Of Interest . . . Cash Flow Variances for more information.

. . . of Interest *Cash Flow Variances*

he difference between actual and budgeted cash inflows and outflows can be analyzed in a series of variances. There are three cash inflow variances as shown in panel A below. The **collection variance** is the difference in the amount of operating cash inflows due to a change in collection patterns.

The **selling price variance** is the difference in operating cash inflows due to a change in selling price. The **selling volume variance** is the difference in operating cash inflows due to a difference between expected and actual sales volume. Determining cash inflow variances is an important part of the analysis and control of accounts receivable and sales.

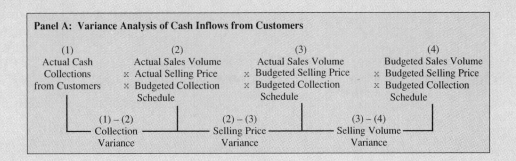

There are also three cash outflow variances as shown in panel B below. The **payment variance** is the difference in the amount of operating cash outflows due to a change in payment patterns. The **purchase price variance** is the difference in operating cash outflows due to a change in purchase price. The **purchase volume variance** is the difference in operating cash outflows due

to the difference between the actual quantity of purchases and the amount of purchases that *should have been made for the actual level of sales volume.* Determining cash outflow variances is an important part of the analysis and control of accounts payable and purchasing.

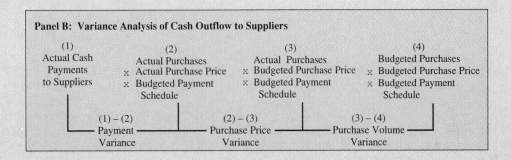

Other Cash Flow Differences

Managers need to analyze the difference between actual and expected cash flows for the other items listed on the statement of cash flows. This information is important to management because inadequate cash inflows can cause delayed payments, inadequate cash reserves, or worse. This information also helps management plan for its future cash needs. Therefore, if any of these differences are significant, managers would investigate to determine their cause(s).

EXHIBIT 24.9 | Cash Flow Variance Analysis

A&E CORPORATION
Cash Flow Variance Analysis
For the year Ended September 30,1995
(In thousands)

	Actual	Budget	Difference
Cash received from customers	$ 201,000	$ 203,500	$ 2,500U
Cash received from renters	1,500	1,500	–0–
Cash paid for inventory	(116,250)	(115,000)	1,250U
Cash paid for insurance	(5,400)	(5,400)	–0–
Cash paid for wages	(9,600)	(9,800)	200F
Cash paid for miscellaneous expense	(8,400)	(8,000)	400U
Cash paid for income taxes	(12,150)	(11,000)	1,150U
Cash paid for interest	(1,920)	(1,920)	–0–
Net cash flows from operating activities	**$ 48,780**	**$ (53,880)**	**$ 5,100U**
Cash received from sale of temporary investment	$3,900	$ –0–	$ 3,900F
Cash received from sale of equipment	1,600	1,000	600F
Cash paid for building	(51,300)	(50,000)	(1,300U
Cash paid for equipment	(12,100)	–0–	12,100U
Net cash flows from investing activities	**$ (57,900)**	**$ (49,000)**	**$ 8,900U**
Cash received from short-term note payable	$ 300	$ 500	$ 200U
Cash received from bond issue	28,200	27,000	1,200F
Cash paid for treasury stock	(25,000)	(20,000)	5,000U
Cash paid for dividends	(10,000)	(10,000)	–0–
Net cash flows from financing activities	**$ (6,500)**	**$ (2,500)**	**$ 4,000U**
Net change in cash during 1995	**$ (15,620)**	**$ 2,380**	**$18,000U**
Add beginning balance of cash	**84,500)**	**84,500**	**–0–**
Ending balance of cash	**$ 68,880**	**$ 86,880**	**$18,000U**

Exhibit 24.9 shows the cash flow variance analysis assuming that A&E Corporation has no other costs that vary with sales.[7] The remaining cash flow differences are simply the difference between actual and budgeted (assumed amount) cash flows for each item shown on the statement of cash flows. Notice that an unfavorable difference arises when cash inflows are less than the amount budgeted or when cash outflows are more than the amount budgeted.

Exhibit 24.9 indicates that cash flows from operating activities were $5,100,000 less than the amount budgeted, cash flows from investing activities were $8,900,000 less than the amount budgeted, and cash flows from financing activities were $4,000,000 less than expected. The ending balance of cash, therefore, was $18,000,000 less than the amount budgeted.

SUMMARY

The statement of cash flows supplements the accrual-based accounting information illustrated in the income statement, balance sheet, and statement of retained earnings. Its purpose is to illustrate the cash flows arising from operating, investing, and financing activities, respectively.

- According to the Financial Accounting Standards Board, the statement of cash flows is useful to (1) assess the entity's ability to generate positive future net cash flows, (2) assess the entity's ability to meet its obligations and pay dividends, and its need for external financing, (3) assess the reasons for differences between income and associated cash receipts and payments, and (4) assess both the cash and noncash aspects of the entity's investing and financing transactions during the period.

---

[7]If A&E Corporation paid its employees a commission, the cash outflows to employees would be adjusted to reflect the change in selling price and sales volume.

- The operating activities section of the statement of cash flows may be prepared using either the direct or indirect format. The direct format illustrates the actual amounts received or paid for operating activities, while the indirect format requires adjustments to accrual-based net income to determine cash flows from operations.

- The investing and financing sections of the statement of cash flows indicate the cash received from or paid for investing and financing events, respectively. The events are further reflected by changes in current nonoperating assets and liabilities, noncurrent assets and liabilities, and owners' equity accounts.

- Internally, companies often prepare a cash variance analysis to determine if actual cash flows met expectations.

KEY TERMS

collection variance The difference in the amount of operating cash inflows due to a change in collection patterns

current operating liabilities Accounts representing operating obligations

direct format The format of the statement of cash flows that shows the actual cash inflows and outflows of operating activities

indirect format The format of the statement of cash flows that shows the differences between accrual-based net income and cash flows from operations

noncash current operating asset A noncash account that represents operating activities

payment variance The difference in the amount of operating cash outflows due to a change in payment patterns

purchase price variance The difference in operating cash outflows due to a change in purchase price

purchase volume variance The difference in operating cash outflows due to the difference between the actual quantity of purchases and the amount of purchases that *should have been made for the actual level of sales volume*

selling price variance The difference in operating cash inflows due to a change in selling price

selling volume variance The difference in operating cash inflows due to a difference between expected and actual sales volume

QUESTIONS

1. Explain the objectives of the cash flow statement.

2. Explain how the cash flow statement, in conjunction with the other financial statements, is useful for external users.

3. Explain the importance of the sections of the statement of cash flows.

4. Explain the difference between the direct and indirect formats for presenting the statement of cash flows.

5. If accounts receivable decreases during the period, which is greater, collections from customers or sales on account? Why?

6. Rent expense as shown on the income statement is $120,000 while cash paid for rent is shown on the statement of cash flows at $135,000. Did prepaid rent increase or decrease during the period? By what amount?

7. Accounts payable for services decreased $67,000 during the year. The statement of cash flows indicates that cash paid for services was $568,000. What was the amount of the related expense shown on the income statement?

8. If the Subscriptions Received in Advance account decreases during the period, which is greater, cash received in advance from customers or subscription revenue? Why?

9. Company A's inventory decreased by $10,000 during the period while its accounts payable for inventory increased by $6,000. Which is greater, cost of goods sold or cash paid for inventory? Why?

10. If the interest expense for the period is $1,500 and the Premium on Bonds Payable account decreases during the period by $50, how much is the cash paid for interest? Why?

11. In the indirect method of presentation of operating cash flows, why is net income adjusted for depreciation, depletion, and amortization shown?

12. If a bond payable is issued at a discount, is the resulting amortization added to, or deducted from, net income to determine cash flows from operations in the indirect method? Why?

13. If an investment in bonds is purchased at a discount, is the resulting amortization added to, or deducted from, net income to determine cash flows from operations in the indirect method? Why?

14. Where and how do gains and losses appear on the statement of cash flows on an indirect basis? Why?

15. When the indirect method is used for the statement of cash flows, how and why is net income affected by changes in current operating assets to determine cash flows from operations?

16. When the indirect method is used for the statement of cash flows, how and why is net income affected by changes in current operating liabilities to determine cash flows from operations?

17. If a company sells a building that cost $150,000 and has $80,000 of accumulated depreciation for $65,000, how does the company reflect this event on the statement of cash flows? Why?

18. Does the amount shown on the statement of retained earnings always equal the amount shown on the statement of cash flows for dividends? Why or why not?

19. If a company exchanges common stock for a building, should it disclose this event on the statement of cash flows? Why or why not?

20. Explain why managers have cash flow information that they do not wish to disclose to external users.

21. Explain the three factors that cause a difference between the actual and expected cash inflows from customers.

22. Explain the three factors that cause a difference between the actual and expected cash outflows to suppliers.

23. Explain why managers evaluate the difference between actual and expected cash flows.

EXERCISES

E 24.1   A variety of transactions is shown below. Identify each transaction as an operating (O), investing (I), financing (F), or other noncash (NC) event. Put the correct letter(s) in the space provided.

_____   *a.* Loan from a bank or other financial institution.
_____   *b.* Payments of accounts payable.
_____   *c.* Purchase of machinery and equipment.
_____   *d.* Collection of an accounts receivable.
_____   *e.* Declaration of dividends to stockholders.
_____   *f.* Sale of land and building.
_____   *g.* Purchase of inventory.
_____   *h.* Sale of common stock.
_____   *i.* Interest received on available-for-sale securities.
_____   *j.* Payment of insurance for one year in advance.

E 24.2   A variety of transactions is shown below. Identify each transaction as an operating (O), investing (I), financing (F), or other noncash (NC) event. Put the correct letter(s) in the space provided.

_____   *a.* Borrowed $50,000 on a long-term note payable.
_____   *b.* Made a sale for $2,500 on open account.
_____   *c.* Reclassified as a short-term liability the long-term notes payable of $30,000 now due within one year.
_____   *d.* Purchased a building for $120,000 with a $20,000 cash down payment and signed a long-term note payable for the balance.
_____   *e.* Paid the maturity value of $1,050 on a short-term note payable with a face value of $1,000.
_____   *f.* Wrote off $500 in uncollectible accounts receivable.
_____   *g.* Paid the liability for accrued wages payable of $700 as well as the current period's wages of $4,500.

_h._	Paid $2,000 on accounts payable.
_i._	Sold marketable securities that cost $12,000 for $12,750.
_j._	Issued 200 shares of $5 par value common stock in payment for equipment having a fair market value of $17,400.

E 24.3 Ingram Company reveals the following information for the past fiscal period.

	Ending Balance	Beginning Balance
Accounts receivable	$ 54,300	$45,600
Inventory	34,000	50,000
Prepaid insurance	8,000	6,400
Accounts payable	82,100	74,560
Taxes payable	15,400	10,500
Wages payable	23,600	32,875
Sales	560,500	
Cost of goods sold	392,350	
Insurance expense	5,000	
Tax expense	8,200	
Wage expense	50,000	

Use the direct format to determine Ingram's cash flow from operating activities for the period.

E 24.4 Searfross Company reveals the following balances in selected accounts.

	May 31, 1996	May 31, 1995
Accounts receivable	$108,600	$ 96,200
Inventory	68,000	100,000
Prepaid rent	16,000	13,200
Accounts payable—inventory	52,100	44,560
Accounts payable—services	24,300	28,700
Wages payable	12,500	14,400
Sales	970,000	
Cost of goods sold	582,000	
Rent expense	78,000	
Miscellaneous expenses	125,600	
Wage expense	144,000	

Determine the operating cash flows using the direct format.

E 24.5 For the year ended December 31, 1996, Chicago Service, Inc., reported net income of $175,000 on the accrual basis of accounting. Using the information supplied below, convert the accrual-based net income to the cash basis.
_a._ The liability for unearned service revenue increased by $12,500 during 1996.
_b._ The liability for equipment rental decreased $5,100 during the year.
_c._ The inventory for supplies on hand increased by $1,700 during 1996.

E 24.6 During 1995, World Tours Company generated a $56,750 net income. Using the information below, determine the adjusted net income.
_a._ Equipment was sold during the period at a loss of $5,000.
_b._ Trading securities (not cash equivalents) were sold during the period at a gain of $2,400.
_c._ Patent amortization expense was $1,800 for the period.
_d._ Bonds were retired at a loss of $3,500.

E 24.7 During 1996, Boston Globe Company recorded interest expense on bonds payable of $15,800 and decreased the premium on bonds payable by $200. If net income was $44,600 during 1996, what is Boston Globe's net income adjustment shown on the statement of cash flows?

E 24.8 Refer to E 24.7. Assume your company purchased Boston Globe Company's bonds when issued and held them during 1996. If your net income is $34,500, what is the net income adjustment to your statement of cash flows?

E 24.9 Feltner Products had a beginning balance in Furniture and Fixtures, net of depreciation, of $186,500. The ending balance in that account was $192,000. Depreciation expense for that period was $18,700, and there were no sales of furniture or fixtures during the period. What was the amount of furniture and fixtures purchases?

E 24.10   Abram's Specialty Meats had $45,900 in its Equipment account at the beginning of 1995. The beginning balance of Accumulated Depreciation—Equipment was $9,000 at that time. During 1995, Abram's recorded depreciation expense of $9,000 and sold a piece of equipment for $2,500 resulting in a gain of $500. At the end of 1995, the Equipment account had a balance of $63,100 and the balance in the Accumulated Depreciation—Equipment account was $14,000. What was the amount of equipment purchases that Abram's made during 1995?

E 24.11   Adams Company purchased a machine on January 1, 1995, for $75,000 in cash. On June 30, 1997, Adams sold the machine at a gain of $5,000. Accumulated depreciation as of June 30, 1997 was $18,250. What is the cash flow shown in the investing section of the statement of cash flows? What adjustment is needed to the net income in the operating section of the statement of cash flows?

E 24.12   On March 1, 1996, Downing Incorporated issued 10-year bonds with a face value of $600,000 and a face interest rate of 10 percent that was paid semiannually. The bonds were sold to yield a market rate of 8 percent. What is the cash inflow shown in the financing section of the statement of cash flows for the year ending December 31, 1996?

E 24.13   Refer to E 24.12. Assuming this is Downing's only debt, what is the amount shown on the cash flow statement for the year ending December 31, 1996, as cash paid for interest using the direct method? Where is this amount shown?

E 24.14   During 1996, Grey Incorporated issued a long-term note for $50,000. In this same time period, Grey paid off another long-term note of $30,000. How would Grey reflect these events on the statement of cash flows? Why? In what section do these events appear?

E 24.15   During 1997, Moriarty Motors' Common Stock and Additional Paid-In Capital accounts increased by $25,000 and $37,500, respectively. If no common stock was retired during 1997, what is the amount shown on the statement of cash flows with respect to common stock? In what section is this disclosed?

E 24.16   Ross Rustproofing had a beginning balance in Retained Earnings of $36,790. During the year, it generated a net income of $5,320. At the end of the year, the Retained Earnings account had a balance of $39,110. In addition, Ross Rustproofing's Dividends Payable account increased by $500 during the year. What is the total amount shown on the statement of cash flows as "cash paid for dividends"? In what section is this disclosed?

E 24.17   During the year Neosho Company sold trading securities costing $6,500 for a gain of $600. What amount of cash did Neosho raise from this transaction, and where would Neosho report it on the statement of cash flows?

E 24.18   During the year Logo, Inc., issued 50,000 shares of $1 par value common stock in exchange for land. The appraised value of the land was $580,000. Logo's common stock was trading at $12 per share at the time of the exchange. Where, and in what amount, would Logo report this transaction on the statement of cash flows for the period?

E 24.19   Manko Company sells Widgets. At the beginning of the period, it expected to sell 150,000 Widgets at $50 each. Based on past experience, it expected to collect 90 percent of its sales. Actual Widget sales were 145,000 at $53 each, and 87 percent of sales was collected. Determine the difference between actual and budgeted cash inflows from customers by calculating the collection, selling price, and selling volume variances.

E 24.20   Newfies, Inc., purchases Newfoundlands from various breeders across the United States. Because the dogs grow quickly, Newfies does not plan to maintain an inventory. On average, each Newfoundland is expected to cost $250 and Newfies, Inc., expects to pay for only 99 percent of its purchases because some breeders offer discounts. At the beginning of the period, Newfies, Inc., expected to sell 2,000 dogs. During the period, 2,400 Newfies were sold, and 2,450 Newfies were purchased at an average price of $240 each. The total cash paid during the period to breeders was $575,400. Determine the difference between actual and budgeted cash outflows to breeders by calculating the payment, purchase price, and purchase volume variances. (See Of Interest . . . Cash Flow Variances.)

PROBLEMS

P 24.1   The financial statements of Buffy's Pet Store are presented below.

BUFFY'S PET STORE
Income Statement
For the Year Ended September 30, 1997

Sales		$485,000
Expenses:		
Cost of goods sold	$331,000	
Salaries	87,000	
Rent	16,000	
Depreciation	7,000	
Other operating expenses	20,000	461,000
Net Income		$ 24,000

BUFFY'S PET STORE
Balance Sheet
As of September 30, 1997, and 1996

	1997	1996
Current assets:		
Cash	$ 23,000	$ 16,000
Accounts receivable	36,000	28,000
Inventory	120,000	135,000
Prepaid rent	4,000	–0–
Total current assets	$183,000	$179,000
Long-term assets:		
Furniture and fixtures	148,000	148,000
Accumulated depreciation	(88,500)	(81,500)
Total long-term assets	$ 59,500	$ 66,500
Total assets	$242,500	$245,500
Current liabilities:		
Accounts payable	$ 28,000	$ 25,000
Salaries payable	5,000	5,500
Accrued liabilities—operating expenses	7,500	4,000
Notes payable	35,000	–0–
Total current liabilities	$ 75,500	$ 34,500
Long-term liabilities:		
Notes payable	–0–	35,000
Total liabilities	$ 75,500	$ 69,500
Owner's equity:		
Buffy, capital	167,000	176,000
Total liabilities and owner's equity	$242,500	$245,500

Required:
   a. Prepare Buffy's statement of cash flows using the indirect method.
   b. Prepare Buffy's statement of cash flows using the direct method.
   c. Determine the percentage of cash collections and cash payments for inventory and the cash flows from operations to net income ratio. What do these indicate?
   d. Which statement do you feel provides the most relevant information for external users? For internal users? Why?

P 24.2   The financial statements of L. B., Inc., are shown below.

L.B., INC.
Income Statement
For the Year Ended December 31, 1996

Sales		$576,000
Cost of goods sold		392,000
Gross margin		$184,000
Operating expenses:		
Depreciation	$ 6,500	
Other operating expenses	155,900	162,400
Net income		$ 21,600

L.B., INC.
Balance Sheet
As of December 31, 1996, and 1995

	1996	1995
Current assets:		
Cash	$ 12,800	$ 15,400
Accounts receivable	21,700	20,300
Inventory	32,100	34,600
Total current assets	$ 66,600	$ 70,300
Property, plant, and equipment:		
Furniture and fixtures	$ 68,700	$ 51,200
Less: Accumulated depreciation	(29,400)	(22,900)
Total property, plant, and equipment	$ 39,300	$ 28,300
Total assets	$105,900	$ 98,600
Current liabilities:		
Accounts payable—merchandise	$ 16,800	$ 18,300
Accounts payable—operating expense	13,400	5,100
Total current liabilities	$ 30,200	$ 23,400
Long-term liabilities:		
Notes payable	$ 25,000	$ 30,000
Total liabilities	$ 55,200	$ 53,400
Stockholders' equity:		
Common stock	40,000	40,000
Retained earnings	10,700	5,200
Total stockholders' equity	$ 50,700	$ 45,200
Total liabilities and stockholders' equity	$105,900	$ 98,600

Required:
a. Prepare L. B.'s statement of cash flows using the indirect method.
b. Prepare L. B.'s statement of cash flows using the direct method.
c. Determine the percentage of cash collections and cash payments for inventory and the cash flows from operations to net income ratio. What do these indicate?
d. Which statement do you feel provides the most relevant information for external users? For internal users? Why?

P 24.3 Go to the library and research the history of the statement of cash flows. Be sure to examine the related FASB discussion memorandum and the exposure draft as well as articles written by academics and professionals at the time. Describe the basic controversy over this statement.

P 24.4 Refer to Disney's statement of cash flows introduced in Chapter 2 and answer the following questions:
a. Is this statement prepared on the direct or indirect basis? How can you tell?
b. Is net cash flow from operating activities greater than or less than net income?
c. What is shown on the statement of cash flows regarding changes in current operating assets during the period?
d. What is shown on the statement of cash flows regarding changes in current operating liabilities during the period?
e. How much cash did Disney pay for interest during the period? Where did you find this information?
f. How does the company define cash equivalents? Where did you find this information?
g. How much cash did Disney pay for income taxes during the period? Where did you find this information?
h. What were the principal investing events during the year?
i. What were the principal financing events during the year?
j. Did the company report any noncash investing/financing events during the year? If so, where did you find this information?
k. If you were an investor, would you be interested in Disney? Why or why not?

P 24.5 Refer to the Boston Celtics' statement of cash flows introduced in Chapter 7 and answer the following questions:

    a. Is this statement prepared on the direct or indirect basis? How can you tell?

    b. Is net cash flow from operating activities greater than or less than net income?

    c. What is shown on the statement of cash flows regarding changes in current operating assets during the period?

    d. What is shown on the statement of cash flows regarding changes in current operating liabilities during the period?

    e. How much cash did the Celtics pay for interest during the period? Where did you find this information?

    f. How does the company define cash equivalents? Where did you find this information?

    g. How much cash did the Celtics pay for income taxes during the period? Where did you find this information?

    h. What were the principal investing events during the year?

    i. What were the principal financing events during the year?

    j. Did the company report any noncash investing/financing events during the year? If so, where did you find this information?

    k. If you were an investor, would you be interested in the Boston Celtics? Why or why not?

P 24.6 Refer to Anheuser-Busch's statement of cash flows introduced in Chapter 10 and answer the following questions:

    a. Is this statement prepared on the direct or indirect basis? How can you tell?

    b. Is net cash flow from operating activities greater than or less than net income?

    c. What is shown on the statement of cash flows regarding changes in current operating assets during the period?

    d. What is shown on the statement of cash flows regarding changes in current operating liabilities during the period?

    e. How much cash did Anheuser-Busch pay for interest during the period? Where did you find this information?

    f. How does the company define cash equivalents? Where did you find this information?

    g. How much cash did Anheuser-Busch pay for income taxes during the period? Where did you find this information?

    h. What were the principal investing events during the year?

    i. What were the principal financing events during the year?

    j. Did the company report any noncash investing/financing events during the year? If so, where did you find this information?

    k. If you were an investor, would you be interested in Anheuser-Busch? Why or why not?

P 24.7 Refer to Harley-Davidson's statement of cash flows introduced in the annual reports booklet and answer the following questions:

    a. Is this statement prepared on the direct or indirect basis? How can you tell?

    b. Is net cash flow from operating activities greater than or less than net income?

    c. What is shown on the statement of cash flows regarding changes in current operating assets during the period?

    d. What is shown on the statement of cash flows regarding changes in current operating liabilities during the period?

    e. How much cash did Harley-Davidson pay for interest during the period? Where did you find this information?

    f. How does the company define cash equivalents? Where did you find this information?

    g. How much cash did Harley-Davidson pay for income taxes during the period? Where did you find this information?

    h. What were the principal investing events during the year?

    i. What were the principal financing events during the year?

    j. Did the company report any noncash investing/financing events during the year? If so, where did you find this information?

    k. If you were an investor, would you be interested in Harley-Davidson? Why or why not?

P 24.8 Refer to Archer Daniel Midland's Statement of cash flows in the annual report booklet and answer the following questions:
  a. Is this statement prepared on the direct or indirect basis? How can you tell?
  b. Is net cash flow from operating activities greater than or less than net income?
  c. What is shown on the statement of cash flows regarding changes in current operating assets during the period?
  d. What is shown on the statement of cash flows regarding changes in current operating liabilities during the period?
  e. How much cash did Archer Daniel Midland pay for interest during the period? Where did you find this information?
  f. How does the company define cash equivalents? Where did you find this information?
  g. How much cash did Archer Daniel Midland pay for income taxes during the period? Where did you find this information?
  h. What were the principal investing events during the year?
  i. What were the principal financing events during the year?
  j. Did the company report any noncash investing/financing events during the year? If so, where did you find this information?
  k. If you were an investor, would you be interested in Archer Daniel Midland? Why or why not?

P 24.9 Use a database such as Disclosure or LEXIS/NEXIS or consult a financial magazine such as *Business Week* or *Fortune* and identify a company that is experiencing financial difficulty. Analyze this company's financial statements, including the statement of cash flows, for the past five years. Describe your findings.

P 24.10 Use a database such as Disclosure or LEXIS/NEXIS or consult a financial magazine such as *Business Week* or *Fortune* and identify a company that has experienced rapid growth. Analyze this company's financial statements, including the statement of cash flows, for the past five years. Describe your findings.

COMPUTER APPLICATIONS

CA 24.1 For fiscal 1996, Winston Enterprises indicated the following cash flow information.

Cash collections from customers	$81,323,055
Cash paid for inventory	58,072,646
Cash paid for operating expenses	18,580,476
Cash paid for income taxes	1,805,517
Cash paid for purchase of equipment	3,665,801
Cash received from long-term debt	5,650,000
Cash received from stock issue	7,564,967

At the beginning of the fiscal 1996 period, Winston Enterprises budgeted the following cash flows:

Cash collections from customers	$83,356,131
Cash paid for inventory	57,491,918
Cash paid for operating expenses	19,416,597
Cash paid for income taxes	1,000,000
Cash received from sale of equipment	1,769,407
Cash paid for purchase of equipment	4,000,000
Cash received from long-term debt	5,000,000
Cash received from stock issue	8,000,000

Required: Use a computer spreadsheet. Assume independent situations.
  a. Determine the difference between actual and budgeted cash flows for each cash flow item listed, and label the differences as favorable or unfavorable.
  b. Determine the difference between actual and budgeted cash flows assuming that the budgeted amounts were 5 percent larger than those given. Label these differences as favorable or unfavorable.

c. Determine the difference between actual and budgeted cash flows assuming that the budgeted amounts were 8 percent smaller than those given. Label these differences as favorable or unfavorable.

d. Give an explanation for each cash flow variance calculated in *a* above.

CA 24.2   Stardust Company has determined its budgeted and actual cash flows from operations as shown below.

	Budget	Actual
Cash paid for rent	$ 60,000	$ 62,000
Cash paid to employees	345,000	325,000
Cash received for rent	5,000	6,000
Cash paid for raw materials	129,000	127,500
Cash paid for interest	12,000	12,000
Cash received from dividends	1,500	1,600
Cash paid for overhead	417,000	467,000
Cash paid for taxes	6,500	6,500
Cash received from customers	1,250,000	1,500,000

Required: Use a computer spreadsheet. Assume independent situations.

a. Determine the difference between actual and budgeted cash flows, and label these differences as favorable or unfavorable.

b. Assume that all the actual amounts were 10 percent greater than those shown above. Determine the difference between actual and budgeted cash flows, and label the differences as favorable or unfavorable.

c. Assume that all the actual amounts were 7 percent less than those shown above. Determine the difference between budgeted and actual cash flows, and label the differences as favorable or unfavorable.

d. Give an explanation for each variance calculated in *a* above.

CASES

C 24.1   Refer to the annual report of the company you selected in Chapter 1 (C 1.1) and answer the following questions:

a. Is this statement prepared on the direct or indirect basis? How can you tell?

b. Is net cash flow from operating activities greater than or less than net income?

c. What is shown on the statement of cash flows regarding changes in current operating assets during the period?

d. What is shown on the statement of cash flows regarding changes in current operating liabilities during the period?

e. How much cash did the company pay for interest during the period? Where did you find this information?

f. How does the company define cash equivalents? Where did you find this information?

g. How much cash did the company pay for income taxes during the period? Where did you find this information?

h. What were the principal investing events during the year?

i. What were the principal financing events during the year?

j. Did the company report any noncash investing/financing events during the year? If so, where did you find this information?

k. If you were an investor, would you be interested in this company? Why or why not?

C 24.2   Using a database such as LEXIS/NEXIS or NAARS, determine how many companies prepared their statement of cash flows on a indirect basis and how many prepared their statement of cash flows on a direct basis during the current year. Do the companies in each category have anything in common? Describe what you discovered.

CT 24.1   The statement of cash flows shown below is incorrectly presented. Analyze this statement and explain the problems you found. Do not prepare a new statement.

MANDRAKE COMPANY
Statement of Cash Flows
As of December 31,1996

Sources (inflows) of cash:		
Net income		$ 88,000
Add (deduct) items to convert from the		
accrual to cash basis:		
Depreciation	$ 15,800	
Inventory increase	10,000	
Prepaid expense increase	(4,000)	
Extraordinary gain on land	(36,000)	
Extraordinary loss on bonds	(2,000)	
Accounts receivable increase	(60,000)	
Accounts payable increase	30,000	
Amortization of bond discount	200	
Wages payable decrease	3,000	
Cash inflows from operations		$ 45,000
Sales of land		106,000
Issuance of bonds		10,000
Total sources of cash		$171,000
Uses (outflows) of cash:		
Cash dividends		30,000
Machinery purchased		20,000
Common stock issued to retire bonds		42,000
Preferred stock issued to purchase building		20,000
Purchase of trading securities		10,000
Total uses of cash		$122,000
Increase in cash		$ 49,000

CT 24.2   Prior to the issuance of *SFAS No. 95*, companies commonly prepared a "funds" statement that reported the changes in working capital during the period. We present a funds statement below. Analyze this statement and describe its strengths and weaknesses as a communication tool.

BORLAND ENTERPRISES
Statement of Changes in Financial Position—Working Capital Basis
For the Year Ending December 31, 1981

Sources of working capital:		
Income from continuing operations:		
Net income		$132,000
Add (deduct) items to convert to		
working capital:		
Depreciation expense	$ 23,700	
Amortization of bond discount	300	
Gain on sale of equipment	(54,000)	
Loss on sale of land	3,000	
Working capital from operations		$105,000
Sale of equipment		159,000
Sale of land		15,000
Total working capital sources		$279,000
Uses of working capital:		
Cash dividends paid		$ 45,000
Machinery purchased		30,000
Trading securities exchanged for note payable		12,000
Total uses of working capital		87,000
Increase in working capital during 1981		$192,000

ETHICAL CHALLENGES

EC 24.1   M. Conway is the manager of Hartwick Company. Conway receives an annual salary plus a bonus of 15 percent of net income before taxes. Hartwick Company uses the LIFO inventory costing method. During 1995 when prices were increasing, M. Conway switched to the FIFO inventory method.

Required: Prepare an example that illustrates the effect on the income statement of switching from LIFO to FIFO. In addition, show the effect of the switch on the balance sheet and the statement of cash flows.
  a. Did net income increase or decrease?
  b. Did ending inventory increase or decrease?
  c. Did cash flows increase or decrease?
  d. Could a change in inventory methods entitle M. Conway to a larger bonus than she was otherwise entitled to? Explain.
  e. In this situation, was the change economically beneficial to the Hartwick Company? Explain.

EC 24.2   K. Stein is the manager of Hoskin Enterprises. Stein receives an annual salary and a bonus of 20 percent of net income before taxes. Hoskin's uses the FIFO inventory costing method. During 1996, the prices of inventory began to rise and K. Stein suggested that the firm should switch to the LIFO inventory method. This change was made during 1996. At the end of the year, K. Stein was very upset because her year-end bonus was small. She argues that her bonus should be increased because she saved Hoskin Enterprises money.

Required: Prepare an example that illustrates the effect on the income statement of switching from FIFO to LIFO. In addition, show the effect of the switch on the balance sheet and the statement of cash flows.
  a. Did net income increase or decrease?
  b. Did ending inventory increase or decrease?
  c. Did cash flows increase or decrease?
  d. Could a change in inventory methods prevent K. Stein from receiving as large a bonus? Explain.
  e. In this situation, was the change economically beneficial to Hoskin Enterprises? Explain.
  f. Was K. Stein treated fairly? Explain.

CHAPTER 25

Firm Performance: A Comprehensive Evaluation

Learning Objectives

1. Describe the relationships among product and service markets, capital markets and information markets.
2. Use financial accounting ratios to assess a company's profitability, and short-term and long-term risk.
3. Explain why and how financial information and market information can be used to assess a company's investment potential.

In 1975 there was virtually no personal computer industry. Since then, the personal computer industry has grown to the point where worldwide shipments in 1993 were 36 million units. Analysts predict that the home market for personal computers in the 1990s will resemble the videocassette recorder market in the 1980s. The ever-increasing computing power and functionality of personal computers has made them indispensable in the workplace and commonplace in homes.

Apple Computers was among the early personal computer manufacturers, and it continues to be a major force in the industry today. Apple's share of the personal computer market in 1993 was 10.2 percent, which ranked second behind IBM's 11.8 percent market share.

When it began, Apple marketed its products by targeting sales toward educational institutions. Apple found that as students graduated they were inclined to buy, for their work or homes, the kind of computer with which they were familiar from school. Now Apple looks to become a major competitor in the business computing market.

How did Apple grow from a small company that focused on educational institutions to such a strong contender in the personal computer industry? Apple

Computers had products that consumers wanted, and it was able to attract investors who provided the capital for the company to expand its capacity as consumer demand grew. The investors use financial statement analysis as part of their investment decisions. This chapter describes the role of financial statement analysis in helping creditors and investors decide whether to invest in companies like Apple Computers.

In Chapter 12 we described how management uses financial statements to evaluate operating decisions such as those associated with credit sales and the payment of trade payables. This chapter examines how external stakeholders, particularly creditors and investors, use financial statement analysis to evaluate *overall firm performance*. In addition to assessing operating, investing, and financing activities of a business like Apple Computers, both management and external stakeholders also need measures of the business's liquidity, longer term risk, and profitability. The difference in financial statement analysis performed by managers and external stakeholders is that external stakeholders need to assess the investment value of the business as a whole.

In Chapter 16, we discussed how businesses choose among investment alternatives. Creditors and investors face the decision of whether to provide capital to businesses. A business needs creditors and investors as sources of capital for its investments because operating activities typically cannot provide enough capital to both sustain operations and finance a business's growth.

The entire group of creditors and investors who provide capital to business make up the **capital market,** in which businesses find financing for their investments. Creditors and investors choose the businesses in which to invest based on their perception of the risk and potential return for each business. How do creditors and investors find out what they need to know? They use financial statements issued by companies as their principal source of information.

Financial statements are a result of analyzing, classifying, and summarizing the numerous interrelated events of a business in a useful and meaningful fashion. The statements report the events; however, they do not evaluate them. In this chapter, we show how external stakeholders evaluate the information contained in financial statements to assess a business's risk and its potential return.

Also note that there is another important use for financial statement information—as a means for managers to report how they have used the capital acquired from creditors and investors. Current creditors with outstanding loans to the company want to know how managers have handled the capital they have provided. As you know, creditors often include restrictions called debt covenants as part of the lending agreement on instruments such as bonds or mortgages. By requiring that a company maintain or have certain account balances or financial ratios, debt covenants attempt to ensure that managers do not jeopardize loan repayment or interest payments by paying investors prior to meeting a business's credit obligations. Creditors use financial statements to obtain information about whether management has violated such agreements.

Current stockholders want to know how managers are using the stockholders' investments. Stockholders have the option of selling a company's stock if they do not approve of its management's activities. This action resembles an investment decision. Though current creditors and stockholders face a slightly different evaluation problem, the financial statement analysis they conduct is essentially the same as the evaluations they make for lending and investing.

This chapter begins with a discussion of the nature of the decisions that creditors and investors make and how capital markets function in allocating investment capital. Then, we apply financial statement analysis to the financial statements of Apple Computers to show how external parties might assess Apple's risk and potential return. Finally, we show how analysts combine the information found on financial statements with other information to assess the overall performance of firms.

EXTERNAL STAKEHOLDER'S DECISION: WHETHER TO INVEST

Throughout the text we have discussed the economic interests of external stakeholders in business activities. In the broadest sense, many external parties face the decision about whether to invest in a company.[1] We focus on the decisions of two groups of external stakeholders: creditors and investors. Creditors loan money to the business and expect to receive interest payments plus repayment of the loaned money in return. Investors[2] invest money in companies expecting return in the form of dividends and/or higher prices for the stock they hold.

Different Investment Perspectives: Lenders and Investors

There are important differences in the ways that creditors and investors view any investment decision. Creditors lend a fixed amount of money over a limited term as part of a loan agreement. For example, banks and other financial institutions often lend money for periods ranging from a few days to 30 or 40 years. The fixed term and return (cash flows) aspects of debt make the risk of not receiving interest payments or principal repayment a major concern of creditors when they assess an investment prospect. On the other hand, investors have no limited or fixed term when it comes to their investments. They commit funds to a business until the business ceases to operate or until they sell their stock to another investor.[3]

Another important difference between creditors and investors is the legal nature of the risk they face. Creditors usually have legal documents like promissory notes, bonds, and mortgages that give them legal recourse in recovering their investment from the businesses to which they lend. Investors, however, have few guarantees for the money that they invest. The Securities Acts of 1933 and 1934 passed by Congress following the stock market crash of 1929 provide some recourse for investors. However, the principal thrust of the Securities Acts is to ensure that investors have sufficient reliable information on which to base their investment decisions.

PAUSE & REFLECT

Preferred stockholders usually have dividends of fixed amounts, but no fixed term. Would you consider them to be more like creditors or investors? What are preferred stockholders' legal rights compared to creditors and investors?

Stepping back from the analysis of individual investments to look at the capital market as a whole gives an important perspective on its role in society. Creditors and investors are the owners of society's capital, and capital markets serve as a way of allocating that capital for investment in business. Next we briefly describe how capital markets serve as a mechanism to allocate capital.

THE SOCIETAL ROLE OF CAPITAL MARKETS

In a **free market economy,** consumer demand determines the nature of businesses that exist and how much of a given product or service is available. Free market economies do not rely on a government dictating what kinds of businesses there should be and the level of investment that businesses should receive. As shown on the

---

[1]Employees invest their time and effort, and, although they are compensated, they have a vested interest in seeing the company succeed. Their investment typically is less tangible than that of external parties, yet they have given part of their lives to the company and expect jobs in the future in return.

[2]Throughout this chapter, we use the term *investors* to describe both current stockholders or potential stockholders. It can also apply to partners and prospective partners in a partnership.

[3]Another possibility is that the corporation can buy back stock and either retire it or hold it as treasury stock.

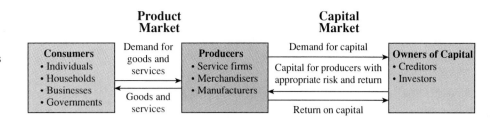

EXHIBIT 25.1

**The Relationship between
Product and Capital Markets**

left side of Exhibit 25.1, a free market economy creates a product market (goods and services) where consumers, whether they are individuals, households, other businesses, or governments, determine the types of goods and services they need and want. This demand for products, in turn, creates opportunities for producers to provide these items to consumers.

How does society decide where to invest its resources? The capital market serves an important role in the decision about what kinds of businesses receive the capital necessary to expand and succeed. The capital market exists between those who produce goods and services and the creditors and investors who own the capital, as shown on the right side of Exhibit 25.1. Producers whose product is in demand by consumers seek to expand, or new producers of that product want to begin production. How do they finance the necessary investment? The owners of capital are the principal source of funds for the producers' potential investment. In return for the use of the capital, owners want the highest return possible, as long as the related level of investment risk is not too high.

The capital market determines which businesses get the capital they need as follows. The level of consumer demand determines the price and the profitability of products. The higher the demand for certain products, the higher the prices consumers are willing to pay, making products that are in high demand more profitable than those in low demand. Producers with more profitable products can afford to pay more, or provide a higher return, for the use of the capital they need to allow them to expand. Since the amount of capital is limited, capital owners choose to invest in producers that offer them the highest return. Thus, consumers' demand for products indirectly determines the businesses and industries that receive capital in a free market economy.

Consider the effect of the greater numbers of people working outside their homes since about 1970. This shift in the work force created demand for convenience foods and day care for children. As these demands have risen, it has become more profitable for some businesses to provide meals that are either ready to eat with little preparation, or no preparation as in the case of fast food restaurants. In addition, the expansion of the work force has resulted in opening of chains of day care centers. The resulting increased profitability for these types of businesses induced these providers of day care services to expand and encouraged other new providers of such services to enter the market. Since these types of services have become more profitable, their providers can compete for capital in the capital market by offering sufficient return to attract investors away from other investments.

*Trading in Capital
Markets*

Any market is comprised of buyers and sellers who choose whether to buy or sell. Whether the market is for gold coins, food, or autos, it brings together those people who want a product with those who want to sell it. Capital markets function like other markets. Those individuals or businesses with capital and those in need of capital come together and agree on terms allowing the owners of capital, or creditors and investors, to exchange the use of their capital for some return. For creditors, that return is the interest rate charged to the borrower. For debt that is not held to maturity, the return to creditors also includes the amount of change in the market value of

| EXHIBIT | 25.2 |

Financial Information Market

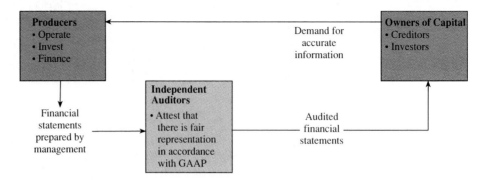

the debt.[4] Return for investors consists of the dividends they receive in addition to the change in the value of stocks they hold.

We need to be clear that there is not one big capital market where all the owners of capital and all those needing capital physically come together to trade. The capital market is segmented into different markets by factors like geography or size of transactions. A small local retailer who needs a loan to remodel the interior of a store is likely to view its capital market as the banks and savings and loan companies in the town. On the other hand, a large multinational company seeking a major expansion would consider as its capital market large banks in major cities or its own ability to issue bonds or stocks on a large scale.

In capital markets, owners of the capital have choices among alternatives. Not all potential investments offer the same risk and return. And, not all creditors and investors share the same investment goals, nor do they have the same tolerance for risk. Creditors and investors use the information available from financial statements and other sources to assess firms' liquidity, longer term debt-paying ability, and profitability. Then, they try to find investments with characteristics that match their investment goals and risk preferences.

For example, a retired couple whose active earning years are over is likely to have the investment goals of steady income and low risk of losing their capital. Thus, they focus on finding investments that offer lower risk, even if that means a commensurately lower return. A young, successful professional might, on the other hand, be willing to accept more risk with the prospects of a higher potential earnings. Therefore, the young professional might look for high potential returns even though the risk of losing some or all of the investment is higher.

**Information for
Capital Markets**

In order for creditors and investors to make good decisions, they need to answer certain questions about the businesses to which they might provide capital. Creditors want to know: "Will I receive interest payments when they are due?" and "Will I recover the principal loaned to the borrower?" The situation with investors is a bit different. Investors are not guaranteed dividends nor is there any repayment of amounts invested because there is no fixed term for the investment. So, investors need to answer the questions "What return will the sum of the dividends I receive and the change in stock price provide?" and "What is the risk that this investment will provide a lower return than I expect?"

Unlike managers who have ready access to lots of information about the activities within a business, external investors and creditors cannot observe business activities firsthand, nor do they have much information about those activities. As Exhibit 25.2 shows, this creates another market—a market for financial information. Owners of capital create the demand for accurate financial information on which to base their investment decisions. Producers (businesses) supply information to investors and creditors using GAAP to determine the necessary level of information

---

[4]We discuss organized markets for trading in bonds and stocks later in the chapter.

disclosure. As we explain below, independent auditors play an important role by attesting, or indicating, that there is fair representation of the information communicated between businesses and investors.

Issues to Consider Regarding Financial Information   There are two problems with this market for financial information. One problem is that, once information is published, anyone can use it. Annual reports issued by corporations, which include the four required financial statements plus other information like management's forecast of sales, are available to anyone. Since consumers receive this information for free, it is impossible to use price to determine the quantity of information demanded. Because the information market does not work as a typical product market in which price determines the quantity demanded, therefore, the Securities and Exchange Commission mandates certain disclosures in order to maintain standards and consistency of public information. The content of those disclosures is determined by GAAP.[5]

PAUSE & REFLECT

Many financial analysts publish newsletters that provide investment advice, which they sell to investors. Why do investors pay for these newsletters when the companies analyzed issue financial reports for free and all the reports filed with the Securities and Exchange Commission by these companies are also available for free?

The other problem with the financial information market is that investors cannot tell whether the information that management reports is accurate. Investors cannot see the events about which management reports and, in addition, investors tend to believe that managers bias their reports to reflect well on management. So investors can either assume that the information that managers provide is at least partially wrong and, as a result, they can subjectively adjust for the expected bias, or they can hire someone to help ensure the information's accuracy.

The Role That Auditors Play   An important role for independent auditors is to provide the users of financial statements with assurance that the financial statement information is a fair representation of the economic circumstances of the company that issues it.[6]

While published financial statements are an important source of information, they are not the only source. Industry trade publications and government statistics can reveal broader economic factors not related specifically to the business being analyzed. Exhibit 25.3 lists a few of the trade publications for the computer industry compiled by *Standard & Poor's Industry Surveys*, 1994. Some of the publications, like *Computerworld*, are sources of technological information about computer-related products and their performance. Others, like *Electronic News*, are oriented more toward the business aspects of the computer industry. In these publications, creditors and investors can find information about Apple Computers and its competitors (for example), which they can use along with financial information prepared by the company they are interested in to project financial performance of the firms.

We have explained the nature of creditors' and investors' decisions in capital markets. In addition, we have shown why information from financial statements, as well as other sources, is critical for making good investment decisions. The next section of this chapter refers to the financial statements of Apple Computers to show how creditors and investors might use ratio analysis to evaluate Apple as an investment opportunity.

---

[5]In 1994, the American Institute of Certified Public Accountants issued a special report, "Improving Business Reporting—A Customer Focus," that called for financial reporting to include more information about the plans, opportunities, risks, and uncertainties that businesses face. It also called for more nonfinancial information indicating how key business processes are performing.

[6]Often stockholders represented by the audit committee of the board of directors hire the independent auditor, though the auditor's fee is paid by the company. Banks also request audited financial statements before making major loans.

EXHIBIT | 25.3 | Some Trade Publications in the Computer Industry

Publication	Frequency of Publication	Publisher	Content
Computer Reseller News	Weekly	CMP Publications Inc.	News coverage of the computer hardware and software industries
Computerworld	Weekly	Kevin McPherson	Computer hardware and software updates
Datamination	Bimonthly	Cahners Publishing Co.	News on all aspects of the information service industries
Electronic Business	Bimonthly	Cahners Publishing Co.	Computer hardware and software news
Electronic News	Weekly	Fairchild Publications	News coverage of the computer hardware and software industries
Information Week	Weekly	CMP Publications Inc.	News and features on the computer hardware and software industries
InfoWorld	Weekly	InfoWorld Publishing Co.	Coverage of the computer hardware and software industries
PC Week	Weekly	Ziff-Davis Publishing	News and developments in the desktop computing area

Source: Standard & Poor's, *Industry Surveys,* November 24, 1994.

STATEMENT ANALYSIS FOR EXTERNAL USERS

Chapter 12 indicates that those who evaluate firms based on financial statements generally use a combination of three methods of analysis: (1) horizontal analysis, which examines the changes in one financial statement item over time, either in numbers of dollars, as a percentage, or both; (2) vertical analysis, which shows each item on a financial statement as a percentage of one particular item on the statement; and (3) ratio analysis, which expresses two or more selected items on the statements in relation to one another.

Recall that horizontal and vertical analyses use changes in items on financial statements and the relative importance of those items to reflect a company's performance. Applications of these two methods of analyses are essentially the same whether they are used to evaluate a company's operating activities or its overall performance. In this chapter we extend the ratio analysis introduced in Chapter 12 by focusing on ratios that external analysts use to evaluate lending and investment decisions. We organize the discussion around four important dimensions: (1) activity, (2) liquidity, (3) long-term debt-paying ability, and (4) profitability. First we present some general points to remember when analyzing a company.

First, Study the Statements

The first step in financial statement analysis is to read carefully the comparative financial statements. **Comparative financial statements** report two or more years' financial statements side by side in columnar form. The purpose of studying comparative financial statements is to become familiar with the firm's reporting practices, the accounts and classifications it uses, and the general range of amounts it reflects. Analysts must observe the company in the total context of its comparative statements before they can examine intelligently the specific aspects of its operations. Using comparative financial statements to study a firm's performance is a well-established practice, and published annual reports of large companies frequently contain comparative data for as many as 10 years.

A careful evaluation of the changes in reported financial data over time helps determine the general trend of operations and assists in deciding whether the company

EXHIBIT | 25.4

Consolidated Balance Sheets

(Dollars in thousands)

September 30, 1994, and September 24, 1993	1994	1993
Assets:		
Current assets:		
Cash and cash equivalents	$ 1,203,488	$ 676,413
Short-term investments	54,368	215,890
Accounts receivable, net of allowance for doubtful accounts of $90,992 ($83,776 in 1993)	1,581,347	1,381,946
Inventories	1,088,434	1,506,638
Deferred tax assets	293,048	268,085
Other current assets	255,767	289,383
Total current assets	4,476,452	4,338,355
Property, plant, and equipment:		
Land and buildings	484,592	404,688
Machinery and equipment	572,728	578,272
Office furniture and equipment	158,160	167,905
Leasehold improvements	236,708	261,792
	1,452,188	1,412,657
Accumulated depreciation and amortization	(785,088)	(753,111)
Net property, plant, and equipment	667,100	659,546
Other assets	159,194	173,511
	$ 5,302,746	$ 5,171,412
Liabilities and Shareholders' Equity:		
Current liabilities:		
Short-term borrowings	$ 292,200	$ 823,182
Accounts payable	881,717	742,622
Accrued compensation and employee benefits	136,895	144,779
Accrued marketing and distribution	178,294	174,547
Accrued restructuring costs	58,238	307,932
Other current liabilities	396,961	315,023
Total current liabilities	1,944,305	2,508,085
Long-term debt	304,472	7,117
Deferred tax liabilities	670,668	629,832
Commitments and contingencies		
Shareholders' equity:		
Common stock, no par value; 320,000,000 shares authorized; 119,542,527 shares issued and outstanding in 1994 (116,147,035 shares in 1993)	297,929	203,613
Retained earnings	2,096,206	1,842,600
Accumulated translation adjustment	(10,834)	(19,835)
Total shareholders' equity	2,383,301	2,026,378
	$ 5,302,746	$ 5,171,412

is better or worse off than in previous periods. It also enables the analyst to see trends as they develop. Creditors, actual or potential, may obtain the same information from their analysis and can use it as a factor when making decisions about the amount of credit to extend to a firm.

Obviously, analysts should not project historical trends indiscriminately into the future. Nonetheless, historical trends provide an excellent starting point for financial statement analysis because the more that is known about a company's past, the greater the chances of predicting the future accurately. A major thrust of financial statement analysis is to use what has transpired in the past to predict the future.

The 1993 and 1994 Apple Computer comparative balance sheets, income statements, and statements of cash flows are shown in Exhibits 25.4, 25.5, and 25.6, respectively. We will use these to analyze Apple as an investment prospect.

The computer industry is competitive and constantly changing, so it is not a surprise that a number of important things happened to Apple in the years immediately following these statements. By the fourth quarter of 1994, Apple's share of the personal computer market was 8.2 percent, a decrease of approximately 2 percent from 1993. Although 1995's Christmas season was one of the best that the personal

Consolidated Statements of Income

(In thousands, except per share amounts)

Three fiscal years ended September 30, 1994	1994	1993	1992
Net sales	$ 9,188,748	$ 7,976,954	$ 7,086,542
Costs and expenses:			
Cost of sales	6,844,915	5,248,834	3,991,337
Research and development	564,303	664,564	602,135
Selling, general and administrative	1,384,111	1,632,362	1,687,262
Restructuring costs	(126,855)	320,856	—
	8,666,474	7,866,616	6,280,734
Operating income	522,274	110,338	805,808
Interest and other income (expense), net	(21,988)	29,321	49,634
Income before income taxes	500,286	139,659	855,442
Provision for income taxes	190,108	53,070	325,069
Net income	$ 310,178	$ 86,589	$ 530,373
Earnings per common and common equivalent share	$ 2.61	$ 0.73	$ 4.33
Common and common equivalent shares used in the calculations of earnings per share	118,735	119,125	122,490

computer industry ever had, Apple's market share slipped further, to 7.1 percent. Apple's management made what are widely considered to be serious marketing mistakes during 1995. They underestimated demand for their Macintosh models, which were based on a super-fast PowerPC chip. So, as the rest of the computer industry grew rapidly, Apple was hampered by its shortages of computers to sell. The biggest backlog of computer orders came in September of 1995 when $1 billion worth of orders were waiting to be filled.

However, not all the events for Apple were bad. In mid-1994 Apple signed licensing agreements with some smaller computer manufacturers to make Macintosh clones (computers made with the same operating system as the Macintosh, and, thus, that use the same software). In 1996, these Mac clones started to hit the market. Apple will benefit by any growth in sales of these clones in terms of both revenue from the licensing agreements and the increased portion of the market that uses their operating system. As the number of personal computers that use Apple's operating system increases, it becomes more attractive for software writers to write programs that run on their operating system. The increase in software makes buying a Mac-based computer more attractive, so the cycle of increasing market share fueling software development feeds itself.

A Basis for Evaluation

Without some standard for judgment, there is not a good basis for making evaluations about whether the firm is a good or bad investment. Remember that sources for external standards are available in college and public libraries. Generally, external standards provide both an average and a range of quantitative values for ratios of firms in the same or similar industries. This information gives a good comparison among investment alternatives.

The *RMA Annual Statement Studies* (published by Robert Morris Associates) summarizes financial information by industry using Standard Industry Classification (SIC), which groups companies based on the nature of their business (e.g., service companies, manufacturers), and by the types of product they produce. Apple Computers is grouped into the manufacturers—electronic computers industry (SIC #3571). The right-hand column of Exhibit 25.7 shows the condensed common-size (vertical analysis) statements for manufacturers—electronic computers—in 1993 complied from compustat. These percentages reflect the averages across all the companies classified as part of the industry. The middle column in Exhibit 25.7 shows the common-sized statements of Apple compiled from Compustat, which we describe subsequently.

Consolidated Statements of Cash Flows

(In thousands)

Three fiscal years ended September 30, 1994	1994	1993	1992
Cash and cash equivalents, beginning of the period	$ 676,413	$ 498,557	$ 604,147
Operations:			
Net income	310,178	86,589	530,373
Adjustments to reconcile net income to cash generated by			
(used for) operations:			
Depreciation and amortization	167,958	166,113	217,182
Net book value of property, plant, and equipment retirements	11,130	13,145	14,687
Changes in assets and liabilities:			
Accounts receivable	(199,401)	(294,761)	(180,026)
Inventories	418,204	(926,541)	91,558
Deferred tax assets	(24,963)	(68,946)	23,841
Other current assets	33,616	(96,314)	(87,376)
Accounts payable	139,095	315,686	69,852
Income taxes payable	50,045	(54,724)	100,361
Accrued restructuring costs	(249,694)	202,894	(57,327)
Other current liabilities	39,991	(13,383)	96,915
Deferred tax liabilities	40,836	19,029	100,933
Cash generated by (used for) operations	736,995	(651,213)	920,973
Investments:			
Purchase of short-term investments	(312,073)	(1,431,998)	(2,121,341)
Proceeds from sale of short-term investments	473,595	2,153,051	1,472,970
Purchase of property, plant, and equipment	(159,587)	(213,118)	(194,853)
Other	(3,737)	(15,169)	(69,410)
Cash generated by (used for) investment activities	(1,802)	492,766	(912,634)
Financing:			
Increase (decrease) in short-term borrowings	(530,982)	638,721	35,895
Increase (decrease) in long-term borrowings	297,355	(10,624)	(391)
Increases in common stock, net of related tax benefits			
and changes in notes receivable from shareholders	82,081	85,289	120,388
Repurchase of common stock	—	(273,454)	(212,625)
Cash dividends	(56,572)	(55,593)	(57,196)
Other	—	(48,036)	—
Cash generated by (used for) financing activities	(208,118)	336,303	(113,929)
Total cash generated (used)	527,075	177,856	(105,590)
Cash and cash equivalents, end of the period	$ 1,203,488	$ 676,413	$ 498,557
Supplemental cash flow disclosures:			
Cash paid during the year for:			
Interest	$ 34,387	$ 11,748	$ 8,778
Income taxes, net	$ 45,692	$ 226,080	$ 97,667
Schedule of noncash transactions:			
Tax benefit from stock options	$ 12,235	$ 16,553	$ 36,836

Comparing Apple's statements with the averages that represent the typical firm in its industry reveals important differences. For example in 1993, Apple had a higher proportion of total current assets (83.9% versus 76.0%) than the average for the industry. This is due to the significantly higher percentages of its cash and equivalents (17.3% versus 13.1%) and other current assets (10.8% versus 2.8%). Having more cash means that Apple is in a stronger position to meet its near-term obligations, such as trade payables, which are lower than the industry average. These higher percentages invested in cash and other assets more than offset the lower percentage in trade receivables that Apple has (26.7%) versus the industry (31.6%). Apple's lower-than-average level of receivables implies that they are doing a good job of collecting their credit sales.

	Apple Computers	Industry Average Manufacturers— Electronic Computers (SIC #3571)
Cash and equivalents	17.3%	13.1%
Trade receivables	26.7	31.6
Inventory	29.1	28.5
Other current assets	10.8	2.8
Total current assets	83.9	76.0
Fixed assets	12.7	15.8
Intangibles (net)	0.0	3.1
Other noncurrent assets	3.4	5.1
Total assets	100.0%	100.0%
Notes payable—short term	15.9%	11.8%
Current maturity of long-term debt	0.0	2.3
Trade payables	14.4	16.3
Income taxes payable	0.5	1.7
Other current liabilities	17.9	11.8
Total current liabilities	48.7	43.9
Long-term debt	0.0	7.4
Deferred taxes	12.1	0.7
Other noncurrent liabilities	0.0	4.0
Net worth	39.2	44.0
Total liabilities and net worth	100.0%	100.0%
Net sales	100.0%	100.0%
Gross profit	34.2%	46.7%
Operating profit	1.3%	5.4%

Apple's current liabilities include a higher proportion of short-term notes payable than the average for the industry. Companies often fund one-time operating expenditures like big promotional campaigns with short-term debt. One explanation for Apple's strong cash position may be that they intentionally accumulated cash to pay for some major event in the subsequent year.

Another important difference between Apple and the typical computer manufacturer is that in 1993 Apple had virtually no long-term debt,[7] while the typical firm in its industry had 7.4 percent of its total liabilities and net worth in long-term debt.

PAUSE & REFLECT

What economic reasons would a company like Apple have for not using long-term debt in its capital structure? What other reason can you think of for companies not wanting debt financing?

Apple has much higher percentage of deferred taxes than the average firm in the industry (12.1 versus 0.7). Deferred taxes arise from recognizing expenses faster and recognizing revenue slower for income tax purposes than for financial accounting purposes. It would require some careful comparison of Apple's financial statements over the last few years to explain why Apple's deferred taxes are so much higher. When considering a company as a long-run investment, investigating such differences can be worthwhile.

[7]Actually, Apple had over $7 million in long-term debt at the end of 1993. When their long-term debt is calculated as a percentage of over $5 billion of total liabilities and net worth, as is done in the common-sized statements in Exhibit 25.7, it is less than 0.2 of 1 percent, which is virtually zero!

Comparing Apple's income statement items with those of the industry reveals cause for concern about Apple's profitability. Apple's gross profit is only 34 percent compared with the 46.7 percent industry average. This implies that the price of Apple's computers does not exceed production cost by as much as others in the computer industry, which means that Apple does not have as much flexibility in price competition.

Sources of Comparative Standards

We stated previously that amounts reported in financial statements are difficult to interpret without external standards against which they can be compared. Below we discuss a few additional sources of external standards.

Moody's Investor Services issues a number of publications, including *Moody's Handbook of NASDAQ Stocks* and *Moody's Handbook of Common Stocks*. These handbooks provide one-page summaries of the history and principal products as well as detailed financial tables for many of the companies whose stock is traded in the United States. Exhibit 25.8 shows the page from *Moody's Handbook of NASDAQ Stocks*[8] that describes Apple Computer. As you can see, it lists financial data for seven years and includes a discussion of developments that are likely to affect Apple's performance in the near future. For example, the growth in international revenues was driven by shipments to Japan; analysts would consider whether or not sales to Japan would continue when they forecast revenues for the next few years. Also, notice that information about Apple's business includes the comment that Apple develops specific versions of processors (CPUs) for individual geographic markets. This information, too, is used to assess future sales of Apple computers.

Another source of financial information is a menu-driven database distributed on compact disk by Standard & Poor's Compustat Services, Inc. The information in this database is taken from the reports that companies are required to file with the Securities and Exchange Commission. A company's financial statements as well as data on ownership and information on 29 key financial ratios are available for the companies on Compustat. (The common-sized statement data for Apple in 1993 shown in Exhibit 25.7 was taken from the Compustat PC compact disk.)

External sources of comparative financial standards, like many published financial statements, use some titles and descriptions that differ from those used in this book. For example, the *RMA Annual Statement Studies* uses net worth instead of stockholders' equity. These differences can be confusing initially, but, with some effort, it is easy to understand them.

Exhibit 25.9 presents a table of 1993 financial ratios taken from the Compustat database. We chose these seven companies (including Apple) from a broad set of industries to show how ratios can differ among industries. As we discuss the various ratios throughout the remainder of the chapter, we will compare Apple's ratios to those of the other companies selected.

RATIO ANALYSIS FOR LENDING AND INVESTING

As you know, careful analysis of current and past financial statements helps provide some of the answers about why things happened in certain companies the way they did. Ratio analysis makes it easy to compare relationships: (1) for a firm over time, (2) of different firms, and (3) with standards such as industry averages. Exhibit 25.10 shows some of the ratios commonly used in analyzing financial statements.

Activity Ratios

Creditors and investors ask the important question about whether the normal flow of funds from cash to inventory to accounts receivable and back to cash is sufficient and regular enough for the firm to pay its debts on time or to pay dividends. One means of assessing business operations is by using **activity ratios,** which are financial ratios that are helpful in judging a firm's efficiency in using its current assets and liabilities.

---

[8]NASDAQ is the acronym for one of the organized stock markets discussed later in this chapter.

EXHIBIT 25.8 Apple's Listing in *Moody's Handbook of NASDAQ Stocks*

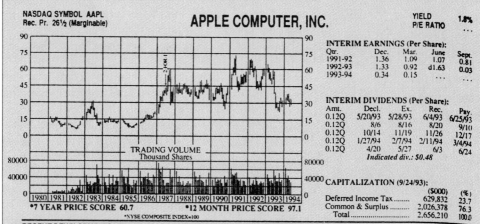

NASDAQ SYMBOL AAPL
Rec. Pr. 26½ (Marginable)

APPLE COMPUTER, INC.

YIELD 1.8%
P/E RATIO ...

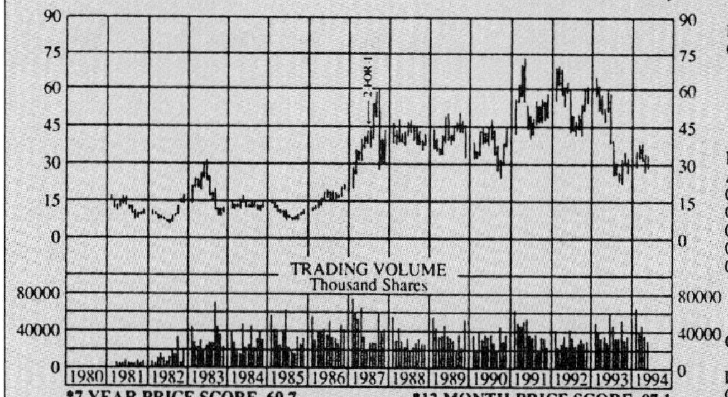

*7 YEAR PRICE SCORE 60.7 *12 MONTH PRICE SCORE 97.1
*NYSE COMPOSITE INDEX=100

INTERIM EARNINGS (Per Share):

Qtr.	Dec.	Mar.	June	Sept.
1991-92	1.36	1.09	1.07	0.81
1992-93	1.33	0.92	d1.63	0.03
1993-94	0.34	0.15	...	...

INTERIM DIVIDENDS (Per Share):

Amt.	Decl.	Ex.	Rec.	Pay.
0.12Q	5/20/93	5/28/93	6/4/93	6/25/93
0.12Q	8/6	8/16	8/20	9/10
0.12Q	10/14	11/19	11/26	12/17
0.12Q	1/27/94	2/7/94	2/11/94	3/4/94
0.12Q	4/20	5/27	6/3	6/24

Indicated div.: $0.48

CAPITALIZATION (9/24/93):

	($000)	(%)
Deferred Income Tax	629,832	23.7
Common & Surplus	2,026,378	76.3
Total	2,656,210	100.0

Recent developments provide a basis for forecasting trends in sales for various products.

RECENT DEVELOPMENTS: For the quarter ended 4/1/94, revenues were $2.08 billion, an increase of 5% over $1.97 billion reported for the same quarter last year. Net income was $17.4 million compared with $110.9 million for the 1993 quarter. Macintosh unit shipments increased 9% compared with the year-ago period. AAPL also shipped 145,000 of its new Power Macintosh® personal computers during the quarter. International revenues were 52% of total revenues during the quarter, up from 47% in the year-ago period. The growth in international revenues was driven by strong shipments in Japan. AAPL's financial results for the second quarter also reflected a $127.4 million reduction in operating expenses. During the quarter, AAPL introduced several new products, including Macintosh Application Environment, for use with SPARCstations and Hewlett-Packard 9000 Series 700 workstations; a new version of Newton® MessagePad; and several new imaging products.

Knowing the nature of the company's industry and its strategies allows analysts to make appropriate comparisons with competitors in the company's industry.

BUSINESS

APPLE COMPUTER, INC. develops, manufactures and markets personal computer systems for use in business, education, science, engineering, government, and the home. The Company offers an extensive line of personal computers, peripherals and system software designed to address individual needs. The Macintosh family of computers---the Macintosh Plus, the Macintosh SE, and the Macintosh II---and the Apple II family---the Apple IIc, the Apple IIe and the Apple IIgs---comprise Apple's line of central processors (CPU). The Company develops international versions of all CPUs in order to meet the specific demands and requirements of individual geographic markets. Apple also develops a full line of computer peripherals, including the LaserWriter and ImageWriter printers, disk drives, and color and monochrome monitors. In addition, new system software products, such as MultiFinder, HyperCard and an Apple's implementation of the Unix operating system extend the usefulness of Apple computers. Communications products such as modems, the Apple Talk local area network and AppleShare file server allow individual users to gain access to share information with other computers.

ANNUAL EARNINGS AND DIVIDENDS PER SHARE

	9/24/93	9/25/92	9/27/91	9/28/90	9/29/89	9/30/88	9/25/87
Earnings Per Share	0.73	4.33	2.58	3.77	3.53	3.08	1.65
Dividends Per Share	0.48	0.48	0.48	0.45	0.41	0.34	[1] 0.20
Dividend Payout %	65.8	11.1	18.6	14.3	11.6	11.0	12.1

[1] 2-for-1 stk split, 6/87

ANNUAL FINANCIAL DATA

RECORD OF EARNINGS (IN MILLIONS):							
Total Revenues	7,977.0	7,086.5	6,308.8	5,558.4	5,284.0	4,071.4	2,661.1
Costs and Expenses	7,700.5	6,063.6	5,657.1	4,643.7	4,524.9	3,373.4	2,219.1
Depreciation & Amort	166.1	217.2	204.4	202.7	124.8	77.7	70.5
Operating Income	110.3	805.8	447.3	712.0	634.3	620.3	371.4
Income Bef Income Taxes	139.7	855.4	499.7	778.5	744.3	656.2	410.4
Income Taxes	53.1	325.1	189.9	303.6	290.3	255.9	192.9
Net Income	86.6	530.4	309.8	474.9	454.0	400.3	217.5
Aver. Shs. Outstg. (000)	119,125	122,490	120,283	125,813	128,669	129,900	131,615
BALANCE SHEET (IN MILLIONS):							
Cash & Temp Cash Invests	...	...	...	...	...	545.7	565.1
Accounts Receivable, Net	1,381.9	1,087.2	907.2	761.9	792.8	638.8	405.6
Inventories	1,506.6	580.1	671.7	355.5	475.4	461.5	225.8
Gross Property	1,412.7	1,135.6	1,036.0	844.9	643.4	420.3	289.1
Accumulated Depreciation	753.1	673.4	588.0	446.7	309.1	213.0	158.7
Net Stockholders' Equity	2,026.4	2,187.4	1,766.7	1,446.8	1,485.7	1,003.4	836.5
Total Assets	5,171.4	4,223.7	3,493.6	2,975.7	2,743.9	2,082.1	1,477.9
Total Current Assets	4,338.4	3,558.4	2,863.6	2,403.3	2,294.4	1,783.0	1,307.4
Total Current Liabilities	2,515.2	1,425.5	1,217.1	1,027.1	895.2	827.1	478.7
Net Working Capital	1,823.2	2,132.9	1,646.6	1,376.3	1,399.2	955.9	828.7
Year End Shs Outstg (000)	116,147	118,479	118,386	115,359	126,270	122,768	126,088
STATISTICAL RECORD:							
Operating Profit Margin %	1.4	11.4	7.1	12.8	12.0	15.2	14.0
Book Value Per Share	17.45	18.46	14.92	12.54	11.77	8.17	6.63
Return on Equity %	4.3	24.2	17.5	32.8	30.6	39.9	26.0
Return on Assets %	1.7	12.6	8.9	16.0	16.5	19.2	14.7
Average Yield %	1.1	0.9	0.8	1.3	1.0	0.8	0.5
P/E Ratio	89.4-30.1	16.2-9.6	28.4-15.6	12.7-6.4	14.3-9.2	15.5-11.5	36.2-12.1
Price Range	65¼-22	70-41½	73¼-40¼	47¾-24¼	50⅜-32½	47¾-35½	59¾-20

Statistics are as originally reported.

Financial data over a 7-year time frame allows analysts to put recent performance in perspective.

We use the accounts receivable turnover as an example of how creditors and investors might apply activity ratios in order to assess a potential investment. Recall from Chapter 12 that the accounts receivable turnover represents the relationship between accounts receivable and credit sales, and it measures how many times the company collected the average accounts receivable balance in the period.

EXHIBIT 25.9	1993 Common Financial Ratios for Seven Companies						
Ratio	Apple	Compaq	Nordstrom	Albertsons	Amgen	Microsoft	Worthington
Current	1.73	2.65	2.1	1.13	2.56	5.06	2.48
Quick	0.91	1.61	1.08	0.18	2.15	4.67	1.27
Cash flow per share	$(5.47)	$2.44	$2.97	$2.12	$3.16	$1.93	$1.06
Inventory turnover	5.03	5.45	4.22	9.75	2.6	4.65	6.11
Accounts receivable turnover	6.46	6.08	6.04	109.85	8.58	12.34	6.99
Total asset turnover	1.7	1.99	1.7	3.62	.88	1.16	1.71
Gross profit margin	34.20%	9.62%	34.08%	26.48%	87.55%	86.81%	18.51%
Return on assets	1.84%	11.31%	6.64%	10.89%	23.86%	29.57%	10.12%
Return on equity	14.10%	17.41%	12.66%	24.46%	35.58%	35.07%	14.16%
Interest coverage before taxes*	12.84	10.78	6.64	11.0	59.52	1,402.0	31.7
Long-term debt to equity	0.35%	0.00%	28.84%	47.86%	15.46%	0.00%	12.84%
Total debt to total assets†	15.92%	0.00%	21.99%	23.00%	16.58%	0.00%	8.28%
Earnings per share	$0.73	$1.82	$1.71	$1.34	$2.67	$1.575	$1.06

* Equivalent to times interest earned.

† Equivalent to debt to equity for measuring long-term risk.

Using the data from Exhibits 25.4 and 25.5, we calculate Apple's accounts receivable turnover for 1994[9] as follows:

$$\text{Accounts receivable turnover} = \frac{\text{Net credit sales}^{10}}{\text{Average net accounts receivable}} = \frac{\$9,188,748}{\$1,481,647^{11}} = 6.20$$

Exhibit 25.9 shows that Apple had an accounts receivable turnover ratio of 6.46 in 1993. So Apple appears to be collecting its accounts receivable a little more slowly in 1994 (6.20) than it did in 1993. However, the difference is not great and does not indicate a substantial change in Apple's accounts receivable collection rate.

Comparing the 1993 accounts receivable turnover ratio with those of the other six firms in Exhibit 25.9, we see that Apple's accounts receivable turnover ratio of 6.46 is close to Compaq (6.08), Nordstrom (6.04), a chain of large specialty stores, and Worthington Industries (6.99), the steel and plastic product manufacturer described in Chapter 6. The two companies that appear most different are Microsoft Corporation (12.34), the largest computer software company in the world, and Albertsons (109.85), a large chain of retail grocers.

Recall that the average collection period is found by dividing 365 days by the accounts receivable turnover ratio. We explain the difference between Apple and Microsoft by assuming that they have different credit policies. Apple appears to allow a 60-day collection period (365/6.46 = 56.5 days) and Microsoft appears to allow only 30 days (365/12.34 = 29.57 days) for its collections.

Albertsons' incredibly high accounts receivable turnover ratio is due to the nature of the Compustat database from which the ratios were taken. Compustat's ratios use total sales, the combination of both cash and credit sales, and are calculated the same way for all firms in the database. Since most of a retail grocer's sales are cash sales,

---

[9]For ratios that require two years' data to calculate, we use averages for the balance sheet items, and we calculate 1994 ratios for Apple. Otherwise we calculate only 1993 ratios to compare with those of the other companies.

[10]Most companies do not separate sales into cash and credit sales. We will explain the implications of this later in the chapter.

[11][$1,581,347 (ending balance) + $1,381,946 (beginning balance)] ÷ 2.

EXHIBIT | **25.10** | **Important Financial Ratios**

What is Measured	Ratios	Means of Calculation
Activity	Accounts receivable turnover	$\dfrac{\text{Net credit sales}}{\text{Average net accounts receivable}}$
	Inventory turnover	$\dfrac{\text{Cost of goods sold}}{\text{Average inventory}}$
	Payables turnover	$\dfrac{\text{Total cash expenses}}{\text{Average current liabilities (except bank loans)}}$
Liquidity	Current ratio	$\dfrac{\text{Current assets}}{\text{Current liabilities}}$
	Cash flow per share	$\dfrac{\text{Cash flow from operations} - \text{Preferred dividends}}{\text{Weighted-average number of shares of common stock}}$
	Quick ratio	$\dfrac{\text{Cash} + \text{Temporary investments} + \text{Accounts receivable}}{\text{Current liabilities}}$
Long-term debt–paying ability	Times interest earned	$\dfrac{\text{Net income before interest and taxes}}{\text{Interest expense}}$
	Debt to equity	$\dfrac{\text{Total liabilities}}{\text{Total shareholders' equity}}$
Profitability	Gross margin ratio	$\dfrac{\text{Gross margin}}{\text{Net sales}}$
	Return on sales	$\dfrac{\text{Net Income}}{\text{Net Sales}}$
	Return on assets	$\dfrac{\text{Net income}}{\text{Average total assets}}$
	Return on owners' equity	$\dfrac{\text{Net income}}{\text{Average owners' equity}}$
	Return on common equity	$\dfrac{\text{Net income} - \text{Preferred stock dividends}}{\text{Stockholders' equity} - \text{Liquidating value of preferred stock}}$
	Asset turnover	$\dfrac{\text{Net sales}}{\text{Average total assets}}$
	Return on sales	$\dfrac{\text{Net income}}{\text{Net sales}}$
	Du Pont ROI	$\dfrac{\text{Net sales}}{\text{Average total assets}} \times \dfrac{\text{Net income}}{\text{Net sales}}$ or Asset turnover × Return on sales
	Earnings per share	$\dfrac{\text{Net income} - \text{Preferred dividends}}{\text{Weighted-average number of shares of common stock}}$
	Dividend payout ratio	$\dfrac{\text{Dividends paid to common stockholders}}{\text{Earnings available to common stockholders}}$
	Price-earnings ratio	$\dfrac{\text{Current market price}}{\text{Earnings per share}}$
	Dividend yield	$\dfrac{\text{Dividends paid per share of stock}}{\text{Market price per share of stock}}$

when its average accounts receivable balance (which is low) is divided into its total sales, it appears that the receivables turnover is incredibly high. Credit versus total sales is the appropriate numerator to use in computing this ratio. Since credit sales are much lower for a grocer than total sales, the accounts receivable turnover ratio would be much lower than 109.85!

This leads us to raise two notes of caution about the computation of the accounts receivable turnover ratio. First, it assumes that all the sales were made on open account. If this is not the case, the numerator in the turnover ratio should be net credit sales, not total net sales.

Second, care must be exercised in using the average of beginning and ending accounts receivable balances. Many businesses are seasonal and have periods of high sales accompanied by large receivable balances. Ideally, the average accounts receivable balance should be the average of the beginning balances for each of the 12 months in the fiscal year. Keep in mind that the managers of the corporation who perform financial statement analysis have access to the data necessary to make these computations accurately. However, when the detailed data on credit sales and monthly balances are not available, the analyst needs to understand the potential deficiencies involved. When only total sales data are available, and the analyst believes the proportion of credit sales is low, then the accounts receivable turnover ratio should be used with caution. Using year-end balances rather than monthly data means that seasonal businesses with unusually high (low) accounts receivable balances at year-end appear to have an accounts receivable turnover that is slower (faster) than it is.

Inventory turnover and payables turnover discussed in Chapter 12 are also activity ratios. Investors use these ratios to assess management's operating efficiency with respect to the purchasing and payment activities.

Assessing Short-Term Liquidity and Solvency

When assessing a business as a potential investment, its liquidity is an important consideration, particularly for creditors whose return relies exclusively on cash flow from the company. Recall that liquidity refers to the cash position of a company and its ability to generate cash inflows through normal operations. Firms rarely have sufficient cash on hand to pay off all their liabilities. Therefore, they depend on the timing of cash inflows in relation to the timing needs of the outflows to pay liabilities. Liquidity and solvency analysis is concerned with cash flows and the adequacy of current assets to meet current liabilities. We discussed two ratios commonly used for liquidity, or solvency, analysis—current and quick ratios—in Chapter 12. Using the amounts from Exhibit 25.4, at the end of 1993 Apple's current ratio was:

$$\text{Current ratio} = \text{Current assets/Current liabilities}$$
$$= \$4,338,335/\$2,508,085$$
$$= 1.73$$

The quick ratio provides a stricter test of the adequacy of current assets to meet current liabilities because it excludes, in the numerator, current assets that are not readily convertible to cash, such as inventory and prepaid items. Apple's 1993 quick ratio of 0.91 was calculated by dividing readily-convertible-to-cash assets of $2,274,249 (cash and equivalents, $676,413; short-term investments, $215,890; and accounts receivable, $1,381,946) by current liabilities of $2,508,085.

We evaluate Apple's liquidity based on its current and quick ratios (1.73 and 0.91, respectively) by comparing them to the ratios of the other firms listed in Exhibit 25.9. Apple and Albertsons appear to be the least liquid of the seven companies. Microsoft appears to be in the strongest liquidity position, with current and quick ratios of 5.06 and 4.67, well above the rest. Note the very low quick ratio for Albertsons (0.18). This occurs because inventory is the major component of Albertsons' current assets, and inventory is not part of the quick ratio calculation. There are very few other current assets available to pay Albertsons current liabilities.

Grocers like Albertsons rely on selling inventory quickly, so their inventory could be considered as more liquid than that of other types of firms. Note that Albertsons inventory turnover ratio (9.75) is the highest of the seven companies, which supports the contention that the grocer relies on selling its inventory to pay for its current liabilities. Thus, we do not consider Albertsons' liquidity position to be unusual for its industry.

Analysts also can use cash flows from the statement of cash flows to assess a firm's liquidity.[12] One such measure is **cash flow per share,** which we calculate as follows:

$$\text{Cash flow per share} = \frac{\text{Cash flow from operations} - \text{Preferred dividends}}{\text{Weighted average number of shares of common stock}}$$

---

[12]See "Developing Ratios for Effective Cash Flow Statement Analysis," by Charles A. Carslaw and John R. Mills, in *Journal of Accountancy*, November 1991, pp. 63–70.

Using the amounts shown in Exhibits 25.5 and 25.6, we find Apple's cash flow per share was an *outflow* of $5.47 ($651,213/119,125). Notice that Apple had no preferred stock and that the denominator in the ratio is the number of common and common equivalent shares used to calculate the earnings per share shown on Apple's income statement (Exhibit 25.5). Apple's cash flow per share supports the weak liquidity indicated by its quick and current ratios. The other six firms had positive cash flows from operations ranging from $1.06 for Worthington to $3.16 for Amgen. Apple's negative cash flow from operations cannot continue for very long because cash flow from operations funds future operations, such as acquiring materials for production, and provides a return for stockholders and repayment of debt, though Apple had almost no debt to be repaid in 1993.

Long-Term Debt Repayment

You already know that investors have an interest in companies' long-term ability to repay debt, but the creditors, both current and potential, have the risk of not recovering their funds. They, therefore, want to know about the firm's debt structure and how that will affect the firm's ability to meet both its short- and long-term debt obligations. We discuss three ratios typically used by creditors to evaluate a firm's creditworthiness below.

Times Interest Earned   Creditors, especially long-term creditors, judge the ability of a borrower to pay interest based on the relationship of borrower's before-interest earnings to the amount of the interest charges for the period. The **times interest earned ratio** compares earnings before deducting interest and taxes to the amount of the interest charges. A company whose income before interest is barely sufficient to cover its interest expense is riskier from a creditor's point of view than one with a high times interest earned ratio. We calculate the times interest earned ratio as follows:

$$\text{Times interest earned} = \frac{\text{Net income before interest and taxes}}{\text{Interest expense}}$$

Using the amounts from Exhibits 25.4 and 25.5, we calculate Apple's 1993 times interest earned ratio as follows:

$$
\begin{aligned}
\text{Net income before interest and taxes} &= \text{Net income} + \text{Interest expense} + \text{Tax expense} \\
&= \$86,589 + \$11,800^{13} + \$53,070 \\
&= \$151,459
\end{aligned}
$$

$$\text{Times interest earned} = \$151,459/\$11,800 = 12.84$$

Of the seven firms we are comparing, Nordstrom has the lowest times interest earned ratio (6.64),[14] which indicates that it presents creditors with more risk in 1993 than the other six firms. Apple, Albertsons, and Compaq, another computer manufacturer, have ratios almost twice as high as Nordstrom, thus, they present much lower risk for creditors. The unusually high interest coverage before taxes for Microsoft is due to its high earnings with virtually no interest expense.

Debt-to-Equity Ratio   Recall that the debt-to-equity ratio expresses the total liabilities as a percentage of the total owners' or shareholders' equity and, thus, measures a company's risk as an investment by the extent to which it relies on debt rather than ownership financing. Using the amounts from Exhibit 25.4, we calculate Apple's 1993 debt-to-equity ratio as follows:

$$\text{Debt-to-equity ratio} = \frac{\text{Total liabilities}}{\text{Total shareholders' equity}} = \frac{\$3,145,034}{\$2,026,378} = 1.55$$

---

[13]This amount was disclosed in the notes that accompany the financial statements of Apple Computer's 1994 annual report.

[14]Compustat's "interest coverage before taxes" is equivalent to the times interest earned ratio.

This means that about three-fifths [\$3,145,034/(\$3,145,034 + \$2,026,378)] of Apple's financing at the end of 1993 came from liabilities.[15]

Long-Term Debt to Equity A similar way of measuring risk is by comparing long-term debt to equity. The focus on long-term debt instead of total liabilities is a measure of the extent to which long-term financing comes from debt. The use of total liabilities would also include the proportion of debt that comes from operations (short term) *and* financing from other long-term liabilities like pension obligations.

Apple's long-term debt at the end of 1993 was only about \$7.1 million. So, its long-term debt-to-total-equity ratio was 0.35 percent (\$7,117/\$2,026,378), a very small amount. Albertsons, with a long-term debt-to-total-equity ratio of 47.86, is by far the most risky of the seven firms we compare. Compaq and Microsoft present virtually no risk associated with the extent of long-term debt in their capital structure because their respective ratio is 0!

PAUSE & REFLECT   Many of the risk measures we have discussed focus on the risk to creditors of not receiving cash flows from their debtors. What is the nature of the economic risk that stockholders face? Can it be measured the same way as creditors' risk? If not, how?

Profitability: The Source of a Firm's Value

Our analysis and evaluation to this point has been concerned with the company's ability to pay its debts on time. In a broader, more long-term sense, if the company is not profitable, it eventually will not meet its maturing obligations. Thus, profitability is important to lenders. However, future profitability is also central to any investor's analysis of a firm's value as an investment because both the value of the company and the potential for dividend payments depend on a firm's profitability.

Profitability is the return on funds invested by the owners and achieved by the efforts of management. Profitability results from numerous operating, investing, and financing decisions over periods of time. Effectively measuring profitability requires more than examining the amount of net income in a particular period. The absolute dollar amount of profits in one period reveals very little about the effectiveness of operations and a company's long-term prospects.

Both current and potential owners of a business are interested in the business's long- and short-term profitability. They also are interested in the firm's disposition of its earnings, which could be either distributed to them as dividends or reinvested in the firm. If the company's stock is publicly traded, owners are concerned also with the stock market's perception of the firm's profitability and its dividend policy. We discuss the role of market price in providing investors' return later in the chapter. Now we describe a few of the financial ratios that investors use to evaluate a firm's profitability.

Gross Margin Ratio Chapter 12 describes how to use ratios to assess management's product pricing decisions, which directly affect profitability. If management prices a product too high, it will sell fewer units. On the other hand, a price that is too low may not provide the firm with a sufficient gross margin to cover operating expenses. Thus, we use the gross margin ratio as a measure of profitability.

$$\text{Gross margin ratio} = \frac{\text{Gross margin}}{\text{Net sales}}$$

---

[15]Compustat does not offer the debt-to-equity ratio. Instead it presents interest coverage before taxes and total debt to total assets as measures of long-term risk.

Using the amounts from Exhibit 25.5, we find Apple's 1993 gross margin (gross profit) as follows:

$$\text{Gross margin} = \text{Net sales} - \text{Cost of sales}$$
$$= \$7,976,954 - \$5,248,834$$
$$= \$2,728,120$$

Then, we calculate Apple's gross margin ratio of 34.2 percent as shown here:

$$\text{Gross margin ratio} = \text{Gross margin/Sales}$$
$$= \$2,728,120/\$7,976,954$$
$$= 34.2\%$$

Apple's margin indicates that the company has 34.2 percent of its products' prices available to use to meet its other expenses like research and development and advertising, and also to provide net profit. Comparing the gross margins of the seven firms in Exhibit 25.9, reveals that Apple's competitor, Compaq Computer, has the lowest gross margin ratio (9.62% versus Apple's 34.2%). Thus, if these two companies were to engage in price competition, Compaq would have much less flexibility to cut prices and still remain profitable.

Worthington's 18.51 percent gross margin ratio is in great contrast to the gross margins of Microsoft (86.81%) and Amgen (87.55%), the largest biotechnology company in the United States. The difference makes sense if you consider the relatively high product costs of Worthington's steel products versus the lower costs of computer software and biopharmaceutical products. It might be more meaningful to determine whether Worthington's gross margin was too low relative to other companies in its industry where the product costs are more comparable to Worthington's.

Return on Assets   Many analysts consider the **return on assets (ROA) ratio** singularly important because it includes the two fundamental profitability elements—earnings and investments in assets.

The investment-in-assets element represents the total investment of the business, and the ratio of net income to those assets measures the effectiveness of management in utilizing the resources at its command. Since a company earns net income over a

span of time, meaningful analysis compares net income to the firm's average amount of investments over that same time period, as shown below.

$$\text{Return on assets} = \frac{\text{Net income}}{\text{Average total assets}}$$

Using the amounts from Exhibits 25.4 and 25.5, we compute Apple's 1994 return on assets as follows:

$$\text{ROA} = \frac{\$310,178}{\$5,237,079^{16}} = 5.92\%$$

Comparing Apple's 1993 return on assets with the six other firms in Exhibit 25.9, we find that Apple's 1.84 percent ROA and Nordstrom's 6.64 percent ROA were substantially lower than the other five companies. The two firms with the highest profit were Amgen (23.86%) and Microsoft (29.57%). These companies are likely to have fewer resources invested in fixed assets due to the easy-to-manufacture nature of the products they produce.

Return on Owners' Equity   Another measure of profitability is **return on owners' equity,** which measures the return earned (net income) relative to the portion of the firm that belongs to the owners. Return on owners' equity is:

$$\text{Return on owners' equity} = \frac{\text{Net income}}{\text{Average owners' equity}}$$

We calculate Apple's 1994 return on owners' equity using the amounts from Exhibits 25.4 and 25.5 as follows:

$$\text{ROE} = \frac{\$310,178}{\$2,204,839.5^{17}} = 14.1\%$$

When comparing Apple's 1993 return on owners' equity of 14.1 percent with the six other firms shown in Exhibit 25.9, we see that Apple is more profitable than Nordstrom and has a return on equity ratio that is comparable to Worthington's. The highest-profit firms were Amgen (35.58%) and Microsoft (35.07%),

---

[16] $\frac{\$5,171,412 \text{ (beginning total assets)} + \$5,302,746 \text{ (ending total assets)}}{2}$.

[17] $\frac{\$2,026,378 \text{ (beginning equity)} + \$2,383,301 \text{ (ending equity)}}{2}$.

but the difference between those two companies and the others is much less than it was when comparing the return on assets ratios due to the fact that both Amgen and Microsoft have very little debt.

Since Amgen's and Microsoft's equities are higher than the other firms featured, the differences between their return on assets and return on equity is less than the differences in these ratios for the other four firms, which have more debt. In other words, Amgen and Microsoft are less highly leveraged, and the returns they earn are not based on borrowed capital. This situation benefits the stockholders of Amgen and Microsoft because profits are not reduced by interest paid to debtholders.

Return on equity is generally computed for the common stockholders only. If there is preferred stock outstanding, adjustments are made for preferred dividend components of the calculation, as shown below, to derive a **return on common equity:**

$$\text{Return on common equity} = \frac{\text{Net income} - \text{Preferred stock dividends}}{\text{Stockholders' equity} - \text{Liquidating value of preferred stock}}$$

The net income in the numerator is reduced by the amount of preferred stock dividends, and the denominator is reduced by the liquidating value of the preferred stock, which is the amount that the corporation would have to pay to purchase all the preferred stock from the preferred stockholders.

Since Apple does not have any preferred stock, there is no difference between its return on equity and its return on common equity.

Asset Turnover   **Asset turnover ratio** is an activity ratio that measures profitability because it relates a firm's ability to generate sales to the amount of assets that the firm employs. The ratio involves dividing net sales by the average assets for the period. A high ratio indicates that management is utilizing the assets under its control well.

$$\text{Asset turnover} = \frac{\text{Net sales}}{\text{Average total assets}}$$

Using the amounts from Exhibits 25.4 and 25.5, we calculate Apple's asset turnover ratio for 1994 as:

$$\text{Asset turnover} = \frac{\text{Net sales}}{\text{Average total assets}} = \frac{\$9,188,748}{\$5,237,079^{18}} = 1.75$$

Exhibit 25.9 shows that Apple had an asset turnover ratio of 1.7 in 1993. So Apple appears to be utilizing its assets to generate sales comparably in 1994 (1.75). Comparing Apple's 1993 asset turnover ratio with those of the other firms in Exhibit 25.9 shows that, because Albertsons relies on a high volume of sales, it has a very high asset turnover ratio (3.62). Amgen, due to the nature of the biotech industry, has a large investment in assets that does not yet generate a high volume of sales. Therefore, it has a low asset turnover ratio (.88). Apple is virtually the same as Nordstrom and Worthington in terms of asset utilization, and fares better than Compaq, a firm in its own industry.

Du Pont Method of Return on Investment   The Du Pont Company was one of the early examples of a very diversified company. It produced a number of different

---

[18]$\frac{\$5,171,412 \text{ (beginning total assets)} + \$5,302,746 \text{ (ending total assets)}}{2}$.

products requiring different raw materials and production processes. In order to assess the profitability of various production facilities, Du Pont developed a return on investment (ROI) measure that is a combination of return on sales, a profitability measure, and the asset turnover ratio, an activity measure.

For our purposes, return on investment is the same as return on assets, which we discussed earlier. The **Du Pont return on investment** (return on assets) is:

$$ROA = \frac{\text{Net income}^{19}}{\text{Average total assets}}$$

$$= \frac{\text{Net sales}}{\text{Average total assets}} \times \frac{\text{Net income}}{\text{Net sales}}$$

$$= \text{Asset turnover} \times \text{Return on sales}$$

By breaking the return on assets expression into two components, we can look at two potential causes for changes in a company's return on assets from period to period. We calculated Apple's return on assets for 1994 to be 5.92 percent, and Exhibit 25.9 shows that, in 1993, its return on assets was 1.84 percent. Was this 1994 improvement in ROA due to changes in utilization of assets or profitability?

Using the Du Pont method, we can isolate the asset utilization measured by the asset turnover ratio from profitability measured by return on sales. Earlier we calculated Apple's 1994 asset turnover ratio to be 1.75, and Exhibit 25.9 shows that Apple had asset turnover ratio of 1.7 in 1993. We calculate Apple's return on sales for 1993 and 1994 as follows:

$$1993 \text{ Return on sales} = \frac{\$86,589}{\$7,976,954} = 1.08\%$$

$$1994 \text{ Return on sales} = \frac{\$310,178}{\$9,188,748} = 3.38\%$$

Looking at the components of Apple's ROA for 1993 and 1994, we see that the improvement in ROA from 1993 to 1994 was driven almost totally by an improvement in profitability (return on sales). The calculations supporting this observation are as follows:

	ROA	=	Asset turnover	×	Return on sales
1993	1.84%	=	1.70	×	1.08%
1994	5.92%	=	1.75	×	3.38%

Earnings per Share   We know that earnings per share (EPS) is such an important measure of profitability that it is required to be presented as part of the income statement. Apple's 1993 EPS is calculated below.

$$\text{Earnings per share} = \frac{\text{Net income} - \text{Preferred stock dividends}}{\text{Weighted average number of common shares outstanding}}$$

$$= \frac{\$86,589}{119,125}$$

$$= \$.73$$

---

[19]Often, this ratio reflects income from continuing operations in place of net income.

In 1993, Apple's $.73 EPS was lowest of the seven firms we compare, while Amgen had the highest EPS of $2.67 per share (Exhibit 25.9). From the stockholders' perspective, the EPS of the firms in which they invest are best evaluated relative to the market price of firm's stock. Later we discuss how analysts use a stock's market price to assess earnings.

Dividends: Cash Flows for Investors

As part of their financing and operating decisions, some firms pay dividends to their stockholders, while others do not. Investors differ in their investment objectives, and not all investors want to receive dividends. Part of investors' evaluation of a potential investment is assessing the corporation's dividend policy.

The dividend payout ratio reveals a firm's dividend payment philosophy. The **dividend payout ratio** relates the amount of dividends paid to the period's earnings. As shown below, this is determined only for common stockholders.

$$\text{Dividend payout ratio} = \frac{\text{Dividend paid to common stockholders}}{\text{Earnings available to common stockholders}}$$

The dividend payout ratio enables financial statement users to assess the prospects for future cash flows paid directly to them by the corporation, which is not the same as the amount of cash flows received by the business. Rather, dividend payout shows the portion of the firm's assets distributed to the common stockholders as well as the remaining portion of earnings that is reinvested in the firm. Therefore, the dividend payout ratio gives the financial statement reader an indication of management's policy on reinvesting the earnings of the firm.

PAUSE & REFLECT   Some corporations pay dividends and others do not. What are some of the reasons why these different dividend policies exist?

Apple's statement of cash flows (Exhibit 25.6) shows that it paid $55,593 as dividends in 1993. Since Apple had no preferred stock, its earnings available to common stockholders are calculated as follows:

$$\text{Dividend payout ratio} = \frac{\text{Dividends paid}}{\substack{\text{Earnings available} \\ \text{to common stockholders}}} = \frac{\$55,593}{\$86,589} = 64.2\%$$

Exhibit 25.11 shows the dividend and market-related data for the seven companies we have discussed in this chapter. Comparing Apple's dividend payout to the other six firms reveals some interesting differences in dividend policy among the firms. The three other high-tech companies, Compaq, Amgen, and Microsoft, do not pay dividends. Instead, stockholders in these three companies receive their return solely from increases in the value of the stock held. This suggests that Compaq, Amgen, and Microsoft believe that they can offer sufficient returns to stockholders through increases in their stocks' prices without paying dividends. These companies also have low-debt capital structures (Exhibit 25.9), which suggests that they find equity a less expensive way to finance their businesses. Apple, which paid out the highest portion of its earnings, still has a low-debt capital structure, and, therefore, appears to have less need for cash to finance growth.

We have shown how creditors and investors use information presented in a company's financial statements to assess activity, liquidity and solvency, long-term debt-paying ability, and profitability for companies, in addition to dividend policies. But external stakeholders use information about the market value of their investments as well as the information they receive from a company's financial statements. In the next section, we describe how investors use market information when evaluating companies.

EXHIBIT	25.11	1993 Dividend and Market-Related Data for Seven Companies						
		Apple	Compaq	Nordstrom	Albertsons	Amgen	Microsoft	Worthington
Dividend payout		64.2%	0.0%	19.88%	32.84%	0.0%	0.0%	44.40%
Dividend yield		2.05%	0.0%	0.97%	1.64%	0.0%	0.0%	1.66%
Market price at 1993 year-end		$23.28	$24.63	$35.00	$26.75	$49.5	$44.00	$19.75

USING STOCK PRICE INFORMATION FOR INVESTING

Stock markets are an important part of the world's capital markets. They allow numerous transactions involving the purchase and sale of corporate stock on a daily basis. In addition to offering investors a place to exchange stock, stock markets also provide corporations with a place to sell additional stock to raise capital and to repurchase their stock easily. In addition to the NYSE, AMEX, and NASDAQ[20] in the United States, there are major stock exchanges throughout the world in places like London and Tokyo.

Organized Stock Markets

One important feature of stock exchanges is that the buyers and sellers are rarely present. Sales are made by brokers who represent the parties in the transaction. This allows large volumes of trades to occur. The typical volume on the NYSE alone is between 200 and 400 million shares on an average day.

Another important feature of these exchanges is that they set trading rules to protect buyers and sellers. Since the parties to the buy and sell transactions are not present at the time of the transaction, they would be reluctant to trade if there was not some protection for their cash and investments.

Stock Prices

In the stock market, investors buy and sell ownership interest in corporations (stock) at a mutually agreeable price. When there are prospects for a firm to be more profitable and, thus, more valuable, stock prices go up. In such circumstances, the price the holders of stock demand and the price the buyers of that stock offer both go up. When the prospects for firm performance take a downturn, the opposite happens. This process results in establishment of the market price of a stock.

Exhibit 25.12 shows the portion of *The Wall Street Journal* (WSJ) that includes Amgen's and Apple's price information for May 1, 1995. Both are traded on the NASDAQ exchange. Apple is listed as AppleCptr. Notice that Apple's stock ended the day (close) selling for 38 1/4 ($38.25) per share. The highest price for its stock in the preceding 52 weeks was 48 1/16, and the lowest price was 24 5/8. Also note that Amgen's price was 1 15/16 ($1.938) less than its closing price on the previous trading day, while Apple's price was unchanged. The range of prices and the daily changes allow investors to assess the risk of the stock as measured by the volatility of, or change in, its price.

Using Information from Stock Markets

Investors use the *price-earnings* and the *dividend yield* ratios to evaluate the stocks they are considering. Both of these ratios use the market price of the stocks as part of the calculation.

Price-Earnings Ratio The **price-earnings (PE) ratio** reflects the relationship between the current market price of the firm's common stock and the earnings of the firm. It appears below:

$$\text{Price-earnings ratio} = \frac{\text{Current market price}}{\text{Earnings per share}}$$

---

[20]The NASDAQ is a securities exchange sponsored by the National Association of Securities Dealers.

EXHIBIT 25.12

Apple's Market Disclosures from *The Wall Street Journal*, May 2, 1995

Hi, Lo, Close and Net Chg refer to the day's trading for the stock.

Yld% and PE are based on the most recently reported annual earnings and the day's closing price.

Symbols that represent the stocks are found on the stock ticker, where prices are reported (almost) as they occur on stock exchanges.

52 Weeks Hi	52 Weeks Lo	Stock	Sym	Div	Yld %	PE	Vol 100s	Hi	Lo	Close	Net Chg
24 7/8	19	AMFED Fnl	AMFF	.24	1.1	13	305	22 3/4	22 1/4	22 5/8	+ 1/8
76 1/8	40 1/2	Amgen	AMGN		...	29	7953	73	70 3/4	70 3/4	– 1 15/16
2 7/8	1 1/8	Amistar	AMTA		...	8	1	2 5/8	2 5/8	2 5/8	+ 1/16
n 7 7/8	7	AmpaceCp	PACE		...	...	88	7 15/32	7 3/8	7 7/16	+ 1/16
9 1/4	5 1/2	AMRESCO	AMMB	.20	2.9	10	122	7 1/4	7	7	– 1/8
11 7/8	5 1/2	Amrion	AMRI		...	20	47	9 7/8	9 5/8	9 5/8	...
3 1/16	**11/16**	**AmserHlthcr**	**AMSR**		**...**	**dd**	**143**	**2 1/2**	**2 1/4**	**2 3/8**	**– 1/8**
20 3/4	6 3/4	AmtechCp	AMTC	.08	1.1	13	850	7 1/8	6 7/8	7	+ 1/8
10 3/4	6	Amtran	AMTR		...	28	89	8 3/4	8 1/4	8 1/4	...
x 18 3/4	13 1/2	AMTROL	AMTL	.20	1.1	12	335	18 1/4	17 1/2	17 1/2	– 5/8
11 1/2	3 1/2	AmylinPharm	AMLN		...	...	2083	4 5/8	4	4 5/8	+ 1/8
n 15 1/4	13 1/4	ANADIGICS	ANAD		...	...	731	14	13 1/4	13 3/4	+ 3/8
21	14 3/4	Analogic	ALOG	.04p	...	15	54	18	17 1/2	17 1/2	– 1/4
27	14 1/2	AnlyInt	ANLY	.52	2.0	18	256	25 5/8	25 1/4	25 5/8	+ 3/8
6 5/8	2 1/4	AnlySurvy	ANLT		...	17	116	6 1/4	5 7/8	5 7/8	– 1/8
s 16	13 1/4	Anangel	ASIPY	1.00e	6.7	19	1	15	15	15	+ 1/8
3 5/8	1 7/8	Anaren	ANEN		...	dd	13	3 1/4	2 3/4	3 1/32	+ 1/32
38 3/4	25 1/4	AnchrBcpWis	ABCW	.40f	1.2	10	51	32 3/4	32 1/4	32 3/4	– 3/8
19 1/2	10 1/2	AnchorGaming	SLOT		...	12	24	16 1/4	15 7/8	15 7/8	– 3/8
21 3/4	13 1/2	AndovrBcp	ANDB	.40	2.3	7	31	18	17 3/4	17 3/4	...
s 50	21 21/32 ♣	AndrewCp	ANDW		...	36	1822	50	48 3/4	49	– 1/2
19 1/2	13 1/2	Andros	ANDY		...	14	257	16 7/8	16 1/2	16 7/8	...
n 7 1/4	4 3/4	AndyneCptg	ADYNF		...	...	9	5 3/8	5 1/4	5 3/8	+ 1/8
5 1/2	**1 3/4**	**Anergen**	**ANRG**		**...**	**...**	**219**	**3**	**2 1/2**	**3**	**+ 3/8**
10 1/8	4 3/8 ♣	Anesta	NSTA		...	...	66	7 3/8	7	7 3/8	+ 1/4
38 1/2	**15**	**ANTEC Cp**	**ANTC**		**...**	**...**	**4088**	**25**	**23 1/4**	**23 3/8**	**– 1 3/8**
14 7/8	3 5/16	ApertusTech	APTS		...	dd	1631	14	13 3/4	14	+ 1/16
17 1/4	6 7/8	Aphton	APHT		...	...	20	13	12 1/2	13	...
18 1/2	11 1/2	ApogeeEnt	APOG	.32	1.8	18	36	17 3/4	17 1/4	17 3/4	+ 1/2
n 22 3/4	12	Apogee	APGG		...	dd	203	19	18	18	– 1/4
nx 21 15/32	8 1/4 ♣	ApolloGp A	APOL	.56	2.7	...	663	20 3/4	20 3/8	20 5/8	+ 1/8
48 1/16	**24 5/8**	**AppleCptr**	**AAPL**	**.48**	**1.3**	**9**	**15889**	**38 3/4**	**38**	**38 1/4**	**...**
s 18 3/4	10 3/4	AppleSouth	APSO	.02f	.1	27	3104	14 5/8	14 3/8	14 5/8	+ 1/8
24	11	Applebee	APPB	.05e	.2	39	4039	22 1/4	21 3/4	21 3/4	– 1/4
12 3/4	3 3/8	ApplncRecyc	ARCI		...	dd	202	5 1/2	5 1/8	5 1/8	...

The importance of the price-earnings ratio is reflected by the fact that it is included in the stock listings of *The Wall Street Journal.* Keep in mind that the PE ratio changes frequently as the price of the stock changes each day, or as annual earnings are announced.

The price-earnings ratio is an overall approximation of the market's assessment of a company's prospective earnings performance. A high PE ratio suggests that the market anticipates higher earnings for the firm in the future.

The price-earnings ratio is often referred to as the **earnings multiple** and is a measure used by investors to decide whether to buy, sell, or hold a particular stock. For example, if the price-earnings multiple is considered to be low by an investor, then the investor would view the stock price as low relative to its earnings potential and might buy the security. On the other hand, if an investor holds a company's stock that has an earnings multiple the investor considers too high, then the investor might sell the stock in anticipation of the decline in its market price.

The earnings multiple can vary widely by industry and by company. Determining whether a PE ratio is too high or too low is based on the belief of the investor making the investment decision.

PAUSE & REFLECT **What are the PE ratios for the seven firms in Exhibit 25.11?**

Dividend Yield   The **dividend yield ratio** measures the return that an investor would receive on a company's stock at the current price, if dividends paid in the recent past continue into the foreseeable future. It is applied to both preferred and common stock, as shown.

The dividend yield does not measure the return from appreciation of the stock price. Rather, it measures the cash return as a percentage of the stock's current price. It is calculated by dividing the dividend per share of stock by the current market price of the stock.

$$\text{Dividend yield} = \frac{\text{Dividends paid per share of stock}}{\text{Market price per share of stock}}$$

Comparing the companies shown in Exhibit 25.11, we see that Apple has the highest dividend yield (2.05%). This points out the importance of using market prices in investment analysis. Recall that Apple had the lowest EPS (Exhibit 25.9), which would have been misleading on its own without its market price per share as a measure of the amount invested.

Amgen and Microsoft are considered growth companies, which have small or no dividends issued because they are reinvesting the earnings of the firm in the company, rather than paying them out.

For stock of companies with established dividend policies, the dividend yield is an important component of the return that investors expect. For example, preferred stock typically has a specified dividend amount, and investors who buy preferred stock realize that this set dividend yield will provide most of their return. If the amount of the specified dividend, which is the principal source of return on preferred stock, is not satisfactory, the investor will not buy the preferred stock.

It is important to remember that the information provided in a company's financial statements is only part of the information that prudent creditors and investors need. In addition to sources of industry and economic information, investors also should include in their assessment the value that a stock's market price implies.

SUMMARY

Creditors and investors own the capital that businesses need to finance their investments. Financial statement analysis provides creditors and investors with important information they need in order to choose businesses in which they will invest their capital. However, the data from financial statements is not sufficient for a thorough understanding of investment opportunities.

- Consumer demand for products indirectly determines which businesses will be able to attract the capital they need from the capital markets. Creditors and investors need reliable information on which to base their investment decisions.

- Financial statement analysis requires a thorough understanding of the statements themselves and the accounting classifications used by the business. A careful reading of the statements should precede the computations of analytical ratios.

- The ratios used as part of financial statement analysis are classified into these categories: activity, liquidity and solvency, long-term debt-paying ability ratios, and profitability ratios. Activity ratios focus on the efficiency with which management uses the company's current assets and liabilities. Liquidity and solvency ratios reveal the firm's ability to pay its current debts on time. Assessing long-term debt-paying ability requires ratios that measure the risk of not receiving interest or principal repayment. Profitability ratios focus on the long-term earnings potential of a business.

- Investors earn returns on investments in stock from either dividends paid to them by the corporation or from changes in the stocks' prices while they own it.

- Stock markets are places where buyers and sellers of the stock of many companies typically engage in transactions through brokers. Stock markets provide information about the value of a firm that investors use in addition to the information from financial statement analysis to make their investment decisions.

KEY TERMS

activity ratios Financial ratios that are helpful in judging a firm's efficiency in using its current assets and liabilities

asset turnover ratio An activity ratio that measures profitability by relating a firm's ability to generate sales to the amount of assets that the firm employs

capital market The entire group of creditors and investors who provide capital to businesses to allow them to finance their investments

cash flow per share A measure of a firm's liquidity using the amount of cash flow from operations less preferred dividends on a per share basis

comparative financial statements Two or more years' financial statements reported side by side in columnar form

dividend payout ratio A ratio that reveals a firm's dividend payment philosophy by relating the amount of dividends paid to the period's earnings

dividend yield ratio A ratio that measures the return an investor would receive on a company's stock at the current price, if recent dividend payments continue into the foreseeable future

Du Pont return on investment A return on investment (ROI) measure that is a combination of return on sales and asset turnover

earnings multiple (price-earnings ratio) A measure used by investors to decide whether to buy, sell, or hold a particular stock (see price-earnings ratio)

free market economy An economy in which consumer demand determines the nature of businesses that exist and how much of a given product or service is available

price-earnings (PE) ratio A ratio that reflects the relationship between the current market price of the firm's stock and the earnings of the firm

return on assets ratio A profitability ratio of net income to average total assets, or earnings to the amount invested in assets

return on common equity ratio A profitability ratio for common stockholders that adjusts the ratio of net income to stockholders' equity for their respective preferred dividend components

return on owners' equity A profitability ratio that measures the return earned (net income) relative to the portion of the firm that belongs to the owners

times interest earned ratio A comparison of earnings before deducting interest and taxes to the amount of interest expense for the period

QUESTIONS

1. Who are the major user groups of financial statements, and how do their perspectives on the analysis of financial statements differ?

2. What is meant by comparative financial statements and how are they used in horizontal analysis?

3. What is the advantage of analyzing a company's financial statements over a series of years rather than just for the current period?

4. Name three sources of external standards to which a firm may be compared.

5. What is a ratio?

6. Briefly explain what is meant by liquidity analysis, and state why it is important.

7. If you know a company has a current ratio of 2 to 1, why is that not enough information to judge its liquidity?

8. Explain what is meant when it is stated that a company has a quick ratio of 1.75.

9. What do activity ratios measure?

10. Explain why the following items are omitted from the calculation of the payables turnover:

   a. Depreciation expense.

   b. Notes payable to the bank.

11. What is meant by profitability analysis?

12. When a firm's return on assets increases and its asset turnover decreases, has the return on sales increased, decreased, or remained constant? Explain.

13. Why is there a difference between return on assets and return on owners' equity?

14. What is meant by earnings per share?

15. What is meant by the price-earnings ratio?

16. Does the dividend payout ratio tell you anything different from the information included in the computation for dividends per share?

17. Why do analysts use ratios to evaluate firm performance?

EXERCISES

E 25.1 Using the data in the abbreviated income statements below, prepare a horizontal analysis showing both the dollar amount and percentage change from year 1 to year 2.

	Year 2	Year 1
Sales	$432,000	$400,000
Cost of goods sold	264,000	240,000
Gross margin	$168,000	$160,000
Operating expense	127,200	120,000
Net income	$ 40,800	$ 40,000

E 25.2 Prepare a vertical analysis (common-size statement) for the condensed balance sheet of Blankenship, Inc., shown below.

	Year 2	Year 1
Cash	$ 60,000	$ 54,000
Accounts receivable	142,500	126,000
Inventory	195,000	168,000
Property, plant, and equipment	352,500	252,000
Total assets	$750,000	$600,000
Accounts payable and accrued liabilities	$127,500	$150,000
Long-term liabilities	150,000	–0–
Stockholders' equity	472,500	450,000
Total liabilities and stockholders' equity	$750,000	$600,000

E 25.3 Using the balance sheet information from Blankenship, Inc., in Exercise 25.2, compute the current ratio for each year.

E 25.4   The summarized data below were obtained from the accounting records of Falmera Company at the end of its fiscal year, September 30. Compute the following for 1996.
   a. Current ratio
   b. Quick ratio

	1996	1995
Cash	$ 24,180	$ 27,240
Accounts receivable	119,500	120,160
Inventory	143,390	101,690
All other assets	348,780	353,580
Accounts payable	95,340	89,590
Bank note payable, due in 90 days	48,000	26,000
Note payable, due in 8 years	27,500	27,500
Sales	940,240	838,240
Cost of goods sold	689,590	641,780
Operating expense (includes depreciation of $5,160 in both years)	28,510	25,330

E 25.5   Make the appropriate computations for each situation described below.
   a. The firm's average days per receivable turnover is 40, and its sales are $276,300. What is the average Accounts Receivable balance?
   b. If a company maintains an average inventory of $60,000, which it plans to turn over every 45 days, what will be the amount of its cost of goods sold?

E 25.6   Refer to the information for Falmera Company in Exercise 25.4 and compute the following for 1996.
   a. Return on sales.
   b. Return on assets.
   c. Asset turnover.
   d. Ratio of debt to equity.
   e. Return on owners' equity.

E 25.7   The following three independent situations concern return on sales, asset turnover, and return on assets.
   a. The return on sales is 8 percent, and the asset turnover is 1.5. What is the return on assets?
   b. The return on assets is 15 percent, and the asset turnover is 3. What is the return on sales?
   c. The return on sales is 4 percent, and the return on assets is 10 percent. What is the asset turnover?

E 25.8   Maurice Products has $690,000 in total assets at the beginning of the period. The firm expects to declare and pay $90,000 in dividends during the year. The forecasted net income is $200,000, and it expects to show a 25 percent return on year-end assets. Determine the expected amount of year-end assets assuming no changes in total liabilities.

E 25.9   After a fire destroyed the accounting records and most of the offices of BAL Company, the owner decided to ask the bank for a short-term loan to supplement the insurance settlement. The owner remembers the following information and asks you to determine the current ratio so that she may give that information in her loan application.

Current assets	$60,000
Long-term liabilities	–0–
Net income	$20,000
Return on assets	10%
Ratio of debt to equity	.3333

E 25.10   Leverage Company has total liabilities of $75,000 and total owners' equity of $100,000. The firm had net income of $13,000 after deducting interest expense of $4,500. This is a proprietorship and, as such, does not pay income tax on its net income. Compute the return on assets and the return on owners' equity. What is the debt-to-equity ratio? What is the times interest earned?

E 25.11   Using the information shown below, determine the missing amounts.

	Case 1	Case 2	Case 3
Assets	$400,000	?	$100,000
Sales	$600,000	?	?
Net income	?	$ 45,000	?
Return on sales	6%	?	?
Return on assets	?	15%	20%
Asset turnover	?	3	5

E 25.12   Yang Si Imports has total stockholders' equity of $970,000 on September 30, 1996. The firm issues only no-par common stock and had 300,000 shares outstanding on that date. During the fiscal year ended September 30, 1996, the firm earned net income of $116,400 and paid dividends totaling $77,600. The stock was selling for $15 per share. Compute the following.

a. Return on common equity.
b. Dividend payout ratio.
c. Earnings per share.
d. Price-earnings ratio.
e. Dividend yield.

PROBLEMS

P 25.1   Similon Products presently has a current ratio of 2.2 to 1 and a quick ratio of 1.4 to 1. For each of the following transactions, specify the effect of the transaction on these two ratios. Use I for increase, D for decrease, and NC for no change. Consider each transaction separately.

	Current	Quick
a. Collection of an account receivable.	_____	_____
b. Recording accrued but unpaid interest.	_____	_____
c. Purchase of inventory on account.	_____	_____
d. Payment of an account payable.	_____	_____
e. Borrow from the bank on a short-term note.	_____	_____
f. Purchase of temporary investments.	_____	_____
g. Payment of insurance premium of six months in advance.	_____	_____
h. Additional contributions of cash by owners	_____	_____
i. Purchase of equipment with a cash down payment and long-term note payable.	_____	_____
j. A cash refund to a customer for merchandise returned.	_____	_____

P 25.2   For each transaction or change listed below, determine the effect on the return on sales, asset turnover, and return on assets. Consider each event by itself and fill in the blanks with I for increase, D for decrease, and NC for no change.

	Return on Sales	Asset Turnover	Return on Assets
a. Pay long-term liability.	_____	_____	_____
b. Purchase equipment for cash.	_____	_____	_____
c. Increase gross margin percentage.	_____	_____	_____
d. Increase average inventory by purchase on open account.	_____	_____	_____
e. Decrease operating expenses as a percentage of sales.	_____	_____	_____
f. Issue additional capital stock for cash.	_____	_____	_____
g. Decrease number of units sold.	_____	_____	_____
h. Purchase buildings with partial payment and issue a mortgage payable for the balance.	_____	_____	_____

P 25.3   Beaver Ridge, Inc., had $1,000,000 in net income for 1997 after deducting interest expense of $200,000 and income taxes of $240,000. The price of the stock at the fiscal year-end was $25. The firm's stockholders' equity is presented below.

Preferred stock, 6%, $10 par value, authorized 200,000 shares, 150,000 issued and outstanding	$1,500,000
Common stock, $5 par value, authorized 1,000,000 shares, 700,000 shares issued and outstanding	3,500,000
Paid-in capital in excess of par, common stock	800,000
Total contributed capital	$5,800,000
Retained earnings	1,475,000
Total stockholders' equity	$7,275,000

Required: *a.* Determine the times interest earned.
b. Compute the earnings per share.
c. Compute the degree of financial leverage.
d. Calculate the return on common equity.
e. Determine the price-earnings ratio at the fiscal year-end.

P 25.4   Summarized data from the records of Tanning Enterprises at the end of the fiscal year appear below.

	1997	1996
Cash	$ 250,140	$ 231,860
Temporary investments	–0–	520,370
Accounts receivable	2,925,540	2,589,950
Inventory	3,480,210	3,684,970
All other assets	4,219,750	2,494,730
Accounts payable	1,054,950	1,142,630
Other current liabilities from operations	685,160	571,320
Current bank loans payable	1,850,000	1,037,880
Long-term liabilities	2,000,000	2,000,000
Sales	22,838,400	23,804,700
Cost of goods sold	18,910,190	20,543,450
Operating expense (includes depreciation of $296,500 in each year)	2,968,995	2,332,870

Required: Calculate the following.
a. Current ratio.
b. Quick ratio.
c. Return on sales.
d. Return on assets.
e. Asset turnover.
f. Ratio of debt to equity.
g. Return on owners' equity.

P 25.5   A condensed, common-size income statement and some other information for Sybil Company are presented below.

Other Information:

Operating expenses	$96,000
Asset turnover	2.5
Ratio of debt to equity	.5
Current ratio	1.8

Income Statement

Sales	100%
Cost of goods sold	62
Gross margin	38
Operating expenses	32
Net income	6

Required:
 a. Determine the dollar amount for all items shown on the income statement.
 b. Compute the dollar amounts for the following balance sheet items.
  (1) Current assets.
  (2) Property, plant, and equipment.
  (3) Total assets.
  (4) Current liabilities (there are no long-term liabilities).
  (5) Owners' equity.
  (6) Total liabilities and owners' equity.

P 25.6 The following information is a condensed set of financial statements for Vruman Company.

VRUMAN COMPANY
Statement of Financial Position
September 30

	1999	1998	1997
Cash	$ 35,000	$ 20,000	$ 16,000
Accounts receivable	78,000	80,000	83,000
Inventory	97,000	98,000	102,000
Prepaid expenses	15,000	12,000	4,000
Long-term assets, net	375,000	410,000	425,000
Total assets	$600,000	$620,000	$630,000
Current liabilities*	$ 95,000	$120,000	$105,000
Long-term liabilities	65,000	80,000	100,000
Owners' equity	440,000	420,000	425,000
Total liabilities and owners' equity	$600,000	$620,000	$630,000

*Does not include a note payable; all current liabilities result from operations.

VRUMAN COMPANY
Income Statement
For the Years Ended September 30

	1999	1998	1997
Sales	$900,000	$920,000	$970,000
Cost of goods sold	545,000	580,000	590,000
Gross margin	$355,000	$340,000	$380,000
Operating expenses*	285,000	290,000	300,000
Net income	$ 70,000	$ 50,000	$ 80,000

*Includes depreciation expense of $42,000 for each of the three years and interest expense of $7,600 for 1999 and $9,500 for 1998 and 1997.

Required:
 a. Make the following financial statement analysis calculations for 1999 and 1998.
  (1) Current ratio.
  (2) Quick ratio.
  (3) Gross margin.
  (4) Return on sales.
  (5) Asset turnover.
  (6) Return on assets.
  (7) Return on owners' equity.
  (8) Ratio of debt to equity.
  (9) Times interest earned.

P 25.7 Refer to the financial statement information for Vruman Company in P 25.6.

Required:
 a. Prepare a vertical analysis of the financial statements for the three years.
 b. Prepare a horizontal analysis of the financial statements for the three years.

P 25.8
The following information was taken from the accounting records of Callum Company for the year ended December 31:

	1997	1996	1995
Current assets:			
Cash	$ 35,000	$ 31,000	$ 26,000
Trading securities	12,000	8,000	10,000
Accounts receivable	175,000	176,000	169,000
Inventories	225,000	215,000	212,000
Prepaid expenses	5,000	4,000	4,000
Total current assets	$ 452,000	$ 434,000	$ 421,000
Property, plant, and equipment:			
Land	$ 50,000	$ 50,000	$ 50,000
Building, net of depreciation	141,000	149,000	157,000
Equipment, net of depreciation	32,000	47,000	52,000
Total property, plant, and equipment	$ 223,000	$ 246,000	$ 259,000
Total assets	$ 675,000	$ 680,000	$ 680,000
Current liabilities:			
Accounts payable	$ 96,000	$ 77,000	$ 80,000
Notes payable	40,000	60,000	60,000
Other current liabilities	32,000	41,000	39,000
Total current liabilities	$ 168,000	$ 178,000	$ 179,000
Long-term liabilities	75,000	75,000	75,000
Total liabilities	$ 243,000	$ 253,000	$ 254,000
Owners' equity	432,000	427,000	426,000
Total liabilities and owners' equity	$ 675,000	$ 680,000	$ 680,000
Sales	$1,920,000	$2,085,000	$1,880,000
Cost of goods sold	1,152,000	1,209,000	1,110,000
Gross margin	$ 768,000	$ 876,000	$ 770,000
Operating expenses	688,000	771,000	678,000
Net income	$ 80,000	$ 105,000	$ 92,000

Required:
   a. Prepare a vertical analysis of the balance sheet accounts for the years 1997 and 1996.
   b. Using the ratios in the chapter, analyze the liquidity position of the company for 1997 and 1996.
   c. Compare the results of your vertical analysis with the results of the ratio and turnover calculations and point out areas that reveal essentially the same information or where the information from the calculations supplements each other.

P 25.9
Use the information in Problem 25.8 for Callum Company.

Required:
   a. Prepare a vertical analysis of the income statement accounts for the years 1997 and 1996.
   b. Using the appropriate formulas discussed in the chapter, analyze the profitability of the company for 1997 and 1996.
   c. Compare the results of your vertical analysis in this and the previous problem with the results of your profitability calculations and point out areas that reveal essentially the same information or where the information from the calculations supplements each other.

P 25.10
Use the information in Problem 25.8 for Callum Company.

Required:
   a. Perform a horizontal analysis on the statements.
   b. Discuss any trends that appear to be significant. If you have worked Problems 25.8 and 25.9 on the Callum Company, compare your trends from the horizontal analysis with the ratios and turnovers from the other two problems to determine where similar information is revealed.

P 25.11 The condensed financial statements of Belleville Company for 1994 and 1995 are shown below.

BELLEVILLE COMPANY
Income Statement
For the Years Ended December 31

	1995	1994
Sales	$280,000	$260,000
Cost of goods sold:		
Inventory, 1/1	$ 22,700	$ 20,500
Purchases	166,000	153,000
Goods available for sale	$188,700	$173,500
Inventory, 12/31	23,500	22,700
Total cost of goods sold	$165,200	$150,800
Gross margin	$114,800	$109,200
Operating expenses*	84,000	83,200
Income before taxes	$ 30,800	$ 26,000
Tax expense	5,600	3,900
Net income	$ 25,200	$ 22,100

*Includes $5,000 of depreciation expense

Belleville Company
Statement of Financial Position
December 31

	1995	1994
Assets		
Cash	$ 9,800	$ 8,400
Accounts receivable	18,200	17,600
Inventory	25,300	22,700
Property, plant, and equipment	58,700	49,300
Total assets	$112,000	$98,000
Liabilities and Stockholders' Equity		
Current liabilities	$ 24,200	$19,500
Long-term liabilities	12,000	12,000
Stockholders' equity	75,800	66,500
Total liabilities and stockholders' equity	$112,000	$98,000

Additional Information:

Ending balances, December 31, 1993:

Accounts receivable, $17,200.

Total assets, $96,000.

Stockholders' equity, $61,800.

Common stock issued and outstanding: 50,000 shares.

Market price of the stock: 12/31/1995 $23, and 12/31/1994 $18.

Dividends paid: 1995 $10,000, and 1994 $15,000.

Required: *a.* Prepare common-size income statements for 1994 and 1995.

b. Prepare the ratios that managers, owners and potential owners, and creditors would prepare if they were interested in the Belleville Company.

CASES

C 25.1 Select a company listed on the New York Stock Exchange and conduct a ratio analysis on the company. Organize the analysis from the perspective of management, common or potential stockholders, and creditors. Once the ratios are calculated, use either Dun & Bradstreet's *Key Business Ratios* or Robert Morris Associates' *Annual Statement Studies* to compare your company's results with other companies with similar operations.

C 25.2 The original Pan American Airlines went out of business. Determine when the airline went out of business and then find the annual reports for Pan American for the last three years of its existence. From these annual reports, calculate the ratios listed below, and then describe the trends in these ratios.
a. Return on assets.
b. Return on common equity.
c. Debt-to-equity ratio.
d. Quick ratio.
e. Earnings per share.
f. Price-earnings ratio.
Explain whether investors knew about Pan American's bankruptcy before it happened.

COMPUTER APPLICATIONS

CA 25.1 The following list of accounts was taken from the 1993 annual report of International Dairy Queen.

Cash and cash equivalents	$ 21,188,062
Marketable securities	9,989,490
Notes receivable, current, net	3,411,747
Accounts receivable, net	23,247,355
Inventories	4,560,714
Prepaid expenses	1,086,561
Miscellaneous current assets	1,301,043
Notes receivable, long term, net	21,406,772
Miscellaneous long-term assets	1,610,849
Franchise rights, net	83,770,710
Rental properties, net	3,241,108
Miscellaneous revenue-producing assets	39,036
Property, plant, and equipment, net	9,349,670
Drafts and accounts payable	16,791,824
Committed advertising	2,092,851
Other current liabilities	6,761,960
Income taxes payable	962,626
Current maturities of long-term debt	1,913,481
Deferred franchise income	278,917
Deferred income taxes	4,955,000
Long-term debt	23,901,770
Class A common stock	156,594
Class B common stock	90,291
Paid-in capital	3,957,075
Retained earnings	122,340,728
Net sales	241,611,862
Service fees	51,601,113
Franchise sales and other fees	7,625,539
Real estate finance and rental income	8,988,027
Other revenue	1,267,434
Cost of sales	217,154,994
Expenses applicable to real estate	8,441,375
Selling, general, and administrative expense	37,515,701
Interest income	1,425,788
Income taxes	19,520,000

Required: **Use a computer spreadsheet program to determine each of the following ratios.**
  a. Current ratio.
  b. Quick ratio.
  c. Accounts receivable turnover.
  d. Collection period.
  e. Inventory turnover.
  f. Selling period.
  g. Payables turnover.
  h. Payment period.

CA 25.2   Refer to the account information on International Dairy Queen in CA 25.1.

Required: **Use a computer spreadsheet program to determine each of the following ratios and comment on your results.**
  a. Debt to equity.
  b. Return on equity.
  c. Return on sales.
  d. Return on assets.
  e. Asset turnover.
  f. Du Pont formula for return on investment.
  g. Long-term debt to equity.

CRITICAL THINKING

CT 25.1   Consider the differences between the investment decisions of internal stakeholders and those of external stakeholders. Describe any differences in the nature of their investment objectives. Relate those differences to the types of information they would use to make investment decisions.

CT 25.2   The market value of a corporation as a whole can be estimated by multiplying the number of shares of common stock times the market value at any given time. The corporation's book value is simply the book value of its assets less the book value of its liabilities, or its recorded equity value. Discuss reasons why these two values might differ for the same firm, and why the difference might be greater or less for different firms.

ETHICAL CHALLENGE

EC 25.1   Assume that you work for a corporation and discover that the new product that it had developed, news of which had contributed greatly to the recent rise in its stock price, has been rendered obsolete by the new product of a competitor. You own a substantial number of shares of the corporation's stock. The news of the competitor's discovery has not been made public. Should you sell the stock? Why or why not?

EC 25.2   The auditing profession relies on its reputation for integrity. If people do not trust the auditors to provide unbiased opinions about the presentation of financial information, demand for audit services will decline and so will audit fees. To avoid this, auditors must be independent of their clients. However, presently the auditors' fee is paid by the client. Does this keep the auditor from conducting an independent audit? What can auditors do to show that they are independent? Is there an alternative to the auditors' fee being paid by the client they audit?

Present and Future Value Tables

TABLE 1 | **Future Amount of $1**

Periods	1.0%	1.5%	2.0%	2.5%	3.0%	4.0%	5.0%	6.0%	7.0%	8.0%	9.0%
1	1.0100	1.0150	1.0200	1.0250	1.0300	1.0400	1.0500	1.0600	1.0700	1.0800	1.0900
2	1.0201	1.0302	1.0404	1.0506	1.0609	1.0816	1.1025	1.1236	1.1449	1.1664	1.1881
3	1.0303	1.0457	1.0612	1.0769	1.0927	1.1249	1.1576	1.1910	1.2250	1.2597	1.2950
4	1.0406	1.0614	1.0824	1.1038	1.1255	1.1699	1.2155	1.2625	1.3108	1.3605	1.4116
5	1.0510	1.0073	1.1041	1.1314	1.1593	1.2167	1.2763	1.3382	1.4026	1.4693	1.5386
6	1.0615	1.0934	1.1262	1.1597	1.1941	1.2653	1.3401	1.4185	1.5007	1.5869	1.6771
7	1.0721	1.1098	1.1487	1.1887	1.2299	1.3159	1.4071	1.5036	1.6058	1.7138	1.8280
8	1.0829	1.1265	1.1717	1.2184	1.2668	1.3686	1.4775	1.5938	1.7182	1.8509	1.9926
9	1.0937	1.1434	1.1951	1.2489	1.3048	1.4233	1.5513	1.6895	1.8385	1.9990	2.1719
10	1.1046	1.1605	1.2190	1.2801	1.3439	1.4802	1.6289	1.7908	1.9672	2.1589	2.3674
11	1.1157	1.1779	1.2434	1.3121	1.3842	1.5395	1.7103	1.8983	2.1049	2.3316	2.5804
12	1.1268	1.1956	1.2682	1.3449	1.4258	1.6010	1.7959	2.0122	2.2522	2.5182	2.8127
13	1.1381	1.2136	1.2936	1.3785	1.4685	1.6651	1.8856	2.1329	2.4098	2.7196	3.0658
14	1.1495	1.2318	1.3195	1.4130	1.5126	1.7317	1.9799	2.2609	2.5785	2.9372	3.3417
15	1.1610	1.2502	1.3459	1.4483	1.5580	1.8009	2.0789	2.3966	2.7590	3.1722	3.6425
16	1.1726	1.2690	1.3728	1.4845	1.6047	1.8730	2.1829	2.5404	2.9522	3.4259	3.9703
17	1.1843	1.2880	1.4002	1.5216	1.6528	1.9479	2.2920	2.6928	3.1588	3.7000	4.3276
18	1.1961	1.3073	1.4282	1.5597	1.7024	2.0258	2.4066	2.8543	3.3799	3.9960	4.7171
19	1.2081	1.3270	1.4568	1.5987	1.7535	2.1068	2.5270	3.0256	3.6165	4.3157	5.1417
20	1.2202	1.3469	1.4859	1.6386	1.8061	2.1911	2.6533	3.2071	3.8697	4.6610	5.6044
21	1.2324	1.3671	1.5157	1.6796	1.8603	2.2788	2.7860	3.3996	4.1406	5.0338	6.1088
22	1.2447	1.3876	1.5460	1.7216	1.9161	2.3699	2.9253	3.6035	4.4304	5.4365	6.6586
23	1.2572	1.4084	1.5769	1.7646	1.9736	2.4647	3.0715	3.8197	4.7405	5.8715	7.2579
24	1.2697	1.4295	1.6084	1.8087	2.0328	2.5633	3.2251	4.0489	5.0724	6.3412	7.9111
25	1.2824	1.4509	1.6406	1.8539	2.0938	2.6658	3.3864	4.2919	5.4274	6.8485	8.6231
26	1.2953	1.4727	1.6734	1.9003	2.1566	2.7725	3.5557	4.5494	5.8074	7.3964	9.3992
27	1.3082	1.4948	1.7069	1.9478	2.2213	2.8834	3.7335	4.8223	6.2139	7.9881	10.2451
28	1.3213	1.5172	1.7410	1.9965	2.2879	2.9987	3.9201	5.1117	6.6488	8.6271	11.1671
29	1.3345	1.5400	1.7758	2.0464	2.3566	3.1187	4.1161	5.4184	7.1143	9.3173	12.1722
30	1.3478	1.5631	1.8114	2.0976	2.4273	3.2434	4.3219	5.7435	7.6123	10.0627	13.2677
31	1.3613	1.5865	1.8476	2.1500	2.5001	3.3731	4.5380	6.0881	8.1451	10.8677	14.4618
32	1.3749	1.6103	1.8845	2.2038	2.5751	3.5081	4.7649	6.4534	8.7153	11.7371	15.7633
33	1.3887	1.6345	1.9222	2.2589	2.6523	3.6484	5.0032	6.8406	9.3253	12.6760	17.1820
34	1.4026	1.6590	1.9607	2.3153	2.7319	3.7943	5.2533	7.2510	9.9781	13.6901	18.7284
35	1.4166	1.6839	1.9999	2.3732	2.8139	3.9461	5.5160	7.6861	10.6766	14.7853	20.4140
36	1.4308	1.7091	2.0399	2.4325	2.8983	4.1039	5.7918	8.1473	11.4239	15.9682	22.2512
37	1.4451	1.7348	2.0807	2.4933	2.9852	4.2681	6.0814	8.6361	12.2236	17.2456	24.2538
38	1.4595	1.7608	2.1223	2.5557	3.0748	4.4388	6.3855	9.1543	13.0793	18.6253	26.4367
39	1.4741	1.7872	2.1647	2.6196	3.1670	4.6164	6.7048	9.7035	13.9948	20.1153	28.8160
40	1.4889	1.8140	2.2080	2.6851	3.2620	4.8010	7.0400	10.2857	14.9745	21.7245	31.4094
41	1.5038	1.8412	2.2522	2.7522	3.3599	4.9931	7.3920	10.9029	16.0227	23.4625	34.2363
42	1.5188	1.8688	2.2972	2.8210	3.4607	5.1928	7.7616	11.5570	17.1443	25.3395	37.3175
43	1.5340	1.8969	2.3432	2.8915	3.5645	5.4005	8.1497	12.2505	18.3444	27.3666	40.6761
44	1.5493	1.9253	2.3901	2.9638	3.6715	5.6165	8.5572	12.9855	19.6285	29.5560	44.3370
45	1.5648	1.9542	2.4379	3.0379	3.7816	5.8412	8.9850	13.7646	21.0025	31.9204	48.3273
46	1.5805	1.9835	2.4866	3.1139	3.8950	6.0748	9.4343	14.5905	22.4726	34.4741	52.6767
47	1.5963	2.0133	2.5363	3.1917	4.0119	6.3178	9.9060	15.4659	24.0457	37.2320	57.4176
48	1.6122	2.0435	2.5871	3.2715	4.1323	6.5705	10.4013	16.3939	25.7289	40.2106	62.5852
49	1.6283	2.0741	2.6388	3.3533	4.2562	6.8333	10.9213	17.3775	27.5299	43.4274	68.2179
50	1.6446	2.1052	2.6916	3.4371	4.3839	7.1067	11.4674	18.4202	29.4570	46.9016	74.3575

10.0%	11.0%	12.0%	13.0%	14.0%	15.0%	16.0%	17.0%	18.0%	19.0%	20.0%	Periods
1.1000	1.1100	1.1200	1.1300	1.1400	1.1500	1.1600	1.1700	1.1800	1.1900	1.2000	1
1.2100	1.2321	1.2544	1.2769	1.2996	1.3225	1.3456	1.3689	1.3924	1.4161	1.4400	2
1.3310	1.3676	1.4049	1.4429	1.4815	1.5209	1.5609	1.6016	1.6430	1.6852	1.7280	3
1.4641	1.5181	1.5735	1.6305	1.6890	1.7490	1.8106	1.8739	1.9388	2.0053	2.0736	4
1.6105	1.6851	1.7623	1.8424	1.9254	2.0114	2.1003	2.1924	2.2878	2.3864	2.4883	5
1.7716	1.8704	1.9738	2.0820	2.1950	2.3131	2.4364	2.5652	2.6996	2.8398	2.9860	6
1.9487	2.0762	2.2107	2.3526	2.5023	2.6600	2.8262	3.0012	3.1855	3.3793	3.5832	7
2.1436	2.3045	2.4760	2.6584	2.8526	3.0590	3.2784	3.5115	3.7589	4.0214	4.2998	8
2.3579	2.5580	2.7731	3.0040	3.2519	3.5179	3.8030	4.1084	4.4355	4.7854	5.1598	9
2.5937	2.8394	3.1058	3.3946	3.7072	4.0456	4.4114	4.8068	5.2338	5.6947	6.1917	10
2.8531	3.1518	3.4785	3.8359	4.2262	4.6524	5.1173	5.6240	6.1759	6.7767	7.4301	11
3.1384	3.4985	3.8960	4.3345	4.8179	5.3503	5.9360	6.5801	7.2876	8.0642	8.9161	12
3.4523	3.8833	4.3635	4.8980	5.4924	6.1528	6.8858	7.6987	8.5994	9.5964	10.6993	13
3.7975	4.3104	4.8871	5.5348	6.2613	7.0757	7.9875	9.0075	10.1472	11.4198	12.8392	14
4.1772	4.7846	5.4736	6.2543	7.1379	8.1371	9.2655	10.5387	11.9737	13.5895	15.4070	15
4.5950	5.3109	6.1304	7.0673	8.1372	9.3576	10.7480	12.3303	14.1290	16.1715	18.4884	16
5.0545	5.8951	6.8660	7.9861	9.2765	10.7613	12.4677	14.4265	16.6722	19.2441	22.1861	17
5.5599	6.5436	7.6900	9.0243	10.5752	12.3755	14.4625	16.8790	19.6733	22.9005	26.6233	18
6.1159	7.2633	8.6128	10.1974	12.0557	14.2318	16.7765	19.7484	23.2144	27.2516	31.9480	19
6.7275	8.0623	9.6463	11.5231	13.7435	16.3665	19.4608	23.1056	27.3930	32.4294	38.3376	20
7.4002	8.9492	10.8038	13.0211	15.6676	18.8215	22.5745	27.0336	32.3238	38.5910	46.0051	21
8.1403	9.9336	12.1003	14.7138	17.8610	21.6447	26.1864	31.6293	38.1421	45.9233	55.2061	22
8.9543	11.0263	13.5523	16.6266	20.3616	24.8915	30.3762	37.0062	45.0076	54.6487	66.2474	23
9.8497	12.2392	15.1786	18.7881	23.2122	28.6252	35.2364	43.2973	53.1090	65.0320	79.4968	24
10.8347	13.5855	17.0001	21.2305	26.4619	32.9190	40.8742	50.6578	62.6686	77.3881	95.3962	25
11.9182	15.0799	19.0401	23.9905	30.1666	37.8568	47.4141	59.2697	73.9490	92.0918	114.4755	26
13.1100	16.7386	21.3249	27.1093	34.3899	43.5353	55.0004	69.3455	87.2598	109.5893	137.3706	27
14.4210	18.5799	23.8839	30.6335	39.2045	50.0656	63.8004	81.1342	102.9666	130.4112	164.8447	28
15.8631	20.6237	26.7499	34.6158	44.6931	57.5755	74.0085	94.9271	121.5005	155.1893	197.8136	29
17.4494	22.8923	29.9599	39.1159	50.9502	66.2118	85.8499	111.0647	143.3706	184.6753	237.3763	30
19.1943	25.4104	33.5551	44.2010	58.0832	76.1435	99.5859	129.9456	169.1774	219.7636	284.8516	31
21.1138	28.2056	37.5817	49.9471	66.2148	87.5651	115.5196	152.0364	199.6293	261.5187	341.8219	32
23.2252	31.3082	42.0915	56.4402	75.4849	100.6998	134.0027	177.8826	235.5625	311.2073	410.1863	33
25.5477	34.7521	47.1425	63.7774	86.0528	115.8048	155.4432	208.1226	277.9638	370.3366	492.2235	34
28.1024	38.5749	52.7996	72.0685	98.1002	133.1755	180.3141	243.5035	327.9973	440.7006	590.6682	35
30.9127	42.8181	59.1356	81.4374	111.8342	153.1519	209.1643	284.8991	387.0368	524.4337	708.8019	36
34.0039	47.5281	66.2318	92.0243	127.4910	176.1246	242.6306	333.3319	456.7034	624.0761	850.5622	37
37.4043	52.7562	74.1797	103.9874	145.3397	202.5433	281.4515	389.9983	538.9100	742.6506	1020.6747	38
41.1448	58.5593	83.0812	117.5058	165.6873	232.9248	326.4838	456.2980	635.9139	883.7542	1224.8096	39
45.2593	65.0009	93.0510	132.7816	188.8835	267.8635	378.7212	533.8687	750.3783	1051.6675	1469.7716	40
49.7852	72.1510	104.2171	150.0432	215.3272	308.0431	439.3165	624.6264	885.4464	1251.4843	1763.7259	41
54.7637	80.0876	116.7231	169.5488	245.4730	354.2495	509.6072	730.8129	1044.8268	1489.2664	2116.4711	42
60.2401	88.8972	130.7299	191.5901	279.8392	407.3870	591.1443	855.0511	1232.8956	1772.2270	2539.7653	43
66.2641	98.6759	146.4175	216.4968	319.0167	468.4950	685.7274	1000.4098	1454.8168	2108.9501	3047.7183	44
72.8905	109.5302	163.9876	244.6414	363.6791	538.7693	795.4438	1170.4794	1716.6839	2509.6506	3657.2620	45
80.1795	121.5786	183.6661	276.4448	414.5941	619.5847	922.7148	1369.4609	2025.6870	2986.4842	4388.7144	46
88.1975	134.9522	205.7061	312.3826	472.6373	712.5224	1070.3492	1602.2693	2390.3106	3553.9162	5266.4573	47
97.0172	149.7970	230.3908	352.9923	538.8065	819.4007	1241.6051	1874.6550	2820.5665	4229.1603	6319.7487	48
106.7190	166.2746	258.0377	398.8813	614.2395	942.3108	1440.2619	2193.3464	3328.2685	5032.7008	7583.6985	49
117.3909	184.5648	289.0022	450.7359	700.2330	1083.6574	1670.7038	2566.2153	3927.3569	5988.9139	9100.4382	50

TABLE 2 Present Value of $1

Periods	1.0%	1.5%	2.0%	2.5%	3.0%	4.0%	5.0%	6.0%	7.0%	8.0%	9.0%
1	0.9901	0.9852	0.9804	0.9756	0.9709	0.9615	0.9524	0.9434	0.9346	0.9259	0.9174
2	0.9803	0.9707	0.9612	0.9518	0.9426	0.9246	0.9070	0.8900	0.8734	0.8573	0.8417
3	0.9706	0.9563	0.9423	0.9286	0.9151	0.8890	0.8638	0.8396	0.8163	0.7938	0.7722
4	0.9610	0.9422	0.9238	0.9060	0.8885	0.8548	0.8227	0.7921	0.7629	0.7350	0.7084
5	0.9515	0.9283	0.9057	0.8839	0.8626	0.8219	0.7835	0.7473	0.7130	0.6806	0.6499
6	0.9420	0.9145	0.8880	0.8623	0.8375	0.7903	0.7462	0.7050	0.6663	0.6302	0.5963
7	0.9327	0.9010	0.8706	0.8413	0.8131	0.7599	0.7107	0.6651	0.6227	0.5835	0.5470
8	0.9235	0.8877	0.8535	0.8207	0.7894	0.7307	0.6768	0.6274	0.5820	0.5403	0.5019
9	0.9143	0.8746	0.8368	0.8007	0.7664	0.7026	0.6446	0.5919	0.5439	0.5002	0.4604
10	0.9053	0.8617	0.8203	0.7812	0.7441	0.6756	0.6139	0.5584	0.5083	0.4632	0.4224
11	0.8963	0.8489	0.8043	0.7621	0.7224	0.6496	0.5847	0.5268	0.4751	0.4289	0.3875
12	0.8874	0.8364	0.7885	0.7436	0.7014	0.6246	0.5568	0.4970	0.4440	0.3971	0.3555
13	0.8787	0.8240	0.7730	0.7254	0.6810	0.6006	0.5303	0.4688	0.4150	0.3677	0.3262
14	0.8700	0.8118	0.7579	0.7077	0.6611	0.5775	0.5051	0.4423	0.3878	0.3405	0.2992
15	0.8613	0.7999	0.7430	0.6905	0.6419	0.5553	0.4810	0.4173	0.3624	0.3152	0.2745
16	0.8528	0.7880	0.7284	0.6736	0.6232	0.5339	0.4581	0.3936	0.3387	0.2919	0.2519
17	0.8444	0.7764	0.7142	0.6572	0.6050	0.5134	0.4363	0.3714	0.3166	0.2703	0.2311
18	0.8360	0.7649	0.7002	0.6412	0.5874	0.4936	0.4155	0.3503	0.2959	0.2502	0.2120
19	0.8277	0.7536	0.6864	0.6255	0.5703	0.4746	0.3957	0.3305	0.2765	0.2317	0.1945
20	0.8195	0.7425	0.6730	0.6103	0.5537	0.4564	0.3769	0.3118	0.2584	0.2145	0.1784
21	0.8114	0.7315	0.6598	0.5954	0.5375	0.4388	0.3589	0.2942	0.2415	0.1987	0.1637
22	0.8034	0.7207	0.6468	0.5809	0.5219	0.4220	0.3418	0.2775	0.2257	0.1839	0.1502
23	0.7954	0.7100	0.6342	0.5667	0.5067	0.4057	0.3256	0.2618	0.2109	0.1703	0.1378
24	0.7876	0.6995	0.6217	0.5529	0.4919	0.3901	0.3101	0.2470	0.1971	0.1577	0.1264
25	0.7798	0.6892	0.6095	0.5394	0.4776	0.3751	0.2953	0.2330	0.1842	0.1460	0.1160
26	0.7720	0.6790	0.5976	0.5262	0.4637	0.3607	0.2812	0.2198	0.1722	0.1352	0.1064
27	0.7644	0.6690	0.5859	0.5134	0.4502	0.3468	0.2678	0.2074	0.1609	0.1252	0.0976
28	0.7568	0.6591	0.5744	0.5009	0.4371	0.3335	0.2551	0.1956	0.1504	0.1159	0.0895
29	0.7493	0.6494	0.5631	0.4887	0.4243	0.3207	0.2429	0.1846	0.1406	0.1073	0.0822
30	0.7419	0.6398	0.5521	0.4767	0.4120	0.3083	0.2314	0.1741	0.1314	0.0994	0.0754
31	0.7346	0.6303	0.5412	0.4651	0.4000	0.2965	0.2204	0.1643	0.1228	0.0920	0.0691
32	0.7273	0.6210	0.5306	0.4538	0.3883	0.2851	0.2099	0.1550	0.1147	0.0852	0.0634
33	0.7201	0.6118	0.5202	0.4427	0.3770	0.2741	0.1999	0.1462	0.1072	0.0789	0.0582
34	0.7130	0.6028	0.5100	0.4319	0.3660	0.2636	0.1904	0.1379	0.1002	0.0730	0.0534
35	0.7059	0.5939	0.5000	0.4214	0.3554	0.2534	0.1813	0.1301	0.0937	0.0676	0.0490
36	0.6989	0.5851	0.4902	0.4111	0.3450	0.2437	0.1727	0.1227	0.0875	0.0626	0.0449
37	0.6920	0.5764	0.4806	0.4011	0.3350	0.2343	0.1644	0.1158	0.0818	0.0580	0.0412
38	0.6852	0.5679	0.4712	0.3913	0.3252	0.2253	0.1566	0.1092	0.0765	0.0537	0.0378
39	0.6784	0.5595	0.4619	0.3817	0.3158	0.2166	0.1491	0.1031	0.0715	0.0497	0.0347
40	0.6717	0.5513	0.4529	0.3724	0.3066	0.2083	0.1420	0.0972	0.0668	0.0460	0.0318
41	0.6650	0.5431	0.4440	0.3633	0.2976	0.2003	0.1353	0.0917	0.0624	0.0426	0.0292
42	0.6584	0.5351	0.4353	0.3545	0.2890	0.1926	0.1288	0.0865	0.0583	0.0395	0.0268
43	0.6519	0.5272	0.4268	0.3458	0.2805	0.1852	0.1227	0.0816	0.0545	0.0365	0.0246
44	0.6454	0.5194	0.4184	0.3374	0.2724	0.1780	0.1169	0.0770	0.0509	0.0338	0.0226
45	0.6391	0.5117	0.4102	0.3292	0.2644	0.1712	0.1113	0.0727	0.0476	0.0313	0.0207
46	0.6327	0.5042	0.4022	0.3211	0.2567	0.1646	0.1060	0.0685	0.0445	0.0290	0.0190
47	0.6265	0.4967	0.3943	0.3133	0.2493	0.1583	0.1009	0.0647	0.0416	0.0269	0.0174
48	0.6203	0.4894	0.3865	0.3057	0.2420	0.1522	0.0961	0.0610	0.0389	0.0249	0.0160
49	0.6141	0.4821	0.3790	0.2982	0.2350	0.1463	0.0916	0.0575	0.0363	0.0230	0.0147
50	0.6080	0.4750	0.3715	0.2909	0.2281	0.1407	0.0872	0.0543	0.0339	0.0213	0.0134

10.0%	11.0%	12.0%	13.0%	14.0%	15.0%	16.0%	17.0%	18.0%	19.0%	20.0%	Periods
0.9091	0.9009	0.8929	0.8850	0.8772	0.8696	0.8621	0.8547	0.8475	0.8403	0.8333	1
0.8264	0.8116	0.7972	0.7831	0.7695	0.7561	0.7432	0.7305	0.7182	0.7062	0.6944	2
0.7513	0.7312	0.7118	0.6931	0.6750	0.6575	0.6407	0.6244	0.6086	0.5934	0.5787	3
0.6830	0.6587	0.6355	0.6133	0.5921	0.5718	0.5523	0.5337	0.5158	0.4987	0.4823	4
0.6209	0.5935	0.5674	0.5428	0.5194	0.4972	0.4761	0.4561	0.4371	0.4190	0.4019	5
0.5645	0.5346	0.5066	0.4803	0.4556	0.4323	0.4104	0.3898	0.3704	0.3521	0.3349	6
0.5132	0.4817	0.4523	0.4251	0.3996	0.3759	0.3538	0.3332	0.3139	0.2959	0.2791	7
0.4665	0.4339	0.4039	0.3762	0.3506	0.3269	0.3050	0.2848	0.2660	0.2487	0.2326	8
0.4241	0.3909	0.3606	0.3329	0.3075	0.2843	0.2630	0.2434	0.2255	0.2090	0.1938	9
0.3855	0.3522	0.3220	0.2946	0.2697	0.2472	0.2267	0.2080	0.1911	0.1756	0.1615	10
0.3505	0.3173	0.2875	0.2607	0.2366	0.2149	0.1954	0.1778	0.1619	0.1476	0.1346	11
0.3186	0.2858	0.2567	0.2307	0.2076	0.1869	0.1685	0.1520	0.1372	0.1240	0.1122	12
0.2897	0.2575	0.2292	0.2042	0.1821	0.1625	0.1452	0.1299	0.1163	0.1042	0.0935	13
0.2633	0.2320	0.2046	0.1807	0.1597	0.1413	0.1252	0.1110	0.0985	0.0876	0.0779	14
0.2394	0.2090	0.1827	0.1599	0.1401	0.1229	0.1079	0.0949	0.0835	0.0736	0.0649	15
0.2176	0.1883	0.1631	0.1415	0.1229	0.1069	0.0930	0.0811	0.0708	0.0618	0.0541	16
0.1978	0.1696	0.1456	0.1252	0.1078	0.0929	0.0802	0.0693	0.0600	0.0520	0.0451	17
0.1799	0.1528	0.1300	0.1108	0.0946	0.0808	0.0691	0.0592	0.0508	0.0437	0.0376	18
0.1635	0.1377	0.1161	0.0981	0.0829	0.0703	0.0596	0.0506	0.0431	0.0367	0.0313	19
0.1486	0.1240	0.1037	0.0868	0.0728	0.0611	0.0514	0.0433	0.0365	0.0308	0.0261	20
0.1351	0.1117	0.0926	0.0768	0.0638	0.0531	0.0443	0.0370	0.0309	0.0259	0.0217	21
0.1228	0.1007	0.0826	0.0680	0.0560	0.0462	0.0382	0.0316	0.0262	0.0218	0.0181	22
0.1117	0.0907	0.0738	0.0601	0.0491	0.0402	0.0329	0.0270	0.0222	0.0183	0.0151	23
0.1015	0.0817	0.0659	0.0532	0.0431	0.0349	0.0284	0.0231	0.0188	0.0154	0.0126	24
0.0923	0.0736	0.0588	0.0471	0.0378	0.0304	0.0245	0.0197	0.0160	0.0129	0.0105	25
0.0839	0.0663	0.0525	0.0417	0.0331	0.0264	0.0211	0.0169	0.0135	0.0109	0.0087	26
0.0763	0.0597	0.0469	0.0369	0.0291	0.0230	0.0182	0.0144	0.0115	0.0091	0.0073	27
0.0693	0.0538	0.0419	0.0326	0.0255	0.0200	0.0157	0.0123	0.0097	0.0077	0.0061	28
0.0630	0.0485	0.0374	0.0289	0.0224	0.0174	0.0135	0.0105	0.0082	0.0064	0.0051	29
0.0573	0.0437	0.0334	0.0256	0.0196	0.0151	0.0116	0.0090	0.0070	0.0054	0.0042	30
0.0521	0.0394	0.0298	0.0226	0.0172	0.0131	0.0100	0.0077	0.0059	0.0046	0.0035	31
0.0474	0.0355	0.0266	0.0200	0.0151	0.0114	0.0087	0.0066	0.0050	0.0038	0.0029	32
0.0431	0.0319	0.0238	0.0177	0.0132	0.0099	0.0075	0.0056	0.0042	0.0032	0.0024	33
0.0391	0.0288	0.0212	0.0157	0.0116	0.0086	0.0064	0.0048	0.0036	0.0027	0.0020	34
0.0356	0.0259	0.0189	0.0139	0.0102	0.0075	0.0055	0.0041	0.0030	0.0023	0.0017	35
0.0323	0.0234	0.0169	0.0123	0.0089	0.0065	0.0048	0.0035	0.0026	0.0019	0.0014	36
0.0294	0.0210	0.0151	0.0109	0.0078	0.0057	0.0041	0.0030	0.0022	0.0016	0.0012	37
0.0267	0.0190	0.0135	0.0096	0.0069	0.0049	0.0036	0.0026	0.0019	0.0013	0.0010	38
0.0243	0.0171	0.0120	0.0085	0.0060	0.0043	0.0031	0.0022	0.0016	0.0011	0.0008	39
0.0221	0.0154	0.0107	0.0075	0.0053	0.0037	0.0026	0.0019	0.0013	0.0010	0.0007	40
0.0201	0.0139	0.0096	0.0067	0.0046	0.0032	0.0023	0.0016	0.0011	0.0008	0.0006	41
0.0183	0.0125	0.0086	0.0059	0.0041	0.0028	0.0020	0.0014	0.0010	0.0007	0.0005	42
0.0166	0.0112	0.0076	0.0052	0.0036	0.0025	0.0017	0.0012	0.0008	0.0006	0.0004	43
0.0151	0.0101	0.0068	0.0046	0.0031	0.0021	0.0015	0.0010	0.0007	0.0005	0.0003	44
0.0137	0.0091	0.0061	0.0041	0.0027	0.0019	0.0013	0.0009	0.0006	0.0004	0.0003	45
0.0125	0.0082	0.0054	0.0036	0.0024	0.0016	0.0011	0.0007	0.0005	0.0003	0.0002	46
0.0113	0.0074	0.0049	0.0032	0.0021	0.0014	0.0009	0.0006	0.0004	0.0003	0.0002	47
0.0103	0.0067	0.0043	0.0028	0.0019	0.0012	0.0008	0.0005	0.0004	0.0002	0.0002	48
0.0094	0.0060	0.0039	0.0025	0.0016	0.0011	0.0007	0.0005	0.0003	0.0002	0.0001	49
0.0085	0.0054	0.0035	0.0022	0.0014	0.0009	0.0006	0.0004	0.0003	0.0002	0.0001	50

TABLE 3 — Future Amount of an Ordinary Annuity of $1

Payments	1.0%	1.5%	2.0%	2.5%	3.0%	4.0%	5.0%	6.0%	7.0%	8.0%	9.0%
1	1.0000	1.0000	1.0000	1.0000	1.0000	1.0000	1.0000	1.0000	1.0000	1.0000	1.0000
2	2.0100	2.0150	2.0200	2.0250	2.0300	2.0400	2.0500	2.0600	2.0700	2.0800	2.0900
3	3.0301	3.0452	3.0604	3.0756	3.0909	3.1216	3.1525	3.1836	3.2149	3.2464	3.2781
4	4.0604	4.0909	4.1216	4.1525	4.1836	4.2465	4.3101	4.3746	4.4399	4.5061	4.5731
5	5.1010	5.1523	5.2040	5.2563	5.3091	5.4163	5.5256	5.6371	5.7507	5.8666	5.9847
6	6.1520	6.2296	6.3081	6.3877	6.4684	6.6330	6.8019	6.9753	7.1533	7.3359	7.5233
7	7.2135	7.3230	7.4343	7.5474	7.6625	7.8983	8.1420	8.3938	8.6540	8.9228	9.2004
8	8.2857	8.4328	8.5830	8.7361	8.8923	9.2142	9.5491	9.8975	10.2598	10.6366	11.0285
9	9.3685	9.5593	9.7546	9.9545	10.1591	10.5828	11.0266	11.4913	11.9780	12.4876	13.0210
10	10.4622	10.7027	10.9497	11.2034	11.4639	12.0061	12.5779	13.1808	13.8164	14.4866	15.1929
11	11.5668	11.8633	12.1687	12.4835	12.8078	13.4864	14.2068	14.9716	15.7836	16.6455	17.5603
12	12.6825	13.0412	13.4121	13.7956	14.1920	15.0258	15.9171	16.8699	17.8885	18.9771	20.1407
13	13.8093	14.2368	14.6803	15.1404	15.6178	16.6268	17.7130	18.8821	20.1406	21.4953	22.9534
14	14.9474	15.4504	15.9739	16.5190	17.0863	18.2919	19.5986	21.0151	22.5505	24.2149	26.0192
15	16.0969	16.6821	17.2934	17.9319	18.5989	20.0236	21.5786	23.2760	25.1290	27.1521	29.3609
16	17.2579	17.9324	18.6393	19.3802	20.1569	21.8245	23.6575	25.6725	27.8881	30.3243	33.0034
17	18.4304	19.2014	20.0121	20.8647	21.7616	23.6975	25.8404	28.2129	30.8402	33.7502	36.9737
18	19.6147	20.4894	21.4123	22.3863	23.4144	25.6454	28.1324	30.9057	33.9990	37.4502	41.3013
19	20.8109	21.7967	22.8406	23.9460	25.1169	27.6712	30.5390	33.7600	37.3790	41.4463	46.0185
20	22.0190	23.1237	24.2974	25.5447	26.8704	29.7781	33.0660	36.7856	40.9955	45.7620	51.1601
21	23.2392	24.4705	25.7833	27.1833	28.6765	31.9692	35.7193	39.9927	44.8652	50.4229	56.7645
22	24.4716	25.8376	27.2990	28.8629	30.5368	34.2480	38.5052	43.3923	49.0057	55.4568	62.8733
23	25.7163	27.2251	28.8450	30.5844	32.4529	36.6179	41.4305	46.9958	53.4361	60.8933	69.5319
24	26.9735	28.6335	30.4219	32.3490	34.4265	39.0826	44.5020	50.8156	58.1767	66.7648	76.7898
25	28.2432	30.0630	32.0303	34.1578	36.4593	41.6459	47.7271	54.8645	63.2490	73.1059	84.7009
26	29.5256	31.5140	33.6709	36.0117	38.5530	44.3117	51.1135	59.1564	68.6765	79.9544	93.3240
27	30.8209	32.9867	35.3443	37.9120	40.7096	47.0842	54.6691	63.7058	74.4838	87.3508	102.7231
28	32.1291	34.4815	37.0512	39.8598	42.9309	49.9676	58.4026	68.5281	80.6977	95.3388	112.9682
29	33.4504	35.9987	38.7922	41.8563	45.2189	52.9663	62.3227	73.6398	87.3465	103.9659	124.1354
30	34.7849	37.5387	40.5681	43.9027	47.5754	56.0849	66.4388	79.0582	94.4608	113.2832	136.3075
31	36.1327	39.1018	42.3794	46.0003	50.0027	59.3283	70.7608	84.8017	102.0730	123.3459	149.5752
32	37.4941	40.6883	44.2270	48.1503	52.5028	62.7015	75.2988	90.8898	110.2182	134.2135	164.0370
33	38.8690	42.2986	46.1116	50.3540	55.0778	66.2095	80.0638	97.3432	118.9334	145.9506	179.8003
34	40.2577	43.9331	48.0338	52.6129	57.7302	69.8579	85.0670	104.1838	128.2588	158.6267	196.9823
35	41.6603	45.5921	49.9945	54.9282	60.4621	73.6522	90.3203	111.4348	138.2369	172.3168	215.7108
36	43.0769	47.2760	51.9944	57.3014	63.2759	77.5983	95.8363	119.1209	148.9135	187.1021	236.1247
37	44.5076	48.9851	54.0343	59.7339	66.1742	81.7022	101.6281	127.2681	160.3374	203.0703	258.3759
38	45.9527	50.7199	56.1149	62.2273	69.1594	85.9703	107.7095	135.9042	172.5610	220.3159	282.6298
39	47.4123	52.4807	58.2372	64.7830	72.2342	90.4091	114.0950	145.0585	185.6403	238.9412	309.0665
40	48.8864	54.2679	60.4020	67.4026	75.4013	95.0255	120.7998	154.7620	199.6351	259.0565	337.8824
41	50.3752	56.0819	62.6100	70.0876	78.6633	99.8265	127.8398	165.0477	214.6096	280.7810	369.2919
42	51.8790	57.9231	64.8622	72.8398	82.0232	104.8196	135.2318	175.9505	230.6322	304.2435	403.5281
43	53.3978	59.7920	67.1595	75.6608	85.4839	110.0124	142.9933	187.5076	247.7765	329.5830	440.8457
44	54.9318	61.6889	69.5027	78.5523	89.0484	115.4129	151.1430	199.7580	266.1209	356.9496	481.5218
45	56.4811	63.6142	71.8927	81.5161	92.7199	121.0294	159.7002	212.7435	285.7493	386.5056	525.8587
46	58.0459	65.5684	74.3306	84.5540	96.5015	126.8706	168.6852	226.5081	306.7518	418.4261	574.1860
47	59.6263	67.5519	76.8172	87.6679	100.3965	132.9454	178.1194	241.0986	329.2244	452.9002	626.8628
48	61.2226	69.5652	79.3535	90.8596	104.4084	139.2632	188.0254	256.5645	353.2701	490.1322	684.2804
49	62.8348	71.6087	81.9406	94.1311	108.5406	145.8337	198.4267	272.9584	378.9990	530.3427	746.8656
50	64.4632	73.6828	84.5794	97.4843	112.7969	152.6671	209.3480	290.3359	406.5289	573.7702	815.0836

10.0%	11.0%	12.0%	13.0%	14.0%	15.0%	16.0%	17.0%	18.0%	19.0%	20.0%	Payments
1.0000	1.0000	1.0000	1.0000	1.0000	1.0000	1.0000	1.0000	1.0000	1.0000	1.0000	1
2.1000	2.1100	2.1200	2.1300	2.1400	2.1500	2.1600	2.1700	2.1800	2.1900	2.2000	2
3.3100	3.3421	3.3744	3.4069	3.4396	3.4725	3.5056	3.5389	3.5724	3.6061	3.6400	3
4.6410	4.7097	4.7793	4.8498	4.9211	4.9934	5.0665	5.1405	5.2154	5.2913	5.3680	4
6.1051	6.2278	6.3528	6.4803	6.6101	6.7424	6.8771	7.0144	7.1542	7.2966	7.4416	5
7.7156	7.9129	8.1152	8.3227	8.5355	8.7537	8.9775	9.2068	9.4420	9.6830	9.9299	6
9.4872	9.7833	10.0890	10.4047	10.7305	11.0668	11.4139	11.7720	12.1415	12.5227	12.9159	7
11.4359	11.8594	12.2997	12.7573	13.2328	13.7268	14.2401	14.7733	15.3270	15.9020	16.4991	8
13.5795	14.1640	14.7757	15.4157	16.0853	16.7858	17.5185	18.2847	19.0859	19.9234	20.7989	9
15.9374	16.7220	17.5487	18.4197	19.3373	20.3037	21.3215	22.3931	23.5213	24.7089	25.9587	10
18.5312	19.5614	20.6546	21.8143	23.0445	24.3493	25.7329	27.1999	28.7551	30.4035	32.1504	11
21.3843	22.7132	24.1331	25.6502	27.2707	29.0017	30.8502	32.8239	34.9311	37.1802	39.5805	12
24.5227	26.2116	28.0291	29.9847	32.0887	34.3519	36.7862	39.4040	42.2187	45.2445	48.4966	13
27.9750	30.0949	32.3926	34.8827	37.5811	40.5047	43.6720	47.1027	50.8180	54.8409	59.1959	14
31.7725	34.4054	37.2797	40.4175	43.8424	47.5804	51.6595	56.1101	60.9653	66.2607	72.0351	15
35.9497	39.1899	42.7533	46.6717	50.9804	55.7175	60.9250	66.6488	72.9390	79.8502	87.4421	16
40.5447	44.5008	48.8837	53.7391	59.1176	65.0751	71.6730	78.9792	87.0680	96.0218	105.9306	17
45.5992	50.3959	55.7497	61.7251	68.3941	75.8364	84.1407	93.4056	103.7403	115.2659	128.1167	18
51.1591	56.9395	63.4397	70.7494	78.9692	88.2118	98.6032	110.2846	123.4135	138.1664	154.7400	19
57.2750	64.2028	72.0524	80.9468	91.0249	102.4436	115.3797	130.0329	146.6280	165.4180	186.6880	20
64.0025	72.2651	81.6987	92.4699	104.7684	118.8101	134.8405	153.1385	174.0210	197.8474	225.0256	21
71.4027	81.2143	92.5026	105.4910	120.4360	137.6316	157.4150	180.1721	206.3448	236.4385	271.0307	22
79.5430	91.1479	104.6029	120.2048	138.2970	159.2764	183.6014	211.8013	244.4868	282.3618	326.2369	23
88.4973	102.1742	118.1552	136.8315	158.6586	184.1678	213.9776	248.8076	289.4945	337.0105	392.4842	24
98.3471	114.4133	133.3339	155.6196	181.8708	212.7930	249.2140	292.1049	342.6035	402.0425	471.9811	25
109.1818	127.9988	150.3339	176.8501	208.3327	245.7120	290.0883	342.7627	405.2721	479.4306	567.3773	26
121.0999	143.0786	169.3740	200.8406	238.4993	283.5688	337.5024	402.0323	479.2211	571.5224	681.8528	27
134.2099	159.8173	190.6989	227.9499	272.8892	327.1041	392.5028	471.3778	566.4809	681.1116	819.2233	28
148.6309	178.3972	214.5828	258.5834	312.0937	377.1697	456.3032	552.5121	669.4475	811.5228	984.0680	29
164.4940	199.0209	241.3327	293.1992	356.7868	434.7451	530.3117	647.4391	790.9480	966.7122	1181.8816	30
181.9434	221.9132	271.2926	332.3151	407.7370	500.9569	616.1616	758.5038	934.3186	1151.3875	1419.2579	31
201.1378	247.3236	304.8477	376.5161	465.8202	577.1005	715.7475	888.4494	1103.4960	1371.1511	1704.1095	32
222.2515	275.5292	342.4294	426.4632	532.0350	664.6655	831.2671	1040.4858	1303.1253	1632.6698	2045.9314	33
245.4767	306.8374	384.5210	482.9034	607.5199	765.3654	965.2698	1218.3684	1538.6878	1943.8771	2456.1176	34
271.0244	341.5896	431.6635	546.6808	693.5727	881.1702	1120.7130	1426.4910	1816.6516	2314.2137	2948.3411	35
299.1268	380.1644	484.4631	618.7493	791.6729	1014.3457	1301.0270	1669.9945	2144.6489	2754.9143	3539.0094	36
330.0395	422.9825	543.5987	700.1867	903.5071	1167.4975	1510.1914	1954.8936	2531.6857	3279.3481	4247.8112	37
364.0434	470.5106	609.8305	792.2110	1030.9981	1343.6222	1752.8220	2288.2255	2988.3891	3903.4242	5098.3735	38
401.4478	523.2667	684.0102	896.1984	1176.3378	1546.1655	2034.2735	2678.2238	3527.2992	4646.0748	6119.0482	39
442.5926	581.8261	767.0914	1013.7042	1342.0251	1779.0903	2360.7572	3134.5218	4163.2130	5529.8290	7343.8578	40
487.8518	646.8269	860.1424	1146.4858	1530.9086	2046.9539	2739.4784	3668.3906	4913.5914	6581.4965	8813.6294	41
537.6370	718.9779	964.3595	1296.5289	1746.2358	2354.9969	3178.7949	4293.0169	5799.0378	7832.9808	10577.3553	42
592.4007	799.0655	1081.0826	1466.0777	1991.7088	2709.2465	3688.4021	5023.8298	6843.8646	9322.2472	12693.8263	43
652.6408	887.9627	1211.8125	1657.6678	2271.5481	3116.6334	4279.5465	5878.8809	8076.7603	11094.4741	15233.5916	44
718.9048	986.6386	1358.2300	1874.1646	2590.5648	3585.1285	4965.2739	6879.2907	9531.5771	13203.4242	18281.3099	45
791.7953	1096.1688	1522.2176	2118.8060	2954.2439	4123.8977	5760.7177	8049.7701	11248.2610	15713.0748	21938.5719	46
871.9749	1217.7474	1705.8838	2395.2508	3368.8380	4743.4824	6683.4326	9419.2310	13273.9480	18699.5590	26327.2863	47
960.1723	1352.6996	1911.5898	2707.6334	3841.4753	5456.0047	7753.7818	11021.5002	15664.2586	22253.4753	31593.7436	48
1057.1896	1502.4965	2141.9806	3060.6258	4380.2819	6275.4055	8995.3869	12896.1553	18484.8251	26482.6356	37913.4923	49
1163.9085	1668.7712	2400.0182	3459.5071	4994.5213	7217.7163	10435.6488	15089.5017	21813.0937	31515.3363	45497.1908	50

| TABLE | 4 | Present Value of an Ordinary Annuity of $1 |

Payments	1.0%	1.5%	2.0%	2.5%	3.0%	4.0%	5.0%	6.0%	7.0%	8.0%	9.0%
1	0.9901	0.9852	0.9804	0.9756	0.9709	0.9615	0.9524	0.9434	0.9346	0.9259	0.9174
2	1.9704	1.9559	1.9416	1.9274	1.9135	1.8861	1.8594	1.8334	1.8080	1.7833	1.7591
3	2.9410	2.9122	2.8839	2.8560	2.8286	2.7751	2.7232	2.6730	2.6243	2.5771	2.5313
4	3.9020	3.8544	3.8077	3.7620	3.7171	3.6299	3.5460	3.4651	3.3872	3.3121	3.2397
5	4.8534	4.7826	4.7135	4.6458	4.5797	4.4518	4.3295	4.2124	4.1002	3.9927	3.8897
6	5.7955	5.6972	5.6014	5.5081	5.4172	5.2421	5.0757	4.9173	4.7665	4.6229	4.4859
7	6.7282	6.5982	6.4720	6.3494	6.2303	6.0021	5.7864	5.5824	5.3893	5.2064	5.0330
8	7.6517	7.4859	7.3255	7.1701	7.0197	6.7327	6.4632	6.2098	5.9713	5.7466	5.5348
9	8.5660	8.3605	8.1622	7.9709	7.7861	7.4353	7.1078	6.8017	6.5152	6.2469	5.9952
10	9.4713	9.2222	8.9826	8.7521	8.5302	8.1109	7.7217	7.3601	7.0236	6.7101	6.4177
11	10.3676	10.0711	9.7868	9.5142	9.2526	8.7605	8.3064	7.8869	7.4987	7.1390	6.8052
12	11.2551	10.9075	10.5753	10.2578	9.9540	9.3851	8.8633	8.3838	7.9427	7.5361	7.1607
13	12.1337	11.7315	11.3484	10.9832	10.6350	9.9856	9.3936	8.8527	8.3577	7.9038	7.4869
14	13.0037	12.5434	12.1062	11.6909	11.2961	10.5631	9.8986	9.2950	8.7455	8.2442	7.7862
15	13.8651	13.3432	12.8493	12.3814	11.9379	11.1184	10.3797	9.7122	9.1079	8.5595	8.0607
16	14.7179	14.1313	13.5777	13.0550	12.5611	11.6523	10.8378	10.1059	9.4466	8.8514	8.3126
17	15.5623	14.9076	14.2919	13.7122	13.1661	12.1657	11.2741	10.4773	9.7632	9.1216	8.5436
18	16.3983	15.6726	14.9920	14.3534	13.7535	12.6593	11.6896	10.8276	10.0591	9.3719	8.7556
19	17.2260	16.4262	15.6785	14.9789	14.3238	13.1339	12.0853	11.1581	10.3356	9.6036	8.9501
20	18.0456	17.1686	16.3514	15.5892	14.8775	13.5903	12.4622	11.4699	10.5940	9.8181	9.1285
21	18.8570	17.9001	17.0112	16.1845	15.4150	14.0292	12.8212	11.7641	10.8355	10.0168	9.2922
22	19.6604	18.6208	17.6580	16.7654	15.9369	14.4511	13.1630	12.0416	11.0612	10.2007	9.4424
23	20.4558	19.3309	18.2922	17.3321	16.4436	14.8568	13.4886	12.3034	11.2722	10.3711	9.5802
24	21.2434	20.0304	18.9139	17.8850	16.9355	15.2470	13.7986	12.5504	11.4693	10.5288	9.7066
25	22.0232	20.7196	19.5235	18.4244	17.4131	15.6221	14.0939	12.7834	11.6536	10.6748	9.8226
26	22.7952	21.3986	20.1210	18.9506	17.8768	15.9828	14.3752	13.0032	11.8258	10.8100	9.9290
27	23.5596	22.0676	20.7069	19.4640	18.3270	16.3296	14.6430	13.2105	11.9867	10.9352	10.0266
28	24.3164	22.7267	21.2813	19.9649	18.7641	16.6631	14.8981	13.4062	12.1371	11.0511	10.1161
29	25.0658	23.3761	21.8444	20.4535	19.1885	16.9837	15.1411	13.5907	12.2777	11.1584	10.1983
30	25.8077	24.0158	22.3965	20.9303	19.6004	17.2920	15.3725	13.7648	12.4090	11.2578	10.2737
31	26.5423	24.6461	22.9377	21.3954	20.0004	17.5885	15.5928	13.9291	12.5318	11.3498	10.3428
32	27.2696	25.2671	23.4683	21.8492	20.3888	17.8736	15.8027	14.0840	12.6466	11.4350	10.4062
33	27.9897	25.8790	23.9886	22.2919	20.7658	18.1476	16.0025	14.2302	12.7538	11.5139	10.4644
34	28.7027	26.4817	24.4986	22.7238	21.1318	18.4112	16.1929	14.3681	12.8540	11.5869	10.5178
35	29.4086	27.0756	24.9986	23.1452	21.4872	18.6646	16.3742	14.4982	12.9477	11.6546	10.5668
36	30.1075	27.6607	25.4888	23.5563	21.8323	18.9083	16.5469	14.6210	13.0352	11.7172	10.6118
37	30.7995	28.2371	25.9695	23.9573	22.1672	19.1426	16.7113	14.7368	13.1170	11.7752	10.6530
38	31.4847	28.8051	26.4406	24.3486	22.4925	19.3679	16.8679	14.8460	13.1935	11.8289	10.6908
39	32.1630	29.3646	26.9026	24.7303	22.8082	19.5845	17.0170	14.9491	13.2649	11.8786	10.7255
40	32.8347	29.9158	27.3555	25.1028	23.1148	19.7928	17.1591	15.0463	13.3317	11.9246	10.7574
41	33.4997	30.4590	27.7995	25.4661	23.4124	19.9931	17.2994	15.1380	13.3941	11.9672	10.7866
42	34.1581	30.9941	28.2348	25.8206	23.7014	20.1856	17.4232	15.2245	13.4524	12.0067	10.8134
43	34.8100	31.5212	28.6616	26.1664	23.9819	20.3708	17.5459	15.3062	13.5070	12.0432	10.8380
44	35.4555	32.0406	29.0800	26.5038	24.2543	20.5488	17.6628	15.3832	13.5579	12.0771	10.8605
45	36.0945	32.5523	29.4902	26.8330	24.5187	20.7200	17.7741	15.4558	13.6055	12.1084	10.8812
46	36.7272	33.0565	29.8923	27.1542	24.7754	20.8847	17.8801	15.5244	13.6500	12.1374	10.9002
47	37.3537	33.5532	30.2866	27.4675	25.0247	21.0429	17.9810	15.5890	13.6916	12.1643	10.9176
48	37.9740	34.0426	30.6731	27.7732	25.2667	21.1951	18.0772	15.6500	13.7305	12.1891	10.9336
49	38.5881	34.5247	31.0521	28.0714	25.5017	21.3415	18.1687	15.7076	13.7668	12.2122	10.9482
50	39.1961	34.9997	31.4236	28.3623	25.7298	21.4822	18.2559	15.7619	13.8007	12.2335	10.9617

10.0%	11.0%	12.0%	13.0%	14.0%	15.0%	16.0%	17.0%	18.0%	19.0%	20.0%	Payments
0.9091	0.9009	0.8929	0.8850	0.8772	0.8696	0.8621	0.8547	0.8475	0.8403	0.8333	1
1.7355	1.7125	1.6901	1.6681	1.6467	1.6257	1.6052	1.5852	1.5656	1.5465	1.5278	2
2.4869	2.4437	2.4018	2.3612	2.3216	2.2832	2.2459	2.2096	2.1743	2.1399	2.1065	3
3.1699	3.1024	3.0373	2.9745	2.9137	2.8550	2.7982	2.7432	2.6901	2.6386	2.5887	4
3.7908	3.6959	3.6048	3.5172	3.4331	3.3522	3.2743	3.1993	3.1272	3.0576	2.9906	5
4.3553	4.2305	4.1114	3.9975	3.8887	3.7845	3.6847	3.5892	3.4976	3.4098	3.3255	6
4.8684	4.7122	4.5638	4.4226	4.2883	4.1604	4.0386	3.9224	3.8115	3.7057	3.6046	7
5.3349	5.1461	4.9676	4.7988	4.6389	4.4873	4.3436	4.2072	4.0776	3.9544	3.8372	8
5.7590	5.5370	5.3282	5.1317	4.9464	4.7716	4.6065	4.4506	4.3030	4.1633	4.0310	9
6.1446	5.8892	5.6502	5.4262	5.2161	5.0188	4.8332	4.6586	4.4941	4.3389	4.1925	10
6.4951	6.2065	5.9377	5.6869	5.4527	5.2337	5.0286	4.8364	4.6560	4.4865	4.3271	11
6.8137	6.4924	6.1944	5.9176	5.6603	5.4206	5.1971	4.9884	4.7932	4.6105	4.4392	12
7.1034	6.7499	6.4235	6.1218	5.8424	5.5831	5.3423	5.1183	4.9095	4.7147	4.5327	13
7.3667	6.9819	6.6282	6.3025	6.0021	5.7245	5.4675	5.2293	5.0081	4.8023	4.6106	14
7.6061	7.1909	6.8109	6.4624	6.1422	5.8474	5.5755	5.3242	5.0916	4.8759	4.6755	15
7.8237	7.3792	6.9740	6.6039	6.2651	5.9542	5.6685	5.4053	5.1624	4.9377	4.7296	16
8.0216	7.5488	7.1196	6.7291	6.3729	6.0472	5.7487	5.4746	5.2223	4.9897	4.7746	17
8.2014	7.7016	7.2497	6.8399	6.4674	6.1280	5.8178	5.5339	5.2732	5.0333	4.8122	18
8.3649	7.8393	7.3658	6.9380	6.5504	6.1982	5.8775	5.5845	5.3162	5.0700	4.8435	19
8.5136	7.9633	7.4694	7.0248	6.6231	6.2593	5.9288	5.6278	5.3527	5.1009	4.8696	20
8.6487	8.0751	7.5620	7.1016	6.6870	6.3125	5.9731	5.6648	5.3837	5.1268	4.8913	21
8.7715	8.1757	7.6446	7.1695	6.7429	6.3587	6.0113	5.6964	5.4099	5.1486	4.9094	22
8.8832	8.2664	7.7184	7.2297	6.7921	6.3988	6.0442	5.7234	5.4321	5.1668	4.9245	23
8.9847	8.3481	7.7843	7.2829	6.8351	6.4338	6.0726	5.7465	5.4509	5.1822	4.9371	24
9.0770	8.4217	7.8431	7.3300	6.8729	6.4641	6.0971	5.7662	5.4669	5.1951	4.9476	25
9.1609	8.4881	7.8957	7.3717	6.9061	6.4906	6.1182	5.7831	5.4804	5.2060	4.9563	26
9.2372	8.5478	7.9426	7.4086	6.9352	6.5135	6.1364	5.7975	5.4919	5.2151	4.9636	27
9.3066	8.6016	7.9844	7.4412	6.9607	6.5335	6.1520	5.8099	5.5016	5.2228	4.9697	28
9.3696	8.6501	8.0218	7.4701	6.9830	6.5509	6.1656	5.8204	5.5098	5.2292	4.9747	29
9.4269	8.6938	8.0552	7.4957	7.0027	6.5660	6.1772	5.8294	5.5168	5.2347	4.9789	30
9.4790	8.7331	8.0850	7.5183	7.0199	6.5791	6.1872	5.8371	5.5227	5.2392	4.9824	31
9.5264	8.7686	8.1116	7.5383	7.0350	6.5905	6.1959	5.8437	5.5277	5.2430	4.9854	32
9.5694	8.8005	8.1354	7.5560	7.0482	6.6005	6.2034	5.8493	5.5320	5.2462	4.9878	33
9.6086	8.8293	8.1566	7.5717	7.0599	6.6091	6.2098	5.8541	5.5356	5.2489	4.9898	34
9.6442	8.8552	8.1755	7.5856	7.0700	6.6166	6.2153	5.8582	5.5386	5.2512	4.9915	35
9.6765	8.8786	8.1924	7.5979	7.0790	6.6231	6.2201	5.8617	5.5412	5.2531	4.9929	36
9.7059	8.8996	8.2075	7.6087	7.0868	6.6288	6.2242	5.8647	5.5434	5.2547	4.9941	37
9.7327	8.9186	8.2210	7.6183	7.0937	6.6338	6.2278	5.8673	5.5452	5.2561	4.9951	38
9.7570	8.9357	8.2330	7.6268	7.0997	6.6380	6.2309	5.8695	5.5468	5.2572	4.9959	39
9.7791	8.9511	8.2438	7.6344	7.1050	6.6418	6.2335	5.8713	5.5482	5.2582	4.9966	40
9.7991	8.9649	8.2534	7.6410	7.1097	6.6450	6.2358	5.8729	5.5493	5.2590	4.9972	41
9.8174	8.9774	8.2619	7.6469	7.1138	6.6478	6.2377	5.8743	5.5502	5.2596	4.9976	42
9.8340	8.9886	8.2696	7.6522	7.1173	6.6503	6.2394	5.8755	5.5510	5.2602	4.9980	43
9.8491	8.9988	8.2764	7.6568	7.1205	6.6524	6.2409	5.8765	5.5517	5.2607	4.9984	44
9.8628	9.0079	8.2825	7.6609	7.1232	6.6543	6.2421	5.8773	5.5523	5.2611	4.9986	45
9.8753	9.0161	8.2880	7.6645	7.1256	6.6559	6.2432	5.8781	5.5528	5.2614	4.9989	46
9.8866	9.0235	8.2928	7.6677	7.1277	6.6573	6.2442	5.8787	5.5532	5.2617	4.9991	47
9.8969	9.0302	8.2972	7.6705	7.1296	6.6585	6.2450	5.8792	5.5536	5.2619	4.9992	48
9.9063	9.0362	8.3010	7.6730	7.1312	6.6596	6.2457	5.8797	5.5539	5.2621	4.9993	49
9.9148	9.0417	8.3045	7.6752	7.1327	6.6605	6.2463	5.8801	5.5541	5.2623	4.9995	50

Answers to the Pause and Reflects

Chapter 1

p. 8 Many people think the corporation actually hindered the development of accounting because it forced standardization before accounting concepts were fully developed. On the other hand, use of the corporate form of business helped accountants recognize the need for standardized accounting principles.

p. 9 Standardization is necessary because the financial results of a company are reported to many different users who use this information for many different purposes. Since reports cannot be prepared to meet the specific needs of all the users, a general approach to reporting is necessary and, therefore, rules must be established to limit the reporting options available to businesses. However, there are times when the rules hinder a company's ability to describe its financial results, particularly in times of inflation or deflation. In addition, some relevant information is not disclosed on the financial statements, therefore, footnotes are very important to annual report readers.

p. 10 The SEC allows the accounting profession to establish GAAP because accounting professionals are the experts in accounting. The SEC is not equipped to take on this role.

p. 14 Often corporations pass on the income tax to consumers by charging higher prices for their products. To the extent they are able to do this, then consumers ultimately pay the tax. However, not all corporations are able to pass the tax on in higher prices, therefore, it is appropriate to state that corporations do pay tax in both a financial and economic sense.

Chapter 2

p. 31 Yes. An accounting event does not have to involve cash, but it must be measurable in financial terms. Since the value of the land can be determined, this is an accounting event.

p. 33 When a buyer purchases something on account, the buyer has an obligation to transfer resources in the future to the seller, a liability known as accounts payable. The seller has a right to these resources, an asset known as accounts receivable.

p. 35 The income of Disney is $38,000 ($50,000 − $12,000).

p. 41 Disney also paid back some loans and repurchased some of their common stock during the period.

p. 42 The asset was purchased at the end of the year, therefore, it was not used to generate revenues during Period #1.

p. 44 Revenues of $4,500 were not collected in cash. Wage expense of $1,000 was not paid in cash and depreciation expense does not require cash.

p. 45 The answer is provided in Exhibit 2.10.

p. 49 External parties cannot have access to the same information as management because most management accounting information is confidential. Therefore, owners monitor managers and offer compensation packages to encourage managers to act in the best interests of the stockholders.

Chapter 3

p. 66 When a car dealer buys trucks it is an operating activity because trucks are inventory to be sold to customers. If the dealer finances the acquisition on a short-term basis, it does not change the analysis. However, if the dealer finances the acquisition on a long-term basis, it is also a financing event.

p. 70 Most companies have multiple classifications. In some respects, McDonalds' is a manufacturing firm (it makes hamburgers), a merchandising firm (it sells merchandise), and a service firm (it provides fast service to its customers). A company which sells appliances with warranties is a merchandising firm and a service firm regardless of how it packages the warranty.

p. 71 Electronic transmission of documents is faster and often cheaper. However, internal control is more difficult because the paper trail does not exist. In addition, paper documentation is not subject to electronic theft.

p. 77 Events involved with paying employees require documentation. The employees usually must document the time worked, perhaps with a time card. The employer must document the time worked, the amount paid to the employee, the amounts withheld from the employee's check, and the amounts owed by the employer as payroll taxes (discussed in Chapter 8).

p. 80 Suppliers will usually ship partial orders, and bill accordingly, so that the customer does not have to wait for the order any longer than necessary.

Chapter 4

p. 107 If Wendy's thinks a particular sandwich will be offered by its competitors it would probably use penetration pricing. On the other hand, if it thinks a particular sandwich will be offered only by Wendy's, at least for awhile, it would use price skimming.

p. 110 The expected cost of rent, in total, is the same, $5,000. On a per-unit basis, at 6,525 hamburgers, the rent cost is $.766 per hamburger.

p. 110 No, because workers are paid by the hour, not by the hamburger, so the relationship between wage costs and hamburgers is not proportional.

p. 112 As activity decreases, a mixed cost decreases in total and increases per unit.

p. 117 No, because both these levels are outside the relevant range, and therefore, predictions cannot be made.

p. 121 Building depreciation will not change with changes in volume, therefore, it is a fixed cost.

p. 124 If only 365 hamburgers are sold, the loss will be $9.50 ($1.90 × 5).

p. 124 The breakeven point in units when multiplied by the selling price per unit equals the breakeven point in dollars.

p. 125 No effect. At breakeven, profit is zero, therefore, no taxes are paid.

Appendix:

p. 131 Wendy's would approach CVP in the same manner as the concession stand business. For every product, it would need to estimate the sales mix and the contribution margin. Then, Wendy's would need to determine its fixed cost component. After these estimates are made, breakeven can be determined using the weighted average contribution margin.

Chapter 5

p. 149 Standards should be set to motivate and control individuals. Whether ideal or normal standards are set depends on the environment the company is in, the product life-cycle phase it is in, and the type of employees it has.

p. 154 $\$270,000,000 \times .6 \times .98 = \$158,760,000$
$\quad\quad +270,000,000 \times .3 \quad\quad = \quad\quad 81,000,000$
$\quad\quad +280,000,000 \times .1 \quad\quad = \quad\quad \underline{28,000,000}$
$\quad\quad\quad\quad\quad\quad\quad\quad\quad\quad\quad\quad\quad\quad \$267,760,000$

p. 154 The quantity of each model of car to be sold is based on demographic analyses and last year's sales levels. Ford Motor Company's customers are Ford, Lincoln, Mercury, Jaguar, and other dealerships throughout the world. Ford would estimate its cash receipts based on the last budget period's cash collection schedules and any anticipated changes for the current period.

p. 157 Ford would not want to have any ending inventories of finished cars at the end of the budget period because the new models would be due out in the coming period. Throughout the budgeting period, Ford would probably want to maintain minimal inventories to ensure an adequate supply of cars for its dealers. Cars are produced in anticipation of demand. Since many new cars are sold early in the fall, they need to be on the dealers' lots as soon as the new model year begins, typically August. Conversion cycle planning is probably done by a number of people throughout the conversion process and in many different manufacturing plants throughout the world. The activities of all the different plants must be organized so that parts are available when needed.

p. 158 Direct materials planning is probably done by the purchasing departments of Ford in consultation with the production departments. Purchases must be planned in advance so that suppliers can be contacted and supply lines established. The direct materials in an automobile include steel, tires, engines, electronic (computer) assemblies, airbags, exhaust systems, interior items such as stereos, seats, and consoles, and convertible tops. Indirect materials for an automobile include paints, trim pieces, striping kits, carpet, screws, bolts, door locks, and many other small items.

p. 160 Since Ford is unionized, labor is fairly fixed within the budgeting period. Thus, Ford must schedule production to ensure that laborers are kept busy and overtime is kept to a minimum. Direct laborers in an automobile manufacturer would include assembly line workers who install various items as the cars move down the assembly line and painters who paint the cars. Indirect labor would include all other workers in the manufacturing facilities such as supervisors, janitors, quality control inspectors, production accountants, and those workers in charge of moving materials to where they are needed. Manufacturing overhead includes indirect materials, indirect labor, and all the other manufacturing overhead costs incurred. Other manufacturing overhead costs would include depreciation on the buildings and equipment, utilities, property taxes on the buildings and equipment, insurance on the buildings and equipment, repairs and maintenance of the buildings and equipment, and many other miscellaneous costs.

p. 160 Selling and administrative costs planning is probably done by the accounting, purchasing, selling, and administrative departments and considers last year's costs, anticipated increases, and this year's anticipated sales level. The selling and administrative costs would include advertising, salaries, utilities, warranties, transportation, building and equipment depreciation, building and equipment insurance, building and equipment property taxes, commissions, income taxes, and many other miscellaneous costs.

p. 162 Purchases from August:
$3,491,600 \times .8 \times .97$	=	2,709,482
$3,491,600 \times .2$	=	698,320
+ labor & overhead	=	178,356,280
+ selling & administrative	=	$\underline{1,230,200}$
		182,994,282

p. 168 The amount of the next order would be equal to the regular amount plus the amount of safety stock used. It does not affect the calculation of EOQ.

Chapter 6

p. 188 When employees work overtime, capacity does not change, but labor costs become relevant to the decision. Machine setup costs are relevant if the number of setups changes in which case these costs are included in the analyses.

p. 190 Opportunity costs become irrelevant if the opportunity ceases to exist. Therefore, if a decision maker takes too long to make a decision, the opportunity may disappear. When trying to determine whether additional information is needed, the decision maker must always consider the time required to gather the information.

p. 195 Other customers could have been included in the analysis. A counteroffer could have been considered. If the company could estimate what their competitors would charge for such a special order, the company could use this information to determine a counteroffer price. Information on other customers' buying habits would be useful to analyze the impact of accepting the special offer.

p. 197 There are many factors they should consider such as the effect this decision may have on other customers, the impact on employees, and quality of work done, and whether it sends a signal to the company that special "deals" can always be made.

p. 199 There are many factors they should consider such as the impact on employees, related sales, and overall market share.

p. 201 There are many factors to consider such as the impact on employees, the quality of the products made versus those bought, whether a factory will eventually have to be shut down, and whether the proposed supplier is reliable.

p. 209 There may be situations where the optimal solution is not followed because the costs which cannot be measured in linear programming are important. For example, a potential, very important customer may want the product. In this case, losing this customer has long-term consequences which are not measured by the linear programming model, and it may be in the company's best interests to satisfy the customer even though the optimal solution is not followed.

Chapter 7

p. 222 The Balance Sheet for the Boston Celtics shows a number of assets which probably have a fair market value differing significantly from the dollar amount shown. These include:
1) Program Broadcast Rights (These represent the rights to films and tapes.)
2) Property and Equipment
3) National Basketball Association Franchise
4) Network Affiliation and Other Intangible Assets (The Celtics owned a TV station at June 30, 1993.)

It is impossible to know exactly what a National Basketball Association Franchise is worth, but this question should stimulate some interesting responses.

p. 226 The account balances resulting from events (a) & (b) will be:
1) Cash = $60,000 (debit of $200,000 from (a), and credit of $140,000 from (b))
2) Land = $100,000 (debit from (b))
3) Hockey Rink = $200,000 (debit from (b))
4) Capital Stock = $200,000 (credit from (a))
5) Note Payable = $160,000 (credit from (b))

Total Assets = Liabilities + Owners' Equity, as shown below:
Total
Assets = $60,000 + $100,000 + $200,000 = $\underline{\$360,000}$
Total Liabilities
& Owners' Equity = $200,000 + $160,000 = $\underline{\$360,000}$
Total debit and credit balances are equal:
All the asset accounts have debit balances, while the Note Payable and Capital Stock accounts have credit balances. Totals for both are $360,000.

p. 228 A company which has large amounts of uncollected revenues may not be able to pay bills currently due. As companies grow, many go through periods of "tight" cash. Some are even forced to declare bankruptcy while their income statements show revenues in excess of expenses.

p. 236 The type of adjusting entries discussed in Chapter 7 will never affect the cash account. No cash receipt or disbursement should be unrecorded as of the end of a period.

Adjusting entries will always affect net income. Net income consists of revenues and expenses, which affect owners' equity, therefore, every adjusting entry will affect both the Income Statement and the Balance Sheet.

p. 238 Of those accounts shown on the Celtics' Balance Sheet, the following were probably affected by adjusting entries:

1) **Accounts Receivable** (Note: The text has not yet discussed the adjustment of doubtful accounts expense. The instructor may want to discuss it briefly at this point, or ignore it until later.)

2) **Program Broadcast Rights** - This is an intangible asset which is amortized each year. According to notes to the Celtics' financial statements, the current portion shown on the Balance Sheet is the amount to be amortized during the next twelve months.

3) **Prepaid Expenses** - This asset includes things such as Prepaid Insurance, which must be adjusted every year.

4) **Property & Equipment** - Subject to depreciation each year.

5) **National Basketball Association Franchise** - Subject to amortization each year.

6) **Network Affiliation . . . .** - Subject to amortization each year.

7) **Accrued Expenses** - This represents the liability recorded as a result of accrued expense adjustments at year-end.

8) **Deferred Compensation** - This has to be adjusted each year to record (the present value of) future payments owed to players as a result of their performance during the current year.

The following revenues and expenses may have required adjustments at year end:

1) **Ticket Sales** (There may be a required adjustment to record the portion of revenue earned from sales of "season tickets." However, because the Celtics have a year end of June 30, which is "off-season", it is probable that no adjustment is needed at year end.)

2) **All Other Revenues shown** - All revenue accounts might conceivably require an adjustment to record the portion earned, but not yet billed or collected.

3) **Amortization of Program Broadcast Rights** - This expense represents the estimated allocation relative to the Program Broadcast Rights shown on the Balance Sheet.

4) **Depreciation** - This relates to the Property and Equipment shown on the Balance Sheet.

5) **Interest Income** and **Interest Expense** - These amounts might include an accrued portion. Note that although interest does not affect the balance of Notes Receivable and Notes Payable on the Balance Sheet, there is a direct relation between these items.

6) **All Other Expenses shown** - Students may come up with other plausible suggestions for adjustments.

p. 240 Whether the Lobsters' first year was successful is a matter of judgment. They did, however, earn a profit which is a positive sign, especially in light of the fact that their year ended during the middle of their first season. Many new businesses, especially sports franchises, take several years before becoming profitable.

Cash from operations exceeded income by $33,700 ($44,000 – $10,300). To help students understand the difference between cash and accrual basis, it would be helpful to have them attempt to explain specifically what caused this difference:

Difference between cash receipts from ticket sales and revenue on income statement	$20,000
Difference between cash receipts from adv. sales and adv. sales revenue	(500)
Difference between cash paid for utilities and utilities expense	900
Difference between cash paid for interest and interest expense	12,800
Difference between cash paid for supplies and supplies expense	500
Difference between cash paid for depreciation and depreciation expense	10,000
Difference between cash paid for insurance and insurance expense	(10,000)
Total difference	$33,700

It appears the Lobsters may have some trouble paying off their loan when it matures at the end of three years. Although their cash balance increased by a hefty $94,000, most of that increase resulted from one time financing activities (including the loan itself). This should not, however, be a major cause for concern. They are generating positive cash flows from operating activities which may, in fact, grow over the next two years by the amount needed to repay the loan. If not, they should be able to refinance given the positive nature of operations. (NOTE: Some students may also point out that the loan came from Mr. Clause's father, so perhaps some deal could be worked out.)

p. 241 When revenues and expenses are closed to the Income Summary account, an excess of expenses over revenues would yield a debit balance in the Income Summary account.

To transfer the loss to the Retained Earnings account, Income Summary would be credited, and the Retained Earnings account debited.

A net loss would indicate two things:
1) Expenses exceeded revenues for the period.
2) The Owners' Equity declined as a result of operations.

Chapter 8

p. 264 It is important because they represent different types of events. Financial statement users want to know if the reduction of the firm's assets is the result of operating activities consuming the firm's assets or are caused by events not associated with the operations of the firm. This distinction between expense and loss provides this information.

p. 266 When the cost of the warranty work in subsequent periods exceeds the amount in the estimated warranty liability account, the excess is debited to the warranty expense account of the subsequent year. When the warranty period runs out and the estimated warranty liability account still has a balance, the estimated warranty liability account is debited for the remaining account balance and the warranty expense account for the current year is credited. Adjusting the current year's warranty expense account is done because this is a change in estimate and, therefore, gets prospective treatment.

p. 267 This would be impractical because many people would not send in their withholding and also because the volume and frequency of payments to the federal and state government would dramatically increase the cost of administering the program.

p. 271 This is called the Gross Method. The entries that reflect this system are described below.

Inventory	1,000	
A/P		1,000
(Terms: 2/10, n/30)		
A/P	1,000	
Inventory		20
Cash		980
(If paid within discount period)		
A/P	1,000	
Cash		1,000
(If paid after discount period)		

This method describes the discounts taken by the company. This system works when cash discounts are not available to the firm. However, if the firm has a policy of taking all cash discounts, its weakness is that the firm does not know when it failed to take advantage of a discount.

p. 278 There will be no difference between FIFO and LIFO. These cost flow assumptions only differ when the prices for an item of inventory change over an accounting period.

p. 288 When ending inventory is too small, cost of goods sold is too big, and net income too small. When ending inventory is too big, cost of goods sold is too small, and net income is too big. Therefore, ending inventory has a direct effect on net income. When the understated/overstated income is closed to retained earnings, the retained earnings account will also be understated/overstated as a result of the inventory error.

When beginning inventory is too small, cost of goods sold is too small, and net income is too big. When beginning inventory is too big, cost of goods sold is too big, and net income is too small. Therefore, beginning inventory has an inverse relationship to net income. When the overstated/understated net income is closed to retained earnings the retained earnings account will be correct. This is because the error in the prior year caused by the ending inventory is offset by the error in the beginning inventory in the current year.

After two years inventory errors wash out. That is, they will have no effect on the financial statements of the company after two years. For example, if ending inventory is too big then net income is too big but the next year the net income will be too small by the same amount as a result of the ending inventory becoming the beginning inventory. Therefore, the error, if not corrected, will correct itself in two years.

Chapter 9

p. 304 A revenue that increases owners' equity by means of an increase in assets is a revenue recorded at the same time the cash is collected, or a revenue recorded before the cash is collected.

A revenue that increases owners' equity by means of a decrease in liabilities is a revenue earned and recorded after the cash is collected.

p. 311 Some of the factors to consider are:
1) How long a period of time has the customer been taking the discount improperly?
2) Has the customer been confronted with the problem and what was the customer's response?
3) How large a customer is it? Will their business be missed if a firm stand is taken, causing them to take their business elsewhere?
4) How many other customers are following the same practice?
5) What will happen if the other customers find out about this customer's behavior?

p. 312 Technically, it is a contra-revenue because it represents sales that are not expected to be collected and, therefore, the earnings process is not complete.

p. 313 The percentage of "customer receivables owned" that J. C. Penney estimated to be uncollectible at the end of each fiscal year shown in Table 9.1 is as follows:
- 1991: 79/3,303 = 2.39%
- 1992: 69/2,918 = 2.36%
- 1993: 59/3,685 = 1.60%

The percentage is decreasing meaning that the quality of these receivables is improving. This represents a favorable development for the company, indicating the company expects to collect a larger percentage of these receivables.

p. 315 An aging analysis determines what the *year-end balance* of Allowance for Doubtful Accounts should be. Any balance in the account prior to adjustment must be taken into consideration in calculating the amount of the adjusting entry.

1) If the Allowance for Doubtful Accounts had a $500 credit balance immediately prior to adjustment, the entry to increase the account to a $3,650 credit balance would be:

Uncollectible Accounts Expense	3,150	
Allowance for Doubtful Accounts		3,150

($3,650 – $500 = $3,150)

2) If the Allowance for Doubtful Accounts had an $850 debit balance immediately prior to adjustment, the entry to increase the account to a $3,650 credit balance would be:

Uncollectible Accounts Expense	4,500	
Allowance for Doubtful Accounts		4,500

($3,650 + $850 = $4,500)

Since the year-end adjusting entry for uncollectible accounts is based on an estimate, the amount removed from this account when recording actual write-offs in the subsequent period will probably differ. Consequently, one would expect there to be a balance leftover in the account at the end of each subsequent year, prior to adjustment.

p. 317 The liability called "Advances in excess of related costs" shown on Boeing Company's 1994 balance sheet represents unearned revenue. The notes included in Boeing's 1994 Annual Report do not specify exactly what it relates to, but the copy of the note included on page 8 of the chapter gives a hint. It probably relates to long-term contracts where cash payments received from customers exceed cost associated with the project but the revenues are not yet earned because specific "performance milestones" have not been achieved yet.

Chapter 10

p. 338 It is important because the purchase of raw materials would be recorded as increases to each of the respective raw material subsidiary ledgers while the issuance of materials into production is recorded as a decrease to the respective subsidiary ledger.

p. 338 Since direct materials and direct labor can be traced to the product, it implies that these items are more expensive and management is expected to control and monitor their use.

p. 342 Square feet is appropriate because these costs relate to using the facilities but they do not vary with the number of units produced, number of production runs, or any similar cost driver. Other costs which might be included are salary of the security guard, rent, insurance, and maintenance.

p. 343 It is an appropriate cost driver because the costs are assumed to vary with the number of production runs. Every production run requires an additional machine setup and production is inspected by the batch. If every unit is inspected, then the number of units is a better cost driver for inspection costs.

p. 347 If the entry is not made at all, then cost of goods sold is understated by $41,250. However, if the entire amount of underapplied overhead was closed to cost of goods sold, it would be overstated by $48,750.

Chapter 11

p. 374 Future cash flows are affected by the amount of sales and the rate at which they are collected as well as the amount of expenses and the rate at which they are paid. Understanding cash flows in the past is the first step to predicting the future. In addition, economic information (inflation, etc.) would be useful to predict cash flows.

p. 380 When notes are discounted without recourse the discounting rate is higher because the purchasing company assumes the risk of collection, and, therefore, wants a higher discounting rate.

p. 382 If segregation of duties is not possible, it is important that the owner/manager be actively involved in the business. Also, employees must be required to take vacations so that someone else must do their jobs while they are gone.

p. 386 It takes the bank a period of time to process all the checks and deposits it receives. No, this is not an internal control weakness, these items are a normal part of business.

Chapter 12

p. 400 It might be best to fill the rush order to keep the customer happy. The company needs to monitor its inventory purchasing procedures. When the manager discusses this with the employees she/he must be careful not to place blame on any one individual or department.

p. 401 External standards are important as benchmarks to judge the company against. If no external standards are available, the company can look for improvements over time to measure the success.

p. 401 Companies may be unwilling to reveal more information than that required if they fear competitors will use the information to gain a competitive advantage.

p. 410 Maintaining the same dollar amount of inventory during periods of inflation means that the physical quantity of inventory held is becoming smaller, and, therefore cost of goods sold will be higher. Since cost of goods sold is larger, the inventory turnover ratio will be higher. This decision also has implications for future sales (inventory is smaller) and, therefore, cash inflows.

p. 411 It depends. For some businesses, a 25-day selling period is good. For others, this selling period is too long.

p. 413 No Answer: If the company's vendors are not complaining or are not charging interest then this practice might continue. However, if the vendors are complaining they might discontinue providing their goods or charge interest on the late payments.

p. 415 Since its collection period is shorter than its credit terms it might want to relax its credit policies slightly in an effort to increase sales.

Chapter 13

p. 435 If department managers are evaluated using the master budget they will be unfairly penalized for exceeding the budget when production exceeds what was expected. On the other hand, they may be unjustly rewarded if production is less than expected.

p. 436 If a wage increase (unfavorable price variance) results in increased production, it may be considered a favorable result.

p. 437 If management uses ideal standards, variances will normally be unfavorable. It is up to management to decide how large of an unfavorable variance is acceptable.

p. 438 If cheaper, inferior quality materials are purchased (favorable price variance), it may result in poor quality products which would be considered an unfavorable result.

p. 440 If inventory is at a level considered acceptable by management, a zero variance would be acceptable. However, if inventory levels are too high, a zero variance, indicating that inventory levels remained constant during the period, is not acceptable.

p. 442 If the variance is significant they would investigate by checking prices first since the prices are already recorded in the accounting records. If this did not explain the variance they would need to look further to see if waste occurred, or if the predetermined cost was incorrect.

p. 443 Since the first step to controlling overhead costs is understanding what causes them, variance analysis is very useful. It can help direct management to areas which need additional investigation.

p. 451 Yes, if the company spends so much time and money ensuring a quality product, they may not get the product to the market, or it may be so high priced that no one can afford it.

p. 452 Filing an income tax return is a value-added activity because it is required by law.

Chapter 14

p. 475 Risk-seeking investors would be willing to pay $100,000 for Investment B only if they were the only person interested in the investment or all other investors were also risk-seekers. However, because the market consists of investors with a variety of risk preferences, risk-seekers would not pay $100,000 when they could pay $63,636 and also be compensated for Investment B's expected cash flows.

p. 477 Short-term interest rates became lower than long-term interest rates because lenders considered long-term lending riskier than short-term lending. Long-term loans were considered riskier because inflation during this time period was very volatile and the inflation rate at some time during the life of a long-term loan might exceed the interest earned on the loan. Therefore, to compensate for inflation risk the interest rate for long-term loans was increased. Short-term loans had less risk than long-term loans because if inflation increased the loan would come due in a short period of time and the money could be loaned again but at a higher rate.

Chapter 15

p. 501 Corporations call their preferred stock and liquidate the preferred stockholders' interest in the corporation when this action will benefit the common stockholders of the corporation. By eliminating preferred stockholders, the common stockholders will receive the dividends normally given to preferred stockholders.

In some cases, the preferred stock is called in order to use another less expensive source of financing. For example, if a company had issued 10% preferred stock and can now issue long-term debt at 7% it may be to the firm's advantage to call the preferred stock and replace the equity financing with cheaper debt financing.

p. 502 Redeemable preferred stock is legally an equity instrument but in economic substance it is a liability because it obligates the corporation to make a cash payment, the redemption price, to the preferred stockholder at some point in the future. It is like equity in that the corporation is not legally required to pay preferred stockholders dividends and are paid after all creditors are paid in the event the corporation is liquidated. It is interesting to note that the SEC requires corporations who issue preferred stock to report it on the "Mezzanine" of the balance sheet, that is, between liabilities and owners' equity because it shares characteristics of both debt and equity.

p. 503 When a corporation purchases its own stock it liquidates the ownership interest of a stockholder. Therefore, if the corporation buys all its stock back it would have no stockholders and, therefore, the creditors would own the corporation.

p. 505 When a corporation issues a stock dividend, stockholders have more shares but no greater interest in the corporation. However, in many cases the total market value of the shares held increases. For example, if a stockholder held 100 shares of a corporation with a market price of $20 per share and the corporation declared a 10% stock dividend the stock price should drop to $18.18 per share and the total market value of all the shares should remain at $2,000 after the dividend because the assets, liabilities, and stockholders' equity has not changed as a result of the stock dividend. However, in many cases the price per share does not decrease and, therefore, the total market value of the shares held increases. For example, if the price per share did

not change after the stock dividend, the stockholder described above would have stock worth $2,200 ($20 × 110 shares).

The corporation issues stock dividends when it wants to reward stockholders without distributing cash to the stockholders. This only works when the stock market views the stock dividend as a positive event. That is, the market believes the corporation is doing well and wants to reinvest earnings to generate more profits rather than distribute it to stockholders.

p. 510 Most people would want to invest in LEVER because it generates a 21% rather than a 12% rate of return. However, LEVER investors assume greater risk than NODEBT investors because the interest on the debt must be paid even if the return on the assets is less than the interest on the debt.

p. 514 To find the face value of a noninterest-bearing note once the cash proceeds needed from the note are determined, we must find the future value of the proceeds. To determine the future value (face value) of the note we must know the maturity date of the note and the firm's market interest rate. In this case the face value is $96,630 if the noninterest-bearing note is due in 5 years and the firm's market interest rate is 10% as calculated below.

$$
\begin{array}{rcccl}
PV & \times & a_{ni} & = & FV \\
\$60,000 & \times & a_{5,10\%} & = & FV \\
\$60,000 & \times & 1.6105 & = & FV \\
& & \$96,630 & = & FV
\end{array}
$$

p. 521 Most students will say that a secured bond issue will have a lower interest rate because it specifies assets that will be sold to pay bondholders if the corporation defaults on the debt and, therefore, lower risk than a bond that is merely a promise to repay the bond. In general, however, debentures typically have lower interest rates because they usually have lower risk. Corporations that issue secured bonds do so because they are already at risk and bondholders need more than the corporation's promise to repay the debt before creditors are willing to loan the money. On the other hand, corporations that issue debentures are able to do so because they have a history of stable operating performance and good credit histories and, therefore, creditors believe there is little risk that the corporation will fail to meet its financial obligations. An exception to this is the issuance of junk bonds, which are debentures that have high interest rates.

p. 521 This is based on information in Exhibit 15.16. Kmart has five debentures and four notes that reflect the publicly financed portion of its long-term debt. It also has a mortgage note which means the note is secured by Kmart real estate.

Chapter 16

p. 540 Although the total of the cash flows are the same in Exhibit 16.5 and Exhibit 16.9, the present value of the uneven cash flows is greater because more cash was received closer to the present value date than the even cash flows.

p. 545 Cash flows from land are not shielded from taxation because land is not depreciated. Land is not depreciated because we assume that land is not used up over time.

p. 550 If the negative NPV is based on very conservative numbers, it is reasonably possible that more realistic numbers would yield a positive NPV. Unless the decision maker is a very risk-averse person it would be reasonable to accept this project. The situation is just the opposite with very optimistic projections. Unless the decision maker was a risk seeker the project would probably be rejected.

Chapter 17

p. 565 Actually public accounting firms have overtime typically during the busy audit season (January through March) and the busy tax season (mid-January through April 15th). Recently they have tried to reduce that amount of overtime to lower employee turnover because training costs are very high. Some firms hire temporary employees to do tax returns. It is harder to use part-time employees to perform audits.

p. 568 Vesting means that the employee has received an irrevocable right to receive the benefits. Even if the employee is dismissed with cause the employee has a right to receive vested benefits.

p. 572 In order to protect employees Congress passed the Employee Retirement Income Security Act (ERISA) in 1974. It establishes minimum funding, participation, and vesting requirements. It also created the Pension Benefits Guaranty Corporation (PBGC), which ensures payment of minimum benefits by defined benefit plans and administers plans that are terminated. Employees have claim to their contributions in contributory plans.

p. 580 Employees can engage in collective bargaining to settle disputes about wages, hours, job security, and other matters. It may be assisted by a neutral third-party mediator. An arbitrator resolves disputes by imposing a decision on both sides. The arbitrator's decision may be compelled by the government or be part of voluntary agreement.

Chapter 18

p. 594 The market interest rate on noncash transactions is set by the management of a company. It is a fairly subjective process but should be based on the incremental borrowing rate of the firm. That is, the interest rate that a firm would incur to borrow cash on a long-term basis at the time of the noncash transaction. However, because the firm is not actually borrowing cash at the time of the transaction, management makes an informed judgment about its incremental borrowing rate. Any interest rate that is less than two-thirds of a firm's incremental borrowing rate is considered unrealistic. In applying the 2/3 test the incremental borrowing rate is determined by an independent third party rather than management.

p. 600 The interest payable account remains the same because it is a portion of the cash interest established by the bond indenture. The amount of cash interest is the same each year and is determined by multiplying the face interest rate times the face or maturity value of the bond.

p. 600 Note 6 says the interest expense reported in 1995 is $170,886,000 and made cash interest payments of $181,000,000. This difference exists because much of ADM's long-term debt was issued at a discount as indicated in Note 4.

p. 603 ADM has eight bond issues outstanding in 1995, all of which are issued at a discount. The zero coupon bond has the largest discount. According to the financing section of the cash flow statement, ADM raised $17,626,000 from long-term debt in 1995 and paid $32,304,000 to retire long-term debt in the same year.

p. 606 Anheuser-Busch's convertible debentures have an 8 percent face rate and are due in 1996. The carrying value as of December 31, 1994, is $233,200,000. This debt is convertible into preferred stock at a price of $47.60 per share. See note 6.

p. 608 According to Note 5, ADM is leasing agricultural processing and transportation equipment. ADM has incurred $43,902,000 ($27,438,000 for agricultural processing and $16,464,000 for transportation equipment) of debt related to capital leases. Rent expense for 1992 is $113,803,000.

Chapter 19

p. 625 Profit and loss agreements are designed to equitably distribute the profits and losses of the partnership and are based on what the partners contribute to the partnership. In some limited cases this distribution will result in what appears to be an inequitable distribution. However, if all partners are aware of these potential outcomes and they feel the profit and loss agreement is fair they will accept these paradoxical outcomes. When a partner is unaware of the implications of a profit and loss agreement, problems arise.

When a partnership incurs a loss, it is possible for one partner to increase his or her partnership account. This will occur when the loss is less than the salary allowances of one or more of the partners.

p. 627 Mr. Nemazi would pay $30,000 for $20,000 interest if he felt the firm is worth more than the book value of the assets or that the firm's future earning's potential is exceptional.

Mr. Hays would sell if the firm's assets were overvalued, if he was trying to encourage a new partner who had exceptional skills to join the firm, or if he was anxious to leave the firm.

p. 629 If the fair value of the partnership assets are less than its book value and they are not revalued before the admission of a new partner, the new partner will be paying too much for her or his interest in the partnership.

p. 629 Assuming that the assets have been properly revalued, this could happen if the remaining partners are anxious to get rid of the departing partner.

Assuming that the assets have been properly revalued, this would also happen if the departing partner was anxious to get out of the partnership. When this occurs, the excess capital is divided among the remaining partners.

p. 631 Overvaluing the assets in a noncash stock transaction is called watering the stock. This overstates the value of the assets and the financial position of the firm.

A corporation creates secret reserves when it undervalues the assets in a noncash stock transaction. This understates the value of the assets and the financial position of the firm and creates a unreported buffer against the negative effects of poor corporate performance.

Both watered stock and secret reserves are not appropriate because both distort the financial position of the corporation.

p. 632 By making no entry, the benefits of tax abatements are realized in the year the taxes are not paid or when they are realized. In the year the taxes are forgiven net income is higher by the amount of the taxes not paid.

Those who argue that this future benefit should be recognized as an asset when the abatement is granted would make the following entry.

| Tax Abatement | 5,000,000 | |
| Contributed Capital | | 5,000,000 |

The consumption of the benefit over the life of the abatement would create an expense that would lower net income in the years the tax abatement was granted.

| Tax Abatement Amortization | 1,000,000 | |
| Tax Abatement | | 1,000,000 |

Currently the benefits of tax abatements are not recognized as an asset when granted but in the year when the benefit is taken.

p. 632 While Kroger's stockholders have the right to vote and, therefore, to select the management team to run the corporation they do not have an equity position financially because the firm's assets are less than the liabilities of the firm. At this point, only the creditors have a claim to Kroger's assets. However, because the firm is able to service its debt, the creditors cannot foreclose their debt and must allow the management selected by the board of directors (who are elected by the stockholders) to operate the firm.

Chapter 20

p. 654 SFAS No. 34 specifically requires the capitalization of interest costs incurred during construction of certain assets. Insurance, and other costs incurred as part of the costs of a long-term construction project are also capitalized if incurred during construction.

However, once construction is complete and the asset is placed in service, the same interest and insurance costs are revenue expenditures which are expensed as incurred. SFAS No. 34, paragraph 18, states that the capitalization period for interest ends "when the asset is substantially complete and ready for its intended use." The same would apply to other indirect costs such as insurance.

The reason for the rule is simple. Interest and insurance costs incurred during construction will provide future benefits and are therefore capital expenditures but, once the asset is in use, interest and insurance expenditures provide current benefits.

p. 655 Companies generally want to maximize depreciation deductions on their tax returns in order to minimize tax payments. Because land cannot be depreciated, companies benefit from assigning the smallest possible portion of the total purchase price to the land.

p. 657 The fact that plant assets are often reported on the balance sheet at carrying values substantially below their current fair market values causes at least two major problems:

1) It is not easy for investors and creditors to determine the real net worth of the business, especially for companies like Union Pacific where operational investments represent a majority of the dollar amount of reported assets, and many of the assets may be older.

2) It is difficult to compare the real net worth of related companies when one company may own relatively new assets with carrying values relatively close to their current fair market values, while the other may own older assets with carrying values significantly different than their current fair market values.

If businesses were required to report current fair market values for all plant assets, the values would be somewhat subjective. This fact can easily be demonstrated by asking several people to state what they think various well-known buildings might be worth.

p. 665 Fully depreciated plant assets are reported on the balance sheet with other plant assets at their carrying value (original cost less accumulated depreciation)—even if this carrying value equals zero. Companies must report them as part of an effort to fully disclose the company's financial position (including *all* plant assets owned) in accordance with GAAP.

Assets are removed from the balance sheet if and when the company disposes of them, not simply because they are fully depreciated.

p. 671 The newly acquired building will generate $100,000 of depreciation over its useful life (assuming a salvage value equal to zero), which will reduce income by a total of $100,000.

If the $700,000 gain were recorded, the new building would have been assigned a cost equal to its current fair market value of $800,000. The entry would have been:

Building (Acquired in Exchange)	$800,000	
Accumulated Depreciation—Building	$400,000	
Building (Given up in Exchange)		$500,000
Gain on Exchange		$700,000

The gain would have increased income by $700,000, but resulting depreciation over the useful life of the new asset would have been $800,000. Thus, the net effect on income would still have been a reduction of $100,000, the same as when the gain was not recorded.

Therefore, we can say that the unrecorded gain on exchanges of similar assets is recognized in the form of *reduced depreciation* over the life of that asset, and the final impact is essentially the same as if the gain had been recognized.

p. 672 Expense recognition requires the realization of the benefit that corresponds with the expense. When we recorded depreciation, we assumed we were getting current benefits from using the plant asset. However, in the case of depletion we assumed the depletion was part of the cost of producing a natural resource, and that this resource had not yet been sold (which is necessary to get any benefit from its production).

If depreciation is directly associated with the cost of manufacturing inventory (such as depreciation on a factory building and manufacturing equipment), it should be added to the cost of the inventory rather than expensed as incurred. Recall our discussion of product costs in Chapter 13.

p. 672 In both cases the answer depends on what the demand for the service is expected to be. An exclusive right is a very valuable asset, however, franchises typically are expensive to obtain.

p. 673 For a company to be able to acquire goodwill as part of the purchase of another business, the goodwill must be attached to the business or the business's product, not the prior owner of the business.

If a sole practitioner doctor sells his/her business and retires, the doctor cannot generally sell any goodwill because the goodwill cannot be separated from the individual who is retiring. When the retiring doctor leaves the practice, he/she cannot leave behind any goodwill for the benefit of the new doctor. The same is true for accountants, lawyers, and other professionals.

This point has been established over the years in a number of court cases relating to professionals who attempted to "sell" goodwill in order to take advantage of applicable tax benefits.

However, if the doctor practices as part of a clinic, or some other group practice, and the goodwill attaches to the reputation of the clinic, rather than any individual doctor, it might be possible to purchase goodwill as part of the purchase of the clinic.

p. 678 Putting a new roof on a building is generally considered a capital expenditure because it prolongs the life of the asset, thus providing future benefits extending well beyond the current accounting period.

However, an individual may argue that a new roof is a revenue expenditure on the basis that it merely maintains the building in good working order. Painting a building is not generally considered a capital expenditure, and yet the paint job often lasts 5–8 years. The primary difference between a new roof and a paint job is one of degree. A new roof is usually more expensive and lasts considerably longer than a paint job.

If the new roof is expensed, income for the current year will decrease by $100,000. However, if the roof is capitalized, income will decrease by $10,000 ($100,000/10 years). The difference is $90,000.

Chapter 21

p. 692 The benefit of making the distinction between interest income and the gain or loss on the investment does not exceed the cost of the process of determining the difference.

p. 694 The price of debt securities change primarily with the change in interest rates. The price of equity securities change with investor's expectations about the future earnings of a corporation. Expectations about a corporation's future earnings are affected by a variety of factors such as: interest rates, the health of the national economy, consumer demand for the corporation's products, quality of the corporation's management, the corporation's prior earnings performance. There are more factors that impact a firm's performance so the stock price is more volatile than bond prices.

p. 696 The Unrealized Loss or Gain recorded in conjunction with Trading Securities is a function of the changes in the market adjustment account. If the market adjustment account needs to be debited to get from its existing balance to its desired balance, an Unrealized Gain is recognized. If the market adjustment

account needs to be credited to get from its existing balance to its desired balance, an Unrealized Loss is created. The ending balance in the market adjustment account will only correspond to the unrealized gain or loss reported on the income statement when the market adjustment account has a zero balance before the adjusting entry takes place. This type of adjusting entry is called a balance sheet push because the adjusting entry is driven or pushed by the need to report a specific account balance on the balance sheet.

If the fair value of the securities was $75,600,000, the adjustment would be a credit of $5,000 because the adjustment account would have a balance of $2,000 (debit) before adjustment and it must have an ending credit balance of $3,000.

p. 697 The amortization schedule would only be the same as that of the issuing company if Genentech purchased the bonds from Chappuy when they were issued. If Genentech purchases the bonds in the secondary market after they are issued, the bonds will probably have a different effective interest rate than when the bonds were issued. As a result, the bond amortization schedule for Genentech will be different than that of the issuing company.

p. 698 There are two ways an investor can lose money on its investment in another company's bonds.

1. An investor company can lose money when it sells bonds if the price of the bond is lower than what it invested in the bonds. The price of a bond in the secondary market will decrease if the market interest rate for the bond increases. Therefore, when a bondholder intends to sell its bonds in the secondary market before the bonds mature, it is possible for the price to drop below the purchase price of the bonds and the bondholder to sell the bonds at a loss.

2. If an investor company intends to hold the bonds of another company until maturity, it can lose money on the bond if the issuing company defaults on the bond issue. That is, the company fails to pay the cash flows promised by the bond indenture.

Chapter 22

p. 720 Harley-Davidson's income statement is a multistep format because it separates cost of goods sold from selling, administrative and engineering expenses. Other information such as the earnings of various divisions of Harley-Davidson, Inc. is reported in the notes.

p. 725 Harley-Davidson's earnings per share for 1994, 1993, and 1992, respectively, were $1.37, $(.16), and $.75. Its diluted earnings per share for 1994, 1993, and 1992, respectively, were $1.37, $(.16), and $.72. Students should note that the net loss in 1993 is due to the cumulative effects of accounting changes, $(32,124,000) and $1,796,000.

p. 725 Extraordinary loss was calculated as $1,100,000/23,000,000 and cumulative effect of an accounting change was calculated as $880,000/23,000,000. Harley-Davidson indicates earnings per share on (1) income from continuing operations, (2) extraordinary item, (3) accounting changes (notice loss per share), and (4) net income (loss).

p. 726 The effect of the correcting entries would be to decrease owners' equity (retained earnings) by $16,500, decrease assets (prepaid rent) by $30,000, and increase liabilities (taxes payable) by $13,500.

p. 728 Not entirely. Although cost of goods sold is reported at a more current cost, large holding gains result from inventory held during the period which is shown on the balance sheet.

p. 732 The income from operations shown on Exhibit 22.7 matches the income from operations shown on Exhibit 22.1.

p. 734 Realized holding gains can be reliably reported because the event has already occurred. However, unrealized holding gains may be more relevant to users because they impact future earnings and cash flows.

Chapter 23

p. 749 Current assets are those that the company expects to convert to cash and that would require the outlay of cash in the upcoming year. Long-term assets are used in operations in two or more accounting periods. The purpose of classifying assets as current is to disclose which assets are available to meet current obligations. Long-term assets in the last year of their useful lives are not available to meet current obligations, so they should not be classified as current.

p. 750 These checks were taken by the company in payment for another's obligation to it. Since the checks did not liquidate the debt, the firm should record receivables instead of cash. It should record the amount of the check plus any fees that its bank assessed as a result of the NSF check. If the company believes that the receivable is uncollectible, then it is inappropriate to record it as a receivable and it does not belong on the balance sheet.

p. 754 Classifying assets as intangible means they are long-lived assets that indirectly benefit operations, while showing receivables is one of the most direct sources of cash from operations. Showing receivables is one of the most important disclosures that a company can make. The most important characteristic that most intangibles have is that they represent legal rights held exclusively by their owner, which are the source of their value. For example, a patent has economic value because it allows the owner exclusive legal rights to the patented process or procedure.

p. 758 Long-term debt represents contractual obligations between the company and its debt holders. Other long-term liabilities include pension obligations and deferred taxes. Thus, the legal obligation to make cash payments differs between the two classifications, since funding of pensions and the payments for deferred taxes are much less certain than the principal and interest payments required in a debt agreement. Making the distinction allows statement readers to better estimate the legal obligations to make payments and the risk of violating debt covenants, which may lead to bankruptcy.

p. 761 Legally corporations can issue authorized but unissued stock, or they can issue treasury stock which is issued but not outstanding. They might reacquire stock rather than issuing additional stock in order to avoid changing ownership control or further diluting the ownership of the net assets.

Chapter 24

p. 789 Cash received from customers, $824,103
Other operating cash receipts and payments, net, $9,819

p. 790

Beginning prepaid insurance	$ 1,500	
Add cash paid for insurance in advance	?	[$5,400]
Less insurance expense for the period	6,000	
Ending prepaid insurance	$ 900	
No related account, thus expense = payment	$ 8,400	
Beginning taxes payable	$ 1,300	
Add tax expense for the period	11,700	
Less cash paid for income taxes	?	[$12,150]
Ending taxes payable	$ 850	
Beginning interest payable	$ 600	
Add interest expense	1,800	
Less discount amortized	30	
Less cash paid for interest	?	[$1,920]
Ending interest payable	$ 450	

p. 790 Cash paid to suppliers and employees, $510,319
Interest paid, $42,090
Income taxes paid, $50,088
Taxes other than income taxes paid, $41,898

p. 790 Receivables increased during the period and were subtracted from net income, $(30,550) because the revenue associated with this account was greater than the related cash inflow. Fuel inventory increased during the period and was subtracted from net income, $(28,956) because the expense associated with the account was less than the associated purchase. Other working capital accounts (net) increased during the period and were subtracted from net income, $(114,436) because the expense associated with the accounts was less than the cash outflow or the revenue associated with these accounts was greater than the cash inflow.

p. 792 Depreciation—equipment and patent amortization expenses should be added to net income to determine cash flows from operations.

p. 792 When notes or bonds are issued at a premium, the cost of borrowing is less than the cash interest paid. Therefore, the interest expense of the period is less than the cash payment and the difference (premium amortization) must be subtracted from net income to determine cash flows from operations.

p. 793 Cumulative effect of a change in accounting principle $(35,415)
Chance in rate deferrals, $390,177
Depreciation, amortization, and decommissioning, $690,841
Deferred income taxes and investment credits, $31,006
Allowance for equity funds, $(9,629)

p. 793 When a noncash current operating asset decreases during the period, it means that the revenue related to the account was less than the cash inflow or that the expense associated with the account was greater than the cash outflow. Since the revenue or expense is part of net income, net income must be increased by the amount of the change to determine cash flows from operations.

p. 793 Since the inventory account increased during the period, the change in the account should be deducted from net income to determine cash flows from operations. Since the prepaid insurance account decreased during the period, the change in the account should be added to net income to determine cash flows from operations. Yes, it is appropriate because insurance expense which was subtracted to calculate net income was $6,000, while the cash paid for insurance was only $5,400.

p. 794 When a current operating liability decreases during the period, it means that the revenue related to the account was greater than the cash inflow or that the expense associated with the account was less than the cash outflow. Since the revenue or expense is part of net income, net income must be decreased by the amount of the change to determine cash flows from operations.

p. 794 Since the accounts payable account increased during the period, the change in the account should be added to net income to determine cash flows from operations. Since the interest payable, taxes payable, and wages payable accounts decreased during the period, the changes in the accounts should be subtracted from net income to determine cash flows from operations. Yes, it is appropriate because wage expense was $9,000 while the cash paid for wages was $9,600.

p. 794 Accounts payable decreased during the period and was subtracted from net income, $(19,124) because the expense associated with this account was less than the cash outflow. Taxes accrued increased during the period and were added to net income, $115,250 because the expense associated with this account was greater than the cash outflow. Interest accrued decreased during the period and was subtracted from net income $(194) because the expense associated with this account was less than the cash outflow. Reserve for rate refund decreased during the period and was subtracted from net income $(48,117) because the expense associated with this account was less than the cash outflow. Note that three other net income adjustments

Answers to the Pause and Reflects

to determine operating cash flows are reported: (1) refunds to customers, (2) decommissioning trust contributions, and (3) other.

p. 795 One reason is that the direct format requires additional disclosures which, in essence, is the indirect format. Probably more important, however, is the issue of privacy. When a company uses the indirect format, it reveals less about its actual cash flows.

p. 795 These events are separately reported because they each provide information which might be lost if they were aggregated.

Beginning accumulated depreciation	$ 30,900	
Add depreciation expense for the period	6,300	
Less decrease due to equipment sales	?	[$3,900]
Ending accumulated depreciation	$ 33,300	
Equipment sold	$?	[$10,000]
Less related accumulated		
depreciation (above)	3,900	
Less loss on sale of equipment	4,500	
Cash received from sale of equipment	$ 1,600	
Beginning equipment	$101,700	
Add purchases of equipment	?	[$12,100]
Less equipment sold (above)	10,000	
Ending equipment	$103,800	

p. 796 Southwestern Public Service Company reports two investing activities, cash used for construction expenditures, $(94,662) and cash used for nonutility property, $(28,219). Entergy Company reports construction expenditures, $(618,436) less an allowance for equity funds used, $9,629. It used cash to purchase nuclear fuel, $(207,501) and received cash from the sale/leaseback of this fuel, $226,607. It used cash to invest in nonregulated utilities, $(172,814).

p. 796 Southwestern Public Service Company issued long-term debt, $76,204, retired long-term debt, $(16,880), and decreased short-term debt, $(14,994). It also paid dividends, $(94,898). Entergy Company received cash from two sources: (1) general mortgage bonds, $109,285, and (2) bank notes, $273,542. It used cash to retire debt: first mortgage bonds, $(225,800), general mortgage bonds, $(69,200), and other debt, $(221,043). It also redeemed preferred stock, $(46,564) and paid dividends $(408,553). Finally it decreased its cash by changing its short-term borrowing $(126,200).

p. 797 Entergy reports a change in unrealized appreciation of $16,614. See also note #8 "Commitments and Contingencies," note #10 "Postretirement Benefits," and note #11 "Restructuring Costs," which may have future cash flow implications.

Chapter 25

p. 814 Preferred stock falls in between debt and stock. It is closer to one or the other depending on the characteristics of the preferred stock. For example, cumulative preferred stock is closer to debt because the firm must pay dividends just like interest payments, while convertible preferred stock would be more like being a common stockholder. The legal rights of preferred stockholders also fall in between. They cannot force the corporation into bankruptcy like debtholders nor can they vote in stockholder meetings like common stockholders.

p. 817 Companies that publish investment newsletters have expertise in interpreting disclosures that most investors do not have. In addition, they often go to companies they report on and gather information that is not part of the corporation's disclosures. They use information about the industry and the general economy as part of the evaluation also. Corporate financial disclosures are made at most quarterly and financial analysts monitor changes in a corporation's activities more often than quarterly.

p. 822 If Apple believes that it can raise capital at a lower cost by issuing stock than it can by borrowing, then it makes sense to not have long-term debt. Corporations can also avoid the risk associated with the fixed payments of debt by using equity capital.

p. 829 The risks that stockholders face principally result from potential declines in stock prices while they own the stock. Stockholders can use diversification of their investments as a way of avoiding the risk of price fluctuations of individual stocks. They still face price changes that affect the whole stock market. One measure of the risk of an individual stock's price is beta, which measures the covariation of that stock's price with the rest of the stock prices. Betas higher than one represent stocks that are more risky than the market in general.

p. 834 Dividend payment policies depend on factors like the stage of the corporation's industry and the desires of the stockholders. In growing companies management often needs its cash for investment and chooses not to pay dividends. Some stockholders invest in stocks and live on the dividends they receive, those investors prefer stocks that pay reliable dividend payments. This is a complex decision that is explored more fully in most introductory finance courses.

p. 837 From Exhibits 25.10 and 25.11

Apple	23.28/.73	=	31.89
Compaq	24.63/1.82	=	13.53
Nordstrom	35.00/1.71	=	20.47
Albertson's	26.75/1.34	=	19.96
Amgen	49.50/2.67	=	18.54
Microsoft	44.00/1.575	=	27.94
Worthington	19.75/1.06	=	18.63

Photo Credits

Index

AT&T, 12
Attitudes toward risk, 473
Auditing, 10, 18
Auditors, 817
    report in annual report, 763,
        766-68
Authority, 67-68
Authorized shares, 502, 523
Authorized signature, 73
Automation, 85, 87-88, 566
Automobiles, depreciation of, 663
Available-for-sale (AFS) securities,
    691, 696-99, 704
    on balance sheet, 702
    on financial statements, 703
    value of, 698-99
Average collection period ratio, 408,
    414-15, 421
Average selling period ratio, 408,
    410-11, 421
Avoiders of risk, 473, 475

B

Babylonia, 5-6
Backflush costing, 352, 354-56
Balance column, in general ledger,
    230
Balance sheet, 38-9, 40, 50, 745
    accounting events reflected on, 42
    assets on, 750-54
    bonds on, 600
    carrying value of bond on, 602-3
    dollar amounts on, 221
    information from classifications,
        749-50
    installment note impact on, 593
    for internal reports, 768-69
    interrelationship with other
        financial statements, 284
    investment information on, 66,
        702
    liabilities on, 754-58
    manufacturing inventories on, 349
    market adjustment account on,
        695, 696
    operational investments reported
        on, 676-77
    for partnership, 622
    preparation in accounting cycle,
        239
    problem from LIFO, 289
    pro forma, 163-64
    purchase of goods and services on,
        281
    report considerations, 317-18
    status of company short-term
        liquidity, 746
    stockholders' equity on, 638-39,
        759-60
    summary of investments on, 703
    treasury stock on, 636, 637, 639
Balance statement approach to
    estimating uncollectible
    accounts expense, 314, 322
Bank reconciliation, 383-86, 388
    internal control considerations,
        384
Banks, 6
    compensating balance
        requirement of, 750
    loans payable in cash flows
        statement, 794
    records of, 382-83
    as source of debt financing, 518
    statements from, 383, 385, 388
Barron's, 504
Barter, 7
Basic accounting principles, 221-22
Batch-related activity level, 341
    overhead costs, 442
Batch-related overhead price
    variance, 441

Batch-related overhead usage
    variance, 443
Bearer bonds, 520, 523
Before-tax profit, 125, 128
Bellsouth, 13
Benefits in management accounting,
    45-47, 50
Betterments, 665, 679
Bidding, 78
Billing
    credit customers, 79-82
    progress, 82
Bill of lading, 79, 81
Bill of materials, 84, 85, 86
Binding constraint, 207
Blue Ribbon Sports, 4
Boeing Company, 73, 303
    annual report, 316
    balance sheet, 309
    note on revenue recording
        process, 306
Bond amortization table, 599, 601
Bond certificate, 519, 523
Bondholders, covenants to protect,
    760
Bond indenture, 519, 523
Bond register, 520
Bonds, 11, 19, 519-21, 523, 596-603
    available-for-sale, 697-98
    calling feature of, 604-5
    carrying value of, 596
    converting to stock, 605-6
    early retirement of, 603-6
    impact on financial statements,
        602-3
    market rate equal to face rate,
        596-97
    market rate greater than face rate,
        598-600
    market rate less than face rate,
        600-3
    present value of cash flows, 599,
        601
    provisions, 520-21
Bonds payable, on balance sheet, 755
Bonds Payable account, 605
Bonuses, 578-79, 580
    to existing partners, by new
        partner, 627-28
    negative impact of business
        decisions on, 549
    to new partner, 628
Book value, 237, 546
    of equipment, 656-57
Book value method, of recording
    bond conversion, 605-6
Borrowed funds
    perception of return and risk on,
        477
    reasons for, 508-11
Boston Celtics, 220, 573
Bottom-up budgeting, 149
Breakeven point, 122, 128
    determining, 123-24
Brokerage fees, 694
    inclusion in asset cost, 532
Broker's commission, in debt
    securities cost, 693
BRX, Inc., balance sheet,
    stockholder's equity section,
    638-39
Budget analysis, production levels
    and, 433
Budgetary slack, 147, 165
Budget committee, 146, 165
Budget director, 146, 165
Budgeted cash flows, vs. actual,
    798-800
Budgeting, 144, 165; *see also* Capital
    budgeting
    accuracy in, 147
    benefits, 145-46
    costs of, 146-48

Budgeting—*Continued*
    labor intensive companies, 159*n*
    for sales, 151-53
    strategies for, 148-50
Budgets, 144, 165
    direct labor and manufacturing
        overhead, 159
    and individual motivation and
        behavior, 147-48
    problems from rigid adherence,
        146-47
    types, 150-51
Business, 5, 19
    basic functions, 15-16
    changes in environment, 86-88
    formula for success, 15-16
    noncorporate forms of, 619;
        see also Partnerships *and* Sole
        proprietorships
    purpose of, 11
Business activities, 63, 92
Business cycle, temporary seasonal
    overtime for, 565
Business entity concept, 7, 19, 31
Business goals, 67
    for expenditure cycle, 72
Business risk, 476, 490
Business segment information,
    in annual report, 761, 763,
    764, 765
Business transactions, phases, 68

C

CAD (computer-assisted design), 87
Callable bonds, 520, 523, 604-5
Callable preferred stock, 501, 523
Cambell Taggart, Inc., 332
CAM (computer-assisted
    manufacturing), 87
CAP (Committee on Accounting
    Procedure), 10
Capital
    accounting for contributions to
        corporation, 630-31
    cost of, 533-35
    donated, 631, 640, 760
Capital accounts, 243, 245
    balance after closing, 620
    for partners, 621, 625, 628
Capital budgeting, 532-36, 553
    cash outflows for, 541
    evaluating investments, 536
    financing investments, 535-36
    identifying long-term
        opportunities, 532-33
    illustration, 547-48
    informed speculation in, 550-52
    qualitative factors, 552
    selecting investments, 533-35
    sensitivity analysis in, 551
Capital contributions, by
    stockholders, 630
Capital expenditure budget, 535, 553
Capital expenditures, 653, 679
    errors in reporting, 678
    vs. expenses, 830
    to extend asset life, 665
Capitalize, 679
Capitalized cost, used equipment as,
    655
Capital leases, 518-19, 523
    accounting for, 606-8
    on balance sheet, 753
    impact on debt-to-equity ratio,
        607-8
Capital market, 813, 838
    information for, 816-17
    relationship to product market,
        815
    segmentation in, 816
    societal role of, 814-17
    trading in, 815-16

Capital stock
    initial issue, 507
    shares of, 499
    values, 503-5
Carrying costs, of inventory, 155, 167
Carrying value, 237, 245
Carrying value of asset, 656-57
    loss when discarding asset, 666
Carrying value of bond
    on balance sheet, 602-3
    vs. purchase price on secondary
        market, 604
Carrying value of note, 513, 523
Cartel, 105, 128
Cash
    as asset on balance sheet, 750
    investment of idle, 374-76
    need for, 373
    revenue recognition timing and
        collection, 307, 308-9
    shortage of, 376
Cash accounts, 318
    imprest, 386-87
Cash balance, 382-86
Cash-based ratios, 417
Cash budget, 162, 165
Cash disbursements; *see* Cash
    payments
Cash disbursements schedule, 150,
    161, 165
Cash discount, 161
Cash dividend, 505, 523
Cash equivalent determination
    future value of $1, 479-80
    present value of $1, 480-81
    unknown rates calculated, 482-83
    unknown time period calculated,
        482-83
Cash equivalent value, 32, 306, 478
Cash flow adequacy ratio, 417
Cash flow analysis, 535
    for internal users, 797-800
Cash flow per share, 826, 827-28,
    838
Cash flows
    budgeted vs. actual, 798-800
    effect of uneven on net present
        value, 539-40
    forecasting, 374
    and income taxes, 542-44
    present value of bond's, 599, 601
    source of, 541-42
    variances, 799-800
Cash flow statement, 39-41, 51,
    282-83, 781-801
    accounting events reflected on, 42
    bond impact on, 596-97, 600
    cash flows from investing
        activities, 795-96
    determination and analysis of
        operating cash flows, 784-95
    Financial Accounting Standards
        Board on, 800
    financing cash flows, 796-97
    GAAP and, 781-84
    interrelationship with other
        financial statements, 284
    investment information on, 702-3
    note issuance and, 593
    operating activities on, 66
    operational investments and,
        677-78
    preparation in accounting cycle,
        240
    purpose of, 781-82
    ratios from, 417
    report considerations, 318-19
    sections in, 782-84
Cash flow to sales ratio, 417
Cash inflows, 541, 783
    actual vs. budgeted, 798
    after-tax, 542-43
    vs. revenues, 787-89

Cash interest, vs. effective interest, 515
Cash management, 372-89
  internal controls, 380-87
  need for, 373-80
Cash outflows, 783
  after-tax, 543-44
  for capital budgeting, 541
  vs. expenses, 789-90
  to suppliers, actual vs. budgeted, 798
Cash payments
  controls over, 382
  as expenditures, 263
  expense recognized at time of, 264
  expense recognized before, 265
  vs. expenses, 227
  for inventory, and cost of goods sold, 283
  planning, 161-62
  "small," 386
  in statement of cash flows, 282
Cash position, evaluating, 418-20
Cash receipts
  controls over, 380-81
  planning, 153-54
Cash receipts schedule, 150, 153, 165
Cash sales, 78, 318
Cells in manufacturing facilities, 83, 92
Central operations, 305
Certificates of deposit (CDs), 375, 376, 388
Certified Internal Auditor (CIA), 18
Certified Management Accountant (CMA), 18
Certified public accountant (CPA) certificate, 18
Certified public accountants (CPA), 10, 19
CFO (chief financial officer), 17
Chart of accounts, 231, 245
Checks, reversing entry for bad, 385-86
Chief financial officer (CFO), 17, 19
Chronological record, general journal as, 229
Chrysler Motors, 73
CIA (Certified Internal Auditor), 18
CIM (computer-integrated manufacturing), 87
"Clean" opinion, 18
Closing entries, 240-42
  Dividends account to Retained earnings, 634
  for partnerships, 622
  for sole proprietorship, 620
  for sole proprietorship and partnership, 243
Closing process, 241-42, 245
CMA (Certified Management Accountant), 18
Coca-Cola, 13
Code of Hammurabi, 5
Codes of ethical conduct, 48
Collateral, 518, 523
Collecting from customers, 82
Collection variance, 799, 801
Collective bargaining, 579
Commercial paper, 378, 388
Commission basis, 577, 580
Committee on Accounting Procedure (CAP), 10
Common carriers, 79
Common stock, 37, 39, 500, 523
  bonds exchanged for, 521
  preferred stock convertible to, 502
Common Stock account, 630
Common stockholders, earnings available to, 724
Communication, in budgeting process, 145

Company best interest, decisions in, 550
Company performance, financial statement analysis to evaluate, 813-38
Compaq
  dividend policy, 834
  financial ratios, 825
  gross margin ratio, 830
Comparability of information, 718
Comparative financial statements, 818-20, 838
Comparative standards, information sources for, 823
Comparison
  actual results to flexible budget, 434-35
  actual results to master budget, 432-33
Compensating balance requirement of bank, 750, 770
Compensation
  bonuses as, 578-79
  deferred, 572-76
  impact on business decisions, 564-66
  nonmonetary, 576
  risks in future, 577-78
Compensation expense, recording for granted stock option, 574
Competition, and selling price, 103, 104
Competitive advantage, 15
Competitive trends, analysis of, 152
Compounding, 478
  calculating number of periods to accumulate future value, 482-83
  impact on future value, 481
Compound interest, 478-79, 490
  annuities and, 486
Comprehensive income, 717, 734; see also Net income
  elements of, 718
Compustat PC compact disk, 823, 825
Computer-assisted design (CAD), 87
Computer-assisted manufacturing (CAM), 87
Computer industry, 819-20
  trade publications, 818
Computer-integrated manufacturing (CIM), 87
Computerized accounting systems, 71
Computers, depreciation of, 663
Computerworld, 817
Conservatism principle, in exchange of similar assets, 668
Consistency of information, 718
  in depreciation policy, 675
Consolidated financial statements, 701, 704
Consolidated statement of income, 37, 38
Constant, from regression analysis, 115
Constraints, 203, 204, 205-6
Construction costs, accounting for, 654
Consumer demand, in capital market, 815
Contingent liabilities, 763, 770
Continuing operations, income from, 720
Contra-asset account, 237, 238, 245
  accumulated depreciation account as, 656
  Sales Returns and Allowances as, 309
Contra equity accounts
  drawing account, 620
  Treasury Stock account as, 636
Contra liability accounts, 609
  discount account as, 594
  Discount on Bonds Payable, 600

Contra-revenue account, 310, 323
  Sales Discounts as, 311
Contributed capital, 34, 50
  on balance sheet, 759-60
  in excess of par, 504
Contribution margin, 128, 398
  as approach for breakeven point calculation, 124
Contribution margin per unit, 121, 123, 128
Contribution margin ratio, 124, 128
Contributory pension plans, 570, 580
Control, budgeting for, 146
Control accounts, 335
Control of corporation, through stock ownership, 700, 701
Controller, 17, 19
Conversion cycle, 69, 82-85, 92
  activities in, 333-34
  analysis and control, 430-54
  communicating results of events, 347-51
  vs. expenditure or revenue cycles, 70
  planning, 154-57
  recording and communicating in, 332-56
Convertible bonds, 521, 523
  effect on earnings per share, 724
Convertible preferred stock, 502, 523
  effect on earnings per share, 724
Converting bonds to stock, 605-6
Coordination, in budgeting process, 145
Copyright, 238, 672, 679
Corporations, 8, 19, 629-39
  accounting for earnings, 632-36
  acquiring significant influence or control of, 700-1, 703
  changing proprietorship or partnership to, 507
  characteristics, 14
  equity events reporting, 637-39
  limited liability of owners, 499
  market value of stock as reflection of financial condition, 505
  purchase of own shares, 503
  stock types issued by, 500-2
  taxation of, 9, 13
Cost
  of capital, 533-35, 553
  of debt securities, 693
  of equity financing, 533-34
  of land, 654-55
  linking containment to bonus plan, 578
Cost accumulation, importance, 333
Cost allocations, as income statement limitation, 728
Cost-based pricing policy, 105
Cost behavior, 107-12
Cost drivers, 108, 128
  choosing, 117-19
  cost pool for, 340
  estimated amount of overhead per, 339
  estimating amount to use, 342
  for Hewlett-Packard, 446
  in high/low cost estimation, 113
Cost estimation
  comparison of methods, 116-17
  high/low method, 113-14
  linear regression analysis, 114-16
Cost flow assumptions, 273-79, 291
  comparison of, 278-79
Cost of goods manufactured, 347, 352
  report, 348-49, 352
Cost of goods sold, 35, 50, 269
  and cash paid for inventory, 283
  on income statement, 333, 349
  in multistep income statement, 316
  notes in income statement on, 720

Cost of Goods Sold account, 263, 279
Costing, full-absorption, 729-30
Cost pool, 340, 344, 352
  combining costs in, 342
  for Hewlett-Packard, 446
  overhead price variance for, 441
Costs, 45-47, 50
  in cost-volume-profit analysis, 120
  fixed, 109
  of investigating variances, 447-48
  mixed, 110-12
  variable, 110
Cost-volume-profit (CVP) analysis, 119-27, 128
  assumptions of, 119-20
  graphical approach, 122-23
  mathematical approach, 123-25
  multiple-product, 129-31
  sensitivity analysis, 126-27
Coupon bonds, 520
Covenants, 511, 519, 523, 813
  to protect bondholders, 760
CPA (certified public accountants), 10
Credit, 6, 223, 245
  customer approval, 78-79
  debit/credit rules, 224-28
  entries in journal, 229
Credit card, use as cash sale, 78
Credit customers, billing, 79-82
Credit decisions, 413-15
Creditors
  information needs, 26, 28, 813, 816-17
  investment decisionmaking by, 814
  stockholders' equity retained to protect, 503-4
Credit policy, 311
Credit sales, 78, 318
  controlling cash from, 381
Crunching numbers, 16
Cumulative accounting adjustments, 722-23, 734
Cumulative preferred stock, 501, 523
Currency, 7
Current assets, 32, 51, 469, 746, 7 50-52
  on balance sheet, 281
  comparing company with industry, 821
Current cost income report, 731, 732-33, 734
Current cost net income, vs. realized income, 733
Current liabilities, 33, 51, 511, 746
  adjustments for changes in, 793-94
  on balance sheet, 754-55
  comparing company with industry, 822
  note payable as, 596
Current operating liabilities, 793, 801
Current ratio, 408, 418-19, 421, 756, 826, 827
  classification of current items and, 749
  and collection period length, 415
Current replacement cost, for balance sheet internal users, 768-69
Customer-focused operations, 87
Customer ill will, 449
  optimal defect level with, 450
  risk of, 196
Customer orders, generating, 78
Customers, 156
  collecting from, 82
  information needs, 29
  involvement in product development, 88

Legal title to goods, 79
Letter to stockholders, in annual report, 761, 770
Liabilities, 33, 51, 287, 508; *see also* Debt financing
accrued expenses and, 265-66
on balance sheet, 754-58
from cash collection, 235
classifying as short-term or long-term, 746, 749
contingent, 763, 770
from customer advance payments, 309
in determination of financing cash flows, 796
for dividends declared, 634
employee wage withholdings as, 266-67
limits on corporation owners, 499
payments in statement of cash flow, 283
unlimited, of proprietorships and partnerships, 499
Liability account, 223
normal balance of, 231
Life cycle, and budgeting strategy, 149
Life-cycle pricing, 106, 128
Life insurance
for employees, 567
vs. retirement benefits, 572
LIFO (last-in, first-out) inventory costing method, 262, 273, 276-77, 291
and income taxes, 278-79
misleading aspects of, 288-89
LIFO reserve, 289
Limited liability, 8, 19
for corporate owners, 619
Limited liability partnership (LLP), 14, 19
Limited partnership, 13-14, 19
Linear programming, 193, 203, 204-8
graph, 208
Linear regression analysis, 114-16, 128
Line of credit, 376-77, 388
Liquid assets, 374
Liquidating dividends, 505
Liquidity, 282, 291
clasification of assets and liabilities and appearance of, 749
status of company short-term, 746
Liquidity analysis, 417
Liquidity ratios, 826, 827-28
Liquidity risk, 476-77, 490
Loans;: *see also* Notes payable *and* Promissory notes
short-term from financial institutions, 376
Local income taxes, 266
Lockbox collection system, 381, 388
Long-term assets, 32, 51, 469
Long-term debt financing, 511-17, 590-609
accounting for long-term notes payable, 591-603
on balance sheet, 755-56
covenant limits on, 519
early retirement of bonds, 603-6
information for decision makers, 608-9
leases, 606-8
lump-sum payment notes, 513-14
periodic payment and lump-sum note, 514-17
periodic payment notes, 512
ratios to evaluate repayment, 826, 828-29
sources of, 518-21

Long-term debt to equity, 829
Long-term investments
financing, 535-36
identifying opportunities, 532
reasons for, 533
selecting, 533-35
Long-term liabilities, 33, 51, 511, 746, 749
Long-term noncancellable lease, 758
Long-term notes payable
accounting for, 591-603
lump-sum payment, 593-96
periodic payment, 591-93
Long-term operational investment, expenditures included in cost, 532
Loss, 263-64, 291
cash flow adjustments for, 792
on disposal of assets, 546-47
on exchange of assets in trade-in, 669
from operational investments, 677
from sale of equity investments, 694-95
Loss area on graph, 123
Lotus 1-2-3, for regression analysis, 118
Lump sum, relationship of annuity payments to, 487
Lump-sum payment long-term notes payable, 593-96
Lump-sum payment notes, 513-14, 524
on income statement, 595-96
private sources of, 603
Luxury items, 104

M

McConnell, John P., 186
McDonnell, Jim, 431
Machine setups, 83
MACRS (modified accelerated cost recovery system), 663, 679
method of depreciation allowable under, 664
Major operations, 305
Make-or-buy decisions, 200-201, 204
Maker of note, 376, 388
Management accounting, 29, 45-49, 51
vs. financial accounting, 49
Management-by-exception, 431
variance reports, 446, 454
Management cycle, 89-91
Management view of business, in annual report, 761, 762
Mandated budgeting, 148, 166
Manufacturing
cells in facilities, 83
planning, 158-60
Manufacturing costing systems, 353-56
Manufacturing efficiency, 187
Manufacturing firms, 8, 12, 19
budgeting, 165
operating cycles in, 70-71
revenue-generation, 36
short-term operating decisions in, 200-203
Manufacturing inventories, 335-36
Manufacturing overhead, 337*n*, 338, 352
actual, 339
applied, 339-40
applied to work-in-process, 343
items included in, 84-85
Marketable securities
as asset on balance sheet, 750
reclassifying as trading securities, 746
Market adjustment account, 705
on balance sheet, 695, 696

Marketing, 15, 19, 78
pricing responsibility, 103
Marketing department, 145
planning by, 151
Market interest rate of bond
equal to face rate, 596-97
greater than face rate, 598-600
less than face rate, 600-3
Market interest rate of note, 512, 524
equal to face rate, 517
greater than face rate, 514-16
less than face rate, 516-17
Market price of share of stock, 504-5
with stock split, 507
Market rate of interest, 513
Market share, 90
Market value of ending inventory, 281
Mark to market, 695, 704
Markup, 105, 128
Master budget, 150-51, 166
comparing actual results to, 432-33
converted to flexible budget, 798
vs. flexible budget, 434
Matching principle, 222, 246
Material amounts, 718
Materiality concept of accounting, 656, 679
Materials requisition form, 84, 86
Mattel, 26
Maturity date of bond, paying off bond before, 604
Maturity date of promissory note, 308, 323
Maturity phase, in product life cycle, 88
Measurement in accounting events, 32
Merchandise inventory, 263, 291
acquisition of, 269-72
costs included in, 269
Merchandise purchase budget, 158*n*
Merchandising company, 6, 12, 19
budgets, 165
cycles in, 69-70
merchandise purchase budget, 158*n*
standard costs for, 432
Method of Venice, 7
Microsoft, 13
accounts receivable turnover, 825
dividend policy, 834
employee compensation, 563-64
financial ratios, 825
gross margin ratio, 830
liquidity, 827
return on assets, 831
Midyear convention for depreciation expense, 662, 664, 680
Mixed costs, 110-12, 128
Modified accelerated cost recovery system (MACRS), 663, 675
method of depreciation allowable under, 664
Monetary unit concept, 7, 19, 31, 221
Money market accounts, 375-76, 388
Monopolistic competition, 104, 128
Monopoly, 128
Moody's Handbook of Common Stock, 823
Moody's Handbook of NASDAQ Stocks, 823, 824
Moody's Investor Services, 823
Mortgage, 524
Mortgage bonds, 521, 524
Motivation of employees
economics of, 576-77
and performance-based labor costs, 576
standards and, 148
in teams, 578
Muda (waste), 156

Multiple-product cost-volume-profit analysis, 129-31
Multistep income statement, 279, 316-17, 323, 719-20
Mutual agency, 13, 19
Mutual funds, 12, 19

N

NAFTA (North American Free Trade Agreement), 86
NASDAQ (National Association of Securities Dealers Automated Quotations), 11, 503, 507, 835
Natural Frozen Foods Company, 403-4, 405
operating cycle, 417
vertical analysis, 406-7
Natural resources, 238, 670-71, 680
on balance sheet, 753
Need for goods, in expenditure cycle, 72
Negative rate of return, 471
Net cash flow, 540
vs. net income, 42
Net credit sales, in accounts receivable turnover, 414
Net income, 35, 51, 498-99, 717, 734
bonuses based on, 579
in financial statements, 784
impact on retained earnings, 632-33
vs. net cash flow, 42
vs. profit, 120*n*
reduction by preferred stock dividends in earnings per share calculation, 724
Net loss, impact on retained earnings, 632-33
Net-of-tax cash flows from asset sold with a gain, 547
Net-of-tax cash flows from asset sold with loss, 547
Net pay, 266, 291
Net present value, 553
advantage of, 540
effect of uneven cash flows, 539-40
of equipment, 548-49
Net present value method of discounted cash flow analysis, 536-38
Net price method, 270, 291
NetProfitII (Sampling, Inc.), 347
Net realizable value, 312, 323
Net worth, 246
cash flow and, 228
revenue to increase, 304
New partners
admission of, 626-28
asset revaluation before admission, 628-29
New York Stock Exchange, 503, 507
Nike, 4, 14, 86, 500
Nominal accounts, 240, 246
Noncash assets, recording from partners, 621
Noncash current operating assets, 801
adjustments for changes in, 793
Noncash expenses, 544-46
Noncash financing, in cash flow statement, 784
Noncash stock issue, 631
Noncontributory pension plans, 570, 581
Nonfinancial information, in management accounting, 47
Noninterest-bearing notes, 378, 389, 513, 691-92
on balance sheet, 756
Noninventoriable goods and services, 263, 291
accounting for, 264-69
errors in accounting for, 287